PENGUIN REFERENCE

The Penguin Dictionary of Literary Terms and Literary Theory

J. A. Cuddon was a writer, schoolteacher and academic. Best known for his *Dictionary of Literary Terms*, he also produced the large *Dictionary of Sport and Games*, as well as several novels, plays and travel books. He also edited two anthologies of supernatural fiction. He died in 1996.

M. A. R. Habib is Professor of English at Rutgers University. His publications include *An Anthology of Modern Urdu Poetry in Translation* (2003) and *The Early T.S. Eliot and Western Philosophy* (1999). He is also author of the highly acclaimed books *A History of Literary Criticism: from Plato to the Present* (2005), *Modern Literary Criticism and Theory: A History* (2007), *Literary Criticism from Plato to the Present: An Introduction* (2011), and the *Cambridge History of Literary Criticism: Vol. VI: The Nineteenth Century* (ed., 2013). He is currently writing a book entitled *Hegel and the Foundations of Modern Literary Theory*.

Matthew Birchwood is Senior Lecturer in English Literature at Kingston University, London; Vedrana Velickovic is Lecturer in English at Brighton University; Martin Dines is Senior Lecturer in English Literature at Kingston University, London; Shanyn Fiske is Associate Professor of English at Rutgers University, Camden.

The Penguin Dictionary of

LITERARY TERMS AND LITERARY THEORY

J. A. Cuddon

Revised by
M. A. R. Habib

Associate Editors
Matthew Birchwood, Vedrana Velickovic,
Martin Dines and Shanyn Fiske

PENGUIN BOOKS

PENGUIN BOOKS

Published by the Penguin Group

Penguin Books Ltd, 80 Strand, London WC2R 0RL, England
Penguin Group (USA) Inc., 375 Hudson Street, New York, New York 10014, USA
Penguin Group (Canada), 90 Eglinton Avenue East, Suite 700, Toronto, Ontario, Canada M4P 2Y3
(a division of Pearson Penguin Canada Inc.)
Penguin Ireland, 25 St Stephen's Green, Dublin 2, Ireland
(a division of Penguin Books Ltd)
Penguin Group (Australia), 707 Collins Street, Melbourne, Victoria 3008, Australia
(a division of Pearson Australia Group Pty Ltd)
Penguin Books India Pvt Ltd, 11 Community Centre, Panchsheel Park,
New Delhi – 110 017, India
Penguin Group (NZ), 67 Apollo Drive, Rosedale, Auckland 0632, New Zealand
(a division of Pearson New Zealand Ltd)
Penguin Books (South Africa) (Pty) Ltd, Block D, Rosebank Office Park,
181 Jan Smuts Avenue, Parktown North, Gauteng 2193, South Africa
Penguin Books Ltd, Registered Offices: 80 Strand, London WC2R 0RL, England

www.penguin.com

First published by André Deutsch Ltd 1977
Second edition published by André Deutsch Ltd 1979
Third edition published by Basil Blackwell Ltd 1991
Fourth edition published by Blackwell Publishers Ltd 1998
This edition first published in hardback by Wiley-Blackwell 2013
Published in paperback by Penguin Books 2014

017

Copyright © The Estate of J. A. Cuddon, 2013

The moral right of the author has been asserted

All rights reserved

Typeset by Toppan Best-set Premedia Ltd
Printed in Great Britain by Clays Ltd, Elcograf S.p.A

978-0-141-04715-7

www.greenpenguin.co.uk

MIX
Paper from
responsible sources
FSC
www.fsc.org   FSC® C018179

Penguin Books is committed to a sustainable
future for our business, our readers and our planet.
This book is made from Forest Stewardship
Council™ certified paper.

Contents

Preface to the Fifth Edition

While our editorial aim has been to produce an updated and more comprehensive version of the fourth edition of J. A. Cuddon's *Dictionary of Literary Terms and Literary Theory*, we have tried to remain mindful of the fact that we are revising a volume that has hitherto enjoyed great success and has effectively created a wide audience. Hence, while we have endeavoured to update and modernize the book, it seemed unbefitting to transform it beyond recognition and to discard its distinctive characteristics of (a) historical range, (b) conciseness and wit, (c) intercultural breadth, and (d) readability, appealing as it does to a broad spectrum of people. And we wished to avoid turning it into yet another glossary of contemporary critical terms. While we acknowledge that current debates concerning literary theory are moving in many directions, we have sought not to dilute the range or depth of what Cuddon has already accomplished.

Nonetheless, after consulting with many people, we concurred that there were clearly areas where the book could be improved and made more effective as a resource. For example, some of the extant entries reflect Cuddon's esoteric interests, as in the discussions of unwieldy length on topics such as 'ghost story' and 'spy story'. These have been retained but in a much abbreviated form. Furthermore, a number of very obscure terms have been removed altogether.

One of the factors that rendered Cuddon's dictionary so accessible and usable was the conciseness of *most* entries. And this made it a work of reference different in kind from, say, the *Johns Hopkins Guide to Literary Theory and Criticism* (a splendid book in its own right), where often it will take an hour or more to read a single entry. But again, some of the entries in the Cuddon *Dictionary* were disproportionately lengthy, as for example, the forty pages on the novel. Any reader who wants that kind of detailed information on the novel can easily go to fuller sources. Hence we have tried to keep the longest entries to a maximum of about three pages; this also had the advantage of creating room for numerous new entries, as well as for expanding and updating some of the existing ones, without the book's length being substantially altered. Some of the entries that needed revising and updating, such as those on 'dialectic', 'logocentrism', 'estrangement' and 'essentialism', have been reconceived from what we hope is a more philosophically informed perspective. Other entries have been modified in the light of more recent theoretical developments.

There are a number of areas in which we thought that additional entries needed to be included: gender studies and queer theory; postcolonial theory; poststructuralism; postmodernism; narrative theory; cultural studies; terms from other literatures (Chinese, Arabic, Persian, Urdu, Indian); and a number of miscellaneous terms, including cybercriticism, life writing, world literature, and dub poetry.

Even with such a range of additions, the dictionary can hardly claim to be exhaustive or as comprehensive as we might have wished. We have had to exercise a great deal of selectivity in choosing terms from these various fields. Finally, such is our admiration for Cuddon's work that it is only with a great deal of tentativeness that we hope to have produced a dictionary which both retains the merits of the original and is firmly grounded in the twenty-first century.

Preface to the Fourth Edition

> I make not therefore my head a grave, but a treasure of knowledge; I
> intend no monopoly, but a community in learning; I study not for my
> own sake only, but for theirs that study not for themselves.

Thomas Browne, Religio Medici

Charles Cuddon was the author of twelve plays, three libretti, five novels, two travel books, two dictionaries, and many short stories and essays; he was the editor of ghost and horror stories, a schoolmaster, a talented sportsman, and even, in his youth, a photographic model. When this remarkable man died in the spring of 1996, he left, among these many works, the incandescent *Owl's Watchsong* (1960) (his astonishing elegy to Istanbul), the colossal and witty *Dictionary of Sport and Games* (1980), and the present work, the *Dictionary of Literary Terms and Literary Theory* (1976), which he was readying for its fourth edition. The number and quality of his literary remains are his own memorial: they are the testimonial of the range of his interests, his lucid scholarship, his large intelligence, his delightful sense of humour, and his elegant prose. Above all, they are a record of his generosity, to friends, students, scholars, and all who have benefited, and will benefit, from his labours.

Like one of his favourite writers, Sir Thomas Browne, Charles Cuddon would not make his head a grave; at his death in March 1996, he was far advanced in the revisions which are contained in this new edition of his *Dictionary*; the task of incorporating the new entries and the corrections to existing ones which he left among his extensive notes has therefore been pleasant and easy. Charles also left proposals for many new entries which he could not himself finish, and a substantial number of these have been adopted and written, often according to rough drafts he had already sketched out.

Over the years, Charles and his *Dictionary* prompted correspondence from readers and friends who suggested improvements and additions; fortunately, a number of these were willing to be dragooned into the project of completing the fourth edition, and their help was indispensable. Anna Cuddon, Jean Gooder, Eric Griffiths, Kevin Jackson, John Kenyon, John Kerrigan and Ato Quayson fielded random queries and supplied vital information. Three others produced major rewriting as well as entirely new entries for the *Dictionary*: John Lennard wrote 'Rhyme', 'Punctuation' and 'Crime fiction'; Clive Wilmer wrote 'Verse novel', 'Dramatic monologue', 'Sonnet cycle', and a number of shorter entries; and Anne Henry wrote 'Ellipsis'. I should like to record special thanks to Anna Cuddon, Charles' widow, for her constant encouragement; and to Clive Wilmer for his interest and enthusiasm for the *Dictionary*, both in its new form and over the long years of his friendship with Charles.

C. E. Preston Sidney Sussex College Cambridge

As is usual in the making of anything, one of the main problems at the outset in compiling this dictionary was to decide what to put in and what to omit. In the first place, it is not easy to decide what a literary term really is, because, by most standards, it is a vague classification. Epic is one, hexameter is, and so is elegy. But are pornography, pattersong and apocrypha? In the *Shorter Oxford Dictionary* the main definition of 'literary' runs thus: 'Of or pertaining to, or of the nature of, literature, polite learning, or books and written compositions; pertaining to that kind of written composition which has value on account of its qualities of form.' If we accept this as a working indication of what is meant by 'literary', then what is to be done about the terms (and there are many) used by printers and compositors? What about the language of grammarians and the proliferating terminology of linguisticians? Most or all of these are related, however tenuously in some cases, to the literary, and to literature. After a good deal of deliberation on these matters, I decided to be judiciously selective and include a few terms of printers, grammarians, philologists and linguisticians. So, for instance, I have included **quarto** and **folio** but left out **line-block** and **galley**. **Paragraph** and **loose** and **periodic sentence** are in; **supine** and **declension** are not. **Keneme** and **morpheme** are in; **diphthong** and **labial** are not.

Another poser was whether to include all literary terms from all or most languages and literatures and to provide illustrations and examples, but this would surely have seemed like assuming the function of the encyclopaedist, and greatly lengthened the book. In any case, some terms are so obscure (and rare) as to be of interest only to the specialist.

What I have endeavoured to do, then, is to provide a serviceable and fairly comprehensive dictionary of those literary terms which are in regular use in the world today; terms in which intelligent people may be expected to have some interest and about which they may wish to find out something more. If by any chance they do not know (or have forgotten) what a *haiku* is, or *verso tronco*, or how blue-stockings came to be so named, then I hope that this dictionary will provide them with the basic information.

I say 'fairly comprehensive' because any work of orismology is bound to be limited by the author's reading and knowledge. No man or woman can be expected to have read even a tithe of everything. I am familiar with Classical, European, Slavonic and Near Eastern literatures and have some knowledge of the literatures of North America and of Commonwealth nations. But my knowledge of Oriental literatures and those of Spanish America and South America is limited. There are, therefore, inevitably, considerable gaps.

Most of the terms are drawn from Greek, Latin, English, French, German, Spanish, Italian, Russian, Arabic, Japanese, Old French, Old Provençal and Old Norse. A few are Serbian, Chinese, Persian, Turkish, Welsh or Korean.

Twelve main categories can be distinguished at the outset, as follows:

1. Technical terms (e.g. iamb, pentameter, metonymy, *ottava rima*).
2. Forms (e.g. sonnet, *villanelle*, limerick, *tanka*, clerihew).
3. Genres or kinds (e.g. pastoral, elegy, *fabliau*, *Märchen*, *conte*).
4. Technicalities (e.g. pivot word, tenor and vehicle, communication heresy, aesthetic distance).
5. Groups, schools and movements (e.g. Pléiade, Parnassians, Pre-Raphaelites, School of Spenser).
6. Well-known phrases (e.g. willing suspension of disbelief, negative capability, *discordia concors*, *in medias res*, *quod semper quod ubique*).
7. -isms (e.g. realism, primitivism, Platonism, plagiarism, structuralism, orientalism).
8. Motifs or themes (e.g. *ubi sunt*, *carpe diem*, Faust-theme, *leitmotif*).
9. Personalities (e.g. *scop*, *jongleur*, villain, *gracioso*, *guslar*).
10. Modes, attitudes and styles (e.g. *dolce stil nuovo*, irony, Marinism, grotesque, sentimental comedy).
11. Objects/artefacts (e.g. *coranto*, holograph, manuscript, gazette, buskin, book).
12. Concepts (e.g. sincerity, the sublime, concrete universal, noble savage, decorum).

These twelve categories account for a fair proportion of literary terms but there are scores which do not belong to any particular family or phylum, and any kind of taxonomical approach soon breaks down as one begins to classify. The following haphazard list suggests the difficulty of satisfactory division: abstract, *belles lettres*, brief, censorship, forgery, Freytag's pyramid, *hamartia*, inspiration, juvenilia, Grub Street, palindrome, quotation titles – to mention no others.

The plan of the dictionary is simple. It is alphabetical and runs from Abbey Theatre (though it would have been more suitable to start with *ab ovo*) to zeugma; and, so to speak, from epic to limerick. Each term is given a brief description or definition. In some cases, but by no means always, when I thought it might be helpful and/or of interest, I give some brief etymology of the term. This is particularly necessary when a term comes from one thing but now denotes another. For instance, the Spanish *estribillo*: the word signifies 'little stirrup', being the diminutive of *estribo* 'stirrup'. It here denotes a refrain or chorus (also a pet word or phrase) and is a theme, verse or stanza (of from two to four lines) of a *villancico*; and there is more to it than that. *Fit* (a division of a poem, a canto or stave) and *slang* are other interesting examples.

Many indications of origin are added in brackets. Where it was not possible to do this in a simple fashion I have shown the history at greater length within the definition of the term. Often this description explains the etymology and what the term denotes. For literary forms and genres I have provided a *résumé* of origins, history and development, and I have also provided details of notable examples and distinguished practitioners. I have not included bibliographies; to have done so would have been to lengthen the book by perhaps a third as much again. But, where appropriate, I have referred to the classic work on a particular theme or subject (e.g. C. S. Lewis's *The Allegory of Love*, A. O. Lovejoy's *The Great Chain of Being*, Maud Bodkin's *Archetypal Patterns in Poetry*).

I would have liked to provide an example in full to illustrate every poetic form and genre (e.g. **rondeau**, **ode**, **elegy**, **lyric**), but this was not feasible either. I would also have liked to include a quotation for every kind of metrical scheme, but this again would have expanded the book inordinately. It would have entailed quoting in at least sixteen different languages and this would have required translation in many instances. Moreover, it would have involved using seven alphabets (Greek, Japanese, Hebrew, Arabic, Cyrillic, Sanskrit and Chinese) in addition to the Roman. Thus, in the interests of simplicity and brevity, I have settled, whenever possible, for a quotation in English verse.

Apropos versification I am obliged to mention the matter of terms used in Classical prosody. Miscellaneous hierophants have pointed out that Classical prosody, its systems and classifications, bear little relationship to English verse. This may well be so, but we have inherited the terms (as have other nations and languages); they have been in use for some hundreds of years; and it will be found that the vast majority of poets have a very thorough knowledge and understanding of them. Moreover, if in doubt about their utility, one might ask: is it easier to say (or write) 'an iambic pentameter', or 'a line of verse consisting of five feet with a rising rhythm in which the first syllable of each foot is unstressed and the second stressed'? The Greeks in fact *did* have a word for almost everything and we have inherited these terms whether we like them or not. And it seems to me much simpler to understand and use them rather than to pretend they do not exist, or find verbose alternatives.

Some entries were peculiarly difficult to condense, and none more so than **novel**. The chief problem here was what to include out of the thousands of possible examples. In the end I decided to go by that principle which guided me throughout the making of the dictionary and to include only those writers whose books I am familiar with and which have seemed to me to be of particular merit. Naturally enough, the selection must often coincide with what, in all probability, most other people would choose. Some novelists have to go in whether you like them or not because the general consensus over the years has confirmed that their novels are outstanding or at any rate of notable quality. On the whole, as far as the novel is concerned, I have mentioned most of those who I believe are major novelists, and I have provided a selection of minor novelists. Inevitably, the treatment of the novel (like the treatment of travel books, short stories, detective stories, spy, ghost and horror stories) has involved long lists.

I have some misgivings about the lists but I have kept them fairly detailed in order to be fair, as it were, and also in the hope that the browser or reader may encounter things that they have not met before or which they have forgotten existed. For instance, the works of some authors of distinction have, unhappily, sunk leaving few traces. A mention of their neglected books may help to revive interest.

With regard to works of fiction in general, I would have liked to include more evaluative comments, however brief, but to have done this would have been to double or even triple the length of the entries.

As for dates – these, as we all know, can become boring. On the other hand, their absence can be frustrating. Accordingly, I have attempted a compromise. It seemed otiose to put in the dates of every author each time I referred to him or her, especially the famous. There are, for instance, many references to Aristotle, Plato, Horace, Dante, Chaucer, Sir Philip Sidney, Shakespeare, Molière, Dryden, Pope, Goethe, Keats, Thomas Mann, James Joyce, W. B. Yeats and T. S. Eliot – to cite only a handful. When referring to the famous I assume that the reader is familiar with the approximate period in which they flourished. When referring to the not-so-famous, but, nonetheless, important (e.g. Archilochus, Lucian, Cavalcanti, Dunbar, Clément Marot, Thomas Campion, Tieck, Lady Winchilsea, James Sheridan Knowles, Théophile Gautier, Queiros) I have, in many instances, included some indication of their dates. In any event it is clear as a rule when they lived because I refer to the century, or I give the dates of their works whenever it is helpful or necessary to do so. The dates given refer, unless otherwise indicated in the text, to the first performance of plays, the first publication in one volume of prose works, and the first collected publication of poems. I diverge from this system only where it might be misleading. I have cited in English those titles of works which are less familiar in their original form to an English-speaking reader. The dates given in such cases refer to the first publication in the original language.

The whole dictionary is cross-referenced so that the user can move easily from one entry to another. The references are the plumbing and wiring of the book. If, for example, you look up **ballad** you will be referred to REFRAIN,

ORAL TRADITION, HOMERIC EPITHET, KENNING, INCREMENTAL REPETITION, NARODNE PESME, BROADSIDE, FOLKSONG, LAY and NARRATIVE VERSE.

In the twenty years since this book was first published a great deal has happened in the world of literature. Thousands of novels have been published in many languages, thousands of short stories, poems, biographies and autobiographies; several hundred new plays have been produced – and so on. Since the early 1970s the full impact of structuralist theory has been experienced and has been succeeded or added to by poststructuralism, of which deconstruction is a vital part. Feminist criticism has burgeoned; so, to a lesser extent, have Marxist criticism and psychoanalytic and Freudian criticism. Reader-response and reception theories have developed. Such concepts as narratology and grammatology have become established. Indeed, literary theory has proliferated, sometimes counter-productively in so far as there are commentaries about commentaries about commentaries so that we approach that state of affairs so vividly predicted by E. M. Forster in his admonitory short story *The Machine Stops*. A select bibliography of books, essays and miscellaneous discourses concerned with literary theory during the last fifteen to twenty years (in the major languages of the world) may run to five hundred or more entries.

With the theories and the theories about theories have come a considerable number of what might be called 'technical terms' (e.g. *aporia*, *différance*, dissemination, *écriture féminine*, indeterminacy, intertextuality, logocentrism, metalanguage, phallogocentrism, *plaisir/jouissance*, readerly/ writerly, *supplément*, *qq.v.*).

In this revised and expanded edition I have attempted a *résumé* and clarification of these matters which, very often, are extremely complex and not infrequently abstruse to the point of being arcane: to such an extent, in fact, that sometimes one is reminded of 'the lone scholars' sniping at each other from the walls of learned periodicals.

However, the *raison d'être* of a dictionary is, I take it, to provide information – be it commonplace or recondite. A decent dictionary of geography, for instance, will tell us what exfoliation, jungle and *Karst* are. It should also inform us about katabatic winds, *poljes* and diastrophism. So, in this edition, in response to quite a large number of letters (one from a man who requested a list of *all* the rare technical terms left out of earlier editions) I have included a good many esoteric technical terms and semitechnical terms, plus information about important theatres and theatrical companies which have had a potent influence in the world of drama.

I have also devoted a good deal of space to some of the more 'popular' forms or modes. In earlier editions there were no entries for **ghost story** or **horror story**. In view of the wide and apparently increasing interest in these I have now included quite long accounts. The original entry for **detective story** was totally inadequate and that has been much expanded. I have also expanded the entries on, for example, **gothic novel**, **limerick**, **nonsense**, **spy story** and **thriller**, and included entries for, among other things, **censorship**, **literary forgery**, **literary prizes**, **police procedural**, **roman policier** and **Western**.

I should also add that, as this is a personal book, I have, occasionally, spread myself with entries on subjects of particular interest to me; for example, conceit, *danse macabre*, the limerick, nonsense, primitivism, revenge tragedy and table talk – to name but a few. But every author and reader has his or her favourite themes and subjects. It is probable that, from time to time, I have allowed my opinions (and perhaps some prejudices) an easy rein; but when one has read many thousands of volumes of verse, plays and fiction, essays, discourses, sermons, courtesy books, encyclopaedias, *novelle*, *Festschriften*, tracts and interpretations (and what not?) perhaps one is entitled to ventilate a few opinions. They are unlikely, I feel, to do any harm in such circumstances, and they may have the beneficial effect of provoking argument, comment or disagreement.

I have also taken the liberty of contributing a few items of my own: firstly, a double-dactyl verse – under that heading; secondly an example of synthetic rhyme – under that heading; and thirdly, three neologisms – namely *birocrat*, *sufferingette* and *verbocrap* (all under **neologism**). At any rate, I put in a modest claim for having devised these ghost-words.

I wrote above that this is a 'personal' book, but, naturally, in the course of making it, I have consulted a number of friends and I would like to take this opportunity of thanking them for giving me the benefit of their knowledge and advice. They are: Mrs Heywood, Margaret J. Miller, Mr John Basing, Dr Derek Brewer, Mr Paul Craddock, Mr Vincent Cronin, Professor Ian Jack, Mr Kevin Jackson, Dr Harry Judge, Mr Paul Moreland, Mr T. R. Salmon, Mr Philip Warnett, Professor and Mrs Singmaster, Mr and Mrs McNally, Dr David Stockton, Mr Hardcastle, Mr Clive Wilmer, Mr Michael Charlesworth, Mr Alastair Ogilvie, Mr Colin Chambers, Mr Steve Gooch, Mr Andrew Brown, Mr Stuart Thomson, Mr Harry Jackson, Mr Barry Duesbury and Mr Kenneth Lowes.

I remain much indebted to my original editors in the Language Library Series, the late Professor Simeon Potter and the late Eric Partridge. Professor Potter showed much patience and gave me the unstinting help of his wide learning and experience; Eric Partridge, often by means of his famous postcards, sustained my sometimes flagging spirits with help, praise and encouragement.

I am also much indebted to Mr Martin Wright who devoted many hours to checking the manuscript of this edition and to making suggestions for improving it, and to Mr Michael Rossington who also gave much time and thought to many entries. Finally, my thanks also to my current editors for their help: Mr Alyn Shipton, Mr Philip Cartwright, Miss Helen Jeffrey and Miss Caroline Richmond.

J. A. Cuddon

Acknowledgements

I should like to thank the following for the benefit of their expertise and
advice during the preparation of this fifth edition: David Lyle Jeffrey, David
Rabeeya, Gloria Mazziotti, Lewis Eron, Carol Singley, Laurie Bernstein, Ed
Bryant, William Fitzgerald and J. T. Barbarese. I would especially like to
thank the associate editors of this volume, Matthew Birchwood, Vedrana
Velickovic, Martin Dines and Shanyn Fiske, for their thorough, intelligent
and timely work. Finally, it has been a pleasure, as always, to work with Emma
Bennett and her colleagues at Wiley-Blackwell, including Ben Thatcher,
Bridget Jennings, and copy-editor Ann Bone.

M. A. R. Habib

List of Abbreviations

A	Arabic
abbrev.	abbreviation, -ated
AL	Anglo-Latin
AN	Anglo-Norman
Ar	Armenian
c.	century, or centuries
c.	*circa* (as in *c.* 1150, meaning the approximate date)
cf.	*confer* 'compare'
Ch	Chinese
Du	Dutch
e.g.	*exempli gratia* 'for example'
Eng	English
et al.	*et alii* 'and others'
F	French
fl.	*floruit* 'he flourished'
G	German
Gk	Greek
Heb	Hebrew
HG	High German
i.e.	*id est* 'that is'
It	Italian
J	Japanese
K	Korean
KJV	King James Version of the Bible
L	Latin
LDu	Low Dutch
LG	Low German
LL	Late Latin
MDu	Middle Dutch
ME	Middle English
MedL	Medieval Latin
MHG	Middle High German
MLG	Middle Low German

List of Abbreviations

ModL	Modern Latin
NGk	Neo-Greek
NT	New Testament
OE	Old English
OED	Oxford English Dictionary
OF	Old French
OHG	Old High German
ON	Old Norse
OT	Old Testament
P	Persian
Pg	Portuguese
pl.	plural
Pr	Provençal
Pt	Part
publ.	published
qq.v.	*quae vide* 'which see' (pl.)
q.v.	*quod vide* 'which see' (sing.)
R	Russian
S	Serbian
sing.	singular
Skt	Sanskrit
Sp	Spanish
Sw	Swedish
T	Turkish
trans.	translation, -ated
viz.	*videlicet* 'namely'
W	Welsh

A

Abbey Theatre Celebrated Dublin home of the Irish dramatic movement founded in 1899 by W. B. Yeats, Augusta Gregory and Edward Martyn, first incarnated as the Irish Literary Theatre and later the Irish National Theatre Society. Other early important contributors were two local acting brothers, William and Frank Fay, the playwright-director John Synge and wealthy tea heiress Annie Horniman whose patronage allowed for the acquisition of the Abbey Street site, incorporating the old city morgue. The theatre first opened in 1904.

According to its published manifesto, the movement aimed 'to bring upon the stage the deeper thoughts and emotions of Ireland' and to 'show that Ireland is not the home of buffoonery and easy sentiment, but the home of an ancient idealism'. This early synthesis of national ideological and cultural aims would characterize the spirit of the Abbey Theatre throughout the turbulent century to come. On its opening night Synge's *Playboy of the Western World* (1907) was greeted with riots on account of its allegedly immoral and unpatriotic portrayal of Irish women. Periodically attracting popular acclaim and criticism in equal measure, in its early years the Abbey continued to commission and produce the work of important playwrights, including Padraic Colum, George Bernard Shaw and Lennox Robinson.

The fortunes of the theatre declined following Horniman's financial withdrawal from the enterprise in 1909, but were partly relieved through three famous plays by Sean O'Casey. Premiering in 1923 at the height of the Irish Civil War, *Shadow of a Gunman* was followed by *Juno and the Paycock* (1924) and *The Plough and the Stars* (1926). The last of these was once again the cause of civil disorder, this time in reaction to O'Casey's pacifist critique of the nationalist struggle. In 1925, the theatre received a grant from the Irish government and became the first state-supported theatre in the English-speaking world.

A Dictionary of Literary Terms and Literary Theory, Fifth Edition. J. A. Cuddon.
© 2013 The Estate of J. A. Cuddon. Published 2013 by Blackwell Publishing Ltd.

In the period following Yeats's death in 1939, the theatre lapsed into relative decline with few original productions to rival the ground-breaking works of its earlier years. Following a fire in July 1951, the company was forced to relocate to the old Queen's Theatre. Exiled from its Abbey street location for fifteen years, it was not until the 1960s with the rebuilding of a second theatre on the original site that the playhouse reinvoked its experimental heritage, showcasing the work of playwrights such as Hugh Leonard, Brian Friel and Tom Murphy. More recently, plans were announced to move and expand this iconic theatre once again.

abecedarius A type of ACROSTIC (*q.v.*) following an alphabetical pattern.

Abenteuerroman (G 'adventure novel') A form of fiction related to the picaresque novel in which the hero conventionally undergoes a series of testing and episodic adventures, often involving travel to colourful and exotic locations. The tradition has its roots in medieval verse tales such as *Herzog Ernst*, *König Rother* and *Salman und Morolf* and is discernible in Arthurian romance cycles. An influential example, the German chapbook *Volksbuch Fortunatus* (1509), centring upon a hero whose wanderings are funded by a magically inexhaustible purse, found its way into several European versions, including Thomas Dekker's *Old Fortunatus* (1600). The so-called *Simplicianische Schriften* series of novels by Johann Grimmelhausen is often cited as the apogee of the tradition, in particular *Der abenteuerliche Simplicissimus* (1609). The popularity of the form continued into the late 17th and 18th c. in the writings of Johann Beer (1655–1700) and *Die Insel Felsenburg* (1731–43) by Johann Schnabel. Thomas Mann's *Bekenntnisse des Hochstaplers Felix Krull* (partly published in 1922) is a conscious variation on this theme, relating the unlikely escapades of a roguish anti-hero. *See also* GOTHIC NOVEL/FICTION; PICARESQUE NOVEL; ROBINSONADE; VOLKSBUCH.

abjection A psychoanalytic concept developed by Julia Kristeva in *Powers of Horror* (1980) to explain the formation and maintenance of subjectivity. For Kristeva, subject formation – that is, the development of a discrete 'I' – occurs in early infancy, prior even to Lacan's 'mirror stage'. The infant creates borders between the 'I' and other by abjecting – violently throwing out, jettisoning – that which seems improper; Kristeva's rather visceral examples include sour milk, excrement and an all-engulfing mother. Despite being radically excluded, that which is abjected continues to linger at the fringes of consciousness. Indeed, while utterly repulsive, because it threatens our sense of ourselves as separate and autonomous beings, the abject is at the same time deeply alluring, since it invokes a comforting state of unity with the maternal. Thus the abject exists as a constant companion through life, always challenging – and requiring maintenance of – the tenuous borders of selfhood. Kristeva argues that much literary production, from the Old Testament, with its insistence on purification, to Céline's anti-Semitic writings, relates this perpetually anguished struggle. Abjection has since become a key concept in the study of Gothic literature. The horror or fascination associated with threshold states, for example between life and death, or between the human and the non-human, has similarly been understood to be a consequence of the essentially insecure nature of selfhood. *See also* GOTHIC NOVEL/FICTION; PSYCHOANALYTIC CRITICISM.

abolitionist literature The term 'abolitionist' refers to the 18th and 19th c. black British, African-American, and white European and American men and women who campaigned for the abolition of slavery in the British Empire and North America. The origins of abolitionist literature can be found in the long history of slave rebellions, particularly in the Caribbean colonies in the 17th and 18th c. Such literature takes a moral stand against slavery, exposes the horrors of the slave trade and the inhumanity of slavery, and calls for the abolition of this institution. It often uses sentimental and biblical rhetoric to attract sympathy for the abolitionist cause. It comprises miscellaneous writings and documents, including poetry, novels, songs, pamphlets, speeches, court rulings, anti-slavery periodicals and slave narratives (*q.v.*). Slave narratives – the autobiographical accounts of former and runaway slaves – were a particularly popular genre in the antebellum period and had a considerable impact on the struggle to end slavery in America.

Abolitionist literature comprises a diverse body of writing and material culture, ranging, for example, from the famous inscription 'Am I Not a Man and a Brother?' (1787) on Josiah Wedgwood's medallions, which were distributed during the 18th c. anti-slavery campaign in Britain, to the speech 'Ain't I a Woman?' by the African-American former slave and women's rights activist Sojourner Truth (1797–1883). Well-known instances in 18th c. English Literature include slave narratives by early black British writers and abolitionists such as Ignatius Sancho, Olaudah Equiano and Ottobah Cugoano, political writings and speeches by the white abolitionists such as James Ramsey, Thomas Clarkson and William Wilberforce, and anti-slavery writings by the Quakers. Their joint efforts helped end the British slave trade in 1807 and slavery in British colonies in 1833. American abolitionist literature is equally diverse. It includes the writings of the American Anti-Slavery Society (1833–70), the narratives by former slaves and abolitionists such as Frederick Douglass's *Narrative of the Life of Frederick Douglass* (1845) and Harriet Jacobs's *Incidents in the Life of a Slave Girl* (1863), and Harriet Beecher Stowe's best-selling sentimental novel (*q.v.*) *Uncle Tom's Cabin* (1852). By writing about the harsh reality and persistence of slavery, many of these authors exposed the inherent flaws in the idea of 'universal rights' guaranteed by the US Declaration of Independence. Together, these writings sparked debates about the moral, political and economic nature of slavery in America, which was one of the key factors leading to the Civil War (1861–5) and the abolition of slavery in 1865. *See also* SENTIMENTAL NOVEL.

ab ovo (L 'from the egg') This term may refer to a story which starts from the beginning of the events it narrates, as opposed to one which starts in the middle – *in medias res* (*q.v.*). Horace used the expression in *Ars Poetica*.

abridged edition An abbreviated or condensed version of a work. Abridgement may be done in order to save space or to cut out passages which are thought unsuitable for some sections of the reading public. School editions of Shakespeare were often abridged (and still are occasionally) lest the sensibilities of adolescents be offended. *See also* BOWDLERIZE.

absence/presence Terms or concepts given a particular meaning by the French philosopher Jacques Derrida (1930–2004). Speech and the spoken word imply the immediate presence of somebody: a speaker, orator, actor or politician, for example. Writing does not require the writer's presence. Thus, the originator of the word is absent.

absolutism The principle or doctrine that there are immutable standards by which a work of art may be judged. The absolutist contends that certain values are basic and inviolable. *See* RELATIVISM.

abstract (a) A summary of any piece of written work, especially a long poem, prose narrative, proposal, conference proceeding, article or dissertation; (b) not concrete but rather dealing with the conceptual or general. In the history of criticism, the perceived abstractness or concreteness of the prevailing imagery of a given work has often been taken as a measure of literary worth. Sidney's *Defence of Poesie* (1595) praised the poet's unique ability to combine the 'general notion with the particular example' (as opposed to the philosopher, who deals with abstractions, or the historian, who is necessarily mired in the particular and often accidental details of situations). Similar positions (though argued very differently) were advanced by many thinkers, including Kant and Hegel, as well as by Romantics such as Wordsworth and Coleridge who professed a preference for a fusion of the abstract and concrete over the conventionalized abstractions of 18th c. neoclassicism. Modernist poetry, influenced by the French symbolists, exhibited a preoccupation with 'the dry hardness' of poetic language (in T. E. Hulme's words), especially in the literary criticism and poetic practice of Ezra Pound and T. S. Eliot. *See also* ABSTRACT POEMS; IMAGISTS; NEOCLASSICISM.

abstract poem More generally known as 'Sound Poetry', a form of verse which depends primarily upon patterns of sound rather than conventional syntactic or grammatical structures to constitute meaning. Edith Sitwell coined the term 'abstract poem' to describe her collection *Façade* (1950), inviting a comparison with the revolutions of abstract art. Gerard Manley Hopkins also made daring use of onomatopoeic and melopoeic devices; so did the French poet Rimbaud. Among writers using English, Roy Campbell (1901–57) was perhaps the most outstanding and prolific experimenter. This example is taken from his series *Mithraic Frieze*, published in *Mithraic Emblems*:

> Of seven hues in white elision,
> the radii of your silver gyre,
> are the seven swords of vision
> that spoked the prophets' flaming tyre;

their sistered stridencies ignite
the spectrum of the poets' lyre
whose unison becomes a white
revolving disc of stainless fire . . .

abusio The misapplication of a word (L, from rhetoric). *See* CATACHRESIS.

academic Four basic meanings may be distinguished: (a) that which belongs to the school of thought of Plato – from academy (*q.v.*); (b) a person or work that is scholarly and erudite; (c) concerned with the rules of composition rather than with the result of the act of creation; (d) of little importance or note. In the second and fourth senses the word is often used pejoratively.

academic drama A dramatic institution of the late 15th and early 16th c. in England, in which plays written by schoolmasters or other scholars were performed by students at schools, universities or Inns of Court. Translations of Roman playwrights such as Terence and Plautus were popular and, along with original dramatic compositions in Latin, were performed as part of the curriculum. Following a pedagogical ideal influenced by European humanism, imitations of these classical models also appeared in English from the mid 16th c., with the comedy *Ralph Roister Doister* (*c.* 1552) by the Westminster schoolmaster Nicholas Udall surviving as an early example. Relatively neglected in comparison to the public theatres of the age, academic drama also constituted an important link between crown and academe, with Elizabeth both receiving plays at court and commissioning their performance as royal entertainment during state visits to the universities. *See also* SCHOOL DRAMA.

academy The word is derived from the name of a park near Athens where Plato's Academy was situated from 387 BC to AD 529. The name was adopted in Italy by scholars during the Renaissance and now usually applies to some sort of institution devoted to learning, even if it be only the trade of war – as at the Royal Military Academy. There are a large number of academies scattered round the world. Most of them are concerned with research and culture and have limited memberships. Some are very exclusive. Probably the most famous is the Académie Française, founded by Richelieu in 1635. This is primarily a literary academy, one of whose main tasks is the compilation and revision of a dictionary of the French language. The British Academy was founded in 1902 for the promotion of moral and political sciences. The exclusiveness of many academies may account for the pejorative use of the word 'academic'. The Académie Française, for instance, has been described as the 'hôtel des invalides de la littérature'. The pejorative use may equally derive from the anti-intellectualism of modern culture. *See also* ACADEMIC.

acatalectic (Gk 'not lacking a syllable in the last foot') It denotes, therefore, a metrical line which is complete. If a line lacks one or more unaccented syllables, it is truncated (*see* CATALEXIS). If a line contains an extra syllable it is then hypercatalectic (or hypermetrical, redundant or extrametrical). In the following stanza from William Blake's *Art and Artists* the first line is catalectic, the third acatalectic, and the fourth hypercatalectic:

> When Sr Joshua Reynolds died
> All Nature was degraded;
> The King dropp'd a tear into the Queen's Ear,
> And all his Pictures Faded.

See BRACHYCATALECTIC; CATALEXIS; DICATALECTIC.

accelerated rhyme A term referring to the decreased spacing of rhymes. As with delayed rhymes, accelerated rhymes may be used to modify an established pattern. See RHYME.

accent The emphasis or stress (*q.v.*) placed on a syllable, especially in a line of verse. It is a matter of vocal emphasis. Where the accent comes will depend on how the reader wishes to render the sense. In the following lines the metrical stress is fairly clear, but the accents can be varied:

> All human things are subject to decay,
> And, when Fate summons, Monarchs must obey.

The variables are 'all', 'human', 'and', 'when', 'Fate', 'Monarchs', 'must', and 'obey'. At least half a dozen emphases are possible. Obviously, where the metrical scheme is very strict, then accent variation is limited. In blank verse (*q.v.*), however, many subtleties of accent are possible. *See* BEAT; HOVERING ACCENT; ICTUS; LEVEL STRESS; LOGICAL STRESS; QUANTITY.

accentual verse Verse in which the lines are defined by the number of stressed syllables in each line, rather than the number of syllables taken altogether. Anglo-Saxon poetry is accentual in this sense. Perhaps the most renowned example of Old English accentual poetry is *Beowulf*. Although syllabic verse (*q.v.*) became the favoured form for much English poetry from the late Middle Ages on, the meter survived in popular forms such as ballads and nursery rhymes. In the early 20th c., the possibilities of accentual verse were brought to the attention of a number of modernist poets following the lead of Gerard Manley Hopkins, who coined the term 'sprung rhythm' (*q.v.*) for his own version of accentual verse. *See also* ALLITERATIVE VERSE; METER; SPRUNG RHYTHM; SYLLABIC VERSE.

accidence That branch of grammar which deals with 'accidents'; that is, the inflexions or the variable endings of words.

acclamatio An expression of enthusiastic public approval (or disapproval) deriving from the popular cries of the Roman Republic.

acephalous (Gk 'headless') A metrical line whose first syllable, according to strict meter, is wanting. An iambic line with a monosyllabic first foot would be acephalous.

acervatio (L 'heaping together') A term used by the Roman rhetorician Quintilian to describe the compounding of various ideas and clauses. *See also* POLYSYNDETON.

acmeism The Acmeists were a group or school of Russian poets, who, early in the 20th c., began a new anti-symbolist movement. Much of their work and their theories were published in the magazine *Apollon*. They were in favour of an Apollonian (*q.v.*) lucidity and definiteness and strove for texture (*q.v.*) in their verse. The movement did not last very long (it seems to have faded out by *c.* 1920) but it included some distinguished poets: principally, Nikolai Gumilyev (1886–1921), Osip Mandelstam (1891–1940?) and Anna Akhmatova (1889–1967), who is still highly regarded as a writer of lyric (*q.v.*) poems.

acroama (Gk 'something heard') Two meanings may be distinguished; (a) a dramatic entertainment or a recital, during a meal or on some such occasion; (b) a lecture to the initiated; for instance, a discourse given by a *guru*, professor or comparable Gamaliel.

acronym (Gk *acron*, 'tip, end' + *onyma*, 'name') A word formed from or based on the initial letters or syllables of other words. For example: ENSA (*E*ntertainments *N*ational *S*ervices *A*ssociation); NAAFI (*N*avy, *A*rmy and *A*irforce *I*nstitute); NATO (*N*orth *A*tlantic *T*reaty *O*rganization); NIMBY (*N*ot *I*n *M*y *B*ack *Y*ard); OPEC (*O*rganization of *P*etroleum *E*xporting *C*ountries); PEN (*P*oets, *P*laywrights, *E*ditors, *E*ssayists and *N*ovelists); RADAR (*Ra*dio *D*etection *a*nd *R*anging). The economy of characters offered by acronymic phrasing has made them a convention of email, mobile phone texting and new communications media generally. As well as the ubiquitous 'asap' ('as soon as possible'), common informal shorthands include 'imho' (in my humble/honest opinion) and 'lol' ('laughing out loud'), among many others.

acrostic Apart from puzzles in newspapers and magazines the commonest kind of acrostic is a poem in which the initial letters of each line make a word or words when read downwards. An acrostic might also use the middle (mesostich) or final (telestich) letter of each line. In prose the first letter of each paragraph or sentence might make up a word.

The acrostic may have been first used as a kind of mnemonic device to aid oral transmission. In the Old Testament most of the acrostics belong to the alphabetical or abecedarian kind. The forming of words from the initials of words is also a form of acrostic. Chaucer used a simple acrostic device in *ABC*, a twenty-four stanza poem in which the first letter of the first word in each stanza is the appropriate letter of the alphabet, from A to Z. Some dramatists have put the titles of their plays in acrostic verses which give the argument (*q.v.*) of the play. A well-known instance is Ben Jonson's *Argument* prefacing *The Alchemist*.

A famous example of an 'all round' acrostic, which is a form of palindrome (*q.v.*), is the Cirencester word square, Roman in origin:

R O T A S
O P E R A
T E N E T
A R E P O
S A T O R

There has been much learned debate as to the possible meanings of this acrostic, which is known in a second form from an Egyptian papyrus of the late 4th or early 5th c. AD, thus:

S A T O R
A R E P O
T E N E T
O P E R A
R O T A S

Various permutations suggest that one meaning may be: 'the sower Arepo holds the wheels carefully'.

This, like many acrostics, may have magic and/or religious significance. In Ethiopia in the 6th c. the five words, corrupted to Sador, Alador, Danet, Adera and Rodas, were used as the names of the five nails of Christ's Cross.

The word square is known to have been used in France as a form of charm (*q.v.*); a citizen of Lyon was cured of madness by eating three crusts of bread (each inscribed with the square) while making five recitations of the Pater Noster in remembrance of the five wounds of Christ and the five nails. In the 19th c. in South America it was used as a charm against snake bites and also to aid childbirth. *See also* LOGOGRIPH.

acryology Incorrectly used or obsolete diction. *See* EUPHEMISM.

act A major division in a play. Each act may have one or more scenes. Greek plays were performed as continuous wholes, with interpolated comment from the Chorus (*q.v.*). Horace appears to have been the first to insist on a five-act structure. At some stage during the Renaissance the use of five acts became standard practice among French dramatists. Plays by Shakespeare and his contemporaries have natural breaks which can be taken as act divisions. In shaping their plays Elizabethan dramatists were influenced by Roman models (e.g. Seneca). The act divisions were marked as such by later editors. Ben Jonson was largely responsible for introducing the five-act structure in England. From the second half of the 17th c. the vast majority of plays were in five acts. The introduction of the proscenium and the curtain (unknown in the Elizabethan theatre) during the Restoration period (*q.v.*) had some influence on structure. In the Restoration period the curtain rose at the end of the prologue (which was spoken on the forestage) and stayed out of sight until the end of the play. By c. 1750 the curtain was dropped regularly to mark the end of an act. Ibsen (1828–1906) cut the number of acts to four. Dramatists like Chekhov (1860–1904) and Pirandello (1867–1936) also used four. Since early in the 20th c. most playwrights have preferred the three-act form, though the two-act play is not uncommon. In modern productions, especially in the cases of five- and four-act plays, there is only one curtain-drop and interval. Thus the first three or two acts are run together without a break. Many modern plays are written and presented in a sequence of scenes. Pirandello, Shaw, Brecht and Beckett, among others, have been responsible for an increased flexibility. T. W. Baldwin gives an illuminating account of Elizabethan methods in *Shakespeare's Five-Act Structure* (1947). *See* SCENE.

actant In narratology (*q.v.*), a term used by A. J. Greimas to describe the paired roles he argued as common to all stories: subject/object, sender/receiver, helper/opponent. *See* NARRATOLOGY.

action Two basic meanings may be distinguished: (a) the main story (in cinematic jargon 'story-line') of a play, novel, short story, narrative poem, etc.; (b) the main series of events that together constitute the plot (*q.v.*). Action is fundamental to drama, and implies motion forward. Much action is achieved without physical movement on stage, or even without anything being said. An essential part of action is the unfolding of character and plot. *See* CONFLICT.

activism At the end of the First World War activism (in German *Aktivismus*) denoted active political commitment or engagement among and by intellectuals. Historically it is closely associated with expressionism (*q.v.*), and as far as drama was concerned it required realistic solutions to social problems. It is particularly associated with Kurt Hiller, who organized the Neuer Club for expressionist poets, and with the magazine *Aktion*, founded in 1911 by Franz Pfempfert. Now, activism is predominantly a political term.

actual reader In reader-response theory (*q.v.*), the individual reader who brings his or her personal experience to a text and who combines with the implied reader (*q.v.*) to construct the meaning of a given text. *See* IMPLIED READER/ACTUAL READER.

adage A maxim or proverb (*qq.v.*). A well-known collection of adages was made by Erasmus and published as *Adagia* (1500).

adaptation The process by which one narrative form or medium is converted into another, for example a novel to film, a stage play to screenplay, or a classical poem to graphic novel. Adaptation theory has recently sought to develop its purpose and methodology beyond the straightforward identification of how close a retelling might be to the original. The move away from so-called 'fidelity' criticism, with its implicit attendant critical judgement (the film is rarely deemed as 'good as the book'), has opened up a theoretical debate concerning the nature of appropriation, authorship and the canon. Prominent examples include 'reimaginings' of Shakespeare, with Baz Luhrmann's film resetting *Romeo and Juliet* at Verona Beach a much-discussed example, popular television adaptations of classics in Austen and Dickens, and fictionalized versions of documented political events such as the Watergate scandal in *Frost/Nixon* or the death of Princess Diana in the film *The Queen*.

addendum (L 'something to be added') An addition or an appendix to a book (pl. addenda).

Addisonian In the manner or style of Joseph Addison (1672–1719): equable, relaxed, good-humoured and urbane. Some would also add complacent. Addison is chiefly famous for his contributions to the periodical essay (*q.v.*).

address A statement or speech of some formality, which may be delivered or written. It also denotes the kind of audience or reader an author intends. He may be self-communing or addressing a single person or a group of people.

adjunctio *See* ZEUGMA.

adnominatio *See* POLYPTOTON.

adonic A line consisting of a dactyl (*q.v.*) followed by a spondee (*q.v.*). The fourth and last line of the Sapphic (*q.v.*) are usually adonic.

adversaria (L *adversaria scripta*, 'things written on the side') Miscellaneous collections of notes. The kind of things that most writers accumulate in a notebook, day book, journal or diary. *See* ANNOTATION; COMMONPLACE BOOK; DIARY AND JOURNAL.

adynaton (Gk 'not possible') A form of hyperbole (*q.v.*) which involves the magnification of an event by reference to the impossible. There are famous examples in Marvell's poem *To His Coy Mistress* and his *The Definition of Love*, which begins:

> My Love is of a birth as rare
> As 'tis for object strange and high:
> It was begotten by despair
> Upon Impossibility.

Another famous example is Christ's statement: 'It is easier for a camel to go through the eye of a needle, than for a rich man to enter into the kingdom of God' (Matthew 19: 24, KJV).

ae freislighe In Irish prosody (*q.v.*), a quatrain (*q.v.*) of seven-syllable lines, rhyming abab. The poem should end with the same first syllable, line or word with which it begins.

Aeolic The name derives from the Greek dialect which Alcaeus and Sappho used for their poetry. Thus it applies to particular meters in which dactyls and trochees (*qq.v.*) are brought close together so that the choriambs (*see* CHORIAMBUS) are very noticeable. *See* ALCAICS; SAPPHIC ODE.

Aeschylean In the manner or style of Aeschylus (525–456 BC), the oldest of the great Greek tragedians whose works are currently extant (e.g. the Oresteian trilogy). Thus – sombre, magnificent, lofty, possessing grandeur.

aesthetic distance The term implies a psychological relationship between the reader (or viewer) and a work of art. It describes the attitude or perspective of a person in relation to a work, irrespective of whether it is interesting to that person. A reader may dislike a poem, for instance, for subjective reasons but this should not vitiate his objective reaction. The reader or critic has at once to be involved with – and detached from – what he is concentrating on. The work is 'distanced' so that it may be appreciated aesthetically and not confused with reality. The writer bears the responsibility for gauging and determining the distance (not in any spatial sense) at which his work should be viewed. If he bullies the reader into attending, then his reader may be repelled; if he undertakes too much, then his reader may not get the point.

The concept of aesthetic distance became established in the 20th c., though it appears to be inherent in 19th c. aesthetics; and, as long ago as 1790, Kant, in his *Critique of Judgement*, had already described the disinterestedness of our contemplation of works of art. In 1912, E. Bullough published an essay entitled *Psychical Distance as a Factor in Art and an Aesthetic Principle* (*British Journal of Psychology*, V) in which he defined 'psychical distance'. This is an important essay in the history of the concept. Since Bullough a number of critics have addressed themselves to the matter, including David Daiches in *A Study of Literature for Readers and Critics* (1948). More recently, Hans Robert Jauss, in developing his theory of the 'horizon of expectations' (*q.v.*), has given the term a very different additional significance. In his theory literary value is measured according to 'aesthetic distance', the degree to which a work departs from the 'horizon of expectations' of its first readers. *See* ALIENATION EFFECT; SUBJECTIVITY AND OBJECTIVITY; VIEWPOINT.

aestheticism A complex term 'pregnant' with many connotations. The actual word derives from Greek *aisthēta*, 'things perceptible by the senses'; and the Greek *aisthētēs* denotes 'one who perceives'. In 1750 A. T. Baumgarten published *Aesthetica*, a treatise (*q.v.*) on the criticism of taste considered as a philosophical theory. Gradually, the term *aesthetic* has come to signify something which pertains to the criticism of the beautiful or to the theory of taste. An *aesthete* is one who pursues and is devoted to the 'beautiful' in art, music and literature. And *aestheticism* is the term given to a movement, a cult, a mode of sensibility (a way of looking at and feeling about things) in the 19th c. Fundamentally, it entailed the point of view that art is self-sufficient and need serve no other purpose than its own ends. In other words, art is an end in itself and need not be (or should not be) didactic, politically committed, propagandist, moral – or anything else but itself; and it should not be judged by any non-aesthetic criteria (e.g. whether or not it is useful).

The origins of this movement or cult are to be found in the work of several German writers of the Romantic period (*q.v.*) – notably Kant, Schelling, Goethe and Schiller. They all agreed that art must be autonomous (that is, it should have the right of self-government) and from this it followed that the artist should not be beholden to anyone. From this, in turn, it followed that the artist was someone special, apart from others. Tennyson expressed the post-Romantic idea that the poet was superior to ordinary mortals:

> Vex not thou the poet's mind
> With thy shallow wit:
> Vex not thou the poet's mind;
> For thou canst not fathom it.

This attitude helps to explain why, later in the 19th c., the artist developed the image of being a Bohemian and a non-conformist. This was the long-term result of Romantic subjectivism and self-culture; of the cult of the individual ego and sensibility.

The influence of the Germans referred to above was very considerable, especially that of Goethe. Their ideas were diffused in Britain by Coleridge and Carlyle; in America by Edgar Allan Poe and Ralph Waldo Emerson; and in France by what we would now call 'culture vultures' in the shape of Madame de Staël, Victor Cousin and Théophile Jouffroy.

Approximately concurrent with the new aesthetic (or 'science of beauty') we have the doctrine of 'art for art's sake' (*q.v.*), and the movement known as Parnassianism.

Gautier's Preface to *Mademoiselle de Maupin* (1835) is often quoted as one of the earliest examples of a new aesthetic point of view. Thereafter, Poe and Baudelaire between them (and later Flaubert and Mallarmé) virtually launched aestheticism as a cult and their combined influence on the *symboliste* poets in France was very great (*see* SYMBOL AND SYMBOLISM). In England aestheticism was the result of French influence and native ideas.

The major implication of the new aesthetic standpoint was that art had no reference to life, and therefore had nothing to do with morality (Poe, for instance, had condemned the 'heresy of didacticism'), and in the later Victorian period we find Swinburne (who was much influenced by Baudelaire) proclaiming the art for art's sake theory. Walter Pater advocated the view that life itself should be treated in the spirit of art. His collection of essays *The Renaissance* (1873) had a deep influence on the poets of the 1890s, especially Wilde, Dowson, Lionel Johnson and Symons.

Art, not life. Art instead of life, or as an alternative to life. Life as art, or as a work of art. The outstanding example of the aesthete's withdrawal from life is J.-K. Huysman's *A rebours* (1884), in which the hero, Des Esseintes, seeks to create an entirely artificial life. The work 'illustrates' Wilde's flippant dictum that 'The first duty in life is to be as artificial as possible. What the second duty is no one has yet discovered.' Much of the attitude was neatly summarized by Villiers de l'Isle-Adam when he had his hero in *Axel* (1890) say: 'Live? Our servants will do that for us.'

In part aestheticism seems to have been a kind of reaction against the materialism and capitalism of the later Victorian period; and also against the Philistines who embodied what has been described as the 'bourgeois ethos'. Certainly one can detect a widespread disenchantment in the literature of the 'aesthetes', and especially in their poetry. By contrast it is noticeable that many novelists of the period (e.g. Dickens, Zola, Gissing and Samuel Butler) *were* dealing with reality in a forthright and unsqueamish fashion.

Aestheticism in poetry (as in art) is closely identified with the Pre-Raphaelites (*q.v.*) and shows a tendency to withdrawal or aversion. Many poets of the period strove for beautiful musical effects in their verses rather than for sense. They aspired to sensuousness and to what has become known as 'pure poetry' (*q.v.*). They also revived archaistic modes and archaic language (in this respect they were heavily influenced by Spenser and Keats) and revived an extensive use of Classical mythology as a framework for expressing ideas. Medievalism (*q.v.*) and the interest in chivalry and romance was an important part of the aesthetic cult. Tennyson, William Morris, D. G. Rossetti and Swinburne are the major writers in these respects. Tennyson's *The Lotos-Eaters* embodies many of the feelings inherent in the aesthetic ideal. Ah, why *should* life all labour be?

Among English/American artists Burne-Jones, D. G. Rossetti, William Morris, James McNeill Whistler and Aubrey Beardsley were the main exponents of aestheticism. It should also be noted that George Moore (an enthusiast for pure poetry), Arthur Symons and Edmund Gosse did much to popularize the works of French poets and painters in England in the 1890s.

Aestheticism is particularly associated with that decade; with Aubrey Beardsley, with Oscar Wilde (long the 'folk hero' or 'cult hero' of the aesthetic movement), with *The Yellow Book* (*q.v.*), with dandyism, with affectation, and with Max Beerbohm. But by the 1890s it was becoming less intense. As Beerbohm drolly observed: 'Beauty had existed long before 1880. It was Oscar Wilde who managed her début.' With this period, too, are associated ideas about the Bohemian and immoral life of the artist. The cult of Bohemianism (itself a kind of rejection of a commercially oriented society) had been influenced earlier in the century by Henri Murger's *Scènes de la vie de Bohème* (1851).

At its best aestheticism was a revitalizing influence in an age of ugliness, brutality, dreadful inequality and oppression, complacency, hypocrisy and Philistinism (*q.v.*). It was a genuine search for beauty and a realization that the beautiful has an independent value. At its worst it deteriorated into posturing affectation and mannerism, to vapid idealism and indeed to a kind of silliness which is not wholly dead. Nothing could be more 'Bohemian' than the postwar cultural revolution of the so-called 'freaked-out' society. 'Pop' is another kind of aestheticism, another kind of reaction against a corrupt and commercial world. *See* DECADENCE; PARNASSIANS.

affect/affect theory/affective criticism Affect theory is a recent interdisciplinary field devoted to the study of the role of affect and emotions and their various manifestations in human behaviour, culture and society. Gregory J. Seigworth and Melissa Gregg define affect as 'the name we give to those forces – visceral forces beneath, alongside, or generally *other than* conscious knowing, vital forces insisting beyond emotion – that can serve to drive us toward movement and extension'. Affect theory draws much on the work of psychologist Silvan Tomkins (1911–99) and his notion of positive, negative and neutral affects. For Tomkins, affect is a biological manifestation of emotion which starts in the face rather than inwardly, so the affect of shame, for example, is manifested through blushing. Not all theorists of affect make a distinction between affect and emotion, or their biological and cultural manifestations, and critics such as Sara Ahmed insist rather on their messiness and interrelatedness. Affect theory has also been influenced by a number of critical approaches, including psychoanalytic criticism (*q.v.*), experimental psychology, phenomenological accounts of subjectivity as embodied, Gilles Deleuze's theory of assemblages between bodies and worlds, and cognitive and neurosciences, particularly the work of neuroscientist Antonio Damasio.

The 1995 essays by Eve Kosofsky Sedgwick and Adam Frank, *Shame in the Cybernetic Fold: Reading Silvan Tomkins*, and Brian Massumi's *The Autonomy of Affect* mark the so-called 'affective turn' in criticism, which represents an attempt to turn away from the poststructuralist 'linguistic turn' (*q.v.*) in the latter half of the 20th c. and produce more politically engaged work. Recently, there have been a string of books, published mainly by queer, feminist, postcolonial and disability theorists, that centre on examining negative affects in particular and how certain affects are racialized or gendered, attachments and matters of belonging and not belonging, ordinary feelings, and public affects such as happiness, guilt and melancholia. Some of the most important publications include Lauren Berlant, *Cruel Optimism* (2011); Eve Kosofsky Sedgwick, *Touching Feeling: Affect, Performativity, Pedagogy* (2003); Paul Gilroy, *After Empire: Melancholia or Convivial Culture?* (2004); Sara Ahmed, *The Cultural Politics of Emotion* (2004); Sianne Ngai, *Ugly Feelings* (2005); Elspeth Probyn, *Blush: Faces of Shame* (2005); and Brian Massumi, *Parables for the Virtual: Movement, Affect, Sensation* (2002). *See also* CULTURAL MATERIALISM; ETHICAL CRITICISM; QUEER THEORY.

affectation The adoption of a mode or style of writing unsuited to the matter, form or occasion. In the 18th c. writers were particularly sensitive to inappropriateness of this kind. *See* DECORUM.

affective fallacy A term defined by Wimsatt and Beardsley (*The Verbal Icon*, 1954) as 'a confusion between the poem and its results (what it is and what it does)'. It is said to be a critical error of evaluating a work of art in terms of 'its results in the mind of the audience'. It would be a mistake, therefore, for a reader to conclude that Spenser's *Faerie Queene* was a bad poem because it inspired in him a repugnance to Protestantism. The principles involved in this fallacy can also be applied to prose works. *See* INTENTIONAL FALLACY.

affective stylistics *See* READER-RESPONSE THEORY.

afflatus (L 'blown upon') As far as poetry is concerned, the equivalent of inspiration (*q.v.*). The usual phrase is 'divine afflatus'. The implications are that a writer's inspiration is vouchsafed to him by some supranormal or supernatural power, like a Muse (*q.v.*) or the gods. *See* DONNÉE; FANCY AND IMAGINATION; INVENTION; LIGNE DONNÉE.

African-American Studies An interdisciplinary academic field (previously more widely known as 'Black Studies') devoted to the study of the culture, history, politics and sociology of African-Americans. The field has its roots in attempts by African-American historians in the 19th c., such as W. E. B. Du Bois, to consider slavery and its aftermath from the perspective of blacks. African-American Studies became institutionalized in American universities during the 1960s and 1970s in the wake of the Civil Rights Movement and rising Black Nationalism. Many programmes, usually entitled 'Black Studies', were implemented in response to the demands of black students for greater inclusion in mainstream American life and for an education more relevant to their needs. Implicit in the assertion of the value of African-American/Black Studies is an indictment of American scholarship's claims to objectivity and universality. Such presumptions were deemed ideological, veiling content and perspectives which were largely white. Indeed, practitioners in the field are typically motivated not only by the goal of achieving academic objectivity but also by a sense of social responsibility; they aim to enhance understanding of black experience in order to help transform the social conditions of African-Americans. Literary analysis has always had an important place in African-American Studies, with black writing considered an important, enduring vehicle for self-expression in virtually all historical periods of African-American experience. As well as focusing on prominent writers and key literary movements such as the Harlem Renaissance and the Black Arts Movement (*qq.v.*), scholars have also sought to recover and explicate earlier materials such as slave narratives (*q.v.*). *See also* BLACK THEATRE; ETHNIC STUDIES.

afsana Most commonly translated as 'short story', but can also be rendered as 'tale' or 'romance'. The most popular current literary form in Urdu and Hindi literature, it was pioneered by Munshi Premchand and its major practitioners include Saadat Hasan Manto, Ahmed Nadeem Qasmi and Krishan Chander.

after-piece A short play, often a one-act farce or comedy (*qq.v.*), presented after the main play in a programme, and regardless of whether that play was a tragedy or comedy or any other form of drama. They became popular in the 18th c. as a result of the introduction of the half-price system – an entrance fee for latecomers. Theatrical managers had to pad out a programme for these patrons and felt justified in charging them. Originally, they had been allowed in for nothing. The half-price arrangement prevailed in London and elsewhere until at least the 1870s. In the 18th c. not a few playwrights wrote notable after-pieces. David Garrick (1717–79), Samuel Foote (1720–77) and Arthur Murphy (1727–1805) excelled at them. Murphy wrote some very good two-act after-pieces, including *The Apprentice* (1756), *The Upholsterer* (1758), *The Citizen* (1761) and *What We Must All Come To* (1764). *See* CURTAIN RAISER.

agent, literary The first agents began to appear towards the end of the 19th c. and A. P. Watt (1834–1914) is often taken to have been the first. Among his clients were Thomas Hardy, Rudyard Kipling and Rider Haggard. Other notable agents were J. B. Pinker (1863–1922), Curtis Brown (1866–1945) and John Farquharson. For many years there was a good deal of opposition to agents, and authors were by no means in agreement as to their desirability and usefulness. Nowadays it is rare to find an author who has not got one. An agent's job is many-sided and includes the placing of manuscripts with publishers/editors/theatrical managements, etc., negotiating contracts and rights, dealing with legal matters and advising in general. It has been said that a successful relationship between author and agent is comparable to a successful marriage.

age of reason A term applied to the Restoration and Augustan periods (*qq.v.*). So named because it was a period when the workings of reason were revered. Form, balance, restraint, harmony, decorum (*q.v.*) and order are some of the main characteristics of the literature of the period. The term also has strong political connotations deriving from the title of Thomas Paine's 1794 pamphlet *The Age of Reason*, which attacked institutionalized religion. *See* ENLIGHTENMENT; NEOCLASSICISM.

agitprop drama The term 'agitprop' is a conflation of the words 'agitation' and 'propaganda' (*q.v.*) and derives from the name of the Department of Agitation and Propaganda created in September 1920 as part of the Central Committee Secretariat of the Communist Party of the Soviet Union. The Bolsheviks wished to use art as a weapon in the revolutionary struggle, and the agitprop department mobilized culture across the vast and largely illiterate country to stimulate people's understanding of and involvement in such important matters as health, sanitation, literacy or the military situation. In drama, the Blue Blouse movement, named after the industrial clothes a worker would wear, drew on visual forms, such as cinematic montage and folk art, as well as on avant-garde (*q.v.*) techniques to develop its own accessible and popular forms, which included 'Living Newspapers' and revues (*qq.v.*). The troupes typically performed away from conventional theatres, in pubs and clubs, on wagons and platforms. They were predominantly amateur and reached the height of their influence in the mid-1920s, but were eclipsed by the rise of official, dogmatic socialist realism (*q.v.*).

In the wake of the Russian Revolution, agitprop drama spread to Europe and North America. Agitprop was seen as a proletarian antidote to bourgeois drama and in each country it evolved as a mix of the imported model and indigenous traditions. Germany developed a powerful agitprop movement until its suppression by the Nazis. German troupes were noted for their cabaret forms and choral speaking, and such forms of dramatic presentation influenced the development of epic theatre and the *Lehrstück* (*qq.v.*), or didactic play. Hard-hitting agitprop, often linked to workers' campaigns, resurfaced in Europe and America at another period of international and political turmoil in the late 1960s and 1970s. Theatre movements inspired by agitprop methods also arose in developing countries, such as the Theatre of the Oppressed, which originated in Brazil but now is global in its scope. *See also* DOCUMENTARY THEATRE.

agnominatio A meaningful play on words which depends upon the repetition of a word with a subtly altered sound or letter. An example is Derrida's coined term *différance* as distinct from *différence*. *See* PARONOMASIA; PUN.

agon (Gk 'contest') In Greek drama a verbal conflict between two characters, each one aided by half the Chorus (*q.v.*). By extension, the term might also be used to refer more generally to the impelling conflict of any dramatic work. *See* ANTAGONIST; PROTAGONIST.

agrarian movement A 'back to grass roots', 'back to the soil', and 'back to nature' cult that had some vogue in Germany and America early in the 20th c. Sherwood Anderson was one of its examplars. *See* NEW CRITICISM.

aiodos An itinerant Greek singer of songs and poems. Often used to denote the composer of works in the classical oral tradition such as the *Iliad* and *Odyssey*. *See also* GUSLAR; MINNESINGER; SCOP; SKALD; TROUBADOUR; TROUVÈRE.

air It usually denotes a song (*q.v.*), tune or melody, or all three. Frequently used in the late 16th c. and during the 17th when many collections were published. For example: John Dowland's *Second Book of Airs* (1600); Robert Jones's *First Book of Songs and Airs* (1600). In *The Tempest*, Caliban uses the word in this sense: 'Be not afeard. The isle is full of noises,/ Sounds and sweet airs that give delight and hurt not' (III, ii, 148–9).

akhyana An Indian beast epic or folk tale (*qq.v.*) in prose. The central part, or that which deals with the climax, is in verse.

alazôn The braggart in Greek comedy, a stock character who is easily duped by the more intelligent and dissembling *eirôn* (*q.v.*). Examples of the type in drama are the *miles gloriosus* of Plautus, Molière's Tartuffe and, conceivably, Falstaff. *See also* BRAGGADOCIO; STOCK CHARACTER.

alba Provençal for aubade (*q.v.*).

album (L *albus*, 'white') For the Roman an *album* was a white tablet or register on which the praetor's edicts and other such public notices were recorded. The modern album dates from the 16th c. and comprises a blank book for the insertion of photographs, autographs, newspaper cuttings, excerpts, etc.

In short, it is a kind of scrapbook. One of the earliest examples is the *album amicorum*, a 'book of friends' which might comprise a collection of emblems, epigrams or salutations, passed between early modern academics.

Alcaics   A four-lined stanza or strophe (*qq.v.*) named after the Greek poet Alkaios (Alcaeus, a native of Lesbos, late 7th to early 6th c. BC). The arrangement, predominantly dactylic, is:

$$7 \ / \ \cup \ / \ 7 \ / \ \cup \ \cup \ / \ \cup \ \cup$$
$$7 \ / \ \cup \ / \ 7 \ / \ \cup \ \cup \ / \ \cup \ \cup$$
$$7 \ / \ \cup \ / \ 7 \ / \ \cup \ / \ /$$
$$/ \ \cup \ \cup \ / \ \cup \ \cup \ / \ \cup \ / \ 7$$

The mark indicating an unstressed syllable placed above a stress mark denotes a possible variation.

The scheme was often used between the 16th and 18th c. by Italian poets, but has seldom been popular in England. However, Swinburne, Clough, Tennyson and R. L. Stevenson experimented with Alcaics. A well-known example is Tennyson's sixteen-line poem on Milton which begins:

> Ó míghtў- | moúthĕd ĭn | véntŏr ŏf | hármŏniĕs,
> Ó skílled to síng ŏf | Tíme ŏr Ĕ | térnĭtў,
> Gód-gíftĕd | órgăn- | vóice ŏf | Énglănd,
> Míltŏn, ă | náme tŏ rĕ | sóund fŏr | ágĕs.

See AEOLIC; DACTYL; SAPPHIC ODE.

Alcmanic verse   A metrical form used by and named after Alcman (7th c. BC). It consists of a dactylic tetrameter (*q.v.*) line. It was used in Greek dramatic poetry, and is occasionally found in Latin dramatic poetry. The Alcmanic strophe (*q.v.*) combines a dactylic hexameter (*q.v.*) with an Archilochian (*q.v.*) verse. *See* DACTYL.

aleatory writing   (L *aleatorius*, from *aleator, alea*, 'dice') 'Aleatory' means depending on the throw of a die, and it here refers to writing (as well as to the composition of music, sculpture and painting) achieved by some random means, by leaving things to chance or accident. No doubt many creative artists have depended on the element of luck and chance, the totally unexpected; and the history of inspiration (*q.v.*) provides many instances of fortuitous experience which have helped in the creative act. In fact, one might go so far as to say that it may be a fundamental part of the process of inspiration and invention.

Those who practise aleatoric techniques are somewhat more deliberate. They do not leave things to chance; they create the opportunities of chance. There is a certain 'method' in their 'madness', as it were. For example, a writer may write down a large number of words on different pieces of paper, throw the pieces of paper into the air, see how (like dice) they fall – and then join the words together according to their random disposition. Or, he might shuffle them like cards and then record the sequence that ensues. There are a number of ways of setting about it.

William Burroughs, for example, is well known for his 'cut-up' technique in which he snips up pages and allows the random fall of the words and phrases to guide him. B. S. Johnson composed *The Unfortunates* – a 'novel in a box'. It consists of a box of separately bound chapters which the reader is invited to rearrange as he or she pleases and to read in any order. Tom Phillips's *Humument* is the result of taking a Victorian novel called *A Human Document* by W. H. Mallock and inking out words and letters to find a book within a book. Ian Hamilton Finlay has also made various experiments of an aleatory kind in the creation of concrete poetry (*q.v.*). Mallarmé's *Coup de dés* is a good example of a poem which at any rate *appears* to be the result of aleatoric techniques. It is a long poem about a shipwreck in which phrases are repeated in lines stretched right across the page; the original version was printed on very large pages. Dream sequences have also been used as aleatoric guides. De Chirico's novel *Hebdomeros* comprises a series of linked dream sequences. Many other experimental efforts might be cited. In music and painting, too, we find aleatoric methods. The composer John Cage has been successful with them; Jackson Pollock tried them with many paintings. *See also* ALTERNATIVE LITERATURE; ANTI-NOVEL; POSTMODERNISM.

alejandrino A Spanish verse form of two hemistichs (*q.v.*) with seven syllables each. It derives from Alexander the Great, whose legendary deeds were celebrated in this meter in the *Libro de Alejandre* (c. 1240), a *mester de clerecía* (*q.v.*) poem.

aleluyas (Heb *hallelu*, 'praise ye' + *Jāh*, 'Jehovah') Thus *hallelujah*, *alleluiah*. A Spanish term for verses printed below wood-block prints or other illustrations on broadsheets or broadsides (*q.v.*). At first they were basically religious; later they became secular. They were popular from the end of the 15th c. until some way into the 19th c. *See also* PLIEGO SUELTO.

Alexandrianism The term refers to the works, styles and critical principles of the Alexandrian (Greek) writers who flourished between c. 325 and 30 BC. Some of the main forms they used were: elegy, epigram, epyllion, lyric (*qq.v.*). They also wrote drama. Much of their work was marked by ornateness and obscurity (*q.v.*).

alexandrine In French prosody a line of twelve syllables and known as *tétramètre* (*q.v.*). It has been the standard meter of French poetry since the 16th c., especially in dramatic and narrative forms. The equivalent in English verse is the iambic hexameter (*q.v.*). The earliest alexandrines occur in *Le Pèlerinage de Charlemagne à Jérusalem*, an early 12th c. *chanson de gestes* (*q.v.*), but the term probably takes its name from a later poem – the *Roman d'Alexandre* (towards the end of the 12th c.). The meter was used by Ronsard and members of the Pléiade (*q.v.*) and was perfected by the great 17th c. French dramatists. These two lines are from Racine's *Andromaque* (1, ii, 173–4):

> La Grèce en ma faveur est trop inquiétée:
> De soins plus importants je l'ai crue agitée.

It has never been a popular meter in English verse, largely because it is rather unwieldy, just a little too long; though Spenser used it to good effect for the last line of his Spenserian stanza (*q.v.*) in *The Faerie Queene*. Other English poets to use it fairly successfully were Drayton in *Poly-Olbion*, Browning in *Fifine at the Fair*, and Bridges in *The Testament of Beauty*. A classic example of its use occurs in Pope's *Essay on Criticism*:

> A needless Alexandrine ends the song,
> Thát, líke | ă wóund|ĕd snáke, | drágs ĭts | slów léngth ălóng.

See TRIMETRE.

alienation As defined by Marx in the *Economic and Philosophical Manuscripts* (1844), alienation is a specific historical condition in which man experiences a separation from nature, other human beings and especially the products of his labour. Since man creates himself through labour, all of these forms of alienation imply an alienation of man from himself. Alienation for Hegel had been a philosophical concept expressing one aspect of the process of self-objectification: in the dialectical process, Spirit objectified itself in nature (a stage in which it was alienated from itself) and then returned to itself. Marx regards alienation as a product of the evolution of division of labour, private property and the state: when these phenomena reach an advanced stage, as in capitalist society, the individual experiences the entire objective world as a conglomeration of alien forces standing over and above him. In this sense, alienation can only be overcome by the revolutionary abolition of the economic system based on private property.

  Alienation has also been a central concept in sociology, a centrality deriving in part from Max Weber's recognition of the individual's feeling of helplessness in a 'disenchanted' world governed by rational, bureaucratic and impersonal institutions. Existentialists, notably Heidegger and Sartre, have also centralized this concept, viewing it not as the symptom of given historical configurations but as a defining condition of existence. The concept of alienation has also reverberated widely through the various branches of psychology.

alienation effect Loose English translation of the German *Verfremdungseffekt*, Brecht's term for a key principle of his dramatic theory of epic theatre (*q.v.*), sometimes abbreviated to A-effect. The theory dictated that both audience and actors ought to maintain a critical detachment from the play rather than submitting to the staged illusion or easy emotional identification with character and situation. Techniques deployed to disrupt the impulse towards realism might include the use of songs, captions, montage, artificial narrative interventions, and role reversals. Together, such techniques persistently draw attention to the work as a dramatic illusion and construct. The purpose of such 'distancing' or 'estrangement' is to resist passive escapism and instead to compel reflection on the characters as participants in broader historical, social and political processes. *See also* COMMITMENT; CONVENTION; EPIC THEATRE; ESTRANGEMENT; ILLUSION; SOCIALIST REALISM.

alinéa An indented line used to indicate a new paragraph. *See* PUNCTUATION.

aljamiado A composition in a Romance language, usually Spanish, written in Arabic characters. Aljamiado are particularly associated with the Moriscos of late 16th c. Iberia and developed as a means of preserving Islamic tradition following the prohibitions of Philip II of Spain concerning the Arabic language.

allegory (Gk *allegoria*, 'speaking otherwise') An allegory is a story or image with several layers of meaning: behind the literal or surface meaning lie one or more secondary meanings, of varying degrees of complexity. The origins of allegory as a narrative strategy are ancient and certainly pre-date literate culture. Much myth (*q.v.*), for example, adopts allegory in its endeavours to explain phenomena through analogy and correspondence. Allegory is closely related to other literary forms, for example the fable, parable and exemplum (*qq.v.*), and it has sometimes been viewed as extended metaphor (*q.v.*). In these various guises, allegory may be satirical, salutary or moralistic in purpose. The form may be narrative or pictorial (or both, as in emblem-books, *q.v.*)

In literature, early examples of allegory include Plato's celebrated story of the cave in *The Republic* and the influential *Psychomachia* by Prudentius (4th c. AD) which instituted a mode of psychological allegory, the externalization of a struggle within. In medieval literature, allegory underpins the dream vision genre (*q.v.*) in which the narrator customarily falls asleep at the outset of the tale and undergoes an experience with strong symbolical and allegorical overtones. The morality plays (*q.v.*) of the same period are essentially dramatized allegories in which personified virtues and vices act out the cosmic struggle for the soul of Mankind. John Bunyan's *The Pilgrim's Progress* (1678) draws upon this same tradition to produce an extended allegory of Christian salvation. In early modern English literature, Spenser's epic *The Faerie Queene* is perhaps the most ambitious allegory, or 'dark conceit' as the poet terms it in his prefatory letter. More overtly radical in their signification are the allegorical satires of Dryden, exemplified in his *Absalom and Achitophel* (1681) and *The Hind and the Panther* (1687) which treat contemporary controversies in religion and politics. With its general privileging of realism over stylized signification, there are perhaps fewer incontrovertible examples of allegory in the novel, although notable exceptions include an early example of the form in Swift's *Gulliver's Travels* (1726) and Orwell's 20th c. fable *Animal Farm*.

In general, the use of allegory is fundamental to the scriptures of all the major religions. It is highlighted in the New Testament, where much of Christ's teaching is conducted in parables, and in the Qur'an, where, on numerous occasions, God is said to speak in parables to humankind. Allegory, largely typological, pervades both the Old and New Testaments. The events in the Old Testament were considered 'types' or 'figures' of events in the New Testament. In *The Song of Solomon*, for instance, Solomon is seen as a 'type' of Christ and the Queen of Sheba represents the Church, as explained by Matthew (12:42). The Paschal Lamb was also seen as a 'type' of Christ.

Scriptural allegory was mostly based on a vision of the universe as bifurcated into two worlds, the spiritual and the physical. The visible world was seen as a revelation of the invisible. St Thomas Aquinas analysed this kind of allegory in his *Summa* (13th c.) in terms of four levels of meaning or interpretation. This fourfold exegesis can be applied, for instance, to the City of Jerusalem. On the literal level, it is the Holy City; allegorically, it stands for the Church militant; morally or as a trope, it signifies the just soul; and anagogically (*q.v.*) or mystically, it represents the Church triumphant. In his *Convivio* and his *Letter to Can Grande Della Scala* Dante elaborated this theory in literary terms.

allegro   A musical term which, when used as a literary term, means much the same thing: in a lively and brisk manner. The rhythm and movement of Milton's *L'Allegro*, from which these lines are taken, indicate the meaning:

> Haste thee nymph, and bring with thee
> Jest and youthful Jollity,
> Quips and cranks, and wanton wiles,
> Nods, and becks, and wreathèd smiles,
> Such as hang on Hebe's cheek,
> And love to live in dimple sleek;
> Sport that wrinkled Care derides,
> And Laughter holding both his sides.
> Come, and trip it as you go
> On the light fantastic toe.

alliteration   (L 'repeating and playing upon the same letter') A figure of speech in which consonants, especially at the beginning of words or stressed syllables, are repeated. It is a very old device indeed in English verse (older than rhyme) and is common in verse generally. It is used occasionally in prose. In OE poetry, alliteration was a continual and essential part of the metrical scheme and until the late Middle Ages was often used thus. However, alliterative verse (*q.v.*) becomes increasingly rare after the end of the 15th c. and alliteration – like assonance, consonance and onomatopoeia (*qq.v.*) – tends more to be reserved for the achievement of the special effect.

There are many classic examples, like Coleridge's famous description of the sacred river Alph in *Kubla Khan*:

> Five miles meandering with a mazy motion

Many others are less well known, like this from the first stanza of R. S. Thomas's *The Welsh Hill-Country*:

> Too far for you to see
> The fluke and the foot-rot and the fat maggot
> Gnawing the skin from the small bones,
> The sheep are grazing at Bwlch-y-Fedwen,
> Arranged romantically in the usual manner
> On a bleak background of bald stone.

Alliteration is common in tongue-twisters (*q.v.*) and jingles (*q.v.*). It is also used in nonsense verse (*q.v.*), as in:

> Be lenient with lobsters, and ever kind to crabs,
> And be not disrespectful to cuttle-fish or dabs;
> Chase not the Cochin-China, chaff not the ox obese,
> And babble not of feather-beds in company with geese.

See also ASSONANCE; CACOPHONY; INTERNAL RHYME; RHYME.

alliterative prose A good deal of OE and ME prose alliterates and uses some of the techniques of alliterative verse (*q.v.*). In OE Aelfric (*c.* 955–*c.* 1010) and Wulfstan (d. 1023) wrote outstanding alliterative prose. Notable instances in ME belong to what is called 'The Katherine Group': five works of devotional prose, in MS Bodley 34, dating from *c.* 1190–1225. They are *Seinte Marherete, Seinte Iuliene, Seinte Katerine* (hence the group name), *Sawles Warde* and *Hali Meiðhad*. They come from Herefordshire.

alliterative revival A general term for a collection of poems composed in the second half of the 14th c. Alliteration had been the basic device in OE poetry and was then again used, especially by Langland in *Piers Plowman* and by the author of *Sir Gawain and the Green Knight*. See ALLITERATION; ALLITERATIVE VERSE.

alliterative verse Alliterative meter is an essential feature of Germanic prosody. Alliteration (*q.v.*) was a basic part of the structure. Nearly all OE verse is heavily alliterative, and the pattern is fairly standard – with either two or three stressed syllables in each line alliterating. This example is from *Beowulf* (8th c.):

> þa waes on burgum   Beowulf Scyldinga,
> leof leodcyning   longe þrage
> folcum gefræge   fæder ellor hwearf,
> aldor of earde –,   oþ þaet him eft onwoc
> heah Healfdene.

In succeeding centuries the systematic pattern is gradually loosened. These lines from the beginning of Passus III of Langland's *Piers Plowman* (14th c.) show some of the changes:

> Now is Mede þe mayde · and namo of hem alle
> With bedellus & wiþ bayllyues   brouȝt bifor þe kyng.
> The kyng called a clerke   can I nouȝt his name,
> To take Mede þe mayde   and make hire at ese.

Another but similar alliterative style is adopted in *Sir Gawain and the Green Knight* (c. 1350–75):

> The brygge watz brayde doun, and þe brode ȝatez
> Vnbarred and born open vpon boþe halue.
> þe burne blessed hym bilyue, and þe bredez passed;
> Prayses þe porter bifore þe prynce kneled.

The poem *Pearl* (c. 1375) is also elaborately alliterative, and many of the Medieval Mystery Plays (*q.v.*) were written in rough alliterative verse. These lines come from the start of the York version of *The Harrowing of Hell*:

> ⟨Iesus. M⟩anne on molde, be meke to me,
> And haue thy Maker in þi mynde,
> And thynke howe I haue tholid for þe
> With pereles paynes for to be pyned.

The use of alliteration dwindled steadily during the 15th c. and the only notable poet to make much use of it in Tudor times was John Skelton. Shakespeare used it occasionally, as in Sonnet XXX:

> When to the sessions of sweet silent thought
> I summon up remembrance of things past,
> I sigh the lack of many a thing I sought,
> And with old woes new wail my dear time's waste.

It was not until late in the 19th c. that Gerard Manley Hopkins revived the alliterative tradition. He experimented a great deal. These lines from *Spring* suggest how:

> Nothing is so beautiful as Spring –
> When weeds, in wheels, shoot long and lovely and lush;
> Thrush's eggs look little low heavens, and thrush
> Through the echoing timber does so rinse and wring
> The ear, it strikes like lightnings to hear him sing;

Later Ezra Pound also experimented with it. In 1912 he published *Ripostes*, which contained a fine rendering of the OE elegiac lyric *The Seafarer*. These are the opening lines:

> May I for my own self song's truth reckon,
> Journey's jargon, how I in harsh days
> Hardship endured oft.
> Bitter breast-cares have I abided,
> Known on my keel many a care's hold,

> And dire sea-surge, and there I oft spent
> Narrow nightwatch nigh the ship's head
> While she tossed close to cliffs.

Three more recent poets have shown mastery of this form: Richard Eberhart, C. Day Lewis and W. H. Auden. Eberhart's *Brotherhood of Men* is a distinguished experiment; so are C. Day Lewis's *As One Who Wanders into Old Workings* and *Flight to Australia*. The latter, particularly, shows the influence of the OE meter and the style of Langland. The third stanza runs:

> Fog first, a wet blanket, a kill-joy, the primrose-of-morning's
>   blight,
> Blotting out the dimpled sea, the ample welcome of land,
> The gay glance from the bright
> Cliff-face behind, snaring the sky with treachery, sneering
> At hope's loss of height. But they charged it, flying blind;
> They took a compass-bearing against that dealer of doubt,
> As a saint when the field of vision is fogged gloriously steels
> His spirit against the tainter of air, the elusive taunter:
> They climbed to win a way out,
> Then downward dared till the moody waves snarled at their
>   wheels.

W. H. Auden made skilful use of alliterative meters, as in *The Age of Anxiety*:

> To the Cross or to *Clarté* or to Common Sense
> Our passions pray but to primitive totems
> As absurd as they are savage; science or no science,
> It is Bacchus or the Great Boyg or Baal-Peor,
> Fortune's Ferris-wheel or the physical sound
> Of our own names which they actually adore as their
> Ground and goal.

allonym A substitute name, often historical, used by an author. *See* PSEUDONYM.

allusion Usually an implicit reference, perhaps to another work of literature or art, to a person or an event. It is often a kind of appeal to a reader to share some experience with the writer. An allusion may enrich the work by association (*q.v.*) and give it depth. When using allusions a writer tends to assume an established literary tradition, a body of common knowledge with an audience sharing that tradition and an ability on the part of the audience to 'pick up' the reference. However, the allusiveness of some poets, particularly those in the modernist (*q.v.*) tradition such as Pound or Eliot, might be considered to be more specialized, even deliberately esoteric, challenging the reader and critic to untangle multiple references. In this sense, allusion is one marker of intertextuality (*q.v.*). The following kinds may be roughly distinguished: (a) a reference to events and people (e.g. there are a number in Dryden's and Pope's satires); (b) reference to facts about the author himself (e.g. Shakespeare's puns on Will; Donne's pun on Donne, Anne and Undone); (c) a metaphorical allusion (there are many examples in T. S. Eliot's work); (d) an imitative allusion (e.g. Johnson's to Juvenal in *London*); (e) a structural allusion (e.g. Milton's division of the 1674 edition of *Paradise Lost* into twelve books after Virgil's *Aeneid*).

almanac A book or table which comprises a calendar (*q.v.*) of the year which shows: days, weeks and months; a register of feast days and saints' days; a record of astronomical phenomena. Sometimes it contains meteorological forecasts and agricultural advice on seasonal activities. The word may be connected with late Greek *almenikhiaká* and we find it in medieval Latin as *almanac*. In Roger Bacon's *Opus Majus* (*c.* 1367) the term denoted permanent tables which showed the apparent movements of the stars and planets.

Among the earliest were the 'clog' almanacs of the Danes and Normans. These crude tables consisted of blocks of wood on which the days of the year were notched. The first printed almanac dates from 1457. Most English almanacs were published by the Stationers' Company, and they became very popular in 17th c. England, especially in the period 1640–1700. Besides astronomical and astrological tables they contained a wide range of information, including feast days, agricultural notes, prophecies and verses. Particularly well-known compilers and publishers were Richard Allestree, John Gadbury and William Lilly (1602–81), the astrologer, who all published almanacs for some forty years. These often sold in huge quantities (up to 300,000 per year). The best known to us now is the *Vox Stellarum* (1700) of Francis Moore (1657–1714), a physician and astrologer. This was a collection of weather predictions and was intended to promote the sales of his pills. It survives as *Old Moore's Almanac* and still sells in large numbers. *Whitaker's Almanack* (first published in 1868) is a compendious volume of general information about the world.

A different kind is the *Almanach de Gotha*, which has been published annually since 1763. It gives royal and aristocratic genealogies and statistics of the world.

a lo divino (Sp 'in religious terms') A literary treatment through which popular secular themes were transformed into religious themes by the use of Christian allegory, metaphor or symbol (*qq.v.*). It was particularly common during the Golden Age (*q.v.*). *See also* SYMBOL AND SYMBOLISM.

als ob (G 'as if') In 1876 Hans Vaihinger put forward the idea that it was a prerequisite of any idealism that we must act on the assumption that something presented as art is as it appears. Thus it is *as if* we were watching a real representation. *See* WILLING SUSPENSION OF DISBELIEF.

altar poem Also known as a *carmen figuratum* (L 'shaped poem'), it is a poem in which the verses or stanzas are so arranged that they form a design on the page and take the shape of the subject of the poem. The device is believed to have been first used by Persian poets of the 5th c. and it was revived during the Renaissance period when it was practised by a number of poets – including Wither, Quarles, Benlowes, Herrick and Herbert. Puttenham, in his *The Arte of English Poesie* (1589), devoted a complete chapter to the shaped poem and provided a number of interesting illustrations. Herbert's *The Altar* and his *Easter Wings* are two particularly well-known instances. The latter is arranged thus:

> Lord, who createdst man in wealth and store,
> Though foolishly he lost the same,
> Decaying more and more,
> Till he became
> Most poore:
> With thee
> O let me rise
> As larks, harmoniously,
> And sing this day thy victories:
> Then shall the fall further the flight in me.

The second stanza is arranged in the same fashion.

A well-known recent example is Dylan Thomas's *Vision and Prayer*, a series of twelve devotional poems; but the device has been exploited with other motifs. Rabelais, for example, wrote a bottle-shaped song, his *epilenie*, in honour of Bacchus; and Apollinaire wrote a poem called *Il pleut* (in *Calligrammes*) which was printed so that the letters trickled down the page like falling tears. *See also* CONCRETE POETRY; EMBLEM-BOOK; PATTERN POETRY.

altercatio (L 'argument') A Roman legal term signifying rapid cross-questionings and replies. Applied to literature, it refers to a series of short questions and answers. Common in drama, dialogue and debate. *See* STICHOMYTHIA.

alterity A term denoting difference, employed to distinguish between notions of the 'other' as opposed to the 'self'. Levinas first extrapolated the concept to incorporate cultural 'selves' and 'others'. By extension, the term is now used widely in postcolonial discourse to refer to the ways in which disparate cultures, nations and religions both perceive and represent one another. In this sense, alterity can describe the process and rationale by which cultures perceived as 'marginal', whether by dint of race, gender or class, are subordinated to the dominant culture. *See also* DOMINANT/EMERGENT/RESIDUAL.

alternance des rimes In French prosody the term refers to the rules regulating the alternation of masculine and feminine rhymes (*qq.v.*). The principles were more or less established in the 16th c. and were accepted until well on in the 19th c. *Les symbolistes* tended to ignore them. In the 20th c. they have often been ignored. One of the more rigid rules was that in alexandrine verse a couplet with a masculine rhyme must be followed by a couplet with feminine rhyme (or vice versa). Also known as *rimes plates* or *rimes suivies*. *See also* ALEXANDRINE; RHYME; RIMES CROISÉES; RIMES EMBRASSÉES; RIMES MÊLÉES.

alternate rhyme The rhyme of the stanza form abab. *See* QUATRAIN.

alternative literature A term used to describe literature thought to be outside the mainstream or in some way resistant to the dominant culture. To some degree historically contingent, examples of alternative literature might be identified in the poetry of the Beat generation (*q.v.*), as the product of the so-called 'counterculture' of the 1950s, or in the subversive experiments of futurism (*q.v.*) in the early 20th c. Notably, many such instances have latterly moved away from the margins, if they have not been entirely absorbed into the canon. Alternative literature might also self-consciously reject traditional forms, a recent example being the 'hyper novel', a method of non-linear story-telling structured around the multiple links of a webpage. *See also* ALEATORY WRITING; ALTERNATIVE THEATRE; POSTMODERNISM.

alternative theatre A term loosely applied to any kind of dramatic presentation which is basically non-conformist and non-traditional and thus outside the standard repertory productions one would expect to find in the West End of London, on Broadway, in boulevard theatres or in regional theatres in cities and large towns. It tends to be avant-garde (*q.v.*), experimental and off-beat. *See* AGITPROP DRAMA; CELEBRATORY THEATRE; FRINGE THEATRE; OFF-BROADWAY; THIRD THEATRE; TOTAL THEATRE.

ambiguity Ever since William Empson published *Seven Types of Ambiguity* (1930) this term has had some weight and importance in critical evaluation. In brief, Empson's theory was that things are often not what they seem, that words *connote* at least as much as they *denote* – and very often more. Empson explained thus: 'We call it ambiguous . . . when we recognise that there could be a puzzle as to what the author meant, in that alternative views might be taken without sheer misreading . . . An ambiguity, in ordinary speech, means something very pronounced, and as a rule witty or deceitful.' He uses the word in an extended sense and finds relevance in any 'verbal nuance, however slight, which gives room for alternative reactions to the same piece of language'. 'The machinations of ambiguity', he says, 'are among the very roots of poetry.'

He distinguishes seven main types, which may be summarized as follows:

1. When a detail is effective in several ways simultaneously.
2. When two or more alternative meanings are resolved into one.
3. When two apparently unconnected meanings are given simultaneously.
4. When alternative meanings combine to make clear a complicated state of mind in the author.
5. A kind of confusion when a writer discovers his idea while actually writing. In other words, he has not apparently preconceived the idea but come upon it during the act of creation.

6. Where something appears to contain a contradiction and the reader has to find interpretations.
7. A complete contradiction which shows that the author was unclear as to what he was saying.

In varying degrees Gerard Manley Hopkins's poem *The Bugler's First Communion* exemplifies all seven types. *See also* ALLUSION; ASSOCIATION; CONNOTATION; DENOTATION; PLURISIGNATION.

amblysia (Gk 'blunting') A device related to euphemism (*q.v.*) where language is reduced or modified by way of preparation for the announcement of something tragic or alarming. Often used by the bearers of bad news, it is the equivalent of saying 'I am afraid you must prepare yourself for a shock'. In Classical tragedy the Messenger had the task. Two good examples are Ross (in *Macbeth*) making ready to break the news to Macduff of the murder of the latter's wife and children; and the Messenger in Milton's *Samson Agonistes* gradually working his way up to the description of how Samson destroyed the temple.

American Renaissance The writing of the period before the Civil War (1861–5), beginning with Emerson (1803–82) and Thoreau (1817–62) and the Transcendentalist movement (*q.v.*), and including Whitman (1819–92), Hawthorne (1804–64), and Melville (1819–91). These writers are essentially Romantics of a distinctively American stripe. See F. O. Matthiessen's *The American Renaissance* (1941).

amoebean (Gk 'interchanging') This term relates to verses, couplets or stanzas spoken alternately by two speakers. A device very similar to *stichomythia* (*q.v.*) and highly effective in creating tension and conflict. It is common in pastoral (*q.v.*) and not unusual in drama. A good example is to be found in *October*, the tenth Eclogue in Spenser's *Shepheard's Calendar*, where Piers and Cuddie have a debate. Such an exchange (at its best the amoebean verse involves competition) is reminiscent of the *débat* and poetic contest (*qq.v.*).

amour courtois *See* COURTLY LOVE.

ampersand A corruption of *and per se and*. *Per se* means 'standing by itself'. Thus: 'and', standing by itself, means 'and'. Ampersand is the name of the sign & (formerly *&*), the ligature of *et*.

amphiboly (Gk 'thrown on both sides') An ambiguity (*q.v.*) produced either by grammatical looseness or by double meaning. For example: (a) He spoke to the man laughing; (b) Having received the essay, the professor promised to waste no time reading it. *See* DOUBLE ENTENTE.

amphibrach (Gk 'short at both ends') A metrical foot consisting of a stressed syllable flanked by two unstressed ones: ∪ / ∪. It is not common in English verse and very seldom indeed functions as the main foot of a poem. However, occasional amphibrachs (mixed with other feet) occur quite often in stress groups. Matthew Prior's *Jinny the Just* is a fairly well-known instance of a poem which has a basis of amphibrachs. This is the first verse:

Rĕléas'd frŏm | thĕ nóise ŏf | thĕ Bútchĕr | ănd Bákĕr
Whó, m̆y óld | Friénds bĕ thánked, | dĭd séldŏm | fŏrsáke hĕr,
Ănd fróm thĕ | sŏft Dúns ŏf | m̆y Lándlŏrd | thĕ Quákĕr,

Many three-syllable words in English are amphibrachs. For example: dĕpéndĕnt, ărrángemĕnt, cŏntúsiŏn. Amphibrachic meter also frequently occurs in limericks (*q.v.*). *See also* AMPHIMACER.

amphigory (Gk 'circle on both sides') The term has come to mean a kind of burlesque or parody (*qq.v.*), especially a kind of nonsense verse (*q.v.*) which appears to be going to make sense but does not. A well-known example is Swinburne's *Nephelidia*.

amphimacer (Gk 'long at both ends') The opposite of an amphibrach (*q.v.*), thus: / ∪ /. Also known as the Cretic foot, it is believed to have originated with the Cretan poet Thaletas (7th c. BC). Rare in English verse, except when mixed with other feet. Tennyson used it in *The Oak*:

Líve thy̆ Lífe,
Yóung ănd óld,
Líke yŏn óak,
Bríght ĭn spríng,
Lívĭng góld.

And Coleridge described and imitated it:

Fírst ănd Lást | béiňg lóng, | míddlĕ, shórt | Ámphĭmácĕr
Stríkes hĭs thún | dĕriňg hoóves | lĭke ă próud | hígh-bréd Rácĕr.

In the second line the pattern is not so regular, and unless 'like a' is counted as one syllable and '-bred' is unstressed the meter does not really fit.

amphisbaenic rhyme The term derives from the Greek word *amphisbaina*, 'a monster with a head at each end'. It denotes a backward rhyme. For example: liar/rail. A rare poetical device.

amplification A device in which language is used to extend or magnify or emphasize. A part of rhetoric (*q.v.*) and common in oratory. Often used to attain a particular effect, as in this passage from *Our Mutual Friend* by Dickens:

Mr and Mrs Veneering were bran-new people in a bran-new house in a bran-new quarter of London. Everything about the Veneerings was spick and span new. All their furniture was new, all their friends were new, all their servants were new, their plate was new, their carriage was new, their harness was new, their horses were new, their pictures were new, they themselves were new, they were as newly-married as was lawfully compatible with their having a bran-new baby, and if they had set up a great-grandfather, he would have come home in matting from the Pantechnicon, without a scratch upon him, French-polished to the crown of his head.

-ana As in Shakespeareana, Victoriana, etc. A suffix adopted in continental literature and deriving from the neuter plural of Latin adjectives ending in *-anus*. Johnson defined '-ana' in his *Dictionary* thus:

Books so called from the last syllables of their titles; as Scaligerana, Thuaniana; they are loose thoughts, or casual hints, dropped by eminent men, and collected by their friends.

A particularly important example is *Thraliana*, a mixed bag of poems, jokes, diary entries and anecdotes, compiled by Mrs Hester Thrale, Dr Johnson's dear friend, between 1776 and 1809. This collection was edited and published in 1942. Other examples are *Baconiana* (1679); *Blackguardiana* (c. 1785); *Addisoniana* (1803); *Boxiana* (1818–29); *Feminiana* (1835). *See* ANECDOTE; BIOGRAPHY; TABLE-TALK.

anabasis (Gk 'a going up') The rising of an action to a climax or dénouement (*qq.v.*). In drama, for instance, the approach to the climax in *Othello* when the Moor murders Desdemona in Act V.

anachorism (Gk 'something misplaced') Action, scene or character placed where it does not belong. *See* ANACHRONISM.

anachronism (Gk 'back-timing') In literature anachronisms may be used deliberately to distance events and to underline a universal verisimilitude and timelessness – to prevent something being 'dated'. Shakespeare adopted this device several times. Two classic examples are the references to the clock in *Julius Caesar* and to billiards in *Antony and Cleopatra*. Shaw also does it in *Androcles and the Lion* when the Emperor is referred to as 'The Defender of the Faith'. *See* ANACHORISM.

anaclasis (Gk 'back bending') When the positions of a long and short syllable in verse are interchanged.

anacoluthon (Gk 'lacking sequence') Beginning a sentence in one way and continuing or ending it in another. 'You know what I – but let's forget it!'

anacreóntica A Spanish poetic genre named after the Greek poet Anacreon of Teos (6th c. BC). It was a kind of pastoral (*q.v.*) or nature poem particularly popular in the 18th c. *See* ANACREONTIC VERSE.

anacreontic verse Named after Anacreon of Teos (6th c. BC). The *Anacreontea* or *Anacreontics* consist of sixty-odd short poems on love, wine and song. They had a considerable influence on Ronsard and Belleau in France; on Tasso, Parini and Leopardi in Italy; and on some 18th c. German lyricists. There are not many examples in English literature, though Abraham Cowley wrote some *Anacreontiques*, and so did Thomas Moore in a translation called the *Odes of Anacreon*. But this example is by Thomas Campion (1567–1620):

> Follow, follow,
> Though with mischief
> Armed, like whirlwind
> Now she flies thee;
> Time can conquer
> Love's unkindness;
> Love can alter
> Time's disgrace;
> Till death faint not
> Then but follow.
> Could I catch that
> Nimble traitor,
> Scornful Laura,
> Swiftfoot Laura,
> Soon then would I
> Seek avengement.
> What's th'avengement?
> Even submissely
> Prostrate then to
> Beg for mercy.

See ANACREÓNTICA.

anacrusis (Gk 'striking up') One or more initial syllables in a line of verse which are unaccented, as in Blake's *The Tyger*:

> When the stars threw down their spears
> And watered heaven with their tears.

The 'and' is unaccented.

anadiplosis (Gk 'doubling') The repetition of the last word of one clause at the beginning of the following clause to gain a special effect. For example, Samson at the beginning of Milton's *Samson Agonistes*:

> I seek
> This unfrequented place to find some ease,
> Ease to the body some, none to the mind
> From restless thoughts.

It is not uncommon in prose, as in this instance from Dr Johnson's *Rambler* No. 21: 'Labour and care are rewarded with success, success produces confidence, confidence relaxes industry, and negligence ruins the reputation which diligence had raised.' *See* EPANADOS; EPANALEPSIS.

anagnorisis (Gk 'recognition') A term used by Aristotle in *Poetics* to describe the moment of recognition (of truth) when ignorance gives way to knowledge. According to Aristotle, the ideal moment of anagnorisis coincides with peripeteia (*q.v.*), or reversal of fortune. The classic example is in *Oedipus Rex* when Oedipus discovers he has himself killed Laius. *See* TRAGEDY.

anagogical (Gk 'mystical sense') The anagogical meaning of a text – especially, for example, in the Bible – is its spiritual, hidden, allegorical or mystical meaning. Thus, anagogy or anagoge is a special form of allegorical interpretation. *See* ALLEGORY.

anagram (Gk 'writing back or anew') The letters of a word or phrase are recombined to form a new arrangement. For instance, the word 'dictionary' can be turned into 'idiocy-rant'. This is a common feature of crosswords. Samuel Butler's title *Erewhon* is an anagram of 'nowhere'.

analects (Ch *Lun Yu*) Also translated as 'Sayings' of the Chinese philosopher Confucius (K'ung Fu-Tzu; *c.* 551–*c.* 479 BC). The *Analects* was one of a group of works that, between the Han Dynasty (206 BC–AD 220) and the Song Dynasty (960–1279), came to be attributed to Confucius or his disciples, and to be regarded as the core of Confucian doctrine. These works, known as the Confucian canon, included six 'classics': the *Book of Changes* (*I Ching*), containing a system of divination; the *Book of Documents* (*Shu Ching*), a series of official documents and speeches; the *Book of Songs* (*Shih Ching*) (*q.v.*), an anthology of lyric poems and songs; the *Spring and Autumn* (*Ch'un-ch'iu*), or annals concerning Confucius's home state of Lu; the *Book of Rites* (*Li Ching*); and the *Book of Music* (*Yueh Ching*), which was largely destroyed in the 3rd c. BC.

In addition to these six classics was a series of four books in which the *Analects* was grouped. The other three were the *Book of Mencius*, a collection of dialogues of the 4th c. BC scholar, and two chapters of the *Book of Ritual*, known as the *Great Learning* (*Ta Hsueh*) and the *Doctrine of the Mean* (*Chung Yung*). Most of these texts were not actually authored by Confucius, and it is likely that portions of the *Analects* were compiled by his disciples.

The core doctrines of the *Analects* are deeply conservative, espousing the attainment of wisdom through learning, informed by reverence for the past, tradition, parents, state, and early exemplary rulers in Chinese history. Some of these values are exhibited in the following extracts:

> The Master said, Govern the people by regulations, keep order among them by chastisements, and they will flee from you, and lose all self-respect. Govern them by moral force, keep order among them by ritual and they will keep their self-respect and come to you of their own accord. (II, 3)
>
> The Master said, At fifteen I set my heart upon learning. At thirty, I had planted my feet firm upon the ground. At forty, I no longer suffered from perplexities. At fifty, I knew what were the biddings of Heaven. At sixty, I heard them with docile ear. At seventy, I could follow the dictates of my own heart; for what I desired no longer overstepped the boundaries of right. (II, 4)
>
> Chi K'ang-tzu asked whether there were any form of encouragement by which he could induce the common people to be respectful and loyal. The Master said, Approach them with dignity, and they will respect you.

Show piety towards your parents and kindness towards your children, and they will be loyal to you. Promote those who are worthy, train those who are incompetent; that is the best form of encouragement. (II, 20)

The Master said, I have transmitted what was taught to me without making up anything of my own. I have been faithful to and loved the Ancients. (VII, 1)

The Master said, I once spent a whole day without food and a whole night without sleep, in order to meditate. It was no use. It is better to learn. (XV, 30)

(Translated by Arthur Waley)

Confucius's influence in China and Japan was vast; his doctrines underlay the Chinese civil service and education systems for many centuries. *See also* BOOK OF SONGS.

analogue A word or thing similar or parallel to another. As a literary term it denotes a story for which one can find parallel examples in other languages and literatures. A well-known example is Chaucer's *The Pardoner's Tale*, whose basic plot and theme were widely distributed in Europe in the Middle Ages. The tale is probably of oriental origin and a primitive version exists in a 3rd c. Buddhist text known as the *Jatakas*; but the version usually taken to be the closest analogue to Chaucer's tale is in the Italian *Libro di Novelle e di Bel Parlar Gentile* (1572), which is nearly two hundred years later than Chaucer's story.

analogy The illustration of an idea by means of comparison to a recognizable parallel.

analysis A detailed splitting up and examination of a work of literature. A close study of the various elements and the relationship between them. An essential part of criticism. As T. S. Eliot put it, the tools of the critic are comparison and analysis. Analytical criticism helps to make clear an author's meaning and the structure of his work. It is argued that analysis spoils an intuitive and spontaneous response to a work of literature. Those in favour of 'deep' analysis contend that, on the contrary, it enhances the reader's enjoyment.

analytical language A language, like English, which employs specific words (particles) to express grammatical relations between syntactical units, rather than inflections (as are used in Latin, for example).

anamnesis (Gk 'recalling to mind') The recollection of ideas, people or events (in a previous existence). This is common in memoirs and autobiography (*qq.v.*), but it may also pervade a work of fiction or a poem. It is a special kind of harking back, and the maieutic processes of the writer often involve it. Proust's *A la recherche du temps perdu* is a good example in fiction. Among poets, the anamnesic element is particularly noticeable in the work of W. B. Yeats, Ezra Pound, T. S. Eliot and W. H. Auden. In philosophy, the term refers to a Platonic theory which posits that knowledge is innate and 'remembered' by the process of education, rather than learned.

ananym (Gk 'behind name') A name or word written backwards.

anapaest (Gk 'beaten back') A metrical foot comprising two unstressed syllables and one stressed: ∪ ∪ /. The opposite of a dactyl (*q.v.*). It is a running and galloping foot and therefore used to create the illusion of swiftness and action. As Coleridge illustrates it in *Metrical Feet*:

> Wĭth ă leáp | ănd ă boúnd | thĕ swĭft Á | năpaĕsts thróng.

Originally it was a martial rhythm used in Greek verse, and was adapted by the Romans for drama. In English literature it is mostly found in popular verse until early in the 18th c. Thereafter it was used fairly frequently for 'serious' works by poets like Cowper, Scott, Byron, Morris and Swinburne. In the 20th c. Belloc, Chesterton, Masefield and Betjeman all employed it successfully. Most poets at some time or another have occasion to use anapaests in combination with other feet. A famous anthology piece which illustrates the anapaestic rhythm is Byron's *Destruction of Sennacherib*. The following example comes from William Morris's *The Message of the March Wind*:

> Bŭt ló, | thĕ ŏld ínn, | ănd thĕ líghts, | ănd thĕ fíre
> Ănd thĕ fídd|lĕr's ŏld túne | ănd thĕ shúff|lĭng ŏf feét;
> Sóon fŏr ús | shăll bĕ quí|ĕt ănd rést | ănd dĕsíre,
> Ănd tŏmór|rŏw's ŭprí|sĭng tŏ déeds | shăll bĕ swéet.

anaphora (Gk 'carrying up or back') A rhetorical device involving the repetition of a word or group of words in successive clauses. It is often used in ballad and song, in oratory and sermon (*qq.v.*), but it is common in many literary forms. A fine example in verse occurs six verses from the end of Chaucer's *Troilus and Criseyde*:

> Swich fyn hath, lo, this Troilus for love!
> Swich fyn hath al his grete worthynesse!
> Swich fyn hath his estat real above,
> Swich fyn his lust, swich fyn hath his noblesse!
> Swich fyn hath false worldes brotelnesse!
> And thus bigan his lovyng of Criseyde,
> As I have told, and in this wise he deyde.

An equally fine instance in prose is the opening of Charles Dickens's *A Tale of Two* Cities,

It was the best of times, it was the worst of times, it was the age of wisdom, it was the age of foolishness, it was the epoch of belief, it was the epoch of incredulity, it was the season of Light, it was the season of Darkness, it was the spring of hope, it was the winter of despair, we had everything before us, we had nothing before us, we were all going direct to Heaven, we were all going direct the other way . . .

See also INCREMENTAL REPETITION; RHYME.

anaphoric rhyme *See* RHYME.

anastrophe (Gk 'turning back') The inversion of the normal order of words for a particular effect. The word order in these lines, from the beginning of Belial's speech in the Council of Pandemonium in *Paradise Lost*, is deliberately confused to suggest Belial's speciousness:

> I should be much for open war, O Peers,
> As not behind in hate, if what was urged
> Main reason to persuade immediate war
> Did not dissuade me most, and seem to cast
> Ominous conjecture on the whole success.
> When he who most excels in fact of arms,
> In what he counsels and in what excels
> Mistrustful, grounds his courage on despair
> And utter dissolution, as the scope
> Of all his aim, after some dire revenge.

Anastrophe is also common in prose. This example comes from Richard Whateley's *Elements of Rhetoric* (1828): 'The question between preaching extempore and from a written discourse, it does not properly fall within the province of this discourse to discuss on any but what may be called rhetorical principles.'

anatomy (Gk 'cutting up') A detailed analysis of a subject; an exhaustive examination. Well-known examples are: Lyly's *Euphues or the Anatomy of Wit* (1579); Philip Stubbes's *Anatomie of Abuses* (1583); Thomas Nashe's *Anatomie of Absurditie* (1589), a reply to Stubbes; Robert Burton's *Anatomy of Melancholy* (1621), perhaps the most famous of all. Among more recent instances one should mention Rosamund Harding's *Anatomy of Inspiration* (1940). In his *Anatomy of Criticism* (1957) Northrop Frye treats 'anatomy' as a form of fiction associated with Menippean satire (*q.v.*), and thus a compendious, if not encyclopaedic, satirical analysis of human behaviour, attitudes and beliefs.

ancients and moderns The phrase refers to two literary parties which grew up in France and England in the late 17th c. Originally, in France, there were arguments over the relative merits of French and Latin for literary purposes, an issue discussed by du Bellay long before in his *Deffense et Illustration* (1549). The increasing influence of the French Academy in the 17th c. helped to provoke further argument. Fundamentally, it was a case of progress and the modern rationalistic spirit of inquiry versus reverence for Classical rules and precepts. Some moderns thought they were better than the ancients; others did not. A number of distinguished writers joined the fray, including

Perrault, Bayle, La Fontaine and Boileau. By 1700 the quarrel was over, but the issues were still unresolved. Neoclassicism (*q.v.*) was to prevail in France for a very long time (far longer than anywhere else) and the moderns did not really gain their victory until the 19th c. was well advanced.

In England the *casus belli* was an essay by Sir William Temple, published in 1690, on the comparative merits of ancient and modern learning. Temple praised ancient learning at the expense of the moderns. In so doing he praised the spurious *Epistles* of Phalaris. This provoked the indignation and criticism of William Wotton and Richard Bentley.

However remote and even esoteric such intellectual and literary fracas may now seem, this one at any rate had good side-effects. Among other things it produced Swift's *The Battle of the Books* (1704), a prose satire in which the ancients have the advantage.

androgyny (Gk *anēr* 'man' and *gunē* 'woman') Denotes 'having characteristics of both genders', or 'the merging of male and female attributes'. It has often been considered as a synonym for hermaphroditism and bisexuality. The idea of androgyny has a long tradition. It can be found in Hindu mythology, Daoist philosophy of yin and yang, which is based on the unity of opposites, the writings of Plato, the story of Tiresias in Ovid's *Metamorphoses*, in the work of Renaissance writers and in Freud. In Plato's Symposium (*c.* 384 BC), for example, Aristophanes tells the story of the 'double' beings who were male-male, female-female and male-female before they were split in half by Zeus out of fear of competition. Since then, humans have longed to return to this primal state of wholeness and have yearned to be reunited with their other 'lost half'.

John Donne's love poetry is characterized by such androgynous reunion, and this is particularly evident in his poems on the merging of lovers (e.g. 'An Epithalamion', 'The Canonization', 'The Extasie', 'The Undertaking'). The theme of androgyny is also prominent in Shakespeare's plays (e.g. Ariel in *The Tempest*, the cross-dressing in *As You Like It* and *Two Gentlemen of Verona*), and in the work of Virginia Woolf (e.g. *Orlando*, *A Room of One's Own*, *To the Lighthouse*). Among more recent instances one should mention Ursula Le Guin's science-fiction novel *The Left Hand of Darkness* (1969), which presents the people called the Gethenans, who 'do not see one another as men or women', Jeanette Winterson's novels *The Passion* (1987) and *Written on the Body* (1992), and Jeffrey Eugenides's novel *Middlesex* (2002). *See also* GENDER THEORY.

anecdote A brief account of or a story about an individual or an incident. The anecdotal digression is a common feature of narrative in prose and verse. In the history of English literature and of literary characters the anecdote has a specific importance. In his *Dictionary* Johnson defined the term as 'something yet unpublished; secret history'. During the 18th c. an interest in 'secret' histories increased steadily, and no doubt there is some connection between this and the growing popularity of -ana, table-talk and biography (*qq.v.*) at that time. During the second half of the 18th c. there was almost a 'craze' for

'secret' histories. In the last thirty years of it over a hundred books of anec-
dotage were published in England. Isaac Disraeli, father of Benjamin, became
one of the best-known and most assiduous gleaners of anecdotes. In 1791 he
published three volumes titled *Curiousities of Literature, consisting of Anecdotes, Characters, Sketches, and Observations, Literary, Historical and Critical*. These he followed with other collections: *Calamities of Authors* (1812–13)
in two volumes, and *Quarrels of Authors* (1814) in three volumes. In 1812
John Nichols published the first of nine volumes in a series titled *Literary
Anecdotes of the 18th c.* Such works remained popular during the Victorian
period. Nor is the appetite for collections of anecdotes assuaged. In 1975
there was *The Oxford Book of Literary Anecdotes*.

Anglo-Norman period (1100–1350) During this time, Anglo-Norman, a
western type of French, was spoken and written in Britain. It continued to
be used for official documents and in English courts of law long after it
was no longer spoken. Some literature of merit in Anglo-Norman survives,
notably the mystery play (*q.v.*) *Mystère d'Adam* (c. 1150) and *The Voyage of
Brendan* (first half of the twelfth century).

Anglo-Saxon period (or Old English period) The period from the invasion
of Celtic England by the Angles, Saxons and Jutes in the first half of the 5th c.
up till the conquest in 1066 by William of Normandy. After their conversion
to Christianity in the 7th c. the Anglo-Saxons began to develop a written
literature (prior to that period it had been oral). The Benedictine monastic
foundations played an important part in the development of culture, literacy
and learning. Two outstanding scholars of the period were the Venerable Bede
(c. 673–735) and Alcuin (c. 735–804). From the Anglo-Saxon period dates
what is known as Old English literature (composed in the vernacular Anglo-
Saxon). It includes the epic (*q.v.*) *Beowulf* and some fine lyric poems such
as *The Wanderer, The Seafarer* and *Deor*. Much of the literature that survives
is anonymous, but the names of two poets are known: Caedmon (fl. late 7th
c.) and Cynewulf (late 8th and early 9th c.). They wrote on biblical and religious themes. Alfred the Great (c. 848–99), who was king of Wessex, 871–99,
was largely responsible for the restoration of learning in England after the
Viking invasions. He translated into Old English various books in Latin and
is believed to have been responsible for planning the *Anglo-Saxon Chronicle*
which continued from his reign, in the Peterborough version, until 1134. This
is written in Old English prose and is an invaluable source of Anglo-Saxon
history.

angry young man A term which became current in the late 1950s, though
it was probably first used as the title of an autobiography by Leslie Paul
published in 1951. Apart from journalists, the writer mainly but indirectly
responsible for the term's popularity was John Osborne, whose play *Look
Back in Anger* (1957) spoke for a generation of disillusioned and discontented
young men strongly opposed to the social and political mores of the establishment. 'Angry young man' was used to refer both to the protagonists of

hard-hitting fiction and drama and to their authors, who frequently shared with their characters a provincial, working-class background. But while critical of the privileges of the metropolitan elite and the fatuousness of consumer society, these angry young men rarely articulated anything approaching a political vision, and were prone to expressions of nihilistic despair and bouts of misogyny. *See also* KITCHEN-SINK DRAMA.

anisometric (Gk 'of unequal lengths') A stanza composed of lines of unequal lengths; as in the first stanza of John Donne's *The Message*:

> Send home my long strayd eyes to mee,
> Which (Oh) too long have dwelt on thee;
> Yet since there they have learn'd such ill,
> Such forc'd fashions,
> And false passions,
> That they be
> Made by thee
> Fit for no good sight, keep them still.

annals (L 'year books') Notable examples are: the *Anglo-Saxon Chronicle*, made in a number of recensions, of which seven survive, from the 9th c. to the middle of the 12th; and the *Annales Cambriae*, the ancient annals of Wales whose earliest extant manuscript dates from the second half of the 10th c. *See also* CHRONICLE; YEAR BOOK.

annotation Textual comment in a book. It may consist of a reader's comment in the margin, hence the term marginalia (*q.v.*), or printed explanatory notes provided by an editor. *See also* ADVERSARIA.

anomoiosis *See* CONTRAST.

anonymous There is a great body of anonymous literature, especially that belonging to early or primitive societies, most of which is of the oral tradition (*q.v.*). Much Homeric poetry was anonymous in origin; so was OE poetry (of which *Beowulf* is a notable example), and the South Slav *narodne pesme* (*q.v.*). Folk literature of all kinds tends to be anonymous; so are many sagas, ballads, medieval *chansons de gestes*, *fabliaux*, proverbs, nursery rhymes, etc. (*qq.v.*). *See also* PSEUDONYMOUS LITERATURE.

anonymuncule (L 'nameless little man') A derogatory term for a petty type of anonymous writer. A mean, shifty writer who hides behind anonymity.

antagonist In drama or fiction the antagonist opposes the hero or protagonist (*q.v.*). In *Othello* Iago is antagonist to the Moor. In *The Mayor of Casterbridge*, Farfrae is antagonist to Henchard.

antanaclasis (Gk 'breaking back against') A figurative device in which a word is used twice or more in two or more of its possible senses. When Othello is about to murder Desdemona (*Othello*, V, ii) he says: 'Put out the light, and then put out the light'. The first 'light' refers to a candle or taper; the second to Desdemona's life. *See* PUN; PARONOMASIA.

anthimeria (Sources differ on the etymology of this term, some deriving it from the Gk *anthos*, 'flower', and others from *anti*, 'instead of' + *meros*, 'part'.) The substitution of one part of speech for another, for example a verb for a noun or vice versa; often a form of metaphor *(q.v.)*. This example comes from Shakespeare's *Coriolanus* (V, v, 5):

> A mile before his tent fall down, and *knee*
> The way into his mercy.

And this from Edward Young's *Complaint, or Night Thoughts*:

> That ghastly thought would drink up all your joy,
> And quite *unparadise* the realms of light.

anthology (Gk 'collection of flowers') In Classical times anthologies tended to be collections of epigrams, elegiac and otherwise, and date back to the *Garland of Meleager* (*c.* 60 BC). Philippus of Thessalonica (*c.* AD 40) made a further collection of Greek epigrams. The first major anthology is known as the *Palatine* or the *Greek Anthology*, compiled *c.* 925 by Constantinus Cephalas, a Byzantine Greek. In the 16th c. anthologizing became commonplace. From this period date two important Latin anthologies: *Catalecta veterum poetarum* (1573) and *Epigrammata et poemata vetera* (1590). In England several notable collections appeared: Tottel's Miscellany (*Songes and Sonettes*) (1557); *Very Pleasaunt Sonettes and Storyes in Myter* (1566); *The Paradice of Dainty Devices* (1576); *A Gorgious Gallery of Gallant Inventions* (1578); *The Phoenix Nest* (1593); *Englands Parnassus* (1600); *Englands Helicon* (1600); *Poetical Rhapsody* (1602); then little of note until Percy's *Reliques* (1765). In 1831 Southey put out *Select Works of the British Poets*, and in 1861 came Palgrave's *Golden Treasury*, probably the most famous of all English anthologies. Others worthy of mention are T. H. Ward's *English Poets* (1883) and Arthur Quiller-Couch's *Oxford Book of English Verse* (1900). In the last fifty years anthologies have proliferated endlessly, especially anthologies of verse. Many are little more than commercial publishing packages which provoke the invention of anaemic academic 'joke' titles such as *The Oxford Book of Cambridge Light Verse*, *The Cambridge Book of Oxford Light Verse*, *The Oxbridge Book of Heavy Verse* – and so forth.

anthropomorphism (Gk *anthropos* 'human', *morphe* 'shape') Describes the attribution of human characteristics to non-human entities or concepts, for example animals, inanimate objects or abstract ideas or forces. Prominent examples in literature and art are to be found in the fable *(q.v.)* tradition in which animals are made anthropomorphic in order to illustrate moral lessons or other maxims. The gods and goddesses in epics such as *Gilgamesh* and the *Iliad* and *Odyssey* are often both supernatural forces and anthropomorphic beings. Other natural phenomena frequently subject to anthropomorphic treatment include celestial bodies (the 'man in the moon') or weather conditions ('Jack Frost', 'The West Wind'). *See also* PERSONIFICATION.

antibacchius *See* PALIMBACCHIUS.

anticlimax According to Dr Johnson's definition (and he appears to have been the first to record the word) it is 'a sentence in which the last part expresses something lower than the first'. In fact, a bathetic declension from a noble tone to one less exalted. The effect can be comic and is often intended to be so. A good example occurs in Fielding's burlesque (*q.v.*), *Tom Thumb*:

> King [Arthur, to his queen Dolallola]
> ... Whence flow those Tears fast down thy blubber'd cheeks,
> Like swoln Gutter, gushing through the Streets?

The effect can also be unintentionally comic. There is a well-known example in Crashaw's *Saint Mary Magdalene, or the Weeper*:

> And now where e'er He strays,
> Among the Galilean mountains,
> Or more unwelcome ways,
> He's followed by two faithful fountains;
> Two walking baths; two weeping motions;
> Portable, & compendious oceans.

See BATHOS.

anti-hero A 'non-hero', or the antithesis of a hero of the old-fashioned kind who was capable of heroic deeds, who was dashing, strong, brave and resourceful. It is a little doubtful whether such heroes have ever existed in any quantity in fiction except in some romances (*q.v.*) and in the cheaper kind of romantic novelette (*q.v.*). However, there have been many instances of fictional heroes who have displayed noble qualities and virtuous attributes. The anti-hero is the man who is given the vocation of failure.

The anti-hero – a type who is incompetent, unlucky, tactless, clumsy, cackhanded, stupid, buffoonish – is of ancient lineage and is to be found, for instance, in the Greek New Comedy (*q.v.*). An early and outstanding example in European literature is the endearing figure of the eponymous knight of *Don Quixote* (1605, 1615). But perhaps the first anti-hero who fits the modern image is Hylas, in d'Urfé's very successful *Astrée* (1627), who is a contrast to the conventional hero Céladon. Another notable instance is Tristram Shandy – in Sterne's *Tristram Shandy* (1760–67). One can find isolated representatives in European literature from the 18th c. onwards, for example Hašek's Schweik in *The Good Soldier Schweik* (1920–23). A case could be argued that Leopold Bloom in Joyce's *Ulysses* (1922) is a kind of anti-hero. Camus's Meursault in *L'Etranger* (1942) is an example. Charles Lumley in John Wain's *Hurry on Down* (1953) is another. When Kingsley Amis created Jim Dixon in *Lucky Jim* (1954) the postwar anti-hero type was established, and the anti-hero Jimmy Porter of John Osborne's play *Look Back in Anger*

(1957) produced a succession of personalities of the same kind. Other examples are Sebastien in J. P. Donleavy's *The Ginger Man* (1955), Herzog in Bellow's *Herzog* (1964), and Yossarian in Joseph Heller's *Catch-22* (1961). The principal male characters in several of Graham Greene's novels are also anti-heroes. *See* ANGRY YOUNG MAN; ANTI-NOVEL; NOUVEAU ROMAN.

antihumanism A philosophical position which rejects many of the primary convictions of humanism (*q.v.*), particularly the assumption of a universal 'human nature', and a belief in the rational, autonomous individual. The term was coined in an essay of 1964 by Louis Althusser, who sought to defend Marxism from what he perceived to be the malign influence of humanism. For Althusser, to speak of 'humanity' is to deny the primacy of historical forces, and obscures the principal dynamic by which society is organized, namely, class. The term 'antihumanism' has been applied retrospectively to earlier critics of humanism, such as Heidegger, for whom 'humanity' was a metaphysical construct which misconstrues the nature of being. Antihumanists also draw on theories of the unconscious: Freud's arguments about how individuals are driven by irrational desires beyond their control would seem to undermine humanism's trust in the rationality and agency of the individual. Althusser's student Foucault was another prominent antihumanist. In *The Order of Things* (1966) Foucault notoriously declared the 'death of man', echoing Nietzsche's (and Hegel's) earlier pronouncement of the 'death of God'. The concept of 'humanity', Foucault contended, emerged as a modern substitute for religion, but was now obsolete. A new epoch was emerging, characterized by a decentred subject, one of the key concepts of poststructuralist thought. A further critique is articulated by Alain Badiou, for whom humanism is inevitably conservative and oppressive. Badiou argues that confinement to an established model of humanity precludes other ways of being and thinking. *See also* MARXIST CRITICISM; POSTHUMANISM; POST-MODERNISM; POSTSTRUCTURALISM; PSYCHOANALYTIC CRITICISM.

anti-literature A term coined by the poet David Gascoyne (1916–2001) in 1935 to describe literature which turns traditional rules and conventions upside down. Gascoyne was a staunch advocate of surrealism (*q.v.*) and in 1935 published *A Short Survey of Surrealism*. *See also* ALTERNATIVE LITERATURE; ANTI-HERO; ANTI-NOVEL.

antilogy (Gk 'against knowledge') An illogicality or contradiction in terms.

anti-masque An innovation by Ben Jonson in 1609. It took the form of either a buffoonish and grotesque episode before the main masque (*q.v.*) or an interlude, similarly farcical, during it. When performed beforehand, it was known as an ante-masque. One form of it was a burlesque (*q.v.*) of the masque itself, in which case it had some affinity with the Greek satyr play (*q.v.*).

antimetabole (Gk 'opposite change/variety') The repetition of words in successive clauses, in reverse grammatical order. As in this example by Dr

Johnson in one of his *Rambler* essays: 'It ought to be the first endeavour of a writer to distinguish nature from custom, or that which is established because it is right from that which is right only because it is established.' *See also* CHIASMUS.

antinomy (Gk 'contradictory law') A kind of division or contradiction between laws or principles, yet the term also contains the idea that the contradictions are reconcilable. In Kantian philosophy, the term is used to articulate the difficulties of establishing principles of rationality via methods of applied reason, which are, by their very nature, empirical and subjective. Reason can make equal claim to contradictory proofs. For instance, Kant proposes that, on the subject of taste (*q.v.*), there can be no argument, and at the same time there can be. *See* APOLLONIAN/DIONYSIAN; CLASSICISM/ ROMANTICISM; HEBRAISM/ HELLENISM; NAIV UND SENTIMENTALISCH.

anti-novel This kind of fiction tends to be experimental and breaks with the traditional story-telling methods and form of the novel (*q.v.*). Often there is little attempt to create an illusion of realism or naturalism (*qq.v.*) for the reader. It establishes its own conventions and a different kind of realism which deters the reader from self-identification with the characters, yet at the same time persuades him to 'participate' but not vicariously. One has only to compare novels by, say, Thomas Hardy and Henry James, with those by, say, Nabokov and Samuel Beckett, to see how the work of the latter writers comes into the anti-novel category; though anti-novel is a thoroughly misleading term.

We can see the process of anti-novel innovation at work in the major experiments of James Joyce in *Ulysses* and *Finnegans Wake*, in several novels by Virginia Woolf (e.g. *Mrs Dalloway*, *The Waves* and *To the Lighthouse*) and in the early fiction of Samuel Beckett (e.g. *Molloy* and *Murphy*). However, it may be that the possibilities were perceived long before by Laurence Sterne. *Tristram Shandy* (1760–7) might be cited as a kind of anti-novel. Horace Walpole described it as 'a kind of novel . . . the great humour of which consists in the whole narration always going backwards'.

Some of the principal features of the anti-novel are lack of an obvious plot; diffused episode; minimal development of character; detailed surface analysis of objects; many repetitions; innumerable experiments with vocabulary, punctuation and syntax; variations of time sequence; alternative endings and beginnings. Some of the more extreme features are detachable pages; pages which can be shuffled like cards; coloured pages; blank pages; collage effects; drawings; hieroglyphics.

Of notable and influential contributions to the anti-novel – apart from those referred to above – one should mention Sartre's *La Nausée* (1938); Camus's *L'Étranger* (1942); Robbe-Grillet's *La Jalousie* (1957); and Nabokov's *Pale Fire* (1962).

It is worth noting that as far back as 1627 Charles Sorel subtitled his novel *Le Berger extravagant* an *anti-roman*. *See also* ANTI-HERO; AVANT-GARDE;

EXPRESSIONISM; FABULATION; NOUVEAU ROMAN; NOUVELLE VAGUE; STREAM OF CONSCIOUSNESS.

antiphon Either a hymn (*q.v.*) in alternative parts or a lyric (*q.v.*) containing responses, as in this example from George Herbert, which again is a kind of hymn:

CHORUS Let all the world in every corner sing, My God and King.
VERSICLE The heavens are not too high,
    His praise may thither fly;
    The earth is not too low,
    His praises there may grow.
CHORUS Let all the world in every corner sing, My God and King.
VERSICLE The church with psalms must shout,
    No door can keep them out:
    But above all, the heart
    Must bear the longest part.
CHORUS Let all the world in every corner sing, My God and King.

The Divine Office is sung antiphonally.

antiphrasis (Gk 'expressed by the opposite') The use of a word in a sense opposite to its proper meaning. Common in irony and litotes (*qq.v.*).

anti-play A dramatic work which not only ignores the traditional conventions but actively distorts them. There is no observable plot and little development of character. Dialogue is often inconsequential or totally disconnected. Playwrights of the Theatre of the Absurd (*q.v.*) have used anti-play techniques. Sometimes they have been very successful. *See* HAPPENING.

antipophora (Gk 'against answer') A figurative device in which a person (or character) asks a question of himself and then answers it himself. There is a succession of them in Falstaff's famous disquisition on 'honour' in *Henry IV*, Pt I (V, i). *See* RHETORICAL QUESTION.

antisagoge (Gk 'leading into against') A complex figurative device in which an order or precept is given and a reward offered if it is obeyed, and punishment threatened if it is ignored. As when Leontes speaks to Camillo in *The Winter's Tale* (I, ii):

    Do't, and thou hast the one half of my heart;
    Do't not, thou split'st thine own.

antispast (Gk 'drawn in the contrary direction') A metrical foot comprising two stressed syllables flanked by two unstressed ones: ◡ // ◡. In other words, an iamb and a trochee (*qq.v.*). It is by no means certain that this foot (*q.v.*) actually existed in Classical prosody.

antistoichon (Gk 'balanced opposition of ideas') An antithetical device in which statements counterbalance each other. *See* ANTITHESIS.

antistrophe (Gk 'counter-turning') In Greek drama the return movement of the Chorus from left to right. It also refers to the choric song accompanying this movement. It was also the second of a pair of movements or stanzas in an ode (*q.v.*), exactly the same metrically as the preceding strophe (*q.v.*). *See also* EPODE.

antisyzygy *See* OXYMORON.

anti-theatre The term was devised some time in the 1950s and denotes any form of drama which is not naturalistic, traditional, conventional or 'legit'; thus, theatre which disobeys or actively goes against accepted laws and rules of dramaturgy. It has been used to describe the Theatre of the Absurd (*q.v.*). *See also* AGITPROP DRAMA; ALTERNATIVE THEATRE; ANTI-HERO; ANTI-LITERATURE; ANTI-NOVEL; THIRD THEATRE.

antithesis (Gk 'opposition') Fundamentally, contrasting ideas sharpened by the use of opposite or noticeably different meanings. For example, Bacon's apophthegm (*q.v.*): 'Crafty men contemn studies; simple men admire them; and wise men use them.'

It is common in rhetoric (*q.v.*) and was particularly favoured by the Augustan poets and users of the heroic couplet (*q.v.*). These lines from Dryden's *Absalom and Achitophel* are strongly antithetical:

> Rais'd in extremes, and in extremes decry'd;
> With Oaths affirm'd, with dying Vows deny'd.
> Not weighed, or winnow'd by the Multitude;
> But swallow'd in the Mass, unchew'd and Crude.
> Some Truth there was, but dash'd and brew'd with Lyes;
> To please the Fools, and puzzle all the Wise.
> Succeeding times did equal folly call,
> Believing nothing, or believing all.

Pope was an expert at the antithetical, as this compact example in his *Moral Essays* shows:

> Les wit than mimic, more a wit than wise.

It is also used frequently in prose to telling effect, as in this example from Dr Johnson (in the *London Chronicle*, 2 May 1769) on the character of the Reverend Zacariah Mudge: 'Though studious, he was popular; though argumentative, he was modest; though inflexible, he was candid; and though metaphysical, yet orthodox.' *See* EPIGRAM; OXYMORON.

antode (Gk 'opposite song') In Greek Old Comedy (*q.v.*), during the parabasis (*q.v.*) the antode was the lyric song sung by one half of the Chorus in response to the ode (*q.v.*) sung earlier by the other half.

antonomasia (Gk 'naming instead') A figure of speech in which an epithet, or the name of an office or dignity, is substituted for a proper name. So 'the Bard' for Shakespeare; 'a Gamaliel' for a wise man; 'a Casanova' for a womanizer; and 'a Hitler' for a tyrant. *See also* AUNT EDNA; METONYMY; SYNECDOCHE.

antonym A word of opposite meaning to another: fierce/mild; ugly/beautiful; abstract/concrete. *See* SYNONYM.

anxiety of influence A phrase coined by the American critic Harold Bloom in the eponymous book (1973) to describe his conception of the Oedipal relation of individual poets to their literary precursors, who fulfil the function of the father in the Freudian family drama. Bloom explains the artistic development of the great poet as a progress moving from admiration and imitation of the poetic forebear to rejection and displacement, and finally to a crucial 'misprision' (misreading) by which the new poet deforms and recasts the work of the precursor to make something quite new. The struggle of Wordsworth with Milton, Shelley with Wordsworth, and Wallace Stevens with Whitman are some of Bloom's exemplary cases of the strong originality born in the overthrow of the earlier influential writer in the creative psyche of the nascent later one. *See* BELATEDNESS; PSYCHOANALYTIC CRITICISM.

apestail A name for the symbol '@', adapted from its Dutch name, 'aape-staartje' (*aap*, ape + *staart*, tail; cf. Serbo-Croat, in which this symbol is called the 'monkey'). In email addresses English speakers usually designate @ as an emphatically pronounced 'at'.

aphaeresis (Gk 'a taking away') The suppression of an initial, unstressed syllable, usually a vowel: 'mongst' for *amongst*; 'mid' for *amid*; 'tween' for *between*. *See also* APHESIS.

aphesis (Gk 'letting go') The loss of an unstressed initial vowel: 'squire' from *esquire*. *See also* APHAERESIS.

aphorism (Gk 'marking off by boundaries') A terse statement of a truth or dogma; a pithy generalization, which may or may not be witty. The proverb (*q.v.*) is often aphoristic; so is the maxim (*q.v.*). A successful aphorism exposes and condenses at any rate a part of the truth, and is an aperçu or insight. For instance, the anonymous 'Conscience is a cur that will let you get past it, but that you cannot keep from barking'.

The aphorism is of great antiquity, timeless and international. The Classical, Hebraic and Oriental worlds have all made great contributions, and the common stock of wisdom and knowledge everywhere has scattered these nuggets of truth in the writings and sayings of many civilizations. Of the thousands who have added to the store the following deserve special mention: Aristotle, Plato, St Augustine; Montaigne, Pascal, La Rochefoucauld, Chamfort, La Bruyère, Vauvenargues, Joubert, de Tocqueville, Valéry, de Chazal, Remy de Gourmont, Proust, Camus; Chaucer, Francis Bacon, Sir Thomas Browne, George Halifax, Pope, Dr Johnson, Lord Chesterfield, William Blake, Coleridge, Walter Bagehot, Hazlitt, Samuel (*Erewhon*) Butler, Oscar Wilde, Bernard Shaw, A. N. Whitehead, W. H. Auden; Ralph Waldo Emerson,

Thoreau; Goethe, Schopenhauer, Lichtenberg, Nietzsche, Karl Kraus; Kierke-gaard; Chekhov; Cesare Pavese; Ortega y Gasset; Santayana. John Stuart Mill composed a short piece on aphorisms and John Morley wrote a brief discourse on them. Two valuable modern collections are *The Faber Book of Aphorisms* (1964) compiled by W. H. Auden and *The Oxford Book of Aphorisms* (1983) compiled by John Gross. *See also* SENTENTIA.

apocalyptic literature The term 'apocalyptic' derives from Greek *apocalypse*, 'to disclose', and Apocalypse is the name given to the last book of the New Testament, The Revelation of St John. Such literature comprises prophetic or quasi-prophetic writings which tend to present doom-laden visions of the world and sombre and minatory predictions of mankind's destiny. An early example is Wulfstan's homily to the English (*c.* 1014). In the later Middle Ages chiliastic movements in Europe evoked a large number of diatribes against the wickedness of humanity and the imminence of the end of the world. Sermon literature abounds in apocalyptic visions. The apocalyptic imagery in much of Blake's poetry combines religious visions with a more secular anger directed at the injustices and depravations of the modern world; subsequently, apocalyptic writing has tended to blame man rather than God for bringing about the end of civilization. In the 20th c., and in the postwar period especially, visions of man-made apocalypses brought about by war, pandemic or environmental catastrophe are not uncommon, and abound in science fiction (*q.v.*). Examples of apocalyptic literature might include James Thomson's poem *The City of Dreadful Night* (1874), H. G. Wells's *Mind at the End of its Tether* (1945), perhaps George Orwell's *Nineteen Eighty-Four* (1949), Norman Mailer's *The Armies of the* Night (1968) and Doris Lessing's *The Four-Gated City* (1969). Many such narratives focus on the post-apocalyptic aftermath, which facilitates an exploration of what humanity might be like without the support – or constraints – of civilization as we know it. Thus recent apocalyptic writing has close parallels with dys-topian literature and desert island fiction (*qq.v.*).

apocope (Gk 'cutting off') The dropping of a letter or letters from the end of a word. Fairly common in verse to achieve an elision, especially with the word 'the'. Other examples are: taxi(cab); edit(or); curio(sity); cinema (tograph).

Apocrypha (Gk 'things hidden') Writings of unknown or uncertain author-ship. Fourteen books of the Greek version of the Old Testament, contained in the Septuagint but not in the Hebrew Bible, were rejected from the Canon (*q.v.*). Writings ascribed on insufficient evidence to certain authors (e.g. Chaucer and Shakespeare) are also called apocryphal.

Apollonian/Dionysian Terms derived from the names of the Greek gods Apollo and Dionysus. Apollo was the messenger of the gods, and the presid-ing deity of music, medicine, youth and light, and was sometimes identified with the sun. Dionysus was the god of vegetation and wine and, it might be said, of 'permissiveness'. Nietzsche used the terms in *The Birth of Tragedy out of the Spirit of Music* (1872). He was making a distinction between reason and instinct, culture and primitive nature; possibly brains as opposed to loins and heart. Apollonian is also often thought to signify 'sunny' and 'serene', whereas the Dionysian means 'stormy' and 'turbulent'. Nietzsche argued that these elements formed a unity in Greek tragedy where dialogue provided the Apollonian element and the dithyrambic choral songs the Dionysiac. In the 19th c. this antinomy (*q.v.*) was much elaborated, particularly in the work of Schopenhauer, but it was Schiller who originally made the distinction between *naiv* and *sentimentalisch* (*q.v.*). Among more modern writers D. H. Lawrence was deeply interested in it. He might be described as a Dionysiac writer whereas Stendhal and André Gide were Apollonian. Of course, a combination is possible, as in Shakespeare's sonnets, or the love poems of Donne and Burns. *See also* CLASSICISM/ROMANTICISM; EMOTIVE LANGUAGE; HEBRAISM/HELLENISM.

apologue *See* FABLE.

apology (Gk 'defence') A work written to defend a writer's opinions or to elaborate and clarify a problem. A well-known example is Plato's *Apology* in which Socrates defends himself against the governing body of Athens. Another notable instance is Sir Philip Sidney's *Apologie for Poetrie*, or *Defence of Poesie* (1595), an essay which examines the art of poetry and discusses the state of English poetry at the time. Shelley also wrote a *Defence of Poetry* (1821), a remarkable achievement in which he vindicates his views on the elements of love and imagination in poetry. A very different work was Lamennais's apologia, *Paroles d'un Croyant* (1834), a 'reply' to a papal Encyclical. The most famous example of more recent times is John Henry Newman's *Apologia Pro Vita Sua* (1864): a masterly exposition of Newman's beliefs, and a refutation of Charles Kingsley's accusation that Newman did not regard truth as a necessary virtue.

apophasis (Gk 'from speaking') Affirming by apparent denial, a stressing through negation. A famous example is contained in Hamlet's parting words to Gertrude at the end of the 'bedroom scene' (III, iv):

> Not this, by no means, that I bid you do:
> Let the bloat King tempt you again to bed;

He goes on to emphasize a series of injunctions.

apophthegm (Gk 'speaking out plainly') A terse, pithy saying – akin to proverb, maxim and aphorism (*qq.v.*). A well-known collection from antiquity was the *Apophthegmata Patrum*, a compilation of anecdotes and sayings from the Egyptian Desert Fathers. The work was probably compiled late in the 5th c. Francis Bacon made a collection entitled *Apophthegms New and Old* (1624), which contained the saying 'Hope is a good breakfast, but it is a bad supper'. *See also* GNOMIC VERSE; SENTENTIA.

aporia (Gk 'impassable path') A term used in the theory of deconstruction (*q.v.*) to indicate a kind of impasse or insoluble conflict between rhetoric and thought. *Aporia* suggests the 'gap' or lacuna between what a text means to say and what it is constrained to mean. It is central to Jacques Derrida's theory of *différance* (*q.v.*). In his excellent book on Derrida's critique of philosophy (*Derrida*, 1987) Christopher Norris discusses this central feature of deconstruction as 'the seeking-out of those "aporias", blindspots or moments of self-contradiction where a text involuntarily betrays the tension between rhetoric and logic, between what it manifestly means to say and what it is nonetheless constrained to mean'.

aposiopesis (Gk 'becoming silent') A rhetorical device in which speech is broken off abruptly and the sentence is left unfinished. A memorable example occurs in a speech by King Lear (II, iv) in which he fulminates against Regan and Goneril:

> – No, you unnatural hags,
> I will have such revenges on you both,
> That all the world shall – I will do such things, –
> What they are, yet I know not; but they shall be
> The terrors of the earth.

apostrophe (Gk 'turning away') A figure of speech in which a thing, a place, an abstract quality, an idea, a dead or absent person, is addressed as if present and capable of understanding. Classic instances are Goldsmith's opening of *The Deserted Village*: 'Sweet Auburn, loveliest village of the plain . . .'; Antony's cry in *Julius Caesar*: 'O Judgement! thou art fled to brutish beasts . . .'; and Wordsworth's passionate appeal in *London 1812*: 'Milton! Thou should'st be living at this hour . . .'

Apostrophe is also the name of the symbol ', used to indicate elision and (with or without 's') the possessive case. *See also* PUNCTUATION.

apparatus (or **apparatus criticus**) A feature of scholarly editions of literary works, historical documents, etc. It includes textual footnotes, emendations, variant readings, marginalia, appendices, glossaries, and so forth.

appositum *See* EPITHET.

aptronym A name that fits the nature and character of a person and/or their occupation. This is how names were originally acquired or bestowed (e.g. Hunter, Farmer, Cooper, Smith, Mason, Miller, Draper). Aptronymic titles have often been used in literature as a kind of label (William Archer called them 'label names'). They were common in the Morality Plays (*q.v.*), in allegories like Spenser's *Faerie Queene* and Bunyan's *Pilgrim's Progress*, in novels (especially those of Fielding, Dickens and Thackeray) and in dramatic comedy (e.g. plays by Jonson, Congreve, Sheridan and Goldsmith). Famous instances are Mr Worldly Wiseman, Mrs Malaprop and Mr Gradgrind. *See* ALLEGORY; COMEDY OF HUMOURS; HUMOURS.

Arcadia Originally a mountainous district in the Peloponnese. For Classical poets Arcadia was the symbol of rural serenity, the harmony of the legendary Golden Age. Virgil's *Eclogues* illustrate an ideal way of pastoral life in Arcadia, where shepherds and shepherdesses, removed from 'real life', devote themselves to their flocks and their songs. During the Renaissance the idea was popularly revived by a number of writers, especially Sannazzaro, who published a series of verses linked by prose called *L'Arcadia* (1501), and by Sir Philip Sidney who published a prose romance, also called *Arcadia* (1590). Spenser's pastoral (*q.v.*) poems also depict this ideal existence.

archaism This term denotes what is old or obsolete. Its use was common in poetry until the end of the 19th c. The reasons are various. Sometimes the older form of a word was more suitable metrically. Many archaisms were used because of their associations with the past, especially those linked to the age of chivalry and romances (*q.v.*). Spenser, who much admired Chaucer, was the person chiefly responsible for the fashion – particularly in *The Faerie Queene* (1589, 1596). Spenser, in order to try to re-create the spirit and atmosphere of chivalry and devotion in the Middle Ages (as seen from his point of view), used a sort of poetic diction (*q.v.*) which was partly archaic and partly of his own devising. Milton, who greatly admired Spenser, used them sparingly; but in Milton we find a different kind of archaism – namely the use of a syntax and word order characteristic of Latin, which was by his day a dead language. The 18th c. 'Spenserians' continued the tradition; so did Keats (much influenced by Spenser), Coleridge and William Morris. Tennyson used archaisms for the same purposes as Keats and Spenser. Late in the 19th c. Gerard Manley Hopkins also resuscitated a number of archaisms, but they were seldom of the Spenserian type. He was interested in 'working' words, rather than the decorative or atmospheric.

This stanza from Thomas Parnell's *A Fairy Tale* (c. 1700) illustrates a grotesque use of the Spenserian variety:

> With that Sir Topaz, hapless youth!
> In accents faultering, ay for *ruth*
>   Intreats them pity *graunt*;
> For *als* he been a mister *wight*,
> Betray'd by wandering in the night
>   To tread the circled haunt.

The italicized words were all archaisms by the time this was written.

On the other hand, in Keats's *The Eve of Saint Mark* (c. 1819) we find a deliberate archaism to suggest something written in the 14th c. The maiden fair Bertha is reading the 'legend page' of 'Holy Mark':

> 'Gif ye wol stonden hardie wight –
> Amiddes of the blacke night –
> Righte in the churche porce, pardie
> Ye wol behold a companie
> Appouchen thee full dolourouse

> For sooth to sain from everich house
> Be it in city or village
> Wol come the Phantom and image
> Of ilka gent and ilka carle
> Whom coldè Deathè hath in parle
> And wol some day that very year
> Touchen with foulè venime spear
> And sadly do them all to die –

And so on for a further nineteen lines before he reverts to normal language thus:

> At length her constant eyelids come
> Upon the fervent martyrdom;
> Then lastly to his holy shrine,
> Exalt amid the tapers' shine
> At Venice, –

Except in parody (*q.v.*), archaism is rare in prose. A noteworthy example is C. M. Doughty's *Travels in Arabia Deserta* (1888). In this extraordinary work Doughty used a mixture of Chaucerian and Elizabethan English combined with Arabic.

archetypal criticism The investigation and analysis of archetypal and mythical narrative patterns, character types, themes and motifs in literature and their recurrence in literature. It owes much to the original work of the school of comparative anthropology at Cambridge, to J. G. Frazer's monumental study *The Golden Bough* (1890–1915), which traces elemental patterns of myth and ritual, and to the depth psychology of C. G. Jung. The term has often been used since Maud Bodkin's remarkable book *Archetypal Patterns in Poetry* (1934). Northrop Frye's *Anatomy of Criticism* (1957) is perhaps the classic work. *See* ARCHETYPE; MYTH; NARRATOLOGY.

archetype (Gk 'original pattern') A basic model from which copies are made; therefore a prototype. In general terms, the abstract idea of a class of things which represents the most typical and essential characteristics shared by the class; thus a paradigm or exemplar. An archetype is atavistic and universal, the product of 'the collective unconscious' and inherited from our ancestors. The fundamental facts of human existence are archetypal: birth, growing up, love, family and tribal life, dying, death, not to mention the struggle between children and parents, and fraternal rivalry. Certain character or personality types have become established as more or less archetypal. For instance: the rebel, the Don Juan (womanizer), the all-conquering hero, the braggadocio (*q.v.*), the country bumpkin, the local lad who makes good, the self-made man, the hunted man, the siren, the witch and *femme fatale*, the villain, the traitor, the snob and the social climber, the guilt-ridden figure in search of expiation, the damsel in distress, and the person more sinned against than sinning. Creatures, also, have come to be archetypal emblems. For example, the lion, the eagle, the snake, the hare and the tortoise. Further archetypes are the rose, the paradisal garden and the state of 'pre-Fall' innocence. Themes include the arduous quest or search, the pursuit of vengeance, the overcoming of difficult tasks, the descent into the underworld, symbolic fertility rites and redemptive rituals.

The archetypal idea has always been present and diffused in human consciousness. Plato was the first philosopher to elaborate the concept of archetypal or ideal forms (Beauty, Truth, Goodness) and divine archetypes. Since the turn of the 19th c. the idea and subject have been explored extensively. Practitioners of the two sciences of comparative anthropology and depth psychology have made notable contributions. The major works in this venture of discovery include: J. G. Frazer's *The Golden Bough* (1890–1915); C. G. Jung's 'On the Relation of Analytical Psychology to Poetic Art' (1922) in *Contributions to Analytical Psychology* (1928) and 'Psychology and Literature' in *Modern Man in Search of a Soul* (1933); Sigmund Freud's *A General Introduction to Psychoanalysis* (1920); Maud Bodkin's *Archetypal Patterns in Poetry* (1934); G. Wilson Knight's *Starlit Dance* (1941); E. Cassirer's *Language and Myth* (trans. 1946); Robert Graves's *The White Goddess* (1948); Richard Chase's *Quest for Myth* (1949); J. Campbell's *The Hero with a Thousand Faces* (1949); Philip Wheelwright's *The Burning Fountain* (1954) and his *Metaphor and Reality* (1962); B. Seward's *The Symbolic Rose* (1960); Northrop Frye's *Anatomy of Criticism* (1957) and 'The Archetypes of Literature' in *Fables of Identity* (1963), plus several other inquiries. *See also* IMAGERY; MYTH; STOCK CHARACTER; STOCK RESPONSE; STOCK SITUATION; SYMBOL AND SYMBOLISM.

archi-écriture *See* PHONOCENTRISM.

Archilochian verse So called after the Greek satirist Archilochus (*c.* 700 BC). He is believed to have invented lines or couplets in which different meters were combined. The main forms are: Greater Archilochian – a dactylic tetrameter (*q.v.*) plus a trochaic tripody (*q.v.*); and the Lesser Archilochian – a dactylic trimeter catalectic. He also used the dactylic tetrameter catalectic, the iambelegus and the elegiambus. In addition he is credited with four different kinds of strophe (*q.v.*). His work had a major influence on Horace. *See* CATALEXIS; DACTYL; TROCHEE.

archive A repository of documents or other primary source material. As opposed to library holdings, archival repositories tend to be unique and may represent the accumulated collections of individuals or institutions. Respective examples of these kinds are the Churchill archive in Cambridge, comprising the speeches, correspondence and other biographical material relating to Winston Churchill, or the BBC archive which aims to preserve radio and television broadcasts for posterity. The National Archives at Kew are the British government's official archive and contains documents from a period spanning a thousand years. In literary studies, particularly following the rise of new historicism (*q.v.*), the use of archival material has become an increasingly common method employed to read texts via their interpretative contexts. Developments in electronic technology have enabled the digitization of a growing number of archives, promising to open up hitherto relatively inaccessible collections. By the same token, it seems inevitable that future archives will be constituted by electronic documents and other media to a significant degree.

arch-rhyme *See* RHYME.

argot A French word of unknown origin. It means slang or cant (*qq.v.*) and usually refers to the slang used by social outcasts or those who are disapproved of socially. Much abstruse *argot* of this kind has been assembled by Auguste le Breton in *Langue verte et noirs desseins* (1960). *See also* PATOIS; RHYMING SLANG.

argument (a) In literary use an abstract or summary of a plot prefacing a work. For instance, each book of *Paradise Lost* is preceded by an explanation of what is going to happen. This used to be common practice with a long poem, a novel or a treatise of some length and substance. The practice survives in the summaries sometimes found in the contents pages of a book. (b) An argument is also a division of a speech. (c) The term is also used to describe the dialectic (*q.v.*) in a poem. The argument in this fine poem by Thomas Beedome, for instance, is set forth in four different but interlocked statements and is concluded in the resolution of the final couplet:

> *The Question and Answer*
>
> When the sad ruines of that face
> In its owne wrinkles buried lyes
> And the stiffe pride of all its grace,
> By time undone, fals slack and dyes:
>   Wilt thou not sigh, and wish in some vext fit,
>   That it were now as when I courted it?
>
> And when thy glasse shall it present,
> Without those smiles which once were there,
> Showing like some stale monument,
> A scalpe departed from its haire,
>   At thy selfe frighted wilt not start and sweare
>   That I belied thee, when I call'd thee faire?
>
> Yes, yes, I know thou wilt, and so
> Pitty the weaknesse of thy scorne,
> That now hath humbled thee to know,
> Though faire it was, it is forlorne,
>   Love's sweetes thy aged corps embalming not,
>   What marvell if thy carkasse, beauty, rot?

> Then shall I live, and live to be
> Thy envie, thou my pitty; say
> When e're thou see mee, or I thee,
> (Being nighted from thy beautie's day),
>   'Tis hee, and had my pride not wither'd mee,
>   I had, perhaps, beene still as fresh as hee.
>
> Then shall I smile, and answer: 'True thy scorne
> Left thee thus wrinkled, slackt, corrupt, forlorne.'

argumentum ad (L 'appeal to') There are several phrases: (a) *ad baculum* ('to the stick', and thus the argument according to force); (b) *ad crumenam* ('to the wallet', the argument which appeals to a person's material instincts); (c) *ad hominem* ('to the man', that is, personal); (d) *ad ignorantiam* ('to ignorance', that is, the argument which depends upon the person being ignorant or uninformed); (e) *ad populum* ('to the people', that is the argument which is intended to rouse the feelings of the crowd); (f) *ad verecundiam* ('to modesty', that is an argument so constructed that the other person has to make a cautious reply in order to avoid being indecorous).

ars est celare artem (L 'art is to conceal art') The implication is that the best art seems spontaneous though in all probability it is the outcome of extremely hard work. Or 'hard writing makes easy reading'. *See* INSPIRATION; SPONTANEITY.

arsis and thesis (Gk 'lifting up' and 'setting down') The terms describe the upward and downward beat keeping time in Greek verse. The long syllable of a dactyl (*q.v.*) was the *thesis*; the *arsis* comprised the two short beats. *See* THESIS.

arte mayor (Sp 'major art') In the first place an eight-syllable verse in stanzas of eight lines; later of twelve syllables. It was usually employed for longer poems and there were several variations on the basic form. The twelve-syllable line would have a caesura (*q.v.*) after the sixth syllable and therefore this scheme amounted to a pair of *versos de redondilla menor*. But whereas the latter was only stressed on the fifth syllable, in *arte mayor* there is a stress on the second syllable. The rhyme scheme was usually abba acca. Intimations of *arte mayor* begin with Juan Ruiz, the Archpriest of Hita (*c.* 1280–*c.* 1351), and stories in the *Conde Lucanor*. Juan de Mena (1411–56) brought a new seriousness to Spanish poetry and was one of the masters of *arte mayor*. *See* ARTE MENOR; REDONDILLA.

arte menor (Sp 'minor art') A Spanish metrical term denoting lines of two to eight syllables with accent on the penultimate, and either assonance or rhyme. This type of line being relatively easy to compose, *arte menor* can be said to be a rather vague term. Popular poetry of many types falls readily into this category. It is found in traditional narrative poetry, popular song, and dramatic work. *See* ARTE MAYOR.

art for art's sake The phrase connotes the idea that a work of art has an intrinsic value without didactic or moral purpose. This concept seems to have been first put forward by Lessing in *Laokoon* (1766), and became something of an artistic battle-cry or slogan (*q.v.*) following the publication of Gautier's Preface to *Mademoiselle de Maupin* (1835). Throughout the 19th c. it became a guiding principle for many writers. Oscar Wilde was one of its leading advocates. *See* AESTHETICISM; DECADENCE; PARNASSIANS; REALISM.

articulus *See* BRACHIOLOGY.

artificial comedy *See* COMEDY OF MANNERS.

art nouveau (F 'new art') Primarily a style of architecture and decoration which had a wide vogue in Europe and America in the 1890s and up to *c.* 1914. It was ornate, decorative, asymmetrical and somewhat fantastic. As far as the literary scene is concerned it had a considerable influence on book production and periodicals in the 1890s, a decade which saw such productions as *The Century Guild Hobby Horse* (1884), *The Dial* (1889–97), *The Yellow Book* (1894–7) and *The Savoy* (1889–97). The *art nouveau* book was adorned by distinguished illustrators: principally, Aubrey Beardsley (1872–98), Charles Ricketts (1860–1931), Laurence Housman (1865–1959), Charles Conder (1868–1909) and Thomas Sturge Moore (1870–1940).

arts, the seven liberal *See* QUADRIVIUM.

Arzamas A short-lived Russian literary group which flourished 1815–18. Its members were in favour of literary and stylistic reforms and included Karamzin, Zhorkiski, Batynashkov, Vyazemski and Pushkin.

ascending rhythm *See* RISING RHYTHM.

Asclepiad A meter named after the Greek poet Asclepiades (*c.* 290 BC) of Samos. It comprised one spondee (*q.v.*), two or three choriambs (*see* CHORI-AMBUS) and one iamb (*q.v.*). It was used for lyric and tragic verse and was much employed by Horace. It is rare in English verse. W. H. Auden was probably the first poet since Campion to use accentual Asclepiads (in *In Due Season*).

aside In drama a few words or a short passage spoken in an undertone or to the audience. It is a theatrical convention and by convention the words are presumed inaudible to other characters on stage; unless of course the aside be between two characters and therefore clearly not meant for anyone else who may be present. It was in continual use until early in the twentieth century (especially in comedy and melodrama, *qq.v.*). The advent of 'naturalistic drama' (*q.v.*) led to its almost complete exclusion. However, it is still liberally used in pantomime (*q.v.*) and in farce (*q.v.*).

association The shared connection between an object and ideas. Coleridge spoke of it in *Biographia Literaria*: 'Ideas by having been together acquire a power of recalling each other; or every partial representation awakes the total representation of which it had been a part.'

Any sensory perception or idea may be associated with something from the past. Proust's *A la recherche du temps perdu* is a sustained exercise in the use of associations. Nearly all poetry is strongly associative. *See* AMBIGUITY; CONNOTATION; DISSOCIATION OF SENSIBILITY; SUGGESTION.

assonance Sometimes called 'vocalic rhyme', it consists of the repetition of similar vowel sounds, usually close together, to achieve a particular effect of euphony (*q.v.*). There is a kind of drowsy sonority in the following lines from Tennyson's *Lotos-Eaters* which is assonantal:

> The Lotos blooms below the barren peak:
> The Lotos blows by every winding creek:
> All day the wind breathes low with mellower tone
> Thro' every hollow cave and alley lone,
> Round and round the spicy downs the yellow Lotos-dust is
> blown.

In *Strange Meeting* Wilfred Owen uses a vocalic or half rhyme (*q.v.*) to similar effect:

> It seemed that out of battle I escaped
> Down some profound dull tunnel, long since scooped
> Through granites which titanic wars had groined.
> Yet also there encumbered sleepers groaned,
> Too fast in thought or death to be bestirred.

See also ALLITERATION; CONSONANCE; EUPHONY; MELOPOEIA; ONOMATO-POEIA; PHANOPOEIA; RHYME; VOWEL RHYME.

asteismus (Gk 'clever talk, wit') A contrived turning or twisting of the meaning of something said so that it implies something else. Related to the *double entente* and pun (*qq.v.*).

asterisk *See* PUNCTUATION.

astracanada A form of Spanish farce (*q.v.*), often broad and bawdy. It developed *c.* 1900 and remains popular. Two playwrights were largely responsible for the creation of this genre: Pedro Muñoz Seca (1881–1936) and Enrique García Álvarez (1873–1931).

asynartete (Gk 'disconnected') Applied to a poem whose divisions have different rhythms and meters. The creator of this sort of verse was Archilochus (7th c. BC) who used dactylic, trochaic and iambic verse. Hence the term Archilochian verse (*q.v.*).

asyndeton (Gk 'unconnected') A rhetorical device where conjunctions, articles and even pronouns are omitted for the sake of speed and economy. Puttenham, in *The Arte of English Poesie* (1589), calls it 'loose language', but it has been particularly popular in modern poetry (e.g. the work of W. H. Auden, Robert Lowell and John Berryman) as a means of achieving compact expression. Milton often used it, in *Paradise Lost* especially:

> The first sort by their own suggestion fell
> Self-tempted, self-depraved; man falls, deceived
> By the other first; man therefore shall find grace,
> The other none . . .

See ELLIPSIS.

asyntactic (Gk 'not arranged') Applied to prose or verse which is loose, ungrammatical in structure and therefore which breaks the normal conventions governing word order. *See* SYNTAX.

Atellan fables *See* FABULA.

atmosphere The mood and feeling, the intangible quality which appeals to extra-sensory as well as sensory perception, evoked by a work of art. For instance, the opening scene in *Hamlet* where the watch is tense and apprehensive, even 'jumpy'. By contrast, the beginning of Ben Jonson's *The Alchemist* indicates clearly that the play is going to be comic to the point of knockabout. An excellent example in the novel is Hardy's depiction of Egdon Heath in *The Return of the Native*.

atmosphere of the mind A phrase invented by Henry James to denote what the subjective writer of the novel tries to convey to the reader. After a time we in a sense 'inhabit' the writer's mind, breathe that air and are permeated by his vision.

atonic (Gk 'without tone or stress') Generally used to describe the unaccented syllables of a word; or, in verse, the unstressed syllables of a word or foot (*q.v.*).

Atticism A style adopted by Greek and Roman orators; distinguished by its simplicity and directness and by its lack of rhetorical device.

aubade (F 'dawn song') The Provençal and German equivalents are *alba* and *Tagelied* respectively. The dawn song is found in almost all the world's early literatures and expresses the regret of parting lovers at daybreak. The earliest European examples date from the end of the 12th c. There is a theory that the *aubade* grew out of the night watchman's announcement from his tower of the passing of night and the renewal of day. The exchange between Romeo and Juliet at the end of their wedding night is a good example. Perhaps the most beautiful and moving one in English literature occurs in Book III of Chaucer's *Troilus and Criseyde*:

> Myn hertes lif, my trist, and my plesaunce,
> That I was born, allas, what me is wo,
> That day of us moot make disseveraunce!

> For tyme it is to ryse and hennes go,
> Or ellis I am lost for evere mo!
> O nyght, allas! why nyltow over us hove,
> As longe as whan Almena lay by Jove?

Thus Criseyde begins when she hears the cock crow, and the exchange continues between the lovers for a further fourteen stanzas. An interesting modern example is William Empson's *Aubade* (1940). *See* DRAMATIC MONOLOGUE.

Aufklärung A German term for Enlightenment (*q.v.*).

Augustan age During the reign of the Emperor Augustus (27 BC–AD 14) many distinguished writers flourished, notably Virgil, Horace, Ovid and Tibullus. The term has been applied to that period of English history in which Dryden, Pope, Addison, Swift, Goldsmith, Steele and, to some extent, Johnson lived and imitated their style: that is the final decades of the 17th c. and the first half of the 18th c. So the phrase suggests a period of urbane and classical elegance in writing, a time of harmony, decorum (*q.v.*) and proportion. Goldsmith contributed an essay to *The Bee* on 'the Augustan Age in England', but he confined it to the reign of Queen Anne (1702–14). In French literature the term is applied to the age of Corneille, Racine and Molière. *See also* ENLIGHTENMENT; NEOCLASSICISM.

Aunt Edna The typical theatre-goer invented by Terence Rattigan and called by Kenneth Tynan 'a mythical, middle-class admirer . . . backbone of the theatre . . . she follows, never leads, intelligent taste'. An instance of antonomasia (*q.v.*).

aura A term used by the Marxist cultural critic Walter Benjamin in his essay *The Work of Art in the Age of Mechanical Reproduction* (1936) to denote the unique existence of a work of art in time and space. This uniqueness embraces the work's authenticity, authority, and its intrinsic embedding within the fabric of history, ritual and tradition. Reproduction of the work of art, especially for mass consumption, erodes this aura, detaching the reproduced object from tradition, substituting a plurality of copies for a unique existence, and enabling the reproduction to meet the beholder or listener in her own particular situation.

Benjamin says that the concept of aura can apply also to natural objects: when we view elements of nature directly, we experience their aura, which withers in their reproduction in magazines or film. To thus 'pry an object from its shell, to destroy its aura', is the mark of a historical stage of perception premised on the universal equality of things, a perception which adjusts 'reality to the masses and . . . the masses to reality'.

The concept of aura is also used by Max Horkheimer and Theodor Adorno to indicate a work of art's unique stylistic and epistemological orientation, which is abrogated by the filter of the culture industry (*q.v.*), where style becomes a function of social hierarchy. Here, art's unique 'self-negation', whereby it imbues a new shape to the very social and aesthetic forms it ostensibly embodies and expresses, is supplanted by the striving of inferior works (and of human beings) for bland similarity, accessible and ideologically effective without the exercise of intellectual effort. In this era of 'pseudo individuality' art 'renounces its own autonomy and proudly takes its place among consumption goods'. This 'purposelessness' of art (as allegedly characterized by Kant) is subsumed under the purposes of the market. Hence, the 'work of art, by completely assimilating itself to need, deceitfully deprives people of precisely that liberation from the principle of utility which it should inaugurate'. No object, including art, has an inherent value, and an object is valued only in so far as it can be exchanged.

aureate language A kind of poetic diction (*q.v.*) used by Scottish and English poets in the 15th c. It was a rather ornate and ornamental language, often consisting of vernacular coinages from Latin words. It is particularly noticeable in the poems of Dunbar and Henryson in Scotland, and Lydgate, Hawes and King James I of Scotland (1394–1437). James I was detained in England for nineteen years and there composed *The Kingis Quair* (written 1423–4) in aureate style. However, Dunbar was probably its best exponent. These lines by Dunbar give some indication of the style:

> Hale, sterne superne, hale in eterne
> In Godis sicht to schyne;
> Lucerne in derne for to discerne
> Be glory and grace devyne:
> Hodiern, modern, sempitern,
> Angelicall regyne,
> Our tern inferne for to dispern,
> Helpe, rialest rosyne.
> *Ave Maria, gracia plena*,
> Haile, fresche floure femynyne;
> Yerne us, guberne, virgin matern,
> Of reuth baith rute and ryne.

author, death of In *The Death of the Author*, an essay first published in *Mantéia V* in 1968, Roland Barthes attacks the common and traditional view of the author as the ultimate 'explanation' of a work. Barthes (and poststructuralist theory) contends that the author can no longer be regarded as the omniscient and all-pervading presence and influence in a work of literature; indeed, he implies that the reader takes over as the prime source of power in a text. At the end of the essay Barthes suggests that 'the birth of the reader must be at the cost of the death of the Author'. The author becomes little more than an hypothesis, a 'person' projected by the critic from the text, and a convenient catch-all for the critic, whereas the reader is at liberty to see the plurality of the text.

Barthes explains the idea of 'the death of the author' via a specific French literary tradition – that of Mallarmé and Valéry. Mallarmé's poetics consists in suppressing the author in the interests of writing. In a memorable phrase, he wrote of the poet's role being to 'cede the initiative to words'. Barthes also refers to the 'modern scriptor', implying a comparison between 'classic realist' and 'modern/postmodern' fiction. It should be remembered that his essay (1968) is close to *S/Z* (1970) and the essay *From Work to Text* (1971), which are, *inter alia*, critiques of bourgeois ideology.

Readers have become conditioned by the idea and 'construct' of an Author – be the author dead or alive. Barthes is at pains to dismantle this idea; and deconstructive practice, for example, has shown anyway that authors are extremely unreliable; they often do not know what they are doing; and there is a big discrepancy between intention and result. Authorial authority is highly questionable.

A key passage in Barthes's essay is:

the image of literature one can find in contemporary culture is tyrannically centred around the author, his person, his history, his tastes, his passions; criticism still consists for the most part in saying that Baudelaire's *œuvre* is the failure of Baudelaire the man, that Van Gogh's *œuvre* is his madness, and Tchaikovsky's his vice: the explanation of the *œuvre* is always sought on the side of the man who has produced it as if, through the more or less transparent allegory of the fiction, it was always in the end the voice of one person alone, the author, who was giving us his confidences.

Foucault's essay *What is an Author?* (1969) should also be noted. Foucault historicizes the notion of authorship in a sceptical way and envisages anonymous texts at the end. But this is distinct from Barthes's point of view.

Finally, it should be said that, arguably, the 'death of the author' was initiated in Anglo-American literary criticism by the New Critics (*see* NEW CRITICISM), who, like deconstructionists, advocated the primacy of the text (though with totally different results). Barthes has argued that the New Critics have consolidated the position of the author. *See* DECONSTRUCTION.

autobiographical novel   Many novels are in part autobiographical. Some are more obviously so than others. Fairly well-known representative examples are: Goethe's *Die Leiden des jungen Werthers* (1774), E. J. Trelawny's *The Adventures of a Younger Son* (1831), Thomas Aldrich's *The Story of a Bad Boy* (1870), Somerset Maugham's *Of Human Bondage* (1915), Gertrude Stein's *The Autobiography of Alice B. Toklas* (1933), Henry Miller's *Tropic of Cancer* (1934) and Maureen Duffy's *That's How It Was* (1962). The most famous instance in English literature is probably Joyce's *A Portrait of the Artist as a Young Man* (1916), which developed from *Stephen Hero* begun by Joyce *c.* 1904 (publ. 1944). *See* MEMOIR-NOVEL; NOVEL; WERTHERISM.

autobiography   A person's own account of his or her life. Unlike private records such as journals or diaries (*qq.v*), which such a definition might also describe, autobiographies are always written for a public audience. Indeed, autobiography is ideally understood by both its authors and its readers to be exemplary, as a reliable and true portrayal of a life from which others can learn.

The term was first used in English in 1797 by William Taylor, though the genre has its roots in antiquity. Sappho, Herodotus and Xenophon are among several poets and historians of the Classical era who wrote about their own lives. But the first autobiography as we would recognize it today was St Augustine's *Confessions*, produced in the 4th c.: an intensely personal account of spiritual experience and an extraordinary instance of self-exploration. There are, however, marked differences between the *Confessions* and autobiographical writing of the modern era. Whereas Augustine sees himself as a model servant of God, Enlightenment writers such as Montaigne understood themselves first and foremost as individuals. The rise of anthropocentric humanism certainly encouraged people to explore and analyse themselves in greater detail, and helps to explain the proliferation of autobiography in the Enlightenment period.

The genre's overall development might be seen as reflecting shifts in conceptions of the individual. Late medieval and Renaissance work, such as Benvenuto Cellini's *Vita* (1556–8) and John Bunyan's *Grace Abounding to the Chief of Sinners* (1666), tended to present lives chronologically to portray the emergence of a coherent self which develops into spiritual wholeness. Many autobiographies of the Romantic era, including Rousseau's *Confessions* (1781, 1788) and Hazlitt's *Liber Amoris* (1823), were influenced by developments in epistemology but also focused more intensely on their writers' emotional experiences. In the 20th c., modernist sensibilities produced autobiographies, such as Yeats's *Autobiographies* (1955), which foregrounded the fragmented nature of the self. Increasingly, veracity was subordinated to the requirements of expression, as the distinctions between fiction and autobiography became blurred. The crossing of these boundaries, though, is not in itself new. During the 18th c. we can discern some connection between autobiography and the relatively new form of the novel. For example, Defoe's *Robinson Crusoe* (1719) and Sterne's *Sentimental Journey* (1768) were both presented as factual representations of their authors' lives. But if fiction could be cast as autobiography, autobiography was rarely presented as fiction until the 20th c.

The last one hundred years or so has undoubtedly been the genre's period of greatest formal innovation. One key development is the autobiographical novel *(q.v.)*, such as James Joyce's *A Portrait of the Artist as a Young Man* (1916) which presents its subject in the third-person. Some writers, including Yeats, Maya Angelou and Edmund White, have produced different versions of their lives, from a variety of perspectives, or in different modes of writing. In the 20th c., autobiography has provided crucial vehicles for minority voices who have sought to claim significance for certain marginalized lives: for example, those of immigrants (e.g. Mary Antin, *The Promised Land*, 1912), African-Americans (e.g. Richard Wright, *Black Boy*, 1945), and gay/lesbian writers (e.g. Audre Lorde, *Zami: A New Spelling of My Name*, 1982).

Autobiography has been a largely Western tradition. While there are some prominent examples of autobiographical writing from elsewhere – including Murasaki Shikubu's 'The Tale of Genji', from 10th c. Japan – it rarely seems to have caught on as it has done in the West. In colonized cultures which originally had no tradition of writing about individual lives or indeed of writing at all, autobiography has sometimes taken on interesting, hybrid forms. Many Native American autobiographies such as Leslie Marmon Silko's *Storyteller* (1981) attempt to articulate communal, oral traditions (*q.v.*) by presenting their material as the product of many voices. *See also* BIOGRAPHY; COMING-OUT STORY; MEMOIR; LIFE WRITING; SLAVE NARRATIVE.

autoclesis (Gk 'self-invitation') A rhetorical device by which an idea is introduced in negative terms in order to call attention to it and arouse curiosity. A classic example is Mark Antony's use of the will in *Julius Caesar* (III, ii) in order to rouse the mob's interest.

automatic writing Writing which is attempted without conscious control. It is more likely to be possible in states of hypnosis or under the influence of drugs. When Dadaism and surrealism (*qq.v.*) were fashionable, the disciples of the creeds 'went in for' automatic writing. It produced the equivalent of a 'happening' (*q.v.*). Nothing of any importance survives.

autorhyme *See* RHYME.

autos sacramentales An allegorical and didactic genre of Spanish religious drama intended to expound the doctrines of the Church. The allegories were taken from biblical, Classical and historical themes. The plays were put on by the civic authorities and staged with pomp. Calderón (1600–81), the most famous of the playwrights who composed them, is credited with over eighty. *Autos* were performed until 1765, when they were banned by Charles III. *See also* ALLEGORY; MYSTERY PLAY.

autotelic (Gk 'self-completing') A jargon term employed in the New Criticism (*q.v.*) to denote that a poem, for instance, has no other end or purpose but to *be*; therefore it has no didactic, moral or any other additional purpose. The origins of the idea are found in the work of the 18th c. Swiss critics J. J. Bodmer and Breitinger. It helped to promote the doctrine of art for art's sake (*q.v.*) and also seems to have influenced those involved in the avant-garde (*q.v.*) *creacionismo* (*q.v.*) movement which developed *c.* 1916 in the Spanish-speaking world and in France. The main theorist was Vicente Huidobro (1893–1948), the Chilean poet, who had some influence on the development of concrete poetry (*q.v.*). In France, Pierre Reverdy, a friend of Huidobro, was the main theorist.

auxesis *See* AMPLIFICATION.

avant-garde An important and much used term in the history of art and literature. It clearly has a military origin ('advance guard') and, as applied to art and literature, denotes exploration, pathfinding, innovation and invention; something new, something advanced (ahead of its time) and revolutionary.

In 1845, Gabriel-Désiré Laverdant published a work called *De la mission de l'art et du rôle des artistes*. In it he wrote:

> Art, the expression of society, manifests, in its highest soaring, the most advanced social tendencies: it is the forerunner and the revealer. Therefore, to know whether art worthily fulfils its proper mission as initiator, whether the artist is truly of the avant-garde, one must know where Humanity is going, what the destiny of the human race is . . .

In 1878 Bakunin founded and published for a short time a periodical devoted to political agitation called *L'Avant-garde*. Even at this period it is rare to find the term applied to art and literature alone. Baudelaire treats it with scorn. In his personal notebook, *Mon cœur mis à nu*, he refers to 'les littérateurs d'avant-garde', and elsewhere he speaks of 'la presse militante' and 'la littérature militante'. He is referring to radical writers, to writers of the political Left.

During the last quarter of the 19th c. the term and concept appear in both cultural and political contexts. Gradually the cultural-artistic meaning displaced the socio-political meaning. For a long time it has been commonplace to refer to avant-garde art or literature. Nowadays we are accustomed to think of the symbolist poets Verlaine, Rimbaud and Mallarmé as the first members of the avant-garde; likewise the playwrights of the Theatre of the Absurd (*q.v.*) and novelists like Alain Robbe-Grillet, Michel Butor, Nathalie Sarraute. *See* ANTI-NOVEL; NOUVEAU ROMAN; NOUVELLE VAGUE.

aversio *See* APOSTROPHE.

B

bacchius A metrical foot consisting of one unstressed syllable followed by two stressed ones: ⌣ / /. The name may derive from the use of the foot in Greek drinking songs and verses devoted to the god Bacchus. Rare in English verse; not many three-syllable words take such quantities. *See* PALIMBACCHIUS.

Baconian theory The theory that Francis Bacon (1561–1626) wrote the plays ascribed to Shakespeare. This hypothesis began to achieve some vogue in the middle of the 19th c. but is not now taken seriously.
  In 1920 the unfortunately named T. J. Looney identified Edward de Vere, 17th Earl of Oxford (1550–1604), as the author of Shakespeare's plays. Since then the so-called 'Oxfordians' have tried to promote the claim.

bailes (Sp 'dances') A term used in Golden Age (*q.v.*) literature to denote compositions for music, song and dance, usually performed between the second and third acts of three-act *comedias*. A notable example is *Las flores* by Alonso de Olmedo, used as an interlude (*q.v.*) in Calderón's *Hado y divisa* (1680). *Bailes* were composed by many authors.

Bakhtinian *See* CARNIVALIZATION/CARNIVALESQUE; HETEROGLOSSIA.

balada A dance song of Provençal origin. It was not a fixed form but it had a refrain (*q.v.*) that was often repeated.

ballad Like *ballade* (*q.v.*) and ballet, the word derives from the late Latin and Italian *ballare* 'to dance'. Fundamentally a ballad is a song that tells a story and originally was a musical accompaniment to a dance. The ballad is an ancient poetic form which, in Europe, flourished from the late Middle Ages, treating topics from legend and folklore as well as from local and national history. As a primarily oral form, however, its antecedents may be discerned in the Germanic story-telling tradition of the *Beowulf* poet and beyond to the Homeric cycle.

A Dictionary of Literary Terms and Literary Theory, Fifth Edition. J. A. Cuddon.
© 2013 The Estate of J. A. Cuddon. Published 2013 by Blackwell Publishing Ltd.

We can distinguish certain basic characteristics common to large numbers of ballads: (a) the beginning is often abrupt; (b) the language is simple; (c) the story is told through dialogue and action; (d) the theme is often tragic (though there are a number of comic ballads); (e) there is often a refrain (*q.v.*). To these features we may add: a ballad usually deals with a single episode; the events leading to the crisis are related swiftly; there is minimal detail of surroundings; there is a strong dramatic element; there is considerable intensity and immediacy in the narration; the narrator is impersonal; stock, well-tried epithets are used in the oral tradition (*q.v.*) of kennings and Homeric epithets (*qq.v.*); there is frequently incremental repetition (*q.v.*); the single line of action and the speed of the story preclude much attempt at delineation of character; imagery is sparse and simple.

We may distinguish further between two basic kinds of ballad: the folk or traditional ballad and the literary ballad. The former is anonymous and is transmitted from singer to singer by word of mouth. It thus belongs to oral tradition (*q.v.*). In this manner ballads have been passed down from generation to generation over centuries. Inevitably, this has led to many variations of one particular story. In the British Isles the border conflicts between English and Scots produced many stirring ballads. The legends of Robin Hood were also circulated in ballad form from at least the late Middle Ages. The latter kind of ballad is not anonymous and is written down by a poet as he composes it. Here is an example of a stanza from a traditional oral ballad:

> As I was walking all alone,
> I heard twa corbies making a mane;
> The tane unto the t'other say,
> 'Where sall we gang and dine to-day?'

And here is a stanza from a literary ballad by a modern poet, Charles Causley:

> Mother, get up, unbar the door,
> Throw wide the window-pane,
> I see a man stand all covered in sand
> Outside in Vicarage Lane.

These literary (or sometimes 'lyrical') ballads represent a revival of interest in the earlier oral form and are particularly associated with the Romantic poets. Coleridge's *Rime of the Ancient Mariner* is a prime example.

Many historians and critics distinguish a third kind of ballad – the popular. This has much in common with the traditional or folk ballad. However, it tends to be associated with semi-literate or literate *urban* rather than rural communities, and is often very realistic, unheroic and comic or satirical. It is sometimes called the broadside ballad or street ballad and, like the traditional ballad, has influenced many poets (e.g. Pope, Byron, Wordsworth, Blake, Coleridge, Shelley and Oscar Wilde).

Since early in the 18th c. there have been attempts to classify the form, as evident from the appearance of several published collections of ballads. In the 20th c., Cecil Sharp's *Folk Songs of England* (5 vols, 1908–12), A. Quiller-Couch's *The Oxford Book of Ballads* (1910) and *The Faber Book of Ballads* (1965) have been important examples. *See also* BALLAD METER; BALLAD OPERA; FOLKSONG; LAY; NARRATIVE VERSE; ROMANTICISM.

ballade An OF verse form, particularly popular during the 14th and 15th c. The commonest type consists of three eight-line stanzas rhyming ababbcbc, with a four-line *envoi* (*q.v.*) rhyming bcbc. The last line of the first stanza serves as the refrain (*q.v.*) repeated in the last line of each stanza and of the *envoi*. Its rhyming complexity makes the *ballade* a difficult form.

The *ballade* was standardized in the 14th c. by French poets like Guillaume de Machaut and Eustache Deschamps, and perfected in the next century, principally by Villon (especially in, for instance, *Ballade des pendus* and *Ballade des dames du temps jadis*). By the 17th c. there was little regard for the form; it was mocked by Molière and Boileau.

Medieval English poets (especially Chaucer and Gower) occasionally imitated it but it never became popular. It was not until the 19th c. that English poets – notably Dobson, Lang, W. E. Henley and Swinburne – revived it with mixed success. Since then the few who have attempted it include Chesterton, Belloc and Sir John Squire. *See also* BALLAD; BALLAD METER; CHANT ROYAL; TERN.

ballad meter Traditionally a four-line stanza or quatrain (*q.v.*) containing alternating four-stress and three-stress lines. The rhyme scheme is usually abcb; sometimes abab. A refrain (*q.v.*) is common. Here is the opening stanza of *Earl Brand*:

> Rise up, rise up, my seven brave sons,
> And dress in your armour so bright;
> Earl Douglas will hae Lady Margaret awa
> Before that it be light.

ballad opera It may be considered an early form of musical (*q.v.*). It combines dialogue in dramatic prose (which is spoken rather than 'sung' or chanted in any way) with music and songs, usually set to traditional and contemporary melodies. It was virtually invented by John Gay when he composed *The Beggar's Opera* (1728), a play with music and songs interpolated (the music was arranged by J. C. Pepusch). This has remained a regular favourite with amateur and professional theatre companies (cf. Alan Ayckbourn's *Chorus of Disapproval*, 1987). There were many imitations of Gay's work in the 18th c. and ballad opera was very popular for some twenty years. Gay wrote a sequel, *Polly*, to *The Beggar's Opera*, and this was eventually produced in 1777. Other 18th c. works of note which are very like ballad opera were Arne and Bickerstaffe's *Thomas and Sally* (1760) and *Love in a Village* (1762). Sheridan also made a contribution to this form with *The Duenna* (1775). In the 20th c. Bertolt Brecht experimented with the form and produced one outstanding example in the shape of *The Threepenny Opera* (1928), a reworking of Gay's theme and story. Thereafter the main practitioner was Ewan MacColl (1915–89), who wrote several. His *Johnny Noble* (1945) was particularly fine. *See* BALLAD; OPERA.

barbarism An impropriety of language. The term may refer to a mistake in the form of a word or the unwarranted use of foreign words.

barcarole (It *barca*, 'boat') A poem or song whose subject matter is in some way connected with boats or water; also one whose aural effects can suggest the movement of water. Dates from the Middle Ages.

bard (Welsh, *bardd*; Irish, *bard*) Among the ancient Celts a bard was a sort of official poet whose task it was to celebrate national events – particularly heroic actions and victories. The bardic poets of Gaul and Britain were a distinct social class with special privileges. The 'caste' continued to exist in Ireland and Scotland, but nowadays are more or less confined to Wales, where the poetry contests and festivals, known as the Eisteddfodau, were revived in 1822 (after a lapse since Elizabethan times). In modern Welsh a *bardd* is a poet who has taken part in an Eisteddfod (*q.v.*). In more common parlance the term may be half seriously applied to a distinguished poet – especially Shakespeare.

bardolatry Excessive praise and veneration of Shakespeare, most commonly associated with the development of the cult of Shakespeare in the mid-eighteenth century, particularly with David Garrick's 1769 Shakespeare jubilee at Stratford. Hence, 'bardolater' (by analogy with 'idolater'), anyone who idolizes the Bard.

baroque The term probably derives from the word *baroco*, often used in the late Middle Ages to describe any form of grotesque pedantry. It is a term more commonly used of the visual arts (and music) than literature, but it may be used judiciously to describe a particularly ornate or sumptuous style. It can be applied, for example, to the prose of Sir Thomas Browne and to the more extravagant conceits (*q.v.*) of Crashaw and Cleveland, all writers who flourished in the Baroque period. *See* EUPHUISM; GONGORISM; MANNERISM; SECENTISMO.

barzelletta (It 'joke, funny story') An Italian verse form. Originally it was a mixture of disconnected and nonsensical matter presented in variable meters and rhymes. It the 14th c. it denoted epigram and didactic verse. Later it was used by love poets but seems to have remained a very flexible form with which a poet might do much as he pleased. *See also* NONSENSE.

base and superstructure The main premise of Marx's materialist conception of history is that man's first historical act is the production of means to satisfy his material needs. The production of life, through both labour and procreation, is both natural and social: a given mode of production is combined with a given stage of social cooperation. Only after passing through these historical moments, says Marx, can we speak of men possessing 'consciousness', which is itself a 'social product'. Hence the realms of ideology, politics, law, morality, religion and art (which collectively comprise the 'superstructure') are not independent but are an efflux of a people's material behaviour, as embodied in the economic 'base' or infrastructure of a given society: 'Life is not determined by consciousness, but consciousness by life.'

basic English A language devised by Ogden and Richards and presented in 1930. Its carefully selected vocabulary consisted of only 830 words – of which 600 were nouns, and 150 were adjectives. The remainder were what they called 'operators': that is, verbs, adverbs, prepositions and conjunctions. Though the range of expression was limited it was serviceable.

batch An early English word for a stanza (*q.v.*). *See also* FIT; STAVE.

bathos (Gk 'depth') In a mock critical treatise called *Peri Bathous, or, Of the Art of Sinking in Poetry* (1728), Pope assures the reader that he will 'lead them as it were by the hand . . . the gentle downhill way to Bathos; the bottom, the end, the central point, the non plus ultra, of true Modern Poesy!'

Bathos is achieved when a writer, striving at the sublime, over-reaches himself and topples into the absurd. Pope illustrates bathos himself with the lines:

> Ye Gods! annihilate but Space and Time
> And make two lovers happy.

There is a fine collection of the bathetic in *The Stuffed Owl* (1930, rev. edn 1948), an anthology of bad verse selected by Wyndham Lewis and C. Lee. *See* ANTICLIMAX.

battle of the books *See* ANCIENTS AND MODERNS.

beast epic An allegorical tale, often, but by no means always, long, in which animals are characters and in which the style is pseudo-epic. The 1st c. collection of Latin fables made by Phaedrus was, after Aesop, the source and inspiration of a very large number of fables in European literature. The prototypal beast epic is almost certainly *Roman de Renart*, composed late in the 12th c. by Pierre de Saint-Cloud. The first episode is the Chanticleer story later used by Chaucer in the *Nun's Priest's Tale* (*c.* 1395). Spenser continued the tradition in *Mother Hubbard's Tale* (1590). Goethe used it in his *Reineke Fuchs* (1794). The intention of this form was often satirical, like many fables. Orwell's *Animal Farm* (1945) is in the same tradition. *See also* ALLEGORY; BESTIARY; EPIC; FABLE; MOCK-EPIC.

beat Metrical emphasis in poetry, sometimes used as a synonym for stress (*q.v.*). *See also* ACCENT; METER.

Beat generation The term 'beat', in this restricted sense, is generally believed to have been devised by Jack Kerouac (1922–69). It bears connotations of down-beat, off-beat, down-and-out, drop-out and beatitude, and denotes a group of American writers (especially poets) who became prominent in the 1950s. They are particularly associated with San Francisco, USA, and their generally accepted father-figures were Kenneth Rexroth, Henry Miller and William Burroughs. The Beat writers (and many of the 'Beat generation') developed their own slang and a highly idiosyncratic style. Their convictions and attitudes were unconventional, provocative, anti-intellectual, anti-hierarchical and anti-middle-class (the 'squares'). They were influenced by jazz, by Zen Buddhism and by American Indian and Mexican Peyote cults, and their Bohemian life-style was popularly associated with drugs, 'free' sex, drink and permissive living in general. It was in some respects anarchic and provoked considerable hostility. Allen Ginsberg's *Howl and Other Poems* (1956) represents as well as anything the disillusionment of the Beat movement with modern society, its materialism and militarism and its outmoded, stuffed-shirt, middle-class values and mores. Ginsberg's *Kaddish* (1960), an elegy for his mother, and *Reality Sandwiches* (1963) were other important publications. So were Lawrence Ferlinghetti's *Pictures of the Gone World* (1955) and *A Coney Island of the Mind* (1958), Gregory Corso's *Gasoline* (1958) and *Bomb* (1959), and Gary Snyder's collection of work songs and *haikus* (*q.v.*) in *Riprap* (1959). Jack Kerouac himself made memorable contributions to the Beat movement and literature with his prose works *On the Road* (1957), *The Dharma Bums* (1958) and *Big Sur* (1962). The novels of William Burroughs (e.g. *Junkie*, 1953, *The Naked Lunch*, 1959, *Minutes to Go*, 1960) and John Clellon Holmes (e.g. *Go*, 1952, *The Horn*, 1958) are also closely associated with the Beat movement, whose influence was to go far beyond the English-speaking world. It is discernible, for instance, in the work of the Russians Yevtushenko and Voznesensky. It created a cult and affected pop culture. *See also* BLACK MOUNTAIN POETS; JAZZ POETRY; SUBCULTURE.

beginning rhyme This is rare. An example occurs in Thomas Hood's *Bridge of Sighs:*

> *Mad* from life's history,
> *Glad* to death's mystery.

belatedness In Harold Bloom's theory of the anxiety of influence (*q.v.*), belatedness denotes the state of mind and predicament of the poet who feels that his predecessors have already said anything worth saying, that there is no room for further creativity.

belles lettres (F 'fine letters') The term is the literary counterpart of *beaux arts*. Formerly, it was the equivalent of the 'humanities' or *literae humaniores* (literally, 'the more human letters' *q.v.*). Swift appears to have been the first to use the term in English literature, in *Tatler* No. 230 (1710), where he refers to '. . . Traders in History and Politicks, and the Belles lettres'. Now it is applied almost exclusively to literary studies, the aesthetics of literature and, conceivably, what may be described as 'light' literature, but not fiction or poetry. Often the essay (*q.v.*) is the favoured form of the belle-lettrist. The works of Max Beerbohm provide good examples. So do those of Aldous Huxley, many of whose collections of essays (*Themes and Variations, Vulgarity in Literature, Music at Night*, etc.) are listed as *belles lettres*. They are witty, elegant, urbane and learned – the characteristics one would expect of *belles lettres*.

bergette A single-strophe (*q.v.*) *rondeau* (*q.v.*) without a refrain (*q.v.*). Now used sometimes for light verse (*q.v.*).

Berliner Ensemble An important and influential theatrical company founded in East Berlin in 1949. It moved to the Theater am Schiffbauerdamm in 1954. A new theatre was opened in 1980. Bertolt Brecht was a vital influence on its work and many of his plays were performed by it; Brecht's wife, the actress Helene Weigel, made an invaluable contribution. Manfred Wekwerth (1929–) has been its most notable director.

Besserungsstück (G 'recovery' or 'improvement' play) A minor dramatic genre of Viennese provenance which was popular in the early part of the 19th c. The themes of such plays were concerned with the remedy and cure of some evil or malady or grave shortcoming in the main character. Among notable examples are *Die Musikanten am hohen Markt* (1815) and *Der Berggeist* (1819), both by Joseph Gleich (1772–1841). *See also* VOLKSSTÜCK.

bestiary A medieval didactic genre in prose or verse in which the behaviour of animals (used as symbolic types) points a moral. The prototype is very probably the Greek *Physiologus* (2nd–4th c. AD), a compendium of some fifty fabulous anecdotes. This was widely translated, especially into Latin. During the 12th c. additions were made to Latin versions, and these derived from the *Etymologiae* of Isidore of Seville (570–636). The period of greatest popularity for bestiaries in Europe was from the 12th to the 14th c., especially in French. The development and combination of story and moral in the bestiaries had some influence on the evolution of the *exemplum* and the fable (*qq.v.*). Literary sleuths have surmised that such stories as Orwell's *Animal Farm* (1945) and Richard Adams's *Watership Down* (1972) are modern developments of the bestiary. *See also* BEAST EPIC.

best-seller This term first came into frequent use in the 1920s, and in its proper sense denotes a book that at any given time (in a particular country) is selling more copies than any other work. It is one that captures popular interest and imagination; for example, Voltaire's *Candide* (1759) or Byron's *Don Juan* (1819). More recent instances are J. K. Rowling's Harry Potter series, Ian McEwan's *Atonement* (2001), Zadie Smith's *White Teeth* (2001) and Khaled

Hosseini's *The Kite Runner* (2003). *Jane's Fighting Ships, Aircraft Recognition* and the Bible are perennial best-sellers.

Bhagavad Gita (Skt 'Song of God') A part of the *Mahābhārata* (*q.v.*) and likewise regarded as revealed scripture, but often treated as a great poem in its own right. It is sometimes called the *Gītopaniṣad*, thus emphasizing its status as an *Upaniṣad*. It is cast as a dialogue on the battlefield of Kuruksetra between Lord Krishna and Prince Arjuna who is about to fight his own cousins. In this scripture, Krishna, who is revered by Hindus as a manifestation of the Divine (*Bhagavan*), imparts a philosophy based on *yoga* (the attainment or realization of one's ultimate inner self as pure consciousness distinct from both body and mind), and *Vedanta* (which deals with the nature of Brahman or absolute truth). Attainment of such spiritual insight is premised on devotion to the Divine, selfless action, and transcendent knowledge. The central teaching of the *Bhagavad Gita* is that Krishna is the supreme absolute truth. It is through Krishna that the true Self is immortal and cannot perish with the body; that pleasure, pain, gain and loss, victory and defeat, should all be held in equal indifference; that serenity lies in freedom from wealth, and in mastery of one's consciousness; that one's interest should lie in work or action as the performance of duty, not in its fruits; it is such selfless action, not mere renunciation, which brings release, since work arises from Brahman; that one must abandon all desires and all attachment to the world, which is but a 'thicket of delusion'; that seeking solace in the immortal Self alone must govern the phenomenal self.

There has existed a rich tradition of commentary on the *Gita*, with widely diverging interpretations of the war and other elements of the poem. In modern times it has been interpreted allegorically, notably by Gandhi, who offered a reading of it that reflected both its importance in his own life and its foundational potential for the Indian independence movement. *See also* MAHĀBHĀRATA; VEDAS.

bhakti (Skt 'serve, enjoy') The term denotes popular religious poetry in the vernacular languages of medieval India.

bibelot Derived from French, a miniature book or, more generally, a trinket.

Bible, the (Gk *biblia*, 'books') A collection of books which is divided into Old and New Testaments ('covenants'). The former comprises the primary scripture of Judaism, while both are included in the Christian Bible. The text of the Jewish scripture or Tanakh (what Christians call the Old Testament), was written predominantly in Hebrew, and took shape over a period of more than a thousand years, achieving a standard accepted form only in the 1st c., and its precise composition still varies widely between different denominations and sects.

The official version of the Jewish scriptural canon or Tanakh is known as the Masoretic text (*masorah*, 'tradition'), redacted between the 7th and

10th c. This text differs from the Septuagint, a Greek translation of the Hebrew scriptures, completed in 132 BC. The Tanakh is divided into three parts: the Law, the Prophets and the Writings. The Law comprises the Pentateuch or first five books (lit. 'five scrolls'), which are Genesis, Exodus, Leviticus, Numbers and Deuteronomy. These books expound the central religious themes and history of the Israelites, beginning with the Creation and God's covenant with Abraham, and progressing through the exodus from Egypt, the disposition of the law at Mount Sinai, and the passage of the Hebrews through the wilderness to Moses's final address to his people.

The Prophets are divided into Former and Latter, the former including the Books of Joshua, Judges, Samuel and Kings. The latter consist of the Books of the 'Major Prophets' Isaiah, Jeremiah and Ezekiel, and the Book of the Twelve or 'Minor Prophets'. The books of the Prophets recount the rise and struggles (internal and external, military and doctrinal) of the Hebrew kingdom, as well as the prophets' abjuration of unjust Israelite rulers, ending with accounts of the conquest of the Hebrews by the Assyrians and Babylonians, the destruction of the Temple in Jerusalem and its reconstruction after the Persians' subjugation of Babylon. The books of the Writings comprise a more heterogeneous collection of philosophical and poetic material which includes the Books of Ruth, Job, Lamentations and Daniel, as well as the Psalms and the Song of Solomon. Many of the Psalms are attributed to David, and the Song of Solomon, Proverbs and Ecclesiastes to Solomon.

There has also developed in Judaism an oral tradition of exegesis which is regarded as essential for the interpretation of the written Torah. The Oral Torah comprises the Halakha (laws), Aggadah (homiletic stories, parables, narrative theology) and the Kabbalah (esoteric knowledge). Parts of this oral tradition have been recorded in writing in the Talmud, a collection of Rabbinic disquisitions and discussions on law, ethics, and history, which is itself divided into the Mishnah (which deals with specific examples) and the Gemara (Rabbinic commentary on the Mishnah). Other texts such as the Midrash (a collection of homiletic commentaries on the Tanakh, accumulated between the 2nd and 7th c.), are also essential in mainstream Judaism.

Thereafter, various models of scriptural interpretation developed, in addition to the Midrashic or homiletic method (*d'rash*), notably *p'shat*, *remez* and *sod*. The first of these, *p'shat* (plain) sought to determine scriptural meaning through recourse to historical, linguistic and literary context. *Remez* (hint) explored the allegorical meaning, and *sod* (secret) the mystical significance. Some of the main pioneers and exponents of scriptural interpretation were Saadiah Gaon (882–942), Jonah Ibn Janach (*c.* 990–*c.* 1050), Rabbi Shlomo Yitzhaki (the foremost exegete, known as Rashi, 1040–1105), Rashbam (died *c.* 1174), Avraham ibn Ezra (1089–1164), Moses Maimonides (1135–1204), Nahmanides (known as Ramban, 1194–*c.* 1270), Abrabanel (1437–1508), Malbim (1809–79), Nechama Leibowitz (1905–97) and Martin Buber (1878–1965). Many contemporary Jewish scholars read the Tanakh using a wide range of modern historical and literary methods.

As the foregoing range of methods suggests, the Hebrew scriptures contain a broad spectrum of literary types, from poetry, myths, hymns and laments, through history, law and oracle, to parable, allegory and the sensual/spiritual love-song of Solomon. The Book of Job is remarkable in its depth of exploration of man's questioning of God; and the Psalms have rarely been matched as religious poetry. Psalm 19 embodies their spirit:

> The heavens declare the glory of God; and the firmament
>   sheweth his handywork.
> Day unto day uttereth speech, and night unto night sheweth
>   knowledge.
> There is no speech nor language, where their voice is not
>   heard.
> Their line is gone out through all the earth, and their words
>   to the end of the world. In them hath he set a tabernacle
>   for the sun,
> Which is as a bridegroom coming out of his chamber, and
>   rejoiceth as a strong man to run a race.
> His going forth is from the end of the heaven, and his circuit
>   unto the ends of it: and there is nothing hid from the heat
>   thereof.
> The law of the Lord is perfect, converting the soul: the
>   testimony of the Lord is sure, making wise the simple.
> The statutes of the Lord are right, rejoicing the heart: the
>   commandment of the Lord is pure, enlightening the
>   eyes.
> The fear of the Lord is clean, enduring for ever: the
>   judgments of the Lord are true and righteous altogether.
> More to be desired are they than gold, yea, than much fine
>   gold: sweeter also than honey and the honeycomb.
> Moreover by them is thy servant warned: and in keeping of
>   them there is great reward.
> Who can understand his errors? cleanse thou me from secret
>   faults.
> Keep back thy servant also from presumptuous sins; let them
>   not have dominion over me: then shall I be upright, and I
>   shall be innocent from the great transgression.
> Let the words of my mouth, and the meditation of my heart,
>   be acceptable in thy sight, O Lord, my strength, and my
>   redeemer.

> (KJV)

The Christian Bible is composed of the Old and New Testaments. The Old Testament is viewed by Christians as part of their scripture, though its order is somewhat different from that of the Tanakh; and its precise composition differs between Roman Catholics and various Protestant and other denominations. The Old Testament has been regarded by Christians since the time of Christ as allegorically or otherwise foreshadowing some of the central themes and events of Christianity.

Although Jesus preached in Aramaic, the New Testament was written in Greek, the *lingua franca* of the region. It is divided into twenty-seven books, all written within a period of a hundred years in the 1st c. They comprise a number of literary types. The first four books, attributed to Matthew, Mark, Luke and John, are 'gospels' ('good news'), which deal with the life, ministry and miracles of Jesus. The next book, the Acts of the Apostles, recounts the early dissemination of the Christian faith in the years after Christ, especially Paul's journeys to Greece and Asia Minor. The next twenty-one books are in the form of letters, the most renowned of these written by St Paul to Christian communities in Corinth, Thessalonica, Rome and other cities The final book, Revelation, has usually been interpreted in eschatological terms, though some read it as foretelling the impending apocalypse, offering a stark vision of the end of the world and the second coming of Christ.

The Gospels of Matthew, Mark and Luke are generally acknowledged to have drawn on the same source, hence these three are known as the 'Synoptic' gospels (Gk 'common seeing'). The Gospel of John, written later, draws on different sources and differs in content, recounting Jesus's early ministry and disquisitions to his disciples. Many other Gospels and accounts of Jesus existed; but these four Gospels were made canonical by the Church in the 3rd and 4th c., the others being relegated to the status of 'apocrypha' ('hidden' or 'spurious').

The Vulgate, a definitive Latin translation commissioned by Pope Damasus, and produced by St Jerome around 400, was enduringly influential in this process, and its authority was sanctioned by the Council of Trent (1545–63). Authoritative translations into English have included: a number of versions produced in the 14th c. under the influence of the reformer John Wycliffe, and, in the Reformation period, a translation by William Tyndale (1526–31); the Geneva Bible (1560), which included annotations from a Calvinist perspective; the Roman Catholic Douai-Reims Bible (NT, 1582; OT, 1609); the 'authorized version' commissioned by King James I (1611); the American Standard Version (1901); and the Revised Standard Version (NT, 1946; OT, 1952). The following passage, from Jesus's Sermon on the Mount, illustrates well his spiritual ethic of other-worldliness:

> Blessed are the poor in spirit: for theirs is the kingdom of
>   heaven.
> Blessed are they that mourn: for they shall be comforted.
> Blessed are the meek: for they shall inherit the earth.
> Blessed are they which do hunger and thirst after
>   righteousness: for they shall be filled.
> Blessed are the merciful: for they shall obtain mercy.

> Blessed are the pure in heart: for they shall see God.
> Blessed are the peacemakers: for they shall be called the
>   children of God.
> Blessed are they which are persecuted for righteousness' sake:
>   for theirs is the kingdom of heaven.
> Blessed are ye, when men shall revile you, and persecute you,
>   and shall say all manner of evil against you falsely, for my
>   sake.
> Rejoice, and be exceeding glad: for great is your reward in
>   heaven: for so persecuted they the prophets which were
>   before you.
>
> (Matthew, 5: 3–12, KJV)

And the following embodies Christ's central insistence on 'inward' faith as opposed to merely outward show:

> And when thou prayest, thou shalt not be as the hypocrites
>   are: for they love to pray standing in the synagogues and in
>   the corners of the streets, that they may be seen of men.
>   Verily I say unto you, They have their reward.
> But thou, when thou prayest, enter into thy closet, and when
>   thou hast shut thy door, pray to thy Father which is in
>   secret; and thy Father which seeth in secret shall reward
>   thee openly.
>
> (Matthew, 6: 5–6, KJV)

As with the Hebrew scriptures, the Christian Bible has been subjected to numerous traditions of exegesis, interpretation and hermeneutics. Theologians and philosophers in these traditions, ranging from the Church Fathers and Augustine through Aquinas to the German 'Higher' biblical critics such as David Strauss and modern existentialist theologians such as Paul Tillich and Rudolph Bultmann, have commented on the historical context of scripture, its peculiar uses of language, its literary and rhetorical forms, and its various meanings, ranging from literal sense through the various levels of allegory. Certain English literary figures were influenced by the German Higher Criticism. These included George Eliot, who translated David Strauss's *Das Leben Jesu* (1836; *The Life of Jesus*, 1846) which had rejected Christ's divinity and the literal truth of the Gospels, and Matthew Arnold, who attempted to formulate a kind of secular and rational religion, divested of miracles such as the Incarnation, in books such as *Literature and Dogma* (1873). A number of literary scholars, including Northrop Frye, Frank Kermode, Robert Alter and David Lyle Jeffrey, have played a significant role in making the English Bible important to the literary curriculum. *See also* SACRED BOOKS; SERMON.

biblio-   A number of words, apart from bibliography (*q.v.*), which relate to literature, are built on this stem. The main ones are: **biblioclasm** (Gk 'breaking of a book'): the destruction of a book or books for religious, ideological or other reasons; **biblioclast**: a destroyer of books; **bibliogony** (Gk 'book making'): the production of books; **bibliolatry** (Gk 'book worship'): an excessive devotion to or reverence for a book or books (the bibliophile (*q.v.*) is susceptible to it; so are worshippers of the Bible and other sacred books (*q.v.*)); **bibliomancy** (Gk 'divination by book'): the practice of opening the Bible or a comparable work at random and interpreting the first verse or verses as a form of prophecy or precognition; **bibliomania** (Gk 'book madness'): a manic devotion to the collection and possession of books; **bibliophile** (Gk 'book lover'): one who collects, cherishes and preserves books for their value as physical objects, as well as for other reasons; **bibliopole** (Gk 'book merchant'): a book-seller or book dealer; **bibliotaph** (Gk 'book' and 'tomb'): a burier of books; a concealer and hoarder; one who keeps them under lock and key; **bibliotecha** (Gk 'book' and 'repository'): a collection of books; a library; a bibliographer's catalogue.

bibliography (Gk 'book writing') A list of books, essays and monographs on a subject; or a list of the works of a particular author. More strictly the historical study of the make-up and form of books as physical objects. The study of printing and the physical composition, format, of books is known as 'analytical' or 'critical bibliography'; the detailed and formal description of books is 'descriptive bibliography'; and the application of the methods and the evidence to textual criticism (*q.v.*) is 'textual bibliography'.

bibliothèque bleu The forerunner of the *livre poche* (*q.v.*). Early in the 17th c. publishers produced small books wrapped in blue sugar paper. These were sold by *colporteurs*. The trade was centred on Troyes. It spread through Rouen, Paris and elsewhere. They were mostly written by hacks (*q.v.*) and literary journeymen who recycled legends, adventures, lives of saints, popular tales and so forth. The booklets were very cheap, sold in huge numbers and made an important contribution to the development of literacy. Like almanacs they were intended for the non-bookbuying classes. They might be read aloud to semi-literate audiences such as village *veilées*. Comparable to the English chapbook (*q.v.*). *See* COLPORTAGE.

Biedermeier In the first place this was a grotesque figure who originated in *Fliegende Blätter*, the German *Punch*. The caricature symbolized narrow-minded Philistinism and a head-in-the-sand attitude. Ludwig Eichrodt parodied the type in nonsense verses published in 1869 as *Biedermeiers Liederlust*. Later the name *Biedermeierstil* was given to the type of early Victorian furniture and décor common in Germany between 1815 and 1848. The term was also extended to describe painting, sculpture, music and literature.

bienséances, les A French term closely related to *vraisemblance* (*q.v.*), which means and implies appropriate decorum, of which there are two kinds: external and internal. The former requires that a character behave as his rank, position, title, etc. demand; the latter that a character behave in character as he or she is depicted within the play, novel or story. *See also* CONSISTENCY; VERISIMILITUDE.

Bildergedicht (G 'picture poem') *See* ALTAR POEM; CONCRETE POETRY/VERSE; LETTRISM; MERZ; PATTERN POETRY.

Bildungsroman (G 'formation novel') This is a term more or less synonymous with *Erziehungsroman* – literally an 'upbringing' or 'education' novel (*q.v.*). Widely used by German critics, it refers to a novel which is an account of the youthful development of a hero or heroine (usually the former). It describes the processes by which maturity is achieved through the various ups and downs of life. The earliest example is usually taken to be Wieland's *Agathon* (1765–6). The most famous (and most often imitated) examples are Goethe's *Die Leiden des jungen Werthers* (1774) and his *Wilhelm Meisters Lehrjahre* (1795–6) – which became well known in Britain through Thomas Carlyle's translation of 1824. Other celebrated examples in German are Tieck's *Sternbalds Wanderungen* (1798), Keller's *Der grüne Heinrich* (1854), Freytag's *Soll und Haben* (1855), Stifter's *Der Nachsommer* (1857), and Raabe's *Der Hungerpastor* (1864). Plus, in the 20th c., Thomas Mann's *Königliche Hoheit* (1904), *Der Zauberberg* (1924) and *Joseph und seine Brüder* (1933–42). In France Flaubert's *L'Education sentimentale* (1869) is an instance. Novels in English that might be put into this category are Defoe's *Moll Flanders* (1722), Fielding's *Tom Jones* (1749), Jane Austen's *Emma* (1816), Dickens's *David Copperfield* (1849–50), Meredith's *The Adventures of Henry Richmond* (1871) and Samuel Butler's *The Way of All Flesh*, though autobiography, too (1903). Joyce's *A Portrait of the Artist as a Young Man* (1916) has also been so classified but Germans would call this a *Künstlerroman* (*q.v.*), or 'artist novel'. A recent instance is Doris Lessing's five-volume work *Children of Violence* (1952–69), whose heroine is Martha Quest. *See also* AUTOBIOGRAPHICAL NOVEL; ZEITROMAN.

binary opposition The term 'binary' denotes 'composed of two', 'twofold'; as in a binary star, 'one of a pair of stars held together by gravitation'. Language, too, has countless binary oppositions: up/down; slow/fast; sense/nonsense; truth/falsehood; black/white; man/woman – and so on. The concept of binary opposition is central to structuralism (*q.v.*) and structuralist practice. As a structuralist concept it derives especially from Lévi-Strauss's studies of mythology. Linguistics and structuralist analysis use the notion of binary opposition not only in terms of words or concepts but in terms of the conventions or codes of a text. For deconstruction and poststructuralism (*qq.v.*), the notion of binary opposition is unsatisfactory because it represents a nostalgia for 'self-presence' or 'centring'. Derrida's *Structure, Sign and Play in the Discourse of the Human Sciences* (1966) criticizes Lévi-Strauss's hankering for essences in his interpretation of myth. The very idea of a binary opposition implies a centring or imposition of order: such binary signification is stable and systematic to structuralists, and unstable and decentred to poststructuralists. Deconstructive practice seeks to undermine, loosen, such analogical oppositions (which tend to over-simplify meaning) and reveal how a text undermines the imposition of binary structure on it through *aporia* and indeterminacy (*qq.v.*) and through its inherent 'disseminations' (i.e. the 'surplus' or 'overspill' of meaning). *See* DISSEMINATION.

biography An account of a person's life, and a branch of history. Dryden defined it as the 'history of particular men's lives'. As a literary form it has become increasingly popular since the second half of the 17th c., before which period it is rare.

Almost any form of material is germane to the biographer's purpose: the subject's own writings (especially diaries and letters), laundry bills, official archives, memoirs of contemporaries, the memories of living witnesses, personal knowledge, other books on the subject, photographs and paintings.

The origins of biography are no doubt to be found in the early accounts of monarchs and heroes; in, for example, the Old Testament stories, and the Greek, Celtic and Scandinavian epics and sagas. The sayings of wise and holy men are also a branch of biography; and we can learn a lot about Socrates, for instance, from Plato's teaching; as we can from Xenophon's *Memorabilia*. However, the Roman historians Plutarch, Tacitus and Suetonius were the pioneers of the form. Plutarch's *Parallel Lives* (1st c. AD) covered twenty-three Greeks and twenty-three Romans, arranged in pairs. They proved an important source of plots for many plays, including some by Shakespeare. Sir Thomas North produced a version of them from a French translation in 1579. Incidentally, Plutarch seems to have been the first writer to distinguish between biography and history. The main biographical work of Tacitus is contained in his *Histories* (c. 104–9), which deal with the reigns of the emperors from Galba to Domitian. An outstanding work by Tacitus is his account of Agricola, his father-in-law. Suetonius wrote *Lives of the Caesars* (from Julius Caesar to Domitian) and also lives of Terence, Horace and Lucan. The lives of the Caesars are particularly readable because they are full of gossip and scandal, but as history they are unreliable.

There was little in the way of biography in the Middle Ages, for, with few exceptions, the lives of the saints were idealized according to predictable patterns. However, hagiology does contain some notable instances of good biography. One should mention especially Bede's account of St Cuthbert, and St Adamnan's account of St Columba. Eadmer wrote an admirable biography of St Anselm. Secular biographies from the Middle Ages include: Asser's Life of Alfred (c. 900); Aelfric's lives of St Oswald and St Edmund; and various lives of Edward the Confessor in both prose and verse. A remarkable work dating from the later Middle Ages is Boccaccio's *De Casibus Virorum et Feminarum Illustrium* (late 14th c.).

At the Renaissance, biography, like autobiography (*q.v.*), acquired considerable interest. Notable achievements in the 16th c. were Sir Thomas More's *History of Richard III* (1543, 1557) and Vasari's important *Lives of the Painters* (1550, 1568); William Roper's account of his father-in-law,

The Life of Sir Thomas More (written c. 1558 but not published until 1626), is an early example of a biography drawn from contemporary experience.

The 17th c. was the most important period for the development of English biography. From this age date Aubrey's *Brief Lives* (not published until 1813) and Izaak Walton's *Lives* of Donne, Sir Henry Wotton, Richard Hooker, George Herbert and Robert Sanderson (the first four were written over a long period and published in one volume in 1670; the last appeared in 1678).

In the 18th c. the principal works are Roger North's *The Lives of the Norths* (1740–4), Mason's *Life of Gray* (1774), Johnson's *Lives of the Poets* (1779–81) and Boswell's *Life of Johnson* (1791). Johnson was one of the most influential and accomplished of biographers, inaugurating a new candour in approach. Between them, Johnson and Boswell virtually decided the course of biography in the early 19th c., when biographies began to appear in great numbers.

In the mid-Victorian period a certain prudishness and gentility pervaded biographical works for the worse. The truth was glozed by the need for 'respectability', and reticence candied over anything scandalous or disagreeable. However, there were honourable exceptions, like Carlyle's portrait of Abbot Samson in *Past and Present* (1843) and his account of *The Life and Times of Frederick the Great* (1858–65). Earlier, in 1824, Carlyle had published a good biography of Schiller. Mrs Gaskell's *Life of Charlotte Brontë* (1857) is also a distinguished work; as is Forster's *Life of Charles Dickens* (1872–4). Eventually Carlyle's friend and disciple Froude produced a major biography of Carlyle himself (1882–4).

Soon after the First World War, Lytton Strachey brought about something of a revolution in the art of biography. Like Carlyle and Froude, he despised panegyric and prolixity, as exemplified in his *Eminent Victorians* (1918) and *Queen Victoria* (1921), among others. Apart from Strachey, among English biographers during the 20th c., Harold Nicolson is generally regarded as one of the ablest.

Since the 1950s the art of biography has burgeoned, and biography has become a major publishing industry. Scores of new biographies continue to appear each year. There is a vast quantity of historical and political biography, and the majority of those who have become prominent in the performing arts and in sport have also had biographies written about them. Literary biography has become immensely popular. The importance of biography to literary studies generally is evidenced in the interest now generated by 'life writing' (*q.v.*) and its attendant disciplines.

Biographers and scholars alike have also begun to be much more exercised about some of the theoretical and ethical problems that biography raises. One concern is the question of biography's accuracy: there is often a tension between the need to appeal to evidence and the drive to generate personality in order to make the work more interesting. However, the recent assertion of poststructuralism (*q.v.*) – that personal identity is illusory, merely a product of language – would suggest that such concerns about the authenticity of biography are misconstrued. Others are more concerned that biography tends to overrepresent the dominant class and its interests. In *A Room of One's Own* (1929), for instance, Woolf complained that biography is 'too much about great men', and called for more coverage of the 'lives of the obscure'. Certainly the lives of women, the poor and non-white subjects are rather marginalized in biography.

Among biographical collections some of the more valuable and important works are *Biographia Britannica* (1744); *Biographie universelle ancienne et moderne* (1843–65); *Nouvelle Biographie générale* (1852–66); and *Dictionary of National Biography* (1885–1900) with later Supplements. *See also* -ANA; ANECDOTE; LIFE WRITING; TABLE-TALK.

black arts movement   African-American cultural nationalist movement active from the mid-1960s to the mid-1970s. Prominent figures include Amiri Baraka (LeRoi Jones), Nikki Giovanni, Haki Madhubuti (Don Lee) and Sonia Sanchez. The black arts movement sought to create 'black art': art steeped in black experience which spoke to a people in need of racial uplift. In so doing, the movement turned away from protest art, typified by the writings of Richard Wright, which attempted to convince white audiences of the injustices of racism and the worthiness of black citizens. The slow implementation of civil rights, the violent response from many whites to reform and the entrenched social and economic disadvantages experienced by blacks suggested that there was little benefit from continuing with such a strategy. The aim of black art was to help forge an independent black identity (as opposed to a Negro identity, which was considered a negative product of white society). Such art was shaped by a 'black aesthetic', which was conceived as being inherently and necessarily political, indeed revolutionary. It was an aesthetic which, while rooted in black history, envisaged a better future, and furnished the tools for achieving it. Black arts movement writers favoured poetry and drama, viewing such forms as more direct and immediate: poems and plays were quicker to compose and could be performed and read in all manner of social situations; they could readily employ vernacular speech and music and were thus considered to be more authentic and affective. Many writers consciously drew on West African oral traditions and ethics; several also expressed solidarity in their work with postcolonial movements around the globe. *See also* AFRICAN-AMERICAN STUDIES; HARLEM RENAISSANCE; NÉGRITUDE.

black comedy   The term is a translation of *comédie noire*, which we owe to Jean Anouilh (1910–88), who divided his plays of the 1930s and 1940s into *pièces roses* and *pièces noires*. It is more than likely that the term also in part derives from André Breton's *Anthologie de l'humeur noire* (1940), which is concerned with the humorous treatment of the shocking, horrific and macabre. Black comedy is a form of drama which displays a marked disillusionment and cynicism. It shows human beings without convictions and with little hope, regulated by fate or fortune or incomprehensible powers. In fact, human beings in an 'absurd' predicament. At its darkest such comedy is pervaded by a kind of sour despair: we can't do anything so we may as well laugh. The wit is mordant and the humour sardonic.

This form of drama has no easily perceptible ancestry, unless it be tragicomedy (q.v.) and the so-called 'dark' comedies of Shakespeare (for instance, *The Merchant of Venice*, *Measure for Measure*, *All's Well that Ends Well* and *The Winter's Tale*). However, some of the earlier works of Jean Anouilh (the *pièces noires*) are blackly comic: for example, *Voyageur sans bagage* (1936) and *La Sauvage* (1938). Later he wrote what he described as *pièces grinçantes* ('grinding, abrasive'), of which two notable examples are *La Valse des toréadors* (1952) and *Pauvre Bitos* (1956). Both these plays could be classified as black comedy. So might two early dramatic works by Jean Genet: *Les Bonnes* (1947) and *Les Nègres* (1959). Edward Albee's *Who's Afraid of Virginia Woolf?* (1962), Pinter's *The Homecoming* (1965) and Joe Orton's *Loot* (1965) are other examples of this kind of play. The television dramatist Giles Cooper also made a very considerable contribution.

In other forms of literature 'black comedy' and 'black humour' (e.g. the 'sick joke') became more and more noticeable in the 20th c. It has been remarked that such comedy is particularly prominent in the so-called 'literature of the absurd'. Literary historians have found intimations of a new vision of man's role and position in the universe in, for instance, Kafka's stories (e.g. *The Trial*, *The Castle*, *Metamorphosis*), surrealistic art and poetry and, later, the philosophy of existentialism (q.v.). Camus's vision of man as an 'irremediable exile', Ionesco's concept of life as a 'tragic farce', and Samuel Beckett's tragi-comic characters in his novels are other instances of a particular Weltanschauung (q.v.). A baleful, even, at times, a 'sick' view of existence, alleviated by sardonic (and, not infrequently, compassionate) humour is to be found in many works of 20th c. fiction; in Sartre's novels, in Genet's non-dramatic works also, in Günter Grass's novels, in the more apocalyptic works of Kurt Vonnegut (junior). One might also mention some less famous books of unusual merit which are darkly comic. For example Serge Godefroy's *Les Loques* (1964), Thomas Pynchon's *V* (1963) and his *The Crying of Lot 49* (1966), Joseph Heller's *Catch-22* (1961), D. D. Bell's *Dicky, or The Midnight Ride of Dicky Vere* (1970) and Mordecai Richler's *St Urbain's Horseman* (1966). *See* NONSENSE; SURREALISM; THEATRE OF CRUELTY; THEATRE OF THE ABSURD.

Black Mountain poets So called after Black Mountain College in North Carolina, USA. In the early 1950s the college became a centre for 'poetics' and also for a 'school' of poets. Charles Olson, Rector of the college from 1951 to 1956, encouraged a new approach to writing poetry. In 1950 Olson published *Projective Verse*, a statement of aims of Black Mountain poetics: anti-academic, anti-intellectual, anti-traditional; pro-spontaneity and pro the dynamism that may derive from using breathing exercises. Robert Creeley and Robert Duncan have been among the more celebrated poets in this 'school'. The quality of the work produced by the Black Mountain poets has been variable. It may be assessed in the magazine *Origin* (1951–6) and in the *Black Mountain Review* (1954–7).

black theatre   Drama which, initially, was concerned with the consciousness and identity of black Americans, and a kind of movement which has had considerable influence outside America and which has in turn been affected by the Black Power and the Civil Rights movements. During the 1960s the black theatre movement became progressively more radical and there was an increasing tendency among black playwrights to dissociate themselves from the white American theatre and put on performances for black audiences only. A kind of effect has been the use of all-black casts for plays by Shakespeare and other dramatists, including Beckett (*Waiting for Godot*, for instance). The movement had some influence in England, for example in the Dark and Light Theatre in Brixton, London. The first major work by a black dramatist is generally reckoned to be Hansberry's *A Raisin in the Sun* (1959). Other black playwrights of note have been James Baldwin, LeRoi Jones (who changed his name to Amamu Amiri Baraka), Ed Bullins and Aimé Césaire, the Martinique-born writer. West African dramatists – especially Wole Soyinka – and more recently, black British dramatists – especially Kwame Kwei-Armah and Winsome Pinnock – have also made a contribution. *See also* BLACK ARTS MOVEMENT; NÉGRITUDE.

blank   Unrhymed. Though most commonly found in the term 'blank verse' (*q.v.*) the term may be applied to any unrhymed verse form: thus Robert Lowell's unrhymed sonnets may also be termed blank sonnets.

blank verse   This was introduced by the Earl of Surrey in the 16th c. in his translation of the *Aeneid* (*c.* 1540) and consists of unrhymed five-stress lines; properly, iambic pentameters (*q.v.*). Surrey probably took the idea from the *versi sciolti* ('freed verse') of Molza's Italian translations of the *Aeneid* (1539). It has become the most widely used of English verse forms and is the one closest to the rhythms of everyday English speech. This is one of the reasons why it has been particularly favoured by dramatists. It was almost certainly first used for a play by Sackville and Norton in *Gorboduc* (1561), and then became the standard verse for later Tudor and Jacobean dramatists who made it a most subtle and flexible instrument: for instance, Thomas Heywood in *A Woman Killed with Kindness* (1603):

> O speak no more!
> For more than this I know, and have recorded
> Within the red-leaved table of my heart.
> Fair, and of all beloved, I was not fearful
> Bluntly to give my life into your hand,
> And at one hazard all my earthly means.
> Go, tell your husband; he will turn me off,
> And I am then undone. I care not, I:
> 'Twas for your sake. Perchance in rage he'll kill me,
> I care not, 'twas for you. Say I incur

> The general name of villain through the world,
> Of traitor to my friend; I care not, I.
> Beggary, shame, death, scandal, and reproach,
> For you I'll hazard all: why, what care I?
> For you I'll live, and in your love I'll die.

Thereafter it was used a great deal for reflective and narrative poems, notably by Milton in *Paradise Lost* (1667). During the late 17th c. and the first half of the 18th c. it was used much less often. Dryden, Pope, indeed the majority of 18th c. poets, preferred the heroic couplet (*q.v.*). However, Thomson used it in *The Seasons* (1726–30); so did Young in *Night Thoughts* (1742) and Cowper in *The Task* (1785). Wordsworth especially, and Coleridge, made much use of it. All the poets of the Romantic period (*q.v.*) wrote blank verse extensively, and so did most of the great poets of the 19th c. It is still quite widely practised today and dramatists like Maxwell Anderson and T. S. Eliot experimented with it in freer forms in their plays. *See* RHYME.

blazon (F 'coat-of-arms' or 'shield') As a literary term it was used by the followers of Petrarchism (*q.v.*) to describe verses which dwelt upon and detailed the various parts of a woman's body; a sort of catalogue of her physical attributes. Such a catalogue was a convention established in the 13th c. by Geoffrey of Vinsauf and often used after Marot published his *Blason du Beau Tétin* (1536). Elizabethan sonneteers and lyric poets frequently listed the physical beauties of their mistresses. A well-known instance occurs in Spenser's *Epithalamion* (1595):

> Her goodly eyes like sapphires shining bright,
> Her forehead ivory white,
> Her cheeks like apples which the sun hath rudded,
> Her lips like cherries charming men to bite,
> Her breast like to a bowl of cream uncrudded,
> Her paps like lilies budded,
> Her snowy neck like to a marble tower,
> And all her body like a palace fair.

Such inventories or litanies are also to be found in Thomas Watson's *Hekatompathia* (1582), Sir Philip Sidney's *Astrophil and Stella* (1591) and Thomas Lodge's *Phillis* (1593). As a rule, there was nothing original in this form of conceit (*q.v.*). Most of the images were used long before by the elegiac Roman poets and the Alexandrian Greek poets.

Almost inevitably the convention became a cliché and we find poets parodying this kind of conceit in the *contreblazon*. Sir Philip Sidney, for example, copied Francesco Berni's device of using conventional descriptions for the 'wrong' parts of the body, thus producing a sort of grotesque mutant. Mopsa's forehead is 'jacinth-like', her cheeks are opal, her twinkling eyes are 'bedeckt with pearl' and her lips are 'sapphire blue'. Shakespeare turned the *blazon* upside down in his famous sonnet which begins: 'My mistress' eyes are nothing like the sun'; and Greene, in *Menaphon* (1589), reduced the *blazon* to absurdity:

> Thy teeth like to the tusks of fattest swine,
> Thy speech is like the thunder in the air:
> Would God thy toes, thy lips, and all were mine.

It was only a few years earlier that Sidney had written one of the most famous *blazons* of all, beginning:

> What tongue can her perfections tell?

See also CATALOGUE VERSE.

blog The term 'blog', and the related terms 'to blog', 'blogging', 'bloggers' (people who run blogs) and 'blogosphere' (an online realm for the daily dissemination and exchange of blog information), is a conflation of the words 'web' and 'log', and it is used to describe web sites that regularly publish dated entries in reverse chronological order. They can be run by an individual blogger or a group. Blogs often allow the public to submit comments after each blog post.

When blogs first appeared in the mid-1990s, they were mainly associated with online diaries and journals, but with the development of blogging software and tools, such as 'blogger', 'blogspot' and 'wordpress', blogs now serve a variety of purposes and cover a range of topics. They can come in a traditional form of personal journals, or can be used to disseminate news and information. Blogging is now a global phenomenon. Bloggers can post comments on political and social affairs, or indeed, use blogs for the purposes of literary criticism and self-publishing of books, poetry and scholarly texts. Many newspapers and journals now feature book review blogs such as *The Guardian* Books Blog. There are other creative uses of blogs such as photo blogs or video blogs. Blogs can also be subversive and used for political purposes and the fight against censorship, as the use of blogging in China testifies, where many so-called 'dissident' bloggers have been jailed by the government. Recently, micro-blogging services, such as Twitter, that allow users to send and exchange short text-based posts, have been increasingly popular. *See also* INTERNET.

Bloomsbury Group A coterie of writers who lived in the Bloomsbury area, London, before, during and after the First World War. The main figures were Virginia Woolf, Leonard Woolf, Lytton Strachey, Clive Bell, Vanessa Bell, Roger Fry, Duncan Grant, Maynard Keynes, E. M. Forster and David Garnett. Indirectly (they did *not* form a 'school') they had a considerable influence in the world of letters, art and philosophy.

blue blouse movement *See* AGITPROP DRAMA.

blue book A cheap (blue-covered) kind of thriller (*q.v.*), spine-chiller, shocker, horror story, romance (*q.v.*) which sold in large quantities at the end of the

18th c. and the beginning of the 19th. A relation of the penny dreadful, the dime novel (*qq.v.*), and others. Also, most commonly, a Parliamentary report.

blues, the   A musical tradition deriving from folksongs of African-Americans in the Southern US at the end of the 19th c. Many blues songs are based on a three-line lyric and are often expressive of despair, grief and a general feeling of hopelessness.

blues stanza   A form of triplet (*q.v.*) stanza (*q.v.*) which derives from traditional jazz among black Americans. Customarily, the mood is one of lament or complaint (*qq.v.*). The first two lines are identical rhymes (e.g. dark/dark). A line usually comprises a flexible iambic pentameter (*qq.v.*) measure, with incremental repetition (*q.v.*) of the first line in the second.

blue stocking circle/society   The Blue Stockings were a group of intelligent, well-educated and gifted women who, from early in the 1750s, held receptions or soirées, in the French salon (*q.v.*) tradition, at their homes in London, and continued to do so through most of the second half of the 18th c. The first hostess was almost certainly Mrs Vesey. Other regular hostesses were Mrs Montagu, Mrs Carter, Mrs Chapone, Mrs Boscawen, Mrs Delaney and, later, Hannah More, who wrote an agreeable poem, *Bas bleu* (1786), which described the pleasures and activities of the Blue Stocking Society. Those who attended the meetings were fashionable and literary and included a number of famous men such as: Joshua Reynolds, David Garrick, Horace Walpole, James Boswell, James Beattie, Samuel Richardson, George Lyttleton and Dr Johnson. Members of the aristocracy were frequent attenders. The main object of the meetings was conversation; there were no cards and no alcohol, and politics, swearing and scandal were forbidden. Their title derives from the worsted blue stockings of Bishop Benjamin Stillingfleet. He could not afford evening clothes and attended in his ordinary everyday gear. Traditionally it was Admiral Boscawen who nicknamed the group thus. When used pejoratively, as it often has been (and was in the 18th c.), the term 'bluestocking' denotes a woman who affects literary tastes and behaves in a dilettante fashion; a female pedant. Henry James described George Eliot as 'a horse-faced bluestocking'.

blurb   A brief description of the contents of a book printed on the dust jacket. Often couched in enthusiastic and, at times, extravagent terms. The word is believed to have been coined by the American author Gelett Burgess who defined it as 'a sound like a publisher'. Earlier the term 'puff' was used, probably after Mr Puff in Sheridan's *The Critic* (1779). *See also* PUFFERY.

boasting poem   Common in oral literatures in many parts of the world, especially in the epic and ballad (*qq.v.*) traditions. A warrior or hero 'blows his own trumpet' about his exploits. It is debatable whether there is an example of a boasting poem in English literature, though there are instances of something akin to it in *Beowulf* – especially the slanging match between Unferth and Beowulf himself, when Unferth taunts the hero at being defeated by

Breca in a seven-day swimming match at sea. Beowulf defends himself by giving the true account of the Breca episode. A further example occurs when Beowulf tells Hygelac how he overcame the monster Grendel. *See also* FÂRSA; GIERASA.

bob and wheel A metrical device found in alliterative verse (*q.v.*). The first short line of a group of rhyming lines is known as the 'bob', and the following four as the 'wheel'. Often the group ends a strophe (*q.v.*). The bob contains one stress preceded by one and sometimes two unstressed syllables. Each line of the wheel contains three stresses. The device is used throughout *Sir Gawain and the Green Knight*. For example:

> On many bonkkes ful brode Bretayn be seetez
> > wyth wynne,
> > Where werre and wrake and wonder
> > Bi syþez hatz wont þerinne,
> > And oft boþe blysse and blunder
> > Ful skete hatz skyfted synne.

Here 'wyth wynne' is the bob; the final four lines form the wheel.

Boedo Street group A literary group of the 1920s named after a lower-class area in Buenos Aires largely inhabited by Creole immigrants. Little of the writers' work survives. *See* FLORIDA STREET GROUP.

Boerde A MDu term for tales which tend to be bawdy or satirical, akin to the French *fabliau* (*q.v.*) and the Italian *novelle* (*q.v.*), and the kind of tale that Chaucer and Boccaccio delighted in. Many of them hail from Indian and Arabic legends.

bombast Originally the word described the cotton or horse-hair used in tailoring for padding. The term came to mean inflated and extravagant language. In *Othello* (I, i), Iago, complaining to Roderigo of how the Moor has passed him over for promotion, says:

> But he, as loving his own pride and purposes,
> Evades them [i.e. three great ones of the city] with a
> > bombast circumstance
> Horribly stuff'd with epithets of war;
> And in conclusion
> Nonsuits my mediators.

There are many instances of ranting and bombastic speeches in late Tudor drama (especially in Marlowe's plays) and few better than Hotspur's tirade in *Henry IV*, Pt I (I, iii):

> By heaven methinks it were an easy leap
> To pluck bright honour from the pale-fac'd moon

But Shakespeare burlesqued bombast in the play in *Hamlet*. Sometimes bombast has been used for humorous effect, as in Fielding's *Tom Thumb* (1730). *See also* FUSTIAN; HEROIC DRAMA; HYPERBOLE.

bonnes lettres, la société des There were several such societies after the restoration of the monarchy in France and their members were mostly young men who had religious and monarchical sympathies. They had literary as well as political and altruistic interests and they had quite close links with the *Congrégations* (the lay and clerical associations which originated from the Jesuits in the 16th c. were suppressed during the Revolution, and were regarded with some suspicion when they were revived during the Empire).

book The word probably derives from *boks*, 'beech' (Germanic), the wood of that tree usually providing the tablets on which runes (*q.v.*) were carved (cf. 'Barbara fraxineis pingatur runa tabellis', Venantius Fortunatus VI). A book is either a written document or a record; or a written or printed literary composition. It may also be a volume of accounts or notes. It has a further meaning when it denotes a subdivision of a work (e.g. *Paradise Lost* is made up of twelve books). Occasionally, novels are divided into separate books, or parts. *See also* LEDGER; MANUSCRIPT; ROLL.

Booker McConnell Prize *See* MAN BOOKER PRIZE.

book of hours *See* CALENDAR.

Book of Songs (*Shih Ching*) A collection of 305 poems, whose compilation around 600 BC is sometimes attributed to Confucius. Many of the poems are revisions of ballads and folk poetry (*qq.v.*). They deal with a wide variety of themes, ranging from war and life's hardships to love. They are essentially composed in the form of odes, often in quatrains (*qq.v.*), and are often musical or song-like in character, making much use of refrain and rhyme. Some of these lyric poems anticipate Western Romanticism in their use of nature to depict or complement states of mind or feeling, as in these lines from No. 28:

> Cold blows the northern wind,
> Thick falls the snow.
> Be kind to me, love me,
> Take my hand and go with me.
> Yet she lingers, yet she havers!
> There is no time to lose.

The theme of lovers meeting (or being disappointed) is also common, as in No. 57:

> By the willows of the Eastern Gate,
> Whose leaves are so thick,
> At dusk we were to meet;
> And now the morning star is pale.

Some of the poems are used to express social or political discontent, as in the following lines, whose pertinence has endured across time and cultures:

> Minister of War,
> Truly you are not wise.
> Why should you roll us from misery to misery?
> (No. 127; translations by Arthur Waley)

Other poems concern the court, the life of the various classes, and the history of China. The *Book of Songs* is regarded as one of the five classics comprising the 'Confucian canon', embodying the wisdom of the 5th c. BC Chinese thinker. *See also* ANALECTS.

Booktrust   Founded in 1924 as the National Book Council by the Society of Bookmen, a group formed by Hugh Walpole, John Galsworthy, publisher Stanley Unwin and others to promote literature by cooperation across the book trade. The Council was renamed the National Book League, and later Booktrust. In 1992 it launched Bookstart, a national programme which gives free books to children, and since 2005 it has been responsible for the management of the Children's Laureate. Among the literary prizes Booktrust administers are the John Llewellyn Rhys Prize, the David Cohen Prize for Literature and the Independent Foreign Fiction Prize.

boulevard drama   In 1791, the French theatres were given their freedom, the Boulevard du Temple became a centre of theatrical activity and many theatres were opened. Popular drama was presented, often of a melodramatic kind. Guilbert de Pixerécourt (1773–1844), who wrote at least fifty melodramas, was one of the most prolific and popular dramatists. Alexandre Dumas *père* (1802–70), was another. Many of the melodramas presented were about contemporary crime. Boulevard drama also fostered the Romantic movement in the French theatre. Eventually boulevard drama became a generic term for popular French drama from the mid-19th c. onwards. The plays consisted for the most part of farce and domestic comedy (*qq.v.*) and were a distinctly commercial entertainment. Two of the best-known dramatists were Eugène Labiche (1815–88) and Ludovic Halévy (1834–1908). *See* MELODRAMA.

bourgeois   (From OF *burgeis*, 'town dweller') In pre-Revolutionary France, 'bourgeois' denoted a citizen class, often traders, who held a middle station between the peasantry and the aristocracy. With the expansion of trade, this class had been increasing in size and importance, but it was the rise of industrial capitalism in the late 18th c. which consolidated its economic power. In Marxist thought, the term refers to the ruling class in capitalist societies, specifically, those who own the 'means of production', or the economic resources such as factories, materials and capital. Marx also employed the adjective 'bourgeois' to describe the kind of society precipitated by the capitalist mode of production, as well as the ideology (*q.v.*) which sustains it. Since the 18th c. the term has frequently been used to express contempt for the materialism, moral hypocrisy, conformism and philistinism of the middle classes. Bourgeois culture has been satirized repeatedly in literature, notably in Zola's series of novels *Les Rougon-Macquart* (1871–93). On the other hand, Marxist literary critics have argued that the form of the novel has served to legitimize bourgeois rule. The 'petit-bourgeoisie', which roughly corresponds with 'lower-middle class', was defined by Marx as the class which does not have ownership of the means of production, but which nevertheless supports the rule of the bourgeoisie. *See also* MARXIST CRITICISM.

bourgeois drama   Now a slightly pejorative term describing modern naturalistic drama (*q.v.*) concerned with middle-class social problems. Many dramatists were engaged in writing this kind of play during the first forty years or so of the twentieth century. An outstanding example was Galsworthy, especially such works of his as *Strife* (1909), *Justice* (1910), *The Skin Game* (1920) and *Loyalties* (1922).

boustrophedon   (Gk 'ox-turning' when ploughing up and down a field) Lines written alternately from right to left and left to right, as in ancient Greek inscriptions.

bouts-rimés   (F 'rhymes without lines') A versifying game which appears to have originated in 17th c. Paris. It became a vogue and spread to England. The idea was, given certain rhymes, to compose lines for them and make up a poem which was natural. For instance, given the rhyming words 'might', 'dog', 'sleight' and 'fog', compose a four-line poem. The diversion remained fashionable in France, England and Scotland until the 19th c.

bovarysme   From Flaubert's *Madame Bovary* (1857). A tendency towards escapist daydreaming in which the dreamer imagines himself or herself to be a hero or heroine in a romance. Madame Bovary suffered from such a condition.

bowdlerize   Derived from the name of Thomas Bowdler, MD (1754–1825), who in 1818 produced *The Family Shakespeare*.
  Bowdler removed from the plays whatever in his opinion was 'unfit to be read by a gentleman in the company of ladies'. Other editors, for example A. W. Verity, when producing school editions of Shakespeare, cut out passages which they regarded as indecent. *See also* ABRIDGED EDITION; CENSORSHIP.

boys' companies   Also known as children's companies, troupes of boy actors which flourished during the 16th c. Early records show that the choristers of the Chapel Royal had performed plays by 1516. Choristers at St Paul's in London also performed them *c.* 1525. In 1576 Richard Farrant, Master of the Children of the Chapel at Windsor, leased premises in Blackfriars to present commercial theatrical performances.
  Increasingly associated with the performance of politically dangerous material, the boys' companies fell foul of Archbishop Whitgift's crackdown following the attack on the Established Church which generated the Marprelate controversy (1588–9). The companies were prohibited soon after, in 1590. However, at the beginning of the 17th c. they were revived and a number of

well-known dramatists composed plays for them, including Beaumont and Fletcher, Chapman, Dekker, Ben Jonson, Marston, Middleton and Webster. They were clearly deemed serious competition for the adult companies, as suggested by Hamlet's topical reference to the popularity of 'an eyrie of children, little eyases [hawks]' (II, ii, 340) who force the players to seek an audience at Elsinore.

The children's companies were prominent antagonists in the War of the Theatres (1599–1601), a notorious episode of professional rivalry which set the Children of Paul's (Marston and Dekker) against the Children of the Chapel (Jonson). These latter initially found royal favour with King James, being redubbed the Children of the Queen's Revels with his accession in 1603. However, when the controversy surrounding a purportedly seditious reference in Jonson, Marston and Heywood's *Eastward Ho* (1605) led to the imprisonment of the authors, the company lost its patronage. The influence of the boys' companies declined thereafter, and although the fashion enjoyed a brief resurgence later in the century under William Beeston (Beeston's Boys 1637–42), the phenomenon of the turn of the century was not to be repeated. *See also* JESUIT DRAMA; SCHOOL DRAMA.

braces *See* PUNCTUATION.

brachiology (Gk 'short speech') Terse and condensed expression. Characteristic of the heroic couplet (*q.v.*). *See* ASYNDETON.

brachycatalectic (Gk 'short left off') A metrical line which lacks two syllables or a foot and is therefore an incomplete line. *See* ACATALECTIC.

brackets *See* PUNCTUATION.

Bradleyan Characteristic of the method and style of A. C. Bradley's criticism of Shakespeare's plays, as typified in his celebrated book *Shakespearean Tragedy* (1904). Bradley (1851–1935), who displayed remarkable insight and perception, tended to a naturalistic interpretation, treating characters as if they were real people and ignoring dramatic and stage convention (*q.v.*). Later criticism, more concerned with myth, symbol, patterns of imagery (*qq.v.*), etc., and with convention, was a reaction against his approach.

braggadocio The term came into English *c.* 1590 from the verb *to brag*, to which the Italian augmentative suffix was added. It denotes a swaggering, idle man; usually a coward. Spenser created a character called Braggadochio in *The Faerie Queene*, a typical braggart who is finally shown to be what he really is. Falstaff is probably the most famous *braggadocio* type in English literature. *See also* ALAZON; MILES GLORIOSUS.

Bread and Puppet Theatre Founded in 1961 by Peter Schumann, who regarded bread and theatre as equally sacramental and distributed home-made bread to the audiences. The type of work presented was close to performance art (*q.v.*) and visual impact was all-important, not least in the use of huge puppets (up to twenty feet high). Anti-materialist in spirit,

Schumann's presentations were often in the open air. Notable productions were: *A Man Says Goodbye to His Mother* (1968), *The Cry of the People for Meat* (1969), *A Monument for Ishi* (1975) and *Ave Maris Stella* (1978).

Brechtian Characteristic of the style and technique of the plays of Bertolt Brecht (1898–1956), the German poet, playwright and director. He is particularly associated with the alienation effect, epic theatre, *Lehrstück* and the Berliner Ensemble (*qq.v.*).

bref double In French prosody, a fixed form (*q.v.*) and a kind of quatorzain (*q.v.*). It may be an ancestor of the sonnet (*q.v.*) and is a fourteen-line poem, in three quatrain stanzas ending with a couplet (*qq.v.*). There are only three rhymes in such a poem but every line is rhymed. The *a* rhyme appears somewhere in the three quatrains and once in the couplet. Likewise, the *b* rhyme. Rhyme *c* ends each quatrain.

breve *See* MORA.

breviary (L 'summary, abridgement') The book contains the Divine Office for each day and is used by Roman Catholic priests. It contains: Calendar; Psalter; Proprium de Tempore (i.e. collects and lessons); Proprium de Sanctis (i.e. collects for Saints' Days); Hours of the Virgin; burial services.

brief We may distinguish the following meanings: (a) a summary; (b) a list or memorandum; (c) a letter; (d) a papal communication on disciplinary matters; (e) a summary of a law case prepared for counsel.

Briefroman (G 'letter novel') In Germany there were two kinds of epistolary novel (*q.v.*): (a) those in which all the letters are by one person; (b) those in which the letters are by two or more people (though most of them are by the main character). Examples of (a) are: Goethe's *Die Leiden des jungen Werthers* (1774), Hölderlin's *Hyperion* (1797, 1799) and the anonymously published *Briefe die ihn nicht erreichten* (1903) – which was written by Baroness von Heyking. Examples of (b) are: Johann Hermes's *Sophiens Reise von Memel nach Sachsen* (1769–73) and Sophie von La Roche's *Geschichte des Fräuleins von Sternheim* (1771).

broadside A sheet of paper printed on one side only and usually distributed by hand. Broadsides were used largely for disseminating news and information and also for the publication of songs and ballads. They were hawked about Britain from early in the 16th c. until the 1920s. *See also* BALLAD.

brochure (F *brocher*, 'to stitch') A pamphlet or comparably short work which is stitched, not bound. Nowadays brochures are mostly used for a variety of commercial and advertising purposes.

broken rhyme This occurs when a word is 'broken' or split in order to get a rhyme. Not unusual in light verse or for some comic effect, but rare in serious verse. However, Gerard Manley Hopkins uses it successfully in several poems, as here from *To What Serves Mortal Beauty*?:

> To what serves mortal beauty | – dangerous; does set dancing
>   blood – the O-seal-that-so | feature, flung prouder form
> Than Purcell tune lets tread to? | See: it does this: keeps warm
> Men's wits to the things that are; | what good means – where
>   a glance
> Master more may than gaze, | gaze out of countenance.

brut   A transferred use, in French or in Welsh, of *Brutus*, the name of the legendary and eponymous founder of Britain and the reputed grandson of Aeneas. The *Roman de Brut* and Laȝamon's *Brut* (of the late 12th c.) were well-known accounts of English history that went back to Brutus. Thus, a chronicle (*q.v.*).

bucolic   *See* PASTORAL.

bucolic diaeresis   So called because it was so common in bucolic poetry and occurred after a dactyl (*q.v.*) in the fourth foot. *See* DIAERESIS.

bugarštice   The term probably derives from the Serbo-Croatian word *bugar-iti*, 'to chant', and denotes a long line of verse of fifteen or sixteen syllables, with a caesura (*q.v.*) usually after the seventh. They were used in the composition of heroic songs or epic ballads which for the most part dealt with combat against the Turks in Dalmatia and other parts of what was Yugoslavia from the 15th c. onwards. *See* GUSLAR; NARODNE PESME; PEVACI.

bull   (L 'bubble, round object') The lead seal on an official document, especially one of papal origin, and thus the document itself. It is also used to denote a tall story (*q.v.*), or a story which strains credulity; for example, a cock-and-bull story (*q.v.*). More generally it may apply to a literary incongruity or howler.

bulletin   The term derives (via French) from the Italian word *bulletino*, 'a little document', from *bullo*, a 'bubble', 'seal' or 'document with a seal' which is the origin of papal bull (*see* BULL). As a literary term bulletin may denote a literary or scholarly periodical (it may be the name of a periodical), and it is often used to describe a summary or catalogue of activities or events. It also, of course, denotes news, which may be spoken or recorded in print.

bululú   A single ambulatory actor in 16th and 17th c. Spain. In some respects a descendant of the *juglar* or *jongleur* (*q.v.*). Where two travelled and played as a pair they were known as *ñaque*; if four as a *gangarilla*; and there was a standard company of six – five men and one woman – known as a *cambaleo*. The *cambaleo* has been recorded as late as the 1930s.

bunkum   Originally nonsensical oratory; now applicable to almost anything said or written if it is regarded as rubbish. It derives from the name of Buncombe County in North Carolina, because a member of that district, while attending the 16th Congress debate on the 'Missouri Question', persistently declared, when pressed for a 'Question', that he was obliged to make a speech for Buncombe.

burden (Or bourdon or burthen) The word probably derives from the late Latin *burdo*, 'drone bee'. The term denotes either the refrain (*q.v.*) or chorus (*q.v.*) of a song, or its theme or principal sentiment.

bürgerliches Trauerspiel A genre of German dramatic tragedy (*q.v.*) – the term originated mid-18th c. to describe the kind of play which did not deal with the fall of nobles and princes but dealt rather with that of middle-class people (burghers) in a middle-class environment (i.e. *bürgerlich*). Such plays were written in prose. Probably the earliest example is Lessing's *Miss Sara Sampson* (1755). Lessing was influenced by George Lillo's tragedy *The London Merchant* (1731), a rarity then because it made ordinary commercial life the theme of tragedy. Diderot was also influenced by it in his *Le Fils naturel* (1757). See DOMESTIC TRAGEDY.

burlesque The term derives from the Italian *burlesco*, from *burla*, 'ridicule' or 'joke'. It is a derisive imitation or exaggerated 'sending up' of a literary or musical work, usually stronger and broader in tone and style than parody (*q.v.*). For the most part burlesque is associated with some form of stage entertainment. Aristophanes used it occasionally in his plays. The satyr plays (*q.v.*) were a form of burlesque. Clowning interludes in Elizabethan plays were also a type.

An early example of burlesque in England is the play of Pyramus and Thisbe performed by Bottom and his companions in *A Midsummer Night's Dream* (c. 1595). Here Shakespeare was making fun of the Interludes (*q.v.*) of earlier generations. A few years later Francis Beaumont created one of the first full-length dramatic burlesques – namely *The Knight of the Burning Pestle* (c. 1607). In 1671 George Villiers, Duke of Buckingham, had produced *The Rehearsal*, generally regarded as an outstanding example of a full-scale dramatic burlesque. In it he ridiculed contemporary actors and dramatists as well as the heroic tragedies of the period. Later Henry Carey did the same thing with his *Chrononhotonthologos* (1734). He also burlesqued contemporary opera in *The Dragon of Wantley* (1734). Fielding did much the same thing with *Tom Thumb* (1730) and his *Historical Register for the Year 1736*. Samuel Foote employed the same kind of caustic, but his plays and sketches ridiculed people rather than contemporary drama. One of the most famous works in this genre is Gay's *The Beggar's Opera* (1728), in part a burlesque of Italian opera. His work anticipates the kind of entertainment that became popular in the 19th c. in the hands of Gilbert and Burnand. Other dramatic burlesques of note from this period are: *The What d'ye Call it* (1715) by Gay; *Three Hours After Marriage* (1717) by Gay, Pope and John Arbuthnot; *The Covent Garden Tragedy* (1732) by Henry Fielding; *Distress upon Distress* (1752) by George Alexander Stevens; *The Critic* (1779) by Sheridan; *The Rovers* (1798) by George Canning, John Hookham Frere and George Ellis; and *Bombastes Furioso* (1810) by William Rhodes. In the USA a theatrical burlesque is an entertainment with songs, dances, routines and extensive use of a chorus line and leg-show.

Burlesque was not confined to drama. In the mid-17th c. the French dramatist Scarron wrote a burlesque in verse called *Virgile travestie* (1648), and a little later Samuel Butler published *Hudibras* (1662), a mock-heroic (*q.v.*) poem ridiculing romance, chivalry and Puritanism. In 1674 Boileau wrote a famous mock-epic (*q.v.*), *Le Lutrin*, in which, with much irony and grave epic decorum (*q.v.*), he made fun of Classical epic. Dryden burlesqued the animal fable in *The Hind and the Panther* (1687); and, later, Pope showed great mastery of the possibilities of burlesque in his mock-epic *The Rape of the Lock* (1714) and in *The Dunciad* (1728, 1742, 1743). From this period also dates an agreeable burlesque by Swift – *Baucis and Philemon* (1709). A curiosity is William Blake's fragment *An Island in the Moon* (originally untitled), which he wrote *c.* 1784–5, a kind of 'send-up' of cultural and scientific pretensions. In fiction, Peacock came close to burlesque of the Gothic novel (*q.v.*) with his *Nightmare Abbey* (1818). *See also* ANTI-MASQUE; CARICATURE; FARCE; IRONY; INVECTIVE; SATIRE.

burletta Like burlesque (*q.v.*), the term derives from the Italian *burla*, 'joke' or 'fun'. A *burletta* is a comic play with music, or a play spoken to music, popular in the 18th and 19th c. theatre. It is of minor importance in the history and development of drama, except that, in company with musical burlesques and the later musical comedies, it may well have had some influence on the conception of the modern musical.

Burns stanza Also known as Burns meter, 'Scottish stanza' and 'Habbie stanza'. In fact, Burns did not invent it. It has been found in 11th c. Provençal poems and in medieval English romances. However, it takes its name from the frequent use Burns made of it. It comprises a six-line stanza rhyming aaabab. The first, second, third and fifth lines are tetrameters (*q.v.*) and the others dimeters (*q.v.*) as in *To a Mountain Daisy*:

> Ev'n thou who mourn'st the Daisy's fate,
> That fate is thine – no distant date;
> Stern Ruin's ploughshare drives elate
>   Full on thy bloom
> Till crush'd beneath the furrow's weight
>   Shall be thy doom.

business novel *See* MONEY NOVEL.

buskin The derivation is disputed, but it occurs in a number of European languages. It denotes a thick-soled half boot (*cothurnus*) worn by actors in Athenian tragedy, and contrasted with the low shoes (*soccus*) or 'sock' worn by comic actors. Thus it describes figuratively the spirit or style of tragedy. There is a famous reference in Ben Jonson's poem of praise to Shakespeare:

To hear thy buskin tread,
And shake a stage: or, when thy socks were on,
Leave thee alone, for the comparison
Of all, that insolent Greece, or haughty Rome
Sent forth, or since did from their ashes come.

Milton, in *L'Allegro*, refers to Jonson's 'Learned sock'.

Butzenscheibenpoesie (G 'archery target poetry') A type of late 19th c. poetry which displays a kind of decadent or degenerate romanticism (*q.v.*) with an emphasis on medieval themes and nationalistic attitudes and values. Prominent practitioners were J. V. von Scheffel, Rudolf Baumbach and Julius Wolff. *Butzenscheibenpoesie* was a derogatory term invented by Paul Heyse (1830–1914).

bylina (R *byl* 'that which happened') A type of Russian epic (*q.v.*) folksong and poetry often associated with an historical event or movement. The term *bylina* is of academic provenance and came into use in the 1830s; the peasants use the word *starina* ('what is old'). These songs are mostly about the exploits of the *bogatyrs*, warrior heroes at the court of Prince Vladimir (978–1015) in Kiev, and the very earliest examples may pre-date Vladimir's era. For many centuries they belonged to oral tradition (*q.v.*). People were beginning to write them down in the 16th and 17th c. Possibly the first collector was an Englishman, Richard James, who was chaplain to the English embassy in Moscow in 1619. The main garnering belongs to the 19th c. when, anyway, there was widespread interest in Europe in collecting and studying these ballad and epic forms of verse. In fact, many *byliny* still belong to oral tradition among peasants, particularly in areas where literacy is minimal. The same is true of the *narodne pesme* (*q.v.*) among the South Slavs.

Byliny vary in length from, say, a hundred lines to a thousand or more. There are two basic categories: (a) the heroic, concerned with deeds of valour; (b) the romantic, concerned with love, deceit, infidelity, magic and wealth. The former far outnumber the latter. Traditionally, they are sung or chanted, without musical accompaniment, by specialist narrators/singers called *skaziteli* ('narrators'). Some *skaziteli* are blind and in many respects are close kin of the Anglo-Saxon *scopas*, the Scandinavian *skalds* and the South Slav *guslari*. Like these bards of honoured and ancient vocation, the *skaziteli* are often poets as well as reciters, and a skilled one will amplify, embellish and improvise on traditional material with words, phrases and lines of his own devising. The verse tends to be free, with a pattern of a fairly fixed number of stresses and considerable flexibility in the number of unstressed or 'slack' syllables. Rhyme is occasional. Strong, plain similes, of the 'white as a swan', 'brown as a berry', 'fresh as a daisy' ilk, are a conspicuous feature. Fixed or Homeric epithets (*q.v.*) are frequent and obligatory. Incremental repetition (*q.v.*) is also common; as are periphrastic figures, and figures comparable to the kenning (*q.v.*) of skaldic and Old English verse. *See also* BALLAD; GUSLAR; SKAZ.

Byronic stanza   *See* OTTAVA RIMA.

Byzantine age   A period which runs approximately from the beginning of the 6th c. until 1453, the year in which Constantinople fell to the Turks.

C

caccia (It 'hunt') An Italian verse form which may have evolved from the madrigal (*q.v.*). A poem of short lines with a refrain (*q.v.*) but no rhyme. The name suggests that at some stage the subjects of the *caccia* were connected with hunting. The form was used mostly in the 14th and 15th c.

cacoethes scribendi (Gk 'evil disposition' + L 'of writing') An uncontrollable urge to write. This phrase goes back to Juvenal's *insanabile* (incurable) *scribendi cacoethes* (*Satires*, VII, 52).

cacophony (Gk 'dissonance') The opposite of euphony (*q.v.*). Harsh sounds are sometimes used deliberately by writers, especially poets, to achieve a particular effect. A well-known example occurs in Tennyson's *Morte D'Arthur*:

> Dry clashed his harness in the icy caves
> And barren chasms, and all to left and right
> The bare black cliff clanged round him, as he based
> His feet on juts of slippery crag that rang
> Sharp-smitten with the dint of armed heels –
> And on a sudden, lo! the level lake,
> And the long glories of the winter moon.

The alliteration and assonance (*qq.v.*) of the first five lines are self-evidently rough; the last two lines, containing the same devices, are mellifluously smooth and euphonious. *See also* ONOMATOPOEIA.

cadence In particular it refers to the melodic pattern preceding the end of a sentence; for instance, in an interrogation or an exhortation; and also the rhythm of accented units. In more general terms it refers to the natural rhythm of language, its 'inner tune', depending on the arrangement of stressed and unstressed syllables; so, now, a rising and falling. It is present in prose

---

A Dictionary of Literary Terms and Literary Theory, Fifth Edition. J. A. Cuddon.
© 2013 The Estate of J. A. Cuddon. Published 2013 by Blackwell Publishing Ltd.

as well as verse. Almost every writer with any individuality of style at all has particular cadences which are really his own 'voice', the inherent and intrinsic melody of linked syllables and words, of phrases, sentences and paragraphs, which at once transcends and supports the meaning. Sense and sound are inseparable. The cadences of prose writers as various as Sir Thomas Browne, Edward Gibbon, Jack London and Samuel Beckett are instantly apparent. In verse, even within traditional metrical arrangements, differing cadences are apparent, especially in free verse (*q.v.*). *See* RHYME; RHYTHM.

caesura (L 'a cutting') A break or pause in a line of poetry, dictated by the natural rhythm of the language and/or enforced by punctuation. A line may have more than one caesura, or none at all. If near the beginning of the line, it is called the initial caesura; near the middle, medial; near the end, terminal. The commonest is the medial. An accented (or masculine) caesura follows an accented syllable, an unaccented (or feminine) caesura an unaccented syllable. In OE verse the caesura was used rather monotonously to indicate the half line:

> Ða waes on burgum || Beowulf Scyldinga
> leof leodcyning || longe þrage.

So long as alliterative verse (*q.v.*) was the favoured form, there was not a great deal of variation, as these lines from Langland's *Piers Plowman* show:

> Loue is leche of lyf || and nexte owre lorde selue,
> And also þe graith gate || þat goth in-to heuene.

The development of the iambic pentameter (*q.v.*) in Chaucer's hands produced much more subtle varieties:

> With him ther was his sone, || a yong Squier
> A lovyere || and a lusty bacheler,
> With lokkes crulle || as they were leyd in presse.
> (*Prologue to the Canterbury Tales*)

Blank verse (*q.v.*) allowed an even wider range in the preservation of speech rhythms, as these lines from Shakespeare suggest:

> I have ventur'd
> Like little wanton boys || that swim on bladders,
> This many summers || in a sea of glory;
> But far beyond my depth. || My high-blown pride
> At length broke under me, || and now has left me,
> Weary and old with service, || to the mercy
> Of a rude stream || that must for ever hide me.
> (*King Henry VIII*, III, ii, 359)

The identical placement of caesurae in successive lines produces a regular caesura-to-caesura line ('My high-blown pride/ At length broke under me', 'and now has left me,/ Weary and old with service') which counterpoints the actual verse lines, and produces a *rocking lineation* which is the motor of much Shakespearean blank verse, a terminal couplet commonly acting as a brake. In the heroic couplet (*q.v.*) end-stopping tends to prevent the development of rocking lineation, and the often regular caesurae act instead to enforce balance, as Dryden shows:

> In squandering wealth || was his peculiar art:
> Nothing went unrewarded, || but desert.
> Beggar'd by fools, || whom still he found too late:
> He had his jest, || and they had his estate.
> > (*Absalom and Achitophel*, Pt I, 559)

In more modern verse there is a great deal of variation in the placing of the caesura, as can be seen in the work of outstanding innovators like Gerard Manley Hopkins, W. B. Yeats, Ezra Pound and T. S. Eliot. Take, for instance, these lines from Yeats:

> That is no country for old men. || The young
> In one another's arms, || birds in the trees
> – Those dying generations – || at their song,
> The salmon-falls, || the mackerel-crowded seas,
> Fish, flesh, or fowl, || commend all summer long
> Whatever is begotten, || born, || and dies.
> Caught in that sensual music || all neglect
> Monuments of unageing intellect.
> > (*Sailing to Byzantium*)

It will be noticed that the last line has no caesura.

It can be seen from these few examples that the caesura is used, basically, in two contrary ways: (a) to emphasize formality and to stylize; and (b) to slacken the stiffness and tension of formal metrical patterns.

calembour *See* PUN.

Calderonian honour *El honor calderiano* implies an exaggerated concept of honour. A product of 17th c. Spanish drama, and particularly of the plays of Calderón (1600–81). The following are especially noteworthy: *El médico de su honra, A secreto agravio, secreta venganza, El Pintor de su deshonra, El mayor monstruo, los celos*. The usual situation is that the play's climax centres on the sacrifice of the wife, who is either really or supposedly unfaithful. The atmosphere of the dénouement (*q.v.*) is harsh and even bloody. For instance, in the first of the above four plays the jealous husband engages a blood-letter to perform the deed in his wife's bedroom where she is apparently ill, thus purging his own besmirched honour by 'surgery'.

calendar The term derives from Latin *calendae* (calends, or kalends), the first day of the month and the date on which accounts were due. Hence Latin *calendarium*, 'an account book'. The ordinary calendar is a table giving the divisions of the year. Some of the major calendars are: the Julian, the

Gregorian, the Jewish, the Chinese, the French Republican and the Moham-
medan. The perpetual calendar provides the year, the dominical letter (i.e.
the *dies dominica*, Latin for 'Sunday'; a convention adopted in tables to
indicate that day in January on which the first Sunday falls in any particular
year), followed by the regnal years, their beginning and ending. It also
shows the fixed feasts and saints' days, which are important in the dating of
documents.

Another kind of calendar is the book of hours (*les heures*), an illustrated
prayer-book based on the priest's breviary (*q.v.*) and ordered according to
the hours of the Divine Office in monasteries. Such books made their appearance in the 12th c. and quite soon became popular, especially in France and
the Netherlands. Some of them were of remarkable beauty and exquisitely
illustrated. A very well-known example is the Duc de Berry's *Très Riches
Heures* of the 15th c. which was illustrated by the Limbourg brothers. Such
a work contains the usual *calendarium*, the Little Office of Our Lady, the
Penitential Psalms, the Litanies, the Office for the Dead, the Adoration of
the Cross, Devotions to the Holy Ghost, and others.

A notable instance of the form of the calendar being used for a poetic work
is Spenser's *Shepheard's Calendar* (1579), which comprises twelve eclogues
– one for each month of the year. John Clare attempted something similar in
The Shepherd's Calendar (1827).

Another type of calendar is a sort of register (*q.v.*). An unusual example
is *The Newgate Calendar, or Malefactors' Bloody Register* (*c.* 1774), a work
which gave an account of the more infamous crimes perpetrated from 1700
to 1774. A further series came out *c.* 1826.

A curiosity in the genre is Nicholas Breton's *The Fantasticks* (1626), a
collection of observations arranged in calendar form according to hours, days
and seasons. *See* ALMANAC.

calligramme A design using the letters of a word; more particularly a poem
written and printed in a specific shape. Guillaume Apollinaire (1880–1918)
published *Calligrammes* (1918), which contains the well-known *Il pleut*,
printed with letters trickling down the page like 'tears'. Rabelais had done
something comparable with his *epilenie*: a song in honour of Bacchus printed
in the shape of a bottle. *See* ALTAR POEM; CONCRETE POETRY/VERSE.

calypso Usually an improvised song or ballad (*qq.v.*) composed and sung by
West Indians on festive and public occasions – like carnivals, elections and
test matches. The word happens to be the same as the name of the nymph
who detained Ulysses on the island of Ogygia, but there appears to be no
connection.

Cambridge Festival Theatre This theatre existed from 1926 to 1933 and
became a centre of innovative theatre design and production in Britain.
Notable features were its thrust stage and revolving stage and remarkable
experiments with lighting. The inspiration of the enterprise was Terence
Gray, assisted by Harold Ridge. Gray's other collaborators included Ninette

de Valois, his cousin, and Humphrey Jennings. The Festival Theatre was eventually sold to the Cambridge Arts Theatre, founded by J. M. Keynes. In 1998 the theatre was sold to commercial developers.

Cambridge School   A term applied to a group of critics associated with Cambridge University in the 1920s and 1930s. Its luminaries were I. A. Richards (1893–1979), F. R. Leavis (1895–1978), Q. D. Leavis (1906–81), and William Empson (1906–84). They had a profound influence on the development of literary criticism and its techniques, especially in practical, analytical criticism. The Leavises had much influence through the periodical *Scrutiny* (1932–53). *See* PRACTICAL CRITICISM.

camp   Although often used simply to refer to male effeminacy, the term, whose origins are obscure, also relates something more complex and elusive. 'Camp' is variously understood as a sensibility, an aesthetic, or a style which values artifice, excess and, perhaps most of all, misplaced seriousness. It is closely associated with gay male subculture and is characteristic of the writing of numerous literary homosexuals: Oscar Wilde, Ronald Firbank, Christopher Isherwood and Tennessee Williams for sure; and perhaps also Jean Genet and Joe Orton. However, since 'camp' is more a way of seeing than an inherent quality, many cultural objects, from the trashy to the high-minded, can be comprehended through the term. Examples might include the early Flash Gordon comics or Bellini's operas, Tiffany lamps and Shirley Bassey.

Some claim that 'camp' is more potent when used by gay men, but given the term's indifference to the authentic, it is perhaps inappropriate to insist on any group's rightful ownership. It certainly bears similarities to postmodern irony (*q.v.*); indeed, sometimes 'camp' is similarly derided as being little more than defensive, depoliticizing playfulness. Others, however, particularly since the emergence of queer theory (*q.v.*), have stressed the transgressive potential of 'camp', in particular its tendency to ridicule normative codes of gendered and sexual behaviour. *See also* GAY AND LESBIAN CRITICISM; KITSCH; PERFORMATIVITY.

campus novel   A novel which has a university campus as its setting. This genre is largely an Anglophone tradition. Mary McCarthy's *The Groves of Academe* (1952) is usually thought to be the first campus novel, though there are earlier works which feature university settings, or whose protagonists are university students. The latter are usually known as 'varsity novels'; Evelyn Waugh's *Brideshead Revisited* (1945) is a famous example. Campus novels frequently satirize academic life, in particular the intellectual pretensions of scholars. Many, such as Kingsley Amis's *Lucky Jim* (1954), David Lodge's *Changing Places* (1975) and Malcolm Bradbury's *The History Man* (1975), are comedies, and sometimes resemble farce (*q.v.*). Others are more serious in tone, for example J. M. Coetzee's *Disgrace* (1999) and Philip Roth's *The Human Stain* (2000), tackling issues such as social mobility, political correctness and sexual and racial harassment. The genre frequently exploits the cloistered nature of campus life; in such cases the university is presented either as a microcosm of society or as a world removed from it. Perhaps because of their relative isolation, there is a strong tradition of setting murder mysteries on university campuses, which replace the country house setting of 'Golden Age' crime fiction (*q.v.*).

canción   The term is now generally applied to any Spanish poem consisting of strophes (*q.v.*) with alternate lines of eleven and seven syllables. This, the Italianate *canción*, was introduced into Spain near the middle of the 16th c. *See* LIRA; REMATE; SILVA.

cancrine   (L 'crab-wise') Verses that read both ways, and which thus form a palindrome (*q.v.*).

canon   A body of writings established as authentic. The term usually refers to biblical writings accepted as authorized – as opposed to the Apocrypha (*q.v*). The term can also apply to an author's works which are accepted as genuine, as, for example, the Shakespeare Canon. In recent history, the term has been used to refer to a traditional body of texts deemed by the literary establishment to be authoritative in terms of literary merit and influence.

canso   Also *chanso* and *chanson* (*q.v.*) A Provençal love-song or lyric (*q.v.*). The lyrical *canso* has five or six stanzas with an *envoi* (*q.v.*). Metrical virtuosity in the *canso* was much prized. The themes were almost invariably those of courtly love (*q.v.*). *See* ODE; SONNET.

cant   The jargon or slang (*qq.v.*) of a particular class, group, trade, calling or profession. Usually associated with pedlars, thieves, gipsies, tinkers and vagabonds. Professional tramps or roadmen, for instance, have a variety of cant terms – like: *blagging hard* – travelling fast; *castle* – the house, flat or office of a wealthy person; *croker* – fourpence; *dead hard mark* – a place only approachable by an expert tramp; *dollcie* – well-off; *front the gaff* – call at the entrance of a large house; *gry* – a horse (of Romany origin); *lurk* – a tramp's favourite stopping place; *mark* – a house, its resident or the sign outside; *merry* – a girl; *postman* – a fast-moving tramp; *sham* – a gentleman; *steamer* – a mug, a simpleton; *top-cock* – a master tramp; *wheeler* – a pauper who circles near institutions and who is despised by the real roadmen or 'pikers' who refer to the road as 'the stem', 'the grit', 'the white'. Also, hollow, dogmatic or hypocritical talk.

cantar   In Spanish literature the word has often been used vaguely to denote words for a song. In modern times it has come to mean an octosyllabic quatrain (*q.v.*), with certain characteristics: assonance (*q.v.*) and, occasionally, consonance (*q.v.*) in the even-numbered lines, and unrhymed oxytones (*q.v.*) in the odd ones.

cantar de gesta   (Sp 'song of deeds') The Spanish equivalent of the French *chanson de gestes* (*q.v.*), but differing in some respects from the French *chansons*, which tend to be in assonanced *laisses* (*q.v.*) of ten syllables whereas the Spanish type is usually in longer lines, but of varying length with a leaning towards fourteen syllables, in four-accent *laisses* with all four having the same assonance. The most complete and most famous *cantar de gesta* is the *Poema de mío Cid* (c. 1140) whose composer probably had the advantage of reading the French *chansons*, including *Roland*.

cantares Spanish narrative poems of the epic (*q.v.*) genre which derive from oral tradition (*q.v.*), originally sung or accompanied by music. Two notable examples of *cantares de gesta* are *Poema de mío Cid* (c. 1140) and *Bernardo del Carpio* (c. 1200). During the Romantic period there was renewed interest in this genre. *See also* ROMANTIC REVIVAL.

canticle A form of hymn (*q.v.*) with biblical words, other than those from the Psalms.

canticum In Roman drama that part of a play which was declaimed or sung, as opposed to the *diverbium* (*q.v.*) or spoken dialogue. There are a large number of *cantica* in the plays of Plautus; few in Terence.

canto (It 'song') A subdivision of an epic (*q.v.*) or narrative poem; comparable to a chapter in a novel. Outstanding examples of its use are to be found in Dante's *Divina Commedia*, Spenser's *Faerie Queene*, Pope's *The Rape of the Lock* and Byron's *Childe Harold*.

canzone An Italian and Provençal form of lyric (*q.v.*) which consists of a series of verses in stanza form but without a refrain (*q.v.*). Usually written in hendecasyllabic lines with end-rhyme (*q.v.*). There were three main styles: tragic, comic and elegiac. William Drummond of Hawthornden was one of the few British writers to use it. The *canzone* had considerable influence on the evolution of the sonnet (*q.v.*). *See* CANZONET; OTTAVA RIMA.

canzonet *Canzonetta* is a diminutive of the Italian *canzone* (*q.v.*), and a *canzonet* is 'a little song'; a light-hearted song akin to the madrigal (*q.v.*).

capa y espada (Sp 'cloak and sword') The term describes 16th and 17th c. comedies about more or less melodramatic love and conspiracy among the aristocracy. Two of the main playwrights were Lope de Vega and Calderón. *See also* CLOAK-AND-DAGGER STORY; COMEDY; COMEDY OF INTRIGUE.

caricature In literature (as in art) a portrait which ridicules a person by exaggerating and distorting his most prominent features and characteristics. Quite often the caricature evokes genial rather than derisive laughter. English literature is exceptionally rich in examples. The following are a few of the more outstanding: Sir Andrew Aguecheek, Malvolio and Sir Toby Belch (*Twelfth Night*); Pistol and Fluellen (*Henry V*); Falstaff (*Henry IV* and *The Merry Wives of Windsor*) – all by Shakespeare. Other examples are Sir Giles Overreach in Massinger's *A New Way to Pay Old Debts*; Sir Epicure Mammon in Ben Jonson's *The Alchemist*; and Jonson's Volpone in *Volpone*; Sir Fopling Flutter in Etherege's *The Man of Mode*; Captain Brazen in Farquhar's *The Recruiting Officer*; Sir Lucius O'Trigger in Sheridan's *The Rivals*; Tony

Lumpkin in Goldsmith's *She Stoops to Conquer*; Lady Bracknell in Wilde's *The Importance of Being Earnest*; Drinkwater in Shaw's *Captain Brassbound's Conversion*.

There are many in satirical poems: for instance, Dryden's caricature of Shadwell in *Mac Flecknoe*; and Pope's of Cibber in *The Dunciad*.

There are so many in novels that the list would be almost endless. The works of Fielding, Smollett, Dickens, Thackeray and Surtees are especially rich in them.

On the whole caricature belongs to the province of comedy (*q.v.*). However, a caricature is occasionally to be found in tragedy – among minor characters. For instance, the weak and gullible Roderigo in *Othello*; and Osric, the pansy courtier, in *Hamlet*.

carmen (L 'song') Usually a song or lyric (*qq.v.*) but the word has been applied to a wide variety of forms ranging from epic (*q.v.*) to legal formula. Now almost an archaism (*q.v.*) and, if used, likely to be very nearly facetious, except when referring to Catullus's *Carmina* or Horace's *Odes* or a *carmen figuratum* (*q.v.*).

carmen figuratum *See* ALTAR POEM.

carnivalization/carnivalesque Originally, a carnival was a feast observed by Roman Catholics before the Lenten fast began. The word *carnival* derives, apparently, from the Latin *carnem levare*, 'to put away flesh'. Traditionally, meat was not eaten during the Lenten fast; thus, a carnival would be the last occasion on which meat was permissible before Easter. Broadly speaking, a carnival is an occasion or season of revels, of merrymaking, feasting and entertainments (e.g. a Spanish fiesta). In times past there were carnivals which were symbolic of the disruption and subversion of authority; a turning upside down of the hierarchical scale (e.g. the Feast of Fools, the Abbot of Misrule, the Boy Bishop). Mikhail Bakhtin (1895–1975) coined the word 'carnivalization' (he introduces it in the chapter 'From the Prehistory of Novelistic Discourse', in his book *The Dialogic Imagination* – translated in 1981) to describe the penetration or incorporation of carnival into everyday life, and its shaping effect on language and literature.

Early examples of literary 'carnival' are the Socratic dialogues (in which what appears to be logic is stood on its head and shown to be illogical) and Menippean satire (*q.v.*). A carnivalesque element is also characteristic of burlesque, parody and personal satire. Bakhtin puts forward the theory that the element of carnival in literature is subversive; it disrupts authority and introduces alternatives. It is a kind of liberating influence and he sees it as part of the subversion of the sacred word in Renaissance culture. He cites Rabelais as an example of a writer who used carnival (e.g. in *Gargantua* and *Pantagruel*, 1532–46).

In his book *Problems of Dostoevsky's Poetics* (1929) he develops the idea of the carnivalesque in making a contrast between the novels of Tolstoy and Dostoevsky. In Tolstoy's fiction he sees a type of 'monologic' novel where all is subject to the author's controlling purpose and hand, whereas Dostoevsky's fiction is 'dialogic' or 'polyphonic'. Many different characters express varying, independent views which are not 'controlled' by the author to represent the author's viewpoint (*q.v.*). They are 'not only objects of the author's word, but subjects of their own directly significant word as well'. Bakhtin sees this quality as a kind of dynamic and liberating influence which, as it were, conceptualizes reality, giving freedom to the individual character and subverting the type of 'monologic' discourse characteristic of many 19th c. novelists (including Tolstoy).

Dostoevsky's tale *Bobok* (1873) is a particularly good example of carnival. The dead, disencumbered of natural laws, can say what they like and speak the truth for fun. But Bakhtin does not pretend that an author is not still in control of his material while allowing his characters to be subversive. He acknowledges the role of the author as directing agent. *See* AUTHOR, DEATH OF; DIALOGIC/MONOLOGIC.

carol The word derives from the Italian *carola*. It seems very probable that originally a carol was a kind of ring or round dance, then the song accompanying the dance. Now a carol denotes a light-hearted song sung in a spirit of joy at Christmas time (and also, occasionally, at Easter). Thus, a festive religious song. It appears to have been an ancient practice in the Church to sing carols, and throughout the Middle Ages the clergy wrote many of them – usually in sequences like the *Laetabundus*. Most of the carols we know today are not earlier than the 15th c. In 1521 Wynkyn de Worde, a pupil of Caxton, printed the first collection of Christmas carols. Counterparts of the carol elsewhere are the *noël* in France (dating from the 16th c.), and the *Weihnachtslied* in Germany. After the Reformation the practice of composing carols dwindled, though in the 17th c. several poets (Southwell, Herbert, Vaughan, Crashaw and Milton) wrote poems and songs which belong to the carol genre. Milton's *Nativity* hymn is an outstanding example; so is Southwell's *The Burning Babe*. Among well-known carols mention should be made of *The Seven Joys of Mary*; *I saw Three Ships*; *God Rest You Merry, Gentlemen*; *The Virgin Unspotted*; *Jesus Born in Bethlehem*; and *The Twelve Days of Christmas*. Other kinds of carol have moral and satirical themes. There are also love carols. *See also* LYRIC; SONG.

Caroline period Of the time of Charles I (1625–49), from the Latin *Carolus*, 'Charles'. During this period the Civil War was fought and a large number of distinguished writers were active. The following were pre-eminent: Donne, Burton, Shirley, Massinger, Milton, Edward and George Herbert, Sir Thomas Browne, Thomas Carew, Crashaw, Vaughan, Quarles, Thomas Killigrew (the elder), Herrick, Sir John Suckling and Lovelace. *See also* CAVALIER DRAMA; CAVALIER POETS.

carpe diem (L 'snatch the day') The phrase occurs in Horace's *Odes* (I, xi):

> *Dum loquimur, fugerit invida*
> *Aetas: carpe diem, quam minimum credula postero.*

In short: 'Enjoy yourself while you can'. Horace elaborates on the motif (*q.v.*) in *Odes* III, xxix. It is found in Greek as well as Latin poetry, recurs frequently in many literatures and obviously arises from the realization of the brevity of life and the inevitability of death. It might be assessed as the motto of epicureanism.

At some point, possibly in the work of the 4th c. Roman poet Ausonius, the rose became the symbol of the beauty and transitoriness of life, a thought finely expressed by Ausonius in *De Rosis Nascentibus*. Whatever its origin the symbolism persisted through the Middle Ages and is to be found associated with the *carpe diem* motif in Goliardic verse (*q.v.*) and in much French and English poetry. At some stage the rose came to represent virginity; and its death, loss of virginity. The 15th and 16th c. love poets incorporated both theme and symbolism in their appeals to their mistresses not to deny them or disdain them. The Cavalier poets (*q.v.*) were among the last to elaborate the idea (for example, Herrick's poem *To the Virgins, to Make Much of Time* begins: 'Gather ye Rose-buds, while ye may'), but it has never entirely lost its hold on the poet's imagination – as is evident in the work, for instance, of Yeats.

The *carpe diem* motif, in more specifically Christian and didactic writings, appears in many sermons and much devotional literature during the Middle Ages and thereafter, but the import tends to be admonitory: life is short – prepare to meet thy doom. However, it is the more pagan and epicurean spirit of the motif that has made the greatest appeal to writers, and in few places is it better expressed than in a poem about a Syrian dancing girl, in the *Appendix Vergiliana*, which concludes:

> Pone merum et talos, pereat qui crastini curat.
> Mors aurem vellens, 'vivite', ait, 'venio'.

See also UBI SUNT; SYMBOL AND SYMBOLISM.

carwitchet *See* PUN.

casbairdne In Irish prosody, a quatrain (*q.v.*) stanza of heptasyllabic lines. The second and fourth lines rhyme and the first and third lines consonate with them. There are at least two cross-rhymes in each couplet (*q.v.*).

catachresis (Gk 'misuse') The misapplication of a word, especially in a mixed metaphor (*q.v.*). Puttenham, in *The Arte of English Poesie* (1589), described catachresis as a figure of 'plain abuse, as he that bade his man go into his library to fetch his bow and arrows'. A famous instance occurs in Milton's *Lycidas*:

> Blind mouths! that scarce themselves know how to hold
> A sheep-hook, or have learned aught else the least
> That to the faithful herdman's art belongs!

catalects Literary works which are detached (or detachable) from the main body of a writer's work. *See* ANALECTS.

catalexis The omission of the last syllable or syllables in a regular metrical line. Often done in trochaic and dactylic verse to avoid monotony. The second and fourth lines of this verse from Hood's *The Bridge of Sighs* illustrate the point:

> Óne mŏre ŭn | fórtŭnăte,
> Wéarў ŏf | breáth,
> Ráshlў ĭm | pórtŭnăte,
> Góne tŏ hĕr | deáth!

It may, however, be argued that the second and fourth lines are choriambic feet. *See* ACATALECTIC; CHORIAMBUS.

catalogue raisonné A descriptive and annotated catalogue of books or works of art. Often divided into subject groups.

catalogue verse The term describes a list of people, things, places or ideas. It is a device of ancient origin and found in many literatures. Sometimes its function has been didactic. In any event its usual object is to reinforce by elaboration. There are many instances in epic (*q.v.*) poetry, like this from Milton's *Paradise Lost* (X, 695):

> Now from the north
> Of Norumbega, and the Samoed shore
> Bursting their brazen dungeon, armed with ice
> And snow and hail and stormy gust and flaw,
> Boreas, and Caecias and Argestes loud
> And Thrascias rend the woods and seas upturn;
> With adverse blasts upturns them from the south
> Notus and Afer black with thunderous clouds
> From Serraliona; thwart of these as fierce
> Forth rush the Levant and the Ponent winds
> Eurus and Zephir, with their lateral noise,
> Sirocco, and Libecchio.

See also BLAZON; EPIC SIMILE.

catastasis Two meanings may be distinguished: (a) the narrative part that comes in the introduction of a speech (*q.v.*); (b) the third of the four divisions of a tragedy (*q.v.*) – the first, second and fourth being *protasis*, *epitasis* and *catastrophe* (*qq.v.*). *See also* FREYTAG'S PYRAMID.

catastrophe (Gk 'overturning') The tragic dénouement (*q.v.*) of a play or story. For example, the Moor's murder of Desdemona and his own suicide at the climax (*q.v.*) of *Othello*. *See* CATASTASIS; FREYTAG'S PYRAMID.

catch In verse the term denotes an extra unstressed syllable at the beginning of a line when the regular meter requires a stress. A famous example occurs in Gray's poem *On Vicissitude*:

> New-born flocks, in rustic dance,
> Frisking ply their feeble feet;
> Forgetful of their wintry trance,
> The birds his presence greet –

In contrast to 'new-born' and 'frisking', the word 'forgetful' takes a stress on the second syllable.

A catch is also a 'round' for three or more voices. A singer starts a line, another follows him. They take each other up and harmonize. A good example occurs in *Twelfth Night* (II, iv) when Sir Toby Belch, Sir Andrew Aguecheek and Feste are fooling about and getting drunk.

catharsis (Gk 'purgation') Aristotle uses the word in his definition of tragedy (*q.v.*) in Chapter VI of *Poetics*, and there has been much debate (still inconclusive) on exactly what he meant. The key sentence is: 'Tragedy through pity and fear effects a purgation of such emotions.' So, in a sense, the tragedy (*q.v.*), having aroused powerful feelings in the spectator, has also a therapeutic effect; after the storm and climax there comes a sense of release from tension, of calm.

cauda (L 'tail') The short line or tail which, in a stanza (*q.v.*) of longer lines, usually rhymes with another short line. The use of *caudae* was common in medieval metrical romances (*q.v.*). *See also* TAIL-RHYME.

caudate sonnet A form of sonnet (*q.v.*) in which the normal pattern of fourteen lines is modified by one or more *codas* or 'tails'. The practice is believed to originate from Francesco Berni, the 16th c. Italian poet. The form is rare in English verse, though it has been used for satirical purposes: for instance, Milton's poem *On the New Forces of Conscience Under the Long Parliament*. *See* TAIL-RHYME.

causerie (F *causer*, 'to talk, converse') It denotes an informal talk, essay or article particularly on literary topics. The term comes from Sainte-Beuve's *Causeries du lundi*, his contributions to *Le Globe* and *Le Constitutionnel* in the 19th c. *See also* ESSAY; PROPOS.

Cavalier drama In the 1630s the Queen gave patronage to a type of court play called Cavalier drama. It was a decadent form, artificial and ponderous in style, unoriginal in subject matter. The main playwrights were Sir John Suckling, James Shirley and Thomas Killigrew. The Civil War put an end to it.

Cavalier poets A group of English lyric poets who were active, approximately, during the reign of Charles I (1625–49). The label is much later than the 17th c., but it is fair to include in the group Lovelace, Sir John Suckling, Herrick, Carew and Waller; plus some minor ones like Godolphin and Randolph. These poets virtually abandoned the sonnet (*q.v.*) form which had been the favoured medium for love poems for a century. They were considerably influenced by Ben Jonson. Their lyrics are light, witty, elegant, and, for the most part, concerned with love. They show much technical virtuosity. Good representative examples are: Suckling's *Why so pale and wan, fond lover?*; Herrick's *Delight in Disorder*; Lovelace's *To Althea, from Prison*. *See* CAROLINE PERIOD.

celebratory theatre A form of festive and popular theatrical entertainment which may celebrate and dramatize some important event or events. It may combine elements of pageant, tableau, *son et lumière* (*qq.v*), the circus and the tattoo. It may also include song, music, dance, mime, acrobatics and ritual. There is an emphasis on spectacular and ceremonial presentation. A notable example was the celebration of the French Revolution in Le Théâtre du Soleil's *1789*, created by Ariane Mnouchkine in 1970. Peter Brook (1925–) has been a pioneer of celebratory theatre in Britain and abroad. *See also* CARNIVALIZATION/CARNIVALESQUE; LIVING THEATER.

Celtic revival A recrudescence of interest in culture, myth, legend and literature of Celtic people took place in the second half of the 18th c. and was to continue through the Romantic period, and indeed on into the 20th c. Interest in the Gothic and in early Celtic culture was becoming apparent by *c.* 1760. It is evident in, for example, Thomas Gray's Pindaric ode *The Bard* (1757) and in *The Triumphs of Owen* (1768). Gray was influenced by a big collection of Welsh poetry, namely *Some Specimens of the Poetry of the Ancient Welsh Bards. Translated into English . . .* (1764) by Ieuan Brydydd. Interest was also stimulated by James Macpherson's Ossianic poems, which were forgeries (*see* LITERARY FORGERIES) but which were enormously popular and widely influential. In the 19th c. a number of translations of Celtic works began to appear, including Charlotte Guest's version of the *Mabinogion* (1838–49) and Hersart de la Villemarqué's *Barzaz Breiz* (1839) and *Les Bardes bretons du sixième siècle* (1850). In 1854 Ernest Renan published his celebrated study *La Poésie des races celtiques*, which may have caught the attention of Matthew Arnold. In 1865–6 Arnold delivered a series of lectures on Celtic literature at Oxford; this linked all Celtic literatures and helped to promote the foundation of a Chair of Celtic at Oxford in 1877. During the 19th c. several English writers were affected by Celtic culture; notable instances are Thomas Love Peacock, Tennyson and Gerard Manley Hopkins. So, too, were Welsh, Scottish and Irish writers. Among the Scots we should mention particularly the novelist William Black (1841–98) and the poet and novelist William Sharp (1855–1905), whose verse and prose romances on Celtic themes were published under the pen-name Fiona Macleod, a literary *alter ego* or heteronym (*q.v.*). Irish writers of the Irish literary renaissance (*see* CELTIC TWILIGHT) looked back to Celtic origins. In 1893 W. B. Yeats published *The Celtic Twilight*, a collection of stories in folklore. The creation of the Abbey Theatre (*q.v.*) and its promotion of Irish plays by Irish dramatists can be considered as an aspect of the Celtic revival. Renewed interest in the study of Gaelic was another aspect, and continues to be.

Celtic twilight A vague term used to describe that atmosphere, that romantic and somewhat dreamy sense and evocation of the past, which was
cultivated and admired in Ireland towards the end of the 19th c. Irish writers,
in what has been called the Irish literary Renaissance, wishing to dispel the
influence of English literature, turned to their own heritage in search of myth
and legend and the glories of a putative 'golden age' represented by such
heroic figures as Finn MacCool. It was an attempt, partially successful, at a
revival of Irish Celtic culture.

Three influential works in this recrudescence were: O'Grady's *History of
Ireland: Heroic Period* (1878); W. B. Yeats's *The Wanderings of Oisin* (1889)
and his *The Celtic Twilight* (1893). Yeats, with other distinguished writers,
founded the Irish Literary Society in London and the Irish National Literary
Society in Dublin. In 1899 he, George Moore and Edwin Martin founded the
Irish Literary Theatre; and, in 1901, the Abbey or National Theatre Society
was established. Yeats, Lady Gregory and Synge supported it. As the movement gained popularity, libraries were created, books on Irish subjects
published, lectures delivered and the Gaelic language revived. Other notable
writers associated with the movement were: 'AE' (pseudonym of George
William Russell), Oliver St John Gogarty, Sean O'Casey and James Stephens.
Many people ridiculed the movement and James Joyce dismissed it with the
scornful phrase 'cultic twalette'.

cénacle F 'supper room') The *cénacles* were groups or coteries which formed
round the early leaders of the Romantic movement. The first is believed to
have been formed in the *salon* of Charles Nodier (1780–1844) at the Bibliothèque de l'Arsenal. The second gathered at Victor Hugo's house. Later a
group of 'disciples' sat at the feet of Sainte-Beuve.

censorship Forms of censorship began to be introduced very soon after the
invention of printing. Rulers, governments and the Church quickly realized
the power of the printed word to spread sedition and heresy. Proclamations
against seditious and heretical works began in England under Henry VIII in
1529. In 1538 laws were introduced that books must be licensed for printing
by the Privy Council or other royal nominees. Thereafter, throughout the
16th c., there was a series of proclamations and prohibitions. British monarchs were particularly concerned about the importation of foreign books.
In Europe there were similar measures. Underground and illegal printing
presses were soon in operation. Thus a pattern was set for the next 450 years.

In 1557 there was an important development when the Stationers'
Company got a 'charter of incorporation', after which only members of
the company (or others holding a special patent) were allowed to print any
work for sale in the kingdom. In 1586 the Star Chamber devised an ordinance
which directed that no printing press might be set up in any place other than
London – apart from one each in the university towns of Oxford and Cambridge. The Star Chamber continued to exercise considerable power and in
1637 imposed harsh penalties on offending printers. The Star Chamber was
abolished by the Long Parliament in 1641, but this did not mean the press

was liberated. In fact, restrictions and controls became, if anything, even tougher. During the 1640s there were numerous suppressions, prosecutions and imprisonments. In 1655 Cromwell stopped all unofficial periodicals (e.g. the *corantos*, *q.v.*, and other forms of newsletter). The Rump Parliament of 1659 permitted licensed newsbooks but their issue was restricted.

During the Restoration period (*q v.*) control and licensing of the press continued. In 1662 a Licensing Act was passed in Parliament, initially for two years; it was renewed and extended to 1679. In that year it lapsed, to be renewed in 1685. In 1694 Parliament declined to renew again. Later, the Secretary of State was responsible for dealing with any libellous or offensive matter. This covered anything published which might constitute a breach of the peace, or bring king, government or Parliament or the administration of justice into contempt. The authorities had wide-ranging powers. Offenders might be imprisoned and prosecuted. Standard punishments were the pillory, imprisonment and fines, as suffered by Daniel Defoe for his pamphlets on ecclesiastical issues. During the 18th c. interference with and restrictions on the press were gradually reduced but people still had to be careful what they wrote and published. When Thomas Paine published *The Rights of Man* (1791–2) both he and his book were regarded as subversive and he had to flee the country.

Censorship and control of the theatre, plays and performers were established in the 16th c. Some companies of players were attached to the court and to noble households, and there were also wandering troupes of players who had no patrons. In the interests of public order some controls over stage performances were in operation by *c.* 1550. The licensing of individual plays began in 1549 (or earlier). By an Act in 1572 all players (actors) were deemed 'rogues and vagabonds' unless they belonged to a baron of the realm (or somebody of higher rank), or were licensed by two justices. Plays were popular at court (Queen Elizabeth herself enjoyed them), but the City Fathers opposed them. There were ways of evading civic regulations. For example, the first theatre to be built in London was in Finsbury Fields (an area outside the Lord Mayor's control). In *c.* 1574 the post of Master of the Revels was created. He was a court official and no play could be performed in England without his licence. In 1581 he was given powers to imprison offenders. From 1606 he had the power to license the printing as well as the performance of plays. During the reigns of James I and Charles I the London theatrical companies worked under royal patents. The authorities were concerned with matters of religion and government, but not morals.

The Puritans were hostile to all forms of theatre and regarded the stage as immoral. In 1642 the Long Parliament prohibited all dramatic performances. The theatres were closed. Even so, there were various evasions, such as the drolls (*q.v.*). At or after the Restoration Charles II issued patents (*see* PATENT THEATRES) to Davenant and Thomas Killigrew (the Elder), creating a monopoly of two companies. In 1699 a royal order forbade the presentation of anything contrary to religion and good manners and the Master of the Revels was prohibited from licensing plays which might offend propriety.

In due course it became the Lord Chamberlain's job to exercise controls and in 1737 the Licensing Act was passed. This was the result of Walpole's efforts and was intended to control dramatic performance. A series of committee enquiries and renewed ordinances in the 19th c. served to maintain the status quo. Most importantly, the Lord Chamberlain maintained his role as official censor, exercising the power to prohibit plays up until the 1960s. Finally, in 1968, the Theatres Act was passed, repealing Walpole's legislation and ushering in a new era of experimental and taboo-breaking theatre. However, the pressure to censor on the grounds of sexual, moral or religious grounds continues to arise periodically in relation to controversial theatrical performances.

In general, Britain may be said to have escaped fairly lightly in matters of censorship. However, in the 1920s DORA (Defence of the Realm Act) had some influence. Clauses in this Act provided for forms of censorship, which, in the hands of a reactionary or puritanical Home Secretary, might be invoked.

Elsewhere, during the 20th c., censorship controls of the most stifling kind were imposed by all totalitarian and repressive regimes. Censorship departments in Communist-bloc countries (especially the USSR, Czechoslovakia, Hungary, Romania and Albania) were extremely careful about what they would allow to be published, and equally careful in their control of the importation of foreign books, papers and magazines. In the 19th c., Russian writers had long been accustomed to rigorous censorship under the Czarist regime.

In 1972 a periodical named *Index on Censorship* was founded by Writers and Scholars international: a group of writers, scholars, intellectuals and artists. This group was formed primarily at the instigation of the English poet and critic Stephen Spender and the Soviet dissident Pavel Litvinov. The group is concerned with the promotion of intellectual freedom in countries which suffer from repressive regimes, and the periodical publishes work by writers who are restricted or suppressed in their own countries. It also contains accounts of censorship and the imprisonment of authors.

Globally, regimes have sought to exercise control over many forms of artistic and political expression via censorship. Alongside suppression of traditional modes such as literature, cinema and theatre, control of electronic media, including access to web resources is fast becoming one of the most contested forms of government control. *See* PROPAGANDA; SAMIZDAT.

cento (L 'patchwork') A collection of bits and pieces from various writers. A patchwork poem made up of verses by different writers. Such works were common in later antiquity (e.g. Falconia Proba dedicated to Honorius a *Cento Vergilianus* dealing with events of the Old and New Testaments). Perhaps the most outstanding example of a *cento* is that by Decimus Magnus Ausonius (*c.* AD 310–90). His *Cento Nuptialis* runs to 131 lines, the lines or half lines being taken from, variously, Virgil's *Aeneid*, *Georgics* and *Eclogues*. He derives the term from Greek *kentrōn*, and in his introductory exposition to Paulus defines and explains it:

It is a poem compactly built out of a variety of passages and different meanings, in such a way that either two half-lines are joined together to form one, or one line and the following half with another half. For to place two (whole) lines side by side is weak, and three in succession mere trifling. But the lines [i.e. the lines of the poet from whose works the *cento* is compiled] are divided at any of the caesurae which heroic verse admits, so that either a penthemimeris can be linked with an anapaestic continuation, or a trochaic fragment with a complementary section, or seven half-feet with a choric anapaest, or after a dactyl and a half-foot is placed whatever is needed to complete the hexameter: so that you may say it is like the puzzle which the Greeks have called *ostomachia*.

(*Ostomachia* is a puzzle in which fourteen different pieces of bone representing different geometrical shapes are placed in combinations to represent various objects.) Ausonius's poem is a kind of epithalamion (*q.v.*). These are the opening lines (with references):

> Accipite haec animis laetasque advertite mentes,[1]
> ambo animis, ambo insignes praestantibus armis;[2]
> ambo florentes,[3] genus insuperabile bello.[4]

(1. *Aeneid*, V, l. 304; 2. *Aeneid*, XI, l. 291; 3. *Eclogues*, VII, l. 4; 4. *Aeneid*, IV, l. 40.)

An ingenious modern example is that by A. Alvarez in his introduction to *The New Poetry* (rev. edn 1966). The synthesis contains lines from eight different modern poets:

> Picture of lover or friend that is not either
> Like you or me who, to sustain our pose,
> Need wine and conversation, colour and light;
> In short, a past that no one now can share,
> No matter whose your future; calm and dry,
> In sex I do not dither more than either,
> Nor should I now swell to halloo the names
> Of feelings that no one needs to remember:
> The same few dismal properties, the same
> Oppressive air of justified unease
> Of our imaginations and our beds.
> It seems the poet made a bad mistake.

See COLLAGE; PASTICHE.

Centre 42 A scheme which was the brain-child of Arnold Wesker (1932–), the dramatist. He planned to create an arts centre supported by the trade unions and Labour movement. In 1960 the Trades Union Congress passed a resolution (No. 42) by which the arts should be supported. Festivals were held in 1962 and for a while it was hoped that the Round House in London would be the centre. Eventually, lack of money meant the whole plan was aborted. *See also* THEATRE WORKSHOP.

Centre for Contemporary Cultural Studies (CCCS) Founded in 1964 as a postgraduate research centre at the University of Birmingham by the sociologist Richard Hoggart. Other key figures in the Centre were literary critic Raymond Williams, historian E. P. Thompson and sociologist and cultural theorist Stuart Hall, who became director of the CCCS in 1968. The Centre is notable for having established a new interdisciplinary field known as cultural studies (*q.v.*) in Britain. Its three key areas of inquiry, as Hoggart noted, have been the historical and philosophical, the sociological and the literary critical. Staff, students and associates of the Centre worked together on a wide range of areas, including literature, the media, education, popular culture and race and gender politics. Their interdisciplinary and intersectional methodological approach initiated a study of culture that is not divorced from politics and lived experience. Drawing on Marxist thought, CCCS scholars theorized culture as a site of conflict and struggle, negotiation and resistance, and initiated a critical analysis of cultural forms in contemporary societies. This led to an engaged critique of cultural and political changes in postwar Britain, and resulted in a number of studies dealing with questions such as class, gender, race, youth culture, diaspora, Thatcherism and consumerism.

The Centre published a number of influential books, articles and its own journal. Notable examples are collections of essays *The Empire Strikes Back: Race and Racism in '70s Britain* (1982), *Off-Centre: Feminism and Cultural Studies*, edited by notable feminist CCCS scholars Sarah Franklin, Celia Lury and Jackie Stacey, and Stuart Hall's *Policing the Crisis* (1978), which examined the discourses around 'mugging' and race, and the subsequent construction of black youth criminality in Britain in the 1970s. The CCCS became a Department of Cultural Studies in 1988 and it was dramatically closed in 2002, despite an international campaign to save it. Its legacy, however, has continued to inspire scholars around the world.

centres dramatiques Theatres (in some cases combined with a drama school) established in the purlieus of Paris and some provincial towns from 1945. The idea was to take theatre and drama 'to the people': to the workers and those of the lower-middle-class bracket. Work done by the directors had discernible leftist tendencies and many of the directors belonged to the Left. A number of these centres were combined with *maisons de la culture* and not a few were highly successful. In Britain they have had counterparts comparable in some respects. For instance, the Unity Theatre, Centre 42, Theatre Workshop (*qq.v.*).

centrifugal/centripetal The terms were coined by Mikhail Bakhtin (1895–1975) in his essay *Discourse in the Novel* to describe the two forces at work in all languages, or in any utterance. Adopting the terms from physics, Bakhtin argues that centripetal forces operate by pulling all aspects of language and its numerous rhetorical modes towards a central point in order to produce one standard language, or an 'official' language that everyone would have to speak and use. Centripetal force is regulatory, unifying, centralizing and monologic. By contrast, centrifugal forces push the elements of language away from the centre and produce multiplicity. Centrifugal force is thus decentralizing, stratifying and anti-canonical. It is a distinct feature of Bakhtin's notion of heteroglossia (*q.v.*). At any given moment, Bakhtin claims, language is stratified not only into dialects, but also into languages that reflect a profession, a genre, a generation group, an age group and so forth. The dialectic between the centripetal and centrifugal forces displays the dynamic of language and ensures that it remains in constant flux. Bakhtin also argues that poetry and poetic language are marked by centripetal forces, while the novel and novelistic language are centrifugal and dialogic. *See also* DIALOGIC/MONOLOGIC; HETEROGLOSSIA.

chain verse A rhyming scheme, like *rime riche* (*q.v.*), where the last syllable of a line is repeated in the first syllable of the next line; but though the sound is the same, the sense is different. It is rare in English verse.

The term is also applied to a verse in which the last line of each stanza becomes the first line of the next. Again, this is rare. *See* VILLANELLE.

chanson A form of love-song, particularly among the Provençal troubadour (*q.v.*) poets. The *chanson* had five or six stanzas, all of the same construction, and an *envoi* (*q.v.*) or *tornada* (*q.v.*). A high degree of originality and technical virtuosity was required, but the themes and subjects were usually the same: devotion to a lady or mistress in the courtly love (*q.v.*) tradition.

chanson à danser Song from the Middle Ages (the earliest extant dates from the first half of the 13th c.) composed as an accompaniment to dance. The metrical forms varied considerably. The principal dance was the *carole*, from which evolved the poetic form *rondet de carole* – similar to a *triolet* (*q.v.*). The *ballette* was another dance song consisting of three stanzas and a refrain (*q.v.*). *See also* CAROL.

chanson à personnages Medieval song in dialogue form. Popular themes were a dispute between husband and wife, an exchange between lovers parting at dawn, a meeting between a knight and a shepherdess. *See* AUBADE; DÉBAT; PASTOURELLE; REVERDIE.

chanson de gestes (F 'song of deeds') OF epic poems which relate the heroic deeds of Carolingian noblemen and other feudal lords. Some describe wars against the Saracens; others are devoted to intrigue, rebellion and war among the nobles. They exhibit a combination of history and legend (*q.v.*) and also reflect a definite conception of religious chivalry. There are three main cycles: the cycle of Guillaume d'Orange; the cycle of Charlemagne; the third mostly develops the themes of a lord's revolt against his *seigneur*. They were very popular (a literature of entertainment) between the 11th and 14th c., and over eighty survive. Easily the most famous is the *Chanson de Roland* (The Song of Roland), probably composed in the second half of the 11th c. *See also* EPIC; NARRATIVE VERSE; ROMANCE.

chanson de toile *Toile* is 'linen, canvas, cloth'. The *chansons de toile* are associated particularly with northern medieval France, the idea being that they were sung by women while they were sewing, pinning or the like. They were short poems in the form of monorhyme stanzas with a refrain (*q.v.*) and related some love episode or sorrow. They tended to be simple, and touching by their immediacy of feeling.

chansonnier A collection of Provençal troubadour (*q.v.*) poems in manuscript form.

chant (OF *chanter*, L *cantare*, 'to sing') The term may denote almost any song or melody, particularly the melody to which the Psalms are sung. It may denote the Psalm itself. Chants are commonest in liturgical services. Gregorian plain song or *cantus firmus* is the most famous form of chant and has been the most influential. Anglican chant and the chants of the Orthodox churches are also notable. When a poem is chanted the musical elements are subordinate to the verbal. This produces a stylized quality, noticeable in the recitation of the choral pieces in Classical drama, or choral pieces modelled on the Classical style. Also in the recitation of epic ballads. The *guslari* (*q.v.*), for instance, chant their poems to the accompaniment of a one-string fiddle called a *gusle*.

chante fable (Pr) A romance (*q.v.*) of adventure composed of alternating prose and verse. *Aucassin and Nicolette* (early 13th c.) is believed to be the only survivor of a genre which probably had some popularity in the 12th and 13th c.

chantey *See* SHANTY.

chant royal A metrical and rhyming scheme related to *ballade* (*q.v.*) forms. It consists of five eleven-line stanzas rhyming ababccddedE, followed by an *envoi* (*q.v.*) rhyming ddedE. It also has a refrain (*q.v.*) as indicated by the capital letters, at the end of each stanza and including the last line of the *envoi*. A further complication is that no rhyme word may be used twice except in the *envoi*. The formidable technical difficulties involved make it a rare form except in the 14th c. when distinguished poets like Eustache Deschamps, Charles d'Orléans and Jean Marot used it.

chapbook A form of popular literature hawked by pedlars or chapmen, mostly from the 16th to the 18th c. Chapbooks consisted of ballads, pamphlets, tracts, nursery rhymes and fairy stories (*qq.v.*). They were often illustrated with wood-blocks and were sold at a penny to sixpence. Old romances like *Bevis of Hampton* and *Guy of Warwick* were favourites.

chapka (K 'miscellaneous songs') Long narrative poems sung by professional Korean minstrels.

character The person portrayed in a narrative or dramatic work. Also, a short prose sketch of a particular individual type. As a literary genre, the 'character' became popular early in the 17th c. At this time there was an increasing interest in the analysis of character (we may have here the beginning of the novelist's approach to character) but the 'Character' had already a long history, in one form or another, in European literature: in exemplum, allegory, fable, tale (*qq.v.*) (for instance, the character studies in Chaucer's *General Prologue to the Canterbury Tales*), and in the dramatic and psychological doctrine of humours (*q.v.*), influenced by Horace's precepts on dramatic types. Moreover, it seems there was a disposition towards and an interest in Charactery because of the by then well-established idea that man, as a 'little world' (microcosm), was an embodiment of the universe (macrocosm).

In his *Advancement of Learning* (1605) Francis Bacon discusses the ancient opinion that 'man was *microcosmus*, an abstract or model of the world'. And in his *History of the World* (1614) Sir Walter Ralegh wrote: 'because in the little frame of man's body there is a representation of the Universal; and (by allusion) a kind of participation of all the parts there, therefore was man called *Microcosmos*, or the little World'. Later, Sir Thomas Browne, in *Religio Medici* (1642), observed: 'We carry within us the wonders we seek without us: there is all Africa and her prodigies in us; we are that bold and adventurous piece of Nature, which he that studies wisely learns in a *compendium* what others labour at in a divided piece and endless volume.'

Writers and thinkers of the period were very attracted to the microcosm/macrocosm concept, but the popularity of the 'Character' may also be attributed to the publication in 1592 of a Latin translation, by Isaac Casaubon, of the *Characters* of Theophrastus of Lesbos (371–287 BC) – the prototypal work – which was followed in 1593 by an English version of Casaubon's Latin by John Healey. Other works which very probably had some influence were pamphlets by Nashe and Greene and Nicholas Breton's *The Fantasticks* (1626).

The first major collection of character studies was Joseph Hall's *Characters of Virtues and Vices* (1608). A minor work by 'W. M.' called *The Man in the Moon* came out in 1609. The next major work was Sir Thomas Overbury's *Characters* (1614), some of which are believed to have been written by Webster, Dekker and Donne. Another minor work was Geffray Mynshul's *Essays and Characters of Prison and Prisoners* (1617). By now the connection between the essay (*q.v.*) and the 'Character' is becoming clear, and one may suppose that the influence of Montaigne is to be detected here. Then, in 1628, John Earle published *Microcosmographie*. Earle is the truest descendant of Theophrastus and his characters are generally thought to be the best.

The subjects of Characterology fall into roughly three categories: (a) a type – a self-conceited man, a blunt man; (b) a social type – an antiquary, an old college butler; (c) a place or scene: a tavern or cockpit. The idea was to create an individual while formulating a type. There was usually an attempt at universality. For instance, a pretender to learning might be found in any part of the world at any time. The miniature portraits were aphoristically terse, a style particularly congenial in the 17th c.

Hall, Overbury and Earle had many imitators. The more notable authors and works were: Donald Lupton's *Long and Country Carbonadoed* (1632); Richard Flecknoe's *Enigmatical Characters* (1658); Francis Osborn's *A Miscellany of Sundry Essays* (1659). An elaborate extension of the whole idea of 'charactery' is George Halifax's *The Character of a Trimmer* (1688).

One of the most famous of all such collections wax La Bruyère's *Les Caractères* (1688), in the great French tradition of Montaigne, Pascal and La Rochefoucauld. He combined translations of Theophrastus with his own observations – which are shrewd, tartly laconic, aphoristic (like La Rochefoucauld's *Maxims*) and presented with Baconian terseness.

The practice of 'charactery' was carried on in the following century in the periodical essay (*q.v.*), especially by Steele, Addison, Goldsmith and Johnson. They took the process a stage further by naming the characters (for instance. Sir Andrew Freeport, Will Honeycomb, Dick Minim), and these essay characters, though types, were also particular individuals. The essay character gave place to and made possible the character of the novel (*q.v.*), as can be seen in Fielding's novels *Joseph Andrews* (1742) and *Tom Jones* (1749).

Modern 'charactery' tends to be the portrayal of individuals, though many of Dickens's characters are also typical – just as virtues and vices are typical in most parts of the world. Something in between the characters of Earle and the novel character is to be found in such works as Dickens's *Sketches by Boz* (1839), Thackeray's *Book of Snobs* (1848) and George Eliot's *Theophrastus Such* (1879). *See also* MAXIM; PENSÉE.

charm A spell or incantation, which may consist of song, verse or mere mumbo jumbo and abracadabra to invoke supernatural or supranormal powers. It is one of the earliest forms of written literature and appears to be almost universal. The OE *Charms* are among the first extant written works in our language. There are several: For a sudden stitch; Against a dwarf; Against wens; For taking a swarm of bees; A land remedy; A journey spell; Against the theft of cattle; The nine herbs charm. Examples of charms incorporated in a more literary context are to be found in Elizabethan and Jacobean plays. Famous instances are the Weird Sisters' charms in *Macbeth* (*c.* 1606). Quite as good are those in Ben Jonson's *The Masque of Queens* (1609), and the lyric of Campion's which begins:

> Thrice toss these oaken ashes in the air;
> Thrice sit thou mute in his enchanted chair;
> Then thrice three times tie up this true love's knot,
> And murmur soft: 'She will, or she will not.'

See INCANTATION.

chastushka (R 'part-song') A form of Russian folksong. It usually consists of two, four or six lines (four being the commonest) which rhyme. Often humorous and epigrammatic, most of them are love-songs. Some *chastushki* are concerned with political events such as the Revolution and the Second World War, and not a few express anti-Soviet attitudes. As a kind of brief lyric poetry, they are sung solo or chorally and may be accompanied by guitar, balalaika or accordion.

Chaucerian stanza   *See* RHYME ROYAL.

cheville   (F 'plug, stopgap') A word or phrase used by poets to secure the necessary number of syllables in a line of verse so that it scans properly. Chaucer frequently uses such 'plugs' with 'I trow' or 'ywis'.

Chevy Chase stanza   The verse form of alternating lines of iambic tetrameter and pentameter, in quatrains, associated with the ballad, after *The Ballad of Chevy Chase*. *See* BALLAD METER.

chiasmic rhyme   *See* RHYME.

chiasmus   (Gk 'a placing crosswise') A reversal of grammatical structures in successive phrases or clauses. As in this example from Dr Johnson's *The Vanity of Human Wishes*:

> By the day the frolic, and the dance by night.

And this from Pope's *Essay on Man* (Epistle I):

> His time a moment, and a point his space.

The device is related to antithesis (*q.v.*). *See also* ANTIMETABOLE; RHYME; ZEUGMA.

Chicago School   Also known as the Neo-Aristotelians, a group of critics who began formulating their central ideas around the same time as the New Critics were voicing their manifestoes. In the 1930s, departments of humanities at the University of Chicago were undergoing a radical transformation in an attempt to revive them and make them institutionally more competitive with the sciences. Six of the figures later known as the Chicago critics were involved in these changes: R. S. Crane, Richard McKeon, Elder Olson, W. R. Keast, Norman Maclean and Bernard Weinberg. These critics later produced the central manifesto of the Chicago School, *Critics and Criticism: Ancient and Modern* (1952), which both attacked some of the important tenets of the New Criticism (*q.v.*) and elaborated an alternative formalistic method of criticism derived in part from Aristotle's *Poetics*. In an earlier essay of 1934, Crane had anticipated (and influenced) John Crowe Ransom's call that professional criticism should move from a primarily historical towards an aesthetic focus.

However, Crane and the Chicago School generally diverged from the New Criticism in their insistence that literary study should integrate both systematic theory of literature (being informed by the history of literary theory) and the practice of close reading and explication of literary texts. Moreover, the Chicago School drew from Aristotle's *Poetics* a number of characteristic critical concerns, such as the emphasis on literary texts as 'artistic wholes', the analytical importance of locating individual texts within given genres, and the need to identify textual and generic (as opposed to authorial) intention. Whereas the New Critics had focused attention on specifically poetic uses of language, irony, metaphor, tension and balance, the Chicago School followed Aristotle in emphasizing plot, character and thought. In general, the Neo-Aristotelians offered an alternative formalist poetics which acknowledged the mimetic, didactic and affective functions of literature.

children's books Until about the middle of the 18th c. there was little in the way of books specifically for children, except for didactic works of one sort and another like textbooks, books of etiquette and works of moral edification. For entertainment and diversion they had Aesop's *Fables*, romances, travel books, chapbooks, broadside ballads (*qq.v.*) and any 'adult' reading they could lay their hands on. Notable examples of this are Bunyan's *Pilgrim's Progress* (1678), Defoe's *Robinson Crusoe* (1719) and Swift's *Gulliver's Travels* (1726). In France, children had been a little better off because of Fénelon's *Télémaque* (1699), Perrault's fairy tales, and *The Arabian Nights*, which came to England via a French translation early in the 18th c.

In England one of the first people to realize that there was a demand for children's books was John Newbery (1713–67), a bookseller who issued a variety of works illustrated with woodcuts or engravings at low prices. His two best-known publications were *A Little Pretty Pocket-Book* (1744) and *The History of Little Goody Two-Shoes* (1765?). From this point on we find an ever increasing number of publications for children in Europe and America.

School stories have also proved a very popular form of fiction among children and adolescents. A few of the more or less classic works in this field are Sarah Fielding's *Governess* (1749); Harriet Martineau's *Crofton Boys* (1841); and Thomas Hughes's *Tom Brown's Schooldays* (1857).

The fairy tale (*q.v.*) is a widespread form of fiction for children. Again there are a number of classic works, like *The Arabian Nights*, Perrault's tales, the stories by the Grimm brothers and Hans Andersen, Chandler Harris's *Uncle Remus* (1880), Lewis Carroll's *Alice's Adventures in Wonderland* (1865), A. A. Milne's *Winnie the Pooh* (1926) and Carlo Lorenzini's *Pinocchio* (1883).

There are also a large number of what may be described as animal stories. Notable instances are Anna Sewell's *Black Beauty* (1877) and Kipling's *Jungle Books* (1894–5).

Some notable instances of children's verse are Christina Rossetti's *Sing-Song* (1872); R. L. Stevenson's *A Child's Garden of Verses* (1885); and T. S. Eliot's *Old Possum's Book of Practical Cats* (1939). This last is a kind of nonsense verse (*q.v.*), a genre to which (for children) several famous writers have made outstanding contributions – especially Lewis Carroll and A. A. Milne. Subsequently, Puffin published some of the best anthologies of children's verse, namely, *Junior Voices* (in four different books) and *Voices* (in three books).

In the 20th c. there were a number of works in the fairy tale category which became classics. Obvious examples are J. M. Barrie's *Peter Pan* (1904),

Kipling's *Just So Stories* (1902) and Hugh Lofting's Dr Dolittle series (begun in the 1920s). To these should be added the many Beatrix Potter stories, the first being published in 1902.

Since the 1950s literature intended specifically for children has become a publishing industry in its own right. There are specialist guides, and, in the more reputable newspapers, specialist reviewers. The whole approach has become highly professional. Different age groups are carefully catered for, and so are the sexes. Close attention has been given to racism and sexism, and also to what is acceptable or unacceptable politically and ideologically. Not a few prize awards have been created: for example, the Kate Greenaway Medal for illustration, the Newbery Medal, the Eleanor Farjeon Medal and the Carnegie Medal.

Some authors have become enormously popular and have what is almost a cult following. A notable example is J. R. R. Tolkien (1892–1973), who published *The Hobbit* in 1937 and followed this with *The Lord of the Rings* in three volumes (1954–5). C. S. Lewis (1898–1963) has been equally popular with his Narnia series: seven stories beginning with *The Lion, the Witch and the Wardrobe* (1950) and ending with *The Last Battle* (1956). In the 1970s the author and illustrator Raymond Briggs (1934–) achieved fame with a series of outstanding stories, principally *Father Christmas* (1973), *Fungus the Bogeyman* (1977) and *The Snowman* (1979). Besides his verse for children, Roald Dahl also wrote many notable stories, including *Charlie and the Chocolate Factory* (1964), *The BFG* (1982) and *Esio Trot* (1990).

Of the dozens of other writers who have produced distinguished literature for children since the 1950s we should mention particularly Nina Bawden, Maurice Sendak, Ian Serraillier, Philippa Pearce, Alan Garner, Rosemary Sutcliff, Leon Garfield, Margaret J. Miller, Joan Aiken, William Mayne, Robert Westall, Stan Barstow, Bill Naughton, John Prebble, Penelope Lively, Barry Hines, J. K. Rowling, Philip Pullman, Graham Oakley and Eoin Colfer. Plus the Americans Virginia Hamilton, Paula Fox, Ursula Le Guin, Betsy Byars, Lee McGiffin, Rick Riordan, Suzanne Collins and David Wiesner; and the Australians Patricia Wrightson and Ivan Southall. *See also* COMICS.

children's literature *See* CHILDREN'S BOOKS.

chora The term derives from Greek and is usually translated as 'womb' or 'receptacle'. It is a psychoanalytic concept developed by Julia Kristeva in *Revolution in Poetic Language* (1974) to describe a space, or a stage which is prior to the child's acquisition of language and even to Lacan's proposed mirror stage (*q.v.*). Kristeva borrows the term from Plato's *Timaeus* to explicate the earliest stage in psychosexual development and the ways in which an infant's psychic environment is oriented to its mother's body. Kristeva firstly associates the *chora* with the interaction between the child and the mother's body, and with an exchange of blood, milk, tears and touch that takes place between them. In this early psychic stage, the infant is unable to distinguish the difference between itself and the mother, and so the mother's body provides a soothing space for the potentially disorienting and destructive drives and instincts that the infant experiences.

The *chora* thus signifies a stage before the child develops borders of identity and realizes that it is both separate from and dependent on the mother. Secondly, the *chora* signifies something that precedes language – that is, the space before the child begins to use language to refer to objects, and later symbolically through grammar and syntax. Kristeva uses the term 'semiotic chora' to describe the ways in which a child uses different expressions to release energy, such as coos and babbles, without knowing that they can express something. Reflecting Plato's discussion of *chora* as both the container and the producer, Kristeva's notion of *chora* is thus a space that both receives and generates energy.

In *Khôra* (1993), Jacques Derrida takes the definition of the *chora* further as that which philosophy is unable to name. *Khôra*, thus transcribed, resists definition and representation. It is neither a static place nor a receptacle, neither the sensible nor the intelligible, but something that precedes the birth of the cosmos and spatiality. *See also* ABJECTION; ÉCRITURE FÉMININE.

choree *See* TROCHEE.

choriambus (Gk 'chorus iamb') An iamb and a trochee (*qq.v.*) combined to make a metrical foot of two stressed syllables enclosing two unstressed: / ◡ ◡ /. In English verse, rare as the basic scheme of a poem; but not infrequently found in combination with other feet. Swinburne, a skilled and indefatigable experimenter in meter, shows its use well in *Choriambics*:

> Sweét thĕ | kíssĕs ŏf deáth | sét ŏn thў líps
> Cóldĕr ăre théy | thăn míne;
> Cóldĕr | súrelў thăn pást | kíssĕs ŏf lóve
> Póured fŏr thў líps | ăs wíne.

choric/choral character Usually in a play, the choric character or 'presenter' comments on the action and perhaps also introduces it. This character is related to the Chorus (*q.v.*) in Greek drama. The choric character may not take much part in the main action, and the commentary is likely to be omniscient or ironical. Well-known choric characters are Thersites in Shakespeare's *Troilus and Cressida* (c. 1602), Wong in Brecht's *The Good Woman of Szechuan* (1938–41), and the lawyer in Arthur Miller's *A View from the Bridge* (1955). *See* CONFIDANT.

chorography (Gk 'writing about countries') An archaic term for the description of place, particularly of nations or regions. It is perhaps distinct from *topographical poetry* (*q.v.*), which is concerned with particular features such as towns rather than with larger districts; but the two terms are largely interchangeable. The foremost chorographers in English are William Camden, *Britannia* (1586), and Michael Drayton, *Poly-Olbion* (1612, 1622). *See also* TOPOTHESIA.

Chorus (Gk 'dance') Originally the Chorus was a group of performers at a religious festival, especially fertility rites. By some process of grafting or symbiosis Greek tragedy (*q.v.*) acquired (or grew out of) these choral rites. At any rate, the Chorus became an essential and integral part of Greek tragic drama. In the works of Aeschylus the Chorus often took part in the action; in Sophocles it served as a commentator on the action; and in Euripides it provided a lyric element. The Romans copied the idea of a Chorus from the Greeks, and Elizabethan dramatists took it over from the Romans. However, a full-scale Chorus has seldom been used in English drama, or indeed European drama.

Usually the Chorus has been reduced to one person, as in *Henry V* (1599), *Pericles* (c. 1608) and *The Winter's Tale* (c. 1609–10). Milton used a full Chorus in his closet drama (*q.v.*) *Samson Agonistes* (1671), but thereafter there are few instances until T. S. Eliot's *Murder in the Cathedral* (1935), in which the remarkable Chorus of the women of Canterbury takes part in the action, comments on it and provides mood and atmosphere. Eliot also used a Chorus of the Eumenides in *The Family Reunion* (1939). There have been occasional uses of a single Chorus as commentator on the action (moving in and out of the play). Notable instances are the scurrilous Thersites, in Shakespeare's *Troilus and Cressida* (c. 1602), the Fool in *King Lear* (1606), and Antony's henchman Enobarbus in *Antony and Cleopatra* (c. 1606–7). Other important instances in drama are to be found in Brecht's *The Caucasian Chalk Circle* (1943–5), Anouilh's *Antigone* (1944), Tennessee Williams's *The Glass Menagerie* (1945) and Arthur Miller's *A View from the Bridge* (1955). The use of a kind of group Chorus is also to be found occasionally in novels. For example, there are the rustics in George Eliot's *Silas Marner* (1861), the Mellstock musicians in Thomas Hardy's *Under the Greenwood Tree* (1872) and the rustics in his *The Return of the Native* (1878). A not dissimilar use of Chorus is to be found in some of William Faulkner's novels: for instance, *The Hamlet* (1940), *The Mansion* (1959) and *The Reivers* (1962).

chosism (F 'thingism') It denotes the highly detailed description of objects, things (often inanimate) – their shape, colour, texture, density – that some French novelists associated with the *nouveau roman* (*q.v.*) tended to go in for. It had its fascination but when overdone it could become counterproductive. Alain Robbe-Grillet and Michel Butor, among others, were particularly skilled at it. *See also* TROPISM.

chrestomathy (Gk 'useful learning') An anthology (*q.v.*) of passages in prose or verse (or both); particularly one to be used for learning a language.

Christabel meter The meter of Coleridge's poem *Christabel*. It comprises free couplets with a pattern of four stresses. Much of the time the feet are iambs or anapaests (*qq.v.*). Coleridge claimed that the meter was based not on a syllable count but on an accent count, that this was a new principle and that the length of the line varied with the amount of passion expressed. In fact the principle was *not* new, but it is true that the passion does vary occasionally. One feature of the poem is that in a few lines he manages mono-syllabic feet.

chronicle   A register of events in order of time, often composed contemporaneously with the events it records. Early examples are the Roman *Fasti
Consulares* or *Capitolini* compiled in the reign of Augustus. There were many
medieval chronicles, in verse and prose, which are important sources for the
historian. Among the earliest are the 6th c. chronicle of Gildas, *De Excidio
et Conquestu Britanniae*, Bede's *Ecclesiastical History* (c. 731), the *Historia
Brittonum* of Nennius (c. 796), Asser's 9th c. chronicle covering the period
849–87, and the *Historia Remensis Ecclesiae* by Flodoard of Rheims which
covers the period 919–66. From the second half of the 10th c. dates the
Annales Cambriae. The *Anglo-Saxon Chronicles* are very valuable records of
events in England from the beginning of the Christian era until the middle
of the 12th c. Several Latin chronicles belong to the 12th c., including Flor-
ence of Worcester's *Chronicon ex Chronicis*, which he took down to 1117
and which was then extended by others until 1295. Eadmer's *Historia
Novorum in Anglia* goes as far as 1122. William of Malmesbury, one of the
best and most famous chroniclers, compiled several records: particularly
the *Gesta Regum Anglorum* (449–1127) and *Historia Novella*, which covers
English history as far as 1142. From the 12th c. also date Geoffrey of Mon-
mouth's *Historia Regum Britanniae*, Roger of Hoveden's *Cronica*, Jocelin de
Brakelond's chronicle of his abbey, several records by Giraldus Cambrensis
and William of Newburgh's *Historia Rerum Anglicarum* (1066–1198). In the
13th c. some schools of history developed, particularly at St Denis where a
large number of Latin chronicles were produced which eventually became
the *Grandes Chroniques de France*; and at St Albans where Matthew of Paris
compiled his great chronicles (1235–59). From the 13th and 14th c. we should
also note Robert Gloucester's chronicle from earliest times down to 1272,
Richard of Cirencester's *Speculum Historiale* (447–1066), Froissart's *Chroniques* (1325–1400) and Andrew of Wyntoun's *The Orygynale Cronykil*. In
the 15th c. John Capgrave made several important chronicles, and in the
16th c. we find an increasing number of such records: Robert Fabyan's *Concordance of Histories* (1516), an anonymous *History of Richard III* (1534),
which was something of a landmark in history and biography (*q.v.*), Polydore
Vergil's *Anglicae Historiae Libri xxvi* (1534–55), Camden's *Britannia* (1586),
Holinshed's *Chronicles* (1577), Edward Hall's *The Union of the Noble and
Illustre Families of Lancastre and York*, a number of very valuable *Chronicles*
by John Stow (especially his account of London), and William Harrison's
Description of England (included in Holinshed's *Chronicles*). Early in the
17th c. John Speed published *Historie of Great Britain* (1611), and between
1599 and 1636 Sir John Hayward published several biographies. By this stage
the writing of history and the making of records was very different from
what it had been earlier. Biography, autobiography (*q.v.*), memories, diaries,
logbooks, travel books, narratives of sea voyages and exploration were
becoming commonplace and thereafter the chronicle was no longer a form

of any note. The writing of history, as is evident from, for instance, Sir Walter Ralegh's *History of the World* (1614), was to become a much more specialized business. *See* ANNAL; CHRONICLE PLAY; DIARY AND JOURNAL; TRAVEL BOOK.

chronicle novels *See* BILDUNGSROMAN; ROMAN CYCLE; ROMAN-FLEUVE; SAGA NOVEL.

chronicle play Also known as a History Play, and therefore based on recorded history rather than on myth or legend (*qq.v.*). Early examples are *The Persians* by Aeschylus, and *Octavia*, ascribed to Seneca.

Early chronicle plays in England were like pageants interspersed with battle scenes. However, some dramatists saw the possibility of the history play. Bale wrote what is generally regarded as the first: *King John* (c. 1534). Two other important works in the transition from Interlude (*q.v.*) and Morality Play (*q.v.*) to historical drama were Sackville and Norton's *Gorboduc* (1561) and Preston's *Cambises* (1569). Later, Marlowe also saw the possibilities of such presentation and, using Holinshed, dramatized the life of Edward II (1593). Shakespeare followed with a succession of chronicle plays which covered the English monarchy from Richard II to Henry VIII. Shakespeare also wrote *King John* (probably adapted before 1598 from an earlier work and not printed until the Folio (*q.v.*) of 1623). After him Fletcher, with *Bonduca* (1619), and Ford, with *Perkin Warbeck* (1634), continued the tradition successfully.

Thereafter chronicle plays are fairly rare, though a number of dramatists attempted Roman historical subjects in the 18th and 19th c. James Sheridan Knowles, Darley, Tennyson, Browning and Swinburne all turned to history for their subjects but with little success – largely because they were out of touch with the requirements of the theatre and insufficiently familiar with the stage. Thomas Hardy also attempted a dramatization of history in the shape of *The Dynasts* (1904, 1906, 1908), which also proved unstageable. By general agreement Schiller in the *Wallenstein Trilogy* (1799) and *Maria Stuart* (1800) was the only subsequent dramatist to manage this kind of play with much success.

Since the Second World War there have been several notable chronicle plays. For example, Arthur Miller's *The Crucible* (1953), Robert Bolt's *A Man for All Seasons* (1960) and *State of Revolution* (1977), and Rolf Hochhuth's *The Representative* (1966) and *Soldiers* (1967). *See* CHRONICLE; EPIC THEATRE.

chronogram (Gk 'time writing') An inscription in which letters form a date in Roman numerals.

Ciceronian In the style of Cicero (106–43 BC). Thus, dignified, balanced, melodious, well ordered and clear. Cicero had much influence on the writing of prose from the Renaissance onwards.

cielito (Sp 'little heaven') In gaucho literature (*q.v.*) an octosyllabic quatrain (*q.v.*) rhyming in the second and fourth lines. A well-known practitioner was

Bartolomé Hidalgo (1788–1822), the Uruguayan poet, who was primarily responsible for the creation of gaucho literature.

cinquain A five-line stanza with a variable meter and rhyme scheme. It may be of medieval origin. The American poet Adelaide Crapsey worked out a particular kind of *cinquain* consisting of five lines with a fixed number of syllables: two, four, six, eight and two respectively.

cipher A mode of writing which employs the substitution or transposition of letters. A private and secret means of communication. Interesting if childish examples occur in Mary Leith's letters to Swinburne. For instance:

Cy merest dozen,
Ansk thawfully for your kyind letter. Since you and Mr Watts kyindly give us the choice of days (or doice of chays) may we name Wednesday all things being propitious? . . .
This little delay has allowed me more time to devote to your most interesting Eton book . . . even tho' it be only the tavings of a rug, or even the topping of a mug, it is exceptionally amusing to your mi', tho' I could dish that it wealt with a pater leriod.

See SPOONERISM.

circumambages The devices of periphrasis (*q.v.*). A rare term.

circumlocution Roundabout speech or writing. Using a lot of words where a few will do. *See* EUPHEMISM; PERIPHRASIS; TAUTOLOGY.

circumstance, tragedy of A tragedy (*q.v.*) in which some kind of external force like fate or the gods brings about the doom of the hero or heroine (and other characters).

citizen comedy A type of play which had some vogue early in the 17th c. It was usually about life in contemporary London and the characters were based on those likely to be found among the middle or lower-middle classes. Well-known examples of the genre are Dekker's *The Shoemaker's Holiday* (1600), Middleton's *A Chaste Maid in Cheapside* (c. 1613) and Ben Jonson's *Bartholomew Fair* (1614).

civic critics A name given to Russian critics (especially those of the 19th c.) who tended to evaluate literature in terms of its social and political ideas and attitudes and were concerned with whether or not it was progressive. They were opposed to the Parnassians and Parnassianism (*q.v.*) and the aesthetic of art for art's sake (*q.v.*).

civic poetry The name given to 19th c. Russian poetry which is chiefly concerned with the expression of political and social consciousness and thus with the way of life that people lead (e.g. the peasantry). Its originator was probably Kondrati Ryleyev (1795–1826), much of whose poetry was about the Cossacks, whose democratic ideals and standards he admired. Other poets of note who were practitioners of this kind of verse were Nikolai Ogaryov (1813–77), Nikolai Nekrasov (1821–78), Ivan Aksakov (1823–86), Ivan Nikitin (1824–61), Alexei Pleshcheyev (1825–93), Nikolai Vilenkin (1855–1937) and Semyon Nadson (1862–87). Civic poetry as a tradition came more or less to an end in the 1890s with the advent of symbolism. *See* SYMBOL AND SYMBOLISM.

claque (F *claquer*, 'to clap') An early form of 'rent-a-crowd'. A band of people hired by a theatre manager to applaud during plays at specific points and passages. A contract, drawn up between the manager and the *chef de claque*, was called '*un entreprise de succès dramatique*'. The origins of the claque are said to date from the Emperor Nero's period. When he performed before the people applause was carefully orchestrated.

classic A number of meanings may be distinguished, but principally: (a) of the first rank or authority; (b) belonging to the literature or art of Greece and Rome; and (c) a writer or work of the first rank, and of generally acknowledged excellence.

Originally a *scriptor classicus* wrote for the upper classes; a *scriptor proletarius* for the lower classes. Gradually, for the Romans, the term 'classic' came to signify an author of the first-class quality. During the Middle Ages the word merely meant a writer who was studied (in the classroom) regardless of his merit. At the Renaissance (*q.v.*) only the major works by Greek and Latin authors were regarded as of first-class importance, and the humanistic ideal established the view that the best Classical authors had reached perfection. Nowadays we tend to use classic in one of three senses: (a) first-class or outstanding (we have 'classic' races); (b) ancient; (c) typical (for instance, a classic example of a disease).

The adjective 'Classical' usually applies to anything pertaining to Greece and Rome. Nearly always there is the implication of the 'best', a standard of excellence worthy of emulation. When applied to literature the word Classical suggests that the work has the qualities of order, harmony, proportion, balance, discipline . . . In short, nothing can be taken away from it or added to it without doing it some injury. *See* CLASSICISM/ROMANTICISM; NEOCLASSICISM.

classicism In general when we speak of classicism we refer to the styles, rules, modes, conventions, themes and sensibilities of the Classical authors, and, by extension, their influence on and presence in the works of later authors. Classicism implies an emphasis on the virtues of reason, moderation, balance and harmony, as well as a view of human beings as essentially social in their nature. For the Romans classicism was coterminous with Greek influence. Seneca, for example, imitated the Greek tragedians; Virgil was much influenced by Homer. Then, in the 12th c., we find Graeco-Roman models used by writers of the French and German courtly romances. The imitation of the rules of Classical poetics is another very important development. Aristotle's *Poetics* and Horace's *Ars Poetica* were two major influences in the 15th and

16th c. Aristotle's shadow lies heavily over much drama from the 16th c. to the end of the 18th c.

Many commentators on Aristotle in the 16th c. diffused his theories of imitation (q.v.). His views of tragedy and epic were regarded as almost gospel. The principal commentators on Aristotle were mostly Italian: Robortelli, Segni, Maggi Vettori and Castelvetro. In England, Scaliger's *Poetica* (1561) was a key work. Horace's remarks on decorum (q.v.), the propriety of language and style, the mutual propriety of action and character, and his insistence on craftsmanship, were also analysed and disseminated by commentators in the 16 c., principally Vida, Robortelli, Joachim du Bellay, Pierre de Ronsard and Sir Philip Sidney (in *Apologie for Poetrie*, 1595).

Another major Classical influence on drama was Seneca, especially in tragedy; to such an extent that we have a subspecies known as Senecan tragedy (q.v.).

Classicism was strongest in France in the 17th and 18th c. but it was also very strong in England. In France, the main authors to follow Classical precepts were Corneille, Racine, Molière, Voltaire, Boileau and La Fontaine. The most influential treatise by a Frenchman in this respect is undoubtedly Boileau's *Art poétique* (1647). The major English authors to follow Classical rules and modes were Ben Jonson, Dryden, Pope, Swift, Addison and Dr Johnson. The influence of classicism is also very noticeable in the work of many German writers in the second half of the 18th c. (notably, Winckelmann, Lessing, Goethe, Schiller and Hölderlin), and also in the work of some Italian authors – especially Alfieri. The Germans, however, were not interested in French neoclassicism (q.v.) or the Roman authors. They went back to the Greeks and imitated Greek forms.

Classicism in literature is by no means extinct. In the 20th c. there was a considerable revival of interest in Classical themes in drama, fiction and verse, especially in French drama, and particularly in the plays of Sartre, Cocteau, Giraudoux and Anouilh. *See also* NEOCLASSICISM.

classicism/romanticism An antinomy (q.v.) devised by Friedrich von Schlegel (1772–1829) and expressed in *Das Athenaeum* (1798). Schlegel saw classicism (q.v.) as an attempt to express infinite ideas and feelings in a finite form and romanticism (q.v.) as an attempt to express a kind of universal poetry in the creation of which the poet made his own laws. Mme de Staël (1766–1817) first publicized this idea in *De l'Allemagne* (1813) and it was through this work, as much as through Schlegel's, that English and French writers became acquainted with the theory. Mme de Staël rejected classicism. Once this antinomy was established, many people modified and expanded it. The most notable person to do so was Goethe who equated classicism with health and romanticism with sickness. This over-simplified antinomy has been much debated ever since.

clausula A form of prose rhythm invented by Greek orators as a punctuation for oral delivery. Latin authors, particularly Cicero, adopted the device and introduced *clausulae* in the writing of prose. Prose is scannable, in the same way that verse is; thus writers developed the trick of concluding sentences and periods with regularized cadences.

clef *See* LIVRE À CLEF.

clench/clinch A quibbling form of pun (*q.v.*). Also a statement that settles an argument; one that clinches it. *See* PARONOMASIA.

clerihew A four-line verse consisting of two couplets, invented by Edmund Clerihew Bentley (1875–1956). He is supposed to have devised the form during a boring chemistry lesson – hence this:

> Sir Humphrey Davy
> Abominated gravy.
> He lived in the odium
> Of having discovered sodium.

At their best they are witty, deft and epigrammatic. For instance:

> George the Third
> Ought never to have occurred.
> One can only wonder
> At so grotesque a blunder.

Many people have composed good clerihews and making them up has become a parlour game. The inventor's son, Nicolas Bentley, is the author of a famous one:

> Cecil B. de Mille
> Rather against his will
> Was persuaded to leave Moses
> Out of the Wars of the Roses.

See also BOUTS-RIMÉS; DOUBLE DACTYL; LIMERICK.

cliché (F 'stereotype plate') A trite, over-used expression which is lifeless. A very large number of idioms (*q.v.*) have become clichés through excessive use. The following sentence contains eight common ones: 'When the grocer, who was as fit as a fiddle, had taken stock of the situation he saw the writing on the wall, but decided to turn over a new leaf and put his house in order by taking a long shot at eliminating his rival in the street – who was also an old hand at making the best of a bad job.' Hackneyed literary phrases (often misquoted) are another form of cliché. Pope remarked caustically on these in his *Essay on Criticism* (II, 350ff) when criticizing the stereotyped mannerisms of 18th c. poetasters (*q.v.*):

> Where'er you find 'the cooling western breeze',
> In the next line it 'whispers through the trees';
> If crystal streams 'with pleasing murmurs creep',
> The reader's threatened (not in vain) with 'sleep'.

Eric Partridge's *A Dictionary of Clichés* is one of the best guides to these literary tares. *See* COLLOQUIALISM; DEAD METAPHOR; SLANG.

climax That part of a story or play (for that matter, many forms of narrative) at which a crisis (*q.v.*) is reached and resolution achieved. *See also* ANTICLI-MAX; CATASTROPHE; DÉNOUEMENT; FALLING ACTION; FREYTAG'S PYRAMID; RISING ACTION; TURNING POINT.

clinch A statement that settles an argument; one that clinches it.

cloak-and-dagger story Usually applied to the novel of adventure which involves disguise, espionage, daring exploits, acts of sabotage and anarchy, and, in general, subversive and illegal activity. The phrase has strong associa-tions with 19th c. and Victorian melodrama (*q.v.*), in which saturnine and double-dyed villains (often heavily disguised) wore cloaks and carried weapons such as swordsticks and poignards (plus poison and explosives). There may be some connection between cloak-and-dagger and the genre of Spanish drama known as *comedias de capa y espada* (*q.v.*). English literature is rich in cloak-and-dagger tales, by such authors as Anthony Hope, Baroness Orczy, Rafael Sabatini, A. E. W. Mason, John Buchan, Edgar Wallace, Sydney Horler, Sapper, Dornford Yates, Dennis Wheatley, Leslie Charteris, Eric Ambler, Len Deighton and Frederick Forsyth – to name only a handful. *See* SPY STORY; THRILLER.

clogyrnach A form of syllabic Welsh verse in a sestet (*q.v.*) stanza. The number of syllables in each line is eight, eight, five, five, three and three. The rhyme scheme is aabbba.

closed couplet Two metrical lines (almost invariably rhyming) whose sense and grammatical structure conclude at the end of the second line. It is very common in the heroic couplet (*q.v.*), as in these lines from Johnson's *London*:

> In vain, these Dangers past, your Doors you close,
> And hope the balmy blessings of repose:
> Cruel with Guilt, and daring with Despair,
> The midnight Murd'rer, bursts the faithless Bar;
> Invades the sacred Hour of silent Rest
> And leaves, unseen, a Dagger in your Breast.

See also END-STOPPED LINE; ENJAMBEMENT; OPEN COUPLET.

closet drama A play (sometimes also called a dramatic poem) designed to be read rather than performed. The term may also apply to a play which was intended to be performed but hardly ever is, and yet has survived as a piece of worthwhile literature. In the 17th c., closet dramas developed as an impor-tant facet of female publication and authorship as, for example, in Margaret Cavendish's writing. The closure of the public theatres at the outbreak of the English Civil War in 1642 also gave particular impetus to the form. Having written for the Caroline stage, Thomas Killigrew resorted to closet drama as a means of dramatic expression. Later well-known examples are Milton's *Samson Agonistes* (1671); Landor's *Count Julian* (1812); Byron's *Manfred* (1817); Shelley's *Cenci* (1819); Keats's *Otho the Great* (1819); Shelley's *Prometheus Unbound* (1820); Swinburne's *Bothwell* (1874); and Hardy's *The Dynasts* (1904, 1906, 1908). *See also* SENECAN TRAGEDY.

clou (F 'nail') A situation or episode upon which everything hangs. The meaning is implicit in the phrase 'And thereby hangs a tale.'

cobla In Old Provençal, the normal word for stanza (*q.v.*). It may also denote a poem composed of a single stanza. From the 12th c. onwards *coblas* are fairly common. Their themes are similar to those of the *sirventes*. In some compositions one *cobla* is 'answered' by another, in which cases it is akin to the *tenson* (*q.v.*). *See also* DÉBAT; POETIC CONTESTS.

cock-and-bull story A long, rambling and improbable story, related to the tall story (*q.v.*). The origin of the phrase is obscure, but it is plausible that it derives from fables (*q.v.*) in which cocks and bulls were characters. There are a number of references in literature. In his *Anatomy of Melancholy* Burton refers to men who delight to talk 'of a cock and a bull over a pot'. *See also* BEAST EPIC; BESTIARY; BULL.

cockney rhymes False rhymes brought about by London pronunciation, like time and name: time/nime.

cockney school of poetry This term was first used in *Blackwood's Magazine* (Oct. 1817) and thereafter employed derisively of a group of writers who were Londoners by birth or adoption. They included Keats, Leigh Hunt, Shelley and Hazlitt. Leigh Hunt was a favourite target. *See also* LAKE POETS.

coda (L *cauda*, 'tail') Basically a musical term denoting a passage which forms the completion of a piece and rounds it off to a satisfactory conclusion. In literature it is pretty well the equivalent of an epilogue (*q.v.*). At the end of the play *Jumpers* (1972) by Tom Stoppard there is a good example of a coda.

code A variety of meanings may be distinguished: (a) a collection or digest (*q.v.*) of laws; (b) a system of rules or regulations; (c) a volume; (d) a system of signals; (e) a cipher; (f) a system of words, letters or symbols for the purpose of secrecy or economy in transmission; (g) a set of rules and characters for the conversion of one form of data to another (as in computing), and the resulting representation of data; (h) in socio-linguistics, the language system of a community or a particular variety within a language.

In structuralism (*q.v.*) the term code has acquired rather specific senses. It denotes a culture's system of signification through which reality is mediated. The theory of structuralism is that all cultural phenomena are the product of codes or a code, and it maintains that it is the relationship between the elements of such a system which gives it signification, and *not* the relationship between the elements and 'reality'.

In his celebrated analysis of Balzac's short story *Sarrasine*, Roland Barthes posits five codes: hermeneutic, semic, symbolic, proairetic and cultural. Through these the text is constituted and these codes are shared by author and reader. According to Barthes each code is 'one of the voices of which the text is woven'. Barthes suggests that the text itself supplies the codes which enable him to correlate, grammatically and semantically, the various elements of the story. He does not impose any 'hierarchy' on the codes; they are all held to be equal.

Each code may be described approximately thus: (a) the *hermeneutic code*: this comprises 'all the units whose function it is to articulate in various ways a question, its response, and the variety of chance events which can either formulate the question or delay its answer; or even constitute an enigma and lead to its solution'. This is the story-telling code, which poses questions, and brings about suspense and mystery by means of the narrative; (b) the *proairetic code* (Gk *proairesis*, 'action of choosing'): this code describes the way a code of actions is constructed for the reader: the sequential logic of action and behaviour. As Barthes puts it: 'The proairetic sequence is never more than the result of the artifice of the reading.' So it governs the reader's construction of plot; (c) the *symbolic code*: this gathers together the patterns of antithesis in the text; these 'groupings' are repeated by various modes and means in the text; (d) the *semic code*: the code of semes and signifiers and thus of recurrent connotations or themes in the text; this code makes use of hints or 'flickers of meaning' generated by certain signifiers; (e) the *referential or cultural code*: this code groups all the references in the text to the cultural and social background and knowledge of Balzac's period; thus it is concerned with the assumptions that Balzac makes.

In the analytical application of these codes Barthes breaks down the text into *lexies* – that is, reading-units of varying length. *See also* SIGNIFIER/ SIGNIFIED.

codex   The term derives from the Latin *codex*, a block of wood split into leaves or tablets and then covered with wax for writing on. When paper and parchment replaced wood, the word was retained for a book. Thus, a volume of manuscript. The *Vercelli Book*, which contains several important Anglo-Saxon works, is a famous example.

codicology   The study of manuscript (*q.v.*) volumes. *See* CODEX.

cofradía   A travelling company or guild of Spanish actors in the 16th and 17th c. They gave performances in the main towns on Sundays and feast days in order to make money for charities. At first they performed in existing courtyards (*corrales*) then in the new theatres, of which there were three in Madrid by 1584. Before the time of Lope de Vega they played *comedias* (simply, plays) based on authors like Plautus and Seneca.

cognitive language   *See* EMOTIVE LANGUAGE.

coin   To invent and put into use a new word or expression. *See* NEOLOGISM.

cola The plural of colon (*q.v.*).

collage (F 'sticking' or 'pasting things on') A term adopted from the vocabulary of painters to denote a work which contains a mixture of allusions, references, quotations, and foreign expressions. It is common in the work of James Joyce, Ezra Pound and T. S. Eliot. The influence of surrealism (*q.v.*) in this respect has been considerable. These collage lines come from David Jones's *Anathemata*:

> Her menhirs
>> DIS MANIBUS of
> many of a *Schiller*'s people
> many men
> of many a Clowdisley's ship's company:
> for she takes nine
>> in ten!
>> But what Caliban's Lamia
> rung him for his Hand of Glory?
> (And where the wolf in the quartz'd height
>> – O long long long
> before the sea-mark light! –
> saliva'd the spume
>> over Mark's lost hundred.
> Back over the hundred and forty *mensae* drowned
> in the un-apsed *eglwysau*, under.
> Back to the crag-mound
>> in the drowned *coed*
>> under.)

Collage techniques have also been employed by modern novelists, particularly in the so-called anti-novel (*q.v.*). *See* CENTO; DADAISM.

colloquialism A colloquial word, phrase or expression is one in everyday use in speech and writing. The colloquial style is plain and relaxed. This sentence is colloquial: 'The man, a dodgy customer with a shifty look in his eye, was clearly up to no good.' *See* CLICHÉ; IDIOM; KING'S ENGLISH; SLANG; STANDARD ENGLISH.

colloquy A dialogue (*q.v.*) or discussion. A *colloquium*. As a title and as a form there are a few instances: the *Colloquia* of Erasmus (*c.* 1526), and Southey's *Sir Thomas More: Colloquies on the progress and prospects of Society* (1829).

colon A short metrical unit comprising a number of feet or metra with a recurring pattern. For punctuation, *see* PERIOD (3).

colophon (Gk 'summit, finish') A publisher's emblem which appears on the title page of a book (or at the end of it), and/or information about the date, place, printer and edition.

colportage The literature of *colportage* comprises the miscellaneous publications hawked through town and counry by *colporteurs* (pedlars) during the French ancien regime (i.e. pre-Revolutionary) and into the 19th c. Almanacs, broadsheets, pamphlets and the booklets of the *bibliothèque bleu* (*qq.v.*) were the usual kind of stock. Their counterparts in England were chapbooks (*q.v.*) hawked by chapmen.

comedias de capa y espada (Sp 'cloak and sword plays') A species of Spanish Golden Age (*q.v.*) drama (also known as *comedias de ingenio*), thus called because the protagonists were normally gentlemen or nobles who wore a cloak and carried a sword. Any plebeian characters wore everyday dress. They were mostly about domestic intrigue. One of the first known as *Comedia Himenea* by Bartolomé de Torres Naharro (1485?–1524?). Many Golden Age dramatists wrote them, incuding Pedro Calderón de la Barca. *See also* CLOAK-AND-DAGGER STORY.

comedias de figurón A genre of Spanish drama. The plays tended to have stock themes and stock characters (*q.v.*), particularly the pompous and pretentious fool (male or female). The style and comic ideas and situations were closely associated with *commedia dell'arte* (*q.v.*). An early and well-known example is *Entre bobos anda el juego* (1645) by Francisco de Rojas Zorrilla. Augustín Moreto (1618–69) also wrote some *comedias de figurón. See* COMEDY.

comedias de ruido (Sp 'noisy plays') Thus named in Spanish Golden Age (*q.v.*) drama because they required many stage props, contraptions and mechanical devices. By the 17th c. stage machinery had become very ingenious and spectacular effects were achieved, but it *did* make rather a lot of noise. Many of the *comedias* had as their main theme the life of a saint. Others had mythological and historical themes. Lope de Vega (1562–1635) is believed to have written over two hundred of them.

comédie Originally in France this did not necessarily denote a play that was comic, but rather a play that was not a tragedy (*q.v.*). It might be a serious play which contained some comedy (*q.v.*). A good example in English dramatic literature is Eugene O'Neill's *Long Day's Journey into Night* (1956). *See* DRAME.

comédie-ballet Molière developed this dramatic form from ballet by interspersing ballet between the acts of a comedy (*q.v.*). It was a satirical or farcical interlude related to the theme of the play. The first instance is *Les Fâcheux* (1661). Molière wrote fourteen plays of this kind. *See also* ANTI-MASQUE; SATYR PLAY.

comédie de mœurs French for 'comedy of manners' (*q.v.*).

Comédie-Française The first state theatre of France; also known as Le Théâtre Français and La Maison de Molière. Its origins were in the company of actors created by Molière (1622–73) in 1658 at the Théâtre du Petit-Bourbon. After Molière's death the company merged with that of the Théâtre du Marais and became known as the Théâtre Guénégaud (after the street of that name). In 1680 the companies of the Théâtre Guénégaud and the Hôtel de Bourgogne (*q.v.*) amalgamated to form the Comédie-Française.

During the Revolutionary period from 1789 the company became divided into factions: Republican and Royalist. The pro-Revolutionary group formed the Théâtre de la République, but this had become defunct by 1799. The Royalist faction were put in prison. Ultimately the government re-formed the original company, which had its headquarters in the rue de Richelieu in the theatre known as the Théâtre Français; this took place in 1799 and the company still occupies it. Napoleon himself redrafted its constitution in 1812, and there have been few changes since. While on probation its members are known as *pensionnaires*; thereafter they become *sociétaires* or full members.

The theatre's contribution to French drama and the French theatrical tradition and history is immeasurable. It has had enormous influence in France and Europe and most of the leading French dramatists have had plays performed by it.

comédie larmoyante (F 'tearful comedy') The French counterpart to 18th c. sentimental comedy (*q.v.*) in England. In France, its leading exponents were Nivelle de la Chaussée and Diderot: in Germany, Gellert and Lessing.

comédie noire *See* BLACK COMEDY.

comédies rosses *See* THÉÂTRE LIBRE.

comedy (Gk *komos*, 'revel, merrymaking') In common literary usage a work, particularly a dramatic work, which is designed to amuse and divert through its depiction of (traditionally) everyday characters and situations and its delivery of a happy resolution. As a genre, however, comedy encompasses every form and may be found in both prose and poetry. Individual types of comedy include *comédie-ballet*; *comédie larmoyante*; comedy of humours; comedy of ideas; comedy of intrigue; comedy of manners; comedy of morals; *commedia dell'arte*; *commedia erudita*; burlesque; black comedy; drawing-room comedy; domestic comedy; farce; high comedy; musical comedy; romantic comedy; satirical comedy; sentimental comedy; tragicomedy (*qq.v.*); and, in addition, all those plays which may be classified under the heading of Theatre of the Absurd (*q.v.*).

In the European tradition, comedy can be traced back to Classical Greece and the plays of Aristophanes (*c.* 448–*c.* 380 BC) and his successor Menander (*c.* 343–*c.* 291 BC). Menander's comedies tended away from Aristophanes's satiric portrayal of contemporary political and literary society towards a romantic comedy based upon the vicissitudes of young love. This shift is marked in the distinction between the so-called Old Comedy (*q.v.*) and New Comedy (*q.v.*). The Roman comic writers to follow, chiefly Terence (190–159 BC) and Plautus (*c.* 254–184 BC), took their cues from these Greek antecedents, and particularly from Menander, whose work has not largely survived but whose influence can be read in the use of stock characters (*q.v.*) and amorous entanglements.

In the late Middle Ages, comedy might be discerned in the development of farce and comic interludes (*q.v.*) in the Mystery Plays (*q.v.*). Only known through a Latin translation of an Arabic manuscript by Ibn Rushd (Averroes), the writings of Aristotle on comedy in his *Poetics* were also beginning to be circulated in this period. Although his chief interest is tragedy, Aristotle identifies comedy as representing 'low' or morally defective characters in contrast with the elevated characters of tragedies. In a commentary on his *Divina Commedia*, Dante saw comedy as distinguished from tragedy by its use of colloquial vernacular language and its felicitous outcome as embodied in the movement from difficulty towards happiness in the narrator's journey from Inferno to Paradiso. In the equivalent landmark for an English literary vernacular, Chaucer's *Canterbury Tales* encompasses both this sense of happy resolution and a satirical bent discernible in English comic writers since.

Renaissance comedy maintained both impulses. In his *Defence of Poesie* (1595), Philip Sidney rearticulated Aristotle's theory in contemporary terms: 'Comedy is an imitation of the common errors of life, which he representeth in the most ridiculous and scornful sort that may be; so that it is impossible that any beholder can be content to be such a one.' However, this theory of the morally improving nature of comedy can hardly be said to have been strictly observed by Sidney's contemporaries. Following what is regarded as the first English dramatic comedy, Nicholas Udall's *Ralph Roister Doister* (c. 1553), it was another forty years before English playwrights would turn to comedy in earnest. In the heyday of the new public theatres, William Shakespeare and Ben Jonson led the way.

Shakespeare's early experiments were *The Comedy of Errors* (c. 1590), based on the *Menaechmi* of Plautus, *The Taming of the Shrew* (c. 1594), *The Two Gentlemen of Verona* (c. 1594–5) and *Love's Labour's Lost* (c. 1595). These were followed by *A Midsummer Night's Dream* (c. 1595–6), another romantic comedy (*q.v.*), and *The Merchant of Venice* (c. 1596), a romantic comedy combined with serious elements. *Much Ado About Nothing* (c. 1598), a departure in so far as it might be considered a comedy of manners (*q.v.*), was followed by another romantic comedy, *As You Like It* (c. 1599). *The Merry Wives of Windsor* featured one of Shakespeare's most celebrated comic characters in Falstaff, who had already appeared in earlier history plays, both parts of *Henry IV*. This easy cross-over should alert us to the dangers of placing Shakespeare's work too rigidly within any straightforward generic categories. Both *Twelfth Night* (c. 1600) and *The Tempest* are romantic comedies which incorporate aspects of tragicomedy (*q.v.*) in complex tonal balancing acts. Finally, *All's Well that Ends Well* (c. 1602–3), *Measure for Measure* (c. 1604), *The Winter's Tale* (c. 1609–10) and *Cymbeline* (c. 1610) are all plays which were deemed to be comedies by the compilers of the First Folio (1623) but which have troubled critics due to their several undoubtedly dark undertones.

By contrast, Ben Jonson's comic writing developed from an early interest in the so-called comedy of humours (*q.v.*), with its forensic dissection of human vices via recognizable stock characters (*q.v.*), for example, *Every Man in His Humour* (1598) through to sophisticated and virulent satires on contemporary mores and society as in *Volpone* (1606) and *The Alchemist* (1610). In this period, Robert Greene, Thomas Dekker, John Marston, Philip Massinger and Thomas Heywood also all catered to the popular taste for dramatic comedies.

In the period following the restoration of the theatres in 1660, five important dramatists ensured the continued importance of comedy on the English stage: George Etherege, William Wycherley, John Vanbrugh, William Congreve and George Farquhar. Their plays are multifarious but might be characterized by an interest in urbane wit, social positioning and sexual intrigue, sometimes licentiously treated. Moreover, recent criticism of plays such as Aphra Behn's *The Rover* (1677) demonstrates the ways in which Restoration comedy (*q.v.*) can be read as both reflecting and critiquing the court, its morality and politics.

In the 18th c., sentimental comedy (*q.v.*), burlesque (*q.v.*) and political or social satire predominate, as in the works of Steele, Gay and Goldsmith, and especially Marivaux, Voltaire and Beaumarchais in France. The 19th c. continued a strain of social critique in the plays of Dumas *fils*, and in Musset's comedy of manners, but also exhibited a taste for melodrama (*q.v.*) and farce (*q.v.*) in comic theatre. The last decades of the 19th c. saw innovations by Ibsen and Chekhov which would profoundly influence the radical experiments in 20th c. drama to follow. Notoriously difficult to gauge in tone (Chekhov insisted that his *Cherry Orchard* was a comedy, his first director Stanislavsky read it as a tragedy), Chekhov's work paved the way for a new and troubling kind of tragic-comedy which would find its ultimate expression in the absurdist works of Samuel Beckett.

Two other important exponents of dramatic comedy also emerged around 1900: Oscar Wilde, whose plays are characterized by their urbane wit (and which are in some ways a revival of the comedy of manners, *q.v.*, described above), and George Bernard Shaw, who introduced a moral seriousness and overt political meaning into many of his plays, sometimes called a 'comedy of ideas'. The comedy of manners was continued in the 20th c. by Noel Coward, S. N. Behrman and Philip Barry. Other notable 20th c. dramatists included J. M. Synge and Sean O'Casey, also Irish, the Marxist Bertolt Brecht in Germany, Eugène Ionesco and Beckett in France, the English playwrights Joe Orton, Harold Pinter, Edward Bond, Tom Stoppard and Caryl Churchill, as well as the Americans Lillian Hellman, Edward Albee, Amiri Baraka and Neil Simon.

Many writers and thinkers have theorized about the nature of comedy and sometimes its relation to tragedy. Notable works include G. Meredith's *An Essay on Comedy* (1877), F. Nietzsche's *The Gay Science* (1882), H. Bergson's *Laughter* (1912), M. Bakhtin's *Rabelais and His World* (1965) and M. C. Bradbrook's *The Growth and Structure of Elizabethan Comedy* (1973).

comedy of humours A form of drama which became fashionable at the very end of the 16th c. and early in the 17th. So called because it presented 'humorous' characters whose actions (in terms of the medieval and Renaissance theory of humours (q.v.)) were ruled by a particular passion, trait, disposition or humour. Basically this was a physiological interpretation of character and personality. Though there were ample precedents for this in allegory (q.v.), Tudor Morality Plays (q.v.), and Interludes (q.v.), Ben Jonson appears to have been the first person to have elaborated the idea on any scale. His two outstanding works in this kind of comedy are *Every Man in His Humour* (1598) and *Every Man Out of His Humour* (1599); plus minor works like *The Magnetic Lady: or Humours Reconciled* (1632). Following the practice of the Moralities and Interludes, Jonson named *dramatis personae* aptronymically: Kitely, Dame Kitely, Knowell, Brainworm and Justice Clement (in *Every Man in His Humour*); Fastidious Brisk, Fungoso, Sordido, and Puntarvolo the vainglorious knight, and so forth (in *Every Man Out of His Humour*). The indication of character in this fashion became a common practice and continued to be much favoured by dramatists and novelists in the 18th and 19th c.

John Fletcher, a contemporary of Jonson's, wrote a number of 'humour' comedies, and other plays of note from the period are Chapman's *All Fools* (c. 1604), Middleton's *A Trick to Catch the Old One* (1605) and Massinger's *A New Way to Pay Old Debts* (1625). Shadwell revived comedy of humours late in the 17th c. with *The Squire of Alsatia* (1688) and *Bury Fair* (1689).

The use of an individual to formulate a type in this way was also practised by those who wrote books of Characters, as in Earle's *Microcosmographie*. See APTRONYM; CHARACTER; ESSAY.

comedy of ideas A term loosely applied to plays which tend to debate, in a witty and humorous fashion, ideas and theories. Shaw is an outstanding exponent in *Man and Superman* (1905), *The Doctor's Dilemma* (1906), *Androcles and the Lion* (1912) and *The Apple Cart* (1929).

comedy of intrigue A form of comedy which depends on an intricate plot full of surprises and tends to subordinate character to plot. This distinguishes it from comedy of manners (q.v.), though the latter may also have complex plots. The form originated in Spain and was largely the work of a group of four famous dramatists: Lope de Vega (1562–1635), Tirso de Molina (1571–1648), Alarcón (1581–1639) and Moreto (1618–69). It has not appealed much to English dramatists, but Mrs Aphra Behn made some distinguished contributions: *The Rover* (1677–81) and *The City Heiress* (1682). In France, Beaumarchais's *Le Barbier de Séville* (1775) deserves special mention.

comedy of manners This genre has for its main subjects and themes the behaviour and deportment of men and women living under specific social codes. It tends to be preoccupied with the codes of the middle and upper classes and is often marked by elegance, wit and sophistication. In England Restoration comedy (q.v.) provides the outstanding instances. But Shakespeare's comedies *Love's Labour's Lost* (c. 1595) and *Much Ado About Nothing* (c. 1598–9) are also comedies of manners. Molière's *Les Précieuses ridicules* (1658), Sheridan's

The School for Scandal (1777) and Wilde's *Lady Windermere's Fan* (1892), *A Woman of No Importance* (1893) and *The Importance of Being Earnest* (1895) are other outstanding examples of the genre. Some of the 'drawing-room' comedies of Somerset Maugham might be so classified; and so might several plays by Noël Coward, especially *Private Lives* (1930). *See* COMEDY; DOMESTIC COMEDY; DRAWING-ROOM COMEDY.

comedy of menace   A term first used by David Campton by way of subtitle to his four short plays *The Lunatic View* (1957). It denotes a kind of play in which one or more characters feel that they are (or *actually* are) threatened by some obscure and frightening force, power, personality, etc. The fear and the menace become a source of comedy, albeit laconic, grim or black. Harold Pinter, among others, exploited the possibilities of such a situation in such plays as *The Birthday Party* (1958) and *The Dumb Waiter* (1960). *See also* BLACK COMEDY; THEATRE OF THE ABSURD.

comedy of morals   Satirical comedy (*q.v.*) designed to ridicule and correct vices like hypocrisy, pride, avarice, social pretensions, simony and nepotism. Molière is the supreme playwright in this genre. Ben Jonson and Shaw are other notable instances.

comic relief   Comic episodes or interludes, usually in tragedy (*q.v.*), aimed to relieve the tension and heighten the tragic element by contrast. They are or should be an essential and integral part of the whole work. If not actually extended into an episode or interlude, the relief may take the form of a few remarks or observations (or some form of action) which help to lower the emotional temperature. The humour involved tends to be wry or sardonic. Good representative examples are Iago's gulling of Roderigo in *Othello*, the drunken porter scene in *Macbeth* (regarded as a *locus classicus*), Hamlet's laconic and witty treatment of Polonius, Rosencrantz and Guildenstern and Osric in *Hamlet* (and the Gravediggers 'scene' in *Hamlet*) and the Fool's mockery in *King Lear*. Other outstanding examples are to be found in Marlowe's *Dr Faustus*, Webster's *The Duchess of Malfi* and *The White Devil*, and Tourneur's *The Revenger's Tragedy* and *The Atheist's Tragedy*.

There was good precedent for such relief in some Mystery Plays (*q.v.*). A remarkable example is the York Mystery Cycle version of the *Crucifixion* in which the four soldiers talk in the colloquial, matter-of-fact style of everyday life as they go about their business of nailing Christ to the Cross. In a different vein is the almost slapstick (*q.v.*) and buffoonish comedy that occurs in Marlowe's *Dr Faustus*, which itself is a counterpoint and contrast to the wry ironies of Mephistopheles.

Since the 16th c. hardly a tragedian of any note has failed to make use of the possibilities of comic relief. *See also* BLACK COMEDY; COMEDY; FARCE; LOW COMEDY; TRAGICOMEDY.

comics   Scholars of comics disagree over the precise definition of a comic, though in his seminal study *Comics and Sequential Art* (1985) Will Eisner asserts that comics always involve 'the arrangement of pictures or images and words to narrate a story or dramatize an idea'. The satirical pictures of

William Hogarth (1697–1764) are sometimes understood to be precursors of the modern comic. *The Rake's Progress* (1726), for instance, is a series of eight canvases which make up a narrative; these were subsequently reproduced together as prints. Speech bubbles appeared later that century, for example in some of James Gillray's pungent caricatures depicting events from around the time of the French Revolution. In the early 19th c. Swiss artist Rudolphe Töpffer popularized the use of sequences of pictures in separate frames. His work was widely published across Europe and in the United States. From the mid 19th c. satirical 'cartoons' began to appear in magazines in Europe, America and later also in China. Often these consisted of single images, but some appeared as 'strips'.

The publication with the best claim to being the first comic is probably the British *Ally Sloper's Half Holiday* (1884–1923). The recurring titular character Ally Sloper was a kind of anti-hero (*q.v.*) and the prototype of the stock character (*q.v.*) in the comic. Subsequently, *Comic Cuts* (1890–1953) and *Chips* (1890–1953), among other titles, established a British tradition of juvenile comics. Two of the most famous titles established in the interwar period, *The Dandy* (1937–) and *The Beano* (1938–), are still very much alive and some of the original characters survive. (*The Dandy* is about to cease publication in print because of low circulation, though it will continue on-line.) *The Eagle* (1950–69) featured such classic series as 'Dan Dare' and 'Heros the Spartan'. In the United States there is a stronger tradition of intrigue, action and adventure-themed publications. *Detective Comics* (1937–) is the longest-running comic in the world; the initial issue of *Action Comics* (1938–), depicting Superman on its front cover, was the first comic to feature superheroes, and spawned one of the most successful of all comic genres. In continental Europe, comics are taken somewhat more seriously. In Francophone Europe they are referred to rather soberly as *bandes dessinées* ('drawn strips'). The earliest and easily the most famous Belgian comic was Hergé's *The Adventures of Tintin* (1929–76). Many French-language comics, like *Tintin*, were produced in longer magazine or book-like formats; in the Anglophone world it is increasingly common to refer to longer publications as graphic novels (*q.v.*). From the 1960s in France (and also Italy) a great number of titles were produced for adult readers, many of them (especially after 1968) politically radical or avant-garde (*q.v.*). In Japan and other parts of East Asia since the Second World War, comics – or 'manga' to use the widely adopted Japanese term – have occupied a salient cultural position. They are read by most elements of society and cover a broader range of genres than elsewhere in world, including romance, historical drama and even business.

Since the 1980s comics have increasingly been considered a topic worthy of academic study, and 'comic studies', which draws on cultural studies, semiotics (*qq.v.*) and composition studies, has begun to emerge as a distinct discipline. *See also* CHILDREN'S BOOKS.

coming-out story The act of 'coming out' usually refers to an individual's declaration of a minority sexual identity (the phrase derives from that which describes a young woman making her social debut). A coming-out story, usually told by the individual in question, recounts that disclosure and its consequences. The coming-out story is one of the most salient genres of gay and lesbian literature since the 1980s. Some works in this genre are fictions; often they are at least partly autobiographical. They tend to focus on an individual coming to terms with his or her homosexuality (or more rarely, bisexuality or transgenderism) without necessarily ending with a public declaration. Typically the protagonist is shown negotiating adolescence, though usually the narrative voice is retrospective and that of an adult. Thus, the coming-out story may be considered a kind of *Bildungsroman* (*q.v.*). The coming-out story is largely an Anglophone and particularly an American phenomenon. Influential examples include Edmund White's *A Boy's Own Story* (1981) and Jeanette Winterson's *Oranges Are Not the Only Fruit* (1985). *See also* AUTOBIOGRAPHY; GAY AND LESBIAN CRITICISM; NOVEL.

comma(ta) *See* PERIOD (3).

commedia dell'arte In medieval Italy the *arti* were groups of artisans or guilds; hence the term means 'comedy of the professional actors'. The absolute origins of this dramatic genre are obscure, but they are probably Roman. *Commedia dell'arte*, as we understand it now, developed in 16th c. Italy and had a considerable influence on European drama. The troupes or companies who performed the plays travelled widely through Europe, especially in France. The plots of *commedia dell'arte* were usually based on love intrigues involving people of all ages; masters and servants, mistresses and confidantes. Both plot and dialogue were often improvised after basic rehearsal (improvisation was important because performance could be adapted to local and contemporary needs) and the success of a piece depended very largely on the comic ingenuity of the performers, who would include mime, farce (*qq.v.*), clownish buffoonery and music in the presentation. Characters were stock types. The main male characters were: Pantaloon, the Captain, a Doctor, the Inamorato, the servants Harlequin, Brighella and Scapino. The main female characters were also stock types. There was Inamorata, her confidante the Soubrette – as like as not in love with one of the servants – plus Canterina and Ballerina who provided interludes in the main action. In spirit, if not in fact, a play like Shakespeare's *Comedy of Errors* (1594) owes something to the traditions of *commedia dell'arte*, and one can detect the influence of the form in the work of Ben Jonson, Molière and Goldoni; in pantomime, farce (*qq.v.*), puppet plays and ballet. *See* COMEDY.

commedia erudita (It 'learned comedy') A form of comedy (*q.v.*) favoured in Italy in the 16th c. It was often a learned imitation of Classical comedies, particularly those by Terence and Plautus. Ariosto was one of the main developers of the form: Machiavelli and Aretino were two of the best-known dramatists to follow him. Machiavelli's *La Mandragola* (*c.* 1520) is widely regarded as an outstanding example.

commitment A committed or *engagé* writer (or artist) is one who, through his work, is dedicated to the advocacy of certain beliefs and programmes, especially those which are political and ideological and in aid of social reform. In order to achieve this he needs to detach himself from the work in order to calculate its effect. Notable dramatists who have been 'committed' are Shaw, Brecht, Sartre and Arnold Wesker. There have been many novelists, among whom one should mention: Sartre, Malraux, James Aldridge, Doris Lessing and Günter Grass. Commitment is common in the work of writers who belong to the so-called Communist bloc. *See also* ALIENATION EFFECT; EPIC THEATRE; PROPAGANDA; SOCIALIST REALISM; THESIS NOVEL.

common measure The quatrain (*q.v.*) of the ballad meter (*q.v.*), also called the hymnal stanza (*q.v.*). The common measure of the hymn books. *See also* HEPTAMETER.

commonplace book A notebook in which ideas, themes, quotations, words and phrases are jotted down. Many writers have kept commonplace books both as an aide-memoire to be used in future works and as a record of the writer's developing literary consciousness. In a properly organized one the matter would be grouped under subject headings. A famous example is Ben Jonson's *Timber: Or Discoveries* (1640), which comprises a draft for a treatise on the art of writing and on types of literature, miniature essays, *sententiae*, *pensées* (*qq.v.*) and so forth. Two examples are Maurice Baring's *Have You Anything to Declare?* (1936), the work of an exceptionally civilized and well-read man, and John Julius Norwich's *Christmas Crackers* (1980). The modern phenomenon of blogging might be seen as an extension of the commonplacing tradition.

common rhythm *See* RUNNING RHYTHM.

Commonwealth literature Since the 1950s, the term has been used broadly by literary critics to refer to a fast-growing and diverse body of writing in English from the former colonies. Early critics of Commonwealth literature helped establish the field and some of the first university English courses devoted to the study of Commonwealth writers. They also organized a number of conferences. Of particular importance was the 1964 conference at the University of Leeds which saw the creation of the Association of Commonwealth Literature and Language Studies (ACLALS) and the subsequent inauguration of the *Journal of Commonwealth Literature* in 1965. In 1971, Anna Rutherford founded the European Association (EACLALS) and the journal *Kunapipi*.

By the 1980s, and with the advent of the term postcolonialism (*q.v.*), critics began to identify the problematic aspects of the term 'Commonwealth literature'. As John McLeod explains in *Beginning Postcolonialism* (2000), the term incorporated writers from the European settler colonies as well as African, Caribbean and South Asian writers from the newly, or soon-to-be, independent nations. Both critics and writers challenged the homogenizing tendencies of the term and the implied common grounding of writings from such divergent locations, and with different histories and experiences of colonialism. In 1984, Salman Rushdie famously wrote that 'Commonwealth Literature Does Not Exist' and discussed the term in relation to the English literary canon. He challenges the centrality of English literature, as a term that seems to be reserved only for writers who are white, and the hierarchies that are then created between English literature 'proper' and 'Commonwealth literature', which is displaced to the periphery. Rushdie prefers the term 'young' or 'new' English literatures, and claims that 'Commonwealth literature' marginalizes and ghettoizes the non-white writers. Rushdie's essay also echoes other debates on the usefulness of the term 'Commonwealth literature', most notably its positioning only in relation to the former colonial centre, and the selective discussion of 'Commonwealth literature' as simply being an expression of an author's ethnicity or newly forged national identity. *See also* POSTCOLONIALISM.

Commonwealth period Strictly speaking, denotes the period from the execution of King Charles I (1649) to the inauguration of the Protectorate under Cromwell's personal rule (1653). However, the term is often loosely applied to the entire period of republican government (1649–60) brought to an end by the restoration of Charles II (also known as the interregnum or the Puritan period). The period is characterized by a proliferation of printed polemic, proto-newspapers (*see* NEWSBOOKS) and the suppression of dramatic activities. With the outbreak of Civil War in 1642, public theatres were closed by Parliament and did not fully reopen until the return of monarchy, although there is evidence for a tentative revival towards the very end of Cromwell's regime. The writings of Milton and Marvell have traditionally dominated literary accounts of the period, although more recently attention has been paid to women writers such as Anne Fanshawe and Lucy Hutchinson. This time of creativity and ferment is notable for a number of diverse writers, including Clarendon, Bunyan, Hobbes, Thomas Browne, Edmund Waller, Davenant, Cowley and Vaughan.

communication fallacy A term used by the American poet Allen Tate to describe poetry which attempts to convey ideas and feelings which would be better served by and expressed in prose; at any rate, *not* in poetry. Propaganda (*q.v.*) verse, for instance, may stimulate reactions which have little to do with the aesthetic qualities of the verse.

communication heresy A term used by the American critic Cleanth Brooks. It refers to the belief that the function of a poem is to convey an idea, whereas Brooks's contention is that the reader should have a *total* aesthetic experience of the poem. In short, the substance and form of a poem are not separable; though, of course, one may analyse both style and matter individually.

communicative reason A notion formulated by the German thinker Jürgen Habermas (1929–). As against poststructuralist critics who claim that Enlightenment reason is relative, coercive and exclusive, Habermas argues that communicative reason or rationality is inherent in the very process of communication, on the basis of which 'communicative action' will be possible. Such a communal and consensual notion of rationality is necessary, he urges, for the continuation of cultural traditions and for social integration.

community theatre Theatre seen as responding to the concerns and serving the needs of the community to which it is performed. 'Community' in this sense may be defined either geographically or as a 'constituency of interest' (e.g. working-class, ethnic, women, the elderly).

It originated in the mid-1970s with theatre companies such as: the Half Moon, Common Stock and the Brighton Combination at the Albany in London; Pentabus and Theatre Foundry in the West Midlands; Perspectives in the East Midlands; Pit Prop in Lancashire; DAC in Yorkshire; Solent People's Theatre in Southampton; Avon Touring in the South-west and Bruvvers in the North-east.

Venues which have housed community-oriented theatre include Chapter Arts in Cardiff, Croydon Warehouse, Phoenix Arts in Leicester, the Tron in Glasgow and the Leadmill in Sheffield.

Community theatre is more a way of relating content and a democratic method of organization to perceived community concerns than a specific aesthetic model. Productions have ranged from virtual cabaret through musicals and plays with songs to serious drama.

Examples of plays include: *Taking Our Time* by Red Ladder (1978); *My Mother Says I Never Should* by the Women's Theatre Group (1975); the plays of Les Miller for Inner City, among them *Finger in the Pie* (1985) and *Hot Stuff* (1987); the plays of John McGrath for 7:84 and the Liverpool Everyman, for example, *The Cheviot, The Stag and the Black, Black Oil* and *Fish in the Sea*; and the plays of Steve Gooch, including *Will Wat, If Not, What Will?* (1972) and *Female Transport* (1973). Steve Gooch also wrote an excellent book on community theatre: *All Together Now* (1984).

Both organizationally and aesthetically, community theatre shares much common ground with socialist touring theatre (7:84, Belt & Braces, Monstrous Regiment, etc.), as well as with Theatre-in-Education and Young People's Theatre – many companies providing both 'community' and 'young people's' productions. It is always a form of professional theatre (unlike in the USA) and has little in common with 'the community play', a term for the production model established by Ann Jellicoe's Colway Theatre Trust; the Trust employs professional directors and playwrights (e.g. Howard Barker, Nick Darke, David Edgar) to work with large numbers of amateur performers drawn from the local (usually rural) community, to which the play (usually on a local historical subject) is also performed. In 2000, Colway Theatre relocated and became Claque under the stewardship of Jon Oram. An interesting example of a community play is Edgar's *Entertaining Strangers* (1988), eventually given a full-scale production with professional actors at the National Theatre (*q.v.*).

commus *See* KOMMOS.

commutatio *See* CHIASMUS.

compar *See* ISOCOLON; PARISON.

comparatio *See* ANTITHESIS.

comparatist One who follows the comparative method in linguistics (*q.v.*) or literature. Comparative philology began in the 18th c. and entails the study and identification of those characteristics which different languages have in common and the hypothetical reconstruction of parent languages (e.g. 'Indo-European'). The great editors of *The Oxford English Dictionary* were all concerned with tracing the probable origins of words in English as far back as possible. Comparative methods in literature involve making comparisons between literary works and architecture, music and paintings, and also comparisons between different literatures. Among modern writers, Sacheverell Sitwell (1897–1988) was adept at this.

comparative criticism *See* CRITICISM AND THEORY.

comparative linguistics *See* LINGUISTICS.

comparative literature Traditionally, the examination and analysis of the relationships and similarities of the literatures of different peoples and nations. Just like languages, literatures have always been in contact with one another, and as Haun Saussy remarked, even the Ancient Greek critic Longinus analysed passages of Greek and Hebrew literatures. However, comparative literature as a discipline is relatively recent and emerged with the rise of the nation-states in the 19th c. Among the early important figures who contributed to the discipline were Goethe and his notion of *Weltliteratur* (q.v), Mme de Staël, whose work *De l'Allemagne* (1810/1813) proposed that national differences are reflected through literature, and the Transylvanian philologist Hugo Meltzl de Lomnitz, who founded the first journal of comparative literature, *Acta Comparationis Litterarum Universarum* (*Zeitschrift für vergleichende Literatur*, 1877–88). The main focus of these early approaches was the study of foreign literatures and the universality of the human experience, the relationship between linguistics and literature, and an examination of myths and epics in order to trace the perceived 'origins' of a national literature. In the early 20th c., the work of Russian Formalists (*q.v.*) and the scholars from the Prague Linguistic Circle also contributed to the evolution of the discipline. In the postwar years, comparative literature was institutionalized in France and the United States.

Today, the discipline has its well-established journals, departments and scholarly associations, such as the British Comparative Literature Association (BCLA, founded in 1975) and American Comparative Literature Association (ACLA, founded in 1960). Recent critical interventions in cultural and postcolonial studies (*qq.v.*) have allowed comparative literature scholars to rethink the traditional Eurocentric (*q.v.*) focus of the field on mainly European and American literature, shift the emphasis from national literatures to world literature (q.v.) and promote the study of literature along international and cross-cultural lines. *See also* WELTLITERATUR; WORLD LITERATURE.

compensation An adjustment for an omitted syllable or foot (q.v.) in a metrical line. It is either made up for by an additional foot in the next line, or compensated for by an added foot in the same line. A pause or rest (q.v.) sometimes compensates for a missing foot or part of a foot.

competence/performance A distinction in linguistics made by Noam Chomsky (1928–), the American linguistics professor. 'Competence' denotes a person's knowledge of his or her language and its rules (grammar, syntax, usage), while 'performance' denotes individual and specific utterance: thus, the use of the knowledge. Chomsky's distinction revises/develops Saussure's distinction between *langue* and *parole* (q.v.). Jonathan Culler's notion of 'literary competence' extends this idea from linguistics to the knowledge of the conventions acquired for reading literary texts.

complaint A plaintive poem; frequently the complaint of a lover to his inconstant, unresponsive or exacting mistress. For example, Surrey's *Complaint by Night of the Lover not Beloved*. The theme or burden of complaint became a convention, and finally a cliché, of a great deal of love poetry, but it was still being worked successfully in the middle of the 17th c. by the Cavalier poets (q.v.), and particularly well by poets like Thomas Carew and Thomas Stanley.

There are other types of complaint; most of them lament the state of the world, the vicissitudes of Fortune and the poet's personal griefs. An early and fine example is *Deor*, an OE poem about a minstrel who is out of favour and has been supplanted by another. To this may be added two of the best, both by Chaucer: *A Complaint Unto Pity*, in which the poet seeks some respite for his unhappy state; and the more light-hearted *Complaint of Chaucer to his Purse*. Spenser's minor verses and juvenilia contain some complaints, including *The Ruines of Time*. Complaint can be a distinctive female genre.

There are a number of curiosities in this genre. For instance, Sir David Lindsay's poem *The Dreme*, an allegorical lament on the misgovernment of the country, and the same poet's *Complaynt to the King*, and his *Testament and Complaynt of Our Soverane Lordis Papyngo* – both of similar import and tone as *The Dreme*.

Thomas Sackville's *The Complaint of Buckingham* in *Mirror for Magistrates* is another notable example. So is Cowley's ode *The Complaint*, and Young's long didactic poem, in elegiac mood, *The Complaint, or Night Thoughts*. *See* DIRGE; DRAMATIC MONOLOGUE; ELEGY; LAMENT.

complex metaphor *See* TELESCOPED METAPHOR.

composite verses Those composed of different kinds of feet. For instance, those which combine dactyl and trochee (qq.v.).

composition In its literary sense, any work of writing or a term denoting the technical make-up of a piece of writing, particularly in terms of style and effect. Textbooks on this subject distinguish four kinds of prose composition: exposition, argument, description and narrative.

conceit Originally meaning simply a 'concept', conceit now refers to an extended, often elaborate metaphor which invites an unexpected comparison or parallel, particularly in poetry. A conceit might augment the major theme of a poem or constitute the governing principle of an entire poem as in the famous compass image in Donne's *A Valediction Forbidding Mourning*:

> Our two souls therefore, which are one,
>   Though I must go, endure not yet
> A breach, but an expansion,
>   Like gold to airy thinness beat.
>
> If they be two, they are two so
>   As stiff twin compasses are two;
> Thy soul, the fixed foot, makes no show
>   To move, but doth, if the other do.
>
> And though it in the centre sit,
>   Yet when the other far doth roam,
> It leans and hearkens after it,
>   And grows erect, as that comes home.
>
> Such wilt thou be to me, who must,
>   Like th' other foot, obliquely run;
> Thy firmness makes my circle just,
>   And makes me end where I begun.

These so-called 'metaphysical conceits' were popular among poets of the 17th c. and plundered a wide range of discourses, including the (pseudo) scientific, geographical and mercantile, for their effect. Particularly common in the Elizabethan sonnet tradition is the 'Petrarchan conceit' which deploys conventional (often clichéd) comparative figures in praise of a mistress. Within this category, there are many types, including the conceit of oxymoron, a classic example occurring in Wyatt's 'Description of the Contrarious Passions in a Lover' after Petrarch's Sonnet 134, which begins:

> I find no peace and all my war is done;
> I fear and hope, I burne and freeze like ice.

There is also the jealousy conceit, as in Romeo's exclamation:

> O! That I were a glove upon that hand,
> That I might touch that cheek.
>   (*Romeo and Juliet*, II, i)

and the *blazon* (*q.v.*) conceit, exemplified in Spenser's

> Her lips did smell like unto Gilly flowers,
> Her ruddy cheeks like unto Roses red:
> Her snowy brows like budded Bellamoures,
> Her lovely eyes like Pinks but newly spread.
> (*Amoretti*, 64)

All are easily parodied, as in Shakespeare's celebrated 'My mistress' eyes are nothing like the sun' (Sonnet 130). Overuse along with the meretriciousness associated with sustained use of conceits meant that they fell out of critical favour after their 17th c. heyday, although it is instructive to note that they were reincarnated to some degree in the modernist verse of the early 20th c.

conceptio *See* SYLLEPSIS.

conceptismo (Sp *concepto*, 'conceit') A literary practice and attitude in 17th c. Spain and very closely associated with the *culteranismo* (*q.v.*) of the same time. For the sake of convenience Góngora may be taken as the best representative of *culteranismo* and Lope de Vega of *conceptismo*. But the leader of the *conceptismo* party was Francisco Gómez de Quevedo y Villegas (1580–1645), usually referred to as Quevedo. He was the sworn enemy of *culteranismo*, and between 1626 and 1635 wrote many satires against this movement and its devotees. The *conceptistas* disapproved of obscure references, arcane (and archaic) language and any kind of hermeticism (*q.v.*). They insisted that language should be precise, correct and idiomatic in the pure sense. Yet they *did* favour the use of conceits – especially the metaphor and pun – hence their title. Lope de Vega was not a prominent or active theorist. He practised the art of pleasing beloved of Molière. He liked and believed in good taste, sense, sensibility, order and balance, and lacked the aggressive spirit of Góngora. The different kinds of conceit were classified by Gracián in *Agudeza y arte de ingenio* (1642). *See* GONGORISM.

concordance An alphabetical index of words in a single text, or in the works of a major author. It shows, therefore, the number of times a particular word is used and where it may be found. There are concordances for the Bible and for Shakespeare's works. *See also* DICTIONARY; GLOSSARY.

concrete poetry/verse A recent development of the altar poem (*q.v.*) and the *carmen figuratum*. The object is to present each poem as a different shape. It is thus a matter of pictorial typography which produces 'visual poetry'. It may be on the page, or on glass, stone, wood and other materials. It is extremely difficult to do well but the technique lends itself to great subtlety, as Apollinaire demonstrated in *Calligrammes* (1918). The modern concept of concrete poetry was developed under the influence of Max Bill (1908–1994) and Eugen Gomringer (1925–) and presented at an exhibition of concrete art at São Paulo in 1956. This was the work of Brazilian designers and poets. The Brazilian Noigandres Group was also a pioneer influence. A vogue or movement was created which has since become widespread and has led to further developments and refinements, such as 'emergent poetry' (which involves cryptographic tricks with letters), 'semiotic poetry' (which uses symbols), 'kinetic poetry' (q.v.) and logograms. In Germany a school of concrete poets has grown, called the *Konkretisten*. The group includes the Austrian Ernst Jandl, Achleitner, Heissenbüttel, Mon and Rühm, and Gomringer himself, who edited an anthology of such poetry: *Konkrete Poesie. Deutschsprachige Autoren* (1972). Since the Second World War notable experiments have been made by several British poets, including Simon Cutts, Stuart Mills, Dom Sylvester Houédard and Ian Hamilton Finlay. Finlay is regarded by many as the best. In the more way-out examples of this kind of verse sense is abandoned; there is no syntax or grammar. Good representative collections are *An Anthology of Concrete Poetry*, edited by E. Williams (1967), and *Concrete Poetry: An International Anthology*, edited by S. Bann (1967). *See* NONSENSE; PATTERN POETRY.

concrete universal The term derives from idealist philosophy. Hegel expanded his theory of the concrete universal as a solution to the problem of the nature and reality of universals. As far as a work of art is concerned, it refers to the unification of the particular and the general; perhaps a general idea expressed through a concrete image. As Sir Philip Sidney put it: 'the poet coupleth the general notion with the particular example'. This term has produced much discussion. Two of its principal debaters have been W. K. Wimsatt in *The Verbal Icon* (1954) and John Crowe Ransom in *The World's Body* (1938). *See* ABSTRACT.

condition of England novel This rather clumsy title denotes fiction which developed in the 1840s as a result of a disturbance of the social conscience among the middle classes about the way of life of those working in industrial cities and in factories. The industrial revolution, especially in the Midlands and the North, resulted in poor housing, over-crowding and inadequate or non-existent sanitation. Factory conditions, in what Blake had described as 'dark Satanic mills', were barbarous. Such environments generated pollution, filth and vermin. Poverty, ill-health, disease and misery were widespread. A great many people (particularly factory owners and bosses) grew rich at the expense of the working classes, both adults and children, and gave scant attention to the lot of their workers who were paid miserly wages.

Anxiety and concern about this state of affairs were primarily stimulated by Thomas Carlyle (1795–1881), who inveighed against the mechanical age and its effects at length in two important books: *Chartism* (1839) and *Past and Present* (1843). Using apocalyptic language, he described the conditions, warned of the consequences (above all, revolution) and prescribed various remedies – especially factory legislation.

Prominent novelists turned their attention to the matter and their interest produced a spate of novels, many of which offered miscellaneous solutions. Some of the main works were: Disraeli's *Coningsby* (1844) and *Sybil* (1845); Mrs Gaskell's *Mary Barton* (1848) and *North and South* (1855); Charles

Dickens's *Dombey and Son* (1848) and *Hard Times* (1854); Charles Kingsley's *Yeast* (1848) and *Alton Locke* (1850); Charlotte Brontë's *Shirley* (1849); Dinah Mulock's *John Halifax, Gentleman* (1857); and George Eliot's *Felix Holt* (1866). *See also* REGIONAL NOVEL.

conduct book A species of guide (*q.v.*) to good behaviour, concerned with morality, deportment, manners and religion. It is quite closely related to the courtesy book (*q.v.*) and a sort of successor to that as well as being a precursor of books of etiquette, which proliferated in the 19th c.

Among the first of the conduct books, which were to become very popular during the 18th c. and were often devoted to the conduct of girls and young women, was Richard Allestree's *The Whole Duty of Man* (1658), which he later followed with *The Ladies' Calling* (1673). *The Whole Duty* was a kind of devotional work which expounded man's duties to God and his fellow men. Two years later came Hannah Woolley's *The Gentlwoman's Companion* (1675) and in 1694 the anonymous *The Ladies' Dictionary*.

Many followed, and they give a fascinating insight into the attitudes, assumptions, mores and conventions of the period. Some of the attitudes, accompanied by pompous and complacent moralizing, would be enough to drive modern feminists quite distracted and it is no wonder that the unhappy Mary Wollstonecraft was to inveigh against the position of women in her book *A Vindication of the Rights of Woman* (1792).

Some of the best-known conduct books are as follows: Mary Astell's *A Serious Proposal to the Ladies for the Advancement of Their Time and Great Interest* (1701); Lady Sarah Pennington's *An Unfortunate Mother's Advice to Her Absent Daughters* (1761), which she followed later with *The Polite Lady, or, A Course of Female Education in a Series of Letters, from a Mother to Her Daughter* (1775); Fordyce's *Sermons to Young Women* (1767); George Edmond Howard's *Apophthegms and Maxims on Various Subjects for the Good Conduct of Life &c* (1767) and *Instructions for a Young Lady in Every Sphere and Period of Life* (1773); Hester Chapone's *Letters on the Improvement of the Mind* (1773); Dr John Gregory's *Legacy to His Daughters* (1774); Clara Reeve's *Plans of Education: With Remarks on the Systems of Other Writers. In a Series of Letters between Mrs Darnford and Her Friends* (1792); Laetitia Matilda Hawkins's *Letters on the Female Mind, its Power and Pursuits* (1793); Thomas Gisborne's *An Enquiry into the Duties of Men in the Higher and Middling Classes of Society* (1794) and *An Enquiry into the Duties of the Female Sex* (1796); Jane West's *Letters to a Young Man* (1802) and *Letters to a Young Woman* (1806); Miss Hatfield's *Letters on the Importance of the Female Sex: With Observations on Their Manners, and on Education* (1803); Hannah More's *Coelebs in Search of a Wife* (1809); Elizabeth Appleton's *Private Education, or, A Practical Plan for the Studies of Young Ladies. With an Address to Parents, Private Governesses, and Young Ladies* (1815).

Numerous books of etiquette have been the successors of these erudite disquisitions. These concentrate on the do's and don'ts and are often guides for social climbers. They cover such weighty matters as how to address a marquis and the degree of hand pressure permissible by her partner on the waist of a young lady dancing a waltz.

conduplicatio *See* PLOCE.

confessional literature Into this rather vague category we may place works which are a very personal and subjective account of experiences, beliefs, feelings, ideas, and states of mind, body and soul. The following widely different examples are famous: St Augustine's *Confessions* (4th c.); Rousseau's *Les Confessions* (1781, 1788); De Quincey's *Confessions of an English Opium Eater* (1822); James Hogg's *The Private Memoirs and Confessions of a Justified Sinner* (1824); Alfred de Musset's *Confession d'un enfant du siècle* (1836); Chateaubriand's *Mémoires d'outre-tombe* (1849–50); George Moore's *Confessions of a Young Man* (1888). *See* AUTOBIOGRAPHY; CONFESSIONAL NOVEL; DIARY AND JOURNAL; TESTAMENT.

confessional novel A rather misleading and flexible term which suggests an 'autobiographical' type of fiction, written in the first person, and which, on the face of it, is a self-revelation. On the other hand it may not be, though it looks like it. The author may be merely assuming the role of another character. An outstanding modern example is Camus's *La Chute* (1956) in which the judge penitent 'confesses' to the reader. Subsequently this type of novel has become common.

Another form of confessional novel is that which employs a variation of the 'frame story' (*q.v.*) technique: a story in which the novelist is actually writing the story we are reading. This device was used by André Gide in *Tentatives amoureuses* (1891) and in *Les Faux-monnayeurs* (1926). *See* CONFESSIONAL LITERATURE.

confessional poetry It may be argued that much poetry, especially lyric (*q.v.*) poetry, is, *ipso facto*, 'confessional' in so far as it is a record of a poet's states of mind and feelings and his vision of life (for example, much that was written by Wordsworth, John Clare and Gerard Manley Hopkins). However, some poems are more overtly self-revelatory, more detailed in their analytical exposition of pain, grief, tension and joy.

The term is now usually confined to the works of certain writers in the UK and USA in the late 1950s and 1960s. The work of four distinguished American poets may be cited in illustration: Robert Lowell's *Life Studies* (1959), W. D. Snodgrass's *Heart's Needle* (1959), Anne Sexton's four volumes *To Bedlam and Part Way Back* (1960), *All My Pretty Ones* (1962), *Live or Die* (1966), *Love Poems* (1969), plus a number of poems by Sylvia Plath. *See* CONFESSIONAL LITERATURE.

confidant A character in drama and, occasionally, in fiction (feminine *confidante*) who has little effect on the action but whose function is to listen to the intimate feelings and intentions of the protagonist (*q.v.*). He is a trusted friend, like Horatio in *Hamlet*. From fiction one example is Maria Gostrey, the confidante of Strether in Henry James's *The Ambassadors*. James also used the term *ficelle* (French for the string which a puppeteer uses to manipulate his puppets) to denote a confidant. He describes Maria Gostrey as a 'ficelle', who is not so much Strether's friend but, rather, the reader's friend. The confidant is also a common feature of the detective story (*q.v.*). Dr Watson, in Arthur Conan Doyle's Sherlock Holmes stories, is an outstanding example. *See* COMMEDIA DELL'ARTE; FICELLE; IDEAL SPECTATOR.

conflict The tension in a situation between characters, or the actual opposition of characters (usually in drama and fiction but also in narrative poetry). In *Othello*, for instance, the conflicts between Iago, Roderigo, Othello and Desdemona. There may also be internal conflict, as in Hamlet's predicament of wishing to avenge his father and yet not knowing when and how to do it. Conflict may also occur between a character and society or environment. An example is Jude's efforts in Thomas Hardy's *Jude the Obscure* to overcome the social obstacles which keep him from university.

conformatio *See* PERSONIFICATION.

congé (F 'leave, quittance') A lyric poem of farewell. The first known instances are by Jean Bodel (late 12th c.–early 13th c.), who, when he developed leprosy and was obliged to withdraw from the world, said goodbye to his friends with a poem of forty-two stanzas (one stanza per friend). This was later imitated by Adam de la Halle (*c.* 1240–*c.* 1288) but *his* withdrawal was for political reasons and his valediction was a satire at the expense of his fellow citizens.

connotation The suggestion or implication evoked by a word or phrase, or even quite a long statement of any kind, over and above what they mean or actually denote. For example: 'There is a cockroach' may inspire a shudder of distaste in one person; but a scientific inquiry like 'What is it? *Blatta orientalis* or *Blatta Germanica*?' in another person.

A connotation may be personal and individual, or general and universal. Probably nearly all words with a lexical meaning can have public and private connotations. The sentence 'The Fascist activities were continuous' would be likely to have different connotations for a Jew and a professional historian. *See* ASSOCIATION; DENOTATION; KENEME; MEANING.

consciousness, stream of *See* STREAM OF CONSCIOUSNESS.

consistency In the structure, style and tone of a literary work, consistency implies an *essential* coherence and balance. An untimely comic episode in a tragedy might be disastrous to its consistency. Inappropriate words and usage may mar consistency of style. A character suddenly acting completely 'out of character' might produce inconsistency. So might a breach of literary convention (*q.v.*); for instance, the use of soliloquy in a naturalistic drawing-room comedy. *See also* BIENSÉANCES.

consonance The close repetition of identical consonant sounds before and after different vowels. For example: slip – slop; creak – croak; black – block. *See also* ASSONANCE; EYE-RHYME; HALF-RHYME; ONOMATOPOEIA; RHYME.

constructionism A critical position, articulated in much modern philosophy (as in that of Hume, Hegel, Marx, Schopenhauer and Nietzsche), and predominant in the humanities and social sciences since the rise of poststructuralism (*q.v.*), which holds that identities, beliefs and social practices are *constructions*, that is, they are socially constructed, or are products of historically contingent discourse. Constructionism thus stands in opposition to essentialism (*q.v.*), the presumption that particular entities or concepts maintain a core 'essence' across cultures and history. A typical (and formative) constructionist assertion would be that made about gender by Simone de Beauvoir (1908–86) in *The Second Sex* (1949): 'One is not born a woman; rather, one becomes a woman.' Another very influential constructionist position is to be found in the writings of Michel Foucault (1926–84). In *The History of Sexuality*, vol. I (1976) Foucault argues that a distinct homosexual identity is a very modern construction, arising in the late 19th c. as a consequence of the medicalization of sexuality. Previously, notions of sex and sexual deviance had largely been produced through the discourses of sin and criminality. Medical discourse, however, began to identify 'the homosexual' as a specific psychological and physical type. Subsequently, individuals who found themselves so described not only accepted these medicalized formulations, but used them to demand acceptance. Foucault's arguments, then, prompt scepticism towards any attempt to ascribe a homosexual identity to individuals prior to the medicalization of sexuality. Equally, it would be erroneous to describe Plato's *Phaedrus* or those sonnets by Shakespeare which are addressed to a man as instances of 'gay literature'; only careful study of how ideas about sex and sexual desire were produced in the periods and cultures in which these texts were written will facilitate an accurate understanding of their significance with regard to such matters. *See also* FEMINIST CRTICISM; GAY AND LESBIAN CRITICISM; IDENTITY POLITICS; POST-COLONIALISM; QUEER THEORY.

constructivism The constructivists were a group of young Russian poets who flourished in the 1920s and were influenced by futurism (*q.v.*). They were inspired by technology (like the Futurists) and were anti-traditional. They held that a poem should be a 'construction' (like a piece of engineering) and that all images, devices, language, etc. in a poem should be closely related to the theme and subject of the poem. The chief poets were Vera Inber (1890–1972) and Ilya Selvinski (1899–1968). The members of the constructivist movement were pro-Bolshevik and in favour of the proletarian writers. By *c.* 1930 the movement had fallen into desuetude. *See also* PROLETARSKAYA KUL'TURA; SMITHY POETS.

contact zone The term was first used by Mary Louise Pratt in her essay *Arts of the Contact Zone* (1991). As Pratt explains, she developed this term to examine 'social spaces where cultures meet, clash, and grapple with each other, often in contexts of highly asymmetrical relations of power, such as colonialism, slavery, or their aftermaths as they are lived out in many parts of the world today'. In her later book *Imperial Eyes: Travel Writing and Transculturation* (1992), the contact zone signifies the space of colonial encounters. Here, Pratt examines another phenomenon of the contact zone – transculturation. This term was first coined by Cuban sociologist Fernando Ortiz in his book *Cuban Counterpoint: Tobacco and Sugar* (1940) to describe the complex transformation of the Afro-Cuban culture by colonialism. Pratt adopts the term to examine the ways in which marginal groups in metropolitan spaces appropriate and absorb the materials from a dominant group. She also deploys the term in *Imperial Eyes* to ask how metropolitan modes of representation are appropriated by the people at the receiving end of empire. Pratt examines these relations in terms of interaction and reciprocity, rather than viewing them as a one-way process imposed by the colonizer or the dominant group. Since Pratt, the contact zone has proved a useful term for theorizing contemporary postcolonial encounters, migration, borderlands and the relations between the settler and indigenous groups. *See also* HYBRIDITY; LIMINALITY; TRAVEL BOOK.

contamination   Generally, might refer to the blending of legends or other narratives to create new composite versions. More specifically, it refers to the Roman practice of adapting and combining Greek New Comedy (*q.v.*). Such a work was known as a *fabula palliata*. The main authors of *palliatae* were Andronicus, Naevius, Plautus and Terence. *See* FABULA.

conte   (F 'tale, story') The term denotes a kind of fictitious narrative somewhat different from the *roman* and the *nouvelle* (*qq.v.*). The true *conte* tended to be a little fantastic (not realistic), droll and witty. They were often allegorical and moral. Well-known examples are La Fontaine's *Amours de Psyché et Cupidon* (1669), Perrault's *Contes de ma mère l'Oye* (1697) and Voltaire's *Candide* (1759). In this category one might also include Swift's *Gulliver's Travels* (1726), Voltaire's *Zadig* (1747), Johnson's *Rasselas* (1759), and the anonymous Japanese romance *Wasōbyōe* (1774–9), which has affinities with *Gulliver's Travels*. It was a popular form of fiction in the 18th c. when the other main authors were Hamilton, Crébillon *fils* and Voisenon. From the 19th c. the term has tended to denote merely a short story (*q.v.*). For example, Flaubert's *Trois Contes* (1877). Maupassant called his short stories *contes*. *See also* ALLEGORY; CONTE DÉVOT; LAI; TALE.

conte dévot   (F 'pious tale') A French genre of the 13th and 14th c. A tale in verse or prose designed to instruct and therefore having affinities with hagiography (*q.v.*) and the moral tale. A good many *contes dévots* were inspired by the collections of tales called the *Vitae Patrum* and the *Miracles Nostre Dame*. Two well-known examples are: *Tombeor Nostre Dame* and *Conte del'hermite et del jongleour*. *See* CONTE.

contests *See* POETIC CONTESTS.

contextual criticism A mode of critical analysis of a literary text characteristic of the New Criticism (*q.v.*), especially as practised by Murray Krieger and Eliseo Vivas. Krieger discusses the method in *The New Apologists for Poetry* (1956) and *Theory of Criticism* (1976). He describes contextualism as the claim 'that a poem is a tight, compelling, finally closed context' and suggests that it is necessary to analyse and judge such a work as an 'aesthetic object' without reference to anything outside or beyond it. There is an obvious connection here with Jacques Derrida's dictum that 'there is nothing outside the text'. The emphasis on close reading in contextual theory has had considerable influence on critical methods. *See also* DECONSTRUCTION.

contextualism A jargon term current in the New Criticism (*q.v.*) which denotes a particular kind of aesthetic experience of (and response to) a work of literature. The work is experienced as a self-contained artefact and possessed of 'mutually opposing energies of a tension-filled object that blocks our escape from its context and thus from its world' (*sic*).

contractions In verse there are two kinds: synaeresis and syncope. They are forms of elision (*q.v.*) used to keep the syllable count regular. Synaeresis occurs when a poet joins two vowels to make a single syllable, as in this line from Dryden's *Absalom and Achitophel*:

> Titles and Names 'twere tedious to Reherse

'Tedious' counts as a two-syllable word.

Syncope occurs when a vowel flanked by two consonants is not pronounced, as in this line from the same poem:

> Him Staggering so when Hell's dire Agent found,

'Staggering' is taken as a disyllable.

Such contractions were common between 1660 and 1800. The metrical demands of the heroic couplet (*q.v.*) encouraged them.

contrapositum *See* SYNECIOSIS.

contrapuntal reading A term coined by Edward Said in his book *Culture and Imperialism* (1993), referring to a mode of reading which reveals how some literary texts are deeply implicated in the ideologies of imperialism and colonialism. Borrowing the term from music, Said argues that such reading demands looking for what is not said and examining the significance of small plot lines and other marginal elements of a text. In doing so, the critic provides a counterpoint to the long-accepted reading of a text and uncovers its colonial implications. For example, a contrapuntal reading of Charlotte Brontë's *Jane Eyre* can reveal how St John Rivers's wish to go to India is implicated in the idea of a 'civilizing' mission. *See also* ORIENTALISM; POSTCOLONIALISM.

contrast The juxtaposition of disparate or opposed images, ideas, or both, to heighten or clarify a scene, theme or episode. A famous example is the life-in-death image in Andrew Marvell's *To His Coy Mistress*:

> Thy beauty shall no more be found;
> Nor, in thy marble Vault, shall sound
> My echoing song: then Worms shall try
> That long preserv'd Virginity:
> And your quaint Honour turn to dust;
> And into ashes all my Lust.
> The Grave's a fine and private place,
> But none I think do there embrace.

See IMAGERY; METAPHYSICAL.

conundrum A word of very obscure origin, it denotes a form of riddle (*q.v.*) whose answer involves a pun (*q.v.*).

convention In literature, a device, principle, procedure or form which is generally accepted and through which there is an agreement between the writer and his or her readers (or audience) which allows various freedoms and restrictions. The term is especially relevant to drama. The stage itself, as a physical object and area, establishes a convention by creating boundaries and limitations. The audience is prepared to suspend disbelief and to experience a representation of scenery and action, of lighting and words. The use of verse, blank or rhymed, dance, song (*q.v.*), a Chorus (*q.v.*), the unities (*q.v.*), the aside (*q.v.*), the soliloquy (*q.v.*) are all examples of dramatic convention. Working within the conventions and using them to the best possible advantage is essential to the art of the dramatist. The people in the audience are party to the agreement and their acceptance makes possible dramatic illusion.

Dr Johnson summarizes the matter in a famous passage in his *Preface to Shakespeare*:

> Delusion, if delusion be admitted, has no certain limitation; if the spectator can be once persuaded, that his old acquaintance are Alexander and Caesar, that a room illuminated with candles is the plain of Pharsalia, or the bank of Granicus, he is in a state of elevation above the reach of reason, or of truth, and from the heights of empyrean poetry, may despise the circumscriptions of terrestrial nature. There is no reason why a mind thus wandering in extasy should count the clock, or why an hour should not be a century in that calenture of the brains that can make the stage a field. The truth is, that the spectators are always in their senses, and know, from the first act to the last, that the stage is only a stage, and that the players are only players.

In fact every writer accepts conventions as soon as he begins. It can be argued that conventions are essential to all literature as necessary and convenient ways of working within the limitations of the medium of words. And we may not, as Maritain puts it, abuse the limitations of our medium. Thus, in literature, as in the other arts, there are recurring elements.

However, conventions also pertain to the composition (and reception) of poetry and prose. For example, by convention the sonnet (*q.v.*) has fourteen lines (though there are exceptions), and *terza rima* (*q.v.*) rhymes aba, bcb, cdc, and so on. The ballad (*q.v.*) tends to have a particular kind of diction and stanza form, and the pastoral elegy (*q.v.*) traditional essentials. The epic (*q.v.*) tends to begin *in medias res* (*q.v.*) and the Cavalier lyric (*q.v.*) presents certain attitudes towards love. The stock character (*q.v.*) is also a convention. So is tragic love in grand opera, and the flashback (*q.v.*) in the novel (*q.v.*).

A convention may be established as an invention: for instance, Gerard Manley Hopkins's sprung rhythm (*q.v.*) and Chaucer's rhyme royal (*q.v.*). One may be revived – as alliterative verse (*q.v.*) was revived in the 14th c. by Langland and other poets, and again in the 20th c. by W. H. Auden and C. Day Lewis. Or one may be abandoned – as the heroic couplet (*q.v.*) was towards the end of the 18th c. (though there have been more recent revivals by Roy Campbell in *The Georgiad* and by Nabokov (as a parody) in *Pale Fire*). Periodically conventions are broken or replaced. Wordsworth's rejection of 18th c. poetic diction (*q.v.*) is an obvious instance; so is the substitution, in drama, of naturalistic conventions for the traditional dramatic ones. In this sense, it is important to note that although former conventions may be rejected, they are not eradicated. A structuralist (*q.v.*) approach would posit the essentially 'conventional' nature of all literature, made up as it is of recognizable codes, commonly agreed by the culture.

Ignorance of convention may lead to misunderstanding and misinterpretation. To criticize a work for *not* being what it was never *intended* to be is a fault. A classic example is Johnson's misunderstanding of Milton's *Lycidas*. He condemned it for its 'inherent improbability', mainly because (apart from disliking pastoralism) he was not aware of the pastoral conventions. *See also* ALIENATION EFFECT; DECORUM; NATURALISM; NEOCLASSICISM; ORIGINALITY; REALISM; TRADITION.

conversation piece A form of poem which has a relaxed and fairly informal style and tone, may even be 'chatty', tends to display a personal mood, but nevertheless has quite serious subject matter. Horace's *Epistles* and *Satires* are generally taken to be conversation pieces (Pope caught the tone of Horace very well in his *Imitations*). The two English poets who have excelled at them are Coleridge and Wordsworth. Coleridge's *This Limetree Bower My Prison*, for example; and Wordsworth's *Tintern Abbey*. Other poets who have mastered this genre are Robert Browning, Robert Frost and W. H. Auden. Auden's *Letter to Lord Byron* is an outstanding example.

copla (Sp 'couple') In prosody a couplet, strophe or stanza. A metrical combination of great antiquity which has been used by many Spanish poets and still is. There are various kinds of *copla*, for instance, *copla de arte mayor* (*q.v.*), *copla de pie quebrado* (*q.v.*), *coplas de calaínos* (meaning 'useless', from the character of Calaínos in the Spanish books of chivalry), and *coplas de ciego* (literally 'blind man's *coplas*' and therefore bad verses).

Generally the *copla* will be of four octosyllabic lines assonanced in pairs. But it can also be rhymed and may have a length of eleven or twelve syllables; or again octosyllables may alternate with heptasyllables. It may consist of three, four, five or even more lines and is found in the *villancico*, the *redondilla*, the *quintilla* and the *sextilla* (*qq.v.*).

copyright Until the middle of the 16th c. authors had little or no protection against plagiarism (*q.v.*) or downright filching and pirating. When this became a serious problem printers' guilds were granted rights to protect their members, although their primary function was to regulate legal publication and thereby maintain state control and censorship, as, for example, was the case with the Stationers' Company (*q.v.*). The first English copyright law dates from 1709 and marks a fundamental shift in perceptions of authorship. Since then, various amendments and pieces of updated legislation have sought to consolidate copyright law under internationally agreed criteria. Under the 1956 Act the copyright covered an author's lifetime and fifty years thereafter. The 1988 Act stipulates that copyright lasts until seventy years after the author's death. However, fast-paced developments in the internet and electronic media have put considerable strain on traditional intellectual property rights.

coq-à-l'âne Derived from an OF proverbial expression *C'est bien sauté du cocq a l'asne*, which signified incoherent speech or writing. The term denotes a satirical genre of verse devoted to ridiculing the vices and foibles of society. Clément Marot is believed to have created the form in 1530. At any rate he composed a number of poems which come into this category. *See also* FATRASIE.

coquillards (from F *coquille*, 'shell') The shell was the traditional emblem of pilgrims and the term came to be applied to the dispossessed members of a band of vagrants, rogues, vagabonds, deserters, discharged soldiers *et al.* who, after the Hundred Years War, were itinerant in France. They evolved what was almost a subculture (*q.v.*) of their own and had a secret language called *jargon* (*q.v.*). François Villon (1431–?) composed for them his *Ballades en jargon*.

coranto The term appears to derive from the French word *courant*, 'runner'. It was the name applied to periodical news-pamphlets issued between 1621 and 1641 giving information about foreign affairs taken from foreign newspapers. One of the earliest forms of English journalism. The *corantos* were followed by the newsbook (*q.v.*). *See also* GAZETTE.

coronach The Gaelic word means 'wailing together'; thus a funeral lament or dirge (*qq.v.*). Such laments originated in Ireland and the Scottish Highlands. *See also* COMPLAINT; ELEGY.

corpus   (L 'body') A term used to denote the body (i.e. the bulk or all) of a writer's work. For example, the *corpus* of T. S. Eliot's poetry. It may also denote a particular collection of texts, such as the *corpus* of Old English literature. *See* ANGLO-SAXON PERIOD.

correctio   *See* EPANORTHOSIS.

correctness   Adherence to and conformity with rules, convention and decorum (*qq.v.*). In the 18th c. a much prized ideal and standard which writers frequently discussed, especially with regard to verse.

correlative verse   Verse in the shape of abbreviated sentences where there is a linear correspondence between words, as in the last two lines of this stanza from a sonnet by George Peele:

> His golden locks time hath to silver turned;
> Oh time too swift, Oh swiftness never ceasing!
> His youth 'gainst time and age hath ever spurned,
> But spurneth in vain; youth waneth by increasing:
> Beauty, strength, youth, are flowers but fading seen;
> Duty, faith, love, are roots, and ever green.

correspondence of the arts   The idea that all the arts have certain features in common and resemble each other. In Classical times it was believed that art imitated nature but that each art was a separate and distinct activity. In the 19th c., and not, apparently, before, the belief that the arts contained certain correspondences began to take hold. This was encouraged by experiment with drugs and the synaesthetic experiences they produced. The French Symbolist poets, especially, made use of the knowledge of these effects. *See* PARAGONE; POESIS; SYMBOL AND SYMBOLISM; SYNAESTHESIA; UT PICTURA.

cosmists   *See* SMITHY POETS.

cosmopolitanism   (Gk *kosmoit polites*, 'citizen of the world') Some of the earliest examples of cosmopolitan ideas can be found in ancient Greece. The Cynic philosopher Diogenes of Sinope (*c.* 400–323 BC) is commonly reputed to have said 'I am a citizen of the world' whenever someone asked him where he came from. Since the Classical period there have been many other attempts to define cosmopolitan sensibility, particularly in legal and moral terms, as in Kant's notions of cosmopolitan right and the laws of hospitality. Many modernist writers with their transatlantic (*q.v.*) connections considered themselves cosmopolitan. The term has gained currency in the post-Cold War and postcolonial (*q.v.*) discussions of migration, cultural diversity and globalization (*q.v.*) as an alternative means of identity and belonging beyond the narrow frontiers of the nation-state. There have been numerous discussions of the term in the work of diverse scholars: Jacques Derrida and his notion of hospitality, Paul Gilroy and his 'planetary humanism' and 'conviviality', Bruce Robbins's 'comparative cosmopolitanisms', Ulrich Beck's 'cosmopolitan vision' as a counter-discourse (*q.v.*) to sovereignty, and Judith Butler's notion of 'precarious life', to name but a few.

A significant recent contribution to the debate has come from the philosopher Kwame Anthony Appiah. In his book *Cosmopolitanism: Ethics in a World of Strangers* (2007), Appiah develops a notion of 'rooted cosmopolitanism'. Although the term may at first sound paradoxical, since cosmopolitans are considered to be those individuals who put worldwide above local concerns, Appiah reminds us that individuals are nevertheless rooted in the place where they live or come from, and shows that cosmopolitanism's claims to universality and belonging to a world community may often mask allegiance to Western norms. Appiah's ethical notion of cosmopolitanism is an attempt to negotiate between the obligations to those near to us and the obligations to strangers who are both within and outside national borders. He also challenges the notion of the irreconcilable cultural differences promoted in books such as Samuel Huntington's *The Clash of Civilizations* (1996). *See also* COSMOPOLITAN WRITING; WORLD LITERATURE.

cosmopolitan writing As the epithet 'cosmopolitan' (Gk *kosmos*, 'order, world, universe' + *politikos*, 'citizen') suggests, such writing is concerned with global/universal themes and issues (political, social and otherwise) and also with the attitudes and language involved in any discourse on such themes and issues. It is concerned too with individual persons: for instance, immigrants. The postcolonial (or decolonized) world has seen the advent of emergent countries and nations and what came to be known as the 'Third World', and also massive immigration and transmigration to erstwhile imperial 'centres'. Not least to Britain, where there has been a big influx of non-white peoples from South Asia, Africa and the Caribbean, and to North America from Asia and Latin America. To a lesser extent there has been comparable immigration to France, to Canada and Australia. This diaspora has been described by Gordon Lewis as 'colonialism in reverse'. Large ethnic minorities now exist in these countries and these multi-ethnic microcosms have influenced the national cultures and brought about a kind of 'neo-colonialism' (*q.v.*).

In the past there have been many 'national' novels seeking to depict the community that is or was the nation (witness the numerous blockbusting 'epic' narratives produced by American authors). There have also been what are described as 'novels of Empire', works of fiction set in a colonial world or with a kind of 'colonial' background. Obvious examples are Rudyard Kipling's *Kim* (1901), Conrad's *Heart of Darkness* (1902) and E. M. Forster's *A Passage to India* (1924). Such fiction has only in part represented, and often misrepresented, the attitudes, way of life and so forth of the indigenous peoples.

Cosmopolitan writing is an attempt to cross the boundaries and frontiers of nations and nationalism; it stresses the global nature of everyday life and tries to depict societies and individuals as globally representative. The use of myth, fable and parable (*qq.v.*), which tend to have universal parallels and analogies, is a feature of such writing. Cosmopolitan writing can now also begin to be seen as an attempt to come to terms with the state and position of the immigrant.

In postwar and post-imperial Britain, there has been next to no fiction which is concerned with immigrants, their difficulties in adjustment to an alien culture, etc. An obvious exception to this generalization is the work of Colin MacInnes (1914–76), in particular the novel *City of Spades* (1957), an original attempt to depict teenage and immigrant black culture in London. Later, Salman Rushdie tried to come to terms with cosmopolitanism in Britain, especially in connection with the Muslim community, in his novel *The Satanic Verses* (1988). His earlier novels, *Midnight's Children* (1981) and *Shame* (1983), might be viewed as cosmopolitan in so far as they are efforts to present a more truthful picture of the subcontinent of India to the West and in terms widely relevant to other countries. Rushdie is preoccupied with the 'in-between' state of the cosmopolitan, a person who, as he has put it, is in a state of 'translation', of being borne or carried across. This has also been referred to, if somewhat uncouthly, as a state of 'transculturation'.

Other writers of note who have been described as cosmopolitan are Isabel Allende, Bharati Mukherjee, Derek Walcott, Mario Vargas Llosa, Gabriel Garcia Márquez, W. G. Sebald and Kazuo Ishiguro. Derek Walcott, for instance, in his poetry, using a mixture of patois (plural), dialect and standard or Queen's English, has essayed a kind of synthesis or 'alchemy' of African, Indian and European influences and origins (with their historical and racial conflicts and contradictions) to achieve something characteristically Caribbean.

In Gabriel Garcia Márquez's *Cien años de soledad* (1967) the mythical town of Macando is a global and cosmopolitan urban image of decay, corruption, poverty and isolation, and the various misfortunes which befall it and its inhabitants are represented by biblical analogies. *See also* MAGIC REALISM; NOVEL; POSTCOLONIALISM; WORLD LITERATURE.

coterie A literary group, set or circle, sometimes exclusive, joined by friendship and interest. Commoner in France than in other countries, hence the *cénacle* and salon (*qq.v.*). The Bloomsbury Group (*q.v.*) might be taken as an instance of an English coterie, as might the Great Tew Circle of poets in the 17th c. The term refers, by extension, to the literature produced by such groups, which is not designed for popular consumption. The masques (*q.v.*) made by Ben Jonson and Inigo Jones for the court of James I and Charles I are coterie entertainments.

counter-memory Foucault's term for an alternative memory which tends towards subverting or displacing the dominant collective memory.

counterplot *See* SUBPLOT.

counterpoint A term adopted by literary critics. In music it means the simultaneous combination of two or more melodies. When applied to verse it denotes metrical variation – which is very common. If the basic meter of a

poem is iambic and there are dactylic and trochaic variations, then a counterpoint is achieved. The counterpoint effects in this stanza from George
MacBeth's *The God of Love* are very noticeable:

> Ĭ foúnd thĕm bĕtwéen fár hílls, bў ă frózĕn láke,
> Ŏn ă pátch ŏf báre gróund. Thĕy wĕre gróuped
> Ĭn ă sólĭd ríng, lĭke árk ŏf hórn. Ănd aroúnd
> Thĕm círclĕd, slówlў clósĭng ín,

> Thĕir tóngues lóllĭng, thĕir eárs fláttĕned ăgaínst thĕ wínd,

> Ă whírlpoŏl ŏf wólves

See SUBSTITUTION; TENSION.

counter-turn Describes the function of the antistrophe (*q.v.*) and the response
to the strophe (*q.v.*) in choral song. It may also refer to the surprise dénouement (*q.v.*) at the end of a short story ('the twist in the tail'), and, conceivably,
a wholly unexpected development in a play or story; unexpected, that is to
say, by either the characters or the reader/audience. *See* COUP DE THÉÂTRE.

country house poem A minor genre of verse which had some vogue in the
17th c. It was a type of complimentary poem which extolled the good qualities of a patron and also the fruitfulness, sound management, and beauties of
his house and estate. An influential early instance is Ben Jonson's *To Penshurst* (1616). Penshurst Place in Kent belonged to the Sidney family (Sir
Philip Sidney was born there). Jonson paid an elegant tribute to the gardens
and landscape, the 'high huswifery' of its lady, the generosity of its lord and
the virtues of the whole household. However, Aemilia Lanyer's *Description
of Cookham* (1611), composed in praise of Margaret Clifford and her estate
as a haven of female fellowship and learning, actually pre-dated Jonson's
efforts. Later examples of the genre are Thomas Carew's *To Saxham* (1640)
and Andrew Marvell's *Upon Appleton House* (written *c.* 1650–2).

coup de théâtre An unexpected and theatrically startling event which twists
the plot and action. For instance, the sudden leap into activity of the supposedly invalid and bedridden wife of General St Pé in Jean Anouilh's play *La
Valse des toréadors*. *See* COUNTER-TURN; DEUS EX MACHINA.

couplet Two successive rhyming lines, as here from the beginning of Chaucer's *Merchant's Tale*:

> Whilom ther was dwellynge in Lumbardye
> A worthy knyght, that born was of Pavye,
> In which he lyved in greet prosperitee;
> And sixty yeer a wyflees man was hee,
> And folwed ay his bodily delyt
> On wommen, ther as was his appetyt

The couplet is one of the main verse units in Western literature and is a form
of great antiquity. Chaucer was one of the first Englishmen to use it, in *The*

Legend of Good Women and for most of *The Canterbury Tales*. Tudor and Jacobean poets and dramatists used it continually; especially Shakespeare, Marlowe, Chapman and Donne. The dramatists at this time employed it as a variation on blank verse (*q.v.*), and also (very often) to round off a scene or an act. This is virtually a convention (*q.v.*) of the period. The couplet composed of two iambic pentameter (*q.v.*) lines – more commonly known as the heroic couplet (*q.v.*) – was the most favoured form. This was developed particularly in the 17th c. and perfected by Dryden, Pope and Johnson; but Chaucer had already shown many of its possibilities. It was also used for heroic drama (*q.v.*) during the Restoration period (*q.v.*) in England.

The octosyllabic couplet (or iambic tetrameter) has also been much used. Outstanding instances are Milton's *L'Allegro* and *Il Penseroso*, Samuel Butler's *Hudibras* and Coleridge's *Christabel*.

The couplet in all forms of meter (even monometer, dimeter and trimeter, *qq.v.*) has proved an extremely adaptable unit: in lines of different lengths; as part of more complex stanza forms; as a conclusion to the sonnet (*q.v.*); as part of *ottava rima* and rhyme royal (*qq.v.*); and for epigrams (*q.v.*).

In French poetry the rhyming alexandrine (*q.v.*) couplet has been a major unit, and used with especial skill by Corneille, Racine, Molière and La Fontaine. During the 17th and 18th c., partly owing to French influence, this unit was used extensively for German and Dutch narrative and dramatic verse. Later Goethe and Schiller revived the *Knittelvers* (*q.v.*), a tetrameter couplet.

In the 20th c. the couplet fell somewhat into desuetude, but it is still used periodically in combination with other metrical units. *See* CLOSED COUPLET; END-STOPPED LINE; ENJAMBEMENT; OPEN COUPLET; RHYME.

courtesy book Basically, this is a book of etiquette, but many of the early courtesy books (especially those of the 16th and 17th c.) were much more than this in that they embodied a philosophy of the art of living (elegantly, with *virtù*) and a guide to it. Moreover, many of them were extremely well written and are an invaluable source for the history of education, ideas, customs and social behaviour.

Some very early examples date from the 13th c: Thomasin von Zirclaria's *Der wälsche Gast*, Bonvincino da Riva's *De le zinquanta cortexie da tavola* and two poems by Francesco da Barberino. The best known of the early English books was the *Babees Book* (a collection of pieces from the 15th and 16th c.), which, like Master Rhodes's *Book of Nurture*, was a useful primer for youths who went to serve in the houses of noblemen in order to learn how to behave. Two 15th c. works in verse, *The Boke of Curtasye* and *Urbanitatis*, were also popular. Though often crudely naive in their delineation of the principles of civilized conduct, they all aimed to encourage good manners, chivalry, courtly behaviour and the knightly ideal exemplified in Chaucer's description of the Knight in the *Prologue to the Canterbury Tales*; an ideal which, it may be argued, owes much to the early medieval tradition of the Christian knight whose paragon and exemplar was Christ. Courtesy meant rather more than merely good manners.

After the year 1400, behaviour, especially that of the better educated, was profoundly affected by the invention of gunpowder and printing. Firearms eventually reduced the importance of skill-at-arms with the sword and altered the ideals of chivalry. Printing made available a large number of books from which people might learn to behave in a more civilized manner.

In the Tudor period there developed the conception of a 'gentleman', a civilized 'all-rounder' or 'universal man' (sometimes called 'Renaissance man'). We can broadly distinguish two types. Type A: Sir Thomas Wyatt, Sir Philip Sidney, Sir Walter Ralegh, Cellini. Type B: Leonardo da Vinci, Erasmus and Sir Thomas More. All these men, like others less known, in many ways exemplified the attainments and ideals of humanism (*q.v.*).

Italian scholarship and culture had much to do with this humanist conception of many-sided excellence, and the most influential of all the courtesy books was Castiglione's *Il Libro del Cortegiano* (The Book of the Courtier) published in Venice in 1528, and translated into English by Sir Thomas Hoby in 1561. Hoby's translation inaugurated a vogue for the importation of such works and in 1576 came a translation of Della Casa's *Galateo* (still much read in Italy). The other most famous and influential Italian work was Guazzo's *La civil conversatione*, translated into English in 1581. From Castiglione came the influential notion of *sprezzatura*, which may be translated as a kind of 'studied carelessness' or appearance of effortless grace in all situations.

However, before these events English writers had addressed themselves to manuals of instruction. Sir Thomas Elyot's *Boke named the Governour* (1531) was the first treatise on education to be printed in England. About the same time appeared Thomas Lupset's *Exhortation to Yonge Men, perswading them to walke in the pathe way that leadeth to honeste and goodnes*; and in 1555, the anonymous *Institution of a Gentleman*.

In its portrayal of a chivalric ideal, Spenser's *Faerie Queene* (1589, 1596) also aimed to teach by example, a purpose made clear in his prefatory letter to Ralegh: 'The generall end therefore of all the booke is to fashion a gentleman or noble person in vertuous and gentle discipline.' It was the most ambitious courtesy book of all.

In the early 17th c. appeared James Cleland's *Institution of a Young Nobleman* (1607); Richard Brathwaite's *The English Gentleman* (1630) and *The English Gentlewoman* (1631); and Henry Peacham's *The Compleat Gentleman* (1622), which included direction upon matters of taste in art and music.

It is important that the vast majority of these works were concerned with worldly and secular matters (this secular morality is particularly noticeable in Della Casa) and not with religious morals. The medieval conception of the Christian knight and chivalrous hero had been modified.

Other 17 c. works of note were Obadiah Walker's *Of Education, especially of Young Gentlemen* (1673), Gailhard's *The Compleat Gentleman* (1678); two influential books translated from French, Antoine de Courtin's *The Rules of Civility* and an anonymous work *Youth's Behaviour*; and George Halifax's *Advice to a Daughter* (1688).

By this time, manners, dress and generally polished behaviour were tending to become an end in themselves, and thus leading to affectation and posturing, all too apparent in Restoration comedy (*q.v.*). The Tudor ideals of amateur *virtù*, of 'the glass of fashion and the mould of form', were being reduced. Nevertheless, the 18th c. produced one noteworthy contribution in the shape of Lord Chesterfield's *Letters to His Son* (1774), which may well be regarded as the last of the traditional courtesy books concerned with the principles of gentlemanly behaviour as well as with the details.

Long before Chesterfield's *Letters* the courtesy book had in part been replaced by the conduct book (*q.v.*).

courtly love The term *amour courtois* (Italian *amore cortese;* Provençal *domnet*) was coined by Gaston Paris in 1883 to describe the cult of love which emerged in the literature and aristocratic culture of southern France, celebrated in the poetry of the troubadours (*q.v.*).

Essentially, courtly love elevates desire to a spiritual plane to the extent that the pursuit of love is seen as an ennobling exercise, even a pseudo-religious quest. Within this formula, the woman is conventionally idolized and aloof, while the man is tormented and abject in his appeals for 'mercy'. Paradoxically, although the ideal lover is a staunch Christian exemplar, adultery frequently occurs. One explanation is that since medieval marriages were often practical alliances rather than love matches, adulterous couplings might be made to stand for authentic love, freely given.

The literary origin of this very remarkable development in the relationship of the two sexes is to be found in Ovid's *Ars Amatoria* (published at the very beginning of the Christian era), and most of the rules were laid down by a monk, Andreas Capellanus, late in the 12th c. in *De Amore* – also known under the title *De Arte Honeste Amandi*.

The feudal concept of vassalage to an overlord and the medieval tradition of devotion to the Virgin Mary also influenced the evolution of courtly love. It is noticeable that the later devotional lyrics of the Middle Ages become more and more secular in their attitude and language as the earthly mistress replaces the celestial goddess and Queen of Heaven. By the time the sonneteers are producing their sequences we have almost an 'overlady', and, on the face of it, the equivalent of a masochistic devotion to beauty.

The troubadour tradition spread to Italy, where it attained its sublime form in the work of Guinicelli and Cavalcanti, the gentlest of the *dolce stil nuovisti* (*q.v.*) and acknowledged influences upon Dante's treatment of courtly love. It also permeated to northern France where it is established in the work of the *trouvères* (*q.v.*), and in the romances (*q.v.*) – particularly in the work of Chrétien de Troyes in the late 12th c. and in the widely read *Roman de la Rose*, a 13th c. poem itself translated into English by Chaucer. In Germany its ideals are presented in the poetry of the Minnesingers. In England the tradition appears in Chaucer, especially in *Troilus and Criseyde* (though Chaucer is in a way rejecting it); and in the work of Gower and Usk. But the ideals of courtly love do not really manifest themselves in English literature until the 16th c. (via Petrarch) in the great sonnet (*q.v.*) sequences of Sidney, Spenser and Shakespeare.

Courtly love is an example of an idea about heterosexual relationships which became widely diffused in various cultures and environments and was susceptible to a variety of different interpretations and expressions. Nevertheless, there appear to be some fundamental elements which are fairly universal: (a) the four marks of courtly love are humility, courtesy, adultery and the religion of love; (b) the love is desire; (c) it is an ennobling and dynamic force; (d) it generates a cult of the beloved.

It will be found that, over a very long period, its ideals, and the attitudes towards women implied in them, have gradually influenced the changing conception of woman's position in society. Several outstanding books have been written on the subject of courtly love, including C. S. Lewis's *The Allegory of Love* (1936), A. F. Denomy's *The Heresy of Courtly Love* (1947), M. J. Valency's *In Praise of Love* (1958) and James A. Schultz's *Courtly Love: The Love of Courtliness and the History of Sexuality* (2006).

courtly makers A group of poets at Henry VIII's court who imported Italian and French poetic forms. The best known are Sir Thomas Wyatt, who wrote the first English sonnets (*q.v.*), and Henry Howard, Earl of Surrey, who introduced blank verse (*q.v.*). Much of the work of the court poets was published in Tottel's Miscellany (1557), a collection which had a considerable influence on Elizabethan writers.

Cowleyan ode An ode (*q.v.*) in which the stanzas or verse paragraphs are irregular in rhyme, line length and number of lines. It is named after Abraham Cowley (1618–67) and has been used a good many times since. Notable instances are: Dryden's *Song for St Cecilia's Day* and Wordsworth's *Intimations of Immortality*.

cradle books Books printed before 1501 are known by this name, or Latin *incunabula*, 'swaddling clothes': G *Wiegendrücker*.

crambe Applied to unnecessary and disagreeable repetition. From Juvenal's phrase *crambe repetita*, 'rehashed cabbage'.

cratylic Referring to the imagined innateness or 'truthfulness' of proper names, from Plato's dialogue *Cratylus*, in which the eponymous character successfully argues that names express their bearers, against the view that names are (like all words) conventional, 'accidental' designations of persons. The debate is centred on the existence of a natural language, and, in the Christian era, of a specifically Adamic, Edenic one. Defenders of cratylism include the Old and New Testaments, Jerome, Augustine, Isidore of Seville, and Gérard Genette; some anti-cratylists are Aristotle (*On Interpretation*), Wittgenstein, and A. J. Ayer.

creacionismo An avant-garde (*q.v.*) movement which began *c.* 1916. Its founding luminary was the Spanish-born Chilean poet Vicente García Huidobro

(1893–1948). Among his followers were Gerardo Diego (1896–1987) and Juan Larrea (1895–1980). When in Paris, Huidobro had some influence on French avant-garde writers such as Pierre Reverdy. Huidobro was a novelist and playwright as well as a poet, and to some extent influenced the development of modern concrete poetry (*q.v.*). He went in for typographical eccentricities in the manner of Apollinaire's *Caligrammes*. Reverdy was associated with cubism and surrealism (*qq.v.*) and founded the review *Nord-sud* (*c.* 1917). The 'creationists' were in favour of 'poetic' vocabulary, striking metaphors and the bizarre juxtaposition of images which did not so much reflect the natural order by any form of 'imitation' (*q.v.*) but, rather, conveyed a magical vision of creation. *See also* ULTRAISM.

creative non-fiction A genre of writing which includes all factually accurate prose that employs literary styles and techniques normally associated with fiction and poetry. The term has gained considerable currency since it first began to be used in the 1970s, though writers have been producing creative non-fiction for centuries. The essay (*q.v.*) has provided one of the most versatile and enduring vehicles. In the 20th c. much creative non-fiction was reportage, for instance, George Orwell's *Down and Out in Paris and London* (1933), or the New Journalism (*q.v.*) of the 1960s and 1970s associated with Tom Wolfe, Norman Mailer and others. Travel writing, biography and memoir (*qq.v.*) have been favoured forms in recent years. Some creative nonfiction has experimented with narrative form and crossed generic boundaries, such as the diverse writings of John MacPhee. When a work has a discernible story arc, it is sometimes referred to alternatively as 'narrative non-fiction'.

While the genre has few established conventions, one cardinal rule is that the subject matter of a piece of creative non-fiction must be verifiably true; while authors should write imaginatively, they must not make anything up. There is some flexibility here, though; indeed, many writers admit that a degree of creative 'invention' in their work is inevitable, for certain things simply cannot be known. However, there have been numerous instances where works purporting to be factual have been proven to contain substantial inaccuracies or fabrications. One recent example is James Frey's *A Million Little Pieces* (2003). Though this was initially promoted as a memoir detailing the author's experience of drug abuse, many of the events described in the novel were later revealed not to have occurred. *See also* AUTOBIOGRAPHY; LIFE WRITING; NON-FICTION NOVEL.

Créolité/créolisation A theory of French West Indian literature and culture as distinctly 'Créole', comprising African, European, Asian and Amerindian influences. The theory has Francophone and Anglophone adherents: Jean Bernabé (*Éloge de la Créolité*, 1989), and Patrick Chamoiseau and Raphael Coupant (*Lettres créoles*, 1991); Kamau Brathwaite (*Contradictory Omens: Cultural Diversity and Integration in the Caribbean*, 1974), and Wilson Harris (*The Womb of Space: The Cross-Cultural Imagination*, 1983). By contrast, 'négritude' (*q.v.*) stresses the importance of the survival of African culture in the West Indies. *See* NÉGRITUDE.

crepuscolari The *poeti crepuscolari* ('twilight poets') were a group of Italian writers who flourished at the end of the 19th and the beginning of the 20th c. The term *crepuscolari* was first applied to Marino Moretti (1885–1979) by Giuseppe Borgese (1882–1952). However, the main five were Cesare Pascarella (1858–1940), Salvatore di Giacomo (1860–1934), Guido Gozzano (1883–1916), Corrado Govoni (1884–1965) and Sergio Corazzini (1886–1907). They were so called because their poetry was subdued, sombre and melancholy in tone, and the poets dwelt on the grim realities of life – not least the approach of death. An atmosphere of doom and helplessness pervaded much of their work, and two of them *did* die young.

cretic *See* AMPHIMACER.

crime fiction The commission and detection of crime, with the motives, actions, arraignment, judgement and punishment of a criminal, is one of the great paradigms of narrative. Textualized theft, assault, rape and murder begin with the earliest epics, and are central to Classical and much subsequent tragedy (*q.v.*). The most important Classical detective is Oedipus, whose dual roles of investigator, and subsequently as revealed criminal, exemplified the blurring of the boundary between morality and immorality. A similar trajectory may be ascribed to Hamlet, since Hamlet begins by investigating the murder of a king and ends by killing one, having been directly or indirectly responsible for at least four other deaths in the process. Other late Elizabethan and Jacobean plays are notably obsessed both with horrific crime and with aspects of criminal psychology, and the same period produced some of the earliest 'true crime' in ballads of murder, robbery, kidnap and piracy. Prose fiction in the 18th c. was dominated rather by financial shenanigans, child theft, rape and prostitution. The obsession with sexual violence, highly sensationalized and often coupled with the supernatural, was central to the Gothic novel (*q.v.*), as well as to some of the greatest Romantic poetry. Particularly in the early Victorian period, 19th c. novels tended to be less explicit, but were no less concerned with financial crime, and also began to explore the criminal underworld of the new industrial cities in a manner reminiscent of Jacobean drama.

Critical work on the genre has overwhelmingly concentrated on the detective story, defined by the adoption of the investigator as protagonist. Poe's 'The Murders in the Rue Morgue' (1841), the first of his Dupin stories, is often considered the first detective story. Other notable pioneers include Dickens, principally for Inspector Bucket in *Bleak House* (1853); Wilkie Collins for *The Moonstone* (1868) and *The Woman in White* (1859); and Émile Gaboriau, for a series of short stories, particularly *Le Petit Vieux de Batignolles* (1876). Fyodor Dostoevsky's *Crime and Punishment* (1866) is sometimes claimed to be the greatest of all crime fictions. All agree that the detective story came of age in the creation by Arthur Conan Doyle (1859–1930) of Sherlock Holmes. The short stories Doyle published in the 1890s attracted an enormous and devoted audience which they have never lost. When Holmes was joined by Father Brown, the creation of G. K. Chesterton

(1874–1936), the first Golden Age of Detection, centred on the short story, began. This period ended in 1914, and while short stories about detectives have continued to be written in large numbers, the second Golden Age, beginning in the late 1920s and ending in 1939, centred on the novel, the form which has been dominant ever since. The second Golden Age is notable for two particular features: the pre-eminence of the three 'Queens of Crime', Agatha Christie (1890–1976), Dorothy L. Sayers (1893–1957), and Margery Allingham (1904–66), establishing a female presence in crime writing; and the growth of detective fiction in other countries, particularly America.

The American 'hard-boiled' writing of Dashiell Hammett (1894–1961), James M. Cain (1892–1977) and Raymond Chandler (1888–1959), many of whose works were rapidly made into very influential films, marks a dramatic break with the established tradition of detective fiction. The Golden Age novels were hermetically sealed, typically by location in a country house (though any isolated setting will do), while their structure was remarkably consistent, featuring a discovery (the body), a sequence of red herrings (a parade of suspects), and a dénouement (the detective announces whodunnit). Consequently they are, for the most part, profoundly unreal, as the persistently amateur status of their detectives, and the omission of any forensic or proper police investigations, attest. The hard-boiled school reacted against this highly artificial model with stark and violent stories, usually in grim urban settings, which feature both lone but professional investigators and police, and blurred the moral distinctions between criminals and law enforcers.

Since 1945 crime fiction has become one of the principal forms of prose in UK and the US, as well as many other European countries and Japan, bolstered by a symbiotic relationship with the mass media of entertainment and information. Notable developments include the police procedural (q.v.), a kind of novel giving extensive details of official investigative methodology, and most recently of the advanced forensic technologies and profiling techniques necessary to apprehend serial killers; the persistent investigation of sexuality, both in the presentation of sexual crime and in the creation of gay and lesbian victims and protagonists; the continuing success and importance to crime fiction of female authors; the prevalence of themes of corruption and conspiracy in high places; and the very popular (though not always distinguished) group of historical and particularly medieval detectives.

criollismo A literary movement in Venezuela and Colombia c. 1900 which encouraged the development of regional literature. Among the moving spirits were Tomás Carrasquilla (1858–1940), Blanco-Fombona (1874–1944) and Ricardo Güiraldes (1886–1927).

crisis That point in a story or play at which the tension reaches a maximum and a resolution is imminent. There may, of course, be several crises, each preceding a climax (q.v.). In Othello, for instance, there is a crisis when Iago provokes Cassio to fight Roderigo, another when Othello is led to suspect his wife, a third when Othello accuses Desdemona of infidelity. Several other minor crises precede the murder of Desdemona. *See* DÉNOUEMENT.

critical theory An umbrella term which denotes a range of theories, schools of thought, thinkers and concepts originating in sociology and the humanities. The term was first used in the 1920s to characterize the work of the Frankfurt School (*q.v.*), whose central figures such as Theodor Adorno (1903–69), Max Horkheimer (1895–1973), Herbert Marcuse (1898–1979) and Walter Benjamin (1892–1940) engaged in a critique of political, social and cultural institutions which would facilitate the enlightenment and liberation of society. These thinkers drew on Hegel, Marx and Freud in attempting to revive the 'negative dialectics' or negative, revolutionary potential of Hegelian Marxist thought. They sharply opposed the bourgeois positivism which had risen to predominance in reaction against Hegel's philosophy, and insisted, following Hegel, that consciousness in all of its cultural modes is active in creating the world. In general, these theorists saw modern mass culture as regimented and reduced to a commercial dimension; and they saw art as embodying a unique critical distance from this social and political world.

Since the 1960s, the term 'critical theory' has overlapped somewhat with 'literary theory' and has been associated with the work of such theorists as Michel Foucault, Julia Kristeva, Louis Althusser, Judith Butler, Gayatri Spivak, Alan Badiou and Slavoj Žižek. This more recent use of the term was developed in the wake of structuralism and poststructuralism (*qq.v.*) in Anglo-American literary departments. Critical theory is now more broadly associated with forms of literary analysis which use writings from outside the field of literary studies – for instance, the reading of philosophical and political writings alongside literary texts. This form of textual analysis resulted in significant interventions into questions of the literary canon, textuality, culture, identity and representation. *See also* DECONSTRUCTION; FEMINIST CRITICISM; MARXIST CRITICISM; NEW HISTORICISM; POSTCOLONIALISM; POST-STRUCTURALISM; PSYCHOANALYSIS; STRUCTURALISM.

criticism and theory Literary criticism and theory have encompassed the study of a number of issues in its attempt to interpret, evaluate and contextualize literature. These include the concept of 'mimesis' or imitation; the concept of beauty and its connection with truth and goodness; the ideal of the organic unity of a literary work; the social, political and moral functions of literature; the connection between literature, philosophy and rhetoric; the nature and status of language; the impact of literary performance on an audience; the definition of figures of speech such as metaphor, metonymy and symbol; the notion of a 'canon' of the most important literary works; and the development of various genres such as epic, tragedy, comedy, lyric poetry, and song.

At the most basic level, it might be said that the practice of literary *criticism* is applied to various given texts. Literary *theory* is devoted to examining the principles behind such practice. Theory might be characterized as a systematic explanation of practice or a situation of practice in a broader framework; theory brings to light the motives behind our practice; it shows us the connection of practice to ideology, power structures, our own unconscious, our political and religious attitudes, our economic structures; above all, theory shows us that practice is not something natural but is a specific historical construct.

It is worth remembering that 'theory' is not new but began at least two and a half thousand years ago, and has been conducted by some of the greatest Western thinkers and writers, ranging from Plato and Aristotle, through Augustine and St Thomas Aquinas, Johnson, Pope and the great Romantics to the great modern thinkers such as Locke, Hume, Kant, Hegel, Freud and W. B. Yeats.

Many of the parameters of literary criticism and theory (and philosophy generally) were laid down by Plato and Aristotle. Plato banned poetry from his ideal republic on the grounds that it was three times removed from truth, being merely an imitation of an imitation: it imitated the world of physical appearances, which was itself an imperfect copy of the eternal world of Forms or essences. He also saw poetry as appealing to our lower nature, exciting the mob of passions to rebel against the rule of reason. Aristotle saw poetry as a productive art, and assigned it essentially a moral purpose. He laid down the formulation of tragedy as an action which was complete (and linear, with beginning, middle and end) and serious, involving significant moral choice. Its language was elevated, and it produced the emotions of pity and terror in an audience through their sympathy and identification with the fall of the hero into misfortune, not through some evil nature but through an overarching human fault or mistake. Classical literary criticism also includes the Roman poet Horace, who urged that poetry must be both pleasing and (morally and intellectually) useful. This insight, regulated into the formula that literature must 'teach and delight', dominated much literary criticism until the 18th c.

Neoplatonic literary criticism, such as that of Plotinus, saw literature as a direct expression of eternal essences; as such it provided access to the higher spiritual realms and to the divine. The Neoplatonists elaborated notions of allegory which enabled a harmony between the Old and New Testaments, the new being allegory prefigured in the old. Augustine attempted to trace the appropriate connections between literal and figurative language in the reading of scripture. Medieval criticism, such as that of Aquinas and Dante, refined these notions of allegory: the meanings of language encompassed not just the literal level, but the allegorical (hidden), moral and anagogical or mystical levels. In general, medieval aesthetics emphasized the beauty, order and harmony of God's creation. It saw literature as one part of an ordered hierarchy of knowledge leading to the divine, whose apex was theology.

Renaissance criticism, such as that of Sir Philip Sidney, became more humanistic and secular, reviving Classical learning: Italian writers such as Giraldi and Castelvetro reassessed the classical heritage; the French writers du Bellay and Ronsard defended the vernacular as a medium of poetic expression;

Sidney found it necessary to defend poetry from the many attacks being levelled against it. In general, Renaissance writers re-examined the notions of imitation, the didactic role of literature, and the classification of genres.

The neoclassicists of the 18th c., such as Pope, Dryden and Johnson, were even more stringent in observing Classical virtues such as rationality, moderation, balance and decorum (the harmony of form and content), and the dramatic unities of time, place and action. The use of 'wit', a broad term referring to intellectual virtuosity and ability, was much advocated and its meaning disputed. At the same time, Enlightenment thinkers such as John Locke – whose philosophy is one of the foundations of modern bourgeois liberalism – opposed the use of wit, which was metaphorical and ambiguous, and urged instead a language that was clear, distinct and unambiguous (we have inherited these ideals of writing in our composition courses, designed for success in a world ruled by corporate ethics).

Romantic literary criticism and theory reacted against these strict tendencies; influenced by Kant, it valued Imagination as a higher and more comprehensive faculty than reason, one which united what is given to our senses with the categorizing capacity of our intellect. In his *Critique of Judgement* Kant articulated for the first time a systematic formulation of the autonomy of art and literature, as a domain free of the constraints of morality or utility. Throughout the19th c., this notion of autonomy developed, in the Romantics, the theories of Poe, Baudelaire and the French symbolists, the aestheticians such as Pater and Wilde, and writers such as Henry James.

A number of other critical currents arose in the mid to late 19th c.: realism (which included requirements of probability and lifelike detail); naturalism, which attempted to model itself on scientific observation of both the internal (psychological) and external worlds; and Marxism, which placed literature in an economic and broad cultural setting; and a number of historical theories, influenced by Hegel, of the evolution of literature and its internal shaping by its unique historical circumstances. The history of literary criticism has yielded a number of enduring concerns, which have persisted into the 21st c.: the notion of mimesis, the truth value of literature, its connections with tradition, the issue of literature as the production of art or genius, the connection between literal and figurative language, the moral, social and ideological function of literature, the definition of beauty, literature as a form of knowledge, and its connections with philosophy and rhetoric.

Since the early 20th c., literary criticism and theory have comprised a broad range of tendencies and movements: a humanistic tradition, descended from 19th c. writers such as Matthew Arnold and continued into the 20th c. through figures such as Irving Babbitt and F. R. Leavis, surviving in our own day in scholars such as Frank Kermode and John Carey; a neo-Romantic tendency, expressed in the work of D. H. Lawrence, G. Wilson Knight and others; the New Criticism, arising initially in the 1920s and subsequently formalized and popularized in the 1940s; the tradition of Marxist criticism (*q.v.*), traceable to the writings of Marx and Engels themselves, being revived first during the depression of the 1930s through figures such as Christopher Caudwell and then again with the political unrest of the 1960s, in the works of Terry Eagleton and Fredric Jameson; psychoanalytic criticism, whose foundations were laid by Freud and Jung; Russian Formalism (*q.v.*), arising in the aftermath of the Russian Revolution; the first wave of feminism, articulated by thinkers such as Simone de Beauvoir and Virginia Woolf; structuralism, which emerged fully in the 1950s, building on the foundations established in the early 20th c. by Saussure and Lévi-Strauss. In addition to these were the various forms of criticism which are sometimes subsumed under the label of 'poststructuralism': Lacanian psychoanalytic theory, which rewrote Freudian concepts in terms of linguistic categories; deconstruction (*q.v.*), as initiated by Jacques Derrida, which emerged in the 1960s, as did the later waves of feminism in writers such as Elaine Showalter, Julia Kristeva and Hélène Cixous; reader-response theory, whose roots went back to Husserl and Heidegger; and the New Historicism, which arose in the 1980s through Stephen Greenblatt, again tracing its roots to Michel Foucault. This decade gave birth to another pervasive mode of criticism, postcolonialism (*q.v.*), which traced its roots through Edward Said back to colonial struggles earlier in the century and their theorists such as Frantz Fanon. The 1990s saw the concerted emergence of gender studies along with gay and lesbian criticism (*q.v.*), in figures such as Judith Butler and Eve Kosofsky Sedgwick.

The attacks of September 11, 2001 on the World Trade Center, and other political and economic circumstances, somewhat shifted the parameters of literary theory: some critics, both liberal and radical, moved explicitly into the political domain, while more conservative critics and some liberal critics reaffirmed a commitment to the aesthetic. Among the most prominent left-wing critics are Slavoj Žižek, who has reformulated, in Lacanian categories, some Marxist imperatives in the light of present political exigencies, such as the Palestinian-Israeli conflict; Antonio Negri and Michael Hardt, who have formulated a new conception of 'Empire'; Marxists such as Terry Eagleton and writers affiliated with poststructuralism such as Jean Baudrillard have analysed the meanings of 'terror'; recent liberal humanist writers include Elaine Scarry, Martha Nussbaum and John Carey, who have analysed the public status of the arts, the notions of beauty, justice and the meanings of democracy and good citizenship; recent formalistic critics have reasserted the desire to reserve a space for the aesthetic, for what they call the study of literature *as* literature.

critique A full-dress, detailed review and assessment of a literary work. The term may also denote a treatise (*q.v.*), such as Kant's *Critique of Judgement* (1790).

cross-rhyme Also known as interlaced rhyme, this occurs in long couplets (*q.v.*) – especially the hexameter (*q.v.*). Words in the middle of each line rhyme. Swinburne used the device successfully in *Hymn to Proserpine*, as these lines suggest:

> Thou hast conquered, O pale Galilean; the world has grown
>   grey from Thy breath;
> We have drunken of things Lethean, and fed on the fullness of
>   death.
> Laurel is green for a season, and love is sweet for a day;
> But love grows bitter with treason, and laurel outlives not
>   May.

See also LEONINE; RHYME.

crotchets *See* PUNCTUATION.

crown of sonnets A sequence of seven, so linked as to form a 'crown' or panegyric (*q.v.*) to the person concerned. The last line of each of the first six sonnets is the first of the succeeding one, and the last line of the seventh repeats the opening line of the first. The best known English example introduces Donne's *Holy Sonnets*. The crown is a prologue to the main sequence. The seven are named *La Corona, Annunciation, Nativitie, Temple, Crucifying, Resurrection* and *Ascension. See* SONNET; SONNET CYCLE.

cruelty, theatre of *See* THEATRE OF CRUELTY.

cubo-futurism The term for a movement in art and poetry which began in Russia just before the First World War and lasted through the early stages of the Bolshevik Revolution. It was to have some influence on the poetry of Vladimir Mayakovsky (1893–1930) and also on the practitioners of *zaum* (*q.v.*), and was part of the Futurist movement launched by Filippo Marinetti in Italy. The cubo-futurist poets tended to be 'iconoclastic' in attitude and published manifestos which advocated the rejection and abandonment of most, if not all, literary conventions. They were more interested in the possibilities of sound than of sense. *See also* DADAISM; EGO-FUTURISM; FUTURISM; PURE POETRY.

culteranismo In 17th c. Spain there came to a head a difference of practice and attitude between two schools of writing and poetry, conveniently known as '*culteranismo*' and '*conceptismo*' (*q.v.*). It is easier now to compile the names of the opposing teams than it would have been for some of the protagonists themselves. Though famous personalities were involved, this is not to say they were team leaders. It is therefore an over-simplification to say that it boiled down to Góngora versus Lope de Vega. In practice most of the propaganda was produced by others of less distinction, but sometimes of clearer aim and warmer feeling.

Góngora (1561–1627) began to write in a style which called for a knowledge of earlier literatures and their languages if his references, couched in refined and stylized terms, were to be appreciated or understood. Two outstanding examples were the *Soledades* and the *Fábula de Polifemo y Galatea*. The learned and elaborate language can be compared with that in the movement known as *la préciosité* (*q.v.*) in France. One of the elements of *culteranismo* which provoked opposition was its slavish imitation of Latin syntax. Among writers who were trying to reach a wide audience, such a tendency would have been suicidal. Lope de Vega, a natural enemy of such a tendency and regarded as the leader of the *conceptismo* movement, asserted that poetry should cost great trouble to the poet but little to the reader. *See* GONGORISM.

cultural capital   A salient term in cultural studies (*q.v.*), coined by the French sociologist Pierre Bourdieu (1930–2002), which relates how classes strive to achieve distinction from one another through consumption practices. Bourdieu argues that material wealth is not the only means by which individuals achieve status and power. Cultural capital, the possession of specific forms of cultural knowledge – e.g. of classical music, Shakespeare or modern art – comprises an equally important resource. Such cultural competence is often understood to be a matter of taste and a product of education; it is therefore difficult to acquire without being brought up within a particular class. Thus these cultural distinctions enforce class hierarchies. More recently, however, scholars have become interested in how different groups have sought to generate and exercise cultural capital on various bases. 'Subcultural capital' describes the way specific subcultures – say, aficionados of certain genres of popular music – make distinctions based not only on knowledge of certain subcultural texts, but also through various consumer practices, such as possessing the 'right' equipment and clothing. *See also* CULTURE; SUBCULTURE.

cultural code   *See* CODE.

cultural imperialism   Though imperialism is usually understood as a strategy whereby a state aims to extend its control forcibly beyond its own borders over other states and peoples, such control is usually not just military but economic and cultural. A ruling state will often impose not only its own terms of trade, but its own political ideals, cultural values, and often its own language, upon a subject state. Cultural imperialism, as propounded by Rudyard Kipling (in poems such as 'The White Man's Burden') and the historian Thomas Babington Macaulay – and questioned by writers such as Conrad – rests on political or moral grounds: imperialism was allegedly a means of bringing to a subject people the blessings of a superior civilization, and liberating them from their benighted ignorance.

In 1975 the American media critic Herbert Schiller defined cultural imperialism as 'the sum of the processes by which a society is brought into the modern world system and how its dominating stratum is attracted, pressured, forced, and sometimes bribed into shaping social institutions to correspond to, or even promote, the values and structures of the dominating center of the system'. Critics of this period also employed subcategories such as 'media imperialism' and 'electronic imperialism'.

Important work in this area includes Edward Said's landmark work *Orientalism* (1978) and his *Culture and Imperialism* (1993), which were somewhat influenced by Foucault. Said argues essentially that the Orient and Eastern cultures generally (as well as the 'West' itself) were constructs of European or American scholarship and ideology. A number of postcolonial critics such as Gayatri Spivak and Homi Bhabha have produced important insights into cultural imperialism.

More recently, thinkers such as Slavoj Žižek, Antonio Negri and Michael Hardt have produced new accounts of cultural imperialism by rethinking some of the former Marxist categories of analysis, sometimes within newly defined concepts of empire and globalism. Žižek has attempted to reconceive the implications of the Hegelian Dialectic, while Hardt and Negri have tried to reconceive sovereignty, which they see as composed of 'a series of national and supranational organisms united under a single logic of rule'. Empire is the name for this new global form of sovereignty, but it differs from imperialism in being decentred and in possessing no fixed boundaries. *See also* POST-COLONIALISM; WORLD LITERATURE.

cultural materialism   A relatively new strand of literary and cultural criticism which interrogates the material circumstances in which culture is produced and disseminated, with a particular focus on the ways texts are both shaped by and contest exploitative relationships. Cultural materialism is often seen as the British equivalent of new historicism (*q.v.*), a mode of criticism situated largely within the American academy. They indeed have much in common: both emerged in the early 1980s; both are informed by poststructuralism and Marxist criticism (*qq.v.*); both seek to comprehend literary texts alongside other contemporaneous discourses and in the context of the historical and social conditions under which they emerged; and both are largely focused on the literature of the English Renaissance.

However, one key difference between the two is that cultural materialists are also keenly interested in the significance and value ascribed to particular texts, and the uses made of them, in present-day culture. Thus it should be no surprise that cultural materialists are so preoccupied with Shakespeare plays (Alan Sinfield and Jonathan Dollimore's edited collection *Political Shakespeare*, published in 1985, is considered a seminal text). For one thing, Shakespeare criticism has traditionally been conservative and liable to ignore questions of exploitation and political dissidence. Also, the iconic figure of 'the Bard' has been regularly exploited in the service of the status quo in different ways, for instance, to defend British imperialism or to insist on a 'traditional' syllabus for schoolchildren. Cultural materialists are as likely to engage in textual analysis of the original play in order to counter dominant interpretations as they are to interrogate all manner of present-day material which invokes the Bard and his plays, from interviews with politicians to advertisements.

Another distinct contribution of cultural materialists is their scrutiny of hierarchies, oppression and forms of dissidence, including those of class, gender, sexuality and race. Cultural materialism thus differs from traditional Marxist criticism, which insists on the primacy of class in any analysis of social hierarchy. A cultural materialist understanding of history is partly Foucauldian. Foucault contends that certain concepts (such as sexuality) will, in any given epoch, be shaped in their entirety by particular paradigms. However, Raymond Williams, who first employed the term 'cultural materialism', argues that various discursive formations or cultural practices will be in play at any one time. One will be dominant; others, though, might be defined as 'residual' (beliefs and practices which reflect an earlier social formation), 'emergent' (those which relate to new emerging modes of social interaction) or 'oppositional' (those which directly challenge the dominant). These various and shifting currents enable cultural materialists to envisage how different kinds of dissidence might be possible at any historical moment. *See also* CANON; DOMINANT/EMERGENT/RESIDUAL; FEMINIST CRITICISM; LIBERAL HUMANISM; STRUCTURE OF FEELING.

cultural relativism The principle that a person's beliefs, values, customs, and world view do not possess absolute or universal validity but are shaped by her particular cultural circumstances. What is revered or considered to be morally good in one culture might be assessed quite differently in another. The notion of cultural relativism arguably has roots going back to the Sophists of 5th c. BC Athens, and has been expressed by various thinkers, including the Muslim historiographer Ibn Khaldun (1332–1406) and Montaigne (1533–92). In modern times it arose in the work of Franz Boas and other anthropologists, and in the work of numerous literary and cultural theorists. It overlaps also with the theories of linguistic relativism proposed by linguists such as Benjamin Whorf (1897–1941) and his mentor Edward Sapir (1884–1939). Hence, the implications of cultural relativism may extend into the spheres of epistemology, ethics, morality, linguistics, literature and politics.

All of these implications of relativism were hotly contested during the so-called 'culture wars' of the 1990s in the US in both politics and literature, between those who basically asserted the need for a broad cultural and educational consensus, and those who, inspired by theoretical developments, embraced a relativistic and pluralistic outlook. *See also* CULTURAL IMPERIALISM; MULTICULTURALISM; POSTCOLONIALSIM.

cultural studies A field of critical enquiry that emerged in Britain in the late 1950s, now very much an international activity, which takes all aspects of culture (*q.v.*), broadly defined, as its subject. Many academic disciplines, including anthropology, literary studies, history and sociology, have traditionally focused on culture, with each employing a distinct methodology. Cultural studies, by contrast, is purposely interdisciplinary and harnesses approaches associated with all of these fields, including content analysis, ethnography (*q.v.*) and semiotics (*q.v.*).

In the early stages of its development, cultural studies was shaped considerably by Marxist thought and the New Left. Formative figures such as Richard Hoggart (1918–), Raymond Williams (1921–88), and E. P. Thompson (1924–93) examined the emergence and evolution of culture at particular moments in modern British history. They understood working-class culture to be a site of struggle for status and legitimacy and therefore sought to defend the authentic culture of common people against the elitism of the middle and upper classes. In 1964, Hoggart established the Centre for Contemporary Cultural Studies (q.v.) at the University of Birmingham, to which the discipline owes its name as well as many of its intellectual frameworks. Throughout the 1970s much of the Centre's work was decisively influenced by ideas of the Italian Marxist Antonio Gramsci (1891–1937), particularly his notion of hegemony (q.v.), which attempts to explain how societies are bound together less by one class forcibly imposing its will on another than through negotiation and consent. Cultural studies practitioners understood popular culture to be a principal arena through which the hegemony of the dominant class was established, but they also held that the same culture provided subordinate groups with resources and strategies for organization and resistance. During the late 1970s much of the Centre's work addressed youth subcultures. Several studies examined the ways in which particular groups sought to mark themselves off from mainstream culture while simultaneously accommodating themselves to parts of it. The late 1970s also saw interventions by feminists and black critics who argued that cultural studies' Marxist emphasis on class had led to a blindness regarding other matters, such as domination over women and non-white people.

The work of Stuart Hall (1932–), who was director of the Centre throughout the 1970s, has had a profound and lasting impact on cultural studies. One of Hall's many important contributions was to argue that television texts – and by extension all cultural texts – consist of semiotic codes which may be *de*coded by audiences in various ways. If an individual decodes a text in ways that accord with the manner in which it was encoded, then her understanding of it is likely to remain 'dominant-hegemonic'. However, 'negotiated' and indeed 'oppositional' readings are equally possible. Hall's arguments challenge the assumptions of the Frankfurt School (q.v.) theorists, who insisted that mass media audiences were uniformly passive and therefore likely to adopt the ideology (q.v.) of the ruling class. Hall's work has been influential in the development of audience studies. One notable piece of ethnographic research, Janice Radway's *Reading the Romance* (1984), investigated the experiences of female readers of romance fiction. Such novels are typically denounced by feminist critics as an avenue through which patriarchal values are inculcated. However, Radway showed that not only did these women sometimes negotiate hegemonic gender representations, but also the very practice of their reading enabled them to resist some of the traditional obligations expected of them in the family home.

In the 1980s, the discipline migrated to other parts of the world, including Australia, France, North America and South Asia, and was adapted to different political and cultural contexts. Sometimes these local developments, notably in the United States, rather abandoned cultural studies' earlier commitment to directing intellectual endeavour towards political change. In India, by contrast, various schools of cultural studies have remained politicized, and have sought, for instance, to recover 'subaltern' (q.v.) histories, that is, accounts of subordinate peoples who have developed their own cultural resources for resisting elite power.

From the 1980s to the present the scope of cultural studies has widened considerably to include consideration of the relationship between cultures and space, the regulation of the body and sexuality, and the impact of globalization and new technologies on the production and consumption of culture. *See also* CULTURE INDUSTRY; CULTURAL CAPITAL; CULTURAL MATERIALISM; FEMINIST CRITICISM; MARXIST CRITICISM; POSTCOLONIALISM; POSTMODERNISM; QUEER THEORY.

culture According to Raymond Williams (1921–88), one of the founders of cultural studies (*q.v.*), 'culture' is one of the most difficult words to define. This is because it has today several different though related meanings which have emerged at particular moments throughout its long history. The word derives from the Latin *colere*, which itself had various meanings, including to cultivate, inhabit, protect or worship. The first of these meanings was taken up by the Latin *cultura*, and subsequently the French *culture*. In the Renaissance, culture's sense of tending crops (which still exists in terms such as 'horticulture' and 'bacterial culture') was extended through metaphor to the purely human endeavour of 'culturing' – i.e. cultivating – the mind and manners. By the late 18th c. the term – particularly its equivalent in French and German – was increasingly used as an abstract and independent noun to designate the process of becoming cultured or civilized, and was employed as a synonym for 'civilization'. During the Romantic period (*q.v.*), however, the assumption that human history progressed in a unilinear fashion towards a civilized future came under increasing criticism; the notion that *distinct* cultures, or ways of life, characterized different peoples and periods (e.g. folk culture; French culture) gained currency. Also during this period, the term became associated with practices which an increasingly materialist, industrial civilization was judged not to value: art, literature, music, religion and so on. In the Victorian era, Matthew Arnold famously defined culture in his *Culture and Anarchy* as 'the best that has been thought and said' in the world.

All four meanings outlined above are still signified by the term 'culture' in the present day: (a) husbandry; (b) the process of becoming civilized; (c) a particular way of life; and (d) a set of practices which might today be overseen by a 'Minister for Culture'. We might add the distinction, initially made in the late 19th c., between 'high' and 'low' (or popular) culture. The term 'mass culture' follows the development of new forms of media and spectatorship in the early 20th c. Until the 1960s, literary scholars largely saw their subject as operating within high culture, and consequently understood it to be a force for moral and social good. Today, in many disciplines within the humanities and social sciences, 'culture' is understood first and foremost as a symbolic system. Usually, however, scholars are equally interested in the material circumstances out of which a system of signs arises and in which it operates. Thus how people become part of a culture, and the relationships between culture and power, including the reasons why some forms of culture are valued over others, are considered important issues for investigation. Many thinkers and critics, notably F. R. Leavis, Edward Said, Max Horkheimer, Theodor Adorno, Herbert Marcuse and Walter Benjamin, have stressed, from their various political perspectives, that culture has often been defined in a hierarchical and exclusive manner. *See also* CULTURAL CAPITAL; DOMINANT/EMERGENT/RESIDUAL; SUBCULTURE.

culture industry The term used by members of the Frankfurt School (*q.v.*) to describe the operations of mass media, which they argued instilled into (largely working-class) audiences the values and beliefs of the dominant capitalist order. The word 'industry' was used to characterize the generation of mass culture as a uniform product, in contradistinction to forms of authentic culture arising from the working classes themselves. *See also* CULTURAL STUDIES; MARXIST CRITICISM.

cultures, the two In 1959 C. P. Snow delivered the Rede Lecture in Cambridge and in the course of it deplored the increasing gap between the humanities and technology, between the arts and science, the two cultures. This lecture caused a great deal of controversy.

cup-and-saucer drama A term applied to the plays of T. W. Robertson (1829–71) and his imitators. Robertson wrote plays in which he paid attention to realistic domestic detail, hence the slightly pejorative label. The six comedies that he had produced in 1865–70 (among the best were *Society*, 1865, *Ours*, 1866, and *Caste*, 1867) set standards for such realism that were to have a considerable influence on a revival of serious drama. *See also* COMEDY; DOMESTIC COMEDY.

cursus (L 'running') A term applied to the rhythm (*q.v.*) or pattern of prose. *See* CADENCE.

curtain raiser An entertainment, often of one act, which precedes the main part of the programme. They are rare now, but in the late 19th and early 20th c. were often used to divert audiences while late-comers arrived. In this way, the main programme would not be interrupted. *See* FARCE; ONE-ACT PLAY; QUART D'HEURE; SOTIE.

curtal sonnet Literally a sonnet (*q.v.*) cut short. Gerard Manley Hopkins used the term in his Preface to *Poems* (1918) to describe a curtailed form of sonnet of his invention. He reduced the number of lines from fourteen to ten, divided into two stanzas: one of six lines, the other of four – with a half-line tail-piece. In *Poems* there are curtal sonnets called *Peace* and *Pied Beauty*. The latter is as follows:

> Glory be to God for dappled things –
>   For skies of couple-colour as a brinded cow;
>   For rose-moles all in stipple upon trout that swim;
> Fresh-firecoal chestnut-falls; finches' wings;

Landscape plotted and pieced – fold, fallow, and plough;
    And áll trádes, their gear and tackle and trim.

All things counter, original, spare, strange;
    Whatever is fickle, freckled (who knows how?)
    With swift, slow; sweet, sour; adazzle, dim;
He fathers-forth whose beauty is past change:
                    Praise him.

See QUATRAIN; SESTET; TAIL-RHYME.

cut-up A technique probably first used by the writer William S. Burroughs (1914–1997) in some of his books. A text, typed or written, is cut up into fragments, segments (words, phrases, sentences, etc.) and then reassembled at random in an 'accidental' order which is eventually printed. Burroughs's *The Ticket that Exploded* (1962) is an instance of the technique. *See* ALEATORY; COLLAGE.

cybercriticism An emerging field of study devoted to the understanding of cyberculture, that is, the culture which has developed from the technological developments of the late 20th c., in particular those associated with the computer and the networks facilitated by the internet. A key concern of cybercriticism is to recognize the rapidly changing and dynamic interaction between biological entities (e.g. humans) and machines with all the profound consequences for constituting identity that this implies. Such concerns have occupied science fiction writers most evidently but the wider theoretical issues raised by 'cybercritics' may be seen to chime with the tendencies of postmodernism more generally: the virtual space generated by the networked system opens up the possibility of multiple, non-linear connections between texts and subjects (so intertextuality (*q.v.*) may be recast as hypertextuality). As Stacy Gillis puts it, 'cyberspace situates the subject as multiple points on a map of virtual reality and cyberculture catches the "subjectless" subject within a web of interactive networks, displacing autonomy' ('Cybercriticism' in *Introducing Criticism at the Twenty-First Century*, ed. Julian Wolfreys, 2002).

cyberpunk/steampunk A subspecies of science fiction (*q.v.*) which emerged in the early 1980s. The word is a conflation of *cybernetics* and *punk*. *Punk* is a word of unknown origin with a variety of meanings, though in this case the term alludes to contemporaneous punk subculture and styles which emphasized customization. *Cybernetics* derives from Greek *kybernetes* ('a steersman') and denotes the science of regulatory systems, whether electronic, mechanical, biological, social or psychological. Cybernetics is commonly understood to be about the combination of artificial and biological systems, i.e. cyborgism. In the bleak near-future visions of cyberpunk fiction, cyborgs – artificially augmented humans – are commonly featured, but the genre is as much interested in the implications of other self-regulating systems such as artificial intelligence, all-powerful corporations, arcologies and marginalized urban subcultures. Among the most well-known and influential practitioners of cyberpunk fiction are William Gibson, K. W. Jeter and Walter Jon Williams. In one of his early short stories Gibson introduced the concept of 'cyberspace', now a ubiquitous term for the internet, but which specifically connotes an abstract notion of the 'space' within a network of computer and telecommunications systems. In his novel *Neuromancer* (1984) Gibson refers to cyberspace as a 'collective hallucination' in which interactions between people and data are imagined to take place.

Steampunk is another, related subgenre of science fiction (the name is a droll adaptation of 'cyberpunk'). Steampunk fiction is usually set in the Victorian era – the age of steam – but its writers envisage alternative histories in which technologies, such as flight, space travel or information technology, have been invented 'before their time'. William Gibson and Bruce Sterling's novel *The Difference Engine* (1990) is a seminal work of steampunk fiction. It imagines what the consequences might have been had the 19th c. inventor Charles Babbage built his planned mechanical computer. *See also* CYBORG; POSTHUMANISM; SYSTEMS THEORY.

cyborg An important term and concept from the feminist theorist Donna Haraway, on how our bodies now combine with technology, and it appears in literary characters. The term 'cyborg' is a conflation of the words 'cybernetic' and 'organism', coined in 1960 by the scientists Manfred Clynes and Nathan Kline. It refers to an organism which has both biological and artificial features and the ways in which our bodies now combine with technology. Haraway's conception of the cyborg was developed in her seminal essay *A Manifesto for Cyborgs: Science, Technology, and Socialist Feminism in the 1980s* (1985), where she describes the cyborg as a 'hybrid of machine and organism, a creature of social reality as well as a creature of fiction'.

Despite being an 'illegitimate offspring of militarism and patriarchal capitalism, not to mention state socialism', the cyborg is, for Haraway, a potentially transgressive and utopian concept as it blurs the boundaries between human and machine, nature and culture, gender and origin. It is a particularly useful concept for feminism as it challenges these binaries, and, according to Haraway, enables us to imagine a world beyond gender categories and what human beings might become. Haraway further developed these ideas in her 1991 book *Simians, Cyborgs, and Women: The Reinvention of Nature*, by examining the connections between humans, machines and animals such as primates. Cyborgs often appear in science fiction (*q.v.*) books and films. William Gibson's *Neuromancer* trilogy (1984–8), Marge Piercy's *He, She, It* (1991), Martin Caidin's *Cyborg* (1978), and the films *Bladerunner* (1982) and *RoboCop* (1987) are some of the well-known instances. *See also* CYBERPUNK/STEAMPUNK; POSTHUMANISM.

cycle A group of poems, stories or plays which are united by a central theme. The term 'epic cycle' was first used by the Alexandrine grammarians to describe a group of epic poems which, by *c.* 800 BC, had grown up in connection with the battle for Troy. The individual epics, in some cases fairly short ballads, were elaborated and eventually joined with others to form an epic cycle. The result we now know as Homer's *Iliad*.

This kind of accretive process has been repeated in many civilizations. Conceivably, quite a large number of the Old Testament stories were originally separate and gradually formed a more or less homogeneous unit. The same may well be true of stories about Buddha and other great religious leaders and rulers; and also the accounts of the lives of some saints. Legend and fact intermingle.

Old Irish epic poetry bears all the marks of cyclical structure. The Scandinavian, Arthurian and Charlemagne cycles are analogous. Russian *byliny* and *stariny* are also grouped about a particular hero or town. The South Slav *narodne pesme* (*q.v.*) – still part of living oral tradition (*q.v.*) – are similar, and form an outstanding example of the cycle. One should mention also the Albanian *Geg Mujo-Halil* cycle, and other Albanian cycles which survive in south-eastern Italy and are concerned with the exploits of the hero Skandarbeg.

Into the cyclic category may also be placed such collections of tales as Boccaccio's *Decameron* and Chaucer's *Canterbury Tales*. A series of lyrical poems may also form a cycle. For instance: Dante's *Vita Nuova*, Petrarch's *Canzoniere* and Shakespeare's *Sonnets*.

Finally there are the cycles of the Mystery Plays (*q.v.*), which attempt an encyclopaedic dramatization of the Old and New Testaments. *See* BALLAD; CHRONICLE PLAY; EPIC; SONNET SEQUENCE.

D

dactyl (Gk 'finger') A metrical foot consisting of one stressed syllable followed by two unstressed ones: / ∪ ∪. Just like finger joints. Dactylics were often used in Classical verse, but not often by English poets until the 19th c. when Scott, Byron, Tennyson, Browning and Swinburne (among many others) experimented with them. Tennyson, for example, used them in his *Charge of the Light Brigade*. One of the best-known instances of dactylic verse is Browning's *The Lost Leader*:

> Júst fŏr ă | hándfŭl ŏf | sílvĕr hĕ | léft ŭs,
> Júst fŏr ă | ríbănd tŏ | stíck ĭn hĭs | cóat –
> Fóund thĕ ŏne | gíft ŏf whĭch | fórtŭne bĕ | réft ŭs,
> Lóst ăll thĕ | óthĕrs shĕ | léts ŭs dĕ|vóte.

Dactylics are not unusual in light verse (*q.v.*), as in these 'Railway Dactyls' by G.D.:

> Hére wĕ gŏ | óff ŏn thĕ | 'Lóndŏn ănd | Bírmĭnghăm',
> Bíddĭng ă | diéu tŏ thĕ | fóggў mĕ|trópŏlĭs!
> Stáyĭng ăt | hóme wĭth thĕ | dúmps ĭn cŏn|fírmĭng 'ĕm: –
> Mótiŏn ănd | mírth ăre ă | fíllĭp tŏ | lífe.

The dactyl, like the trochee (*q.v.*), produces a falling rhythm (*q.v.*) and, as this is not the natural rhythm of English verse, poems composed entirely of dactylics are rare. But the dactyl, like the trochee, is often used in combination with other feet to provide counterpoint (*q.v.*) and to act as a substituted foot. *See also* ANAPAEST; ELEGIAC DISTICH; IAMB; PYRRHIC; RISING RHYTHM; SPONDEE; SUBSTITUTION.

Dadaism (F *dada*, 'hobby-horse') A nihilistic movement in art and literature, started in Zurich in *c.* 1916 by a Romanian, Tristan Tzara, an Alsatian, Hans Arp, and two Germans, Hugo Ball and Richard Huelsenbeck. The term was

---

meant to signify everything and nothing, or total freedom, anti rules, ideals and traditions. Dadaism became popular in Paris immediately after the First World War. The basic word in the Dadaist's vocabulary was 'nothing'. In art and literature manifestations of this 'aesthetic' were mostly collage (*q.v.*) effects: the arrangement of unrelated objects and words in a random fashion. In England and America its influence is discernible in the poetry of Ezra Pound and T. S. Eliot and in the art of Ernst and Magritte. By 1921 Dadaism as a movement was subsumed by surrealism (*q.v.*). However, its influence was detectable for many years. *See also* CUBO-FUTURISM; EXPRESSIONISM; ULTRAISM.

dämonisch A term used adjectivally of a daemon (or daimon) who is a spirit which occupies a middle place between the gods and men (e.g. the daemon or good genius of Socrates) and is associated with inspiration (*q.v.*). During the Romantic revival (*q.v.*) not a few writers (especially poets) ascribed their inspiration and energy to the operations of such a spirit that 'drove' them, and it might easily be destructive or self-destructive (hence the concept of a daemonic/demonic agency). In his autobiography (*q.v.*) *Dichtung und Wahrheit* (1811–33) Goethe suggests that *dämonisch* describes a kind of irrational phenomenon or power which controls or directs a person's destiny, as in the case of the eponymous hero in *Egmont* (1791). *See also* HETERONYM; MUSE; STORM OF ASSOCIATION.

danse macabre Also known as the Dance of Death. The etymology of the word *macabre* is obscure. It seems likely that the first use of the word dates from 1376 when it appeared in a poem written by Jehan Le Fèvre called *Respit de la Mort*: 'Je fis de macabre la dance'.

The Dance of Death (in art and literature) depicted a procession or dance in which the dead lead the living to the grave. It was a reminder of mortality, of the ubiquity of death and of the equality of all men in that state. It was also a reminder of the need for repentance. Apart from its moral and allegorical elements it was very often satirical in tone. The dead might be represented by a number of figures (usually skeletons) or by a single personification of death. The living were usually arranged in some kind of order of precedence – Pope, cardinal, archbishop; emperor, king, duke, etc. – almost, in Johnson's fine phrase, in the 'cold gradations of decay'. Many different media were employed: verse, prose, manuscript illustrations, printed books, paintings on canvas, wood and stone, engravings on stone and metal, woodcuts, sculpture, tapestry, embroidery, stained glass and so on. Its many and various versions were also widespread geographically – chiefly in France, Spain, Germany, Switzerland, Italy, Istria and Britain – and were shaped and altered by numerous classes of people in a variety of social milieux: by printers, publishers, artists, merchants, friars, scribes, lay and church men.

The theme or subject was especially popular in the late Middle Ages and the 16th c. and the influence has continued to our own time. It appealed particularly to artists. The two major works were Holbein's engravings, and the pictures and verses in the cloisters of the church of the Holy Innocents in Paris. In Britain there survive the stone screen in the parish church of Newark-on-Trent and the paintings in Hexham Priory.

There are many precursors and analogues in medieval European literature which are affiliated to the *memento mori* tradition, including Chaucer's *Pardoner's Tale*. The motif (*q.v.*) of the dance is echoed in many *ubi sunt* (*q.v.*) poems, and we find macabre elements in the work of succeeding writers: in the sombre tragedies of Webster and Tourneur, in the work of Poe, Baudelaire and Strindberg, and particularly in Espronceda's eerie poem *El Estudiante de Salamanca* (1839), whose Don Juan hero dances with a corpse. Shakespeare's *Richard II* sums up the grotesquely humorous quality ascribed to death in these personifications:

> for within the hollow crown
> That rounds the mortal temples of a king
> Keeps Death his court, and there the antick sits,
> Scoffing his state, and grinning at his pomp.
>
> (III, ii)

An outstanding modern variation on the traditional medieval idea of the dance of death was achieved in the National Theatre's spectacular version of the Wakefield Mysteries in 1985. *See also* BLACK COMEDY; CARPE DIEM; DIRGE; ELEGY; LAMENT.

dark comedy A term coined by J. L. Styan in the title of his book *The Dark Comedy* (1962). It denotes comedy which is tragic-comic in tone and form; plays in which laughter, grief, wretchedness and despair are intermingled. The plays of Chekhov (1860–1904) are outstanding examples. *See* BLACK COMEDY; TRAGICOMEDY.

deachnadh mor An Irish syllabic verse form, similar to the *rannaigheacht* (*q.v.*), but the first and third lines are octosyllabic and the second and fourth lines are hexasyllabic. All line endings are in disyllabic words.

dead metaphor A metaphor which has been so often used that it has become lifeless and lost its figurative strength. In other words, a cliché (*q.v.*). There are some hundreds, possibly thousands, in the English language. For example: 'green with envy', 'the heart of the matter', 'top dog', 'to beat about the bush', 'pride of place', 'at one fell swoop'. *See also* IDIOM.

débat A form particularly popular in the 12th and 13th c. It was usually a kind of poetic contest (*q.v.*) in which some question of morality, politics or love was discussed. A typical *débat* began with an introduction of the matter to be discussed and/or a description of the circumstances. There followed the discussion, which had some dramatic quality. At the end the issue was referred to a judge.

This form has a long history. There are some early instances in the plays of Aristophanes, especially *Frogs* and *Clouds*. The eclogues of Theocritus and

Virgil contain pastoral contests of wit. This kind of debate survives into the 4th c. in the work of Calpurnius, Nemesianus and Vespa.

A well-known example of a debate on a love theme is the 12th c. *Altercatio Phyllidis et Florae*. There are a good many examples in Provençal and OF literature. A famous instance is the *Débat du corps et de l'âme* (12th c.). Later Villon wrote a *Débat du coeur et du corps*. In English literature the theme of the soul versus the body is found in OE literature and later. Probably the most noteworthy in England is the 13th c. debate of *The Owl and the Nightingale* ascribed to Nicholas of Guildford. The solemn owl and the gay nightingale represent the religious poet and the love poet. In the debate they discuss the benefits they confer on men.

Débat, in various forms, was an important influence in the early stages of the development of drama; probably as important an influence as the *exemplum* (*q.v.*) in the sermon (*q.v.*). The debate was especially concerned with the war between God and the Devil. In the 4th c. Prudentius represented the conflict of good and evil for the soul of man in *Psychomachia*. In the 12th c. Bernard of Clairvaux and Hugo of St Victor made the debate of the *Four Daughters of God* in which Mercy and Peace plead against Truth and Righteousness for Man's Soul (or Mansoul). It was not such a long step from this to more complex allegory (*q.v.*) and also to rudimentary psychological drama of the kind we find in the Mystery Plays (*q.v.*).

Notable *débat* works which influenced the development of drama were the 13th c. *Interludium de Clerico et Puella*; the *Ludus de Bellyale* (1471), based upon the treatise of Jacobus de Theramo called *Processus Belial* (1381); and the *Processus Sathanae* (1570–80), but this is almost certainly a much earlier work.

Various versions of the *Four Daughters of God* appear in the Mystery and Morality Plays (*qq.v.*). One should mention also what is generally regarded as the first secular play – namely, Medwall's *Fulgens and Lucrece* (late 15th c.), which is a dramatized *débat*. An interesting example of a metaphysical poem in *débat* form is Andrew Marvell's *A Dialogue between The Resolved Soul and Created Pleasure* (*c.* 1640).

Dramatic debate makes a reappearance in the work of George Bernard Shaw; especially in *The Apple Cart* (1929) and *Man and Superman* (1901). *See also* AMOEBEAN VERSES; CHANSON A PERSONNAGES; DIALOGUE; DIT; FABLIAU; JEU PARTI; PASTORAL; PREGUNTA.

decadence The term usually describes a period of art or literature which, as compared with the excellence of a former age, is in decline. It has been applied to the Alexandrian period (300–30 BC), and to the period after the death of Augustus (AD 14). In modern times it is used of the late 19th c. symbolist movement in France, especially French poetry. The movement emphasized the autonomy of art, the need for sensationalism and melodrama, egocentricity, the bizarre, the artificial, art for art's sake (*q.v.*) and the superior 'outsider' position of the artist *vis-à-vis* society – particularly middle-class or bourgeois society. Much 'decadent' poetry was preoccupied with personal experience, self-analysis, perversity, and elaborate and exotic sensations.

In France the 'high priest' of decadence was Baudelaire (about whom Gautier wrote one of the most perceptive analyses of decadence), and Baudelaire's *Les Fleurs du mal* (1857) was a sort of manifesto of the movement or cult. *Le Décadent* (1886–9) was the journal of the movement. Huysmans's novel *A rebours* (1884) was what Arthur Symons described as its 'breviary'. Des Esseintes, the hero, exemplifies the decadent figure who is consumed by *maladie fin de siècle*. He devotes his energy and intelligence to the replacement of the natural with the unnatural and artificial. His quest was for new and more bizarre sensations.

Other notable figures who showed allegiance to this aesthetic cult and spirit were Villiers de l'Isle-Adam, Rimbaud, Verlaine, and Laforgue. Disenchantment, world-weariness and ennui pervaded their work. Verlaine's remarks on the word decadent itself display the truth of the matter:

Ce mot suppose . . . des pensées raffinées d'extrême civilisation, une haute culture littéraire, une âme capable d'intensives voluptés . . . Il est fait d'un mélange d'esprit charnel et de chair triste et de toutes les splendeurs violentes du Bas-Empire.

The preoccupation with decay and with ruins, with sadness and despair, was apparent much earlier in the Ossianic poetry of James Macpherson in the 1760s. Some would contend also that Leopardi, the great Italian lyric poet, was a decadent. The more morbid and flamboyant aspects of Poe's stories reveal a decadent element.

The cult did not catch on much in England, but the influences of the French movement are clear in the work of Oscar Wilde (for instance, *The Picture of Dorian Gray*, 1891), in Dowson's *Cynara*, and in various works by Rossetti, Swinburne and Aubrey Beardsley. Decadent verse was published in *The Yellow Book* (*q.v.*). Gilbert and Sullivan satirized decadence and the aesthetic movement in *Patience* (1881). *See* AESTHETICISM; ESPRIT DÉCADENT; SYMBOL AND SYMBOLISM.

decastich (Gk 'ten rows') A poem or stanza (*q.v.*) of ten lines.

decasyllable A line of verse of ten syllables. It seems to have first been used *c*. 1050 in France. It became an increasingly popular form and was used by Dante, Petrarch and Boccaccio. Chaucer's discovery of it is important because he worked out a five-stress line which became fundamental to the development of the sonnet, the Spenserian stanza, the heroic couplet and blank verse (*qq.v.*). In practice, often enough, a decasyllabic line has eleven syllables (occasionally nine) but the extra one is often negotiated by an elision (*q.v.*). This couplet from Pope's *Moral Essays* illustrates the two kinds of line:

> To observations which ourselves we make,
> We grow more partial for th'observer's sake.

décima   A much used and classic Spanish stanza form. It consists of ten octo-syllabic lines rhyming abbaaccddc.

decires   A genre of Spanish poetry of the 15th c. The themes tended to be didactic, courtly or political, in contrast to the amorous themes of the *cantigas* and *canciones* (*qq.v.*).

deconstruction   The term denotes a particular kind of practice in reading and, thereby, a method of criticism and mode of analytical inquiry. Its origin lies partly in the philosopher Martin Heidegger's concepts of *destruktion* (destruction) and *abbau* (dismantling). In her book *The Critical Difference* (1981), Barbara Johnson clarifies the meaning of deconstruction:

> Deconstruction is not synonymous with 'destruction', however. It is in fact much closer to the original meaning of the word 'analysis' itself, which etymologically means 'to undo' – a virtual synonym for 'to de-construct'. The deconstruction of a text does not proceed by random doubt or arbitrary subversion, but by the careful teasing out of *warring forces of signification within the text itself* [emphasis added]. If anything is destroyed in a deconstructive reading, it is not the text, but the claim to unequivocal domination of one mode of signifying over another. A deconstructive reading is a reading which analyses the specificity of a text's critical difference from itself.

One could say that while poststructuralism (*q.v.*) develops as a response to, and displacement of, structuralism (a European phenomenon largely), deconstruction focuses on rhetoric and reflexivity (i.e. the self-referential aspects of language) in a way that the American New Critics (*see* NEW CRITICISM) had encouraged earlier in the century.

Deconstruction owes much to the theories of the French philosopher Jacques Derrida (1930–2004), whose essay *Structure, Sign and Play in the Discourse of the Human Sciences* (1966) – which he was to follow with his book *Of Grammatology* (1967) – began a new critical movement. Deconstruction, so far, has been the most influential feature of poststructuralism because it defines a new kind of reading practice which is a key application of poststructuralism.

Derrida shows that a text (any text – be it a polemic, a philosophical treatise, a poem, or, for that matter, an exercise in deconstructive criticism) can be read as saying something quite different from what it appears to be saying, and that it may read as carrying a plurality of significance or as saying many different things which are fundamentally at variance with, contradictory to and subversive of what may be (or may have been) seen by criticism as a single, stable 'meaning'. Thus, a text may 'betray' itself. A deconstructive criticism of a text reveals that there *is nothing except the text*. In *Of Grammatology* Derrida makes the now well-known axial proposition that this is so (his key words are 'il n'y a rien hors du texte', or, alternatively, 'il n'y a pas de hors-texte'). That is, one cannot evaluate, criticize or construe a meaning for a text by reference to anything external to it.

Derrida carries his logic still further to suggest that the language of any discourse is at variance with itself and, by so being, is capable of being read as yet another language. Thus, hypothetically, one may envisage an endless regression of dialectical interpretations and readings without any stable, essential meaning. In short, a text may possess so many different meanings that it cannot have a meaning. There is no guaranteed essential meaning. An immediate deconstructive practice would be to question the foregoing sentence by asking what is meant by 'guaranteed', 'essential' and 'meaning' in that context.

The implications are that any form of traditional literary criticism which employs the practical tools of comparison and analysis patiently and attentively to elucidate meaning is a self-defeating practice since the rhetoric of both the literary text under analysis and literary criticism is inherently unstable.

The initial stage of Derrida's deconstructive theory is the contention that both speech and writing are signifying processes which lack 'presence'. Derrida destabilizes and displaces the traditional 'hierarchy' (he calls it a 'violent hierarchy') of speech over writing to suggest that speech can only ever be subject to the same instabilities as writing; that speech and writing are forms of one science of language, grammatology (*q.v.*). This is not a reversal of the priority, since Plato, of speech over writing but a displacement which produces a state of 'indeterminacy' (*q.v.*).

Derrida has devised a number of terms to isolate and clarify what he is driving at. He uses the term *supplément* (*q.v.*) to denote the unstable or indeterminate relationship between speech and writing. The French word *suppléer* means 'to take the place of' as well as 'to supplement', and it is his contention that writing both supplements *and* takes the place of speech, though this is by no means the only opposition to which *supplément* applies.

The inherent, subversive, self-contradictory and self-betraying elements in a text 'include' what is not in the text, what is outside the text (*dehors de texte*), what is not said. But despite the presence of what is absent, Derrida's dictum that 'il n'y a pas de hors-texte' must be seen as a *sine qua non* of deconstruction. The elements referred to above would 'include' assumptions and propositions. What is *not* said constitutes a 'gap', 'lacuna' or *aporia* (*q.v.*).

The rigorous probing and analysis of a text, the process of dismantling it or taking it apart, also reveals what Derrida refers to as 'dissemination' and 'trace' (*qq.v.*). The former is the scattering or dispersal of meaning; the latter is something that is absent in a sign (e.g. a signifier) but which, by virtue of the absence of its signified, suggests a nostalgia for 'self-presence'.

Derrida's deconstructive theory also involves the key distinction of *différance* (*q.v.*) and *différence*, which concerns the principle of the continuous (and endless) postponement or deferral of meaning.

Deconstructive theory among American critics has been much in Derrida's debt. Paul de Man's main collections of essays are *Blindness and Insight* (1971), *Allegories of Reading* (1979) and *The Resistance to Theory* (1986). Derrida and de Man met in 1966 and found that they were working on the same obscure text of Rousseau – *On the Origin of Languages* – but de Man worked for the most part independently of Derrida. De Man produced a famous critique (*The Rhetoric of Blindness*) of Derrida's early text *Of Grammatology*, in which he deconstructs Derrida's own reading of Rousseau. In *Blindness and Insight* de Man works out a complex theory that critics achieve insight at the cost of critical 'blindness'. In *Allegories of Reading* he attempts a deconstruction of figurative and rhetorical strategies in Rousseau, Nietzsche, Proust and Rilke, and contends that literary language is fundamentally self-reflexive rather than referential and that texts deconstruct themselves.

Other deconstructive theories have been elaborated by Geoffrey Hartman (e.g. *Saving the Text*, 1981; *Easy Pieces*, 1986) and Harold Bloom (e.g. *The Anxiety of Influence*, 1973; *A Map of Misreading*, 1975). In *The Critical Difference* Barbara Johnson analyses the networks of differences in both literary and critical texts, and deconstructs Roland Barthes's celebrated analysis of Balzac's *Sarrasine*, in which he applies the implications of his distinction between the readerly and the writerly text. Basically, Johnson shows that Barthes makes his 'writerly' analysis by making the story 'readerly' and that Barthes constructs castration as the meaning of the story in a way which *Sarrasine* refuses (i.e. Barthes constructs a version of the story which the story resists). *See* POSTSTRUCTURALISM; READERLY/WRITERLY.

decorum In literature, and especially in poetry, decorum is consistency with the canons of propriety (*q.v.*); a matter of behaviour on the part of the poet *qua* his poem, and therefore what is proper and becoming in the relationship between form and substance. Action, character, thought and language all need to be appropriate to each other. At its simplest, the grand and important theme (for instance that of *Paradise Lost*) is treated in a dignified and noble style; the humble or trivial (for example, Skelton's *The Tunning of Elynour Rumming*) in a lower manner.

Decorum was of considerable importance to Classical authors. Aristotle deals with it in *Poetics*; Cicero in *De Oratore*; Horace in *Ars Poetica*. What they said had wide influence during and after the Renaissance, though there were many who did not subscribe to their dictates.

Many Elizabethan plays, for example, show an awareness of certain rules of decorum. An obvious instance is *Much Ado About Nothing* (c. 1598–9). It being a comedy of manners (*q.v.*), all the comic passages, especially the badinage between Beatrice and Benedick, are written in colloquial dramatic prose; the romantic episodes and themes are always rendered in verse. As soon as Benedick and Beatrice realize they are in love, the emotional temperature rises and they speak in verse.

Decorum became of great importance towards the end of the 17th c. and during the 18th when Classical rules and tenets were revered. The use of correct language was of particular interest. For instance, Johnson observed that the words 'cow-keeper' and 'hog-herd' might not be used in our language; but he added that there were no finer words in the Greek language. Though the subject matter of 18th c. writers was often what they thought of as 'low', if not vulgar, they managed to dress it in appropriate language. Pope combines elegance, wit and grace with an almost brutal forcefulness and succeeds in writing of the crude, the corrupt and the repulsive without offending.

Wordsworth and Coleridge found the doctrines of neoclassicism (q.v.) too restrictive; hence Wordsworth's attempt, as expressed in the Preface to *Lyrical Ballads*, to rebel against 'false refinement' and 'poetic diction' (q.v.).

Since then writers have always considered matters of literary decorum, though in a more flexible way. Dickens is a good example of a writer who adjusts his style to the needs of the moment. Fundamentally, most people have an awareness of the need to adjust their language to the occasion, whether they are writing or speaking. *See* AFFECTATION; CONVENTION; PERIPHRASIS; STYLE.

deep structure A term originating in the linguistics (q.v.) of Noam Chomsky. Deep structure and surface structure are the complementary concepts upon which his Transformational Grammar is based. According to this still disputed theory, all statements have two structures: a visible surface structure and a deep structure underlying it. The deep structure can usually be transformed into several surface structures. For example, the deep structure of Shakespeare's line 'That time of year thou may'st in me behold' could be transformed into a variety of alternatives: 'Thou may'st behold that time of year in me', 'In me thou may'st behold that time of year', 'That time of year in me thou may'st behold', and so on.

Literary critics and theorists have broadened the application of the term to such an extent that their use of it should be understood figuratively. Thus, it is possible to say that two novels of Jane Austen's have the same deep structure. This would imply that they share the same basic plot, or a common theme, or the same set of closely related issues.

defamiliarization A concept and term introduced by Viktor Shklovsky (1893–1984), an important member of the Russian School of Formalism (q.v.). It is a translation of the Russian *ostranenie* 'making strange'. To 'defamiliarize' is to make fresh, new, strange, different what is familiar and known. Through defamiliarization the writer modifies the reader's habitual perceptions by drawing attention to the artifice of the text. This is a matter of literary technique. What the reader notices is not the picture of reality that is being presented but the peculiarities of the writing itself. In his essay *Art as Technique* (1917) Shklovsky makes his point pretty clear:

> The purpose of art is to impart the sensation of things as they are perceived, and not as they are known. The technique of art is to make objects 'unfamiliar', to make forms difficult, to increase the difficulty of length and perception, because the process of perception is an aesthetic end in itself and must be prolonged. *Art is a way of experiencing the artfulness of an object; the object is not important.*

Linked with this is the idea of 'laying bare', or exposing, the techniques and devices by which a work of art is constructed. The classic example analysed by Shklovsky is Sterne's *Tristram Shandy* (1760–7). Russian Formalists tend to be interested in texts which are 'anti-realist'; hence they privilege *Tristram Shandy* or modernist works.

The concept of defamiliarization is closely connected with the concepts of foregrounding and literariness (*qq.v.*). *See also* DOMINANT; READERLY/WRITERLY; REFLEXIVE NOVEL.

defective foot A metrical foot lacking one or more unstressed syllables. In the line:

> This is the forest primeval

one would expect a final dactyl (*q.v.*) but it ends with a trochee (*q.v.*). Only the purists would regard this kind of variation as a fault. *See* CATALEXIS.

definitio *See* HORISMUS.

definitive edition Either an author's own final text which he wishes to be regarded as the accepted version, or a work which is deemed to be 'the last word' on a subject. It may, for example, be the edition of a text, a biography or a work of reference.

deibhidhe An Irish syllabic/accentual verse form. It comprises a quatrain (*q.v.*) stanza rhyming in couplets (*q.v.*). In each line two words alliterate. There are at least two cross-rhymes between the third and fourth lines and each line has seven syllables.

deixis (Gk 'to show') In grammar and linguistics, the use of words relating to the person, time and place of utterance. For example, personal pronouns (I/you, it/them), demonstrative adjectives and adverbs (this, that, here, there, now, then) (adjectival form: 'deictic').

delayed rhyme *See* RHYME.

demotic (Gk 'of the people') The language of the common people, thus of the market, the street, the pub, etc. It also denoted a popular and simplified form of the ancient Egyptian script (as opposed to the hieratic (*q.v.*), or priestly script.

demotion In prosody (*q.v.*) the use of a stressed syllable where, in a regular iambic verse line, an unstressed syllable would normally be used. Demotion usually slows the rhythm of a line, as in the trochaic inversion in 'And sometimes like a gleaner thou dost keep/Steady thy laden head across a brook' (Keats, *To Autumn*, 1819), where the trochee (*q.v.*) 'steady' occupies a place in the line which would normally contain an iamb (*q.v.*). *See* SUBSTITUTION.

denotation The most literal and limited meaning of a word, regardless of what one may feel about it or the suggestions and ideas it connotes. *Apartheid* denotes a certain form of political, social and racial regime. It *connotes* much more. *See* CONNOTATION; MEANING.

dénouement (F 'unknotting') It may be the event or events following the major climax (*q.v.*) of a plot, or the unravelling of a plot's complications at the end of a story or play. *See* CRISIS; DESENLACE; DISCOVERY.

de regimine principum (L 'concerning the rule of princes') A form of didactic literature of the discourse or treatise (*qq.v.*) kind which gives advice to rulers (e.g. kings, princes) on how to rule. There was a particularly large number of them in Portuguese and Spanish. However, easily the best known is Machiavelli's *Il principe* (1513).

descending rhythm *See* FALLING RHYTHM.

descort Either a synonym for the Provençal *lai* (*see* LAY), or a term for a poem whose stanzas are in different languages. Also a Galician verse form expressing the 'discord' felt by the poet when he is suffering the pangs of unrequited love. Line length and meter are variable.

desenlace (Sp 'untying, unlacing') Directly comparable both in original meaning and in usage with its virtual synonym in French, dénouement (*q.v.*).

desert island fiction A form of fiction in which a remote and 'uncivilized' island is used as the venue of the story and action. It has a particular attraction because it can be placed right outside the 'real' world and may be an image of the ideal, the unspoilt and the primitive. It appeals directly to the sense of adventure and exploratory instinct in most people, and also to a certain atavistic nostalgia.

The publication of Defoe's *Robinson Crusoe* in 1719 marked the inception of a literary genre which has attained universal popularity. In 1719 Defoe also published *The Farther Adventures of Robinson Crusoe*, and in the same year an imitation appeared, called *The Adventures and Surprising Deliverance of James Dubourdieu and his Wife from the Uninhabited Part of the Island of Paradise*. French and German editions of *Robinson Crusoe* came out in 1720, and since that time there have been around 200 English editions, some 130 translations into two dozen different languages, about 120 adaptations and approximately 280 imitations (many of which have been translated). These adaptations and imitations soon came to be known as 'Robinsonades' (*q.v.*).

The theme of Crusoe has appeared in numerous other works, of which some of the more notable are *The Hermit, or ... The Adventures of Mr Philip Quarll* (1727); Johann Schnabel's *Die Insel Felsenburg* (1731–43); Johann Campe's *Robinson der Jüngere* (1779–80); and the classic *Der Schweizerische Robinson* by Wyss, which was translated into English as *The Swiss Family Robinson* in 1814. The increasing popularity of children's books (*q.v.*) in the 19th c. produced a good many developments of the Crusoe theme, like J. Taylor's *The Young Islanders* (1841), Madame de Beaulieu's *Le*

Robinson de douze ans (1824) and Jules Verne's *L'Île mystérieuse* (1875). One should note several other works in the Wyss tradition, namely, Marryat's *Masterman Ready* (1841), R. M. Ballantyne's *The Coral Island* (1858) and his *Dog Crusoe* (1861), R. L. Stevenson's *Treasure Island* (1883), and, more recently, William Golding's *Lord of the Flies* (1954), a story which reverses the image of an unspoilt and semi-paradisal existence. By contrast, Aldous Huxley depicted a utopian way of life in *Island* (1966). In the 20th c. many authors reworked the Crusoe story, and were motivated to do so by psycho-analytic, feminist and postcolonial concerns, as well as the threat of nuclear war and environmental catastrophe. Some notable examples include Gerhart Hauptmann's *Die Insel der grossen Mutter* (1924), Michel Tournier's *Vendredi* (1967) and J. M. Coetzee's *Foe* (1986). *See also* APOCALYPTIC LITERATURE; NOBLE SAVAGE; PRIMITIVISM; UTOPIA.

detective story *See* CRIME FICTION.

detractio *See* ECLIPSIS.

deus ex machina (L 'god out of the machine') In Greek drama a god was lowered onto the stage by a *mēchanē* so that he could get the hero out of difficulties or untangle the plot. Euripides used it a good deal. Sophocles and Aeschylus avoided it. Bertolt Brecht parodied the abuse of the device at the end of his *Threepenny Opera*. Today this phrase is applied to any unanticipated intervener who resolves a difficult situation, in any literary genre.

deuteragonist In Greek drama, a second actor – often the same as the antagonist (*q.v.*). *See* PROTAGONIST.

Deutsches Theater A famous and very important Berlin theatre founded in 1893. It is particularly associated with Max Reinhardt (1873–1943), who developed many techniques in the use of stage devices, machinery, etc., and who had a powerful influence on presentation and performance in general. In 1933 the Nazis took it over and in 1945 it became the main theatre in the Soviet sector of Berlin. Brecht's Berliner Ensemble (*q.v.*) developed from it.

diachronic/synchronic (Gk 'through/across time' and 'together time') A term coined *c.* 1913 by Ferdinand de Saussure (1857–1913). A diachronic approach to the study of a language (or languages) involves an examination of its origins, development, history and change. In contrast, the synchronic approach entails the study of a linguistic system in a particular state, without reference to time. The importance of a synchronic approach to an understanding of language lies in the fact that for Saussure each sign has no properties other than the specific relational ones which define it within its own synchronic system. *See* SIGNIFIER/SIGNIFIED.

diacope (Gk 'cutting through') The separation of a compound word. For instance: *never the less*; *what so ever*.

diacritic A sign under or above a letter to distinguish different values or sounds. For example: è, é, ê, ç, ö, ž.

diaeresis (Gk 'taking apart') A sign put over the second of two vowels to indicate that they are pronounced separately. For example: noël.

dialect A language or manner of speaking peculiar to an individual or class or region. Usually it belongs to a region, like the West Riding or East Anglia. A dialect differs from the standard language of a country, in some cases very considerably. Greek, German and Sicilian dialects, for instance, show great variations from the standard.

A good deal of literature is in dialect, especially that created in the earlier stages of a country's civilization. As far as England is concerned, all English medieval verse is in dialect. For example: Robert Mannyng's *Handlyng Synne* (North-east Midland or Lincolnshire); *Sir Orfeo* (South-west); *Ayenbite of Inwyt* (Kentish); *Sir Gawain and the Green Knight* (West Midland or Lancashire or Cheshire); *The Pearl* (West Midland); Langland's *Piers Plowman* (South Midland); Sir John Mandeville's *Travels* (South-east Midland); not to mention many of the medieval Mystery Plays (*q.v.*) and romances (*q.v.*).

Chaucer (who wrote in the East Midland dialect, and thus helped to establish it as the vernacular of educated people) uses words from other dialects quite often; sometimes to suggest local characteristics, sometimes to secure a rhyme.

Since the 16th c., dialect in writing has been used less and less because of the development of Standard English. Scottish poetry has been the most conservative and retentive of dialect forms, as can be seen by comparing the work of Henryson and Dunbar with that of Burns and Edwin Muir. Burns was easily at his best when using the Ayrshire dialect. William Barnes is probably the most distinguished example of an English dialect poet since the 14th c. Most of his *Poems of Rural Life* (in three series, 1844, 1859, 1863) are in the Dorset dialect. Thomas Hardy also used the dialect successfully in *Wessex Poems and Other Verses*. Tennyson experimented with it in *Northern Farmer – Old Style*. James Russell Lowell's *Bigelow Papers* rather comically take off New England rural speech; and, if cockney is accounted a dialect, then Kipling's *Barrack-Room Ballads* provide good examples of its use. A large number of novelists have used dialect forms, particularly to give verisimilitude (*q.v.*) to dialogue. Dickens, George Eliot, Thomas Hardy and D. H. Lawrence are notable instances; recent examples are Irvine Welsh and Roddy Doyle. *See also* SLANG; VERNACULAR.

dialectic (Gk *dialegomai*, 'to converse') A method of philosophical inquiry and reasoning. As a method of argument that proceeds by question and answer – by dialogue – it is attributed to Socrates, the main interlocutor in Plato's dialogues. Through this method, Socrates exposes the flaws in conventional understandings of various notions such as 'piety' and 'justice'. In his *Republic*, Plato sees the 'science of dialectic' as revealing the first principles and essences of things and situating them in an ordered structure of knowledge. In his *Rhetoric*, Aristotle uses the term 'dialectic' to refer to logical argument in general. Kant uses the term 'dialectic' in his *Critique* *of Pure Reason* to denote a systematic refutation of various philosophical fallacies.

In modern thought, the term is most closely associated with Hegel. The dialectic did not comprise the commonly cited triad of thesis, antithesis and synthesis: Hegel cited this formula only twice and Marx never used it. In Hegel's hands, the dialectic had both logical and historical dimensions. The three-stage dialectic formalized into a principle the imperative that thought was a *process* rather than a mechanical tool as it had been in the hands of previous one-sided attempts to understand the world, such as materialism or empiricism. In the first stage an object was apprehended in its sensuous immediacy; the second stage adopted a broadened perspective which saw the object as 'externalized', as having no independent identity but constituted by its manifold relations with its context. The third stage, from a still wider standpoint, viewed the object as a 'mediated' unity, its true identity now perceived as a principle of unity between universal and particular, between essence and appearance. In this way, 'plant' could be viewed as the unifying principle of its own developing stages, bud, blossom and fruit. Hegel's historical treatment of the dialectic is extremely complex but he basically sees societies, from the Oriental world through the Greek and Roman to the modern German world, developing through successive stages of the dialectic: this movement entails a historical increase in degree of self-consciousness culminating in the realization that the external world is a construction out of human subjectivity.

These insights crucially moulded the materialism of both Marx and Engels. It was Engels who coined the phrase 'historical materialism', and the Russian Marxist Plekhanov who termed the Marxist philosophy 'dialectical materialism'. Both terms cover the same materialist disposition peculiar to Marxism, though the former stresses materialism both as a historical phenomenon and as the primary basis of historical development, while the latter indicates a methodological emphasis in the apprehension of reality. The dialectical method views reality not as a conglomerate of fixed entities but as a changing totality of related parts at whose core is a dynamic interaction between human labour and the natural world. Marx's own reflections on materialism, both traditional and dialectical, are focused primarily in his writings of 1844–6.

Engels perpetuated Marx's insistence that materialism must be dialectical, particularly in his *Anti-Dühring* (1878) where he defended the Hegelian aspects of Marxism against attacks from Eugen Dühring. In this work he drew upon Hegel's philosophy of nature to formulate certain dialectical laws of nature: the law that quantitative changes abruptly become qualitative (which Engels also saw happening in terms of economic and political history); the law of interpenetration of opposites, whose tension generates change; and the law of the negation of the negation, which Engels held to apply not only through nature but also in history and philosophy. Marx had already viewed socialism as the negation of capitalist society, which itself had negated feudalism. But, even more than Marx himself, Engels stressed the importance of an organic connection between the natural sciences and philosophy. Hence in his manuscripts posthumously published as *Dialectics of Nature* (1925) he saw Hegel as anticipating the development of the 19th c. sciences which viewed things as part of a larger process of change and evolution rather than as static and isolated atoms. We might add that Hegel's dialectic anticipates the thought of Jacques Derrida and many feminist and poststructuralist thinkers. *See also* DECONSTRUCTION; MARXIST CRITICISM; POSTSTRUCTURALISM.

dialectical theatre *See* EPIC THEATRE.

Dialektdichtung German literature composed either wholly or partly in dialect. There was much of it during the 19th c. and a good deal during the 20th c. An early example of a collection of dialect poetry is *Alemannische Gedichte* (1803). Some five hundred writers have used the High German dialect in their works, and twenty or more the Low German. *See also* VOLKSSTÜCK.

dialogic/monologic Terms used by the Soviet critic Mikhail Bakhtin (1895–1975) in his discussions of language and discourse in literature in which he examines the different 'voices' and suggests how the use of discourse in, for example, a novel may influence and, in a sense, 'disrupt' the authority of a single voice. In his book *Problems of Dostoevsky's Poetics* (1929) he makes a contrast between Dostoevsky's novels and Tolstoy's. In his view Dostoevsky's novels are in the dialogic (or polyphonic) form, which allows characters to speak 'in their own voices', as it were. In Bakhtin's words, they are liberated to speak 'a plurality of independent and unmerged voices and consciousness, a genuine polyphony of fully valid voices . . .' which are not subject to the authoritative control of the author. By contrast, characters in Tolstoy's novels *are* subject to such control. However, Bakhtin's distinction does not imply that characters are necessarily differentiated by an idiosyncratic style of speech or by their idiolect (*q.v.*). In fact, Tolstoy's characters (e.g. in *War and Peace*) are more easily distinguishable in this respect than are Dostoevsky's (e.g. in *The Possessed*). Bahktin claims that his approach in this theory is translinguistic rather than linguistic. In an essay published in translation in *The Dialogic Imagination* (1981) he elaborates his earlier opinions and avers that the dialogic/polyphonic form tends to be typical of the novel. *See* CARNIVALIZATION/CARNIVALESQUE.

dialogue Two basic meanings may be distinguished: (a) the speech of characters in any kind of narrative, story or play; (b) a literary genre in which 'characters' discuss a subject at length.

Of the latter, the earliest examples are believed to be the mimes of Sophron of Syracuse (*c.* 430 BC), but only fragments survive. To the 4th BC belong Plato's Socratic *Dialogues*, which are philosophical debates or dramas which employ the heuristic and dialectical method of question and answer. These are supreme examples of dialogue. Aristotle used the form for more specifically didactic purposes. Lucian's Greek *Dialogues of the Dead* (2nd c. AD) were modelled on Plato's, but Lucian used dialogue for comic and satirical ends and as a form of entertainment (rather as Plato did in *The Symposium*). Plato's method was imitated in the Renaissance by Juan de Valdés and Tasso, and Lucian's in the 17th and 18th c. by Fontenelle and Fénelon.

Notable instances in English of dialogues are: Thomas Starkey's *A Dialogue between Reginald Pole and Thomas Lupset* (c. 1533–6); Dryden's *Essay of Dramatic Poesy* (1668); Hume's *Dialogues concerning Natural Religion* (1779); Landor's *Imaginary Conversations* (1824–9), followed by his *Imaginary Conversations of Greeks and Romans* (1853); and Oscar Wilde's *The Critic as Artist* (1891). Shaw used the form dramatically in *The Apple Cart* (1929). An interesting minor example of a Platonic dialogue is that by Gerard Manley Hopkins: *On the Origin of Beauty* (1865).

In France the Platonic form was revived by Valéry and his Socratic debates are generally thought to be outstanding for their structure and lucidity. The two works were: *L'Ame et la danse* and *Eupalinos ou l'Architecte* (1923). *See also* DÉBAT.

dialysis (Gk 'dismembering') The term denotes a method of analysis, argument or inquiry by which all the possible reasons for or against something are put forward and then disposed of rationally. *See also* DÉBAT; DIALECTIC; DIALOGUE.

diary and journal Diaries and journals can be roughly divided into two categories: the intimate and the anecdotal. Examples of the first are Swift's *Journal to Stella*, the journals of Benjamin Haydon, Amiel, Shelley, Mary Godwin, Constant, Tolstoy and André Gide. Into the second category come Pepys's *Diary*, Evelyn's *Journal*, Boswell's *Journal of a Tour to the Hebrides*, and the diaries of Charles Greville and Thomas Creevey.

It seems that keeping a diary became habitual in the 17th c., though one may assume that there are similar records from earlier times which have been lost; and there are a few which are extant from the 16th c., like the diary kept by King Edward VI as a boy. Sir William Dugdale (1605–86), historian and topographer, kept a journal of great interest. Other minor English diarists of the 17th c. were Edward Lake, Henry Teonge and Roger Lowe. Late in that century Celia Fiennes began a diary (c. 1685) which she finished in approximately 1703 (parts of which were first published by Southey in 1812). But the two great 17th c. diarists (by many considered the greatest of all) were John Evelyn (1620–1706) and Samuel Pepys (1633–1703). Evelyn's *Journal* covers much of his life but was not published until 1818. Pepys's diary, which also covers a long period, was written in a cipher which was not deciphered until 1825, and not published in its entirety until 1893–9.

Many diaries and journals survive from the 18th c., a period when women kept them regularly. Some of the more notable female diarists were Mary, Countess Cooper (1685–1724), Elizabeth Byrom (1722–1801), Fanny Burney (1752–1840), Lady Mary Coke (1756–1829), Mrs Lybbe Powys (1756–1808). From the 18th c., too, dates one of the most agreeable and interesting diaries in English literature – Parson Woodforde's. Titled *The Diary of a Country*

Parson, it was published in five volumes (1924–31). It gives memorable pictures of life in college and in a country parish. Pre-eminent in this period are Fielding's *Journal of a Voyage to Lisbon* (1755), Swift's *Journal to Stella* (1766, 1768) and Boswell's *Journal of a Tour to the Hebrides* (1785), plus his very detailed accounts of his travels published in many volumes in the 20th c. A curiosity of the 18th c. is Defoe's *A Journal of the Plague Year* (1722), a historical reconstruction of the Great Plague of London 1664–5.

From the end of the 18th c. and throughout the 19th we find many other examples of diaries. Again, some of the best were kept by women; for instance: Lady Holland (1770–1845), Mary Frampton (1773–1846), Lady Charlotte Bury (1775–1861), Ellen Weeton (1776–1850), Elizabeth Fry (1780–1845), Caroline Fox (1819–71) and Margaret Shore (1819–39). These are works of minor importance.

From near the end of the 18th c. and for many years, Dorothy Wordsworth kept detailed diaries and journals which tell us much about Wordsworth. The separate works are: *The Alfoxden Journal* (1798); the *Journal of a Visit to Hamburgh* and *A Journey from Hamburgh to Goslar* (1798); the *Grasmere Journal* (1800–3); *Recollections of a Journey made in Scotland* (1803); *Journal of a Mountain Ramble by Dorothy and William Wordsworth* (1805); *Journal of a Tour on the Continent* (1820); *A Tour in Scotland* (1822); and *A Tour in the Isle of Man* (1828). The complete journals were published in 1941.

Two other important women published diaries in the 19th c., namely George Eliot and Queen Victoria. The Queen's contribution was *Leaves from the Journal of Our Life in the Highlands* (1862), and *More Leaves* (1883). George Eliot's *Journals* came out in 1885.

Diaries and journals by men of note in the 19th c. are numerous. Here there is space to mention only a few of the more remarkable ones, like the journal of Benjamin Haydon (1786–1846), the painter, whose records were published as an autobiography in 1853. Of greater importance, especially from the point of view of the biographer and the social historian, are the diaries of Creevey and Greville. Thomas Creevey (1768–1838) kept extensive diaries which were published as the *Creevey Papers* in 1903. Charles Greville (1794–1865) had published three series of 'Greville Memoirs'. The first (1874) covered the reigns of George IV and William IV; the second (1885) covered the years 1837–52; and the third (1887) covered the period 1852–60. Lord Byron also kept copious journals. In addition to these one should mention a work of great charm and interest, the diaries of the clergyman Francis Kilvert (1840–79), which were edited by William Plomer and published in 1938. At the very end of the 19th c. George and Weedon Grossmith published the novel *Diary of a Nobody* (1894), a minor classic. It is a record of Charles Pooter, an assistant in a mercantile business towards the end of the 19th c., and is an unpretentious and immensely readable account of social, domestic and business problems.

Most of the works mentioned have not been by poets, novelists or dramatists, though some have been the records of what may be called occasional writers. There are, however, a large number of works which are part diary, part journal and part notebook. Some of the more valuable and interesting examples are: Shelley's *Notebooks* (not published until 1911); Samuel Butler's *Notebooks* (1912); W. N. P. Barbellion's *The Journal of a Disappointed Man* (1919); the *Journal* of Katherine Mansfield (1927); C. E. Montague's *A Writer's Notes on his Trade* (1930); Arnold Bennett's *Journals* (1933–4), a remarkable work in which Bennett kept a detailed record almost daily from 1896 until his death in 1931; and Somerset Maugham's *A Writer's Notebook* (1949).

Sometimes authors keep a journal of the creation of a book. An interesting recent example in English literature is Graham Greene's *In Search of a Character* (1962). This is a short journal of his travels in the Congo and contains the basis of his novel *A Burnt-Out Case* (1961).

In France the habit (especially among writers) of keeping diaries, journals and notebooks is deeply engrained. Here there is space to mention only a few instances. French writers, exhibiting a certain Gallic thrift, have a predilection for the *journal intime*. Among the more famous are: Constant's *Journal Intime* (1895, 1952) and his *Cahier Rouge* (1907); Amiel's *Journal Intime*, which he kept for thirty-odd years from 1847; *Le Journal des Goncourts*, kept by the Goncourt brothers from 1851 to 1870, and thereafter kept by Edmond, the survivor; André Gide's *Journal*, which he started in 1885 and was still adding to in 1947. Among the many other well-known Frenchmen who have kept this kind of journal are: Baudelaire, Léon Bloy, Du Bos, Renard and De Vigny. The painters Gauguin and Delacroix also kept diaries and journals which are of much value and interest. *See* AUTOBIOGRAPHY; CONFESSIONAL LITERATURE.

diasporic literature   This very broad term encompasses literature that deals with experiences of migration and exile, and cultural or geographical displacement, most often in the context of postcolonialism (*q.v.*), but also arising from dispersals caused by traumatic historical events such as war and forced transportation. *See also* COSMOPOLITAN WRITING.

diatribe   (Gk 'rubbing through') It now has the more or less exclusive meaning of a rather violent attack on a person or work, couched in vitriolic language. *See* FLYTING; INVECTIVE; LAMPOON.

dibrach   A metrical foot of two short unstressed syllables: ◡ ◡. Also a pyrrhic (*q.v.*). Very rare in English verse.

dicatalectic   A metrical line which lacks a syllable of the basic meter in the middle and at the end. *See* ACATALECTIC; CATALEXIS.

diction   *See* POETIC DICTION.

dictionary   The word derives from medieval Latin (*liber*) *dictionarius* or (*manuale*) *dictionarium*, from *dictio*, 'saying'. It is primarily a book containing the words of a language arranged alphabetically. It contains definitions of the meanings of words, which are often accompanied by some etymological explanations. In some dictionaries quotations are given to illustrate meanings and usage over the years. Two-language dictionaries provide corresponding words, phrases and meanings in other tongues – again arranged alphabetically. Special dictionaries (like this one) give information about one particular subject.

Dictionaries of language are relatively recent. Neither the Greeks nor the Romans had anything like a modern dictionary. On the other hand, the glossary (*q.v.*) appeared quite early. Apollonius's Homeric *Lexicon* was compiled in the 3rd c. BC.

In 1532 Robert Estienne completed his great *Dictionarium seu linguae latinae thesaurus*, and in 1572 his son Henri Estienne published his *Thesaurus graecae linguae*, a landmark in Greek lexicography and a work on which others have built steadily. In 1678 Charles du Fresne du Cange produced his monumental dictionary of medieval Latin titled *Glossarium ad Scriptores Mediae et Infimae Latinitatis*; and, ten years later, a companion work on medieval Greek.

All the major dictionaries of modern ethnic languages were first compiled in the 17th c. Notable examples are the Italian *Vocabolario degli Accademici della Crusca* (1612) and the great dictionary of the French Academy in 1694. In the following century the Academy of Madrid published its Spanish dictionary (1726–39). In England the most outstanding work of that century was Johnson's *Dictionary* (1755), on which he worked single-handed for many years. The forerunner of this was Nathan Bailey's *Dictionary* (1721). Johnson's work is remarkable for its range and knowledge, for the compression and adroitness of its definitions, and also because Johnson allowed his prejudices and opinions to appear in the definitions. His *Preface* is one of the finest pieces of prose in the language.

In 1854 Jakob and Wilhelm Grimm began their *magnum opus* on the German language. The work has been carried on by others ever since. A majestic achievement in French lexicography was Émile Littré's *Dictionnaire de la langue française*, which came out in four volumes (1863–78). In that latter year was begun the monumental *New English Dictionary on Historical Principles* (1884–1928), edited by Sir James Murray, Dr Henry Bradley, Sir William Craigie and Dr C. T. Onions. Later known as the *Oxford English Dictionary*, or *OED*, it is a work without parallel in the history of lexicography and gives all the uses of every English word since at least the 12th c. It also provides illustrative quotations to show shifts and changes of meaning. In 1989 a second edition of this majestic work was published, followed in 2000 by the appearance of the *Oxford English Dictionary Online*, a digitized version of the second edition. Under the chief editorship of John Simpson a third edition is under way and updates and revisions become periodically available via these digitial versions. This latest overhaul is estimated to be completed by 2020 at the earliest.

Other dictionaries of great note which should be mentioned here are Webster's *American Dictionary of the English Language* (1828); Webster's *New International Dictionary* (1934, 1961); *A Dictionary of American English on Historical Principles* (1938–44) edited by Craigie and Hulbert; and *The Oxford Dictionary of English Etymology* (1966) edited by C. T. Onions – a remarkable work for which its editor has the reputation of never making a mistake.

Other special dictionaries are Ebenezer Brewer's *Dictionary of Phrase and Fable* (1870) and Eric Partridge's *A Dictionary of Slang and Unconventional English* (1937). The advent of online dictionaries, including open-access projects such as *Wiktionary*, has prompted a revolution in dictionary compilation, with the vast resources of the internet promising ever-broadening coverage and availability while simultaneously threatening the quality control and editorial expertise of traditional scholarship. *See* CONCORDANCE; ENCY-CLOPAEDIA; THESAURUS.

didactic (Gk 'that which teaches') Any work of literature which sets out to instruct may be called didactic. Didactic poetry is almost a special category of its own. Early works are Greek; for instance, Hesiod's *Works and Days* and *Theogony* (8th c. BC). The former combines a farming manual with moral precepts; the latter is an account of the gods and creation. The major works in Latin verse are Lucretius's *De Rerum Natura* (1st c. BC) and Virgil's *Georgics* (1st c. BC). Lucretius expounded the Epicurean system and Virgil expatiated on husbandry and moral principles.

The Middle Ages produced the bulk of the didactic literature in Europe and most of it was in verse. Proverbs, charms, gnomic verses (*qq.v.*), guides to the good life, and manuals of holy living were abundant. In English literature the 12th c. *Poema Morale* and the 13th c. *Ormulum* and *Proverbs of Alfred* were essentially didactic. In *Handlyng Synne* (1303), Robert Mannyng of Brunne (Bourne in Lincolnshire) told stories to illustrate the ten commandments, the seven deadly sins, and the seven sacraments. Gower's *Confessio Amantis* (1388) contained a good deal of instruction.

Consciously didactic poetry had a revival in the 18th c. A number of poems, somewhat in the Virgilian tradition, combined pastoral life with ethics; but they cannot be taken very seriously today. Indeed, at times they appear naively comic. Notable examples are John Philips's *Cyder* (1708), Armstrong's *Art of Preserving Health* (1744) and Dyer's *Fleece* (1757). Near the end of the century came Erasmus Darwin's *Botanic Garden* (1789, 1791), which was in heroic couplets in the style of Pope. Part I dealt with the 'Economy of Vegetation', Part II with 'The Loves of the Plants'.

It has been argued that all poetry is, by implication, didactic; that it should and does instruct as well as delight. Horace's *Ars Poetica*, Boileau's *Art Poétique*, in imitation of Horace, and Pope's *Essay on Criticism* were intended to instruct poets in their craft. *See also* ALLEGORY; COURTESY BOOK; EXEM-PLUM; PROPAGANDA.

diegesis A narrative (as opposed to a *mimetic* (*q.v.*)) account. In drama and in film diegesis can take the form of voice-over, choric intervention, and on-stage description of mimetic action. Similarly, music or sound-effects not emanating from the mimetic action but superimposed on it: sonnets and songs performed by characters in Shakespeare are mimetic; atmospheric background music is diegetic. *See* MIMESIS.

différance A word coined by the French philosopher Jacques Derrida which he uses in opposition to logocentrism (*q.v.*). It is intentionally ambiguous (and virtually untranslatable) and derives from the French *différer*, meaning 'to defer, postpone, delay' and also 'to differ, be different from'. Derrida uses *différance* as a way of pushing Saussure's theory of language to its 'logical' conclusion (it was Saussure who posited that 'signs' in language are arbitrary and differential), and argues that to differ or differentiate is also to defer, postpone or withhold. The word itself illustrates Derrida's point that writing does not copy speech; the distinction between the two different forms *différance* and *différence* does not correspond to any distinction in their spoken form. In his view the process of deferring applies to the written and spoken word: deferral/*différance*. Thus, meaning is continuously and (in theory) endlessly deferred since each word leads us on to yet another word in the system of signification. Derrida sees a text as an endless sequence of signifiers (*q.v.*) which can have no ultimate or determinate meaning.

Two key passages in Derrida's discourse on '*Différance*' may help to clarify:

> The verb 'to differ' [différer] seems to differ from itself. On the one hand it indicates difference as distinction, inequality, or discernibility; on the other, it expresses the interposition of delay, the interval of a *spacing* and *temporalizing* that puts off until 'later' what is presently denied, the possible that is presently impossible. Sometimes the *different* and sometimes the *deferred* correspond [in French] to the verb 'to differ'.

Later in the same essay he writes:

> What we note as *différance* will thus be the movement of play that 'produces' (and not by something that is simply an activity) these differences, these effects of difference. This does not mean that the *différance* which produces differences is before them in a simple and in itself unmodified and indifferent present. *Différance* is the nonfull, nonsimple 'origin'; it is the structured and differing origin of differences.

(Cf. *Bulletin de la Société française de philosophie*, LXII, No. 3, July–Sept. 1968; reprinted in *Speech and Phenomena and Other Essays on Husserl's Theory of Signs*, trans. by D. B. Allison, 1973). *See also* APORIA; DECONSTRUCTION.

digest Either a publication which abridges books or articles (or both) which have already been published; or, the abridgement itself. *See* ABRIDGED EDITION; BOWDLERIZE.

digital humanities A broad multidisciplinary (*q.v.*) field dedicated to understanding the intersection between information technology and the traditional humanities. Areas covered include the digitization of texts and the use of computers as tools for linguistic and textual analysis, although its potential scope is considered more far-reaching by its practitioners. The growing importance of the digital humanities is reflected in the number of conferences and journals devoted to the subject as well as dedicated university centres and programmes. An important theorization of this developing field was made by Lev Manovich in *The Language of New Media* (2001).

digression   Material not strictly relevant to the main theme or plot of a work. Sterne proved himself an incorrigible digressionist in *Tristram Shandy*.

di-iamb   A metrical foot which consists of two iambs (*q.v.*): ∪ / ∪ /. It is taken as one unit.

dilogy   An expression of statement with a double meaning, like *double entente* (*q.v.*). *See* AMBIGUITY; AMPHIBOLY.

dime novel   A cheap form of melodramatic and exciting fiction, so called because it cost a dime. Most of the stories are concerned with romance, historical episodes, warfare and violent action. Many of them were set in America, during the Civil War, Revolution and frontier periods. There was a great vogue for them from 1860 to *c.* 1895, beginning with the publication of Ann Sophia Stephens's *Malaeska: The Indian Wife of the White Hunter*. They were superseded by pulp (*q.v.*) magazines and series about Tom Swift, Frank Merriwell and the Rover Boys. Such stories celebrated the robustness and individualism of Americans. Among the more famous authors were E. Z. C. Judson, Prentiss Ingraham, Edward L. Wheeler (the creator of 'Deadwood Dick') and J. R. Coryell (the creator of 'Nick Carter'). The dime novel was akin to the shilling shocker and the penny dreadful (*q.v.*). *See* BLUE BOOK; THRILLER; WESTERN.

dimeter   A line of verse containing two feet. The third and fourth lines of the limerick (*q.v.*) are dimeters.

diminishing metaphor   A figure of speech in which there is a kind of discrepancy or conjunctive discord between tenor and vehicle (*q.v.*). It occurs when a thought and the image which embodies it are brought together in such a way that they are not wholly congruous. The result is often witty, arresting and intellectually stimulating. Such metaphor is common in metaphysical poetry (*q.v.*) and a good deal of modern poetry. A famous example begins T. S. Eliot's *The Love Song of J. Alfred Prufrock*:

> Let us go then, you and I
> When the evening is spread out against the sky
> Like a patient etherised upon a table;

See DISCORDIA CONCORS; DISSOCIATION OF SENSIBILITY; METAPHOR; OBJECTIVE CORRELATIVE.

Dinggedicht   (G 'thing poem') A form of poetry which attempts to describe objects from within rather than externally. Notable examples are to be found in Rilke's *Neue Gedichte* (1907). *See* IMAGISTS.

dinumeratio   *See* EUTREPISMUS.

Dionysian   *See* APOLLONIAN/DIONYSIAN.

dipody   A pair of any metrical feet which are taken as a single unit. It also denotes verse constructed rhythmically so that in scansion (*q.v.*) pairs of feet must be considered together. It is common in children's rhymes, nursery rhymes (*q.v.*) and ballads (*q.v.*). Occasional in other verses. For example, in John Masefield's *Cargoes*:

> Quinquireme of Nineveh || from distant Ophir
> Rowing home to haven || in sunny Palestine

Here the sound of the rhythm requires grouping of feet in each half line. The same effect occurs in Chesterton's *Lepanto*:

> The cold queen of England || is looking in the glass.
> The shadow of the Valois || is yawning at the Mass.

See FOOT.

dirge   A song of lament, usually of a lyrical mood. The name derives from the beginning of the antiphon of the Office of the Dead: *Dirige, Domine . . .* 'Direct, O Lord . . .' As a literary genre it comes from the Greek *epicedium* (*q.v.*), which was a mourning song sung over the dead and a threnody (*q.v.*) sung in memory of the dead. In Roman funeral processions the *nenia*, a song of praise for the departed, was chanted; and the professional wailing women (*praeficae*) were hired for the task on some occasions. Later the dirge developed into a lyric poem, as in Sir Philip Sidney's poem included in *Arcadia* (1590), which begins, 'Ring out your bells, let mourning shews be spread', and Henry King's *Exequy* on his young wife, 'Tell me no more how fair she is.' Both are very fine poems.

   Occasionally dirges occur in plays. There are two particularly famous ones by Shakespeare: Ariel's song for Ferdinand's dead father in *The Tempest* (I, ii), and Fidele's dirge in *Cymbeline* (IV, ii). Very nearly as famous as these is Cornelia's song over Marcello in Webster's *The White Devil* (V, iv). *See* COMPLAINT; ELEGY; LAMENT; LYRIC; MONODY; SONG; UBI SUNT.

disability studies   An interdisciplinary field developed in the 1990s and focusing on the representation of disabled persons and the concept of disability in the humanities (*q.v.*), sciences and social sciences. Central areas of focus include the study of disability as a physical or functional impairment; examination of the environmental causes of disability; and enquiry into the social, political and historical constructions of difference that affect the relationship between able-bodied and disabled individuals and communities. An important project of this discourse (*q.v.*) has been to destigmatize disability (and even to promote disability activism) as well as to offer disabled persons theoretical frameworks for self-representation across a multidisciplinary landscape. Major voices in this emerging field include Lennard Davis, Tobin Siebers and Sharon Snyder.

discordia concors A phrase used by Johnson in his *Life of Cowley* when referring to metaphysical poetry (*q.v.*). The relevant passage is: 'Wit, abstracted from its effects upon the hearer, may be more rigorously and philosophically considered as a kind of *discordia concors*, a combination of dissimilar images or discovery of occult resemblances in things apparently unlike. Of wit thus defined they [Donne and the other Metaphysicals] have more than enough.' (It is an inversion of Horace's *concordia discors* 'harmony in discord.') *See* DIMINISHING METAPHOR.

discourse Usually a learned discussion, spoken or written, on a philosophical, political, literary or religious topic. It is closely related to a treatise and a dissertation (*qq.v.*). In fact, the three terms are very nearly synonymous. A famous example is Descartes's *Discourse on Method* (1637).

In linguistics 'discourse' denotes a 'stretch of language' larger than a sentence. Basically, it is language which is understood as utterance and thus involves subjects who speak and write – which presupposes listeners and readers who, in a sense, are 'objects'. Discourse has an object and is directed to or at an object. Thus, in theory at any rate, discourse might include any modes of utterance as a part of social practice. They are differentiated by their intention. Thus, discourse may be poetry or prose. It may be a poem, a philosophical essay, a political tract, a biblical commentary, a speech on the hustings, a funeral address, a polemic, a dialogue or an exercise in deconstructive criticism.

Latterly, the term has acquired much wider meanings and implications. It can refer to the specific type of language and the set of problematics that define and delimit a given field, as in 'philosophical discourse' or 'medical discourse'. In Mikhail Bakhtin's work, 'discourse' may denote utterance, a word, or language 'in its concrete and living totality', and is intrinsically dialogic (*q.v.*), that is, always in interaction with discourses of others. For Jacques Lacan, the unconscious is a form of discourse. Foucault and Marxist thinkers have used the term 'discursive formation' to describe systems of thought and practice marked by certain epistemic assumptions and ideological implications. Indeed, the term can harbour an intrinsic ideological orientation, as in 'republican discourse' or 'liberal discourse'. Many recent thinkers, including Foucault, Lacan and Judith Butler, have investigated the role of particular kinds of discourse in the operations of power and in the construction of subjectivity and the social world. *See also* POWER/KNOWLEDGE.

discovery In a literary work the revelation of facts hitherto unknown to one of the principal characters. It often comes at the time of the dénouement (*q.v.*) or climax (*q.v.*). There are two good examples in *The Winter's Tale*: first, when Leontes discovers the identity of Perdita; second, when Polixenes realizes that Perdita is Leontes's daughter.

disemic (Gk 'of two time-units') A term applied in Classical prosody when a long syllable was regarded as two short ones. *See* MORA.

disinterestedness A concept that is associated with a number of writers, especially Henry James (1843–1916) and Matthew Arnold (1822–88). Henry James's literary critical views were influenced by Goethe, Matthew Arnold and Saint-Beuve. From these writers he acquired the idea of critical 'disinterestedness', which he saw as effecting a mediation between history and philosophy (his brother was the pragmatist philosopher William James), since criticism deals with both ideas and facts. James's own influence spanned both sides of the Atlantic, extending to figures such as Ezra Pound and T. S. Eliot.

Matthew Arnold strongly advocated the concept of critical 'disinterestedness', by which he meant 'keeping aloof' from 'the practical view of things', by allowing criticism to follow 'the law of its own nature, which is to be a free play of the mind on all subjects which it touches; by steadily refusing to lend itself to any of those ulterior, political, practical considerations about ideas'. Criticism must attempt to know 'the best that is known and thought in the world, and by in turn making this known, to create a current of true and fresh ideas . . . but its business is to do no more'. Criticism must be entirely independent of all interests. The purpose of criticism is to lead man 'towards perfection, by making his mind dwell upon what is excellent in itself, and the absolute beauty and fitness of things'. Criticism should embrace 'the Indian virtue of detachment', the Hindu ideal of ascetic renunciation of all worldly concerns. The task of both criticism and culture, for Arnold, is to place the pragmatic bourgeois philistine vision of life in a broader historical and international context.

dispersed rhyme *See* RHYME.

dispondee Two spondees (*q.v.*) combined into a single unit. It is rare, and a series of spondees is extremely rare.

dissemination The verb *to disseminate* means 'to sow or scatter abroad', 'to propagate', 'to diffuse'; hence the idea of scattering, spreading and impregnating; especially the spreading of seed (L *semen*, 'seed'). 'Dissemination' basically suggests that 'plurisignification', or a multiplicity of meanings, is not something that is under control as it is in the New Criticism (*q.v.*), where the fact that a text can be interpreted in more than one way is treated as a dimension of its inherent and organic 'greatness'. 'Dissemination' has a deliberately sexual and procreative connotation. It suggests a textual 'free play' which is both joyous, unstable and 'excessive' – close, in fact, to the Nietzschean idea of the Dionysian in art, which Jacques Derrida, the French philosopher, is clearly influenced by. Derrida uses 'dissemination' in a special sense with regard to language. By it he refers to the 'spilling' or 'diffusion' of meaning: the 'surplus' or excess of meaning which is inherent in the use of all language. Homi Bhabha's essay *DissemiNation: Time, Narrative and the Margins of the Modern Nation* (1990) argues that nations and cultures are narrative constructions, embodying dissemination in the Derridean sense. *See also* CONNOTATION; DENOTATION; TRACE.

dissertation   Like a discourse (*q.v.*) a dissertation is usually a substantial and erudite disquisition, now particularly written to fulfil an academic assessment. Sir Thomas Browne's *Vulgar Errors* (1646) and Burke's *Thoughts on the Present Discontent* (1770) are early examples falling within the broader definition. Occasionally such work may be droll, as Lamb's *Dissertation upon Roast Pig* in *Essays of Elia* (1823). *See* TREATISE.

dissident writers   Those who do not conform to the political and cultural ideology of their country and who seek to criticize the governing regime and dominant social formation through their writing. Very many have been harassed, censored, imprisoned, exiled or murdered for their views. During the Cold War period the term was closely associated with the insurgent writings of Soviet bloc authors, such as the Russians Boris Pasternak, Anna Akhmatova and Alexander Solzhenitsyn, the Czechs Václav Havel and Milan Kundera, and the Bulgarian Georgi Markov. This association, however, tends to obscure the fact that the capitalist West has produced many powerful dissident voices, such as the Italian poet and filmmaker Pier Paolo Pasolini and the American linguist Noam Chomsky. Since the end of the Cold War, dissident writers from other parts of the world have come to be 'celebrated', notably the Nigerian Wole Soyinka. Following the fall of its Cold War enemy, the West has become increasingly attentive to the situation, if not always the work, of dissident writers from China (most of all Liu Xiaobo, winner of the 2010 Nobel Prize for Literature), the Indian subcontinent and the Middle East.

dissociation of ideas   In 1901 Remy de Gourmont published *La Culture des idées*, which contained an essay called *Dissociation des idées* in which he put forward the point of view that it was necessary to avoid the unquestioning acceptance of ideas and associations of ideas which have become everyday commonplaces.

dissociation of sensibility   The phrase was used by T. S. Eliot in his essay *The Metaphysical Poets* (1921) to signify the separation of thought and feeling which he identified as an endemic weakness in English poetry from Milton onwards. Eliot identified Donne as the exemplar of the sensible poet for whom thought and feeling were one:

> A thought to Donne was an experience; it modified his sensibility. When a poet's mind is perfectly equipped for its work, it is constantly amalgamating disparate experience; the ordinary man's experience is chaotic, irregular, fragmentary. The latter falls in love, or reads Spinoza, and these two experiences have nothing to do with each other, or with the noise of the typewriter or the smell of cooking; in the mind of the poet these experiences are always forming new wholes.

In the poetry following the English Revolution, Eliot perceived a 'dissociation of sensibility . . . from which we have never recovered'. Eliot contended that modern poets like Corbière and Laforgue had avoided such a 'dissociation of sensibility'. Certainly they had a considerable influence on Eliot, and the combined effect of the influence of Hopkins, Yeats, Pound and Eliot has been potent. *See* ASSOCIATION; SENSIBILITY.

dissonance   The arrangement of cacophonous sounds in words, or rhythmical patterns, for a particular effect. A very common device in much poetry. The following stanzas from Browning's *Childe Roland to the Dark Tower Came* illustrate the possibilities of dissonance:

> If there pushed any ragged thistle-stalk
>> Above its mates, the head was chopped; the bents
>> Were jealous else. What made those holes and rents
> In the dock's harsh swarth leaves, bruised as to baulk
> All hope of greenness? 'tis a brute must walk
>> Pashing their life out, with a brute's intents.
>
> As for the grass, it grew as scant as hair
>> In leprosy; thin dry blades pricked the mud
>> Which underneath looked kneaded up with blood.
> One stiff blind horse, his every bone a-stare,
> Stood stupefied, however he came there:
>> Thrust out past service from the devil's stud!

A more subtle effect, using the same means, is achieved by Crabbe in these lines from *Peter Grimes*:

> Here dull and hopeless he'd lie down and trace
> How sidelong crabs had scrawl'd their crooked race,
> Or sadly listen to the tuneless cry
> Of fishing gull or clanging golden-eye;
> What time the sea-birds to the marsh would come,
> And the loud bittern, from the bull-rush home,
> Gave from the salt-ditch side the bellowing boom:

Particularly good examples can also be found in the work of more modern poets like John Berryman and Robert Lowell. *See* ASSONANCE; CACOPHONY; CONSONANCE.

distant reading   Coined by the Italian literary scholar Franco Moretti, the term refers to a method of understanding and interpreting literature through the aggregation and analysis of large quantities of data (rather than through the study of individual texts). In contrast with the practice of close reading, distant reading views literature as 'a collective system' and aims to uncover the broader scope of this system by using computer technologies that are able to map similarities and trace resonances between texts at a speed and magnitude beyond unaided human capability. The practice of distant reading is uniquely demonstrated by the Stanford Literary Lab, which Moretti founded in 2010. The research conducted by the Lab is characteristically digital, quantitative and collaborative.

distich (Gk 'two rows') A pair of metrical lines of different lengths, usually rhymed and expressing a complete idea. Commonly used in Classical elegiacs (*q.v.*). Often it consisted of a dactylic hexameter (*q.v.*) followed by a dactylic pentameter (*q.v.*).

distributed stress *See* HOVERING STRESS.

dit (F 'something said') A rather vague term used of some types of medieval didactic poetry (*q.v.*), related to the *débat*, the *fabliau*, *conte* and *lai* (*qq.v.*). *See also* EXEMPLUM.

dithyramb Originally a Greek choric hymn, with mime (*q.v.*) describing the adventures of Dionysius. It may have been introduced into Greece early in the 7th c. BC, and thereafter, for at least three hundred years, it underwent various developments. In modern literature dithyrambs are very rare. Dryden, in *Alexander's Feast*, is one of the few poets to have used the form successfully. The opening stanza gives an indication of the shape and mood:

> 'Twas at the Royal Feast, for Persia won,
>> By Philip's warlike son:
>> Aloft in awful State
>> The God-like Heroe sate
>> On his Imperial Throne;
> His valient Pèers were plac'd around;
> Their Brows with Roses and with Myrtyles bound.
>> (So should Desert in Arms be Crown'd:)
> The lovely Thais by his side
> Sate like a blooming Eastern Bride
> In Flow'r of Youth and Beauty's Pride,
>> Happy, happy, happy Pair!
>>> None but the Brave,
>>> None but the Brave,
> None but the Brave deserves the Fair.

Dithyrambic is an adjective which may be applied to any form of rather 'wild' song or chant.

ditrochee Also dichoree. Two trochees (*q.v.*) / ∪ / ∪ taken as one metrical unit. Also called trochaic monometer (*q.v.*).

ditty A composition to be sung; perhaps a *lai* (*q.v.*) or any short song, even a ballad (*q.v.*). It can denote many kinds of composition in verse. It may also refer to the words of a song, its theme or burden (*qq.v.*). *See* ROUNDELAY; SONG.

divan (P *dēvān*, 'brochure, account, custom-house') An oriental council of state or council chamber; also the long seat against the wall of a room. But *also* a collection of poems. It has a large number of other meanings. *See also* GHAZAL.

diverbium   The spoken dialogue in Roman drama, as distinguished from the *canticum* (*q.v.*) – the sung part.

divertissement   (F 'entertainment, amusement, recreation') A French term for a ballet given as a kind of interlude between longer pieces. In effect, the *comédie-ballet* (*q.v.*) developed by Molière. More generally the term is used to describe a literary trifle, something slight and gay.

divisional pause   *See* CAESURA.

dizain   A French poem or stanza of ten octosyllabic or decasyllabic lines, such as Maurice Scève's poem *Délie* (1544) which contains 449 connected *dizains*. In some cases three or five *dizains* combined with an *envoi* (*q.v.*) formed a *ballade* (*q.v.*) or *chant royal* (*q.v.*).

dochmiac   (Gk 'slanted') In Classical prosody a metrical foot of two unstressed syllables and three stressed, normally occurring thus: ∪ // ∪ /. Dochmiacs were confined to Greek tragedy and were used for the very emotional passages. It has been argued that some five-syllable English words like 'originally' are dochmiacs.

document   Something written that provides information or evidence in the shape of a record: yearbooks, annals, gazettes, registers, diaries (*qq.v.*) and so forth; also state papers, wills, certificates, archives, files and dossiers. *See also* DOCUMENTARY NOVEL; NON-FICTION NOVEL/DOCUMENTARY FICTION.

documentary theatre   A form of drama, related to epic theatre (*q.v.*), which may take an overtly political stance, and is characterized by use of relatively recent history and documentary evidence of the kind provided by newspapers, reports, archives, official histories, diaries and journals. Exemplifications in the 20th c. are Hochhuth's *The Representative* (1966), which examined the role of the Pope and the Papacy in the Second World War, and his *Soldiers* (1967), which investigated part of Sir Winston Churchill's career during the same period; Kipphardt's *In the Matter of J. Robert Oppenheimer* (1968), which investigated the USA's atomic energy commission; Peter Brook's *US* (1969); and Ben Hecht and Charles MacArthur's *Front Page* (1928), a tough comedy drama about newspaper life. More recent instances which might be thought of as quasi-documentary dramas are David Hare's 2004 play *Stuff Happens*, narrating the lead-up to the Iraq War, a self-styled 'history play', and Peter Morgan's *Frost/Nixon* (2006), which fictionalized contemporary footage and documentary records of the Watergate scandal. *See* NON-FICTION NOVEL/DOCUMENTARY FICTION; LIVING NEWSPAPER.

doggerel   Probably from *dog*, with contemptuous suggestion as in *dog-Latin*. After Chaucer has broken off his burlesque (*q.v.*) *Tale of Sir Thopas* the Host makes a remark about 'rym dogerel'. This seems to be the earliest reference to doggerel, a term which originally applied to verse of a loose and irregular measure, as in Skelton's *Colyn Cloute* (1519) and Butler's *Hudibras* (1663–78). Now it has come to describe rough, badly made verse, monotonous in rhythm and clumsy in rhyme, usually on a trivial subject. *See* HUDIBRASTIC VERSE; JINGLE; MACARONIC; NONSENSE; TUMBLING VERSE.

dog-Latin Mongrel Latin. Rough, impure, cross-bred, unidiomatic Latin. *See also* DOGGEREL.

dogma A dogma is a tenet, doctrine, law or principle. Something laid down as being so. Dogmatism in criticism is as emphatic. The dogmatic critic ascribes to himself a kind of *ex cathedra* authority.

dolce stil nuovo (It 'sweet new style') The style of Italian lyric poetry in the second half of the 13th c. The term was first used by Dante, in the *Purgatorio*, of his own literary style; but, more importantly, it represented an attitude towards women and earthly love which derived from the troubadour (*q.v.*) tradition. Woman, represented as the embodiment of God's beauty, was believed to inspire gentle love which should lead the lover to Divine love. The *stilnuovisti* poets (other notable ones were Guinicelli and Cavalcanti) attempted to reconcile or, in a sense, combine sacred and profane love. *See* COURTLY LOVE.

domestic comedy A counterpart to domestic tragedy (*q.v.*), it is a form of drama about, predominantly, upper-middle- or middle-class life and characters. It has been particularly fashionable since late in the 19th c., and, as the words suggest, is often concerned with family situations and problems. An early example is Massinger's *A New Way to Pay Old Debts* (*c.* 1621). Goldsmith's *She Stoops to Conquer* (1773) might also be taken as an instance. In the 19th c. a most talented playwright in this form was T. W. Robertson whose best works are *Ours* (1866), *Caste* (1867), *Play* (1868) and *School* (1869). Harold Brighouse's *Hobson's Choice* (1915) is another excellent play in the genre. Several plays by Somerset Maugham in the 1920s were highly successful domestic comedies; particularly *Our Betters*, *Home and Beauty*, *The Constant Wife* and *The Breadwinner*. Domestic comedy continued to fill the theatres in the 1930s and during the postwar period. Other notable dramatists in the genre are Noël Coward, Tennessee Williams, Jean Anouilh, N. C. Hunter, Terence Rattigan, Alan Ayckbourn and Bill Naughton. *See* BOULEVARD DRAMA; COMEDY; DRAWING-ROOM COMEDY; NATURALISTIC DRAMA.

domestic tragedy A play about middle- or lower-middle-class life which concentrates on the more personal and domestic element of tragedy (*q.v.*), as opposed to tragedy in the grand manner which involves kings, princes and enterprises 'of great pitch and moment'. There are a number of examples in Tudor and Jacobean drama. For instance: the anonymous *Arden of Faversham* (1592); the anonymous *A Warning for Fair Women* (1599); Thomas Heywood's *A Woman Killed with Kindness* (1603); the anonymous *A Yorkshire Tragedy* (1608); and Middleton and Rowley's *The Changeling* (1623). There was some domestic tragedy in the 18th c. like Lillo's *The London Merchant* (1731). Hebbel's *Maria Magdalena* (1844) is also taken to be in this genre. The term might also be judiciously applied to some of the work of

Ibsen, Strindberg, Eugene O'Neill, Tennessee Williams and Arthur Miller. *See also* DOMESTIC COMEDY; DRAME.

dominant, the A concept of some importance in the literary theory of formalism developed in the Prague School (*q.v.*) of linguistics and thus of later provenance than Russian Formalism (*q.v.*). Roman Jakobson defined it (in 1935) as 'the focusing component of a work of art: it rules, determines, and transforms the remaining components'. The dominant gives a work its *Gestalt* (*q.v.*), its organic unity; thus bringing about the unified whole of a work.

The concept of 'the dominant' can be seen to emerge as a development and response within the Prague School to Shklovsky's earlier definition of 'defamiliarization' (*q.v.*) in *Art as Technique*. Whereas Shklovsky has suggested that form or technique was in itself a defamiliarizing agent, later Formalists, including Yuri Tynyanov writing in the 1920s, stressed that the defamiliarizing effect of a device depended on its function in the work in which it appeared. Thus a work may include some automatized elements which are subordinate to the defamiliarizing or foregrounded elements. This foregrounding (*q.v.*) of a group of elements comes to be seen later by Jakobson as 'the dominant'. The dominant emphasizes the distinction between those formal elements which function to defamiliarize and those which function passively. This view of the literary text as inherently dynamic and dialectical is developed in the work of the Prague School; to acknowledge that a device which was once defamiliarizing can become automatized is to recognize one aspect of the momentum in literary history. Both Russian Formalism and the Prague Linguistic Circle refine their theories through acknowledging the fact of literary history.

dominant/emergent/residual The tripartite schema, which gives accounts of the relationships between culture (*q.v.*) and power, was devised by Marxist literary critic Raymond Williams, a foundational figure in both cultural studies and cultural materialism (*qq.v.*). Williams's model, which he discusses in detail in his *Marxism and Literature* (1977), represents a move away from the strictly epochal approach of Hegel and Marx, for whom each historical period was characterized by a distinct 'spirit' or form of society. For Marx, culture was inherently ideological, since it sustained the mode of organization which produced it by promoting the interests of the ruling class. Thus, under capitalism, art and literature inevitably articulate bourgeois (*q.v.*) values. Williams argues that such a model fails to render adequately the complexity of the relationship between culture, economics and power. Also, Marx's approach precludes the possibility that art and culture might provide resources for resisting the ruling class.

Williams's model captures how several, often conflicting, cultural concepts and practices may be available at any given historical moment. Usually one set, the 'dominant', is embedded across most of society. Typically, the dominant expresses the perspectives and interests of the establishment. Other beliefs and practices, though, may relate to earlier modes of organization; these Williams calls 'residual'. They may well still hold some currency – as aristocratic values have often done in industrial capitalist society – in which case the ruling class will attempt to co-opt them. Behaviour and ideas which correspond to new forms of social interaction are termed 'emergent' by Williams; these are often in conflict with the dominant, though they may ultimately become established as a new dominant formation. Cultural materialists have since expanded Williams's principal focus on class to consider also how gender, race and sexuality are similarly characterized by multiple, competing and shifting conceptualizations *See also* HEGEMONY; IDEOLOGY; MARXIST CRITICISM; STRUCTURE OF FEELING.

donnée A French word which signifies something 'given' in the sense that it is an idea or notion implanted in the mind or imagination: the seed, so to speak, of a creative work; what Henry James called 'the speck'. It may be a phrase, a conversation, the expression on a person's face, a tune, indeed almost any kind of experience which starts a series of thoughts and ideas in the writer's mind. What species of creative magic brings such an event about is not really known. *See* AFFLATUS; FANCY AND IMAGINATION; INSPIRATION; LIGNE DONNÉE; MUSE; SPONTANEITY.

Doric Doris is a region of Greece, south of Thessaly. Doric denotes the rustic and unsophisticated as opposed to the Attic – the urban and urbane. Milton's lines in *Lycidas*:

> He [the uncouth swain] touch'd the tender stops of various quills,
> With eager thought warbling his Doric lay.

suggest the pastoral (*q.v.*) connotations of the word.

double dactyl A metrical form comprising two dactyls: / ∪ ∪ / ∪ ∪. A fixed form in light verse in which there are two stanzas of four double dactyl lines. The rules, such as they are, require the last lines of each stanza to rhyme and the last lines to be truncated. The first line should be a jingle, the second line a name, and one line in the second stanza should consist of one word, as in this trifle by J. A. Cuddon:

> Higgledy-piggledy
> Nicholas Williamson
> Sat in the bathtub and
> Scratched at his nose.
>
> Seldom was schoolboy so
> Anthropocentrically
> Gifted with flexible
> Bendable toes.

See JINGLE; NONSENSE.

double-decker novel A term which came into use in the 19th c. to describe novels which were published in two parts or volumes. Novels of the period tended to be long and many of them were published in serial form first. A three-decker novel came out in three volumes. *See* NOVEL.

double entente, un mot à A French term signifying an ambiguity (*q.v.*). A word or expression so used that it can have two meanings; one of which is usually frivolous or bawdy. There are a large number of *doubles ententes* in Wycherley's *The Country Wife* involving the word 'china'. It is commoner now to use the phrase *double entendre*. *See* IRONY; PUN.

double rhyme *See* FEMININE RHYME.

drab A term first used by C. S. Lewis in a restricted sense in his introduction to *English Literature in the Sixteenth Century* (1954) to describe the poetry and prose of the later medieval period up to the early Renaissance (*q.v.*). He was distinguishing it from a 'golden' period style (*c.* 1580–1603). It is generally agreed that much that was written in the 15th c. and the early Tudor period was drab. But the period also includes John Skelton (1460?–1529) and Sir Thomas Wyatt (1503–42), who were far from drab.

drama In general any work meant to be performed on a stage by actors. A more particular meaning is a serious play; not necessarily tragedy. Diderot and Beaumarchais were responsible for this restricted usage. *See* COMÉDIE; COMEDY; DRAME; TRAGEDY.

drama of ideas *See* COMEDY OF IDEAS; THESIS PLAY.

drama of sensibility *See* SENTIMENTAL COMEDY.

dramatic irony When the audience understand the implication and meaning of a situation on stage, or what is being said, but the characters do not. Common in tragedy and comedy (*qq.v.*). Oedipus does not realize his crime. Sir Peter Teazle (in *School for Scandal*, IV, iii) does not know his wife is behind the screen when he is talking about her to Joseph Surface.

Another kind of dramatic irony occurs when a character's words 'recoil' upon him. For instance, Macbeth's 'bloody instructions' which 'return / To plague th' inventor'. In the event he is the one thus plagued. *See* IRONY.

dramatic lyric *See* DRAMATIC MONOLOGUE.

dramatic monologue A poem in which there is one imaginary speaker addressing an imaginary audience. In most dramatic monologues, some attempt is made to imitate natural speech. In a successful example of the genre, the persona (*q.v.*) will not be confused with the poet.

In its most fully developed form, the dramatic monologue is a Victorian (*q.v.*) genre, effectively created by Tennyson and Browning, yet the idea of a lyric in the voice of an imagined persona seems to be very ancient. The idylls (*q.v.*) of Theocritus, for instance, written in the 3rd c. BC and acknowledged by Tennyson as a primary source, are dramatic in form and include long speeches; these tend to be self-revelatory and are conversational in idiom. Ovid's *Heroides* (1st c. BC) is a collection of letters or speeches ascribed to various figures from myth and literature. Very often these figures are female characters who look at the actions of their heroic men from an emotional or domestic viewpoint: they are therefore among the first works of literature to focus on interiority at the expense of action. Such poems, especially Ovid's, were influential throughout Europe during the Middle Ages and the Renaissance. The influence is to be noted in the tradition of the complaint (*q.v.*); many complaints, though written by men, purport to be spoken by women.

With the advent of romanticism (*q.v.*), the dramatic potential of lyric utterance takes on a new importance. Several of the Romantic poets draw on the use of monologue and dialogue in the traditional ballad (*q.v.*). Perhaps more significant in the history of dramatic monologue, though, is the use of the dramatic in personal poems, in particular such 'conversation pieces' (*q.v.*) as Coleridge's *Frost at Midnight* and Wordsworth's *Tintern Abbey*. In these poems one is conscious of the following characteristics of the full-blown dramatic monologue: a distinctive manner of speech; the presence of a silent interlocutor; and the poet's changing responses to the very immediate circumstances in which, and of which, he is writing.

It is the role of the interlocutor, more than anything else, that gives the Victorian monologue its innovatory distinctiveness, though this is less true of Tennyson than of Browning. With a few exceptions – *The Holy Grail* being the most important – Tennyson represents the speaker addressing a not very closely defined audience. By contrast, Browning's silent interlocutor is always a specific personage, whose role and reactions are inferred from the speaker's words. The outstanding example of Browning's is *My Last Duchess*, in which an Italian Renaissance duke, addressing the envoy of a prospective father-in-law, appears to confess to the murder of the wife he is hoping to replace. This sort of self-revelation is the hallmark of the Browning monologue. In certain other poems of Browning's, the speaker is not himself the object of interest, but either addresses in imagination the character who is, or describes the character to an unnamed person. Browning's poems *A Toccata of Galuppi's* and *How It Strikes a Contemporary* are examples of the former and latter respectively.

Many other Victorian and early 20th c. poets contributed to the genre in its Browningesque or Tennysonian modes. The subsequent history of the genre, however, emerges by way of the French Symbolist poets (*see* SYMBOL AND SYMBOLISM), many of whom transform the dramatic monologue into what Valéry Laubaud was to call the interior monologue (*q.v.*). These interior reveries are the source for many important modernist (*q.v.*) poems, such as T. S. Eliot's *The Love Song of J. Alfred Prufrock* and *Gerontion*. Today the dramatic monologue is accepted as one of the fundamental poetic genres, so much so that its existence is barely noticed. However, few poets attempt the sort of dramatic illusion associated with Browning. Most modern dramatic monologues are indistinguishable from interior monologues. It is not uncommon for poets to create personae distinct from, and yet connected with, themselves; this is especially true of Philip Larkin's poems (e.g. *Mr Bleaney* and *Dockery and Son*). *See also* MONODRAMA; MONOLOGUE; STREAM OF CONSCIOUSNESS.

dramatic proverb *See* PROVERBE DRAMATIQUE.

dramatic romance *See* DRAMATIC MONOLOGUE.

dramatis personae The characters in a play. Usually the names of these characters are printed at the beginning of the text.

dramatization The act of making a play out of a story in another genre; from a chronicle, novel, short story (*qq.v.*) and so forth. In medieval drama the Bible was dramatized into the Mystery Plays (*q.v.*). In the Tudor period dramatists 'lifted' plots, stories and ideas from historians like Plutarch and Holinshed, and novelists like Lodge and Nashe. But it was not until the 18th c. that dramatization really began to flourish. Then novels provided the material. For example, Richardson's *Pamela*, dramatized by James Dance, was extremely popular. There followed dramatization of novels by Mrs Radcliffe, Walpole, Godwin, 'Monk' Lewis and Clara Reeve. In the 19th c. Dickens and Scott were the authors most used; so were Lord Lytton, Charlotte Brontë, Charles Reade, Wilkie Collins, and many more. The arrival of a group of original dramatists towards the end of the century saved the theatre from this deadening activity. But it is a practice by no means extinct, as television and recent theatrical history amply demonstrate.

dramaturgy (Gk *dramatourgia*, 'playwright'; *drama* + *ergon*, 'a work') The term denotes the principles of dramatic composition and theatrical art, and a dramaturge or dramaturgist is a playwright. In German a *Dramaturg* is a member of a theatrical company who selects the repertoire and may help in the arrangement and production of plays; a kind of literary adviser.

drame A term given in France to the kind of play which was neither tragedy nor comedy, but a serious play somewhere between the two. Diderot expatiated on this genre in the prefaces to his plays *Le Fils Naturel* (1757) and *Le Père de Famille* (1758). There were earlier examples by Voltaire, and by Nivelle de la Chaussée, who was the main dramatist of *comédie larmoyante* (*q.v.*). Diderot's theory was that such plays were serious dramas concerned with middle-class domestic problems. Their counterpart in England was domestic tragedy (*q.v.*). *See* DRAME ROMANTIQUE; METATHEATRE.

drame romantique A 19th c. French dramatic form, in prose and verse. Works in this genre tend to be melodramatic, emotionally torrid, and intricate in plot at the expense of characterization. Apart from Hugo's *Hernani* (1830) the most famous example is unquestionably Rostand's *Cyrano de Bergerac* (1897), which is a fine play by any standards and arguably the best of the *drames romantiques*. *See also* DRAME.

drápa (From ON *drepa*, 'to strike' [the chord of a musical instrument]) A complex form of skaldic heroic poem. The stanza was usually the *dróttkvætt* (*q.v.*) and there was a refrain (*q.v.*) of two or more half lines. Such a poem normally consisted of an introduction (*upphaf*), a middle section (the *stef* or *stefjamál*) and a conclusion (the *slæmr*).

drawing-room comedy A species of drama which had a considerable vogue in the early 20th c. Sometimes known disparagingly as 'French-window comedy', owing to the frequency with which the main set has such windows opening on to a garden or balcony, it is often concerned with the comic predicaments of the English middle classes and is therefore akin to domestic comedy (*q.v.*). Out of the scores of examples extant the following are well known: Shaw's *Candida* (1895); Coward's *Hay Fever* (1925); Terence Rattigan's *The Browning Version* (1948); N. C. Hunter's *The Waters of the Moon* (1951); Enid Bagnold's *The Chalk Garden* (1955). *See also* COMEDY OF MANNERS.

dream vision A form of literature extremely popular in the Middle Ages. By common convention the writer goes to sleep, in agreeable rural surroundings and often on a May morning. He then beholds either real people or personified abstractions involved in various activities. The commentary of Macrobius (*c.* AD 400) on Cicero's *Somnium Scipionis*, and the work itself, are generally agreed to have had a great influence on the genre. Very often the vision was expressed as an allegory (*q.v.*). Probably the best-known example of all is the *Roman de la Rose* (13th c.), which had a wide influence in this period and was translated, probably by Chaucer. Chaucer made use of the dream convention in *The Book of the Duchess* (1369), the *Parlement of Foules*, *The House of Fame* and the prologue to *The Legend of Good Women* (all believed to have been written between 1372 and 1386). However, Langland's vision of *Piers Plowman* (1366–99) is probably the best-known English vision poem, to be compared with the anonymous *The Pearl* (*c.* 1350–80), and many visions of heaven, hell and purgatory; and accounts of journeys there and back. These were almost a form of travel literature and have been taken by some to be the precursors of science fiction (*q.v.*). A common figure of these works is the guide: Virgil in Dante's *Divina Commedia*, an angel in the 12th c. *Vision of Tundale*. The angelic guide became a kind of convention in itself, splendidly parodied by Chaucer in the prologue to *The Summoner's Tale* when the vengeful Summoner gets his own back on the Friar.

The dream vision device has been used many times since and its evergreen popularity can be judged by the tens of thousands of compositions from schoolchildren who use it.

Three later examples are John Bunyan's *Pilgrim's Progress* (1678), Keats's *second* version of *Hyperion* (1818–19) and Lewis Carroll's *Alice's Adventures in Wonderland* (1865). James Joyce's *Finnegans Wake* has also been taken as a kind of cosmic dream.

droighneach An Irish syllabic verse form. A line may consist of nine to thirteen syllables and it always ends in a trisyllabic word. The rhyme is ababcdcd and so on. Cross-rhymes and alliteration occur in each couplet.

drolls Also known as droll-humours. They were brief farces and comic scenes adapted from plays or merely improvised and invented by actors, and traditionally presented in public houses or in taverns during the Commonwealth period (*q.v.*) when the theatres were shut and stage plays forbidden. Some of these entertainments were collected and published by Francis Kirkham in a work titled *The Wits, or Sport upon Sport* (1662, 1673).

dróttkvætt (ON *drótt*, 'The King's bodyguard' + *kvædi*, 'poem song') Also known as the *dróttkvæðr háttr*, this is the normal meter of the ON *drápa* (*q.v.*). It consists of eight-line stanzas, each line having three main stresses and internal rhyme. Each line has a regular trochaic ending. The commonest and most intricate of the skaldic poetic forms, it survives in contemporary Icelandic poetry; and, originally, was the noble meter, suitable for recitation before the *drótt*, the chosen body of warriors in the king's personal following. *See* KENNING; SKALD.

drowned-in-tears, school of the A derisive term applied to those early Romantic poets who were inclined to dwell on the sadder and more morbid aspects of life. *See* GRAVEYARD SCHOOL OF POETRY.

dualism *See* ANTINOMY.

duan A Gaelic term for a poem or a canto (*q.v.*).

dub poetry The term 'dub poetry' was originally coined by the Jamaican poet Oku Onuora in the 1970s to refer to the new forms of artistic expression emerging in Jamaica after Independence. This new art form soon spread to Britain, the Caribbean, Canada, South Africa and the US. A combination of elements – including reggae music, Rastafari and the Black Power movement – gave rise to dub poetry. The term 'dub' denotes 'a drumbeat', and when one reads a dub poem, as Onuora explains, one can 'distinctly hear the reggae rhythm coming out of the poem'. Christian Habekost writes in his book *Verbal Riddim: The Politics and Aesthetics of African-Caribbean Dub Poetry* (1993) that dub poetry is 'word, sound and power'. It fuses together the written and the spoken word, African oral traditions and musical styles such as reggae, calypso and other black rhythms. It may be performed live, presented as a text, or recorded as an album or a track. A well-known example is Linton Kwesi Johnson's critically acclaimed album *Dread Beat and Blood* (1975). Dub poetry reflected black diasporic struggles for equality; in Britain, it constituted a form of political resistance against the socio-economic conditions and racialized oppression in the 1970s and the 1980s. Besides Kwesi Johnson and Onuora, other notable poets who wrote dub poetry include Jamaicans Mutabaruka, Louise Bennett, Jean 'Binta' Breeze and Valerie Bloom, and the British poets Benjamin Zephaniah, Patience Agbabi and SuAndi.

dumb show A mimed dramatic performance whose purpose was to prepare the audience for the main action of the play to follow. The dumb show was popular in Tudor England and at first tended to be allegorical, using symbolic characters rather than those from the play. Elizabethan playwrights were quick to see its possibilities. Early and important examples may be found in

Gorboduc (1561), where it plays a considerable part throughout, and in Kyd's *The Spanish Tragedy* (III, xvi). Peele used it in *The Old Wives' Tale* (1595), and it also appears in the anonymous *A Warning for Fair Women* (1599). Perhaps the most famous instance occurs in *Hamlet* (III, ii), where the players wordlessly enact the murder of a king. In *Hamlet* it is strange that the precise action of the dumb show is repeated in words immediately afterwards. Conceivably, Shakespeare was using it in an archaic way since the fashion for introductory dumb shows was by then over (*c.* 1602).

In such plays as Peele's *Battle of Alcazar* (1594) and Greene's *Friar Bacon and Friar Bungay* (1594) the dumb show provided the dramatist with the means of including more action in his play (without using more dialogue) and of varying the action by showing the audience, as well as characters on stage, something that is happening elsewhere. There are good examples in the latter (II, iii; IV, iii): in the one in Act IV, two young men, with the aid of Bacon's magic glass, see how their fathers meet and kill each other. Closely parallel to this is Webster's use of the dumb show in *The White Devil* (II, ii). By contrast, in Middleton and Rowley's *The Changeling* (IV, i), the dumb show merely represents details necessary to the play's action which it would be tedious or dramatically difficult to present on stage in the normal way. During the Jacobean age (*q.v.*) the dumb show was increasingly used in the masque (*q.v.*).

From the 1630s the dumb show seems to have fallen into desuetude. Later, dumb show was to reappear in a different guise – in harlequinade and pantomime (*qq.v.*). It also had a function in melodrama (*q.v.*) in the 19th c. There is a dumb character in Thomas Holcroft's *A Tale of Mystery* (1802), and it became something of a standard device among writers of melodrama to use a mute to convey essential facts by dint of dumb show. Not a few 19th c. plays made use of dumb show in various ways (e.g. *The Dumb Boy*, 1821; *The Dumb Brigand*, 1832; *The Dumb Recruit*, 1840; *The Dumb Driver*, 1849; *The Dumb Sailor*, 1854). The use of dumb show and mime was a well-known feature of Mme Céleste's performances. Between 1830 and 1840 the house playwrights at the Adelphi, London, composed a number of dumb shows for her.

Two 20th c. instances occur in André Obey's *Le Viol de Lucrèce* (1931) and in Tom Stoppard's *Rosencrantz and Guildenstern Are Dead* (1966). The dramatic possibilities of dumb show are provocatively explored in Beckett's *Waiting for Godot* (1953). *See* MIME; REVENGE TRAGEDY.

duodecimo (L *in duodecimo* 'in a twelfth') The size of a book in which one page is one twelfth of a sheet (abbreviated 12mo). *See* FOLIO; OCTAVO; QUARTO.

duologue A conversation between two characters in a play, story or poem. *See* DIALOGUE.

duple meter This comprises two syllables to a metrical foot, as with the iamb, spondee and trochee (*qq.v.*). Duple meter is rare. A fairly well-known example is Herrick's *Upon his departure hence*:

> Thus I
> Passe by,
> And die:
> As One,
> Unknown,
> And go.

Here he combines iamb, spondee and trochee. *See* MONOMETER.

duple rhythm This occurs when the metrical scheme requires two-syllable feet. It is thus common in iambic and trochaic verse. *See* IAMB; TRIPLE RHYTHM; TROCHEE.

duration One of the four characteristics of the spoken word, the others being pitch, loudness and quality. In poetry the duration of syllables (that is, their phonetic time value) is of particular importance. In these lines, for instance, from D. J. Enright's poem *The Laughing Hyena, by Hokusai*, the varying duration of the syllables contributes subtly to the general effect:

> For him, it seems, everything was molten. Court ladies flow
>   in gentle streams,
> Or, gathering lotus, strain sideways from their curving boat,
> A donkey prances, or a kite dances in the sky, or soars like
>   sacrificial smoke.
> All is flux: waters fall and leap, and bridges leap and fall.
> Even his Tortoise undulates, and his Spring Hat is lively as a
>   pool of fish.
> All he ever saw was sea: a sea of marble splinters –
> Long bright fingers claw across his pages, fjords and islands
>   and shattered trees –

See MORA; ONOMATOPOEIA.

dysphemism (Gk 'not fair speech') The opposite of euphemism (*q.v.*), it emphasizes defects – as in saying 'a filthy dirty face'.

dystopia *See* UTOPIA.

E

ebook Or electronic book, which may refer to a digital version of a printed book, or a digital publication with no printed equivalent. Ebooks are designed to be read on personal computers or portable digital reading devices. The first ebooks were developed in the 1970s and were mainly conceived as a means to convey technical materials to specialist audiences. Project Gutenberg, initiated in 1971, is the oldest digital library. Its founders sought to provide public access to the 10,000 most consulted texts at minimal charge by the end of the millennium; this figure has since been surpassed by a considerable margin.

echo The repetition of the same sound, or a combination of sounds, fairly close together, so that they 'echo' each other. A common device in verse to strengthen meaning and structure, and also to provide tune and melody. Assonance, alliteration, consonance, the various kinds of rhyme (*qq.v.*) and also the refrain (*q.v.*) are all varieties of echo. *See also* ECHO VERSE.

echo verse Normally a poem in which the final syllables are repeated as by an echo (*q.v.*) with a change of meaning. Early examples are to be found in the *Greek Anthology* (compiled *c.* 925). The form became popular again in French, Italian and English verse in the 16th and 17th c. Sir Philip Sidney, George Herbert and Swift, among others, composed notable echo verses. The following is an extract from Herbert's *Heaven*:

> O who will show me those delights on high?
> ECHO. I.
> Thou, Echo, thou art mortall, all men know.
> ECHO. No.
> Wert thou not born among the trees and leaves?
> ECHO. Leaves.
> And are there any leaves that still abide?
> ECHO. Bide.

A Dictionary of Literary Terms and Literary Theory, Fifth Edition. J. A. Cuddon.
© 2013 The Estate of J. A. Cuddon. Published 2013 by Blackwell Publishing Ltd.

> What leaves are they? impart the matter wholly.
> ECHO. Holy.

See also ECHO.

Eckenstrophe A twelve-line stanza with a rhyming pattern of aab, aab, cd, cd, ee, used in the MHG epic poems *Eckenlied*, *Goldemar*, *Sigenot* and *Virginal*.

eclipsis (Gk 'a leaving out') The omission of essential grammatical elements.

eclogue (Gk 'selection') A short poem – or part of a longer one – and often a pastoral (*q.v.*) in the form of a dialogue or soliloquy (*qq.v.*). The term was first applied to Virgil's pastorals or bucolic poems. Thereafter it describes the traditional pastoral idyll (*q.v.*) that Theocritus, and other Sicilian poets, wrote. The form was revived by Dante, Petrarch and Boccaccio and was particularly popular during the 15th and 16th c. A major influence came from the *Eclogues* of Mantuan. Alexander Barclay wrote some distinguished eclogues while at Ely (1515–21). Spenser's *The Shepheard's Calendar* (1579) was outstanding. Later Pope attempted it in his *Pastorals*, and Gay burlesqued it in *Shepherd's Week* (1714). By the 18th c. the term merely referred to the form, and there were non-pastoral eclogues. A good example is Swift's *A Town Eclogue*, 1710. *Scene, The Royal Exchange*. In modern poems like Frost's *Build Soil*, MacNeice's *Eclogue from Iceland* and Auden's *The Age of Anxiety: a Baroque Eclogue*, it is the medium for any ideas the poet feels a need to express. *See also* GEORGIC.

eco-criticism A field of criticism defined by its attempt to delineate the relationship between literature and the natural environment. Eco-critics have taken their cue from broader environmentalist movements which might be traced to the activism of the 1960s and 1970s. The image of the earth from space afforded by the 1969 Apollo moon landing or, for example, the ensuing Gaia Theory postulated by James Lovelock as a new way of perceiving the globe as a self-regulating organism might both be seen as contributory factors towards this heightened consciousness in the latter half of the 20th c. More recently, environmental awareness has emerged as a popular political force and, in turn, the subject of literary criticism. Pioneering treatments of eco-criticism were provided by Cheryll Glotfelty and Harold Fromm in *The Ecocriticism Reader* (1996) as well as by Lawrence Buell's influential book *The Environmental Imagination* (1995). As devotees of Nature, the Romantic poets provided an early object of study for eco-critics, although recent work has broadened this purview to include Shakespeare, the pastoral (*q.v.*) and green spaces in literature more broadly. The Association for the Study of Literature and the Environment (ASLE) represents current thinking in the field.

école parnassienne *See* PARNASSIANS.

economic novel *See* MONEY NOVEL.

ecphonema (Gk 'outcry') An exclamation: of joy, woe, amazement.

ecphrasis *See* EKPHRASIS/ECPHRASIS.

écriture artiste A term used by the Goncourt brothers, Edmond (1822–96) and Jules (1830–70), to describe their mannered, sensitive, impressionistic and 'nervous' style, which is particularly evident in their *romans documentaires* (*q.v.*). They were hypersensitive and very fastidious men and, as Remy de Gourmont put it, possessed 'un don particulier et une sensibilité spéciale'. They were latter-day 'précieux', and described themselves as 'historiens des nerfs'. *See also* PRÉCIOSITÉ.

écriture féminine (F 'feminine writing') A concept proposed by the French feminist Hélène Cixous. It denotes writing which is typically, characteristically feminine in style, language, tone and feeling, and completely different from (and opposed to) male language and discourse – though she does say in *The Laugh of the Medusa* (1976) that this is not to do with biological determinism; women often write in male discourse and men can write in a feminine way. She cites the 'source' of *écriture féminine* in the mother and in the mother–child relationship before the child acquires 'conventional' language. She proposes that this potential language when eventually used in writing (*by men or women*) subverts logic and the rational and any element which may constrain the free play of meaning.

On the other hand, Luce Irigaray posits a 'woman's language', which is multiple, fluid, diverse and heterogeneous and which evades male phallocentric monopoly. This theory has a morphological basis associated with the structure and shape of the genital organs.

A third and related point of view is proposed by Julia Kristeva: a 'language' which is pre-Oedipal and pre-linguistic and is fundamentally semiotic (associated with the *chora* (*q.v.*) – Greek for 'womb') as opposed to male-controlled language which she describes as symbolic (*see* POSTSTRUCTURALISM for her theory of the semiotic element). All of these writers revaluate the significance of the maternal, viewing this as empowering rather than as oppressed. Other feminists, however, such as Christine Fauré, Catherine Clément and Monique Wittig, have challenged this emphasis on the body as biologically reductive, fetishistic and politically impotent. Monique Wittig wishes to do away with the linguistic categories of sex and gender. *See also* FEMINIST CRITICISM.

écrivain/écrivant In an essay of 1960 called *Ecrivains et écrivants*, Roland Barthes distinguishes between two sorts of writer (and two sorts of writing). He suggests that the author performs a function and the writer an activity; that there are (a) the 'transitive' writer (*écrivant*) and (b) the 'intransitive' writer (*écrivain*). The former writes about things and the language he uses is the means to an extra-linguistic end, to a meaning or reality which is, in a sense, 'beyond' the writing; the latter does not intend to take the reader beyond his writing but to call the attention of the reader to *the activity of* *writing itself.* The *écrivain* has 'nothing but writing itself, not as the "pure" form conceived by an aesthetic of art for art's sake [*q.v.*] but, much more radically, as the only area for the one who writes'. Thus, one might surmise that Flaubert, Zola and Ernest Hemingway are 'transitive' writers, and Proust, Joyce and Samuel Beckett are 'intransitive' writers. Barthes's taxonomy here is closely connected with his distinction between the *lisible* and the *scriptible*, or the readerly/writerly (*q.v.*).

écrivant   *See* ECRIVAIN/ECRIVANT.

edda   A term used metaphorically for two collections of ON literature written down in Iceland during the 13th c., which draw on much earlier materials. There are several suggestions for the derivation of *edda*: from ON for 'great-grandmother', with the implication that material is composed of ancient tales; from the place name Oddi, where Snorri Sturlusson (1179–1241) – the Icelandic chieftain and historian to whom is attributed authorship of the prose *Edda* – grew up; and from the word *oðr*, 'poetry', since the prose *Edda* is largely a handbook of poetics.

The prose *Edda* was intended as a book of instruction for skalds (*q.v.*). One section for instance is called *Háttatal*, 'list of meters', and contains a poem consisting of 102 stanzas in 100 different meters which is followed by a full practical commentary in prose. Also contained in the prose *Edda* is a section of specifically poetic words, the so-called *heiti* and kennings (*q.v.*). Many of these circumlocutions can only be understood with a knowledge of some of the tales to which they refer. So, in the section *Skáldskaparmál* ('poetic diction'), Snorri retells many of the old mythological stories. Similarly, the best-known section, *Gylfaginning* ('the beguiling of Gylfi'), recounts how the wise king of Sweden, Gylfi, travelled to Asgardr – the dwelling of the gods – to question them about the world's origin, the gods, and the destruction of the world. The work becomes a comprehensive survey of ON mythology, indispensable to the student of the old Scandinavian world.

The poetic *Edda* (also called the *Elder Edda*) is a collection of poems found in a manuscript *c.* 1270 and which, from linguistic and literary evidence, originate from a period earlier than the settlement of Iceland (870). The poetry of the *Elder Edda* falls into two groups: the mythological lays and the heroic lays.

The mythological poetry is composed of lays about gods in various meters and of various ages. Some, such as *Vafðrudismal*, are didactic and can be regarded as treatises on pagan belief and legend. The heroic lays represent a form of poetry which was at one time current among all Germanic tribes from the Black Sea to Greenland. Such lays were probably designed, in the first place, to be declaimed in the halls of chieftains, often to the accompaniment of the harp. They differ in many ways from epics, with which they might naturally be associated, not only in length but also in scope and choice of subject. They deal not with the whole life of the hero but with one or two incidents in that life, usually of a tragic or moving nature.

edition The total number of copies of a book printed from one set of type. If the original type is changed and the book is reprinted then the term *second edition* is used. One edition may have several impressions or printings. The term *issue* usually describes a book to which new material has been added or which is somehow altered in format. The term *re-issue* may describe the reprinting of a book without changes. The term *edition* is also used to describe, say, the edited collected works of an author. For example: the *Twickenham Edition* of Pope's works. E-dition or electronic edition is used to refer to a digital version of a hard-copy version, or one which provides supplementary material online for purchasers of a hard-copy publication, or a digital publication for which there is no hard-copy distribution.

Edwardian Pertaining to King Edward VII's reign (1901–10), though sometimes the years up to the close of the First World War in 1918 are considered part of the same period. With regard to literature, the Edwardian age is notable for some of the early stirrings of what was to be later understood as modernism (*q.v.*); the period also saw the consolidation of the distinction between popular and 'highbrow' literature.

EEBO Early English Books Online, a resource providing scholars with online access to around 100,000 texts, from the earliest books published in English to those produced in the time of Shakespeare.

ego-futurism A jargon term coined by the Russian poet Igor Severyanin (1887–1942) to describe a movement in early 20th c. Russian poetry. The ego-futurists were anti-traditionalist and wrote highly personal verse in which they went in for neologisms (*q.v.*). The movement did not last long. *See also* CUBO-FUTURISM.

egotism (L 'I') Generally, the term refers to the experience of oneself and one's own interests as primary and the centre of focus. Scientifically, this has been understood by psychologists as a necessary developmental stage towards sociality in the course of a child's life. In cultural and literary contexts, what was traditionally regarded as a vice – closely aligned with narcissism – became, in the 19th c., an aesthetic that viewed the self as a generative, creative and authorizing force. This concept received considerable attention and development from the German Idealists, most notably Johann Gottlieb Fichte (1762–1814) and Friedrich Wilhelm Joseph Schelling (1775–1854). Fichte posited – against Kant's idea of 'things in themselves' or purely intelligible objects (*noumena*) – the knowing subject (or ego) as the producer of the phenomenal world through its representations, ideas and mental images. Schelling argued the necessity of the 'not I' to Fichte's concept of the ego. The work of the German Idealists had profound influence on Romantic and Victorian writers, as perhaps best exemplified in England by what Keats critically called Wordsworth's 'egotistical sublime' and by Stendhal's autobiographical *Memoirs of an Egotist* (1892), in which the self-recording first person acts as the organizational nucleus around which fragmentary impressions gravitate. *See also* AUTOBIOGRAPHY; LIFE WRITING.

egotistical sublime A phrase coined by John Keats (1795–1821) and applied to William Wordsworth's qualities of genius (*q.v.*). *See also* NEGATIVE CAPABILITY; SUBLIME.

eidyllion *See* IDYLL.

eight-and-six meter *See* FOURTEENER.

Einfühlung *See* EMPATHY.

eirôn A stock character in ancient Greek comedy, the counterpart of the braggart or *alazôn* (*q.v.*), whom he or she easily deceives. An example of the type in later drama might include Elmire in Molière's *Tartuffe*. *See also* STOCK CHARACTER.

Eisteddfod A Welsh term denoting an assembly of bards. Basically a form of contest at which literary, musical and dramatic works are presented. The main prizes are a carved oak chair awarded for the best poem in strict Welsh meters (known as the chair ode), and a silver crown for the best poem in free meters (known as the crown poem).

The Eisteddfod is an event of some antiquity: there are records of a bardic festival as long ago as 1176 at Cardigan. After the 16th c. the Eisteddfodau seem to have degenerated into rather casual gatherings in village inns. The event was restored to its original dignity and splendour in the 19th c., since when it has become the supreme cultural festival of Wales. *See also* BARD; POETIC CONTESTS.

ekphrasis/ecphrasis (Gk 'description') The intense pictorial description of an object. This very broad term has been limited by some to the description of art-objects, and even to the self-description of 'speaking' art-objects (objects whose visual details are significant). A more generous account would define *ekphrasis* as virtuosic description of physical reality (objects, scenes, persons) in order to evoke an image in the mind's eye as intense as if the described object were actually before the reader. The Horatian (and Renaissance) dictum *ut pictura poesis* (*q.v.*) seemed to suggest that poetry should yield, in George Puttenham's phrase, 'resemblaunce by imagerie, or pourtrait, alluding to the painters terme, who yeldeth to th'eye a visible representatio[n] of the thing he describes and painteth in his table'. Critical expositions of *ekphrasis* include Gotthold Lessing, *Laokoön* (1766), Jean Hagstrum, *The Sister Arts: The Tradition of Literary Pictorialism and English Poetry from Dryden to Gray* (1958), W. J. T. Mitchell, *Iconology: Image, Text, Ideology* (1986), Murray Krieger, *Ekphrasis: The Illusion of the Natural Sign* (1992). *See also* ICON.

elegantia Regarded by the Romans as one of three essential attributes of a discourse, the others being *compositio* and *dignitas*. They subdivided *elegantia* into *Latinitas* and *explanatio*. The former required the absence of linguistic faults, like solecisms; the latter made the matter of the speech or discourse clear.

elegant variation A term used by H. W. and F. G. Fowler to denote a particular fault of style: namely, the too obvious avoidance of repetition.

elegiac distich The Greek *elegeion* was a distich (*q.v.*) or couplet comprising a dactylic hexameter (*q.v.*) followed by a pentameter (*q.v.*). It seems to have been first used in the 8th or 7th c. BC, especially by Archilochus. The form was used for many purposes by Greek and Latin poets, but is rare in English. Poets who have imitated it are Sidney, Spenser, Clough, Kingsley, Swinburne and Sir William Watson, from whose *Hymn to the Sea* the following lines are taken:

> While, with throes, with raptures, with loosing of bonds, with
> unsealings,
> Arrowy pangs of delight, piercing the core of the world,
> Tremors and coy unfoldings, reluctances, sweet agitations,
> Youth, irrepressibly fair, wakes like wondering rose.

It will be noticed that the lines are not wholly dactylic and that they alternate double and single terminals. The form is also known as elegiacs. *See* DACTYL; ELEGY; EPICEDIUM.

elegiac meter The meter used in the elegiac distich (*q.v.*).

elegiac stanza Also known as Hammond's meter, heroic quatrain (*q.v.*) and elegiac quatrain. It seems that a quatrain (*q.v.*) of iambic pentameters (*q.v.*), rhyming abab, has acquired the name elegiac stanza from its use by Gray in *Elegy Written in a Country Churchyard* (1750). James Hammond's *Love Elegies* (1743) is probably the earliest example. *See* ELEGY.

elegy (Gk 'lament') In classical literature an elegy was any poem composed of elegiac distichs (*q.v.*), also known as elegiacs, and the subjects were various: death, war, love and similar themes. The elegy was also used for epitaphs (*q.v.*) and commemorative verses, and very often there was a mourning strain in them. However, it is only since the 16th c. that an elegy has come to mean a poem of mourning for an individual, or a lament (*q.v.*) for some tragic event.

Near the turn of the 16th c., the term *elegie* still covered a variety of subject matter. For example, Donne wrote *Elegie V: His Picture*, and *Elegie XVI: On his Mistris*. Later the term came to be applied increasingly to a serious meditative poem, the kind that Coleridge was hinting at when he spoke of elegy as the form of poetry 'natural to a reflective mind'. English literature is especially rich in this kind of poetry, which combines something of the *ubi sunt* (*q.v.*) motif with the qualities of the lyric (*q.v.*) and which, at times, is closely akin to the lament and the dirge (*qq.v.*). Examples include the OE poems *The*

Wanderer, The Seafarer and *Deor's Lament*, several medieval lyrics, Thomas Nashe's song 'Adieu, farewell earth's bliss', Johnson's *Vanity of Human Wishes*, Goldsmith's *The Deserted Village*, Gray's *Elegy Written in a Country Churchyard*, Young's *Night Thoughts*, Keats's *Ode to Melancholy* and Walt Whitman's *When Lilacs Last in the Dooryard Bloomed* – to name only a handful of the scores that exist.

Many elegies have been songs of lament for specific people. Well-known examples are Thomas Carew's elegy on John Donne, John Cleveland's on Ben Jonson, Henry King's *Exequy*, Pope's *Verses to the Memory of an Unfortunate Lady*, Dr Johnson's *On the Death of Mr Robert Levet*, Tennyson's *Ode on the Death of the Duke of Wellington*, and, more recently, Auden's *In Memory of W. B. Yeats*. In addition to these there are *Astrophil* and *Daphnaïda*, and the four major elegies in English literature – Milton's *Lycidas*, Shelley's *Adonais*, Tennyson's *In Memoriam* and Matthew Arnold's *Thyrsis*.

Three of the four major elegies belong to a subgenre known as pastoral elegy, the origins of which are to be found in the pastoral laments of three Sicilian poets: Theocritus (3rd c. BC), Moschus (2nd c. BC) and Bion (2nd c. BC). Spenser was one of the earliest English poets to use what are known as the pastoral conventions, namely in *Astrophil* (1586), an elegy for Sir Philip Sidney. It is a minor work but important in the history of the genre. Spenser also wrote *Daphnaïda* (1591), on the death of Sir Arthur Gorges's wife.

The conventions of pastoral elegy include the following: (a) the scene is pastoral; the poet and the person he mourns are represented as shepherds; (b) the poet begins with an invocation to the Muses and refers to diverse mythological characters during the poem; (c) Nature is involved in mourning the shepherd's death; Nature feels the wound, so to speak; (d) the poet enquires of the guardians of the dead shepherd where they were when death came; (e) there is a procession of mourners; (f) the poet reflects on divine justice and contemporary evils; (g) there is a 'flower' passage, describing the decoration of the bier, etc.; (h) at the end there is a renewal of hope and joy, with the idea expressed that death is the beginning of life.

After Spenser, Milton established the form of the pastoral in England with *Lycidas* (1637), a poem inspired by the death of Henry King. In the same tradition as *Astrophil* and *Lycidas* are *Adonais* (1821), Shelley's lament for Keats, and *Thyrsis* (1867), Matthew Arnold's lament – he calls it a monody – for A. H. Clough. They all possess a hopeful conclusion and all except Spenser's dwell on the poets' own problems and anxieties.

In Memoriam (1850), Tennyson's elegy for Arthur Hallam, differs from the others in that it lacks the pastoral conventions. But most of the other features are retained and the element of personal reflection is much more marked.

Since *In Memoriam*, many poets have written elegiac poems (e.g. Gerard Manley Hopkins's *Wreck of the Deutschland*), but the formal pastoral elegy has not been favoured. Indeed, many elegies written in response to the dire conflicts and traumas of the 20th c. – war, terror, genocide, epidemic – mourn multiple subjects rather than individuals. Moreover, the elegy's public role has shifted away from commemoration and consolation towards political protest. Some salient examples are Wilfred Owen's First World War poems, Anna Akhmatova's *Requiem* (1940), Paul Celan's 'Death Fugue' (1948), Robert Lowell's *For the Union Dead* (1960), Carolyn Forché's *The Country between Us* (1981) and Thom Gunn's *The Man with Night Sweats* (1992). *See also* ELEGIAC STANZA; EPICEDIUM; GRAVEYARD SCHOOL OF POETRY; OCCASIONAL VERSE.

elision The omission or slurring of a syllable, as in the following lines from *Paradise Lost* describing the opening of the gates of Hell:

> On a sudden open fly
> With impetuous recoil and jarring sound
> Th'infernal doors, and on their hinges grate
> Harsh thunder

The 18th c. poets often practised elision in order to secure a level decasyllabic line. The omission of one or two adjacent vowels is also called synelepha. *See* CONTRACTION; SYNAERESIS; SYNCOPE.

Elizabethan period A classification sometimes loosely applied to the second half of the 16th c. and the early part of the 17th but strictly designating the period of Elizabeth I's reign, 1558–1603. In government, Elizabeth consolidated the centralized bureaucracy of the earlier Tudors and avoided embroilment in the religious wars raging on the continent. The significant foreign confrontation was with Spain, culminating in the near-miss of a full-scale invasion in 1588 by the Spanish Armada. Nevertheless, the relative peace and prosperity of Elizabeth's reign has led to the popular epithet The Golden Age. The forty-odd years of Elizabeth's reign alone were remarkable for their creative activity and output in English literature, especially drama. At this time there flourished some dozens of dramatists, many of whom were prolific writers. Apart from drama, almost every literary form was exploited, developed and embellished. Among the more famous writers of the age were Marlowe, Sir Philip Sidney, Greene, Kyd, Nashe, Spenser, Daniel, Sir Francis Bacon, Lodge, Shakespeare, Sir Walter Ralegh and Ben Jonson.

ellipsis (Gk 'leaving out') A rhetorical figure in which one or more words are omitted. In classical and medieval texts ellipses were unmarked, but the practice of marking them originated in late 16th c. drama as a manifestation of the imperfections of the voice: the omissions, pauses, and interruptions fundamental to spoken language. From their inception ellipsis marks were variable in appearance, and a continuous rule (—), a series of hyphens (---), or a series of points (. . .) were all used, depending upon the resources and inclination of the printer. Asterisks (***) were first employed to display hiatuses in the printer's copy-text, but as rules and points came to be used for other forms of omission (such as censorship or citation) strings of asterisks became interchangeable with alternative forms of ellipsis marks.

It was not until the late 19th c. that clear distinctions began to be made between the marks. The dash, or continuous rule, had become the most common of the symbols, signalling abrupt changes or breaks, whereas points began to imply a longer, more hesitant pause. Points also became the preferred mark for indicating omissions from quotations, leaving the asterisk the primary role of marking footnotes. Such standardization became increasingly pervasive throughout the 20th c. due to the uniformity imposed on writers and printers by the house-styles of large publishing firms, a resulting dependence on style manuals, and latterly the spread of the word-processor. These influences have also standardized appearance: hyphens now rarely make up a rule, dashes are usually one em in length, and an 'ellipsis mark' is comprised of three points (or four if a full-stop is added), rather than the indiscriminate number of points, rules, or asterisks that previously signified ellipses.

El Teatro Campesino (Sp 'the farmworkers' theatre') A theatrical group created in 1965 by Luis Valdez as part of a trade union. Valdez was particularly concerned with the plight of the Chicanos, an impoverished and underprivileged North American racial group of Spanish and American Indian ancestry, and he wished to use theatre in support of a Chicano farm labourers' strike. The aims were political and documentary. A permanent base for the company was established at San Juan Bautista in 1971. By c. 1980 there were believed to be some eighty Chicano theatre companies. *See also* DOCUMENTARY THEATRE.

emblem-book A book of symbolic pictures with a motto. The pictures were usually woodcuts or engravings to illustrate the word or motto, plus an *explicatio*, or exposition. Among the earliest emblem-books was the *Emblematum Liber* (1531) by the Milanese writer Alciati. The earliest English emblem-book was probably Geoffrey Witney's *Choice of Emblemes* (1586); and the most famous was certainly Francis Quarles's *Emblemes* (1635). About the same time George Wither produced a *Collection of Emblemes*. Some makers of emblems wrote verses in the shape of objects like crosses and altars – hence altar poem (*q.v.*) and *carmen figuratum*. Wither actually wrote a dirge (*q.v.*) in rhomboidal form. The early emblem-books were plundered for images by Elizabethan and 17th c. poets. William Blake revived the emblem form in *The Gates of Paradise* (1793). A notable work on the subject is Rosemary Freeman's *English Emblem Books* (1948). *See also* CONCEIT; GNOMIC VERSE.

emendation The correction or alteration of text or manuscript where it is, or appears to be, corrupt.

emotive language Language intended to express or arouse emotional reactions towards the subject. To be distinguished from referential or cognitive language, which aims only to denote; for instance, the language of the scientist and the philosopher. In *The Meaning of Meaning* (1923) C. K. Ogden and

I. A. Richards made the distinctions clear. *See* APOLLONIAN/DIONYSIAN; ASSO-CIATION; CONNOTATION; DENOTATION.

empathy The word was introduced in 1909 by Titchener when translating the German word *Einfühlung*. The idea of empathy was developed in Germany by Lotze in *Mikrokosmus* (1858). When we experience empathy we identify ourselves, up to a point, with an animate or inanimate object. One might even go so far as to say that the experience is an involuntary projection of ourselves *into* an object. Thus the contemplation of a work of sculpture might give us a physical sensation similar to that suggested by the work. This is related to the common experience of lifting a leg when watching a man or a horse jumping. In a different way, reading, for instance, Gerard Manley Hopkins's *The Windhover*, one might empathically experience some of the physical sensations evoked in the description of the movement of the falcon.

Sympathy, on the other hand, suggests a conformity or agreement of feelings and temperament, and an emotional identification with a person.

emplotment Term coined by Hayden White in his 1973 work *Metahistory* to describe the way in which historians necessarily fashion their source material into narrative. Historiography (*q.v.*), White argues, encodes historical data, which themselves do not constitute a story, into one of four possible intelligible plot types: tragic, comic, romantic or ironic. A single historical event – the French Revolution for instance – will be emplotted in different ways to produce different interpretations. Which type is deployed depends on the trope of figurative representation that dominates the historian's language and culture. These tropes, which correspond to the four emplotment types, include metaphor, metonymy, synecdoche and irony (*qq.v.*). Even before the historian has emplotted historical events in an attempt to render the unfamiliar familiar, he or she must describe them by means of these tropes. Thus the nature of historical events and the relationships between them are not inherent in the events themselves; rather, they are constituted through the very language used to describe them.

enallage (Gk 'exchange') A figurative device which involves the substitution of one grammatical form for another. Common in metaphor. For example: 'to palm someone off'; 'to have a good laugh'; 'to be wived'; 'to duck an appointment'. *See also* HYPALLAGE

enchiridion (Gk 'manual') A book that can be carried by hand. *See* GUIDE-BOOK; HANDBOOK; MANUAL; VADE MECUM.

encomium (L from Gk 'praise') Formal eulogy in prose or verse glorifying people, objects, ideas or events. Originally it was a Greek choral song in celebration of a hero, sung at the *komos* or triumphal procession at the end of the Olympic games. Pindar wrote some encomiastic odes praising the winners. Many English poets have produced encomiastic verse: Milton's *Ode on the Morning of Christ's Nativity* (1629); Dryden's *Song for St Cecilia's Day* (1687); Gray's *Hymn to Adversity* (1742); Wordsworth's *Ode to Duty*

(1805). Encomium can also be the vehicle of irony (*q.v.*) as Erasmus demonstrated in *Moriae Encomium* 'The Praise of Folly' (1509), a satire directed against the follies of theologians and churchmen. A curiosity in this genre is the *Panegyrici Latini*, a collection of encomia on Roman emperors dating from 289 to 389. *See also* EPINICION; OCCASIONAL VERSE; ODE; PANEGYRIC.

encyclical An official statement by a Pope. They are known by their opening words (in Latin). Famous recent examples have been: *Rerum Novarum* (1891) by Pope Leo XIII; *Quadragesimo Anno* (1931) by Pope Pius XI, so called because it came forty years after Pope Leo's; *Pacem in Terris* (1963) by Pope John XXIII, a landmark in the *Aggiornamento*; and *Redemptor Hominis* (1979) by Pope John Paul II.

encyclopaedia The term derives from the Greek *enkyklios* 'circular' or 'general' and *paideiā* 'discipline' or 'instruction'. Though not known to Classical writers, the term embraced that 'circle' of instruction which included grammar, rhetoric, music, mathematics, philosophy, astronomy and gymnastics. The first use of the term in English appears to be that in Sir Thomas Elyot's *Boke named the Governour* (1531), a treatise on education. We again find the term in the title of Paul Scalich de Like's *Encyclopaediae seu orbis disciplinarum tam sacrarum quam profanarum epistemon* (1559).

There are three basic kinds of encyclopaedia: (a) those which are encyclopaedic in intent but not universally comprehensive; (b) comprehensive encyclopaedias; (c) special encyclopaedias.

Some famous early encyclopaedic works are Varro's *Rerum Humanarum et Divinarum Antiquitates* (1st c. BC), the Elder Pliny's *Historia Naturalis* (1st c. AD), Isidore of Seville's *Originum seu Etymologiarum Libri* (7th c.), Martianus Capella's *De Nuptiis Mercurii et Philologiae* (5th c.) and Rabanus Maurus's *De Universo* (9th c.). The greatest medieval encyclopaedia was the tripartite *Speculum* of Vincent de Beauvais (13th c.): *Speculum Historiale*, *Speculum Naturale* and *Speculum Doctrinale*. Also to the 13th c. belongs Bartholomaeus Anglicus's *De Proprietatibus Rerum*, later translated into English by John of Trevisa (1398).

During the Renaissance period and the 17th c. other encyclopaedic works were Johann Heinrich Alsted's *Encyclopaedia Cursus Philosophici* (1608), which was later developed by the author into *Encyclopaedia septem tomis distincta* (1620). This was one of the last encyclopaedic works in Latin. Hereafter it was customary to use the vernacular. Later in this century there appeared Moréri's *Grand Dictionnaire Historique* (1643–80), Hofmann's *Lexicon Universale* (1677), Thomas Corneille's *Dictionnaire des Arts et des Sciences* (1694) and Pierre Bayle's *Dictionnaire historique et critique* (1697) – all major works.

In the 18th c. a large number of important works in English, French and German were published. Some of the principal ones were: *Universal, Historical, Geographical, Chronological and Classical Dictionary* (1703); John Harris's *Lexicon Technicum, or an Universal English Dictionary of Arts and Sciences* (1704); Ephraim Chambers's *Cyclopaedia, or an Universal Diction-*

ary of Arts and Sciences (1728). Upon this monumental work was based the *Encyclopédie ou Dictionnaire raisonné des Sciences, des Arts et des Métiers* (1751–76), which was compiled by D'Alembert and Diderot in 35 volumes.

In 1771 appeared the first edition of the *Encyclopaedia Britannica*. The ten-volume edition – and this was the first attempt in the English language to encompass the sum of human knowledge – appeared soon afterwards (1777–84). Eminent scholars and scientists have contributed to it. It remains, in its various successive editions, and continuous revisions, one of the best of all encyclopaedias.

In the 19th and 20th c. there were an increasing number of encyclopaedias which attempted to cope with the vast quantities of knowledge accumulating daily. Some of the more famous are: *Encyclopédie méthodique ou par ordre de matières*, a work in 200 volumes which came out between 1781 and 1832; a successor to Chambers's work called the *New Encyclopaedia* (1802–20), in 45 volumes; Brewster's *Edinburgh Encyclopaedia* (1809–31); the *Encyclopaedia Metropolitana* (1817–45); Ersch and Gruber's *Allgemeine Encyclopädie der Wissenschaften und Künste* (this was first published in 1818 and thereafter 167 volumes were produced); the *Penny Encyclopaedia*, begun in 1833; the *Encyclopaedia Americana* (1829–32); another version of Chambers's *Encyclopaedia* (1860–68); Larousse's *Le Grand Dictionnaire du XIXe siècle* (1866–76); the *Encyclopédie Française* (1935); the *Encyclopedia Italiana* (1929–39); the *Bolshaya Sovietskaya Entsiklopedia* (1928–47), in 65 volumes; the *Enciclopedia universal ilustrada europeoamericana* (1905–30), in 70 volumes.

There are also many specialist encyclopaedias. The following are especially notable: the *Encyclopaedia of Gardening* (1822) by Loudon; *A Dictionary of Music and Musicians* (1878–90) by Sir George Grove, most recently reworked as *The New Grove* (1980); the *Dictionary of National Biography* (1882–1901), to which there are many supplements; the *Jewish Encyclopaedia* (1901–6); the *Catholic Encyclopaedia* (1907–14); the *Dictionary of Applied Chemistry* (1891, revised in various editions since); *Allgemeines Lexicon der bildender Künstler* (1907–47), in 37 volumes; the *Encyclopaedia of Religion and Ethics* (1908–26); and the *Encyclopaedia of the Social Sciences* (1930–5).

The arrival of the internet has spurred the development of free encyclopaedias. Wikipedia, launched in 2001, is now the largest encyclopaedia in existence, comprising more than 19 million articles in nearly three hundred languages. Some online encyclopaedias, including Wikipedia, are collaborative: they allow anyone to compose or edit most if not all entries. In consequence, they are able to respond quickly to new developments, and have been heralded as a departure from traditional printed encyclopaedias reliant on professionalized experts. However, despite attempts to regulate editing, collaborative encyclopaedias are often criticized for bias, inaccuracy and unreliability. *See* DICTIONARY.

endecha (Sp 'dirge, lament') The term may derive from Latin *indicia*, 'manifestations'. A metrical combination used repeatedly in compositions on sombre themes and made up of six- or seven-syllable lines, usually with assonance. The strophic form of the *endecha real* or 'royal lament', introduced in the 16th c., was usually of four lines. The *endecha* is sometimes called a *romancillo*. A well-known example is Lope de Vega's *Pobre barquilla mía*.

end-rhyme This occurs at the end of a line of verse, and is distinguished from head-rhyme or alliteration (*qq.v.*) and internal rhyme (*q.v.*).

end-stopped line A term applied to verse where the sense and meter coincide in a pause at the end of a line. End-stopped couplets were characteristic of a great deal of 18th c. poetry. This passage from Pope's *Essay on Man* illustrates both the end-stopped line and the open-ended line:

> All nature is but art unknown to thee,
> All chance, direction which thou canst not see;
> All discord, harmony not understood;
> All partial evil, universal good;
> And, spite of pride, in erring reason's spite,
> One truth is clear: Whatever is, is right.

The incidence of the end-stopped line has been used to date Shakespeare's plays and other works. *See* CLOSED COUPLET; COUPLET; ENJAMBEMENT; HEROIC COUPLET; OPEN COUPLET; SINGLE-MOULDED LINE.

engagement *See* COMMITMENT.

English sonnet *See* SONNET.

English Stage Company Founded in 1956 by George Devine (1910–66) at the Royal Court Theatre, London. The Royal Court had opened in 1888 and was originally named The Court. Early on it became distinguished in theatrical history because it was there that Harley Granville Barker (1877–1946) established George Bernard Shaw in the theatre, besides presenting classics, Shakespeare, new plays and the work of European playwrights, all in the course of the years 1904–7. Devine's contribution to a revival of British drama was immeasurable, and it was he who established dramatists such as John Osborne, Arnold Wesker, Edward Bone, David Storey, N. F. Simpson, Christopher Logue, Samuel Beckett, John Arden *et al.* Classics were also presented, plus the plays of some European dramatists such as Jean-Paul Sartre, Jean Genet, Brecht and Eugène Ionesco. After his death Devine's adventurous policy was continued under various directors and yet more dramatists were introduced, including Heathcote Williams, Joe Orton, Christopher Hampton, E. A. Whitehead, David Hare, Athol Fugard, Brian Friel, Howard Barker, Howard Brenton and Caryl Churchill. In 1969 the studio Theatre Upstairs was opened.

englyn A group of strict Welsh meters. The *englyn* monorhyme (*q.v.*) is the most popular of all the strict meters.

enjambement (F 'in-striding' from *jambe*, 'leg') Running on of the sense beyond the second line of one couplet (*q.v.*) into the first line of the next. The device was commonly used by 16th and 17th c. poets but much less frequently in the 18th c. The Romantic poets revived its use. This was part of the reaction against what were felt to be restrictive rules governing the composition of verse. This example is from Keats's *Endymion*, a poem in which he used it often:

> Who, of men, can tell
> That flowers would bloom, or that green fruit would swell
> To melting pulp, that fish would have bright mail,
> The earth its dower of river, wood, and vale,
> The meadows runnels, runnels pebble-stones,
> The seed its harvest, or the lute its tones,
> Tones ravishment, or ravishment its sweet
> If human souls did never kiss and greet?

See CLOSED COUPLET; END-STOPPED LINE; REJET; RUN-ON LINE.

Enlightenment A term used to describe a literary and philosophical movement in Europe between *c.* 1660 and *c.* 1770. In German the term is *Aufklärung* and the period is referred to as the *Zeitalter der Aufklärung*. In England it is sometimes referred to as 'the Age of Reason'. The period was characterized by a profound faith in the powers of human reason and a devotion to clarity of thought, to harmony, proportion and balance. Most of the best writers and philosophers of the period expressed themselves in lucid and often luminous prose. The Enlightenment was facilitated by what the 20th c. German philosopher Jürgen Habermas has identified as the creation of the 'bourgeois public sphere': new forms of urban sociability (salons, coffee houses and debating societies) facilitating open discussion of ideas, and an explosion of print culture. Some of the most notable figures were: (a) in Germany – Kant (1724–1804), who included *What is Enlightenment?* (1784) among his many works; Moses Mendelssohn (1729–86); and Lessing (1729–81); (b) in France – Voltaire (1694–1778) and Diderot (1713–84); (c) in Britain – Locke (1632–1704); Newton (1642–1727); Berkeley (1685–1753); Johnson (1709–84); and Hume (1711–76). *See also* AUGUSTAN AGE; DECORUM; NEOCLASSICISM.

énoncé/énonciation Technical terms in structuralist thoery. The *énoncé* is the utterance; *énonciation* is the act or process of utterance. The latter half of this distinction has allowed poststructuralist theorists to differentiate between the narratorial voice and the voice of its subject, particularly in first-person narratives, where, in the sentence 'I must admit that when I was young I found it difficult not to credit the existence of ghosts', the narrator's voice is the *énonciation* and that of the reported earlier belief in ghosts is the *énoncé*. *Énonciation* is much more marked in first- (and second-) person narratives, where the difference between the narrating voice and its past self (or that of its other subjects) is obvious and pronounced; third-person narratives can often occlude the distinction by emphasizing the *énoncé*, as in the phrase 'When he was young he found it hard not to credit the existence of ghosts', where the narrative voice, though undoubtedly present, is not so clearly marked out by personal pronouns. *See* NARRATOR.

enoplius A term in Classical Greek prosody which has the meaning and force of being 'in martial arms', or 'up in arms'. The verse scheme was either:

∪ / ∪ ∪ / ∪ ∪ / /

or:

∪ ∪ / ∪ ∪ / ∪ ∪ / /.

ensalada (Sp 'salad, medley, mix-up') Colloquially, a 'hotchpotch' and, in literature, a poem comprising lines and strophes of varying lengths and various rhyme schemes. Usually a composition of a lyric nature. Possibly the earliest known example in Spanish is by Fray Ambrosio Montesinos *c.* 1500.

ensenhamen An Old Provençal form of didactic poem. They were usually composed in a non-lyrical meter. Their burden (*q.v.*) was normally advice or instruction, on a variety of topics. *See* DIDACTIC POETRY.

entelechy A term used by Aristotle to denote the realization or complete expression of something that was potential. Later it was used by writers to signify what helped to develop perfection.

entertainment As a specific literary classification, a term used by Graham Greene to distinguish his serious novels from his more light-hearted ones. For instance, he classes *The Power and the Glory* and *The End of the Affair* as novels; *A Gun for Sale* and *Our Man in Havana* as 'entertainments'.

entr'acte (F 'between act') A short interlude, often musical, to divert an audience between the acts of a play.

entremés A Spanish term deriving from French *entremets*. A diversion (dramatic or otherwise) between the courses of a banquet. In Catalonia they were called *entrameses* and the term was later applied to dramatic interludes during the Corpus Christi procession. In Castilian, during the 16th and 17th c., they were brief comic interludes performed between the acts of a play. Many were written by well-known dramatists, including Cervantes, Lope de Vega and Calderón. In the 18th c., similar entertainments were named *sainete*; and in the 19th c., the *género chico* was comparable. *See also* ENTR'ACTE; INTERLUDE; INTERMEZZI.

entremets *See* ENTREMÉS.

envelope When the envelope device is used a line or a stanza is repeated, either in the same form or with a slight variation, to enclose the rest of the poem. There are several variations. Keats uses the first four lines of *The Mermaid Tavern* to envelop the rest of the poem at the end.

An envelope stanza also denotes a group of lines which has enclosed rhymes – say, abba. Tennyson used this stanza form in *In Memoriam*.

envoi (F 'a sending on the way') Also *envoy*. A final stanza, shorter than the preceding ones, often used in the *ballade* (q.v.) and *chant royal* (q.v.). In a *ballade* there are usually four lines, in *chant royal* five or seven. The *envoi* also repeats the refrain (q.v.) of the poem. Among English poets Chaucer used it in *Lenvoy de Chaucer à Scogan* and in *Lenvoy de Chaucer à Bukton*. But Chaucer's *envoi* to Scogan was equal in length to the other stanzas. Scott, Southey, Swinburne and Wilde, among others, also employed the device. More recently, Chesterton, in *A Ballade of an Anti-Puritan*:

> Prince Bayard would have smashed his sword
> To see the sort of knights you dub –
> Is that the last of them – O Lord!
> Will someone take me to a pub?

epanados (Gk 'a repeating of words') A figure of speech in which a word or a phrase is repeated at the beginning and middle, or at the middle and end of a sentence. As in this line from Philip Sidney's *Arcadia*: 'Hear you this soul-invading voice, and count it but a voice?' *See* EPANALEPSIS.

epanalepsis (Gk 'a taking up again') A figure of speech which contains a repetition of a word or words after other words have come between them. There is good example at the beginning of *Paradise Lost*:

> Say first, for Heaven hides nothing from thy view,
> Nor the deep tract of Hell, say first what cause
> Moved our grand Parents, in that happy state . . .

See ANADIPLOSIS; EPANADOS; REPETITION.

epanaphora *See* ANAPHORA.

epanorthosis (Gk 'setting straight again') A figure of speech in which something said is corrected or commented on.

epic A long narrative poem, on a grand scale, about the deeds of warriors or heroes, incorporating myth, legend, folk tale (qq.v.) and history. Epics are often of national significance in the sense that they embody the history and aspirations of a nation in a lofty or grandiose manner.

Epics are understood to belong to one of two categories: (a) primary – also known as oral or primitive; and (b) secondary – or literary. The first is composed orally; only much later, in some cases, is it written down. The second is written down at the start.

Gilgamesh, the Sumerian epic (c. 3,000 BC), is the earliest extant work in the oral tradition. It recounts the adventures of the king of that name and his search for glory and eternal life. Next come the Homeric epics, the *Iliad* and the *Odyssey* (c. 800 BC), whose heroes are Achilles and Odysseus respectively. The *Iliad* recounts the story of the war between the Greeks and the Trojans; the *Odyssey* relates the adventures of Odysseus during his return from the Trojan war to his island home in Ithaca. *Beowulf* (from roughly the

10th c., though it was probably composed some two hundred years earlier) narrates the exploits of a legendary Geatish hero who first rids the Danish kingdom of Hrothgar of two demonic monsters, Grendel and his mother, and then slays a dragon.

Primary epics have features in common, such as beginning *in medias res*, a central figure of heroic, even superhuman calibre, perilous journeys, a strong element of the supernatural, epic similes, descriptive formulae and epithets, kennings (*qq.v.*) and in general a lofty tone.

An example of secondary epic is the *Aeneid* (*c.* 30–19 BC) by Virgil, the first national poet of Rome, which records and celebrates the foundation of Rome by Aeneas after many hazardous adventures following the fall of Troy. Ovid's *Metamorphoses* (1st c. AD) has been viewed as an anti-epic in its use of episodic scenes, its variety of perspectives and its absence of any central character.

Apart from the *Ilias Latina*, a Latin version of the *Iliad* composed in the 1st c. AD, there is little of note in epic in Europe for the best part of a thousand years. Outside Europe, however, there are the great Indian epics, the *Mahābhārata* and the *Rāmāyana* – both of very uncertain date. Towards the end of the first millennium the Persian poet Firdowsi composed *Shah-Nameh*, a national epic. In the 11th and 12th c. across Europe a considerable body of epic poetry, oral in origin, was being written down in order to preserve it – notable examples include the *chansons de gestes* and the Icelandic sagas (*qq.v.*).

In general, from early in the 13th c. literary epic becomes the main form – and in this Virgil is the principal influence. This is particularly apparent in the works of the two great Italian poets Dante and Petrarch. Early in the 14th c. Dante wrote his *Divina Commedia* (*c.* 1310) in Italian; later in the century Petrarch wrote his epic *Africa* in Latin. The *Divina Commedia* is a kind of autobiographical and spiritual epic. *Africa* records the struggle between Carthage and Rome.

Spenser's The *Faerie Queene* (1589, 1596) was the greatest narrative poem in 16th c. English Literature. It is a mixture of epic and romance for which Spenser designed what has become known as the Spenserian stanza (*q.v.*). Spenser organized the poem as an extended and elaborate allegory or 'darke conceit', as he put it, using the material of the Arthurian legends and the Charlemagne romances. The hero of each book represents a virtue, and the poem is throughout a didactic work of astonishing complexity, richness and allusiveness.

If the *Faerie Queene* brings to an end the tradition of the epic of chivalry, *Paradise Lost*, which Milton began composing in 1658 but which was not published until 1667, is often considered the last major epic. Written in blank verse (*q.v.*) and ultimately organized into twelve books, *Paradise Lost* is focused on the Fall of Man, and while its averred purpose is to 'justify the ways of God to men', it has been understood as questioning the authority of the Church. Famously, it offers a compelling portrait of its anti-hero (*q.v.*), Satan.

In the late 17th c. there set in a reaction against the heroic which resulted in 'mock-epic' (*q.v.*). In general, poets tended to modify and reduce the scale and scope of narrative poems, even while retaining the mode and manner of the full-dress epic with all or much of its conventional apparatus – for example, Dryden's *Absalom and Achitophel* (1681) and Pope's *The Rape of the Lock* (1714) and *The Dunciad* (1728, 1735).

The next major poet to attempt an epic-type poem was Byron, whose *Don Juan* (1819–24) has many of the trappings and features of epic even though it is satire (*q.v.*). Later in the 19th c. Matthew Arnold, William Morris, Tennyson and Browning all wrote epic works. In the 20th c. several poets composed works on an epic scale, such as Pound's *Cantos* (1925–69). Pound, along with many of his contemporaries, employed the stream of consciousness method and collage construction associated with modernist writing. Many thinkers, notably Georg Lukács, have seen the epic form as the product of a relatively early and harmonious civilization, a form which is no longer feasible in a modern world riven by various modes of fragmentation. Lukács sees the novel as the epic of a world abandoned by God. *See*: EPYLLION; NARRATIVE VERSE; ROMANCE.

epicedium (Gk 'funeral song') A song of mourning in praise of a dead person, sung over the corpse. A *threnos* (or dirge, *q.v.*), on the other hand, might be sung anywhere. *See* ELEGIAC DISTICH; ELEGY; MONODY.

epic simile An extended simile (*q.v.*), in some cases running to fifteen or twenty lines, in which the comparisons made are elaborated in considerable detail. It is a common feature of epic (*q.v.*) poetry, but is found in other kinds as well. A good example will be found in Milton: 'as when a wandering fire . . . So glistered the dire snake' (*Paradise Lost*, IX, 634–44). *See also* CATALOGUE VERSE.

epic theatre A form of drama and a method of presentation developed in Germany in the 1920s. It originated in the *neue Sachlichkeit* (*q.v.*) period in Berlin and the term was first used of the early plays of Arnolt Bronnen, particularly *Vatermord* (1922), which very nearly caused a riot, and of Alfons Paquet's *Fahnen* (1924), which was subtitled 'epic' and was produced by Erwin Piscator for his socialist theatre. Piscator was the founder and director of this influential movement. Since then the term 'epic theatre' has been most closely associated with Bertolt Brecht (1898–1956). Epic theatre was a break with established dramatic styles. In Brecht's words, the 'essential point of epic theatre is that it appeals less to the spectator's feelings than to his reason'. It denotes a form of narrative/chronicle play which is didactic, which is not restricted by the unity of time and which presents a series of episodes in a simple and direct way: a kind of linear narration ('each scene for itself'). Notable features are the use of a Chorus (*q.v.*), a narrator, slide projection, film, placards and music. Much epic drama was devoted to the expression of political ideas and ideals, though not overtly propagandist. In many ways it has much in common with documentary theatre (*q.v.*).

Brecht discusses the concept in various works. He summarized it in his *Mahagonny* notes in 1930, and wrote at length of it in his essay *Über die Verwendung der Musik für eine epische Bühne* (1935). He also expressed views about it in his unfinished dialogue *Der Messingkauf*, written between 1937 and 1951, and in 1949 published *Kleines Organon für das Theater*, his main theoretical work on the topic.

Piscator's dramatizations of Hašek's novel *The Good Soldier Schweik* (in 1928) and *War and Peace* (in 1942) are two of the major works in epic drama. Brecht's *Threepenny Opera* (1928) and *Mother Courage and Her Children* (1941) are two others. Many dramatists have been influenced by Piscator's work and by Brecht's theory, and the practice of that theory in his plays. Among playwrights writing in German one should mention Dürrenmatt, Dorst, Frisch, Hacks, Hildesheimer, Walser and Weiss. *See also* AGITPROP DRAMA; ALIENATION EFFECT; CHRONICLE PLAY; COMMITMENT; EXPRESSIONISM; PROPAGANDA; TOTAL THEATRE.

epideictic (Gk 'shown upon') Epideictic oratory was a branch of classical rhetoric (*q.v.*) used to praise or blame somebody or something in public. For example, a funeral oration, a panegyric (*q.v.*). So anything epideictic is intended for public display. Such poetry is for a special public occasion. For example, occasional verse (*q.v.*). *See* ENCOMIUM; EPITHALAMION; ODE.

Epigon (Gk *epi*, 'after' + *gon*, 'birth') A term generally used in German to describe writers who are derivative and who work in and are influenced by the manner and tradition of distinguished predecessors. Hence the idea of a later generation which follows on. Its use is associated with Karl Immermann's popular novel *Die Epigonen* (1836).

epigram (Gk 'inscription') As a rule a short, witty statement in verse or prose which may be complimentary, satiric or aphoristic. Coleridge defined it as:

> A dwarfish whole,
> Its body brevity, and wit its soul.

Originally an inscription on a monument or statue, the epigram developed into a literary genre. Many of them are gathered in the *Greek Anthology* (compiled *c.* 925). Roman authors, especially Martial, also composed them.

The form was much cultivated in the 17th c. in England by Jonson, Donne, Herrick, William Drummond of Hawthornden, Dryden and Swift, and in the 18th c. by Pope, Prior, Richard Kendal, Burns and Blake. Coleridge also showed adroitness in the form, as in these lines on John Donne:

> With Donne, whose muse on dromedary trots,
> Wreathe iron pokers into true-love knots;
> Rhyme's sturdy cripple, fancy's maze and clue,
> Wit's forge and fire-blast, meaning's press and screw.

In the 19th c. Landor is generally regarded as the expert of the genre. He wrote a good many, and this is one:

> Go on, go on, and love away!
> Mine was, another's is, the day.
> Go on, go on, thou false one! now
> Upon his shoulder rest thy brow,
> And look into his eyes until
> Thy own, to find them colder, fill.

Mention should also be made of Belloc and Walter de la Mare, both of whom made distinguished contributions to this form. For example, Belloc's:

> When we are dead, some Hunting-boy will pass
> And find a stone half-hidden in tall grass
> And grey with age: but having seen that stone
> (Which was your image) ride more slowly on.

And de la Mare's:

> '*Homo*? Construe!' the stern-faced usher said.
>   Groaned George, 'A man, sir'. 'Yes,
> Now *sapiens*?' . . . George shook a stubborn head,
>   And sighed in deep distress.

Occasionally in verse an epigram takes the form of a couplet or quatrain (*qq.v.*) as part of a poem, as in this example by Pope in the *Essay on Criticism*:

> We think our fathers fools, so wise we grow,
> Our wiser sons, no doubt, will think us so.

In more recent times the verse epigram has become relatively rare, but very many (especially from the 16th c. onwards) have used the form in prose or speech to express something tersely and wittily. These are fairly recent examples: A Protestant, if he wants aid or advice on any matter, can only go to his solicitor (Disraeli); Forty years of romance make a woman look like a ruin and forty years of marriage make her look like a public building (Oscar Wilde); He [Macaulay] has occasional flashes of silence that make his conversation perfectly delightful (Sydney Smith); The optimist proclaims that we live in the best of all possible worlds; and the pessimist fears this is true (J. H. Cabell); God made women beautiful so that men would love them; and he made them stupid so that they could love men (attributed to La Belle Otero, the 19th c. courtesan).

Some other famous epigrammatists have been Lord Chesterfield, Byron, George Bernard Shaw, F. E. Smith (Lord Birkenhead) and Ogden Nash. *See also* ANTITHESIS; EPITAPH.

epigraph Four meanings may be distinguished: (a) an inscription on a statue, stone or building; (b) the writing (legend) on a coin; (c) a quotation on the title page of a book; (d) a motto (*q.v.*) heading a new section or paragraph.

epigraphy (Gk *epi*, 'upon' + *graphein*, 'to write') The study of inscriptions incised on a durable material (e.g. marble, stone, metal, steel) and found on tombs, statues, plaques, tablets, public buildings, sarcophagi, etc. Inscriptions are a vital source of knowledge about the ancient world. *See* EPIGRAPH.

epilogue Three meanings may be distinguished: (a) a short speech to be delivered at the end of a play. It often makes some graceful and witty comment on what has happened and asks for the approval, if not the indulgence, of the audience; (b) the end of a fable (*q.v.*) where the moral is pointed; (c) the concluding section or paragraph of any literary work, sometimes added as a summary, but more often as an afterthought. *See also* PROLOGUE.

epimythium A summary of the moral of a fable (*q.v.*) placed at the end of the fable. If at the beginning it was called a *promythium*. *See* EPILOGUE.

epinicion A triumphal ode (*q.v.*) commemorating a victory at the Olympic Games. As a rule it comprised a number of groups of three stanzas each, arranged as strophe, antistrophe and epode (*qq.v.*) and gave an account of the victor's success. Simonides, Pindar and Baccylides all composed *epinicia*. Euripedes also wrote one for Alcibiades. *See* ENCOMIUM.

epiphany (Gk 'manifestation') The term primarily denotes the festival which commemorates the manifestation of Christ to the Gentiles in the persons of the Magi. The feast is observed on January 6th, 'Twelfth Night', the festival of the 'Three Kings'. More generally, the term denotes a manifestation of God's presence in the world. James Joyce gave this word a particular literary connotation in his novel *Stephen Hero*, part of the first draft of *A Portrait of the Artist as a Young Man*, which was first published in 1916. The relevant passage is:

> This triviality made him think of collecting many such moments together in a book of epiphanies. By an epiphany he meant a *sudden spiritual manifestation* [my italics], whether in the vulgarity of speech or of gesture or in a memorable phase of the mind itself. He believed that it was for the man of letters to record these epiphanies with extreme care, seeing that they themselves are the most delicate and evanescent of moments. He told Cranly that the clock of the Ballast Office was capable of an epiphany.

A little further on he says:

> Imagine my glimpses of that clock as the gropings of a spiritual eye which seeks to adjust its vision to an exact focus. The moment the focus is reached the object is epiphanized.

Joyce elaborates this theme at considerable length. The epiphany is a symbol of a spiritual state. This aspect of aesthetic theory is left out of *A Portrait*, but a knowledge of it is essential for an understanding of Joyce as an artist. *Dubliners, A Portrait, Ulysses* and *Finnegans Wake* are a series of increasingly complex and revealing insights of grace as well as intuitions of immortality. However, Joyce's description of such an experience does not imply a *discovery* on his part. Many writers, especially mystics and religious poets, have conveyed their experience of epiphanies. Striking instances are to be found in the poems of George Herbert, Henry Vaughan and Gerard Manley Hopkins. And there are particularly fine passages in Wordsworth's *Prelude* (Book VIII, 539–59, and VII, 608–23) which describe epiphanies (the term he uses is 'spots of time'). Shelley calls these visionary occasions 'moments'; De Quincey, 'involutes'.

epiphonema (Gk 'after show') A terse summary of an argument (*q.v.*); often expressed by means of epigram or *sententia* (*qq.v.*). Shakespeare concludes his sonnets with a neat rhyming couplet which sums up the argument.

epiplexis (Gk 'on-stroke') A form or style of argument which seeks to shame the interlocutor into seeing the point. For example: 'If you had any sense at all, you would understand that. . . . '

epiploce (Gk 'plaiting together') A term used by Classical prosodists to denote the various possibilities in the scansion (*q.v.*) of metrical lines.

epirrhema (Gk 'that said afterwards') A speech delivered in the *parabasis* (*q.v.*) of Old Comedy (*q.v.*) by the leader of one half of the Chorus (*q.v.*) after that part of the Chorus had sung an ode (*q.v.*). It was usually satirical, didactic or exhortatory.

epische Oper A term devised by Bertolt Brecht (1898–1956) to contrast his concept of opera (*q.v.*) with 'dramatic opera'. The principles and characteristics of epic opera are similar to those of epic theatre (*q.v.*). The music had a didactic function. Brecht invented the word 'Misuk' to denote this and to distinguish it from 'Musik'.

episode Two meanings may be distinguished: (a) an event or incident within a longer narrative; a digression (*q.v.*); (b) a section into which a serialized work is divided.

episteme (Gk 'knowledge' or 'science'; 'epistemology' = the science or study of knowledge) A term used by Plato and Aristotle to denote the universally valid knowledge gained through reason or logic, as opposed to mere opinion or belief (indicated by the word *doxa*).

In modern thought, the term *épisteme* is most commonly associated with Michel Foucault, for whom it refers to the apparatus of enabling conditions, tacit assumptions and rules that structure the discourses of knowledge in a given epoch.

epistemology Literally, 'science of knowledge'. Branch of philosophy concerned with understanding the nature and limitations of knowledge.

epistle A poem addressed to a friend or patron, thus a kind of 'letter' (*q.v.*) in verse. There are approximately two types: (a) on moral and philosophical themes (e.g. Horace's *Epistles*); (b) on romantic or sentimental themes (e.g. Ovid's *Heroides*).

In the Middle Ages the Ovidian type was the more popular. It influenced the theories of courtly love (q.v.) and may have inspired Samuel Daniel to introduce the form in, for instance, *Letter from Octavia to Marcus Antonius* (1603). During the Renaissance and thereafter it was the Horatian kind which had the greater influence. Petrarch, Ariosto and Boileau all wrote such epistles, and there were two outstanding Spanish ones; Garcilaso's *Epístola a Boscán* (1543); and the *Epístola Moral a Fabio* (early 17th c.) ascribed to various authors. In England Jonson appears to have been the first to use the Horatian mode, in *The Forest* (1616). Vaughan, Dryden and Congreve also produced epistles of the Horatian kind. Pope proved to be the most skilled practitioner of this form, especially in his *Moral Essays* (1731–5) and *An Epistle to Dr Arbuthnot* (1735). More recent poets have revived the form, which was not much favoured in the 19th c. Auden's *Letter to Lord Byron* is a good example; so is his *New Year Letter*. Louis MacNeice wrote *Letters from Iceland*.

epistolary novel A novel (q.v.) in the form of letters. It was a particularly popular form in the 18th c. Among the more famous examples are: Richardson's *Pamela* (1740) and *Clarissa Harlowe* (1747, 1748); Smollett's *Humphry Clinker* (1771); Rousseau's *La Nouvelle Héloïse* (1761); and Laclos's *Les Liaisons dangereuses* (1782). Less well known are Harriet Lee's *Errors of Innocence* (1786), John Moore's *Mordaunt* (1800) and Swinburne's *Love's Cross Currents* (1877). Such a technique has not often been favoured, but John Barth's *Letters* (1979), where the author writes to characters from his previous novels, Alice Walker's *The Color Purple* (1982) and Lionel Shriver's thriller *We Need to Talk about Kevin* (2003) are notable recent examples. It is not unusual for letters to make up *some* part of a novel. A number of novels written recently are partly or entirely comprised of email correspondence; David Llewelyn's *Eleven* (2005) is one example. *See also* BRIEFROMAN.

epistrophe (Gk 'upon turning') A figure of speech in which each sentence or clause ends with the same word.

episyntheton (Gk 'compound') Meter composed of different cola (q.v.).

epitaph (Gk '[writing] on a tomb') Inscription on a tomb or grave; a kind of valediction which may be solemn, complimentary, witty or even flippant. Simonides of Ceos (556–468 BC) wrote epitaphs of simplicity and power, including the famous one on the Three Hundred who fell at Thermopylae:

> Go, tell the Lacedaimonians, passer-by,
> That here obedient to their laws we lie.

The major collection of Classical epitaphs is to be found in Book IV of the *Greek Anthology*, a collection of poems from the Classical to the Byzantine period of Greek letters. These epitaphs vary from comic to serious and had considerable influence on Roman and Renaissance writers.

Famous epitaphs include John Wilmot, Earl of Rochester, on King Charles II:

> Here lies a great and mighty king
> Whose promise none relies on;
> He never said a foolish thing,
> Nor ever did a wise one.

And Dr Johnson on Oliver Goldsmith:

> To Oliver Goldsmith, Poet, Naturalist, and Historian, who left scarcely any style of writing untouched, and touched nothing that he did not adorn.

Not a few writers have composed their own epitaphs. Thomas Gray, for example, appended his own to his *Elegy* (1750). Sir Walter Ralegh is said to have written his on the eve of his execution in 1618:

> Even such is Time, that takes in trust
> Our youth, our joys, our all we have,
> And pays us but with earth and dust;
> Who, in the dark and silent grave,
> When we have wandered all our ways,
> Shuts up the story of our days.
> But from this earth, this grave, this dust,
> My God shall raise me up, I trust.

Then there is Alexis Piron's:

> Here lies Piron, a complete nullibiety
> Not even a Fellow of a Learned Society.

Some epitaphs approximate to elegy or lament or dirge (*qq.v.*). There is the marvellous dirge in Shakespeare's *Cymbeline*:

> Fear no more the heat o' the sun . . .

And Gerard Manley Hopkins's poem *Felix Randall* and Matthew Arnold's *Requiescat. See also* DIRGE; ELEGY; EPICEDIUM; EPIGRAM; LAMENT; UBI SUNT.

epitasis (Gk 'near intensification') That part of a play when the dénouement or climax (*qq.v.*) approaches, when the plot thickens. It precedes the catastrophe (*q.v.*). *See also* CATASTASIS; FREYTAG'S PYRAMID; PROTASIS.

epithalamion (Gk 'at the bridal chamber') A song or poem sung outside the bride's room on her wedding night. Sappho is believed to have been the first poet to use it as a literary form. Theocritus wrote one; so, among other Latin poets, did Catullus. At the Renaissance, poets revived the form and many created memorable *epithalamia*: Tasso, Ronsard and du Bellay, to name three Europeans; and in England Sir Philip Sidney, Spenser, Donne, Ben Jonson, Herrick, Marvell, Crashaw and Dryden. By general agreement one of the finest of all is Spenser's. The traditional conventions of this form required the circumstances of a wedding, the events of the wedding day, and the celebration by the poet of the married couple's experience. Spenser may have written his in honour of his own wedding (1594). Sir John Suckling (1609–42) wrote an agreeable parody of such songs called *A Ballad upon a Wedding*. After Dryden the epithalamion went out of fashion. Much later, at the beginning of the 19th c., Shelley wrote an *Epithalamium* (the *-ium* ending is the Latin form) and Tennyson closed *In Memoriam* with an epithalamion. There was also A. E. Housman's song 'He is here, Urania's son'. *See* PROTHALAMION.

epithet Usually an adjective or phrase expressing some quality or attribute which is characteristic of a person or thing. For example: Long John, Dusty Miller, Chalky White, Nobby Clark, Richard the Lionheart. *See also* HOMERIC EPITHET; POETIC DICTION.

epitome (Gk 'cutting short') An abridgement or summary. A long scientific treatise or historical work may be compressed into a single book. A good modern example is the one-volume edition (1922) of Frazer's *The Golden Bough*, which originally appeared in twelve volumes (1890–1915).

epitrite (Gk 'a third as much again') In Classical prosody a metrical foot containing one unstressed and three stressed syllables: ∪ / / /. Like the paeon (*q.v.*), the epitrite had three other forms: / ∪ / /; / / ∪ /; and / / / ∪. They were known as first, second, third and fourth epitrites. Rare in English verse; occasionally used in combination with other feet. Gerard Manley Hopkins, who experimented with paeonic feet, sometimes used them. *See also* SPRUNG RHYTHM.

epizeuxis (Gk 'fastening together') A figure of speech in which a word or phrase is repeated emphatically to produce a special effect. *See* INCREMENTAL REPETITION; REFRAIN.

epode (Gk 'additional song') In a lyric ode (*q.v.*) by a Classical writer the epode completed the strophe and antistrophe (*qq.v.*) and its metrical form was different. It is not often found in English verse, but there is an interesting example of its use in Gray's Pindaric ode *The Progress of Poesy*.

eponymous (Gk 'giving the name to') An eponymous hero, heroine or protagonist (*qq.v.*) gives his or her name to the title of the work. For instance: *King Lear, Pamela, Silas Marner, Dr Zhivago*.

epopee (Gk 'poem making') An epic (*q.v.*) poem or epic poetry.

epos (Gk 'word, song') A name given to early epic (*q.v.*) poetry in the oral tradition (*q.v.*).

epyllion (Gk 'little epos', 'scrap of poetry') The sense of 'little epic' appears to date from the 19th c., when it was used to describe a short narrative poem in dactylic hexameters. The genre included mythological subjects and love themes. The poems are usually learned, elaborate and allusive. They were popular in the Alexandrian period and the late Republican and early Augustan periods. The Byzantine poets also wrote *epyllia*. As a form of narrative verse (*q.v.*) it has some affinities with the Russian *byliny* (*q.v.*), the South Slav *narodne pesme* (*q.v.*) and Greek *kleftic* songs. There are a great many poems in English literature which might be described as *epyllia*. In Renaissance poetry they tended to be a kind of erotic treatment of a mythological narrative. For example, Shakespeare's *Venus and Adonis*, Marlowe's *Hero and Leander*, Thomas Lodge's *Scillaes Metamorphosis* (1589) and Francis Beaumont's *Salmacis and Hermaphroditus* (1602). More generally the term might apply to such poems as Arnold's *Sohrab and Rustum* and C. Day Lewis's *Flight to Australia*. *See* EPIC; NARRATIVE VERSE.

equivalence In quantitative verse the rule that two short syllables equal one long.

equivoque *See* PUN.

erasure A term used in the theory of deconstruction (*q.v.*). It involves paradox (*q.v.*) and the idea is to suggest *suspicion* of an idea/concept by marking it as crossed and thus erased. This is a 'signal' that the idea/concept is at once unreliable *and* indispensable. In French it is called *sous rature* ('under erasure').

erotesis (Gk 'question') A rhetorical device in which a question is asked in order to get a definite answer – usually 'no'.

erotica Broadly, any material principally focused on human sexual relations. Today, the term also has a more precise use, with a distinction frequently made between erotica and pornography (*q.v.*). The former is often understood to be more sophisticated; the latter more formulaic and instrumental (the consumption of pornography is largely about achieving sexual gratification). Erotica may sometimes be art; pornography never so. The distinction is implicitly moral and probably overstated. In any case, the wider meaning of erotica encompasses all kinds of writing, including pornography in its original sense, the 'writing of prostitutes'.

Some of the earliest erotica are sex manuals. The oldest may be the Chinese so-called *Handbooks of Sex* by Emperor Huangdi (*c.* 2697–*c.* 2598 BC), who is also considered to have written *The Tao Love of Coupling*. Philaenis of Samos (early 2nd c. BC), apparently a Greek courtesan, wrote a manual on courtship and sex, of which fragments survive. It was reputably widely read in the ancient world and influenced Ovid's burlesque *Ars Amatoria* (*c.* AD 2). The most famous sex manual of all is the Indian *Kama Sutra* (compiled *c.* 2nd c. AD), attributed to Vātsyāyana. The Sanskrit text is only partly about sex, and also instructs on love and virtuous living. *The Perfumed Garden for the Soul's Recreation* was a 16th c. Arabic work by Sheikh Nefzaoui.

After the development of printing, sex manuals, like other forms of erotica, were subject to censorship (*q.v.*) in the West, and the only ones available were translations of the earlier works like *The Perfumed Garden*, which had to be distributed clandestinely in small numbers. The instructional writing on sexuality by the American advocate for free speech and women's rights Ida Craddock (1857–1902), such as *The Wedding Night* and *Right Marital Living*, were ground-breaking. While not explicit by today's standards, they were banned, and Craddock was convicted of obscenity, which precipitated her suicide. Several books instructing on marital sex were published in Europe from after the First World War onwards, including Marie Stopes's *Married Love* (1918). David Reuben's *Everything You Always Wanted to Know about Sex (But Were Afraid to Ask)* (1969) was the first modern publication to describe sexual acts in explicit terms; Alex Comfort's *The Joy of Sex* (1972) was the first of many manuals published by a mainstream publisher.

Erotic poetry has a long and venerable history. There is a considerable body of Greek erotic verse, particularly by Sappho of Lesbos (*c.* 620–*c.* 570 BC) and Staton of Sardis (1st–2nd c. AD). The major Roman authors are Catullus, Propertius and Ovid. Much erotic poetry survives also from Indian and Arab cultures. In the early Sanskrit literature there is *Medhaduta* (5th c.) and the *Sringsataka* (7th or 8th c.). From Arab civilization we have two major collections of poems: the *Hamā'sa* and the *Mu'allaqāt* (*q.v.*) (both 10th c.). During the Renaissance period erotic poetry was not uncommon, though often it was not written for publication. Notable examples are Shakespeare's *Venus and Adonis* (1593) and Marlowe and Chapman's *Hero and Leander* (1598). In the 17th c. a considerable amount of obscene verse was written by Restoration rakes like John Wilmot, Earl of Rochester (1647–80). Poems such as Rochester's *A Ramble in St. James's Park*, which uncovers all manner of debauchery, were posthumously published in various compilations. In the 19th c. in England the Pre-Raphaelite poets dedicated themselves considerably to erotic themes. Swinburne, perhaps the most notorious, wrote a number of poems that dwelt on flagellation. Much of the poetry of the French symbolists was homoerotic, and many important poets of the 20th c. wrote homoerotic verse, including C. P. Cavafy, Federico Garcia Lorca, W. H. Auden, Allen Ginsberg and Maureen Duffy.

The tradition of prose erotica is almost as rich and long. From the classical era there is Petronius's *Satyricon* (late 1st c. AD) and from the medieval period Boccaccio's *Decameron* (1353). The latter helped foster a tradition of bawdy narrative, as exemplified by Chaucer's *Miller's Tale* (late 14th c.) and the *Facetiae* (15th c.) by Bracciolini. Many erotic works were produced throughout the 16th through to the 19th c.; notable landmarks include what is perhaps the first erotic novel, John Cleland's *Fanny Hill* (1748), the autobiography *Histoire de ma vie* by Casanova (1725–98), and the Marquis de Sade's libertine novels, including *120 Days of Sodom* (written 1785, published 1902), an uncompromising exploration of sexual abuse. Classic works of 20th c. erotic fiction include Georges Bataille's *Story of the Eye* (1928), Henry Miller's *Tropic of Cancer* (1934), Pauline Réage's *The Story of O* (1954), Vladimir Nabokov's *Lolita* (1955), Richard Amory's *Song of the Loon* (1966), Anaïs Nin's *Delta of Venus* (1978) and Nicholson Baker's *Vox* (1992).

Since the late 20th c., several publishers have produced imprints of erotic fiction geared towards particular markets. Black Lace (1993–2010), for instance, published erotica written by and for women. The majority of erotic fiction now being written is online. A large proportion of this is fan fiction, or fanfic, which typically explores the erotic possibilities between characters which appear in popular literature, television and film, such as *Star Trek* or the *Harry Potter* books.

Erwartungshorizont *See* HORIZON OF EXPECTATIONS.

Erzählung (G 'narration, narrative') The term denotes the actual process of telling a story and has also been used to describe a short story (*q.v.*) and a *Novelle* (*see* NOVELLA).

Erziehungsroman *See* BILDUNGSROMAN.

escape literature *See* LITERATURE OF ESCAPE.

Esperanto One of several artificial 'international' languages compounded of words from different tongues. The word appears to derive from the Spanish *esperanza*, 'hope'. L. L. Zamenhof invented the language and published it in 1887.

espinella A Spanish stanza form believed to have been invented by the poet Vicente Espinel (1550–1624). It is an octosyllabic ten-line stanza which rhymes abba: accddc. Since its innovation it has been widely used.

esprit décadent A phrase associated with decadence (*q.v.*) in the period *c.* 1880–*c.* 1890. It has been attributed to the poet Jules Laforgue and he may have 'derived' it from Verlaine's sonnet *Je suis l'Empire à la fin de la décadence*. It refers to the state of mind and spirit which prevailed among and was affected by a large number of poets and men of letters in France in that era. It is particularly associated with small literary societies which flourished briefly at the time, and which met for the discussion of poetry and literature in general, art, politics, philosophy, etc. Decadence (which has nothing to do with *decade*, from the Greek word for ten) implies decay, degeneration, a wasting away of moral (and physical) fibre and vigour. *L'esprit décadent* verged on a posture of affectation, and was the expression of disenchantment and disillusionment – the *fin de siècle* malaise – with life. A species of ennui and pessimism expressive of the futility of life, a disdain of the everyday and ordinary (and natural), and a repugnance to moral and religious convention and taboo. *See* SYMBOL AND SYMBOLISM.

essay (F *essai*, 'attempt') A composition, usually in prose (Pope's *Moral Essays* in verse are an exception), which may be of only a few hundred words (like Bacon's *Essays*) or of book length (like Locke's *Essay Concerning Human Understanding*) and which discusses, formally or informally, a topic or a variety of topics. It is one of the most flexible and adaptable of all literary forms.

It was known to the Classical writers (Bacon observes that 'the word is late, but the thing is ancient') and the *Characters* of Theophrastus (3rd c. BC), the *Meditations* of Marcus Aurelius (2nd c. AD) and Seneca's *Epistle to Lucilius* (1st c. AD) all qualify for inclusion in this genre.

Montaigne coined the word *essai* when, in 1580, he gave the title *Essais* to his first publication. In 1597 Bacon described his *Essays* as 'grains of salt which will rather give an appetite than offend with satiety'. Whereas Montaigne was discursive, informal and intimate (writing on such topics as Liars, The Custom of Wearing Clothes and The Art of Conversation), Bacon was terse, didactic and aloof, though choosing not dissimilar topics (Of Envy, Of Riches, Of Negotiating, Of the Vicissitude of Things). Montaigne's essays often run to many thousands of words; Bacon's seldom exceed a few hundred.

Towards the end of the 17th c., with the proliferation of pamphlets and periodicals, the essay was becoming an increasingly popular form of diversion. No fewer than ninety different periodicals came out between 1709 and 1720. Daniel Defoe's journalistic essays and pamphlets, and especially his *Review* (1704–13), influenced the evolution of the essay, but even more important was the type of periodical essay established by Addison and Steele in the *Tatler* (1709–11) and the *Spectator* (1711–12). They wrote on such subjects as the Tombs in Westminster Abbey, Ladies' Headdress, and Recollections of Childhood, as well as serious moral issues, and literary faculties such as Wit and Imagination.

In the middle of the 18th c. Johnson made his contribution to the essay with *The Rambler* and *The Idler*. He also contributed to other publications like the *Gentlemen's Magazine*. Johnson for the most part was moral and didactic (though there are moments of levity in some of *The Idler* papers) and his prose was lapidary; a very considerable contrast to Addison and Steele, who set out to divert and whose style was urbanely relaxed.

The essay has flourished ever since. Distinguished essayists have included Coleridge, Carlyle, Ruskin, Arnold, Pater, Emerson, Poe, Thoreau, Santayana, Sainte-Beuve, Montesquieu, Bertrand Russell, Sartre, Camus and Aldous Huxley. In the second half of the 20th c. fewer familiar and informal essays were published, in part because there were fewer periodicals to take them. At the same time the literary and critical essay and the essay of ideas have become commonplaces, especially in the numerous academic publications. From time to time distinguished authors produce a volume of them. Some examples include Virginia Woolf's *A Room of One's Own* (1929), which has become a classic of feminist criticism (*q.v.*), George Orwell's *Critical Essays* (1946), Philip Roth's *Reading Myself and Others* (1975) and Chinua Achebe's *Hopes and Impediments* (1989). *See also* CAUSERIE; PROPOS.

essence   In philosophy, essence is the attribute (or set of attributes) that makes a thing what it is – without which it would lose its identity. For example, the essence of a pen might be its ability to write; its colour or precise shape would be merely an accidental, not essential, quality. We encounter more difficulties, however, when we try to define the essence of 'goodness' or 'love' or 'man' or 'woman' or the 'ideal state'. The notion of essence has been challenged and undermined by many thinkers since the Enlightenment. Most of these have viewed essence as a verbal, ideological and social construction. *See also* EXISTENTIALISM; PLATONISM.

essentialism The belief or presumption that people, cultures or literature each possess an 'essence', that is, a core, defining and unchanging quality or set of qualities. For instance, women of all cultures and classes are frequently held to be essentially nurturing. Similarly, some claim that homosexual men throughout history can be shown to be in possession of a 'gay sensibility'. One essentialist definition of literature might be 'any writing that speaks of the "human condition"', an assertion which is commonly made by liberal humanist critics. Long before modern literary theory emerged, essentialism had been undermined by many thinkers, ranging from Locke and Hume through Hegel to the Anglo-Idealist philosophers Bradley and Bosanquet, as well as by the heterological tradition of thought running from Schopenhauer through Nietzsche to Freud and Bergson.

In recent times, two theoretical developments may be understood as working against essentialist thought. Marxist criticism (*q.v.*), deriving some of its formative insights from Hegel, holds that culture is contingent on the particular economic structures that organize a society in a given epoch; it is therefore erroneous to claim that, say, literature exhibits the same qualities across history. Poststructuralist thinkers have argued that social identities do not pre-exist language and culture; rather they are a product of dominant discursive formations. Thus recently it has become quite conventional in academic circles to argue that identities are historically, socially and linguistically *constructed*. Constructionism (*q.v.*) is not without its problems, however. An insistence on the artificiality of identity categories potentially removes the basis for identity politics (*q.v.*). It also becomes more difficult to speak of a particular group's 'ownership' of specific traditions, e.g. black writing. In response, some have suggested that 'strategic essentialism' offers the best way forward (the postcolonial theorist Gayatri Spivak coined the term). Such an approach entails not only an acknowledgement of the limitations of identity categories, and in particular their tendency to generalize people, but also a recognition that these categories must be strategically retained, since they offer crucial tools for collective organization. *See also* FEMINIST CRITICISM; GAY AND LESBIAN CRITICISM; LIBERAL HUMANISM; POSTCOLONIALISM; POSTSTRUCTURALISM; QUEER THEORY.

estancia A general and ultimately vague Spanish term for a series of verses forming a rhythmic whole. Some are regular, following an ordered plan; some irregular and giving an effect of caprice or disorder. Often of four, six, eight or ten lines; six or eight syllables or even alexandrines (*q.v.*) may be found. The poet chose his form according to his feelings as he composed.

estates satire Traditionally, the estates of the realm are three: Lords Spiritual, Lords Temporal, and Commons. The ancient Parliament of Scotland comprised the king and three estates: (a) archbishops, abbots and mitred priors; (b) the barons and commissioners of shires and stewartries; (c) the commissioners from the royal burghs. In France, the three estates were nobles, clergy and the plebs (they remained separate until 1780). The fourth estate is, colloquially, the press. The concept of a strictly gradated society is ancient and perhaps universal; certainly it dominated medieval thinking about society.

Satires on the estates (many in Latin) were a kind of exposition of the duties and responsibilities of different members and the characteristics of individual groups plus criticism of their shortcomings. To a certain extent, Chaucer does this in the 'General Prologue' to his *Canterbury Tales*, which contains some quite scathing portraits of individual types (e.g. Friar, Summoner and Pardoner). Langland drew on the same tradition in *Piers Plowman*, and its use is discernible in, for example, the anonymous ME poem *Mum and the Sothsegger*. Much later we find an interesting development of the tradition in Sir David Lindsey's curious morality play (*q.v.*) *Ane Pleasant Satyre of the Thrie Estaites* (1540).

The general concept of a hierarchical system of 'estates' is also inherent in the theory of the 'Great Chain of Being' (*q.v.*).

estrambote In Spanish verse a term denoting an addition of a few lines which may be made to a stanza or a sonnet (*qq.v.*). Sometimes used for a comment or gloss (*q.v.*) on what has gone before.

estrangement This term has undergone a considerable history of attempted clarification, conducted especially with a view to distinguishing it from alienation (*q.v.*), its habitual synonym. Although the concept is present in earlier writers such as Rousseau, it first acquires a central status in the writings of Hegel and Marx. The German word used by Hegel in *The Phenomenology of Spirit* to denote 'estrangement' (*Entäusserung*) overlaps in its meaning with the terms used to designate 'externalization' and 'objectification'. All of these notions belong to the second stage of Hegel's dialectic: an entity which in the first stage is apprehended as merely given and self-identical is viewed in the second stage as 'self-estranged' or 'externalized', its identity being comprised by the totality of relations into which it enters. The third stage abrogates this estrangement and restores identity, in a larger, mediated and universal sense.

In his *Economic and Philosophical Manuscripts* (1944), Marx praises this dialectic for recognizing that human beings create the objective world through labour but criticizes it for its purely speculative supersession of estrangement; Marx makes a crucial distinction between mere objectification or externalization and estrangement or alienation. The latter is a specific social condition associated with the bourgeois world, and especially private property: the individual experiences the products of his own labour, and the entire 'objective' world including the state, as alien to him. This estrangement, says Marx, can be abolished only 'practically', by revolution. The concept of estrangement has also had a wide currency in sociology, psychology and certain areas of philosophy such as existentialism. In the drama of Brecht, the concept of alienation derives from *Verfremdungseffekt*. *See* ALIENATION; ALIENATION EFFECT.

estribillo (Sp 'little stirrup'; diminutive of *estribo*, 'stirrup') The equivalent of the French *ritournelle*; in Spanish it denotes a refrain or chorus (also a pet word or phrase). It is a theme-verse or stanza (of from two to four lines) of a *villancico* (*q.v.*) and may have originated in the Arabic *zéjel* (*q.v.*). We first come across it in the 11th c. in the form of the romance *jarcha* (*q.v.*) of a Hebrew poem. After *villancicos* ceased to be written they developed another lease of life as the *copla* (*q.v.*) of modern times. The *estribillo* is thus a diachronic element in Spanish popular lyric poetry. Sometimes the *estribillo* formed an introductory stanza, stating the theme of a poem, and then was repeated at the end. Also used in ballad. *Estribote* is an augmentative from *estribo*.

estridentismo A literary movement in Mexico initiated in 1922 by Manuel Maples Arce (1898–1980). Those associated with it espoused and glorified the industrial future at the expense of the 'classical' or 'romantic' past. Their symbols tended to be engines, machinery, industrial plant, etc. The movement soon fizzled out. *See* FUTURISM.

estrofa (Sp 'strophe') The equivalent to the English usage of stanza (*q.v.*).

estrofa mauriqueña A type of *copla de pie quebrado* named after Jorge Maurique (*c.* 1440–79), with the rhyme pattern ABc ABc, where c is the short broken line. The effect is produced by having the two octosyllabic lines (A and B) followed by a four-syllable line (c). *See* COPLA; PIE QUEBRADO.

ethical criticism A mode of literary discussion about the relationship between criticism, literature and ethics, which developed in the latter half of the 20th c., and in response to poststructuralism (*q.v.*). It attempts to bring together the realm of ethics with the realm of the aesthetic, and explores such issues as the ethical nature of literary works, and the role of moral and cultural values that govern the creation and the interpretation of literary works. In North America, it is often associated with the work of critics such as John Gardner, Martha C. Nussbaum, Wayne C. Booth and J. Hillis Miller. In Europe, it has foundations in the continental moral philosophy of Emmanuel Levinas and various works of Jacques Derrida, as well as of Derek Attridge and the Australian philosopher Peter Singer.

ethnic studies In the United States, a term which designates the interdisciplinary study of specific racial or ethnic minority groups, including African-Americans, Asian-Americans and Native Americans. The field emerged on the back of a surge of cultural nationalism among racial minorities in the mid to late 1960s. The establishment of ethnic studies departments was motivated by what activists perceived as mainstream academia's persistent Eurocentrism (*q.v.*) and marginalization of the histories of non-white Americans. Ethnic studies faculties and programmes were envisaged as providing crucial political and cultural resources to non-whites, enabling individual groups to examine the challenges they faced, including racism, on their own terms. One of the earliest ethnic studies faculties was established in San Francisco State University in 1969, following a long strike by activist students. (The first Black Studies department was established in the same institution two years earlier.) A handful of comparative ethnic studies faculties have since been set up; by contrast, departments of African-American Studies (*q.v.*), Asian-American Studies, Native American Studies, and Chicana/o Studies (alternatively Mexican-American or Raza Studies) have become ubiquitous.

In the 1970s, during the so-called 'white-ethnic' revival which occurred in the wake of the Civil Rights era, similar demands were made by those who traced their ethnic heritage to immigrants arriving in America from Europe in the 19th and early 20th c. A small number of Italian-American and Irish-American Studies departments have been established, mainly in the north-east. In the 1990s, whiteness became the subject of particular academic scrutiny. 'White studies', however, is not concerned with establishing racial whiteness as just another ethnicity; rather, it interrogates how white hegemony (*q.v.*) is facilitated by socio-economic and political structures, as well as the ways in which whiteness is always inflected by other factors, such as class.

While ethnic studies has become successfully established in the American academy, it has often been the target of criticism, particularly from the right. Ethnic studies, like identity politics (*q.v.*) more generally, is frequently held to be culturally and racially separatist and to prevent its students from engaging in national and universal narratives. (Ethnic studies and white studies scholars might counter by arguing that whiteness and universality are all too often elided.) Sometimes attacks on ethnic studies have been made through legal channels. For instance, in 2010 legislation was passed in the State of Arizona that specifically outlaws any educational programme or class which promotes ethnic solidarity, or which is specifically designed to be taught to members of the same ethnic group. One Mexican-American studies programme has since been found to be in contravention of the new law, and a number of books on Mexican-American history have been banned from the classroom, as well as numerous works of literature, including even Shakespeare's *The Tempest*.

ethnocentrism Coined by the American political scientist William G. Sumner in 1906, ethnocentrism means literally that one's nation or ethnic group is at the centre of the world. The term denotes a belief in the cultural superiority of one's own ethnic group to all others. It fosters stereotypes, prejudice, and often hostile attitudes towards other nations or ethnic groups. *See also* EUROCENTRISM.

ethnography (Gk *ethnos*, 'nation' or 'people', and *graphia*, 'writing') Literally, a written account of a people's customs and behaviours. Ethnography has traditionally been the study of cultures other than the ethnographer's own. Its methodology involves fieldwork, observation and some contact with native inhabitants. We find examples of some of the earliest ethnographic accounts in Herodotus's *Histories* about the societies and manners of the Greeks and the Egyptians. However, ethnography's emergence as a discipline is usually traced to the European 'voyages of discovery' and the period of high colonialism when there was a proliferation of ethnographic accounts of indigenous cultures written by Western travellers, traders, missionaries and colonizers. In these writings, native peoples and non-European cultures were constructed as inferior, primitive and in the early stages of civilizational development. In the 1980s and early 1990s, postcolonial scholars mounted a critique of the discipline's implication in the colonial project. The role of the observer and his or her subject position was also under scrutiny since it was previously thought that an ethnologist is a neutral observer, writing an objective, truthful and value-free account of another culture. In *Writing Culture* (1986), James Clifford was the first to analyse ethnography as a form of discourse (*q.v.*) and a literary form. He suggested that that we should analyse ethnographies as literary texts, and urged ethnographers to address critically 'the contingencies of language, rhetoric, power and history' in their writing.

etymology   (Gk 'true sense') The study of the history of words: their origins and how their form and meaning have changed over time. The earliest etymologies were written by the grammarians of Sanskrit of ancient India. Modern etymology emerged in Europe in the 18th c. The principal approaches to etymology include philological, which involves the study of changes recorded in written texts, and comparative – often used when textual evidence exists – where two or more related languages are systematically analysed together in order to make inferences about a shared parent language. Words appear in a language through a limited number of means: the borrowing of 'loanwords', onomatopoeia (*qq.v.*), and derivation and compounding. Etymologists are often equally concerned with semantic change, whereby the meaning of a given word shifts over time through a variety of mechanisms, including metaphor, synecdoche (*qq.v.*), auto-antonymy (where a word develops a meaning which is an antonym of its established use) and specialization. Philosophers – notably Nietzsche and Derrida – have examined etymologies in order to interrogate and critique salient concepts in Western thought, such as 'good' and 'evil'. *See also* LINGUISTICS.

Eugene Onegin stanza   *See* ONEGIN STANZA.

euhemerism   Euhemerus was a Sicilian who served Cassander of Macedonia (311–298 BC). In his *Sacred History* he put forward the questionable theory that the Greek gods had formerly been kings or heroes who enjoyed posthumous deification from those they had ruled. Such a treatment of myth (*q.v.*) was thus called 'euhemerism'.

euphemism   (Gk 'fair speech') The substitution of an offensive or disagreeable term by one considered more acceptable: 'pass away' for die; 'gosh' to avoid taking the Lord's name in vain; 'downsizing' for making forced redundancies. Probably the most infamous instance of euphemism in literature is to be found in George Orwell's *Nineteen Eighty-Four*: 'Newspeak' (*q.v.*) is the official language heavily reliant on euphemism which the novel's totalitarian regime wishes to implement in order to prevent seditious thought. *See also* DYSPHEMISM; METALEPSIS; PERIPHRASIS.

euphony (Gk 'sweetness of sound') The term denotes pleasing, mellifluous sounds, usually produced by long vowels rather than consonants; though liquid consonants can be euphonious. The almost voluptuously drowsy vowel sounds in the following lines from Keats's *Hyperion* soothe the ear:

> As when upon a trancèd summer night,
> Those green-robed senators of mighty woods,
> Tall oaks, branch-charmèd by the earnest stars,
> Dream, and so dream all night without a stir,

Consider also the effect of the liquid sounds in this stanza from Gerard Manley Hopkins's *Wreck of the Deutschland*:

> Is out with it! Oh,
> We lash with the best or worst
> Word last! Now a lush-kept plush-capped sloe
> Will, mouthed to flesh-burst,
> Gush! – flush the man, the being with it, sour or sweet,
> Brim, in a flash, full! – Hither then, last or first,
> To hero of Calvary, Christ's feet –
> Never ask if meaning it, wanting it, warned of it – men go.

See ASSONANCE; CACOPHONY; DISSONANCE; MELOPOEIA; ONOMATOPOEIA; TONE COLOUR.

euphuism An ornately florid, precious and mazy style of writing (often al-literative, antithetical and embellished with elaborate figures of speech) which takes its name from a two-part work by John Lyly, namely, *Euphues, the Anatomy of Wyt* (1578) and *Euphues and his England* (1580). In Greek, eu-phues means 'well endowed by nature'. Gabriel Harvey dubbed Lyly's style 'euphuism' in *Advertisement for Papp-Hatchet* (1589). Euphuism appears in Shakespeare's *Comedy of Errors*, *Two Gentleman of Verona* and *Love's Labour's Lost*. Shakespeare parodied the style in *Henry IV*, Pt 1. The more ornate and baroque (*q.v.*) prose styles of some of the early 17th c. writers suggest that Lyly's influence was considerable.

eupolidian (Gk 'well varied') In Classical prosody a term denoting a varied metrical form: a tetrameter (*q.v.*) with mixed choriambic and trochaic feet. *See* CHORIAMBUS; TROCHEE.

Eurocentrism The assumption that Europe constitutes the centre of the world, which is, for example, reflected in Europe's central position on the map of the world. This belief in Europe's centrality and cultural superior-ity dates back to the spatial ordering of the world during European coloniza-tion in 18th and 19th c. In his ground-breaking study *Orientalism* (1978), Edward Said examines how Eurocentrism has played a major role in the perception and construction of other cultures. As he explains, 'European culture was able to manage – and even produce – the Orient politically, sociologically, militarily, ideologically, scientifically, and imaginatively during the post-Enlightenment period'. As far as literature is concerned, literary scholars may examine how Eurocentric assumptions have shaped literary works. *See also* ETHNIC STUDIES; ETHNOCENTRISM; ORIENTALISM.

eutrepismus   (Gk 'turning about') The numbering of the different parts of an argument (*q.v.*).

excursus   (L 'running out') A detailed examination and analysis of a point, often added as an appendix to a book. An incidental discussion or digression.

exegesis   In Roman times the exegetes were professional and official interpreters of charms, omens, dreams, sacred law and oracular pronouncements. Thus the term has come to mean an explanation or interpretation and is often applied to biblical studies. As far as literature is concerned, it covers critical analysis and the elucidation of difficulties in the text. A variorum edition (*q.v.*), for example, contains a great deal of exegesis.

exemplum   (L 'example') A short narrative used to illustrate a moral. The term applies primarily to the stories used in medieval sermons. Occasionally the *exemplum* found its way into literature. Two good examples in Chaucer are *The Pardoner's Tale* and *The Nun's Priest's Tale* (late 14th c.). Gower, in *Confessio Amantis* (c. 1385), makes use of *exempla* when illustrating sins against Venus. In the Middle Ages theological handbooks for preachers contained large numbers of *exempla*. Two particularly important works of this kind were John Bromyard's *Summa Praedicantium* and the *Liber Exemplorum ad Usum Praedicantium* (14th c.). One of the most famous sourcebooks was the 13th c. Latin *Gesta Romanorum*. *See also* FABLE; FABLIAU; GESTA; SHORT STORY.

exergasia   (L 'amplification') A device by which a number of figures of speech amplify a point and embellish a passage. *See also* EUPHUISM.

Exilliteratur   (G 'exile literature') Literature composed by German authors while in exile when they sought refuge abroad during the period of the National Socialist regime. Among the more famous were Bertolt Brecht, Lion Feuchtwanger, Heinrich Mann, Thomas Mann and Stefan Zweig.

existentialism   (Or *Existenzphilosophie*) In philosophy, the terms *exist* and *existence* denote something active rather than passive and thus are closely dependent on the Latin root *ex*, 'out' + *sistere* from *stare*, 'to stand'. The term existentialism means 'pertaining to existence'; or, in logic, 'predicating existence'. Philosophically, it now applies to a vision of the condition and existence of man, his place and function in the world, and his relationship, or lack of one, with God. It is generally agreed that existentialism derives from the thinking of Søren Kierkegaard (1813–55), and especially in his books *Fear and Trembling* (1843), *The Concept of Dread* (1844) and *Sickness Unto Death* (1848). In these and other works Kierkegaard was for the most part re-stating and elaborating upon the belief that through God and in God man may find freedom from tension and discontent and therefore find peace of mind and spiritual serenity; an idea that had prevailed in much Christian thinking over many centuries. Kierkegaard became the pioneer of modern Christian existentialism. After him existential thought was greatly expanded at the beginning of the 20th c. by Heidegger and Jaspers (German philosophers), whose ideas in turn influenced a large number of European philosophers (e.g. Berdyaev, Unamuno, J. de Gautier and B. Fondane) and in whose work are to be found the sources of atheistic existentialism.

An important feature of atheistic existentialism is the argument that existence precedes essence (the reverse of many traditional forms of philosophy) for it is held that man fashions his own existence and only exists by so doing, and, in that process, and by the choice of what he does or does not do, gives essence to that existence.

Jean-Paul Sartre is the hierophant of modern existentialism and his version, expressed through his novels, plays and philosophical writings, is the one that has caught on and been the most widely influential. In Sartre's vision man is born into a kind of void (*le néant*), a mud (*le visqueux*). He has the liberty to remain in this mud and thus lead a passive, supine, acquiescent existence (like Oblomov and Samuel Beckett's sad tatterdemalions) in a 'semiconscious' state and in which he is scarcely aware of himself. However, he may come out of his subjective, passive situation (in which case he would 'stand out from'), become increasingly aware of himself and, conceivably, experience *angoisse* (a species of metaphysical and moral anguish). If so, he would then have a sense of the absurdity of his predicament and suffer despair. The energy deriving from this awareness would enable him to 'drag himself out of the mud', and begin to exist. By exercising his power of choice he can give meaning to existence and the universe. Thus, in brief, the human being is obliged to make himself what he is, and has to be what he is. A now classic statement on this situation is Sartre's description of the waiter in *L'Etre et le néant*.

In *L'Existentialisme est un humanisme* (1946) Sartre expressed the belief that man *can* emerge from his passive and indeterminate condition and, by an act of will, become *engagé*; whereupon he is committed (through *engagement*) to some action and part in social and political life. Through commitment man provides a reason and a structure for his existence and thus helps to integrate society.

In 1946 Sartre founded the review *Les Temps modernes*, a medium for existentialist writings. Apart from Sartre, some of the main exponents of *existentialisme* have been Albert Camus, Simone de Beauvoir, Merleau-Ponty and Jean Wahl. The main exponent of Christian existentialism has been Gabriel Marcel, the philosopher and dramatist, who has written some brilliant critical analyses of Sartre's point of view, and who, in his *Existence et objectivité* (1925), was very probably the first to introduce the term *existentialisme* into the vocabulary of French philosophy. Marcel's influence has been discernible in the work of some French novelists, notably Jean Cayrol and Luc Estang. *See also* COMMITMENT; THEATRE OF THE ABSURD.

exordium   The introductory part of a speech (*q.v.*) as laid down by the Classical rhetoricians. *See also* RHETORIC.

experimentalism   Intellectual/imaginative/creative activity which entails the exploration of new concepts, techniques, etc., which go beyond convention. Avant-garde (*q.v.*) movements come into this category. The 20th c. saw an enormous amount of experimentalist activity. *See* DADAISM; EXPRESSIONISM; MODERNISM; NOUVEAU ROMAN; VORTICISM.

experimentelen   (Du 'experimentalists') Members of a Duch movement in art and literature who were active in the 1950s. The term was invented by the painter Asgar Jorn.

explication   A formal and close analysis of a text: its structure, style, content, imagery – indeed every aspect of it. As a method of elucidation it is commonly practised in French schools, and to a certain extent now in England since the 1920s. Key works in the development of this kind of critical analysis are: *A Survey of Modernist Poetry* (1928) by Laura Riding and Robert Graves; *Practical Criticism* (1929) by I. A. Richards; and *Seven Types of Ambiguity* (1930) by William Empson. *See also* NEW CRITICISM.

expolitio   *See* EXERGASIA.

exposition   At the beginning of his play the dramatist is often committed to giving a certain amount of essential information about the plot and the events which are to come. He may also have to give information about what has 'already happened'. All this comes under the heading of exposition. A skilful dramatist is able to introduce this material without holding up the action of the play and without recourse to the obvious devices of narrative. *See also* PROTATIC CHARACTER.

expressionism   The term (probably used by Vauxcelles after a series of paintings by Julien-Auguste Hervé in 1901 under the title *Expressionismes*) refers to a movement in Germany very early in the 20th c. (*c.* 1905) in which a number of painters sought to avoid the representation of external reality and, instead, to project themselves and a highly personal vision of the world. The term can be applied to literature, but only judiciously.

Briefly summarized, the main principle involved is that expression determines form, and therefore imagery, punctuation, syntax, and so forth. Indeed, any of the formal rules and elements of writing can be bent or disjointed to suit the purpose.

The theories of expressionism had considerable influence in Germany and Scandinavia. In fact, expressionism dominated the theatre for a time in the 1920s. Theatrically it was a reaction against realism (*q.v.*) and aimed to show inner psychological realities. The origins of this are probably to be found in Strindberg's *The Dream Play* (1907) and *The Ghost Sonata* (1907). Wedekind's plays of the same period were also strongly expressionistic. He wrote violent anti-bourgeois plays, three of which are chiefly remembered: *Spring Awakening* (1891), *Lulu* (in two parts, 1895) and *Pandora's Box* (1902). At the age of nineteen Reinhard Sorge wrote what is regarded by some as the first drama of German expressionism, namely *Der Bettler* (1912). However, Carl Sternheim has a rival claim with his *Die Hose* (1910), which he followed with *Der Snob* in 1914. Ernst Toller is accepted as a spokesman of German expressionism in the theatre. He was something of an extremist and a revolutionary in style. His first major play was *Die Wandlung* (1919) which, presented in thirteen tableaux, depicted the horrors of war as he had experienced them. This he followed with *Masse Mensch* (1920) and *Massenschlacht* (1921). Another dramatist to make a great impression at the time was Fritz von Unruh, author of *Offiziere* (1911), *Prinz Louis Ferdinand von Preussen* (1913) and *Ein Geschlecht* (1917). During the 1920s he wrote several other expressionistic plays. Georg Kaiser was the most prolific dramatist of this movement and is credited with no fewer than seventy plays. Among his main works were *Von morgens bis mitternachts* (1916) and his trilogy which comprises *Die Koralle* (1917), *Gas I* (1918) and *Gas II* (1920). Walter Hasenclever also made an impact with *Der Sohn* (1914) and *Antigone* (1917). Most of these dramatists were to influence Brecht and in some of their plays we can see the makings of epic theatre (*q.v.*).

By the mid-1920s expressionism in the theatre was nearly extinct and it did not catch on much outside Germany – nor was it much understood. In France the influence has been negligible. In England and America the dramatists are really the only writers to have been affected; particularly Eugene O'Neill, Elmer Rice and Thornton Wilder. Up to a point T. S. Eliot, W. H. Auden and Christopher Isherwood have also been influenced.

It can be argued that expressionistic theories have also had some effects on writers like Wyndham Lewis and Virginia Woolf, as they certainly had upon Kafka, Schickele and Edschmid. The more involved and exaggerated prose experiments of James Joyce, William Faulkner and Samuel Beckett also bear signs of it. The long-term influences are discernible in the anti-novel (*q.v.*).

Merely sonic and colour effects in poetry and attempts at synaesthesia (*q.v.*), where much of the sense is sacrificed for the sake of sound (as in some of the work of Gerard Manley Hopkins and Roy Campbell), might also be described as expressionistic. Edith Sitwell wrote some whimsical expressionistic poems (like *I Do Like to be Beside the Seaside*) and the possible range of expressionism appears to remain very wide. Much more recently, for example, Christopher Middleton has written poems which might be described as expressionistic. *See also* ULTRAISM.

expressive form, fallacy of A term adopted by R. P. Blackmur (1904–65) from observations made by the poet and critic Yvor Winters (1900–68). Winters wrote of the 'heresy of expressive form' apropos Coleridge's concept of organic form (*q.v.*) and gave the view that it was not possible or desirable artistically to express or describe the disintegration of a belief or a civilization in a chaotic form. For example, he thought that Joyce's *Ulysses* (1922) was 'disintegrated', whereas it should have been disciplined and integrated. Critics pointed out that the transformation of inchoate material into the apparently chaotic was a matter of appearances, the result of the art that conceals art. T. S. Eliot's poem *The Waste Land* (1922) was not *actually* chaotic; it only *appeared* to be. The fallacy of expressive form refers to the idea that if a poet feels with sufficient intensity then this will be enough to create a successful poem. But, if a poet depends only on inspiration (*q.v.*), then this will not be adequate. He or she must also judge, compare, analyse. *See also* ARS EST CELARE ARTEM; SPONTANEITY.

expurgated edition An edition of a book from which passages have been deleted, to purify it of anything which might be deemed offensive, noxious or erroneous. *See* BOWDLERIZE; INDEX EXPURGATORIUS.

extenuatio *See* MEIOSIS.

external rhyme *See* RHYME.

extravaganza The word derives from the Italian *stravaganza* which means, approximately, 'influenced by extravagance'. It is a form of 19th c. English drama which consisted of an elaborately presented fairy tale (*q.v.*) or some mythical story: a sort of mixture of musical, pantomime (*q.v.*) and ballet. The spirit was always light, gay, even farcical, and reminiscent of burlesque (*q.v.*). The most talented writer of this form of entertainment was J. R. Planché who got his inspiration from a French diversion described as 'féerie folie'. It was at the Olympic Theatre, London, that a Madame Vestris perfected the form. A famous extravaganza was *Chu-Chin-Chow* (1916), by Frederick Norton and Oscar Asche. It was based on the story of Ali Baba and the Forty Thieves and ran for 2,238 consecutive performances (a record which stood for many years). Nowadays the nearest thing to an extravaganza is a revue (*q.v.*).

eye-rhyme *See* RHYME.

F

fable   (L *fabula*, 'discourse, story') A short narrative in prose or verse which points a moral. Non-human creatures or inanimate things are normally the characters. The presentation of human beings as animals is the characteristic of the literary fable and is unlike the fable that still flourishes among primitive peoples.

The genre probably arose in Greece, and the first collection of fables is ascribed to Aesop (6th c. BC). His principal successors were Phaedrus and Babrius, who flourished in the 1st c. AD. Phaedrus preserved Aesop's fables and in the 10th c. a prose adaptation of Phaedrus's translation appeared under the title *Romulus*, a work whose popularity lasted until the 17th c. A famous collection of Indian fables was the *Bidpai*, which were probably composed originally in Sanskrit *c.* AD 300. Many versions of these were made in prose and verse in different languages between the 3rd c. and 16th c. The best of the medieval fabulists was Marie de France who, *c.* 1200, composed 102 fables in verse. After her came La Fontaine who raised the whole level of the fable and is generally acknowledged as the world's master. He took most of the stories from Aesop and Phaedrus but translated them in his verse. His *Fables choisies* were published in twelve books (1668, 1678–9, 1694).

La Fontaine had many imitators: principally, Eustache de Noble, Pignotti, John Gay, J. P. C. de Florian and Tomás Iriarte. Later, Lessing followed the style of Aesop. John Gay's *Fifty-One Fables in Verse* were published in 1727. In Russia the greatest of the fabulists was Ivan Krylov, who translated a number of La Fontaine's fables and between 1810 and 1820 published nine books of fables. More recently Kipling made a notable contribution to the genre with *Just So Stories* (1902). Mention should also be made of James Thurber's droll *Fables of Our Time* (1940) and George Orwell's remarkable political satire *Animal Farm* (1945), which is in fable form. *See also* ALLE-GORY; BEAST EPIC; BESTIARY; CONTE.

A Dictionary of Literary Terms and Literary Theory, Fifth Edition. J. A. Cuddon.
© 2013 The Estate of J. A. Cuddon. Published 2013 by Blackwell Publishing Ltd.

fabliau   A short narrative in octosyllabic (*q.v.*) verse, usually of 300 to 400 lines. The genre flourished in France between 1150 and 1400 AD. About 150 are extant. The earliest known is *Richeut* (1159), but it seems likely that they existed earlier because disapproval of them was expressed in Egbert's *Poenitentiale* of the 8th c.

   Fabliaux tended to be ribaldly comic tales. They were satirical, in a rough and ready fashion, often at the expense of the clergy. Their caustic attitude towards women may have been a reaction against the apotheosis of women in the tradition and cult of courtly love (*q.v.*). The form is primarily French, but there are examples in English literature, like Chaucer's *Miller's Tale* and *Reeve's Tale* (late 14th c.). *See also* FABLE; LAY.

fabula   (L 'narrative, story, tale') The Latin *fabulae* were forms of drama among which we may distinguish the following: (a) *Fabula Atellana*, so called after the Oscan town Atella. A kind of southern Italian farce (*q.v.*) popular in Rome until the period of Augustus (63 BC–AD 14). They were bawdy pantomimes (*q.v.*) with stock characters (*q.v.*) who were represented by masks. Some of the main dramatis personae (*q.v.*) were: Bucco, the clown; Maccus, the fool; Pappus, the grandfather or foolish dotard; Manducus, a glutton; Dossenus, a hunchback. (b) *Fabula crepidata*, Roman tragedies based on Greek themes. The Roman word for *cothurnus* worn by the tragic actors was *crepida*; a term rendered in English by *buskin* (*q.v.*). (c) *Fabula palliata* (*palliata* from Latin *pallium*, 'cloak'). A type of comedy first introduced in Rome by Livius Andronicus in the 3rd c. BC. It remained popular for well over a hundred years and consisted for the most part of adaptations of Greek New Comedy (*q.v.*). The only extant *palliatae* were created by Plautus and Terence. (d) *Fabula praetexta*, so called from the *toga praetexta* – a garment worn by priests and magistrates and bordered with a purple stripe. Such *fabulae* were dramas based on Roman history which presented well-known Roman personalities. Thus, a kind of history play (*q.v.*). The invention of the form is attributed to Naevius of the 3rd c. BC. (e) *Fabula saltica*, so called from *saltire*, 'to jump', they were a form of Roman ballet and pantomime. (f) *Fabula stataria*, so called because it tended to be a static form of drama, in distinction from the *motoria* or rapidly moving comedy (or what we should now call farce) with stock characters. (g) *Fabula togata*, so named from the *toga* – the traditional Roman garment. Such dramas were a form of comedy based on Greek models but dealing with Roman life and characters. The main dramatist was Afranius and this type of comedy had some vogue in the latter part of the 2nd c. BC. *See also* FORMALISM, RUSSIAN.

fabulation   A term used to describe the anti-novel (*q.v.*). It appears to have been introduced by Robert Scholes in *The Fabulators* (1967). Fabulation involves allegory (*q.v.*), verbal acrobatics and surrealistic effects. However, it is not entirely a new term; Caxton used *Fabulator* in 1484.

facetiae   A bookseller's term for humorous or obscene books.

faction A portmanteau word (*q.v.*) of obvious composition which originated *c.* 1970 and denotes fiction which is based on and combined with fact. Notable examples are Truman Capote's *In Cold Blood* (1966), Norman Mailer's *Armies of the Night* (1968) and Alex Haley's *Roots* (1976). It is a vague term at the best of times and its usefulness has been questioned. It might easily apply, for instance, to historical novels which combine a great deal of period fact with fictional treatment, or to novels which incorporate actual living personalities (e.g. the President of the USA, the British Prime Minister or the General Secretary of the United Nations) in a narrative about recent events which pertain to historical fact. Faction has proved to be quite a controversial matter, particularly in connection with television. *See* NON-FICTION NOVEL.

fairy tale Fairy tales belong to folk literature (*q.v.*) and are part of the oral tradition (*q.v.*). And yet no one bothered to record them until the brothers Grimm produced their famous collection of *Kinder- und Hausmärchen* or *Household Tales* (1812, 1814, 1822).

In its written form the fairy tale tends to be a narrative in prose about the fortunes and misfortunes of a hero or heroine who, having experienced various adventures of a more or less supernatural kind, lives happily ever after. Magic, charms, disguise and spells are some of the major ingredients of such stories, which are often subtle in the interpretation of human nature and psychology.

The origins of fairy tales are obscure. Some think they may have come from the East. *The Thousand and One Nights* or *Arabian Nights' Entertainments* were written in Arabic and were translated into French in the 18th c.

In European literature there are three major collections: (a) Charles Perrault's *Contes de ma mère l'Oye* (1697), which were translated into English by Robert Samber in 1729; (b) the collection made by the Grimm brothers already mentioned; (c) Hans Christian Andersen's *Fairy Tales* (*Eventyr*) published in 1835. Other fairy tales have been composed by Ruskin, Thackeray, Charles Kingsley, Jean Ingelow and Oscar Wilde. Stories about Prince Charming, Red Riding Hood, Puss in Boots and Cinderella have a European background. *See* CONTE; SHORT STORY; SUPERNATURAL STORY.

Falkentheorie A theory of the *novella* (*q.v.*) worked out by the German writer Paul Heyse (1830–1914). This theory is based on the ninth tale of the fifth day of Boccaccio's *Decameron* (*c.* 1349–51). It is the story of Federigo who wasted his substance in the fruitless wooing of a rich mistress; wasted it to such an extent that he had only his favourite falcon left. This, too, he sacrificed – and his mistress was so moved by the act that she surrendered. The falcon is thus symbolic and denotes the strongly marked silhouette – as Heyse puts it – which, according to him, distinguishes one *novella* from another and gives it a unique quality. An interesting but elaborate theory, which is only another way of saying that each story is different from the others.

falling action That part of a play which follows the dénouement or climax (*qq.v.*). *See* FREYTAG'S PYRAMID; RESOLUTION; RISING ACTION.

falling rhythm This occurs when the stress pattern is thrown backwards in a line of verse so that it falls on the first syllables of the feet. The dactyl and the trochee (*qq.v.*) are the two basic feet in falling rhythm. The following example (basically trochaic) comes from Shakespeare's *The Passionate Pilgrim*:

> Crábbĕd áge ănd yoúth
> Cánnŏt líve tŏgéthĕr;
> Yoúth ĭs fúll ŏf pleásănce,
> Áge ĭs fúll ŏf cáre;
> Yoúth lĭke súmmĕr mórn,
> Áge lĭke wíntĕr's weáthĕr;
> Yoúth lĭke súmmĕr bráve,
> Áge lĭke wíntĕr báre;
> Yoúth ĭs fúll ŏf spórt,
> Ágĕ's breáth ĭs shórt.

See RISING RHYTHM.

false masque *See* ANTI-MASQUE.

familiar verse *See* LIGHT VERSE.

fancy and imagination Two much used and much debated terms in the history of critical theory. As on so many matters relating to literature, its forms and principles, issue was joined again during the Middle Ages and at the Renaissance in the names of the two critical world-champions – Aristotle and Plato. Medieval thought on matters of invention was dominated by Aristotle. Renaissance thought was dominated by Plato. Shakespeare represents the Platonic point of view in *A Midsummer Night's Dream* (V, i):

> And imagination bodies forth
> The forms of things unknown, the poet's pen
> Turns them to shapes, and gives to airy nothing
> A local habitation and a name.

For the Elizabethans poetry had something in it of the divine; it enabled one to express things that were beyond the rational powers. Intuitive perception gave insight by the 'feigning' of poetry. As Bacon put it in Book II of *The Advancement of Learning*, poetry was always thought

> to have some participation of divinesse, because it doth raise and erect the Minde, by submitting the shewes of things to the desires of the Mind, whereas reason doth buckle and bowe the Mind unto the Nature of things.

In his *Apologie for Poetrie* (1595), Sir Philip Sidney puts the point that poetry pleases and instructs by *mimesis* (*q.v.*), by metaphor, by counterfeiting, and at the same time the poet transforms what he finds in Nature, creates forms that did not exist.

Halfway through the 17th c. Hobbes addressed himself to the matter of the poetic imagination in *Leviathan* (1651). All knowledge, he avers, comes from sensory experience. Images of objects are stored in the memory. Judgement and fancy (or imagination) between them develop from this store. In *Leviathan* he expresses the view that fancy is a faculty which finds likeness, and that judgement distinguishes differences. Judgement, which, for Hobbes, was very nearly the same thing as memory, needs to hold fancy in check.

Dryden's views about poetic composition were very similar to those of Hobbes (see Dryden's preface to *Annus Mirabilis*). Hobbes's theory was very influential indeed.

The next major contribution to this topic came from John Locke in his *Essay Concerning Human Understanding* (1690). He describes 'wit' in very much the same terms as Hobbes had used for 'imagination', and their views of the function of judgement are almost identical. Locke also developed the theory of the 'association of ideas'. Locke's influence was also great, and it can be said that between them Locke and Hobbes laid the basis of psychological theory in aesthetics and literary criticism which was to prevail in the 18th c. Addison, too, made a vital contribution in his *Spectator* papers on *The Pleasures of the Imagination.* These were widely read. Addison amplified the associative theory and showed that the connotations of words were quite as important as their denotations.

During much of the 18th c. the creative and inventive processes of the mind were analysed in considerable depth, particularly by Hartley in *Observations on Man* (1749), by Joseph Priestley in *Hartley's Theory of the Human Mind*, by Hume in *Treatise of Human Nature* (1739) and his *Enquiry Concerning Human Understanding* (1748), by Shaftesbury in *Characteristicks* (1711), by Alexander Gerard in *Essay on Genius* (1774), and by William Blake, who took a wholly different point of view from the empiricists. Blake's view was different because the last thing he believed or wanted to believe was that the world was a great machine and God its divine mechanic. Blake held that the human soul existed before birth and had intuitive knowledge and understanding of the spirit world from which it came. To Blake the natural order was an external manifestation of the spiritual and transcendent world. Everything in the natural world had for him a spiritual meaning and thus it was full of symbols, symbols of ideal forms. As Baudelaire was later to express it in *Correspondances*:

> La Nature est un temple où de vivants piliers
> Laissent parfois sortir de confuses paroles;
> L'homme y passe à travers des forêts de symboles

To Blake, the function of the imagination was to decipher these codes, symbols and celestial hieroglyphics, these outward signs of an inward universal grace, and render their meaning in poetry. Thus Blake did not have an intellectual and philosophical system. He trusted to intuition rather than analysis.

But, fundamentally, during the 18th c. fancy and imagination were usually taken to be, if not synonymous, very nearly the same thing, and judgement was regarded as the superior and stronger faculty because it controlled (or ought to control) the fanciful and imaginative processes. Scattered about Johnson's various writings, for example, we continually find strictures on flights of fancy and admonitions to guard against them. Johnson was deeply suspicious of the potency of the fancy and imagination, but it may be said that in general people would have agreed with him. Moreover, judgement was the power of reason, of sobriety, of restraint, of balance and order. The neo-classicists prized these qualities.

It was eventually Coleridge who made the most telling and lasting observations on this topic. His theory of imagination is contained in *Biographia Literaria* (1817). Coleridge was in search of the unified personality and believed that the imagination was the means to attain it. The imagination, he wrote, was the 'synthetic' and 'magical' power which could bring about the fusion of human faculties.

From being a follower of Locke and Hartley, Coleridge turned to Platonism (*q.v.*) and then became a follower of Berkeley, whose main philosophical principle was that to be is to be perceived and that everything exists as an idea in the mind of God. Thus Nature is part of God and is the language of God. Having discovered this 'eternal language' of Nature, Coleridge was at pains to work out the function of the imagination. In this venture he was considerably influenced by Kant, Schelling and Spinoza and he finally expressed his theories in Chapter XIII of *Biographia Literaria*. He decided that fancy was a mode of memory 'emancipated from the order of time and space' which received all its materials 'made from the law of association'. The real imagination is either primary or secondary. The primary mediates between sensation and perception and is the living power and 'prime agent of all human perception', and this faculty is common to all percipient human beings. The secondary or poetic imagination is:

> an echo of the former, co-existing with the conscious will, yet still as identical with the primary in the *kind* of its agency, and differing only in *degree*, and in the *mode* of its operation. It dissolves, diffuses, dissipates, in order to recreate: or where this process is rendered impossible, yet still at all events it struggles to idealize and to unify.

In the preface to his *Poems* (1815) Wordsworth takes a rather different point of view. He regards imagination as the superior faculty, the transubstantiator of experience; while fancy (a contraction of fantasy; L *phantasia*, a transliteration from the Greek) is a kind of assistant to imagination. *See also* AFFLATUS; DONNÉE; INSPIRATION; INVENTION; LIGNE DONNÉE; MUSE; WIT.

farce (L *farcire*, 'to stuff') As applied to drama the term derives from the OF *farce*, 'stuffing'. Farce is a kind of 'low' comedy, and its basic elements are exaggerated physical action (often repeated); exaggeration of character and situation; absurd situations and improbable events (even impossible ones and therefore fantastic); and surprises in the form of unexpected appearances and disclosures. In farce, character and dialogue are nearly always subservient to plot and situation. The plot is usually complex and events succeed one another with almost bewildering rapidity.

The origins of farce are obscure, though it may be reasonably supposed that it precedes anything merely literary. At its simplest, perhaps, it could be described as a form of prehistoric horseplay. In Classical literature farcical elements are to be found in the plays of Aristophanes and Plautus. The Aristophanic plot combined low comedy (*q.v.*) with serious satire (*q.v.*) and invective (*q.v.*). Plautus also used absurd situation (especially that arising from mistaken identity), knockabout and bawdy. The farcical is also discernible in the Greek satyr play (*q.v.*) and in the Roman *fabula* (*q.v.*).

The first plays to be described as *farces* were French and belong to the late Middle Ages. The 'stuffing' consisted of comic interludes between scenes in religious or liturgical drama. These interpolations were usually written in octosyllabic couplets, and an average length was 500 lines. They poked fun at the foibles and vices of everyday life (particularly at commercial knavery and conjugal infidelity) and are related to the *fabliau* and the *sotie* (*qq.v.*). This kind of comedy is well illustrated in Chaucer's *Miller's Tale* (late 14th c.).

Later in the French theatre, these farcical interludes developed into a form of their own: a one-act farce. The influence of French farce is discernible in Italy, Germany and in England where the first writer of note to use the form was John Heywood. No doubt Heywood influenced Tudor dramatists, who began to introduce farcical episodes into their plays. Something approaching farce was sometimes used in tragedy (*q.v.*) for comic relief (*q.v.*).

However, in this period, apart from *The Comedy of Errors* and *The Taming of the Shrew*, there is little that could be described as farce without some reservations. Later we have Jonson's *Bartholomew Fair* (1614). And then, in the middle of the 17th c., Molière showed himself to be a master of the genre – especially with *Le Malade imaginaire* (1672). In Restoration comedy (*q.v.*) and 18th c. comedy there are plentiful farcical episodes, particularly in burlesque (*q.v.*) plays. In the 18th c. also we find a number of short farces used as curtain raisers (*q.v.*).

Fully developed and mature farce finally established itself in the 19th c.: in France with the work of Labiche and Feydeau; in England with the work of Pinero. W. S. Gilbert also helped to popularize the form. Since Labiche and Feydeau, and thanks to them, what is known as the 'bedroom farce', whose themes are sexual fidelity and amorous escapades both in and out of wedlock, has been one of the most popular forms. In the 20th c. the genre continued to flourish, and sometimes demonstrated a harder satirical edge, for instance in the work of Joe Orton, Alan Bennett and Dario Fo. *See also* BLACK COMEDY; COMEDY; SLAPSTICK; THEATRE OF THE ABSURD; VAUDEVILLE.

fârsa A type of boasting poem (*q.v.*) found among the African Galla tribe. Such poems recite a litany of heroes and their heroic deeds. *See also* GIERASA.

farsas Medieval Spanish religious plays, often with a comic interlude (*q.v.*), as in *Farsas y églogas al modo y estilo pastoril y castellano* by Lucas Fernández (1474–1542). The modern Spanish *farsa* has the same intention as farce (*q.v.*).

fashionable novel A form of fiction which was popular in the period 1825–50. The novels were mostly about wealthy, fashionable members of the upper classes. Theodore Hook (1788–1841), an accomplished writer of light verse (*q.v.*), was one of the principal practitioners. Some of his better-known novels were: *Sayings and Doings* (1842–8), *Maxwell* (1830), *Gilbert Gurney* (1836), *Jack Brag* (1837) and *Gurney Married* (1838). Bulwer Lytton's *Pelham* (1828) was also very popular, as was Plumer Ward's *Tremaine, or a Man of Refinement* (1825). Other authors particularly associated with the fashionable novel were: Susan Ferrier (1782–1854), Mrs Gore (1799–1861), T. H. Lister (1800–42) and Disraeli (1804–81). Ouida (1839–1908) – the pseudonym of Marie Louise de la Ramée – also wrote a number of fashionable novels later in the 19th c.

Fastnachtspiel (G 'Shrove Tuesday play') A dramatic genre whose origins are to be found in 15th c. Shrovetide masquerades. They were mostly short – not much more than 'playlets' – and were presented and performed by townspeople. They might, in fact, be considered as early instances of community theatre (*q.v.*). Some of the main themes were domestic – such as marital problems – and they were often devised as a kind of trial or court process. Some are comedies in the form of dramatized *Schwänke*. Many were composed in *Knittelvers* (*q.v.*). The earliest known writer of them is Hans Rosenplüt (15th c.). Other notable dramatists were: Hans Folz (*c.* 1400–*c.* 1575), Hans Sachs (1494–1576), Hans Rudolf Manuel (1525–71) and Jakob Ayrer (1543–1605), who wrote thirty-six *Fastnachtspiele*.

fate drama *See* SCHICKSALSTRAGÖDIE.

fatrasie (F 'medley, rubbish, farrago') A French medieval verse form, usually of eleven lines. They were popular from the 13th to the 15th c. and are one of the earliest forms of nonsense (*q.v.*) verse. It seems that they were intended to be travesties of traditional fixed forms and the conventional rules of prosody, and are sometimes to be found in the form of macaronics (*q.v.*). *See* COQ-À-L'ÂNE; SERMON JOYEUX; SORAISMUS.

Faust theme At some time during the 16th c. a late medieval legend about a man who sold his soul to the Devil became linked with the man called Johann Faust (*c.* 1488–1541), an itinerant conjuror. The first known account of the man's life, the *Historia von D. Johann Fausten*, was published in 1587 and described a magician's pact with the Devil. The publication coincided with a noticeable increase of interest in demonology and Satanism in Europe, an interest which was to continue late into the 17th c. and produced an astonishing number of demonologies, as well as ecclesiastical and civil measures against Satanism.

Christopher Marlowe appears to have been the first major writer to perceive the possibilities of the Faust theme and he dramatized them in his *Tragical History of Dr Faustus* (c. 1588–93), a drama which owes much to the Morality Play (*q.v.*). Marlowe's version travelled to Germany via a troupe of players known as the 'English Comedians'. Later in the 17th c. the story of Faustus was rendered in puppet theatres, but in these presentations Faust was a buffoon and the Devil a bogeyman.

However, it is not until the 18th c. – a period during which there was a singular absence of interest in anything to do with devilry – that we find the theme taken up in earnest. In 1707 Lesage published *Le Diable boiteux*, a kind of picaresque novel (*q.v.*) in which the demon Asmodée becomes the servant of Don Cléophas Zambullo. In 1775 Paul Weidmann produced *Johann Faust: ein allegorisches Drama*, and somewhat later, the writers of the *Sturm und Drang* (*q.v.*) movement used the legend for satirical purposes and combined domestic tragedy with the Faust story. Meanwhile, Goethe had been working on the theme. In 1775 he published *Faust*, and in 1790 and 1808 Part I of *Faust*. (Part II was not published until 1832.) Goethe's version of the story is regarded as one of the greatest.

During the 19th and 20th c. the theme appeared no less attractive to many writers. Byron was influenced by Goethe's *Faust* and treated the theme in *Manfred* (1817). Around this time the Faust legend and the Don Juan legend became mingled and Faust became a Don Juan type profligate. Later notable works include Woldemar Nürnberger's epic poem *Josephus Faust* (1842); Dorothy L. Sayers's play *The Devil to Pay* (1939); and Thomas Mann's long novel *Doktor Faustus* (1947). A number of 19th c. composers were also inspired by the theme in various ways, including Wagner, Berlioz and Liszt.

Fazetie (L *facetia*, *facetus*, 'merry, witty') A German term for a clever, witty, well-phrased anecdote which may or may not be bawdy and/or erotic. *Fazetien* are to be found in humanistic Latin literature of the Renaissance period (*q.v.*). For example: *Facetiae Latinae et Germanicae* (1486), *Facetiae* (1508–12) and *Facetiae* (c. 1600). Not common in German vernacular, but the bawdy and humorous *Schwank* is related to them. *See* FACETIAE.

Félibres, les In c. 1854 a movement known as *le Félibrige* began in order to restore Provençal as a living language and to revive interest in Provençal literature, history, customs, etc. There was even a move to get Provençal taught in schools. In 1855 *les Félibres* founded the annual *L'Armana prouvençau* which published Provençal literature. The founders of the movement were: Paul Giéra (1816–61), Joseph Roumanille (1818–91), Jean Brunet (1823–94), Anselme Mathieu (1828–1925), Théodore Aubanel (1829–86), Frédéric Mistral (1830–1914), Remy Marcellin (1832–1908) and Alphonse Tavan (1833–1905). They all wrote in Provençal.

fellow travellers Those who are sympathetic to a cause (typically revolutionary socialism) but eschew active involvement or membership. The phrase was used by Trotsky (1879–1940) to describe those Soviet authors who accepted the 1917 Revolution without necessarily accepting Bolshevik ideology. In fact they maintained that literature should not be subject to political tenets or coercion. *See also* SERAPIONOVY BRATYA.

feminine caesura A caesura (*q.v.*) which comes after an unstressed syllable, as after 'open' in this line from John Berryman's *Homage to Mistress Bradstreet*:

> The winters close, Springs open, ‖ no child stirs

See MASCULINE CAESURA.

feminine ending An extra unstressed syllable at the end of a line of verse. Common in blank verse, with the slack eleventh syllable, as in the third line of these three from George Chapman's *De Guina* (the first two have masculine endings, *q.v.*):

> O incredulity! the wit of fools,
> That slovenly will spit on all things fair,
> The coward's castle, and the sluggard's cradle.

See FEMININE RHYME.

feminine rhyme When words of two or more syllables rhyme it is known as feminine or double rhyme. It is particularly common in humorous verse, as in the first two lines of this flippant epitaph:

> Here lie I and my four daughters,
> Killed by drinking Cheltenham waters.
> Had we but stuck to Epsom salts,
> We wouldn't have been in these here vaults.

See FEMININE ENDING; MASCULINE RHYME; RHYME.

feminist criticism A development and movement in critical theory and in the evaluation of literature which was well under way by the late 1960s and which has burgeoned steadily since. It is an attempt to describe and interpret (and reinterpret) women's experience as depicted in various kinds of literature – especially the novel, and, to a lesser extent, poetry and drama.

It questions the long-standing, dominant, male, phallocentric ideologies (which add up to a kind of male conspiracy), patriarchal attitudes and male interpretations in literature (and critical evaluation of literature). It attacks male notions of value in literature – by offering critiques of male authors and representations of men in literature and also by privileging women writers. In addition it challenges traditional and accepted male ideas about the nature of women and about how women feel, act and think, or are *supposed* to feel, act and think, and how in general they respond to life and living. It thus questions numerous prejudices and assumptions about women made by male writers, not least any tendency to cast women in stock character (*q.v.*) roles.

The inquiry (or discourse, *q.v.*) has posed a number of questions. For example, the possibility or likelihood of *écriture féminine* (*q.v.*): writing that is essentially, characteristically, feminine or female in language and style. And, if such a thing exists, whether or not it is a fruitful idea to make distinctions between male and female writing; whether or not the making of such distinctions would merely result in 'sexual polarization'.

There is debate in feminism itself about how productive are (a) the notion of an essential difference expressed in writing – a kind of separatism; (b) a radical desire to recognize that male representations of women are as important as women's writing, and also to recognize that the notion of an *écriture féminine* surrenders to a traditional marginalization of women's voices.

Here perhaps one may amplify to make a crude but serviceable distinction between the 'essentialists' and the 'relativists'. The essentialist position holds the view that there is a fundamental distinction (based not on biological determinism so much as on social and economic factors and their psychological consequences) between the way women and men think and write – to such a degree that there is such a thing as *écriture féminine*: that is, a way that women have of expressing themselves totally opposed to the representative aspects of male language and discourse. This position is associated with French feminists. The relativist position – broadly associated with Anglo-American critics – is that the analysis of the representation of men and women by male and female authors is important. No fundamental difference separates men's and women's writing except the way male critics and authors have undervalued the latter.

Feminism has its origins in the struggle for women's rights which began late in the 18th c., more particularly with Mary Wollstonecraft's *A Vindication of the Rights of Woman* (1792). Later came John Stuart Mill's *The Subjection of Women* (1869) and the American Margaret Fuller's *Woman in the Nineteenth Century* (1845). The suffragette movement at the beginning of the 20th c. carried on the campaign. In the 1920s there were clear signs of new and different approaches in relation to women writers and literature. This was noticeable in the critical work of, for example, Rebecca West, and in Virginia Woolf's essays on women authors who suffered from economic and cultural disadvantages in what she termed a 'patriarchal' society. Her book *A Room of One's Own* (1929) was to become a classic 'document' (*q.v.*) of the feminist critical movement. She addressed herself to the issue of why there were so few women writers and why it is frequently difficult or impossible for a woman to write. There was also Dorothy Richardson's very important twelve-volume stream of consciousness (*q.v.*) novel *Pilgrimage*, the first volume of which appeared in 1915 (and the last, posthumously, in 1967). This centres on the female consciousness of the heroine Miriam Henderson, is conducted in unpunctuated female prose and caused Virginia Woolf to observe that Richardson had invented 'the psychological sentence of the feminine gender'.

An important landmark in the evolution of feminist criticism in the post-war period was Simone de Beauvoir's *Le Deuxième* Sexe (1949), a seminal work which questioned the whole position and role of women in society and was a critique of women's cultural identification. She also addressed herself to the matter of the representation of women by various male writers, such as Stendhal and D. H. Lawrence. Her writing was 'political' in tone and she was one of the first to examine ways in which men depict women in fiction.

In the late 1960s there began a spate of diverse criticism, often of a polemical nature. Much of it – especially that on literature (e.g. work by Mary Ellman, Germaine Greer, Kate Millett, Elaine Showalter *et al.*) – was often political and expressed anger and a sense of injustice that women had been oppressed and exploited by men. Indeed, a substantial amount of feminist criticism goes well beyond literature to explore the socio-economic status of women; and, where literature is concerned, to look at women's economic position as authors and the problems they have with allegedly prejudiced male publishers and critics.

In America the spate began with Mary Ellman's *Thinking about Women* (1968), a witty and at times scathing analysis of the ways women are represented in literature by men. In 1969 Kate Millett published *Sexual Politics*, in which she examines how power relations work and how men manipulate and perpetuate male dominance over women. She addressed herself to such writers as Norman Mailer, Henry Miller and D. H. Lawrence.

Indeed, an enduring concern has been the connection of feminism and Marxism. In her seminal text *Women's Oppression Today* (1980), Michele Barrett outlines some of the central problems facing any attempt to forge a coalition of Marxist and feminist perspectives. How can a Marxist analysis, conceived on the basis of 'a primary contradiction between labour and capital', be reconciled with a feminist approach, which must begin with the relations of gender? Barrett focuses on three concepts that have been central to the Marxist feminist dialogue: patriarchy, reproduction and ideology. According to Barrett, the most significant elements of the oppression of women under capitalism are 'the economic organization of households and its accompanying familial ideology, the division of labor and relations of production, the educational system and the operations of the state', as well as the processes of creation and re-creation of gendered subjects. Other works in this vein include Judith Newton and Deborah Rosenfelt's *Feminist Criticism and Social Change* (1985), which also argues for feminist analysis which takes account of social and economic contexts.

In 1979 Sandra Gilbert and Susan Gubar published *The Madwoman in the Attic: The Woman Writer and the Nineteenth Century Imagination*. This study is about, among many other things, the typical motifs and patterns in the works of 19th c. women writers. One of their main arguments is that these writers chose (as Toril Moi puts it in her essay on feminist literary criticism in *Modern Literary Theory*, 1982, edited by Jefferson and Robey) 'to express their own female anger in a series of duplicitous textual strategies whereby both the angel and the monster, the sweet heroine and the raging madwoman, are aspects of the author's self-image, as well as elements of her treacherous anti-patriarchal strategies'. A notable example of the psychological duplicity is the grotesque counter-figure to the heroine. For example, Bertha Rochester, the madwoman in Charlotte Brontë's *Jane Eyre* (1847). Such a figure is, as Gilbert and Gubar put it, 'usually in some sense the *author's* double, an image of her own anxiety and rage'.

Such analyses come into the category of what has been called by Elaine Showalter 'gynocriticism': that is, criticism concerned with writings by women (including letters and journals) and all aspects of their production and interpretation. Showalter herself made a notable contribution in the shape of *A Literature of Their Own: British Women Novelists from Brontë to Lessing* (1977). Other notable works in this mode include *The Female Imagination* (1975) by Patricia Meyer Spacks and *Literary Women* (1976) by Ellen Moers. Toril Moi's *Sexual/Textual Politics: Feminist Literary Theory* (1985) is a long, in-depth description, critique and analysis of Anglo-American and French feminist theory and criticism.

Whereas Anglo-American critics and theorists have been primarily concerned with thematic studies of writings by and about women, French feminist critics have been concerned with the theory of the role of gender in writing. They have been influenced by theories of poststructuralism, semiotics and deconstruction (*qq.v.*). They have been interested in a critique of language. They maintain that all or most Western languages are male-dominated and male-engendered, and that discourse is predominantly 'phallogocentric' (*q.v.*), as Jacques Derrida puts it. They are thus concerned with the possibility of a woman's language and of *écriture féminine*. Among the main French theorists are Julia Kristeva (author of *Desire in Language: A Semiotic Approach to Literature and Art*, 1980), Luce Irigaray (author of *Speculum of the Other Woman*, 1985, and *This Sex Which Is Not One*, 1985) and Hélène Cixous (author of *The Newly Born Woman*, 1986). The concept of an *écriture féminine* which is not 'contaminated' by or appropriated into phallogocentric language is a most interesting and valid one.

An important achievement of the whole movement of feminism and feminist theory and criticism has been the rediscovery of a hidden tradition of women's writing and the rediscovery and republication of numerous novels (and other works) by women which had long since sunk more or less without trace – except in library catalogues. For example, books by Susan Ferrier, Harriet Martineau, Margaret Oliphant, Elizabeth Gaskell, Christina Rossetti, Mary Sinclair and Edith Durham. Three publishing houses in particular (Virago, Pandora and the Women's Press) have been responsible for this recovery.

A notable development has been the attempt to think through feminism from black and minority perspectives, as in Alice Walker's *In Search of Our Mothers' Gardens* (1983) and Barbara Smith's *Toward a Black Feminist Criticism* (1977). Islamic feminists such as Fatima Mernissi and Leila Ahmed have produced important contributions in their respective books *The Veil and the Male Elite* (1992) and *Women and Gender in Islam* (1992). More recently, feminists such as Donna Haraway and N. Katherine Hayles have explored the construction of subjectivity in a virtual and digital world; and Chandra Talpade Mohanty has re-examined the fundamental issues posed by Western feminism in a global and postcolonial context.

Other miscellaneous works of importance in feminist criticism (in chronological order) are *Psychoanalysis and Feminism* (1975) by Juliet Mitchell; *The Laugh of the Medusa* (in *Signs*, vol. I, 1976) by Hélène Cixous; *The Resisting Reader* (1978) by Judith Fetterly; *The Dialectic of Sex* (1979) by Shulamith Firestone; *Women Writing and Writing about Women* (1979), edited by Mary Jacobus; *Women and Language in Literature and Society* (1980), edited by Ginet-McConnell, Borker and Furman; *On Lies, Secrets, and Silence: Selected Prose* (1980) by Adrienne Rich; *Women's Oppression Today: Problems in Marxist Feminist Analysis* (1980) by Michele Barrett; *New French Feminisms: An Anthology* (1981), edited by Elaine Marks and Isabelle de Courtivron; *Writing and Sexual Difference* (1982), edited by Elizabeth Abel; *Feminism and Psychoanalysis: The Daughter's Seduction* (1982) by Jane Gallop; *Contemporary Feminist Thought* (1984) by Hester Eisenstein; *The New Feminist Criticism: Essays on Women, Literature, and Theory* (1986), edited by Elaine Showalter; *Feminist Literary Theory: A Reader* (1986), edited by Mary Eagleton; *Gender and Theory: Dialogues in Feminist Criticism* (1989), edited by Linda Kauffman; *Feminisms* (1998), edited by Sandra Kemp and Judith Squires; Chandra Talpade Mohanty, *Feminism without Borders: Decolonizing Theory, Practicing Solidarity* (2003). *See also* DIFFÉRANCE; GYNOCRITICISM; PLAISIR/JOUISSANCE; READERLY/WRITERLY; READER-RESPONSE THEORY.

fescennine verse A very early form of bawdy Latin verse which probably originated in festivals celebrating the gathering of the harvest and the grape crops. They were also wedding songs. They are important as possible ancestors of drama (because some were in dialogue form) and of satire (*q.v.*) – because some of them were caustic as well as coarse. The derivation of the word is obscure. It may be a corruption of *fascinium*, a phallic emblem worn as a charm; on the other hand it may come from the town of Fescennium in Etruria.

Festschrift (G 'celebration writing') The term denotes a symposium (*q.v.*) compiled in honour of a distinguished scholar or writer. The first 'homage volume' of this kind was presented to Friedrich Ritschl, classical scholar, in 1867; but yet more famous was that compiled in honour of the eminent historian Theodor Mommsen under the title *Commentationes Philologicae* (1877).

fête des fous *See* SERMON JOYEUX.

fetishism The term 'fetish' comes from the French word *fétiche*, which comes from the Portuguese for 'charm', *feitiço*, which in turn derives from the Latin word *facticius*, 'artificial'. Broadly speaking, fetishism is the attribution of power or value to an object, and it is a much used concept in literary and cultural theory.

In *Das Kapital* Marx describes 'commodity fetishism' as the transference in capitalist societies of value arising from social relations, specifically labour, onto products which are circulated as commodities. For Marx, commodity fetishism mystifies and obscures the exploitative nature of production, a situation which can only be resolved by economic revolution.

Fetishism was a common term used in early sexological work appearing in the late 19th and early 20th c. to describe a specific 'perversion': sexual fixation on an object. For Freud, such fetishism arises as a consequence of repression. In his essay *Fetishism* (1929), Freud argues that the male child manages the traumatic knowledge of the mother's lack of a penis (traumatic because such a fate, he supposes, might equally befall him) by transferring the fear onto some object, a reassuring presence which acts as a substitute for that troubling absence.

Following Marx and Freud, theorists have utilized the concept variously. Feminists have understandably objected to Freud's focus on male psycho-sexual development and the assumption that the absence of male genitals generates only horror. In response, many have attempted to theorize the relationships between fetishism and female bodies and sexuality. Elizabeth Grosz argues that femininity itself may be produced by women as a fetish for their apparent lack; Laura Mulvey focuses on the fetishization of women in film in order to offer a critique of the male viewing subject. Lesbian feminists, such as Judith Butler, seek to reappropriate the phallus for other desiring subjects, or, like Teresa de Lauretis, conceptualize forms of fetishism that are altogether independent of 'phallocentric' understandings of sexuality.

The concept of fetishism is frequently deployed in postcolonialism (*q.v.*) to theorize the containment of anxieties and desires arising from colonial and postcolonial encounters. Once again, such troubling relations are often dealt with through substitution; theorists such as Frantz Fanon and Homi Bhabha explore how racial stereotypes provide the means by which such anxieties are managed. *See also* FEMINIST CRITICISM; MARXIST CRITICISM; PSYCHOANALYTIC CRITICISM; POSTCOLONIALISM; REIFICATION.

feuilleton (F 'literary article/story'; *feuille*, 'leaf, sheet of paper') A supplement issued with a newspaper. The best known of the early *feuilletons* was that produced by Julien-Louis Geoffroy (1743–1814), the dramatic critic of the *Journal des Débats*. It was a kind of appendix, printed on the bottom part of a page and detachable. Other journals copied the idea, printing literary and dramatic *feuilletons* and, later, *romans-feuilletons* (*q.v.*).

ficción (Sp 'fiction') A genre invented by the Argentine poet and critic Jorge Luis Borges. A *ficción* is a story-essay which glosses human dreams and illusions. It is ironical in tone and also didactic. Borges published a collection called *Ficciones* in 1944.

ficelle Henry James's term (from the French for 'puppet strings') for the confidante character whose role within the novel is to elicit information, which is conveyed to the reader without narratorial intervention. Some examples of the *ficelle* are Mrs Heaney in Edith Wharton's *The Custom of the Country* (1913), and, brilliantly, James's own Maisie Farange in *What Maisie Knew* (1897), the naive but preternaturally wise child in whom all the warring parents, step-parents and lovers casually confide, and through whose eyes the story is told. *See* CONFIDANT; NARRATOR.

fiction A vague and general term for an imaginative work, usually in prose. At any rate, it does not normally cover poetry and drama though both are a form of fiction in that they are moulded and contrived – or feigned. Fiction is now used in general of the novel, the short story, the *novella* (*qq.v.*) and related genres.

figurae causae In Classical rhetoric (*q.v.*) the term denotes the stylistic shape and pattern of a speech in relation to the speaker's purpose.

figurate poem *See* ALTAR POEM; PATTERN POETRY.

figurative language Language which uses figures of speech; for example, metaphor, simile, alliteration (*qq.v.*). Figurative language must be distinguished from literal (*q.v.*) language. 'He hared down the street' or 'He ran like a hare down the street' are figurative (metaphor and simile respectively). 'He ran very quickly down the street' is literal. *See* HYPERBOLE; METONYMY; SYNECDOCHE.

fin de siècle *See* DECADENCE.

finida (Sp 'finish') One or more lines of verse providing the conclusion of a *cantiga* or *decir* (*qq.v.*). The equivalent of the Provençal *tornada* (*q.v.*).

fit The division of a poem, a canto (*q.v.*). The term may have acquired its meaning from the ON *fit* 'a hem', or the German *Fitze*, a skein of yarn or the thread with which the weavers marked off a day's work. Lewis Carroll's *The Hunting of the Snark* consists of eight fits. Now hardly ever used. *See* STANZA; STAVE.

fixed form The term denotes a form in poetry for which there are prescribed and established rules with regard to the number of lines, the meter, line length, rhyme and so forth. For example, the sonnet, *rondeau* and *villanelle* (*qq.v.*). There are many of them. Most OF forms are fixed. Before *c.* 1800 most poetry was written according to traditional and received patterns and it was believed that particular forms were appropriate for certain subjects and ideas. The 18th c. English poets had great respect for traditional structure and conventional models, hence the liking for imitation (*q.v.*). This respect for established form did not prevent them from achieving a high degree of originality.

Late in the 18th c. and at the beginning of the 19th c. there was a pronounced turning away from traditional structures to what is known as 'organic form' (*q.v.*), where the structure follows the ideas and content. This is particularly noticeable in the development of the ode (*q.v.*). Later there was to come free verse (*q.v.*) and seemingly endless developments in organic forms. The limerick (*q.v.*) is one of many examples. *See* OLD FRENCH AND PROVENÇAL FORMS.

flamenca *See* SEGUIDILLA.

flashback A term which probably derives from the cinema, and which is now also used to describe any scene or episode in a play, novel, story or poem which is inserted to show events that happened at an earlier time. It is frequently used in modern fiction.

flat and round characters Terms used by E. M. Forster in *Aspects of the Novel* (1927) to describe two basically different types of character – and characterization. A 'flat' character does not change in the course of a story or play; a 'round' one develops and thus alters. Forster cites Mrs Micawber as a flat character and Becky Sharp as a round one. Shakespeare's *Henry IV* (Pts I and II) provides a suitable contrast in the shape of Hotspur and Prince Hal. The former is a 'flat' character; the Prince changes and develops considerably in the course of the play. *See also* BURLESQUE; CARICATURE.

fleshly school of poetry A derogatory term used by Robert Buchanan, writing under the pseudonym Thomas Maitland, in *The Contemporary Review* (Oct. 1871) to describe Rossetti, Swinburne and William Morris. Buchanan regarded these writers as decadent, morally irresponsible, aesthetic (in the pejorative sense) and over-interested in the carnal or sensual. Buchanan was a misguided man and his vituperations caused considerable controversy. Swinburne replied to him with some venom. *See also* AESTHETICISM; PRE-RAPHAELITES.

Florida Street group A literary group of the 1920s named after a cosmopolitan and urbane street in Buenos Aires. Their attitudes were avant-garde (*q.v.*) and they tended to learn from the practice of European writers. Jorge Luis Borges (1899–1988) was the best known. *See also* BOEDO STREET GROUP.

Flugschriften The German term for broadsheets or broadsides (*q.v.*). Frequently used for propaganda (*q.v.*) purposes in religious and political controversy during the 16th and 17th c. They were often polemical and scurrilous and were illustrated by woodcuts.

flyting (from OE *flitan*, 'to contend, strive or wrangle') A *flyting* (or *fliting*) is a cursing match in verse; especially between two poets who hurl abuse at each other. An early instance of a kind of *flyting* is the vehement exchange between the leader of the Vikings and Byrhtnoth, the English leader, in the OE poem *The Battle of Maldon*. The 16th c. Scottish poets were particularly fond of the form. A well-known example is the *Flyting of Dunbar and Kennedie*. Skelton appears to have been influenced by this kind of invective (*q.v.*). In drama, particularly that of the early modern period, the flyting tradition may be seen in the recurrent set-piece scenes made up of confrontations between antagonistic characters who fling bombastic invective at one another, as for example in Tamburlaine's vaunting defiance of the Ottoman sultan Bajazet in Marlowe's play *Tamburlaine* (1588) or Vittoria's trial in Webster's *The White Devil* (1612). Modern freestyle 'rap battles' might be seen as the direct descendants of flyting. *See also* DIATRIBE; LAMPOON; POETIC CONTESTS.

focalization An important term in narratology (*q.v.*), introduced by Gérard Genette in his book *Narrative Discourse: An Essay in Method* (1972) to distinguish between the narration and perception of the events in a story, and as a replacement for 'point of view'. According to Genette, who *speaks* and who *sees* are distinct issues. Focalization is 'internal' when the narrative is presented through the perspective of one character, and 'external' when the events are told by a detached narrator. For example, in Edmund White's *A Boy's Own Story* (1982), the action is seen through the boy's eyes, but told by an adult narrator. 'Zero focalization' corresponds to the perspective of an omniscient narrator. *See also* NARRATOR.

folía (Sp *un folio*, 'a folio'; *foliar*, 'to number pages') A Spanish stanza form of four lines in which the lines may be octosyllabic or shorter. Of uncertain origin, they are known to have existed before 1600 and are related to a kind of Portuguese dance-song. The term has also been applied variously to: light music and popular music; the sound and the figure of the Spanish dance which used to be danced only with castanets; a fiesta in certain provinces, with evening bonfires, etc. *See* SEGUIDILLA.

foliation To number the leaves, not the pages, of a volume.

folio (L *folium*, 'leaf') Made by folding a printer's sheet once only, to form two folios or four pages. It also refers to editions of Shakespeare's plays published after his death: the First Folio appeared in 1623. There were three others in 1632, 1663 and 1685. *See* DUODECIMO; LEAF; OCTAVO; QUARTO.

folk drama This kind of drama almost certainly has its origins in fertility rites so ancient that it is not possible to do much more than guess at them. However, folk drama is a common and living phenomenon in many parts of the world – especially in Europe – and often shows affinities with the sword dance (*q.v.*). In the British Isles there are two basic folk plays: *The Mumming Play* (or *St George Play*) and *The Plough Monday Play* (*qq.v.*). *See also* REVESBY PLAY.

folk literature Under this general and somewhat vague term one may include folksong, ballad, fairy tales, drama, proverbs, riddles, charms and legends (*qq.v.*). For the most part, folk literature (or, perhaps, more properly, folklore) is the creation of primitive and illiterate people – and therefore much of it belongs to oral tradition (*q.v.*). It becomes literature in the correct sense of the word only when people gather it together and write it down. When this happens, it is usually a sign that the folk literature in question is in decline.

There were few systematic attempts to gather such literature together until the 19th c., when, for example, the brothers Grimm made their famous collection of fairy tales, and the great Serbian scholar Vuk Karadžić collected many of the epic ballads or *narodne pesme* (*q.v.*) which the *guslari* (*q.v.*) had been reciting and passing down in oral tradition since the 14th c.

Since then, increasingly, individual scholars, cultural societies, academies, universities and many other organizations have laboured to preserve folk literature from oblivion. *See* FOLK DRAMA; FOLKSONG; FOLK TALE.

folksong This kind of song belongs to oral tradition (*q.v.*) and is thus passed on from mouth to mouth. It is a communal form of expression and appears to be universal. Many of them have now been written down. The category includes ballad, carol, sea shanty and lullaby (*qq.v.*). Marching songs, work songs, hobo songs and Negro spirituals are also forms of folksong. To these should be added the *bylina* and the *narodne pesme* (*qq.v.*).

Other special kinds of folksong are the *serenade* or *serenata* – the song the lover sings when he visits his beloved at night; the *aubade* (*q.v.*), or song the lover sings on leaving his beloved at dawn; the *pastourelle* (*q.v.*) or wooing song; and the *coronach* (*q.v.*), a type of lament (*q.v.*).

folk tale Like the folksong (*q.v.*) many folk tales belong to oral tradition (*q.v.*). Some thousands have been collected in the British Isles alone. They include legends, fables, tall stories, shaggy dog stories, fairy stories, ghost stories (*qq.v.*), stories of giants and saints, devils and spirits; husband and wife tales; master and man tales; and what are known as 'rhozzums' (*q.v.*), short humorous tales, often about local characters. *See also* FOLK LITERATURE; MÄRCHEN; SUPERNATURAL STORY.

folly literature The title given to a variety of literature that had some vogue between the 15th and the 17th c. Most of the works in this category are a form of satire (*q.v.*) and can be regarded as early instances of 'the absurd'. They combine elements of fantasy, nonsense and the zany, but have a serious intent to expose, ridicule and 'send up' the more risible aspects of human behaviour. Like the nonsense verse (*q.v.*) of more recent times, and the Theatre of the Absurd (*q.v.*), they display an attempt to correct overmuch seriousness as well as to combat the pretensions and hypocrisies of this world. A way of 'laughing things off'; so it is also called 'Fool Literature'.

An early and classic example is Brandt's *Narrenschiff*, 'The Ship of Fools' (1494), a 'travel' tale reminiscent of Lucian's fantasies. Brandt filled his ship with 112 different kinds of recognizable fool, but became so interested in showing the characters that the ship never left port; rather as if Chaucer's pilgrims never left the Tabard Inn. The success of the work was instant. In 1497 Locher Philomusus translated it into Latin under the title *Stultifera Navis*. In the same year Pierre Rivière translated it into French under the title *La Nef des Folz du Monde*. Other translations followed in rapid succession. Alexander Barclay did an English version (in verse) in 1509, and adapted the original so that it should fit with the English scene. It gives a picture of contemporary English life (dwelling in particular on affectations of manners, customs and clothing, social evils, venal officials and corrupt courts), and provides an early collection of satirical types. Later, comedy of humours and the character (*q.v.*) sketch were to be a development of this kind of treatment of individuals and types.

Another English work of note belonging to the 16th c. is *Cocke Lorell's Bote*, a satire in which various tradespeople embark on a ship and 'sail' through England. The captain of the ship is Cocke Lorell, a tinker. This work in verse gives a vivid picture of 'low life' in England at that time.

In 1509, also, Erasmus wrote his *Moriae Encomium*, 'The Praise of Folly', which was published in 1511. This had enormous success (forty editions came out in the author's lifetime). In 1549 Dedekind wrote *Grobianus: De Morum Simplicitate*, a poem which burlesqued social conditions in Germany. He took his title from Brandt's St Grobianus (in *Narrenschiff*), who was symbolic of boorish behaviour. This work was translated into English and German.

Such books, among several others, influenced the jest-book and the emblem-book (*qq.v.*), both of which had considerable popularity in the 16th and 17th c. Dekker's *Gull's Hornbook* (1609), for instance, was a satire at the expense of fops, gallants and other forms of fool.

Folly literature very probably helped writers to develop character in drama and romance (*q.v.*) and also probably influenced the picaresque (*q.v.*) narrative. Later instances of folly literature are *Gulliver's Travels* (1726) and *Candide* (1759). In 1962 Katherine Anne Porter published *Ship of Fools*, a novel which updated the themes and ideas of Brandt's *Narrenschiff*. The celebration of folly is still a popular activity as we can see in the books of, for example, Spike Milligan. *See* BIEDERMEIER.

foot   A group of syllables forming a metrical unit; a unit of rhythm. The Classical prosodists and poets established nearly all the known foot formations. We measure feet in terms of syllable variation: long and short syllables, stressed and unstressed. The following are the names of the principal feet, illustrated with their stress patterns: / denotes a long syllable or a stressed one; ◡ denotes a short or unstressed syllable:

amphibrach ◡ / ◡
amphimacer / ◡ /
anapaest ◡ ◡ /
antibacchius / / ◡
antispast ◡ / / ◡
bacchius ◡ / /
choree / ◡
choreus (by resolution) ◡ ◡ ◡
choriamb / ◡ ◡ /
cretic (alternative for amphimacer) / ◡ /
dactyl / ◡ ◡

dibrach ◡ ◡
di-iamb ◡ / ◡ /
dispondee / / / /
ditrochee / ◡ / ◡
dochmiac ◡ / / ◡ / (plus any other combinations of the same
   pattern)
epitrite ◡ / / / (known as first, second, third or fourth according
   to the position of the unstressed syllable)
iamb ◡ /
ionic majore / / ◡ ◡
ionic minore ◡ ◡ / /
mollossus / / /
paeon / ◡ ◡ ◡ (known as first, second, third or fourth according
   to the position of the stressed syllable)
palimbacchius (alternative for antibacchius) / / ◡
proceleusmatic ◡ ◡ ◡ ◡
pyrrhic (alternative for dibrach) ◡ ◡
spondee / /
tribrach ◡ ◡ ◡ (and see choreus)
trochee (alternative for choree) / ◡

The commonest feet in English prosody are: iamb, trochee, dactyl, anapaest
and spondee, in that order. *See* FALLING RHYTHM; RISING RHYTHM; ROCKING
RHYTHM; SCANSION; SPRUNG RHYTHM.

foregrounding The English rendering of the Czech word *aktualisace*. The
term denotes the use of devices and techniques which 'push' the act of
expression into the foreground so that language draws attention to itself.
This draws attention, in turn, to the way that literary language represents
reality. Foregrounding occurs especially in poetic language. The Czech linguist Jan Mukařovský (in his essay *Standard Language and Poetic Language*)
observes: 'The function of poetic language consists in the maximum foregrounding of the utterance . . . it is not used in the services of communication, but in order to place in the foreground the act of expression, the act of
speech itself.' In a sense, foregrounding is the art which reveals art rather
than concealing it. Sterne's *Tristram Shandy* (1760–7) is often cited as a good
example of this sort of literariness (*q.v.*), which is closely connected with
Viktor Shklovsky's concept of 'making strange' and 'defamiliarization' (*q.v.*).
Sterne, by various literary devices, persistently calls the reader's attention to
what he is doing. So have many more recent writers as diverse as, for
example, Rimbaud, James Joyce, William Faulkner, Flann O'Brien, B. S.
Johnson, Claude Simon and Samuel Beckett. Beckett, in answering Joyce's
detractors, once wrote: 'You complain that this stuff is not written in English.
It is not only to be read. It is to be looked at and listened to. *His writing is
not about something; it is that something itself* [my italics].' This, perhaps,
gives an idea of the nature of foregrounding, which Coleridge had been

aware of long before. In the *Biographia Literaria* (1817) he speaks of the 'prime merit' of literary genius as the representation of 'familiar objects' in order to evoke 'freshness of sensation'. Coleridge and Wordsworth (in the preface to *Lyrical Ballads*) can be said to have been alert to this important aspect of literary theory. However, Coleridge (like Wordsworth) was a romantic and here he is thinking of the display of new light on things perceived, rather than the literary means and effect. *See also* ARS EST CELARE ARTEM; READERLY/WRITERLY.

forensics A term applied to poetry which is concerned with debate and argument (e.g. the French *débat* and the Spanish *pregunta*, *qq.v.*). Robert Herrick's *Upon Love, by Way of Question and Answer* (in the form of a *pregunta*) gives an idea of the method. It begins:

> I bring ye love: *Quest.* What will love do?
>   *Ans.* Like, and dislike ye;
> I bring ye love: *Quest.* What will love do?
>   *Ans.* Stroke ye to strike ye;

foreshadowing The technique of arranging events and information in a narrative in such a way that later events are prepared for or shadowed forth beforehand. A well-constructed novel, for instance, will suggest at the very beginning what the outcome may be; the end is contained in the beginning and this gives structural and thematic unity.

foreword (Modelled on G *Vorwort*) Usually a short introductory piece to a book. It is similar to a preface (*q.v.*) and an introduction, but is generally composed not by the author but by someone else.

forgery A literary forgery occurs when someone deliberately tries to pass off a piece of writing as being by someone else, or as something else. There have been many famous instances: the *Letters of Phalaris* (2nd c. AD); Psalmanazer's *Historical and Geographical Description of Formosa* (1704); William Lauder's attempts to discredit Milton in *An Essay on Milton's Use and Imitation of the Moderns* (1750); Chatterton's *Rowley Poems* (1769); the Ossianic forgeries by James Macpherson (1760, 1762, 1765); and Thomas Wise's forgeries of bibliographies in the 19th c. which led to a large number of bogus first editions. There have been a large number of Shakespearean forgeries of various kinds. *See* LITERARY FORGERIES; PLAGIARISM; PSEUDEPIGRAPHA.

form When we speak of the form of a literary work we refer to its shape and structure and to the manner in which it is made (thus, its style, *q.v.*) – as opposed to its substance or what it is about. Form and substance are inseparable, but they may be analysed and assessed separately.

A secondary meaning of form is the *kind* of work – the genre (*q.v.*) to which it belongs. Thus: sonnet, short story, essay (*qq.v.*).

Formalism, Russian A literary theory which developed in Russia in the early 1920s. Practitioners and followers were called 'Formalists', a pejorative term to imply limitations. 'Russian Formalism' was also a pejorative label. It was finished by 1930 because of Stalinist and Socialist–Marxist pressures on the individuals involved. The terms 'formalism' and 'formalist' are applied generally, not exclusively, to 'literary', 'linguistic' theoretical approaches.

The theory of Russian Formalism had begun earlier, in the Moscow Linguistic Circle (founded in 1915) and in OPOJAZ (an acronym for 'The Society for the Study of Poetic Language', based in St Petersburg), founded in 1916. The main figure in the Moscow Linguistic Circle was Roman Jakobson (1896–1982), who helped to found the Prague School (*q.v.*) in 1926.

The Russian Formalists were primarily interested in the way that literary texts achieve their effects and in establishing a scientific basis for the study of literature. In their early work, human content in literature (e.g. emotions, ideas, actions, 'reality' in general) did not possess, for them, any significance in defining what was specifically 'literary' about a text. Indeed, the Formalists collapse the distinction between form and content. And they regard the writer as a kind of cipher merely reworking available literary devices and conventions. The writer is of negligible importance. All the emphasis is on the 'literariness' (*q.v.*) of the formal devices of a text. OPOJAZ went so far as to suggest that there are not poets or literary figures: there is just poetry and literature. Viktor Shklovsky (1893–1984) summarizes the attitude in his definition of literature as 'the sum total of all the stylistic devices employed in it'.

The early phases of Formalism were dominated by Shklovsky's ideas, which were partly influenced by the Futurists (*see* FUTURISM). One of his important contributions was the concept of *ostranenie* or 'making strange', later to be called 'defamiliarization' (*q.v.*).

The Formalists also developed a theory of narrative, making a distinction between plot and story. *Syuzhet* ('the plot') refers to the order and manner in which events are actually presented in the narrative, while *fabula* ('the story') refers to the chronological sequence of events.

Boris Tomashevsky, another of the Formalists, used the term 'motif' (*q.v.*) to denote the smallest unit of plot and distinguished between 'bound' and 'free' motifs. The 'bound' motif is one which the story absolutely requires, while the 'free' is inessential.

The concept of 'motif' is clearly linked to 'motive' and thus to 'motivation'. Formalists tended to regard a poem's content as subordinate to its formal devices. This dependence on external 'non-literary' assumptions was called 'motivation'. Shklovsky defined the motivation of a text as the extent to which it was dependent on 'non-literary' assumptions, and he cited Sterne's *Tristram Shandy* as an example of a work totally without motivation.

In later development of Formalist theory the concept of 'device' gave way to the concept of 'function' in a work of literature, depending on the purpose or mode or genre (*q.v.*). It was no longer the device *per se* which was defamiliarizing but its function in the work. One of the key works in the evolution of the theories of 'function' and 'structure' is the *Jakobson–Tynyanov Theses* (1929). As important is Tynyanov and Jakobson's essay

Problems in the Study of Literature and Language (1927). The Prague School was to unite Russian Formalism and Saussurean linguistics. It developed a concept of structure close to Saussurean linguistics and, via Jakobson, was to contribute to structuralism (*q.v.*). *See also* MARXIST CRITICISM; READERLY/WRITERLY; SEMIOTICS/SEMIOLOGY.

format The physical make-up of a book (*q.v.*), i.e. its dimensions and construction (for example, quarto, manuscript, paperback, hardback).

fornyrðislag An ON Eddic metrical form which comprises a four-line stanza in which each line is divided by a caesura (*q.v.*) into two half lines. Each half has two accented or stressed syllables, and two or three unstressed syllables. As in OE verse, alliteration (*q.v.*) is a notable feature of the form. Most of the Eddic poems are composed in this measure. *See also* KVIÐUHÁTTR; LJOÐAHÁTTR; MÁLAHÁTTR.

Forsterian Characteristic of the style, tone and attitudes of E. M. Forster (1879–1970). Thus, relaxed, informal, ironical, liberal and humanistic.

foul papers An author's working drafts, particularly those of English Renaissance dramatists.

Four Ages of Poetry The title of a provocative essay by Thomas Love Peacock published in 1820. With a certain amount of drollery Peacock classified Poetry into four periods: iron, gold, silver and brass. Shelley took the matter seriously and replied with *Defence of Poetry* (1821); and in 1926 I. A. Richards published an equally serious refutation in *Science and Poetry*.

four levels of meaning The origins of the four levels of meaning are not certain, but an awareness of them is manifest in the Middle Ages. It was Dante who explained most clearly (in the *Epistle* to his patron Can Grande della Scala) what they consisted of. He was introducing the matter of the *Divina Commedia* and he distinguished: (a) the literal or historical meaning; (b) the moral meaning; (c) the allegorical meaning; (d) the anagogical meaning.

Such criteria applied to, for instance, Orwell's *Animal Farm* (1945), might suggest the following: (a) the story is about the revolt of the animals against their human overlords, and the outcome of that revolt; (b) 'power tends to corrupt'; (c) Major = Lenin; Napoleon = Stalin; Snowball = Trotsky; Jones = corrupt capitalist landowners – and so forth; (d) human (*and* animal) nature does not change. *See* ALLEGORY.

four meanings In *Practical Criticism* (1929) I. A. Richards distinguishes four different meanings in a poem: (a) the sense – what is actually said; (b) feeling – the writer's emotional attitude towards it; (c) tone – the writer's attitude towards his reader; (d) intention – the writer's purpose, the effect he is aiming at.

fourteener Also known as a heptameter and a septenary. A line of seven feet and fourteen syllables; usually seven iambics (*q.v.*). It was used in Greek and

Latin verse and flourished in English narrative verse (*q.v.*) in the later Middle Ages and in Tudor times. The Elizabethans coined the term 'fourteener'. Before the advent of blank verse in drama (*q.v.*), rhyming fourteeners were common constituents of English plays. Starting in 1598, George Chapman opted to use the fourteener for his celebrated translation of the *Iliad*. It has not been much used since, largely because it is rather unwieldy, as the following lines in so-called 'poulter's measure' (*q.v.*) (alternating with hexameters) from Surrey show:

> In winter's just return, when Boreas gan his reign.
> And every tree unclothèd fast, as nature taught them plain.
> In misty morning dark, as sheep are then in hold,
> I hied me fast, it sat me on, my sheep for to unfold.

The rhyming couplet of the fourteener, written as four lines, became what is known as the eight-and-six meter of the common ballad (*q.v.*) stanza (*q.v.*).

fourth wall The invisible 'wall' dividing a theatre audience from a performance, especially that taking place in a three-walled box set of a proscenium theatre. The idea of such a division is usually attributed to Diderot, who wrote in 1758: 'When you write or act, think no more of the audience than if it had never existed. Imagine a huge wall across the front of the stage, separating you from the audience, and behave exactly as if the curtain had never risen.' Diderot was concerned that theatrical performance and dramatic content should be attuned to real life; enacting a separation between audience and performance seemed to assure that the latter would be more faithful to everyday reality. Indeed the term is closely associated with the rise in the 19th c. of realism (*q.v.*) in European theatre.

Many in the 20th c. have been critical of the concept of the fourth wall as it precludes all kinds of productive devices – soliloquy, chorus, aside (*qq.v.*) – which require performer and audience to occupy the same theatrical space. 'Breaking the fourth wall' relates to any practice which seeks to dispel the illusion that the audience is watching a slice of 'real life'. The same expression is also used in relation to film and fiction to describe a text's acknowledgement of its own artifice, which is usually achieved by a direct address to the audience. *See also* ALIENATION EFFECT.

frame story A frame story is one which contains either another tale, a story within a story, or a series of stories. Well-known instances are the *Arabian Nights* (of uncertain date, but mentioned in the 9th c. AD); Boccaccio's *Decameron* (*c.* 1349–51); Chaucer's *Canterbury Tales* (late 14th c.); Marguerite of Navarre's *Heptaméron* (1558). Much later Goethe used this Boccaccio technique in *Unterhaltungen deutscher Ausgewanderten* (1795). Other notable writers who have used this structure are: Tieck, Hoffmann, Keller, R. L. Stevenson and G. F. Meyer. *See also* DIGRESSION; RAHMENERZÄHLUNG.

Franciscan literature The considerable body of writings which were produced in many countries during and after St Francis of Assisi's life. A well-known collection is the *Fioretti di S. Francesco* compiled by an anonymous Tuscan in the first half of the 14th c.

Frankfurt School A group of theorists whose members were initially based at (or otherwise associated with) the Frankfurt Institute for Social Research, established in 1923 in Weimar Germany. The key members were Max Horkheimer, Theodor Adorno, Erich Fromm, Leo Löwenthal and Herbert Marcuse. Walter Benjamin was an important associate. The Frankfurt School sought to develop 'critical theory': a critique of political, social and cultural institutions which would facilitate the enlightenment and transformation of society. Broadly, members were critical of orthodox Marxism, especially Soviet communism; they sought to combine Marxist thinking with other intellectual developments such as German Idealism and Freudian theory in order to understand how capitalist societies had advanced in ways not countenanced by classical Marxism.

The School went into exile after the Nazis' rise to power. Several members resettled in the United States where they witnessed the rise of mass-produced forms of popular culture controlled by powerful corporations. Adorno and Horkheimer produced a seminal critique of these 'culture industries' (*q.v.*), which they understood as having a crucial role in stabilizing capitalist societies by reproducing for mass audiences the values of American capitalism. Benjamin, however, contested Adorno and Horkheimer's pessimism. Writing in Paris in the 1930s, he argued that mass-produced culture's loss of the 'halo' of originality possessed by the 'high' art of a previous era enabled audiences to respond more creatively and critically to the works in question. Working closely with Brecht, Benjamin also discerned the potential for radical interventions by oppositional cultural producers: theatre and film need not be geared entirely towards audience pleasure, but could be employed to provoke and enlighten. In short, Benjamin saw scope for both producers and consumers of mass culture to develop the critical tools necessary for social transformation.

Although their account has been repeatedly criticized in recent decades for its pessimism, elitism and simplicity, Adorno and Horkheimer and other Frankfurt School members provided the first sustained critique of the relationship between capitalism and the new forms of mass culture which emerged in the mid 20th c. In doing so, they laid foundations for modern cultural studies (*q.v.*) and media studies. *See also* IDEOLOGY; MARXIST CRITICISM.

free association A term commonly used in psychology but which has achieved some currency in literary criticism and theory. The point involved is that a word or idea acts as a stimulus or trigger to a series or sequence of other words or ideas which may or may not have some logical relationship. Some writing *looks* like free association. Much writing that looks like it is probably the result of carefully thought-out and contrived arrangement. In his *Ulysses* (1922) James Joyce was one of the principal pioneers of this kind of technique. In the following passage, for instance, words and images are 'freely' associated:

Ineluctable modality of the visible: at least that if no more, thought through my eyes. Signatures of all things I am here to read, seaspawn and seawrack, the nearing tide, that rusty boot. Snotgreen, bluesilver, rust: coloured signs. Limits of the diaphane. But he adds: in bodies. Then he was aware of them bodies before of them coloured. How? By knocking his sconce against them, sure. Go easy. Bald he was and a millionaire, *maestro di color che sanno*. Limit of the diaphane in. Why in? Diaphane, adiaphane. If you can put your five fingers through it, it is a gate, if not a door. Shut your eyes and see.

See STREAM OF CONSCIOUSNESS.

free indirect style/discourse   The presentation of thoughts or speech of fictional characters which seems by various devices to combine the character's sentiments with those of a narrator. In its most primitive form, indirect discourse is signalled by the narratorial 'framing'of the thought or utterance, as in 'Archer tried to console himself with the thought that he was not quite such an ass as Lefferts' (the unframed, direct version would be 'Archer thought: "I am not quite such an ass as Lefferts"'). The free indirect style can produce more complex effects, however, in what has been called 'the commitments and abstentions of the authorial voice'. Fruitful ambiguity is created when the author's hand in the passage is not clearly marked out from the voice of the character in the following lines: '"Nice" women, however wronged, would never claim the kind of freedom he meant, and generous-minded men like himself were therefore . . . the more chivalrously ready to concede it to them. Such verbal generosities were in fact only a humbugging disguise of the inexorable conventions that tied things together . . .' (Edith Wharton, *The Age of Innocence*, 1920).

free meter   A term rarely used in matters of English prosody; but among the Welsh it refers to all those meters which are not 'strict'. The 'strict meters' (*q.v.*) were those laid down in the 15th c. Among the better known are: *awdl*, *cywydd* and *englyn*.

free verse   Called *vers libre* (*q.v.*) by the French, it has no regular meter or line length and depends on natural speech rhythms and the counterpoint (*q.v.*) of stressed and unstressed syllables. In the hands of a gifted poet it can acquire rhythms and melodies of its own.

Its origins are obscure. There are signs of it in medieval alliterative verse (*q.v.*) and in the Authorized Bible translations of the Psalms and *The Song of Songs*. Milton was clearly experimenting with it in *Lycidas* and *Samson Agonistes*. Interest in its possibilities was renewed in Europe after the period of neoclassicism (*q.v.*). Heine and Goethe (in Germany), Bertrand, Hugo and Baudelaire (in France), Macpherson, Smart, Blake and Arnold (in England) were some of the better-known writers who experimented. It was very probably Walt Whitman, the American poet (who influenced Baudelaire), who did more than anyone else to develop it. The other main innovator in the 19th c. was Gerard Manley Hopkins. In the 20th c. many poets employed it, including Ezra Pound, T. S. Eliot, D. H. Lawrence and William Carlos Williams. The following example comes from Whitman's *After the Sea-ship*:

> After the sea-ship, after the whistling winds,
> After the white-grey sails taut to their spars and ropes,
> Below, a myriad myriad waves hastening, lifting up their
> 　necks,
> Tending in ceaseless flow toward the track of the ship,
> Waves of the ocean bubbling and gurgling, blithely prying,
> Waves, undulating waves, liquid, uneven emulous waves,
> Toward that whirling current, laughing and buoyant, with
> 　curves,
> Where the great vessel sailing and tacking displaced the
> 　surface . . .

See also PROSE POEM; SPRUNG RHYTHM; VERSE PARAGRAPH; VERS LIBÉRÉS.

Freie Bühne A Berlin theatrical company or society founded in 1889. It was a subscription theatre and sponsored private performances of plays banned by the censor and plays which were unlikely to succeed in the commercial theatre. It lasted for only four years but in that time had considerable influence, presenting plays by Ibsen, Hauptmann, Holz, Schlaf, Bjørnson and Strindberg. The society also published an influential monthly journal.

French forms *See* OLD FRENCH AND PROVENÇAL FORMS.

Freytag's pyramid The German critic Gustav Freytag, in *Die Technik des Dramas* (1862), analysed the structure of a typical five-act play thus: (a) introduction; (b) inciting moment; (c) rising action; (d) climax; (e) falling action; (f) catastrophe. The climax is the apex of the pyramidal structure. The pattern can be applied to a large number of plays. *See* CATASTROPHE; CLIMAX; FALLING ACTION; RISING ACTION; TURNING POINT.

fringe theatre A general term (often equated with and synonymous with alternative theatre, *q.v.*) for drama which is presented away from the main centres (e.g. Broadway and the West End of London). It was first used in the late 1950s to describe drama which was staged on the edges, so to speak, of the Edinburgh Festival. Often avant-garde (*q.v.*) and anti-establishment in earlier days, fringe theatre is now very well established. Numerous small theatres (particularly in pubs) present a wide range of dramatic work, including plays that have long been a part of the standard repertoire. *See* AGITPROP DRAMA; OFF-BROADWAY.

frontier writing Literature organized around the experiences of settler peoples on a colonial frontier. Most frontier writing has emerged from North and South America. *See also* GAUCHO LITERATURE; WESTERN.

Frühromantik *See* ROMANTICISM.

fu A Chinese prose poem, but one which contains rhyme and lines of constant length which are not metrical. It was perfected in the 2nd c. BC, but used thereafter.

Fugitives, the A group of poets and critics from the Southern States who gathered at Vanderbilt University in the early 1920s where they published a magazine called *The Fugitive*. In politics and poetry they were traditionalists and regionalists, opposed to the industrial and urban development of the North. The group was distinguished and had among its members Allen Tate, John Crowe Ransom, Donald Davidson and Robert Penn Warren.

full rhyme *See* RHYME.

functional metaphor *See* ORGANIC METAPHOR.

fustian (from MedL [*pannus*] *fustaneus*, 'cloth of Fostat, suburb of Cairo') Formerly a coarse cloth made of cotton and flax; now a thick, twilled cotton cloth. In the 16th c. it was used to describe inflated, turgid language. Pope mentioned it in the *Epistle to Arbuthnot*:

> And he, whose fustian's so sublimely bad,
> It is not poetry, but prose run mad.

See BOMBAST.

futurism Initially, a literary movement which originated in Italy at the beginning of the 20th c. Its long-term influences were to be seen in other arts, particularly painting and music (hence neo-impressionism and *bruitisme*). Its main protagonist was Filippo Marinetti (1876–1944), who founded the periodical *Poesia* in 1905. The first and major manifesto (*q.v.*) of futurism was drawn up by him and published in *Le Figaro* in Paris in 1909. Several other manifestos followed. They advocated a complete break with tradition and aimed at new forms, new subjects and new styles in keeping with the advent of a mechanistic age. They extolled dynamism, the machine (and machinery in general), speed (there was a speed cult) and the splendour of war and patriotism. Early in the 1920s the movement became politically Fascistic, and also had some indirect effect on Dadaism, expressionism and surrealism (*qq.v.*). It seems not to have had all that much influence on literature except in Russia, where it provoked vociferous activity from *c.* 1910 under the leadership of Viktor Khlebnikov (1885–1922). The Russian Futurists were against symbolism (*q.v.*), mysticism and the cult of 'pure' beauty. They set out to shock people and *épater les bourgeois*. The manifesto of 1912 was titled 'A Slap in the Face of Public Taste' and was intended as a literary and cultural purge. Pushkin, Dostoevsky, Tolstoy *et al.* were to be chucked 'overboard'. It was vituperative in tone and followers were enjoined to develop a new vocabulary called *zaumny yazyk* (*see* ZAUM) and cleanse themselves of the 'filth' and 'slime' of such writers as Leonid Andreyev (1871–1919). After the October Revolution many Futurists had official positions in control of literature but the Party did not care for their avant-garde (*q.v.*) policies. The movement died out in the 1920s. *See* CUBO-FUTURISM; EGO-FUTURISM; FORMALISM, RUSSIAN.

fyrtiotalisterna   In the 1940s a group of modernist Swedish poets founded a literary magazine called *40-tal* ('the forties'). So the term means 'poets of the *40-tal*'. The leaders of the group were Erik Lindegren (1910–68), Karl Vennberg (1910–95), Stig Sjödin (1917–93), Karl Aspenström (1918–97), Sven Alfons (1918–96) and Ragnar Thoursie (1919–2010). Their work is marked by extreme pessimism and great stylistic complexity in the use of free association (*q.v.*), allusion (*q.v.*) and startling images. They appear to have been influenced by T. S. Eliot and the French surrealist poets.

G

galliambic A meter associated with the worship of Cybele, the mother goddess. The term derives from the name of the priests – the Galli. Its technical name is ionic tetrameter (*q.v.*) catalectic; thus, four ionic feet per line with the final syllable missing. The *Attis* poem of Catullus is the most famous example of this meter, which was used by George Meredith in *Phaethon* and by Tennyson in *Boadicea*.

gatha A form of metrical hymn (*q.v.*), of usually four, five or seven words to the line. Found in Buddhist writings; and, in group form, in the *Avesta*.

gathering A printed sheet folded into pages is called a signature (*q.v.*). The signatures are then gathered – hence the term.

gaucho literature Verse and prose in Spanish which derived from a particular interest in the way of life of the gauchos on the plains of the River Plate in the Argentine. The gaucho songs (to the guitar) were of special interest. However, the composers of this literature were *not* cowboys. Gaucho poetry and fiction described and celebrated the nomadic existence of the herdsmen, laying stress on their courage, endurance, skills and their love of horses and cattle. A lost poem titled *Corro* by Juan G. Godoy (1793–1864) is generally regarded as the first example of this literature. Other very well-known works are the novel *Don Segundo Sombra* (1926) by Ricardo Güiraldes (1886–1927) and the narrative poem *Martín Fierro* (1869) by José Hernández (1834–86). In Uruguay, Bartolomé Hidalgo (1788–1822) also made an important contribution to gaucho literature.

gay and lesbian criticism A transdisciplinary mode of study which places sex and sexuality at the centre of its analysis. Gay and lesbian criticism (or studies), in a manner that parallels African-American studies and women's studies (*qq.v.*), seeks to advance the interests of lesbian and gay

---

A Dictionary of Literary Terms and Literary Theory, Fifth Edition. J. A. Cuddon.
© 2013 The Estate of J. A. Cuddon. Published 2013 by Blackwell Publishing Ltd.

(and often also bisexual and transgendered) people by contributing intellectually to a lesbian and gay movement, and is informed by resistance to homophobia and heterosexism. It is concerned with a number of topics, the most salient of which are the emergence of sexual identities – in particular, how these have been constructed by capitalist economics and medical discourse; the recovery of gay and lesbian texts and histories which have often been obscured by mainstream literary criticism and official heritage discourse – the homoeroticism which pervades much First World War poetry, for instance, or the queerness of the Bloomsbury Group (*q.v.*); gay and lesbian literary and cultural representations – from detecting covert homosexual desire in ostensibly mainstream texts to evaluating identifiably gay and lesbian narratives, such as the coming-out story (*q.v.*); and the relationships between dominant Western Anglophone gay subcultural formations and non-white and non-metropolitan groups. Some of the most influential figures in gay and lesbian criticism are Jonathan Dollimore, Richard Dyer, Gayle Rubin, Alan Sinfield, Jeffrey Weeks and Bonnie Zimmerman.

The field draws upon a number of recent intellectual developments: feminist criticism (*q.v.*), particularly lesbian feminist criticism, which emerged as a distinct strand in the 1970s as a consequence of mainstream feminism's sidelining of lesbian experience; new historicism and cultural materialism (*qq.v.*), which have been crucial for understanding sexuality as a historical and social construction and for helping to conceive of ways in which texts might lend themselves to alternative readings by sexual dissidents; and queer theory (*q.v.*), an anti-essentialist approach to sexuality and gender which draws heavily on poststructuralist thinking.

Sometimes queer theory and gay and lesbian criticism are understood to be more or less coterminous. Actually, some antagonism exists between the two modes of inquiry. Gay and lesbian criticism is sometimes characterized by queer theorists as being assimilative and exclusive, focusing on established (and relatively privileged) identifications, i.e. gay men and lesbians. One response to this would be that gay and lesbian criticism (or indeed the more inclusive 'LGBT studies') better captures the diversity of the field, and the necessity of strategic alliances between groups which have many things in common, but which also face their own separate issues. The 'queer' of queer theory or queer studies, by contrast, risks positing a false coherence. Also, queer theory is sometimes deemed elitist in its insistence on using highly theoretical language which cannot be readily digested by a political movement, and for turning its back on a constituency which still uses identity categories such as 'gay' and 'lesbian'. However, such differences may easily be exaggerated: gay and lesbian criticism similarly draws on poststructuralist thought, particularly the work of Foucault, and stresses the contingency of sexual identity categories. Reciprocally, leading queer theorists, for example Judith Butler, while emphasizing the regulatory role of sexual identity categories such as gay and lesbian, acknowledge their continued political necessity. *See also* CAMP; CONSTRUCTIONISM; ESSENTIALISM;

HETERONORMATIVITY; HOMOSOCIALITY; IDENTITY POLITICS; POSTSTRUCTUR-
ALISM; TRANSGENDER.

gaze   A term used in film and media theory which refers to the hierarchical
and ideological ways in which spectators view images of people, as well as to
the gaze or look of those portrayed. Many theorists, including Caroline
Evans and Lorraine Gamman, have explored not only the 'male gaze' which
views women voyeuristically, but many other types of looking. In his celebrated television series *Ways of Seeing* (1972), the novelist and art critic John
Berger stressed that women had always been depicted differently from men,
and that the ideal spectator had always been assumed to be male.

In film theory, feminist critics such as Pam Cook and Claire Johnson
analysed the images of women portrayed in film, the patriarchal culture that
overlooks the making of films, and the nature of sexuality and desire. Laura
Mulvey, Kaja Silverman, Mary Ann Doane and Gaylin Studlar all conducted
important studies about the nature of the male gaze directed at the images of
women. In a seminal article called 'Visual Pleasure and Narrative Cinema'
(1975) Laura Mulvey distinguished between 'voyeuristic' looking, which is
controlling, and 'fetishistic' viewing, which transforms the represented object
into a satisfying fetish. She suggested that the institution of cinema is deeply
structured by the unconscious demands of the male ego which have been
institutionalized.

Mulvey's article stirred some controversy and some opposition from those
such as E. Ann Kaplan and Kaja Silverman who, rejecting the implicit essentialism of Mulvey's characterization of men and women as respectively active
and passive, urged that the gaze could be occupied by both male and female
positions. Teresa de Lauretis argued that the female spectator actually effects
a 'double-identification' with both passive and active positions.

More recently, Caroline Evans and Lorraine Gamman have explored how
more attention needs to be drawn to circumstances of female spectatorship
and ethnic difference. Theorists such as James Elkins have enumerated the
manifold relations between a painting and a spectator; and John Ellis and
others have attempted to distinguish between terms such as 'gaze', 'look',
'glance', 'mutual gaze' and 'reciprocal gaze'. *See also* FEMINIST CRITICISM;
FETISHISM.

gazette   (It *gazzetta* from Venetian *gazeta*, a coin of small value) The *Oxford
Gazette* was the first newspaper, other than a newsletter, published in
England in 1665 when the Court took shelter in Oxford from the plague. It
later became the *London Gazette*, which is no longer a newspaper, but a
record of official appointments, bankruptcies and so forth. *See* CORANTO;
NEWSBOOKS.

gazetteer   A geographical index or dictionary.

Gebrauchs-   (G 'utility-') In Germany this term is associated with functionalism in, for example, anthropology, psychology and architecture and in

particular with the *neue Sachlichkeit* (*q.v.*) period of 'utility music' (*Gebrauchsmusik*) and 'utility poetry' (*Gebrauchslyrik*). The so-called utility poetry tended to be satirical (it had a specific purpose and objective) and was so named in 1928 by Kurt Tucholsky (1890–1935). Erich Kästner (1899–1974), among others, also wrote utility poetry of a satirical kind.

Geistesgeschichte (G 'spirit/mind history') A term with complex connotations and implications coined by Friedrich Schlegel in 1808 which achieved much increased currency with the publication of Wilhelm Dilthey's *Einleitung in die Geisteswissenschaften* (i.e. 'sciences of the spirit') in 1883. It is associated with the concept of *Zeitgeist* (*q.v.*) or 'spirit of the times' and in the 20th c. has been a dominant feature of much study of German literature by German scholars and writers. It involves concentration on and the understanding and interpretation of the prevalent 'spirit' and 'mind' of an epoch or age, its essentially characteristic features and development as expressed and exemplified in its literature, art, music, philosophy, religion and culture and in its social life and institutions. *See also* HERMENEUTICS.

geistliche Tageweise German medieval songs based on the form of the *Minnelied* known as *Tagelied*, or dawn song. In the *geistliche Tageweise* the waking up is symbolic of awakening from a state of sin. Some are adaptations of profane or secular songs. *See* AUBADE; KONTRAFAKTUR.

generación del (or de) 1898 Following the break-up of the Spanish empire, and as a result of an alleged *fin de siècle* (*q.v.*) feeling among Spanish intellectuals, a movement arose among a section of the latter which was a kind of miniature renaissance. Usually referred to as *la generación del 98* ('the 1898 generation') because mention of that year focused attention on the severance of the last remnant of the once vast Spanish empire, and because the Cuban war had produced talk of 'regeneración nacional'.

The movement was supported by prominent Spanish writers and scholars (such as Azorín, Onis, Ortega Munilla and Madariaga), but others, like Baroja, Ramiro de Maeztu and Unamuno, were sceptical. Azorín first drew general attention to the movement in 1913 in his book *Clásicos y modernos*. One of the main precepts was that there should be a rebirth of energy, ideas and achievement in the 20th c., to replace those losses, both material and cultural, which were blamed fairly specifically on the 19th c. – by then already held in scorn.

The idea of a 'generation' had been applied to history both before and elsewhere. Ortega Munilla had called it a new and integral social corpus with its select minority and with its crowd, and having a vital and determined path to follow. The character of each 'generation' would depend on two elements: the received and the spontaneous. If the second predominated, the generation would be one of combat. The generation of '98 in Spain was one such.

The common interests binding a single literary generation were held to include proximity of birth-dates, homogeneity of formation, a state of conscience created by an historical fact and an identity of inspiration. Of particular importance to the protagonists of this '98 generation were a fresh enrichment of the language from outside, the reform of expression and style, the search for naturalness and truth, and a new lyricism.

generación del 1927　A group of Spanish writers (mostly poets) also known as the *Nietos del 98*. In 1927 the tercentenary of Góngora's death produced a number of learned works about him and seems to have inspired a number of poets to launch a new movement which was basically non-traditionalist, anti-realist and anti-Romantic. Their innovations in prosody included new words, new styles, free verse (*q.v.*) and so forth. Among the leading members were: Pedro Salinas, Manuel Altolaguirre, Jorge Guillén, Gerardo Diego, Federico García Lorca, Rafael Alberti, Juan José Domenchina, Dámaso Alonso, Vicente Aleixandre and Emilio Prados. *See also* GENERACIÓN DEL 1898.

general and particular　*See* ABSTRACT.

generative grammar　A concept developed by Noam Chomsky in *Syntactic Structures* (1957). His fundamental theory is that it is possible by the application of a finite number of 'rewrite rules' to predict (that is to say, 'generate') the infinite number of sentences in a language and to specify their structure. Of various models available he discusses three: finite state grammars; phrase structure grammars; transformational grammars.

género chico　(Sp 'lesser genre') The term includes the one-act *zarzuela* (*q.v.*) *menor* and the one-act *sainete* (*q.v.*) as opposed to the *género grande* (i.e. tragedy, comedy, opera).

genethliacum　An occasional poem written in honour of a birth. *See* OCCASIONAL VERSE.

Geneva school　A school of criticism active in the 1940s and 1950s which developed a variety of theories in phenomenology (*q.v.*). The main figures were the Belgian Georges Poulet, the Frenchman Jean-Pierre Richard and the Swiss critics Jean Starobinski and Jean Rousset.

genius　Originally a genius was the tutelary spirit or deity that guarded a person from birth, or presided over a place (*genius loci*). Later it was applied to the general tendency or guiding principle of an age or a nation. In the 18th c. it acquired the meaning of a man's innate ability, as opposed to what he could learn. In the Romantic period (*q.v.*) people were beginning to think of a genius as a person of exceptional powers, and this is the approximate meaning we accept today. We might say, therefore, that a genius is gifted with an intellectual, imaginative and creative ability of an outstanding order, and with remarkable powers of original speculation and invention. *See* KRAFTGENIE.

genre　A French term for a kind, type or class of literature. Generic classifications are organized in all manner of ways, and may coalesce around an aspect or aspects of a literary work's form, mode (*qq.v.*) or content. Yet, confusingly, form, mode and content are usually understood to be distinct from genre. Systems for categorizing genre have developed over time and generic categories have proliferated. Plato held that there were only three genres: lyric, epic and drama (*qq.v.*), which broadly correspond to the modern categories poetry, fiction and drama. Aristotle extended this classification to distinguish epic, tragedy and comedy (*qq.v.*). Some consider satire and pastoral (*qq.v.*), which both developed as traditions in the Classical period, to be genres in their own right. From the Renaissance until well on into the 18th c. genres were carefully distinguished, and writers were expected to follow the rules prescribed for them. Subsequently, the genres of novel and short story emerged, as well as a number of non-fiction genres, notably autobiography, biography and the essay. *See also* CONVENTION; GENRE THEORY.

genre theory A field of study whose origins may be traced back to early Greek attempts to categorize literature as exemplified by Aristotle in his *Poetics*. Subsequent theorists and commentators have variously questioned and complicated the traditional sense of genres as distinct and self-defined literary types. One complication is that broad genres easily collapse under the weight of scrutiny into myriad subgenres, as Polonius unwittingly notes in relation to the drama: 'tragedy, comedy, history, pastoral, pastoral-comical, historical-pastoral, tragical-historical, tragical-comical-historical-pastoral' (*Hamlet* II, ii, 334-5). As this litany suggests, any attempt to organize artistic expression in this way tends to draw attention to the porous nature of generic boundaries.

A renewed attempt to fix these boundaries was made by the critic Northrop Frye in his influential *The Anatomy of Criticism* (1957) which set out to recategorize imaginative writings via the identification of recurrent myths and archetypes. The question of genre is also pivotal to deconstructionist (*q.v.*) thinking as articulated by Derrida's contention in 'The Law of Genre' (1980) that literary texts may not be said to 'belong' to any particular genre but rather to 'participate' in several genres. One result of this train of thinking has been an increased sensitivity to the role of social and ideological context in the construction of genre, since generic identities may be seen to rely upon numerous collections of conventions and formal considerations which, although unstable, depend on mutually agreed expectations. In this sense, questions of genre theory relate to wider debates concerning the role and position of the reader (or communities of readers) in making meaning. No longer confined to literary scholarship, fundamental questions of genre theory have come to inform film, television and media studies (*q.v.*) generally. *See also* CONVENTION; GENRE; INTERPRETIVE COMMUNITIES.

Georgian poetry Poetry which appeared in five anthologies edited by Edward Marsh and published between 1912 and 1922, during the reign of George V. The major poets represented were: A. E. Housman, W. H. Davies, Walter de la Mare, John Masefield, Ralph Hodgson, Edward Thomas, James

Stephens, James Elroy Flecker, J. C. Squire, Andrew Young, Siegfried Sassoon, Rupert Brooke, Wilfred Owen, Robert Graves, Edmund Blunden and D. H. Lawrence.

georgic A poem about rural life and husbandry, so called from the Greek word for 'earth worker, farmer'. This is a form of didactic poetry (*q.v.*) and its principal purpose is to give instructions on how to do something. As Addison put it in his essay on the georgic, it consists in giving 'plain and direct instructions'. The georgic also tends to extol the rural life and nature. A very early example is Hesiod's *Works and Days* (8th c. BC). Virgil's *Georgics* are the best known, and they had a wide influence. James Thomson's *Seasons* (1726–30) and Cowper's *The Task* (1785) were very much in the Virgilian tradition. Other georgics include Poliziano's *Rusticus* (1483); Vida's *De Bombyce* (1527); Alamanni's *La Coltivazione* (1546); Tusser's *Five Hundred Points of Good Husbandry* (1573); and Rapin's *Horti* (1665). *See also* ECLOGUE; PASTORAL.

Gesamtkunstwerk (G 'complete art work') A term coined by Richard Wagner (1813–83) to denote a work of art which combines music, drama, poetry, mime, painting in décor, etc. to create a whole. Ideally, all should proceed from a single creative mind and hand.

Gesellschaftslied (G 'song of fellowship') A form of German song for several voices which originated in the latter half of the 16th c. and whose main themes were love, drinking and dancing.

Gesellschaftsroman (G 'society novel') A term used to describe novels which portray a 'society' as a whole (or in particular) and in which this feature is as important as the characters. Thus, it may be a kind of regional novel (*q.v.*). Some well-known examples are: *Die Ritter vom Geiste* (1850–51) by Karl Gutzkow; *Das Landhaus am Rhein* (1869) by Berthold Auerbach; and *Der Zauberberg* (1924) by Thomas Mann. *See also* ZEITROMAN.

gesta (L 'deeds') The *gesta* were accounts of deeds or tales of adventure. For example: the *Gesta Francorum*, a medieval Latin chronicle (*q.v.*) about the First Crusade; the *Gesta Historiale* of the Destruction of Troy (14th c.); and the *Gesta Romanorum*, the most famous of all medieval collections of such stories, compiled in the 14th c. (*c.* 1330) and first printed *c.* 1472. It was later translated by Wynkyn de Worde *c.* 1510. It remained a popular work until well on in the 16th c. It consisted of legends of the saints, romances, tales from Jewish and Indian lore and so forth, and was often used by preachers for *exempla*. A moral was attached to each tale. *See* CHANSON DE GESTES; EXEMPLUM; ROMANCE.

Gestalt (G 'form, figure, shape') A term imported from German philosophy and occasionally used in literary criticism to denote the unified whole of a literary work; its organic unity. *See* STRUCTURE.

Gestus A term used by Lessing in 1767 to denote something distinct from 'gesture'. In *c.* 1930 the word was taken up and used to indicate something that was a kind of combination of 'gesture' and 'gist'; thus attitude or bearing (the early meaning of *gest*) plus point. According to the dramatist Bertolt Brecht (1898–1956), a play or a scene in a play should have a fundamental 'gest' to it, and so a play would comprise a succession of 'gests' and they would be conveyed through all the means at the dramatist's disposal. Meanwhile, the performers ought to be 'gestic', conveying to the audience not only the meaning but also their attitude to what is being said and done, plus a definable attitude about it.

ghazal (A 'conversation with beloved') A strict verse form, used in Arabic, Persian, Turkish, Urdu, Pashto, Uzbek and now English literature. Its origin extends at least as far back as the Arab poet Abu Nawas (d. 813). The ghazal developed certain conventions: it was typically a love poem or mystical meditation of up to thirty couplets, with the rhyme scheme aa, ba, ca, da, etc., each couplet expressing a complete and isolated thought. The first couplet is called the *matla* and the last couplet is the *maqta*, in which the poet mentions his own pen-name (a convention begun in the 12th c.). The Classical ghazal was usually written under aristocratic or courtly patronage and employed stock elements concerning love and rivalry. Often, the love described is hopeless, hence some of the stock characters in the ghazal were the wretched lover (*ashiq*), the merciless beloved (*mashuq*), the lover's lustful rival (*raqib*), and the cup-bearer at the wine party (*saqi*). Innovation within the ghazal was confined largely to the ingenious and unusual deployment of these conventional elements and images by wordplay, extrapolation of meaning or ironic juxtaposition.

The discreteness of each couplet in terms of thought, emotion and mood is a feature tied to the fact that the ghazal was written primarily to be read aloud at a gathering of poets known as a *mushaira*, a tradition which flourishes to this day.

Another pervasive feature of the ghazal, deriving from its Persian heritage, was the use of Sufi, or Islamic mystical, symbolism. In one of his studies of Sufism, A. J. Arberry offers a list of symbols commonly used in Persian mystical verse: *zulf* (tress), referring to the revealed omnipotent attributes of God; *sharab* (wine), representing ecstatic experience at the revelation of the beloved, destroying the foundations of reason; and *saqi* (wine- or cup-bearer), which stands for Reality as manifesting itself through all its revealed forms. These are just a few of a vast stock of symbols, and it is clear that a central ambiguity lies at the ghazal's foundation: the object of love can be either human or Divine.

Some of the renowned exponents of the ghazal include the 13th c. and 14th c. Persian poets Sa'di and Hafez, and the greatest Urdu poet Ghalib (1797–1869), one of whose ghazals might be translated as follows:

> To unite with our beloved was not in Fate's Design;
> Had we lived on, we'd still wait endlessly and pine.

We have lived on your promise but in disbelief:
Had we trusted, would joy not be deadly (though divine)?

Who can see Him, the peerless and Unique?
Were there trace of Otherness, we'd have known its sign.

These plights of Sufism, O Ghalib! And this your account!
We'd think you a saint, were you not given to wine!

                                        (Editor's translation)

Poets continued to write in ghazal form in the 20th c., and Urdu poets such as Sir Muhammad Iqbal and Faiz Ahmed Faiz, and the Pashto poet Ameer Hamza Shinwari, have extended its scope, infusing its structure and symbolism with fresh significance. Indeed, the ghazal, along with other Indian literary forms, became integrated into a more widespread political movement against British rule. It became a potent weapon of protest in the hands of poets such as Josh Malihabadi, Sahir Ludhianvi and Firaq Gorakpuri. Recent practitioners have included Munir Niazi, Nasir Kazmi and Ahmad Firaz. The ghazal has continued to be adapted to contemporary needs and situations, as in the poetry of Saqi Farooqi. Recently, poets writing in English – including Robert Bly, Adrienne Rich and James Harrison – have begun to experiment with the ghazal form and a collection of ghazals in English has been edited by Agha Shahid Ali.

ghost story A fictional narrative, usually in prose (there are some in verse, such as R. H. Barham's tales in the *The Ingoldsby Legends*, 1837–47), of variable length, though commonly taking the form of a short story (*q.v.*), in which the spirit of a person (or spirits of persons), no longer bound by natural laws, manifests itself, or seems to do so and 'haunts' a place, person or thing as a kind of 'presence'.

Ghost stories probably antedate literature and belong to a primordial world. In primitive religion, mythology and ancient epic (*q.v.*) the interrelationship of the living and the dead, the natural and the supernatural, is commonplace. Such beliefs pervade pre-Christian literature in Europe and the Middle East. There are numerous references to ghosts and anecdotes about ghosts in the Christian era in works designed primarily to entertain, but also in didactic literature. Indeed, the Bible confirmed the existence of the supernatural order repeatedly: The Son of God Himself was the most illustrious ghost in history (to say nothing of the Holy Ghost). Christ made eleven separate appearances after the Resurrection.

The Tudor and Jacobean dramatists perceived the rich possibilities of using ghosts as 'characters' in their plays. Some are malignant and revengeful (e.g. the ghost of Andrea and Revenge in Kyd's *The Spanish Tragedy*, c. 1587–90); some have an important part in the plot (e.g. the ghost of Hamlet's father); some have a premonitory role (e.g. the spectre of Caesar who appears to Brutus before Philippi); and some have walk-on parts, so to speak, to give the audiences an additional *frisson* of fear (e.g. the apparitions of Isabella and Brachiano in Webster's *The White Devil*, 1612).

Among the educated and sophisticated people in the neoclassical period and the Augustan age (*q.v.*), ghosts were not a matter much talked or written about. The arrival of the popular 'graveyard poetry' (*q.v.*) in the 1740s marked the beginning of a shift in sensibility (*q.v.*), and the sepulchral meditations of those later called the 'graveyard poets' were to have a pronounced effect on the evolution of the Gothic novel (*q.v.*), which was soon to appear and, with it, the ghost in fiction (e.g. the monstrous ghost in Walpole's *The Castle of Otranto*, 1764), plus much other supernatural apparatus.

Ghost stories as a distinct genre emerged in the early 19th c. coincidentally with the advent of the short story. Some of the earliest can be found in the work of Heinrich von Kleist and E. T. A. Hoffman, e.g. Kleist's very brief *Das Bettelweib von Locarno* ('The Beggarwoman of Locarno') of 1810 and Hoffman's frankly rather long *Das Majorat* ('The Entail') of 1817. Both authors display that strong sense of the past which was to become central to the development of the ghost story in the next hundred years. Strangely, from their time on, German writers have made a minimal contribution to the genre of the ghost story – which has been dominated by Anglophone writers, most of whom have been English. Popular and influential writers of ghost stories in the early and mid 19th c. include Washington Irving, Sir Walter Scott, Edgar Allan Poe, Charles Dickens (who caused ghost stories to be associated with Christmas; he wrote a succession which appeared in seasonal magazine supplements), Wilkie Collins and Sheridan Le Fanu. In the 1860s and 1870s many ghost-story writers were women, including Amelia Edwards (author of *The Engineer* and *The Phantom Coach*), Rosa Mulholland, Mrs Braddon, Mrs Riddell and Mrs Oliphant, who wrote *The Open Door* (1881).

During the second half of the 19th c. there was a great deal of interest in psychic phenomena, spiritualism, psychotherapy and extreme psychological states. F. W. H. Myers (1843–1901), who was deeply interested in Mesmer's theories, helped to found the Society for Psychical Research (1882). Curiosity about the preternatural and speculation about life after death proved beneficial to mediums – and photographers. Photographic archives of the Victorian period contain many examples of 'spirit photographs' of, apparently, palpable ghosts. The Victorians were fascinated by ghosts, and from the 1860s ghost stories proliferated. In 1898 Henry James published one of the most famous and sophisticated ghost stories of all, *The Turn of the Screw*, though this is less interested in psychological states than it is in the veracity of narrative. In the late 1890s M. R. James (1862–1936) began his celebrated *Ghost Stories of an Antiquary* (first issued under that title in 1904). M. R. James was a student of the 19th c. ghost story (he read hundreds of them). He developed his own rules which appear in brief prefaces to his collections of tales.

In the 20th and 21st c., the genre has continued to flourish, though perhaps not with the style, vigour, variety and originality of the years between, say, 1850 and 1910. Notable purveyors, to mention just three, are Walter de la

Mare, Elizabeth Bowen and Shirley Jackson, author of a number of influential American 'haunted house' novels. *See also* SUPERNATURAL STORY.

ghostword A term invented by W. W. Skeat, the great 19th c. editor of medieval texts, to describe words which have no real existence. Such spurious words are often the result of inadvertent errors made by copyists, printers and editors. *See* PHANTOM WORD.

ghost-writer One who does literary work for someone else who takes the credit. It has become a common practice for professional writers to 'ghost' the autobiographies, memoirs or reminiscences of famous personalities.

gierasa A boasting poem (*q.v.*) akin to the fârsa (*q.v.*) of the African Galla tribe. It extols the strength and accomplishments of a particular warrior hero.

gift The social and ethical dilemmas of gift-giving have been much discussed in the social sciences throughout the 20th c. Theorists including Claude Lévi-Strauss, Georges Bataille and Pierre Bourdieu have considered matters such as the extent to which giving involves self-interest, the question of appropriate reciprocation, and how gifts operate as commodities in capitalist societies. Literary theorists have been preoccupied by the topic as well. In *The Gift* (1983), Lewis Hyde offers an elegant defence of artistic creativity in an era when art and culture are dominated by financial imperatives. In *Given Time* (1992) Derrida argues that a gift is impossible since it is inevitably so freighted with obligations as to no longer operate as a pure present. Paradoxically, a genuine gift cannot be understood as one; thus for Derrida the gift exemplifies *aporia* (*q.v.*).

Glasgow Citizens Theatre Started in 1945 when James Bridie (1888–1951) created a company at the then Royal Princess's Theatre, which was built in 1878 in Glasgow's Gorbals. Up until 1969 the policy was to present new plays (especially Scottish ones) rather than classics. In 1970 the present Citizens' Company was formed, and for more than thirty years it was directed by Giles Havergal, Philip Prowse and Robert David MacDonald. Since its formation the group has based its repertoire on British and foreign classics and has performed 165 productions of plays from the foreign (15 British premières) and British (13 world premières) repertoire. In Britain it has become famous for its originality and enterprise; the company has achieved an international reputation (it has made guest and festival appearances in 22 foreign cities) without in any way losing local support and popularity.

glee (OE *glīw, glēo*, 'minstrelsy, merriment') A *glee* or *glee-song* was a part-song for three or more voices, not necessarily with an accompaniment. They had a particular vogue from *c.* 1750 to *c.* 1850. Choirs of glee-singers are still to be heard in the United States.

globalization The process by which the world is becoming increasingly connected through access to global markets, technology and information, but at the same time homogenized by the very forces of globalization which are still located in the capitalist societies in the West.

While access to markets and information may seem to benefit poorer communities and countries, critics of globalization see it as another form of Western domination over the 'Third World' with detrimental effects upon local communities and culture. The argument that globalization will lead to prosperity, freedom and democracy in less developed societies, and raise ecological awareness worldwide, may actually mask older forms of Western imperial domination. It seems that globalization is more difficult to resist as it is couched in a more subtle narrative of universal prosperity and development than classical forms of imperialism. The pervading influence of American popular culture in the 20th and 21st c. and US political and economic domination is a well-known example, and the rise of China as a new global power is another. However, critics such as Simon During have suggested that globalization has superseded postcolonialism (*q.v*).

A good example in literature of the power of global capital is Dubravka Ugrešić's essay 'Europe, Europe' on the ways in which post-1989 Eastern Europe is being transformed by globalization. She examines how Eastern European cities are becoming homogenized by globalization and 'catching up' with the Western consumerist world:

> Dutch tomatoes, German yoghurt, French cosmetics, and Italian shoes. Who would keep track of all that has occupied eastern Europe? The occupation is sensual, exciting and pleasurable; if it hadn't been, someone would have already objected. Invisible money rustles, clinks and pours from pocket to pocket.

In literary studies, critics have recently examined the consumption of 'ethnic' and postcolonial literature in the West, and the relationship between globalization and the production and reception of literary texts. Graham Huggan's *The Postcolonial Exotic* (2001) and Sarah Brouillette's *Postcolonial Writers in the Global Literary Marketplace* (2007) are some key contributions in this area. In the last couple of decades, there has been a proliferation of books on globalization. Arjun Appadurai's *Modernity at Large: Cultural Dimensions of Globalization* (1996), Zygmunt Bauman's *Globalization: The Human Consequences* (1998), Ulrich Beck's *What Is Globalization?* (1999) and Joseph Stiglitz's *Globalization and its Discontents* (2003) are some of the well-known instances. *See also* CULTURAL IMPERIALISM; POSTCOLONIAL CRITICISM; WORLD LITERATURE.

Globe Theatre One of the most famous of all theatres, it was built in 1599, on Bankside in Southwark, in the shape of a polygon with three storeys. The roof was thatched, with the centre open to the sky. In 1576 James Burbage (c. 1530–97) had leased land in Shoreditch on which he had built (of wood) the first building in England specifically designed for plays. In 1577 it became known as 'The Theatre'. In 1598 the fabric was removed to the Bankside and set up as the Globe. At first it was the home of the Lord Chamberlain's Men

(Shakespeare was one of them), after Queen Elizabeth's death renamed the King's Men. Many of Shakespeare's plays were performed in it and Shakespeare had a share in the theatre. It was destroyed by fire in 1613 when a discharge of cannon during a performance of *Henry VIII* ignited the thatched roof. Rebuilt on the same site, it reopened the next year. It was finally demolished in 1644, but a reconstruction of the theatre was begun in the late 1980s and it opened in 1997.

glosa A Spanish metrical form invented by the court poets late in the 14th c. or early in the 15th. It is a poem of a single line or a short stanza which introduces the theme of the work and which is then followed by a stanza for each line of the introductory *cabeza*. The stanza explains or 'glosses' the line. *See also* CANTIGA; ESPINELLA; GLOSS; MOTE.

gloss In the first place an interlinear (or marginal) comment on or explanation of a word or phrase. Classical Greek manuscripts frequently had glosses in Latin. Occasionally poems have been published with marginal glosses. A good example is Coleridge's *Rime of the Ancient Mariner*, which he glossed himself. Another well-known example is E.K.'s gloss to Spenser's *Shepheard's Calendar*. *See also* GLOSSARY.

glossary An alphabetical list of unfamiliar or difficult words and phrases, sometimes appended to the edition of a particular text, and sometimes published as a separate volume like *A Shakespeare Glossary* by C. T. Onions (1911, 1919). *See also* CONCORDANCE; DICTIONARY; GLOSS.

Glossen (G 'glossaries') Explanations/translations of Latin words or sentences in medieval German literature. Marginal glosses are *Randglossen*; those above the lines are 'interlinear'; those in the lines are *Textglossen*. Such glosses are useful to philologists since they provide evidence about the development of the German language in the Middle Ages and also give some idea of Latin texts in use. *See* GLOSS; GLOSSARY.

glyconic The name of a Greek lyric meter named after Glykon, a poet (date unknown). There are two basic patterns: either: 乁 乁 | / ∪ ∪ / | ∪ 乁 or: 乁 乁 | / ∪ ∪ / | 乁 |. It was used for early Greek lyric poetry and drama.

gnomic verse Gnomic derives from the Greek word for 'opinion' or 'judgement', and a *gnome* has come to mean a short pithy statement of a general truth; thus a maxim or aphorism (*qq.v.*). The adjective *gnomic* was first applied to a group of 6th c. BC Greek poets but there are much earlier examples of *gnomes* in Chinese, Sanskrit and Egyptian. The Book of Proverbs, which follows the Psalms in the Old Testament, is one of the best examples of gnomic utterance. Old English, Irish, Norse and Germanic literature provides many instances. *Beowulf* contains a number of gnomic passages. In more recent times Francis Quarles's *Book of Emblemes* (1633) is one of the best-known collections. *See also* APOPHTHEGM; EMBLEM-BOOK; PROVERB; SPRUCH.

gnosticism (Gk 'knowledge') A modern term for a set of religious trends and movements that emerged in the Middle East and eastern Mediterranean in the 2nd and 3rd c. AD. An essential characteristic of gnosticism is the concept of 'gnosis', esoteric knowledge which leads to salvation. Commonly, Gnostics believe that humans are divine beings trapped in a material world created by a demiurge, or imperfect god. In order to escape the material world, one needs to acquire gnosis of the supreme being, who is transcendent and absolutely good. For some Gnostics, Jesus was an embodiment of this supreme being. Such beliefs were considered heresy when Christianity became Rome's official religion in the 4th c.

Gnosticism declined by the Middle Ages, but in the 19th and 20th c. a number of writers around the world became interested in the esoteric mysticism associated with the religion, including Blake, Schopenhauer, Jung, Borges, Georges Bataille and Aleister Crowley.

gobbledegook An onomatopoeic word which no doubt derives from the noises that poultry make. The term denotes unintelligible language, gibberish, and thus nonsense (*q.v.*). It is often applied derisively to the kind of language cherished by lawyers, bureaucrats, art, music and literary critics and other purveyors of jargon (*q.v.*).

golden age An era when things were at their best. The nations and civilizations of antiquity all had their so-called golden ages, usually associated with particular reigns and dynasties. For example, the T'ang dynasty (626–84) and particularly the reign of Tae-tsong (618–26) in China; and the reigns of Sethos I and Ram'eses II in Egypt (1336–1224 BC). The same is true of modern nations. For instance, the reigns of Elizabeth I of England (1558–1603) and of Czar Peter the Great of Russia (1672–1725). As far as literature is concerned there have been several golden ages: the golden age of Spanish literature (16th and 17th c.), French drama (17th c.), English literature – especially drama – (c. 1580–c. 1630). *See also* AUGUSTAN AGE; DRAB.

The Golden Legend A collection of saints' lives originating as the *Legenda Aurea* of the Italian friar and bishop Jacobus de Voragine (13th c.), subsequently translated with other homiletic material and popularly published in English by Caxton in 1483.

Goliardic verse The Goliards were wandering scholars and clerks of the 12th and 13th c., called *vagi scholares aut goliardi*. It is not certain how they got their name. As there are references to their belonging to the 'household of Golias', some believe this may be the origin. But there was no guild of Goliards, no *ordo vagorum*. The name may have derived from Golias, Goliath of Gath, the giant of lawlessness and evil associated later with the Latin word *gula* 'gluttony'. Much Goliardic verse consists of satire (*q.v.*) against the Church, and extravagant praise of the delights of love-making and drinking. It is full of zest, caustic humour and a rough earthiness; at times almost pagan in its unabashed hedonism. The theme of *carpe diem* (*q.v.*) is recurrent.

Gongorism A style of writing derived from the name of the Spanish poet Luis de Góngora y Argote (1561–1627). It is a baroque (*q.v.*) and affected style whose chief characteristics are: Latinistic vocabulary and syntax, intricate metaphors, excessive hyperbole (*q.v.*), rich colour images, mythological allusions and a general strangeness of diction. Comparable features are to be found in the French *la préciosité* (*q.v.*). Such a style provoked mixed reactions and some considerable opposition, especially from the devotees of *conceptismo* (*q.v.*); but many discerning critics have given the highest praise to Góngora's best work among which the *Soledades* and *La Fábula de Polifemo y Galatea* persist as favourites. Góngora, who did not always write like this, had many imitators. Gongoristic elements are to be found in a number of 17th c. English writers including Sir Thomas Browne and Richard Crashaw. *See also* EUPHUISM; MANNERISM; SECENTISMO.

good sense During what is known as the period of neoclassicism (*q.v.*) in France and England, that is during the latter half of the 17th c. and for much of the 18th, good sense was a much prized criterion of excellence in art and literature. If a work displayed good sense then it possessed order, balance, harmony, restraint, appropriateness of style to subject matter, and a general absence of excess or flamboyance. Good sense implied sane understanding and good manners. *See* CONVENTION; DECORUM.

Gothic novel/fiction A type of romance (*q.v.*) very popular from the 1760s until the 1820s. It had a considerable influence on fiction afterwards (still apparent in the 21st c.), and is of much importance in the evolution of the ghost story and the horror story (*qq.v.*).

One of the earliest examples of the genre is Tobias Smollett's *Ferdinand Count Fathom* (1753), very probably the first novel (*q.v.*) – a form then newly developed – to propose terror and cruelty as its main themes. Much better known than this is Horace Walpole's *The Castle of Otranto* (1764).

Most Gothic novels are tales of mystery and horror, intended to chill the spine and curdle the blood. They contain a strong element of the supernatural and have all or most of the now familiar topography, sites, props, presences and happenings: wild and desolate landscapes, dark forests, ruined abbeys, feudal halls and medieval castles with dungeons, secret passages, winding stairways, oubliettes, sliding panels and torture chambers; monstrous apparitions and curses; a stupefying atmosphere of doom and gloom; heroes and heroines in the direst of imaginable straits, wicked tyrants, malevolent witches, demonic powers of unspeakably hideous aspect, and a proper complement of spooky effects and clanking spectres ... The whole apparatus, in fact, that has kept the cinema and much third-rate fiction going for years, is to be found in these tales. The most popular sold in great quantities and they were read avidly.

After *The Castle of Otranto* there came a succession of such novels, of variable quality. Many of them were dramatized (as was *The Castle of Otranto*). Some of the major examples of the genre are Clara Reeve's *The Old English Baron* (1778), William Beckford's *Vathek* (1786) – Beckford lived in the Gothic extravaganza of Fonthill Abbey – Ann Radcliffe's *Mysteries of Udolpho* (1794), Ann Yearsley's *The Royal Captives* (1795), M. G. ('Monk') Lewis's *The Monk* (1796), C. R. Maturin's *The Fatal Revenge* (1807) and his *Melmoth the Wanderer* (1820) and Mary Shelley's *Frankenstein* (1818) – the all-important progenitor of scores of horror films and science fiction (*q.v.*). Godwin's *Caleb Williams* (1794) has often been classed as Gothic, but has a special importance as an early instance of the propaganda novel (*see* 'THESIS NOVEL') and the novel of crime and its detection.

By the turn of the 18th c. dozens of Gothic novels and tales (many of them hackwork sunk without trace except in the vaults of the major libraries) were being published. The demand for cheap, sensational literature was high. Publishers, scenting large profits, exerted themselves (as they seldom do otherwise). So did the authors of such stories; they wrote fast.

There were many short stories and this was at the time that the short story (*q.v.*) was developing as a form and genre in its own right. Like most of the well-known Gothic novels they are curiosities, 'period pieces', ludicrously melodramatic and wildly overwritten, with resonant titles designed to cause a thrilling shudder of apprehension in the sturdiest of breasts. A good many were written by women and they were very popular among female readers.

By early in the 18th c. readers had supped full with horrors and there was a growing demand for even more lurid and sensational fiction. Decadence (*q.v.*) was setting in. Graveyards, charnel houses, the crepuscular and the necropolitan, the macabre (*see* 'DANSE MACABRE') had become increasingly popular elements; and here, perhaps, one may discern the long-term influence of the so-called graveyard school of poetry (*q.v.*) of the 1740s, which had marked a shift of sensibility (*q.v.*) and something of a reaction against the attitudes and codes of the Augustan age (*q.v.*).

By *c.* 1815–20 the need for something different and rather more sophisticated was starting to be felt. Enough had been as good as a feast, as it were. Jane Austen suggested as much in *Northanger Abbey* (published in 1818, but begun in 1798 and prepared for the press in 1803). In 1818, too, Thomas Love Peacock published *Nightmare Abbey*, which is a kind of burlesque (*q.v.*) of Gothic excesses.

Meanwhile, Gothic had travelled to America, where Isaac Mitchell achieved some reputation with *The Asylum* (1811) and Charles Brockden Brown attained something approaching fame with a succession of Gothic romances: *Wieland* (1798), *Arthur Mervyn* (1799–1800), *Ormond* (1799) and *Edgar Huntly* (1799). Some of the main influences on Brown were Samuel Richardson, William Godwin and Ann Radcliffe. In turn, Brown was to influence Nathaniel Hawthorne, Mary Shelley and Edgar Allan Poe – one of the most Gothic of all 19th c. writers of short stories whose long-term contribution to the horror story, the tale of suspense and mystery and the detective story (*q.v.*) was immeasurable.

During the latter half of the 18th c. German writers were developing their own brand of sensational and Gothic fiction. In the 18th c. considerable interest in English literature arose in German literary circles. In England there was corresponding interest in German literature. 'Monk' Lewis, for example, was well read in German, was a gifted translator and was to influence E. T. A. Hoffman. Translation of the *Schauerroman* and German 'terror fiction' began in the 1890s with the publication of an English rendering of Benedikte Naubert's *Hermann von Unna*.

There was also Gothic drama. Playwrights had no inhibitions about displaying horrors on stage. Dramatized versions of Gothic novels (and there were many of them) set out to frighten audiences. For example there was *Le Comte de Comminges* (1764) by François de Baculard d'Arnaud. This spine-chiller was set in the burial crypt of a Trappist monastery. The necropolitan action was so blood-curdling that members of the audience passed out, to be revived by the management with cordials. And there was von Gerstenberg's *Ugolino* (1768), which was based on the story of Ugolino recounted by Dante in the *Inferno* (Canto XXXIII). Such plays were to have a considerable impact on the development of melodrama (*q.v.*), which was becoming an established popular form of entertainment by *c.* 1830.

The last thirty-odd years of the 18th c. and the first twenty to thirty years of the 19th c. are marked by quite important changes in the ways people thought and felt about the metaphysical and the preternatural, and also what they felt about such matters as madness, states of fear, extremes of suffering, cruelty, violence, crime, torture and murder. It is as if, after a long period of rationalism and apparent mental, spiritual and psychological stability, the rediscovery of 'old worlds' and, more especially, the rediscovery of the world of supernatural or quasi-supernatural evil had a strong disruptive and purgative effect. A whole bag of tricks was opened up, a veritable Pandora's box. Out of it came devils, wizards, magicians and witches, trolls, hobgoblins, werewolves, vampires, doppelgängers – and what not? None of all this had had any place in the 'Age of Reason'. Nor for that matter, had Satanism, possession, black magic, sorcery, exorcism or diabolic pacts. In short, the whole caboodle of the occult. Most conspicuous of all was the ghost, 'revived', after an absence of a great many years (an absence dating back to the Jacobean dramatists), as a figure and 'character'. The ghost story was a natural development from the Gothic novel and Gothic tales in general.

If Gothic fiction had never happened, 19th c. fiction in English would look very different, and so would not a little 20th c. fiction. It would be minus many hundreds of stories of mystery and suspense; minus thousands of ghost and horror stories; minus innumerable tales about vampires, werewolves, succubi, incubi, lamias, doppelgängers and demonic pacts.

Moreover, there is a strong Gothic strain discernible in much mainstream 19th c. fiction. It is very clear in the works of the Brontës (e.g. Charlotte Brontë's *Villette*, 1853), in Sir Walter Scott and Charles Dickens (e.g. *Bleak House*, 1853, and *Great Expectations*, 1861). It is also abundantly clear in much fiction by minor novelists; particularly, G. P. R. James (1799–1860), Bulwer Lytton (1803–73), William Harrison Ainsworth (1805–82) and G. W. M. Reynolds (1814–79).

In the 20th c. Gothic flourished vigorously in the cinema (*Frankenstein*, *Dracula* – and all their progeny) and in popular horror fiction (e.g. the novels of Stephen King). What has been dubbed Neo-Gothic is discernible in the fiction of Isak Dinesen (e.g. *Seven Gothic Tales*, 1934), Mervyn Peake (e.g. *Titus Groan*, 1946, and *Gormenghast*, 1950), William Faulkner (1897–1962), Daphne du Maurier (1907–89), Carson McCullers (1917–67), Flannery O'Connor (1925–64), Diane Johnson (1934–), John Gardner (1933–82), Joyce Carol Oates (1938–), Emma Tennant (1937–) and Angela Carter (1940–92).

A scholarly and academic interest in Gothic literature of the 18th and 19th c. has been manifest for some while, and 'Gothics' have become standard fare on some school examination syllabuses. *See also* GROTESQUE; SUBLIME; SUPERNATURAL STORY; TERROR/HORROR.

Göttinger Dichterbund A group of German poets (also known as the *Hainbund*) who were students at Göttingen University between 1772 and 1776. Disciples of Klopstock, they revived the folksong (*q.v.*) and wrote some notable lyric poetry. *See* STURM UND DRANG.

grace That mysterious, even magical, attribute or quality which is, as it were, the spirit of beauty; beauty being the outward sign of inward grace. Because of its mystery it is a *je ne sais quoi* (*q.v.*). The quality of gracefulness was much prized among Classical writers, at the Renaissance and during the 18th c. Pope in his *Essay on Criticism*, wrote of snatching 'a grace beyond the reach of art', suggesting perhaps the qualities of ease and elegance which, though elusive, might be caught upon the wing.

gracioso (Sp 'graceful, gracious, amusing, droll') A comic actor. On the Spanish stage the *gracioso* is often of much importance; the part may be small but it may have great impact. The usual role is that of parodying the actions of the principal character, and its creation is credited to Lope de Vega. It was also used by Calderón to provide comic relief. The *gracioso* is perhaps comparable to the Fool in Shakespeare. Until the time of Zorrilla (1607–48) the humour in a play was nearly always reserved for the *gracioso*.

gradatio *See* CLIMAX.

grammatology A coinage of the French philosopher Jacques Derrida (1930–2004) to denote a 'science' of the written sign, which he expounded in *Of Grammatology* (1967), *Writing and Difference* (1967) and *Speech and Phenomena* (1967). Grammatology is not to be confused with semiology. In *Modern Literary Theory* (1982), Ann Jefferson emphasizes the difference: 'In Derrida's writing the science of semiology is replaced by grammatology which, as he says, takes the form of a question rather than of a new science . . . of writing.' For Derrida, text and its meaning are not one and the same thing. There can be no science of writing for Derrida since the whole idea of *différance* (in contrast with structuralism) is that there is a permanent instability of reference (*qq.v.*). In his theory of *différance* he argues that the 'deferred' or 'deferring' nature of writing makes it impossible for a text and meaning to have a total and simultaneous identity and coexistence. Moreover, a text cannot have a final and ultimate meaning. In the theory of grammatology Derrida conceives of writing as something that *has its own reality*; something that is *sui generis*; *writing in its own right*, as it were, which is separate from and different from any description of or reproduction of reality, or any version of it. Thus, he is concerned *with writing itself*, and not with writing as any kind of substitute or replacement for voice, or as the transparent medium through which meaning is communicated. The possibilities of such writing are evident in, for example, Joyce's *Finnegans Wake*, in some concrete poetry (*q.v.*) and in ideogrammatic characters used, for instance, in Chinese.

A vital part of Derrida's theory is that 'writing' has always been excluded, degraded, distrusted ever since Plato. Writing has been seen as inferior to speech, and as the improper area in which to discuss language and meaning. Now, Derrida does not seek to 'redress' or 'correct' this 'imbalance' – all words of which he would be suspicious – but his point is that there is *nothing outside writing*; there is no proper priority inherent in speech in terms of either time or ideas. As such, writing is to be evaluated not as a medium for something else, as a 'carrier' or 'bearer' of meaning, but as the only *place* in which the *différance* in language is exposed. *See also* DECONSTRUCTION.

grand guignol Guignol is the name of a French marionette or puppet 'created' in Lyon towards the end of the 18th c. The puppet master Mourguet (1744–1844) may have been the creator. This puppet was believed to represent the main characteristics of the peasant and provincial man in the district of Dauphiné. By some symbiotic process Polinchinelle (or Punch) and this character became one. The brutality and violence of the Punch and Judy show may have been an influence here. At any rate, the name Guignol was given to Paris cabarets which presented decadent shows. Later the Théâtre du Grand Guignol specialized in melodramatic plays whose subjects were horrific: murder, rape and suicide. Since then the term has denoted any kind of play which is bloody, gruesome and sensational. *See* MELODRAMA; THEATRE OF CRUELTY.

grand narrative/master narrative Any theory or intellectual system which attempts to provide a comprehensive explanation of human experience and knowledge. Religion, science, Freudian psychology and political ideologies such as Marxism, nationalism and neoliberalism all produce competing grand narratives (also referred to as master narratives and metanarratives). Grand narratives are particularly associated with Enlightenment (*q.v.*) and modernist thinking, in that they are organized around the 'story' of human progress and perfectibility. Postmodern thinkers, most prominently Jean-François Lyotard, have pointed to what they see as the dangers inherent in such 'totalizing' visions of history. In *The Postmodern Condition: A Report on Knowledge* (1979) Lyotard contends that blind faith placed in the singular explanations provided by the grand narratives of modernity has led to an intolerance of difference. This intolerance led directly to the horrors of the 20th c. Instead, Lyotard argues, we should embrace a multiplicity of theoretical viewpoints in order to appreciate the heterogeneity of human experience, and employ *petits récits*, 'little narratives', to enable a better comprehension of and ability to respond to, local, contingent and temporary circumstances. *See also* POSTMODERNISM.

grand style In his Oxford lectures *On Translating Homer* and *On Translating Homer: Last Words* (1861, 1862), Matthew Arnold used this now famous phrase. Such a style, he maintained, arises when a noble nature 'poetically gifted, treats with simplicity or with severity a serious subject'. Arnold refers to Homer, Pindar, Virgil, Dante and Milton as exponents of the grand style. It was a lofty or elevated style (*q.v.*) suitable for epic: a style which Arnold himself attempted in, for instance, *Sohrab and Rustum* (1853).

Grand Tour The term appears to have been first used in a printed work by Richard Lassels in his *Voyage of Italy* (1670). It came to denote a regular tour of many sights and cities of Europe, especially those in the Netherlands, Germany, France, Austria, Switzerland and Italy. The climax of this journey was a visit to Rome and Naples. The Grand Tour is of some interest and importance in the history of literature because a number of famous writers undertook it, and the journeys produced a substantial variety of entertaining travel reminiscences and travel books (*q.v.*). Indeed, it became so popular that detailed guidebooks (*q.v.*) were compiled to assist travellers. Some of the more interesting examples are: James Howell's *Instructions for Forreine Travell* (1642), the earliest of the continental handbooks; Henry Logan's *Directions for such as shall travel to Rome* (1654); The *Gentleman's Pocket Companion For Travelling into Foreign Parts* (1722); Nemeitz's *Séjour de Paris* (1727), one of the most popular and useful guides of the period; Thomas Nugent's *The Grand Tour containing an Exact Description of most of the Cities, Towns and Remarkable Places of Europe* (1743), in four volumes, an essential *vade mecum*; Thomas Martyn's *A Gentleman's Guide in his Tour through France* (1787); and Johann Ebel's *The Traveller's Guide through Switzerland* (1818).

At least a hundred years before Lassels used the phrase an extensive tour of Europe was regarded as an invaluable part of a gentleman's education; this at a time when there was some premium on education and considerable *cachet* was attached to the importance of learning to behave as a gentleman should. Hence the number of courtesy books (*q.v.*) of the period.

In Elizabethan England tours abroad were recognized as a means of collecting information about foreign countries which might be of use to England. Sir Philip Sidney is a notable example of a man sent abroad for three years to acquaint himself with foreign courts. Trips like this were often subsidized by the Queen.

Curious travellers set off on their own account, even though travel in Europe in those days was dangerous, arduous and expensive. One of the earlier and more adventurous ones was Fynes Morison, who published his *Itinerary* of travels in 1617. During the 17th c. increasing numbers of Englishmen explored Europe, including John Evelyn and Milton. By 1700 the Grand Tour was an established practice, and the influence of continental manners and customs became observable in England; so observable that Restoration dramatists poked fun at imported affectations.

During the 18th c. the tour became more fashionable. Thomas Gray toured the continent with Horace Walpole for three years (1739–41). Other famous tourists were the intrepid Lady Mary Wortley Montagu, Thomas Sterne, Tobias Smollett, Dr Johnson, Boswell, Gibbon, Lord Chesterfield and William Beckford. Among Europeans easily the most famous writer to make the trip was Goethe, who subsequently published his *Italienische Reise* (1786–8).

By the middle of the century, if not before, the Tourist had become an object of caricature; a target not to be missed by Pope who sniped at one kind of traveller in *The Dunciad*:

> Led by my hand, he saunter'd Europe round,
> And gather'd ev'ry Vice on Christian ground;
> Saw ev'ry court, heard ev'ry King declare
> His royal sense of Op'ras or the Fair;
> The Stews and Palace equally explor'd,
> Intrigu'd with glory and with spirit whor'd;
> Try'd all hors d'oeuvres, all liqueurs defin'd;
> Judicious drank, and greatly daring dined;
> Dropt the dull lumber of the Latin store,
> Spoil'd his own language and acquir'd no more;
> All Classic learning lost on classic ground,
> And last turn'd Air, the Echo of a Sound!
> See now, half-cur'd and perfectly well-bred,
> With nothing but a Solo in his head.

Forty-odd years later, in *The Progress of Error*, William Cowper, more genially than Pope, satirized the Oxbridge tourist broadening his mind on the Grand Tour.

The French Revolution and the Napoleonic Wars combined to put an end to the tour as it had been known in the 18th c. After peace came, there began the great railway development. Permanent way was laid over much of Europe and hotels were readily available at railway stations. Soon Thomas Cook started his circular tours of the continent. By the 1860s one could reach Rome in three days, whereas before it had taken three weeks or more.

Grangerize To illustrate a book by the addition of prints, engravings and so forth, and particularly those cut out from other books. In 1769 James Granger (1723–76) published a *Biographical History of England* with blank pages for the addition of engraved portraits or other kinds of illustration. For a time Grangerizing became an innocent hobby.

grapheme The smallest unit of a written language; thus, a letter of the alphabet. The study of graphic signs in a language is called 'graphemics' or 'graphology'.

graphic novel A term used to describe a kind of comic book which is typically published in longer and more durable formats than traditional comics (*q.v.*), and which usually narrates a single story. 'Graphic novel' is often used by publishers to indicate that a work's themes and content are more adult than those of a mere comic book, and to promise literariness. The term first appeared on the book jackets of a number of publications in 1976, including Richard Corben's *Bloodstar*. However, book-like comics have been on the scene throughout the world for much of the 20th c. Comic 'albums', hardbound compilations of comic strips, have appeared since the late 19th c. Many of these constitute single stories, as in the Italian *Corto Maltese* and the French *Asterix* books. In the 1970s several of these were released in book form without being pre-published as serials. During the 1940s in the United States, classic novels and films were adapted to stand-alone comic books. The year 1950 saw the release of the film noir-influenced 'picture novel', *It Rhymes with Lust*, which proclaimed itself 'an original full-length novel'. A number of crime- and horror-oriented 'picto-fictions' appeared in the mid-1950s.

Since the 1960s, what have come to be called graphic novels have proliferated, though the genres which predominate are common to comics: crime, mystery, science fiction (*q.v.*) and superheroes. For this reason, some comic artists, such as Neil Gaiman, consider the term 'graphic novel' both pretentious and unnecessary. More recently a number of graphic life narratives have reached wide audiences, including Art Spiegelman's Pulitzer Prize winning *Maus* (1986–92), a biography of the author's father, a Polish Jew and Holocaust survivor, which portrays Jews as mice, Germans as cats and Poles as pigs; Franco-Iranian Marjane Satrapi's *Persepolis* books (originally published in French, 2000–3); and Alison Bechdel's memoir *Fun Home* (2006). All three regularly appear on university literature courses.

graveyard school of poetry The poets who have been put into this school wrote a type of mournfully reflective poetry with emphasis on the brevity of life and on the sepulchral (and the hope of immortality) which had some vogue in 18th c. England, and in the latter half of the century was a widespread phenomenon in Europe. It was possibly part of a reaction against Augustan principles of decorum (*q.v.*) which did not favour anything melancholy or self-indulgently piteous. One of the earliest examples is Thomas Parnell's *Night-Piece on Death* (1721). The best-known works are Edward Young's *Night Thoughts* (1742) and Robert Blair's *The Grave* (1743). Some would include Gray's *Elegy* (1750) and Ugo Foscolo's *De' Sepolcri* (1807), but the general opinion seems to be that these two poems are not typical of the graveyard school. Indeed, they transcend its limitations. *See* ELEGY; UBI SUNT.

great chain of being   The phrase summarizes an idea of considerable antiquity; namely, that all that exists in the created order is part of natural hierarchy, a *scala naturae* from the lowest possible grade up to the *ens perfectissimum*. It implements the concept that Nature abhors a vacuum. Emerson epitomized the concept adroitly in a well-known couplet:

> Striving to be man, the worm
> Mounts through all the spires of form.

The concept has pervaded philosophy, literature and scientific thought from the time of Plato and Aristotle onwards.

Apart from Ulysses's famous speech on 'degree' in Shakespeare's *Troilus and Cressida* (I, iii), one of the clearest statements of the idea in English literature occurs in Pope's *Essay on Man*:

> Vast chain of being! which from God began,
> Natures aethereal, human, angel, man,
> Beast, bird, fish, insect, what no eye can see,
> No glass can reach; from Infinite to thee,
> From thee to nothing. – On superior pow'rs
> Were we to press, inferior might on ours;
> Or in the full creation leave a void,
> Where, one step broken, the great scale's destroy'd;
> From Nature's chain whatever link you strike,
> Tenth, or ten thousandth, breaks the chain alike.

The classic work on the subject is A. O. Lovejoy's *The Great Chain of Being: A Study of the History of an Idea* (1936).

Greek tragedy   This form of tragedy (*q.v.*) had a definite structure which was more or less prescribed. There were four main parts to a play: (a) The *Prologos* or Prologue: an introductory scene of monologue or dialogue. This exposition established the subject and theme of the play and portrayed one or more characters. (b) *Parados*: the entrance of the Chorus (*q.v.*); the choral song provides further exposition and foreshadows subsequent events. (c) *Epeisodia*: episodes (perhaps four or five) which constitute the main action of the play. One or more characters take part in these with the Chorus. Each episode is separated by a choral ode or *stasimon*. In some plays, a part of the episode may involve a *kommos* – a kind of lamentation in which both characters and Chorus take part. (d) *Exodos*: the conclusion, which follows the last ode (*q.v.*) sung and danced by the Chorus. The *Exodos* includes two features: the messenger's speech and the *deus ex machina* (*q.v.*); but the *deus ex machina* was used only by Euripides.

green baize   From the Restoration period (*q.v.*) until well on into the 19th c. it was traditional to lay a green carpet on the stage when a tragedy was to be performed. The object was to protect the costumes of those characters who had to die in the action.

Greenwich Village An area of New York City which has long-standing literary associations and connections and might be described as a sort of counterpart to Chelsea, London, where painters, writers, musicians, singers *et al.* were wont to congregate. It is particularly associated with Henry James (1843–1916), who lived there; and later, during the 1940s and 1950s, with such figures as Jack Kerouac (1922–69) and Allen Ginsberg (1926–97), two moving spirits of the Beat generation (*q.v.*) or movement. In the 1960s the Village expanded and became associated with the so-called Alternative Society and hence with 'underground literature' (*q.v.*). *See also* ALTERNATIVE LITERATURE; ALTERNATIVE THEATRE.

grotesque (It *grotte*, 'caves', adj. *grottesco*, n. *la grottesca*) The English word 'grotesque' was first used *c.* 1640. Its current meaning is quite removed from its original, more technical use, which was to denote a kind of decorative ornamentation consisting of medallions, fantastic animals, foliage, rocks and pebbles. The word was first used to describe the ornate frescos of Roman ruins discovered in the late 15th c. The interiors had filled with centuries of soil, and so seemed like caves. The term came to be applied to paintings and engravings which depicted the intermingling of human, animal and vegetable themes and forms. Some of the works of Raphael and Arcimboldo are typical grotesques. It has also been used to describe architectural embellishments like gargoyles, hideous diabolic shapes and, again, the complex interweaving of themes and subjects. An outstanding instance is Radovan's main doorway of Trogir cathedral.

The extension of the word to a literary context may well have first occurred in 16th c. France. Rabelais, for example, used it apropos parts of the body. But it does not seem to have been employed regularly in a literary context until the 18th c., the age of reason and of neoclassicism (*qq.v.*), when it was commonly used to denote the ridiculous, the freakish and unnatural; in short, aberrations from the desirable norms of harmony, balance and proportion. Grotesque works of literature were typically those which, rather like the interwoven motifs of the original Roman frescos, were unpleasant chimeras that blurred generic boundaries.

In reaction to neoclassical tastes and strictures the grotesque was utilized by several authors working in the Gothic mode, particularly E. T. A. Hoffman and Edgar Allan Poe. But it has been employed by all manner of writers for satirical purposes, and for comic relief (*q.v.*), including Skelton, Swift, Pope, Smollett, Byron, Dickens, Kafka, Evelyn Waugh, Mervyn Peake and Roald Dahl. In the 20th c. it was particularly associated with the Theatre of the Absurd (*q.v.*) and with 'Southern Gothic' (sometimes termed 'Southern Grotesque'). The latter refers to stories located in the American Deep South which typically feature social outcasts beset by physical disability or deformity, or who exhibit strong traits of the opposite gender. Arguably these grotesques relate the South's decline and degeneration in the wake of the Civil War, and in particular the collapse of the patriarchal Southern plantation family. The most famous purveyors of Southern Gothic are William Faulkner, Carson McCullers and Flannery O'Connor.

Several literary theorists have discussed the grotesque. The Russian critic Mikhail Bakhtin's account of Rabelais is the most influential. In *Rabelais and his World* (1965) Bakhtin identifies and commends the French writer's 'grotesque realism', which elevates the body and its various needs above all else. Thus Bakhtin discerns a literary mode which mocks and even threatens social hierarchy. In her book *The Female Grotesque* (1994), Mary Russo employs Julia Kristeva's concept of 'abjection' (*q.v.*) to argue that the grotesque female body is repeatedly abjected in relation to modern idealized, static bodies. Russo suggests that affirmative depictions of the female grotesque may help to unsettle idealizations of feminine beauty. Literary explorations of the female grotesque abound in the works of many modern writers, including Angela Carter, Jeanette Winterson, Fay Weldon and Jackie Kay. *See also* GOTHIC NOVEL/FICTION.

groundlings The name used to describe audience members of London's Globe Theatre who had purchased the cheapest tickets – costing a penny – to stand in the crowded pit (also called the yard) in front of the stage. Groundlings had a reputation for rowdiness. The reconstructed Globe Theatre on London's South Bank has retained the term for its cheapest standing tickets – though not the penny price.

Group, the A poetry society founded by Edward Lucie-Smith in the late 1950s. It had weekly meetings at which poets read and talked about their work. Among the members were Ted Hughes and Peter Redgrove. It was later called Poetry Workshop. *See also* MOVEMENT.

Group Theatre There have been two main companies bearing this title: (a) A New York theatre company founded in 1931 whose main objective was to present plays which depicted contemporary social conditions. It lasted for ten years and was run by Lee Strasberg, Cheryl Crawford and Harold Clurman. Among their more famous productions were Clifford Odets's *Waiting for Lefty* (1935), Robert Ardrey's *Thunder Rock* (1939) and William Saroyan's *My Heart's in the Highlands* (1939). (b) A company founded in 1932 at the Westminster Theatre, London. It gave the first performances of a number of now well-known verse dramas, including Auden and Isherwood's *The Dog Beneath the Skin* (1936), *The Ascent of F6* (1937) and *On the Frontier* (1939), T. S. Eliot's *Sweeney Agonistes* (1935) and Stephen Spender's *Trial of a Judge* (1938). It closed in 1953.

Grub Street According to Dr Johnson, this was 'originally the name of a street near Moorfields in London, much inhabited by writers of small histories, dictionaries, and temporary poems, whence any mean production is called *grubstreet*.' It now describes anything in the way of literary hackwork. *See* HACK.

Grupo de Guayaquil A literary group of the 1930s that began a revival of the Ecuadorean novel. The novels were mainly about regional Ecuadorean life, in the tradition of *costumbrismo*, and combined social comment and protest. The authors were Joaquín Gallegos Lara (1911–47), Enrique Gil Gilbert (1912–73) and Demetrio Aguilera Malta (1909–81).

Gruppe 47 A group of predominantly left-wing German writers founded by Hans Richter in 1947. They gathered annually between 1947 and 1967 when they read each other's work and offered criticism. During those twenty years they had considerable influence on German literature. Among the more famous were Heinrich Böll, Günter Grass and Johannes Bobrowski. Others were Paul Celan, Uwe Johnson, Erich Fried and Hans Enzensberger.

Gruppe 61 A group of left-wing revolutionary German writers centred on Dortmund *c.* 1961. Their principal objective was to promote writing – particularly fiction – about work by working men. The two most prominent members were Max von der Grün and Josef Reding. It seems that the group fell into desuetude without achieving much.

guidebook A book designed to help travellers. Guidebooks range widely from mere hackwork to elegant writing. An early and distinguished example is the *Hellados Periegesis* of Pausanias (2nd c. AD), a remarkably well-informed and interesting guidebook to Attica, Central Greece and the Peloponnese. From the 12th c. dates the *Mirabilia Urbis Romae*, a guidebook to Rome which was still being kept up to date in the 15th c.

Until travel for diversion and holiday (as opposed to that for exploration, proselytizing and commercial enterprise) became fashionable there was little in the way of organized guidebooks; though since the Middle Ages there have been a very large number of travel books (*q.v.*) and reminiscences, often of considerable literary merit.

In the 17th c. the Grand Tour (*q.v.*) caused a number of writers to produce detailed guides for Europe. Possibly the earliest instance of a handbook for continental travel was James Howell's *Instructions for Forreine Travell* (1642). As the Tour became more and more popular so the number of guidebooks multiplied, and there were many in the 18th c. For the most part they were well written, well organized and still make interesting reading.

However, the guidebook proper really belongs to the last hundred years or so – a period which has produced such series as: *Murray's Handbooks of Travellers*, *Nagel's Guides*, the *Baedeker Guides*, *Fodor Guides*, the *Guides Bleus* (outstanding for their comprehensiveness and accuracy) and the *Michelin Guides* (which also set a high standard of accuracy and detail). These are the result of joint efforts by teams of investigators.

Occasionally an author has produced a more personal type of guidebook. Richard Ford, for instance, who wrote *Handbook for Travellers in Spain* (1845); and Augustus Hare, who wrote *Days near Rome* (1875), and *Cities of Northern and Central Italy* (1876). From recent years one might cite William Collins's *Companion Guides* and Jonathan Cape's *Travellers' Guides*.

Since the Second World War, travel having become a simple undertaking for millions of people, guidebooks have proliferated in large numbers all over the world and there is little sign of any diminution. In many instances the quality, too, has improved. In fact, the guidebook may be good literature which, at its best, is distinguished by learning, an elegant style and a high degree of readability. *See* HANDBOOK AND MANUAL; VADE MECUM.

guignol *See* GRAND GUIGNOL.

guillemets The French equivalent of inverted commas, marked « ». *See* PUNCTUATION.

guslar The *gusle* is a one-stringed fiddle played by a *guslar* (pl. *guslari*). The *guslari* were blind minstrels among the South Slavs; professional and itinerant reciters of national heroic poems of the oral tradition (*q.v.*) called *narodne pesme* (*q.v.*). These men corresponded to the Greek rhapsodists, the Celtic bards, the Old English *scopas*, the Scandinavian *skalds* (*qq.v.*), and the French *trouvères* and *jongleurs* (*qq.v.*). Their profession dates from the 14th c. or before.

Many of them composed heroic poetry as well as reciting it. They are still to be found occasionally in the Central Balkans (especially in Bosnia, Serbia and Macedonia) and they carry on the ancient tradition of making up and chanting (to the accompaniment of the *gusle*) heroic poems. The author has seen and heard a blind *guslar* (in the uplands of Bosnia) making up such a poem. Its subject was an engagement between the Partisans and the Germans in the Second World War. *See also* PEVAČI.

gwawdodyns A Welsh syllabic verse form. It comprises a quatrain (*q.v.*) stanza with lines of nine, nine, ten and nine syllables respectively. The first, second and fourth lines have end-rhyme with each other. The third line may rhyme internally with itself, or a syllable before the end of the line may rhyme into the fourth line.

gynocriticism A branch of feminist literary theory and studies which focuses on women as writers, as distinct from feminist criticism and evaluation of male writers. The term was coined by Elaine Showalter. *See* FEMINIST CRITICISM.

gyre (Gk *guros*, 'circle') A term that can refer to a circular or spiral movement but, in a literary context, is associated with the poetic vision of W. B. Yeats. He envisaged a gyre in the shape of a cone, comprised by a series of broadening concentric circles. In *A Vision* (1925, 1937), Yeats spoke of a 'double cone or vortex', each cone spinning within the other. He saw the one as embodying subjectivity and time, the other as embodying objectivity and space. He also saw the whole model as representing what he called the 'four faculties' of will, mask, creative mind and fate. Yeats traces the concept of the double gyre or cone back to Empedocles, and Heraclitus, to Plato's Timaeus, and Aquinas's vision of the 'ascent and descent of angels', as well as to Swedenborg, and a projected but unwritten short story by Flaubert called 'La Spirale'. Yeats's vision of historical development is couched in this form of two gyres, each revolving within the other. A given movement, such as Christianity, begins at the point and spreads out in concentric circles until it reaches its outermost rotation; it then decreases through descending circles. Meanwhile, an opposing movement, which has been widening concentrically, broadens to engulf it. This is the kind of movement expressed in Yeats's poem *The Second Coming*, where Christianity is eventually overcome by whatever darker forces are represented by the 'rough beast'.

H

Habima   (Heb 'stage') A theatre founded in Moscow in 1917–18 to stage plays in Hebrew. It became one of the studios of the Moscow Art Theatre (*q.v.*) and in 1931 moved to Tel Aviv. From 1953 it has been the national theatre of Israel.

hack   The word derives from *hackney*, 'a hired horse, a hireling', and denotes a person who churns out the written word for a pittance. It suggests a low grade of work. In the 18th c. it was associated with writing for booksellers, and produced terms such as 'hack writer', 'hack worker', 'Grub Street (*q.v.*) hack'.

hadīth   (A 'statement') The term given by Muslims to those traditions which are believed to embody the practice and precepts of the Prophet. Many statements were ascribed to the Prophet after his death and a number of *hadīth* compilations were made. How authentic they were has been much debated.

hagiography   (Gk 'sacred writing') The writing or study of the lives of the saints. Also known as hagiology; it is, as a rule, the specialized study of saints, often inspired by veneration. There are two main groups of such works: the literary and the liturgical. Notable examples of the literary are: Eusebius of Caesarea's record of the martyrs of Palestine (4th c.); Theodoret's account of the monks of Syria (5th c.); Gregory the Great's of the monks of Italy (6th c.); the Byzantine Menology (12th c.) – the menology (*q.v.*) being a sort of calendar of the Greek Church which incorporates biographies of the saints; the Chronicle of Nestor (*c.* 1113), written by a priest of that name and known as the primary *Russian Chronicle*; the *Golden Legend* of Jacobus de Voragine (13th c.). Liturgical sources are documents, very often calendars (*q.v.*), which record information about devotion paid to saints. These were local as well as universal calendars; also known as martyrologies. Well-known examples

---

A Dictionary of Literary Terms and Literary Theory, Fifth Edition. J. A. Cuddon.
© 2013 The Estate of J. A. Cuddon. Published 2013 by Blackwell Publishing Ltd.

were compiled by Hieronymian (5th c.), Bede (8th c.), Adon and Usuard (9th c.). There was also the *Roman Martyrology* of the late 16th c.

To these instances one should add the *Acta Sanctorum*, a series of lives of the saints arranged in order of their feasts in the ecclesiastical year. This was begun by the Bollandists, a body of Belgian Jesuits (named after John Bolland, a Flemish Jesuit), in the 17th c. The first volume appeared in 1643, and the last of the original series in 1786. There are also the *Acta Sanctorum Ordinis Sancti Benedicti*, a history of the saints of the Benedictine Order, published between 1668 and 1701.

A curiosity in this genre in English literature is John Foxe's *Actes and Monuments* (popularly known as *The Book of Martyrs*), first published in Latin in 1559 and in English in 1563. This vast work (about twice the length of Gibbon's *Decline and Fall of the Roman Empire*) was a history of the Christian Church but contains detailed accounts of many martyrs, particularly the Protestant martyrs of Queen Mary's reign. *See also* SACRED BOOKS; SYNAXARION.

haiku A Japanese verse form consisting of seventeen syllables in three lines of five, seven and five syllables. Such a poem expresses a single idea, image or feeling; in fact, it is a kind of miniature 'snap' in words. It was first established as a form in the 16th c. Originally it was called a *hokku* (*haiku*, the current term, is 19th c.) and was the opening verse in a linked sequence or *renga*. Many Japanese poets have used the form, but two were especially gifted: namely, Bashō (pseudonym of Matsuo Munefusa, 1644–94); and Kobayashi Issa (pseudonym of Kobayashi Nobuyuki, 1763–1828). Recently it has attracted the interest of poets associated with T. E. Hulme and the Imagist movement. Ezra Pound made use of the principles of the *haiku* in *Mauberley* and the *Cantos*. Other poets to be influenced by it were Amy Lowell, Robert Frost, Conrad Aiken and W. B. Yeats. But few Western poets have been able to imitate it successfully. James Kirkup is one of the few, as in *Evening*, the last of a sequence called *Four Haiku on the Inland Sea*:

> In the amber dusk
> Each island dreams its own night.
> The sea swarms with gold.

Also notable is the work of Camden poet Nick Virgilio.
See also IMAGISTS; TANKA.

half rhyme *See* RHYME.

hallel (Heb 'praise, celebrate') A hymn of praise consisting of Psalms 113–18, each of which is headed with *Hallelujah*, 'praise ye'. Thus, a song of praise to God, sung at the four main Jewish festivals: Passover, Pentecost, Dedication and Tabernacles. *See* HALLELUJAH METER.

hallelujah meter Named from its frequent use in hymns. It consists of a stanza of six iambic lines: four trimeter, and two tetrameter (*qq.v.*). *See also* HALLEL; HYMNAL STANZA.

hamartia (Gk 'error') Primarily, an error of judgement which may arise from ignorance or some moral shortcoming. Discussing tragedy (*q.v.*) and the tragic hero in *Poetics*, Aristotle points out that the tragic hero ought to be a man whose misfortune comes to him, not through vice or depravity, but by some error. For example: Oedipus kills his father from impulse, and marries his mother out of ignorance. Antigone resists the law of the state from stubbornness and defiance. Phèdre is consumed by her passion for Hippolyte. *See* HUBRIS; TRAGIC FLAW.

handbook and manual (OE *handboc*) (MedL *liber manualis*) A small book for handy use like the manual for ecclesiastical offices and ritual. Many guidebooks (*q.v.*) are handbooks, and there are a very large number of handbooks published by way of general information and reference on nations, technical subjects, arts and crafts. In America *handbook* has another and particular sense of 'betting book'. In most cases manual and handbook are synonymous. In the medieval Church a manual contained the forms to be observed in the administration of the sacraments. Other examples are the manual of daily prayer; and specialist works like the various manuals for military training; or the BR rule book, a remarkable publication which caters for almost every conceivable contingency in a railwayman's life. This is a masterpiece in its way because of its opaque, convoluted and, at times, mandarin prose which might have been written by Henry James while under hypnosis. The section on emergency action in fog is especially noteworthy. *See also* VADE MECUM.

hapax legomenon A Greek phrase meaning 'said once'; thus, a word found once only in literature. *See* NONCE WORD.

happening The term appears to have been first used by the painter Allan Kaprow in the late 1950s and about that period came to denote a form of improvised or spontaneous theatrical performance, often of a non-naturalistic and non-representational kind. Aural and visual effects may be juxtaposed and may include music, dance, film, stroboscopic lights, violent noises, even smells: thus, a form of mixed-media presentation. Such pieces were first developed and staged at Black Mountain College, North Carolina, in the 1950s. Early happenings were also presented in Vienna by the Wiener Gruppe in the 1950s. Devisers of such entertainments appear to have been influenced by Dadaism, the Theatre of the Absurd and the Theatre of Cruelty (*qq.v.*); and also by the German concept of *Gesamtkunstwerk* ('complete art-work', *q.v.*). In the 1960s the 'light show' developed and was a kind of happening. A celebrated example was Andy Warhol's 'Exploding Plastic Inevitable'. In the same period happenings were associated with pop art and also with environmental art. A notorious instance of the latter was the covering of a considerable area of cliff in Australia with huge sheets of polythene.

harangue An exhortatory speech, usually delivered to a crowd to incite them to some action. The fire-and-brimstone sermon (*q.v.*) is a kind of harangue. Henry V's pre-battle speeches in *Henry V* and Mark Antony's oration over

Caesar's body in *Julius Caesar* are two well-known examples of harangue in dramatic literature.

Harlem Renaissance A literary and cultural movement among black Americans which flourished from early in the 1920s to the 1930s. It was also called the 'New Negro Movement' or 'Negro Renaissance'. It was centred on the district of Harlem in New York City, which emerged as a new cultural capital of black America, to which tens of thousands of blacks migrated from all over the United States, the Caribbean and Africa. The movement put considerable emphasis on the African heritage of American blacks. Among the more prominent figures were Claude McKay, Jean Toomer, Countee Cullen and Langston Hughes. They produced novels and poetry, and in 1925 Alain Locke published an anthology of work titled *The New Negro*. *See also* AFRICAN-AMERICAN STUDIES; BLACK ARTS MOVEMENT; NÉGRITUDE.

harlequinade A form of theatrical entertainment derived from *commedia dell'arte* (*q.v.*) and introduced into England early in the 18th c. by John Rich (*c.* 1692–1761), the dancer, acrobat and mime who took over the management of the theatre in Lincoln's Inn Fields, London, in 1714. He adopted the characters of *commedia dell'arte* and specialized in the non-speaking part of Harlequin – the Italian Arlecchino. He presented the courtship of Harlequin and Columbine as a kind of interlude (*q.v.*) during plays. The harlequinade was eventually to develop into a pantomime (*q.v.*). The character of Pulcinella in *commedia dell'arte* had long before (*c.* 1650) arrived in England as Punchinel and subsequently became Punch.

headless line *See* ACEPHALOUS.

head rhyme *See* ALLITERATION.

Hebraism/Hellenism This antinomy (*q.v.*) was elaborated by Matthew Arnold in Chapter IV of *Culture and Anarchy* (1869). Arnold sees the essence of Hebraism as 'strictness of conscience'; that of Hellenism as 'spontaneity of consciousness'. He regards a combination of these two as a necessary prerequisite to a mature life. They are not contradictory because, as he puts it, 'the desire, native in man, for reason and the will of God, the feeling after the universal order', is their common aim. This is one of several antinomies worked out in the 19th c. *See also* APOLLONIAN/DIONYSIAN; CLASSICISM/ROMANTICISM; NAIV UND SENTIMENTALISCH.

hegemony (Gk *hegemon*, 'leader, or ruler of a state') In ancient Greece, hegemony entailed the dominance of one city-state over another. Since the 1930s, the term 'hegemony' has most often been associated with the Italian Marxist thinker Antonio Gramsci (1891–1937) who, developing Marx's own insights, argues that the economic and political ascendancy of a given class is organically connected with and prepared for, by the achievement of cultural and intellectual hegemony. The intellectuals sympathetic to this class have an organizational function: to articulate the world view of the class, thereby giving it a unity and consciousness of its aims; to help structure social institutions in accordance with these aims; and to foster an environment of *consent* to the ideas of the class. Taking cognizance of this, a socialist revolution must have its path prepared by its own core of intellectuals who, by galvanizing the working masses into a politically self-conscious agency and working towards institutional and individual acceptance of its ideas, develop an alternative hegemony. The notion of hegemony thus embodies a more dialectical connection between superstructure and economic base than that allowed by a deterministic reading of Marx, which sees historical change and revolution as generated necessarily by developments at the economic level.

In her book *Masks of Conquest: Literary Study and British Rule in India* (1987), Gauri Viswanathan examines how education, and particularly the study of English literature, became an effective instrument of hegemonic control in India under British colonial rule. With the passing of the English Education Act in 1835, the colonial subjects were required to study English literature, which the colonial administration perceived as an effective vehicle for introducing and assimilating the colonized to so-called Western humanist values. Viswanathan shows how the 'civilizing' mission of English Literature helped the imperial power to strengthen its control over the colonized people through more subtle textual practices which, on one hand, promoted Western cultural hegemony, and on the other, insisted on the inferiority of the colonized. See also IDEOLOGY; MARXIST CRITICISM.

hemiepes (Gk 'half-hexameter') In Classical prosody a dactylic trimeter catalectic (*qq.v.*) ending in a long syllable. *See* DACTYL.

hemistich (Gk 'half line') Half a metrical line divided at the caesura (*q.v.*). Very common in OE, OHG, ON and medieval alliterative verse (*q.v.*). In drama the half line is used to build up tension and create the effect of cut-and-thrust argument. It is a highly effective device. In drama it is called *hemistichomythia*. *See* STICHOMYTHIA.

hendecasyllable (Gk 'eleven syllables') A metrical line of eleven syllables. The usual scheme is either: ∪ ∪ / ∪ ∪ / ∪ / ∪ / / or: ∪ / / ∪ / / ∪ / ∪ / ∪. It was often used by Greek and Latin poets, and also employed by Dante and Petrarch in sonnets, *terza rima* and *ottava rima* (*qq.v.*). It has not often been used by English poets, but Tennyson and Swinburne experimented with it. Landor wrote some Latin hendecasyllabics.

hendiadys (Gk 'one through two') A figure of speech in which one idea is expressed by two substantives, as in 'gloom and despondency' or 'darkness and the shadow of death'.

hephthemimeral A form of caesura (*q.v.*) which occurs within the fourth foot of a hexameter (*q.v.*) line.

heptameter A metrical line of seven feet, also known as a septenarius or a 'fourteener' (*qq.v.*). Greek and Latin poets used it, mostly for comic verse, but it has been little used in English verse since the Tudor period. Thereafter it is rare in English verse, though Tennyson and Elizabeth Barrett Browning both attempted it. This example of trochaic heptameter comes from Tennyson's *Locksley Hall*:

> Cursed be the social wants that sin against the strength of youth!
> Cursed be the social lies that warp us from the living truth!
> Cursed be the sickly forms that err from honest nature's rule!
> Cursed be the gold that gilds the straitened forehead of the fool.

The heptameter readily breaks down into standard ballad meter or common measure (*qq.v.*) of alternating four- and three-stress lines.

heptastich (Gk 'seven lines') A stanza of seven lines, much used by English poets. For example: Chaucer's rhyme royal (*q.v.*) in *Troilus and Criseyde*; Spenser used it in *The Ruines of Time*, *Daphnaïda*, and in his four *Hymns* in honour of Love, Beauty, Heavenly Love and Heavenly Beauty; Cowley in *The Lover to his Lyre*; Shelley in *To Night* and *Mutability*; Robert Browning in *A Lover's Quarrel*; Longfellow in *Olive Basselin*; John Masefield in *The Widow in the Bye Street*, *Dauber* and *Daffodil Fields*; and, more recently, W. H. Auden in *Letter to Lord Byron*.

heptasyllabic A line of seven syllables.

heresy of paraphrase A term introduced and examined by Cleanth Brooks in *The Well-Wrought Urn* (1947). Brooks's thesis is that if paraphrase means 'to say the same thing in other words' then it is not possible to paraphrase a poem, because a poem means more than merely what it says.

hermeneutic code *See* CODE.

hermeneutic of suspicion This phrase (and the related phrase 'circle of suspicion') occurs in psychoanalytical criticism in connection with the act of probing into the 'unconscious' of a text in order to reveal the processes and the 'dream-work' by which it was produced. The method or technique focuses on what are referred to as 'symptomatic places' (e.g. ambiguities, ambivalences, repetitions of words and phrases, evasions, words *not* said, actions *not* performed, and so on) in the text. The probing also endeavours to expose the elements of the 'latent content' and the 'subtext' (*q.v.*) and by so doing concentrates on both what the text says and how it actually works. *See* PSYCHOANALYTIC CRITICISM; HERMENEUTICS; INDETERMINACY; READERLY/WRITERLY.

hermeneutics (Gk *hermeneus*, 'an interpreter') In Christian theology hermeneutics is the finding and interpretation of the spiritual truth in the Bible. This is an important quest, so that the truths of the Gospels, for instance, may be interpreted and reinterpreted from generation to generation and thus made relevant in different eras. In more general terms, more recently, hermeneutics has been concerned with the interpretation and understanding of human action (this includes what people do, say and create) and, particularly, with human action through what sociologists refer to, in particular senses, as institutions (i.e. political, cultural, economic and kinship institutions). As far as literature is concerned it is to do with the way textual meaning is communicated. In literature the main impetus of hermeneutic theory comes out of the conflation of German 'Higher Criticism' of the Bible and the Romantic period (*q.v.*).

The history of hermeneutic theory dates from the work of German Protestant theologians of the 17th c. who developed methods of understanding the Bible to support their theological views. In the Romantic period the most prominent figure was Friedrich Schleiermacher (1768–1834), who introduced the concept of the 'hermeneutical circle'. In an essay titled *Reading and Interpretation* (in *Modern Literary Theory*, 1982, ed. by Jefferson and Robey) Ian Maclean describes this central feature thus:

> The circle is that movement from a guess at the 'whole' meaning of a work to an analysis of its parts in relation to the whole, followed by a return to a modified understanding of the 'whole' of the work. It embodies the belief that part and whole are interdependent and have some necessary organic relationship. In this version of interpretation, the historical gap which separates literary work from critic or reader is a negative feature to be overcome by an oscillating movement between historical reconstruction on the one hand and divinatory acts of empathy on the part of the critic or reader on the other.

It was the German philosopher and historian Wilhelm Dilthey (1833–1911) who imported the term hermeneutics from theological studies to the realm of philosophy in order to define more clearly the methods of *Geisteswissenschaften*, or 'sciences of the human spirit', as opposed to the scientific method of the natural sciences (*Naturwissenschaften*). It was he, too, who revived the term *Geistesgeschichte* (*q.v.*). Dilthey was concerned with essential meaning and essence, and thus with understanding (*Verstehen*). The influence of his methods on scholarly interpretation was profound and lasting, and it is partly through his thinking that hermeneutic interpretation has been developed in literary and critical theory. In this field it relates to a general theory of interpretation, to methods, procedures and principles involved in extracting meaning from texts. It has particular relevance to a reader's involvement in the creation of meaning. A text may have totally different meanings for different readers at different times. Thus, what readers bring to a text (knowledge, assumptions, cultural background, experience, insight, etc.) affects their interpretations. A reader is in a position *to create the meaning of a text*.

In the 20th c. hermeneutical methods and ideas had considerable influence on phenomenology, reader-response theory and reception theory (*qq.v.*) and thus on such prominent theorists as Wolfgang Iser, Hans-Georg Gadamer, E. D. Hirsch and Stanley Fish. *See also* AESTHETIC DISTANCE; HERMENEUTIC OF SUSPICION.

Hermeticism   Hermes Trismegistos, the 'thrice great Hermes' to whom Milton refers in *Il Penseroso*, was the name given by the Neoplatonists to the Egyptian god Thoth who was regarded as identical with the Grecian Hermes and the author of mystical doctrines. Some works have survived. Much attention was paid to Hermes Trismegistos in late medieval and Renaissance literature and Marsilio Ficino (1433–99), the Italian philosopher and scholar, translated the so-called Hermetic corpus. Hermeticism also refers to poetry which uses occult symbolism and the term has been used particularly of the French symbolist poets. Hermeticism in this connection was defined and analysed in 1936 by Francesco Flora in *La poesia ermetica*. In this work Flora takes Baudelaire, Mallarmé, Valéry and Ungaretti as the main Hermetic poets. The Italian poet Arturo Onofri (1885–1928) is usually accepted as the principal influence in Italian poetry. Loosely, the term denotes obscure, difficult poetry in which the language and imagery are subjective and in which the 'music' and the suggestive power of the words are of as great an importance (if not greater) as the sense. *See also* PURE POETRY; SYMBOL AND SYMBOLISM.

hero and heroine   The principal male and female characters in a work of literature. In criticism the terms carry no connotations of virtuousness or honour. An evil man and a wicked woman might be the central characters, like Macbeth and Lady Macbeth.

heroic couplet   It comprises rhymed decasyllables, nearly always in iambic pentameters rhymed in pairs: one of the commonest metrical forms in English poetry but of uncertain origin. It is generally thought that it developed with Chaucer, possibly because he was familiar with the OF decasyllabic rhymed couplets. However, it is just as possible that as the old alliterative meters were adapted and modified so the rhyming couplet emerged. But there can be no doubt that Chaucer was the first poet to make extensive and successful use of this verse form. The 15th c. poets used the couplet occasionally but it is not until the 16th and 17th c. that it becomes firmly established. Then one can see poets gradually exploiting its possibilities and gaining a mastery of it. Of the many poets who used it at some time or another the most memorable are Spenser, Shakespeare, Ben Jonson, Hall, Drayton, Fletcher, Beaumont, Donne, Waller, Denham and Oldham.

Thereafter Dryden, and then Pope, made it their own. One might say that Dryden was the farrier and artificer who wrought it into shape; and that Pope was the silversmith who, with elegance, wit and subtlety, polished and refined it to near perfection. The following quotations suggest some of the differences. The first is taken from the beginning of Dryden's *Mac Flecknoe*:

> All humane things are subject to decay,
> And, when Fate summons, Monarchs must obey:
> This Flecknoe found, who, like Augustus, young
> Was call'd to Empire and had govern'd long:
> In Prose and Verse was own'd, without dispute
> Through all the realms of Non-sense, absolute.

> This aged Prince now flourishing in Peace,
> And blest with issue of a large increase,
> Worn out with business, did at length debate
> To settle the Succession of the State;
> And pond'ring which of all his Sons was fit
> To Reign, and wage immortal War with Wit,
> Cry'd, 'tis resolv'd; for Nature pleads that He
> Should onely rule, who most resembles me:
> Shadwell alone my perfect image bears,
> Mature in dullness from his tender years;
> Shadwell alone of all my Sons is he
> Who stands confirm'd in full stupidity.
> The rest to some faint meaning make pretence,
> But Shadwell never deviates into sense.

Dryden made the couplet a flexible, robust, resonant instrument for satire (as he did for his plays). For the most part his verses move with a stately and deliberate speed, a canonical tread. By contrast, Pope is more nimble, acrobatic and elusive. He is more like a spiky and chuckling magician, whose wit glitters sardonically. These lines come from *Epistle II: To a Lady: Of the Characters of Women*:

> Narcissa's nature, tolerably mild,
> To make a wash, would hardly stew a child;
> Has ev'n been prov'd to grant a Lover's pray'r,
> And paid a Tradesman once to make him stare,
> Gave alms at Easter, in a Christian trim,
> And made a Widow happy, for a whim.
> Why then declare Good-nature is her scorn,
> When 'tis by that alone she can be born?
> Why pique all mortals, yet affect a name?
> A fool to Pleasure, and a slave to Fame:
> Now deep in Taylor and the Book of Martyrs,
> Now drinking citron with his Grace and Chartres.
> Now Conscience chills her, and now Passion burns;
> And Atheism and Religion take their turns;

Throughout the 18th c. the heroic couplet was the most favoured verse form, and some of the best verse was written in it, especially by Johnson, Goldsmith, Crabbe and Cowper. In the 19th c. it was used much less; nevertheless, Byron, Keats, Shelley, Browning, Swinburne and William Morris all made use of it. In the 20th c. the heroic couplet was rare, but mention should be made of Roy Campbell's *Georgiad* – a satire in the Augustan manner; and Nabokov's dazzling parody in his anti-novel (*q.v.*), *Pale Fire*. *See also* RIDING RHYME.

heroic drama A name given to a form of tragedy (*q.v.*) which had some vogue at the beginning of the Restoration period (*q.v.*). It was drama in the epic mode – grand, rhetorical and declamatory; at its worst, bombastic. Its themes were love and honour and it was considerably influenced by French classical drama, especially by the work of Corneille. It was staged in a spectacular and operatic fashion, and in it one can detect the influences of opera, which at this time was establishing itself. The two main early works were by Sir William Davenant who was virtually the pioneer of English opera. His *The Siege of Rhodes* (1656) and *The Spaniards in Peru* (1658) helped to establish heroic drama. The main dramas thereafter were Robert Howard's *The Indian Queen* (1665), Dryden's *The Indian Emperor* (1665), *The Conquest of Granada* (1669–70) and *Aureng-Zebe* (1675). Dryden was the best of the heroic dramatists. This kind of tragedy was satirized and burlesqued by Buckingham in *The Rehearsal* (1672), and much later again by Sheridan in *The Critic* (1779). *See also* BURLESQUE.

heroic quatrain A four-line stanza rhyming either abab, or aabb.

heroic verse The meter (*q.v.*) used for epic poetry. For the Classical writers it was the dactylic hexameter (*q.v.*). In England the unrhymed pentameter (*q.v.*) line was commonly used, as in *Paradise Lost*, or the heroic couplet (*q.v.*). The French epic writers normally used the alexandrine (*q.v.*), and the Italians the hendecasyllabic line (*q.v.*). *See also* EPIC SIMILE; HEROIC QUATRAIN.

heteroglossia (Gk *hetero*, 'other, different' + *glossa*, *glotta*, 'tongue') A term coined by Mikhail Bakhtin (1895–1975) – the Russian is *raznorecie* – to describe the variety and diversity of languages used in epic and in the novel (*qq.v.*). He distinguished between the language used to represent the attitudes and opinions of the author and that used by individual characters in fiction and epic. *See also* DIALOGIC/MONOLOGIC.

heteronormativity A key concept in queer theory and transgender studies (*qq.v.*) which relates how heterosexuality and complementary masculine and feminine gender roles are established, discursively and politically, as normal and natural. Other sexualities and forms of gendered behaviour are deemed irregular and abnormal, and are consequently marginalized. The term was coined in 1991 by Michael Warner, though it draws on Adrienne Rich's notion of 'compulsory heterosexuality' and Gail Rubin's concept of a 'sex/gender system', in which certain sexual practices and gendered behaviours are considered acceptable and others less so or not at all. Queer theorists have identified many areas of culture that are pervaded by heteronormative attitudes. Literature for children is one example. While considerable anxiety is usually evoked with regard to the sexuality of children, they are nevertheless commonly depicted as 'pairing off' in male–female couples, suggesting an inevitable heterosexual future. *See also* GAY AND LESBIAN CRITICISM.

heteronym (Gk 'other name') A term invented by the Portuguese poet Fernando Pessoa (1888–1935) to denote a kind of creative *alter ego*: a separate character and personality who produced poetry and prose. He invented three main personalities, namely Alberto Caeiro, Ricardo Reis and Álvaro de Campos, on whom he bestowed lives and histories of their own. In effect one may conclude that they represented different facets of his own many-sided personality. For him they had a *real* existence; they were not pseudonyms (*q.v.*). In a letter to Adolfo Casais Monteiro (13 Jan. 1935) he describes in detail how they came to exist and how they tended to take over in the creative process.

A number of contemporary poets have also experimented with alternative identities. The poems in Christopher Reid's *Katerina Brac* (1985) purport to be translations from the work of a woman poet who comes from an unnamed country in Eastern Europe. In *Living in Disguise* (1986), the Afro-Caribbean poet E. A. Markham takes on two different identities. The first is an English housewife named Sally Goodman; the second, Paul St Vincent, speaks through a further character known as Lambchops. Most interesting of all, the American poet John Peck, in *The Poems and Translations of Hĭ-Lö* (1911), poses as a Chinese poet living in Europe. Hĭ-Lö not only writes his own poems in English, but translates into English from several other tongues. In sensibility, however, both poems and translations remain Chinese, recalling translations from that language by Ezra Pound and Arthur Waley that have irreversibly modified English poetry. *See also* DÄMONISCH; INSPIRATION; MUSE; STORM OF ASSOCIATION.

hexameter (Gk 'of six feet') A metrical line of six feet. In Greek and Latin verse it is often dactylic, especially in epic (*q.v.*). Often the first four feet were spondees (*q.v.*), the fifth a dactyl (*q.v.*) and the last a spondee. It is not a form that has much suited English poets, though there have been many experiments with it especially in the 19th c. by Southey, Kingsley, Coleridge, Longfellow, Clough, Tennyson and Swinburne. But it has never proved a very wieldy line. The occasional hexameter or alexandrine (*q.v.*) has often been used for a particular effect as in *The Faerie Queene*. Michael Drayton in *Poly-Olbion* (c. 1610) was one of the first poets to write at length in iambic hexameters:

> When Phoebus lifts his head out of the winter's wave,
> No sooner doth the earth her flowery bosom brave,
> At such time as the year brings on the pleasant spring,
> But hunts-up to the morn the feathered sylvans sing:
> And in the lower grove, as on the rising knoll,
> Upon the highest spray of every mounting pole,
> Those quiresters are perched with many a speckled breast.

The basic foot here is the iamb (*q.v.*).

hexastich (Gk 'six lines') A stanza of six lines. A very common stanza form. *See* SESTET; SESTINA; SEXAIN; SONNET.

hiatus Either a gap in a sentence so that the sense is not completed, or a break between two vowels coming together where there is no intervening consonant. The indefinite article takes an 'n' – as in 'an answer'.

hieratic   (Gk 'priestly') A style characterized by elaborate, mandarin language; the opposite of demotic (*q.v.*). It also denoted an ancient Egyptian script used by the elite, priestly class.

High Comedy   A term introduced by George Meredith in *The Idea of Comedy* (1877). By it he meant a form of comedy of manners (*q.v.*) marked by grace, wit and elegance; an urbane form whose appeal was primarily to the intellect. Such creations as Shakespeare's *Much Ado About Nothing*, Molière's *Tartuffe*, Congreve's *Way of the World*, Wilde's *A Woman of No Importance* and Shaw's *Pygmalion* might all be put into this category. At the other end of the scale we have Low Comedy (*q.v.*). The term Middle Comedy (*q.v.*) has a more specialized meaning. The term High Comedy can be applied to both poems and novels: Pope's *The Rape of the Lock*, for instance, in verse. Among novels we might mention Pierre de Laclos's *Les Liaisons dangereuses*; Jane Austen's *Pride and Prejudice*; Thomas Mann's *Der Zauberberg*; and Aldous Huxley's *Crome Yellow*. Not to mention works by George Meredith, Henry James and Evelyn Waugh. *See* COMEDY.

higher criticism   In biblical studies higher criticism is concerned with the date and composition of the Scriptures, their authorship, their interrelationship and their cultural and historical backgrounds. This critical technique has its roots in the University of Göttingen late in the 18th c. During the 19th c. it was extended far beyond biblical studies and adopted as a discipline.

hilarody   A form of ancient Greek mime (*q.v.*) which burlesqued tragedy. *See* BURLESQUE; MAGODY; SATYR PLAY.

histoire du livre   *See* HISTORY OF THE BOOK.

historical novel   A form of fictional narrative which reconstructs and recreates history imaginatively. Both historical and fictional characters may appear. Though writing fiction, the historical novelist typically researches his or her chosen period thoroughly and strives for verisimilitude (*q.v.*). In Britain the genre appears to have developed from Mme de La Fayette's *Princesse de Clèves* (1678) and then via the Gothic novel (*q.v.*). Much Gothic fiction was set in the Middle Ages. Maria Edgeworth's *Castle Rackrent* (1800), usually taken to be the first example of a regional novel (*q.v.*) in English, is the first fully fledged historical novel. Edgeworth followed this with *Adelaide* in 1806. Jane Porter published *The Scottish Chiefs* (1810) and *The Pastor's Fireside* (1815). In 1814 Sir Walter Scott published *Waverley*, the first of his many novels. Because of its enormous success, *Waverley* is often said to be the first historical novel. With its affirmative account of Scottish history, it is certainly the first of a great number of historical novels to appear across Europe and throughout the world to be closely involved with nationalist (and imperialist) projects. Two later examples are the epic historical novels of the Polish writer Henryk Sienkiewicz (1846–1916), and the Norwegian Sigrid Undset's trilogy *Kristin Lavransdattar* (1920–2), which appeared, respectively, shortly before and after their home country's independence. Celebrated historical novels such as these have contributed to nation-building by articulating, in narrative form, a nation's origins, 'character' and conflicts. Some have helped to provide the basis for national languages, for example Alessandro Manzoni's *The Betrothed* (1827/1842), which has been called the most widely read novel written in Italian.

The historical novel is usually associated with 19th c. writers such as Scott, Thackeray, Charles Kingsley, George Eliot, Hardy, James Fenimore Cooper, Balzac and Tolstoy. However, the genre has remained popular in the 20th and 21st c. One of the most prolific and successful authors of historical novels was Georgette Heyer, who wrote a great many historical romances set in the Regency period. Heyer's novels, such as *Devil's Cub* (1934), *Regency Buck* (1935) and *Faro's Daughter* (1941), are notable for their meticulous historical detail. Many authors of historical novels have been motivated to reappraise a historical period or figure, as is the case with Robert Graves's *I, Claudius* (1934). Others have focused on specific periods in order to comment on contemporary society and politics. Mary Renault's novels set in Ancient Greece, for instance, particularly *The Last of the Wine* (1956), demonstrate that homosexual relationships have in the past been considered honourable; her novels implicitly ask that present-day homosexuals be offered respect.

The late 20th c. witnessed the rise of the postmodern historical novel, or 'historiographic metafiction', to use Linda Hutchinson's term. Works such as John Fowles's *The French Lieutenant's Woman* (1969), Gabriel Garcia Márquez's *The General in his Labyrinth* (1989) and Thomas Pynchon's *Mason and Dixon* (1997) often confound linear historical narrative through the liberal use of anachronism, temporal distortion and multiple endings. Such methods are used to challenge the authority of official histories, or are provoked by scepticism as to the possibility of any kind of historical truth. For some writers, though, such radical scepticism is counterproductive, even dangerous. Toni Morrison's modern (or neo-) slave narrative (*q.v.*) *Beloved* (1987), for example, has many of the characteristics of historiographic metafiction, but it is less interested in showing how the past can never be truly known than with how the accounts of the past's countless dispossessed must be recovered and remembered. A more recent notable work of historical fiction is Hilary Mantel's *Wolf Hall* (2009), a novel which sympathetically reconstructs the life of Thomas Cromwell, chief adviser to King Henry VIII. See also HISTORIOGRAPHY; METAFICTION; NOVEL; ROMANCE (i).

historical rhyme   A rhyme which was acceptable and good when composed but is no longer so because of a change in pronunciation. A well-known instance occurs in Pope's *Essay on Criticism*:

> Good nature and good sense must ever join;
> To err is human, to forgive, Divine.

In Pope's day *join* was pronounced *jine*.

historiography   The writing of history, or, the study of the ways history has been written. The earliest history writing, in the form of simple chronologies, was produced in Mesopotamia and Ancient Egypt. The first accounts attributed to a named author and in narrative form emerged in Ancient Greece. The earliest known is *The Histories*, composed by Herodotus of Halicarnassus (484–*c.* 425 BC), which provides accounts of various Mediterranean peoples. *The Histories* is significant also for attributes which have characterized much subsequent historiography: human events organized into a narrative; evidence of research; and attempts to evaluate sources.

However, narrative history – which selects significant events and organizes them into a single coherent account – is by no means the only rhetorical strategy employed by historiographers. Annals (*q.v.*) provide a year-by-year chronological account of events. Generally speaking annals draw no distinctions between events great and small and offer little if any comment or analysis. Unlike histories, then, which usually seek to explain how people caused events, annals emphasize instead how events happen to people. Some of the earliest surviving annals were Chinese. The *Spring and Autumn Annals*, traditionally attributed to Confucius, give details of events that occurred in the state of Lu between 722 BC and 481 BC. Annals are a form of chronicle (*q.v.*), though the entries of a chronicle are not necessarily made annually. In the case of 'live chronicles' events are recorded as they happen. In his book *The Content of the Form: Narrative Discourse and Historical Representation* (1987) Hayden White argues that, unlike annals, chronicles have a 'point of view'; typically, they are situated within broader temporal frameworks. For example, some of the Christian chronicles of the Middle Ages view events like wars and calamities as eschatological prophecy. Biography (*q.v.*), a kind of narrative history framed by the birth and death of an individual, is another significant form of historiography. In the modern era, historical enquiry has increasingly employed methodologies from the social sciences. Some social historians have been critical of the tendency of narrative historians to select materials and examples that confirm a particular 'reading' of events, and argue that statistically verifiable methods are more valuable. *See also* EMPLOTMENT.

history of the book The study of the book as a subject first developed in France; hence *histoire du livre*. Traditionally, it has been in the province of bibliographers, historians (social historians in particular, and those devoted to cultural movements and the history of ideas) and librarians. The term is now commonly used to refer to a broad area of interdisciplinary inquiry encompassing all aspects of authorship, production and circulation of books as objects of study for literary and cultural theorists as well as historians. In terms of material culture, all aspects of the book come within their range: manuscripts, printing, binding, libraries and their organization, information retrieval. They are also concerned with censorship, copyright (*qq.v.*), the role of the book in social life, and catalogues in public and private libraries. Research includes the investigation of what books were read by different people at different times. In this field marginalia and annotation (*qq.v.*) are of special interest. *See also* BIBLIO-; BIBLIOGRAPHY; CATALOGUE RAISONNÉ.

history play   *See* CHRONICLE PLAY.

höfische Dichtung   (G 'courtly poetry') There were two main kinds: (a) lyric and epic (*qq.v.*); (b) poetry of laudation and entertainment. The lyric and epic belong roughly to the period 1150–1250 (the *Blütezeit* or 'blossom period'). The poems were composed by knights and expressed the ideals and values of knightly and courtly life and manners. They were performed in courts by song, chant or declamation. The laudatory poems were composed by court poets (professionals) and designed to praise and flatter princes and nobles. *See also* MINNESINGER; SPRUCH.

höfisches Epos   (G 'courtly epic') A type of MHG courtly poem of epic proportions which was popular in German courts in the 12th and 13th c. They were intended as entertainment and extolled knightly and chivalric ideals and virtues. Many derived from French sources. Three of the most notable poets were: Hartmann von Aue (*c.* 1160–*c.* 1210), Wolfram von Eschenbach (*c.* 1170–*c.* 1220) and Gottfried von Strassburg (fl. 12th *c.*–early 13th c.).

hokku   *See* HAIKU.

holograph   (Gk 'entire writing') A manuscript or letter written entirely by the person in whose name it appears.

holophrasis   (Gk 'entire phrase') The use of one word to express a number of ideas.

holorhyme   (Gk 'whole rhyme') An ingenious form of versification in which whole lines have the same sound but different meanings, as in Victor Hugo's couplet:

> O! fragiles Hébreux! Allez, Rébecca, tombe!
> Offre à Gilles zèbres, oeufs; à l'Erèbe, hécatombe!

More ingenious and elaborate are the following lines, akin to the holorhyme:

> Freine ce romance qu'un trime haine, laine demi yeux hier ce.
> Ail comme tout béret six ares note tout près cime
> De Yves; elle dattes mène d'où livres safre; te sème
> De gourdes, hisse oeuf tines tertre vite, d'air Beaune ce.

When these lines are pronounced aloud *slowly* one recognizes the beginning of a well-known speech:

> Friends, Romans, countrymen, lend me your ears;
> I come to bury Caesar, not to praise him.
> The evil that men do lives after them,
> The good is often interred with their bones.
>
> (*Julius Caesar*, III, ii)

Forty of these sleights of tongue have been devised by John Hulme to make up a book which is a piece of clever and inspired whimsy titled *Guillaume Chequespierre and the Oise Salon* (1985), with critical apparatus of notes, glossary and bibliography (*q.v.*). There are other collections: *Mots d'heures: gousses, rames*; *N'heures souris rames*; and *Mörder Guss Reims*. See NONSENSE.

homeoteleuton (Gk 'similarity of endings') A term first used by Aristotle in *Rhetoric*. It has two basic meanings: (a) a figure consisting of a series of words with the same or similar endings; (b) the occurrence of similar endings in two or more adjacent words, clauses or lines of writing. *See also* RHYME.

Homeric epithet Homer joined adjectives and nouns to make compound adjectives known as 'Homeric epithets' when applied to stock nouns. Two famous examples are 'wine-dark sea' and 'rosy-fingered dawn', but there are a great many in the *Iliad* and the *Odyssey* and they become an important feature of poetry in the oral tradition (*q.v.*). Examples from the *Iliad* are: 'Hector with glancing helm', 'swift-footed Achilles', 'well-greaved Achaeans', 'cloud-gathering Zeus', 'white-armed Hera', 'bronze-clad Achaeans', 'god-like Paris', and 'loud-roaring sea'. Examples from the *Odyssey* are: 'god-like Odysseus', 'much-enduring noble Odysseus', 'Odysseus of many counsels', 'bright-eyed Athene', 'Menelaos dear to Ares', 'sharp sword', 'broad heavens', 'splendid armour', and 'well-built hall'. *See also* INCREMENTAL REPETITION; KENNING; PERIPHRASIS; POETIC DICTION.

Homeric simile *See* EPIC SIMILE.

homily (Gk 'discourse') Either a sermon (*q.v.*) delivered to an assembled congregation, or a written work of an admonitory kind edifying the reader morally. Two well-known books of *Homilies* were published in 1547 and 1563 and appointed by the Church of England to be read at Divine Service.

The *Blickling Homilies* (c. 970) and the *Vercelli Homilies* (c. 1000), collections of nineteen and twenty-three pieces respectively, are valuable OE prose texts, whereas the *Lambeth Homilies* (c. 1200) are important in ME.

homograph (Gk 'same writing') A word written in the same way as another, but having a different pronunciation and meaning, e.g. *row/row*; *tear/tear*; *lead/lead*. *See* RHYME.

homology Term used in structuralism (*q.v.*) to refer to similarities in the properties between different structures, or within different levels of a particular structure. The term 'isomorphism' is also used to mean much the same thing. For example, narratologists may identify homologies at the level of syntax and the level of narrative in a story. In Marxist criticism (*q.v.*) the term has been employed to describe the structural parallels between the formal properties of a literary work and the economic foundations of society. The term (sometimes 'structural homology') has also had some currency in sociology, anthropology and cultural studies (*q.v.*): in these disciplines it is used to describe how different cultural practices parallel the attitudes and behaviour of particular social groups. In cultural studies the emphasis has been on exploring homologies between musical structures and social structures.

homonym (Gk 'same name') A word having the same sound and spelling as another, but a different origin and meaning, e.g. *rest* 'repose'/*rest* 'remainder'; *bay* 'gulf'/*bay* 'laurel'. *See* RHYME.

homophone (Gk 'same sound') A word which is pronounced the same as another but has a different spelling and meaning, e.g.: foul/fowl; wood/would; pearl/purl. *See* RHYME.

homosociality A term which denotes same-sex relationships which are not necessarily sexual. Football terraces, Girl Guide camps, military bases and prisons are usually predominantly or entirely homosocial environments. The term was first used by organizational sociologist Jean Lipman-Blumen in 1976, though it has been popularized by leading queer theorist Eve Kosovsky Sedgwick in her work on 'male homosocial desire' in *Between Men* (1985) and *The Epistemology of the Closet* (1991). Sedgwick argues that the ever-present continuum between male homosociality and homosexuality becomes disrupted in modern society due to new knowledge about sexuality. Sedgwick examines how many literary texts produced in the 19th and early 20th c. are shaped by 'homosexual panic' – an anxiety that the close bonds between men might be construed as, or in fact be, sexual. Such panic is often detectable in literary depictions of love triangles involving two men and one woman, for example between Charley, Bradley and Lizzie in Dickens's *Edwin Drood*. Often in these configurations, the woman operates as a token of exchange between the two men, which implicitly eroticizes their relationship. *See also* GAY AND LESBIAN CRITICISM; QUEER THEORY.

homostrophic A term used in prosody (*q.v.*) to denote a single repeated stanza form. As in some of Horace's odes. Other examples are Marvell's *An Horatian Ode upon Cromwell's Return from Ireland* (1650) and Keats's ode *To Autumn* (1820).

Horatian ode So called after the Roman poet Horace who perfected the form. Each stanza has the same metrical form and pattern. *See* ODE.

Horatian satire Gently derisory, essentially comic ridicule of persons or ideas (in contrast to the more virulent diatribe of *Juvenalian satire*, *q.v.*); originating with Horace, Roman poet and essayist (1st c. BC). Pope's *Epistles* and Ben Jonson's *Bartholomew Fair* are examples of Horatian satire. *See* LUCILIAN SATIRE; MENIPPEAN SATIRE; SATIRE.

horismus (Gk 'marking out by boundaries') A short definition of the attributes of a subject.

horizon of expectations A term (the German is *Erwartungshorizont*) devised by Hans Robert Jauss to denote the criteria which readers use to judge literary texts in any given period. It is a crucial aspect of Jauss's aesthetics of reception, and the term designates the shared set of assumptions which can be attributed to any given generation of readers. The criteria help constitute readers' judgements of, say, a poem (e.g. pastoral or elegy, *qq.v.*) in a trans-subjective way. Horizons of expectation change. The poetry of one age is judged, valued and interpreted by its contemporaries, but the views of that age do not necessarily establish the meaning and value of the poetry defini-tively. Neither meaning nor value is permanently fixed, because the horizon of expectations of each generation will change. As Jauss puts it: 'A literary work is not an object which stands by itself and which offers the same face to each reader in each period. It is not a monument which reveals its timeless essence in a monologue.' Each age reinterprets poetry (and literature in general) in the light of its own knowledge and experience, its own cultural environment. Literary value is measured according to 'aesthetic distance' (*q.v.*), the degree to which a work departs from the 'horizon of expectations' of its first readers.

Jauss's essay *Literary History as a Challenge to Literary Theory* (1967) attempts to provide a theory of literature based on a socio-historical context and a solution to the problem of how texts are evaluated. In 'Reading and Interpretation' (an essay published in *Modern Literary Theory*, 1982, ed. by Jefferson and Robey) Ian Maclean comments helpfully on the concept: 'The "horizon of expectations" . . . is detectable through the textual strategies (genre, literary allusion, the nature of fiction and of poetical language) which confirm, modify, subvert or ironize the expectations of readers.' 'Aesthetic distance' becomes a measure of literary value, 'creating a spectrum on one end of which lies "culinary" (totally consumable) reading, and, on the other, works which have a radical effect on their readers'. *See* HERMENEUTICS; READER-RESPONSE THEORY; RECEPTION THEORY.

hornbook A sheet of paper, bearing the alphabet, combinations of consonants and vowels, the Lord's Prayer and the Roman numerals, which was mounted on a piece of wood resembling a small paddle or old-fashioned butter-patter and then covered with transparent horn. It was used for teaching children to read up until the 18th c., when it was replaced by the primer. In 1609 Dekker published *The Gull's Hornbook*, which was a kind of spoof book of manners, or courtesy book (*q.v.*), for the fops and gallants of the time.

horror story A fictional narrative (usually in prose) of variable length which shocks or even frightens the reader, and/or induces a feeling of repulsion and loathing. Some horror stories are serio-comic or comic-grotesque, but none-theless alarming or frightening. The word *horror* derives from Latin *horrere* 'to make the hair stand on end, tremble, shudder'.

From the late 18th c. until the present day the horror story in its many and various forms has been a feature of British and American literature and is of considerable importance in literary history, especially in the evolution of the short story (*q.v.*). It is also important because of its connections with the tradition of the sublime and the Gothic novel (*qq.v.*), as well as with fiction associated with tales of mystery, suspense, terror and the supernatural, and with the ghost story and the thriller (*qq.v.*).

Often horror stories are noteworthy for their exploration of the limits of what people are capable of experiencing. They venture into the realms of psychological chaos, trauma and taboo desire, and the near side of barbarism; they explore the capacity to experience fear and what lurks on and beyond the shifting frontiers of consciousness. The horror story is part of a long process by which people have tried to come to terms with and find adequate descriptions and symbols for deeply rooted and powerful energies and fears which are related to sexuality and the body, death, afterlife, punishment, darkness and violence.

While the horror story emerged as a distinct genre in the late 18th c., writers have long been aware of the magnetic appeal of the horrific. In Classical literature, Seneca (*c.* 4 BC–AD 65) is an obvious example, and in Classical epic (*q.v.*) numerous scenes are concerned with violence and the horrific. For the poets of the late medieval period the most potent and frightening image was that of hell: the abode of eternal loss, pain and damnation. There are numerous visions of hell in literature, the most famous being the 12th c. *Vision of Tundale* and Dante's *Inferno* (early 14th c.). Gradually during the 16th c. hell was 'moved' from its traditional site in the centre of the earth. It came to be located in the mind; it was part of a state of consciousness. This was the beginning of the growth of the idea of a subjective, inner hell, the chaos of a disturbed and tormented mind. Such a concept is suggested by Mephistophilis in Marlowe's *Dr Faustus* (*c.* 1588) when in the guise of a Friar he says:

> Hell hath no limits, nor is circumscrib'd
> In one self place, for where we are is hell,
> And where hell is, must we ever be.

Towards the end of the 18th c. the Devil received a new lease of life as a personality, and was to become a dominant figure in 19th c. literature, more particularly in tales of horror. It is not at all surprising that the Faust theme (*q.v.*) became of great interest again. Closely associated with the recrudescence of the Devil as a character is that major theme of the Romantic period, the divisibility of human identity, the good and bad man. This duality finds common expression throughout the 19th c. in the figure of the double or *doppelgänger* ('double-goer'), which was derived from German folklore. The double provides a source for some of the most powerful psychological horror stories, in which mental and spiritual states are examined and exposed, and in which fear, madness, cruelty and evil predominate. Examples include James Hogg's *Confessions of a Justified Sinner* (1824), and *William Wilson* (1839) as well as many other short stories by Edgar Allan Poe, perhaps the most infamous and influential of all horror writers. Towards the end of the 19th c., stories featuring doubles reflected an increased interest in occult practices, extreme psychological states and the effects of drugs. Stevenson's *Dr Jekyll and Mr Hyde* (1886) is by far the most famous of these.

Vampirism also became of interest during the Romantic period and has inspired numerous horror stories ever since. John Polidori's *The Vampyre* (1818) was one of the first fictional vampire stories. There is little bloodsucking; it is mainly concerned with sex, as are many vampire stories. However, the aristocratic protagonist (*q.v.*), Lord Ruthven, was to become the model for the vampire in English fiction. Later in the 19th c., the vampire became strongly associated with central and eastern Europe, which provided English readers with a new Gothic locale. The Transylvania of Bram Stoker's *Dracula* (1897) is of course the most famous and lasting example.

The werewolf theme also became a fruitful source of horror stories; one of the most famous werewolf stories is Marryat's *The White Wolf of the Hartz Mountains* (1839). Ghost stories (*q.v.*) have been considerably more prolific, though by no means all are horror stories.

In the 20th and 21st c. the horror story has proliferated. Vampire stories, ghost stories and psychological horror stories all remain popular. Notably, the enormous increase in science fiction (*q.v.*) has diversified horror writing considerably: new maps of hell have been drawn, new dimensions of the horrific exposed and explored, and new simulacra and *exempla* created. Popular modern authors of horror stories have included H. G. Wells, Clive Barker, John Saul and Stephen King. *See also* GOTHIC NOVEL/FICTION; TERROR/HORROR.

Hôtel de Bourgogne The first Paris theatre, completed in 1548. It was built by the Confraternity of the Passion and erected in the ruins of the palace of the dukes of Burgundy. It enjoyed its heyday in the 17th c. with the King's Players. In 1680 they were amalgamated into the Comédie-Française (*q.v.*), and the Italian Players (known as the Comédie-Italienne) occupied the Hôtel de Bourgogne until it became defunct in 1783.

House Un-American Activities Committee A committee founded to eradicate subversive political activity in the USA. The HUAC was originally established in 1938, and is best known for its targeting of suspected Communist sympathizers and activists. The committee affected a large number of writers, including Bertold Brecht, Clifford Odets, Lillian Hallman and Arthur Miller, as well as other artists, particularly in film. The committee's qualifications in matters of literature may be assessed from the fact that when, in 1938, the head of the Federal Theater Project Hallie Flanagan made a reference to the English dramatist Marlowe (1564–93) the committee members wanted to know whether Marlowe was a Communist. During the 1960s the activities of HUAC met considerable criticism and its influence declined, particularly after the censuring of leading anti-Communist Senator Joseph McCarthy. After being renamed in 1969, the committee was finally disbanded in 1975.

hovering stress or accent This occurs when it is not absolutely clear in verse whether a syllable should be stressed or not, or whether it should be half stressed. It is a very common phenomenon, as in these lines from Robert Lowell's *Man and Wife*:

> Tamed by Miltown, we lie on Mother's bed;
> the rising sun in war paint dyes us red;
> in broad day*light* her gilded bed-*posts* shine,
> abandoned, almost Dionysian.
> At last the trees are green on Marlborough Street,
> blos*soms* on our magno*lia* ignite
> the morning with their murde*rous* five *days*' white.

Hovering stress in these lines occurs on the syllables italicized. Also known as distributed stress. *See* LEVEL STRESS; VARIABLE SYLLABLE.

howler A blatant or glaring error, as in these examples from examination papers by schoolboys: (a) 'The worm is an hermaphrodite, but it has to meet another worm before it can do anything'; (b) 'I always wanted to come to – – – school because I thought it was Wandsworth Prison, but that is not the real reason'; (c) 'born of the Virgin Mary, deceived of the Holy Ghost'. Called howlers because they are so 'loud'.

hubris (Gk 'wanton insolence') This shortcoming or defect in the Greek tragic hero leads him to ignore the warnings of the gods and to transgress their laws and commands. Eventually hubris brings about downfall and nemesis (*q.v.*), as in the case of Creon in Sophocles's *Antigone* and Clytemnestra in Aeschylus's *Oresteia* trilogy. *See* HAMARTIA; TRAGEDY.

Hudibrastic verse So called from Samuel Butler's *Hudibras* (1663, 1674, 1678), a mock-heroic satirical poem in octosyllabic couplets. Butler's wit, exuberance and invention in this poem have made it an outstanding instance of what may be called 'low satire'. These lines from Canto I give an idea of the tone and manner (they are about the Metaphysical Sectarian):

> He was in Logick a great Critick,
> Profoundly skill'd in Analytick.
> He could distinguish, and divide
> A Hair 'twixt South and South-West side:
> On either which he would dispute,
> Confute, change hands, and still confute.
> He'd undertake to prove by force
> Of Argument, a Man's no Horse.
> He'd prove a Buzard is no Fowl,
> And that a Lord may be an Owl;
> A Calf an Alderman, a Goose a Justice,
> And Rooks Committee-men and Trustees.

See RHYME.

humanism A broad term which encompasses human-centred philosophies (as opposed to those centred on religion and the supernatural). Though it exhibits some continuities with Renaissance humanism (*q.v.*), modern humanism is a post-Enlightenment intellectual disposition: humanists contend that we are all rational beings, and seek rational solutions to human problems. They generally hold that society is increasingly perfectible, and so trust in science and progress. Humanists tend towards atheism, though there are forms of theological humanism; the terms 'secular humanist' and 'religious humanist' are employed to register the distinction. The latter, however, see their faith as an aspect of human experience and believe in the capacity of religion to achieve betterment for humanity.

The term was first employed in France in the late 18th c. In 1846 the German historian Georg Voigt used 'Renaissance humanism' to describe the turn towards Classical learning by scholars of the Italian Renaissance. The British Humanistic Religious Association was established in 1853, an early forerunner of several national humanist organizations. Several writers of the 19th c. are strongly associated with humanism, including Dickens, George Eliot and Hardy. A great many authors in the 20th and 21st c. have declared themselves humanists, with several, including Thomas Mann, Jean-Paul Sartre, Kurt Vonnegut, Umberto Eco, Salman Rushdie and Margaret Atwood, taking leading roles in humanist organizations. Some modern writers, however, have expressed contempt for humanism. Pound considered humanism to be feminizing; Evelyn Waugh declared that his acerbic satire *A Handful of Dust* (1933) 'contained all I had to say about humanism'. Poststructuralist and postmodernist thinkers – such as François Lyotard – have criticized the abstract notion of 'humanity' as another dangerous 'grand narrative' (*q.v.*) *See also* ANTIHUMANISM; ENLIGHTENMENT; LIBERAL HUMANISM; NEW HUMANISM; POSTHUMANISM.

humanisme A short-lived movement in poetry begun by Fernand Gregh in 1902. Its manifesto (*q.v.*) was published in *Le Figaro*. It represented a reaction against the *symboliste* poets (*see* SYMBOL AND SYMBOLISM) and against the Parnassians (*q.v.*).

humanities A term generally used in Europe and America for literature, languages, philosophy, art, history, theology, music, as opposed to the natural sciences and the social sciences. *See* HUMANISM.

humiliatio *See* TAPINOSIS.

humours The term humour (it derives from Latin *humor*, 'moisture'; hence *humid*) was used in the Middle Ages and during the Renaissance period – in the tradition of Hippocratic pathology and physiology – to denote the four humours of the body. These depended on the four fluids: blood, phlegm, yellow bile and black bile. The admixture or commingling of these determined a person's disposition, character, mind, morality and temperament. The humours released spirits or vapours which affected the brain, and thence a person's behaviour. According to the predominant humour a person was sanguine, phlegmatic, choleric or melancholy. Robert Burton, in his *Anatomy of Melancholy*, I, ii, 3 (1621), gives an excellent description of the qualities of the humours.

Vestigially, the theory of humours survives in such expressions as: 'ill-humoured', 'good-humoured', 'black with rage', 'in a black mood', 'yellow with jealousy', 'green with envy', 'yellow-livered', 'red with remorse', and so forth. And we still use 'sanguine' or 'melancholy' to describe certain temperaments.

The theory of humours had a considerable influence on writers when it came to the creation of characters. Dramatists devised characters based on the theory of the imbalances that occurred between the bodily fluids. Comedy of humours (*q.v.*) developed characters who were dominated by a particular mood, inclination or peculiarity. Ben Jonson is the most notable dramatist to do this – in *Every Man in His Humour* (1598); almost certainly the first play created on the theory of personality and ruling passion. This he followed with *Every Man Out of His Humour* (1599).

It may be no coincidence that at this period writers were also addressing themselves to the depiction of 'characters' in character sketches, and analysing character and temperament.

It is not until the 18th c. that we find 'humour' associated with laughter and being used in contradistinction to wit (*q.v.*). *See* APTRONYM; CHARACTER; MORALITY PLAYS.

hybrid (L 'half-breed, mongrel') A word formed from a stem or word in one language plus a suffix or prefix from another. For example: *television* (Greek and Latin); *gullible* (English and Latin).

hybridity A term used in postcolonial theory, in cultural studies (*qq.v.*) and, most recently, in discussions relating to globalization. Hybridity is the characteristic of a culture or a cultural form produced by the interaction of two (or possibly more) separate 'parent' cultures or forms. The hybrid may feature aspects of either or both of its parents, but is a new and distinct formation. Mikhail Bakhtin (1895–1975) was the first theorist to consider the implications of hybridity; in *Rabelais and his World* (1965) he discusses the capacity of the chaotic pleasures of the medieval carnival to challenge the authority of the Church and feudal law. For Bakhtin, the hybridity of such celebrations resides in their heteroglossia (*q.v.*), or polyphony; similarly, he contends, polyphonic narratives have the potential to call into question authoritative discourse.

Postcolonial theorists have focused on the hybridity which emerges as a consequence of interaction between peoples in colonial and postcolonial contact zones (*q.v.*). Hybridization may take many forms. Linguistic hybrids, such as pidgins and creoles, are a common outcome. Miscegenation produces new, hybrid racial categories. Colonizer and colonized may well adopt (and in many instances be forced to adopt) the cultural practices of the other. The association of hybridity with the capacity to disrupt authority, first outlined by Bakhtin, has rendered it an attractive concept to postcolonial theorists.

Homi Bhabha has argued that it is the *ambivalence* of the colonial subject's hybridity which is so disturbing to imperial authority. In taking on the habits, values and knowledge of the colonizer (which is ostensibly what the 'civilizing' project of colonialism is all about), the colonial subject is able to mimic his or her master, a mimicry which hovers between respect and mockery. The figure of the 'mimic man', who so menaces the authority of colonial discourse, has a strong presence in the fiction of numerous imperial and postcolonial writers, including Rudyard Kipling, E. M. Forster and V. S. Naipaul. *See also* BINARY; LIMINALITY.

Hydropathes, les One of three French literary societies associated with the beginnings of the symbolist movement. The others were *les Hirsutes* and *les Zutistes*. These societies had some vogue in the 1880s. Paul Bourget, Jean Moréas, François Coppée and Guy de Maupassant were among the better known *Hydropathes*. *See also* SYMBOL AND SYMBOLISM.

hymn (Gk 'song in praise of a god or hero') Early examples are the Homeric Hymn to Demeter (*c.* 7th c. BC) and the first Delphic Hymn (*c.* 138 BC). Many Latin hymns date from the Middle Ages: *Pange lingua gloriosi*; *Te lucis ante terminum*; *Iam lucis orto sidere*; *Veni Creator Spiritus*; *Veni Sancte Spiritus*; *Jesu dulcis memoria*; *Stabat Mater*; *Dies Irae*. Most English hymns of repute date from the 17th to the 19th c., their authors being: Nahum Tate, Isaac Watts, John and Charles Wesley, Reginald Heber, John Keble, and John Mason Neale. In the 20th c. there were few contributions, though some of these are notable, e.g. Vaughan Williams's settings of Herbert.

   Among English-speaking poets of note who have attempted the form one should mention George Herbert, Dryden, Milton, William Blake, William Cowper, Henry Wadsworth Longfellow, John Greenleaf Whittier, Tennyson, Christina Rossetti and Rudyard Kipling. *See also* ANTIPHON; CANTICLE; HYMNAL STANZA; LAUDA; LYRIC.

hymnal stanza A four-line stanza in iambics with a rhyming scheme of either abcb or abab. It is also known as common measure. This example is the first stanza of a hymn by Nahum Tate:

> While shepherds watched their flocks by night,
>   All seated on the ground,
> The angel of the Lord came down,
>   And glory shone around.

See also HALLELUJAH METER; HYMN; LONG MEASURE; SHORT MEASURE.

hypallage (Gk 'exchange') Also known as transferred epithet. A figure of speech in which the epithet is transferred from the appropriate noun to modify another to which it does not really belong. Common examples are: 'a sleepless night'; 'the condemned cell'; 'a happy day'. It is a very common poetic device, as in these lines from Part One of T. S. Eliot's *The Waste Land*:

> Winter kept us warm, covering
> Earth in forgetful snow, feeding
> A little life with dried tubers.

Clearly, the snow is not 'forgetful', but rather conceals, muffles, 'shrouds' the earth, so that for a time we forget what the earth looks like. *See also* PROLEPSIS.

hyperbaton (Gk 'overstepping') A figure of speech in which words are transposed from their usual order. A very common poetic device. Milton, for instance, uses it constantly – as in these lines from *Paradise Lost*:

> High on a throne of royal state, which far
> Outshone the wealth of Ormuz or of Ind,
> Or where the gorgeous East, with richest hand
> Showers on her kings barbaric pearl and gold,
> Satan exalted sat.

hyperbole (Gk 'overcasting') A figure of speech which contains an exaggeration for emphasis. For example, Hotspur's rant in *Henry IV*, Pt I (I, iii, 201):

> By heaven methinks it were an easy leap
> To pluck bright honour from the pale-fac'd moon,
> Or dive into the bottom of the deep,
> Where fathom line could never touch the ground,
> And pluck up drowned honour by the locks.

Hyperbole was very common in Tudor and Jacobean drama, and in heroic drama (*q.v.*). It is an essential part of burlesque (*q.v.*). There are plentiful examples in writers of comic fiction; in Dickens, especially.

Everyday instances, of which there are many, are: 'I haven't seen you for ages'; 'as old as the hills'; 'terrible weather', and so on. *See* ADYNATON; BOMBAST; LITOTES; TAPINOSIS.

hypercatalectic (Gk 'beyond the last metrical foot') A line is so called when it has an extra syllable at the end. Also known as hypermetrical and extrametrical. Each of these three lines from Crashaw's *Wishes to His Supposed Mistress* illustrates the point:

> Sydnaean showers
> Of sweet discourse, whose powers
> Can crown old Winter's head with flowers.

hyperdochmiac A trochaic tripody (*q.v.*) which is catalectic (*q.v.*); that is to say, short of half a foot at the end of the line. *See* DOCHMIAC; FOOT.

hypermetric syllable *See* HYPERCATALECTIC.

hyperreal The terms *hyperreal* and *hyperreality* suggest something that is 'above' (Gk *huper*) reality, or in excess or reality, and have been associated with the work of French theorist Jean Baudrillard (1929–2007). In his work *Simulation and Simulacra* (1981), Baudrillard defines the *hyperreal* as 'the meticulous reduplication of the real, preferably through another reproductive medium, such as photography'. He examines postmodern consumerist societies and media culture, particularly branding and marketing, and the instances when a reproduction or a simulation of reality becomes more real than the reality itself and assumes an independent value. Such images or signs have no referent in reality; rather they precede their referents and determine the real in what Baudrillard terms 'the precession of simulacra'. In contrast with earlier periods, when there was a relation and a distinction between the representation and the real, in the postmodern period we have copies without originals. As he explains, simulation is 'a real without origins or reality: a hyperreal'. Baudrillard's famous example of this phenomenon is Disneyland. As he writes:

> Disneyland is a perfect model of all the entangled orders of simulacra. It is first of all a play of illusions and phantasms: the Pirates, the Frontier, the Future World, etc. This imaginary world is supposed to ensure the success of the operation. But what attracts the crowds the most is without a doubt the social microcosm, the religious, miniaturized pleasure of real America, of its constraints and joys.

Other examples of this collapse of the distinction between simulation and reality can be found in signs and images such as Nike, Apple or the McDonald's 'M'. A good example of a recent literary engagement with Baudrillard's notion of *hyperreality* is Julian Barnes's novel *England, England* (1998), in which a corporation turns the Isle of Wight into a heritage theme park – a 'fast forward version' of England – that gradually comes to replace real England. Another well-known example is Umberto Eco's *Travels in Hyperreality* (1987). *See also* POSTMODERNISM; SIMULACRA.

hypertext A text – usually electronic – which enables its reader to move instantaneously to other parts of the same text or to other texts. The most famous deployment of hypertext is of course the world wide web, where 'hyperlinks' enable users to move between different texts or different parts of the same text. 'Hypermedia' is commonly used to refer to compositions which include extra-textual material, such as images, video and audio. Hypertext is an increasingly used tool in literary study: online hypertext editions of literary works can provide efficient systems of annotation and allow scholars to access instantly a potentially vast array of targeted bibliographical material. Hypertext could even be said to realize some of the claims of structuralist and poststructuralist theorists about the nature of texts: that they are inevitably 'open' and are potentially linked to all other texts. There is an emergent genre of hypertext fiction and poetry, which often involves the reader deciding which connections he or she will make, thus producing, or otherwise altering, the narrative and meaning. *See also* EBOOK.

hyphaeresis (Gk 'taking away from beneath') In general the term denotes the omission of a letter from a word: 'o'er' for 'over'; 'e'en' for 'even'; 'heav'n' for 'heaven'. *See* ELISION.

hypocorism The term derives from a Greek word meaning 'to play the child'. Commonly used of pet-names, like 'Mike' for Michael, and the use of familiar terms like these: Will Shakespeare, Jim Boswell, Willie Yeats, Tom Eliot. Also endearments like: 'money spider', 'cherry blossom', 'honey', 'chuck'.

hyporchema (Gk 'song accompanied by dancing') A choral song accompanied by dancers is believed to have been invented by Thaletas of Gortyn, Crete (7th c. BC). The Cretic measure was used for the verse. It was used as a hymn (*q.v.*) in honour of Apollo and was related to the paean and the dithyramb (*qq.v.*).

hypostatization A form of personification (*q.v.*) in which an abstract quality is spoken of as something human. For example: 'Truth insists I tell the story'; 'Decency compels me to admit the truth'. Not uncommon in everyday usage. Also refers to the treatment of an entity or concept as possessing an essence.

hypotaxis (Gk 'under arrangement') Subordination; syntactic relationship between dependent and independent constructions, e.g. 'He who knows will tell us' as against 'Who knows? He will tell us.' *See* PARATAXIS.

hypotyposis A figurative device by which something is represented as if it were present. For example: John of Gaunt's dying speech in *Richard II* (II, i, 31) in which he 'sees' England as a sceptred isle and creates a general word image of the country.

hypozeugma *See* ZEUGMA.

hysteron proteron (Gk 'latter former') A figurative device in which events in the temporal order are reversed. Sometimes used for comic effect, it implies 'putting the cart before the horse'. There is an agreeable example in *Much Ado About Nothing* (IV, ii, 20), when Dogberry is holding forth to the Watch, and investigating the malefactors Conrade and Borachio.

I

iamb The term derives from a Greek word of unknown etymology and denotes a metrical foot consisting of an unstressed syllable followed by a stressed syllable, thus: ᴗ /. For instance: dĕféat. It was probably first used by Archilochus (7th c. BC). In antiquity the iambic rhythm was thought to be the nearest to speech and it is the commonest type of foot in all English verse because it fits the prevailing natural pattern of English words and phrases. Of these lines from Pope's *Prologue* to Addison's *Cato*, the first is in regular iambic meter and the next three have slight variations – as the ear soon informs one:

> Tŏ wáke | thĕ sóul | bў tén|dĕr strókes | ŏf árt,
> Tŏ ráise | thĕ géniŭs, | ănd tŏ ménd | thĕ héart;
> Tŏ máke | mánkínd | ĭn cón|scioŭs vír|tŭe bóld,
> Líve o'er | eăch scéne, | ănd bé | whăt théy | bĕhóld.

iambelegus In Classical prosody, an iamb (*q.v.*) followed by a dactylic colon (*q.v.*).

iambes, les French satiric poems in which a twelve-syllable line alternates with one of eight syllables. The *iambe* came into use with the publication of Chénier's *Iambes* (1787–90) and Barbier's *Les Iambes* (1830–1).

iambic trimeter A line of six iambic feet (each pair of feet taken as a unit or dipody), used for satirical verses by Archilochus (7th c. BC) and Simonides (6th–5th c. BC) and common in Greek and Latin drama. *See also* SYZYGY.

ibidem (L 'in the same place, in that very place') Often abbreviated to *ibid.* or *ib.*, the term indicates a reference to or quotation from 'the same place' in a book or chapter or on a page. *See* IDEM; OPERE CITATO.

A Dictionary of Literary Terms and Literary Theory, Fifth Edition. J. A. Cuddon.
© 2013 The Estate of J. A. Cuddon. Published 2013 by Blackwell Publishing Ltd.

icon (Gk 'image') A quasi-literary term used to describe the depiction of an object or person in figurative language, but in a particular way, as in George Herbert's *The Church-floore*:

> Mark you the floore? That square & speckled stone
>> which looks so firm and strong,
>>> Is *Patience*:
> And th'other black and grave, wherewith each one
>> is checker'd all along,
>>> *Humilitie*:

See also EMBLEM-BOOK; EKPHRASIS.

ictus (L 'blow, stroke') The stress or accent (*qq.v.*) placed on particular syllables in a line of verse. Gerard Manley Hopkins used it quite often to show which syllables he wanted the reader to stress; sometimes syllables which would not normally be so, as in these lines from *Spelt from Sibyl's Leaves*:

> For earth | her being has unbound;
> her dapple is at end, astray or aswarm, all throughther, in
> throngs; | self ín self steepèd and páshed – qúite
> Disremembering, dísmémbering | áll now. Heart, you round
> me right
> With: Óur évening is over us; óur night | whélms, whélms,
> ánd will end us.

See SPRUNG RHYTHM.

ideal reader What every author wants. That imaginary person who, the writer hopes, will understand completely the experience he is trying to convey, and respond to it as he wishes. *See also* IDEAL SPECTATOR; IMPLIED READER/ ACTUAL READER.

ideal spectator Two basic meanings may be distinguished: (a) the 'everyman' for whom the dramatist writes; for all practical purposes synonymous with the average person; (b) a character in a play who either expresses the attitudes and feelings of the dramatist or is representative of the majority of the audience.

The French term is *raisonneur* and both 'characters' are related to the Greek Chorus and the single character acting as chorus (*q.v.*), as well as, possibly, to the confidant (*q.v.*).

The ideal spectator of category (b) is not much involved in the plot but is rather an onlooker; a sort of neutral character, like Horatio in *Hamlet*, Kent in *King Lear*, Lord Goring in *An Ideal Husband* and the lawyer in Arthur Miller's play *A View from the Bridge. See also* IDEAL READER.

idée fixe (F 'fixed idea') A preconception, an unshakable conviction; hence a dominating theme; a monomania. Quite a common term in music; rare as a literary term, but important in connection with Valéry's theories on the subject expressed in *Idée fixe* (1932), a dialogue. Like Heraclitus, Hegel and

William James (among others) Valéry denies that an idea is ever quite the same on two occasions of its occurrence. An idea, it is argued, cannot be fixed because the mental state is transitory. Some ideas have the property of reappearing to consciousness more often than others. Their appearance may be relied on in appropriate contexts; thus they are 'fixed' in the sense that a roulette wheel can be fixed. These are 'privileged' and their privilege is shown, not only in the frequency of their reappearances but also in their status.

It is in the nature of an idea to intervene in the mind's normal state of disorder and inattention, and to accentuate and momentarily arrest (or retard) some element in it. The idea is, in fact, this momentarily favoured element which, by thus being coagulated as it were from the general psychic mass, suggests comparisons and hypotheses, whereby the animal flux of images and instincts becomes transmuted into thinking. When the arrestation becomes habitual and the same idea recurs repeatedly in a variety of mental 'situations', we have what may be called an *idée fixe*. Recurrent symbols, word complexes, images and themes in a writer's work are also associated with the fixed idea.

idée reçue (F 'received idea') This term is perhaps most prominent in connection with Flaubert's *Dictionnaire des idées reçues*, published posthumously in 1913 from a mass of half-completed notes. It attacks the sin of affirming without examining. Flaubert, who had a particular aversion to the platitude, conceived the idea as a youth. There are two main themes: an attack on the cliché (*q.v.*); and the peril of accepted ideas. Writing to George Sand in 1871 Flaubert said 'All our trouble comes from our gigantic ignorance. When shall we get over empty speculation and accepted ideas? What should be studied is believed without discussion. Instead of examining, people pontificate.' Reference to Flaubert's *Bouvard et Pécuchet* (1881), a bitter condemnation of human stupidity, helps to show the relevance of *idées reçues* to everyday life. Flaubert also collected specimens for a *Catalogue des idées chics* in order to complete this unfinished novel.

idem (L 'the same') Often abbreviated to *id.*, it denotes the same word or name or title already referred to. *See also* IBIDEM; OPERE CITATO.

identical rhyme *See* RHYME.

identity politics A term which emerged in the United States in the 1970s to denote the political activism of particular social groups which see themselves as disadvantaged or oppressed. In the West, identity politics is most closely associated with sexual, racial and ethnic minorities, and with second-wave feminism. Identity politics typically involves analysis of the reasons for a particular group's marginalization, and strategies for overcoming oppression, such as consciousness-raising and the reclamation and redefinition of previously stigmatized practices. Literary critics motivated by identity politics have often sought to critique the ways in which writing, whether historical or contemporary, reproduces prejudices about particular groups, or contributes to their erasure. Identity politics has, however, come under sustained criticism from conservatives and Marxists for being divisive, and from poststructuralists for its implied essentialism (*q.v.*), its assumption that social differences produce fixed, coherent identities. *See also* AFRICAN-AMERICAN STUDIES; ETHNIC STUDIES; FEMINIST CRITICISM; GAY AND LESBIAN CRITICISM; POSTCOLONIALISM; POSTSTRUCTURALISM.

ideogramic method   A method of verse composition devised by the modernist (*q.v.*) poet Ezra Pound. It is based on the juxtaposition of words and images and, by avoiding abstraction and consecutive discourse, aims to achieve greater force and immediacy.

Pound hit upon the method around 1914 when reading the notebooks of Ernest Fenollosa, a deceased American orientalist. According to Fenollosa, as Pound understood him, the characters of the Chinese alphabet are ideograms. That is to say, each one is either a simplified picture of the object it refers to, or a composite of such pictures which can stand for an idea. For example, the character which means 'east' is a composite of the characters for 'sun' and 'tree': it represents the rising sun entangled in a tree's branches. Thus, the simple characters are direct representations of things like 'sun' or 'tree', while the complex ones are visual metaphors.

In Chinese poetry, which Pound now began to translate, he found a representational directness, especially in the syntax, which for him registered the physical world with more vigour, economy and directness than anything he knew in Western literature. He ascribed this to the way the Chinese language appeared to derive its concepts, not from abstract symbols, but from concrete particulars. The Chinese poets, moreover, give one image to each line, so the lines are juxtaposed with one another.

The method is present in Pound's poetry from 1914 on, but it does not achieve its full potential until he embarks on his epic poem, *The Cantos* (1925–69). This proceeds by association, not by narrative. Meaning is generated from a matrix or field of juxtaposed objects, events and quotations. By setting these items in productive tension, he provokes their re-connection in the reader's mind. The reader thus becomes a vital part of the creative process: we derive meaning from concrete 'facts', much as we do from the objects of experience.

Pound's understanding of the Chinese alphabet has been seriously impugned – apparently, only 10 per cent of Chinese characters can be construed as pictorial symbols – and the method of *The Cantos* has been condemned as widely as it has been praised. It is nonetheless impossible to ignore the beauty and intellectual stimulation of Pound's achievement. Its revitalizing effect on the English poetic tradition, moreover, has been incalculable. The many poets who have learnt from the ideogramic method include: T. S. Eliot (notably in *The Waste Land*), William Carlos Williams, Basil Bunting, Charles Olson. C. H. Sisson and John Peck.

ideograph A written symbol. A picture of the thing itself or a representation of the idea. The Chinese and Japanese languages are ideographic.

ideology Designates any comprehensive system of political thought (e.g. fascism, neoliberalism, democratic socialism) articulated or otherwise tacitly supported by an individual or institution. The term was first used in the 1790s in France and England to designate modern philosophical thought. It was Napoleon Bonaparte, however, who popularized its use in political discourse. In an attack on the 'contrived' Enlightenment principles of democrats, Bonaparte lent the term the pejorative connotations that it has to date never quite shaken off.

In political, literary and cultural theory the term owes much to the writings of Karl Marx (1818–83) and subsequent Marxist criticism (q.v.). In *The German Ideology* (co-written with Friedrich Engels), Marx asserts that ideology corresponds to the dominant ideas held by any particular society. These ideas are in evidence in every aspect of the society's culture and social organization – in its laws, politics, religion, art and so on. They are always also the ideas of the ruling class, and serve to legitimize its wealth and power. Marx defines ideology as the endeavour to present the ideas of this ruling class as being in the general interests of society or the nation as a whole.

We should therefore expect works of literature produced in, say, capitalist societies to justify and support the economic and social relations that benefit the ruling class. Marxist critics would insist that literature written by bourgeois writers exhibits first and foremost the assumptions and values of the bourgeoisie, such as property ownership. Marx and Engels say next to nothing about how a literary text might do this; indeed there is little in their theoretical writing about literature specifically. Subsequently, Marxist literary critics such as Georg Lukács have argued that the very form of literary texts produced in capitalist societies may well reflect and reinforce capitalist structures. The formal aspects of the realist novel, for instance, with its chronological organization, fixed narrative point of view and complex plotting and characterization suggest an orderly, permanent world that is in no need of, or likely to experience, radical transformation.

ideynost (R 'ideological expression') One of the requirements demanded under socialist realism (q.v.). Literature must embody ideas, especially political and social ideas, of a progressive nature. Censors and critics do not accept literature lacking in ideological content, or literature which is merely intended to divert or entertain. *See* CENSORSHIP; NARODNOST; PARTYNOST.

idiolect The aggregate of speech habits peculiar to an individual.

idiom A form of expression, construction or phrase peculiar to a language and often possessing a meaning other than its grammatical or logical one.

Some languages have thousands of idioms and English is no exception. These are a handful out of the many in existence and use: by chance; far and wide; again and again; spick and span; wear and tear; neither here nor there; off and on; as fit as a fiddle; better late than never; no wonder; to turn adrift; to hang fire; to have the upper hand; to back the wrong horse; at daggers drawn; to lead by the nose. *See* CLICHÉ; COLLOQUIALISM; DEAD METAPHOR; SLANG.

Ido An international language devised by Louis Couturat in 1907. It was a 'child' of Esperanto (*q.v.*), in which language *ido* means 'offspring', but was in many ways a simplification of Esperanto. By many it has been thought to be an improvement on the parent language.

idyll (Gk 'little form') It can refer to either a poem or an episode in a poem, or to a poem which describes some episode or scene in rural life (in which case it is very nearly synonymous with pastoral, *q.v.*), or a description of any scene of tranquil happiness. In common parlance 'idyllic' is used to describe a serene and euphoric state or environment which is remotely attainable and idealized. It is not therefore a definite poetic genre, though having strong association with the bucolic, e.g. the *Idylls* of Theocritus. It has indeed been used for a variety of works, like Victor de Laprade's *Idylles héroïques* (1858), Tennyson's *Idylls of the King* (1842–85), Browning's *Dramatic Idylls* (1879–80) and Barrie's *Auld Licht Idylls* (1888). *See also* ECLOGUE; PASTORAL.

illocutionary act An act which is carried out by a speaker in the actual utterance of words. For example, an order, a promise, the striking of an oath. *See* PERFORMATIVE UTTERANCE; PERLOCUTIONARY ACT.

illusion The semblance of reality and verisimilitude (*q.v.*) in art which most writers seek to create in order to enable readers to think that they are seeing, feeling, hearing, tasting and smelling, or, conceivably, having some extra-sensory or kinaesthetic experience. The creation of illusion is a co-operative act between writer and reader. It brings about in the reader what Coleridge called 'the willing suspension of disbelief' (*q.v.*). However, the writer also destroys illusion, sometimes for a specific purpose: for example, to address the reader directly – a not uncommon practice among 18th and 19th c. novelists. The contrast helps the illusion and at the same time sharpens and clarifies the impression of things happening at a distance. Illusion should be distinguished from *delusion* and *hallucination*.

il n'y a rien hors du texte *See* DECONSTRUCTION.

imagery (L 'making of likenesses') The terms *image* and *imagery* have many connotations and meanings. Imagery as a general term covers the use of language to represent objects, actions, feelings, thoughts, ideas, states of mind and any sensory or extra-sensory experience. An 'image' does not necessarily mean a mental picture.

In the first place we may distinguish between the literal, the perceptual and the conceptual. These lines from Robert Lowell's *Our Lady of Walsingham* illustrate the basic differences:

> There once the penitents took off their shoes
> And then walked barefoot the remaining mile;
> And the small trees, a stream and hedgerows file
> Slowly along the munching English lane,
> Like cows to the old shrine, until you lose
> Track of your dragging pain.
> The stream flows down under the druid tree,
> Shiloah's whirlpools gurgle and make glad
> The castle of God.

The first two lines are a literal image (without figurative language) which may or may not convey a visual image also. The phrase 'hedgerows file slowly' is a perceptual image because of the metaphorical use of the world 'file'. The phrase 'castle of God' is conceptual. One can hardly visualize it but one may have an idea of it.

Many *images* (but by no means all) are conveyed by figurative language, as in metaphor, simile, synecdoche, onomatopoeia and metonymy (*qq.v.*). An image may be visual (pertaining to the eye), olfactory (smell), tactile (touch), auditory (hearing), gustatory (taste), abstract (in which case it will appeal to what may be described as the intellect) and kinaesthetic (pertaining to the sense of movement and bodily effort).

These lines from Peter Redgrove's *Lazarus and the Sea* contain all these kinds of image:

> The tide of my death came whispering like this
> Soiling my body with its tireless voice.
> I scented the antique moistures when they sharpened
> The air of my room, made the rough wood of my bed,
> (most dear),
> Standing out like roots in my tall grave.
> They slopped in my mouth and entered my plaited blood
> Quietened my jolting breath with a soft argument
> Of such measured insistence, untied the great knot of my heart.
> They spread like whispered conversations
> Through all the numbed rippling tissues radiated
> Like a tree for thirty years from the still centre
> Of my salt ovum. But this calm dissolution
> Came after my agreement to the necessity of it;
> Where before it was a storm over red fields
> Pocked with the rain and the wheat furrowed
> With wind, then it was the drifting of smoke
> From a fire of the wood, damp with sweat,
> Fallen in the storm.

It is often the case that an image is not exclusively one thing or another; they overlap and intermingle and thus combine. Thus, the kinaesthetic may also be visual.

In this quotation the first two lines are clearly auditory, but the use of the word 'soiling' may suggest the tactile; on the other hand, for some, the word may have olfactory associations. The third line is olfactory. In the fourth and fifth lines we have a combination of the tactile and visual. The sixth line intermingles the tactile, olfactory and gustatory. The phrases 'quietened my jolting breath' and 'through all the numbed rippling tissues' are kinaesthetic, but are also visual and tactile. 'But this calm dissolution/Came after my agreement to the necessity of it;' is abstract. 'Untied the great knot of my heart' is visual-cum-kinaesthetic. The other images in the poem fall readily into one of the categories mentioned. *See* ARCHETYPE; SYMBOL AND SYMBOLISM.

imaginary, symbolic, real Terms used by the French poststructuralist thinker Jacques Lacan (1901–81), who rewrites Freud's account of the unconscious using linguistic terminology and concepts. Lacan posits three orders or states of human mental disposition: the *imaginary* order, the *symbolic* order, and the *real*. The imaginary order is a pre-Oedipal phase where an infant is as yet unable to distinguish itself from its mother's body or to recognize the lines of demarcation between itself and objects in the world; indeed, it does not as yet know itself as a coherent entity or self. Hence, the imaginary phase is one of unity (between the child and its surroundings), as well as of immediate possession (of the mother and objects), a condition of reassuring plenitude, a world consisting wholly of images (hence 'imaginary') that is not fragmented or mediated by difference, by categories, in other words, by language and signs. The mirror stage – the point at which the child can recognize itself and its environment in the mirror – marks the point at which this comforting imaginary condition breaks down, pushing the child into the symbolic order which is the world of predefined social roles and gender differences, the world of subjects and objects, the world of language. *See also* MIRROR STAGE.

imagination *See* FANCY AND IMAGINATION.

imagined communities Refers to Benedict Anderson's notion of popular groups, in particular national groups, as the product of collective and cumulative bonds forged without actual personal contact. As such, the nation is conceived of as an 'imagined political community that is imagined as both inherently limited and sovereign'. In other words, nationhood itself is imaginary because the majority of participants will not come face-to-face in order to agree upon any course or projected identity. Secondly, it is also limited because nations necessarily abut one another, and it is, by definition, sovereign since the post-Enlightenment nation is predicated upon territory rather than ethnicity or religion. In Anderson's original terms, such a conception of nationhood is made possible by the advent and proliferation of print culture (*q.v.*). In the age of global electronic media, the notion of 'imagined communities' is clearly ripe for reinterpretation. *See also* BLOG; INTERNET.

imaginism A short-lived Russian poetic movement originating in 1919. Its attitudes were fundamentally anti-Bolshevik and expressed disenchantment with the Revolution. The members of the imaginist groups made a cult of a Bohemian and permissive life, which tended towards hooliganism, and wrote poems intended to shock. The only well-known poet in the group was Sergey Yesenin (1895–1925). The movement, such as it was, was defunct by c. 1925. *See also* FUTURISM.

Imagists A group of poets who were prominent immediately before the First World War. The best known were Ezra Pound, Amy Lowell, T. E. Hulme, Richard Aldington and H.D. (Hilda Doolittle). They believed that a hard, clear image was essential to verse. They also believed that poetry should use the language of everyday speech and have complete freedom in subject matter. Pound edited the first anthology, *Des Imagistes* (1914), and in 1915 Amy Lowell published some imagist poets. This work contained a statement of the ideals of imagism (or 'amygism', as it was called). T. E. Hulme's *Above the Dock* is a good example of a poem in the imagist manner:

> Above the quiet dock in midnight,
> Tangled in the tall mast's corded height,
> Hangs the moon. What seemed so far away
> Is but a child's balloon, forgotten after play.

See also ABSTRACT; DINGGEDICHT; HAIKU; SYMBOL AND SYMBOLISM; VORTICISM.

imitation Three basic meanings can be distinguished: (a) copying or plagiarism (*q.v.*); (b) the adoption of the tone, style and attitude of another writer; a re-creation; (c) a representation. Literary theory during and after the Romantic period (*q.v.*) regarded imitation in sense (b) as a somewhat inferior practice, derivative, lacking in originality. Prior to that and for many centuries (especially during the 18th) it had been regarded as a wholly respectable practice. Aristotle advocated it, so did Cicero and Horace. The idea was that a writer should learn everything he could from the masters who were his predecessors. This point of view prevailed during the medieval and Renaissance periods and continued into the 18th c. Pope, who composed some of the best imitations (*Imitations of Horace*), gives the 18th c. view in *An Essay on Criticism* (1711):

> Those RULES of old discover'd, not devis'd,
> Are Nature still, but Nature Methodiz'd;
> Nature, like Liberty, is but restrain'd
> By the same Laws which first herself ordain'd . . .
>   You then whose Judgment the right course wou'd steer,
> Know well each ANCIENT'S proper Character,
> His Fable, Subjects, Scope in ev'ry Page,
> Religion, Country, Genius of his Age:
> Without all these at once before your Eyes,

> Cavil you may, but never Criticize.
> Be Homer's Works your Study, and Delight,
> Read them by Day, and meditate by Night,
> Thence form your Judgment, thence your Maxims bring,
> And trace the Muses upward to their Spring;
> Still with It self compar'd, his Text peruse;
> And let your comment be the Mantuan Muse . . .

Nowadays, imitation is seldom used as a critical term. When it is, it is roughly synonymous with mimesis (*q.v.*). *See* FIXED FORM; NOVELTY.

imperialism (L *imperium*, 'power, authority, dominion, empire') Imperialism might be defined as a strategy whereby a state aims to extend its control forcibly beyond its own borders over other states and peoples. Such control is usually not just military but economic and cultural. A ruling state will often impose its own terms of trade, its own political ideals, its own cultural values, and often its own language, upon a subject state.

In modern times, there have been at least three major phases of imperialism. Between 1492 and the mid 18th c., Spain, Portugal, England, France and the Netherlands established colonies and empires in the Americas, the East Indies and India. Then, between the mid 19th c. and the First World War, there was an immense scramble for imperialistic power between Britain, France, Germany, Italy and other nations. By the end of the 19th c., more than a fifth of the land area of the world and a quarter of its population had been brought under the British Empire: India, Canada, Australia, New Zealand, South Africa, Burma and the Sudan. The next-largest colonial power was France, whose possessions included Algeria, French West Africa, Equatorial Africa and Indochina. Germany, Italy and Japan also entered the race for colonies. In 1855 Belgium established the Belgian Congo in the heart of Africa, a colonization whose horrors were expressed in Conrad's *Heart of Darkness* (1899).

Finally, the periods during and after the Second World War saw a struggle involving the countries just mentioned as well as a conflict between America and the Communist Soviet Union for extended control, power and influence. These imperialistic endeavours have survived into the present day in altered forms and with new antagonists. *See also* POSTCOLONIALISM.

implied reader/actual reader Terms invented by Wolfgang Iser and discussed by him in his books *The Implied Reader* (1974) and *The Act of Reading: A Theory of Aesthetic Response* (1976, trans. 1978). The 'implied reader' is a 'model' or 'role'. Such a reader is active as well as passive; the text structures his or her response, but he or she also produces meaning and has the task of 'consistency building' (the expression used by Iser). The 'actual reader', by contrast, receives mental images while reading; but these images are, inevitably perhaps, modified by the experience and knowledge (and thus other images) which the reader brings to the text. The hypothetical implied and actual reader coexist, are one and the same person responding to a text in different ways and at different levels of consciousness. This view of the reader can be taken in conjunction with Umberto Eco's distinction between the 'open' and 'closed' texts. *See* READER-RESPONSE THEORY; RECEPTION THEORY.

imposed form *See* FIXED FORM.

impression *See* EDITION.

impressionism The term very probably derives from Claude Monet's painting *Impression: Soleil Levant* (first exhibited in Paris in 1874). The Impressionists were a school of painters who were particularly concerned with the transitory effects of light, and they wished to depict the fleeting impression from a subjective point of view. They were not interested in a precise representation; the resulting impression depended on the perception of the spectator. The terms *impressionist* and *impressionism* have crept into literary criticism, but they are vague terms which we might well dispense with. French Symbolist poets have been called *impressionist*; so have English poets like Oscar Wilde and Arthur Symons. The term *impressionism* has also been used to describe the novelist's technique of concentrating on the inner life of the main character rather than on external reality. Abundant examples of this technique are to be found in the work of James Joyce, Marcel Proust, Dorothy Richardson and Virginia Woolf. *See also* STREAM OF CONSCIOUSNESS; SYMBOL AND SYMBOLISM.

imprimatur (L 'let it be printed') The term signifies that the Roman Catholic Church has sanctioned the printing of a work. It is a declaration that a book or pamphlet is free of moral or doctrinal error. But it does *not* imply that those who have given the *imprimatur* agree with the contents of the book. Many religious orders require the approval of their own authorities. This, when given, is attested by the additional words *imprimi potest* ('it may be printed'). Closely related is the phrase *nihil obstat* ('nothing stands in the way'), which implies there is nothing in a book or pamphlet which is objectionable in terms of theology or morals.

imprimi potest *See* IMPRIMATUR.

imprint (a) Publisher's name, place and date of publication at the bottom of the title page; (b) Printer's name with that of the printing press traditionally on the final page.

incantation A formulaic use of words to produce a magical effect and to create an intensifying emotional temperature. The words may be chanted or spoken. It is very common in primitive literatures and is much used by sorcerers and witches, and also for ritual purposes as in a charm (*q.v.*). Famous examples are the incantations of the weird sisters in Shakespeare's *Macbeth*, Faustus's in Marlowe's *Dr Faustus*, and the one in Ben Jonson's *The Masque of Queens*, from which these lines come:

> The owl is abroad, the bat and the toad
> And so is the cat-a-mountain;

The ant and the mole sit both in a hole,
    And the frog peeps out o' the fountain.
The dogs they do bay, and the timbrels play,
    The spindle is now a-turning;
The moon it is red, and the stars are fled,
    But all the sky is a-burning:
The ditch is made, and our nails the spade:
With pictures full, of wax and of wool,
Their livers I stick with needles quick;
There lacks but the blood to make up the flood.
Quickly, dame, then bring your part in!
Spur, spur upon little Martin!
Merrily, merrily make him sail,
A worm in his mouth and a thorn in his tail,
Fire above, and fire below,
With a whip in your hand to make him go!
    O now she's come!
    Let all be dumb.

incremental repetition A term invented by Francis Gummere in *The Popular Ballad* (1907) to describe a rhetorical device of the ballad (*q.v.*) form. It has been widely used in ballads for hundreds of years and is very typical of poetry in the oral tradition (*q.v.*). The following stanzas from the traditional ballad *James Harris* (*The Demon Lover*) illustrate well the use of the device:

'O where have you been, my long, long love,
    This long seven years and mair?'
'O I'm come to seek my former vows
    Ye granted me before.'
'O hold your tongue of your former vows,
    For they will breed sad strife;
O hold your tongue of your former vows,
    For I am become a wife.'
He turned him right and round about,
    And the tear blinded his ee:
'I wad never hae trodden on Irish ground,
    If it had not been for thee.'
'I might hae had a king's daughter,
    Far, far beyond the sea;
I might have had a king's daughter,
    Had it not been for love o thee.'

This kind of repetition is thought by some to be peculiar to English and Scottish ballads, but a very similar device is frequent in South Slav *narodne pesme* (*q.v.*) of the oral tradition. *See* ANAPHORA; REPETITION; SYNTHETIC RHYTHM.

incrementum *See* AMPLIFICATION.

incunabula *See* CRADLE BOOK.

indeterminacy Elements in, say, a novel or short story, which depend for their effect or result on a reader's interpretation and which may be interpreted in a number of different (and, conceivably, conflicting) ways are said to be 'indeterminate'. Indeterminacies tend to multiply in accordance with the length and complexity of a text. *See* RECEPTION THEORY; SUBTEXT.

index (L 'forefinger') The plural is indexes or indices. An alphabetical list of subjects treated in a book, with page references. It is now found at the end, but in older books it may serve as a table of contents at the beginning.

index expurgatorius A list of passages in a book which, by order of the Roman Catholic Church, must be deleted before it can be read by members of the Church. This index was abrogated in 1966. *See also* IMPRIMATUR; INDEX LIBRORUM PROHIBITORUM.

index librorum prohibitorum A list of books (*not* authors) which Roman Catholics are forbidden by the Church to read, or books which may be read only in an expurgated edition (*q.v.*). This index was abrogated in 1966. *See also* IMPRIMATUR; INDEX EXPURGATORIUS.

indirect speech The changing of spoken words (*oratio recta*) into reported speech (*oratio obliqua*). For example: 'I won't go tomorrow,' said Fred – becomes 'Fred said that he would not go on the following day.'

induction An archaism (*q.v.*) for introduction or prologue (*qq.v.*). A good example occurs at the beginning of *The Taming of the Shrew*, where Christopher Sly, a drunken tinker, is brought in by a lord and his huntsmen and is then treated as a lord and persuaded that he has lost his wits. He is then obliged to watch the play of the taming of the shrew performed by a troupe of strolling players. Another well-known example is that by Thomas Sackville in *Mirror for Magistrates* (2nd edn 1563), in which Sorrow leads the poet into the dominions of the dead.

inflection Two basic meanings may be distinguished: (a) A change in the form of a word, to show a change in its grammatical function. Usually at the end of a word; the case in a noun for instance. Inflections are common in Latin and Greek and in Slav languages but there are few in English. (b) The term is also used to describe changes in pitch. For example, the word 'well' as a noun, adjective and exclamation could be said in a number of different ways.

infrahistoria A term coined by Miguel de Unamuno (1846–1936) to denote narratives concerned with the unrecorded lives and traditions of ordinary, humble people (in a sense, 'short and simple annals of the poor') and also ordinary or unimportant places and events. Some writers of the *generación de 1898* (*q.v.*) composed *infrahistoria*.

initial rhyme   *See* ALLITERATION; RHYME.

initiating action   The event or events in a plot which bring about a state of conflict and tension. *See also* CLIMAX; EXPOSITION; FALLING ACTION; RISING ACTION.

inkhorn terms   Pedantic terms and learned borrowings from foreign tongues: Thomas Wilson, in his *Arte of Rhetorique* (1553), observed that the first lesson to be learned was never to affect 'any straunge ynkhorne termes, but to speak as is commonly received'. An inkhorn was a small vessel for ink fastened to the clothing. *See* LOAN WORD.

in medias res   (L 'into the middle of things') The origin is Horace's remark in *Ars Poetica*:

> Semper ad eventum festinat et in medias res
> Non secus ac notas auditorem rapit.

('He always hastens to the issue and hurries his hearers into the midst of the story as if they knew it already.') The phrase has become almost a cliché (*q.v.*) to describe a common method of beginning a story – in other words, starting in the midst of the action at some crucial point, when a good deal has already happened. The writer is then able to shuttle back and forth in time between interrelated incidents. Milton does it very effectively in *Paradise Lost* by beginning his narrative in Hell, after the fall of the rebel angels. *See also* AB OVO.

In Memoriam stanza   So named because Tennyson used it in *In Memoriam* (1850). A four-line iambic tetrameter rhyming abba:

> I held it truth, with him who sings
>   To one clear harp in divers tones,
>   That men may rise on stepping-stones
> Of their dead selves to higher things.

Tennyson claimed to have hit upon the stanza independently, though it had previously been used by two Jacobean poets: Ben Jonson in *An Elegie* ('Though Beautie be the Marke of praise') and Lord Herbert of Cherbury in *An Ode upon a Question moved, Whether Love should continue for ever?* Both these poems exhibit the same indented layout as *In Memoriam*.

inscape and instress   Terms invented by Gerard Manley Hopkins. By 'inscape' he meant the individual 'distinctive' form, the 'oneness' of a natural object. For the energy of being by which things are upheld and for the natural stress which determines an 'inscape', he used the word 'instress'. This is akin to what Shelley called 'the One Spirit's plastic stress', and instress is the 'sensation of inscape' – a kind of mystical illumination or insight into the underlying order and unity of creation. The poet's notebooks and journals, which are of enormous interest, reveal his preoccupation with both terms. *See* SPRUNG RHYTHM.

inspiration There are two basic theories about inspiration: (a) that it comes from outside the writer; (b) that it comes from within. The first is the older. Many Greek and Latin writers attempted to explain it by suggesting that inspiration was of divine origin – the action of a muse (*q.v.*). Invoking the muse was common and became a literary convention (*q.v.*). Homer often did so. Plato and Aristotle both suggest that inspiration is divine. For the most part during the Renaissance period the Classical view was retained – at any rate as a convention.

The external-force theory prevailed and proved the more attractive of the two until late in the 18th c. when writers started to favour the second theory and ascribed inspiration to the workings of individual genius (*q.v.*). Psychology and theories of psychoanalysis suggest that the unconscious or subconscious is the main source of creative activity. Few people now, except those with 'romantic' ideas about it, believe in inspiration. As Willam Faulkner once put it tersely, 'No one ever told me where to find it.' One of the more interesting modern comments on the subject is provided by Graham Greene in *The End of the Affair* (1951), a comment which, in its way, covers both theories. 'So much in writing', he says, 'depends on the superficiality of one's days. One may be preoccupied with shopping and income-tax returns and chance conversations, but the stream of the unconscious continues to flow undisturbed, solving problems, planning ahead: one sits down sterile and dispirited at the desk, and suddenly the words come as though from the air: the situations that seemed blocked in a hopeless impasse move forward: the work has been done while one slept or shopped or talked with friends.' *See also* AFFLATUS; DÄMONISCH; DONNÉE; FANCY AND IMAGINATION; INVENTION; LIGNE DONNÉE; MUSE; STORM OF ASSOCIATION.

instress *See* INSCAPE AND INSTRESS.

intention *See* FOUR MEANINGS.

intentional fallacy The error of criticizing and judging a work of literature by attempting to assess what the writer's intention was and whether or not he has fulfilled it rather than concentrating on the work itself. Modern criticism (since the 1920s) has tended to the point of view that anything except the work itself is irrelevant. This point of view is especially noticeable in the criticism of I. A. Richards and T. S. Eliot in the 1920s and that of the American New Critics (*see* NEW CRITICISM) in the 1940s and 1950s. In 1946 W. K. Wimsatt (in collaboration with Monroe C. Beardsley) published his essay *The Intentional Fallacy* (reprinted in his *The Verbal Icon*, 1954), a document central to the development of modern critical theory. They express the point of view that a poem 'is not the critic's own and not the author's (it is detached from the author at birth and goes about the world beyond his power to intend about it or control it). The poem belongs to the public . . . ' Wimsatt's contentions have often been disputed. Some of the New Critics (for example, Cleanth Brooks and John Crowe Ransom) refer to a 'total intention', meaning the total meaning or organization of a work. *See also* AFFECTIVE FALLACY; PERSONAL HERESY.

interior monologue The technique of recording the continuum of impressions, thoughts and impulses either prompted by conscious experience or arising from the well of the subconscious. The phrase originates in an essay on James Joyce by Valéry Larbaud and is often regarded as synonymous with 'stream of consciousness' (*q.v.*). There is, however, some dispute as to which of the two is the larger term. Some critics argue that stream of consciousness includes all imitations of interiority; according to this view, the interior monologue is one method among many. To other critics, interior monologue is the larger category and stands for all methods of self-revelation, including for instance some kinds of dramatic monologue (*q.v.*); according to this view, stream of consciousness refers to an uninterrupted flow, in which logic, conventional syntax and even at times punctuation are abandoned.

It is certainly the case that the origins of this kind of fictional representation are in poetry, and specifically in the kind of 19th c. poetry that is broadly dramatic in method. The English dramatic monologue, as used by Browning and Tennyson, purports to be spoken, but it is often the case that speech dissolves into reverie. This seems to have been taken up by the French Symbolist (*q.v.*) poets and their associates. Projections of interior musings, often deeply ambiguous, are to be found in the poems of Tristan Corbière, Jules Laforgue, Stéphane Mallarmé, Arthur Rimbaud and Paul Valéry. They in turn influenced the fiction of Edouard Dujardin, Dorothy Richardson, James Joyce and Virginia Woolf, as well as the verse monologues of T. S. Eliot (e.g. *Gerontion*) and W. B. Yeats (e.g. the 'Crazy Jane' poems).

interlaced rhyme *See* CROSS-RHYME.

interlude (L 'between play') A short entertainment put on between the courses of a feast or the acts of a play. During the Middle Ages and up to the 16th c. the term was used to describe a variety of dramatic entertainments. Italian Renaissance drama had *intermezzi*. In France and Spain similar diversions were called *entremets* and *entreméses*. Interludes were particularly popular in England in the 15th and 16th c., and especially between 1550 and 1580. In the *Annals of English Drama* 975–1700 Harbage lists ninety or so plays which could qualify as interludes. It is very likely that they form a link between the Mystery Play, the Miracle Play and the Morality Play (*qq.v.*), and the psychological drama of the Elizabethans. Dividing lines are not clear. Many of them are very similar to Moralities and in some cases are indistinguishable from them. They were often allegorical and didactic (many also were farcical) and written in rough verse; at times so rough that it becomes doggerel (*q.v.*). They were usually about a thousand lines long and there seems little doubt that most were intended as entertainment at banquets at court, in the houses of nobility, at university colleges and at the Inns of Court. Two main types can be distinguished: (a) the popular (e.g. *Youth*, *The Pride of Life* and

Mankind); (b) the aristocratic or courtly (e.g. *Fulgens and Lucrece* and *Appius and Virginia*).

One of the earliest instances is the *Interludium de Clerico et Puella* (1290–1335). A list of the most notable examples (some of these are also classified as Moralities) should include: *The Pride of Life* (c. 1300–25); *Mankind* (1465–70); *The Castell of Perseverance* (1400–25); *Wisdom* (1460–3); Medwall's *Fulgens and Lucrece* (1490–1500); *Youth* (c. 1515–28); Heywood's *The Play of the Wether* (c. 1527); *A Play of Love* (c. 1534); *Thersites* (1537); *The Foure P's* (c. 1545); Redford's *Wit and Science* (c. 1531–47); *Respublica*, possibly by Nicholas Udall (c. 1533); *Appius and Virginia* (c. 1567); *Like Will to Like* (c. 1567). *See* MORAL INTERLUDE.

intermezzi Light, comic interpolations put on between the acts of serious plays in Italy during the 15th and 16th c. They were usually devoted to mythological subjects. They were similar to the *momeries* and *entremets* in France, and the *entreméses* (*q.v.*) in Spain. *See also* ENTR'ACTE; INTERLUDE.

internal evidence A term used in analytical and textual criticism (especially in the dating of a literary work) to refer to features of style (e.g. imagery, syntax, idiom, spelling, rhyme, punctuation), or details of environment, fashion and period, which might give some indication of when the work was written. Sometimes it is possible to date within a few years.

internal rhyme It occurs when two or more words rhyme within a single line of verse as in W. S. Gilbert's libretto for *Patience*:

> Then a sentimental passion of a vegetable fashion
>   must excite your languid spleen,
> An attachment à la Plato, for a bashful young potato,
>   or a not too French French bean!
> Though the Philistine may jostle, you will rank as an
>   apostle in the high aesthetic band,
> If you walk down Piccadilly with a poppy or a lily in
>   your medieval hand.

Shelley also used it very successfully in *The Cloud*. *See also* CROSS-RHYME; LEONINE RHYME; RHYME.

International Centre of Theatre Research Founded in 1970 at the Mobilier National in Paris under the directorship of Peter Brook (1925–). The main objective was to gather actors and actresses of various nationalities and races and create a 'universal language' of the theatre. In 1971 *Orghast* was staged in the open air as part of the Shiraz Festival at Persepolis. In 1972–3 a group travelled through Africa, improvising and developing performances of *The Conference of the Birds*. In 1975 the Centre opened the Théâtre des Bouffes du Nord with *The Ik*, an attempt to display the impact of civilization on an African tribe. *See also* TOTAL THEATRE.

internet First used in the early 1970s as an abbreviation of 'internetwork', that is, a network of networks, today the term denotes the global infrastructure of interconnected computer systems which has come to dominate telecommunications. Sometimes the terms 'internet' and 'world wide web' (or simply 'the web') are used synonymously, though the latter denotes a system of interlinked hypertext (*q.v.*) documents that can be accessed through the internet. Other systems facilitated by the internet but which are not part of the world wide web include email, instant messaging and file transfer protocol (FTP), used to upload and download files.

The internet has its origins in a computer network developed by the American military in 1969. This network was built not, as is commonly thought, as a decentred command-and-control structure that might remain operational in the event of a nuclear attack, but rather to share valuable computing resources among scientists located in different parts of the country. The network was augmented by those created by other federal agencies in the 1980s, most significantly that developed by the National Science Foundation in 1981. Major networks being developed by scientists in Europe, Australia and Asia were connected to the internet in the late 1980s, which was subsequently opened to commercial traffic in the mid-1990s. Today, nearly a third of the world's population (over two-thirds in the West) has regular access to the internet, and it is estimated that 97 per cent of all telecommunicated information is now carried by the internet.

The internet, and in particular the world wide web, has had a profound effect on many spheres of social life, and the relative ease with which information can be disseminated and accessed has transformed commerce, journalism, publishing and scholarship. Due to the possibility of reaching large audiences, the absence of editorial control and the low costs involved, an increasing proportion of non-fiction and fiction writing is now web-based. Writing which originates in digital environments such as the web is sometimes referred to as 'electronic literature'. Some forms, in particular the blog (*q.v.*), hypertext fiction and poetry, and collaborative fiction, notably exploit the capacity of networked computers for interactivity. *See also* CYBERPUNK/STEAMPUNK; EBOOK; DIGITAL HUMANITIES; SYSTEMS THEORY.

interpellation The term commonly associated with Louis Althusser's theory of the subject's construction by ideology (*q.v.*). In his essay *Ideology and Ideological State Apparatuses* (1971), Althusser writes:

> Ideology 'acts' or 'functions' in such a way that it 'recruits' subjects among the individuals (it recruits them all), or 'transforms' the individuals into subjects (it transforms them all) by that very precise operation which I have called interpellation or hailing, and which can be imagined along the lines of the most commonplace everyday police (or other) hailing: Hey, you there!

Althusser uses the example of police hailing to show how subjects are constructed by ideological state apparatuses such as police, education and various other institutions. The subject's entrance into subjectivity occurs in the moment when he or she turns round and recognizes that he or she has been the object of a policeman's hailing. See also HEGEMONY; IDEOLOGY.

interpretant In the science of semiotics (*q.v.*) the term denotes the response to a particular sign, and not to a person (who is the interpreter). The usage was coined by the American semiotician C. S. Peirce (1839–1914), and also by the American behaviourist Charles Morris (1901–79).

interpretive communities A term used by the critic Stanley Fish to denote a notional group, the members of which deploy a particular set of shared assumptions and strategies when interpreting any given text. Generally understood to be a development of 'reader-response theory' (*q.v.*), Fish's identification of interpretive communities follows from his 'affective stylistics', an approach which drew attention to the individual reader's experience of the text as a sequential series of anticipated experiences both fulfilled and contradicted. In *Is There a Text in This Class? The Authority of Interpretive Communities* (1980), Fish argues that every act of reading (and hence of interpretation) is a collective response to certain agreed preconceptions about the text and author and that 'these strategies exist prior to the act of reading and therefore determine the shape of what is read rather than, as is usually assumed, the other way around'. The underlying conviction is that meaning is constituted not by the text, but by the reader, who is in turn complicit with his or her interpretive community. Since there is no vantage point from which the relative value of these interpretive communities may be objectively weighed (since all interpretations are inevitably shaped by a particular community), any claim to a definitive or stable meaning in texts is called into doubt. At the same time it is the very existence of interpretive communities that allows for any meaningful act of reading and authorship in the first place.

intersubjectivity A key term in hermeneutics (*q.v.*) which refers to the capacity for shared understanding of an utterance or a text by different listeners or readers.

intertextuality A term coined by Julia Kristeva in 1966 to denote the interdependence of literary texts, the interdependence of any one literary text with all those that have gone before it. Her contention was that a literary text is not an isolated phenomenon but is made up of a mosaic of quotations, and that any text is the 'absorption and transformation of another'. She challenges traditional notions of literary influence, saying that intertextuality denotes a transposition of one or several sign systems into another or others. But this is not connected with the study of sources. 'Transposition' is a Freudian term, and Kristeva is pointing not merely to the way texts echo each other but to the way that discourses or sign systems are transposed into one another – so that meanings in one kind of discourse are overlaid with meanings from another kind of discourse. It is a kind of 'new articulation'. For Kristeva the idea is part of a wider psychoanalytical theory which questions the stability of the subject, and her views about intertextuality are very different from those of Roland Barthes and other theorists. *See* STRUCTURALISM.

intrinsic/extrinsic criticism A distinction that was formalized by the New Critics of the early 20th c., especially John Crowe Ransom, William K. Wimsatt, Jr and Monroe C. Beardsley. Ransom published a series of essays entitled *The New Criticism* (1941) and an influential essay 'Criticism, Inc.', published in *The World's Body* (1938). This essay succinctly expresses a core of New Critical principles underlying the practice of most 'New Critics', whose views often differed in other respects. He urges that criticism must move away from 'external' or 'extrinsic' emphases such as historical scholarship, morality or linguistic studies to the 'intrinsic' literary subject matter of aesthetic value, the technical study of poetry, metrics, tropes and fictiveness, which should be examined in their independence and autonomy. Ransom's arguments have often been abbreviated into a characterization of New Criticism (*q.v.*) as focusing on 'the text itself' or 'the words on the page'.

The critic Wimsatt and the philosopher Beardsley produced two influential and controversial papers that propounded central positions of New Criticism, *The Intentional Fallacy* (1946) and *The Affective Fallacy* (1949). In the first of these, they give explicit formulation to Ransom's implied distinction between 'internal' and 'external' evidence; they reject the idea – whether inspired by intentionalism or any other mode of criticism – that we can go beyond a poem for 'evidence' of a meaning that is not contained within the poem itself.

There are many possible objections to the arguments of both essays. To begin with, they presuppose that we can treat a poem as an isolated artefact, torn from all of its contexts, including the circumstances of its reading or reception. Clearly, the distinction between what Wimsatt and Beardsley see as 'internal' and 'external' evidence cannot be absolute and will vary according to the reader's knowledge and literary education. *See also* AFFECTIVE FALLACY; INTENTIONAL FALLACY.

introduction Normally an essay (of varying length) which states the author's intention and gives the reader some idea of the theme and scope of a work. It may also refer to the first part of a speech (*q.v.*). *See* FOREWORD; PREFACE.

intrusive narrator A mode of narration in fiction whereby the authorial voice 'intrudes' on the events of the narrative, thus 'breaking the frame', and potentially dispelling the illusion that what we are reading is real. Intrusive narration often involves a first-person voice which directly addresses the reader, and is a device closely associated with the realist novelists of the 19th c. such as George Eliot and Tolstoy, though it is also in evidence in the 18th c. novel, for instance in Henry Fielding's *Tom Jones* (1749). In *The Art of Fiction* (1992), David Lodge argues that from the beginning of the 20th c. the intrusive narrator fell out of favour. For one, it tends to reduce the realism of the characters and events depicted, and perhaps the story's emotional intensity as well. Also, in an increasingly sceptical and relativistic age, people are simply less likely to trust an ostensibly omniscient narrator. Hence the tendency in the early 20th c. for authors to delegate responsibility for narration to their characters. In postmodern metafiction (*q.v.*), however, the intrusive narrator is back with a vengeance. The extended authorial commentary, or even the appearance of the author in works such as Kurt Vonnegut's *Slaughterhouse Five* (1967) and Alasdair Gray's *Lanark* (1981), is motivated by a deep distrust of the mechanics of realism (*q.v.*). See also NARRATOR; NOVEL.

invective Speech or writing which is denunciatory, abusive or vituperative. The term is related to the verb *inveigh*, 'to bring in' or 'introduce' or 'denounce'; as in the phrase 'inveigh against'.

In literature examples of invective are to be found fairly evenly distributed in verse and prose, and it is closely associated with satire, lampoon and caricature (*qq.v.*). Many writers have employed invective for a variety of purposes, the commonest being to express dislike, disgust, contempt and even hatred. It is often directed against a particular person (e.g. Junius on the Duke of Grafton in *The Letters of Junius*); occasionally against a class or group (e.g. Swift on the English nobility in *Gulliver's Travels*); against an institution (e.g. William Prynne on the stage in *Histriomastix*); a scene (e.g. Smollett on the night-life in London in *Humphry Clinker*); and on life itself (e.g. Jeremy Taylor in *Of Holy Dying*).

As a mode of expression invective is very ancient. Archilochus (7th c. BC) had a reputation for being a mordant wit (Eustathius called him 'scorpion-tongued') in his writings, of which, unhappily, few are extant. There are plentiful instances of invective in the plays of Aristophanes, and there are supposed to have been examples in the *Sermones* of Lucilius (180–102 BC), but these last have not survived. Persius (AD 34–62) was influenced by Lucilius, and in his *First Satire* is fairly abusive of the poetasters (*q.v.*) and decadent literary tastes of his period. But the greatest of inveighers in Classical literature is unquestionably Juvenal (1st c. AD), who wrote ferocious attacks on the vices and abuses of the Roman 'life-style'. He was particularly savage at the expense of the rich, and of women – to whom he devoted his *Sixth Satire*: a sustained and bitter diatribe (*q.v.*) in which women are compared unfavourably to many different animals.

There is little in the way of invective in European literature from Juvenal's age until the late Middle Ages and early Tudor times, if we except some Latin verse, some Goliardic poetry, the occasional indignant outburst from the pulpit (like Wulfstan's celebrated homily to the English *c.* 1014), and the flytings (*q.v.*) of some Scottish poets like Dunbar. We find, also, some instances in the poetry of Langland and in the *ballades* of Villon. Then comes John Skelton who lashed out in his good-humoured and boisterous fashion at the evils of society and at the expense of individuals (particularly Cardinal Wolsey). More moderate invective is to be found in the Folly Literature (*q.v.*) of the period; and John Knox's famous *First Blast of the Trumpet against the Monstrous Regiment of Women* (1558) is a splendid example of objurgation.

The late Tudor dramatists and pamphleteers found invective a most effective weapon. Good examples in Shakespeare's plays are to be found in: *Troilus and Cressida* (I, ii); *King Lear* (II, ii; IV, i); *Timon of Athens* (IV, i); *Coriolanus* (III, iii); *Cymbeline* (II, v) and *The Tempest* (I, ii; II, ii). Thomas Lodge, John Marston and Ben Jonson were other writers of the period well capable of exploiting abusive language. A curiosity of this time was King James I's *A Counterblaste to Tobacco* (1604). Among 17th c. writers Samuel Butler and Dryden are two witty exponents of invective; the former in *Hudibras*, the latter in *Mac Flecknoe* and *Absalom and Achitophel*. In the following century one should note Pope (especially in *Epistle to Arbuthnot*, *Epistle to Sir Richard Temple* and *The Dunciad*), Swift in *Gulliver's Travels* and Smollett in *Humphry Clinker*. Thereafter *et passim* in the works of Burns, Byron, Macaulay, Dickens, Thackeray, Carlyle, Swinburne, Shaw, Belloc and G. K. Chesterton, to name only a few.

invention The term derives from the *inventio* of Classical and medieval rhetoric. *Inventio* was the first of the five 'parts' of oratory. Invention equalled discovery. Later it came to be applied generally to original discovery and the organization of any literary work. However, it has had many special and particular meanings at different times. It has been contrasted with 'imitation' (*q.v.*), and with judgement. It has been used to describe things incredible and the products of fancy. Sometimes it has meant the production of fiction as opposed to historical truth; or the combination of fiction and historical truth. One of the key remarks on invention occurs in Johnson's *Life of Pope*, where he describes it as the faculty by which 'new trains of events are formed and new scenes of imagery displayed' and by which 'extrinsic and adventitious embellishments and illustrations are connected with a known subject'. In general one may now take it that invention denotes the discovery of an idea or fact, and the arranging of words and ideas in a fresh and arresting fashion. *See* FANCY AND IMAGINATION; INSPIRATION; ORIGINALITY.

inversion In rhetoric the turning of an argument against an opponent. In grammar the reversal of the normal word order of a sentence; as in these lines from *Paradise Lost*:

> His spear, to equal which the tallest pine
> Hewn on Norwegian hills, to be the mast
> Of some great admiral, were but a wand,
> He walk'd with to support uneasy steps
> Over the burning marle.

In prosody, the turning of feet by substitution (*q.v.*).

invocation An appeal or request for help (for instance: for inspiration, *q.v.*) addressed to a muse (*q.v.*) or deity. In epic, it is a literary convention. It usually comes at or near the beginning of a poem. Good examples are to be found in the *Iliad*, the *Odyssey* and *Paradise Lost*. Mock-heroic (*q.v.*) poetry produced mock invocations (as in Pope's *The Rape of the Lock*). It is seldom used now but a good modern example is to be found in Hart Crane's *The Bridge*.

involute   *See* EPIPHANY.

involuted novel   *See* NARRATOR.

ionic   A verse form believed to have originated with the Ionians of Asia Minor. It is thought that they used it in odes in praise of Dionysus and Cybele. There are two kinds of ionic foot: *a majore*: / / ∪ ∪; and *a minore*: ∪ ∪ / /. Ionics are found in the work of Anacreon, Euripides and Horace. They are very rare in English verse, except as occasional feet in combination with others. Browning attempted lesser ionics in the *Epilogue* to *Asolando* (1889), his last volume of poems, which was published on the day of his death:

> Ăt thĕ mídníght | ĭn thĕ sílénce | ŏf thĕ sleép-tíme,
>   Whĕn yŏu sét yoúr | fáncĭes freé,
> Wíll thĕy páss tŏ whére – bў deáth, foóls thínk,
>   ĭmprísonĕd –
> Lów hĕ líes whŏ ónce sŏ lóved yóu, whŏm yóu lóved só?
>   – Pítў mé?

It can be seen from this how difficult it is to maintain ionics for long without forcing words into an unnatural stress pattern.

Irish dramatic movement   *See* ABBEY THEATRE.

Irish literary renaissance   *See* CELTIC TWILIGHT.

irony   (Gk 'dissimulation') First recorded in Plato's *Republic* (4th c. BC), where it has approximately the meaning of 'a glib and underhand way of taking people in'. In the Platonic dialogues, Socrates himself takes on the role of *eirōn* or 'dissembler' and, assuming a pose of ignorance, asks seemingly innocuous and naive questions which gradually undermine his interlocutor's case and trap him into confronting the truth. Hence what is known as dialectical or Socratic irony (*q.v.*).

    For the Roman rhetoricians (in particular Cicero and Quintilian) *ironia* denoted a rhetorical figure and a manner of discourse in which, for the most part, the meaning was contrary to the words. This double-edged nature appears to be a continuing feature of irony.

    It was not until 1502 that we find the first mention of irony in English: 'yronye' – 'of grammare, by whiche a man sayth one & gyveth to understand the contrarye'. This suggests a common usage. Later we find a gloss by 'E. K.' to the October Eclogue in Spenser's *Shepheardes Calender* (1579) in which he refers to a passage as 'An Ironicall Sarcasmus spoken in derision . . . ' By the late 17th and 18th c., irony, as a mode of thinking, feeling and expression, was beginning to attain a high degree of sophistication, as can be seen in the work of Dryden, Swift, Voltaire, Pope, Fielding and Johnson.

At the turn of the 18th c. the concept of irony inspired some careful thinking in Germany, where A. W. and F. Schlegel, Tieck and Karl Solger all addressed themselves to the extremely difficult task of understanding this subtlest of manifestations of the comic spirit. Friedrich Schlegel, for instance, perceived the irony of King Lear's rejection of the daughter he loved the most, or of events in *Troilus and Cressida*, where the fine speeches and grandiose ideas eventually amount to nothing. Tragic irony, then – which can be considered a subcategory of dramatic irony (*q.v.*) – describes a situation where an audience appreciates the incongruity of a character's words or deeds in the light of his or her fate, whereas the character does not. A. W. Schlegel pointed out the ironical nature of the equilibrium or equipoise maintained between the serious and the comic (e.g. the subplots in Elizabethan and particularly Shakespeare's plays). Comic relief (*q.v.*) itself can, by contrast, intensify the irony of a situation. Karl Solger introduced the idea that true irony begins with a contemplation of the fate of the world, a concept which goes under the titles of world irony or cosmic irony or philosophical irony.

Two further commonly used categories of irony are verbal irony and irony of situation. At its simplest, verbal irony involves saying what one does not mean. Johnson defined it as a mode of speech in which the meaning is contrary to the words, such as 'Bolingbroke was a holy man'. Such ironies are often hyperbole or litotes (*qq.v.*). Situational irony occurs when, for instance, a man is laughing uproariously at the misfortune of another even while the same misfortune, unbeknownst, is happening to him.

However, as irony is such an oblique quality or expression, it would be true to say that in many works we find not so much direct or overt irony, but, rather, an ironic temper or tone, an ironic way of looking at things and feeling about them. Many writers have distanced themselves to a vantage point, a god-like eminence, the better to be able to view things (which they often maintain with a smile). When such detached knowingness is directed towards an author's own work – a form of irony Solgar and the Schlegels identified – it is called romantic irony (*q.v.*).

Indeed, by the end of the 18th c. irony was not just a rhetorical device but denoted an entire way of looking at the world, a broad philosophic vision. Friedrich Schlegel's *Fragments* of 1797 had accorded irony an epistemological and ontological function, seeing it as a mode of confronting and transcending the contradictions of the finite world. Such a theory of irony was further developed by many writers, including Heine, Kierkegaard and Nietzsche. At the heart of irony as conceived by most 19th c. thinkers was a Romantic tendency to confront, rather than dismiss, the disorder, contingency and unintelligibility of the world. An ironic vision acknowledges that the world can be viewed from various irreconcilable perspectives, and rejects any foreclosure of the world's absurdity into some spurious unity. Yet Romantic irony was not entirely negative: while it rejected the 'objective' order imposed upon experience or the world by religion or rational thought, it sought a higher unity and purpose, grounded ultimately in the very core of subjectivity. Modernist irony is usually regarded as a development of Romantic irony, and entails a double posture: both a negation of prevailing values and institutions, and a helpless complicity with them. However, modernist irony is more nihilistic, despairing over the possibility of transcending or changing the status quo. More recently the term postmodern irony has been used to describe the self-awareness exhibited by recent metafiction (*q.v.*) – viz., that the world described by the narrative is a fabrication of the author, that its characters are constructs, and that it is merely a reworking of other texts. *See also* MEIOSIS.

irregular ode   An alternative term for the Cowleyan ode (*q.v.*). *See* ODE.

irregular rhyme   *See* RHYME.

isochronism   (Gk 'equal timing') In Classical prosody the assumption that meter comprises a succession of units (like the foot) which are of the same duration. They are then said to be isochronous.

isocolon   (Gk 'equal list') A sequence of clauses or sentences of identical length.

issue   *See* EDITION.

Italian sonnet   *See* PETRARCHAN SONNET.

iterability/iteration   This term was developed by Jacques Derrida, in his 1971 essays *Signature Event Context* and *White Mythology* to theorize the paradox of the simultaneity of sameness and difference in conceptualization. Derrida specifically examines iterability as the condition of writing, language and oral communication. For Derrida, iterability does not simply signify repetition as in 'reiteration'; rather, every iteration is an alteration, or a modification of the same. At the same time, iteration depends on a minimal remainder and illusion of an identity of the same so that repetition can be recognized in the first place. Iteration introduces new contexts and variety into the constitution of the same. For example, Derrida writes that a sign can never simply have one single meaning, but can exist in an infinity of possible contexts:

> Every sign, linguistic or nonlinguistic, spoken or written (in the current sense of this opposition), in a small or large unit, can be *cited*; put between quotation marks; in so doing it can break with every given context, engendering an infinity of new contexts in a manner which is absolutely illimitable. This does not imply that the mark is valid outside of a context, but on the contrary that there are only contexts without any center or absolute anchoring [*ancrage*]. This citationality, this duplication or duplicity, this iterability of the mark is neither an accident nor an anomaly, it is that (normal/abnormal) without which a mark could not even have a function called 'normal'.

(Translated by Samuel Weber)

See also PERFORMATIVITY.

ithyphallic verse The term derives from the Greek for an 'erect phallus', and denotes an ode (*q.v.*) or dance performed at festivals of Dionysus. It is also applied to the verse form: / ∪ / ∪ / ∪ × ×, which is known as trochaic dimeter brachycatalectic or trochaic tripody. It was used by Archilochus in the 7th c. BC.

itihāsa *See* KĀVYA.

ivory tower In *The Song of Songs* (7:4) Solomon tells his beloved: 'Thy neck is as a tower of ivory'; (F *Ton cou est comme une tour d'ivoire*). Sainte-Beuve (1804–69) is believed to have applied this simile to de Vigny suggesting that he lived in an ivory tower, thereby meaning that he was detached and isolated from the world, haughtily aloof from it. This connotation has survived. If we say that a writer or artist lives in an ivory tower, we imply that he is remote from the world, out of touch with reality, and probably devitalized.

J

jabberwocky A form of nonsense; unintelligible speech or writing. At its worst it degenerates into whimsy, that apparently ineradicable cancer of English humour. Lewis Carroll invented the Jabberwock and wrote a poem called *Jabberwocky* in *Through the Looking-Glass* (1872). Alice discovered the poem printed backwards in a looking-glass book. She held it up to the mirror and read (the first verse):

> 'Twas brillig, and the slithy toves
>   Did gyre and gimble in the wabe:
> All mimsy were the borogoves,
>   And the mome raths outgrabe.

Humpty Dumpty says that 'brillig' means 'four o'clock in the afternoon – the time when you start broiling things for dinner'.

The reader can invent for himself. 'Slithy toves' are, perhaps, slithery creatures. 'Gyre and gimble' perhaps suggests a slow and solemn dance of joy. 'Mimsy' – delicate, and bearing blossoms?

The work had some influence on Joyce's *Finnegans Wake* (1939). *See* GHOSTWORD; JINGLE; NONSENSE; NURSERY RHYMES.

Jacobean age So called from *Jacobus*, 'James', and thus belonging to the reign of James I (1603–25). Succeeding to the English Crown as the existing king of Scotland, James's reign set in train a process of Anglo-Scottish unification, albeit one not made law until 1707. In domestic politics, the Gunpowder Plot (1605) signalled the continuing tensions between the Anglican Church and Catholic opposition, while abroad the founding of Jamestown in Virginia (1607) marked the very beginnings of the colonial project in the New World. This was also a period which, like the Elizabethan age (*q.v.*), was particularly rich in literary activity. The king himself published at least four books: two on poetry, a work on demonology, and the famous *A*

A Dictionary of Literary Terms and Literary Theory, Fifth Edition. J. A. Cuddon.
© 2013 The Estate of J. A. Cuddon. Published 2013 by Blackwell Publishing Ltd.

Counterblaste to Tobacco (1604). Among dramatists, Shakespeare, Ben Jonson, Beaumont and Fletcher, Webster, Tourneur, Ford, Middleton and Rowley were all very active. Both the king and his wife, Anne of Denmark, were active patrons of the theatre as well as proponents of the fashionable court masque (*q.v.*). Donne and Drayton were two of the most famous lyric poets of the period. Bacon and Robert Burton were the best-known prose writers. In 1611 the King James Bible was published, the result of seven years of labour by a committee of forty-seven scholars in an attempt to render the scriptures in a final, state-authorized English version.

jarcha *See* KHARJA.

jargon (OF 'warbling [of birds]') Coleridge still used jargon in this sense in *The Rime of the Ancient Mariner* (1798), but by the end of the 15th c., and perhaps earlier, it came to signify unintelligible or secret language. For example, François Villon (1431–?) composed several *Ballades en jargon* in the cant or secret language of the *coquillards* (*q.v.*). We are accustomed to using it derogatorily now to describe a private or technical vocabulary peculiar to a trade or profession. *See also* COLLOQUIALISM; EUPEHMISM; IDIOM; PERIPHRASIS; REGISTER; SLANG.

jazz poetry Poetry which is recited to the accompaniment of jazz. Its origins appear to be found in the ballads of Vachel Lindsay (1879–1931), particularly the well-known *General William Booth* (1913) and *The Congo* (1914). Langston Hughes (1902–67), in the late 1930s, was one of the first versifiers to collaborate with musicians. Jazz poetry began to take off as a popular form in the USA in the 1950s, particularly in the hands of Kenneth Patchen (1911–72), Kenneth Rexroth (1905–82), Amiri Baraka (1934–) and Ted Joans (1928–2003). The poets of the American Beat generation (*q.v.*) also contributed. The vogue spread to Britain in the mid-1950s and has flourished ever since. Notable jazz poets have been Christopher Logue (1926–2011), a pioneer of the movement, Roy Fisher (1930–), Michael Horovitz (1935–), Pete Brown (1940–), Spike Hawkins (1942–) *et al*. The 1970s and 1980s – era of punk, post-punk and the new wave subcultures – in turn produced a further 'generation' of jazz poets, especially John Cooper Clarke and the Anglo-Jamaicans James Berry and E. K. Braithwaite. *See also* LIVERPOOL POETS; SUBCULTURE; UNDERGROUND LITERATURE/POETRY.

je ne scai (sais) **quoi** (F 'I don't know what') An example of critical jargon popular in France in the 17th c. and used to suggest the existence of some otherwise indefinable merit, quality, property or grace (*q.v.*) in a work of art or literature. The term was first used in England *c.* 1656 to describe a sensation or awareness of illness which had no apparent cause. In the 18th c. it served, as it had in France, to describe otherwise indescribable merits in a poetical work. By the end of that century it no longer functioned as a 'support', as Pope put it, to 'all ignorant pretenders to delicacy'. However, the phrase is still used occasionally (as it was in the 19th c.) for more or less its original purpose. We would put it more crudely now. For example: 'It's got something.'

Jeremiad A tale of woe; a sustained complaint; a prolonged railing against the world, the times, the estate of man and God. By allusion to *The Lamentations of Jeremiah* in the Old Testament. There are several good examples in Shakespeare's *Timon of Athens*; especially in the bitter exchanges between Timon and Apemantus.

jest book A collection of stories of a kind that was particularly popular in England and on the continent during and after the 16th c. Jest books were descendants of such collections of tales as the *Gesta Romanorum* ('jest' derives from *gesta* or *geste*), volumes of moral anecdotes like the *Alphabet of Tales* and *Speculum Laicorum*, and theological handbooks like John Bromyard's *Summa Praedicantium* (a kind of guide to easier preaching). The jests are often reminiscent of the medieval *fabliau* (*q.v.*) and for the most part are brief and didactic, humorous and satirical; sometimes they are ribald. The earliest known example in English is *A Hundred Merry Tales* (*c.* 1526). Later popular works were *The Geystes of Skoggan* (1565–6), an account of the exploits of John Scogan, a famous jester at the court of Edward IV; *Tarlton's Jests* (*c.* 1592); and *The Merry Conceited Jests of George Peele* (1607). A Latin source was the *Facetiae* of Poggio (late 14th c.). The modern counterpart of the old jest books is the compilation of jokes and stories for all occasions.

Jesuit drama The drama of the Jesuit schools was similar to other forms of scholastic drama and had a specific didactic purpose. The first plays were performed as part of the school curriculum. They were in Latin and their subjects were religious (or sacred): for instance, stories of people like Saul, Herod, Absalom, Judith, Esther and St Catherine the martyr. The plays were designed to inculcate moral virtues.

The first recorded performance was at Messina in 1551. In the next ten years or so plays were performed at Cordoba, Ingolstadt, Munich and Vienna. By 1587 (only 53 years after the foundation of the Society of Jesus by St Ignatius Loyola), there were 148 Jesuit colleges in Europe and at least one play was performed at them every year. In 1586 the *Ratio atque Institutio Studiorum* provided for the acting of tragedies and comedies. Gradually, partly because of the influence of secular drama, ballet and opera, the plays became more ambitious and spectacular. Great pains were taken in perfecting the technique of presentation. Though plays were still written in Latin, the use of the vernacular became quite common. The range of subject matter was widened to include themes from national history and classical legend and history (e.g. the defeat of the Saracens at Messina in 1068, the liberation of Vienna in 1683, the lives of Pompey, Brutus, Croesus and Damocles).

This form of drama prospered throughout Europe during the 17th c. Productions became more and more sumptuous and elaborate, and technical effects increasingly ingenious and lavish. Such a standard of excellence was achieved that the plays were performed increasingly for the general public and at courts. During the 18th c. this form of drama fell gradually into desuetude. *See* SCHOOL DRAMA.

jeu d'esprit (F 'play of the mind') An epigram (*q.v.*), witticism or brief flight of fancy, urbanely expressed. Oscar Wilde was particularly adept at them; as in these lines from *A Woman of No Importance* (1893):

> MRS ALLONBY: They say, Lady Hunstanton, that when good Americans die they go to Paris.
> LADY HUNSTANTON: Indeed? And when bad Americans die, where do they go?
> LORD ILLINGWORTH: Oh, they go to America.

See WIT.

jeu parti (F 'play divided') A kind of debate poem, which had some vogue in the 13th c., in which two characters argued over a hypothesis; usually some matter of love. The argument proceeded in alternating stanzas. Normally, at the end, the issue was referred to arbitration – perhaps by a patron. Poetic 'contests' of this kind are common in pastoral (*q.v.*). *See also* DÉBAT; PARTIMEN; TENSON.

Jeux Floraux de Toulouse A form of poetic festival founded in 1323 by seven troubadours (*q.v.*) of Toulouse who formed themselves into a 'college' and in 1324 invited all troubadours to gather and compete with poems on the theme of the Virgin Mary. The prize was a golden violet. The festival turned into an annual event and two other prizes were added: a silver marigold and a silver eglantine. Late in the 15th c. Dame Clémence Isaure endowed the college with property. Well-known poets who competed and won prizes include Du Bartas (1544–90), Philippe Fabre d'Eglantine (1755–94) and Victor Hugo (1802–85). Fabre adopted the name 'Eglantine' because he won the *prix de l'Eglantine* (i.e. a wild rose).

jig A form of dramatic after-piece (*q.v.*). Basically, it was a short farce (*q.v.*) with music and dancing. Common in Tudor and Jacobean drama. There are many references to them in the literature of those periods, and a particularly well-known one in *Hamlet* (II, ii. 494). William Kemp and Richard Tarlton, two famous comic actors, often performed them.

jingle Usually a verse or verses with a catchy rhythm, emphatic rhyme and alliteration. Often jingles verge on nonsense. For example:

> Dingle dingle doosey,
> The cat's in the well

Or:

> One, two
> Buckle my shoe;
> Three, four,

Shut the door;
Five, six,
Pick up sticks.
Seven, eight,
Lay them straight:
Nine, ten,
A good fat hen.

Somewhere between jingle and patter (*q.v.*) or chant (*q.v.*) comes this kind of thing:

Dear Mother, the Army's a bugger: sell the pig and buy me out.
　　Your loving son John
Dear John, pig's gone: soldier on.

Plentiful examples are to be found in Geoffrey Grigson's *Faber Book of Popular Verse* (1972); in *The Oxford Nursery Rhyme Book* assembled by Iona and Peter Opie (1955); and in the Everyman Library *A Book of Nonsense* (1927). *See* DOGGEREL; DOUBLE DACTYL; JABBERWOCKY; NONSENSE; NURSERY RHYME; TONGUE-TWISTER.

Joe Miller A hackneyed joke, named after Joseph Miller (1684–1738), an actor and comedian in the Drury Lane Company who had a considerable reputation as a wit. Many stories and jokes were attributed to him.

jogral A Galician term for the Castilian *juglar*, the equivalent of the French *jongleur* and the English minstrel (*qq.v.*).

Johnsonian In the style or manner of Samuel Johnson (1709–84). That is, characterized by grand, lapidary language, balanced phrases, sentences and periods, Latinistic construction and, often, a didactic tone. However, at its best, Johnson's full-dress manner displays a melodious resonance and a certain martial splendour. Moreover, he was perfectly capable of expressing in a pithy sentence what others might labour over in a paragraph. When verbose and pompous, language and style are sometimes called Johnsonese.

jongleur (F *jongleur*, variant of *jougleur*, OF *jogleor*, L *joculatorem*) Though *jongleur* is a term which dates only from the 8th c., such entertainers were active much earlier. They were the literary descendants of the *mimi* and *histriones* of the Roman world. Besides being minstrels who sang and recited, many *jongleurs* were acrobats, jugglers and exhibitors of animals. As versatile professionals, they made a living where and when they could, and their audiences were plebeian as well as patrician. They reached their apogee of popularity in the 13th c., and thereafter they declined. Individual versatility gave way to specialization. Because they were itinerant, they played a considerable part in disseminating literary forms throughout Europe. *See* GUSLAR; PAYADA; SCOP; SKALD; TROUBADOUR; TROUVÈRE.

joruri A form of Japanese puppet-theatre. Many major Japanese plays have been written for this form, including a number by Chikamatsu (1653–1725).

Originally *joruri* was a kind of epic recitation which, *c.* 1630, was cross-fertilized with the puppet shows to create *ningyo-joruri*. The themes and subjects of these plays were mostly legends and historical events. Productions were lavish and the puppets (usually about two-thirds of life size) were manipulated by several puppeteers. The dialogue, accompanied by music, was delivered by a group from the side of the stage. A comparable form of drama is the Sicilian *opra d'i pupi*, once performed in many puppet theatres all over Sicily. *See also* KARAGÖZ.

jouissance *See* PLAISIR/JOUISSANCE.

journal A paper, periodical (*q.v.*) or magazine (*q.v.*). It is often of a learned nature, like: *The Quarterly Review*; *Journal des Savants*; *Giornale storico della letteratura italiana*. *See* DIARY AND JOURNAL.

journalese This term denotes a manner of writing which employs ready-made phrases and formulas, and which breeds its own clichés in abundance.
  We must distinguish between *journalese* and *headlinese*: the eye-catching and formulaic style of newsman's English. For example: Fire Horror in Spastic Home; Police Probe; Prime Minister Attacked in House; Sea Drama in Channel; Mother of Eight Adopts Monkey. Some carelessly worded headlines have become notorious: Chinese Generals Fly Back To Front; Tank Attacks Peter Out In Desert; Infantry Push Bottles Up German Rear.

journalism The occupation or profession of journalist; journalistic writing. Sometimes used derogatorily, in contradistinction to more exalted and less ephemeral forms of literature. But numerous able and distinguished authors have made a name for themselves as journalists. When newspapers increased their range early in the 19th c. many famous writers contributed to them (e.g. Coleridge, Southey, Hazlitt). Charles Dickens was a highly successful reporter; so were Rudyard Kipling and J. M. Barrie. American writers like Mark Twain and Bret Harte also made a name for themselves as journalists. In the 20th c. it became common practice for novelists and poets to write for newspapers (e.g. Robert Graves, Aldous Huxley, Ernest Hemingway, Graham Greene, Norman Mailer). In France there has long been a closer connection than elsewhere between newspapers and writers eminent in fiction and drama. Men of letters like Jean-Paul Sartre, Albert Camus, François Mauriac and Georges Duhamel have been well known for their contributions to journals and newspapers. *See also* NEW JOURNALISM.

Joycean Characteristic of the style, tone and peculiarities of the writings of James Joyce (1882–1941), with particular reference to *Ulysses* (1922) and *Finnegans Wake* (1939). Principally, a high degree of stylistic and technical inventiveness and originality in the use of the pun, the portmanteau word, symbolism and the stream of consciousness (*qq.v.*) technique. It may also allude to his inclination towards scatology (*q.v.*), his habit of joining up numerous words and using little or no punctuation for many pages on end.

Plus his creation of what is virtually a 'private language', especially in *Finnegans Wake*.

Jugendstil   (G 'youth style') *Die Jugend* was an influential literary journal first published in Munich by George Hirth in 1896. Subsequently the journal gave its name to the style of work printed in it. Like baroque (*q.v.*) and impressionism (*q.v.*), *Jugendstil* is a term which was first used in the history of art, architecture and decoration, then applied to literature. It described a decorative style popular in Germany between 1890 and 1910. An attempt, perhaps, to escape from academic tradition. Its French counterpart is *art nouveau*.

Juvenalian satire   From the extremely splenetic and censorious satires of the Roman poet Juvenal (1st–2nd c.), whose diatribes (unlike the more urbane and witty *Horatian satire*, *q.v.*, and the more entertaining medleys of *Menippean satire*, *q.v.*) have serious moral purpose. The English inheritors of Juvenal are Jonson (e.g., in *Volpone* and *The Alchemist*, and 'Epistle to the Countess of Rutland') and Swift (e.g., in *A Modest Proposal* and Books II and IV of *Gulliver's Travels*). *See* HORATIAN SATIRE; LUCILIAN SATIRE; MENIPPEAN SATIRE; SATIRE.

juvenilia   (L 'works done in one's youth') Such were Dryden's occasional poem *Upon the Death of Lord Hastings* (1649), written when Dryden was still at Westminster School and aged eighteen; Pope's *Pastorals*, composed in 1704 when he was only sixteen, and published in Tonson's *Miscellany* (1709); Byron's *Hours of Idleness* (first called *Juvenilia*) published in 1807 when Byron was nineteen.

K

kabuki   A type of Japanese drama. Popular rather than courtly or lyrical drama like *Nō* (*q.v.*), yet *kabuki* may well have developed from this in the 17th c. At any rate, it has adopted many subjects and conventions from *Nō*. The plays are presented on a stage like a *Nō* stage. It is wide and shallow and has what is called a 'flower way' running from the back of the hall or auditorium to the side of the stage. Along this actors make their exits and entrances. The stage is nearly always a revolving one. Scenery is elaborate and detailed. Costumes are rich and ornate. The characters are not masked (as in *Nō*) but are heavily made up. Female roles are taken by men. The dramas usually have some musical accompaniment, whose precise nature will depend on the kind of play. Scenery is changed by two stage-hands: one hooded and one not. By convention they are invisible, and are a survival from the time when each actor had a 'shadow' behind him who held a light on the end of a bamboo to illuminate the actor's features.

The plays are based on popular legends and myths (sometimes historical subjects) and are usually long and episodic. There are three main classes: *jidaimono*, or histories; *sewamono*, or domestic dramas; and *shosagoto*, or dances. A normal programme would present a variety of plays or scenes from these categories.

Kafkaesque   Characteristic of the style, tone and attitudes of the writings of Franz Kafka (1883–1924), and especially the kind of nightmarish atmosphere which he was capable of creating through the pervasive menace of sinister, impersonal forces, the feeling of loss of identity, the evocation of guilt and fear, and the sense of evil that permeates the twisted and 'absurd' logic of ruling powers. His novels *The Trial* (1925) and *The Castle* (1926) and the short story 'In the Penal Colony' are particularly noteworthy for such features.

A Dictionary of Literary Terms and Literary Theory, Fifth Edition. J. A. Cuddon.
© 2013 The Estate of J. A. Cuddon. Published 2013 by Blackwell Publishing Ltd.

kailyard school A group of writers (the best known are J. M. Barrie, J. J. Bell, S. R. Crockett and Ian Maclaren) who wrote stories about Scottish peasant life late in the 19th c. The term derives from a Scottish Jacobite song 'There grows a bonnie brier bush in our kailyard', which Maclaren chose as a motto for his book *Beside the Bonnie Brier Bush* (1894). A kailyard was a cabbage patch or kitchen garden attached to a cottage.

karagöz A traditional Turkish shadow-puppet play (the equivalent of Punch and Judy) named after the principal character, who represents Turkish Everyman or ordinary man. The antagonist (*q.v.*) or deuteragonist (*q.v.*) is Haçivat, usually represented as a lazy or self-important and officious character; clearly the 'baddy' to the 'good' Karagöz. Both persons are believed to be based on actual characters of the 14th c., from which period the karagöz entertainment dates.

There are thirty-odd traditional stories involving these characters, but one of the most popular themes is confusion arising from the meanings of words. Karagöz uses the colloquial language of the common people; Haçivat uses literary and high-falutin' terms. A third character, Efe (the equivalent of Robin Hood), is often introduced to solve the problem. The stock subjects give ample opportunity for improvisation, which will include jokes, satire, songs, dances, badinage with the audience and comments on current social and political matters. The puppeteer does the dialogue. *See also* JORURI; ORTA OYUNU.

kasa (K 'song words') A Korean verse form composed of octosyllabic lines, each line being subdivided into two 'phrases'. There was no limit to the number of lines.

katauta A Japanese form of debate poem in the shape of question and answer. A standard form of *katauta* consists of three lines of five, seven and seven syllables respectively, all unrhymed. A pair of *katautas* comprise a *mondo*.

kāvya (Skt) One of the genres of Indian poetics. Its meaning, as explained by V. Dharwadker, A. K. Ramanujan and other scholars, has changed through various contexts. Earlier, around 500 BC, it denoted poetry or verse in general; later, between AD 700 and 1200, its usage was expanded to include imaginative literature in general, including prose and drama. As a literary style, it was used by Indian court poets and was distinctive for its aesthetic properties, attained largely through the use of figures of speech such as metaphor and simile (*qq.v.*). It is the form in which the *Rāmāyana* (*q.v.*) was composed. Its practitioners included Ashvaghosha (*c.* 80–*c.* 150), whose poems include *Life of the Buddha*, Bāna (7th c.) and Kalidāsa (5th c.). It was distinguished from the *purana* or 'old text' dealing with creation, the gods and their history, myth and legend; and from the *itihāsa*, a traditional historical account on an epic scale, such as the *Mahābhārata* (*q.v.*). The influence of *kāvya* on Indian literature has been vast and extends into the present.

keneme A neo-Hellenic derivation from Greek *kenós*, 'empty', used to denote a small word (article, conjunction or preposition) with little or no lexical meaning, whose function is mainly or entirely syntactic. For example: *the*, *and*, *at*. Such words are also known as *structure words* or *functors*. By contrast words like *angry* (adjective), *horse* (noun) and *clamber* (verb) have lexical meaning; that is, they do mean something on their own. These are sometimes called *pleremes* (from Greek *plérēs*, 'full'). *See also* MORPHEME.

kenning The term derives from the use of the ON verb *kenna*, 'to know, recognize', in the phrase *kenna eitt við*, 'to express or describe one thing in terms of another'. The *kenning* (pl. *kenningar*) was a favourite figure in skaldic verse, where it is employed most lavishly.

It is a device for introducing descriptive colour or for suggesting associations without distracting attention from the essential statement.

Some Old Norse kennings were fairly complex: (a) *Fróda mjǫl* – 'meal (or corn) of Fródi' and so 'gold' (Fródi was an early and legendary king of Denmark. He had a mill named Grotti which would grind out whatever was asked of it. Gold was the first material for which Fródi asked); (b) *Vidris munstrandar marr* – 'the weather-maker's mind-strand'; that is, 'sea of Odin's breast' and so 'poetry'; (c) *brimils vǫllr* – 'seal's field' and so 'sea'; (d) *malmhrið* – 'metal storm' and so 'battle'; (e) *Odins eiki* – 'Odin's oak' and so 'warrior'.

Old English kennings were simpler: (a) *helmberend* – 'helmet-bearer' and so 'warrior'; (b) *beadoleoma* – 'battle light' and so 'flashing sword'; (c) *swansrad* – 'swan road' and so 'sea'. *See also* HOMERIC EPITHET; PERIPHRASIS; POETIC DICTION; RÍMUR.

key novel *See* LIVRE À CLEF.

kharja A form of popular verse written in Arabic or Romance, in the idiom of the common people (and found in Spain). It produces an effect of sadness or despair or longing. It is probably earlier than the *muwashshab* of which it commonly forms the final part or refrain. It was usually given to a woman to utter, but was generally composed by a man. *See* MOZARABIC LYRIC.

kinaesthetic image Kinaesthesis denotes a sense of movement or muscular effort (from Gk *kineein*, 'to move' + *aisthesis*, 'sensation'). A sense of movement and effort is inherent in the rhythm, momentum and energy of words in such an image. It is the visual/physical counterpart of onomatopoeia (*q.v.*). William Faulkner (1897–1962), for instance, excelled in such images in prose. Gerard Manley Hopkins (1844–89) excelled at them in verse. These lines come from his *Harry Ploughman*:

> By a grey eye's heed steered well, one crew, fall to;
> Stand at stress. Each limb's barrowy brawn, his thew
> That onewhere curded, onewhere sucked or sank –
>   Soared or sank –,
> Though as a beechbole firm, finds his, as at a roll-call, rank

And features, in flesh, what deed he each must do –
His sinew-service where do.

See also KINETIC POEM; PHANOPOEIA.

kind A term widely used in the 17th and 18th c. for a literary type or genre (*q.v.*). Criticism determined the category of a work (e.g. epic, tragedy, elegy) and then decided whether or not it obeyed the rules and conventions. Dryden was one of the first to indicate that a writer must begin by deciding what kind he wished to practise. Writers of the Romantic period (*q.v.*) rejected such an approach. *See* FORM.

kinetic poem A poem whose movement depends on the careful placement and programming of words or letters line by line or page by page in order to achieve a visual pattern. *See* ALTAR POEM; CONCRETE POETRY/VERSE; KINAES-THETIC IMAGE; PATTERN POETRY; PHANOPOEIA.

King's English English as it should be spoken. This term was used as early as the 16th c. Thomas Wilson refers to it in his *Arte of Rhetorique* (1553) thus: 'These fine English clerkes will sai thei speake in their mother tongue, if a manne should charge them for counterfeityng the Kinge's Englishe.' A reference to 'Queene's English' occurs in Nashe's *Strange Newes of the Inter-cepting Certaine Letters* (1593); Shakespeare uses the term in *The Merry Wives of Windsor* (1600–1) and Dekker refers to the 'Kinge's English' in *Satiromastix* (1602). *See* COLLOQUIALISM; SLANG; STANDARD ENGLISH.

Kit-Cat Club A literary club founded early in the 18th c. in London. So called because its members met at the house of a pastry-cook named Christopher Kat or Cat (or Katt or Catling) in Shire Lane (near Temple Bar). Kat's mutton pies were called Kit-cats. Distinguished members of the club were Joseph Addison, Richard Steele, William Congreve, Sir John Vanbrugh and Sir Samuel Garth. They later used the premises of Jacob Tonson, the publisher, at Barn Elms. Many members had their portraits painted by Sir Godfrey Kneller. They are less than half length because the dining room was too low for half-size portraits. This size of canvas has come to be known as kit-cat (36 × 28 inches, it shows the head and one hand).

kitchen-sink drama A term which became popular in Great Britain in the middle and late 1950s. Often used derogatorily, it applied to plays which, in a realistic fashion, showed aspects of working-class life at the time. The implication was that the play centred, metaphorically (or psychologically) and in some cases literally, on the kitchen sink. The works of John Osborne, Arnold Wesker and Alun Owen (among others) were all so described. It is doubtful if the term derives in any way from Wesker's play *The Kitchen* because this was first presented in a production without décor in 1958, and not given a full production until 1961. *See* ANGRY YOUNG MAN.

kitsch (G. *kitschen*, 'to throw together') A pejorative term for art objects which are gaudy, sentimental and often mass-produced for mass consumption.

Though usually employed to describe artworks and artefacts, the term is sometimes used to designate a work of literature which is tasteless and unoriginal, a mere 'potboiler' (*q.v.*). During the 1930s the term was popularized by theorists such as Theodor Adorno, who insisted that kitsch was the antithesis of art. The Austrian Hermann Broch even held that in the value system of art, kitsch represents evil. Strongly influenced by these thinkers, the Czech writer Milan Kundera argues in his philosophical novel *The Unbearable Lightness of Being* (1984) that kitsch is an aesthetic closely associated with totalitarianism, as it posits a sanitized, shared vision of the world which denies contradiction and conflict. Since the rise of postmodernism (*q.v.*), however, some have held the distinction between high art and the kitsch of popular culture to be untenable. Additionally, some would claim to be especially appreciative of kitsch, to possess a 'kitsch sensibility', which could be considered similar to camp (*q.v.*). *See also* CULTURE INDUSTRY.

knickerbocker group A group of early 19th c. New York writers. The term derives from *History of New York to the End of the Dutch Dynasty*, by Washington Irving, under the pseudonym Diedrich Knickerbocker (1809). Two of its more famous members were James Fenimore Cooper and Henry Wadsworth Longfellow. Later a publication called *Knickerbocker Magazine* was produced (1833–65), but by then the group had either died or dispersed.

Knittelvers (G 'cudgel verse') What we would call doggerel (*q.v.*); a term employed derogatorily in the 17th c. of a popular meter used in 15th and 16th c. German poetry. *Knittelvers* consisted of octosyllabic rhyming couplets. The meter was revived in the 18th c. by Gottsched, and then used by Schiller and Goethe.

kommos In classical Greek drama, a type of lyric in dialogue form sung by the Chorus (*q.v.*) to express profound emotion.

Kontrafaktur A German term to denote the adaptation of a secular song (e.g. a folksong) so that it has a religious theme and significance. Such adaptations were common in the 15th c. and there were a good many instances later. Luther's Christmas hymn *Vom Himmel hoch da komm ich her* (1535) is often cited as a notable example of the process.

kosmisty *See* SMITHY POETS.

Kraftgenie (G 'power genius') During the *Sturm und Drang* (*q.v.*) movement this term denoted creative and imaginative originality and dynamic energy. Goethe and some of his associates regarded themselves as *Kraftgenies*. The concept of such a personality/character in literature is to be found in such characters as Götz in Goethe's *Götz von Berlichingen* (1773) and in Simone Grisaldo, the eponymous hero of Klinger's play in 1776. *See also* OUTSIDER.

Künstlerdrama *See* KÜNSTLERROMAN.

Künstlernovelle   *See* KÜNSTLERROMAN.

Künstlerroman   (G *Künstler*, 'artist' + *Roman*, 'novel') A novel (*q.v.*) which has an artist (in any creative art) as the central character and which shows the development of the artist from childhood to maturity and later. This kind of novel was particularly popular in Germany and dates from very late in the 18th c. and the beginning of the 19th c. It thus coincides with the start of the romantic revival (*q.v.*), a period when the artist (whatever his *métier*) was held in high esteem, and the man of genius (*q.v.*) became an exalted figure. This 'exaltation' had been foreshadowed during the *Sturm und Drang* (*q.v.*) period by the German concept of the *Kraftgenie* (*q.v.*).

Fictitious artists were often favoured central figures. Goethe was among the first to develop the *Künstlerroman* with *Wilhelm Meisters theatralische Sendung* (composed *c.* 1777–85, but not discovered until 1909), the original version of *Wilhelm Meisters Lehrjahre* (1795–6), which had a sequel in the shape of *Wilhelm Meisters Wanderjahre oder Die Entsagenden*, his last novel, published in 1821. Other well-known examples are: Tieck's *Franz Sternbalds Wanderungen* (1798); Eduard Mörike's *Maler Nolten* (1832); Franz Grillparzer's *Novelle Der arme Spielmann* (1848); Gottfried Keller's *Der grüne Heinrich* (1854–5); Jakob Wassermann's *Das Gänsemännchen* (1915); Thomas Mann's *Novelle Tonio Kröger* (1903) and his *Doktor Faustus* (1947).

There are also a number of works whose central character is a historical figure. Examples are: Mörike's *Novelle Mozart auf der Reise nach Prag* (1855); Albert Brachvogel's *Friedemann Bach* (1858); Walter von Molo's *Der Schiller-Roman* (1912–16); and Franz Werfel's *Verdi* (1924).

Fictitious or historical *Künstlerdramen* ('artist plays') were also popular. For instance: Goethe's *Torquato Tasso* (1807); Grillparzer's *Sappho* (1818); Hauptmann's *Die versunkene Glocke* (1896), *Michael Kramer* (1900) and *Gabriel Schillings Flucht* (1912).

In English literature the most famous example of a *Künstlerroman* is James Joyce's *A Portrait of the Artist as a Young Man* (1916). The *Künstlerroman* and the *Bildungsroman* (*q.v.*) are closely associated, and literary historians and critics have put Goethe's *Wilhelm Meister* in the latter category. *See also* AUTOBIOGRAPHICAL NOVEL.

L

label names *See* APTRONYM.

Labrador, Juan A stock character (*q.v.*) – the Spanish folk hero and symbol of the hard-working peasant who achieves success through his own efforts. 'Immortalized' by Lope de Vega in his play *El villano en su rincón* (*c.* 1611).

lai *See* LAY.

laisse A stanzaic or verse paragraph (*q.v.*) division in OF epics.

lake poets Wordsworth, Coleridge and Southey. They came to be known as the Lake School or 'Lakers' as a result of the abusive articles written by Francis Jeffrey, a Scottish judge, in the *Edinburgh Review* over a period of twenty years – beginning in 1802. He associated these three poets with the Lake District in Cumbria. *See also* COCKNEY SCHOOL OF POETRY.

lament An expression of deep regret or sorrow for the loss of a person or position. A non-narrative kind of poetry, it appears to grow up alongside heroic poetry and is widespread in many languages. Famous examples are: *The Lamentations of Jeremiah*, David's Lament for Saul and Jonathan, the OE *Deor's Lament*, Dunbar's *Lament for the Makaris*, and Burns's *Lament for Flodden* and *Lament for Culloden*. *See* COMPLAINT; CORONACH; DIRGE; ELEGY; EPICEDIUM; MONODY; UBI SUNT.

lampoon The term derives from the French *lampon*, said to be from *lampons* 'Let us drink', used as a refrain. It dates only from the 17th c. The verb *lamper* means to 'swig' or 'to booze'. This suggests excess, coarseness, a rough crudity; a lampoon in fact is a virulent or scurrilous form of satire (*q.v.*). It is more likely to be found in graphic caricature than in writing but there are a few notable examples in literature, like Pope's attack on Hervey in his *Epistle to Arbuthnot*, and this description by Dryden of the unfortunate

---

A Dictionary of Literary Terms and Literary Theory, Fifth Edition. J. A. Cuddon.
© 2013 The Estate of J. A. Cuddon. Published 2013 by Blackwell Publishing Ltd.

Shadwell (here named Og) in *Absalom and Achitophel* (Pt II) beginning thus
at line 457:

> Now stop your noses, Readers, all and some,
> For here's a tun of Midnight work to come,
> Og from a Treason Tavern rowling home.
> Round as a Globe and Liquored ev'ry chink,
> Goodly and Great he Sayls behind his Link.
> With all this Bulk there's nothing lost in Og,
> For ev'ry inch that is not Fool is Rogue:
> A Monstrous mass of foul corrupted matter,
> As all the Devils had spew'd to make the batter.
> When wine has given him courage to Blaspheme,
> He curses God, but God before curst him;
> And if man cou'd have reason, none has more,
> That made his Paunch so rich and him so poor.

See also DIATRIBE; FLYTING; INVECTIVE; PASQUINADE.

langue and parole Terms introduced by Ferdinand de Saussure (1857–1913).
They make cardinal distinctions and are of fundamental importance to structuralism (*q.v.*). Their English equivalents are approximately, but inadequately,
'language' and 'speech'. *Langue* denotes the system or totality of language
shared by the 'collective consciousness'. Thus, all the elements of a language plus the rules for their combination (grammar, syntax and so forth).
Parole is the use which individuals make of the resources of language, which
the system produces and combines, in speech or writing. Thus, utterance.
Taken in conjunction the terms create an antinomy (*q.v.*) of the social and
shared. A further antinomy or dichotomy is implied in the idea that *langue*
is abstract and *parole* is concrete. *Langue* is what people use when thinking
and conceptualizing (abstract); *parole* what they use in speaking or writing
(concrete).

Saussure makes an evaluative distinction; as Raman Selden puts it: 'The
proper object of linguistic study is the system which underlies any particular
human signifying human practice, not the individual utterance.' That is,
langue is more important than *parole*.

Noam Chomsky (1928–) made a similar dichotomy with his terms 'competence' and 'performance' (*q.v.*). *See also* IDIOLECT; SEMIOTICS/SEMIOLOGY.

langue d'oc/langue d'oïl In Roman Gaul Latin was the lingua franca. In the
course of the Roman occupation the language underwent many changes and
developments in different regions and numerous dialects evolved. Gradually
these dialects formed two basic groups: *langue d'oc* and *langue d'oïl*. They
came to be thus called after the words used in them to represent *oui* ('yes'):
'oc' derived from Latin *hoc*; 'oïl' from a contraction or vocalic glide of Latin
hoc ille. The Provençal language *langue d'oc* was used south of a line which
ran approximately west to east from the Gironde (near Bordeaux) to the Alps.

Langue d'oïl was spoken north of that line. The latter evolved into the French language. Languedoc remains as the name of a large region in the south-east. The troubadours (*q.v.*) used *langue d'oc*; the *trouvères* (*q.v.*) used *langue d'oïl. See also* JONGLEUR.

lapidaires Medieval French works which expounded the talismanic and curative properties of precious stones. The discourse was sometimes accompanied by allegorical interpretations. Examples of *lapidaires* occur in the 12th and 13th c. Philippe de Thaon (12th c.) was the author of one. To about the same period belongs one in Latin by Marbode, the Bishop of Rennes.

Latinism A word, phrase, or grammatical construction based on a Latin form or model. Characteristic of many prose and verse styles from the 17th c. onwards; and particularly in the 18th c. when the influence of the Roman authors was at its strongest. Latinisms are common in Milton, Johnson and Gibbon, to name only three of the major influences.

lauda A religious poem or song adapted from the liturgy. The earliest examples were in Latin and date from the 13th c. Two well-known ones were the *Stabat Mater* and the *Dies Irae*. Later they were composed in the vernacular. St Francis produced a noble work in *Cantico delle Creature*, and Jacopone da Todi composed a fine collection of *laude*. The chanting of *laude* was an important part of the activities performed by *laudesi* fraternities. Religious sects like the *flagellanti* and *disciplinati* also made them a part of their ritual.

laureate *See* POET LAUREATE.

lay (OF *lai*) A short narrative or lyrical poem intended to be sung. The oldest narrative *lais*, mostly in octosyllabics (*q.v.*), are the *Contes* of Marie de France (*c.* 1175). They were stories of romance believed to have been based on Celtic legends. The lyric lays were Provençal and usually had love themes. The oldest in OF were by Gautier de Dargiès (early 13th c.). The term 'Breton lay' was applied to 14th c. English poems with a Breton setting and similar to those by Marie de France. A dozen or more are extant in English, the best known being *Sir Orfeo, Havelok the Dane, Sir Launfal* and Chaucer's *Franklin's Tale*. Since the 16th c. the term *lay* has been used more loosely to denote any historical ballad or narrative of adventure. Good examples are Scott's *Lay of the Last Minstrel* (1805) and Macaulay's *Lays of Ancient Rome* (1842). *See also* BALLAD; CONTE; FABLIAU; NOUVELLE; ROMANCE.

leaflet Related to the pamphlet and the tract (*qq.v.*), a leaflet is a small sheet of paper folded into two or more leaves (but not stitched) and containing printed matter. The leaflet developed late in the 19th c.

Leatherstocking Tales The title given to five novels by James Fenimore Cooper (1789–1851). They are novels of American frontier life, whose hero, Natty Bumppo, was nicknamed 'Leatherstocking'. *See also* WESTERN.

Leavisite A follower of F. R. Leavis (1895–1978); or descriptive of one who uses Leavis's methods and approach in the tasks of teaching and practical criticism (i.e. criticism based on the detailed analysis of a text). The term is used pejoratively by those who disagree with Leavis's methods. *See also* LIBERAL HUMANISM; NEW CRITICISM; PRACTICAL CRITICISM.

lectio difficilior (L 'the harder reading') That principle which may guide an editor in choosing between two manuscript variants of apparently equal authority.

lectionary From the Ecclesiastical Latin *lectionarium*, denoting a book containing extracts from the scriptures to be read at Divine Service.

ledger The word probably derives from OE *licgan*, 'to lie', *lecgan*, 'to lay', and denotes a register (*q.v.*) or account book; especially the principal books of accounts among merchants in which the entries in all the other books are entered. Thus a sort of centralized master-copy. *See also* BOOK; MANUSCRIPT; ROLL.

legend (MedL 'things to be read') Originally legends were the stories of lives of saints, which, in monastic life, might be read in church or in the refectory and therefore belonged to hagiography (*q.v.*). The term came to be applied to a collection of such stories (as well as the book in which they were recorded). An outstanding example of such a collection is the 13th c. *Legenda Aurea* ('The Golden Legend') of Jacobus de Voragine. Chaucer, no doubt, was using *legend* in a similar sense in his *Legend of Good Women*, a group of stories (in the manner of Ovid's *Heroides*) about famous women of antiquity (Cleopatra, Thisbe, Dido, Medea, Lucrece, Ariadne, Philomela *et al.*). Recently Slovene authors like Francé Berk and Ludvik Mrzel have revived the Chaucerian type in the reworking of biblical themes.

Subsidiary meanings of the term are: (a) the title or description beneath an illustration; (b) the explanation of the symbols on a map; (c) a story or narrative which lies somewhere between myth (*q.v.*) and historical fact and which, as a rule, is about a particular figure or person. Famous examples are Faust, the Flying Dutchman, the Wandering Jew, Hamlet, Beowulf, King Arthur, Charlemagne, Robin Hood, Jasonik (the Czech Robin Hood), Skandarbeg (the Albanian national hero), Marko Kraljević (the South Slav warrior hero) and Dhigenis (the Greek warrior hero). Any popular folk heroes (or heroines), revolutionaries, saints or warriors are likely to have legends develop about them; stories which often grow taller and longer with time and which may eventually be written down or recited in song, verse and ballad (*q.v.*), through which means the oral tradition (*q.v.*) is sustained. Two modern examples of such folk heroes are Salvatore Giuliano (the Sicilian Robin Hood-type bandit and political revolutionary) and Che Guevara. Quite often the stories and motifs which accrete to such figures had nothing to do with them in the first place. Recent and familiar examples of this accretive process are the many stories that have gathered about the names and personalities of men like W. G. Grace, Churchill, Rommel and Lord Montgomery – not to mention the statements ascribed to them.

legitimate theatre Often abbreviated in the business to 'legit'. It describes 'straight' drama; that is, a theatrical performance without songs, dances or musical accompaniments and interludes of any kind. The term derives from the old theatre-licensing laws, which were designed to cover only non-musical entertainments. These regulations could be evaded by the addition of musical interludes. *See* PATENT THEATRES.

Lehrstück (G 'didactic play') This term came into use in the 1920s to describe a kind of drama (which was related to music theatre, *q.v.*) whose purpose was to teach rather than to entertain an audience. It was very probably a development of Hindemith's *Gemeinschaftsmusik* ('community music'), presented in 1929 at the Baden-Baden chamber music festival. On that occasion Bertolt Brecht, Kurt Weill and Hindemith presented the *Badener Lehrstück vom Einverständnis* and the *Lindberghflug* (the latter on radio). The didactic element was political and derived from Brecht's study of Karl Marx. In the early 1930s Brecht produced other *Lehrstücke* with a Communist 'message'. They were *Der Jasager und der Neinsager*, *Die Massnahme* and *Die Ausnahme und die Regel*. *Lehrstücke* were an important part of his epic theatre (*q.v.*) and their creation was influenced by Japanese *Nō* drama (*q.v.*). *See also* AGIT-PROP DRAMA.

Lehrtheater *See* EPIC THEATRE; LEHRSTÜCK.

Leich (G 'lyric') A medieval German lyric (*q.v.*) form widely used between 1200 and 1350. It was sung to music and may have been accompanied by dance. Three main types have been distinguished: the *Tanzleich* or dance lyric; the *religiose Leich* or religious lyric; and the *Minneleich* or love lyric. It appears that after the 14th c. the form survived only in religious poetry.

leitmotif (G *Leitmotiv*, 'leading motif') A term coined by Hans von Wolzugen to designate a musical theme associated throughout a whole work with a particular object, character or emotion, as so often in Wagner's operas. Thomas Mann used it as a literary term to denote a recurrent theme (*q.v.*) or unit. It is occasionally used as a literary term in the same sense that Mann intended, and also in a broader sense to refer to an author's favourite themes: for example, the hunted man and betrayal in the novels of Graham Greene.

lemma The argument (*q.v.*) or subject of composition, prefixed as a heading or title.

Leonine rhyme A form of internal rhyme (*q.v.*) in which the word before the caesura (*q.v.*) rhymes with the last word of the line of verse. Traditionally it is named after Leo, a 12th c. canon of St Victor's in Paris, whose Latin verses contained such a device. However, Ovid used it in *Ars Amatoria*, and the OE *Rhyming Poem* is also Leonine. Tennyson used it at random in *The Revenge*, from which these lines come:

> And the stately Spanish men to their flagship bore him then,
> Where they laid him by the mast, old Sir Richard caught at last,

And they praised him to his face with their courtly foreign grace;
But he rose upon their decks, and he cried:
'I have fought for Queen and Faith like a valiant man and true;
I have only done my duty as a man is bound to do:
With a joyful spirit I Sir Richard Grenville die!'
And he fell upon their decks, and he died.

See also CROSS-RHYME; RHYME.

letter Latin rhetoricians made a convenient distinction between the private letter (*personalis*) and the letter of affairs (*negotialis*). A third kind is the open or general letter addressed to an individual or a newspaper editor, and intended for publication. Some manuals of letters survive from Classical times. In the Middle Ages there were a large number of manuals on the subject. Many medieval treatises on rhetoric were also 'guides' to letter writing.

Nearly any sort of letter may be of use to the historian and the biographer. A very famous collection is *The Paston Letters* (*c.* 1422–1509), the correspondence of three generations of a Norfolk family. Other well-known collections of letters are those written by Mozart, Keats, Flaubert and Horace Walpole.

The letter form has been adapted and exploited in various ways since the 17th c. For example, there are Pascal's *Lettres Provinciales* (1656–7), a defence of Jansenism, dealing with divine grace and the ethical code of the Jesuits. Between 1687 and 1694 were published *Letters of a Turkish Spy*, a form of travel book (*q.v.*) in epistolary form which started a new genre in European literature. These pseudo-foreign letters purport to be written by a Turkish spy who sends in reports on various aspects of life in England, France, Spain and Italy. A better-known example of this genre is Montesquieu's *Letters Persanes* (1721). Voltaire made a highly individual contribution with *Lettres philosophiques* (1734), better known as *Lettres Anglaises*. Another similar work was Madame de Graffigny's *Lettres d'une Péruvienne* (1747). Lady Mary Wortley Montague also wrote a series of very entertaining *Turkish Letters* (1763) which gave an account of her travels in the Near East.

In the 18th c. the form of the epistolary novel (*q.v.*) was developed. Such novels included: Richardson's *Pamela* (1740), and his *Clarissa* (1747–8); Smollett's *Humphry Clinker* (1771), one of the best of the genre; and the French classic by Laclos, *Les Liaisons dangereuses* (1782). Lord Chesterfield's *Letters* to his natural son, Philip Stanhope, written almost every day from 1737 onwards, were intended to educate any young man. In fact, the whole collection combined a treatise of education with the kind of advice found in the courtesy book (*q.v.*).

During the 18th c. the letter served other purposes. Examples are: Bolingbroke's *Letter to Sir William Wyndham* (1717), a political polemic; Rousseau's *Lettre à D'Alembert sur les spectacles* (1758), a controversial treatise on the morality of drama; the *Letters of Junius*, a pseudonymous invective against individuals, published in the *Public Advertiser* (1769–71); and Edmund Burke's *A Letter to the Sheriffs of Bristol* (1777), a political address.

In the following century, two remarkable examples of letters are: Sydney Smith's *Letters of Peter Plymley* (1807), a defence of Catholic emancipation; and the correspondence, published as part of Cardinal Newman's *Apologia Pro Vita Sua*, between Charles Kingsley and Newman. Other notable writers of letters have been George Sand, Byron, Chateaubriand, Proust, Gide and Claudel, and D. H. Lawrence. More recently, Albert Camus's *Lettres à un ami allemand* (1948) have shown once again the flexibility of the letter form. This distinguished work is more like an essay, or open letter, in which Camus argues moral issues arising from differing German and French attitudes. *See* EPISTLE.

letters patent *See* PATENT THEATRES.

lettrism A French literary movement founded in Paris in 1946 and particularly associated with Maurice Lemaître and Isidore Isou. Its members experimented with forms of concrete poetry and pattern poems (*qq.v.*). They produced what is called phonetic poetry, and toyed with 'hypergraphy', or picture-writing. Some of it is mere gimmickry.

level stress Also known as even accent (*q.v.*), it occurs when the stress falls evenly on two syllables in the same word, or on two adjacent monosyllables, e.g. *buckwheat*; *gang plank. See* HOVERING STRESS; SPONDEE.

lexicographer A maker of dictionaries. In Johnson's famous phrase 'a harmless drudge'.

lexicography The art or task of making a dictionary (*q.v.*).

lexicon The dictionary (*q.v.*) itself, but usually the term denotes a dictionary for Classical languages; also Hebrew and Arabic. *See also* ONOMASTICON.

lexis In computational stylistics (that is, the analysis of an author's writing by computerized measurement) *lexis* is the term for the actual vocabulary of the author while *taxis* denotes the arrangement of the words. For instance, the lexical/taxical computation of the works of James Joyce would show the frequency of the recurrence of words and parts of speech; an analysis of grammatical structure; the number of times a particular word was used per page; the number of ablative absolutes (for example) per chapter; variations from normal order or structure; length of words by letters and by syllables; and length of sentences. Actually, this branch of linguistic science is not new. A Sanskrit grammar of *c.* 500 BC provides the number of syllables, words and verses in the *Rig-Veda*. Though this might appear to be one of the less fruitful activities of the academic industry, it has been helpful in reconstructing blurred and missing passages in the Dead Sea Scrolls.

liaison (F 'binding' or 'joining', formed from *lier*, 'to bind') In the 17th c. a dramatic principle which required that the parts of a play be linked by various kinds of liaison: (a) *présence* – a character remaining from the preceding scene; (b) *vue ou recherche* – a character entering sees another about to leave and vice versa; (c) *bruit* – a noise on stage which brings in a character in search of an explanation; (d) *discours* – when a character in hiding later speaks.

liberal humanism A term for the kind of 'traditional' literary scholarship that does not subscribe to any theoretical school of thought, e.g. Marxist criticism, feminist criticism or new historicism (*qq.v.*). Indeed, liberal humanist critics are often hostile to what they see as the encroachment of overly politicized and often abstruse theory into the field of literary criticism. Such theorizing, they contend, often fails to comprehend the importance of literary imagination and creativity. The term, which is largely pejorative, was first used in the 1970s following the rise of theory in literary studies. To those committed to one theoretical tendency or another, the 'liberal' articulates the political complacency of traditional scholarship, the 'humanism' the belief in the universality of literature, that good literature benefits all humanity. The numerous and various critics of liberal humanism have argued rather that literature (and indeed language) contains no inherent truth; its meaning and value are always culturally and historically situated. Moreover, literature rarely promotes the interests of all humanity, but usually those of ruling elites. Thus the term – yet another 'ism' – is employed to foreground how traditional literary criticism is not without theoretical underpinnings or political assumptions.

Liberal humanism was one of the predominant dispositions of literary criticism from the rise of literary study as an academic discipline in the mid 19th c until the 1960s. Its primary intellectual impetus came from figures such as Matthew Arnold, Irving Babbitt and F. R. Leavis. Many literary scholars still hold to liberal humanist positions, even if they do not use the term to describe their activities. Polemical responses to what is usually seen as theory's malign influence can be found in such titles as Helen Gardner's *In Defence of the Imagination* (1984), Robert Alter's *The Pleasures of Reading in an Ideological Age* (1989), and George Watson's *The Certainty of Literature* (1989). *See also* HUMANISM; POSTSTRUCTURALISM.

libretto (It 'little book') The text of an opera or operetta (*qq.v.*) or any fairly substantial vocal composition, like an oratorio, which involves dialogue and narrative. The term was first used in England in 1742. Well-known librettists include Quinault, Catzabigi, da Ponte, Schikaneder, Boito, Gilbert, Hofmannsthal, J. B. Priestley and W. H. Auden.

Lied *See* MEISTERGESANG.

life writing A term, first used in the 18th c. and increasingly favoured within academic circles since the 1980s, that is employed to describe all kinds of accounts of individual lives and life experience. The study of life writing is now an established area of literary enquiry. Sometimes 'auto/biography' is used as an alternative term. Life writing, however, incorporates not only narratives which would be recognized as either biography or autobiography (*qq.v.*), but also diaries, journals, blogs, testimonies and private letters. Scholars of life writing have become particularly interested in a number of issues, namely, the ways in which a sense of 'self' is constructed – and, equally, contested – through narrative; the relationship between that self and the rest of society; the significance of 'ordinary' lives; and the precariousness of 'authentic' representation. Throughout the 20th c., and particularly since the rise of postmodernism (*q.v.*), many writers of life narrative have demonstrated an acute awareness that lives and selves are largely, and inevitably, fictionalizations; the coinages 'autobiografiction' (by Stephen Reynolds) and 'biomythography' (by Audre Lorde) denote life writing which purposely blurs fiction and autobiography. *See also* BLOG; CREATIVE NON-FICTION; DIARY AND JOURNAL; LETTER; TESTAMENT.

light comedy A loose term for plays which are airy, graceful, amusing (perhaps witty) and light-hearted, and which make minimal or no demands emotionally or intellectually. Among numerous examples the following are well-known repertory pieces: Noël Coward's *Hay Fever* (1925) and his *Blithe Spirit* (1941), Terence Rattigan's *French without Tears* (1936), William Douglas Home's *The Chiltern Hundreds* (1947) and his *The Reluctant Débutante* (1955). *See also* COMEDY; COMEDY OF HUMOURS; COMEDY OF MANNERS; DOMESTIC COMEDY; FARCE.

light ending *See* FEMININE ENDING.

light rhyme When one of a pair of rhyming syllables is unstressed. Common in ballad (*q.v.*), as in this stanza from the traditional ballad *Young Beichan*:

> O whan the porter came up the stair.
> He's fa'n low down upon his knee:
> 'Won up, won up, ye proud porter,
> An what makes a' this courtesy?'

light stress In verse, stress (*q.v.*) on a word which is not normally accented in speech. In the following lines from Edgar Allan Poe's *The Raven* the trochaic and dactylic meter requires a number of light stresses:

> Ónce ŭpón ă mídnĭght dreárў, whíle Ĭ póndĕrĕd, weák ănd weárў,
> Óvĕr mánў ă quáint ănd cúrĭŏŭs vólŭme ŏf fŏrgóttĕn lóre,
> Whíle Ĭ nóddĕd, néarlў náppĭng, súddĕnlў thére cáme ă táppĭng,
> Ás ŏf sóme ŏne géntlў ráppĭng.

light verse A vague and comprehensively flexible term used to describe poetry that lacks serious intent. Under this heading one might place *vers de société*, occasional verse, nonsense verse, sick verse, satire, burlesque, parody, epitaph, epigram, limerick and clerihew (*qq.v.*), not to mention the acrostic and emblematic poems, the jingle and the riddle (*qq.v.*) and punning verses. The following lines, from A. H. Bullen's *Musa Proterva* (1889), suggest the main attributes of light verse:

> Gay, frolic verse for idle hours,
> Light as the foam whence Venus sprang;

> Strains heard of old in courtly bowers,
> When Nelly danced and Durfey sang.

Wit, elegance, grace, ingenuity and technical virtuosity are among the distinguishing characteristics of light verse, as brilliantly displayed in, say, the libretti of W. S. Gilbert.

Among anthologies of light verse one might mention Thomas D'Urfey's *Wit and Mirth, or Pills to Purge Melancholy* (1719); Locker-Lampson's *Lyra Elegantiarum* (1867); and A. H. Bullen's *Lyrics from the Song-Books of the Elizabethan Age* (1888); as well as his *Speculum Amantis* (1888) and *Musa Proterva* (1889). *The Oxford Book of Light Verse* (1938), edited by W. H. Auden, illustrates better than most the possible scope of the form.

Much light verse is anonymous. Among the many famous and accomplished practitioners in English, mention should be made of Skelton, Campion, Herrick, Lovelace, Samuel Butler, Prior, Goldsmith, Cowper, Hood, Theodore Hook, Oliver Wendell Holmes, C. S. Calverley, W. M. Praed, Edward Lear, Austin Dobson, Lewis Carroll, W. S. Gilbert, Hilaire Belloc, G. K. Chesterton, A. P. Herbert, T. S. Eliot, e. e. cummings, John Betjeman and Ogden Nash.

ligne donnée (F 'given line') Paul Valéry (1871–1945) spoke of the *ligne donnée* of a poem, thereby meaning the line that is 'given' to the poet by God, or by nature, or by a muse (*q.v.*), or by some power outside himself. The implication is that he has to find the other lines for himself. *See* AFFLATUS; DONNÉE; FANCY AND IMAGINATION; INSPIRATION; INVENTION; SPONTANEITY.

limerick A type of light verse (*q.v.*) and a particular popular fixed verse form in English. It usually consists of five predominantly anapaestic lines rhyming aabba, as in:

> Titian was mixing rose madder.
> His model posed nude on a ladder.
> Her position to Titian
> Suggested coition.
> So he nipped up the ladder and 'ad 'er.

From this it will be seen that the first, second, and fifth lines are trimeters (*q.v.*), and the third and fourth dimeters (*q.v.*), though these two may be printed as a single line with internal rhyme (*q.v.*). The origin of the term is obscure. One theory is that it stems from the refrain 'Will you come up to Limerick?' sung at convivial settings where such nonsense verses were fashionable. It may be a much older form than has been supposed. Stephano's drinking song in *The Tempest* (II, ii) has a characteristic limerick rhythm. And the following lines date from an 11th c. manuscript:

> The lion is wondrous strong
> And full of the wiles of wo;
> And whether he pleye

> Or take his preye
> He cannot do but slo [i.e. slay].

The limerick is to be found in the *History of Sixteen Wonderful Old Women* (1820) and in *Anecdotes and Adventures of Fifteen Gentlemen* (1822). Edward Lear, who composed a great many limericks, cited this latter volume as the source of his idea of the form. Lear popularized it in his *Book of Nonsense* (1846). Distinguished writers experimented with the form, and by the end of the 19th c. it was well established in both the clean and bawdy varieties. Early in the 20th c. it became very popular and newspapers even ran weekly competitions inviting readers to submit examples or to complete the final line of a given verse.

Many of the best limericks are ribald, such as:

> A vice both obscure and unsavoury
> Kept the bishop of Leicester in slavery.
> Amidst terrible howls
> He deflowered young owls,
> In a crypt fitted out as an aviary.

Modest form though it be, it has lent itself to not a few developments and intricate variations, including the limeraiku (modelled on the *haiku, q.v.,* and invented by Ted Pauker):

> There's a vile old man
> Of Japan who roars at whores:
> 'Where's your bloody fan?'

And the limick, which Ogden Nash excelled at:

> A young flirt of Ceylon
> Who led the boys on,
> Playing 'Follow the Leda',
> Succumbed to a swan.

And the limerick poem, of which a famous example is the anonymous Old Man of Nantucket –

> Who kept his cash in a bucket.
> His daughter, called Nan,
> Ran away with a man,
> And as for the bucket, Nantucket.

And so on. *See also* MACARONIC.

liminality (L *limen*, 'threshold') A term much used in anthropology and literary and cultural theory to designate a space or state which is situated in between other, usually more clearly defined, spaces, periods or identities. The threshold, the foundational metaphor, occupies a liminal space between the inside and outside of a house; dawn and dusk hold liminal positions between night and day; transgender and intersex people assume liminal identities in relation to the established categories of gender. The latter example is suggestive of how liminality might be disruptive of dominant discursive frameworks: it defies boundaries and erases the differences upon which regulatory frameworks depend. In postcolonial theory (*q.v.*), for instance, the concept has been employed to consider how the contact zone (*q.v.*) exists as a cultural space in between that of the colonizer and the colonized; in these liminal spaces of transcultural exchange, the colonized subject may find resources and strategies for self-transformation that upset the fixed polarities of colonial discourse. *See also* HYBRIDITY; QUEER THEORY.

limited edition An edition of a work which is restricted to a certain number of copies. They are usually numbered and the book is not reprinted in the same form.

line A formal structural division in a poem, normally classified according to the number of feet it contains. For example, a pentameter (*q.v.*) contains five feet, a hexameter (*q.v.*) six feet, and so on. *See* FOOT; METER.

line endings In prosody there are two general types, according to the position of the final stress (*q.v.*) near the end of the line. A masculine ending has the stress on the final syllable; the feminine has the last stress on the penultimate (occasionally the ante-penultimate) syllable. The following verse from Sir John Suckling illustrates the two basic kinds:

> Why so pale and wan, fond lover?
> Prithee, why so pale?
> Will, when looking well can't move her,
> Looking ill prevail?
> Prithee, why so pale?

The first and third lines are feminine; the others masculine.

Blank verse (*q.v.*), especially in Tudor and Jacobean drama, has many feminine endings (*q.v.*), which help to preserve colloquial speech rhythms.

lingo A loosely colloquial term for a foreign language or any strange unintelligible speech; as in 'Do you speak the lingo?' It probably derives from Portuguese *lingoa*, from Latin *lingua*, 'a tongue'.

linguistics The scientific study of language. Descriptive linguistics classifies the characteristics; historical or comparative linguistics deals with its growth and development. The principal branches of linguistics are: etymology, semantics, phonetics, morphology and syntax. *See* DEEP STRUCTURE.

linguistic turn An important development in Western philosophy that took place in the early 20th c. which saw philosophers become increasingly focused on language. The linguistic turn is associated with the emergence of 'analytic philosophy', which has dominated the discipline in the Anglophone academy. The term became established after the publication of Richard Rorty's anthology *The Linguistic Turn* in 1967 (though it was first used by

Austrian philosopher Gustav Bergmann). Gottlob Frege (1848–1925), G. E. Moore (1873–1958) and Bertrand Russell (1872–1970) were all influential figures in the rise of language philosophy. However, the work of Ludwig Wittgenstein (1889–1951) has undeniably been the most important. In his *Tractatus Logico-Philosophicus* (1921) Wittgenstein argued that the logical structure of language defines what can be said meaningfully, and therefore, what can be thought. Thus the limits of language, for Wittgenstein, define the limits of thought. He insisted that most of the problems in philosophy – including metaphysics, ethics and aesthetics – had to do not with empirical error but with mistakes in the use of language. Later, in his *Philosophical Investigations* (published posthumously in 1953), Wittgenstein famously distanced himself from his earlier assertions about language, and argued that the meanings of words are derived from their use in specific language communities (a position which has come to be known as 'ordinary language philosophy'). Yet he still considered many of the problems in the history of philosophy to stem from the misuse, or 'bewitchments', of language and, more profoundly, a misunderstanding of the way language works.

Even though *Philosophical Investigations* is often thought to be the single most important philosophical work of the 20th c., Wittgenstein's influence on literary theory has been modest at best. Since the 1970s, 'the linguistic turn' has been widely used to describe the influence of developments in 'continental philosophy' (as opposed to analytic or 'Anglo-American' philosophy) in the humanities. This focus on language began with structuralism (*q.v.*), which largely gave way to poststructuralism (*q.v.*) in the late 1960s. The ideas of poststructuralist thinkers such as Lacan, Derrida and Foucault, which stress how language structures thought and subjectivity, have been especially influential. *See* also POSTSTRUCTURALISM; PSYCHOANALYTIC CRITICISM.

linked rhyme *See* RHYME.

linked sonnet *See* SPENSERIAN SONNET.

lipogram A work which avoids using a particular letter of the alphabet, such as George Perec's *La Disparition* (1969), translated into English as a lipogram by Gilbert Adair (*A Void*, 1995). Although the exercise is of ancient origin, the lipogram has become the special province of the group of writers known as Oulipo (*q.v.*).

lira (Sp 'lyre') A Spanish stanza form and a special form of the *canción* (*q.v.*). It consists of a combination of five eleven-syllable and seven-syllable lines rhyming ababb. The name derives from Garcilaso de la Vega's fifth *canción*, which begins 'Si de me baja lira'.

lisible (F 'legible') Roland Barthes's term (from *S/Z*, 1970) for the 'readerly' (usually 'classic') text which is experienced with little interpretive effort; the lisible is opposed to the 'scriptible' ('writerly'), the usually modernist work whose texture is complex, possibly even opaque, and requires the analytical intervention of the reader. The 'scriptible' insists on the collusion of the reader in the production of meaning; the lisible relies on established literary conventions recognized (perhaps unconsciously) by the reader, and does not, as part of its aesthetic, attempt to impose its own mechanics as the subject of interpretation. *See also* READERLY/WRITERLY.

litany (Gk 'supplication') A liturgical prayer consisting of a series of petitions or invocations, often chanted by a church choir in procession.

literae humaniores (L 'the more humane letters') The phrase denotes the 'classics', namely Latin and Greek, and is usually used in connection with the study of the Classics. At Oxford University *literae humaniores* (often abbreviated *lit. hum.*) refers to the study of them in a degree course referred to as 'Mods and Greats' (courses lasting five terms for 'Mods' or 'Moderations' and seven terms for 'Greats'). It is not clear when *literae humaniores* came to denote Latin and Greek and their study, but during the Renaissance period it seems to have denoted the works of Classical Latin and Greek authors, as opposed to the theological works of the medieval schoolmen.

Dictionaries provide a reference to *literae humaniores* used as a phrase in 1747. As a degree course at Oxford, *literae humaniores* came into existence with the New Examination Statute of 1800. It was not confined to Classics. Candidates were examined in Divinity, Ethics, Rhetoric, Logic, Mathematics and Natural Philosophy as well as in 'the chief Latin and Greek classics'. The first Honours Examination under the new statute was held in 1802. In 1807 a new Honours School of Mathematics and Physics appeared as a separate entity from *literae humaniores*. Classics were also introduced.

In 1850 a new First Public Examination was introduced to come between Responsions and the Final Schools ('Schools' denotes final exams which are conducted in the 'Schools' building). It soon became known as 'Moderations' or 'Mods' after the Moderators who conducted it, the term 'Examiners' being properly reserved for those who examined the Final Schools. Seven Moderators were appointed, of whom four examined in Greek and Latin literature and three in Maths. It seems that 'Greats' had already been for some time in use as a slang term for the Final Honours School. It is not clear when the pattern of five terms for 'Mods' and seven for 'Greats' became fixed. The present structure may have arisen because undergraduates studied the poets and orators for 'Mods' and the philosophers and historians for 'Greats'. In the latter years of the 19th c. more emphasis came to be laid on philosophy and Greek and Roman history in their own rights. The pattern appears to have been well established by the 1890s. *See also* JESUIT DRAMA; SCHOLASTICISM; SCHOOL DRAMA.

literal Several meanings may be distinguished: (a) the misprint of a letter; (b) taking the meaning of words in their primary and non-figurative sense, as in literal interpretation; (c) giving an exact rendering of something, as in literal translation; (d) an opinion based on what is actually written, as opposed to what is implied. *See* FIGURATIVE LANGUAGE.

literariness The object of literary studies in the early phase of Russian Formalism (*q.v.*). Roman Jakobson defined it thus in 1919: 'The subject of literary science is not literature, but literariness, i.e. that which makes a given work a literary work.' Literariness is closely associated with what is known as defamiliarization (*q.v.*): both concepts emphasize that the defining features of a literary work reside in its form.

literary forgeries The dividing line between a forgery and a hoax may often appear to be thin. However, basically, a forger has a serious intention to deceive and maintain a deception. And he is likely to show much determination in avoiding exposure. Motives are various. Forgery may be for monetary gain, for revenge, to make a fool of someone (or many), or to discredit an authority; or merely to enjoy the vicarious laurels of anonymous fame in secrecy and privacy. Pride, vanity, spite and disappointment may all be motivating forces. A hoaxer, on the other hand, has a more light-hearted approach, regards the deception as a joke and, sooner or later, 'comes clean'.

Early examples of forgery date from pre-Christian times. Heraclides Ponticus (4th c. BC) was alleged to have presented his own tragedies under the name of Thespis, the first Athenian tragic poet; and Lobon of Argos was accused of composing verses that he 'quoted' in a work on poets and poetry. Since those times, there have been celebrated instances of forgery. One of the best known concerns the *Letters of Phalaris* (148 in all), about which there was a dispute in the 17th c. The affair was satirized by Swift in *The Battle of the Books* (1697).

During the early Renaissance, frauds of one kind and another proliferated as a result of the widespread enthusiasm for antiquity and classical learning. Some of the most famous were contained in the *Antiquitatum variorum volumina* of Johannes Annius (1432–1502). These included matter ascribed to Fabius Pictor and Myrilus and the five spurious books of Berosus.

In *c.* 1660 certain erotic dialogues were ascribed to Luisa Sigea, a Spanish bluestocking (*q.v.*). They were in fact composed by one Nicolas Chorier, an antiquarian and a lawyer, who claimed that his Latin was a translation of Luisa's Spanish.

The annals of English literature contain some fine examples of fraudulence in the 18th c. An influential series of forgeries – which had some bearing on the 18th c. cult of primitivism (*q.v.*) – were those perpetrated by the Scot James Macpherson (1736–96). These came to be known as the Ossianic forgeries.

Enthusiasm for Shakespeare's plays in the 18th c. also produced a spate of forgeries. George Steevens forged a letter from Peele to Marlowe on Shakespeare and passed it off for many years. William Henry Ireland (1777–1835) produced a mortgage-deed relating to Shakespeare, then extracts from a play titled *William the Conqueror* and then a complete play – *Vortigern and Rowena* – which Sheridan produced at Drury Lane in 1796. Another prominent forger of Shakespeareana was John Payne Collier (1789–1883), who, as librarian to the Duke of Devonshire, had access to privileged documents and produced a succession of frauds.

In the 19th c., Thomas James Wise (1859–1937), the bibliographer, collector and editor who formed the great Ashley Library, persuaded the printers Richard Clay & Sons to produce editions of short works by established authors that antedated the accepted first editions. His authors included Thackeray, Robert Browning, Elizabeth Browning, Matthew Arnold, George Eliot, Ruskin, Tennyson, Swinburne and Kipling. His masterpiece was Elizabeth Browning's *Sonnets* (Reading, 1847), which he launched in 1893. Wise was ultimately exposed in 1934 in *An Enquiry into the Nature of Certain Nineteenth Century Pamphlets* by John Carter and Graham Pollard. They cited fifty-four fraudulent works. Over thirty more were found in later years.

After the Second World War a sensation was caused by the so-called diary of Hitler's mistress Eva Braun. It was serialized in some newspapers and then found to have been composed of passages taken from *Meine Vergangenheit* by the Countess Larisch (which was first published in England in 1913). The *Hitler Diaries*, purchased by the West German news magazine *Stern* in 1983 for 10 million German marks, were also revealed to be forgeries, copied, for the most part, from Hitler's speeches by a forger named Konrad Kujau. An account of the affair is given in Robert Harris's *Selling Hitler: The Story of the Hitler Diaries* (1986).

Literary forgery has seldom been a subject or theme in fiction, but Rudyard Kipling wrote one ingenious short story, *Dayspring Mishandled* (1928), which treats it cleverly and convincingly. It is also prominent in Peter Ackroyd's novel *Chatterton* (1987).

There have been numerous literary hoaxes. Among the most successful were those achieved by Prosper Mérimée (1803–70), who began his literary career with *Le Théâtre de Clara Gazul* (1825), which purported to be a translation of six short plays by the Spanish actress 'Clara Gazul'. These were published anonymously. Her portrait (a faked portrait of the 22-year-old Mérimée in a mantilla) appeared as the frontispiece. A second augmented edition (1830) included *Le Carrosse du Saint-Sacrement* (1829), a fine one-act play (*q.v.*). Mérimée followed his original success with another work under the improbable and exotic pseudonym of Hyacinthe Maglanowich. *La Guzla* (1827) was more ambitious, for it comprised 'translations' of Illyrian national songs and poems. *See* PLAGIARISM; PSEUDEPIGRAPHA.

literary prizes The prize system in general is a 20th c. phenomenon that pervades all classes of Western society and a wide range of activities. It may be argued that the need and desire to assess, judge, grade and reward human effort and attainment is a malaise of increasingly decadent humanism (*q.v.*) which perceives worldly success and its recognition to be an essential part of this life.

The Booker McConnell prize, which became the Man Booker prize (*q.v.*), has been the best-known literary prize in Britain since 1969. The Whitbread Literary Awards (for novel, first novel, biography, children's novel and poetry) are also well known, as is the Orange Prize for Fiction, for women writers in English. The prestigious Commonwealth Writers' Prize, established in 1987 (now the Commonwealth Book Prize), recognizes the best fiction by new and established writers in the Commonwealth countries – countries formerly part of the British Empire – in order, in part, to ensure that these works reach a wider audience outside of their countries of origin.

In the United States the main prize is the Pulitzer, established in 1917 under the will of Joseph Pulitzer, a newspaper proprietor. The prizes are confined to American citizens and are offered in the interests of poetry, drama, the novel, biography and American history. Several prizes are awarded by the American Academy of Arts and Letters. They include the annual Award of Merit medal (for a novel, poetry, drama, painting and sculpture in rotation), the William Dean Howells Medal for fiction (every five years) and the Emerson–Thoreau Medal for a writer's whole achievement in literature.

In France societies and academies award many of the prizes. The Académie Française awards several each year, including the Prix du Roman. The Prix Goncourt is among the most prestigious and influential awards. It is given by the Académie Goncourt (founded in 1903) and goes to the best imaginative prose work, preferably a novel, published in the preceding year.

The most prestigious international prize is the Nobel Prize (*q.v.*) for Literature, awarded annually by the Swedish Academy, which honours any writer who, in the literary field, has produced 'the most outstanding work in an ideal direction'.

Various genres of fiction have their own special prizes. Science fiction (*q.v.*) has the Hugo and the Nebula awards. The world of crime fiction, mystery, suspense and detection also has its own prizes. The Crime Writers' Association gives annual awards for crime fiction and non-fiction: it currently has nine Dagger awards, including Diamond, Gold and Steel. In the US, the Mystery Writers of America presents the Edgar Awards, named after Edgar Allan Poe.

literati (L 'the learned') This term was introduced by Robert Burton (1577–1640), the author of *The Anatomy of Melancholy* (1621), who used it to describe the literate class in China. Later it denoted writers and readers of 'fashionable' literature and it was also used in reference to the habitués of the literary clubs of 18th c. Edinburgh and to the professional men (e.g. lawyers, clergymen) who were supporters of the Moderate party in the Church of Scotland. More generally, the term is used (sometimes not wholly seriously) to describe men of letters and learned men. The meaning is not dissimilar to *cognoscenti* – 'those who know' or who are 'in the know'.

literature A broad term which usually denotes works which belong to the major genres: epic, drama, lyric, novel, short story, ode (*qq.v.*). Traditionally, if we describe something as 'literature', as opposed to anything else, the term carries with it qualitative connotations which imply that the work in question has superior qualities; that it is well above the ordinary run of written works.

However, there are many works which cannot be classified in the main literary genres which nevertheless may be regarded as literature by virtue of the excellence of their writing, their originality and their general aesthetic and artistic merits. Recent challenges to the canon (*q.v.*), debates about what constitutes artistic merit, and theorization of genres like children's literature (*q.v.*) and graphic novels (*q.v.*) have made this term vastly more comprehensive and far less indicative of aesthetic hierarchy.

literature of escape From the First and Second World Wars came many books about escaping from confinement – mostly from prisoner-of-war camps. They form almost a minor genre of their own, and many of them, apart from being very exciting, are well written. Well-known examples from the First World War are H. E. Hervey's *Cagebirds*; H. G. Durnford's *The Tunnellers of Holzminden*; *Escapers All* by various contributors; and *The Escaping Club*. Probably the most famous from the Second World War is *The Wooden Horse* (1949) by Eric Williams. There have been many others, including T. D. Teare's *The Evader*; André Devigny's *Escape from Montluc*; David James's *A Prisoner's Progress*; Airey Neave's *They Have Their Exits*; George Millar's *Horned Pigeon*; Anthony Deane-Drummond's *Return Ticket*; W. B. Thomas's *Dare to be Free*; Peter Medd's *The Long Walk Home*; W. K. Sexton's *We Fought for Freedom*; and Anthony Farrar-Hockley's *The Edge of the Sword*. More recently, Stephen King's novella *Rita Hayworth and Shawshank Redemption* (1982) exemplifies the suspenseful narration characteristic of literature of escape.

literature of terror *See* GOTHIC NOVEL/FICTION; HORROR STORY.

litotes (Gk from *litós*, 'single, simple, meagre') A figure of speech which contains an understatement for emphasis, and is therefore the opposite of hyperbole (*q.v.*). Often used in everyday speech (frequently with a negative assertion) and usually with laconic or ironic intentions. A stock instance is 'not bad' meaning 'very good'. *See also* IRONY; MEIOSIS; PARADIASTOLE.

littérateur (F 'a man of letters') One who devotes himself to the study of writing of literature. It may also suggest an *amateur* or *dilettante*.

little magazines Minority periodicals which publish poetry, fiction, reviews, etc. by relatively little-known writers, emphasize experimentation, and target a smaller audience in comparison with larger, commercial periodicals and scholarly publications. There have been many of them and they have tended to have rather brief lives. It may be that they received their epithet 'little' after the American literary magazine *The Little Review* (founded in 1914). Some of the early 'little' magazines were *The Savoy* (founded 1896), *Rhythm* (1911–13), *Blast* (1914–15), the organ of Vorticism (*q.v.*), and *New Verse* (1933–9). Other notable examples are *Stand* (1952), *Ambit* (1959), *Agenda* (1959), *The Review* (1962) and *The New Review* (1974–9). Little magazines like *Ploughshares* (1971), *Granta* (1889) and *The Paris Review* (1953) still provide entries into the publishing world for young and new writers.

liturgical drama Drama originating in the medieval church and its ritual forms of worship, especially that of the chanted dialogue between the celebrant and the congregation during Mass. Both medieval practitioners and modern historians have described the Mass as a kind of ritual drama, with setting, impersonation of character, and even comic plot (because it 'begins in adversity and ends in peace'). Secular drama in the form of Passion, Miracle and Mystery Plays (*qq.v.*), developed beyond the church in the communities, probably has its roots in liturgical drama. (See O. B. Hardison, *Christian Rite and Christian Drama in the Middle Ages*, 1965.) As services were elaborated additional melodies (and tropes, *q.v.*, in dialogue form) were interpolated. These plays became more popular, vernacular elements were introduced and the laity as well as the clergy took part in them. They are almost certainly the source of the Mystery Plays (*q.v.*). *See also* MIRACLE PLAY.

Liverpool poets A group of poets native to the city of Liverpool who, in the early 1960s, began to give public recitals of their work, often to the accompaniment of music. Their emergence coincided with that of the pop group the Beatles, and with the advent of the Anglo-American jazz poetry (*q.v.*) movement. The principal poets were Roger McGough, Brian Patten and Adrian Henri. Robustly Liverpudlian, witty, slangy and sometimes bawdy, their work reached a sizeable pop audience. At first they were looked at somewhat askance by serious critics, but by the 1970s they had become more or less famous through various anthologies and it was realized what fine poets they were. Their merits were even appreciated by school examination boards.

Living Newspaper A form of political propaganda (*q.v.*) drama which uses topical material and journalistic techniques in the treatment of current social and political issues. It might also be described as a kind of documentary revue (*q.v.*). Such plays are usually presented in a series of short scenes and they are often satirical. The invention of this dramatic form is usually attributed to the Red Army of Soviet Russia during the Revolution. The Department of Agitation and Propaganda (Agitprop) was created in 1920 as a part of the Central Committee Secretariat of the Communist Party of the Soviet Union. Agitprop was responsible for a wide variety of theatrical presentations in the cause of political propaganda. Agitprop also used all mass media. In the United States the Federal Theater Project created a Living Newspaper unit in 1935. This was highly successful and ran for four years. In England the Living Newspaper was pioneered by the Unity Theatre (*q.v.*), which was founded 1935–6 in London. It was a left-wing amateur group which specialized in socialist and communist plays and what was called 'agitational' drama. During the Second World War Living Newspaper techniques were used for propaganda purposes. *See* AGITPROP DRAMA; DOCUMENTARY THEATRE.

Living Theater An avant-garde (*q.v.*) drama company founded by Julian Beck and Judith Malina in New York in 1947. To start with they presented verse drama (mostly 20th c.) and later concentrated more on improvised drama and what has come to be loosely described as 'alternative theatre' (*q.v.*). The company was itinerant in Europe and developed anarchist views. Audience participation was encouraged and audiences were even harassed. Notable productions were *Paradise Now* (1968) and *Prometheus* (1978). The company dispersed in the mid-1980s. *See also* THIRD THEATRE.

livre à clef (F 'book with a key') Also known as a *roman à clef*, in English as a *key novel* and in German as a *Schlüsselroman*. Usually a work of fiction in which actual persons are presented under fictitious names. The genre developed in 17th c. France, from which time notable examples are Mme de Scudéry's *Le Grand Cyrus* (1649–53) and *Clélie* (1656–60), and La Bruyère's *Caractères* (1688). The 'keys' were provided later. Periodically since, there have been other instances. An early example in English is Mrs Manley's *The New Atlantis* (1709), published with a key to its characters. Thomas Love Peacock's *Nightmare Abbey* (1818) contained caricatures of Coleridge, Byron and Shelley. Disraeli's *Venetia* (1837) suggested notable figures of his period. For *Coningsby* (1844) Disraeli had a key to the characters published separately. Aldous Huxley's *Point Counter Point* (1928) caused some stir. In it the personalities of D. H. Lawrence, Oswald Mosley and Middleton Murry were thinly disguised. Somerset Maugham wrote several *livres à clef* and earned some disapproval for his lack of effort to disguise characters.

livre de poche A cheap paperback format first produced in France in 1953 by Henri Filipacchi. Its forebears include the pamphlet and the *bibliothèque bleu* (*q.v.*). The format was immensely successful. By the 1980s one-third of all books published in France were in the *poche* format and over two-thirds of literary texts.

loan word A word imported into a language from another language, or 'borrowed' from it. Very often such borrowings are permanent. English, a particularly permeable language, has assimilated a huge number of foreign elements, especially French, Scandinavian, Celtic, Latin and Greek. The following common words, for instance, are of Scandinavian origin: (a) substantives – axle, dregs, skill and window; (b) verbs – clasp, droop, glitter, skulk and want; (c) adjectives – awkward, muggy, sly, ugly and wrong. Recent importations which have become a permanent part of the language are the Russian words *glasnost* and *perestroika* and the Indian word *chai*. *See also* NEOLOGISM.

local colour The use of detail peculiar to a particular region and environment to add interest and authenticity to a narrative. This will include some description of the locale, dress, customs, music, etc. It is for the most part decorative. When it becomes an essential and intrinsic part of the work then it is more properly called regionalism. A number of American authors have used local colour successfully, for instance, Joel Chandler Harris, Thomas Nelson Page, Mary N. Murfee, Francis Hopkinson Smith, George Washington Cable and Mark Twain. Zola was also a good local colourist; so were Kipling and Hardy. *See also* REALISM; REGIONAL NOVEL.

loco citato (L 'in the place cited') Often abbreviated to *loc. cit.*, the term indicates a reference to a book or page or passage already mentioned. *See* IBIDEM; IDEM; OPERE CITATO.

logaoedic (Gk 'speech song') A term describing a composition which combines the rhythms of poetry and prose. Applied to Greek meter in which dactyls are combined with trochees and anapaests with iambs (*qq.v.*). It may also apply to any mixed meter.

logical stress Also known as rhetorical or sense stress, it is the emphasis required by the meaning of the verse, as in these lines from T. S. Eliot's *Ash Wednesday*:

> Lady of silences
> Calm and distressed
> Torn and most whole
> Rose of memory
> Rose of forgetfulness
> Exhausted and life-giving
> Worried reposeful
> The single Rose
> Is now the Garden
> Where all loves end

logocentrism A term coined by the French philosopher Jacques Derrida (1930–2004). *Logocentric* means literally 'centred on the word', but in Derrida's usage logocentrism implies all forms of thought based on an authorizing foundation or centre or *Logos*. In its ancient Greek philosophical and Judaeo-Christian meaning, the *Logos* referred both to the Word of God which created the universe and to the rational order of creation itself. In other words, it is in the spoken *Logos* that language and reality ultimately coincide, in an identity that is invested with absolute authority, absolute origin and absolute purpose or teleology.

Derrida's view is that logocentrism has been characteristic of Western thought and philosophy since Plato, and has taken a variety of guises. For Plato, the stabilizing function of the *Logos* was fulfilled by the notion of *eidos* or the Form; what holds Aristotle's metaphysics together, as its foundation, is the concept of substance; similarly we could cite Hegel's 'Absolute Idea' or Kant's categories of the understanding. Modern equivalents in Western society might be concepts such as 'freedom' or 'democracy'. All of these terms function as what Derrida calls 'transcendental signifieds', or concepts invested with absolute authority, which places them beyond questioning or examination. An important endeavour of deconstruction is to show the operation of logocentrism in all of its forms, and to bring back these various transcendental signifieds within the province of language and textuality, within the province of their relatability to other concepts.

Derrida's principal subcategory of logocentrism is 'phonocentrism' ('sound-centring'; hence phonocentric, 'centred on sound/speech'). Phonocentrism describes the precedence of speech over writing, again typified by most Western thought since Plato, which decrees that writing has a tendency to 'contaminate' the purity of the spoken word. Derrida argues against the privileged position of speech. He contends that this 'violent hierarchy', as he puts it, is *not* reversible but that it is possible to displace it by the idea of *différance* (*q.v.*), which is a vital part of his theories of deconstruction. *Différance* does not correct or reverse an imbalance (that would be counter to his view of deconstruction); it can only displace (i.e. make the question of hierarchy *obsolete*). *See also* DECONSTRUCTION; SUPPLEMENT.

logodaedalus (Gk *logos*, 'word' + *daedal*, from Daedalus the mythical artist) An artificer in words (e.g. a poet). *Logodaedaly* is verbal legerdemain.

logogram (Gk *logos*, 'word' + *gramma*, 'letter') A single sign for a word. Abbreviated to logo.

logographer (Gk *logos*, 'word' + *graphein*, 'to write') In Greek literature one of the earliest annalists, especially those before Herodotus. It also denotes a professional speech-writer.

logogriph (Gk 'word riddle') An anagram (*q.v.*) or verses from which anagrams or other word puzzles can be guessed. *See also* ACROSTIC.

logomachy (Gk 'word contest') A dispute or fight about words; or merely in words. *See* FLYTING; INVECTIVE.

logopoeia (Gk 'making of words') A poem both *means* and *is*. In *ABC of Reading* (1934) Ezra Pound discusses language as a means of communication and finds three ways in which language can be charged with meaning: (a) by throwing the object, be it fixed or moving, on to the visual imagination; this is phanopoeia (*q.v.*); (b) by inducing emotional correlations by the sound and rhythm of speech; this is melopoeia (*q.v.*); (c) by inducing both of these effects, thus stimulating the intellectual or emotional associations which have remained in the receiver's consciousness in relation to the actual words or groups of words employed; this is logopoeia. *See also* ONOMATOPOEIA; SYNAESTHESIA; TONE COLOUR.

logorrhoea (Gk 'word flowing') Excessive verbosity and prolixity. Vulgarly known as 'verbal diarrhoea'.

log-rolling More commonly known as 'back-scratching'. The practice by which authors review each other's books favourably. *See* PUFFERY.

long measure The LM of the hymn books. A variant of ballad or common meter. It consists of a tetrameter (*q.v.*) in which the foot pattern is usually iambic (but sometimes dactylic) as in this stanza from Burns's *Lament for James, Earl of Glencairn*:

> The mother may forget the child
> That smiles sae sweetly on her knee;

> But I'll remember thee, Glencairn,
> And a' that thou hast done for me.

long syllable *See* METER; QUANTITY.

loose and periodic sentences In a loose sentence the main clause comes first and is followed by its dependent clauses. In a periodic sentence the main clause is last. In the following passage from Macaulay's *Essay on Milton* the first sentence is loose, the second periodic:

> They [the Puritans] rejected with contempt the ceremonious homage which other sects substituted for the pure worship of the soul. Instead of catching occasional glimpses of the Deity through an obscuring veil, they aspired to gaze full on his intolerable brightness . . .

lost generation, the This term was in regular use after the First World War in reference to the host of young men who were killed in it, and also to the young men who survived and who thereafter were adrift – morally and spiritually (and in many other ways). The phrase is believed to have been invented by Gertrude Stein (1874–1946), a supporter and publicizer of artists and writers who were active in the avant-garde (*q.v.*) movements of her period. The mood of the lost generation (a mood of disenchantment and, sometimes, cynicism) was well represented by some American novelists; particularly Scott Fitzgerald (1896–1940). The group of men who later came to be known as the 'war poets' (*q.v.*) also belonged to the lost generation. Forty or fifty years later men who had spent their late youth and early manhood in the war still referred to themselves as members of the lost generation.

love poetry *See* EROTICA.

low comedy A coarse (often bawdy) type of comedy (*q.v.*), sometimes used as comic relief (*q.v.*). The mirth it provokes is likely to come from the belly rather than the brain. It commonly contains buffoonery, slapstick (*q.v.*), violent action and ribald jokes. It is thus a crudely fundamental form which trades upon people's relish at seeing others humiliated and ridiculed and involved in scabrous episodes. The punch-up, the custard-pie contest and the man caught with his trousers down are common examples of low comedy situations. It is frequent in Aristophanic comedy, farce (*q.v.*), medieval English drama, Tudor and Jacobean drama, and also Restoration comedy (*q.v.*). Notable instances are to be found in *The Merry Wives of Windsor*, the brothel scenes in *Pericles* (IV) and several scenes from Wycherley's *The Country Wife*. Low comedy is also to be found in the satyr play, the *fabula* and the anti-masque (*qq.v.*).

Low comedy is plentiful in other literary forms. Excellent examples occur in Goliardic verse (*q.v.*), Boccaccio's *Decameron* and Chaucer's *Canterbury Tales*. It may also be applied to Samuel Butler's *Hudibras*, Pope's *Dunciad* and a number of scenes in the sporting novels of R. S. Surtees.

Some of the Mack Sennett and early Charlie Chaplin films are masterpieces of low comedy.

Lucilian satire Formal verse satire, originating with the Roman poet Lucilius (2nd c. BC): the occasion of satire is an encounter, in a framing story, between the speaker and an adversary whose remarks elicit the speaker's social observations. This is the satirical form practised by Horace and Juvenal. Anita Loos's *Gentlemen Prefer Blondes* (1925) is a modern example. *See* HORATIAN SATIRE; JUVENALIAN SATIRE; MENIPPEAN SATIRE; SATIRE.

lullaby A soothing bedtime song or chant to send a child to sleep. The first lines of some of the better-known lullabies are 'Rock-a-bye baby, on the tree top' and 'Hush, little baby, don't say a word'.

lunulæ *See* PUNCTUATION.

lü-shih (Ch 'regulated poem') A verse form developed in China during the T'ang and Sung dynasties. It also went under the name *chin-t'i shih* to distinguish it from *ku-shih* or 'old poem'. Notable features of the *lü-shih* are parallelism (*q.v.*) and an elaborate tonal pattern. This kind of formalization also affected the *fu* (*q.v.*) or prose poem.

Lustspiel (G 'pleasure play') A light or amusing play. A light comedy (*q.v.*).

Lyon School From the town of Lyon where, in the 16th c., a group of writers lived and met. They were chiefly poets, and were in some cases involved in the other arts; their particular interest as a group was a theory of spiritual love based on ideas of Plato and Plutarch and enunciated in Antoine Héroët's *Parfaicte Amye* (1542). The group was noteworthy for the number of women who took an active part.

The leader of the Lyon School was Maurice Scève (*c.* 1500–64), architect, musician and painter as well as poet. He is known for the following works: *Délie* [anagram of *l'idée*], *objet de plus haulte vertu* (1544); *Le Microcosme* (1562), an encyclopaedic poem on the fall of man; two eclogues – *Arion* (1536) and *La Saulsaye* (1547). Other members of the group were Claude de Taillemont and women poets such as Jeanne Gaillarde, Pernette de Guillet, Clémence de Bourges, and Scève's sisters Claudine and Sibylle. However, the poet Louise Labé (*c.* 1525–66) was the most prominent of Scève's colleagues. It is said that at sixteen this remarkable woman fought on horseback in the siege of Perpignan on the side of the Dauphin. The daughter of a rope-maker, she married a rope-maker and became known as *La Belle Cordière*. She was a linguist and musician and her house became known as a salon for the cultured. Some of her poetry was published in Lyon in 1555. She also wrote a prose allegory *Le Débat de folie et d'amour*.

lyric The Greeks defined a lyric as a song to be sung to the accompaniment of a lyre (*lyra*). A song is still called a lyric (the words in a song are known

411

as lyrics) but we also use the term loosely to describe a particular kind of poem in order to distinguish it from narrative or dramatic verse of any kind.

A lyric is usually fairly short, not often longer than fifty or sixty lines, and often only between a dozen and thirty lines; and it usually expresses the feelings and thoughts of a single speaker (not necessarily the poet herself) in a personal and subjective fashion. The range and variety of lyric verse is immense, and lyric poetry, which is to be found in most literatures, comprises the bulk of all poetry.

Probably the earliest lyric poetry is Egyptian (c. 2600 BC) and can be found in the Pyramid texts of this period. The most memorable contribution in ancient times – apart from some Hebrew lyric poetry – came from the Greeks. Like the Egyptian and Hebrew, the Greek lyric originated in religious ceremonial. Greek lyrics were sung or chanted, sometimes to the accompaniment of a dance.

There were hints of lyric mood and subject in Hesiod and Homer, but it was not until the 7th c. BC that there appeared lyrics proper. Here we can distinguish between the Aeolian or personal lyrics written by Sappho and Alcaeus; and the Dorian (more impersonal and objective) lyrics by Alcman, Arion, Ibycus and Stesichorus.

The 5th c. in Greece produced some of the best of all lyric poetry – by Simonides, Pindar and Bacchylides; and by the dramatists Aeschylus, Sophocles and Euripides in their beautiful choral odes. Melic poetry then predominated, in the Dorian mood. Some of the main lyric types practised were the dance song, the dirge, the dithyramb ode, hymn and paean (qq.v.).

The Roman lyricists tended to be more subjective and autobiographical in the use of this form (the Aeolian mood), as in the poetry of Catullus, Tibullus, Propertius, Ovid, Virgil and Martial.

The medieval Latin lyric, from about AD 300 onwards, showed a remarkable range of subjects and technical skill. The early Church lyrics were hymns based on the Hebrew Psalter and Greek hymns.

The major poets of the Middle Ages writing lyrics in Latin were Abelard, Ausonius, Fortunatus, Paulinus of Nola, Petronius Arbiter and Prudentius, much of whose work is gathered together in Helen Waddell's *Medieval Latin Lyrics* (1929). The Church lyrics of the 12th and 13th c. were unique in their beauty. Such were the *Stabat Mater* and the *Dies Irae*.

A parallel development of the so-called Patristic lyric was the Mozarabic poetry of Spain. Hymns, psalms and poems arising from religious ceremonial were the chief contributions.

Between c. AD 300 and c. 1200 two other traditions in the lyric form can be distinguished. In the first place is the OE lyric, of which outstanding examples are *The Seafarer*, *The Wanderer*, *The Wife's Lament*, *The Lover's Message* and *Deor*. Contemporaneously, the art of the lyric was being perfected in China and Japan, and between the 12th and the 15th c. was highly developed in Persia. The main influence of the Persian lyric was not felt in England until the 19th c.

An abundance of lyric poetry survives from the later Middle Ages. Much of it was composed by troubadours and *trouvères* (*qq.v.*) and other wandering minstrels, and by the *Minnesinger* (*q.v.*). Many of the lyric forms had specific names, like *chanso*, *planh*, *tenso*, *pastorela* and *aubade* (*qq.v.*). They were intended to be sung, and were often danced to. From the 13th and 14th c. a large number of religious and devotional lyrics in English survive. Many of them are of great beauty. The principal European poets of the period who composed lyrics to be read were Bertrand de Born, Chaucer, Chrétien de Troyes, Walther von der Vogelweide, Rutebeuf, Pierre Vidal and Sordello.

The Renaissance period, however, was the great age of the lyric. Petrarch in Italy and Ronsard in France were the two major poets in this form, especially in the use of the sonnet (*q.v.*). In England Sir Thomas Wyatt and the Earl of Surrey made outstanding contributions with their songs, lyrics and sonnets. Some of the finest songs in the language date from this period. Between *c.* 1550 and the Restoration period scores of poets wrote lyrics, many of which are extant. The major collection of such verse in the 16th c. was Tottel's Miscellany (1557). The principal lyric poets in this period were Sidney, Daniel, Spenser, Shakespeare, Campion, Southwell, Drayton, Donne, Ben Jonson, Herrick, Lovelace, Suckling, Carew, Marvell, Herbert, Vaughan and Milton. To this period belong the great sonnet sequences (*q.v.*) of Sidney, Spenser and Shakespeare, the love poems of the Metaphysicals and the mystical and religious lyrics of Donne, Herbert and Vaughan. Not until the 19th c. do we find a comparable variety of religious lyrical poetry.

The lyric form was not so much favoured by the 18th c. poets except Smart, who was a notable minor lyric poet. Some other minor poets also attempted this form – notably Lady Winchilsea, Thomas Parnell, William Collins and Thomas Gray. The odes of Collins and Gray are particularly distinguished lyrics.

Towards the end of the 18th c. and during the Romantic period (*q.v.*) there was a major revival of lyric poetry throughout Europe. In the British Isles the most accomplished lyricists were Burns, Wordsworth, Blake, Coleridge, Byron, Shelley, Keats, John Clare and Thomas Moore; in Germany, Goethe, Schiller, Hölderlin, Eichendorff and Heine; in France, Lamartine, Victor Hugo, Alfred de Vigny and Alfred de Musset; in Italy, Giacomo Leopardi; in Spain, Espronceda; and in Russia, Pushkin.

Throughout the 19th c. many poets used the lyric form. The principal English poets were Tennyson, Browning, Swinburne, Matthew Arnold and Gerard Manley Hopkins. Like some of the Metaphysicals Hopkins wrote some remarkable religious and mystical poetry. Two minor poets are associated with him in this respect; namely, Francis Thompson and Coventry Patmore. Other minor poets who wrote notable lyrics were Dante Gabriel Rossetti and Christina Rossetti.

In France the major writers of lyric poetry in the later part of the 19th c. were the Parnassians, particularly Leconte de Lisle and Prudhomme. The American poet Edgar Allan Poe had a very considerable influence on Baudelaire, who was the precursor of the *symbolistes*. Baudelaire wrote some of the best lyrics in the French language. The other *symboliste* poets who wrote fine lyrics were Mallarmé, Verlaine and Rimbaud. Since the end of the 19th c. almost every major European and American poet has attempted and enriched the lyric form.

lyrisme romantique   A term used to describe those qualities of French lyrical poetry which appeared to depend greatly upon the individual poet's personal experiences and feelings. Thus, deeply subjective poetry. The four major poets of the French Romantic movement – Hugo, Lamartine, Musset and de Vigny – 'wrote from the heart'.

lysiody   *See* MAGODY.

M

macabre   *See* DANSE MACABRE.

macaronic   The term derives indirectly from the Italian word *maccaroni*, an earlier form of *maccheroni* (denoting a wheaten paste in tubular form).Properly speaking, macaronic verse is made when a writer mixes words of his own language with those of another and twists in his native words to fit the grammar of the foreign tongue (e.g., *standez*, *womenorum*). Broadly speaking, the term applies to any verse which mixes two or more languages together. Latin is the language most often used, and the intention in macaronics is nearly always comic and/or nonsensical.

They are first recorded in *Carmen macaronicum de Patavinis* (1490) by Tisi degli Odassi. The form was popularized by Teofilo Folengo in *Liber Macaronices* (1517). Folengo described his verses as a literary analogue (*q.v.*) of *macaroni* ('a gross, rude, and rustic mixture of flour, cheese, and butter'). There is a good deal of macaronic verse in French and German literature (the Germans call it *Nudelvers*) and some interesting examples in English literature: for instance, several poems by John Skelton, and William Drummond of Hawthornden's 'epic' *Polemo-Middinia*. Many writers of light verse and nonsense verse (*qq.v.*) have diverted themselves by composing macaronics.

Machiavel   A character type deriving his name from Niccolò Machiavelli (1469–1527), the Florentine statesman and political philosopher. Machiavelli became famous for *Il Principe* (written in 1513), a treatise on statecraft which justifies the use of various expediencies (including cruelty, lies and treachery) in the ruling of a state. *Il Principe* was often alluded to in Elizabethan drama and during the Elizabethan period the name of Machiavelli became associated (at any rate in the popular imagination) with treachery, murder, atheism and every kind of double-dyed villainy and viciousness. The sinister, resourceful and unscrupulous villain (*q.v.*) – usually an Italian and often the embodiment

---

A Dictionary of Literary Terms and Literary Theory, Fifth Edition. J. A. Cuddon.
© 2013 The Estate of J. A. Cuddon. Published 2013 by Blackwell Publishing Ltd.

of evil – in revenge tragedy (*q.v.*) of the Elizabethan and Jacobean periods came to be regarded as a Machiavel.

machinery In his preface to *The Rape of the Lock* (1712, 1714), Pope refers to machinery as a term invented by the critics 'to signify that part which the deities, angels or demons are made to act in a poem'. The term is particularly associated with Greek tragedy in connection with the *deus ex machina* (*q.v.*) which the Greeks used to put a god on stage. It is also associated with epic (*q.v.*) because Homer included a large number of gods in the *Iliad*. Thus, supernatural figures were referred to as 'machines'. There is a good deal of supernatural 'machinery' in *Paradise Lost*.

macrology (Gk 'long language') Verbose repetition by way of long words and phrases. *See* JARGON; OFFICIALESE; PERIPHRASIS; TAUTOLOGY; VERBOCRAP.

macron The horizontal sign (¯) put over a vowel to indicate length. *See* MORA.

madrigal (L *matricalis*, 'maternal' and so 'simple, primitive') Originally a pastoral song, it is a short lyric (*q.v.*), especially one to be set to music and intended for several voices. It arose in northern Italy in the 14th c. and Petrarch wrote a number of them. In the 16th c. there was a revival of the form and it became extremely popular in England in Tudor times.

Metrically it showed much variety. In the 14th c. it tended to consist of two or three tercets (*q.v.*) followed by one or two rhyming couplets. By the 16th c. there were few rules, but for the most part madrigals were of ten to fourteen lines and normally ended with a rhyming couplet. The themes were usually love, the pastoral or the satiric. Many Tudor poets attempted it, but its three famous English composers were Thomas Morely, Thomas Weelkes and John Wilbye.

magazine (A *makhazin*, plural of *makhzan*, 'a storehouse') A periodical (*q.v.*) publication. *See* LITTLE MAGAZINE.

magic realism This term was coined by Franz Roh and used in the title of his book *Nach-expressionismus, magischer Realismus: Probleme der neuesten europäischer Malerei* (1925). He was concerned with the characteristics and tendencies discernible in the work of certain German painters of the period, especially the *neue Sachlichkeit* (*q.v.*) artists of Munich. Their work was marked by the use of still, sharply defined, smoothly painted images of figures and objects depicted in a somewhat surrealistic manner. The themes and subjects were often imaginary, somewhat outlandish and fantastic and with a certain dream-like quality. The effects could be powerful. Magic realism was also associated with the 1920s Italian movement *stracittà* (*q.v.*).

Later, early in the 1940s, the idea and term magic realism reappeared in the USA. In 1943 the New York Museum of Modern Art held an exhibition called 'American Realists and Magic Realists'. Among the distinguished painters whose work was hung were Edward Hopper (1882–1967) and Charles Sheeler (1883–1965). Subsequently, Hopper's paintings in particular were to receive considerable publicity in Britain and elsewhere.

Gradually the term came to be associated with certain kinds of fiction. In the late 1940s George Saiko (1892–1962), the Austrian novelist, began to publish fiction of a quasi-surrealistic nature and he expressed his views about what he called *magischer Realismus* in his book *Die Wirklichkeit hat doppelten Boden. Gedanken zum magischen Realismus* (1952).

In due course the term caught on in literary circles and was used by critics. By the 1980s it had become a well-established 'label' for some forms of fiction. It has been applied, for instance, to the work of Luis Borges (1899–1988), the Argentinian who in 1935 published his *Historia universal de la infamia*, regarded by many as the first work of magic realism. The Colombian novelist Gabriel Garcia Márquez (1928–) is also regarded as a notable exponent of this kind of fiction, especially his novel *Cien años de soledad* or *One Hundred Years of Solitude* (1967). The Cuban Alejo Carpentier (1904–80) is another described as a 'magic realist'. Experiments in magic realism effects and techniques are also to be found in the fiction of Italo Calvino (1923–85), John Fowles (1926–2005), Günter Grass (1927–), Emma Tennant (1937–), Angela Carter (1940–92), and Salman Rushdie (1947–).

Some of the characteristic features of this kind of fiction are the mingling and juxtaposition of the realistic and the fantastic or bizarre, skilful time shifts, convoluted and even labyrinthine narratives and plots, miscellaneous use of dreams, myths and fairy stories, expressionistic and even surrealistic description, arcane erudition, the element of surprise or abrupt shock, the horrific and the inexplicable. It is seldom easy to define it as a genre and a plausible case might be made that there are plentiful instances of magic realism in the fiction of Kleist, E. T. A. Hoffmann, Prosper Mérimée, Fournier, Kafka, Ronald Firbank and Edward Upward. See *also* GOTHIC NOVEL/FICTION; HORROR STORY; NOVEL.

magnitizdat *See* SAMIZDAT.

magnum opus (L 'great work') A major literary work, perhaps a writer's masterpiece. Milton's *Paradise Lost* was his *magnum opus*.

magody (Gk 'rude pantomime') Like lysiody (named after Lysis, who wrote songs for actors playing female characters in male attire) and hilarody (Gk 'joyous song'), magody was a form of Greek mime (*q.v.*). The magodist took a comic plot or a theme from comedy and worked out a mime. Wearing female clothes, he played both male and female parts. The lysiodist, by contrast, wore male clothes and played female roles, to the accompaniment of a flute. Hilarody was a kind of parody of tragedy (*q.v.*). The actor wore male clothes and buskins (*q.v.*). Simody was an alternative, and later, name for hilarody. *See also* SATYR PLAY.

Mahābhārata (Skt 'War of the Bharata dynasty) One of the two major epics composed in Sanskrit verse, alongside the *Rāmāyana* (*q.v.*). Classified generically as an *itihāsa* or traditional historical account, it was composed over several centuries before the 5th c. AD when it achieved its present form, but its authorship is conventionally attributed to Vyāsa. It is the longest known poem, extending to 100,000 couplets, divided into eighteen sections. More than seven times the length of the *Iliad* and the *Odyssey* combined, the *Mahābhārata* is widely acknowledged to occupy a central place on the stage of world literature, comparable in importance to the Bible and the Qur'an (*qq.v.*), though it is not a singular book in the way that the Abrahamic scriptures are. Most of the poem is framed as a dialogue (enclosing several other dialogues) and recounts the eighteen-day war of the Bharatas in the plain of Kuru (near modern Delhi). This war is a struggle for succession to the throne of Hastinapur between two branches of the Bharata dynasty, the Kauravas and their cousins the Pandavas. The dialogue which occurs as the two armies face each other on the battlefield is actually the beginning of the *Bhagavad Gita* (Song of God) (*q.v.*), which is often treated as an independent poem.

The *Mahābhārata* also recounts the history of the Bharatas, encompassing in its encyclopaedic scope mythology, cosmology, politics and religion. It also serves as a moral and ethical treatise, and its influence on Indian culture has been inestimable, discernible in a wide variety of literature ranging from folk songs through poetry and fiction to religious sermons. *See also* BHAGAVAD GITA; RĀMĀYANA.

maker This was Philip Sidney's 'saucy' definition of 'poet': 'it cometh of this word ποιειν, which is, to make ... which name, how high and incomparable a title it is ...' (*Defence of Poesie*). Sidney goes on to link the makerliness of poets with that of their Maker, so claiming for poetry supreme power above all other human enterprises. In contemporary northern usage, 'maker' referred specifically to the writing of poetry (the Scottish Chaucerians are self-described 'makars'). Chaucer himself, however, had reserved the word 'poet' for writers in Italian or the Classical languages, with the 'maker' as a kind of English 'rhymester'. More recently, the poet John Berryman has reclaimed the term in 'Dreamsong 184'. *See* POEM; POESIS.

makkaronische Dichtung *See* MACARONIC.

málaháttr (ON *mál*, 'a speech' and *háttr*, 'meter') An ON Eddic meter, quite similar to fornyrðislag (*q.v.*). It consists of a four-line stanza, each line being divided into two half lines, the half lines having two accented and three or four unaccented syllables.

malapropism (F *mal à propos*, 'not to the purpose') So called after Mrs Malaprop, a character in Sheridan's *The Rivals* (1775), who had a habit of using polysyllabic words incorrectly. There are some characteristic examples in the following passage from the opening Act:

> Then, sir, she should have a supercilious knowledge in accounts; – and as she grew up, I would have her instructed in geometry, that she might know something of the contagious countries ... and likewise that she might reprehend the true meaning of what she is saying. This, Sir Anthony, is what I would have a woman know; – and I don't think there is a superstitious article in it.

But malapropisms were by no means new in 1775. Dogberry, the Watch in *Much Ado About Nothing* (c. 1598–9), was addicted to them. So was Mrs Slipslop in Fielding's *Joseph Andrews* (1742). One of the most amusing malapropists was Mrs Winifred Jenkins in Smollett's *Humphry Clinker* (1771), who was capable of writing: 'I have already made very creditable correxions in this here place; where, to be sure, we have the very squintasense of satiety.' Another adept was Mrs Heidelberg in *The Clandestine Marriage* (1766) by George Colman (the Elder).

Fortunately malapropisms are a feature of everyday life and people continue to produce endearing gems. Traditionally, loquacious charwomen are a fruitful source, as these samples testify: 'He rides the motor bike and she sits on the pavilion'; 'I'd like you to meet my daughter's fiasco'; 'I've always been thin. When I was a girl I had infantile paraphernalia'.

Medical conditions have caused bizarre afflictions, such as 'malingering' tumours, 'hysterical rectums', and 'teutonic' ulcers. There have been severed 'juggler' veins and 'Cistercian' childbirths. A middle-aged man believed he had undergone a 'midwife' crisis, and a lady declined to volunteer as a 'blood doughnut'.

Man Booker Prize   Originally known as the Booker McConnell Prize, it is a prize for fiction in English open to any writer from the Commonwealth or the Republic of Ireland. It was founded in 1969 and was financed by Booker McConnell, a multinational conglomerate. It is awarded annually by a panel of judges for what, in their opinion, is the best full-length novel published in the previous twelve months. The award is accompanied by considerable publicity and media razzmatazz. It has become the best-known literary prize in Britain; but some other literary prizes are deemed more prestigious. It became the Man Booker Prize in 2002 and is now sponsored by Man Group plc, an alternative investment management business. The first winner was P. H. Newby. Since 1969 winners have included: 1970, Bernice Rubens; 1971, V. S. Naipaul; 1975, Ruth Prawer Jhabvala; 1978, Iris Murdoch; 1979, Penelope Fitzgerald; 1980, William Golding; 1981, Salman Rushdie; 1985, Keri Hulme; 1986, Kingsley Amis; 1989, Kazuo Ishiguro; 1990, A. S. Byatt; 1991, Ben Okri; 1992, Michael Ondaatje and Barry Unsworth; 1996, Graham Swift; 1997, Arundhati Roy; 2000, Margaret Atwood; 2006, Kiran Desai; 2008, Aravind Adiga; 2010, Howard Jacobson; 2011, Julian Barnes.

The Man Booker International Prize was launched in 2005. It is awarded to a contemporary writer who has published in English, or whose work is available in English translation, for his or her overall contribution to fiction.

Oxford Brookes University houses the Booker Prize Archive.

Manchester School   Originally a term used by Benjamin Disraeli (1804–81) to describe the political party led by Richard Cobden (1804–65) and John Bright (1811–89), both advocates of free trade. Later the term was used of a group of Mancunian dramatists whose plays were produced at the Gaiety Theatre, Manchester, in the period 1907–14 when it was run by Annie Horniman (1860–1937), the founder of the Manchester Repertory Theatre. Three dramatists in particular are associated with this 'school'; namely Allan Monkhouse (1858–1936), William Houghton (1881–1913) and Harold Brighouse (1882–1958). Many of the plays are about the trials and tribulations of Lancashire domestic life and reveal the influence of Ibsen. A handful of them have long since been part of the standard repertoire of theatrical companies, especially Houghton's *The Dear Departed* (1908) and his *Hindle Wakes* (1912) and Brighouse's *Hobson's Choice* (1916).

manifesto (L *manu festus*, 'struck by hand') A public declaration, usually of political, religious, philosophical or literary principles and beliefs. The *Communist Manifesto* (1848) of Karl Marx and Friedrich Engels is a notable political manifesto. The *Declaration of the Rights of Man and Citizen* (1793), a central document of the French Revolution, and the *Unites States Declaration of Independence* (1776) are other political examples. Literary movements are also given to publishing manifestos. For instance, Wyndham Lewis's *Blast: The Review of the Great English Vortex* (1914–15), a manifesto for Vorticism (*q.v.*), and André Breton's *Manifeste du surréalisme* (1924). More recently, documents like Donna Haraway's *Cyborg Manifesto* (1985) have begun to challenge the cultural capital of established institutions or ideological structures – in Haraway's case, traditional notions of feminism.

mannerism A term developed in the 20th c. to describe various manifestations of painting and architecture (chiefly Italian) in the period 1520–1600. The word *maniera* (from which *mannerism* derives) was used by Vasari (author of *Le Vite de' più eccellenti Architetti, Pittori et Scultori Italiani*, 1550) to describe 'the schematic quality of much of the work produced, based on intellectual preconceptions rather than direct visual perceptions. Much of mannerism consists of deliberately flouting the "Rules" deduced from classical art and established during the Renaissance' (*A Dictionary of Art and Artists* by Peter and Linda Murray). Like baroque (*q.v.*), mannerism has been applied to particular styles of writing characterized by ornateness of language, strange syntax, far-fetched images and elaborate sentences. The writers (like the painters and architects) can be called *manneristi*. Two authors in particular are associated with mannerism in the 16th c. They are the Spaniard Antonio de Guevara (1480?–1545) and John Lyly (1554–1606), famous for his euphuism (*q.v.*).

More generally speaking, mannerism may denote the idiosyncratic elements of an author's style; any peculiarity, affectation or quality which sets it apart and makes it easily recognizable. For example, the Latinistic syntax of Milton, the balanced and antithetical cadences of Gibbon, the quaint archaisms of C. M. Doughty, the pseudo-biblical rhythms of Hemingway. *See* GONGORISM.

man of letters A well-educated, well-read, civilized and perhaps learned person – who may also be a writer (e.g. a belle-lettrist). 'A man of capital letters', on the other hand, is one who thinks he is these things but is, in fact, very limited. Pope's victims in *The Dunciad* (1728, 1743) might be called 'men of capital letters'. When literacy was an acquisition only of the economically privileged, the man of letters served as an index of class. In the 19th c., 'men of letters' referred more specifically to essayists, journalists and critics (rather than fiction writers), who multiplied with the increase of periodicals and other publications of cultural mediation. In the 20th c., as literary people moved into academia, the term fell out of usage, to be replaced increasingly with the 'public intellectual' – a writer whose critical discourse has a wider import beyond academia. *See also* BELLES LETTRES; LITERATI.

mantra An Indian religious chant (*q.v.*). The *Mantrapatha*, a prayer-book, contains about six hundred *mantras*. It is a kind of manual of prayer for all occasions, especially domestic ceremonials.

manual *See* HANDBOOK AND MANUAL.

manuscript (L *codex manu scriptus*, 'book written by hand') Strictly a book or document of any kind written by hand rather than printed or typed. While a typewritten document is often called a manuscript, it is, in fact, a *typescript*.

maqāma An Arabic term for stories in rhymed prose. The two great masters of the form were Abu al-Fadl Ahmed ibn al-Husain al-Hamadhani (967–1007) and Abu Mohammed al-Qasim al-Hariri (1054–1122). Most of the tales come into the category of picaresque (*q.v.*).

Märchen A German term for a folk tale or fairy story (*qq.v.*). The classic collection is that made by the Grimm brothers early in the 19th c., the *Kinder- und Hausmärchen* (1812, 1814, 1822).

marginalia Notes written in the margin of a manuscript or book by a reader or annotator. Coleridge (in 1832) was the first English man of letters to use this term. *See also* ANNOTATION.

marginality Used in a variety of literary and social theoretical contexts, the term refers to texts, ideas or peoples existing on the boundaries of a conventionally accepted space. The theory of marginality originated in the early 20th c. within a sociological context to describe the production of marginalized individuals whose immigrant backgrounds suspended them between their native cultures and host societies. The problems of hybrid identities and divided selves introduced by the discourse of marginality have extended beyond the field of sociology and it is frequently employed to question the rules of hegemony and exclusion in gender, culture and literary studies. *See also* HYBRIDITY; POSTCOLONIALISM.

Marian legends Legends about the Virgin Mary were popular and widespread in Europe in the Middle Ages and produced a considerable literature. Collections of Marian legends were formed in Latin in the 11th c. and they proliferated during the next three hundred years. Gradually they were popularized through different vernaculars. *See* LEGEND.

Marienklage A genre of German poetry in monologue form composed in the 13th, 14th and 15th c. Their theme was the suffering and lamentation of the Virgin Mary as she watched her Son suffering on the Cross. *Marienklagen* were sometimes dramatized for performance in church.

Marxist criticism Karl Marx (1818–83) and Friedrich Engels (1820–95) were primarily concerned with economic, political and philosophical issues and worked out explanations of the capitalist theory and mode of production. They did not develop an 'aesthetic' of culture or literature, although they did say quite traditional things about Greek art, which suggest that Marx himself believed in the relative autonomy of art (cf. Marx's *Introduction to the Critique of Political Economy*, 1875, and Hans Robert Jauss's article in *New Literary History*, titled *The Idealist Embarrassment*). However, Marxist principles, attitudes and modes of thought and inquiry have been adapted to create a Marxist theory of literature: what it has been, and what it might and, perhaps, should be. The Marxist critic (who tends to be primarily interested in content) writes from the definite standpoint of Marx's philosophical ideas, and from his view of history in which the class struggle is fundamental, or in terms of socio-historical factors.

Much earlier Marxist criticism has been devoted to a reconstruction of the past on the basis of historical evidence in order to find out to what extent a text (say, a novel) is a truthful and accurate representation of social reality at any given time. As Trotsky suggested in *Literature and Revolution* (1924): 'Artistic creation is a changing and a transformation of reality in accordance with the peculiar laws of art.'

The concept of 'socialist realism' (*q.v.*) marked an important advance in the development of Marxist and, *ipso facto*, Communist views on literature – and art in general. Basically, socialist realism required a writer (or any artist) to be committed to the working-class cause of the Party. And it required that literature should be 'progressive' and should display a progressive outlook on society. This necessitated forms of optimism and realism. Moreover, doctrine demanded that literature should be accessible to the masses. This was particularly true of the novel.

Modernism (*q.v.*) in Western literature was deemed to be decadent (especially by critics such as Georg Lukács) because it was, among other things, subjective, introverted and introspective, and displayed a fragmented vision of the world. By contrast, the 19th c. realist novel was extolled. However, a certain amount of squaring of circles and an element of double-think was involved, especially in relation to such novelists as Dostoevsky and Goncharov, for example, who were profoundly pessimistic and introverted.

A key figure is the first major Marxist critic, namely the Hungarian Georg Lukács (1885–1971). He developed the critical theory of 'reflection', seeing literary works as reflections of a kind of system that was gradually unfolding. In his view, the novel, for instance (and he had much to say about this genre), revealed or ought to reveal underlying patterns in the social order and provide a sense of the wholeness of existence with all its inherent contradictions, tensions and conflicts.

The Frankfurt School (q.v.) of Marxist aesthetics is associated with the Institute of Social Research founded in 1923 and affiliated to the University of Frankfurt. During the Nazi period it was exiled (1933) to New York, from where it returned to Frankfurt in 1949–50. This school (whose chief spirits were Theodor Adorno, Max Horkheimer and Herbert Marcuse) rejected realism more or less completely and developed what is known as Critical Theory. They were much influenced by (a) their experience of a totalitarian regime and Fascism; (b) their experience of American mass culture, capitalism and commercialism. Both the Nazi and American societies were regarded as 'one-dimensional'.

Adorno advanced the theory that literature does not have direct contact with reality. He favoured modernism in literature because it is 'distanced' from the reality it seeks to describe, and this 'distancing' enhances its critical reality. Thus, knowledge of reality is achieved indirectly or obliquely. Horkheimer was in favour of the avant-garde (q.v.) and modernism because they are hostile to passivity, acquiescence and submission to the political and artistic status quo, and thus to any form of inhibitive or repressive ideology. Marcuse suggests that the autonomous work of art embodies one form of subversion in a repressive society.

Walter Benjamin, for a while associated with Adorno, took a contrary view to him. He surveyed the importance of technology in 19th and 20th c. urban and industrialized society, and also the enormous development of the media. As a Marxist he was interested in 'mass culture' and in the way in which culture is packaged and consumed by the masses. In his view the media – in close contact with reality – have the power to eliminate the ritual and bourgeois elitism of art and literature and give it a kind of political 'freedom'. He is more concerned with technique and with artistic forces at work than with the correct position of art and literature socially and economically. So, the emphasis is on the relation of a work of art to the ever changing conditions of the production of art itself.

The French Marxist philosopher Louis Althusser (1918–90) developed a theory of different 'levels' within the social formation and argued that these 'levels' possess no overall unity. They have a 'relative autonomy' – a concept developed by Marxists to account for Marx's view that Ancient Greek art was enduringly attractive.

In his book *The Hidden God* (1964), the Romanian critic Lucien Goldmann developed a theory of 'homologies' or structural parallels between literature, ideas and social groups. He saw literary texts as emerging from 'transindividual mental structures' which belong to groups or classes.

Macherey, a follower of Althusser, in *A Theory of Literary Production* (1966), advances the idea that a literary text distances itself from its ideology by virtue of its form and its fiction, and also by the 'silences' or 'gaps' in the text, by what is *not* said. These silences/gaps, he contends, not only conceal but also expose ideological contradictions. Such absences are suppressions, so to speak, within the text of its own 'unconscious'.

Marxist criticism in Britain has not flourished to the extent it has elsewhere. One influential British Marxist critic has been Raymond Williams (1921–88), who attempted a historical assessment of culture and literature in Marxist terms. The principal theorist of Marxist criticism in Britain is Terry Eagleton, who, developing certain views of Althusser and Macherey, suggests that a basic problem is to make clear the relationship between literature and ideology. In his view, texts do not reflect reality but influence an ideology to produce the effect or impression of reality.

The leading exponent of Marxist criticism in America is Fredric Jameson, who makes eclectic use of a range of theories (including structuralism, deconstruction, archetypal criticism (*qq.v.*), allegorical interpretation and Jacques Lacan's interpretations (or reinterpretations) of Freud), any or all of which he may find useful in the critical interpretation of a literary text. It is his contention that Marxism 'subsumes' other interpretative modes when it comes to a political interpretation which exposes the 'political unconscious' of a text. Like Macherey he is concerned with the 'subtext' but more specifically with that subtext which historically and ideologically constitutes the 'unspoken', the concealed and suppressed. Thus a Marxist interpretation looks for levels of meaning in the mode of allegory (*q.v.*). A more recent Marxist voice has been that of the Slovenian philosopher Slavoj Žižek, who has engaged in a reading of Hegelian dialectics in the light of Lacanian categories in order to undertake a renewed critique of capitalism. *See also* BOURGEOIS; CULTURAL MATERIÁLISM; IDEOLOGY.

masculine caesura A caesura (*q.v.*) which comes after a stressed syllable, as after 'moles' in the second of these lines from Matthew Arnold's *To a Republican Friend*:

> The barren optimistic sophistries
> Of comfortable moles, ‖ whom what they do
> Teaches the limit of the just and true.

See FEMININE CAESURA.

masculine rhyme A single monosyllabic rhyme, like *thorn/scorn* at the end of a line. It is the commonest type of rhyme in English verse. In French verse it frequently alternates with feminine rhyme. *See* FEMININE RHYME; RHYME; TRIPLE RHYME.

masque (F 'mask') What is probably the first use of the term occurs in Hall's Chronicle for 1512 where 'maske' applies to a dance of masked figures. According to Ben Jonson, masques were formerly called 'disguisings'. John Lydgate, in the period 1427–35, composed seven of these entertainments which he called 'mummings' or 'mummings by way of disguisings'. These may well be the first specimens of the genre to survive.

A masque was a fairly elaborate form of courtly entertainment which was particularly popular in the reigns of Elizabeth I, James I and Charles I, as it was in Italy (where the masque first acquired a distinctive form), and in France. In fact, *Circe* (1581), first produced in Paris, had a considerable influence on English masque.

The masque combined poetic drama, song, dance and music. The costumes were often sumptuous. The structure was usually simple. A Prologue introduced a group of actors known to the audience. They entered in disguise or perhaps in some kind of decorated vehicle. Plot and action were slight. Usually the plot consisted of mythological and allegorical elements. Sometimes there might be a sort of 'debate'. At the end there was a dance of masked figures in which the audience joined. In short, it was a kind of elegant, private pageant (*q.v.*).

In the Tudor period masques accompanied many festive occasions. Towards the end of Elizabeth's reign the poetic element, thanks to the influence of Gascoigne and Daniel, began to predominate. In the reign of James I, Ben Jonson perfected the genre with the help of Inigo Jones who (like Brunelleschi in Italy) created lavish sets and costumes and performed many ingenious and spectacular feats with stage machinery. By this time masques had become so elaborate that they could almost be described as forerunners of the musical. They were extremely expensive. For example, Jonson's *Love Freed from Ignorance and Folly* (1611) cost a little under £1,000, and his *Oberon* (1611) cost over £2,000 – huge sums of money for those days.

As time went on they became more and more spectacular, and operatically splendid; to such an extent that even Jonson was disillusioned and felt that they were merely obscuring truth. As he put it in *An Expostulation with Inigo Jones* (1631):

> Oh, to make boards to speak! There is a task!
> Painting and carpentry are the soul of masque!
> Pack with you peddling poetry to the stage!
> This is the money-get, mechanic age.

In the development of the theatre the masque was particularly important because it was Inigo Jones who was responsible for the technique of proscenium staging. Moreover, the masque had considerable influence on contemporary drama, as we can see from Shakespeare's *Love's Labour's Lost* (c. 1593), Dekker's *Old Fortunatus* (1600), John Ford's *The Sun's Darling* (1624) and Nabbes's *Microcosmus* (1637). The most famous instance was the masque of Juno and Ceres within the fourth act of *The Tempest* (c. 1611), rivalled only by Milton's *Comus* presented at Ludlow Castle in 1634.

Further development was prevented by the outbreak of civil war and the closing of the theatres by the Puritans. Almost the last masque of any note before the ban was Davenant's *Salmacida Spolia* (1640). However, when the theatres reopened all that had been learned of staging techniques was applied to the production of plays. And Davenant's was by no means the last masque. Shirley's *Cupid and Death* was presented in 1653, Cockayne's *The Masque at Bretby* in 1658, Crowne's *Calisto* in 1675, Davison's *The Masque of Proteus and the Adamantine Rock* in 1688, and Congreve's *The Judgment of Paris* in 1701.

Mention should also be made of the following contributions to the genre: Sir Philip Sidney's *The Lady of May* (1578); Daniel's *The Vision of Twelve Goddesses* (1604); Jonson's *Hymenaei* (1606), *The Masque of Beauty* (1608), *The Masque of Queens* (1609), *The Masque of Augurs* (1621), *Neptune's Triumph for the Return of Albion* (1624?), *The Fortunate Isles and Their Union* (1624); Chapman's *The Masque of the Middle Temple and Lincoln's Inn* (1613?); the anonymous *The Masque of Flowers* (1614); Townsend's *Albion's Triumph* (1632); Shirley's *The Triumph of Peace* (1634); Carew's *Coelum Britannicum* (1634); Kynaston's *Corona Minervae* (1636); and Nabbes's *The Spring's Glory* (1638). Fletcher, Campion, Beaumont and Middleton also composed masques. *See* ANTI-MASQUE.

masthead A statement printed in each issue of a periodical (*q.v.*) which gives the name, date of foundation, motto or slogan (*qq.v.*), the editors' names, and so forth. The term derives from the use of a flag on a ship's mast.

mathnavi A long narrative epic or heroic poem in rhyming couplets. It was sometimes written about legendary lovers of the past or the poet's own experience of love, though it could also be used for religious and philosophical meditation. The form originated in Persia and the most renowned example of its epic mode is the 11th c. poet Firdausi's *Shāhnāmah* (Book of Kings), a history of Persian dynasties which at times engages in moral lessons and romance. The form was adapted in various ways by the Persian poets Jami (1414–92), Farid uddin Attar (*c.* 1145–*c.* 1221) and Sa'di (*c.* 1200–*c.* 1291), the Indian poet Amir Khusrau (1253–1325) and, in the modern period, the Urdu poet N. M. Rāshed (1910–75). The most famous example in Persian is the mystical poem by the 13th c. poet Rumi, who, interestingly, is the most widely read poet in America today.

maxim (L *propositio maxima*, 'greatest theme') A proposition, often barely distinguishable from an aphorism (*q.v.*) and closely related to a *pensée* (*q.v.*), which consists of a pithy, succinct statement (usually a sentence or two, though it may run to more) which contains a precept or general truth about human nature and human conduct.

maximum scene technique A jargon term for stream of consciousness (*q.v.*) technique.

meaning If we take as an example the following dialogue:

> X: Is this a question?
> Y: If it is, this is the answer.

we find that in this form it possesses referential or cognitive meaning. If we change it to:

> x: Is this a sensible question?
> y: If it is, this is an equally stupid answer.

we introduce an emotive element, and it has what is called emotive meaning.

Under cognitive meaning it is normal to distinguish between two relations: (a) that between a word and the things it names or denotes; hence these things are called the extension or denotation (*q.v.*) of the word; (b) that between a word and certain characteristics; these are the intension of the word, or its connotations (*q.v.*). The word *snake*, for instance, denotes the genus of reptiles; but for many people it also has very strong connotations.

measure Another word for meter (*q.v.*). *See also* COMMON MEASURE; LONG MEASURE; POULTER'S MEASURE.

mechanic form *See* ORGANIC FORM.

mechanism In general, it denotes the construction of a work; the relationship of the parts to the whole. We may also speak of the mechanism of a plot (*q.v.*); that is, how it works.

medial rhyme *See* RHYME.

media studies A broadly and variously defined term. In understanding the nature of media two approaches predominate. First, media studies responds to notions of 'text' that have broadened beyond the literary, or the medium of the written word, and encompass other productive and distributive technologies. These include film, television and, most recently, digital networks. Such domains 'remediate' the written word and the pictorial image much as writing itself remediates prior oral modes of communication (*Remediation*, 2000, by Bolter and Grusin). Media studies consequently focuses on the communicative potential of various media and their social effects, especially mass communication entailing large-scale production and distribution of texts. Central to media studies in this respect are insights of Walter Benjamin into the transformed value of artistic works brought about by mechanical (including electronic) modes of reproduction.

A second, more philosophical approach to media studies is focused less on the content and effects of specific media, and seeks to account in general for the mediated character of all human activity. This approach was anticipated by Plato's assertion, in the *Phaedrus*, of the inferiority of writing to speech on account of its more mediated nature. In the 20th c., media studies was inaugurated by Marshall McLuhan, whose *Understanding Media* (1965) advanced a broad conception of media as a technological extrapolation of the human body in space and time. This tool-based conception of media encompassing modes of transport, habitation, and dress in addition to communication underscores the 'in-between' dimension of mediated performance. Media studies is thus oriented towards identifying the complexity of relations between human beings *through* objects and *with* objects.

So-called 'new' media, centred in digital modes of communication and the modes of interaction among users, bring into relief the implicit logic of all technological innovations in their capacity to shape socialization through the remediation of existing forms of communication.

medievalism In a literary work, an emphasis on the attitudes, way of thought, sensibility, themes, style and matter commonly associated with the Middle Ages (c. 800–c. 1450). The Gothic revival, the Romantic revival and Pre-Raphaelitism (q.v.) were all manifestations of medievalism. Keats, for instance, strongly under the influence of Spenser (and of Milton, who in turn had been much influenced by Spenser, a very 'medieval' poet), exhibits many aspects of medievalism.

meiosis (Gk 'lessening') A figure of speech which contains an understatement for emphasis: often used ironically, and also for dramatic effect, in the attainment of simplicity. In everyday speech it is sometimes used in gentle irony, especially when describing something very spectacular or impressive as 'rather good', or words to that effect. Meiosis may even pervade the tone and manner of a work. A particularly good example is Auden's *The Unknown Citizen* (1939). *See also* IRONY; LITOTES.

Meistergesang German poetry for singing to melodies. The Meistersänger were mostly burghers of the 14th, 15th and 16th c. and were organized into guilds on a hierarchical basis. In effect one graduated to the rank of *Meister*. The meetings were informal occasions and the songs were for the most part religious, didactic and moral. In this respect they differed from the Minnesingers (q.v.), whose literary descendants they were. Meistersingers were particularly common in southern Germany and in the Rhineland. Two of the most famous were Hans Folz and Hans Sachs.

meiurus (Gk 'tapering') A hexameter (q.v.) line in which the first syllable of the last foot is short instead of long. Also known as *teliambos*.

melic poetry Lyric poetry to be sung and danced to. It was mostly composed by Aeolians and Dorians, and the best work dates from the 7th to the 5th c. BC. There were basically two kinds: the monodic and the choral. The former was sung by a single voice and expressed one individual's feelings. The principal writers of monody were Sappho, Alcaeus and Anacreon. The latter expressed the feelings of a group and was sung by a chorus. The main practitioners of this kind were Alcman, Stesichorus, Simonides, Pindar and Bacchylides. *See* LYRIC.

melodrama (Gk 'song drama') The origins of melodrama coincide roughly with the origins of opera (q.v.) in Italy very late in the 16th c. Opera developed from an attempt to revive Classical tragedy, and the mixture of music and drama was either opera or melodrama. In the 18th c. Handel called some of his works opera and some melodrama. Towards the end of the 18th c. French dramatists began to develop melodrama as a distinct genre by elaborating the dialogue and making much more of spectacle, action and violence.

Sensationalism and extravagant emotional appeal became popular. One of the main influences from earlier in the century was very probably the gloomy tragedies of Crébillon (*père*). Some of the more notable examples of inchoate melodrama were Rousseau's *Pygmalion* (1775), Gabiot's *L'Auto-da-fé* (1790) and Gilbert de Pixérécourt's *Coelina, ou l'enfant du mystère* (1800). The French influence, plus the Gothic element in the work of Goethe and Schiller, plus, no doubt, the increasing vogue of the Gothic novel (*q.v.*) and the popularity of M. G. 'Monk' Lewis's melodrama *The Castle Spectre* (1797), all contributed to produce an extraordinary number of melodramas on the English stage during the 19th c., a period during which a very large number of novels (by Scott, Reade, Dickens, Wilkie Collins and others) were adapted for the stage in the form of melodrama.

The flourishing of melodrama in the 19th c. produced a kind of naively sensational entertainment containing protagonists who were excessively virtuous or exceptionally evil, an abundance of blood, thunder, thrills and violent action which made use of spectres, ghouls, witches, vampires and many a skeleton from the supernatural cupboard, and also (in more domestic melodrama) a sordid realism in the shape of extravagant tales of the wickedness of drinking, gambling and murdering.

Melodrama all but died out at the end of the 19th c., and at the beginning of the 20th, plays like George Bernard Shaw's *Passion, Poison and Petrification, or The Fatal Gazogene* (1905) were wont to make fun of the more grotesque features of the Victorian melodrama.

Since about the 1920s the cinema has largely ousted melodrama from the stage, but the melodramatic can still draw big and appreciative audiences (hence the success of the revival of Boucicault's *The Shaughraun* in 1988). *See also* GRAND GUIGNOL; THEATRE OF CRUELTY; THRILLER.

melopoeia (Gk 'song making') The musical element in Classical Greek tragedy. Clearly, from its form, it is related to onomatopoeia (*q.v.*) but refers more to the tune and music of the verses, rather than to the specific sounds for certain effects. *See also* LOGOPOEIA; ONOMATOPOEIA; PHANOPOEIA.

memoir-novel A form of novel (*q.v.*) which purports to be a 'true' autobiographical account but which is wholly or mostly fictitious. Thus, a kind of literary convention or fictional device. Daniel Defoe appears to have been the first practitioner with *Robinson Crusoe* (1719) and *Moll Flanders* (1722). Other examples in the 18th c. are Smollett's *Roderick Random* (1748), Goldsmith's *The Vicar of Wakefield* (1766), Mackenzie's *The Man of Feeling* (1771) and Maria Edgeworth's *Castle Rackrent* (1800). In the 19th c. this kind of fiction was much less popular.

memoirs *See* AUTOBIOGRAPHY; DIARY AND JOURNAL.

Menippean (or Varronian) satire So called after Menippus, its originator, who was a philosopher and a Cynic of the 3rd c. BC. He satirized the follies of men (including philosophers) in a mixture of prose and verse. He was imitated by Varro (thus this type of satire is sometimes called Varronian) and also by Lucian – especially in his *Dialogues*.

Less formally regulated than Lucilian satire (*q.v.*), the classic example of this genre in European literature is *Satire Ménippée*, a pamphlet in prose and verse which ridiculed the *États généraux* of 1593 and was published in 1594. It was written by Jean Leroy with the assistance of Jacques Gillot, Nicolas Rapin, Pierre Pithou, Jean Passerat and Florent Chrétien. Its main features were caricature, parody and burlesque (*qq.v.*). It has been suggested by Northrop Frye in his *Anatomy of Criticism* that Burton's *Anatomy of Melancholy* (1621) is in the tradition of Menippus and Varro. Other works which perhaps owe something to this tradition of *satura* or medley are Rabelais's *Gargantua* and *Pantagruel*, Voltaire's *Candide*, Thomas Love Peacock's *Nightmare Abbey*, Aldous Huxley's *Point Counter Point* and *After Many a Summer* and a number of other intellectual charades and fantasies which, through debate and dialogue, serve to ridicule different intellectual attitudes and philosophical postures. *See* HORATIAN SATIRE; JUVENALIAN SATIRE; LUCILIAN SATIRE; SATIRE.

menology (Gk 'record of the month') A form of calendar (*q.v.*) used especially in the Greek Orthodox Church, with biographies of the saints and martyrs. *See* HAGIOGRAPHY; SYNAXARION.

merde, mystique de la Not exactly the 'mystique of shit', but a term denoting a preoccupation with the seamier, muddier, bloodier aspects of life, as well as, excessively, with sex and money. The term was first used by Robert E. Fitch in 1956, and is a coarser version of *nostalgie de la boue*. Among modern writers, Joyce, Genet, Hemingway, Tennessee Williams and William Burroughs have all, from time to time, exploited the possibilities of *merde*.

merismus (Gk 'division into parts') A rhetorical device in which a subject or topic is divided into its various parts. A fairly well-known instance occurs in Shakespeare's *Troilus and Cressida* (III, iii, 171):

> For beauty, wit,
> High birth, vigour of bone, desert in service,
> Love, friendship, charity, are subjects all
> To envious and calumniating Time.

Merz It apparently derives from the word *Kommerz* (commerce); *Merz* was the word which Kurt Schwitters (1887–1948) used as a title for his Dada movement in Hanover in the 1920s. There is also a suggestion that the term is a kind of portmanteau word (*q.v.*) which recalls the French *merde* (*q.v.*) and the German *ausmerzen* ('to extirpate'). Schwitters was a poet as well as a painter, and his work gave rise to *Merz* and a form of concrete poetry (*q.v.*). *See also* ALTAR POEM; PATTERN POETRY.

mesode (Gk 'middle ode') In Greek drama, part of an ode (*q.v.*) between strophe and antistrophe (*qq.v.*). It has an independent existence.

mesostich *See* ACROSTIC.

messenger In Classical Greek tragedy action which took place off stage was reported by a messenger or herald. In Euripides's *Medea*, for example, a messenger entered to report that the princess was dead, and her death was described in some detail. The messenger often figured in Tudor and Jacobean tragedy and occasionally in comedy. This character – or someone performing the function of messenger – was also employed in French Classical drama.

mester de clerecía (Sp 'art of the clerics') After the *epopeya*, the *cantares de gesta* (*q.v.*) chanted by minstrels or *juglares*, and referred to in contrast as the *mester de juglaría*, came the scholars with their learned poetry. This last is what is meant by *mester de clerecía*. At the beginning of the 13th c. attempts were made by the clerics to improve both style and content of the popular verse. Improvements in form led to the *cuaderna vía* (*q.v.*), via the Latin Goliardic verse used by clerics in many countries. But the vehicle was one thing and the intention another. The clerics wished to spread to the ordinary people knowledge of the lives of the saints and other sacred themes. So they used simple methods of composition, a direct style and, so far as possible, the language of the people. The character of the poetry was narrative and real inspiration was rare – as is often the case in didactic (*q.v.*) poetry.

mester de juglaría (Sp 'occupation, or art, of the minstrel') The term denotes oral and epic (*q.v.*) narrative poetry of the 12th, 13th and 14th c. It was composed and recited by minstrels and *juglares* and intended to entertain, unlike the *mester de clerecía* (*q.v.*), which was didactic.

metafiction Any work of fiction which seems preoccupied by its own fictionality or with the nature of fiction generally. In the same way as a metalanguage reflects on language(s), metafiction is fiction whose subject is fiction. Metafiction differs from realist fiction, which employs all kinds of techniques – linear narrative, cause and effect, detailed description, rich characters and dialogue – to encourage readers to feel that what they are reading corresponds with reality. Metafiction, by contrast, obliges its readers to consider first and foremost its own artifice; it disrupts the illusion that fiction gives direct access to the 'real world'. Common techniques include beginnings and endings which comment on the nature of beginnings and endings; the appearance of the author as a character (who may well discuss the process of writing the narrative); and the realization by characters that they are merely characters. Metafiction is often most closely associated with postmodern literature of the late 20th c., and is commonly understood to be motivated by a perception of the shortcomings of realist fiction. For instance, Kurt Vonnegut's celebrated metafictional Second World War novel *Slaughterhouse Five* (1967) intimates that realist fiction is inadequate for talking about war because it always gives order and sense to something which is in fact senseless. However, metafiction certainly pre-dates the rise of postmodernism (*q.v.*). Lawrence Sterne's reflexive novel (*q.v.*) *Tristram Shandy* (1760–7) is still one of the most famous examples. *See also* POSTMODERNISM; METALANGUAGE.

metalanguage In linguistics it denotes any technical language which describes the properties of language (discussed by Roman Jakobson in his essay *Linguistics and Poetics*, 1960). Literally a 'beyond' language, it is also known as a 'second-order' language, which may be used to describe, explain, interpret or replace a 'first-order' language. Each order of language implicitly relies on a metalanguage by which it is explained. In his book *Elements of Semiology* (1967) Roland Barthes perceives that this could lead to an indefinite regression or *aporia* (*q.v.*), which would ultimately undermine and destroy all metalanguages. *See* DECONSTRUCTION; POSTSTRUCTURALISM.

metalepsis (Gk 'after taking, substitution') A form of metonymy (*q.v.*) in which the general idea substituted is considerably removed from the particular detail. As in these lines from *Henry VIII* (II, i):

> Go with me like good angels to my end;
> And as the long divorce of steel falls on me
> Make of your prayers one sweet sacrifice…

See EUPHEMISM; PERIPHRASIS.

metanarrative (Gk 'meta': 'beyond', 'after', 'about') A second-order, totalizing reflection about a group of narratives or stories, aiming to explain, order, unify or contextualize them. Jean-François Lyotard uses the term 'metanarrative' in his work *The Postmodern Condition: A Report on Knowledge* (1979). For Lyotard, 'metanarratives' represent overarching belief systems since they tend to explain all other 'little stories' and therefore make universal and totalizing claims about reality, knowledge or experience. Science, nationalism and different religious and ideological systems are examples of such 'metanarratives'. Lyotard examines the changing status of knowledge in the West, focusing particularly on science, and argues that the Enlightenment's purportedly objective and scientifically legitimate knowledge of the world has been no more than a powerful metanarrative. In the postmodern, post-Auschwitz world, these 'grand' narratives have lost their legitimacy and so Lyotard defines postmodernity as 'incredulity towards metanarratives'. Like other poststructuralist thinkers, Lyotard wants to deconstruct modernity's assumptions about rationality, knowledge and progress. After the undermining of these metanarratives, Lyotard argues, the existence of universal and eternal truths can no longer be claimed; legitimacy can only reside in what he terms *petits récits*, 'small' or 'localized' narratives which are provisional, contingent and make no claim to universality. *See also* POSTMODERNISM; POSTSTRUCTURALISM.

metanoia (Gk 'after thought, change of mind') A figurative device in which a statement is made, and then withdrawn or lessened in its impact. For example: 'I'll murder you. You will be punished.'

metaphor (Gk 'carrying from one place to another') A figure of speech in which one thing is described in terms of another. The basic figure in poetry. A comparison is usually implicit; whereas in simile (*q.v.*) it is explicit. There are several metaphors in these lines from the beginning of R. S. Thomas's *Song at the Year's Turning*:

> Shelley dreamed it. Now the dream decays.
> The props crumble. The familiar ways
> Are stale with tears trodden underfoot.
> The heart's flower withers at the root.
> Bury it, then, in history's sterile dust.
> The slow years shall tame your tawny lust.

See ORGANIC METAPHOR; TELESCOPED METAPHOR; TENOR AND VEHICLE.

metaphor/metonymy   A theory of binary opposition (*q.v.*) propounded by Roman Jakobson (1896–1982) in *Two Aspects of Language and Two Types of Aphasic Disturbances* (1956). Jakobson uses the distinction developed elsewhere between the two axes of language, syntagmatic and paradigmatic (*q.v.*). The first may be thought of as a horizontal line (here one word is associated with another through contiguity), the second as a vertical line where meanings can be substituted one for another. Through his study of aphasia (a language disorder resulting from memory loss), Jakobson extends this model to metaphor and metonymy (*qq.v.*). Thus, the language disorder acts on the two axes of language in different ways so that those suffering from a 'continuity disorder' tend to use substitution (i.e. metaphor) and those suffering from 'similarity disorder' tend to use association (i.e. metonymy). In Jakobson's words: 'Metaphor is alien to the similarity disorder, and metonymy to the continuity disorder.' Jakobson's point is that some forms of writing use one or the other mode predominantly. Romantic and modernist poetry primarily uses metaphor, and the realist novel uses metonymy. Magic realism (*q.v.*) subverts the mainly metonymic axis of the narrative discourse/novel form, as does postmodernism (*q.v.*). In *The Modes of Modern Writing* (1977) and in *Modern Criticism and Theory* (1988) David Lodge discusses aspects of Jakobson's theories.

metaphysical   (L *al* suffixed to Gk 'beyond [Aristotle's work on] physics') A term now generally applied to a group of 17th c. poets; chiefly Donne, Carew, George Herbert, Crashaw, Henry Vaughan, Marvell, Cleveland and Cowley. It appears that one of the first to use the term was William Drummond of Hawthornden in a letter to Arthur Johnson *c.* 1630. Later Samuel Johnson, in his *Lives of the Poets* (1779–81), established the term more or less permanently as a label. Johnson wrote somewhat disapprovingly of the *discordia concors* in metaphysical imagery, and referred to 'heterogeneous ideas . . . yoked by violence together'.

The marks of 17th c. metaphysical poetry were arresting and original images and conceits (showing a preoccupation with analogies between macrocosm and microcosm), wit, ingenuity, dexterous use of colloquial speech, considerable flexibility of rhythm and meter, complex themes (both sacred and profane), a liking for paradox and dialectical argument, a direct manner, a caustic humour, a keenly felt awareness of mortality, and a distinguished capacity for elliptical thought and tersely compact expression. But for all their intellectual robustness the metaphysical poets were also capable of refined delicacy, gracefulness and deep feeling; passion as well as wit. An example is Marvell's *The Definition of Love*.

The Metaphysicals have had a profound influence on the course of English poetry, thanks, in great measure, to the critical appreciations of Herbert Grierson, T. S. Eliot, J. B. Leishman, H. C. White, Rosemond Tuve, Cleanth Brooks, Louis Martz, George Williamson and Helen Gardner. *See* CONCEIT.

metastasis   (Gk 'a changing') A cursory treatment of a matter; a glossing over as if it were of no importance.

metatheatre   A term coined by Lionel Abel in 1963 to classify 'serious' plays which, he argues, do not qualify as tragedies, such as Arthur Miller's *Death of a Salesman* (1949), Tennessee Williams's *A Streetcar Named Desire* (1949), John Arden's *Serjeant Musgrave's Dance* (1959) and Robert Bolt's *A Man for All Seasons* (1960). *See also* DRAME; TRAGEDY.

metathesis   (Gk 'transposition') The interchanging of consonant sounds, as in *third* from OE *thridda* (cf. G *dritte*).

meter   (Gk 'measure') The term refers to the pattern of stressed and unstressed syllables in verse. In English verse, meter is based on stress rather than quantity (*q.v.*). A line may have a fixed number of syllables and yet have a varying number of stresses. As a rule meter keeps to a basic pattern, within which there are many variations. A common form of variation is substitution (*q.v.*).

In English verse the following meters are the commonest: iambic ⌣ /; trochaic / ⌣; anapaestic ⌣ ⌣ /; dactylic / ⌣ ⌣; spondaic / /; paeonic / ⌣ ⌣ ⌣ (first paeon).

Coleridge's poem *Metrical Feet* helps to illustrate the first five of these feet:

> Tróchĕe tríps frŏm lóng tŏ shórt.
> Frŏm lóng tŏ lóng ĭn sólĕmn sórt
> Slów spóndĕe stálks; stróng foŏt yét íll áblĕ
> Évĕr tŏ cóme ŭp wĭth thĕ dáctўl trĭsýllăblĕ.
> Ĭámbĭcs márch frŏm shórt tŏ lóng.
> Wĭth ă leáp ănd ă boúnd thĕ swĭft ánăpaĕsts thróng.

The following terms denote the number of feet per line: monometer – 1; dimeter – 2; trimeter – 3; tetrameter – 4; pentameter – 5; hexameter – 6; heptameter – 7; octameter – 8 (*qq.v.*). *See also* FOOT; FREE VERSE; PROSODY; SCANSION; SPRUNG RHYTHM.

metonymy   (Gk 'name change') A figure of speech in which the name of an attribute or a thing is substituted for the thing itself. Common examples are 'The Stage' for the theatrical profession; 'The Crown' for the monarchy; 'The Bench' for the judiciary; 'Dante' for his works. *See also* ANTONOMASIA; METALEPSIS; SYNECDOCHE.

metrical romance A story of adventure, love, chivalry, and deeds of derring-do. They quite often contain an element of mystery and the supernatural. A popular form of entertainment from the Middle Ages until the 19th c. when the prose romance, already established in the previous century, gradually superseded it. Among numerous metrical romances, one might mention: *Roman de Troie* (c. 1160); *Roman de la Rose* (13th c.); *Sir Orfeo* (mid-14th c.); *Sir Gawain and the Green Knight* (14th c.); Scott's *Lay of the Last Minstrel* (1805) and *The Lady of the Lake* (1810); Byron's *Giaour* (1813) and *The Corsair* (1814); Tennyson's *Idylls of the King* (1842–85) and *The Lady of Shalott* (1852); William Morris's *The Earthly Paradise* (1868–70). See ROMANCE.

metrical variations The term covers various techniques used in achieving contrasts in the rhythm and meter of verse. Variations are only possible when there is a basic metrical pattern. Substitution (*q.v.*) is the commonest variation. *See* COUNTERPOINT; FOOT; METER.

metron In Classical prosody the unit of measurement.

mezzo-zeugma (It and Gk 'middle yoke') A figurative device by which a word, usually a verb, refers to two parts of an expression or governs it. As in this example from Pope's *Epistle to Arbuthnot*, in which 'ask'd' governs 'Judgment' and 'place':

> Receiv'd of Wits an undistinguish'd race,
> Who first his Judgment ask'd, and then a Place:

See ZEUGMA.

middle-brow novel A term first used in the late 1920s, some fifteen years after the emergence of 'high brow' and 'low brow', terms which described writing that was, respectively, intellectual and literary, and popular and generic. 'Middle brow', first employed by book reviewers, denotes work that somehow falls between trashy romances and adventure stories on the one hand, and challenging works of literature on the other. It is a term laced with contempt: middle-brow writing is conservative, unoriginal and smug. Largely, though, this derision is motivated by snobbery and misogyny, for the middle-brow novel is closely associated with middle-class female writers and readers. Domestic settings and a preoccupation with class and manners predominate. Stella Gibbons, Nancy Mitford and Agatha Christie are considered purveyors of middle-brow fiction. Male authors who have also been deemed middle-brow include E. F. Benson, John Galsworthy and P. G. Wodehouse.

Works of 'high' literature have long been considered material worthy of serious academic study, and popular fiction has been recovered by cultural studies (*q.v.*) or else may be appreciated as kitsch (*q.v.*). The middle-brow novel, though, has had few champions. In the last twenty years, however, literary scholars such as Nicola Humble have sought to rehabilitate the middle-brow novel and defend it from elite condescension. The success of the middle-brow novel in the early to mid 20th c. corresponds with the rise of an affluent suburbanized middle class and the growing independence of women. Such literature has helped to consolidate – but also to interrogate – these emerging gender and class identities.

In any case, 'middle-brow' is an unstable category. What are we to make, for instance, of those female authors such as Ivy Compton-Burnett and Elizabeth Bowen whose work was both formally innovative and largely focused on middle-class family life? Many 19th c. novels, such as those by Austen and Thackeray (defended by elite readers as 'classics'), seem middle-brow. And even the shrillest of 20th c. critics of middle-class culture – Evelyn Waugh and George Orwell, for instance – produced numerous middle-brow novels. In the US, Dwight Macdonald asserts in *Against the American Grain* (1962) that middle-brow culture threatens high culture through adulteration: the respect of 'midcult' for the standards of the avant-garde is mere posture; the vulgarization of high culture will ensue unless it is protected from middle-brow consumption. However, scholar Janice Radway has argued that identifiably middle-brow forums – such as America's Book of the Month Club (founded 1926) – offer readers an alternative to academic and elite standards of literary value by stressing the affective experience – and intellectual challenges – of reading fiction. *See also* FEMINIST CRITICISM; NOVEL; WORKING-CLASS NOVEL.

Middle Comedy This succeeded Old Comedy (*q.v.*) of which the chief writer was Aristophanes. Middle Comedy flourished from *c.* 400 BC to *c.* 330 BC. It contained a good deal of burlesque, parody (*qq.v.*) and literary criticism. Antiphanes and Elixis were the main dramatists in this genre. *See* COMEDY.

middle rhyme *See* INTERNAL RHYME; LEONINE RHYME.

miles gloriosus Originated in a comedy by Plautus (254–184 BC). The *miles gloriosus* was a braggart soldier, the prototype of a stock character (*q.v.*) in comic drama; one who is fundamentally a coward yet boasts of valorous deeds and is often made a fool of by other characters. In English drama he first appeared eponymously in Udall's *Ralph Roister Doister* (*c.* 1553). Bobadill in Ben Jonson's *Every Man in His Humour* (1598) was another such braggart. So was Captain Brazen in Farquhar's *The Recruiting Officer* (1706). The epitome of the braggart was Shakespeare's Falstaff. *See* BRAGGADOCIO.

millennial fiction A recently coined term used to denote the body of contemporary writing published at the turn of the 21st c. In Britain, it came into use with the publication of Zadie Smith's *White Teeth* in 2000. Millennial and post-millennial fiction from 2001 to the present has captured the *Zeitgeist* by exploring a range of themes such as multiculturalism and the impact of the 9/11 attacks in America.

Miltonic sonnet A form devised by Milton. He retained the octave (*q.v.*) rhyme scheme of the Petrarchan sonnet (*q.v.*) but dispensed with a change of meaning or a turning point or *volta* (*q.v.*) at the beginning of the sestet (*q.v.*). His rhyme scheme in the sestet was also flexible. His sonnet *On the Late Massacre in Piedmont* is an example.

mime (Gk 'imitation') A form of drama in which actors tell a story by gestures, originating in Sicily and southern Italy. Sophron of Syracuse (5th c. BC) composed mime plays. So did Herodas (3rd c. BC) who later influenced Plautus, Terence and Horace. Dumb acting continued as a very popular form of entertainment throughout the Middle Ages and achieved a considerable revival in Italy in the 16th c. when it was much practised in *commedia dell'arte* (*q.v.*). The influence spread through Europe and in varying degrees mime has been part of the European dramatic tradition ever since.

Nowadays mime denotes acting without words. In France particularly, mime is regarded as an entertainment in its own right. In the 1920s Étienne Decroux encouraged its development and Jean-Louis Barrault aroused much interest in it through his performance in *Les Enfants du paradis*. Jacques Tati has also displayed its possibilities in the cinema. Marcel Marceau was regarded as the greatest mime in the world and virtually established his own genre of monomime. The 19th c. French mime play *L'Enfant prodigue* (in three acts) is the best-known work of the kind. *See* DUMB SHOW; PANTOMIME.

mimesis It has almost the same meaning as mime (*q.v.*) but the concept of imitation (*q.v.*) in this case has wider connotations. Aristotle, in *Poetics*, states that tragedy (*q.v.*) is an imitation of an action, but he uses the term comprehensively to refer to the construction of a play and what is put into it. We should rather use *mimesis* to mean representation, which relates to verisimilitude (*q.v.*). The outstanding work on this topic is Eric Auerbach's *Mimesis* (1957). *See also* DIEGESIS.

mimicry An important term in postcolonial studies. It is used to describe a structural ambivalence in colonial discourse (*q.v.*) and it is often associated with the work of the postcolonial critic Homi Bhabha (1949–). In his book *The Location of Culture* (1994), Bhabha takes as a starting point the Lacanian concept of mimicry as camouflage and Frantz Fanon's discussion of the menacing effect of masks in his book *Black Skins, White Masks* (1952) to examine the ambivalent relationship between colonizer and colonized. Bhabha shows how the colonizer encourages the colonized to copy, internalize or 'mimic' aspects of the colonizing culture, its behaviours, manners and values. Mimicry thus produces the colonized subject who is 'almost the same, but not quite', but it also opens up a disturbing rupture in 'the civilizing mission' of colonial dominance since the colonizer is never sure if the colonized mimics or mocks. As Bhabha writes, 'mimicry is at once resemblance and menace'. Mimicry produces colonial subjects whose not-quite-sameness distorts and fractures the identity of the colonizer as he sees traces of himself in the colonized. At the same time, he needs to maintain the difference between, for example, his 'real' Englishness and the 'Anglicized' colonial subjects, a difference on which colonialism depends.

By examining the dialectical effects of the colonial encounter, Bhabha aims to show how 'partial' colonial discourse is; that is, it contains the seeds of its own failure. For example, the teaching of Christianity and English Literature in India was always already hybridized by 'local' practices; it also produced a (justified) fear in the colonizer that such teaching might inspire the Indians to fight for their liberty. Bhabha closes his discussion by giving another example: the Bible, as a symbol of Empire's greatness, ended up being used as a wrapping paper in Bengal in 1817. *See also* POSTCOLONIALISM.

Minnesinger (G 'love singer') A German lyric poet who, in the 12th and 13th c., composed poems of courtly love (*q.v.*) or *hohe Minne*. The *Minnesang* was the love-song of homage to a lady. The most renowned of these Minnesingers were Hartmann von Aue and Walther von der Vogelweide. *See also* JONGLEUR; MEISTERGESANG; TROUBADOUR; TROUVÈRE.

minstrel (MedL *ministerialis* 'pertaining to a minister or servant') The original minstrels were itinerant musicians, professional entertainers, some of whom had fairly permanent positions in courts. The minstrel was the descendant of the *scop*, the *gleeman*, and the *jongleur* (*qq.v.*). Minstrels flourished especially in the 13th and 14th c., but there were many fewer after the invention of printing. They sang old, traditional stories like the *chansons de gestes* (*q.v.*), short epics and folk ballads. Some composed what they sang, but the art of the minstrel, like that of the Slav *guslar* (*q.v.*), is such that it is almost impossible to tell where memory ends and invention begins. *See also* ORAL TRADITION; TROUBADOUR; TROUVÈRE.

Miracle Play This dramatic genre was a later development from the Mystery Play (*q.v.*). It dramatized saints' lives and divine miracles, and legends of miraculous interventions by the Virgin. Little of note survives in English literature, but in France there is the famous cycle of the *Miracles de Notre Dame*, forty-two plays belonging to the second half of the 14th c. Written in octosyllabic couplets, each dramatizes some aspect of human activity, and each ends with a miraculous intervention by the Blessed Virgin. Other European examples are the German *Marienklage* and the Dutch *Mariken van Nieumeghen* (c. 1500). *See also* INTERLUDE; LITURGICAL DRAMA; MORALITY PLAY; PASSION PLAY.

mirror stage A concept formulated by the French psychoanalyst Jacques Lacan (1901–81) in a 1949 paper of the same title. Lacan locates the mirror stage in the development of a child between the ages of six and eighteen months. At this stage the child can 'recognize as such his own image in a mirror'. The image reflected in the mirror is what Lacan calls 'the Ideal-I', an idealized, coherent and unified version of itself. But this mirror stage occurs prior to the child's actual acquisition of a sense of self, a sense of itself as subject in distinction from objects in the world: the child experiences, as projected in its mirror image, itself and its surroundings as an integrated unity.

This experience of illusory unity is not entirely left behind even when the child grows beyond the mirror stage. The illusion of unity and enduring identity that occurs in the mirror phase also anticipates the lifelong alienation of the ego, not only from the objects that surround it, objects of its desire, but also from itself. The passing of the mirror stage marks the transition from the child's comforting assumption of his satisfying total image or 'I' in the mirror to his entry into the social world. The child has effectively passed from the Imaginary order to the Symbolic order (*q.v.*). What Lacan seems to be suggesting is that from this point onwards, the child's knowledge or awareness will never be immediate, will never be based on a somehow pure experience which precedes identity formation and the categories of subject and object. Rather it will enter a 'socially elaborated' system where all knowledge will be relational and highly mediated (through social, educational and ideological structures), and where the child as 'subject' will confront elements of the world as 'objects', as forms of otherness or foreignness to his identity. Its relation to these objects will assume the form of desire, which is according to Hegel the form of consciousness itself (since it is desire of a subject for an object that defines their mutual relation as one of mutual demarcation, separation and definition).

Lacan suggests that the ego, far from being the coherent, unified and rational agency that has been bequeathed by Descartes and by Enlightenment philosophy, is characterized by its very failure to achieve unity and self-understanding. *See also* IMAGINARY, SYMBOLIC, REAL; POSTSTRUCTURALISM.

miscellany A medley; a collection of writings in one volume. Probably the most famous in English literature is Tottel's Miscellany (1557). *See also* ANTHOLOGY.

mise en abyme A literary recursion: André Gide's coinage for the literary effect of infinite regression. Gide's own *Les Faux-monnayeurs* (*The Counterfeiters*) (1926) established the device. It has been used by, among others, Italo Calvino in *If On a Winter's Night a Traveller* (1979), a novel about reading *If On a Winter's Night a Traveller*.

mise-en-page (F 'putting-on-the-page') A collective term for those features of a written or printed text which derive from practical considerations of design and layout: thus the choice and order of words, or the lineation of verse, are not a part of the *mise-en-page*, but the choice of fount, the degree of leading, the pagination, and all ancillary material (illustrations, ornaments, page numbers, etc.) are. It follows that the same text (say, *King Lear*) will have a different *mise-en-page* in each edition (Arden, Riverside, Penguin, etc.).

mise-en-scène (Fr 'putting in the scene') Refers to the all the visual aspects of a theatrical production or film, such as the stage design, scenery, costumes and actors. Sometimes the term is used in film theory to denote all that can be encompassed by a single shot of the camera. In general, it can convey an emotional tone, a character's state of mind, or some kind of development in the narrative or action.

misprision *See* ANXIETY OF INFLUENCE.

misreading A term most recently associated with the critics Paul de Man and Harold Bloom. In *Blindness and Insight* (1971), de Man, influenced by Jacques Derrida, argued that the insights produced by critics are intrinsically linked to certain blindnesses, the critics invariably affirming something other than what they intended. De Man's *Allegories of Reading* (1979) explored the theory of tropes or figurative language, affirming that language is intrinsically metaphorical and that literary texts above all are highly self-conscious of their status as such and are self-deconstructing. Hence, criticism inevitably misreads a text, given that figurative language mediates between literary and critical text. Harold Bloom, also centrally concerned with the function of tropes in literature, is best known for his assessment of poetic tradition on the basis of the 'anxiety of influence'. Each writer, asserted Bloom, attempts to carve out an imaginative space free from overt domination by his or her predecessors; to this end, as Bloom argued in *A Map of Misreading* (1975), the writer assumes an Oedipal disposition, creatively misreading those predecessors or 'fathers' by way of certain tropes such as irony, synecdoche and metonymy.

mixed metaphor It arises when there is an incongruity between the two elements of the implied comparison, as in the journalist's assertion that 'a bottleneck is strangling the traffic flow'. *See also* METAPHOR.

mnemonic (Gk *mneme*, 'memory') A memorization device in verse or prose. Well-known examples are (a) Oxidation Is Loss; Reduction Is Gain – the initial letters make OILRIG; (b) Richard Of York Gave Battle In Vain; or Read Over Your Good Books In Verse; here the initial letters give the seven prismatic colours: red, orange, yellow, green, blue, indigo, violet. *See also* ACRONYM.

mock-epic A work in verse which employs the lofty manner, the high and serious tone and the supernatural machinery (*q.v.*) of epic (*q.v.*) to treat of a trivial subject and theme in such a way as to make both subject and theme ridiculous. Almost a case of breaking a butterfly upon a wheel. By extension the epic mode is also mocked but this is a secondary consideration.

The acknowledged masterpiece in this genre is Pope's *The Rape of the Lock* (1712, 1714), which he himself describes as an Heroicomical poem. His subject is the estrangement between two families resulting from Lord Petre's snipping off a lock of Miss Arabella Fermor's hair. With faultless skill Pope minifies the epic scale in proportion to the triviality of his theme:

> What dire Offence from am'rous Causes springs,
> What mighty Contests rise from trivial Things,
> I sing – This Verse to *Caryll*, Muse! is due;

> This, ev'n *Belinda* may vouchsafe to view:
> Slight is the Subject, but not so the Praise,
> If She inspire, and He approve my Lays.
>   Say what strange Motive, Goddess! cou'd compel
> A well-bred *Lord* t'assault a gentle *Belle*?

Pope had precedents in the Homeric *Batrachomyomachia*, or *The Battle of the Frogs and the Mice* (translated by Thomas Parnell as a contemporary satire in 1717); Alessandro Tassoni's *La Secchia Rapita* (The Rape of the Bucket) (1622); Boileau's *Le Lutrin* (1674, 1683); Dryden's *Mac Flecknoe* (1682); and Samuel Garth's *The Dispensary* (1699).

The mock-epic tone of Dryden's opening lines differs from Pope's:

> All humane things are subject to decay,
> And, when Fate summons, Monarchs must obey:
> This Fleckno found, who, like Augustus, young
> Was call'd to Empire, and had govern'd long;
> In Prose and Verse, was own'd, without dispute
> Through all the Realms of Non-sense, absolute.

Mac Flecknoe gave Pope the basic idea for *The Dunciad* (1728–43); also a mock-epic, but more powerful, in a denunciatory manner; and more elaborate than *The Rape of the Lock*. See BURLESQUE; PARODY; SATIRE; TRAVESTY.

mock-heroic In the style of mock-epic (*q.v.*), but the term has a slightly wider application. The heroic manner is adopted to make a trivial subject seem grand in such a way as to satirize the style, and it is therefore commonly used in burlesque and parody (*qq.v.*). Fielding's *Tom Thumb* (1730) is a good example of a mock-heroic play, and John Philips's *The Splendid Shilling* (1705) of a burlesque poem.

mode Sometimes approximately synonymous with kind and form, and related to genre (*q.v.*). It is associated with method, manner and style (*q.v.*). Some incline to describe science fiction (*q.v.*) as a mode rather than a genre. Perhaps, too, the horror story (*q.v.*) may be regarded as a mode rather than a genre.

modernism A comprehensive but vague term for a movement (or tendency) which began to get under way in the closing years of the 19th c. and which had a wide influence internationally during much of the 20th c. The term pertains to all the creative arts, especially poetry, fiction, drama, painting, music and architecture. There have been various theories as to when the movement (or its tendencies) was at its height (some suggest the 1920s for this) and as to whether the modernist movement is actually over. Some have suggested that modernism, as an innovative and revivifying movement, was played out by the late 1940s, and that it was then that postmodernism (*q.v.*) began. In fact, such movements, of their nature, do not just start and stop; the evolution is gradual. The impetus and energy of one diminishes (but continues) as the momentum of another burgeons.

Nevertheless, it is valid to point out certain places and periods where and when modernist tendencies were at their most active and fruitful. For example, in France from the 1890s until the 1940s; in Russia during the pre-revolutionary years and the 1920s; in Germany from the 1890s and on during the 1920s; in England from early in the 20th c. and during the 1920s and 1930s; in America from shortly before the First World War and on during the interwar period. Thus, it was a European and transcontinental movement, and its principal centres of activity were the capital cities.

Within the general movement or tendency, there were subsidiary and now labelled and identifiable movements (e.g. surrealism, formalism, *qq.v.*). Much that is loosely categorized under modernism is or was avant-garde (*q.v.*); but one may distinguish between an 'old' avant-garde (e.g. the French symbolist poets) and a 'new' avant-garde which is postmodernist (e.g. dramatists of the Theatre of the Absurd, *q.v.*, and the practitioners of the *nouveau roman, q.v.*). Professor Frank Kermode made a further distinction: between palaeo-modernism and neo-modernism. The former refers to early manifestations of new movements concluding, perhaps, *c.* 1914–20; the latter to movements since that time.

As far as literature is concerned modernism reveals a breaking away from established rules, traditions and conventions, fresh ways of looking at man's position and function in the universe and many (in some cases remarkable) experiments in form and style. It is particularly concerned with language and how to use it (representationally or otherwise) and with *writing itself*. Thus, structuralism was (and is) from the outset closely connected with modernist tendencies, though the theories of structuralism (*q.v.*) did not gain a strong foothold until the 1960s, by which time postmodernism was well established as a new movement.

Aspects of modernism are touched on in the following entries: CONSTRUC-TIVISM; DADAISM; DECADENCE; EXISTENTIALISM; EXPRESSIONISM; FREE VERSE; FUTURISM; IDEOGRAMIC METHOD; IMAGISTS; NEW HUMANISM; PYLON POETS; STREAM OF CONSCIOUSNESS; SYMBOL AND SYMBOLISM; ULTRAISM; VORTICISM.

modernismo A term coined by the Nicaraguan poet Rubén Darío (1867–1916), it denotes simply 'modernism' (*q.v.*). It was Darío's intention to modernize the language and themes of poetry in the Spanish-American culture. He and his followers were considerably influenced by the Parnassians (*q.v.*).

modernity The word 'modern' has been used very loosely in a number of disciplines. In literature it may refer to both historical periods and literary movements. In general, modernity refers to the historical period commencing roughly with the Enlightenment and the French Revolution; the former ushered in an age where rationality and scientific observation displaced theology; and the latter effectively set the stage for the abolition of a feudal social and political structure, the rise of the bourgeois (*q.v.*) class and early capitalism. Both phenomena were integrally related to the development of science and technology, and the industrial revolutions. Important early thinkers of modernity included Sir Francis Bacon who urged the inductive method and experimentation based on observation as against traditionalistic scholastic deduction, Descartes who proposed a method of inquiry based on rationality rather than theological authority, and empiricists such as John Locke and David Hume who insisted that our knowledge be derived from our actual sense-experience of the world.

Post-modernity designates a society that has evolved beyond the phases of industrial and finance capitalism into consumer capitalism, characterized by the global extension of capitalist markets, mass migration of labour, the predominating role of mass media and images, unprecedented economic and cultural interaction between various parts of the world, and an unprecedented pluralism and diversity at all levels of culture. According to many of the theorists of postmodernism (q.v.), this contemporary social order no longer is based on, or even attempts to pursue, the Enlightenment ideals of progress, justice and the rational acquisition of knowledge aided by scientific and technological advance. Rather, the external world is viewed as an ideological construction, refracted through an endlessly circulating world of signs, through media images and the various technologies and institutional codes (of school, workplace, religious centres) that hold us in their sway. *See also* POSTMODERNISM.

molossus (From a Greek place-name, Molossós) A metrical foot with three stressed syllables: / / /. Very rare anyway it hardly ever exists as an independent foot. However, some might argue that the last foot in the second of these two lines from Gerard Manley Hopkins's *The Caged Skylark* could be scanned as a molossus:

> As a dare-gale skylark scanted in a dull cage
> |Mán's mo'untĭng|spírĭt ĭn hĭs|bóne-hoúse,|meán hoúse, dwélls–

So the line would scan: palimbacchius/ first paeonic/ spondee/ molossus.

moment *See* EPIPHANY.

money novel (Also known as the 'business novel' or the 'economic novel') Narrative constructed around the process of money-making or the machinery of business; secondarily, of the political, social and acquisitive power conferred by these activities. Often cast as rags-to-riches stories (with both men and women as protagonists), money novels make epic or poetic the intricacies of dealing, markets and financial cunning; money novel heroes have epic and sometimes Faustian qualities, their activities being translated into forms of conflict and conquest. The Gilded Age (1860–1900) and its aftermath (especially in America) and the 1980s produced notable examples: Frank Norris's *The Pit* (1902), Theodore Dreiser's 'Trilogy of Desire' (1913–47), and Upton Sinclair's *The Money-Changers* (1909) are ancestors of Tom Wolfe's *The Bonfire of the Vanities* (1987), Po Bronson's *The Bombardiers* (1995), and Caryl Churchill's *Serious Money* (1987).

Monk's Tale stanza A stanza of eight iambic pentameters, rhyming ababbcbc, used by Chaucer in *The Monk's Tale*, an *ABC*, and some other poems. In origin it is a French *ballade* (*q.v.*) stanza. It was used quite a lot in the 15th c. and may well have been the model from which Spenser developed what is now known as the Spenserian stanza (*q.v.*).

monodrama A theatrical entertainment in which there is only one character. Ruth Draper, Cornelia Otis Skinner and Joyce Grenfell excelled in this genre. Tennyson also used the term to describe *Maud* (1855). A more recent example is *Krapp's Last Tape* (1959) by Samuel Beckett. *See* MONOLOGUE; MONOPOLYLOGUE.

monody (Gk 'alone song') An ode (*q.v.*) sung by a single actor in Greek tragedy, or a poem which mourns someone's death. In his introduction to *Lycidas* Milton described the poem as a monody. And Arnold called *Thyrsis* a monody. *See* DIRGE; ELEGY; EPICEDIUM; LAMENT.

monogatari (J 'tales') Japanese legends and stories in collections; mostly dating from the Middle Ages. Notable examples are: *Taketori Monogatari* (*c.* 850–920), one of the earliest extant works of Japanese fiction; *Utsubo Monogatari* (*c.* 850–1000); *Ise Monogatari* (*c.* 939); *Ochikubo Monogatari* (*c.* 950–990), a novel; *Yamato Monogatari* (*c.* 950), stories illustrated by poems; *Eiga Monogatari* (*c.* 1092); *Okagami* (*c.* 1115); *Hōgen Monogatari* (*c.* 1156), a story of the civil war of the Hōgen period; *Heiji Monogatari* (1159–60); *Tsutsumi Chūnagon Monogatari* (12th c.); *Heike Monogatari* (*c.* 1215–50). *See* NOVEL; SHORT STORY.

monograph (Gk 'single writing') An essay or treatise (*qq.v.*) on a particular subject.

monologic *See* DIALOGIC/MONOLOGIC.

monologue A term used in a number of senses, with the basic meaning of a single person speaking alone – with or without an audience. Most prayers, much lyric verse and all laments are monologues, but, apart from these, four main kinds can be distinguished: (a) monodrama (*q.v.*), as in Strindberg's *The Stronger*; (b) soliloquy (*q.v.*), for instance, the Moor's self-revelations in *Othello*; (c) solo addresses to an audience in a play; for instance, Iago's explanations to the audience (in *Othello*) of what he is going to do; (d) dramatic monologue (*q.v.*) – a poem in which there is one imaginary speaker addressing an imaginary audience, as in Browning's *My Last Duchess*. *See also* AUBADE; COMPLAINT; INTERIOR MONOLOGUE; PERSONA; STREAM OF CONSCIOUSNESS.

monometer A line of verse consisting of one metrical foot, as in Ogden Nash's 1931 ditty:

> Candy
> Is dandy
> But liquor
> Is quicker

> Pot
> Is not.

See also DIMETER; HEPTAMETER; HEXAMETER; OCTAMETER; PENTAMETER; TETRAMETER; TRIMETER

monopolylogue An entertainment in which one performer plays many parts, as in some forms of monodrama (*q.v.*).

monorhyme A poem or part of a poem in which all the lines have the same end-rhyme. It is by no means uncommon in Latin, Italian, Arabic, Welsh and Slav poetry. It is very common indeed in Slav poetry of the oral tradition (*q.v.*). In English verse, because English is not a language rich in easy rhymes, monorhyme is fairly uncommon; but Shakespeare achieved a nicely doggerel touch with nine such in 'All that glisters is not gold . . .' (*The Merchant of Venice*, II, vii, 67). *See also* IDENTICAL RHYME.

monostich (Gk 'one line') A single metrical line, or a poem consisting of one line.

mora (L 'delay') A unit of metrical time which denotes the duration (*q.v.*) of a short syllable which is usually represented thus: ∪. This is called a *breve*. The time occupied by a long syllable in quantitative verse is two *morae*. This is represented by /; and this is called a *macron*. *See* FOOT; SCANSION.

moral The lesson to be learnt from a story, poem, fable (*q.v.*), play – or indeed any work which purports to teach anything either directly or obliquely. Thus, the point in any didactic work. As Johnson put it, grandly, in *The Vanity of Human Wishes* (he was referring to the warrior king, Charles XII of Sweden):

> But did not Chance at length her Error mend?
> Did no subverted Empire mark his End?
> Did rival Monarchs give the fatal Wound?
> Or hostile Millions press him to the Ground?
> His Fall was destin'd to a barren Strand,
> A petty Fortress, and a dubious Hand;
> He left the Name, at which the World grew pale,
> To point a Moral, or adorn a Tale.

See DIDACTIC POETRY.

moral interlude A form of drama which has something in common with both the Morality Play and the Interlude (*qq.v.*). It tended to be didactic but contained more humour than the Morality. Two well-known examples are *Hyckescorner* (1512) and Wever's *Lusty Juventus* (c. 1550). But both have been taken to be ordinary Morality Plays.

moralische Wochenschriften German weekly periodicals published throughout much of the 18th c. Their models were English, especially the *Tatler* and the *Spectator*. They were moral in tone and content and concerned with morals, education and matters of taste and aesthetics. They were not political. *See* PERIODICAL.

Morality Play   Basically, a Morality Play is an allegory in dramatic form. Its dramatic origins are to be found in the Mystery and Miracle Plays of the late Middle Ages; its allegorical origins in the sermon literature, homilies, *exempla*, romances and works of spiritual edification like the *Lambeth Homilies* (12th c.); *Ancrene Riwle* (1200–50); the homily *Sawles Warde* (13th c.); *Chasteau d'Amour* (14th c.); the *Abbey of the Holy Ghost* (14th c.); *Aʒenbite of Inwyt* (1340). In essence a Morality Play was a dramatization of the battle between the forces of good and evil in the human soul; thus, an exteriorization of the inward spiritual struggle: man's need for salvation and the temptations which beset him on his pilgrimage through life to death. The main characters in *Everyman* (c. 1500) are God, a Messenger, Death, Everyman, Fellowship, Good Deeds, Goods, Knowledge, Beauty and Strength. Everyman is summoned by Death and he finds that no one will go with him except Good Deeds.

In other plays we find the forces of evil (the World, the Flesh and the Devil, the Seven Deadly Sins and various demons) deployed against Man, whose champions are the forces of good (God and his angels, and the four moral and the three theological virtues). Nearly all the Moralities are didactic illustrations of and commentaries on a preoccupation which dominated Christian thought throughout much of the Middle Ages: namely, the war between God and the Devil.

The writing in the plays is often uneven, the characterization is crude and the psychology naive. Nevertheless, in their simplicity, a number of them have a certain robust and impressive power. The better ones show an increasingly sophisticated analysis of character, and point the way to that examination of human nature and morality in depth which makes the best Tudor and Jacobean drama so remarkable.

The most memorable Morality Plays are: *The Castell of Perseverance* (c. 1425); *Mind, Will and Understanding* (c. 1460); and *Mankind* (c. 1475). These three are considered as a group because they occur in the Macro Manuscript. Then comes *Everyman* (c. 1500), to which there is a slightly earlier Dutch analogue, *Elckerlijk*. To the same period belong the French Moralities *Bien avisé, Mal avisé* and *L'Homme juste et l'homme mondain*, and *La Condemnation de Banquet*. To the early years of the 16th c. belong *The World and the Child*; *Hyckescorner* (1512); Skelton's *Magnificence* (1516); Rastell's *Four Elements* (1519); *Mundus et Infans* (c. 1520); Henry Medwall's *Nature* (c. 1530); Sir David Lindsay's *Satyre of the Three Estaitis* (1540), an example of a political Morality Play; and Wever's *Lusty Juventus* (c. 1550). From about the middle of the 16th c. Morality Plays became less popular, but they were still being written and many plays bore unmistakable marks of their influence, such as Nathaniel Woodes's *The Conflict of Conscience* (1563); Fulwell's *Like Will to Like* (c. 1568); Lupton's *All for Money* (c. 1578); Marlowe's *Dr Faustus* (c. 1588). Even as late as 1625 Ben Jonson's *The Staple of News* showed strong Morality influences, especially in the person of Lady Pecunia, an allegorical figure representing Riches.

The long-term influence of the Moralities is discernible in the pageant and masque (*qq.v.*), and in the label names or aptronymics (*q.v.*) given to characters in 17th and 18th c. comedy (*q.v.*) and also in the names in novels. A modern example of a Morality Play was Jerome K. Jerome's *The Passing of the Third Floor Back* (1908). *See* ALLEGORY; INTERLUDE; MIRACLE PLAY; MORAL INTERLUDE; MYSTERY PLAY.

morology (Gk 'foolish speech') Deliberate foolishness or nonsense for effect. *See* NONSENSE.

morpheme (Gk 'form') A minimal linguistic unit; like *dis-* as a negative prefix. *See also* KENEME.

mosaic rhyme A rhyme of two or more syllables, with more than one word making a part of the rhyme unit. Common in humorous and satirical verse. Swift provides a good example in these lines from *To Dr Sheridan*:

> I went in vain to look for Eupolis,
> Down in the Strand, just where the new pole is;
> For I can tell you one thing, that I can,
> You will not find it in the Vatican.
> He and Cratinus used, as Horace says,
> To take his greatest grandees for asses.
> Poets, in those days, used to venture high;
> But these are lost full many a century.
> Thus you may see, dear friend, ex pede hence,
> My judgment of the old comedians.

See RHYME.

mosaic verse A patchwork poem made up of lines from other poems. An ingenious modern example by A. Alvarez occurs in the introduction to *The New Poetry* (rev. edn 1966). *See* CENTO, where the example by Alvarez is quoted in full.

Moscow Art Theatre Founded in 1898 by Constantin Stanislavsky (1863–1938) and Vladimir Nemirovich-Danchenko (1859–1943). It had its first success with Chekhov's *The Seagull* in 1898. Later the theatre was supported by Lenin, and the world tour of 1922–4 made it very well known. It has continued to be an important theatre whose company has had wide influence.

mot (F 'word') Three phrases commonly used as literary terms employ this word: (a) *bon mot* – an adroitly witty remark; (b) *le mot juste* – the exact or appropriate word for the occasion; (c) *le mot propre* – the precisely necessary term for anything.

mote (Sp 'motto, device, maxim, catchword, nickname') It may also denote a riddle, an enigma and an emblem. In verse, a poem of one or two lines which expresses a complete thought. Often the thought is glossed in verse. The whole composition is then called a *mote* or a *glosa* (*q.v.*). One *mote* may be glossed by several poets, or by one poet in different versions. *See* GLOSS.

motif One of the dominant ideas in a work of literature; a part of the main theme. It may consist of a character, a recurrent image or a verbal pattern. *See* CARPE DIEM; LEITMOTIF; UBI SUNT.

motion The name given to puppet plays in England in the 16th and 17th c. Originally, the themes were taken from Holy Writ but, as forms of theatrical entertainment became increasingly secular, so the themes became more diverse. In *The Winter's Tale* (IV, iii) there is a reference to a 'motion of the Prodigal Son'. Ben Jonson refers to 'motions' several times, as do other playwrights of that period.

motto (L *muttum*, 'murmur') A short sentence or phrase (often in Latin) adopted as representative of a person or family. In such cases it may accompany a shield or coat of arms or other heraldic device. For example: *per ardua ad alta*. Chaucer's Prioresse had the motto *Amor Vincit Omnia* wrought in her gold brooch. Institutions such as schools often have mottoes, as do most regiments and other units of the armed services. They are frequently found on coins and medallions; for instance, the motto on the Welsh one-pound coin is *Pleidiol wyf i'm gwlad* ('Loyal am I to my country'). The term also denotes a passage prefixed to a book or chapter which adumbrates its matter (cf. ARGUMENT) as well as a scrap of verse or prose enclosed in a cracker or accompanying a sweetmeat.

movement A term commonly applied to a trend or development in literature. The Pléiade (*q.v.*), for instance, by dint of their innovations in poetry constituted a movement.

Movement, the A term applied to a tendency rather than a movement which became apparent in the work of a number of British poets in the 1950s. It was a tendency towards traditionalism in form, and also towards empiricism. Some of the main poets associated with the so-called Movement were Kingsley Amis, Donald Davie, Thom Gunn, Elizabeth Jennings, Philip Larkin and John Wain. A representative selection of their work was published in Robert Conquest's anthology *New Lines* (1956).

Mozarabic lyric The Arabic poetic form *muwashshah* was first developed in Spain c. 9th–10th c. Its *kharja* (*q.v.*) or refrain was not in the classical tongue but in Romance or colloquial Arabic, known as the Mozarab dialect. This form was popular in the 11th–12th c.; it may have been the forerunner of the Provençal lyric.

mu'allaqat (A 'the suspended', but the precise meaning of the term is still debated) A group of seven Arabic poems, known as the 'Golden Odes', which represent the only important surviving texts from oral poetic traditions among Bedouin tribes in southern Arabia. They derive their name from a tradition that the best poems were 'suspended' or hung in the Ka'aba, the sacred shrine of Islam in Mecca. Each of the poems is composed as an ode or *qasidah* (*q.v.*), usually in a single meter. The odes, which are lengthy, celebrate the austere life of the desert and arduous journeys; the military virtues of strength, courage and cunning, as well as the virtues of warhorses and camels; love, and the beauty of women; and the proud accomplishments and fates of both individuals and their tribes.

The odes are conventionally attributed to certain poets who lived in the 6th and 7th c.: Imru' al-Qais, Tarafa, 'Antara, Zuhayr, Labīd,' Amr ibn Kulthum and Harith (though other names have sometimes been suggested). Here is an extract from one of the odes (the Ode of Tarafa), illustrating both their intense individualism and their ability to reflect upon life and death:

> Unceasingly I tippled the wine and took my joy,
> unceasingly I sold and squandered my hoard and my patrimony
> till all my family deserted me, every one of them,
> and I sat alone like a lonely camel scabby with mange;
> yet I saw the sons of the dust did not deny me
> nor the grand ones who dwell in those fine, widespread tents.
> So now then, you who revile me because I attend the wars
> and partake in all pleasures, can you keep me alive forever?
> ... I see Death chooses the generous folk, and takes for his own
> the most prized belonging of the parsimonious skinflint;
> I see Life is a treasure diminishing every night,
> and all that the days and Time diminish ceases at last.
>   (Translated by A. J. Arberry)

The compilation of the odes was undertaken by the 8th c. rhapsodist and scholar Hammad ar-Rawiya. *See also* QASIDAH.

mudanza (Sp 'change, alteration, mood') In Spanish verse, a rhymed triplet used in the *zéjel* (*q.v.*) and followed by a fourth line, known as the *vuelta*.

multiculturalism Refers to a broad range of of intellectual and political movements initiated by various ethnic and religious minorities, feminists and gays during the last two or three decades of the 20th c. All of these were in their own way opposed to the American or European self-image of homogeneity as based allegedly on Enlightenment rationality, Anglo-Saxon Christianity, the Judaeo-Christian tradition or the Graeco-Roman Classical heritage. All demanded both political and legal recognition of their unique identities and their potential to contribute in their own ways to the larger political and cultural process.

Multicultural thinking has endeavoured to question and revaluate the literary and cultural canon in Western institutions, ranging from Homer to T. S.

Eliot, and from Plato to Logical Positivism. Paul Berman, Bhikhu Parekh and others have attempted to explain how the unrest of the 1960s and the growth of French literary theory led to the perception that this canon was symptomatic of the oppression of blacks, working-class people, women and gays, as well as of the imperialistic exploitation of Third World countries.

The central conservative argument against multiculturalism was advanced by Allan Bloom, Arthur Schlesinger and others. It assumed, first, that in the past there existed a period of consensus with regard to the aims of education, political ideals and moral values; second, that this consensus, which underlies the national identity of America, is threatened by the irreconcilable voices of multiculturalism. Multiculturalists respond that this past consensus is imaginary: the educational curricula adopted at various stages both in the US and elsewhere have been the products of fierce debate and ideological conflict.

A third assumption of conservatives is that great literature somehow conveys 'timeless truths' and should promote 'disinterested' intellectual inquiry. But multiculturalists argue that 'English literature' was from the beginning imbued with ideological motives – to educate citizens as to their duties, to inculcate national pride and moral values. In 1834 the British politician and historian Thomas Babington Macaulay argued the merits of English as the medium of instruction in India, stating: 'I have never found one . . . who could deny that a single shelf of a good European library was worth the whole native literature of India and Arabia.' One can refrain from commenting on this except to add Macaulay's own subsequent statement that 'I have no knowledge of either Sanscrit or Arabic'.

Recent controversial statements about the literary canon have been made by the Kenyan writer Ngugi Wa Thiong'o in his 'On the Abolition of the English Department' (1968) and *Decolonizing the Mind* (1986). Many writers, notably Chinua Achebe, have struggled with the dilemma of whether to express themselves in their own dialect, to achieve an authentic rendering of their cultural situation, or in English, to reach a wider audience. Today, there are innumerable varieties of English spoken in many countries, and their expression in literature has only recently been institutionally acknowledged. One of the profound effects of multiculturalism is that so-called 'English Departments' – all over the world – teach much more than merely English literature. Their scope has extended to encompass literatures written in English in many parts of the globe; literary criticism and theory with a wide international provenance; literatures in translation; postcolonial literatures; and literatures from various religious traditions. *See also* GLOBALIZATION; POSTCOLONIALISM; WORLD LITERATURE.

multiple or polysyllabic rhyme *See* TRIPLE RHYME.

mumming play A primitive form of folk drama associated with funeral rites and seasonal fertility rites, especially the spring festival. As recently as the middle of the 19th c. it was widespread throughout Britain – there is a description of such a performance in Hardy's *Return of the Native* – and there is reliable evidence that it has been performed regularly as far afield as the islands of Nevis and St Kitts in the West Indies.

Though the 'texts' stem from oral tradition (*q.v.*) there is a good deal of uniformity in the mumming play, which is performed by Mummers. The main characters are St (or Sir) George, a Turkish knight, a doctor, a fool in cap and bells, and a devil (usually Beelzebub). Sometimes there is a Father Christmas and Jack Finney, or Johnny Jack the sweeper. The plot (which is probably not earlier than the 17th c.) and action are very simple: St George introduces himself as a gallant Christian knight and is challenged by the Turk. They duel and one of them (usually St George) is killed. The Doctor then appears and delivers a boastful litany of the ailments he can cure. He finally revives the dead man. There follows a collection of money (often by the devil).

The theme of the mumming play is clearly death and resurrection, which suggests that it may be connected with a pagan spring-festival rite. But there is no evidence for such rites until long after the Middle Ages. *See* PLOUGH MONDAY PLAY; REVESBY PLAY; SWORD DANCE.

muse One of nine Greek goddesses who were the daughters of Zeus and Mnemosyne (or Memory). Each presided over one activity or art: Calliope, epic poetry; Clio, history; Erato, love poetry; Euterpe, lyric poetry; Melpomene, tragedy; Polyhymnia, songs of praise to the gods; Terpsichore, dancing; Thalia, comedy; Urania, astronomy.

It was the tradition for a poet (especially an epic poet) to invoke the aid of a particular muse to help him with his work. *See* INSPIRATION; INVOCATION; STORM OF ASSOCIATION.

musical comedy/musical A form of theatrical entertainment developed in the United States during the 19th c. It combines song, music and spoken dialogue, and descends from light opera, ballad opera and vaudeville (*qq.v.*). Some famous examples of 20th c. musicals are *The Arcadians* (1909), *Lady Be Good* (1924), *Me and My Girl* (1937), *Bless the Bride* (1947), *The Boy Friend* (1953), and *My Fair Lady* (1956), adapted from Shaw's *Pygmalion* (1912). More recently, musicals such as *Les Misérables* (1985), from Victor Hugo's novel (1862), and *Billy Elliot* (2005), set against the background of the 1984 miners' strike in the UK, have taken on darker subjects.

music theatre A form of entertainment related to opera. It is a musical performance presented on a stage with some theatrical props and costume. The emphasis is on the music, but some kind of dramatic text may be included. This sort of entertainment is believed to have originated with the composers György Ligeti and Mauricio Kagel. In 1956 Alexander Goehr and John Cox formed a 'Music Theatre Ensemble' which presented works by Schönberg, Kurt Weill, Peter Maxwell Davies *et al*.

muwashshah *See* MOZARABIC LYRIC.

mycterism (Gk 'turning up of the nose') A subtle form of derision; a sarcasm or irony (*q.v.*) in which the gibe is half hidden.

Mystery Play (L *mi[ni]sterium*, 'handicraft') The Mystery Plays of the Middle Ages were based on the Bible and were particularly concerned with the stories of man's Creation, Fall and Redemption. They antedate Miracle Plays (*q.v.*).

Mystery Plays developed out of the Liturgy of the Church and in particular out of the *quem quaeritis* trope (*q.v.*) of Easter Day. The earliest dramatizations were presented on the greater festivals of the Church: Christmas, Easter, Pentecost and Corpus Christi. At first they were in Latin and performed by the clergy in the church. There then came an increasing admixture of the vernacular, and lay folk also performed in them. This gradual secularization of religious drama was accompanied by a corresponding physical move. The drama moved out of the church through the west door. Thus, what had been sacred drama became, literally, profane (*pro fano*, 'before the temple'). From the churchyard to the market-place was the next logical step. The dramatization became more and more elaborate, the plays were written more or less exclusively in the vernacular and their presentation became the concern of the trade guilds, each of which became responsible for a particular episode or episodes. For example, the masons' guild might present the Noah story, and the weavers the Crucifixion. The object of the cycle of plays was to dramatize the Bible from the Creation to the Last Judgement.

Each play was mounted on a wagon with a curtained scaffold. The lower part of the wagon was a dressing room. After the play had been performed the wagon moved on to where another play had just been acted. Thus, in the course of a day or days, the population of a city like York was able to see the complete cycle.

In time the presentation and setting became extremely elaborate. Heaven and Hell were represented; all sorts of mechanical contrivances contributed to theatrical effects. Costume became lavish, and even lighting, for evening performances, was spectacular.

Most of the plays are anonymous (at any rate, we do not know the authors) and show considerable variation in the quality of the writing. For the most part the verse is rough and characterization crude. However, in the later work the beginnings of sophistication and psychological realism are clearly discernible, and this development is intensely interesting.

The principal English Mystery cycles were those of York (48 episodes); Coventry (42); Wakefield – also known as Towneley (32); and Chester (25). There were also the Cornish plays and the *Ludus Coventriae* (which had nothing to do with Coventry), plus one from Newcastle and one from Norwich. There were other cycles at Beverley, Doncaster, Ipswich and Worcester, but these have been lost.

Mystery Plays were widespread in Europe, and in France they were particularly popular. The French preferred a more fixed setting. The *sedes* or mansions (that is, the stages, platforms or scaffoldings on which the plays were performed) were set in two lines facing each other in the yard, square or market-place outside the west door of the church. Each *sedes* represented a particular place, like Hell, Heaven, the House of Caiaphas, the Sepulchre, etc. They were so sited that there was plenty of room for the spectators to gather round.

Other well-known examples are: (a) the Cyprus *Passion Cycle*, a group of Greek prose-plays depicting the events of Holy Week, which originated in Cyprus in the 13th c.; (b) the Oberammergau *Passion Play* of Upper Bavaria, which dates from 1633; (c) the Spanish *Autos Sacramentales*, a form of religious drama performed on the feast of Corpus Christi. These allegorical plays were still popular in the 17th c., when they were perfected by Calderón. *See* MORALITY PLAY; PASSION PLAY; SACRA RAPPRESENTAZIONE.

myth (Gk *mūthos*, 'anything uttered by word of mouth') In general a myth is a story which is not 'true' and which involves (as a rule) supernatural beings – or at any rate supra-human beings. Myth is always concerned with creation and explains how something came to exist. Myth embodies feeling and concept – hence the Promethean or Herculean figure, or the idea of Diana, or the story of Orpheus and Eurydice. Many myths or quasi-myths are primitive explanations of the natural order and cosmic forces.

The history and meaning of the term are complex. Homer used the word *mūthos* to mean narrative and conversation, but not a fiction. Odysseus tells false stories about himself and uses the term *mūthologenevein* to signify 'telling a story'. Later, Greek *mūthos* is used to mean fiction. Plato refers to *mūthoi* to denote something not wholly lacking truth but for the most part fictitious. It has been surmised that the transition of *mūthos* to mean fiction may have been helped by a kind of association with *muein*, 'to initiate into secrets' (hence, mystic, mystery). The word *mūthikos* ('mythical') went into Latin as *mythicus*. *Mūthos* has also been equated with the Latin *fabula* (*q.v.*). Nowadays a myth tends to signify a fiction, but a fiction which conveys a psychological truth.

Classical writers had a 'ready-made' mythology. Others have not been so fortunate and some have felt a great need to invent or somehow contrive a mythology to be the vehicle of their beliefs. Poets, especially, have continued to fall back on the Greek and Roman myths, and, to a lesser extent, upon Germanic and Scandinavian myths, and in some cases, upon Chinese, Indian, Egyptian and Latin American myths. A good example of a poet who has 'invented' a mythology akin to the traditional kind is William Blake. He said that he felt obliged to create a system: otherwise he would be enslaved by someone else's. Accordingly he combined his own visionary gleams with what he 'lifted' from established mythologies, plus elements of Christianity and ideas from Swedenborg and Neoplatonism (*q.v.*). A more recent example is W. B. Yeats, who was in the fortunate position of being able to make use of a considerable stock of Celtic lore and legend of a more or less mythical kind. Yeats explained his 'mythology' in *A Vision* (1926). Herman Melville (*Moby-Dick*), James Joyce (*Ulysses*) and D. H. Lawrence (*The Plumed*

Serpent) have also used a variety of mythical materials, for the most part those which belong to what Jung described as the 'collective unconscious'. *See* LEGEND; MYTHEME; MYTHOPOEIA; NARRATOLOGY; STRUCTURALISM; SYMBOL AND SYMBOLISM.

mytheme A term coined by Claude Lévi-Strauss, the structuralist anthropologist, by analogy with morpheme and phoneme (*qq.v.*). In his structural analysis of myths a mytheme 'is a set of items which share a single functional trait'. Mythemes are organized in binary oppositions (*q.v.*). Three items in one mytheme for Lévi-Strauss are: (a) Cadmos seeks his sister, ravished by Zeus; (b) Oedipus marries his mother, Jocasta; (c) Antigone buries her brother, Polynices, unlawfully. Lévi-Strauss invented the term 'mytheme' as part of the structural analysis of myths, and it has been of some importance in structuralism (*q.v.*) and in the theory of narratology (*q.v.*). *See also* MYTH.

mythopoeia (Gr 'myth-making') The conscious creation of a myth (*q.v.*). In literature, the appropriation and reworking of mythical material, or the creation of a kind of 'private' mythology.

N

nacimientos Spanish plays and poems about the Nativity of Christ. They were performed/recited at Christmas in churches and private houses, or in the streets. They were common in the 15th c.

naiv und sentimentalisch (G 'naive and sentimental') A category or distinction made by Schiller in his essay *Über naive und sentimentalische Dichtung* (1795). Schiller divides poets into two classes: (a) the naive (e.g. Homer, Shakespeare, Goethe) who attempt to project nature as they embody it; (b) the sentimental (e.g. Schiller, Wordsworth, Southey) who have lost touch with nature and are trying to depict it as a sought-for ideal. Naive poets create instinctually; the sentimental, formally. Schiller pursued his theory to suggest that sentimental poets try to project an ideal of nature whereas the naive poet cannot and does not do this. He is concerned with nature *as it is; not as it may be conceived*. If we compare the work of, say, John Clare, William Barnes, Thomas Hardy, R. S. Thomas and Ted Hughes, with that of, say, John Dyer, John Keats, Robert Browning, A. E. Housman and Edmund Blunden, we find that the first group tend to be instinctual in their responses to nature; the second group, formal.

Schiller also elaborated the idea that the poetic genius (*q.v.*) is a sentimental poet by virtue of his feelings and idealisms, and a naive by virtue of his genius. The combination enables him to convey a total vision of nature: the real and the transcendental. Gerard Manley Hopkins might well come into this category. *See* ANTINOMY; APOLLONIAN/DIONYSIAN; CLASSICISM/ROMANTICISM.

narodne pesme (S 'peoples' songs') The poems (*pesma* also means 'poem') belong to the genre of traditional popular narrative poetry based on historical events and created mainly by individual members of an illiterate or semi-literate society and preserved by oral tradition (*q.v.*) in former Yugoslavia.

A Dictionary of Literary Terms and Literary Theory, Fifth Edition. J. A. Cuddon.
© 2013 The Estate of J. A. Cuddon. Published 2013 by Blackwell Publishing Ltd.

They exist in print now because the 19th c. Serbian scholar Vuk Karadžić spent much of his life collecting them from the *guslari* (*q.v.*) while there were still plenty of these itinerant bards in existence.

There are nine epic cycles of these poems. The most famous is the Kosovo cycle, a group of ballads (*q.v.*) and lays which grew up as a result of the Battle of Kosovo in 1389 when the Serbs were defeated by the Turks. There is a pre-Kosovo cycle which treats of myth and legend, and a Marko Kraljević cycle which mostly concerns the deeds of a semi-legendary warrior of that name. The fourth main cycle (the most recent) comprises all the poems dealing with the struggles against the Turks in the 19th c. The other five deal with (a) the Serbian nobles and their conflicts after the Battle of Kosovo until towards the end of the 15th c.; (b) the exploits of the *hajduks* (bandit-type guerrilla soldiers) against the Turks; (c, d and e) Montenegrin, Bosnian and Dalmatian struggles against invading powers.

The nine cycles constitute one of the most remarkable bodies of oral poetry known. Apart from the Homeric ballads they probably have no equals. *See also* EPIC; PEVAČI; ŽENSKE PESME.

narodnost (R 'national character') A requirement demanded of literature under socialist realism (*q.v.*). Literature should express typical national thought and character through a 'national style'. The term also implies 'folk' and 'popular' character; thus there has been much emphasis on folk and popular literature and language and the importance of the contribution it can make to more exalted forms of literature. *See* IDEYNOST; PARTYNOST.

narratee A term invented by Gerald Prince to denote the person to whom a narrator addresses his discourse. The narratee is not to be confused with the reader, who may be the 'virtual reader' (i.e. the kind of reader the narrator has in mind while composing the discourse), or the 'ideal reader' (i.e. the reader who understands everything the writer/narrator is saying and doing). *See also* IMPLIED READER/ACTUAL READER; READER-RESPONSE THEORY.

narrative verse A narrative poem that tells a story. Such poetry is widespread in many literatures. The three main kinds are epic, metrical romance and ballad (*qq.v.*) but there are a very large number of narrative poems which cannot be easily classified and which certainly do not fit into any of the above categories.

Early examples of narrative poetry are the epic of *Gilgamesh* and the poems of Homer and Hesiod, the narrative odes of Pindar (*c.* 522–442 BC) and the *Argonautica* of Apollonius of Rhodes (end of 3rd c. BC). The Romans often used narrative verse, famous examples including the *Annales* of Ennius (239–169 BC), the *Aeneid* of Virgil (70–19 BC) and the *Metamorphoses* of Ovid (43 BC–AD 18). Narrative poems continued to be written in the following five hundred years in both Greek and Latin. Later, lives of the saints in verse were not uncommon; and historical poems in Latin verse appeared during the Carolingian period. In the early Middle Ages we find the beginnings of romance, but it is not until the 12th c. that this is an established form. Between *c.* 1000 and *c.* 1300, for the first time since the 8th c. BC, oral epics were written down – in Western vernaculars and in Greek. Outstanding examples include *Beowulf*, assigned to the middle of the 8th c. (though the MS dates from *c.* 1000) and a large number of *chansons de gestes* (*q.v.*), of which the best known is the *Chanson de Roland* (the earliest MS *c.* 1170).

Throughout the later Middle Ages narrative poems were widely written in Europe and increasingly in the vernacular: Dante's *Divina Commedia* (*c.* 1310), Chaucer's *Troilus and Criseyde* (*c.* 1372–86) and *Canterbury Tales* (1385–1400), and Langland's *The Vision of Piers Plowman* (*c.* 1360–99).

The Renaissance period produced a succession of epic narratives, notably: *Orlando Innamorato* by Boiardo (1441–94); *Orlando Furioso* by Ariosto (1474–1533); *Gerusalemme Liberata* by Tasso (1544–95); and the *Os Lusiadas* by Camoëns (1524–80). These four works constitute a revival of national epic.

In the 15th and 16th c. in England narrative poetry flourished. The 15th c. poets are little read now but Lydgate and Hawes were prolific writers. Major narrative poems in the 16th c. include Spenser's *The Faerie Queene* (1589, 1596) and Marlowe's *Hero and Leander* (1593). By the end of the 16th c. the tendency was to write shorter narrative poems; what may be called *epyllia* (*q.v.*).

In the 17th c. the two outstanding narrative poems in English literature are Abraham Cowley's unfinished *Davideis* (1656), and the greatest epic in the language – Milton's *Paradise Lost* (1667). In France in the 17th c. the principal narrative works were Boileau's *Le Lutrin*, a mock-epic (*q.v.*) written between 1673 and 1683, and Fénelon's prose poem (*q.v.*) *Télémaque* (1699).

It is noticeable that in the second half of the 17th c. and during much of the 18th c. longer poems tend to be satire (*q.v.*). In a number of cases these satires were a form of narrative verse. Pope's *The Rape of the Lock* (1712, 1714) is a case in point. Rather than write anything original on an epic scale, poets chose to translate. Notable translations of Classical authors were done by Dryden, Pope and Cowper. However, there was one epic work of some merit, namely Voltaire's *Henriade* (1728), a national epic on the religious wars.

Towards the end of the 18th c. we find a recrudescence of the genre. It is probable that the publication of Percy's *Reliques of Ancient Poetry* in 1765 revived interest. It is possible that James Macpherson's Ossianic poems (1760, 1762, 1765) were also an influence. At any rate, towards the turn of the century, and continually thereafter, narrative verse proliferates, with notable writers of the genre including Walter Scott, Wordsworth, Coleridge, Byron and Keats.

Nearly all the major poets of the Victorian period (*q.v.*) wrote narrative verse, including Tennyson (*Idylls of the King*) and Browning (*Childe Roland to the Dark Tower Came*). Since the Victorian period much narrative verse has been written, notable examples including Sir John Betjeman's *A Lincolnshire Tale*, T. S. Eliot's *Journey of the Magi*, C. S. Lewis's *Flight to Australia*, Philip Larkin's *Whitsun Weddings*, and a large number of poems by Robert Frost, as well as long narrative poems by W. H. Auden, Hugh MacDiarmid and many others. *See also* DRAMATIC MONOLOGUE; EPIC; ONEGIN STANZA; SONNET CYCLE; VERSE NOVEL.

narratology Theory, discourse or critique of narrative or narration. The term is an Anglicization of the French *narratologie*, coined in 1969 by the Franco-Bulgarian philosopher Tzvetan Todorov (1939–) in his *Grammaire du Décaméron*. Structuralist analysis of narrative was begun by Claude Lévi-Strauss (1908–2009), who, in *Anthropologie structurale* (1958) and elsewhere, advanced a new theory about myth (*q.v.*). He puts forward the idea that myths are variations on basic themes and that in their totality (and there are thousands of them) their narratives contain certain constant, basic and universal structures by which any one myth can be explained. He sees myths as a kind of 'language' which can be broken down into individual units or 'mythemes' – by analogy with phonemes (*q.v.*). Myths can be read in relation to each other rather than as reflecting a particular version. Hence the concept of a kind of 'grammar' or set of relations underneath the surface of the narrative.

This structuralist theory has been brought to bear on the study of narrative in literature, or narratology. In some respects Lévi-Strauss's theory was prefigured by the Russian Formalist Vladimir Propp, who, in his *Morphology of the Folk Tale* (1928), 'reduced' all folk tales to seven 'spheres of action' and thirty-one fixed elements or 'functions' of narrative. The function is the basic unit of the narrative 'language' and denotes or refers to the actions which constitute the narrative, and the functions tend to follow a logical sequence.

A. J. Greimas, in his *Sémantique structurale* (1966), breaks the scheme down still further, and aims at a kind of universal grammar of narrative by attempting a semantic analysis of sentence structure. More accessible are Gérard Genette's theories propounded in *Narrative Discourse* (1972) in the context of a detailed analysis of Proust's *A la recherche du temps perdu*. Bearing in mind the distinctions made in Russian Formalism (*q.v.*) between *fabula* ('story') and *syuzhet* ('plot'), he distinguishes between *récit* (i.e. the chronological order of events in a text/narrative); *histoire* (the sequence in which events actually occur); and *narration* (the act of narrating itself).

Whereas Genette has a relational approach and sees narrative as a product or result of the interaction of its different component levels, and all aspects of narrative as dependent units, Roland Barthes (in his essay *Introduction to the Structural Analysis of Narrative*, 1977) presumes a hierarchical arrangement of levels and suggests that, up to a point, they can be discussed separately. He describes narrative as 'a long sentence, just as every constative sentence is in a way the rough outline of a short narrative'. He selects basic units of narrative; for example, 'function' and 'index'. The functions constitute a chain of acts; the indices constitute information about characters. Using a linguistic analogy, Barthes suggests that functions are based on metonymic relations and indices on metaphoric relations. This distinction draws upon Roman Jakobson's theory of metaphor/metonymy (*q.v.*).

Lastly, we should mention Northrop Frye's conception of literature, proposed in his *Anatomy of Criticism* (1957). Frye's theory is not strictly structuralist but it can be seen as structuralist in some respects. He sees literature as an 'autonomous verbal structure' unrelated to anything beyond itself, a world which contains 'life and reality in a system of verbal relationships'. In this 'universe' there are four radical 'mythoi' – that is to say, plot forms and basic organizing structural principles – which correspond to the four seasons of the natural order and constitute the four main genres of comedy, romance, tragedy and satire (*qq.v.*). He has developed this archetypal theory in many subsequent discourses on a huge range of texts, including the Bible. *See* ARCHETYPAL CRITICISM; STRUCTURALISM.

narrator Plato and Aristotle distinguished three basic kinds of narrator: (a) the speaker or poet (or any kind of writer) who uses his own voice; (b) one who assumes the voice of another person or persons, and speaks in a voice not his own; (c) one who uses a mixture of his own voice and that of others. Out of the thousands of examples available to illustrate the three voices the following will serve. In his poem *The Statue* the poet John Berryman speaks throughout in his own voice. In *The Prisoner of Chillon*, Byron assumes the voice of François de Bonnivard who was imprisoned in the castle of Chillon in the 16th c. A good example of the combination of three voices can be found in *Paradise Lost*. Milton begins in his own voice in the first person to invoke the 'Heavenly Muse'. In line 34, Book I, the impression is that the Muse (that is, the Holy Spirit) responds to Milton's formal invocation (*q.v.*), thus beginning the main narrative. When Satan first speaks (line 84) the third voice is introduced. Thereafter each different character has his own voice, though all, as it were, are Milton's. At the beginning of Book III Milton draws breath and uses his 'own' voice again.

So anyone telling a story may begin, as narrator, by using his own voice; then introduce a narrator who tells the story – in which there are characters who, in turn, have their own voices and who, in their turn, of course, may narrate. Potentially the progression (or regression) is infinite. Many novelists have employed this technique, one of the most adept being Joseph Conrad.

T. S. Eliot also makes an important distinction in his essay *The Three Voices of Poetry* (1953): 'The first voice is the voice of the poet talking to himself – or to nobody. The second is the voice of the poet addressing an audience, whether large or small. The third is the voice of the poet when he attempts to create a dramatic character speaking in verse; when he is saying, not what he would say in his own person, but only what he can say within the limits of one imaginary character addressing another imaginary character.'

What is known as the 'self-conscious narrator' is one who employs techniques related to the theories of foregrounding and defamiliarization (*qq.v.*). By dint of 'baring the device' (or devices) the writer reveals to and reminds the reader that the narration is a work of fiction while at the same time pointing up or exposing the discrepancies between the fiction and the reality which it purports or seems to represent. Tristram in Sterne's *Tristram Shandy* (1760–7) is a notable instance. Others are Marcel in Proust's *A la recherche du temps perdu* (1913–27) and the narrator in Byron's *Don Juan* (1819–24).

The method of using the self-conscious narrator lends itself to sophisticated and complex refinements in what is known as the 'reflexive novel' (*q.v.*) or the 'involuted novel'. An outstanding example of this is André Gide's *Les Faux-monnayeurs* (1926), in which he uses intricate narrative tactics. This book is the diary of a novelist who is writing a novel – which is going to have the title *Les Faux-monnayeurs* ('The Counterfeiters') – about a novelist who is keeping a diary about the novel he is actually writing. Gide compounded this ingenuity by keeping a journal while he was composing the novel; this was the *Journal of the Counterfeiters*, which he published in the same year as the novel. Vladimir Nabokov's *Pale Fire* (1962) is another and different instance of the involuted narrative method.

There is also what is known as the 'fallible' or 'unreliable narrator'. Such a narrator is one whose perception and interpretation of what he or she narrates do not correspond or coincide with the perceptions, interpretations and opinions of the author who is or purports to be the controlling force in the narration. Thus, there is a kind of contrived discrepancy between the narrator (what James called 'the centre of consciousness') and the actual author. Henry James was a past-master of this technique (e.g. in *The Aspern Papers*, 1888). *See also* AESTHETIC DISTANCE; CONFESSIONAL NOVEL; DIALOGIC/MONOLOGIC; ÉNONCÉ/ÉNONCIATION; EPISTOLARY NOVEL; FICELLE; FREE INDIRECT STYLE/DISCOURSE; NARRATOLOGY; NOVEL; PERSONA; RÉCIT; STREAM OF CONSCIOUSNESS; SUBJECTIVITY AND OBJECTIVITY; VIEWPOINT.

National Book League *See* BOOKTRUST

National Theatre The foundation stone of the British National Theatre was laid on the South Bank of the Thames in 1951. In 1962 a National Theatre board was appointed and Laurence Olivier (1907–89) was put in charge. The Old Vic Theatre (*q.v.*) became the headquarters and an inaugural performance of *Hamlet* was given there in 1962. Eventually the new theatre was built (it took some ten years) with three auditoriums. In March 1976 the Lyttelton opened with a production of Samuel Beckett's *Happy Days*; in October of that year the Olivier opened with a production of Marlowe's *Tamburlaine* (*c.* 1590); and in March 1977 the Cottesloe studio theatre presented Ken Campbell's *Illuminatus*. Before any of the theatres was opened Peter Hall (1930–) had replaced Laurence Olivier as artistic director. Peter Hall held the post from 1973 to 1988 and during those fifteen years a wide variety of plays, from established classics to new work by comparatively unknown dramatists, was presented – often with conspicuous success. Richard Eyre succeeded Peter Hall; Trevor Nunn took over in 1997; and Nicholas Hytner in 2003.

nation language   The term was coined by Caribbean poet and literary critic Edward Kamau Brathwaite in his 1979 lecture *History of the Voice* (first printed in 1984). It is a language from the Caribbean, a creolized form of English based on African oral traditions. As Brathwaite explains, 'English it may be in terms of its lexicon, but it is not English in terms of its syntax.' However, it is not simply a dialect (*q.v.*). Brathwaite deliberately uses the word 'nation language' in order to dismantle the view that languages from the Caribbean are simply dialects of English. A dialect is often considered to be a form of 'bad' English.

When Jamaican poet Louise Bennett published her collection of poetry, ironically entitled *Dialect Verses* (1942), the compositions were dubbed 'dialect' poems since they were not written in 'Standard English'. Like Brathwaite, Bennett argues that Jamaican English is not simply 'a corruption of Standard English' and shows that Standard English is itself a fusion of dialects and foreign languages. In her radio monologue 'Jamaica Language' (1979–81), she explains that while the English would say 'Go away', the Jamaicans would say 'Gweh', which illustrates a strong influence of African rhythms and oral traditions.

Nation language is a language that emerged out of the Caribbean experience of slavery and colonialism. As Brathwaite writes in *The Development of Creole Society in Jamaica, 1770–1820*, 'it was in language that the slave was perhaps most successfully imprisoned by his master and it was in his (mis-) use of it that he perhaps most effectively rebelled'. For Brathwaite, nation language is an effective way of recuperating the African traditions and languages that were submerged during slavery and colonialism, and a useful medium for articulating new and emerging Caribbean cultural identities. *See also* CRÉOLITÉ/CRÉOLISATION.

nativism   The term 'nativism' is used by postcolonial critics to describe the desire to return to pre-colonial cultural values and native traditions. This project of recovering indigenous cultural forms was particularly significant in the decolonization period after the Second World War since native cultures were constructed as 'primitive' or less developed during colonialism. But while the recovery of native practices and traditions was a useful way of reclaiming identity and restoring dignity for decolonized people, some post-colonial critics also pointed to problems in nativist models – most notably, the reinforcement of traditional, patriarchal values through idealization of the pre-colonial culture. An exploration of reconstructing pre-colonial societies in fiction and the related debates on nativism occurs in Chinua Achebe's novel *Things Fall Apart* (1952). *See also* POSTCOLONIALISM.

naturalism In literary criticism, a word sometimes used loosely as a synonym for realism (*q.v.*), and also in reference to works which show a pronounced interest in, sympathy with and love of natural beauty (e.g. much of the poetry of Wordsworth). Properly speaking, it should be used to describe works of literature which use realistic methods and subjects to convey a belief that everything that exists is a part of nature and can be explained by natural and material causes – and not by supernatural, spiritual or paranormal causes.

In literature naturalism developed out of realism. The main influences that went to forming a different point of view were Darwin's biological theories, Comte's application of scientific ideas to the study of society, and Taine's application of deterministic theories to literature. Those in favour of a naturalistic approach to and interpretation of life concentrated on depicting the social environment and dwelt particularly on its deficiencies and on the shortcomings of human beings. The 'naturalist's' vision of the estate of man tended to be subjective and was very often sombre.

The Goncourt brothers appear to have been the first to establish the naturalistic point of view in literature; namely in *Germinie Lacerteux* (1865). This analytical investigation of the rather squalid life of a servant girl was much admired by Émile Zola, the high priest of the naturalist movement in literature. In his preface to *Thérèse Raquin* (1868) he described himself as a *naturaliste*. His method was scientifically clinical, that of the pathologist and physiologist. In his view men's lives and actions were determined by environment and heredity and it was the business of the novelist, as he saw it, to dissect, to perform an autopsy on life.

Zola's influence has been very considerable and is discernible in many plays and novels of the last hundred years. It is particularly noticeable in the work of Maupassant and J.-K. Huysmans, of George Moore and George Gissing. However, he made his greatest impact in Germany, where naturalism as a movement was concentrated in one literary school in Berlin and another in Munich. Here the principal luminaries of the movement were G. M. Conrad, Holz and Schlaf, the Hart brothers, Bleibtreu, and Bölsche. The dramatist Gerhart Hauptmann proved to be the most distinguished exponent of German naturalism. Outside France and Germany naturalism was apparent in the works of Ibsen, Strindberg, Chekhov, Tolstoy, Gorky, and across the Atlantic in the novels of Theodore Dreiser, Frank Norris and Stephen Crane. *See also* NATURALISTIC DRAMA; THEATRICALISM; THESIS NOVEL.

naturalistic drama Drama which seeks to mirror life with the utmost fidelity. It became established and popular late in the 19th c., stemming from the naturalism (*q.v.*) of Zola and his followers, and going beyond the realism (*q.v.*) of Ibsen. The main French dramatist was Henri Becque. In the late 1880s Antoine established naturalistic drama in his Théâtre Libre. There Becque and other playwrights, including Strindberg, had their work performed. The movement of naturalism in the theatre spread to Germany, England, Russia and America. A famous instance of ultranaturalism is Gorky's *Lower Depths* (1902). Gradually, the leading dramatists, like Strindberg and Hauptmann, forsook this kind of play for a more symbolic form. However, naturalism persisted and in its decadence considerably influenced drawing-room comedy (*q.v.*) and much light theatrical entertainment in the 1920s and 1930s. There was a sustained effort to reproduce everyday speech as exactly as possible, and more and more emphasis was placed on surface verisimilitude – especially in décor and setting where no effort was spared to persuade the audience that it was in fact looking at a 'real' set, such an exact representation of a room that they might well use it themselves. Here art was attempting to deceive nature, not reflect it. Thus the theatre was defeating its own ends and, in the abandonment of traditional dramatic conventions, becoming more and more restrictive. Nevertheless, many dramatists exploited the limitations very skilfully. Galsworthy was an outstanding example, and, later, N. C. Hunter and Terence Rattigan. *See* THEATRICALISM.

Natural School, the The name given to an early phase of Russian realism. This particular *-ism* was formulated by Belinsky (1811–48) who was the 'interpreter' of Gogol. It was Belinsky's belief that the writer should eschew anything like romanticism and should depict the social evils of his period, especially the injustices of peasant and serf life. The tenets of the *natural'naya shkola* were strongly opposed to anything artificial or idealistic.

natya A form of Indian dance drama whose plots for the most part derive from the epics *Ramayana* and *Mahabharata* (*qq.v.*).

nazm A term used in Urdu letters. Simply means 'poem', and can range in form from self-conscious adaptation of conventional meters and rhymed verse to what is called *āzād-nazm* or 'free verse'. Unlike the conventional *ghazal* (*q.v.*), the *nazm* usually possesses thematic coherence and continuity. Some poets have also written in a form known as *nasri-nazm* or the prose-poem, which does not follow or adapt any given poetic meter.

near rhyme *See* RHYME.

negation A form of affirmation by denial; sometimes found in litotes (*q.v.*). A famous example occurs in Keats's *Hyperion*:

> No stir of air was there,
> Not so much life as on a summer's day

Robs not one light seed from the feathered grass,
But where the dead leaf fell, there did it rest.

negative capability   A famous phrase used by Keats when writing to his brothers George and Thomas (21 Dec. 1817). The relevant passage is:

> I had not a dispute, but a disquisition, with Dilke upon various subjects; several things dove-tailed in my mind, and at once it struck me what quality went to form a man of achievement, especially in literature, and which Shakespeare possessed so enormously – I mean negative capability, that is, when a man is capable of being in uncertainties, mysteries, doubts, without any irritable reaching after fact and reason. Coleridge, for instance, would let go by a fine isolated verisimilitude caught from the penetralium of Mystery, from being incapable of remaining content with half-knowledge. This pursued through volumes would perhaps take us no farther than this; that with a great Poet the sense of beauty overcomes every other consideration, or rather obliterates all consideration.

> Accept, therefore, the insight into beauty and be cautious of rationalization. In his *Ode on a Grecian Urn* Keats summarized part of his philosophy in this matter:

> > 'Beauty is truth, truth beauty,' – that is all
> > Ye know on earth, and all ye need to know.

See SUBJECTIVITY AND OBJECTIVITY.

Negrismo   A Latin American movement with strong indigenous traditions particularly associated with black culture. In Cuba it is referred to as Afro-Cubanism. It developed during the 1920s and prominent *negristas* have been Emilio Ballagas and Nicolás Guillén of Cuba, Luis Palés Matos of Puerto Rico and Ildefonso Pereda Valdés of Uruguay. The Cuban novelist Alejo Carpentier (1904–80) of Havana (though not black himself) did much to promote black art and literature. Fernando Ortiz (1881–1969) was a leading light in Afro-Cubanism. *See* NÉGRITUDE.

Négritude   The term was coined some time in the 1930s by Aimé Césaire (a French poet and dramatist from Martinique) and the Senegalese poet and politician L.-S. Senghor. It refers to and connotes the attitudes displayed in some recent writing by African authors and, more particularly, by French-speaking Africans. In literature it represents an aesthetic which seeks to maintain and uphold traditional African culture and sensibilities. The idea of Négritude has had considerable vogue since the publication of Césaire's *Cahier d'un retour au pays natal* (1939), and as a result of Senghor's work. The latter is now regarded as the chief luminary and he expressed a part of his philosophy in *Négritude et humanisme* (1964). *See* CRÉOLITÉ.

nemesis (Gk 'retribution') In Greek thought a personification of the gods' resentment and anger at man's insolence, hubris (*q.v.*), towards themselves. Thus nemesis was punishment; what overtook and befell the tragic hero. *See* TRAGEDY.

neoclassicism The neoclassical period is usually taken to be the hundred-odd years *c.* 1660–*c.* 1780; in other words, from Dryden's maturity to Johnson's death (1784). Apart from the dramatists the main English authors in this period were: Dryden (1631–1700), Swift (1667–1745), Addison (1672–1719), Steele (1672–1729), Pope (1688–1744), Lord Chesterfield (1694–1773), Fielding (1707–54), Johnson (1709–84), Goldsmith (1730–74) and Gibbon (1737–94). In literary theory and practice most writers of this period were traditionalist, and they had a great respect for the Classical authors, and especially the Romans, who, they believed, had established and perfected the principal literary genres for all time. Literature was regarded as an art, in which excellence could be attained only by prolonged study. Thus the writers of the period were painstaking craftsmen who had a deep respect for the rules of their art. These rules could best be learnt from close study of the Classical authors (Horace was a favourite) and by careful (if not sedulous) imitation of their works. Their approach was thoroughly professional. They thought that reason and judgement were the most admirable faculties (the 18th c. was, after all, the Age of Reason), and that decorum (*q.v.*) was essential. In prose, as in verse, the most desirable qualities were harmony, proportion, balance and restraint. It follows, therefore, that the neoclassical writers aimed at *correctness*. This was nowhere more evident than in their use of the heroic couplet.

Neoclassical beliefs and ideals generated a definite vision of man and mankind. Man and his activities were regarded as the main subjects of poetry. As Pope put it in *An Essay on Man*:

> Know then thyself, presume not God to scan,
> The proper study of mankind is man.

Man, man in society, man in his social environment – these were to be the preoccupations of the poets. The emphasis tended to be on what men possess in common; the general and representative characteristics of mankind. Johnson summarized it all in *The Vanity of Human Wishes*:

> Let observation with extensive view,
> Survey mankind, from China to Peru;
> Remark each anxious toil, each eager strife,
> And watch the busy scenes of crowded life.

There thus evolved a general view of nature and mankind; a general vision of man's position and function in the universe, his relationship to the natural order and his relationship with and to God – mid-way in the great chain of being (*q.v.*).

Despite all this the neoclassicists were not conservative in any pejorative sense. Though they were inclined to settle for the traditional and the typical, they were ready to accept the novel and the particular, and they were much concerned with the importance of invention, and fancy and imagination (*qq.v.*). Johnson often fulminated against the perils of the fanciful, of letting the imagination run away with one. So long as novelty and invention enhanced the subject, adorned the chosen form, it was acceptable; it was, in a sense, 'safe'. *Aurea mediocritas* (the golden mean) was almost a working motto (Horace himself referred to it in one of his *Odes* [II, x, 5]:

> auream quisquis mediocritatem
> diligit tutus, caret obsoleti
> sordibus tecti, caret invidenda
> sobrius aula.)

but no one could accuse Pope, Swift or Johnson of lack of originality.

The preservation (as well as the establishment) of order, balance and correctness was dear to them; hence their frequent use of satire (*q.v.*) as a corrective. It was a means of controlling excess (which was especially repugnant to them), folly, stupidity and corruption; indeed, any shortcoming in man and society which threatened to be contrary to the maintenance of good moral order and literary discipline. As Pope wrote, 'Order is Heav'n's first law.' Thus the writer was under some moral and aesthetic obligation to instruct as well as to please. *See also* ABSTRACT; AGE OF REASON; AUGUSTAN AGE; HEROIC COUPLET; POETIC DICTION; ROMANTICISM; ROMANTIC REVIVAL.

Neo-Aristotelians *See* CHICAGO SCHOOL.

neo-colonialism The term 'neo-colonialism' was coined by Kwame Nkrumah, the first president of Ghana, in his *Neo-Colonialism: The Last Stage of Imperialism* (1965), and is generally used to describe the ways in which the former colonial powers and the new superpowers, such as the United States and China, use new forms of dominance over the formerly colonized countries even after they gain independence. Nkrumah pointed out that these more subtle, indirect forms of control replace the direct forms of exploitation practised during colonialism. 'New colonialisms' are even more dangerous than traditional colonial domination as they create new patterns of dependency that are difficult to resist. For example, neo-colonialism is perpetuated through the dependence of postcolonial states on various international monetary bodies, aid investment, and multinational corporations, which continue to exploit their resources. *See also* POSTCOLONIALISM.

neologism (NGk 'innovation in language') A newly coined word; sometimes a phrase. Neologisms are entering languages all the time and are a necessary invigorating influence. They are basically of three kinds: (a) a completely new word (e.g. *hep*; cf. *hippie*, *hepcat*, *hepster*) without any discernible etymological origin or pedigree (*pedigree* was formerly a neologism, formed probably from French *pied de grue*: 'crane's foot', from the arrowhead figure in a stemma, *q.v.*); (b) a word formed from an existing root or prefix (e.g. the many from *stereo-*, *para-*, *hetero-*); (c) an established word (e.g. *beat*, *dig*, *high*) which has been given a completely new meaning.

Many neologisms are acronyms (*q.v.*), such as quango, an abbreviation using initial letters from Quasi-Autonomous Non-Governmental Organization. In many instances people have forgotten how or why the word was created in the first place.

Here follow a handful of neologisms of fairly recent invention: (a) *LOL*: laughing out loud (or 'lots of love') in text messaging; (b) *bubble-headed*: frivolous, flighty; (c) *camcorder*: a video camera and sound recorder combined in one unit; (d) *eurocrat*: an official concerned with any organization within the European Union (they tend to use a lingo known as 'euro-babble'); (e) *Grammy*: (from gramophone) an award, corresponding to the cinema Oscar, bestowed by the National Academy of Recording Arts and Sciences, now the Recording Academy; (f) *necklacing*: barbaric form of punishment by which a petrol-soaked tyre is placed round the victim's neck and ignited (used in South Africa by blacks against blacks thought to be government sympathizers); (g) *power breakfast/lunch*: high-level business discussion held during such a meal; (h) *quadrella*: an Australian term for a group of four (especially the last four) horse races at a meeting for which the punter selects the four winners; (i) *Stellenbosch, to*: to relegate to a post where incompetence matters less (from Stellenbosch, Cape of Good Hope, such a dumping ground); (j) *vtol* (pron. vē'tol): an acronym for a system enabling aircraft to land and take off vertically (*vertical take-off and landing*).

Anybody can invent neologisms and anybody does. My own contributions are (a) *birocrat*: a menial subspecies in the phylum bureaucrat; (b) *verbocrap*: polysyllabic circumlocutions (the jargon, *q.v.*, of verbocrats, educationalists, sociologists *et al.*). *See also* GHOSTWORD; INKHORN TERMS; LOAN WORD; NONCE-WORD; PORTMANTEAU WORD; VERBOCRAP.

neo-realism A kind of movement in Italy which began in the late 1940s which is particularly associated with the Italian novel (*q.v.*) and also the cinema industry. It is related to the late 19th c. movement in Italy called *verismo* (*q.v.*). Neo-realist novelists of distinction have been Carlo Levi (1902–75), Elio Vittorini (1908–66), Cesare Pavese (1908–50), Beppe Fenoglio (1922–63) and Italo Calvino (1923–85).

neue Sachlichkeit (G 'new objectivity') Basically, a term for functionalism in architecture. In literature it referred to fiction, journalism and poetry which made social criticism. The inherent attitudes represented a reaction against expressionism (*q.v.*) in the 1920s. *See* GEBRAUCHS-; PROLETARSKAYA KUL'TURA; SOCIALIST REALISM.

New Apocalypse A short-lived British literary movement of the 1940s. The moving spirits were James Findlay Hendry, Henry Treece and G. S. Fraser. They described themselves as 'anti-cerebral' and their poetry and prose was surrealistic in technique and subject matter. There were three main anthologies: *The New Apocalypse* (1939), *The White Horseman* (1941) and *The Crown and the Sickle* (1944). Other poets associated with the movement were George Barker, Dylan Thomas and Vernon Watkins.

New Comedy Greek comedy which flourished in the 3rd and 4th c. BC. It differed from the Old Comedy (*q.v.*) in that there was little or no satire (common in Aristophanes) and both plots and characters were very often stereotyped. The emphasis was on intricate amorous intrigues with a happy ending. Menander, Philemon and Diphilus were the best-known playwrights. They were imitated by the Romans Plautus and Terence, who, in turn, had a considerable influence on Elizabethan comedy. *See also* COMEDY; COMEDY OF MANNERS.

New Criticism A term which refers to a kind of 'movement' in literary criticism which developed in the 1920s (for the most part among Americans). However, it was not until 1941 that John Crowe Ransom published a book called *The New Criticism*. In it he criticized the critics I. A. Richards, William Empson, T. S. Eliot and Yvor Winters, and made a plea for what he called the 'ontological critic'.

The New Critics advocated 'close reading' and detailed textual analysis of poetry rather than an interest in the mind and personality of the poet, sources, the history of ideas and political and social implications. The application of semantics to this criticism was also important.

Other leading figures were Allen Tate, R. P. Blackmur, Kenneth Burke, Cleanth Brooks, W. K. Wimsatt and Robert Penn Warren. The last two, in *Understanding Poetry* (1938), helped to spread the principles of the New Criticism throughout the American academic scene. The latest 'new' criticism is, of course, to be found in structuralism and deconstruction (*qq.v.*). However, the traditional methods of criticism and analysis, as in practical criticism (*q.v.*), are still widely employed; not least because structuralist and deconstructive practice tends to be inaccessible to many, and even very abstruse. *See also* FEMINIST CRITICISM; PSYCHOANALYTIC CRITICISM; MARXIST CRITICISM; NEW HUMANISM; INTENTIONAL FALLACY.

Newdigate Prize A prize at Oxford University for English verse, and in all probability the earliest of the literary prizes (*q.v.*) created in England. It was founded in 1805 by Sir Roger Newdigate (1719–1806). Not a few distinguished writers have won it, but if you put all the prize-winning works together the result would be a corpus of unremarkable verse.

Newgate fiction A minor genre or mode which had some vogue in the 1830s; it has been called 'crime fiction' and is, perhaps, an early form of faction (*q.v.*). The so-called Newgate novelists based their stories on actual criminal cases (there was ample source material in the Newgate Calendar). At the time there was an increasing interest in violent crime and in criminal motives, and some of the novelists aroused moral indignation and adverse criticism for presenting criminals and their deeds in a sympathetic light. The two novelists who are particularly associated with this type of fiction are Edward Bulwer Lytton (1803–73) and William Harrison Ainsworth (1805–82). Lytton wrote *Paul Clifford* (1830) and *Eugene Aram* (1832), and Ainsworth wrote *Rookwood* (1834) and *Jack Sheppard* (1839), which considerably glamorized the famous highwayman.

In fact, this sort of fiction was by no means new. Long before, Fielding had dealt with criminal life in detail in *Jonathan Wild* (1743), based on the life of the notorious thief-taker of that name about whom Defoe had already written a biographical account; while in *Caleb Williams* (1794), an early example of the propaganda or thesis novel (*q.v.*) concerned with crime and its detection, Godwin had depicted the ruthless and arrogant criminal Falkland.

In the 1830s Dickens published *Oliver Twist* (1837–8) and Thackeray published *Catherine* (1839–40), and their view of criminal life constituted something of a reaction against the attitudes expressed in Newgate fiction. A few years later Poe was to publish his remarkable stories about crime and murder, thus becoming one of the main progenitors of the detective story (*q.v.*). *See also* CALENDAR; CRIME NOVEL; NOVEL OF SENSATION.

new historicism This term or appellation is relatively new in literary studies and literary theory. The practice of the approach has been described under other names, such as the 'historical method'. There are many kinds of historical method (e.g. those belonging to Marxist criticism and Jauss's reception theory, *qq.v.*). At its simplest, the historical method is interested not in asserting the transcendent or autonomous aesthetic value of literary texts but, to use Marxist terminology, in researching the contexts of their production, consumption and status. It would certainly be true to say that the 'new historicists' are opposed, above all, to the pure formalism of the New Criticism, structuralism, poststructuralism and hermeneutics (*qq.v.*) as approaches to literature. They also oppose the old Leavisite preoccupation with moral value, and implicitly question the way that the literary canon in schools and universities has been arrived at, namely through exclusion and suppression. It would not be inaccurate to say that the 'new historicist' work has Marxist sympathies and is also informed by some of the relativism of poststructuralism. Thus, 'new historicists' do not always see what they are doing as incompatible with deconstruction (*q.v.*) since the enemy of both schools is an unrefined and simple idea of value implicit in the canon. New historicism is associated with research being done in two periods – especially in the English-speaking world: the Renaissance and the Romantic period (*qq.v.*). Much of the best research is being done in the USA: for instance, in the Renaissance period by Stephen Greenblatt, and in the Romantic period by Jerome McGann and Marjorie Levinson. In Britain, Marilyn Butler is a distinguished example of a 'new historicist' scholar of the Romantic period. The 'new historicists' tend to question labels and titles and are constantly refining their goals in order to resist being made to seem as crude as 19th c.

philological scholars or Marxists trying to give a materialist explanation of literature. They constantly interrogate the relationship between history and literature rather than making dogmatic assertions. *Rethinking Historicism: Critical Readings in Romantic History* (1989), edited by Marjorie Levinson, which includes essays by Marjorie Levinson, Marilyn Butler, Jerome McGann and Paul Hamilton, contains many interesting ideas. There is also *The New Historicism* (1989), a collection of essays, mainly by American academics, edited by H. Aram Veeser.

new humanism A movement in American literary and critical circles which flourished between 1915 and 1933. The prime movers were Irving Babbitt, Paul Elmer More and Norman Foerster. Its programme was intended to uphold human dignity and moral rectitude and extol the importance of the use of reason and the will. New humanists were anti-Romantic, anti-realist and anti-naturalist. Their exemplar and mentor was Matthew Arnold. They had a good deal of influence in their time and some of it was beneficial. In retrospect many of their views seem narrow and bigoted and display the shortcomings of men who, having set themselves up as arbiters, gradually become too big for their books. *See* HUMANISM.

new journalism There have been many developments in journalism (*q.v.*) which have taken the modifier 'new', but since the 1970s the term has been used to refer to a distinct style which became popular in the 1960s and 1970s. Mostly published in periodicals such as *Esquire*, *Harpers* and *Rolling Stone*, rather than newspapers, new journalism was reportage that employed distinctly literary techniques, including narrating a story through scenes and a defined point of view, and providing full dialogue, rather than quotations. Thus new journalism can be considered a form of creative non-fiction (*q.v.*). Another defining quality of new journalism was its subjectivity. The conventional view of the journalist is that he or she should when producing reportage remain as far as possible neutral and invisible. By contrast, in works of new journalism the author's opinions and participation frequently clearly shaped the story. Such involvement was often justified as the writing was conceived as a form of social activism. Some of the leading figures of new journalism were Joan Didion, Norman Mailer, Gay Talese, Hunter S. Thompson and Tom Wolfe. They covered diverse topics, including custom cars, the Vietnam War, individual celebrities and national politics. Several of these writers also published non-fiction novels (*q.v.*).

New Left A broad movement of left-wing politicians, educators, students, intellectuals and activists. Its origins can be traced to the 1950s and 1960s when socialists in France (affiliated with the *nouvelle gauche*), Britain and the US began to distinguish their beliefs and strategies from those of the 'old left', as enshrined in the authoritative and centralized parties of the Communist bloc and the focus in Western nations on trade unions and labour issues. Inspired by thinkers such as Antonio Gramsci, the sociologist C. Wright Mills, and especially the prominent member of the Frankfurt School (*q.v.*) Herbert Marcuse, the New Left envisaged a more democratic, international, and humanistic implementation of Marx's ideas through civil disobedience, pacifism and, not least, intellectual argument. Much of the New Left took root in the widespread discontent of the 1960s, where it shared ground with the Civil Rights Movement, the women's movement, Students for a Democratic Society, the Campaign for Nuclear Disarmament, and student protests against the Vietnam War. Its publishing outlet was New Left Books (now Verso), as well as the highly regarded journal *New Left Review*, founded in 1960. The *NLR* was edited by Stuart Hall, followed by Perry Anderson. Major contributors have included E. P. Thompson, Ralph Miliband, Charles Taylor, Raymond Williams, Terry Eagleton and Slavoj Žižek. Its scope has extended from debates in Western Marxism and analyses of the global disarray of capitalism, through feminism, to the wars in Afghanistan and Iraq and the revolutions shaking the Arab world.

newsbooks Also known as *diurnalls*, they succeeded the *coranto* (*q.v.*). They consisted, first of all, of one printed sheet of eight pages; later of two printed sheets (sixteen pages). They contained domestic or home news and were issued by journalists (under various titles) between 1641 and 1665. They were succeeded by the *Oxford Gazette*, which later became the *London Gazette*. See GAZETTE.

newsletters Manuscript records of parliamentary and court news sent twice weekly to subscribers from the London office of a man called Muddiman (a famous journalist) in the latter half of the 17th c. A relic of these records is the 'London Letter', which still appears in provincial papers.

newspeak A 'language' invented by George Orwell in his novel *Nineteen Eighty-Four* (1949). *See also* EUPHEMISM; JARGON.

New York Intellectuals A group of critics who produced their most significant work between the 1930s and 1960s and who wrote extensively for radical journals such as the *Partisan Review*, *The New Republic*, *The Nation*, *Commentary* and *Dissent*. Major figures in this group included Richard Chase, Irving Howe, Alfred Kazin, Philip Rahv, Lionel Trilling, Elizabeth Hardwick, Sidney Hook, Steven Marcus, Richard Poirier, Meyer Schapiro and Susan Sontag. Taking the work of Edmund Wilson as a model, these writers considered themselves aloof from bourgeois society, commercialism, Stalinism and mass culture; they viewed themselves as democratic socialists and wrote criticism with a social and political emphasis. They promoted literary modernism, and valued complexity, irony and cosmopolitanism in literature. This broad critical movement (if such a diverse range of critical activity can be called such) was never institutionalized though it was continued into the 1980s, confined within small circles.

Nibelungenstrophe The stanza of the 12th c. MHG epic *Nibelungenlied*. It consists of four lines rhyming aabb. The first three lines have six stressed syllables; the last, seven.

nihilism A word invented by Turgenev in his novel *Fathers and Sons* (1862). It denotes a radical or extreme radical attitude which denies all traditional values, and, not infrequently, moral values as well. Turgenev invented it to describe the radical elements in the Russian intelligentsia who were profoundly disillusioned by lack of reform and believed that the only way to achieve anything was to destroy more or less completely all prevailing systems. The main theorist and ideologist was Pisarev (1840–68), who was depicted by Turgenev as Bazarov in *Fathers and Sons*. Nihilistic ideas spread and nihilism threatened for a time to develop into quite a powerful revolutionary force. Several other novelists took nihilism as a theme in their fiction and through it criticized the nihilists. The main nihilist works were: Pisemski's *Troubled Seas* (1863), Leskov's *No Way Out* (1864), Goncharov's *The Precipice* (1869) and Dostoevsky's *The Possessed* (or *The Devils*, 1871–2). Some of the worst aspects of nihilism were exemplified by Dostoevsky in the immoral and unscrupulous character Peter Verkhovensky. Few writers were sympathetic to nihilism, but in *What is to be Done?* (1863) Chernyshevski showed some sympathy for the nihilists and portrayed them as self-sacrificing heroes and radical leaders to be emulated.

nihil obstat *See* IMPRIMATUR.

Nine Worthies Caxton, in his preface to Malory's *Le Morte d'Arthur* (1485) listed the Nine Worthies, or Heroes, of late medieval literature. The pagan heroes are: Hector, Alexander and Julius Caesar; the Jewish: Joshua, David and Judas Maccabeus; the Christian: Arthur, Charlemagne and Godfrey of Bouillon.

Nō (Noh) This form of Japanese drama evolved in the 14th c., probably from ritual dances associated with Shinto worship. They were lyric dramas (there are believed to be about three hundred in all) and were intended for aristocratic audiences. They therefore differed from the 'popular' *kabuki* (*q.v.*). They were traditionally the work of a man named Kwanami and his son Seami. The form became fixed early in the 17th c. It was therefore a 'frozen' or 'fossil' form, like traditional icon paintings, and just about as stylized.

    Nō plays are presented on a square stage, raised slightly from the ground, on which the audience sit on two sides. At one side is a balcony accommodating a chorus of ten singers. Upstage there is a smaller platform occupied by four musicians and two stage-hands. The actors enter and leave on a long slanting walk, a sort of bridge, from stage left. There is little or no scenery except for a framework with a roof and three symbolic trees in front of the slanting walk which represent heaven, earth and humanity.

    There are usually between two and six actors in a *Nō* play: the hero or leading character, *shite* (or *shtay*); his companion, *tsure*; *waki*, a kind of deuteragonist (*q.v.*); and *waki*'s companion. There are also a child, *kokata*, and an extra actor, *ahi*. *Waki* introduces the play with a chant and tells the audience what is going to be performed. *Shite* then appears disguised (in mask and elaborate costume) and delivers a chant. He converses with *waki* so that the theme of the play is clear and the real character of *shite* is revealed. The rest of the play consists of a series of stylized dances, usually in five movements, by the first actor. These dances are preceded by an interlude in which an actor in ordinary clothes tells the story of the play. All the actors (except the man playing *waki*) usually wear masks and elaborate costumes and they chant in low- or high-pitched voices to a musical accompaniment. To Western ears the chanting is reminiscent of the gentle warbling of slightly dispeptic doves, and the gestures which go with it are as arcane as Byzantine cricket.

A full *Nō* entertainment (women never act in it and men take the female roles) lasts about seven hours, and normally consists of five plays separated by three *kyogen* – brief farcical interludes. These are often performed in ordinary costume and actually parody the *Nō* plays themselves; rather as a satyr play (*q.v.*) served as a comic relief to the trilogy in Classical Greek tragedy.

Nō drama has had some influence in the West. W. B. Yeats was very interested in it. Ezra Pound and Fenollosa adapted some *Nō* plays. Arthur Waley did some translations and commentaries. Sturge Moore wrote some *Nō* plays, and Laurence Binyon, Bertolt Brecht and Paul Claudel all used their techniques. Their influence was especially noticeable in the work of Thornton Wilder, particularly in *Our Town* (1938). Two studies by Noel Peri, *Cinq Nō* (1929) and *Le Nō* (1944), have also helped to make *Nō* drama known in Europe.

Nobel Prizes These were established under the will of Alfred Bernhard Nobel (1833–96), the Swedish chemist who made a major contribution to the development of explosives. The terms of his will provided for prizes to be awarded annually for the most important discoveries in physics, chemistry, and physiology or medicine; to the person who has done the most to promote 'the fraternity of nations' (i.e. the Peace Prize); and to the person who has produced 'the most outstanding work of an idealistic tendency' in the field of literature. Recent winners of the Nobel Prize in Literature include Harold Pinter (2005), Orhan Pamuk (2006), Doris Lessing (2007), Jean-Marie Gustave Le Clézio (2008), Herta Müller (2009), Mario Vargas Llosa (2010) and Tomas Tranströmer (2011).

noble savage, the The concept or title which connotes the exemplar of primitive goodness, dignity and nobility uncorrupted by the evil effects of civilization. The origins of the idea of the noble savage are obscure, but one may suppose that they have to do with the belief that in a primitive and 'free' state there existed innocent, prototypal human beings like Milton's Adam and Eve in Eden:

> Two of far nobler shape erect and tall,
> Godlike erect, with native honour clad
> In naked majesty seemed lords of all,
> And worthy seemed, for their looks divine

> The image of their glorious maker shone,
> Truth, wisdom, sanctitude severe and pure.
> (*Paradise Lost*, IV, 288)

We find Montaigne touching upon the idea of the noble savage in his essay *Of Cannibals* (1580), but it is not until well on in the 17th c. that it becomes prominent. The concept is handsomely embodied by Dryden in a resonant triplet (*q.v.*) in his heroic play *The Conquest of Granada*, Pt I, I, i (1670):

> I am as free as nature first made man,
> Ere the base laws of servitude began,
> When wild in woods the noble savage ran.

The idea is especially noticeable in Aphra Behn's *Oroonoko: or, The History of the Royal Slave* (c. 1688). The eponymous hero of this 'romance' is an educated as well as a noble savage (he has learnt French and English), and he is virtuous, young, beautiful, brave and a fine warrior; in short, the 'fair rose i' the state' of his native Africa. Behn dwelt upon primitive innocence and deplored the effects of civilization and man's inventions. She foreshadowed the 'return to nature' philosophy and doctrine which Rousseau was to elaborate seventy years later in *Émile* (1762). 'Everything is well when it comes fresh from the hands of the Maker', wrote Rousseau; 'everything degenerates in the hands of Man'. Chateaubriand also exploited the noble savage idea, and it proved a particularly attractive concept to many writers in the late 18th c. and during the Romantic period (*q.v.*). It was a part of the reaction against the growth of industrialism, materialism and capitalism. *See* PRIMITIVISM.

nom de plume (F 'pen-name') A term used in English, but *not* in French, to indicate a fictitious name employed by a writer. For instance: Beachcomber was J. B. Morton; O. Henry was William Sydney Porter; George Eliot was Mary Ann Cross. The French use *nom de guerre* for an author's pen-name or pseudonym. A very large number of writers have pen-names. *See also* ANONYMOUS LITERATURE; PSEUDONYMOUS LITERATURE.

nonce-word A word invented and used for a particular purpose, expressly; one used for a specific occasion; for the nonce = for that once, temporarily. Lewis Carroll's *Jabberwocky* is a classic example, but over the centuries numerous neologisms have started life as nonce-words. *See* GHOSTWORD; NEOLOGISM.

non-fiction novel/documentary fiction A novel based on real events and people, which largely draws on documentary evidence such as newspaper articles, official papers, personal letters, and interviews. Elements of the story's narrative, however – in particular, the conversations and thoughts of the protagonists – are the author's invention. In the late 1960s the term 'faction', a portmanteau word (*qq.v.*) combining fact and fiction, was coined to describe such work. The first work of faction is commonly said to be Truman Capote's *In Cold Blood* (1966), an account of the notorious murders in 1959 of the Kansas farmer Herbert Clutter and his family. The novel closely examines the motivations and treatment of the murderers, whom Capote was able to interview. Other commonly cited examples of faction include Norman Mailer's *The Armies of the Night* and Tom Wolfe's *The Electric Kool-Aid Acid Test*, both published in 1968. Indeed, faction has much in common with Tom Wolfe's school of 'new journalism' (*q.v.*) in vogue in the 1960s and 1970s, whose purveyors typically employed a noticeably more personalized narrative voice than that used in traditional reportage.

However, while the term was new, faction was not really an invention of the 1960s. The Argentine investigative journalist Rodolfo Walsh published *Operación Masacre* in 1957. Theodore Dreiser's *An American Tragedy* (1925) is an earlier work based on newspaper accounts of a murder trial. Dreiser changes the location where the murder took place and the name of the killer (though his protagonist shares the same initials as the real murderer). The non-fiction novel has much in common with biography (*q.v.*), which typically also utilizes documentary material which is necessarily embellished by the writer. Since the 1980s, the non-fiction novel has been eclipsed by the rise of 'creative non-fiction' (*q.v.*), which noticeably provides less scope for authorial invention.

nonsense There are basically two kinds of nonsense involving the use of words: (a) the unintentional; (b) the intentional. The former is common in speech and much semi-educated writing (e.g. malapropisms, *q.v.*). The latter has become a minor genre in literature, especially during the last 150 years. Setting aside gibberish, true or positive nonsense writing is never intended to make formal sense; nevertheless it has a kind of internal lunatic logic of its own, and often comprises enigmatic variations on the absurd. Most of it is verse, but there is some prose; for example, the patter and punning and intricate witticisms of Shakespearean Fools (especially in *King Lear*), James Joyce's epic *Finnegans Wake* and some passages in Thomas Lovell Beddoes's *Death's Jest Book* (1850). It has a long history in Europe and is to be found in all or nearly all European languages and literatures, and in Russian literature. *See also* BURLESQUE; CARNIVALIZATION/CARNIVALESQUE; DOGGEREL; DOUBLE DACTYL; FOLLY LITERATURE; HOLORHYME; LIGHT VERSE; PALINDROME; PATAPHYSICS; PATTER SONG; PUN; RIDDLE; SURREALISM.

nota (L 'note') Any mark or text in the margins, as distinct from punctuation, which occurs within the body of a text.

notebook *See* DIARY AND JOURNAL.

noucentisme A Catalan literary movement named after the 1900s or 20th c. It started *c.* 1906 when Enric Prat de la Riba published a manifesto (*q.v.*) titled *La nacionalitat catalana*. Members of the movement attempted to create a new humanism (*q.v.*) and they had considerable influence on Catalan literature. Among the main writers were Guereau de Liost, Josep Carner and Carlos Riba.

nouveau roman (F 'new novel') This term appears to have become part of critical jargon in France *c.* 1955 with the publication (in periodicals and reviews) of Robbe-Grillet's essays on the nature and future of the novel (*q.v.*). His theories were later gathered in *Pour un nouveau roman* (1963). The movement, if such it can be called, of the *nouveau roman* was somewhat biblioclastic in the sense that it rejected much that had gone before. In his evangelical role Robbe-Grillet regarded many earlier novelists as *vieux jeu*. Such things as plot, action, narrative, ideas, and the delineation and analysis of character had little or no place in the novel. On the contrary, the novel should be a form of 'resistentialism' – to use Paul Jennings's word. It should be about *things*; an individual version and vision of *things*; a systematized and analytical record of objects. And so, in practice, many of the *nouveux romans* were and are; and hardly anywhere is the practice better displayed than in Michel Butor's novel *La Modification* (1957).

Such a view of the function of the novel was not entirely new. Long before, Huysmans had suggested what might be done about objects and how the novel might be depersonalized; Kafka had shown that the conventional methods of depicting character were not essential; James Joyce had demonstrated that plot was dispensable; and Louis-Ferdinand Céline, in several novels, but especially in *Voyage au bout de la nuit* (1932), had written of themes which later preoccupied the existentialists and the *hodjas* (mentors) of the cult of the absurd, and especially those of the Theatre of the Absurd (*q.v.*). Proust, William Faulkner, Samuel Beckett and Albert Camus had also shown that it was possible to break with a number of the traditional conventions of the novel form.

In 1939 Nathalie Sarraute published *Tropismes* and this has come to be regarded as a probable prototype of the *nouveau roman*. Later, in 1952, she published a collection of essays called *L'Ère du soupçon* in which she discussed this new form. *See* ANTI-HERO; ANTI-NOVEL; TROPISM.

nouvelle The *nouvelle* differs from the *roman* or novel (*qq.v.*) in that it deals with a single situation or episode. The event moves to an unexpected climax, and it may be comic or tragic. It is related to the *novella* and the *récit* (*qq.v.*) and seldom exceeds a hundred pages.

The *nouvelle* followed on from the medieval *lais* and *fabliaux* (*qq.v.*), and the form took definite shape in the collection of tales known as *Cent Nouvelles Nouvelles* (1462). Notable examples from near the end of the 15th c. were *Arrêts d'amour* and *Jehan de Paris*. In the next century a collection of stories titled *Nouvelles Récréations et Joyeux Devis* was published *c.* 1558 and ascribed to Des Périers. Thereafter the *nouvelle* was an established form, and in the 19th c. the term *conte* (*q.v.*) was often used as a synonym. The main authors from this period were Flaubert and Maupassant, Alfred de Musset, Alfred de Vigny, Prosper Mérimée, Joseph-Arthur Gobineau and Anatole France. *See also* SHORT STORY.

nouvelle vague (F 'new wave') A term which appears to have come into regular use in the 1950s and 1960s to describe a new trend in the arts. It was particularly applied to experimental work in the cinema (films by Godard and Resnais, for example), and then to experimental novels (for instance, works by Alain Robbe-Grillet, Michel Butor, Nathalie Sarraute, Alan Burns and B. S. Johnson) and also to playwrights like Harold Pinter, Samuel Beckett, Eugène Ionesco, Arthur Adamov, Jean Genet, N. F. Simpson and Ann Jellicoe. *See also* ANTI-NOVEL; AVANT-GARDE; BLACK COMEDY; NOUVEAU ROMAN; NOVEL; THEATRE OF THE ABSURD.

nouvellistes Members of the Parisian population in the 17th c. who held regular meetings at various points in the city in order to pass on news and discuss it. Eventually they were paid to collect news by those in a position of power and influence who needed to know it. The *nouvellistes* were active even after the establishment of the press. Hand-written newsletters (called *nouvelles à la main* and *gazettes à la main*) were circulated clandestinely. *See also* CORANTO; GAZETTE; NEWSBOOKS; NEWSLETTERS.

novecentismo A Spanish term denoting the 'spirit' of the 20th c., taken from Massimo Bontempelli's magazine *900* (founded in 1926) and introduced by Eugenio d'Ors. It came to be applied to a group of writers of the post-'98 generation which included Ortega y Gasset, Linares Rivas, Martínez Sierra, Pedro Salinas and Pérez de Ayala. *See* GENERACIÓN DE 1898.

novel Derived from Italian *novella*, 'tale, piece of news', and now applied to a wide variety of writings whose only common attribute is that they are extended pieces of prose fiction. But 'extended' begs a number of questions. The length of novels varies greatly and there has been much debate on how long a novel is or should be – to the *reductio ad absurdum* of when is a novel *not* a novel or a long short story or a short novel or a *novella* (*q.v.*). There seem to be fewer and fewer rules, but it would probably be generally agreed that, in contemporary practice, a novel will be between 60,000 words and, say, 200,000.

The actual term 'novel' has had a variety of meanings and implications at different stages. From roughly the 16th to the 18th c. its meaning tended to derive from the Italian *novella* and the Spanish *novela* (the French term *nouvelle*, *q.v.*, is closely related) and the term (often used in a plural sense) denoted short stories or tales of the kind one finds in Boccaccio's *Decameron* (c. 1349–51), Marguerite of Navarre's *Heptameron* (c. 1530), George Pettie's *A Petite Palace of Pettie his Pleasure* (1576) and Cervantes's *Novelas ejemplares* (1613).

Nowadays we would classify all the contents of the above as short stories. Broadly speaking, the term denoted a prose narrative about characters and their actions in what was recognizably everyday life and usually in the present, with the emphasis on things being 'new' or a 'novelty'. And it was used in contradistinction to 'romance' (*q.v.*). In the 19th c. the concept of 'novel' was enlarged.

As to the quiddity of the novel there has been as much debate. However, without performing contortions to be comprehensive we may hazard that it

is a form of story or prose narrative containing characters, action and incident, and, perhaps, a plot (*q.v.*). In fact it is very difficult to write a story
without there being *some* sort of plot, however vague and tenuous. So well
developed is the average reader's need for a plot (at its simplest the desire to
know what is going to happen next) that the reader will look for and find a
plot where, perhaps, none is intended. Moreover, as soon as the reader is
sufficiently interested in one or more of the characters (one can hardly envisage a novel without a character of some kind) to want to know what is going
to happen to them next and to ask why, when and where – then there is a
plot.

The subject matter of the novel eludes classification. No other literary
form has proved so pliable and adaptable to a seemingly endless variety of
topics and themes. No other literary form has attracted more writers (or more
people who are *not* writers), and it continues to do so despite the oft-repeated
cry (seldom raised by novelists themselves) that the novel is dead. If proliferation is a sign of incipient death then the demise of the novel must be
imminent.

At the moment it seems unlikely. Apart from dramatic comedy (*q.v.*) no
other form has been so susceptible to change and development and the literary taxonomist is at once confronted with a wide range of subspecies or
categories. For example, we have the epistolary novel, the sentimental novel,
the novel of sensation, the condition of England novel, the campus novel, the
Gothic novel and the historical novel; we have the propaganda, regional,
thesis (or sociological), psychological, proletarian, documentary and time
novel; we have the novel of the soil and the saga (or chronicle) novel, the
picaresque novel, the key novel or *livre à clef* and the anti-novel; not to
mention the detective novel, the thriller, the crime novel, the police procedural, the spy novel, the novel of adventure and the novelette (*qq.v.*). In
French we have various kinds of *roman*, especially the *roman-fleuve*, the
roman à tiroirs, the *roman-feuilleton*, the *récit*, the *roman policier* (the equivalent of the detective novel), the *nouveau roman* (the equivalent of the
anti-novel) and the *roman à clef*. In German we find the *Bildungsroman*,
the *Künstlerroman*, the *Ritter- und Räuberroman* (the picaresque), the *Briefroman* (epistolary), the *Zeitroman* (*qq.v.*), the *Schauerroman* ('shudder
novel') and the *Schlüsselroman* (key novel). A number of these classifications
shade off into each other. We should also note that in other literatures and
languages similar classifications have been established.

The absolute origins of the genre are obscure, but it seems clear that in the
time of the XIIth Dynasty Middle Kingdom (*c.* 1200 BC) Egyptians were
writing fiction of a kind which one would describe as a novel today. But it
is not until towards the end of the first millennium that we find work more
recognizably like the novels we have become accustomed to in the last two
hundred or so years. These works are in Japanese.

Until the 14th c. most of the literature of entertainment (and the novel is
usually intended as an entertainment) was confined to narrative verse (*q.v.*),
particularly the epic (*q.v.*) and the romance. Romance eventually yielded the

word *roman*, which is the term for novel in most European languages. In some ways the novel is a descendant of the medieval romances, which, in the first place, like the epic, were written in verse and then in prose (e.g. Malory's *Morte D'Arthur*, 1485).

Spain was ahead of the rest of Europe in the development of the novel form. The greatest of all Spanish novels is Cervantes's *Don Quixote de la Mancha* (1605, 1615), which satirized chivalry and a number of the earlier novels. After the death of Cervantes the Spanish novel, having begun so promisingly, went into decline until the 19th c.

In England, early in the 18th c. Defoe published his story of adventure – *Robinson Crusoe* (1719). From now on the novel comes of age and within another seventy years is a major and matured form.

In the early years of the 19th c. two figures dominate English fiction: Sir Walter Scott and Jane Austen. The middle years of the 19th c. witnessed the most astonishingly prolific output of fiction, especially from Dickens, Anthony Trollope, Thackeray and George Eliot, and it is noticeable that much of this fiction has lasted.

The development of the novel as a popular form in the 19th c. was a European phenomenon, and one of the most remarkable features of its history is the speed with which it matured. From nowhere, so it seemed, great novelists sprang up and produced novels which became and remained classics.

In the 20th c., Dorothy Richardson was the first English novelist to introduce the stream of consciousness technique (*q.v.*). In 1916 James Joyce published *A Portrait of the Artist as a Young Man*, in which he also employed the stream of consciousness technique. He perfected this in *Ulysses* (1922), and in *Finnegans Wake* (1939) he pushed it to its probable limits. After Joyce the novel was never quite the same again.

From the mid-1950s – the period when some people began to claim that the novel was 'dead' – until now the novel in Britain and elsewhere continued to show remarkable diversity and resilience, and the form has continued to attract large numbers of gifted writers. Since then, so many excellent books using the techniques of realism, modernism, postmodernism and magic realism (*qq.v.*) have been written by so many gifted writers. The novels of Kurt Vonnegut, John Bart, Thomas Pynchon, William Burroughs and Umberto Eco are some of the well-known examples of postmodern fiction in the period from the 1960s to the late 1980s. More recent writers such as Neil Gaiman, Dave Eggers and Zadie Smith have taken the postmodern novel in new directions. Following decolonization in the 1950s, a number of African, Asian, Caribbean, African-American and other writers have used the novel to 'write back' to colonial and racist representations. Since the 1990s, we also witness a number of rewritings of the Victorian period and the rise of the so-called 'neo-Victorian novel'. Authors such as Sarah Waters, Margaret Atwood, A. S. Byatt and Peter Ackroyd have all used the conventions of the Gothic novel in new ways. In the late 20th and early 21st c., a number of novelists have responded to contemporary events such as migration, cultural hybridity, the impact of technology and the media, and the 9/11 attacks.

Even these few recent examples show the great variety of thematic concerns, genres and styles in the contemporary novel. A 'short' short-list would contain the names of over a hundred novels. *See also* EPISTOLARY NOVEL; NOVEL OF SENSATION; REFLEXIVE NOVEL; REGIONAL NOVEL; VERSE-NOVEL.

novelette   A work of fiction shorter than a novel but longer than a short story (*q.v.*). Often used derogatorily of 'cheap' fiction, sentimental romances and thrillers of popular appeal but little literary merit. In America the term applies to a long short story somewhere between the short story and the *novella* (*q.v.*).

novel-in-verse   *See* VERSE-NOVEL.

novella   (It 'tale, piece of news') Originally a *novella* was a kind of short story, a narrative in prose of the genre developed by Boccaccio. His *Decameron* (*c.* 1349–51) was a collection of such stories. Later there appeared Tommaso Guardati's *Il Novellino* (1467). In the 16th c. Bandello published a collection of 214 *novelle*. Tudor dramatists often used *novelle* as source-books for plots. Thereafter, there was little sign of the *novella* developing for some time; unless one were to include in this category some of the narratives of Deloney and Greene, Nashe's *Unfortunate Traveller* (1594), Emanuel Ford's *Irnatus and Artesia* (1634), Mrs Behn's *Oroonoko* (*c.* 1688) and Congreve's *Incognita* (1713). But such works may also be regarded as romances (*q.v.*), or embryonic novels. It was not until late in the 18th and early in the 19th c. that the *novella* was fashioned into a particular form according to certain precepts and rules. Then the Germans became the most active practitioners, and the *Novelle* has since flourished in Germany more than anywhere else.

Basically, the *Novelle* is a fictional narrative of indeterminate length (a few pages to two or three hundred), restricted to a single event, situation or conflict, which produces an element of suspense and leads to an unexpected turning point (*Wendepunkt*) so that the conclusion surprises even while it is a logical outcome. Many *Novellen* contain a concrete symbol which is the steady point, as it were, at the heart of the narrative.

Goethe attempted to summarize the quiddity of the *Novelle* when he said: 'What else is a *Novelle* about but an event which is unheard of but has taken place?' Or, more concisely, 'an event without precedent' ('eine sich ereignete unerhörte Begebenheit').

The first of its kind, in all probability, was Goethe's *Unterhaltungen deutscher Ausgewanderten* (1795), derived from the *novella* form used by Boccaccio. It is a *Novelle* with a cyclic frame or *Rahmen*. There has been a good deal of debate and theory ever since as to what precisely a *Novelle* is or should be. August Schlegel theorized about it and stressed the importance of the *Wendepunkt* in the narrative. Tieck also stressed the importance of this. Later, Paul Heyse worked out his *Falkentheorie* (*q.v.*) in *Deutscher Novellenschatz* (1871–6). In 1828 Goethe had observed that the genre harboured 'many a wonderful thing'.

Among the principal practitioners were Goethe himself, Kleist (a vital influence in the creation of the short story, *q.v.*, who published his stories as *Erzählungen*), Hoffmann, Tieck, Theodor Storm, Fontane, Paul Heyse, Hermann Hesse and Thomas Mann. The Swiss writers Gottfried Keller and Conrad Meyer were also prolific; as were the Austrians Ferdinand Saar and Arthur Schnitzler.

Nowadays the term is often used to distinguish a long short story from a short story and a short novel from a full-dress novel (*q.v.*). Stories which might be placed in this middle-distance category are Tolstoy's *The Cossacks* (1852) and *The Death of Ivan Ilyich* (1886); Thomas Mann's *Tonio Kröger* and *Tod in Venedig* (1913); Aldous Huxley's *Two or Three Graces* (1916); Alberto Moravia's *Conjugal Love* (1951); Hemingway's *The Old Man and the Sea* (1952); and H. E. Bates's trilogy *The Nature of Love* (1953). Some would also include Conrad's three long short stories *Youth*, *Heart of Darkness* (1902) and *Typhoon* (1903). *See* NOVELETTE.

novellat A form of folk tale of the Semitic tradition which is of a particular time and place. It lacks universality (*q.v.*) and thus differs from the *chimerat* which is not essentially tied to a particular place or period.

Novelle *See* NOVELLA.

novel of adventure Literature in English is particularly rich in this form of fiction, which is seldom to be found in other languages. Daniel Defoe appears to have been its main pioneer with *The Life and Strange and Surprising Adventures of Robinson Crusoe* (1719). This produced many imitations known as 'Robinsonades' (*q.v.*) and a large quantity of what is called 'desert island fiction' (*q.v.*). The novel of adventure is also related to the picaresque novel and the romance (*qq.v.*). Among the numerous British exponents the following are some of the more notable: Captain Marryat, R. M. Ballantyne, G. A. Henty, P. C. Wren, Stanley Weyman, R. L. Stevenson, Anthony Hope, Arthur Conan Doyle, John Buchan, Dornford Yates, Hammond Innes, C. S. Forester, Alistair Maclean, Nevil Shute, Willard Price and John Masters. Two famous Americans in this field are James Fenimore Cooper and Mark Twain.

novel of ideas A vague category of fiction in which conversation, intellectual discussion and debate predominate, and in which plot, narrative, emotional conflict and psychological depth in characterization are deliberately limited. Such a form of novel is perhaps best exemplified by Aldous Huxley's *Crome Yellow* (1921), *Point Counter Point* (1928) and *After Many a Summer* (1939). *See* NOVEL.

novel of sensation A form of fiction that became extremely popular in the 1860s in England and that borrowed its plot lines and techniques from the domestic novel, Gothic fiction, melodrama and the stage. The most well-known sensation novels include Wilkie Collins's *The Woman in White* (1860), Mrs Henry Wood's *East Lynne* (1861) and Mary Elizabeth Braddon's *Lady Audley's Secret* (1862). As a form of light reading, sensation novels were subject to intense criticism from those who feared that the genre encouraged the popular appetite for murder, bigamy and madness – all common themes in these stories. Scholars have argued that the genre appealed to anxieties already existent in Victorian society, particularly those aroused by the effects of industrialism, urbanization, and the shifting of class structures that these forces helped to catalyse. It is more than likely that the novel of sensation was eventually to influence the evolution of the thriller and the detective story (qq.v.). See also CRIME NOVEL; GOTHIC NOVEL/FICTION; NEWGATE FICTION.

novel of sensibility See SENTIMENTAL NOVEL.

novel of the soil A work of fiction whose main theme is the struggle of human beings against the natural forces of the earth as in Ellen Glasgow's *Barren Ground* (1925), the Norwegian O. E. Rolvagg's *Giants in the Earth* (1927), Erskine Caldwell's *Tobacco Road* (1932) and *God's Little Acre* (1933), John Steinbeck's *Grapes of Wrath* (1939) and Patrick White's *The Tree of Man* (1956). Many would include D. H. Lawrence's *The Rainbow* (1915), the novels of Mary Webb and some of the work of Thomas Hardy, as well as Jean Giono's descriptions of pastoral life in Provence (e.g. *Colline*, 1929; *Un de Baumugnes*, 1929; *Regain*, 1930; *Batailles dans la montagne*, 1939). See also NOVEL; THESIS NOVEL.

novelty A good deal was made of the importance of novelty in literature by such writers as Addison, Akenside and Dr Johnson. Johnson approved of it so long as it was a means to an end and provided variation and freshness. Writers of the Romantic period (q.v.) were also preoccupied with the matter. Coleridge takes much the same point of view as Johnson. The judicious test of the value of novelty must be whether or not it is an end in itself or a means to an end. Novelty intended solely to shock or surprise will probably run the risk of being meretricious or melodramatic and may, in some cases, have an unbalancing effect. T. S. Eliot's sober observations in his essay *Tradition and the Individual Talent* (1919) show a sense of proportion on this issue. See IMITATION; ORIGINALITY.

Nudelvers See MACARONIC.

null rhyme See RHYME.

number The term may refer to poems (poetry in general), verses or metrical feet. When Shakespeare writes in the 17th Sonnet:

> If I could write the beauty of your eyes
> And in fresh numbers number all your graces,

he is probably using it in the first sense. On the other hand, when Wordsworth, in *The Solitary Reaper*, writes:

> Will no one tell me what she sings? –
> Perhaps the plaintive numbers flow
> For old, unhappy, far-off things,

he may well be referring to verses.

Pope uses 'numbers' at least twice, and in *Essay on Criticism* is almost certainly using the term in the sense of metrical feet, thus:

> But most by numbers judge a poet's song,
> And smooth or rough with them is right or wrong.

nursery rhyme Such rhymes belong to the oral tradition (*q.v.*) of literature. A nursery rhyme consists of a verse or verses recited or sung by a mother (or other adult) to the very young members of the family. The origins of most nursery rhymes are very obscure and are thought to be of considerable antiquity. Certainly a large number of them are known to have been alive in the oral tradition for two or three hundred years. They range from a very nearly meaningless jingle (*q.v.*) like:

> Tae titly,
> Little fitty,
> Shin sharpy,
> Knee knapy.
> Hinchie pinchy,
> Wymie bulgy,
> Breast berry,
> Chin cherry,
> Moo merry,
> Nose nappy,
> Ee winky,
> Broo brinky.
> Ower the croon,
> And awa' wi' it.

to quite a sophisticated poem in semi-ballad form like 'What can the matter be?'

> O dear, what can the matter be?
> Dear, dear, what can the matter be?
> O dear, what can the matter be?
> Johnny's so long at the fair.
>
> He promised he'd buy me a fairing
>   should please me,
> And then for a kiss, oh! he vowed
>   he would tease me,
> He promised he'd bring me a bunch of blue ribbons
> To tie up my bonny brown hair.

483

Somewhat more than eight hundred nursery rhymes are known to exist in English. Many of them are counting jingles, weather rhymes, songs from games, riddles, tongue-twisters and so forth. Apart from these there are ballads, or rhymes in more or less ballad (*q.v.*) form, like: *Aiken Drum*, *Willy Wood*, *The Lover's Tasks*, *The Twelve Days of Christmas*, *Tom the Piper's Son*, *Cock Robin*, *The Love-Sick Frog*, *The Milk Maid*, *The Derby Ram* and *Bobby Shaftoe*. A score or more of the others could be described as extremely well known and many children are still brought up on them. For example: *Ring-a-Ring o' Roses*, *Humpty Dumpty*, *Goosey Gander*, *Ding, Dong, Bell*, *Old Mother Hubbard*, *Solomon Grundy*, *The Queen of Hearts*, *Little Miss Muffet*, *Little Jack Horner*, *Jack and Jill*, *Simple Simon*, *The House that Jack Built*, *Sing a Song of Sixpence*, *Old King Cole*, *Little Bo-Peep*, *Oranges and Lemons*, *London Bridge*.

The earliest known collection is *Tom Thumb's Pretty Song Book* (1744). *Mother Goose's Melody* (c. 1765) is another famous compilation. Mention should also be made of *Gammer Gurton's Garland* (1784); *Nursery Rhymes of England* (1842); *Popular Rhymes and Nursery Tales* (1849); and *The Oxford Dictionary of Nursery Rhymes* (1951), compiled by Iona and Peter Opie. Another collection by the same editors is *The Oxford Nursery Rhyme Book* (1955). *See* LULLABY.

O

obelus *See* PUNCTUATION.

obiter dicta (L 'things said by the way') A vaguely comprehensive term for remarks 'shed' in conversation (or in writing). The aphorism (*q.v.*) or *aperçu* is often an *obiter dictum*. The table-talk (*q.v.*) of great men like Goethe contains many examples. Boswell was an assiduous gleaner of Dr Johnson's *obiter dicta*. *See* -ANA; ANALECTS; PENSÉE.

objective and objectivity *See* SUBJECTIVITY AND OBJECTIVITY.

objective correlative A term first used apparently by the American painter Washington Allston in *c.* 1840 and subsequently revived and made famous by T. S. Eliot in an essay on *Hamlet* (1919). The relevant passage is: 'The only way of expressing emotion in the form of art is by finding an "objective correlative"; in other words, a set of objects, a situation, a chain of events which shall be the formula of that *particular* emotion; such that when the external facts, which must terminate in sensory experience, are given, the emotion is immediately evoked.' Eliot goes on to suggest that in Lady Macbeth's sleep-walking speech and in the speech that Macbeth makes when he hears of his wife's death, the words are completely adequate to the state of mind; whereas in Hamlet the prince is 'dominated by a state of mind which is inexpressible, because it is in *excess* of the facts as they appear'. These observations have provoked a good deal of debate.

In other (if Thomistic) terms a successful artistic creation requires an exquisite balance between, and coalescence of, form and matter. If the matter (thought, feeling, action) is 'too much for' ('in excess of') the form (in this case words) we have a discrepancy, strain, a lack of unity (that is, insufficient correlation; they don't 'fadge'). Vice versa, another kind of discrepancy and strain: the experience is overwhelmed by the words. Colloquially we say 'I was speechless', 'It was indescribable'. In other words we have not found the 'formula'. In reverse, lacking the 'formula', again we over-describe, say too much. *See* SYMBOL AND SYMBOLISM.

objectivism A term coined by William Carlos Williams (1883–1963) *c.* 1930 and the name bestowed on a short-lived movement among American poets in the 1930s. Williams's early work was imagist. Later he moved to objectivism, which he described thus: 'It looks at the poem with a special eye to its structural aspects, how it has been constructed . . .' It was an attempt at greater precision. Other objectivist poets of the period were George Oppen (founder of the Objectivist Press), Carl Rakosi, Luis Zukovsky and Charles Reznikoff. *See* IMAGISTS.

obligatory scene The English version of the French *scène à faire*. It usually denotes a scene, probably of fairly intense emotional content, which the audience anticipates and which the dramatist feels obliged to include. For instance, one expects, sooner or later, a 'confrontation' between Hamlet and his mother (III, iv). One certainly could hardly expect Shakespeare to have contrived the play without it. When it comes it is an emotional climax.

oblique rhyme *See* HALF RHYME.

obscenity A culturally specific concept which might signify any act or statement deemed offensive or derogatory to the mores of the dominant culture, particularly in terms of the breaking of sexual, moral or religious taboos. The first Obscene Publications Act (1857) inaugurated a series of government attempts to regulate and censor the production and dissemination of obscene works. When finally updated in 1959, legislation introduced the defence of 'public good'. An early test of the new law was the infamous *Lady Chatterley's Lover* trial (1961) which unsuccessfully prosecuted Penguin's publication of D. H. Lawrence's novel. *See* CENSORSHIP; EROTICA.

obscurity Obscurity in literature may be deliberate or involuntary. In either case an 'obscure' writer is one whose meaning is difficult to discern. Some 19th c. French poets like Mallarmé and Rimbaud were found obscure, but seem less so now. In the 20th c. Ezra Pound, T. S. Eliot and David Jones were charged with obscurity. Marks of obscurity are: an elliptical style (loose syntax; anacoluthon; asyndeton, *qq.v.*), recondite allusion and reference, archaic or ornate language, private and subjective imagery, and the use of words and phrases from foreign languages. A writer who wilfully disguises the fact that he has little or nothing to say is usually found out in the end. *See* HERMETICISM.

occasional rhyme *See* RHYME.

occasional verse Verse written for a particular occasion, perhaps to celebrate some incident or event. It may be light or serious. The elegy and the ode (*qq.v.*) have been used to produce some memorable occasional verse. The Poet Laureate (*q.v.*) is obliged to write a certain amount of it (e.g. for a coronation or a royal wedding). Notable examples are: Milton's *Lycidas* (1637) and his sonnet *On the Late Massacre in Piedmont*; Marvell's *Horatian Ode upon Cromwell's Return from Ireland* (1650); Dryden's *Alexander's Feast* (1697); Tennyson's *Charge of the Light Brigade* (1854); Hopkins's *The Wreck of the Deutschland* (c. 1875); Yeats's *Easter 1916*; and Auden's *September 1st 1939.*

octameter A line of eight feet; rare in Classical verse; rarer still in English verse. Swinburne's *March* provides instances; so, in the opinion of some, does Poe's *The Raven*. Tennyson attempted octameters in *Frater Ave atque Vale*:

> Row us out from Desenzano, to your Sirmione row!
> So they rowed, and there we landed – 'O venusta Sirmio!'
> There to me through all the groves of olive in the summer glow,
> There beneath the Roman ruin where the purple flowers grow,
> Came that 'Ave atque Vale' of the Poet's hopeless woe,
> Tenderest of Roman poets nineteen-hundred years ago,
> 'Frater Ave atque Vale' – as we wandered to and fro
> Gazing at the Lydian laughter of the Garda Lake below
> Sweet Catullus's all-but-island, olive-silvery Sirmio!

It can be seen (and heard) at once what a difficult meter it is to manage because of the length of line. The meter is trochaic. Incidentally, the poem also illustrates the use of monorhyme (*q.v.*).

octastich (Gk 'eight rows') A group or stanza of eight lines. Also *huitain*. A poem of eight lines. *See also* OCTAVE.

Octateuch (Gk 'containing eight books') Specifically, the first eight books of the Old Testament; namely, the Pentateuch (*q.v.*) together with Joshua, Judges and Ruth.

octave Also known as octet. A group of eight lines – either in stanza form, in which case it is *ottava rima* (*q.v.*), or as the first eight lines of a sonnet (*q.v.*). The octave in a sonnet usually rhymes abbaabba.

octavo A book in which the printer's sheets have been folded three times to produce eight leaves or sixteen pages. Abbrev. 8vo. *See also* DUODECIMO; FOLIO; QUARTO.

octonarius (L 'of eight each') In Latin verse a line of eight feet. Also a stanza of eight lines. *See also* OCTASTICH; OCTAVE; OTTAVA RIMA.

octosyllabic verse A tetrameter (*q.v.*) line containing eight syllables and usually consisting of iambic and/or trochaic feet. Often used in couplets (*q.v.*). In all probability the octosyllabic couplet derives from late medieval French poetry. It was well established in England by the 14th c. when it was used by Chaucer and Gower. Many British poets have since employed it, including Milton, Jonson, Dyer, Collins, Samuel (*Hudibras*) Butler, Wordsworth, Coleridge, Byron, Scott and William Morris. These lines are from Milton's *Il Penseroso*:

> But let my due feet never fail,
> To walk the studious cloister's pale,
> And love the high embowed roof,
> With antique pillars massy proof,
> And storied windows richly dight,
> Casting a dim religious light.

ode (Gk 'song') A lyric poem, usually of some length. The main features are an elaborate stanza-structure, a marked formality and stateliness in tone and style (which make it ceremonious), and lofty sentiments and thoughts. In short, an ode is rather a grand poem; a full-dress poem. However, this said, we can distinguish two basic kinds: the public and the private. The public is used for ceremonial occasions, like funerals, birthdays, state events; the private often celebrates rather intense, personal, and subjective occasions; it is inclined to be meditative, reflective. Tennyson's *Ode on the Death of the Duke of Wellington* is an example of the former; Keats's *Ode to a Nightingale*, an example of the latter.

The earliest odes of any note – or at any rate poems which could be put into the ode category – were written by Sappho (fl. *c.* 600 BC) and Alcaeus (fl. *c.* 611–580 BC). Fragments of Sappho's *Ode to Aphrodite* and Alcaeus's *Ode to Castor and Polydeuces* still survive.

Next, and more important, was Pindar (522–442 BC), a native of Thebes, whose odes were written for public occasions, especially in honour of victors in the Greek games. Modelled on the choric songs of Greek drama, they consisted of strophe, antistrophe and epode (*qq.v.*); a patterned stanza movement intended for choral song and dance.

Pindar's Latin counterpart was Horace (65–8 BC), but his odes were private and personal. They were stanzaically regular and based on limited metrical patterns, especially Alcaics and Sapphics (*qq.v.*). Between them Pindar and Horace were the begetters of the ode and both influenced the development of the form in Renaissance Europe. Meantime, the Provençal *canso* and the Italian *canzone* came near to the ode. Dante described the *canzone* as a composition 'in the tragic style, of equal stanzas without choral interludes, with reference to one subject'. This form, as used by Dante, Guinicelli and their contemporaries, survived and flourished into that period known as the High Renaissance, when Spenser's *Epithalamion* (1595) and *Prothalamion* (1596) showed the loftiness and majesty of the fully blown ode. *Epithalamion* consists of twenty-three regularly rhymed eighteen-line stanzas, followed by an *envoi* (*q.v.*). The stanzas are of ten-syllable lines interspersed with six-syllable lines and each concludes with an alexandrine (*q.v.*). Precedents for *Epithalamion* (Gk 'at the bridal chamber') can be found in the works of Sappho and Catullus. *Prothalamion* (Gk 'before the bridal chamber') is in the same stanzaic form as *Epithalamion* but without the *envoi*.

Late in the 16th c. and early in the 17th William Drummond of Hawthornden, Samuel Daniel and Michael Drayton all attempted odes, but Ben Jonson was the first to write one in the Pindaric tradition; namely, *Ode to*

Sir Lucius Cary and Sir H. Morison (1629), which contains the following famous lines:

> It is not growing like a tree
> In bulk, doth make man better be;
> Or standing long an Oak, three hundred year,
> To fall a log at last, dry, bald, and sear.
> A Lily of a day
> Is fairer far, in May
> Although it fall and die that night;
> It was the plant and flower of light.
> In small proportions we just beauties see;
> And in short measure, life may perfect be.

Later Andrew Marvell wrote his Horatian *Ode upon Cromwell's Return from Ireland* (1650), and Abraham Cowley published his so-called Pindaric Odes, dispensing with the strophic arrangement. His stanzas were free and varied; so are the lines and meters. This flexibility had much influence on later writers, including Dryden. His four main contributions to the form all come into the Pindaric and public phylum and are among the finest odes in our language. They are: *Threnodia Augustalis* (1685); *Ode to the Memory of Mrs Anne Killigrew* (1686); *Song for St Cecilia's Day* (1687); and *Alexander's Feast* (1697). One would have expected Milton to favour the ode form, but he never described any of his poems as such. However, his *On the Morning of Christ's Nativity* is all that one would expect of an ode, and Milton's conception of the grander type of lyric (*q.v.*) had much influence on poets in the 18th c. and during the Romantic period (*q.v.*).

Because of its architectonic possibilities (the elaborate rules, formality and decorum) one would expect the 18th c. poets to be attracted to the ode form, and indeed that period produced many distinguished examples.

Lady Winchilsea (1661–1720) wrote a Pindaric poem on *The Spleen*, and, early in his life, Pope composed an *Ode on Solitude* in the Horatian style. He also attempted the Pindaric manner in *Ode for Music on St Cecilia's Day*. Congreve, too, surprisingly attempted the ode and even wrote a discourse on the Pindaric ode. Isaac Watts, Akenside and Young also tried with varying degrees of success, but it was Collins and Gray, and, to a lesser extent, Cowper who wrote the great odes of the Augustan Age. Collins experimented with several metrical arrangements. The main works were: *Ode to Evening* and *Ode to Simplicity* (both in the Horatian mood), *Ode to Fear*, *Ode to Mercy*, *Ode on the Poetical Character*, *Ode to Liberty* (all in the Pindaric tradition and all published in 1747). Gray's odes also showed considerable variety and versatility. Four of them were relatively short and in simple stanza forms. These were the *Ode on Spring* (1742), *Ode on a Distant Prospect of Eton College* (1742), *Ode on Adversity* (1742) and *Ode on the Death of a Favourite Cat* (1747). To these should be added his two Pindarics: *The Bard* (1757) and *The Progress of Poesy* (1754).

Then followed: Coleridge's *France* (1798) and *Dejection* (1802); Wordsworth's magnificent *Ode on Intimations of Immortality* (1802–4) and his *Ode to Duty* (1805); Shelley's *Ode to the West Wind* (1819); and six superb odes by Keats (*c.* 1819): *On a Grecian Urn*; *To a Nightingale*; *To Autumn*; *On Melancholy*; *On Indolence*; and *To Psyche*.

After that grand constellation of poems most odes have looked a little pale. However, four notable instances must be mentioned. They are Tennyson's *Ode on the Death of the Duke of Wellington* (1854), in the Pindaric manner; and, much more recently, Allen Tate's splendid *Ode to the Confederate Dead*; and Auden's *In Memory of W. B. Yeats* and *In Praise of Limestone*, both in the Horatian manner.

Other well-known English poets to have essayed this kind of lyric are: Robert Herrick, Walter Savage Landor, Matthew Arnold, Coventry Patmore, Francis Thompson and Algernon Charles Swinburne.

Outside England the ode has flourished particularly in Italy, France and Germany. In Italy experiments in the Pindaric mode were made by Trissinio, Minturno and Alamanni during the Renaissance period; and in France the members of the Pléiade (*q.v.*) tried the form. The most successful of these poets was Ronsard, who, in 1550, published *The First Four Books of Odes*. Later in the 16th c., very probably influenced by Ronsard, the Italian poets Tasso and Chiabrera also published some notable odes. Since their day Manzoni, Leopardi, Carducci and D'Annunzio have all written fine odes. In France the main follower of Ronsard was Boileau (in the 17th c.). In the Romantic period Lamartine, de Musset and Victor Hugo all attempted this lyric form. So, more recently, did Verlaine and Valéry. In Germany the ode was established by Weckherlin early in the 17th c., with *Oden und Gesänge* (1618–19). In the following century Goethe, Klopstock and Schiller revived the use of Classical models. Hölderlin, too, wrote some notable odes. *See also* ANTODE; OCCASIONAL VERSE.

off-Broadway The term denotes drama produced in New York City away from the main theatre 'stem'. It is often experimental drama. There is also a subspecies known as off-off-Broadway, which is clearly even further removed. Much of this kind of drama is in the 'happening' (*q.v.*) category, and may also be skit and revue (*qq.v.*). However, much of it is not. An outstanding repertory company has been the Living Theater (*q.v.*) founded in 1947 by Julian Beck and Judith Malina in order to present new and experimental plays.

officialese A term coined by Sir Ernest Gowers in *Plain Words* (1948) to denote the pompous, abstract, euphemistic, polysyllabic, periphrastic and circumlocutory language often used by officials, bureaucrats, politicians, sociologists, educationists and others. It is a form of verbocrap (*q.v.*), and ranges from semi-literature letters like:

. . . We are in receipt of your esteemed order of the 29th inst. and beg to inform you that the articles in question have been discontinued. We shall cause you to be informed if any such articles are to be found in alternative sources.

to obfuscating 'Whitehallese' like:

The efflorescence of a host of specialists in commerce and industry and the ever widening inroad that the Government is forging into our business lives are carcinogens of effective communication; for the jargon of, on the one hand, such people as computer programmers, systems analysts, cyberneticians, psychologists and, on the other hand, the complex prose of Whitehall constitute an invidious growth which is challenging our ability to express ourselves in clear simple terms.

Other works by Sir Ernest Gowers on the subject are: *The ABC of Plain Words* (1951) and *The Complete Plain Words* (1954). *See* EUPHEMISM; JARGON; LOGORRHEA; PERIPHRASIS.

Old Comedy Greek and of the 5th c. BC, this kind of drama developed from fertility rites in honour of Dionysus. It was fantastic, bawdy and scurrilous, and at times obscene. It featured three stock characters: *bomlochos* (buffoon); *alazon* (impostor or braggart); and *eiron* (a self-derogating character). Invective and satire (*qq.v.*) were essential elements in it. Much of the verse was finely lyrical. The Chorus (*q.v.*) took an important part in the action and represented the dramatist's point of view. In what is known as New Comedy (*q.v.*) the Chorus disappeared. Unhappily only the plays of Aristophanes survive from this period. The best known are *Clouds*, *Knights* and *Frogs*. *See* COMEDY; MIDDLE COMEDY; PARABASIS.

Old French (OF) and Provençal forms From about AD 850 to about 1300 most French and Provençal literature was in verse and belonged to oral tradition (*q.v.*). From the 12th c. many of the main forms were becoming established. Metrically elaborate, a great many of them were worked out by the troubadour (*q.v.*) poets. In succeeding centuries most of them were adopted in England and were particularly used by the Victorian poets. The principal forms are: *ballade*, *chant royal*, *conte*, *dit*, *flamenca*, *lai*, *rondeau*, *rondel*, *sestina*, *villanelle* and *virelai* (*qq.v.*). *See also* CHANSON DE GESTES; FIXED FORM; OCTOSYLLABIC VERSE; ROMANCE.

Old Vic Theatre Opened in 1818, it was formerly known as the Coburg and was for many years associated with melodrama (*q.v.*). It was renamed the Royal Victoria and soon came to be known as the 'Old Vic'. A troubled financial period ensued and it was closed in 1880. Soon after, it was bought by Emma Cons, a crusader of the temperance movement, who turned it into an amusement hall. In 1898 Emma Cons was joined by Lilian Baylis (her niece), who became manager in 1912 and made it famous as a theatre for the production of Shakespeare. Between the wars it flourished. War damage put it out of action, but it was restored and from 1947 to 1952 was the headquarters of the Old Vic School under the director Michel Saint-Denis. Between 1953 and 1958 the complete First Folio of Shakespeare's work was presented, and in 1963 it became the home of the National Theatre Company (*q.v.*), which remained there until 1976. Thereafter it had a chequered career and was empty from 1981 to 1983 when it was bought by the Canadian millionaire Ed Mirvish, who had it completely renovated. After it reopened it began another successful career with a range of classics, musicals and new plays. In 1998 the building was acquired by the Old Vic Theatre Trust and in 2003 Kevin Spacey was appointed artistic director. Alongside an eclectic mix of new works and classics, the theatre launched Old Vic New Voices, to nurture young actors, writers and directors.

Omar Khayyám quatrain   *See* QUATRAIN; RUBAI.

omnibus edition   Such an edition of an author's works includes in one volume everything that he has written. The works of Oscar Wilde and Robert Service, among others, have been concentrated in such a form.

one-act play   Self-evidently a dramatic work consisting of only one act, a one-act play is the dramatic equivalent of a short story and tends to concentrate on a single episode or situation and as a general rule has only two or three characters. In theme, mood and subject the range is considerable – from farce to tragedy. The one-act play is usually short, with a playing time of fifteen to forty minutes.

The one-act play was very rare before late in the 19th c., though there are many earlier examples of shortish plays which could qualify as one-act plays, and the after-piece popular in the 18th c. was a kind of one-act play. However, towards the end of the 19th c. an increasing number of small experimental theatres greatly encouraged the development of the one-act drama as a form in its own right and it was often used as a curtain raiser (*q.v.*). Since that period it has flourished and is as popular as ever, though seldom used as a curtain raiser. A more common practice is to present two or three one-act plays by way of a double or triple bill. Two examples of this are Harold Pinter's *Landscape* and *Silence* (1970) and John Mortimer's *Come As You Are* (1971).

Many famous dramatists have attempted the form, including Chekhov, Strindberg, Shaw, Hauptmann, Synge, J. M. Barrie, Eugene O'Neill, Samuel Beckett and Harold Pinter.

Onegin stanza   The stanza invented by Alexander Pushkin for his verse-novel (*q.v.*) *Eugene Onegin* (1831). Modelled on the sonnet (*q.v.*) but significantly deviating from any of the standard forms, it consists of fourteen iambic tetrameters (*q.v.*) rhyming ababccddeffegg. The a, c and e rhymes are disyllabic and provide the poet with opportunities for bathos and irony in the manner of Byron's *Don Juan*. The Onegin stanza has been described as constituting a 'little chapter', in which the first quatrain introduces the main idea, the second and third develop it and the couplet epigrammatically sums it up.

It has been imitated in several languages, but English, with its poverty of rhyme, has mostly proved resistant to its tightness. Notable exceptions are

Sir Charles Johnston's dazzling translation of *Eugene Onegin* (1977) and Vikram Seth's Californian verse-novel, *The Golden Gate* (1986). The opening stanza of the latter provides a good example:

> To make a start more swift than weighty,
> Hail Muse. Dear Reader, once upon
> A time, say, circa 1980,
> There lived a man. His name was John.
> Successful in his field though only
> Twenty-six, respected, lonely,
> One evening as he walked across
> Golden Gate Park, the ill-judged toss
> Of a red frisbee almost brained him.
> He thought, 'If I died, who'd be sad?
> Who'd weep? Who'd gloat? Who would be glad?
> Would anybody?' As it pained him,
> He turned from this dispiriting theme
> To ruminations less extreme.

Seth's poem is an extraordinary tour de force. It has the plot of an ordinary modern novel, which it tells in 590 of these stanzas. A wide range of tone and mood is achieved: elegiac, comic, satirical and parodic. Even the acknowledgements and the biographical note about the author are in the Onegin form.

onomasticon A Greek term for a book of names or a vocabulary. Formerly used sometimes for lexicon and dictionary (*qq.v.*).

onomastics The study of names and naming practice, especially of the patterns and principles adopted by writers in the selection of proper names; hence 'onomastic', 'of names'.

onomatopoeia (Gk 'name-making') The formation and use of words to imitate sounds. For example, *dong, crackle, moo, pop, whizz, whoosh, zoom*. It is a figure of speech in which the sound reflects the sense. It is very common in verse and fairly common in prose and is found in many literatures at all times. As a rule it is deliberately used to achieve a special effect, as in these lines from T. S. Eliot's *Dry Salvages*:

> When the train starts, and the passengers are settled
> To fruit, periodicals and business letters
> (And those who saw them off have left the platform)
> Their faces relax from grief into relief,
> To the sleepy rhythm of a hundred hours.

The whole passage is subtly onomatopoeic, the rhythm of the second line is a beautifully skilful evocation of the clickety-click of wheels on rails. *See also* ALLITERATION; ASSONANCE; CACOPHONY; CONSONANCE; EUPHONY; LOGOPOEIA; MELOPOEIA; SYNAESTHESIA; TONE COLOUR.

ontology   A philosophical term which denotes the study of being. As a literary term it has a special meaning, thanks to John Crowe Ransom. According to him the texture (*q.v.*) and structure (*q.v.*) of a poem, which, combined, provide the meaning, combine also to give it 'ontology' – that quality or property peculiar to itself which distinguishes it from anything that is *not* poetry.

open and closed texts   A term deriving from the Italian semiotician and philosopher Umberto Eco (b. 1932). According to Eco, a 'closed' text is one which encourages a particular interpretation, whereas an 'open' text invites a diversity of readings. Such a distinction is also implied in Roland Barthes's essay *From Work to Text* (1971), where he makes a distinction between 'work', which is more or less passively consumed, and 'text', which renders the process of reading active, productive and constitutive. The text requires of the reader a 'practical collaboration'.

open couplet   A couplet (*q.v.*) in which the sense is not completed in the second line, but is carried forward into the third or fourth line; or perhaps for several, though this is rare. This example comes from Pope's *Epistle to Augustus*:

> Our rural Ancestors, with little blest,
> Patient of labour when the end was rest,
> Indulg'd the day that hous'd their annual grain,
> With feasts, and off'rings, and a thankful strain.

See CLOSED COUPLET; END-STOPPED LINE; ENJAMBEMENT; HEROIC COUPLET.

open stage   The term was first used by Richard Southern, the theatre historian, in 1953 to describe any form of staging in which the performers are not separated from the audience by a proscenium arch. Open stage techniques were developed in the first part of the 20th c., particularly by William Poel (1852–1934), Max Reinhardt (1873–1943), Vsevolod Meyerhold (1874–1942), Jacques Copeau (1879–1949) and Nikolai Okhlopkov (1900–67). The main forms are: (a) 'thrust stage', with an audience on three sides; (b) 'end stage', with an audience facing it from one end; (c) 'transverse stage', with an audience on two opposite sides. There is also theatre-in-the-round (*q.v.*), where the audience sits all round the acting area.

opera   (L *opera*, 'exertion, service', collective feminine from plural of neuter noun *opus*, 'work') Originally opera was chanted tragedy, and what is generally agreed to be the first, Rinuccini's *Dafne* (1594), was an attempt to revive Classical Greek tragedy – a form which has had a profound influence on opera. The masque (*q.v.*) influenced the development of opera. Surprisingly few writers (and very few poets) have been attracted to opera *as* writers (except, of course, for those whose expertise and business it is to compose libretti). On the other hand, librettists and composers have drawn freely upon plays and other works for their operas. An interesting example of a collaboration between dramatist and composer is that between Bertolt Brecht and Kurt

Weill, which produced *The Threepenny Opera* (1928), *The Rise and Fall of the City of Mahagonny* (1927–9) and *The Seven Deadly Sins* (1933). More recently Auden and Kallman collaborated with Stravinsky to create *The Rake's Progress* (1951). Some notable modern examples of adaptation are Benjamin Britten's operas from Henry James's *The Turn of the Screw* (1953), Herman Melville's *Billy Budd* (1951) and George Crabbe's story of Peter Grimes in his poem *The Borough* (1945). *See also* BALLAD OPERA; LIBRETTO; MELODRAMA; OPERETTA.

opéra-comique A form of drama set to music. Music alternates with spoken dialogue and thus it is akin to ballad opera (*q.v.*). It originated in the *comédies à ariettes* which were comedies (or farces) punctuated with lyrical passages sung to music. They became popular early in the 18th c. and were performed at the Théâtre de la Foire in Paris. In *c.* 1780 the company at the theatre became known as the Opéra-Comique and in 1783 moved to the Salle Favart.

opere citato (L 'in the work cited') Often abbreviated to *op. cit.*, it refers to a book to which reference has already been made. *See* IBIDEM; IDEM; LOCO CITATO.

operetta (It 'little opera') A light drama (for all practical purposes synonymous with F *opéra bouffe*, It *opera buffa*). It consists of musical interludes and spoken dialogue, often satirical. Famous examples are Gay's *Beggar's Opera* (1728), Sheridan's *The Duenna* (1775) and the numerous works of Gilbert and Sullivan. *See also* BALLAD OPERA; OPERA.

oral formulaic theory The systematic study of oral composition, pioneered by Milman Parry in the 1930s, and continued by Albert B. Lord and David E. Bynum. This theory analyses the composition and transmission of oral texts in terms of the concepts of 'formula', 'theme' and narrative pattern. Parry defined a formula as a group of words employed in the same meter to express a given idea. Lord expounded the notions of theme (such as the arming of the hero) and story pattern (such as journey or wedding song) in his renowned work *The Singer of Tales* (1960). Parry was interested in issues such as the poet's ability to improvise, the role of an audience, and the notion of authorship. He saw the epics attributed to Homer, for example, as the result of a long oral tradition of story-telling – which had built up a narrative repertoire – passed down through generations of bards or singers, with each bard modifying his treatment of a given story and theme. Hence oral compositions are characterized by intrinsic textual variability and indefinite authorship. The pioneering insights of these scholars were both confirmed and informed by their study of living oral traditions in Yugoslavia. Oral formulaic theory was anticipated by philologists such as F. Wolf (1759–1824), who furnished archaeological evidence that the Homeric epics must have been composed orally. *See also* ORAL TRADITION.

oral tradition Poetry and stories belonging to such a tradition are composed orally, or made up by the poet or story-teller during a performance according to preconceived formulae and themes. A 'formula' is a group of words used regularly to express a given idea. A 'theme' is a repeated passage recounting an incident or description. Oral composition usually relies on an established framework of story-telling whereby the stories are well known in their basic outlines and passed down through generations of singers or bards. As a rule, they are the products of illiterate or semi-literate societies but have also been important components of English and European literary traditions, as in *Beowulf* and Old English poetry.

The main types of oral narratives are epic and ballad (*qq.v.*). They are often sung or chanted, sometimes to musical accompaniment. Oral compositions are characterized by variability, since the text changes with each performance, and sparse use of *enjambement*, since a thought is usually contained in a given line or built up through additional complete lines. The most renowned examples of oral poetry include the *Iliad* and the *Odyssey*, conventionally attributed to Homer. Characteristics of oral composition also include epithets (such as 'swift-footed Achilles' or 'grey-eyed Athene'), and formalized descriptions of religious rites or the ritual arming of a hero. Oral poetry played an important role in the social life of a people or community, expressing its collective world view, its system of religion, its moral values, its history and its dreams for the future. Many literate cultures have looked to oral traditions in order to consolidate their identity as a distinct people. Numerous postcolonial authors have drawn on oral traditions to develop a mode of writing that is not wholly dependent on the culture of the colonizer. *See also* BALLAD; BYLINA; EPIC; FOLKSONG; NARODNE PESME; ORAL-FORMULAIC THEORY; POSTCOLONIALISM.

oratio obliqua   *See* INDIRECT SPEECH.

oratio recta   *See* INDIRECT SPEECH.

organic form   That form which derives from the nature and materials of a writer's subject and theme, as opposed to mechanic form, which derives from rules and conventions imposed on the nature and materials. Shakespeare and his fellow dramatists might be claimed to favour organic form, while the French Classical dramatists (like Racine) had a predilection for mechanic form (indeed, in France you were *expected* to follow the rules). However, if a poet chooses to express himself by means of a fixed form (e.g. a *villanelle*, *q.v.*) or by means of an established stanzaic or metrical scheme (e.g. *quatrain*, *terza rima*, *qq.v.*) then the result may be a coalescence of organic and mechanic form.

The idea of organic form is to be found in Plato's *Phaedrus* where Socrates draws an analogy between making a speech and the growth of a living creature. It was the German Romantics and Coleridge who worked out the analogy in considerable detail. The implications of organic form are that a work 'grows' from a seminal concept, like a living organism. So declared Henry James, Croce and many others. *See* CONVENTION; DONNÉE; INSPIRATION; LIGNE DONNÉE.

organic metaphor   Also known as a functional or structural metaphor; in this figure of speech the vehicle (*see* TENOR AND VEHICLE) is symbolic and carries an implicit tenor. If we examine the following passage from Robinson Jeffers's poem *Hurt Hawks* we may be able to disentangle sense from this thicket of jargon. He has described the wounded hawk and his feelings about it. He comes to the point where he decides that the creature must be put out of its misery:

> I gave him the lead gift in the twilight.
> What fell was relaxed,
> Owl-downy, soft feminine feathers; but what
> Soared: the fierce rush: the night-herons by the flooded river
> Cried for fear at its rising
> Before it was quite unsheathed from reality.

The periphrasis and euphemism (*qq.v.*) of 'lead gift' clearly denote a bullet. What follows suggests that the released 'spirit' of the hawk soars heavenwards; the reversal of stooping to its prey. 'Unsheathed from reality' suggests parting from this life; the sheath being the heap of 'feminine feathers'. Thus the vehicle is the event of death; the tenor, the image (very nearly abstract in this case), the soaring of the hawk's 'soul'. *See also* METAPHOR; TELESCOPED METAPHOR.

orientalism   A term pertaining to the Orient as discovered, recorded, described, defined, imagined, produced and, in a sense, 'invented' by Europe and the West. As far as literature is concerned it refers to the discourse by the West about the East, which comprises a vast corpus of texts – literary, sociological, scientific, historical, linguistic/philological, political, anthropological and topographical – which has been accumulating since the Renaissance and particularly since the 18th c. and to which there is no counterpart in the East about the West. In all, this discourse aggregates to a 'textual universe', as Edward Said puts it in his book *Orientalism* (1978). It also refers to the attitudes of the West towards the East; to the Occident (the outsiders) looking in/on/at the Orient – in fact 'watching' the East and endeavouring to explain and interpret it.

As for what the East consists of, the profusion, in the West, of topographical/geographical terms suggests a certain difficulty in coping with it, in 'containing' it, so to speak, in giving it shape, boundaries, limits. So vast and multitudinous an area (and, with it, equally broad concepts) has led to vague subdivisions. In Britain we have long been accustomed to such loose categories as the Near East, the Middle East and the Far East (with other subdivisions such as the Levant and Asia Minor). This vagueness is compounded by the vexed and disputed matter of 'where East meets West' (and vice versa). No one has yet proposed a junction point of general satisfaction, though a number have been suggested.

Orientalism as a discourse is believed to have begun its formal existence with the decision of the Church Council of Vienne in 1312 to found a series of chairs in Arabic, Greek, Hebrew and Syriac at Oxford, Paris, Bologna, Avignon and Salamanca. In the Middle Ages (or the late Middle Ages) the East became of increasing interest to the West. It was remote, inaccessible, inscrutable and exotic. Curiosity and speculation were stimulated by travellers' tales and improbably tall stories. Marco Polo (c. 1254–c. 1324) is a prime example of an author who began to introduce the East to the West with his immensely popular book of travels which was translated into many European languages and first 'Englished' by John Frampton in 1579. And there was Sir John Mandeville, the supposed author of a famous travel book also found in many European languages after its first appearance in Anglo-Norman French in 1356–7. Ostensibly a guide for pilgrims to the Holy Land, it peregrinates (with notable fabulations) through India, Egypt, Persia, Turkey and Tartary.

By early in the 17th c. orientalism as a discourse was well under way, with its roots deeply entrenched in the rise of Islam, the Crusades and the growth of the Ottoman Empire. Travellers' accounts of the East (Near, Middle, and Far) began to proliferate during the 18th c. and these influenced literature in Europe and England. A version of the *Arabian Nights' Entertainments*, or *The Thousand and One Nights*, by Antoine Galland appeared in 1704 and 1717 and aroused much interest in Europe. It also contributed to the vogue of the oriental tale (*q.v.*) in the 18th c. The Grand Tour (*q.v.*) became fashionable and the more adventurous travellers went far beyond the generally prescribed itineraries of the Tour. During the latter part of the century Sir William Jones, one of the first great British orientalists, translated many works from Arabic and Persian and these were to influence the oriental themes of Romantic poets such as Byron, Southey and Thomas Moore. Richard Knolles's *The Generall Historie of the Turkes* (1603) was much admired during the 18th c., not least by Johnson, and, later, by Byron.

The rise and expansion of the British Empire vastly increased the archives of oriental studies. So, to a lesser extent, did French colonial enterprises in the Near East and Egypt (during the Napoleonic period); and later, in Indo-China. The 19th c. was the outstanding period of oriental studies. Numerous learned and cultural societies were established in Europe to advance them. The East, as Disraeli suggested in his novel *Tancred* (1847), could be regarded as a 'career'. Countless colonial officials, statesmen, explorers, soldiers, diplomats, doctors, missionaries, travellers, writers, navigators and merchant adventurers contributed memoirs, autobiographies, commentaries, government reports (and what not?) to the corpus of oriental studies. So did scholars, not a few of whom never went anywhere near any part of the East. Encyclopaedic records of oriental studies were published. One of the first important ones was the *Bibliothèque orientale* (1697), a vast compendium of virtually all that was then known about the East, by Barthélemy d'Herbelot (1625–95). Another notable example was Jules Mohl's *Vingt-sept ans d'histoire des études orientales*, a two-volume logbook of everything of note that took place in orientalism between 1840 and 1867. Other outstanding French orientalists were Abraham-Hyacinthe Anquetil-Duperron (1731–

1805), Silvestre de Sacy (1758–1838) and Louis Massignon, who made invaluable contributions in the interwar period in the 20th c. Ernest Renan (1823–92) also achieved fame but was frequently at fault in his judgement and assumptions. German orientalism was largely in the hands of scholars such as Steinthal, Müller, Becker, Goldziher, Brockelmann and Nöldeke. Numerous British adventurers, explorers and scholars have added to the store of oriental studies. For example, Edward Lane, the Arabist, who published his classic work *An Account of the Manners and Customs of the Modern Egyptians* in 1836, Alexander Kinglake, Sir Richard Burton, C. M. Doughty, W. G. Palgrave, T. E. Lawrence, D. G. Hogarth, Gertrude Bell, Ronald Storrs, Wilfrid Scawen Blunt, St John Philby, H. A. R. Gibb, Edward Henry Palmer and Wilfred Thesiger. We should also mention Lafcadio Hearn, half-Irish, half-Greek, who wrote some memorable books about Japan late in the 19th c. French poets and novelists were also particularly attracted to and influenced by the Orient, especially Chateaubriand, Lamartine, Victor Hugo, Gérard de Nerval, Flaubert and Pierre Loti. Chateaubriand, Hugo and Loti were responsible, among others, for fabricating and projecting a 'romantic' view of it, and it is true that much that belongs to the field of orientalism has remarkably little to do with the actualities and realities of life in the Orient – wherever it be. It is the product of 'myth', legend, assumption and theory. It is as if the magnetism of the East, the spell it cast, inspired Europeans to create or re-create an East which would accord with what the West wanted it to be: mysterious, wonderful, bizarre and perhaps even immoral. Chateaubriand 'invented' an Orient which suited him and what Stendhal called his 'stinking egoism'. Hugo's collection of lyrics, *Les Orientales* (1829), evokes a personal view of an Orient which is exotic, languorous and barbaric. Loti used Constantinople as a picturesque setting for sentimental romance novels.

In the 20th c. miscellaneous British novelists – Kipling, E. M. Forster, Anthony Burgess, Paul Scott and J. G. Farrell, for example – attempted to depict the British and Asians under the imperial regime.

The relationship of the United States with the Orient only really began with the Second World War and thus in terms of political and military action. Since that war the military/political factor has been pre-eminent and American orientalism is largely concerned with policies, with data, statistics, trends and commerce. Culture and literature seldom come into it.

The bibliography of European orientalism and oriental studies multiplies yearly. Apart from Edward Said's highly original critical analysis, there have been many scholarly works in recent years. Of special note are Raymond Schwab's *La Renaissance orientale* (1950), Johann W. Fück's *Die arabischen Studien in Europa bis in den Anfang des 20. Jahrhunderts* (1955) and Dorothy Metlitzki's *The Matter of Araby in England* (1977). Plus traditional-type travel books (*q.v.*) by such authors as Freya Stark, Wilfred Thesiger, Colin Thubron, Paul Theroux, William Dalrymple and V. S. Naipaul, whose excursion into Islam, *Among the Believers* (1981), has been criticized as anecdotal and wilfully critical.

Indeed, much of the discourse of orientalism has been partial and prejudiced and often condescending (especially that originating from government servants, colonial officers, political agents/rulers *et al.*). Much, too, reveals a certain arrogance and sense of superiority – a 'we know best' attitude – on the part of the West towards the East. Much of it is marred by racism, naivety, presumption and plain ignorance, and there are often facile generalizations by people who should know better (e.g. Ernest Renan, T. E. Lawrence), as in vague statements about 'the Arab mind', 'the Asian sensibility', 'the Semitic temperament'. Moreover, not a little of it has been repetitive and reductive in so far as writers/scholars have merely recycled the ideas and views of predecessors to create a body of *idées reçues* of the kind that Flaubert called 'bromides': platitudes and trite generalizations which purport to embody a truth.

oriental tale/novel A form of fiction which had a considerable vogue in the 18th c. and early in the 19th c. They tended to be rather exotic and extravagant tales of adventure with 'Eastern' settings (more particularly those of the Near East). The heroes were luminously good and virtuous; the villains suitably double-dyed and wicked. Supernatural and/or magical elements were a prominent feature in this literature of diversion and entertainment.

The vogue is partly explained by the fact that the *Arabian Nights* appeared in an English translation in 1705–8 and these tales became extremely popular. Sir William Jones (1746–94), an outstanding orientalist, also made available translations of Indian and Arabic literature of which most people knew nothing. There was another reason: by c. 1750 there was a sizeable quantity of travel books (*q.v.*) giving accounts of journeys to the Levant and Near East and through the Ottoman Empire, which by that stage was huge. These travels aroused considerable interest in the 'East' and everything to do with it. The more intrepid travellers (e.g. Lady Mary Wortley Montague) who undertook the Grand Tour (*q.v.*) roved as far as Constantinople (as Istanbul was then known) and beyond.

The fiction produced displays variety, and ranges from Johnson's sober didactic romance *The History of Rasselas, Prince of Abyssinia* (1759) to Beckford's improbable fantasia *Vathek* (1786). Other notable examples are: John Hawkesworth's *Almoran and Hamlet* (1761); James Ridley's *Tales of the Genii* (1764); Frances Sheridan's *The History of Nourjahad* (1767); Alexander Dow's *Tales . . . of Inatulla of Delhi* (1768); and James Morier's *The Adventures of Hajji Baba of Ispahan* (1824).

There were also oriental narrative tales in verse, such as Southey's *The Curse of Kehama* (1810), Byron's *The Giaour* (1813) and *The Corsair* (1814), and Thomas Moore's enormously popular *Lalla Rookh* (1817), which had run to twenty editions by 1840. Moore used the frame story (*q.v.*) method with a series of tales in verse which were connected by a narrative in prose.

originality A work may be said to possess this quality if, as a result of the author's invention (*q.v.*), he innovates a new form or mode; or, perhaps, uses hitherto undiscovered or unexploited themes and subjects. *See* CONVENTION; FANCY AND IMAGINATION; INSPIRATION; NOVELTY; PLAGIARISM.

orismology (Gk 'definition of knowledge') The explanation of technical terms, which this dictionary is in aid of. *See* LEXICOGRAPHY.

ornamentalism A term which, in Russian literary history, denotes an intricate, mannered and ostentatious prose style. It is usually related to prose of the early part of the 20th c. and particularly to a school of writers led by Andrei Bely (1880–1934) and Alexei Remizov.

orta oyunu (T 'middle play') A kind of Turkish folk drama (*q.v.*) not dissimilar to *commedia dell'arte* (*q.v.*). The characters are Turkish regional 'types' and the actors imitate their dialects while depicting their occupations. The stage is usually an open space with an audience all round. Occasionally a platform is used. Scenery is limited and the actors normally sit with the audience. Each actor has his own piece of music and introduces himself with a song or a dance. There are two main characters – Pişekâr and Kavuklu. The former wears a brightly coloured costume and carries a club which he uses to hit the other actors. Pişekâr is on stage nearly all the time. The latter is the comic character and the dialogues between them form the basis of the play. There is also a woman (Zenne) played by a man, and perhaps one or two other subsidiary characters. Each *orta oyunu* normally consists of two parts. In the first Pişekâr and Kavuklu do their comic turn (reminiscent of Punch and Judy), and in the second the Turkish character types are 'taken off'. *See* KARAGÖZ.

orthotone A word which is normally unstressed, but which, because it occupies a certain position in a metrical line, may receive stress. Likely words are: and, but, the, a, an, to. Orthotonic words are fairly common in ballad (*q.v.*).

Oscan fable *See* FABULA.

Osiris Players Britain's first all-women professional theatre group. It was founded in 1927 by Nancy Hewins (1902–78), long before radical feminism began. As a touring company it was a forerunner of such companies as Cheek by Jowl and Théâtre de Complicité (*q.v.*). The company never comprised more than seven women (all that could be afforded). They toured Britain until the early 1960s, performing everywhere and anywhere. Nancy Hewins herself put on 1534 performances of 33 plays (16 by Shakespeare) and played 128 different parts. For transportation the company used two Rolls Royces which drew two caravans. All props, costumes, lighting equipment, etc., travelled with them.

Ossianism Ossian is the name normally given to Oisin, a legendary Gaelic warrior and poet, who is supposed to have lived in the 3rd c. In 1760 James Macpherson (1736–96) published *Fragments of Ancient Poetry Collected in the Highlands of Scotland, and Translated from the Gaelic or Erse Language.* In 1762 he produced *Fingal*, and in 1763 *Temora*. Both purported to be translations of epic poems in Gaelic by a poet named Ossian. In fact they were a sort of fabulation of Gaelic ballads mixed with Macpherson's own work. Notwithstanding this, his evocation of a remote past, a Gaelic twilight of myth and legend, had a considerable influence on writers in Europe and made some contribution to romanticism (*q.v.*). Goethe was particularly interested in the Ossianic poems; so were Herder and Schiller. They were widely translated, and the long-term effects of the so-called Ossianic movement are discernible late in the 19th c. *See* LITERARY FORGERIES.

ostranenie *See* DEFAMILIARIZATION.

ottava rima (It 'eighth rhyme') An eight-line iambic stanza rhyming abab-abcc. It is almost certainly of Italian or Sicilian origin, and it may have developed from the *canzone* (*q.v.*) or the *strambotto*. A number of medieval Italian poets employed it, including Boccaccio, who, by using it in *Teseida* (*c.* 1340) and *Filostrato* (*c.* 1340), helped to establish it as the main form for Italian narrative verse (*q.v.*). Other poets who developed it were Boiardo, Pulci and Poliziano in the 15th c. Ariosto used it for *Orlando Furioso* (1516) and Tasso for *Gerusalemme Liberata* (1575). Spanish and Portuguese poets followed their example, particularly Ercilla in *La Araucana* (1569, 1578, 1589) and Camoëns in *Os Lusiadas* (1570). The form was introduced into English verse by Sir Thomas Wyatt early in the 16th c. Later Spenser and Drayton used it. It was not favoured much thereafter until Shelley and Keats experimented. It proved the ideal vehicle for Byron's narrative poems. He used it for *Beppo* (1818) and *The Vision of Judgment* (1822), and, most notably, in *Don Juan* (1819–24). From time to time since, other poets have employed the form. Yeats's *Sailing to Byzantium* is an outstanding example. He also wrote *ottava rima* for *Among School Children*, from which the following stanza (the last) comes:

> Labour is blossoming or dancing where
> The body is not bruised to pleasure soul,
> Nor beauty born out of its own despair,
> Nor blear-eyed wisdom out of midnight oil.
> O chestnut tree, great-rooted blossomer,
> Are you the leaf, the blossom or the bole?
> O body swayed to music, O brightening glance,
> How can we know the dancer from the dance?

See SICILIAN OCTAVE; SPENSERIAN STANZA.

Oulipo Abbreviation for the Ouvroir de Littérature Potentielle (Workshop for Potential Literature) founded 1960 by Raymond Queneau and others; this writers' group was interested initially in incorporating mathematical structures in literature; latterly, it has extended itself to all self-imposed restrictive systems. Oulipian writers specialize in playful language games to generate their works – novels which lack a certain letter of the alphabet (the lipogram, *q.v.*); well-known poems whose substantives are replaced by numerically determined but semantically random selections from the dictionary. Its spin-offs include Oulipopo (Ouvroir de Policière Potentielle, generating detective fiction); Oulipeinpo (painting); Ou-x-po (Ouvroir de x Potentielle, 'Workshop for Potential x'). Its best-known adherent is Georges Perec (*La Disparition*, 1969; *Life, a User's Manual*, 1978). *See* LIPOGRAM.

outrides *See* SPRUNG RHYTHM.

outsider A term and concept which had some vogue in the late 1950s as a result of a much publicized and much talked-of book called *The Outsider* (1956) by Colin Wilson. An 'outsider' may be seen as a person (especially a creative artist) who is, in some respects, above and 'outside' the society in which he or she lives and perhaps even superior to it. There have always been the unconventional, the eccentric and the egregious; the outsider is all these; perhaps even a kind of 'superman'. Those endowed with what is loosely known as genius (*q.v.*) might be regarded as outsiders. The German Romantics seem to have had some concept of such a being with their image of the *Kraftgenie* (*q.v.*). Anybody can make their own selection of outsiders. Among Wilson's are Nietzsche, Kierkegaard, Kafka, T. E. Lawrence and Ernest Hemingway. Another list might include James Joyce, Jean Genet, Samuel Beckett, Wilfred Thesiger, Jack Kerouac and Hunter S. Thompson. In a different way there are outsiders as 'characters' in literature. For example, the hero of Camus's novel *L'Étranger* (1942). A further category might be the *lishni chelovek* or 'superfluous man' (*q.v.*) of 19th c. Russian novelists. In short it is one of those concepts and terms which may be made to serve a variety of theses.

overdetermination The Marxist thinker Louis Althusser (1918–90) uses the concept of overdetermination (taken over from Freud) to express the specificity of the Marxist notion of contradiction and in particular its divergence from Hegel's dialectic. Whereas Hegel's formulation of contradiction as the causal site of historical change is 'simple', embodying a process of cumulative internalization of previous forms of consciousness and history, Marx's notion of contradiction is 'overdetermined': it is determined not uniformly but by a variety of levels and instances of the social formation it animates.

Oxford movement Also known as the Tractarian movement, it originated in July 1833 as a result of a sermon by Keble on the subject of national apostasy; a sermon against the Latitudinarian and Erastian attitudes of the time. Men who shared Keble's views supported him, and in 1833 there appeared the first of the famous *Tracts for the Times*. The most notable figures in the movement were Newman, Froude and Pusey. The main object was to revive the position and role of the Church of England and to re-emphasize its sacramental and divine mission. Ironically, in the course of this reforming effort, doctrines akin to those of Roman Catholicism were adopted.

The movement caused a very considerable disturbance and involved several leading literary figures – especially Charles Kingsley and Matthew Arnold.

Kingsley attacked Newman and the latter replied in *Apologia pro Vita Sua* (1864), a major work in English literature. *See* TRACT.

oxymoron (Gk 'pointedly foolish') A figure of speech which combines incongruous and apparently contradictory words and meanings for a special effect; as in Milton's 'darkness visible' or Lamb's celebrated remark: 'I like a smuggler. He is the only honest thief.'

It is a common device, closely related to antithesis and paradox (*qq.v.*), especially in poetry, and is of considerable antiquity. It was particularly popular in the late 16th c. and during the 17th. A famous example occurs in *Romeo and Juliet*, when Romeo jests about love:

> Here's much to do with hate, but more with love.
> Why then, O brawling love! O loving hate!
> O anything! of nothing first create!
> O heavy lightness! serious vanity!
> Mis-shapen chaos of well-seeming forms!

Probably the most famous instance of sustained oxymoron is Sir Thomas Wyatt's version of Petrarch's 134th sonnet, which begins:

> I find no peace, and all my war is done;
> I fear and hope, I burn and freeze like ice;
> I flee above the wind, yet can I not arise;
> And nought I have and all the world I season.

Other English poets who have used the figure extensively are Keats and Crashaw. The Italian Marino and the Spaniard Góngora also had a predilection for it. *See* PARADOX.

oxytone (Gk 'sharp strain') A word or line of verse with the accent (*q.v.*) on the last syllable. Every iambic or anapaestic line bears the accent or stress on the last syllable. *See* ANAPAEST; FOOT; IAMB.

P

pace-egging play A mumming play (*q.v.*); usually the play of St George (or Sir George) which used to be performed (and occasionally still is) in the north of England, especially Lancashire. The Mummers called themselves 'pace-eggers' after the Eastertide custom of staining hard-boiled eggs and rolling them against one another until they broke, after which they were eaten. Easter Monday is the traditional day for this. *Pace* is northern dialect for *Pasch* from Heb. *pesakh* 'Passover'. *See also* PLOUGH MONDAY PLAY; REVESBY PLAY.

paean (Gk 'striking' from *paiein*, 'to strike') A song or hymn of joy, exultation or praise. In ancient Greece it was an invocation (*q.v.*) or thanksgiving addressed to Apollo the Striker, 'one who strikes blows in order to heal mankind'.

paeon In Classical prosody a foot of one stressed and three unstressed syllables. It is known as the first, second, third or fourth paeon depending on the position of the stressed syllable: (a) / ∪ ∪ ∪; (b) ∪ / ∪ ∪; (c) ∪ ∪ / ∪; (d) ∪ ∪ ∪ /. Paeonic verse is found in Greek poetry, and especially in comedy. Rare in English verse. Gerard Manley Hopkins is one of the few poets to use it successfully and he experimented with it a good deal. This example is taken from *The Windhover: To Christ Our Lord*:

> Ĭ caúght | thĭs mór|nĭng mór|nĭng's mí|nĭŏn, kíng-
> dŏm ŏf dáylĭght's | daúphĭn, | dápplĕ | dáwn-dráwn |
> Fálcŏn, ĭn hĭs | rídĭng
> Ŏf thĕ róllĭng | lévĕl | úndĕr|néath hĭm | stéadў | áir, ănd |
> strídĭng
> Hígh thĕre, hŏw hĕ | rúng ŭpŏn thĕ | reín ŏf ă wímp|lĭng wíng
> Ĭn hĭs écstă|sў! thĕn óff, | óff fórth ón swíng,
> Ăs ă skáte's hĕel | swéeps smóoth | ŏn ă bów-bĕnd: | thĕ
> húrl ănd glídĭng

A Dictionary of Literary Terms and Literary Theory, Fifth Edition. J. A. Cuddon.
© 2013 The Estate of J. A. Cuddon. Published 2013 by Blackwell Publishing Ltd.

Rěbúffed | thě bíg wínd. | Mў héart | ǐn hídǐng
Stírred fǒr ǎ bírd, | – thě ǎchiéve ǒf, | thě mástěrў | ǒf thě thíng!

This is only one of several possible ways of scanning this piece of verse. However it is scanned, it contains pronounced variations. The first line is fairly even iambics with an anapaest to end. The second line scans: paeon c | trochee | trochee | spondee | trochee. 'In his riding' is paeon c. Line three scans: paeon c | followed by six trochees. Line four scans: paeon a | paeon a | choriam | iamb. Line five scans: paeonic | anapaest | spondee | spondee (but 'off forth on swing', depending on how it is read, might be paeonic in two or possibly three different ways. It might also be antispast: ∪ // ∪). Line six scans: paeon c | spondee | paeon c | iamb. 'And gliding' is amphibrach. Line seven scans: iamb | bacchius | iamb | amphibrach. Line eight scans: choriambus | paeon c | paeon b | anapaest. *See also* EPITRITE; SPRUNG RHYTHM.

pageant Originally the movable stage or platform on which the medieval Mystery Plays (*q.v.*) were presented, it was built on wheels and consisted of two rooms: the lower was used as a dressing room, the upper as a stage. Later, the term was applied to plays acted on this platform. In modern usage it describes any sort of spectacular procession which presents tableaux and includes songs, dances and dramatic scenes. This sort of entertainment was fashionable in the early decades of the 20th c., especially in depicting local history. The annual Lord Mayor's Show in London carries on the tradition. A recent and interesting example of a kind of dramatic pageant was John Arden's *Left-Handed Liberty* (1965), a play commemorating the six-hundredth anniversary of the signing of the Magna Carta. *See also* MASQUE; MORALITY PLAY.

palaeography (Gk 'ancient writing') The study of and the art of deciphering ancient manuscripts, inscriptions and writings.

paleface and redskin Terms appropriated in 1939 by Philip Rahv and used by him to distinguish two 'poles' (as in north and south, but in this case in no sense regional). The polarization, which is a kind of antinomy (*q.v.*), sees a grouping of writers according to their attitude, style, subject matter and so forth. Thus, Herman Melville (1819–91) and Henry James (1843–1916) may be regarded as 'palefaces', whereas Walt Whitman (1819–92) and Mark Twain (1835–1910) may be regarded as 'redskins'. 'Palefaces' have cultured and patrician attitudes and write in a mannered style using symbolism and lofty themes. 'Redskins' write of frontier life, working men, the plebs, low life in cities, etc., and are more colloquial and naturalistic in style. Among more recent writers, William Faulkner might be regarded as a redskin; John Updike as a paleface; with writers such as Saul Bellow and Bernard Malamud somewhere in between.

palilogy (Gk 'speaking over again') A deliberate repetition of a word or words for emphasis. A common rhetorical device. The following example is from

Beckett's play *Waiting for Godot*, and comes from Lucky's long speech in Act I:

> . . . so fast I resume the skull to shrink and waste and concurrently simultaneously what is more for reasons unknown in spite of the tennis on on the beard the flames the tears the stones so blue so calm alas alas on on the skull the skull the skull the skull in Connemara in spite of the tennis the labours abandoned left unfinished graver still abode of stones in a word I resume alas alas abandoned unfinished the skull the skull in Connemara in spite of the tennis the skull alas the stones Cunard . . .

palimbacchius Also known as the anti-bacchius. In Greek prosody a foot of two stressed syllables and one unstressed: / / ◡. In other words, the reverse of bacchius (*q.v.*). Rare in English verse, but occasional examples occur in the work of Tennyson, Swinburne, Browning, Gerard Manley Hopkins, Ezra Pound, W. B. Yeats, and more recent poets.

palimpsest (Gk 'again rubbed away') A surface, usually vellum or parchment, which has been used more than once for writing on, the previous writing having been rubbed out or somehow removed. Medieval parchment, being expensive, was often used two or three times.

palindrome (Gk 'running back again') A word or sentence (occasionally a verse) which reads the same both ways. Common words are *civic*, *level*, *minim*, *radar*, *rotor*. Famous examples of such phrases or sentences are (a) 'Madam, I'm Adam', to which the reply was 'Sir, I'm Iris'; (b) Able was I ere I saw Elba (attributed apocryphally to Napoleon who, alas, spoke no English).

The best-known collection of verses was that produced by one Ambrose Pamperis in 1802. It consists of 416 palindromic verses recounting the campaigns of Catherine the Great. *See also* ACROSTIC.

palinode (Gk 'singing over again') A recantation in song or verse. Usually a poem in which a writer retracts or counterbalances a statement made in an earlier poem. The first palinode was a lyric by the Greek poet Stesichorus (*c.* 640–555 BC) in which he withdrew his attack on Helen as the cause of the Trojan war. Ovid is supposed to have written his *Remedia Amoris* in order to retract his *Ars Amatoria*. As a theme the palinode is not uncommon in love poetry. A well-known instance of a palinode in English literature is Chaucer's *Legend of Good Women* (*c.* 1372–86), written to atone for the story of the false Criseyde in *Troilus and Criseyde*.

palinodic Adjective of palinode (*q.v.*). It describes a verse where two similar stanzas or stanzaic groups (e.g. strophe and antistrophe, *qq.v.*) are interrupted by another matched pair.

palliata *See* FABULA.

pamphlet (AL *panfletus*, possibly from a Latin erotic poem *Pamphilus* – from Greek *Pamphilos*, 'beloved of all' – very popular in the Middle Ages) A small unbound book, usually with paper covers. Originally a pamphlet was a sort of treatise or tract (*qq.v.*). It then came to mean a short work written on a topical subject on which an author feels strongly. Many outstanding writers have used the pamphlet to express vigorous political or religious views. The pamphlet has flourished most notably in England in the hands of such authors as Sir Thomas More, Tyndale, Greene, Dekker, Gerard Winstanley, Milton, Defoe, Swift and Shelley, plus the 19th c. Chartists. During the 18th and 19th c. many political controversies were dealt with in pamphlets. In France, too, the pamphlet has been much used – especially during times of unrest like the Revolutionary period from 1789 to 1848.

pandect (Gk *pan*, 'everything' + *dektēs*, 'a receiver') A book that purports to include everything possible on a topic; originally Justinian's encyclopaedia of Roman civil law in fifty volumes.

panegyric (Gk 'pertaining to public assembly') A speech or poem in fulsome praise of an individual, institution or group of people. Originally panegyric was a branch of rhetoric (*q.v.*) whose rules were laid down in the rhetorical works of Menander and Hermogenes. Scaliger also provides its rules in *Poetices Libri Septem* (1561). Two famous examples from Classical times are the festival oration delivered by Isocrates (436–338 BC) on the occasion of the Olympian games in 380, and Pliny the Younger's (AD 61–c. 113) eulogy on Trajan. Mark Antony's funeral oration in Shakespeare's *Julius Caesar* (1599) could be described as panegyric. *See* ENCOMIUM.

panoramic method A term for the omniscient viewpoint (*q.v.*) in authorship, especially in writing fiction.

pantaloon The old man in harlequinade (*q.v.*) who is the butt of the clown's practical jokes. Pantalone was an elderly Venetian in *commedia dell'arte* (*q.v.*) renowned for being greedy, suspicious, gullible and amorous. In Elizabethan times, a term applied to an old man. Hence the reference by Jaques to 'the lean and slippered pantaloon' in his speech on the seven ages of man in *As You Like It* (II, vii, 158).

pantomime (Gk 'all imitator') It may be merely a synonym for mime (*q.v.*), but its principal modern meaning is an exotic and spectacular entertainment particularly suitable for children. It first became popular in England in the 18th c., when it was a variation on the harlequinade. By the 19th c. it had become the main item on a bill. Modern pantomime is based on fairy tales, and it includes popular songs and topical comedy. Tradition requires the hero or principal boy to be played by a girl, and the comic older woman, the dame, to be played by a man. Favourite subjects are Cinderella, Aladdin, Dick Whittington, the Babes in the Wood, and Jack and the Bean Stalk.

The term has also been used to describe mime plays, dumb show, melodrama (*qq.v.*), and 18th c. mythical ballets. In ancient Rome actors sometimes performed a kind of pantomime, with the aid of masks, in the dramatization of fabulous tales called *fabula Atellana*. *See* FABULA.

pantun A verse form of Malayan origin. A poem of no determinate length, composed of quatrains (*q.v.*) with internal assonance (*q.v.*) and rhyming abab. The second and fourth lines of each stanza become the first and third lines of the next. In the last quatrain the first line of the poem reappears as the last, and the third line as the second. *Pantun bĕrkait* and *pantun bĕrikat* are terms which denote sets of quatrains; and a *pantun sindiran* is an epigram (*q.v.*). The form was introduced into Western poetry by Ernest Fouinet in the 19th c. Some distinguished French poets used it, notably Victor Hugo, Leconte de Lisle and Baudelaire. It never proved popular in England. One of the better-known versions is Austin Dobson's *In Town*.

parabasis (Gk 'going aside, stepping forward') Part of the choral performance in Greek Old Comedy (*q.v.*). Usually near the end of a play the Chorus, without masks, came forward and addressed the audience directly in a speech which contained the personal views of the author on some topical matter of religion or politics. *See* ANTODE; EPIRRHEMA.

parable (Gk 'side throwing, comparison') A short and simple story, related to allegory and fable (*qq.v.*), which points a moral. Our Lord's forty parables are recorded in the synoptic Gospels only. *See* EXEMPLUM.

paradiastole (Gk 'side separation') A form of euphemism (*q.v.*) where the force and tone of a description is deliberately weakened – often in irony (*q.v.*). For example: 'unattractive' for 'ugly', 'perceptive' for 'sharp', 'uncivilized' for 'savage'. *See* LITOTES.

paradigm (Gk 'example') A pattern, exemplar or model which, as a literary device, points up a resemblance, as in this stanza from Cleveland's poem *To the State of Love, or, The Senses' Festival*:

> My sight took pay, but (thank my charms)
> I now impale her in my arms,
> (Love's compasses) confining you,
> Good angels, to a circle too.
> Is not the universe strait-laced
> When I can clasp it in the waist?
> My amorous folds about thee hurled,
> With Drake I girdle in the world.
> I hoop the firmament and make
> This my embrace the zodiac.
> > How would thy centre take my sense
> > When admiration doth commence
> > At the extreme circumference?

See CONCEIT; METAPHYSICAL.

paradigmatic *See* SYNTAGMATIC/PARADIGMATIC.

paradox (Gk 'beside/beyond opinion') Originally a paradox was merely a view which contradicted accepted opinion. By round about the middle of the

16th c. the word had acquired the commonly accepted meaning it now has: an apparently self-contradictory (even absurd) statement which, on closer inspection, is found to contain a truth reconciling the conflicting opposites. Basically, two kinds may be distinguished: (a) particular or 'local'; (b) general or 'structural'. Examples of the first are short, pithy statements which verge on the epigrammatic – such as Hamlet's line: 'I must be cruel only to be kind'; and Milton's description of God: 'Dark with excessive bright thy skirts appear'.

The second kind is more complex. For instance, there is a paradox at the heart of the Christian faith: that the world will be saved by failure. A structural paradox is one which is integral to, say, a poem. The works of the metaphysical (q.v.) poets, especially Donne and Marvell, abound in them. In fact Donne has been regarded as the first major English poet to develop the possibilities of paradox as a fundamental structural device which sustains the dialectic and argument (qq.v.) of a poem. Notable examples are to be found in *The Will*, *Good Friday, 1613. Riding Westward* and the sonnet beginning:

> Death be not proud, though some have called thee
> Mighty and dreadful, for, thou art not so . . .

In recent verse one of the most striking series of paradoxes can be found at the beginning of T. S. Eliot's *Little Gidding*:

> Midwinter spring is its own season
> Sempiternal though sodden towards sundown,
> Suspended in time, between pole and tropic.
> When the short day is brightest, with frost and fire,
> The brief sun flames the ice, on pond and ditches,
> In windless cold that is the heart's heat,
> Reflecting in a watery mirror
> A glare that is blindness in the early afternoon.
> And glow more intense than blaze of branch, or brazier,
> Stirs the dumb spirit: no wind, but pentecostal fire
> In the dark time of the year.

Some critical theory suggests that the language of poetry is the language of paradox. This idea has been elaborated persuasively by, among others, Cleanth Brooks in his book *The Well-Wrought Urn* (1947).

A paradoxical vision of the behaviour and state of humankind is inherent in much nonsense (q.v.) poetry and also in plays belonging to the Theatre of the Absurd (q.v.).

The ultimate logic of deconstructive criticism implies a paradoxical state of affairs, for such criticism suggests that the meaning of any text is indefinitely in doubt and it follows, therefore, that by using language in *another* text in order to interpret the meaning and language of the *first* text the meaning of the second text is, *ipso facto*, indefinitely in doubt – and so on.

See DECONSTRUCTION; DEFAMILIARIZATION; FOLLY LITERATURE; METALAN-
GUAGE; OXYMORON; PATAPHYSICS.

paragone (It 'comparison') A contention between the arts, usually spoken by
representative practitioners, to determine supremacy. The most typical *para-
goni* pitch poetry and painting against each other, with the ultimate conclusion that each has an indisputable excellence and supremacy which informs
the excellence and supremacy of the other (hence the famous dictum attributed to Simonides: 'the poem is a speaking picture, the painting mute poetry';
see *ut pictura poesis, q.v.*). *Timon of Athens* opens with a *paragone* between
painter and poet; the anonymous entertainment for Queen Elizabeth at
Mitcham (1598) features a poet, a painter and a musician. The *paragone* is
not, however, restricted to the fine arts: Philip Sidney's *Defence of Poesie* (*c.*
1579) plays with the convention in asserting the power of poetry over that
of personified figures of the historian and the philosopher. Examples of the
paragone are Lodovico Dolce, *Aretino* (1557); Leonardo da Vinci, *Trattato
della Pittura* (*c.* 1500). *See* CORRESPONDENCE OF THE ARTS.

paragram (Gk 'letter joke') A play on words by alteration of a letter or letters.
Quite often a facetious and low form of humour, of traditional 'schoolboy'
kind – for example: 'What's homicidal and lives in the sea?' Answer: 'Jack
the Kipper'. However, it may attain respectability and sense on occasion – for
example: 'The straw that breaks the *hamal's* back' (author's example). *See also*
PUN; SPOONERISM.

paragraph (Gk 'side writing') Originally a short, horizontal stroke drawn
below the beginning of a line in which there was a break in the sense. Now,
for all practical purposes, a passage, or section, or subdivision in a piece of
writing. Usually a paragraph deals with one particular point or aspect of the
subject presented. It may vary greatly in length.

paralipomena (Gk 'things left out') Matter left out of the main body of a work
and included in appendices.

paralipsis (Gk 'leaving aside') A figurative device by which a speaker or writer
feigns to ignore or pass over a matter and thus draws attention to it. A famous
example occurs when Mark Antony is addressing the mob in *Julius Caesar*
(III, ii, 130).

parallelism (Gk 'alongside one another') A very common device in poetry
(especially Hebrew poetry) and not uncommon in the more incantatory types
of prose. It consists of phrases or sentences of similar construction and
meaning placed side by side, balancing each other, as in Isaiah (9:2):

> The people that walked in darkness have seen a great light: they that dwell
> in the land of the shadow of death, upon them hath the light shined.
>   Thou hast multiplied the nation, and not increased the joy: they joy
> before thee according to the joy in harvest, and as men rejoice when they
> divide the spoil.

Parallelism is common in poetry of the oral tradition (*q.v.*) – for instance, in *Beowulf* and the *narodne pesme* (*q.v.*) – and often the effect is that of a litany (*q.v.*). Other interesting examples can be found in the work of Langland, T. S. Eliot, D. H. Lawrence, and especially in the verse of Walt Whitman, who probably used the device more than any other poet.

paraph *See* PUNCTUATION.

paraphrase (Gk 'tell in other words') A version in other words of the sense of any passage or text. It may be a free rendering or amplification of a passage (not to be confused with précis, *q.v.*). As Dryden put it: 'translation with latitude where the author is kept in view . . . but his words are not so strictly followed as his sense'. Paraphrase is often used nowadays in rewriting technical books and articles in language which the layman can understand.

pararhyme The repetition in accented syllables of the final consonant sound but without the correspondence of the vowel sound. Therefore it is a form of consonance (*q.v.*), which is also known as approximate, embryonic, imperfect, near, oblique and slant rhyme. It was common in Icelandic, Irish and Welsh verse. Henry Vaughan appears to have been the first to use it in English, but it was not until Gerard Manley Hopkins and W. B. Yeats that English poets began to use it regularly. Since them there have been many examples in the work of such poets as Wilfred Owen, John Crowe Ransom. T. S. Eliot, Emily Dickinson, Allen Tate and W. H. Auden. The following well-known example comes from Emily Dickinson's *I like to see it lap the miles*:

> I like to see it lap the miles,
> And lick the valleys up,
> And stop to feed itself at tanks;
> And then, prodigious, step
> Around a pile of mountains,
> And, supercilious, peer
> In shanties by the sides of roads;
> And then a quarry pare.

Up/step, peer/pare are the pararhymes. *See also* ASSONANCE; RHYME.

parataxis (Gk 'beside arrangement') Co-ordination of clauses without conjunctions: the opposite of hypotaxis (*q.v.*). Common in Latin and not unusual in English. The effect is terseness and compression. Pope was expert in its use within the exacting form of the heroic couplet (*q.v.*), as these lines from his *Epistle IV: To Richard Boyle* suggest:

> Still follow Sense, of ev'ry Art the Soul,
> Parts answ'ring parts shall slide into a whole,
> Spontaneous beauties all around advance,
> Start ev'n from Difficulty, strike from Chance;

Nature shall join you, Time shall make it grow
A work to wonder at – perhaps a STOW.

See ELLIPSIS; POLYSYNDETON.

paratext Supplementary visual and verbal material that accompanies the main text (such as novels, poems or non-fiction). The term was coined by the French literary theorist Gérard Genette in 1987. Paratexts can include book covers, illustrations, titles, dedications, forewords, epigraphs, the index or table of contents, and other non-authorial material. Paratexts may often influ-ence the reception of a text, and as Genette explains, these devices serve as an important medium between author, editors, publishers and readers.

parenthesis (Gk 'put in beside') A rhetorical figure in which a word or words are intercluded within a clause; in written/printed texts parentheses (such as this one) are usually indicated by lunulae, dashes, or commas.

The rhetorical figure dates from classical antiquity, but the practice of marking only from 1399, when lunulae were invented for the purpose. Gram-marians from the 16th c. to the present have frequently asserted that parentheses are subordinate and/or extraneous, and (esp. in the 18th c.) have judged them to be inelegant or indicative of stylistic incompetence; but both assertion and judgement are mistaken. Conventional Renaissance uses of the parenthesis include not only the indication of vocatives and attributions of speech (which are commonly subordinate), but also of *sententiae* and com-parisons (including metaphors and similes), the cruxes of arguments by authority and analogy – and in these instances parenthesization is a form of visual emphasis and not of grammatical subordination. In satire also, while parentheses may be grammatically subordinate, they are almost always satiri-cally emphatic.

The popularity of parentheses has varied over time, and offers an interest-ing stylistic index of the preoccupations of an age. In Renaissance, 17th c., Romantic and 20th c. writing parentheses are common; in 18th c. and mid-Victorian work (with the exception of satire) relatively much rarer. *See* PUNCTUATION.

parison (Gk 'almost equal, evenly balanced') A sequence of clauses or sen-tences which have a symmetrical structure.

Parnassians Parnassianism was an influential literary movement in France in the second half of the 19th c. It was a kind of reaction against the romanti-cism (*q.v.*) of Victor Hugo, de Vigny and Lamartine, against subjectivism and 'artistic socialism'. Some scholars take Théophile Gautier (1811–72) as the founder and star of the movement. Others hold that Leconte de Lisle (1818–94) was the 'chef d'orchestre'. They both had much influence. In the Preface to *Mademoiselle de Maupin* (1835) Gautier put forward the belief that art was an end in itself, not a means to an end. In Gautier's view a poet was like a sculptor, a craftsman who must be strictly objective and fashion his poem into something almost tangible. Hence analogies with the plastic arts, and imagery drawn from them. And hence the idea of objective poetry from which the personality of the poet is eliminated. This looks forward to Eliot's dictum that the 'progress of an artist is a continual self-sacrifice, a continual extinction of personality'. *L'art pour l'art* can be taken as one of the slogans of *les Parnassiens*. For them poetry achieved the status of a religion.

Most of *les Parnassiens* were born round about 1840, and the main movement started with Catulle Mendès and L.-X. de Ricard in the early 1860s. At their meetings Leconte de Lisle was the oracular figure (one might say the Lenin of the movement, to Gautier's Marx). Apart from him the important figures were: Théodore de Banville (1823–91), Sully Prudhomme (1839–1907), François Coppée (1842–1908), Léon Dierx (1838–1912), Jean Lahor (1840–1909), and J.-M. de Heredia (1842–1905).

By the 1870s the theories of this Parnassian School were beginning to be felt in England, largely through the influence of de Banville whose *Petit traité de poésie française* (1872) was widely known. De Banville corresponded with Austin Dobson, Swinburne, Edmund Gosse and Andrew Lang, and the so-called English Parnassians became enthusiastic followers of the French cult, especially in matters of style and form and in the use of older French forms like *ballade*, *rondeau* and *villanelle* (*qq.v.*). However, the doctrines of 'art for art's sake' (*q.v.*) never really caught on in England. *See also* AESTHETICISM; PERSONAL HERESY; SYMBOL AND SYMBOLISM.

parody (Gk 'beside, subsidiary or mock song') The imitative use of the words, style, attitude, tone and ideas of an author in such a way as to make them ridiculous. This is usually achieved by exaggerating certain traits, using more or less the same technique as the cartoon caricaturist. In fact, a kind of satirical mimicry. As a branch of satire (*q.v.*) its purpose may be corrective as well as derisive.

If an author has a propensity for archaic or long words, double-banked adjectives, long, convoluted sentences and paragraphs, strange names, quaint mannerisms of expression, is sentimental, bombastic, arch or pompous, then these are some of the features that the would-be parodist will seek to exploit.

Parody is difficult to accomplish well. There has to be a subtle balance between close resemblance to the 'original' and a deliberate distortion of its principal characteristics. It is, therefore, a minor form of literary art which is likely to be successful only in the hands of writers who are original and creative themselves. In fact, the majority of the best parodies are the work of gifted writers.

The origins of parody are ancient. Aristotle refers to it in *Poetics* and attributes its invention to Hegemon of Thasos who used an epic style to represent men as being inferior to what they are in real life. Hegemon was supposed to have been the first man to introduce parody in the theatre, in the 5th c. BC. However, the 6th c. poet Hipponax has also been credited with this.

Aristophanes used parody in the *Frogs* where he took off the style of Aeschylus and Euripides. Plato also caricatured the style of various writers in the *Symposium*. Lucian used parody in his *Dialogues*. It was so common among Latin authors that Cicero listed its varieties. In the Middle Ages parodies of the liturgy, hymns and the Bible were fairly frequent. One of the first and best-known English parodies was Chaucer's *Tale of Sir Thopas* (c. 1383), a skit on some of the more absurd characteristics of medieval romances (Chaucer was in turn to be well parodied by Alexander Pope and W. W. Skeat).

Late in the Renaissance period Cervantes parodied the whole tradition of medieval romances in *Don Quixote* (1605, 1615). Erasmus in *Moriae Encomium* (1509) and Rabelais in *Gargantua* and *Pantagruel* (1534, 1532) turned scholasticism upside down. Shakespeare parodied the euphuism (*q.v.*) of John Lyly in *Henry IV*, Pt I (1597), Marlowe's bombastic manner in *Hamlet* (c. 1603) and the general style of Nashe in *Love's Labour's Lost* (c. 1595). Later Sir John Suckling took off Donne splendidly as a love poet, and in 1701 John Philips parodied Milton very cleverly in *The Splendid Shilling*. Somewhat earlier Buckingham produced one of the few dramatic parodies which have survived contemporary interest; namely *The Rehearsal* (1671), which mocked Dryden's *The Conquest of Granada*.

In 1736 Isaac Hawkins's *A Pipe of Tobacco* created a precedent because it was the first collection of parodies of various authors' supposed attempts on a single subject. Fielding's burlesque drama *Tom Thumb* appeared in 1730; and Fielding's *Shamela* (1741) was a complete parodic novel at the expense of Richardson's *Pamela* (1740). To the 18th c. also belongs Sheridan's *The Critic* (1779), a successful parody of sentimental drama and the malicious literary criticism of the period.

The Romantic period and the 19th c. provided a succession of ample targets for literary iconoclasts. In 1812 James and Horace Smith published *Rejected Addresses* in which Scott, Wordsworth, Byron, Coleridge, Dr Johnson and others were parodied very successfully. Thereafter, Burns, Byron, Wordsworth, Poe, Longfellow, Tennyson, Browning, William Morris, the Rossettis, Swinburne, Southey, Whitman, Hopkins and Kipling were quite frequently parodied, often by writers equally distinguished. For example, Keats on Wordsworth, Byron on Wordsworth, James Hogg on Wordsworth, Swinburne on Tennyson, C. S. Calverley on Browning, Lewis Carroll on Swinburne, Hogg on Coleridge – and so forth. The favourite victims were Southey, Wordsworth, Browning and Swinburne.

Max Beerbohm refined parody to art, and his collection of his own parodies in *A Christmas Garland* (1912), which includes pieces in the manner of Kipling, Galsworthy, Hardy, Arnold Bennett, Edmund Gosse and others, is generally agreed to have set a standard which may never be surpassed.

In what has been described as the 'post-Beerbohm' period of parody there is to be found as much variety as in the 19th c. and often as much skill. James Joyce was a gifted parodist, some of whose best efforts can be found in the 'Oxen of the Sun' episode of *Ulysses*. A classic parody of the 1930s was Stella Gibbons's *Cold Comfort Farm* (1932), a clever caricature of the primitivism (*q.v.*) of Mary Webb's novels – and also, for that matter, of the primitivism of

Hardy, J. C. Powys and D. H. Lawrence. More recent and talented instances are C. Day Lewis's parodies in Part V of *An Italian Visit*, Cyril Connolly on Aldous Huxley, Paul Jennings on Resistentialism, Kenneth Tynan on Thornton Wilder – plus a whole school of American parodists much of whose work has appeared in *The New Yorker*. The best known of these are Robert Benchley, Peter De Vries, Wolcott Gibbs, S. J. Perelman, Frank Sullivan, James Thurber and E. B. White. In 1960 Dwight MacDonald published *Parodies: an Anthology from Chaucer to Beerbohm and After*, an admirable collection of vintage pieces. An accomplished contemporary parodist in verse is Wendy Cope. There are some good examples in her collection of poems *Making Cocoa for Kingsley Amis* (1986). *See* BURLESQUE; LAMPOON; MOCK-EPIC; MOCK-HEROIC; SKIT.

parole *See* LANGUE AND PAROLE.

paronomasia A punning play on words which uses similar or identical phonemes for its effect (an 'assonant pun'). Hamlet's 'Little more than kin and less than kind' is an extreme example; less so is J. L. Austin's description of philosophers: 'they split hairs to save starting them', or Greeks' exclamation 'The Trojan's trumpet!' at the entrance of Cressida. *See* ANTANACLASIS; CLENCH/CLINCH; PUN.

paronym (Gk 'beside word') A word from the same root as another, especially a word taken from another language with slight modifications. For example: Gk *ekstasis* – OF *ecstasie* – MedL *extasis* – English *ecstasy*.

paroxytone A word, or line of verse, with the accent on the penultimate syllable. *See* OXYTONE.

partimen A form of *jeu parti* (*q.v.*) and related to the *tenson* (*q.v.*). A kind of poetic debate in which, for example, a poet presents a proposition. A stock instance is: it is better to love a woman than be loved by her. A second poet then defends or rejects the proposition; after which the first again defends his proposition. The issue is then referred to an arbiter for settlement. There are occasional instances of a triple *partimen* with three poets engaged. *See* POETIC CONTESTS.

partitio *See* MERISMUS.

part-song A song whose parts are sung by different voices to create a harmony, with or without instrumental accompaniment.

partynost (R 'party spirit') One of the main requirements in literature in socialist realism (*q.v.*). Writers are expected to express a 'party spirit' in accordance with the objectives and methods of the Communist Party in the Soviet Union. It is believed that Lenin was the first to point out that this was necessary. *See also* IDEYNOST; NARODNOST.

paso (Sp 'passage') A procession representing part of the Passion of Christ. The term has also been applied to a short dramatic piece and a comic interlude.

pasquinade (It *pasquinata*, 'lampoon') *Pasquinata* derives from the name Pasquino or Pasquillo given to a damaged statue discovered in Rome in 1501. The custom developed that it was honoured on St Mark's Day by having satirical Latin verses hung on it. Hence, a lampoon (*q.v.*) hung up in some public place.

Passion Play A religious drama presenting the Crucifixion of Christ, usually performed on Good Friday. The first was performed in *c.* 1200 at Siena. In 1244 *The Passion* and *The Resurrection* were presented together at Padua. In some places Passion Plays were incorporated in the Corpus Christi cycle; in others they remained separate. Long after the Reformation they were performed in Southern Germany, Austria and Switzerland. The most famous survival is at Oberammergau, Bavaria, where the villagers have performed the play every ten years since 1633. *See* MIRACLE PLAY; MYSTERY PLAY.

passus (L 'step') A division in a story or poem; a chapter, a canto (*q.v.*). Langland used the term for the sections of *The Vision of Piers Plowman*.

pastiche (It *pasta*, 'paste') A patchwork of words, sentences or complete passages from various authors or one author. It is, therefore, a kind of imitation (*q.v.*) and, when intentional, may be a form of parody (*q.v.*). An elaborate form of pastiche is a sustained work (say, a novel) written mostly or entirely in the style and manner of another writer. A good modern example is Peter Ackroyd's brilliant *The Last Days of Oscar Wilde* (1983), which is a diary. *See* CENTO; COLLAGE.

pastoral (L 'pertaining to shepherds') A minor but important mode which, by convention, is concerned with the lives of shepherds. It is of great antiquity and interpenetrates many works in Classical and modern European literature. For the most part pastoral tends to be an idealization of shepherd life, and, by so being, creates an image of a peaceful and uncorrupted existence; a kind of prelapsarian world.

The origins of pastoral with many of its conventions are to be found in the works of Theocritus (*c.* 316–*c.* 260 BC), a native of Syracuse in Sicily, who wrote pastorals for the sophisticated Greeks of Alexandria. Theocritus's successors were Bion (*c.* 100 BC) and Moschus (*c.* 150 BC), whose poems were similar. Virgil (70–19 BC) modelled his *Eclogues* on Theocritus and in them evoked that 'golden age' in which innocent shepherds lived in primitive bliss.

The next work of note in the tradition is the Greek pastoral romance *Daphnis and Chloe* (3rd–5th c. AD) by Longus, the model of the romance favoured by writers in the Renaissance.

One may suppose that by the late Middle Ages the pastoral imagery which was an important feature of the Christian and Hebrew teachings may well have had some influence on pastoral. After all, Christ was the shepherd and human beings were His flock. Such knowledge enhanced the conviction that the shepherd's life was a paradigm of tranquillity and harmonious love. In this connection one should note that *The Adoration of the Shepherds* was a popular medieval Mystery Play (*q.v.*). The veneration accorded to Virgil in the Middle Ages resulted from certain lines in the *Fourth Eclogue*, which were interpreted as a prophecy of the advent of Christ, and which accordingly had some influence on the concept of pastoral and the pastoral life.

Petrarch and Boccaccio wrote eclogues in Latin; but more influential than these were the Latin pastorals of Mantuan (1448–1516). By this time, the pastoral 'novel' was also beginning to be established, as in Boccaccio's *Ameto* and Sannazaro's *Arcadia*. The latter was a kind of model for Sidney's pastoral romance *Arcadia* (1590). Meantime, Spenser's *Shepheardes Calendar* was closely modelled on the eclogues of Theocritus, Virgil and Mantuan.

In the late 16th c. many other works amplified the pastoral tradition, such as Marlowe's *The Passionate Shepherd to his Love*, which evoked a memorable reply from Sir Walter Ralegh. Michael Drayton also wrote some eclogues (1593).

At about this time pastoral drama appeared in Italy with Tasso's *Aminta* (1581) and Guarini's *Il Pastor Fido* (1585). The influence of these works is discernible in a number of Shakespeare's plays; also in Ben Jonson's unfinished play *The Sad Shepherd* (1641). In the 17th c. the main practitioner of the pastoral convention was Milton, as evidenced above all in his *Lycidas* (1637).

Fundamentally, pastoral displays a nostalgia for the past, for some hypothetical state of love and peace which has somehow been lost. The dominating idea and theme of most pastoral is the search for the simple life away from the court and town, away from corruption, war, strife, the love of gain, away from 'getting and spending'. In a way it reveals a yearning for a lost innocence, for a pre-Fall paradisal life in which man existed in harmony with nature. It is thus a form of primitivism (*q.v.*) and a potent longing for things past. Hence the myth of the golden age which, in Classical literature, is diffused in Hesiod, Virgil and Ovid. In the Middle Ages Boethius, Jean de Meung, Dante and Chaucer used it as an image or metaphor for the Garden of Eden. During the Renaissance period the expression of a longing for this Arcadian world was worked out in greater detail. But it is probably not entirely a coincidence that, as the mythopoeic attractions of pastoral happiness diminish, so utopia (*q.v.*) begins to acquire a particular interest for people.

In the 18th c. pastoral was further modified. Notable works include Pope's *Windsor Forest* (1713), John Gay's *Shepherd's Week* (1714), Goldsmith's *The Deserted Village* (1770), George Crabbe's *The Village* (1783) and Wordsworth's *Tintern Abbey* (1798). Many of Blake's poems extol the simplicity and innocence of country life, and in Book VIII of *The Prelude* Wordsworth evoked the whole history of pastoral. The 19th c. produced two great pastoral elegies in Shelley's *Adonais* (1821) and Matthew Arnold's *Thyrsis* (1867).

Later attempts at a kind of pastoralism were made by Tennyson, William Barnes, John Davidson, A. E. Housman (*A Shropshire Lad*), Yeats, Ezra Pound, Auden, MacNeice and R. S. Thomas.

pastourelle A short narrative poem of the Middle Ages (in Provençal *pastorela*) whose typical subject is a meeting between a knight and a shepherdess. A kind of 'debate' follows, and the shepherdess may or may not succumb; or she may outwit the knight, or be rescued by shepherds. *Pastourelle* was a popular form of entertainment in OF in the 13th c. *See also* DÉBAT; PASTORAL.

pataphysics A pseudo-philosophical system devised by Alfred Jarry (1873–1907), and known as the 'science of imaginary solutions'. Jarry was a precursor of surrealism (*q.v.*), and after the Second World War a number of devotees founded the *Collège de Pataphysique*. With solemn whimsy they invented rules and regulations and in fact produced a sort of parody of the conventional college of learning. The main spirits in this 'joke' were Ionesco, Raymond Queneau, Boris Vian, Jacques Prévert and Jean Dubuffet. Pataphysics are the metaphysics of nonsense (*q.v.*) and the absurd, and are anti-reason. The influence of the ideas can most clearly be seen in the Theatre of the Absurd (*q.v.*).

patavinity A rare term which denotes dialect peculiarities in writing. It also denotes a 'provincial' style. The word derives from the place-name *Patavium* – where Livy was born. The historian's writings were said to possess such oddities.

patent theatres Letters patent were issued in 1662 by Charles II to William Davenant (1606–68) and Thomas Killigrew (1612–83), which allowed them the sole right to present plays in public within the City of Westminster. After their deaths the letters patent were the source of numerous legal disputes, squabbles and sales; ultimately they were settled on the Drury Lane and Covent Garden theatres. Legitimate (*q.v.*) drama was confined to the patent theatres, but there was much dispute as to exactly what legitimate drama was. The patents existed until 1843 when the Theatres Act made them inoperative.

pathetic fallacy A phrase invented by John Ruskin in 1856 (*Modern Painters*, Vol. III, Pt IV). According to Ruskin a writer was pathetically fallacious when he ascribed human feelings to the inanimate. For Ruskin it was a derogatory term because it applied, so he said, not to the 'true appearances of things to us', but to the 'extraordinary, or false appearances, when we are under the influence of emotion or contemplative fancy'. To illustrate his point Ruskin quotes from Kingsley's *The Sands of Dee*:

> They rowed her in across the rolling foam –
> The cruel, crawling foam.

And from Coleridge's *Christabel*:

> The one red leaf, the last of its clan
> That dances as often as dance it can.

Such passages are, according to Ruskin, 'morbid', however beautiful they may be.

Such a form of personification (*q.v.*) has been used countless times from Homer onwards, and still is. By Ruskin's criterion, therefore, many of the greatest poets would qualify as morbid. Nowadays the phrase is used in a non-pejorative and therefore neutral way to define this common poetic phenomenon.

pathopoeia (Gk 'making of feeling') A scene or passage intended to arouse feelings: anger, grief or passion. For example, Henry V's pre-battle speeches in *Henry V*.

pathos (Gk 'suffering, feeling') That quality in a work of art which evokes feelings of tenderness, pity or sorrow. For example: in *Hamlet*, Gertrude's speech describing the death of Ophelia; in *Othello*, the death of Desdemona.

patois A word of unknown origin which denotes a local dialect, especially in France and French Switzerland. We find it in OF as *patois* 'rough speech'; perhaps from the OF *patoier* 'to handle roughly'. Often used loosely as an equivalent of cant, lingo, slang (*qq.v.*). *See also* ARGOT.

patronage A patron is a person of wealth and position (often of power and rank, also) who bestows bounty on an artist and thus supports him. In return the artist dedicates his work to the patron and thus honours him. Two of the most famous patrons were the Emperor Augustus, and his friend Maecenas. Both were much celebrated for their patronage of learning and letters. Maecenas was benefactor to Virgil and Horace. Patronage was common in classical times and throughout the medieval and Renaissance periods. As the power of printers and publishers increased, patronage became less frequent. Nevertheless, quite a large number of writers continued to enjoy the advantages of benefactors during the 17th and 18th c. *See also* POET LAUREATE.

pattern As a literary term, a model, design, plan or precedent – with the implication of being worthy of imitation. Pope's *Imitations* of Horace are based on the Roman's pattern. *See also* ARCHETYPE; SYMBOL AND SYMBOLISM.

pattern poetry Probably oriental in origin, this kind of poem has its lines arranged to represent a physical object, or to suggest action/motion, mood/feeling; but usually shape and motion. Thus geometric figures are common; other shapes are wings, egg and spear. Pattern poems first appear in the works of Greek bucolic poets, particularly those of Simias of Rhodes (4th c. BC). It seems that the Planudean version of the *Greek Anthology* passed on the idea.

In English literature pattern poems begin to appear in the 16th c.; for instance, in Puttenham's *The Arte of English Poesie* (1589). George Herbert's *Easter Wings* is one of the most famous examples. Among modern poets to attempt the form are Apollinaire, Mayakovsky, e. e. cummings and Dylan Thomas. This example comes from Dylan Thomas's series of twelve pattern poems entitled *Vision and Prayer*:

> Who
> Are you
> Who is born
> In the next room
> So loud to my own
> That I can hear the womb
> Opening and the dark run
> Over the ghost and the dropped son
> Behind the wall thin as a wren's bone?
> In the birth bloody room unknown
> To the burn and turn of time
> And the heart print of man
> Bows no baptism
> But dark alone
> Blessing on
> The wild
> Child.

See ALTAR POEM; CONCRETE POETRY/VERSE; PRUNING POEM; RHOPALIC VERSE.

patter song Usually a kind of comic lyric (*q.v.*) half spoken, half sung – or chanted. In ancient Greek comedy (*q.v.*) it was known as *pnigos*. A large number of patter songs developed during service life in the First World War and lasted thereafter. The cockney tradition of a quick-fire line of guff, and the music hall tradition of a jokey story half sung, half told, were both strong influences. Two famous ones are:

> Today is my daughter's wedding day,
> Ten thousand pounds I'll give away. (Three cheers)
> On second thoughts I think it best
> To put it away in the old oak chest.
> You mingy bastard! Chuck him out! etc. etc.

and

> Help, help, there's a woman overboard!
> Who will save her?
> I will!
> Who are you?
> Ballocky Bill the sailor, just returned from sea!

Such more or less nonsense patters might be recited for no reason at all, perhaps only to relieve tension or create a diversion. Not a few of the best patters are bawdy. One of the most famous is *The Showman* (or *The Wild West Show*). It was known before the First World War, but became very popular during it.

Most patter songs belong to the oral tradition (*q.v.*). An instance of a 'written' one is Gilbert and Sullivan's 'nightmare' in *Iolanthe*.

Patter probably derives from *Pater Noster*; from the rapid recitation of the prayer when, for example, saying the rosary. *See also* JINGLE.

pause In prose fiction a kind of resting point which allows the reader to reflect. Trollope uses the device quite often in his recapitulations. In verse, the equivalent of a caesura (*q.v.*). In drama, an indication that there is to be a silence – often of no determined length. Some modern dramatists (e.g. Jean-Jacques Bernard, Montherlant, Samuel Beckett and Harold Pinter) have made extensive use of the pause: an exploitation of the dramatic principle that what people do not say may be quite as important as what they do say. *See also* THEATRE OF SILENCE.

payada In Spanish-American *una paya* is an improvised song accompanied by a guitar. *Un payo* is 'a rustic', and *un payaso* 'a clown or buffoon'. A *payada* has come to denote a dialogued poetical composition which the *payadores* improvise and accompany on the guitar. Two *payadores* may play in counterpoint; hence *payada de contrapunto*. In the Argentine this is a popular form of contest between gauchos. In Argentina the *payador* is akin to our strolling player, and thus related to the *jongleur*, *trouvère* and troubadour (*qq.v.*).

Peking opera It dates from the 18th c. during the reign of the Emperor Ch'ien Lung (1736–95), who personally collected the best actors and singers in his realm. As a form of drama it incorporates a wide range of traditional theatrical modes, including music, song, dance, dialogue and acrobatics. *See also* WEN AND WU.

PEN An international association of Poets, Playwrights, Editors, Essayists and Novelists founded in 1921 by Mrs Dawson-Scott under the presidency of John Galsworthy. Its function is to promote co-operation among writers worldwide, in the interests of international goodwill and freedom of expression, and literature in general. There are regular conferences in various parts of the world.

penny dreadful A novel or novelette (*qq.v.*) of mystery, adventure, crime and action. Without any literary pretensions. Bound in paper and cheaply printed. A penny, from the cost; dreadful, presumably, because they were regarded as low, vulgar, sensational, etc. Known among schoolboys as 'bloods', and the equivalent of the American dime novel (*q.v.*). G. K. Chesterton wrote a celebrated defence of penny dreadfuls. *See also* BLUE BOOK; DETECTIVE STORY; MELODRAMA; ROMAN À DEUX SOUS; THRILLER.

pensée (F 'thought') A thought (or reflection) put in literary form. It may be only a short sentence – like the average aphorism or maxim (*qq.v.*) – or it may run to several pages. The most famous collection of *pensées* is unquestionably Pascal's. It constituted the notes and framework for an uncompleted *Defence of the Christian Religion* (1670). According to how they are numbered and classified there are between eight hundred and a thousand of Pascal's *pensées*. They display a profoundly original and acute mind and constitute one of the great works of European literature. A brief example is: 'Memory and joy are intuitive; and even mathematical propositions become so. For reason creates natural intuitions, and natural intuitions are erased by reason.'

Many writers keep notebooks, diaries, journals, daybooks and other memoranda in which they jot down thoughts, but relatively few have chosen to make the *pensée* the main vehicle of their thinking. Indeed, had Pascal lived to complete his work the result would have been an *apology* (*q.v.*) for the Christian faith rather than a diversity of thoughts. However, outstanding examples of those who followed in the Pascal tradition are Diderot, whose *Pensées philosophiques* (1746) were intended as a kind of reply to Pascal's work, and Joseph Joubert (1754–1824), who took the *pensée* as his principal form. His observations on a wide variety of subjects were edited by Chateaubriand as *Recueil des pensées* (1838).

English writers have not been given so much to the *pensée* habit, though many of their journals and notebooks abound in them, and many survive in collections of table-talk (*q.v.*). However, there have been some notable contributions. First, Ben Jonson's *Timber, or Discoveries made upon Men and Matters* (1640), a collection of *obiter dicta*, *sententiae* and reflections on miscellaneous subjects. Some are only a line or two; some as long as short essays. George Savile, Marquess of Halifax, composed three collections of 'thoughts' towards the end of the 17th c. but they were not published until 1750, when they appeared as *Political, Moral and Miscellaneous Reflexions*.

To these one may add three other notable collections from more recent years: *Speculations* (1924), the result of Herbert Read's editing of T. E. Hulme's notebooks; Paul Valéry's *Rhumbs* (1926), thus called in reference to the navigational sense of the word *rhumb* or *rumb* (the angular distance between two successive points of the compass); and *The Unquiet Grave* (1944) by Palinurus, alias Cyril Connolly, an assembly of quotations and sage *aperçus* on a wide range of topics. *See also* CHARACTER; COMMONPLACE BOOK; DIARY AND JOURNAL; ESSAY; OBITER DICTA; SENTENTIA.

pentameter (Gk 'of five measures') The five-foot line and the basic line in much English verse; especially in blank verse and the heroic couplet (*qq.v.*). It was probably introduced by Chaucer, and was certainly established by him. For the next five hundred years it was the line unit commonly favoured by scores of poets. Late in the 19th c. poets began to experiment in freer forms, hence free verse (*q.v.*). It was Ezra Pound, as much as anyone, who helped to loosen its traditional hold ('to break the pentameter,' he said, 'that was the first heave'). In the 20th c. poets experimented a great deal with lines of varying length, yet the pentameter has remained a most convenient unit.

The first two lines from this poem, *Mr Edwards and the Spider*, by Robert Lowell, are pentameters; the following three are not.

> Ĭ sáw | thĕ spí|dĕrs már|chĭng thróugh | thĕ áir,
> Swímmĭng | frŏm trée | tŏ trée | thăt míl|dĕwed dáy
> Ĭn láttĕr | Aúgŭst | whĕn thĕ háy
> Cămĕ créakĭng | tŏ thĕ bárn. | Bŭt whére
> Thĕ wínd | ĭs wéstĕrlў . . .

The basic foot in English pentameters is iambic. In antiquity the pentameter was a dactylic-spondaic line of two equal parts: two and a half feet + two and a half feet. Coleridge illustrates this use neatly in *Ovidian Elegiac Meter*:

> Ín thĕ hĕx|ámĕtĕr | rísĕs thĕ | fóuntaĭn's | sílvĕrў | cólŭmn,
> Ín thĕ pĕn|támĕtĕtĕr | áye fáll ĭng ĭn mélŏdў báck.

See DACTYL; HEXAMETER; IAMB.

pentapody (Gk 'five feet') A group or line of five feet.

pentarsic (Gk 'five rises') A line with five metrical beats, like an iambic pentameter (*q.v.*). *See* ARSIS AND THESIS.

pentastich (Gk 'five lines') A stanza or poem of five lines. *See* CINQUAIN; QUINTET.

Pentateuch (Gk 'containing five books') The first five books of the Old Testament: Genesis, Exodus, Leviticus, Numbers and Deuteronomy. They are taken together as a connected group and ascribed (traditionally) to Moses. *See* OCTATEUCH.

penthimimer (Gk 'of five halves') In Greek and Latin verse a metrical unit consisting of two feet; as that forming either half of a pentameter (*q.v.*) or the first part of a hexameter (*q.v.*).

per cola et commata *See* PERIOD (3).

pereval (R 'the pass') A group or society of Russian writers formed in 1923 whose leader was Alexander Voronski (1884–1937?). Their work was published in his journal *Red Virgin Soil*. They were against the concept and practice of proletarian literature. The group was abolished in 1932 when all literary organizations were compulsorily amalgamated in the Union of Soviet Writers (*q.v.*).

perfect rhyme Also known as true or full rhyme, it occurs when there is an exact correspondence between vowel sounds and the following consonants, but not of the consonants preceding the vowel. It may be single, double or triple: haunch – launch; dollar – collar; podium – sodium. *See also* RHYME; RIMES RICHES; RIMES SUFFISANTES.

performance *See* COMPETENCE/PERFORMANCE.

performance art Art which involves a performance presented to an audience. Performance art may take place in any location. Only recognized as a medium of artistic expression in its own right in the 1970s, performance art nevertheless thrived throughout the 20th c. Artists associated with futurism, constructivism, Dadaism and surrealism (*qq.v.*) have all utilized performance art as a way of bringing conceptual ideas to life. Since the late 1960s, such art has proliferated; artists such as Joseph Beuys, Laurie Anderson, and Gilbert and George have used the form to explore the nature of ritual, the relationship between the body and space, and between the media, technology and audiences, and also as a form of social protest. *See also* HAPPENING; PERFORMANCE STUDIES.

performance studies A field of inquiry which takes performance, whether theatrical, social or linguistic, as its object of study and often also as its method of research. Performance studies is profoundly interdisciplinary, and draws on theatre and literary studies, anthropology, linguistics (*q.v.*) (particularly speech-act theory), critical theory and cultural studies (*q.v.*); it has even been described as a 'border discipline' or an 'inter discipline' by some of its practitioners. Consequently, precisely what constitutes 'performance' is contested. Generally, however, performance studies scholars are engaged in a set of recurring issues, including the nature of the relationship between performer and audience; the ubiquity of performance in everyday life; the extent to which performances are performative, i.e. whether they make things happen; the ways in which performance inscribes power and facilitates transgression; and the role of performance in community formation and intercultural communication. Centres for performance studies first emerged in the US in the late 1970s and have since become established internationally. The field is not without its detractors: some consider performance studies to be unstable and even incoherent. However, there have been important correspondences between this field and the development of queer theory (*q.v.*), feminist theory and critical race theory. *See also* PERFORMANCE ART; PERFORMATIVITY.

performative utterance The term developed by the linguistic philosopher J. L. Austin to describe various executive speech acts, in other words, utterances which possess some degree of inherent agency. Simple declarative locutions are not inherently performative, but become so under certain conditions, such as persuasion, oath (illocutionary act, *q.v.*), or ceremonial conventions such as the marriage rite or the Eucharist (perlocutionary act, *q.v.*). See J. L. Austin, *How to Do Things With Words* (1962) and John Searle, *Speech Acts* (1969).

performativity A concept derived from the speech-act theory of philosopher J. L. Austin, in particular his notion of the performative utterance (*q.v.*), i.e. a speech act which does not merely describe something but enacts it. Performativity is most closely associated with the work of poststructuralist theorist Judith Butler. For Butler, both gender and sexuality are not givens; rather, they are 'performances' enacted by continuous repetition. Hence one does not so much *have* a gender as *perform* it. Butler argues that 'gender performativity' opens up the radical possibility that normative codes of masculinity, femininity and heterosexuality may be demonstrated to be contingent, thereby undermining their authority and creating opportunities for expression by marginalized and dissident sexual and gendered subjects. While some have criticized Butler's account for being overly optimistic, or for not properly describing performance contexts, her work – especially *Gender Trouble* (1990) and *Bodies that Matter* (1993) – has profoundly shaped feminist criticism, performance studies and queer theory (*qq.v.*). *See also* POSTSTRUCTURALISM.

period (1) A term commonly used in the history of literature for convenient if sometimes arbitrary classification and reference. For example: Renaissance period, Restoration period, Augustan, Romantic and Victorian periods (*qq.v.*). Renaissance is associated with all the creative arts and the history of art. Restoration has political connotations. Augustan suggests a certain style (*q.v.*) as well as having political connotations. Romantic derives from a literary term and implies a certain attitude and feeling. Victorian is a matter of chronology: roughly coincident with the sovereign's reign. Such classifications have little to do with literary norms and are often misleading.

(2) In the US, an alternative term for the full-stop.

(3) Between classical antiquity and *c.* 1700 the largest unit of syntax, replaced after *c.* 1700 by the sentence. While the sentence is defined either by minimal grammatical completeness (subject + verb + object) or by typography (capital letter to full-stop), the period was primarily a rhetorical unit, closer in many ways to the paragraph than to the modern sentence; and while sentences are usually analysed as one or more clauses, periods were analysed as a sequence of *cola* (the words between two colons, or between a colon and a full-stop), and *cola* as a sequence of *commata* (the words between two commas, or between a comma and a heavier stop). So, for example, the Boatswain's second speech in the first scene of *The Tempest* appears in the First Folio as:

> *Botes.* Heigh my hearts, cheerely, cheerely my harts: yare, yare: Take in the toppe-sale: Tend to th'Masters whistle: Blow till thou burst thy winde, if roome enough.

Despite the capital letters this is clearly punctuated as a single period, and regarded as a whole, since each part is closely related to the others, the Boatswain issuing an unbroken sequence of orders and exhortations. The period is divided by four colons (the marks) into five *cola* (the words between the marks); and the first, second, and fifth *cola* are subdivided by commas into *commata*; but modernized texts will usually change the single period into a sequence of discrete and disjointed sentences, as the *Riverside Shakespeare* does:

> *Boats.* Heigh, my hearts! cheerly, cheerly, my hearts! yare, yare! Take in
> the topsail. Tend to th'master's whistle. – Blow till thou burst thy wind, if
> room enough!

With some difficulty, using medial exclamation-marks and an intra-sentence
dash, the single period has been rendered as four sentences: some clarity may
be gained, but only at the cost of grammatical and dramatic coherence. Shakespearean texts suffer particularly badly from this kind of modernization,
ubiquitous in scholarly editions produced between *c.* 1945 and *c.* 1985, but
almost all texts pre-dating 1700 are affected, and the recovery of periodic
syntax has been a driving force in the resurgence of facsimile, old-spelling,
and unmodernized editions since *c.* 1985.

Both Cicero and Quintilian considered the 'average' period to have four
cola, but the Renaissance reception of these grammarians tended to transform
this observation into a prescription. In consequence the period of four *cola*
is frequent in works adopting a Ciceronian style, and in euphuism (*q.v.*). The
period remained the dominant form of syntax throughout the 17th c. – *Paradise Lost*, for example, is wholly periodic – but began to give way to the
modern sentence in the last quarter of the century, probably under the influence of the stylistic reforms promoted by the Royal Society: while Dryden's
verse is largely periodic, his prose contains many sentences, and the ascendancy of the sentence was assured by its use in novels from Defoe's *Robinson
Crusoe* (1719) onwards.

periodical A magazine or journal published at regular intervals: monthly,
quarterly, etc. The periodical, as we understand it today, dates from the
middle of the 17th c. The exclusively literary periodical is more recent. The
first of any note to appear was the French *Journal des Sçavans* [*Savants*]
in 1665. Then came the Italian *Giornale de Letterati* (1668–81), and the
British *Mercurius Librarius* (1668–1711). The *Athenian Mercury* (1690–7)
and the *Gentleman's Journal* (1692–4) were then precursors of the *Spectator*.
The opening years of the 18th c. were vital in the evolution of the periodical
and the essay (*q.v.*) because of Defoe's *Review of the Affairs of France and
All Europe* (1704–12) – and the *Tatler* (1709–11), the *Spectator* (1711–12)
and the *Guardian* (1713), all three of which were established by Addison
and Steele. In 1731 the *Gentleman's Magazine* first came out and was to
last until 1907. Boswell was one of its more famous contributors. Similar
publications were the *London Magazine* (1732–84), the *Scots* (1739–1817),
which became the *Edinburgh* for seven years after that, the *Oxford* (1768–
82), and the *European* (1782–1826). The *Museum* (1746–7) and the *Monthly
Review* (1749–1845) were landmarks in the development of the literary
periodical. The latter was a Whig journal and from this time politics were
to influence the genre for many years. Three important Tory periodicals
from about the same period were: the *Critical Review* (1756–1817), the
London Review (1775–80) and the *British Critic* (1793–1843). In 1802 was
published the *Edinburgh Review*, one of the most famous and influential of all periodicals. It lasted until 1929. The *Quarterly Review*, a Tory

publication, began in 1809 and is still published. From this period, too, dates the foundation of Blackwood's *Edinburgh Magazine*. From the beginning of the 19th c. there was a steadily increasing number of periodicals until the First World War. Since then, and especially since the Second World War, the number has steadily decreased, largely because they are too expensive to produce. Some of the more famous publications in the 19th c. were the *London Magazine*, *Fraser's Magazine*, *Dublin University Magazine*, the *Cornhill Magazine*, *Longman's Magazine*, *London Quarterly Review*, *The Athenaeum*, *Spectator*, *Saturday Review*, *The Examiner*, *Truth* and *The Speaker*. In the 20th c. some of the landmarks in periodical literature were the publication of the *Times Literary Supplement*, *Saturday Westminster Gazette*, *Week-End Review*, *New Statesman*, *Time and Tide*, *New Age*, *T. P.'s Weekly*, *G. K.'s Weekly* and *John o' London's Weekly*. Sir John Squire's *London Mercury* was a literary magazine of prime importance. Also *Horizon*. In more recent years the *London Magazine* has been revived, and *Encounter* has established itself.

Outside Britain the periodical has flourished also, especially in France, Germany, Italy and America.

peripeteia (Gk 'sudden change') Peripety is a reversal of fortune; a fall. In drama, usually the sudden change of fortune from prosperity to ruin; but it can be the other way about. A much debated term, it was first used by Aristotle in *Poetics* (Chap. VI). The relevant passage, in Bywater's translation, is:

> [Peripety] is the change from one state of things within the play to its opposite of the kind described, and that too in the way we are saying, in the probable or necessary sequence of events; as it is for instance in *Oedipus*: here the opposite of things is produced by the Messenger, who, coming to gladden Oedipus and to remove his fears as to his mother, reveals the secret of his birth.

See ANAGNORISIS; TRAGEDY; TURNING POINT.

periphrasis (Gk 'roundabout speech') A roundabout way of speaking or writing; known also as circumlocution; thus, using many or very long words where a few or simple words will do. For example: Her olfactory system was suffering from a temporary inconvenience (i.e., Her nose was blocked). Much periphrasis comes from an over-nice regard for 'politeness', in the pejorative sense. Semi-literate people are also tempted to this sort of pomp and verbosity. It is also much loved by lawyers, politicians, officials, bureaucrats and verbocrats. What Sir Ernest Gowers described as 'officialese' (*q.v.*) is laden with the periphrastic. It is very often the result of slack thinking, but it may be used deliberately – usually for comic effect, especially in the depiction of character. In the 18th c., particularly, propriety and poetic decorum required periphrastic usage. *See* DECORUM; EUPHEMISM; HOMERIC EPITHET; JARGON; KENNING; METALEPSIS; PLEONASM; POETIC DICTION; TAUTOLOGY.

perlocutionary act An act that is the effect of an utterance. It often involves the use of imperatives. Such acts became a feature of Hitler's rhetorical harangues. See ILLOCUTIONARY ACT; PERFORMATIVE UTTERANCE.

peroration The concluding part of an oration, speech or discourse; a summing or rounding up of what has gone before. It suggests the grand manner favoured by Greek and Roman orators and 18th and 19th c. statesmen. In written works Dr Johnson, Gibbon and Macaulay, for instance, were inclined to perorate.

perqué (It *perché*, 'why') A Spanish verse form comprising a series of octosyllabic couplets to ask rhetorical questions. Usually preceded by a *redondilla* or *quintilla* (*qq.v.*). The first on record is by Hurtado de Mendoza in the 14th c.

persona (L 'mask') Originally a mask or false face of clay or bark worn by actors. From it derives the term *dramatis personae* (*q.v.*) and, later, the word *person*. In literary and critical jargon *persona* has come to denote the 'person' (the 'I' of an 'alter ego') who speaks in a poem or novel or other form of literature. For instance, the narrator of Chaucer's *Canterbury Tales*, the speaker in Keats's *Ode to a Nightingale*, the different speakers in Browning's dramatic monologues, the Gulliver of *Gulliver's Travels*, Marlow in Conrad's *Heart of Darkness* and other stories by him. *See also* AESTHETIC DISTANCE; DRAMATIC MONOLOGUE; MONOLOGUE; NARRATOR; VIEWPOINT.

personal criticism Also known as autobiographical criticism, this is an evolving field that emerged in the 1980s and focuses on the study of life narratives. Of particular interest to scholars in the field are questions about the intersections of self, subject, and text; the relationship between lived and recollected events (and thus, more broadly, the relationship between truth and fiction); and the ability of individual lives to be representative of their historical moments. Influential figures in the field include James Olney, William Spengemann, Philippe Lejeune, and Michael Sprinker. *See* LIFE WRITING.

personal heresy, the In 1934 C. S. Lewis contributed an article on *The Personal Heresy in Criticism* to *Essays and Studies*. In this he expressed disquiet at and disapproval of the then fairly widely held belief that poetry is or should be the expression of a poet's personality. In the course of this he referred to a book by E. M. W. Tillyard on Milton in which, according to Lewis, Tillyard stated the premise that all poetry is about the poet's state of mind. Tillyard 'replied' to this in an essay. Lewis 'replied' to that. And so on. The two men then decided to publish their three essays apiece in one volume (publ. 1939). *The Personal Heresy*, erudite, urbane, courteous and continuously stimulating, is, in its way, a model of how people should agree to differ in their search after truth. *See also* AESTHETICISM; PARNASSIANS; SINCERITY.

personification The impersonation or embodiment of some quality or abstraction; the attribution of human qualities to inanimate objects. Personification is inherent in many languages through the use of gender, and it appears to be very frequent in all literatures – especially in poetry. This example is from Sylvia Plath's *The Moon and the Yew Tree*:

> The moon is no door. It is a face in its own right,
> White as a knuckle and terribly upset.
> It drags the sea after it like a dark crime; it is quiet
> With the O-gape of complete despair. I live here.
> Twice on Sunday, the bells startle the sky –
> Eight great tongues affirming the Resurrection.
> At the end, they soberly bong out their names.

See PATHETIC FALLACY.

Petrarchan sonnet Also known as the Italian sonnet, the form originated in Italy in the 13th c. and was perfected by Petrarch (1304–74). It is a fourteen-line poem divided into two parts: the first eight lines comprise the octave (*q.v.*) or octet and rhyme abbaabba; the following six lines or sestet (*q.v.*) usually rhyme cdecde. Rhyme variations in the sestet are admissible, but rhymes are limited to five. As a rule the octave presents the theme or problem of the poem, the thesis; the sestet resolves it. It was imported to England in the 16th c. This example is by Sir Thomas Wyatt, translating Petrarch:

> The pillar perisht is whereto I leant,
> The strongest stay of mine unquiet mind;
> The like of it no man again can find,
> From East to West still seeking though he went.
> To mine unhap! for hap away hath rent
> Of all my joy the very bark and rind;
> And I, alas, by chance am thus assigned
> Daily to mourn till death do it relent.
> But since that thus it is by destiny,
> What can I more but have a woful heart –
> My pen in plaint, my voice in careful cry,
> My mind in woe, my body full of smart,
> And I myself myself always to hate –
> Till dreadful death do ease my doleful state?

Wyatt here has the traditional rhyming couplet to round off the poem. *See* SONNET.

Petrarchism In a broad sense the imitation of Petrarch's style. Petrarch (1304–74) was considerably plagiarized and imitated during and after his life and he had a considerable influence on European poets: Bembo, Michelangelo, Tasso, Ronsard, du Bellay, Lope de Vega, Góngora, Camoëns, Wyatt, Surrey, Sidney, Spenser and Shakespeare (and some other Elizabethans). The influence was by no means entirely beneficial, as can be seen from the more mannered and elaborate sonnets of Spenser and Shakespeare (especially the former). On the other hand, Petrarch helped to develop the use of the vernacular and established the sonnet (*q.v.*) form. *See* BLAZON; PETRARCHAN SONNET.

pevači Muslim ballad-singers or chanters in Bosnia, where the ballad tradition was under strong Turkish influence. They were professional minstrels of the oral tradition (*q.v.*) and thus kin to the Greek *rhapsodes*, the Old English *scopas*, the Scandinavian *skalds* and the Serbian *guslari* (*qq.v.*). The *pevači* differed from the Christian *guslari* in that they accompanied their chant or recitation on a *tambura*, whereas the *guslar* used a *gusle* – a one-stringed fiddle.

phallocentric Centred on the phallus. Phallocentrism denotes a system which privileges the phallus as the symbol and source of power. A patriarchal society is phallocentric. The term has frequently been used in feminist literary criticism (*q.v.*) – for example, by Julia Kristeva and Hélène Cixous – in attempts to dismantle such binary oppositions (*q.v.*) as male/female, masculine/feminine. *See also* PHALLOGOCENTRIC.

phallogocentric A term invented by the French philosopher Jacques Derrida. It is a conflation of *phallocentric* ('phallus-centred') and *logocentric* ('word-centred'; epistemologically, 'truth-centred'). Terry Eagleton has translated it (happily) as 'cock-sure'. Applied to, for example, society, it denotes one which controls or attempts to control by means of sexual/social influence and power. Thus, a patriarchal society would be predominantly logocentric as well as phallocentric. Poststructuralists would describe modern Western society (or some aspects of such societies) as phallogocentric. As far as literature is concerned, the term might be applied to novels in which the male characters have the upper hand and the female characters are sex objects. The more macho features of Ernest Hemingway's novels might be called phallogocentric. *See* PHALLOCENTRIC.

phanopoeia (Gk 'making something visible') A figurative or verbal device by which the writer conveys the image of the object (be it fixed or moving) to the visual imagination. Ezra Pound discussed this in *ABC of Reading* (1934). In these lines from Philip Larkin's *The Whitsun Weddings* the rhythm and stress sequences skilfully suggest the physical motion of the train and produce a visual image:

> All afternoon, through the tall heat that slept
> For miles inland,
> A slow and stopping curve southwards we kept.
> Wide farms went by, short-shadowed cattle, and
> Canals with floatings of industrial froth;

The heavily stressed paeonic rhythms of the first two lines relax into iambs in the third line (except for the spondaic 'southwards'). The fourth line is also heavily stressed; the fifth is a relatively brisk combination of two iambs and two anapaests. *See* LOGOPOEIA; MELOPOEIA.

phantom word A word that exists through the error of scribe, printer or lexicographer, or merely through some corruptive influence. Examples are: *willy-nilly* for *will he? nill he?*; *whatnot*; *dacious* for *audacious*; *obstropolous* for *obstreperous*; *brecksus* for *breakfast*. *Bacon and eggs* and *ham and eggs* are inclined to appear on European menus as *bekendecks* and *hemenex*, and in other variations. The OED Supplement has a list of such words. *See* GHOSTWORD.

phatic language *Phatic* derives from Greek *phasis*, 'utterance'. A term in linguistics which derives from the phrase 'phatic communion' invented by the anthropologist Bronislaw Malinowski (1884–1942). It was applied to language used for establishing an atmosphere and the communication of feelings rather than of ideas, and of logical and rational thoughts. Phatic words and phrases have been called 'idiot salutations'; and, when they generate to a form of dialogue, 'two-stroke conversations'. Exchanges about the state of the weather and a person's health fall into this category. It seems that the term may also be applied to the kind of noises that a mother makes to her baby, a lover to his mistress and a master to his dog.

phenomenology (Gk *phenomena*, 'things appearing' + *logos*, 'knowledge') A method of philosophical inquiry which lays stress on the perceiver's vital and central role in determining meaning. It derives from the thinking of Edmund Husserl (1859–1938), the German philosopher. In his view the proper object of philosophical inquiry is not the objects in the world that are perceivable through the senses but, rather, the *a priori* contents of our consciousness. Thus, the method demands a close inspection of mental and intellectual states and processes. Using this method, he believed, makes it possible to reveal the underlying nature of consciousness and phenomena, and to do so in an *a*temporal and *a*historical way – the point being to establish a trans-subjective theory of understanding. The implication is that an individual human mind is the centre and origin of meaning. As far as literature and literary theory are concerned, the phenomenologist's critical approach involves an entry to and investigation of the underlying nature and essence of a work of literature under scrutiny and thus a kind of access to the author's consciousness.

A different – and perhaps more 'vulgar' – version of the phenomenological approach is the exploration of the unique personality behind a work of literature. In order to do this the phenomenological critic needs to empty his or her mind of all preconceptions and presuppositions about the author and the text he or she is to study. Having done this, the critic is or ought to be in a highly receptive and sensitive state, a state which may enable him or her to share the mode of consciousness of the author. This state of mind has been described as 'consciousness of the consciousness of another'. It is probably doubtful if any critic could actually bring about such a state of mind. With the best will and intentions in the world the consciousness of the critic would, sooner or later, intervene.

The influence of phenomenology has been widespread since Husserl put forward his theories in 1900 and thereafter. Concepts of phenomenology were developed by Martin Heidegger in Germany and by Maurice Merleau-Ponty and, in turn, by Hans-Georg Gadamer. The Polish theorist Roman Ingarden developed Husserl's ideas in *The Literary Work of Art* (1931, trans.

1973) and in *The Cognition of the Literary Work* of Art (1937, trans. 1973). Important German critics affected by Ingarden are Wolfgang Iser and Hans Robert Jauss. The influence is especially clear in Iser's reader-response theory (*q.v.*) and Jauss's reception theory (*q.v.*). The term 'phenomenological criticism' has also been applied to the theory and practice of the Geneva School of critics. The long-term effects of the various theories are also evident in poststructuralism (*q.v.*). *See* HERMENEUTICS.

philippic A denunciation in speech or writing and couched in vituperative language. The term derives from Demosthenes's orations in denunciation of Philip of Macedon. *See* DIATRIBE; INVECTIVE.

Philistine The Philistines were an alien and aggressive tribe who inhabited the southern coast of Palestine. From there they continually raided the Israelites. The term *Philister* was applied by German students to a person who was a 'townsman' in the sense that he was not a member of the university. From this probably derives the notion that a Philistine is a person devoted to money, material objects, the commonplace, the prosaic and the uncultured. He has little concern for art (of any kind), beauty or the nobler aspirations and achievements of mankind. Matthew Arnold, in his last lecture as Professor of Poetry at Oxford (1867), criticized those whom he regarded as the Philistines of England – namely the bourgeois classes who accepted wealth as the measure of greatness. Arnold argued that culture 'helps us by means of its spiritual standard of perfection, to regard wealth as but machinery . . . If it were not for this purging effect wrought upon our minds by culture, the whole world, the future as well as the present, would inevitably belong to the Philistines.' *See* AESTHETICISM; DECADENCE.

philology (Gk 'love of learning') Primarily refers to the study of the historical development of languages over time or of shared structural features between languages across cultures. In this original usage, philology might be considered synonymous with historical or comparative linguistics (*q.v.*). More broadly, this term may be taken to mean the close and systematic analysis of literary texts in general.

In the 19th c., philology was most closely associated with German scholarship which endeavoured to combine cultural and linguistic studies. The underpinning idea driving this movement was the conviction that language itself might provide the means to excavate the sediments of national histories and cultures. In Britain, the Philological Society was set up in 1842 to 'investigate and promote the study and knowledge of the structure, the affinities, and the history of languages'. This impulse found its ultimate expression in the collaborative scholarship behind *The New English Dictionary on Historical Principles* (1884–1928), now known as the *Oxford English Dictionary*.

In the 20th c., emphasis moved from the study of linguistic changes over time to the analysis of linguistic properties and states regardless of historical contingencies. In Saussure's distinction, a diachronic (*q.v.*) approach was supplanted by a synchronic (*q.v.*) one. The idea of language as a self-sufficient system has been enormously influential. In literary criticism, Erich Auerbach's comparative study *Mimesis: The Representation of Reality in Western Literature* (1946) is one example of criticism in the philological tradition. *See also* LINGUISTICS; SEMANTICS; SEMIOTICS; STYLISTICS.

Philosophes, les Broadly speaking, men of letters, philosophers, writers, scientists *et al.* of 18th c. France. Though many of them differed considerably in their individual attitudes and convictions, they were united in their belief and trust in the power and value of reason. They were also united in their antagonism to outmoded creeds, superstitions and institutions. Many distinguished writers and intellectuals were numbered among them, including: Montesquieu, Voltaire, Diderot, Rousseau, Buffon, Condillac, Turgot, Condorcet, d'Alembert, Morellet, d'Holbach, Marmontel, Helvétius and Raynal. Their *magnum opus* was the *Encyclopédie* (1751–66). They were frequently attacked by different and powerful groups, particularly the Jansenists and Jesuits (who themselves were in a state of dispute). The overall influence of their independence of mind and rebellious spirit was immeasurable and their attitudes and doctrines did much to bring about the Revolution.

phoneme (Gk 'speech sound') The smallest significant unit in the sound system of a language. For example, in English 't' and 'd' are separate phonemes; 'c' and 'k' may be the same or different (compare *cider, caulk, kirk*); 'c' and 's' may be the same or different (compare *sump, cork* and *civet*); 'ph' and 'f' in English are the same.

phonocentrism The word *phonocentric* means 'centred on sound/speech'; hence, phonocentrism denotes 'sound centring' or 'sound-centredness'. Jacques Derrida (1930–2004), the French philosopher, uses the term 'logocentrism' (*q.v.*) to describe all forms of thought which are premised on some version of the 'logos' or immediate coincidence of language and reality. 'Phonocentrism' is a subcategory of logocentrism, indicating an immediate coincidence of sound and meaning and the privileging of speech (where meaning is supposedly immediate) over writing. Derrida counters this traditional precedence (expressed archetypally by Plato) with the idea of language as a kind of writing – what he calls 'archi-écriture'. This is his way of emphasizing that philosophy is only a kind of writing, and is a 'quasi-science' of language. The basic point is that for Derrida language is an endlessly relational network and philosophy or science therefore can make no pretensions to being anything more than 'a kind of writing'. *See also* GRAMMATOLOGY.

picaresque novel (Sp *pícaro*, 'rogue') It tells the life of a knave or picaroon who is the servant of several masters. Through his experience this picaroon satirizes the society in which he lives. The picaresque novel originated in 16th c. Spain, the earliest example being the anonymous *Lazarillo de Tormes* (1553). The two most famous Spanish authors of picaresque novels were Mateo Alemán, who wrote *Guzmán de Alfarache* (1599–1604), and Francisco Quevedo, who wrote *La vida del Buscón* (1626). Both books were widely read in Europe. Other picaresque novels included Thomas Nashe's *The Unfortunate Traveller* (1594), Lesage's *Gil Blas* (1715), Defoe's *Moll Flanders*

(1722), Fielding's *Jonathan Wild* (1743) and Smollett's *Roderick Random* (1748). A more recent example is Thomas Mann's unfinished *Confessions of Felix Krull* (1954). The German term for this kind of story is *Räuberroman*.

picaroon *See* PICARESQUE NOVEL.

Piccolo Teatro, Milan Opened in 1947, the Piccolo was the first Italian theatre to be supported by public funds. For forty years it had continual success under the direction of Giorgio Strehler (1921–97) and achieved an international reputation with a company which has visited over thirty countries. It has been particularly well known for many notable productions of Brecht's plays.

picturesque During the 18th c. there was a steadily increasing interest in rural scenery, and in the 'scenic'. This interest was closely connected with landscape gardening (by, for example, William Kent, 'Capability' Brown and Humphry Repton) and landscape in general, and with a growing amount of travel in Britain and abroad (it is noticeable that travel books, *q.v.*, begin to proliferate in the 18th c.). In due course the Grand Tour (*q.v.*) was also to have an influence on peoples' sensibilities and responses. Artists and writers looked at scenery in new and different ways. The work of three painters in particular became very popular in Britain: namely, Nicolas Poussin (1594–1665), Claude Lorrain (1600–82) and Salvator Rosa (1615–73). Landscape gardeners copied scenes from Claude's compositions. The poet Thomas Gray (1716–71) carried what was called a 'Claude glass', a kind of mirror, convex and blackened, which gave the impression of a 'Claudian' view. Writers re-experienced the natural order through the individual vision of these painters and others. Almost a case of visual defamiliarization (*q.v.*). They began to describe scenery in detail, and the wilder, more remote and unspoilt it was (e.g. Wales, the Lake District), the better they like it. Thus there developed what may be called a 'cult of the picturesque'. Gardens were landscaped to look 'wild' and 'natural', fake ruins were built to adorn them, the grander and more awe-inspiring aspects of the natural order were admired and extolled. It was a matter of aesthetic taste and fashion of which people became connoisseurs, or affected to be connoisseurs. This cult is discernible early in the 18th c. in, for instance, Addison's *Remarks on Several Parts of Italy* (1705) and Pope's *Eloisa to Abelard* (1717). In the course of the 18th c. and early in the 19th c. the cult produced a certain amount of literature of interest. For example, William Mason's poem *The English Garden* (1771–81), Thomas Gray's travel journal (1775), Richard Payne Knight's *The Landscape: A Didactic Poem* (1794), and, of course, the delightful topographical poetry (*q.v.*) of the period which relished the rural scene. There were various essays on the matter, too, among them William Gilpin's *Three Essays: On Picturesque Beauty; On Picturesque Travel; On Sketching Landscape* (1792) and Sir Uvedale Price's *Essay on the Picturesque* (1794). The Gothic novelists went in for descriptions of picturesque scenery and their influence becomes discernible in Walter Scott's novels. Eventually there came those who made fun of it and satirized it. For instance, Jane Austen in *Mansfield Park* (1814), Peacock in *Headlong Hall* (1816) and William Combe in *The Tour of Dr Syntax in Search of the Picturesque* (1809). The cult of the picturesque is related to romanticism and also to the concept of the sublime (*q.v.*). *See also* GOTHIC NOVEL/FICTION.

pièce à thèse *See* THESIS PLAY.

pièce bien faite *See* WELL-MADE PLAY.

pièces noires *See* BLACK COMEDY.

pillow book A form of commonplace book (*q.v.*) which appears to have originated in Japan. It is a compilation of notes, jottings, 'occasional' writings; the sort of thing that might go into an extended diary (*q.v.*) or journal. A classic example, and one of the earliest extant, is *The Pillow Book of Sei Shōnagon*, which is titled *Makura no Sōshi* ('notes of the pillow') and was composed c. 1000. Sei Shōnagon was a lady-in-waiting to the Empress Sadako during the last decade of the 10th c. The story of its origin is that when a bundle of unused notebooks was brought to the Empress she wondered what to do with them. The lady-in-waiting suggested that she should have them and make them into a pillow. That may have meant putting them into the drawers of a wooden pillow. She subsequently filled the notebooks with random facts and jottings, lists and so forth. This early pillow book is the forerunner of a traditional Japanese genre called *zuihitsu* ('occasional writings') which still exists.

pillow dictionary A euphemism (*q.v.*) for a tutor in a foreign language or languages who, as the term implies, gives tuition in bed. A term more commonly used by men of women than vice versa. Those who practise hypnopaedic techniques use a different kind of dictionary. *See also* LEXICON; PILLOW BOOK.

Pindaric ode *See* ODE.

p'ing hua A Chinese term for a type of popular tale or yarn (*qq.v.*) which is dominated by the narrator's presence and by the use of colloquial and idiomatic language. The *p'ing hua* tends to be fantastic in content but is realistic in tone. It is akin to the Russian *skaz* and to the tall story (*qq.v.*).

pivot word A word or phrase which has the effect of modifying what precedes or follows, especially in repetition. A recent example is the use of the word 'something' by Jon Silkin in *Death of a Son (who died in a mental hospital aged one)*. The poem begins:

> Something has ceased to come along with me.
> Something like a person: something very like one.
> And there was no nobility in it
> Or anything like that.

piyyut A form of Hebrew liturgical poem especially written to celebrate a festival. They sometimes take an acrostic (*q.v.*) form. They were common between the 3rd and 7th c. Seven are known to have been written by the Hebrew religious poet Yose ben Yose.

plagiarism (L *plagiarius*, 'kidnapper, seducer, literary thief') Hence *plagiary*, the noun; and *plagiarize*, the verb. C. T. Onions defined plagiarism as 'wrongful appropriation and publication as one's own'. Much plagiarism has been the lifting, filching or pirating of other people's works; a very common practice among dramatists during the Elizabethan period when hack writers blatantly stole the plays of others and presented them as their own. These days, with the proliferation of online media, plagiarism offences have become difficult to determine and are often referred to experts in intellectual property law. The institutions of academe and journalism lay out severe penalties for plagiarism, ranging from suspension to expulsion.

plaint A lament (*q.v.*) in verse. *See* COMPLAINT; DIRGE; ELEGY; PLANH.

plaisir/jouissance Terms used with a special signification by Roland Barthes in his book *Le Plaisir du texte* (1973), a discussion of the *lisible/scriptible* or readerly/writerly (*q.v.*) text. The writerly text, he opines, offers two kinds of enjoyment: *plaisir*, 'pleasure'; and *jouissance*, 'bliss'. *Jouissance* carries connotations of ecstasy and sexual delight, and Barthes offers an aesthetics based on the pleasure of the body. To clarify his distinction he suggests that the *plaisir* taken in a text comes through the more or less straightforward processes of reading, while the *jouissance*, a heightened form of pleasure, derives from a sense of interruption, a 'breakdown' or gap, where, perhaps, something unorthodox or unexpected occurs. The comforts of *plaisir* are compatible with texts which are *lisible*; while the comforts and surprises of *jouissance* arise from the *scriptible*. He elaborates with a kind of erotic analogy, suggesting that the focus of erotic pleasure is the place where naked flesh meets a garment, where 'the garment gapes'. This is analogous to *jouissance*. However, he also suggests that the 'text of bliss' may impose a 'state of loss'; it is a text that discomforts and 'unsettles the reader's historical, cultural, psychological assumptions, the consistency of his tastes, values, memories, brings to a crisis his relation with language'.

planh A funeral lament (*q.v.*) in Old Provençal. Some forty-odd are believed to be extant. Most of them are laments for the death of some distinguished person, a patron or patroness. *See* COMPLAINT; DIRGE; ELEGY.

plateresco (Sp *platero*, 'silversmith') Thus, an ornamental, 'filigreed' style of writing in Spanish 16th c. romances. The English version is *plateresque*, 'silversmith-like'. Primarily an architectural term, and applied to an ornate style of architecture popular in Spain during the 16th c. *See also* BAROQUE; GONGORISM.

platitude A dull, commonplace statement. A trite and obvious remark. Many proverbial expressions and idioms have become platitudes. For example: 'You cannot have your cake and eat it.'

Platonism Paradoxically, Platonism has been a continual, pervasive and powerful influence on poets and poetry (and other forms of literature) down the ages. 'Paradoxically' because Plato would not 'allow' most forms of poetry in his *Republic*. The point is made uncompromisingly clear towards the end of Book X: 'But you will know that the only poetry that ought to be allowed in a state is praise to the gods and paeans to virtuous men; as soon as you go beyond that and admit lyric or epic poetry, then pleasure and pain become your rulers instead of the law and the principles that are commonly accepted as best.' However, Plato believed that poetry might serve the community by helping to educate it, and poetry which praised the gods and good men would show people who and what they should emulate. The didactic virtues of poetry were invoked in late Classical and medieval times to defend the art against those who objected to it on moral grounds. During the Renaissance (*q.v.*) period such a Platonic idea influenced the belief that the poet had a special role as a kind of 'celebrant' of nationalism. Much epic (*q.v.*) in the Renaissance is national epic. For example, Camoëns in *Os Lusiadas* composed a kind of historical manifesto of Portuguese nationalism, and Camoëns would have had a passport to the Republic because he sang the praises of noble men.

Plato saw the world as an imperfect imitation of a divine ideal, a shadowy and even distorted simulacrum of a heavenly prototype. It followed that the poet imitated this (because he imitated nature) and thus his work was merely an imitation of an imitation. As such, in the Platonic view, poetry could not arrive at truth. Aristotle attempted to deal with this problem in *Poetics* and advanced the theory that poetry did indeed convey the truth by a form of acceptable imitation or feigning. Neoplatonic philosophers (the most distinguished was Plotinus, 3rd c.) thought that poetry was the most estimable form of imitation because it 'copied' not nature but a divine archetype. Such theories had much influence at the Renaissance and during the Romantic period (*q.v.*).

Plato, like Homer, also claimed that the poet was an inspired person. The idea of inspiration (*q.v.*) found great favour in later ages and there developed the belief that the poet was different from ordinary mortals; that the Muse had visited him; that he had vatic powers; that, in short, in the creation of poetry, he was in an exalted state as the result of divine insufflation. The image of the poet as visionary and prophet (even, according to Shelley, as an unacknowledged legislator) had a considerable vogue during the Romantic period.

Many of Plato's works (especially *Symposium*, *Timaeus*, *Parmenides* and the *Republic*) also include myths, symbols and images through whose similitudes (*q.v.*) he sought to express his ideas of Truth, Beauty and the Good, all of which, in his view, were One: a form of aesthetic and philosophic Trinity. These concepts were a powerful influence from the early Middle Ages onwards, and especially during the Renaissance when the influence of Platonism was at its greatest, thanks in great measure to Marsilio Ficino's Latin translation of Plato's works towards the end of the 15th c. and his attempted 'reconciliation' of Platonic and Christian philosophy in *Theologia Platonica*. Indeed, it was Ficino who used the term *Amor Platonicus* more or less synonymously with *Amor Socraticus* to denote spiritual love. Platonic love has become the best-known idea or aspect of Platonism, and the ideal of Platonic love has influenced Western literature and life to such an extent that the most unlettered person may be presumed to have some acquaintance with it. In its origin (and the source is Plato's *Symposium*) it was the contemplation of the idea of perfect and absolute beauty; separate, simple and infinite beauty. By contrast, terrestrial beauty was a shadowy reflection of it. The chief Neoplatonist philosophers were Plotinus, Porphyry, Proclus and Hypatia; they combined Platonic ideas with oriental mysticism and drew on the theory of Platonic love, and influenced Christian philosophy through St Augustine. Renaissance thinkers developed it into a theory that physical beauty was an outward expression of the inward grace and spiritual beauty of the soul, and this spiritual radiance was an extension of the effulgent beauty of God Himself. The Platonic lover therefore paid devotion and adoration to a physical beauty of his mistress only in so far as that beauty reflected her soul. From earthly and physical desire he aspired to the contemplation of the beatific vision. Such an attitude informed much lyric and love poetry of the late Middle Ages and during the Renaissance. Spenser elaborated the idea in his *Four Hymns*. There is a notable exposition in the fourth book of Castiglione's *Il Libro del Cortegiano* (The Book of the Courtier; 1528).

During the Romantic period there was a marked revival of interest in the concept of Platonic love, and a great interest in Platonism in general. Blake, Wordsworth, Shelley and Hölderlin especially were strongly influenced by it. This is particularly noticeable in Shelley's *Epipsychidion* and Wordsworth's *Intimations of Immortality*.

Between the end of the 16th c. and the beginning of the Romantic period Platonism as a force and influence is not much marked in Western thought and literature. However, mention should be made of the Cambridge Platonists – a group of philosophers who flourished during the middle of the 17th c. and whose headquarters were at Cambridge University. The main members of the group were Ralph Cudworth, Henry More, John Smith and Nathanael Culverwel. This group reacted against Puritan dogmatism and against the materialistic philosophies of Hobbes and Descartes. They were idealists who believed in the essentially spiritual constitution of the world. Henry More wrote some philosophical poetry which propounded some of the ideas of the group.

Platonism has continued to be a strong fertilizing influence in the minds of various poets, especially Coleridge, Rilke, Yeats and Wallace Stevens. There can be little doubt that Benjamin Jowett's translations of Plato (1871) did much to encourage the study of Platonism throughout the English-speaking world, though nowadays he has come under criticism for inaccuracy and pseudo-archaic English.

Plato's manifold influences have pervaded much political and utopian (*see* UTOPIA) thinking. Modern Fascism and Marxist Communism would have been repugnant to Plato, but his *Republic* depicts a prototypical totalitarian state and has had incalculable influence.

The form in which he chose to express many of his ideas was the dialogue (*q.v.*), of which there have been many celebrated examples since. We should also note the continual influence he has had on modes of thinking, methods of teaching and education in general.

play A dramatic work designed to be presented on a stage (or in a television studio) and performed by actors and actresses. An exception is a closet play (*q.v.*). *See* CHRONICLE PLAY; COMEDY; COMEDY OF MANNERS; HIGH COMEDY; LOW COMEDY; MIRACLE PLAY; MORALITY PLAY; MYSTERY PLAY; PASSION PLAY; THESIS PLAY; TRAGEDY; WELL-MADE PLAY.

Pléiade A group of 16th c. French poets named after the constellation of the seven daughters of Atlas. Ronsard originated the term in 1556. Until that time he had used the term *Brigade*. He adopted *Pléiade* from the Alexandrine group of poets who had borne that name. Membership of the group varied over the years but never exceeded seven. In 1556, besides Ronsard, it included Joachim du Bellay, Pontus de Thiard, Jean-Antoine de Baïf, Jacques Pelletier, Etienne Jodelle and Rémy Belleau. They were innovators who wished to abandon the medieval poetic tradition, and their innovations were based on a study of Greek and Latin poetry. They established the sonnet, the ode and the alexandrine (*qq.v.*) in France. Their theories were expounded in du Bellay's *Deffense et Illustration de la langue françoise* (1549), in Ronsard's preface to his *Odes* (1550) and in his *Abrégé de l'art poétique* (1565).

pleonasm (Gk 'superfluity') Redundant use of words. It may be deliberate but is usually involuntary. A common fault in much writing. For example: 'In this day and age', instead of 'now', 'today' or 'nowadays'. *See* PERIPHRASIS; POETIC DICTION; TAUTOLOGY.

pliego suelto (Sp 'loose sheet') Sheets of paper used for printing Spanish ballads from early in the 16th c. Also known as *literatura de cordel* ('writings hanging from a string') because vendors strung the broadsheets from cords in stationers' shops or tents on market days. Collections of them formed *cancioneros* (*q.v.*), nowadays normally in book form. The first (undated) *cancionero de romances* was published in Antwerp; presumably before 1550 – the date of the second. Followed by *romanceros* (*q.v.*), beginning in 1551 with Sepúlveda's. There were also *silvas de romances* and *rosas de romances*.

ploce (Gk 'plaited, woven') A figurative device in which the same word (or words) is repeated. It also denotes the complication of a dramatic plot. *See also* INCREMENTAL REPETITION.

plot The plan, design, scheme or pattern of events in a play, poem or work of fiction; and, further, the organization of incident and character in such a way as to induce curiosity and suspense (*q.v.*) in the spectator or reader. In the space/time continuum of plot the continual question operates in three tenses:

Why did that happen? Why is this happening? What is going to happen next – and why? (To which may be added: And – is *anything* going to happen?)

In *Poetics*, Aristotle includes plot as one of the six elements in tragedy (*q.v.*). For Aristotle it is the 'first principle' and 'the soul of a tragedy'. He calls plot 'the imitation of the action', as well as the arrangement of the incidents. He required a plot to be 'whole' (that is, to have a beginning, a middle and an end) and that it should have unity, namely 'imitate one action and that a whole, the structural union of the parts being such that, if any one of them is displaced or removed, the whole will be disjointed and disturbed.'

This is the ideal, well-knit plot which Aristotle distinguished from the episodic plot in which the acts succeed one another 'without probable or necessary sequence', and which he thought was inferior. Aristotle also distinguished between simple and complex plots: in the simple the change of fortune occurs without peripeteia (*q.v.*) and without anagnorisis (*q.v.*), whereas in the complex there is one or the other or both. Aristotle also emphasized the importance of plot as opposed to character.

His views will be adequate for some Greek tragedy, some Elizabethan and Jacobean tragedy and some French Classical tragedy, and elements of the application of Aristotle's theories can be found in many plays – and novels.

However, a plot has come to denote something much more flexible than that envisaged by Aristotle. The decline of tragedy, the rise of comedy, the development of the novel – all have contributed to a much looser conception and many varied theories.

A more homely approach than Aristotle's is that of E. M. Forster. In *Aspects of the Novel* (1927) he provided a simple but very serviceable description of plot: 'We have defined a story as a narrative of events arranged in their time-sequence. A plot is also a narrative of events, the emphasis falling on causality. "The king died and the queen died," is a story. "The king died and then the queen died of grief," is a plot. The time-sequence is preserved, but the sense of causality overshadows it. Or again: "The queen died, no one knew why, until it was discovered that it was through grief at the death of the king." This is a plot with a mystery in it, a form capable of high development. It suspends the time-sequence, it moves as far away from the story as its limitations will allow.'

Such a description will suffice to cover a very large number of plots, especially those in which causality among episodes is explicit or implied. It will certainly cover an enormous number of novels. On the other hand no theory or definition of plot can now cover adequately the variety of works by, say, Joyce, Bulgakov, Graham Greene, Ivy Compton-Burnett, Heinrich Böll, Michel Butor, William Burroughs, Robbe-Grillet and Len Deighton – to take a handful of very different writers at random; or, for that matter, Kafka, Arnold Bennett, Malcolm Lowry, Ivo Andrić, Eric Ambler, Nabokov, Saul Bellow, Grass, Bykov, Claude Simon and V. S. Naipaul. *See* SUBPLOT.

Plough Monday play, the   In English folk-festivals Plough Monday is the Monday after Twelfth Night. The play, which is related to the Mumming (or

St George) Play, survives in a few fragmentary texts from the East Midlands. The play differs from the Mumming Play in several respects. The characters are Tom the Fool, a Recruiting Sergeant, a Ribboner or Recruit, three farm servants, a Doctor and Beelzebub; plus two women, the Young Lady and old Dame Jane. The play (like the St George play) in all probability symbolizes the death and resurrection of the year and may well be the survival of a fertility rite. *See also* MUMMING PLAY; PACE-EGGING PLAY; REVESBY PLAY.

pluralist criticism This entails a critical approach to literature by which a text is studied with an open mind and thus without any necessary or apparent commitment to an ideological position or stance. Most importantly it expresses the willingness to hold more than one position. Structuralist critics have expressed disapproval of this approach. Many Marxist critics – who tend to be committed to a position – would also disapprove. *See* MARXIST CRITICISM; STRUCTURALISM.

plurisignation A term (it means, literally, several or many signs or marks) used by Wheelwright in *The Burning Fountain* (1954) to indicate that a word, a passage or a whole work may have various levels and meanings of what is described as 'semantic thrust'. This instrument of critical jargon can be useful in the work of close analysis. *See* ALLEGORY; ALLUSION; AMBIGUITY; FOUR LEVELS OF MEANING.

poem (Gk *poiēma*, 'something made, created'. Thus, a work of art) A composition, a work of verse, which may be in rhyme (*q.v.*) or may be blank verse (*q.v.*) or a combination of the two. Or it may depend on having a fixed number of syllables, like the *haiku* (*q.v.*).

In the final analysis what makes a poem different from any other kind of composition is a species of magic, the secret to which lies in the way the words lean upon each other, are linked and interlocked in sense and rhythm, and thus elicit from each other's syllables a kind of tune whose beat and melody varies subtly and which is different from that of prose (*q.v.*) – 'the other harmony'. *See also* MAKER; POESIS; POETRY.

poëme A genre invented by Alfred de Vigny. In 1837 he defined his *poëmes*, in a preface, as compositions in which philosophic thought is presented under an epic (*q.v.*) or dramatic form. Thus, *poëmes philosophiques*.

poesis (Gk *poiēsis*, from *poiein*, 'to make') Thus poesis denotes 'making' in general, but in particular the making of poetry. The word came into the English language as 'poesie' in the 14th c. Later in that century the word 'poetrie' (from L *poetria*) was also introduced. They were frequently used synonymously. Eventually *poetry* supplanted *poesy*. The latter produced *posy*, 'a motto verse'. *See* MAKER; POEM.

poetaster A hack poet; an inferior versifier. The word is a combination of 'poet' and '-aster'; *aster* being a suffix of substantives and adjectives expressing an incomplete resemblance. The word is always derogatory. Its usage dates from the 16th c.

poète maudit   A phrase which became current as a result of Verlaine's collection of essays *Les Poètes maudits* (1884, 1888). These were brief critical and biographical studies of six poets who, in his view, were insufficiently appreciated and understood. They were: Marceline Desbordes-Valmore (1786–1859), Villiers de l'Isle-Adam (1838–89), Stéphane Mallarmé (1842–98), Tristan Corbière (1845–75), Arthur Rimbaud (1854–91) and 'Pauvre Lelian', Paul Verlaine's anagram of his own name. The phrase 'poètes maudits' may be a reference to Baudelaire's *Bénédiction*, the first poem in *Les Fleurs du mal* (1857). *See also* TEL QUEL SCHOOL.

poetic contests   There are two basic kinds: (a) A formal competition in which poets enter and compete for a prize. This form of competition goes back to the festivals in Athens. In the Middle Ages there were comparable contests, mostly in France at Valenciennes, Arras, Douai, Tournai, Lille, Rouen and Dieppe. In Germany, from the 14th to the 16th c., the Meistersinger guilds held singing contests. The Academy of the Jocs Florals, which originated in Toulouse in the 14th c., still has festivals. Probably the best known of all is the National Eisteddfod (*q.v.*) of Wales, which dates at least from the 13th c. and is still held annually. (b) An imaginary debate or contest in a play or poem. An early example is to be found in Aristophanes's *Frogs*, in which Aeschylus and Euripides argue the merits of their poetry. The device, if such it is, occurs in Latin, Provençal, OF and ME works. One of the most interesting examples of a poetic contest in Europe is to be witnessed at Nuoro in central Sardinia where, at midsummer or later, shepherds compete with one another in the improvisation of poems in dialect. For some time before the final there have been eliminating contests. *See also* BARD; DÉBAT; DIALOGUE; FLYTING; LAUDA; PARTIMEN; PUY; TENSON.

poetic contractions   *See* SYNAERESIS; SYNCOPE.

poetic diction   In general, diction denotes the vocabulary used by a writer. Poetic diction usually refers to that rather particular kind of language and artificial arrangement employed by many poets in the 18th c. who were guided by the theory and practice of neoclassicism (*q.v.*). Thomas Gray observed that 'the language of the age is never the language of poetry', and by this he meant that language must be selected and adapted according to its appropriateness for the work in hand. This is the principle of decorum (*q.v.*). Satire, for instance, a favoured mode of expression in the 18th c., required an urbane, cultivated and somewhat formal language; the style and diction of a gentleman. Pope was the supreme exponent of this. An ode (*q.v.*), on the other hand, or a pastoral (*q.v.*) required a more specialized diction. Probably the most notable characteristic of poetic diction in the 18th c. was periphrasis (*q.v.*) for the sake of elegance and politeness. Stock examples are: 'finny tribe' for 'fish'; 'feathered breed' for 'birds'; 'wingy swarm' for 'bees'; and 'foodful brine' for 'sea'. Taken to extremes this kind of expression could become absurd, a mere contortion. Excessive use of Latinism (*q.v.*) in 18th c. poetic diction *did* on occasion become absurd, as in these examples: 'purple groves pomaceous' for 'orchards' and 'rich saponaceous loam' for 'good soil'. Other features of neoclassical poetic diction were archaism (*q.v.*) and frequent use of personification (*q.v.*).

At its best the judicious use of poetic diction could produce agreeable results, as in these lines from Gray's *Ode on a Distant Prospect of Eton College* (1747):

> Say, Father Thames, for thou hast seen
> Full many a sprightly race
> Disporting on thy margent green
> The paths of pleasure trace;
> Who foremost now delight to cleave
> With pliant arm thy glassy wave?
> To captive linnet which enthrall?
> Why idle progeny succeed
> To chase the rolling circle's speed,
> Or urge the flying ball?

At the turn of the century there set in a strong reaction against poetic diction. This was expressed with vigour by Wordsworth, in his preface to the second edition of the *Lyrical Ballads* (1800). He was for the language of the common man, for everyday colloquial speech in poetry, what Shakespeare meant by 'russet yeas and honest kersey noes'; but even Wordsworth found this difficult to achieve in practice, and the problem of what language is appropriate for poetry and what not has exercised writers ever since Wordsworth and Coleridge addressed themselves to the matter. Throughout the 19th c. we find many poets trying to work out a mode and idiom and, often enough, failing to develop an individual one of their own. Much verse written in that age was laboured and stilted, encumbered by archaism and strange syntax. Gerard Manley Hopkins tried to break free of these clogs and, in his highly idiosyncratic fashion, proved a profoundly influential innovator. But even as late as the 1920s there were poets who had still not solved the problem of how to use colloquial language.

T. S. Eliot asked for an 'easy commerce of the old and new',

> The common word exact without vulgarity,
> The formal word precise but not pedantic

And Wallace Stevens introduced the idea of the 'anti-poetic' as a counter to the concept that there had to be something special about the language of poetry.

It may be argued that any word is a suitable tool for the poet, and that its suitability will depend on how it is used. But this immediately raises the difficulty of technical language, jargon (*q.v.*) and obscure words. *See also* AUREATE LANGUAGE.

poetic justice A term invented by Thomas Rymer in *Tragedies of the Last Age Considered* (1678) to convey the idea that the evil are punished appropriately and the good rewarded as they should be. It was a widely held belief that literature should reflect a moral point of view and that a work of literature should reward the virtuous and punish the wicked. Towards the end of the 17th c. it was going out of fashion. Corneille rejected it; so, later, did Addison. However, it seems that many people still think a work of literature should show *some* sense of justice: at its simplest, that the villain should get his deserts.

poetic licence The liberty allowed to the poet to wrest the language according to his needs in the use of figurative speech, archaism (*q.v.*), rhyme (*q.v.*), strange syntax (*q.v.*), etc. But this liberty depends on the end justifying the means. Dryden defined it as 'the liberty which poets have assumed to themselves in all ages, of speaking things in verse, which are beyond the severity of prose'.

poetic prose Prose (*q.v.*) which approximates to verse in the use of rhythm, perhaps even a kind of meter (*q.v.*), in the elaborate and ornate use of language, and especially in the use of figurative devices like onomatopoeia, assonance and metaphor (*qq.v.*). Poetic prose is usually employed in short works or in brief passages in longer works in order to achieve a specific effect and to raise the 'emotional temperature'. Many writers have attempted it. For example: Lyly, Sir Thomas Browne, Jeremy Taylor, de Quincey, Lautréamont, Melville, Rimbaud, Oscar Wilde, James Joyce, Virginia Woolf, William Faulkner and Lawrence Durrell. There are some examples of it in the narrator's part in Dylan Thomas's radio play *Under Milk Wood* (1954). *See also* EUPHUISM; GONGORISM; POLYPHONIC PROSE; PROSE POEM; PURPLE PASSAGE.

poetics Traditionally, the term refers to the theory of poetry, in particular emphasizing principles of composition and structure, with the *Poetics* of Aristotle (384–322 BC) being the earliest, most well-known, and most influential formulation. Since then, various poets, critics and writers have expounded upon the topic, their treatises often marking a specific literary movement or philosophical trend. Notable examples in the history of poetics include Horace's *Ars Poetica* (18 BC); Longinus's *On the Sublime* (1st / 3rd c.); Sir Philip Sidney's *Defence of Poesie* (1595); Alexander Pope's *An Essay on Criticism* (1711); and William Wordsworth's 'Preface' to his *Lyrical Ballads* (1801, 1802). The term has been expanded in contemporary theory to comprehend the application of a hermeneutical aesthetics to various cultural practices, political discourses and social phenomena, as in Peter Stallybrass's *The Politics and Poetics of Transgression* (1986) and Morris Meyer's *The Politics and Poetics of Camp* (1993).

poetischer Realismus (G 'poetic realism') This -ism, coined by Friedrich Schelling in 1802, is, somewhat surprisingly perhaps, peculiar to German literature. It is a rather vague term associated with, approximately, the period 1840–80 and denoting narrative poetry of a plain and realistic kind, traditionalist in attitude and moral and humane in tone and feeling. The principal writers associated with poetic realism were: Annette von Droste-Hülshoff (1797–1848); Jeremias Gotthelf (1797–1854); Adalbert Stifter (1805–68); Otto Ludwig (1813–65); Theodor Storm (1817–88); Gottfried Keller (1819–90); Conrad Meyer (1825–98); and Wilhelm Raabe (1831–1910).

poet laureate The origin of the term lies in the myth of Apollo who tried to seize Daphne, whereupon she turned into a laurel tree. Apollo ordained that the laurels should be the prize for poets and victors. It is likely that the tradition of the court poet and professional entertainer is the forebear of the modern poet laureate, who is appointed by a government and expected to compose poems for state events and important occasions. On a more abstract level, the poet laureate is, ideally, a poetic representative of the spirit of his age. The epithet laureate was applied to a number of poets (e.g. Petrarch, Chaucer, Skelton, Ben Jonson, Davenant, and others) before the first official appointment was made, namely Dryden in 1668. Other notable poets laureate have been William Wordsworth (1843–50); Alfred Lord Tennyson (1850–92); Robert Bridges (1913–30), John Betjeman (1973–84) and Ted Hughes (1984–98). Recent American poet laureates have included Billy Collins (2001–3), Louise Glück (2003–4) and Philip Levine (2011–12).

poetry (MedL *poetria* based on Gk *poëtēs*, 'doer, creator') It is a comprehensive term which can be taken to cover any kind of metrical composition. However, it is usually employed with reservations, and often in contradistinction to verse. For example, we should describe Shakespeare's sonnets as poetry, and the wittily ingenious creations of Ogden Nash as verse; though both are *in* verse. We speak of 'light verse' rather than 'light poetry'. The implications are that poetry is a superior form of creation; not necessarily, therefore, more serious. Aristophanes, Chaucer, Ben Jonson, Donne, Marvell, Pope, Byron and Auden, to name a few, have all written witty and humorous poems.

Poets' Corner A part of the south transept of Westminster Abbey, London, which contains the tombs (or monuments) of a number of famous English poets: notably, Shakespeare, Edmund Spenser, Ben Jonson, Milton, Michael Drayton, Samuel Butler, Mrs Aphra Behn, John Gay, Lord Byron and W. H. Auden.

point of attack The moment in a play or story when the main action begins.

point of rest *See* PAUSE.

point of turning *See* CLIMAX.

polemic (Gk 'pertaining to war') A vigorous dispute. A controversy, especially in politics and religion. A famous example of a polemic is Milton's *Areopagitica* (1664). British polemicists of note are Richard Bentley, Jonathan Swift, Sydney Smith, Cardinal Newman, Bernard Shaw, Hilaire Belloc and G. K. Chesterton.

police procedural A subgenre of the detective story (*q.v.*), police procedurals deal realistically with crime from the point of view of the police and how they solve crimes and catch criminals. The central figure is a professional police officer. Until the advent of the police procedural, the police were often on the sidelines and were not infrequently depicted as cumbersome, inept and dull-witted (very nearly joke coppers in some instances), in contrast to the sagacious and quasi-omniscient amateur sleuth or detective whose greatest exemplar is Sherlock Holmes.

A move away from what was regarded as the classic type of detective story towards the police procedural took place in the late 1920s with the development of the private eye, an investigator of the 'hard-boiled school'. Raymond Chandler (1888–1959) and Dashiell Hammett (1894–1961) were the pioneers. Later came the stories of professional policemen using traditional police methods and resources. Laurence Treat's *V as in Victim* (1945) is generally regarded as the first American police procedural. The procedural is predominantly a British and American genre.

policier *See* CRIME FICTION.

politico-military thriller *See* THRILLER.

polyphonic prose A kind of poetic prose (*q.v.*) developed by Amy Lowell (1874–1925) and named by John Gould Fletcher (1886–1950). Amy Lowell got the idea from the *Ballades* (1886) of the French poet Paul Fort. Her most notable work is *Can Grande's Castle* (1918). Fletcher also used this style in *Breakers and Granite* (1921). This sort of prose has many of the attributes of verse: elaborate cadences and tuneful rhythms, assonance, alliteration and rhyme (*qq.v.*). *See also* FREE VERSE; PROSE POEM; VERS LIBRE.

polyptoton (Gk *poly*, 'many' + *ptosis*, 'a falling, fall') A rhetorical figure; a case or grammatical inflexion of any kind (e.g. of the adverb from the adjective). The idea is that one ending (e.g. nominative case) 'falls off' the end of the word to be replaced by another (e.g. accusative). So, the term has come to mean the repetition of a word in a different form. For instance: 'The live give life to the living'. A well-known example occurs in Shakespeare's *Troilus and Cressida* (I, i. 7–8):

> The Greeks are strong, and skilful to their strength,
> Fierce to their skill, and to their fierceness valiant;

polyrhythmic (Gk 'of many rhythms') Applied to a poem which has different metrical patterns. Pindar was well known for his polyrhythms.

polyschematic (Gk 'of many forms') In Classical prosody, varying combinations of the trochee and the choriambus (*qq.v.*).

polysyllabic rhyme *See* TRIPLE RHYME.

polysyndeton (Gk 'much compounded') The opposite of asyndeton (*q.v.*) and thus the repetition of conjunctions. Common in poetry and prose. The most frequently used conjunction in English is 'and'. Ernest Hemingway, for instance, was particularly addicted to this device in the use of 'and'. In the more extreme instances of his pseudo-biblical style it becomes the equivalent of a verbal tic. *See* HYPOTAXIS; PARATAXIS.

popular novel A loose term for a novel which has a wide readership; it often carries slightly pejorative connotations which suggest a middle- or low-brow 'audience' and imply that such a novel may not possess much literary merit. Many a best-seller, historical novel, novel of sensation, thriller and novel of adventure (*qq.v.*) has been so described. Some of the well-known British popular novelists have been: Warwick Deeping, Howard Spring, R. F. Delderfield, Dornford Yates, Angela Thirkell, Daphne du Maurier and Dennis Wheatley. Such a list might be greatly extended.

pornography (Gk 'writing of harlots') In all probability the term derives from the sign hung outside a brothel or whore's establishment.

A pornographer is a writer of pornography, and a *pornograph* is a work of fiction (in the broadest sense of that term) in which there is a considerable emphasis on sexual activity and which is, as a rule, written in such a way as to arouse sexual excitement. It may be funny, serious, bizarre or horrific, and, like any other kind of fiction, it may be well or badly written.

We may distinguish two basic sorts of pornography: (a) *erotica* (*q.v.*) – this concentrates on the physical aspects of sexual love and may describe them in great detail; (b) *exotica* – this concentrates on what are known as abnormal or deviationist sexual activities, and thus the emphasis is on sexual perversion. Common subjects for this kind of pornography are sadism, masochism, fetishism, transvestism, voyeurism (or scoptolagnia), narcissism, pederasty and necrophilia. Less common subjects are coprophilia, kleptolagnia, zoophilia and pyrolagnia.

Under phylum (a) we can put such classics as Ovid's *Ars Amatoria* (1st c. BC); Vatsayana's *Kama-Sutra* (4th c. AD) and other Indian love manuals; and Casanova's *Memoirs* (1826–38). Under phylum (b) Sade's *Justine* (1768!) and his *The 120 Days of Sodom* (1785), Sacher-Masoch's *Venus in Furs* (c. 1870) and *The Whippingham Papers* (late 1880s).

As society has become more 'permissive', so the conception of what is obscene (and pornographic) has become more flexible. There was a time when Joyce's *Ulysses* (first published in a limited and numbered edition in 1922), Lawrence's *Lady Chatterley's Lover* (1928) and Radclyffe Hall's *The Well of Loneliness* (1928) were regarded as obscene and pornographic. They provoked abusive and scandalized comment and legal action. Lawrence Durrell's *Black Book* (1936) was also thought pornographic; so, in 1955, was Nabokov's *Lolita*. Anyone who now described these books as pornographic would be regarded as loudly ridiculous.

In general the literature of pornography is vast, and some of it is of considerable antiquity. At the outset, however, we must distinguish between pornography and the pornographic. Actually it is only since the second half of the 18th c. that pornography has been produced on a large scale and much of this has been the pornography of *exotica*. Pornographic elements, however, are to be found much earlier and in many literatures.

There is plentiful material in the Old Testament on the subject of pornography in its original sense. There are pornographic elements in the plays of Aristophanes (especially *Lysistrata*), in *The Satyricon* of Petronius Arbiter (1st c. AD), in *The Letters of Alciphron* (c. 200 AD), the *Deipnosophistai* of Athenaus (2nd c. AD) and the *Dialogues* of Lucian (2nd c. AD). The *Milesian Tales* of Aristides of the 2nd c. BC were also believed to be pornographic, but they do not survive.

In Europe, after the fall of the Roman Empire, there appears to be no pornography and no literature with pornographic elements, though there is quite a lot of erotic poetry, until late in the Middle Ages. Then, we find bawdy or innocuously obscene elements in, for instance, the *fabliaux* (*q.v.*) and some of Chaucer's tales.

The first major work of modern pornography is Boccaccio's *Decameron* (c. 1349–51). Other works of note in the Renaissance period which have been described as pornographic are Poggio's *Facetiae* (15th c.), Rabelais's *Gargantua* (1534) and *Pantagruel* (1532), Cellini's *Memoirs* (begun in 1558), Aretino's *Ragionamenti* (1600), Brantôme's *Vies des dames galantes* (1665–6) and Beroalde de Verville's *Le Moyen de parvenir* (1610). There are also some instances of pornographic scenes in Elizabethan and Jacobean drama, and scurrilous or bawdy elements in much verse (e.g. Skelton's poetry).

The same could be said of some Restoration comedy (*q.v.*) and several 18th c. novels. From the 18th c. dates what many have regarded as the first masterpiece of English pornography, namely John Cleland's *Memoirs of a Woman of Pleasure*, or *Memoirs of the Life of Fanny Hill* (1748–9). After that, an increasing number of pornographic works were published. The full details and titles are to be found in H. S. Ashbee's *Notes on Curious and Uncommon Books* (1877–85) and the *Register Librorum Eroticorum* by R. S. Reade (1936). Some notable examples are *New Atlantis for the Year* (1762), *Useful Hints to Single Gentlemen respecting Marriage, Concubinage and Adultery. In Prose and Verse. With Notes Moral, Critical and Explanatory* (1792); *The Merry Muses of Caledonia, a Collection of Favourite Scots Songs, ancient and modern, selected for us of the Chrochallan Fencibles* (c. 1800); *The Voluptuarian Cabinet* (c. 1820).

Between 1820 and 1840, and then from c. 1860 onwards, a colossal amount of erotic pornography was published (much of it illustrated). Some notable examples are *The Bedfellows: or Young Misses' Manual* (1820); *The Adventures, Intrigues and Amours of a Lady's Maid* (1822); *The Modern Rake* (1824); *The Lustful Turk* (1828); *The Seducing Cardinale* (1830); *A Night in a Moorish Harem* by 'Lord George Herbert' (late 1890s); the works of Edward Sellon, one of the most famous English pornographers – particularly *The New Epicurean* (1865), *The Ups and Downs of Life* (1867) and *Letters from a Friend in Paris* (1874). To these should be added the anonymous *My Secret Life* (c. 1885), and *My Life and Loves* (1925–9) by Frank Harris.

Most of these could be placed in the category of *erotica* (*q.v.*). There are quite as many under *exotica*, or the pornography of perversion. Many are concerned with flagellation practices, incest and various forms of fetishism. Two celebrated names are always associated with this kind of pornography, namely the Marquis de Sade and Leopold von Sacher-Masoch, from whom derive the words *sadist* and *masochist*. Sade's principal works are *Justine* (1781); *The 120 Days of Sodom* (1785); *Aline and Valcour* (1788); *The Philosopher in the Boudoir* (1795); *Juliette* (1796); and *The Crimes of Love* (1800). Sacher-Masoch's *Venus in Furs* (c. 1870) is his masterpiece.

In the 20th and 21st c. so much pornographic literature of every kind has been published that there is no space to give an account of it. Innumerable works, especially novels, contain pornographic elements. Much of it is to be found in 'girlie' and 'cutie' magazines and glossy periodicals. Most such publications combine articles and stories, case histories, diaries and so forth with a variety of photographs. For many of these one might coin a portmanteau word (*q.v.*) like *phorntography* or *porntography*.

A minor and innocuous branch of pornography (or perhaps more accurately scatology) is the bawdy ballads of the oral tradition (*q.v.*) kept alive in the Armed Forces and among sporting fraternities (especially rugby clubs). Whether such verses are obscene or merely bawdy is again largely a matter of opinion and taste, and it is next to impossible (and perhaps not particularly useful) to categorize them. *See also* EROTICA; LOW COMEDY.

portmanteau word (F *porter*, 'to carry' + *manteau*, 'cloak') A word formed by combining two or more words. Also known as a telescope word. Lewis Carroll applied this term to combined words in *Through the Looking-Glass* in explanation of some words in *Jabberwocky* (*q.v.*). James Joyce, in *Finnegans Wake*, coined a large number of such words. The following passage suggests how Joyce did it:

> Hence when the clouds roll by, jamey, a proudseye view is enjoyable of our mounding's mass, now Wallinstone national museum, with, in some greenish distance, the charmful waterloose country and the two quitewhite villagettes who hear show of themselves so gigglesomes minxt the follyages, the prettilees! Penetrators are permitted into the museomound free. Welsh and the Paddy Patkinses, one shelenk! Redismembers invalids of old guard find poussepousse pousseypram to sate the sort of their butt. For her passkey supply to the janitrix, the mistress Kathe. Tip.

See also GHOSTWORD; NEOLOGISM; NONCE-WORD.

postcolonialism 'Postcolonialism' (covering the terms 'postcolonial studies', 'postcolonial theory' and 'postcolonial literature') is an interdisciplinary academic field devoted to the study of European colonialism and its impact on the society, culture, history and politics of the formerly colonized regions such as the African continent, the Caribbean, the Middle East, South-Asia and the Pacific. The term 'postcolonialism' was first used by historians after the Second World War to refer chronologically to the post-independence period. Since the 1990s it has been used by literary critics as an oppositional reading practice to study the effects of colonial representation in literary texts. The field has its roots in anticolonial writings, such as the Négritude (q.v.) movement and related works by Aimé Césaire, Léopold Sédar Senghor and Frantz Fanon, and in colonial discourse analysis inaugurated by Edward Said's *Orientalism* (1978). Other prominent postcolonial theorists include Homi Bhabha, Marxist critics such as Aijaz Ahmad, Robert J. C. Young and Neil Lazarus, and feminist critics such as Gayatri C. Spivak and Anne McClintock.

Postcolonial critics are concerned with the impact of colonialism generally, including its relationship with issues such as gender and class; they challenge how colonialists constructed colonized regions and people as inferior, and also examine how colonialism affects the colonizing nations. They are interested in the wider idea of imperialism: how particular nations construct relationships that secure their superiority. They use literature as a prime example of how colonial ideas are transmitted through writing, which often involves a re-reading of canonical Western texts in order to expose the biases operating in what is claimed to be universal humanism.

Postcolonial literatures seek to reclaim self-representation from stereotypical portrayals in colonial literatures and colonial discourses, and to do so they often use the 'writing back' paradigm, or a rewriting of Western 'master' texts. They reimagine silenced and suppressed histories – of slavery and colonialism – and endeavour to come to terms with the trauma of the Middle Passage. They are often engaged with the problems of identity (individual or national) that have resulted from the cultural disruptions initiated by colonialism (disempowerment, dislocation, diaspora, migration).

Postcolonialism has been a subject of much debate among scholars. For example, the term may imply that colonialism is over when it is not, and it often tends to homogenize into a single category cultural experiences that are very different. There has been much debate as to whether 'postcolonialism' is a useful term for white settler colonies like Canada, Australia and New Zealand, whether it should be used to refer to countries such as Ireland, and most recently, the former Communist countries of Eastern Europe. Finally, the term defines all world cultures by their relationship to European colonialism, and so obliquely perpetuates the European belief in its own centrality. But postcolonialism has also provided timely critiques of the continuing legacies of colonialism in both the colonized and colonizing nations. As Sara Ahmed usefully points out in her book *Strange Encounters: Embodied Others in Post-Coloniality* (2000), postcolonialism opens up 'the complexity of the relationship between the past and present, between the histories of European colonization and contemporary forms of globalization'. *See also* HYBRIDITY; ORIENTALISM; SUBALTERN; GLOBALIZATION.

posthumanism   Sometimes used as a synonym for antihumanism (q.v.), more commonly posthumanism denotes a philosophical position concerned with reconceptualizing what it means to be human. Posthumanism refutes all ideas of naturalness, and denies the existence of a transcendent 'human nature' asserted by humanism (*q.v.*). However, posthumanists share with humanists a commitment to progress and a respect for science and rationality. 'Transhumanists' such as the computer scientist Marvin Minsky are focused particularly on the ways in which humans might transition to the posthuman, through technological augmentation and other enhancements. Indeed, the concept of the posthuman is more or less coterminous with that of Donna Haraway's 'cyborg' (*q.v.*).

While the terms posthumanism and transhumanism are relatively new – the latter was coined in the 1980s by the writer known as FM-2030 – all manner of writers have contemplated the posthuman. The French rationalist Marquis de Condorcet wrote in 1794 that 'no bounds have been fixed to the improvement of faculties . . . the perfectibility of man is unlimited'. Infamously, in *Thus Spake Zarathustra* (1883–5), Nietzsche declaimed that 'man is something to overcome'. Many works of science fiction (*q.v.*), from *Frankenstein* (1818) and H. G. Wells's *The Time Machine* (1895) to Thomas Sturgeon's *More than Human* (1957) and Frank Herbert's *Dune* (1965), explore posthuman possibilities. *See also* CYBERPUNK/STEAMPUNK; DYSTOPIA; POSTMODERNISM; UTOPIA.

post-Impressionism An early 20th c. art movement generally identifiable by the use of bright colours, sharply defined edges and a tendency towards abstraction. First coined by Roger Fry in a 1910 exhibition called *Manet and Post-Impressionism*, the movement both derived its foundations from Impressionism and expanded upon its elements to express individual artists' tastes and temperaments. Notable artists associated with the movement include Vincent Van Gogh (1853–90), Paul Gauguin (1848–1903), Georges Seurat (1859–91), and Paul Cézanne (1839–1906). The Post-Impressionists influenced a number of later movements, including the Nabis, the German Expressionists, the Fauvists, and the American Modernists.

postmodernism A general (and sometimes controversial) term used to refer to changes, developments and tendencies which have taken place (and are taking place) in literature, art, music, architecture, philosophy, etc. since the 1940s or 1950s. Postmodernism is different from modernism (*q.v.*), even a reaction against it. It is no easier to define than many other -isms. Like them, it is amorphous by nature.

To talk of postmodernism is to imply that modernism is over and done with. This is not so. There never is a neat demarcation line. Originally, avant-garde (*q.v.*) movements in literature and the arts in general were modernist; avant-garde influences continue. It might be said that there is a new avant-garde. Besides, postmodernism is still happening. When something else develops from it or instead of it, it will, perhaps, be easier to identify, describe and classify.

As far as literature is concerned it is possible to descry certain features in postmodernism. For instance, there is literature which tends to be non-traditional and against authority and signification. Here one may cite experimental techniques, in fiction as displayed in the *nouveau roman* and the anti-novel (*qq.v.*). In some cases these looked perilously close to mere gimmickry. There have also been experiments with what is called concrete poetry (*q.v.*), though there is nothing particularly postmodernist about that (or even modernist, for that matter) since Simias of Rhodes was experimenting with pattern poems (*q.v.*) in the 4th c. BC. In drama one might cite experiment with form, content and presentation in such developments as the Theatre of the Absurd, Total Theatre, the 'happening' and, latterly, the Théâtre de Complicité (*qq.v.*).

Other discernible features of postmodernism are an eclectic approach, aleatory writing, parody and pastiche (*qq.v.*). Nor should we forget the importance of what is called magic realism (*q.v.*) in fiction, new modes in science fiction (*q.v.*), the popularity of neo-Gothic and the horror story (*q.v.*).

The burgeoning of Marxist, feminist and psychoanalytic criticism since the 1970s is yet another aspect of postmodernism. It also refers to a critical position in criticism, in which a complete relativism exists – hence its proximity to poststructuralism (*q.v.*). Perhaps most important of all are the revolutionary theories in philosophy and literary criticism expressed in structuralism and deconstruction (*qq.v.*) An important analysis of postmodernism is contained in Jean-François Lyotard's *The Postmodern Condition: A Report on Knowledge* (1979).

Another important dimension of postmodern theory has issued from African-American critics such as Cornel West and bell hooks, who have observed that, for all its emphasis on difference, postmodern theory has ignored the work of black writers and intellectuals. While she makes this point in her essay *Postmodern Blackness*, hooks acknowledges that postmodernism's critique of essentialism can be useful to black studies by promoting the notion of multiple black identities and experiences, by resisting colonial paradigms of a monolithic black identity, and by seeing the connections of race with issues such as class mobility. *See also* ALTERNATIVE LITERATURE; ALTERNATIVE THEATRE; FEMINIST CRITICISM; GOTHIC NOVEL/FICTION; MARXIST CRITICISM; SUBCULTURE.

poststructuralism Late in the 1960s, structuralism (*q.v.*) became subject to a rigorous and lasting critique of its thinking and method. Poststructuralism is in part an attempt to work out some of the overlooked possibilities, implications and shortcomings of structuralism and its basis in Saussurean linguistics itself. In a sense it complements structuralism by offering alternative modes of inquiry, explanation and interpretation.

Poststructuralism questions the assumptions of structuralism and, as far as literature is concerned, tends to argue that the meaning of any text is indeterminate. It reveals that signification is, in its very nature, unstable.

Saussure's fundamental distinction between signifier and signified (*q.v.*) is at the heart of the instability. Without realizing it, Saussure, in making the distinction, exposed not coherence between signs, but an inherent incoherence. Poststructuralism pursues further the Saussurean perception that in language there are *only differences without positive terms* and shows that the signifier and signified are, as it were, not only oppositional but plural, pulling against each other, and, by so doing, creating numerous deferments of meaning, apparently endless criss-crossing patterns and sequences of meaning. In short, what are called 'disseminations' (*q.v.*).

A belief in the incommensurate qualities of language (a form of inadequacy) is basic to poststructuralist thinking. Hence the idea of indeterminacy (*q.v.*), which is an important element in deconstructive practice and in Jacques Derrida's theory of *différance* (*q.v.*). The fundamental position of poststructuralist theory is that meaning is inherently unstable, whereas a structuralist would hold that an explanation/understanding is conceivable and possible, provided that the conventions and codes of any literary text or cultural message are analysed.

In poststructuralist theory Roland Barthes is of particular importance because he bridges the structuralist and poststructuralist movements. In his book *Elements of Semiology* (1967) he proposed that structuralism is capable of an explanation of any sign system of any culture (i.e. all systems of signification). But he also perceives that such an explanation necessitates a theory of meaning/explanation. This gives rise to the idea of a 'metalanguage' (*q.v.*); that is to say, a 'beyond' language or 'second-order language' which is used to describe/explain/interpret a 'first-order' language. Given one metalanguage for one explanation, it follows that there may be another in turn, and a metalanguage may replace a 'first-order' language. Each order of language implicitly relies on a metalanguage by which it is explained, and ironically, therefore, deconstruction is placed precariously in the position of becoming (against its principles and design) a metalanguage itself. Thus, discourse upon discourse in regression; and all discourses are exposed to interrogation. This is one aspect of Barthes's poststructuralist thinking and is, fundamentally, deconstructive.

Barthes's later theories (post-1968) lead him to other challenging caveats: (a) that the Author (or the concept of the Author) is dead; this idea he elaborates in his essay *The Death of the Author* (1968); (b) that there are two basic experiences to be had in reading: namely, *plaisir* and *jouissance* (*q.v.*); (c) that texts may be either *lisible* or *scriptible* (i.e. 'readerly' or 'writerly', *q.v.*); and (d) that given the application of certain codes a text may be analysed and interpreted as either 'readerly' or 'writerly' (or even as both).

Further important contributions to poststructuralist theory in the French tradition (and the French have been the principal innovators) have been made by Julia Kristeva. Hers is fundamentally a psychoanalytic approach and, though of considerable complexity, is fascinating. In *La Révolution du langage poétique* (1974) she discusses the relationship between the orderly/rational and the heterogeneous/irrational, between the conscious and the unconscious, the 'normal' and the 'poetic'. She suggests that semiotic material is irrational and illogical, the material of impulse and rhythm; while reason creates logic, syntax and coherence and brings about the symbolic element.

There are implied antinomies such as feelings/thoughts, heart/brain and, to reverse the sequence in the binary opposition (*q.v.*), Apollonian/Dionysiac.

Basically, she conceives the 'semiotic' element (which is linked with the concept of infant – a word which means 'speechless' – in the pre-Oedipal phase) as being opposed to the 'symbolic' and sees it as a means of undermining symbolic order, thus causing confusion, through its fluidity and plurality, its pulsions, in any attempt at precise meaning. Like water, the semiotic element is opposed to anything fixed or static; and it is opposed to any binary opposition such as masculine/feminine. Though, of course, there is more than a hint of binary opposition in fluid/fixed. In a sense, 'semiotic' writing is bisexual (the pre-Oedipal phase is genderless). In English literature, James Joyce and Virginia Woolf are instances of 'semiotic' writers, using a fluid, diffuse, disseminated, 'writerly' mode and style; and in those respects different from anything fixed, rigid, conventional or realistic.

Julia Kristeva goes so far as to relate sound in poetry to primal sexual impulse and suggests that combinations of consonantal sound, for example, may be either feminine or masculine. There is a suggestion that 'semiotic' material might be equated with a feminine tendency, and the symbolic with the masculine. This raises the possibility for feminist theory of the idea of *écriture féminine* (*q.v.*).

Even this very brief résumé of complex matters makes it clear that the approaches of Roland Barthes and Kristeva are very different.

The main aspect of poststructuralist theory used in literary practice is deconstruction, for which Jacques Derrida has been primarily responsible. His essay *Structure, Sign, and Play in the Discourse of the Human Sciences* (1966) was among the first critiques of structuralism and it was he who initiated the techniques of particularly close reading which latterly have been largely practised in the USA. *See also* DECONSTRUCTION.

potboiler A work written merely to gain a livelihood. The term is at least as old as the 18th c. A classic example of the potboiler that transcends its immediate end is Johnson's philosophical 'novel' or didactic 'romance' (*qq.v.*) *Rasselas* (1759), which was written in the evenings of a week to defray the expenses of his mother's funeral and to pay her debts. *See* KITSCH.

poulter's measure Rhyming couplets consisting of one iambic hexameter (*q.v.*) followed by an iambic heptameter (*q.v.*). To be found in the *Towneley Mystery Plays* and some Morality Plays (*q.v.*) and used quite frequently in the 16th c. (by Sir Thomas Wyatt, the Earl of Surrey and Sir Philip Sidney, among others) but little thereafter because it was found that the hexameter and the heptameter are lines too long to be easily manageable. The term derives from the poulterer's traditional practice of giving fourteen eggs in the second dozen, a point recorded by Gascoigne in *Steele Glas* (1576). These lines come from the Earl of Surrey's *Youth and Age*:

> Laid in my quiet bed, in study as I were,
> I saw within my troubled head a heap of thoughts appear.

And every thought did show so lively in mine eyes,
That now I sigh'd, and then I smiled, as cause of thought did rise.
I saw the little boy in thought how oft that he
Did wish of God to scape the rod, a tall young man to be.

povest A Russian term for a fictional narrative. It denotes the sum of facts and events connected with an individual or a particular incident. Alexander Pushkin (1799–1837), who mastered all the Western literary forms and genres, referred to a '*povest* of myself', meaning the sum total of what had happened to him. His *Povesti Belkin* (1830) are notable examples of the form. Terseness and compression are characteristic of *povesti*, which have less complex plots than novels and are shorter. It is perhaps the Russian equivalent of the German *Novelle* (*see* NOVELLA) and by virtue of its length, at any rate, comparable with the French *récit* (*q.v.*). The Bulgarians use the term *povest* for a reasonably long short story; and in Croatian (which has the 'ije' dialect of what is commonly called Serbo-Croatian) the word *povijest* denotes history or records or a chronicle. In Serbian *povest* means history and story.

power/knowledge The term was developed by Michel Foucault in his collection of essays *Power/Knowledge* (1980) to examine the workings of power in the production of knowledge, and is closely related to his concept of discourse (*q.v.*). For Foucault, knowledge and power are joined together through discourse, defined as a system of statements by which dominant groups in society construct bodies of knowledge as well as whole sets of concepts, categories and vocabularies to analyse and explain the 'subject' under study. Power constitutes knowledge and vice versa, hence power and truth are closely linked. Foucault is interested in showing how something gets established as knowledge and 'truth', and how particular disciplines have been developed throughout history. For example, he examines the construction of the homosexual in the 19th c. through particular institutions and discursive practices. Thus, homosexuality has been constructed by religion as a sin, by law as a crime, and by medicine as an illness. Knowledge gives one power to make valid or invalid truth claims about specific 'subjects' as well as to control what can be said about them. Subsequently, homosexuals have used the very vocabulary (such as 'queer') that has disqualified them in order to demand legitimacy and to subvert such language of 'truth' in what Foucault calls 'reverse discourse'.

Edward Said's work on orientalism (*q.v.*) is another instance of power/knowledge. He examines the workings of imperial power and, specifically, the Western construction of knowledge about the 'Orient' as a way of maintaining power and domination over it. As Said famously stated, the West was able to 'manage – and even produce – the Orient politically, sociologically, militarily, scientifically, and imaginatively'. Indeed, Said is particularly interested in how knowledge about the 'Orient' was disseminated in Western literary representations. *See also* DISCOURSE; ORIENTALISM; POSTCOLONIALISM; QUEER THEORY.

power, literature of   In an essay titled *The Poetry of Pope* (published in the *North British Review*, Aug. 1848), Thomas de Quincey made an interesting distinction between the literature of knowledge and the literature of power:

> There is, first, the literature of *knowledge*; and, secondly, the literature of *power*. The function of the first is – to *teach*; the function of the second is – to *move*: the first is a rudder, the second an oar or a sail. The first speaks to the *mere* discursive understanding; the second speaks ultimately, it may happen, to the higher understanding or reason, but always *through* affections of pleasure and sympathy.

De Quincey elaborates the idea at some length. What he is getting at is that an encyclopaedia instructs and is therefore didactic; a great play, on the other hand, moves by appealing to the emotions – and thereby also instructs but in a totally different way.

practical criticism   Criticism based on close analysis of a text in isolation. Such criticism was pioneered by I. A. Richards (1893–1979) and the term was given currency by him. His book *Practical Criticism: A Study of Literary Judgment* (1929) was to revolutionize the teaching and study of English and his methods were to have an immeasurable influence: not least on the acceptance of modernism (*q.v.*) and the development of what came to be called the New Criticism (*q.v.*). Other important books by Richards were *The Meaning of Meaning* (1923), *Principles of Literary Criticism* (1924) and *Science and Poetry* (1926). F. R. Leavis was an outstanding exponent of practical criticism and influenced a complete generation of critics.

praecisio   *See* APOSIOPESIS.

praeposteratio   *See* HYSTERON PROTERON.

pragmatism   (Gk *pragma* 'deed or act') An American philosophical tradition with roots in the 1870s that attempted to reconcile the need for an empiricist epistemology with the existence of moral and religious belief systems. Presented as a 'mediating philosophy', the pragmatic method – by focusing on the practical consequences of a theory or proposition – aimed to clarify understandings of key concepts like truth and free will so as to dissolve seemingly irresolvable metaphysical disputes between science, religion and morality. There are various brands and applications of pragmatism, but all share this desire to align philosophical with scientific inquiry and to privilege the concept of intelligent practice. Key figures in the development of pragmatism include its founder Charles Sanders Peirce (1839–1914), William James (1842–1910), and John Dewey (1859–1952), with Richard Rorty (1931–2007) representing a more recent practitioner with his concept of neopragmatism. Literary theorists like Stanley Fish have also often been cited as incorporating pragmatist practices into their work.

Prague School   Also known as the Prague Linguistic Circle. It was founded in 1926 and remained active in the 1920s and the early 1930s. Leading figures were Roman Jakobson, Boris Eikenbaum, Trubetskoy, Viktor Shklovsky and Mukařovský. They were influenced by Russian Formalism (*q.v.*) and by futurism (*q.v.*), and developed the theory of phonology, in which sounds are analysed in sets of oppositions. *See* RUSSIAN FORMALISM.

praxis A Gk term used by Aristotle in *Poetics* (it is normally rendered by the word 'action') to denote the first principle and soul of tragedy (*q.v.*).

préciosité, la The term denotes that refinement of language and manners which became the concern of civilized and sophisticated French men and women early in the 17th c. The Marquise de Rambouillet appears to have been one of the prime movers in this matter. From 1608, and for forty years thereafter, she established salon (*q.v.*) life at her town house. To this venue came many of those who wished to refine and polish manners and literary style. Honoré d'Urfé's pastoral (*q.v.*) novel *L'Astrée* (1607) inspired many aspects of their urbane code. The main sources for a knowledge of *les précieuses* are A. B. de Somaize's *Dictionnaire des précieuses* (1660), Madeleine de Scudéry's *Le Grand Cyrus* (1649–53) and *Clélie* (1654–60), and Tellemant des Réaux's *Historiettes*. The pursuit of elegance was a civilizing influence, but it also led to affectation. Some of the *habitués* of this salon helped to found the Académie Française in 1635. Their affectations were satirized by Molière in *Les Précieuses ridicules* (1659). *See also* BLUE STOCKING CIRCLE/ SOCIETY; SECENTISMO.

précis A summary or synopsis of a work. A shortened version of a passage.

preface An introduction to a literary work. Some famous examples are: Johnson's *Preface* to his *Dictionary* (1755), one of the finest pieces of prose in the language; Shaw's prefaces to many of his plays (in some cases they were much longer than the plays and contained all that he could not express dramatically); Harley Granville-Barker's *Prefaces to Shakespeare* (4 vols, 1927–48), a most valuable contribution to an understanding of the plays. *See also* FOREWORD.

pregunta (Sp 'question', from *preguntar*, 'to ask') A form of poetic debate practised by Spanish court-poets in the late 14th c. and in the 15th c. A poet put a question (*recuesta*) on some theme concerned with morals, love, philosophy or religion, and a second poet provided an answer (*respuesta*) in exactly the same form and using the same rhymes.

Pre-Raphaelites, the The mid-19th c. self-styled brotherhood of London artists, all young, who united to resist current artistic conventions and to create, or re-create, art forms in use before the period of Raphael (1483–1520). They expressed their views in the magazine *The Germ* (1850). The members of the group were John Everett Millais, William Holman Hunt, Dante Gabriel Rossetti, William Michael Rossetti, Thomas Woolner, Frederick George Stephens and James Collinson. Their 'movement' subsequently influenced the writers William Morris, Christina Rossetti and Swinburne, and the artist

Burne-Jones. The poetry of the Pre-Raphaelites showed a distinct liking for medievalism (*q.v.*), 18th c. ballads, archaic diction, symbolism and sensuousness. The poets were considerably under the influence of Spenser. Tennyson had already stimulated their interest in medievalism. Rossetti and his followers were dubbed 'the fleshly school of poetry' (*q.v.*). *See also* AESTHETICISM; PARNASSIANS; PRIMITIVISM; SYMBOL AND SYMBOLISM.

press (L *pressare*, 'to press') The term denotes, variously: printing; a printing machine; a printing organization; a publishing house; printing activities; newspapers and periodicals collectively; the journalistic profession; a newspaper; a favourable (or unfavourable) reception in a newspaper or periodical (e.g. a review; hence a 'good' press, a 'bad' press).

There are numerous phrases and terms which are derivative: (a) press agent – a person who arranges for newspaper advertising and publicity; (b) press association – an association of newspapers formed to act as a news agency for the members of the association, supplying local news, etc.; (c) press-book – a book printed at a private press (*q.v.*); (d) press-box – an erection provided for the use of reporters (e.g. at sports, games, shows); (e) press conference – a meeting of a public personage with members of the press in order to make an announcement or answer questions; (f) press-cutting – a paragraph or article cut out of a newspaper, periodical (*q.v.*) or magazine; (g) press gallery – a gallery for reporters (e.g. in the House of Commons); (h) pressman – one who works at a printing press, a journalist or reporter; (i) press-mark – a mark on a book to show its place in a library; (j) press-proof – the last proof before printing; (k) press release – an official statement or report supplied to the press; (l) press-room – a room where printing presses are worked or a room for the use of journalists and reporters; (m) press-work – the operation of a printing press; (n) at press, in press – in the course of printing or about to be published; (o) go to press – to begin to print or to be printed; (p) liberty, freedom, of the press – the right of publishing material without submitting it to a government authority for permission; (q) printed matter in general (especially newspapers) and journalists as a group or class.

priamel (L *praeambulum*, 'preamble') It denotes a form of German folk verse which had some vogue from the 12th to the 16th c. It appears to have developed from a kind of improvised epigram (*q.v.*). Basically a *priamel* comprised a variety of disconnected ideas and observations with a surprise conclusion.

priapean From the god Priapus, a god of fertility often represented as a grotesque figure with an exaggerated phallus. He gives his name to a classical Greek meter comprising a glyconic and a pherecretean. Anacreon used the measure, and it was also used for the choruses in satyr plays (*q.v.*).

primary accent and secondary accent The primary accent or 'primary' falls clearly on the first or main syllable of a word. The secondary tends to come on the third syllable. As in *secondary*, where the 'a' is not so heavily stressed. *See also* STRESS.

primer Originally a prayer-book for the laity before the Reformation, and for some time after it. The medieval primer consisted of translations and/or copies from various sections of the breviary (*q.v.*). In the 16th c. the name was given to similar works. After the Reformation the name was used of books in which the offices for daily prayers had been based on orders in the *Book of Common Prayer*. Gradually there developed the sense of an elementary school-book. In his *Dictionary* (1755) Johnson defined a primer as a small prayer-book for teaching children to read.

primer couplet A fixed verse form of dipodic couplets rhyming aa, bb, cc and so on. As in the anonymous *Obadiah*:

> Obadiah
> Jumped in the fire,
> The fire was hot,
> He jumped in the pot . . .

primitivism In the history of art the 'primitives' are taken to be those painters of the Netherlandish and Italian schools who flourished before *c.* 1500. The word 'primitive' is also applied to the work of many artists belonging to many periods and milieux which displays a naive vision, a technically 'simple' conception and presentation of reality, even a certain crudeness of style. Perhaps a kind of untutored art.

As far as literature is concerned primitivism has very different connotations. Fundamentally, the so-called primitivist writer is, in Horace's words, a *laudator temporis acti*, 'an extoller of things in the past' (though not necessarily either testy or querulous), and primitivism is, and expresses, a form of nostalgia for a primitive (or pre-civilized) way of life. The *laudator temporis acti* is an observably common phenomenon since there seems to be a deeply rooted awareness and conviction in mankind that once upon a time there was a paradisal era, a 'golden age', to which there are plentiful allusions in Classical literature. The Bible and many writers of antiquity exalt a prelapsarian state; so do many works of the Renaissance period, when there was a remarkable resurgence of interest in Classical learning and literature.

This kind of atavistic nostalgia has impelled man to look for his origins, for that lost 'innocence', for 'the good old days'. Such impulses moved the Italian primitives and, later, the Pre-Raphaelites (*q.v.*). In fact the apotheosis or glorification of this mythical state of well-being is common in art and literature; and primitive themes are even commoner, as is evident from a study of utopianism (*see* UTOPIA), the pastoral (*q.v.*) tradition and convention, and what may be called 'desert island fiction' (*q.v.*).

Basically, then, the primitivist is anti-civilization, anti-materialism, anti-industrialism, anti-progress and pro-Nature. The cultural primitivist, as he has been called, finds that peoples isolated from civilization are preferable to those living in civilized and urbanized milieux. The cult of the 'noble savage' (*q.v.*) in European and American literature (a cult closely associated with some aspects of romanticism, *q.v.*), is part of the ideal.

Primitivist themes are found in many literatures of the world; they are plentiful in Classical and medieval literature. As far as Europe is concerned, it is very noticeable that, with the growth of civilization, with the advance of technology and with the development of an urban and industrialized way of life, so these themes become more frequent and obvious; just as, with the decline of orthodox Christian beliefs in an afterworld, utopian schemes proliferate. Notable examples are Montaigne's observations on savages in his essay *Of Cannibals* (1580), Sir Philip Sidney's evocation of the 'golden age' in his *Arcadia* (1580), and intimations of an ideal existence in Shakespeare's *The Winter's Tale* and *As You Like It*. Dante, Tasso, Spenser and Milton expressed similar ideas, often in relation to a prelapsarian state. Later, Aphra Behn's *Oroonoko* (c. 1688) enjoyed wide popularity and influence. In the 18th c. Rousseau, perhaps more than anyone, was responsible for a powerful resurgence of primitivist feelings and the cult of the 'noble savage', with such works as *La Nouvelle Héloïse* (1761), *Émile* (1782) and *Du contrat social* (1762). Critical theory of this period – in the work of Vico, Blair, Blackwell and others – underlines a taste for primitivism in its reaction against neoclassicism. Nostalgia for the simple rustic life is also found in the Romantics, notably Wordsworth, as well as Thoreau and Melville. In the 20th c., mythopoeic primitivism can be found in the poems of W. B. Yeats, in T. S. Eliot's *The Waste Land* and in the fiction of Conrad, D. H. Lawrence, William Faulkner, William Golding and many others.

print culture As opposed to the predominantly oral culture (*q.v.*) which preceded it, usually taken to refer to all aspects of printed texts and their wider milieux, the advent of which may be dated to the revolution in textual production and propagation enabled by Johannes Gutenberg's invention of the printing press around the mid 15th c. Although the means to duplicate texts via woodcuts and blocks had existed before that time, Gutenberg's technological advance meant that the number and therefore reach of reproducible texts rose exponentially throughout the European Reformation and Renaissance (*q.v.*) periods. At the same time, scribal and manuscript culture, although it continued to coexist alongside the new means of production, became marginalized, particularly in relation to popular and commercial publication. The proliferation of standardized, relatively economical printed texts had far-reaching consequences for European politics, religion and society as a whole. Critics have argued that print culture is implicated in such seismic shifts as the Protestant Reformation and the scientific revolution of the Enlightenment (*q.v.*). The crucial importance of this transition is maintained by Elizabeth Eisenstein in her seminal study *The Printing Press as an Agent of Change* (1979). Print culture has also been considered instrumental in the formulation of 'imagined communities' (*q.v.*) and thereby the rise of nation-states. Many commentators have pointed to the increasing importance of electronic media and online publication as evidence that print culture is in its next transitional phase. Certainly, the advent of digital technologies means that what traditionally constitutes a 'text' (*q.v.*) is itself open to inquiry. *See* EBOOK.

printer's rhyme   *See* EYE-RHYME; RHYME.

private press   Such a press is usually set up and run by an individual or a small group in order to publish works which might not otherwise get into print. The most famous in England have been: the Strawberry Hill Press established by Horace Walpole in his home in 1757; Dr Daniel's press at Oxford in 1845; the Kelmscott Press founded by William Morris, in 1890; the Golden Cockerel Press (1921); the Nonesuch Press established by Francis Meynell in 1923; and finally Eric Gill's press set up in 1933. There have been few outside England. The best known is probably the Cranach founded at Weimar in 1913. *See also* PRESS.

proairetic code   *See* CODE.

problem play   *See* THESIS PLAY.

proceleusmatic   (Gk 'arousing to action in advance') A metrical foot comprising four unstressed syllables: ◡ ◡ ◡ ◡. Rare in Greek lyric poetry and tragedy; but not uncommon in Latin comedy. *Very* occasional as an isolated foot in English verse.

prochronism   *See* ANACHRONISM.

proem   (Gk 'prelude') Colloquially a 'limbering up' or 'warming up'; a preface; an introduction; a preamble. Milton sounds his proem at the beginning of *Paradise Lost*. It is the literary equivalent of an overture.

Professorenroman   (G 'professor novel') Not, as might be thought, a campus novel (*q.v.*) of the kind that Professors Bradbury, Lodge and Wain have excelled at, but historical novels and novels with archaeological themes and subjects which display a range of recondite erudition but are short on style, character and imaginative re-creation. Exponents were the distinguished German professors Felix Dahn (1834–1912), Georg Ebers (1837–98) and Adolf Hausrath (1837–1909).

prohemio   A Spanish term denoting an introduction to a collection of poems. There is a well-known example by Santillana (1398–1458), addressed to the Constable of Portugal and giving a personal view of Spanish poetry to date.

prolegomenon   (Gk 'something said in advance') A preface (*q.v.*) or introduction; perhaps an introductory treatise. The equivalent of clearing the ground in preparation for building. A good example is R. B. McKerrow's *Prolegomena for the Oxford Shakespeare* (1939).

prolepsis   (Gk 'a taking beforehand, anticipation') A figurative device by which a future event is presumed to have happened. A very famous example occurs in Keats's *Isabella* (stanza 27):

> So the two brothers and their *murder'd man*
> Rode past fair Florence, to where Arno's stream
> Gurgles through straitened banks

Lorenzo, the 'murder'd man', has not yet been murdered but he is being taken into a forest by Isabella's two brothers where he *will* be murdered.

The term also denotes a pre-emptive strike in argument in the shape of raising an objection beforehand in order to dispose of it. Also the summary of a detailed account of something to come. *See also* HYPALLAGE.

proletarian novel A novel (*q.v.*) about the working classes and working-class life; perhaps with the intention of making propaganda (*q.v.*) in pointing out poor economic conditions. An excellent example is Walter Greenwood's *Love on the Dole* (1933). *See also* NON-FICTION NOVEL/DOCUMENTARY FICTION; THESIS NOVEL.

proletarskaya kul'tura (R 'proletarian culture') Abbreviated to the rather barbarous *proletcult*, which refers to a Soviet movement started by Bogdanov in 1917. The group was made up of militant writers strongly in favour of a proletarian culture. The results of such organizations (the Smithy Poets, *q.v.*, was another) were only too apparent in some Communist states, including the renegade Albania. Many of the contributors to their publications were pick and shovel hack writers. *See also* CONSTRUCTIVISM; SOCIALIST REALISM.

prologue (Gk 'before speech') The opening section of a work; a kind of introduction which is part of the work and not prefatory. It was common in drama in the 17th and 18th c., when it was often in verse. Occasionally found in novels. In plays the prologue is usually a Chorus (*q.v.*). The most famous example in English is Chaucer's *General Prologue* to *The Canterbury Tales*. *See also* EPILOGUE; INDUCTION.

promythium *See* EPIMYTHIUM.

pronominatio *See* ANTONOMASIA.

pro-ode In Greek dramatic and lyric poetry a strophe (*q.v.*) without a matching antistrophe (*q.v.*) which preceded the strophe and antistrophe of a choral ode (*q.v.*). It may also denote a short verse before a longer one.

propaganda Term 'lifted' from the title *Congregatio de propaganda fide* (now the APF – Association for the Propagation of the Faith), a committee of the Roman Church responsible for foreign missions and the dissemination of the faith. It was set up in 1622.

When literature is propaganda and when it is not is a much debated issue. If an author sets out to make a case for a particular religious, social or political point of view, through the medium of a play or a novel, for example, and he is *seen* to be doing this, and perhaps in the process he sacrifices verisimilitude (*q.v.*) by contriving character and situation to suit his thesis, then it might be said that the result is a work of propaganda. If what he has to say is worth reading or listening to long after the issue which provoked the propaganda is dead, then his art has transcended the contingent needs of the propagandist.

Basically propaganda is devoted to the spreading of a particular idea or belief. Much pamphlet (*q.v.*) literature and journalism (*q.v.*) has precisely this purpose. It is partial. Pamphleteering in the 18th c., for instance, was openly propagandist. Later, notable polemicists like H. G. Wells, Bernard Shaw, Hilaire Belloc and G. K. Chesterton wrote a lot of propaganda to support and promulgate their political, social and religious beliefs. Though proselytizing is forbidden to the layman, Belloc and Chesterton came very near it at times. Ibsen might fairly be described as propagandist in some of his plays; so might Galsworthy. And Brecht certainly was. There have also been a number of plays presented to spread the doctrines of Moral Re-Armament. Many writers in the Communist bloc have been overtly propagandist in aid of socialism, in novels, as well as in plays and verse. *See* COMMITMENT; COMMUNICATION FALLACY; THESIS NOVEL; THESIS PLAY.

propaganda novel *See* THESIS NOVEL.

propaganda play *See* THESIS PLAY.

propos (F 'chat') A minor form invented by Emile-Auguste Chartier (1868–1951), whose pen-name was 'Alain'. In 1906, this distinguished teacher started a daily series of *Propos d'un Normand* in the *Dépêche de Rouen*. They were short essays of about eight hundred to a thousand words on a wide variety of subjects. He continued them for many years and in 1933 published *Propos de littérature*. *See* CAUSERIE; ESSAY.

proposition That part of a work in which the author states his theme (*q.v.*) or intention, and introduces the burden of the work. It may be explicit or implicit and is likely to come at or near the beginning. Some famous examples of propositions are: (a) the opening lines of Milton's *Paradise Lost*; (b) the first sentence of Rousseau's *Du contrat social*; (c) the opening sentences of Tolstoy's *Anna Karenina*. *See* PROEM.

propriety The canons of propriety are the canons of good taste, good manners and correctness; thus, in writing, conformity with what is suitable and appropriate. A virtue especially prized in the 18th c. when the suiting of style and form to subject matter was studied with more than usual care. Hence the regard for decorum (*q.v.*). *See also* POETIC DICTION.

prose The word derives from the Latin *prosa* or *proversa oratio*, 'straightforward discourse'. Thus, a direct, unadorned form of language, written or spoken, in ordinary usage. It differs from poetry or verse (*qq.v.*) in that it is not restricted in rhythm, measure or rhyme (*qq.v.*). However, there are such things as poetic prose and the prose poem (*qq.v.*).

prose poem A composition printed as prose (*q.v.*) but distinguished by elements common in poetry (*q.v.*): such as elaborately contrived rhythms, figures of speech, rhyme (*q.v.*), internal rhyme (*q.v.*), assonance (*q.v.*), consonance (*q.v.*) and startling images. Aloysius Bertrand (1807–41) appears to have been one of the first writers to establish it as a minor genre. His *Gaspard de la nuit* (1842) was a collection of fantasies in the manner of Rembrandt and Callot written in very ornate and rhythmical language. It contains many dazzling images, a number of which are grotesque. Later, Baudelaire was influenced by this work, as is apparent from his *Petits poèmes en prose* (1869). It is likely that Bertrand's work had some influence on the symbolist poets and on the surrealists. Other writers of note to have attempted the prose poem are Rimbaud, Oscar Wilde, Amy Lowell and T. S. Eliot; plus, latterly, Peter Redgrove and David Wevill. A remarkable recent example is Heathcote Williams's *Whale Nation* (1988), a long work which is a celebration of the existence and way of life of whales and a plea for their preservation. Also notable is Geoffrey Hill's *Mercian Hymns* (1971). *See also* POETIC PROSE; SURREALISM; SYMBOL AND SYMBOLISM.

prose rhythm What Dryden called the 'other harmony of prose' has its own rhythms which vary from writer to writer, according to their nature, style, subject matter and purpose.

prosodion A form of religious song used in devotions to the god Apollo in Ancient Greece. It was sung by a Chorus (*q.v.*) to the accompaniment of music.

prosody The study or science of versification and every aspect of it. It thus includes meter, rhythm, rhyme and stanza (*qq.v.*) forms.

prosopopoeia (Gk 'face making') The term is still used sometimes for personification (*q.v.*).

prospect poem *See* TOPOGRAPHICAL POETRY.

protagonist (Gk 'first combatant') The first actor in a play; thence the principal actor or character. In Greek tragedy (*q.v.*) the playwright was limited to the protagonist (first actor), deuteragonist (second actor) and tritagonist (third actor). It is probable that in the first place Greek drama consisted of a Chorus (*q.v.*) and the leader of the Chorus. Thespis (6th c. BC) is believed to have added the first actor to give greater variety to the dialogue and action. The second and third were added by Aeschylus and Sophocles respectively. The protagonist has come to be the equivalent of the hero (*q.v.*). *See* AGON; ANTAGONIST.

protasis (Gk 'stretching forward') Thus, a proposition or something put forward. In Greek drama the opening section of a play in which the characters are introduced and the situation explained. The protasis is followed by the epitasis and the catastrophe (*qq.v.*). *See* CATASTASIS; FREYTAG'S PYRAMID.

protatic character A character introduced at the beginning of a play, usually for the purpose of exposition (*q.v.*). Probably a development of the Chorus (*q.v.*). In drawing-room comedy often a servant.

prothalamion A term invented by Spenser (by analogy with epithalamion, *q.v.*) for his poem (1596) in celebration of the double wedding of the Lady Elizabeth and the Lady Katherine Somerset. It thus means a 'spousal verse' or something written 'before the bridal chamber'.

protozeugma *See* ZEUGMA.

protreptic A kind of discourse designed to persuade or hortate. Not unusual in Classical literature. Aristotle wrote one called *Protreptikos*.

proverb A short pithy saying which embodies a general truth. It is related in form and content to the maxim and the aphorism (*qq.v.*). Common to most nations and peoples, it is a form of expression of great antiquity. Many writers have made use of them. The best-known collection is the Book of Proverbs which follows the Psalms in the Old Testament. Some examples of proverbs include: Send a fool to close the shutters and he'll close them all over the town (Yiddish); We cannot step twice into the same river (Classical Greek); When you want a drink of milk you don't buy the cow (Cretan). A fine collection of English proverbs is the *Oxford Dictionary of English Proverbs* (1935).

proverbe dramatique A short dramatic sketch which illustrates a proverbial saying. The genre had some vogue in the French salons of the 17th and 18th c. Their precursors were *jeux des proverbes* – parlour games in which a conversation had to be sustained by using proverbs. *Proverbes dramatiques* were then written for private theatricals. In the first place these were much the same as charades and the audience had to guess the proverb. Then writers disclosed the proverb and illustrated it in their little play, which was normally a one-act comedy.

Towards the end of the 17th c. a collection of *Proverbes* by Mme Durand was published. About this time Mme de Maintenon composed *proverbes* to be acted by the young ladies of Saint-Cyr. Such pieces had their greatest vogue in the mid-18th c. Collé, Carmontelle and Moissy were the main authors in this period. After the Revolution the *proverbe* tradition was revived in salons. In the 1820s and 1830s the best-known authors were Antoine-Marie, Baron Roederer, Hyacinthe de Latouche and Octave Feuillet. However, it was Alfred de Musset who mastered this genre in the middle of the 19th c. Two well-known works by him are: *On ne badine pas avec l'amour*, and *Il faut qu'une porte soit ouverte ou fermée*.

pruning poem More accurately a 'pruned' poem. In this verse form, which is very rare, the second and third rhymes of each stanza are formed by pruning the first consonant of the preceding rhyme. George Herbert's *Paradise* is an example. The first two stanzas are:

> I blesse thee, Lord, because I GROW
> Among thy trees, which in a ROW
> To thee both fruit and order OW.

> What open force, or hidden CHARM
> Can blast my fruit, or bring me HARM
> While the inclosure is thine ARM.

See also ALTAR POEM; PATTERN POETRY; RHOPALIC VERSE.

psalm A sacred song or hymn (*q.v.*), especially one of the collection in the Bible: The Book of Psalms.

psalter A book which contains psalms; a psalm-book; not to be confused with psaltery, an ancient or medieval musical instrument. *See* PSALM.

pseudepigrapha (Gk 'false inscription') A term for books or writings which have a false title or are ascribed to an author who is not the real one. *See also* FORGERY.

pseudonym (Gk 'false name') A name other than his own taken by a writer. Also known as a pen-name and a nom de plume (*q.v.*).

pseudonymous literature The use of a pseudonym, pen-name or nom de plume (*q.v.*) is a well-established practice; as well established as publishing work anonymously. Here are just a few: Montcorbier – François Villon; Gerard – Desiderius Erasmus; François-Marie Arouet – Voltaire; Jean Baptiste Poquelin – Molière; Friedrich von Hardenberg – Novalis; Marie-Henri Beyle – Stendhal; the Brontë sisters – Currer, Ellis and Acton Bell; Thackeray – Michael Angelo Titmarsh; Dickens – Boz; Mary Ann Evans – George Eliot; Edward Bradley – Cuthbert Bede; Samuel Clemens – Mark Twain; Louis Marie Julien Viaud – Pierre Loti; Jacques Anatole François Thibault – Anatole France; William Sydney Porter – O. Henry; Edgar Allison Peers – Bruce Truscot; H. H. Munro – Saki; C. Day Lewis – Nicholas Blake; J. I. M. Stewart – Michael Innes.

pseudo-statement A term used by I. A. Richards to distinguish 'scientific' from 'poetic' truth. By 'statement' Richards means a scientific expression of fact which is verifiable as such. A pseudo-statement, on the other hand, is found in poetry and is not necessarily verifiable or even logical. Such statements have the function of ordering and organizing the receptor's (*q.v.*) attitudes and feelings. The implications of this concept and distinction are that poetry tells the truth and its own truth in its own way by feigning. In other words, verisimilitude (*q.v.*) and a kind of truth can be attained and conveyed by emotive as well as referential language (*qq.v.*). The idea that poetry can convey a particular kind of knowledge not conveyable by any other means is of great antiquity.

psittacism (L 'parrot-like speech') Meaningless and repetitive speech.

psychic distance *See* AESTHETIC DISTANCE.

psychoanalytic criticism A body of criticism that emerged in the 20th c. which seeks to explain the significance of literary texts in terms of psychological development and conflict. The theories and writings of Sigmund Freud (1856–1939) provide its foundations. Freudian criticism supposes that much narrative is the expression of desires and anxieties emanating from the unconscious part of the mind; they reside there as a consequence of the earlier repression of troubling episodes typically experienced in childhood. Thus for Freud literature is, like dreams and slips of the tongue, indicative of 'a return of the repressed'. This return of something which the conscious mind had been hiding from itself explains the disconcerting feeling a reader may experience of a story seeming to be strangely familiar, a sensation Freud refers to as 'uncanny'. All kinds of conflicts and taboo desires become repressed, but two of the most famous include the Oedipus complex and castration complex, both of which involve fears and desires of the male child as he emerges from a state of dependence on his parents.

Freud's most general essay about literary interpretation was *Creative Writers and Day-Dreaming* (1907), in which he argued that the creative artist, like the child, engages in a kind of 'play', fashioning a world of fantasy where, as in a dream, his wishes are obliquely fulfilled. While many of his writings which deploy these ideas are actually case studies of his patients, Freud wrote a number of essays about literary texts, including E. T. A. Hoffman's Gothic tale *The Sandman*, Dostoevsky's *The Brothers Karamazov* and Wilhelm Jensen's novel *Gradiva*. Freud frequently discusses the plays of Shakespeare, and in *The Interpretation of Dreams* (1900) makes some famously suggestive observations about Hamlet's relationships with his parents, which were followed up by the psychoanalyst Ernest Jones in *Hamlet and Oedipus* (1949).

Freud is not consistent as to what the object of these literary studies is or should be. Sometimes they constitute studies of 'character-types', which presumably would prove instructive in the treatment of real people. In other instances, such as his examination of the Hoffman tale, they seem to explain anxieties a reader may bring to his reading of a text (though uncomfortably this rather implicates Freud's own reading). Often, a literary work is understood as symptomatic of its author's unresolved traumas and conflicts. This latter approach is known as 'psychobiography' (*q.v.*) and became the dominant mode of psychoanalytic criticism in the middle decades of the 20th c.

More recent psychoanalytic criticism exhibits considerable diversity. For example, in *The Anxiety of Influence* (1973), Harold Bloom advances the idea that every poet is, in a sense, 'belated' and oppressed by anxiety because of 'precursor' poets – the great ones above all. A putative poet stands in the relationship of 'son' to them, or to one of them in particular, and feels oppressed by that relationship. Carrying through the Oedipal idea, Bloom suggests that such a 'son' is a rival to the father poet, who is a 'castrating precursor'. The 'son', powerfully influenced by a parent-poem or poems of the 'father', experiences ambivalent feelings, compounded not only of love and admiration but also of envy and fear – and perhaps even hatred. The fear and hatred are caused by the son's great need to reject and rebel against the 'father', to be autonomous and original and find his own 'voice'.

More difficult (and some might say, obscure) are the methods and theories propounded by Jacques Lacan (1901–81), especially in his *Écrits* (1977). In this work, Lacan sets out to reinterpret Freud in terms of structuralist and poststructuralist theories of discourse. He emphasizes the centrality of language to any understanding of the unconscious: in examining the workings of an individual's unconscious, the analyst is both responding to and using language. Indeed, Lacan insists, the unconscious is itself structured like a language. A crucial aspect of language for Lacan is that words and meanings do not always correspond (a position often simplistically attributed to the structuralist thought of Saussure); signifiers 'float free' of what they refer to. Thus language is detached from a verifiable external reality. Lacan's conclusion is that the unconscious, and that concept so treasured in much Western thought, a unified separate self, are merely effects of language. It should be stressed, however, that many thinkers prior to Lacan had arrived at such insights concerning language, objectivity and subjectivity. The implications of these insights for literary criticism are dramatic: a necessary rejection of the very notion of characterization and indeed the possibility of literary realism. Adopting the conclusions of Lacan and his radical predecessors means that there is no point in looking for evidence of the author's, or indeed the characters', unconscious motivations. Lacanian critics instead typically examine how texts undermine their own realism by revealing the constructedness of unified notions of character, or demonstrate key Lacanian developmental phases, such as the 'mirror stage' (*q.v.*) where a child learns of its identity as it enters the 'symbolic order', in which the world of law and the social community is defined.

Jungian psychology and Jung's theories about the collective unconscious and the archetype (*q.v.*) have also provided a fruitful but less influential development in psychoanalytic criticism. See also ABJECTION; DECONSTRUCTION; FETISHISM; SIGNIFIER/SIGNIFIED; STRUCTURALISM.

psychobabble   A term coined by R. D. Rosen in *Psychobabble: Fast Talk and Quick Cure in the Era of Feeling* (1977) – a critique of DIY ego-psychology – and defined as: 'a set of repetitive verbal formalities that kills off the very spontaneity, candour and understanding it pretends to promote. It's an idiom that reduces psychological insight to a collection of standardized observations, that provides a frozen lexicon to deal with an infinite variety of problems.' Common in everyday speech and re-created/reproduced in fiction (e.g. Cyra McFadden's clever satirical novel *The Serial: A Year in the Life of Marin County*, 1977). It is discussed by David Lodge in a witty essay in *Working with Structuralism* (1981) in which he cites such instances as: 'get centred', 'into the pits', 'flash on', 'blow away', 'off the wall', 'wig out', 'upfront', 'spaced/spaced out/spacey'. All have metaphorical or semi-metaphorical meanings, in some cases a good deal removed from literal sense. For example, 'off the wall' signifies 'spontaneously'. *See also* NEOLOGISM.

psychobiography A form of biography which is clinical in its treatment of its subject, which stresses the subject's psychological development and applies psychoanalytical knowledge and principles. For example, Erik H. Erikson's biography of Martin Luther – *Young Man Luther* (1958) – makes use of Freud's discoveries and theories in examination of Luther's adolescent 'identity crisis'. Notable examples of literary psychobiogaphy are Leon Edel's *Henry James* (1953–72) and Justin Kaplan's *Mark Twain and His World* (1974). *See also* PSYCHOANALYTIC CRITICISM; PSYCHOGRAPHY; LIFE WRITING.

psychography (Gk 'writing of souls') A term apparently applied by George Saintsbury to Sainte-Beuve, who described himself as a 'naturalist of souls'. As a jargon term it refers to the importance of an author's life in a work of art. The psychographer, therefore, will be in search of revealing details in the life of an author in order to see what bearing they may have on his art.

psychological novel A vague term to describe that kind of fiction which is for the most part concerned with the spiritual, emotional and mental lives of the characters and with the analysis of character rather than with the plot and the action. Many novelists during the last two hundred years have written psychological novels.

psychomachy A battle for the human soul, from Prudentius's *Psychomachia* (AD 400), usually with contending virtues and vices, angels, devils, or other external *personae* representing good and evil. Marlowe introduces the warring impulses in Faustus with a visit from his bad and good angels, who argue for and against his involvement with necromancy (*Doctor Faustus*, c. 1593). *Everyman*, the early sixteenth-century morality play, is an extended psychomachy in which personifications of Death, Knowledge, Strength, Discretion, etc., vie for Everyman's attention and loyalty.

public lending right This was secured by an Act of Parliament in 1979. It was the result of a long campaign (twenty-eight years) initiated by the novelist John Brophy in 1951. The Society of Authors (*q.v.*) and the Writers' Action Group were closely associated with it. By this statute authors receive annually a payment for the loan of books from public libraries. The amount depends on the number of books they have in print and the frequency with which they are borrowed. The scheme (which has reciprocal arrangements in other countries) is financed by a central grant from the Treasury and in Britain is administered by a registrar in Stockton-on-Tees.

public sphere A shared space where individuals come together in order to share, test and form collective opinion. As a political force, the public space mediates between private, individual opinion and the monolithic authority of the state. In these terms, the concept derives from the philosopher Jürgen Habermas and the thesis expressed in his 1962 work *Strukturwandel der Öffentlichkeit. Untersuchungen zu einer Kategorie der bürgerlichen Gesellschaft*, translated in 1989 under the title *The Structural Transformation of the*

Public Sphere. Habermas argues that a new bourgeois public sphere, and thereby the foundations of liberal democracy, emerged in 18th c. Europe, enabled by specific historical conditions such as the rise of mercantilism and increased literacy. The coffee houses and literary salons of the time are cited as important forums for the formation and expression of this collective influence, which acts as both a check on the absolutist power of the state and ultimately as a challenge to its traditional authority. The problem arose, according to Habermas, when the success of capitalism led to unequal access to the public sphere, allowing power to shift once again into the hands of the few, not the many, albeit this time in favour of big business, and in particular media owners as gatekeepers to the new public sphere of television and newspapers.

Instrumental though they have been, Habermas's ideas have been subjected to widespread qualification and criticism, leading to the proposal of many alternative models, so-called 'counter publics'. Among these are feminist critiques which point out that Habermas's public sphere fails to take into account many marginal and/or voiceless elements in society, excluding them by virtue of gender, class or economic considerations. Alternatively, critics have argued for the importance of dialogue and rhetoric in constituting the public sphere, in other words positing an emphasis on discourse rather than identity. The rise of the internet and the concomitant notion of the public space as one that may be actual or virtual clearly promises to give renewed impetus to Habermas's original conception. The blog (*q.v.*) is just one area where the formulation of new public spheres may be discerned.

puffery The kind of criticism which is the product of literary cliques. Authors who belong to such cliques laud one another's works. 'To puff' is to overpraise, to 'blow up'. The term no doubt derives from the character Mr Puff, the bogus and verbose critic of Sheridan's play *The Critic*. In publishers' jargon a puff is the equivalent of a blurb (*q.v.*). *See* LOG-ROLLING.

pulp literature (L. *pulpa*, 'flesh') 'Pulp' is a pejorative term for certain kinds of fiction (and its authors). Pulp magazines began to appear in the First World War or earlier and got their name from the fact that they were printed on wood pulp, which gave the content a coarse, grainy appearance. They were about 7 x 10 inches in size, had gaudy covers and comprised about 120 pages. They published short stories and occasional extracts from novels. During the 1920s they became extremely popular (there were well over two hundred in existence) and they remained popular in the 1930s. Eventually, television brought about their demise.

They are of some importance in literary history because the American detective story (*see* CRIME FICTION) was born in them. Well-known examples were *The Black Mask, Dime Detective, Thrilling Detective* and the *Detective Story Magazine*. Pulp magazines also published examples of the horror story (*q.v.*) and many tales of the weird and wonderful, the supernatural and the fantastic. Science fiction (*q.v.*) stories also became very popular through the pulp magazine, especially *Amazing Stories* (first published in 1926), though this was by no means the first SF magazine.

The postwar years saw the emergence of pulp novels in America. These were cheap paperbacks usually featuring stories from popular genres – the romance, western (*qq.v.*), crime story, etc. Occasionally 'serious' fiction or reprints of classics would be published as 'pulps'; more frequently the content would be explicitly pornographic, particularly as censorship laws were relaxed in the 1960s. Pulp literature is often dismissed as trash, though many of the novels have become collectors' items – their lurid covers in particular are often appreciated as a charming form of kitsch (*q.v.*). Cultural studies (*q.v.*) scholars have become interested in pulp readerships, and in particular, how pulp literature has helped foster minority identities and communities. While many postwar pulp novels with lesbian themes were exploitative, and the stuff of male fantasy, those by lesbian authors such as Ann Bannon informed readers of the possibilities and practicalities of lesbian life. *See also* EROTICA; GAY AND LESBIAN CRITICISM; PORNOGRAPHY.

pun A figure of speech which involves a play upon words. The Greek term is paronomasia (*q.v.*); other names are *calembour*, clinch, quibble and carwitchet. One of the earliest types of wordplay, the pun is widespread in many literatures and gives rise to a fairly universal form of humour. Puns are very often intended humorously but not always. Donne, for example, puns elaborately and quite seriously in his *Hymn to God the Father* thus:

> I have a sin of fear, that when I have spun
>   My last thread, I shall perish on the shore;
> But swear by Thy self, that at my death Thy Son
> Shall shine as he shines now, and heretofore;
>   And having done that, Thou hast done;
>   I fear no more.

Here 'Son' means both Christ and 'the sun', and the word 'done' is a pun on the poet's name.

A famous pun in dramatic literature is Mercutio's laconic crack as he is dying: 'Ask for me tomorrow and you shall find me a grave man' (*Romeo and Juliet*, III, i).

A pun form known as *asteismus* involves a reply to earlier words used in a different sense. This example occurs in *Cymbeline* (II, i):

CLOTEN: Would he had been one of my rank!
LORD: To have smell'd like a fool.

A kind of sylleptic pun is contained in the following admonitory notice seen by the author outside a London church: 'Are you going to sleep with the wise virgins, or wake with the foolish ones?'

James Joyce is generally regarded as one of the most compulsive and incorrigible of punners in English literature. *Ulysses* and *Finnegans Wake* abound in them. *See* ANTANACLASIS; CLENCH/CLINCH; PARAGRAM; PARONOMASIA.

punctuation Many people restrict punctuation to marks, but there are also spaces, and the functional analysis of punctuation as *elocutionary*, indicating breaths; *syntactic*, indicating logic; or *deictic*, for emphasis, needs supplementing.

Punctuation is co-extensive with writing, as with reading, but eight spatial levels may be distinguished: (1) letter-forms, punctuating the blank page; *scriptio continua* (*q.v.*), wordswithoutspacesormarksbetweenthem; (2) inter-word spaces, including paragraph-, verse line- and stanza-breaks; (3) the marks of punctuation with their associated spaces; (4) words or other units distinguished by fount, face, case, colour, siglum, or position; the detail of the *mise-en-page* (*q.v.*); (5) the organization of the page and opening; the principles of the *mise-en-page*; (6) pagination or foliation (*q.v.*), punctuating reading; (7) the structure of grouped pages; sections, chapters, prolegomena and appendices, and apparatus; and (8) the book itself, as a complete object punctuating space or constituent volume. At all levels punctuation may be deictic, and at levels 2–7 elocutionary or syntactic, depending largely on whether one reads silently or aloud; but, in general, the higher the level, the more absolute the prescription of punctuation (by author, printer or whomever): punctuation is a tool of authority, limiting as well as generating and inflecting meaning, and has long been of interest to church and state.

Punctuation studies have been impeded, especially in English, by a misconceived search for fixed rules rather than guiding principles. The importance of word-order in analytical (*q.v.*) languages privileges the articulation of syntax; and the art of punctuating is influenced by religion, utility, philosophy and aesthetics at least as much as by logic or theoretical coherence. Individual marks have conventional uses, but are not restricted to them: –); many combinations of marks/spaces are possible, and in every generation some poets, dramatists, prosicians, typographers, printers, critics, and readers have developed the art.

Historical patterns of punctuating cannot yet be properly described or theorized, but much contemporary Western punctuation is clearly recent. Classical readers (so far as we know) mentally divided *scriptiocontinua* into, certainly, words and paragraphs (*q.v.*) (which might be indicated by section-marks, § or ¶), and probably into periods (. to .) composed of *cola* (: to :) subdivided into *commata* (, to ,) (*see* PERIOD (3)). In the late 7th c. some Irish texts show word-separation, which spread to other European vernaculars, and Latin; distinctive marks and layouts also appeared, but varying greatly in shape and function until Carolingian scholars added capital letters and began to codify a general European repertoire of punctuation. At its late medieval zenith that repertoire covered every mode and level of punctuation, but had only four principal marks, the *punctus*, *punctus interrogativus*, *punctus elevatus*, and *virgula* (roughly [.] [?] [:] and [,] or [/]). The Humanists, to complement their newly joined-up handwriting, added the exclamation-mark (1360s), lunulae (1390s), and the semicolon (1490s), as well as an outstanding clarity of script and print. Crotchets appeared soon after; and in the late 16th c. inverted commas appear (but did not reach their exact modern function until the mid-19th). Other marks – ¿ ¡ /...\ | {} * - « », etc. – evolved in different countries at different times, exactitude, clarity, satire and mimesis driving innovation while unwelcome complexity, fashion, and the inertia of conventions in an increasingly mass-market favoured stability. Punctuation is currently in profound flux, however, largely under the pressures of computing (including word-processors and printers, DTP (desk-top publishing), email, the Net, and 'postmodernism'), but also in that many 19th c. practices, especially that of combining marks:– had already been abandoned. The paucity of current general conventions, exposed by the demands of new text media, has led to radical and reactionary innovation, and the establishment of genre- or medium-specific sub-repertoires of punctuation and layout.

The bottom and sidelines remain the punctuation on a QWERTY keyboard: the stops, tonal indicators, inverted commas, a family of brackets and slashes, rules and some special sorts + space, tab and return keys. Upper and lower cases are available, and on word-processors face and fount manipulation. The three principal space-keys and appropriate capitalization can generate words, lines, stanzas (*q.v.*), paragraphs (*q.v.*), and almost every conventional layout (letters, recipes, drama . . .), and the marks are brutally summarized below:

The **stops**, commonly indicating the completion of syntactical or rhetorical units, are the **full-stop** (or in the US, period) [.], **colon** [:], **semicolon** [;], and **comma** [,]. They have a descending order of weight or duration, but the full-stop doubles as a suspension-mark (and in threes as an ellipsis (*q.v.*) [...], indicating omissions, etc.); the connection across a colon is logical, or in series, while that across a semicolon is tangential, or in parallel; and commas may be used in pairs, for mild parentheses (*q.v.*), or singly to end clauses or signal pauses.

The **tonal indicators** are the **question-** and **exclamation-marks** [? and !], broadly conveying (in English) rising pitch and volume respectively. Both often serve as full-stops, but may be used medially, and iterated (?? or !!!) for comedy or emphasis. Spanish convention has since 1754 also used them initially, as '¿How are you?' or '¡Ouch!'.

Inverted commas [" and/or ""], developed, like their French equivalent, *guillemets* [«»], from the diple, a medieval *nota* (*q.v.*) used mainly to indicate scriptural quotations. Deployed within the text for greater clarity and exactitude, they could from the late 16th c. indicate speech (in which they are now supported by *alinéa*, a new line for each new speaker), but continued to indicate quotation and tonal variation (functions from which the finger-waggle has developed). A single, raised comma doubles as the **apostrophe** ['], formally (but decreasingly) used to indicate elision (*q.v.*), and with 's' to indicate genitives.

The family of **brackets** comprises: **lunulæ** (round), used in many conventions; **crotchets** [square], used to distinguish editorial matter or emendation;

braces {curly} used mainly for grouping; and <angled brackets>, often used like the *guillemets* they resemble. All brackets contain and display their contents, for subordination or emphasis, and create textual strata whose meaning is only contextually definable. The family of **slashes**, the common [/], vertical [|], and backslash [\], develop from the virgula, and are also used variedly to signal parallel (not sequential) constructions, or groupings (verse units in prose transcription, computer-language commands).

The common **rules** are the **hyphen** [-], used to join words (or a broken word), and the **dash** [–], used, often with spaces, singly to distinguish, link, or isolate clauses or phrases, and in pairs to signal and inflect parentheses. Longer rules may be created by multiplying dashes.

The **special sorts** vary between keyboards, but commonly include (with standard arabic numerals) minimal mathematical punctuation [+ = %]; the **asterisk** [*], **paraph** [§], **paragraphus** [§], and **obelus** [†], often used for annotation; the special characters of other languages; currency symbols; and two symbols for individual words, the **ampersand** [&] for 'and', and the **apestail** [@] for 'at . . . (each)'.

pure poetry A question-begging term because of the ambiguities and connotations of 'pure', and very nearly as loose, at times, as the banality of 'sheer poetry'. However, if, in Valéry's words, we 'cleanse the verbal situation', we can say with a degree of truth that poetry aspires to the state of purity in the sense that it aspires to an excellence and by so doing is refined to all dross and impurity.

It may also be said to aspire 'towards the condition of music', as Walter Pater, in an essay on Giorgione in 1873, said all art does. If poetry does this, then the idea is suggested that the beauty of the poem's words and its content would be in unsurpassable harmony with the melody and sound the words conveyed.

As it happens, the theory and idea of pure poetry manifests itself in the middle of the 19th c. Edgar Allan Poe was hinting at it in *The Poetic Principle* (1850). Baudelaire, who was much influenced by Poe, was referring to it in his *Notes nouvelles sur Edgar Poe* (1857). Hereafter there seems gradually to have developed the idea that pure poetry was a form of music; that it expressed the essence of whatever it was the poet needed to express. Baudelaire, Mallarmé, Verlaine and Rimbaud, and, later, Valéry, all explored the possibilities of this kind of purity in verse. Thus, the theories of pure poetry are closely associated with symbolism and the symbolist poets.

In the 20th c. the most notable advocates of pure poetry were George Moore and the Abbé Bremond. In an introduction to his anthology of *Pure Poetry* (1924) Moore esteemed the works of Poe because they were 'almost free from thought'. In 1926 Abbé Bremond published *La Poésie pure*. The Abbé associated poetry with prayer; it aspired to an ineffable and incantatory condition.

T. S. Eliot also regarded pure poetry as a notable development in 19th c. verse, as he pointed out in his essay *From Poe to Valéry* (1949). *See* AESTHETI-CISM; CREATIONISM; HERMETICISM; SYMBOL AND SYMBOLISM.

purism At its worst the doctrine of precisionists and pedagogues who, to a fault, are devoted to the maintenance of absolute standards of correctness in writing; and an absolute observance of the rules of expression.

In a wider sense purism refers to those periodic efforts that have been made to purify languages – especially in the exclusion of foreign terms. In this respect the Greek Atticists were purists. The Romans, too, were not sympathetic to Greek coinages. The most notable attempt ever at purism was that made by the Académie Française, which received a commission in 1635 to purify the French language. Its dictionary was published in 1694. In the Preface to his own *Dictionary* (1751) Samuel Johnson expressed the most eloquent of all claims for a language to be free of legislators, insisting that the efforts of academies to regulate the use of language will remain futile.

purple patch In *Ars Poetica* (2, 3, 14–19) Horace refers to *purpureus . . . pannus*, the purple piece of cloth which is an irrelevant insertion of a grandiloquent passage into a work. Thus the term now denotes an ornate, florid or over-written piece of writing which is incongruous. It is nearly always used pejoratively.

puy The title of medieval fraternities of *jongleurs* (*q.v.*) and also the ordinary citizens of towns in northern and western France. The *puys* held poetry contests at which lyric poets competed. The title may derive from the place-name Le Puy-en-Velay (where such contests were believed to have begun), or from *puy* denoting a raised stage on which the poets recited their verses in front of a president and panel of judges. The *puys* date, in all probability, from the 12th c., and the poems usually had a religious theme. For example, at the *puy* of Rouen poets presented poems in honour of the Immaculate Conception. There were similar *puys* at Caen and Dieppe.

puyyut (Gk *poietes*, 'maker, poet') A Hebrew psalm of the early Christian era, mostly associated with the Baghdad region.

pylon poets Nickname for the school of poets who dominated British poetry in the 1930s. The key figures were W. H. Auden, C. Day Lewis, Louis MacNeice and Stephen Spender, their names sometimes conflated as 'MacS-paunday'. Taken from a poem of Spender's called *The Pylons* (1933), the nickname identifies the group with their use of self-consciously 'modern' imagery derived from industry and technology. An obvious source for their method is the metaphysical (*q.v.*) poetry of John Donne, whose 'scientific' images were much admired by T. S. Eliot, who influenced Auden and Spender in particular. A more immediate influence is probably Marxist materialism, which affected them all to a greater or lesser degree. *See* MODERNISM.

pyrrhic (Gk 'war dance') A metrical foot comprising two short syllables: ∪ ∪. Also known as a dibrach. The shortest metrical foot in Classical verse. In

English prosody the pyrrhic of two unstressed syllables often occurs but it is regarded as belonging to adjacent feet or as a substitution (*q.v.*).

pysma A Greek term denoting a question which requires an answer and not merely 'yes' or 'no'. A rhetorical device by which a speaker or writer asks a series of questions which require various forms of answer. The Latin rhetoricians used the term *quaestium*. A well-known example is Hamlet's outburst to Gertrude (*Hamlet*, III, iv):

> Have you eyes?
> Could you on this fair mountain leave to feed,
> And batten on this moor? . . . what judgement
> Would step from this to this?

pythiambic verse A combination of dactylic hexameters (*q.v.*) and iambic dimeters or trimeters (*qq.v.*). There are some examples in Horace's *Epodes*. *See* PYTHIAN METER.

pythian meter Also known as *versus pythius*. A name given to the dactylic hexameter (*q.v.*) because it was the meter used in the Pythian or Delphic oracles. *See* PYTHIAMBIC VERSE.

Q

qasidah   (A 'intention') A long lyric poem or ode written in the rhyme scheme aa, ba, ca, da, characteristically employed as either a panegyric in praise of ('intended for') the poet's patron or a satire upon people or social conditions. The form was developed in a wide range of literary traditions, including Arabic, Persian Urdu and Turkish. The earliest examples in Arabic are the famed seven 'golden odes' or *mu'allaqat* (*q.v.*), which display the tripartite character of the *qasidah* as described by the 9th c. Arab writer Ibn Qutayba: the *nasib* or nostalgic prelude, in which the poet laments over the deserted camp of his beloved; the *rahil* or journey across the desert, citing its hardships; and the *madih* or panegyric in praise of his tribe or himself or his patron. While in many contexts the *qasidah* was displaced in popularity by other forms such as the *ghazal* (*q.v.*), it none the less continues to command relevance. As W. Flagg Miller has stated, it is used in a wide variety of contexts from village weddings and funerals to televised commentaries on world politics. The form was imitated by Tennyson in *Locksley Hall*, using couplets in octameters (*q.v.*).

quadrivium   In the Middle Ages the seven liberal arts were divided into the *quadrivium* and the *trivium*. The former, being the more advanced, comprised the mathematical sciences, namely arithmetic, geometry, astronomy and music; the latter, grammar, logic and rhetoric (which included oratory).

quaestium   *See* PYSMA.

quantity   The duration (*q.v.*) of the sound of a syllable; thus, the time needed for its pronunciation. Most Classical verse is based on quantities in accordance with certain rules. In English verse the duration of the vowels and syllables is important aesthetically but is of no metrical importance. Compare the first line of Virgil's *Aeneid* with the first line of Milton's *Paradise Lost*:

A Dictionary of Literary Terms and Literary Theory, Fifth Edition. J. A. Cuddon.
© 2013 The Estate of J. A. Cuddon. Published 2013 by Blackwell Publishing Ltd.

> Árma̅ vi̅rúmque̅ ca̅nó, Troía̅e̅ qu̅i prímu̅s a̅b óri̅s
> Of Man's first disobedience, and the fruit

The quantities of Virgil's dactylic hexameter (*q.v.*) are fixed; those of Milton's pentameter (*q.v.*) are flexible and the line might be read in more ways than one according to different degrees of emphasis. *See also* ACCENT; BEAT; HOVERING ACCENT; STRESS; VARIABLE SYLLABLE.

quart d'heure (F 'quarter of an hour') A short one-act play (*q.v.*); a curtain raiser (*q.v.*), common in the French theatre, rare in England.

quartet Four lines of verse, either as a separate quatrain (*q.v.*) or as a non-separate part of a poem. For example, the Shakespearean sonnet (*q.v.*), which consists of three groups of four lines concluded by a 'binding' couplet.

quarto (Short for Latin *in quarto*, 'in fourth') (a) A book made from printer's sheets folded twice to form four leaves or eight pages. Abbrev. 4to. (b) The form in which about twenty of Shakespeare's plays were printed. Such versions are known as First Quarto, Second Quarto, and so forth. *See* DUODECIMO; FOLIO.

quaternarius *See* IAMB.

quatorzain Any poem of fourteen lines, which usually follows the sonnet (*q.v.*) pattern, but not always regularly.

quatrain A stanza of four lines, rhymed or unrhymed. The commonest of all stanzaic forms in European poetry, it lends itself to wide variation in meter and rhyme. Most rhyming quatrains fall into the following patterns:

(a) abab, as in Charles Causley's *The Prisoners of Love*:

> Trapped in their tower, the prisoners of love
> Loose their last message on the failing air.
> The troops of Tyre assault with fire the grove
> Where Venus veils with light her lovely hair.

(b) xbyb, as in the same writer's *The Life of the Poet*:

> Lock the door, Schoolmaster,
> Keep the children in.
> The river in spate at the schoolyard gate
> Roars like original sin.

(c) aabb, as in Causley's *Timothy Winters*:

> Timothy Winters comes to school
> With eyes as wide as a football pool,
> Ears like bombs and teeth like splinters:
> A blitz of a boy is Timothy Winters.

(d) abba, the so-called envelope stanza (*q.v.*) which Tennyson used in *In Memoriam*:

> Strong Son of God, immortal Love,
> Whom we, that have not seen thy face,
> By faith, and faith alone, embrace,
> Believing where we cannot prove;

(e) aaxa, a form which is less common but well known as the Omar Khayyám stanza:

> Awake! for Morning in the Bowl of Night
> Has flung the Stone that puts the Stars to Flight:
> And Lo! the Hunter of the East has caught
> The Sultan's Turret in a Noose of Light.

It is also possible to have a monorhymed stanza. Other complexities are alternate use of masculine and feminine rhymes, and irregular line lengths. Some special names have been acquired by some quatrains. The heroic or elegiac stanza (*q.v.*), used by Gray in his *Elegy*, consists of iambic pentameters rhyming abab. Ballad (*q.v.*) meter consists of iambic tetrameter (*q.v.*), trimeter (*q.v.*), tetrameter trimeter, usually rhymed abcb or xbyb. Hymn (*q.v.*) forms have also received special names: common meter, which is the same as ballad meter, or 'eights-and-sixes'; long meter, which is iambic tetrameters; short meter, which is trimeter, trimeter, tetrameter, trimeter.

The quatrain has been used a great deal in European poetry, usually in long and narrative poems. The term can also be applied to the two components of the octave (*q.v.*) of a sonnet (*q.v.*). In epigrammatic utterance the quatrain has been used successfully as a poem by itself by many writers, for example Prior, Landor, Yeats and Ogden Nash. *See also* QUARTET; TETRASTICH.

queer theory A broadly poststructuralist and avowedly radical approach to gender and sexuality. Queer theory became so named in the early 1990s, though it draws considerably on earlier work, particularly the writings of Michel Foucault (1926–84). The use of 'queer' follows the reappropriation of the pejorative term for homosexual by gay activists during the AIDS crisis of the mid- to late 1980s. Many (but by no means all) queer theorists are gay and lesbian, though queerness has come to be associated with all non-normative gendered and sexual experience, including bisexuality, polyamory and transgenderism. Queer theory does not work towards the inclusion of excluded groups within dominant notions of normality, but rather seeks to understand and challenge what Michael Warner has called 'regimes of the normal', i.e. those discourses and institutions that produce certain kinds of behaviour as normal, and others as aberrant. Thus queer theory is motivated by a politically progressive agenda: to help envisage circumstances where sexuality and gender can be lived in less restrictive and more creative ways.

A key assumption of queer theory is that categories of gender and sexuality are neither fixed nor natural. Rather, as Foucault argues in *The History of*

Sexuality, vol. I (1976), they are culturally and historically specific and 'constructed' through particular discourses, such as religion, law and medicine. In the late 19th c. the latter discourse helped produce sexual 'types' and identities, such as the 'homosexual'. Thus to assert a minority identity does not challenge but rather confirms authorized ways of conceiving and speaking about sexuality. Other queer theorists have attempted to articulate practices which might provide a means of destabilizing normative codes of gender and sexuality. Judith Butler's influential concept of performativity (*q.v.*) understands gender and sexuality as established through repeated social and linguistic performances. Parodying these performances establishes their contingency and diminishes their authority.

Queer theorists have been considerably attentive to works of literature. 'Queer reading' seeks to identify queer elements in ostensibly 'straight' texts. This rarely entails attempting to find evidence of a character's, or indeed a writer's, latent sexuality. Rather, queer readings identify anxieties relating to gender and sexuality which unsettle a text. Eve Kosovsky Sedgwick is perhaps the most influential queer theorist to engage in this kind of work. In *Between Men* (1985) and *The Epistemology of the Closet* (1991), Sedgwick examines a number of works from the late 18th to the early 20th c. and argues that male 'homosocial' relations, which help structure patriarchy, became complicated in this period by new forms of knowledge about homosexuality. Many texts exhibit 'homosexual panic', an anxiety that male–male relationships as in bachelor communities have been eroticized. Sedgwick demonstrates how many literary texts attempt to sublimate these concerns by transposing them onto safer, though related, topics. For example, Wilde's *The Picture of Dorian Gray* (1891) and Stevenson's *Strange Case of Dr Jekyll and Mr Hyde* (1886) start off by treating the erotic tensions between men, but end up as cautionary tales of solitary substance abusers. This kind of reading disrupts the straightforward distinction between 'straight' and 'gay' texts; Sedgwick shows that queerness *structures* patriarchal and heterosexual narratives. *See also* AFFECT; CONSTRUCTIONISM; ESSENTIALISM; FEMINIST CRITICISM; GAY AND LESBIAN CRITICISM; HETERONORMATIVITY; HOMOSOCIALITY; IDENTITY POLITICS; POSTSTRUCTURALISM; TRANSGENDER STUDIES.

quem quaeritis trope A trope (*q.v.*) of vital importance in the evolution of European drama. Part of the Easter *Introit*, it was adapted and elaborated into a dialogue and so became the source of liturgical drama. E. K. Chambers goes into the matter in great detail in his classic work *The Mediaeval Stage* (1903).

querelle des anciens et des modernes *See* ANCIENTS AND MODERNS.

question, epic A device in epic poetry by which the poet invokes the aid of a muse, patroness or superior power to explain what has happened. Milton uses it to considerable effect at the beginning of Books I, VII and IX of *Paradise Lost*.

questione della lingua (It 'dispute, problem, question or quarrel of the language') A controversy or debate about the suitability of the vernacular as opposed to Latin as language of literature. It also raised the problem of which Italian dialects should be used. This was a medieval debate in origin, to which Dante contributed. In *De vulgari eloquentia* he rejected all dialects and argued for an eclectic language composed from the best elements of all the dialects. In his *Divina Commedia* he used the Florentine dialect; which Petrarch and Boccaccio also used. The argument went on long after this, even though Florentine had become the literary language of Italians. In the 16th c. Castiglione was in favour of the language spoken in courts; others reverted to Dante's eclectic theory. Two schools of thought developed, and produced an 'ancients versus moderns' conflict. Bembo insisted on 14th c. Florentine in his *Prose della volgar lingua* (1525). Castelvetro and Machiavelli opted for the contemporary Florentine. The debate was still going on in the 19th c. when Leopardi favoured 14th c. Florentine. In the 19th c. Manzoni also tackled the problem.

quibble *See* PARONOMASIA; PUN.

quidproquo (L *quid pro quo*, 'something for something') A term usually limited to the drama in reference to some kind of blunder or misunderstanding on the part of the characters, perhaps from the misinterpretation of a word or situation. Frequent in comedy; for example: situations in Shakespeare's *The Comedy of Errors*, Jonson's *The Alchemist*, Goldsmith's *She Stoops to Conquer* and Sheridan's *School for Scandal*.

quinary A metrical line of five syllables, as in William Blake's *The Sick Rose*:

> O Rose! thou art sick!
> The invisible worm,
> That flies in the night,
> In the howling storm

quintain A stanza or verse group of five lines, as in Jack Clemo's *The Plundered Fuchsias*:

> They lie all around the lawn
>   And on the furrowed wall
> Like little red bombs winged and splayed.
>   No gale has made them fall:
>   A child's whim, that is all.

See also QUINTET.

quintet A five-line stanza of varying rhyme scheme and line length. A common rhyme scheme is ababb. Shelley, for instance, used this in *To a Skylark*:

> Hail to thee, blithe spirit!
> Bird thou never wert,

> That from Heaven, or near it,
> Pourest thy full heart
> In profuse strains of unpremeditated art.

See also QUINTAIN.

quinteto In Spanish prosody a verse of five lines of *arte mayor* (*q.v.*).

quintilla (Sp 'little fifth') A five-line stanza of eight syllables and two rhymes; or any five-line stanza with two rhymes. Verses or lines with other numbers of syllables do exist. In Castilian, the *quintilla* is one of the commonest octo-syllabic strophes. It was used by dramatists (e.g. Lope de Vega), but perhaps the most famous instance is Fernández de Moratín's *Fiesta de toros en Madrid* of the 18th c. *See also* REDONDILLA.

quinzain A fifteen-line stanza. Rare because of its length.

quod semper quod ubique (L 'which always and which everywhere') This remains the hallmark of great literature in time and place. The words occur in the so-called Vincentian canon framed by St Vincent of Lérins (near Cannes) in the 5th c. The sentence runs: *Id teneo quod semper quod ubique et quod ab omnibus creditum est*. It applies the test of eternity, ubiquity and consensus. *See* UNIVERSALITY.

quotation titles Titles of books echoing famous phrases from earlier literature and evoking known associations in the mind of the reader. This kind of title achieved considerable popularity in the 20th c. but was by no means new. Some notable quotation titles include E. M. Forster's *Where Angels Fear to Tread* (1905), recalling Pope's *Essay on Criticism* (l. 625), and William Thackeray's *Vanity Fair* (1848), which echoes Bunyan's *The Pilgrim's Progress*.

Qur'an (A 'recitation') The Islamic holy scripture, which Muslims believe was revealed to the Prophet Muhammad by the Archangel Gabriel over a period of twenty-three years. Its Arabic text has survived unchanged for over fourteen centuries, and it is the primary source of authority in Islam, complement by the Ahadith (traditions or sayings of the Prophet) and the historically developed canons of Islamic law or Shari'a. The Qur'an consists of 114 *suras* or chapters, which are in turn composed of *ayat* or 'verses' (sing. *ayah*). The *suras* are traditionally divided into Meccan and Medinan. The earlier *suras*, revealed at Mecca, the birthplace of Muhammad and Islam, tend to be shorter, proclaiming God's Oneness, establishing the Prophet's credentials, addressing issues of social justice, and reminding people of impending judgement. The later *suras*, revealed after the Prophet's migration to Medina, are longer and more prosaic, and concern laws and regulations of various aspects of domestic and social life such as marriage, inheritance and business transactions, the need to establish a united community, connections with the 'People of the Book', and stories of earlier prophets.

The Qur'an states that Islam confirms what is true in Judaism and Christianity, and it calls itself the 'confirmation of previous scriptures' (XII: 111).

Indeed, the Qur'an urges the Prophet and his followers to proclaim their continuity with Jews and Christians (called 'the People of the Book'):

> Say: 'We believe
> In God, and in what
> Has been revealed to us
> And what was revealed
> To Abraham, Ismā'īl;
> Isaac, Jacob, and the Tribes,
> And in (the Books)
> Given to Moses, Jesus,
> And the Prophets,
> From their Lord:
> We make no distinction
> Between one and another
> Among them, and to God do we
> Bow our will.'
>
> (II: 136; translation by
> Abdullah Yusuf Ali)

This passage in its original Arabic is repeated almost verbatim in the subsequent *sura* (III: 84). On numerous occasions the Qur'an recounts stories of the Old Testament prophets, some of them, such as the story of Joseph, in great detail. It refers to the prophet Abraham as the 'friend of God'. It also narrates the birth and miracles of Jesus.

The literary characteristics of the Qur'an are striking, notwithstanding its expressed desire to dissociate itself from poetry as such and to emphasize its nature as divine revelation (LXIX: 40–3). Among its literary qualities are the use of rhythmic prose (analogous with the Arabic prose form known as *saj'*), irregular rhythm, numerous varieties of rhyme, rhetorical imperatives (as in the passage above, beginning with 'Say'), questions and oaths. The Qur'an states on numerous occasions that it uses the language of metaphor or simile, and in a renowned passage it distinguishes between its own use of 'clear' passages (*mukhamat*) and 'figurative' passages (*mutashabihat*), the true meaning of the latter being known only to God (III: 7). One of the most celebrated instances of a figurative passage is the following:

> God is the Light
> Of the Heavens and of the Earth;
> His Light is a parable, of
> A Lamp within a niche; without the lamp, a glass
> Haloed as a brilliant star, lit
> From an olive tree, blessèd;
> Whose soil is neither East nor West;
> Its very oil would shine forth
> Though untouched by fire:
> Light upon Light.
> God raises to His Light whom He will;

He engenders parables for humankind. He
Whose knowing encompasses all things
(XXIV: 35–6; editor's translation)

Much has been written on the figurative and mystical significance of this passage.

It should be mentioned that the voice of the Qur'an extends over many rhetorical and performative situations: God addressing the Prophet and various other persons as well as humankind in general and the believers in particular; God speaking in parables; sometimes in the first person and sometimes in the third person; God recounting historical events and moral lessons, as well as dialogues between historical figures; and God offering arguments and explaining the signs and manifestations of His existence.

Hence, it would be misconceived to view the Qur'an as an ahistorical text, divorced from interaction with audience or language. The Qur'an itself repudiates such a reductive approach via a number of strategies: its emphasis on parable and metaphor; its attention to its audience; its self-consciousness of its position in history and the contextual import of its own message; its awareness of its own history as a text; its consciousness of its own linguistic force; and its recalcitrance towards any potential confusion of its own unique discourse with other discourses, such as poetry.

There has existed a vast body of exegesis of the Qur'an, ranging from the early commentary of Ibn Jarir al-Tabari (838–922) to the unfinished work of the Egyptian modernist Muhammad 'Abduh (1849–1905) and the interpretations of Abul Kalam Azad (1888–1958) and Kenneth Cragg. The problems – of historical contextualization, etymology and law – occupying these commentators have overlapped to some extent with those confronted by translators of the Qur'an. Characteristic problems have included the abrogation of certain earlier verses by subsequent revelations; the chronology and coherence of the whole; the historical departure of some Arabic words from their original meaning in the Qur'an; and the semantic comprehensiveness or distinctness of certain Arabic words, equally resistant to translation.

On a broader level, the history of translation of the Qur'an reveals that the study of Islam has been a phenomenon of Western politics, scholarship and thought as much as it has been a governing imperative of the Islamic political, cultural and legal world. Modern critical approaches in particular have been conducted largely by Western scholars, especially by Muslims trained in Western as well as Eastern traditions. The first Western translation of the Qur'an was completed in 1143 by the English scholar Robertus Retenensis, under direction from Peter the Venerable, Abbot of Cluny. Motivated by hostile intentions, this version was profoundly inaccurate yet served as the basis for early European translations. Equally distinguished by its inaccuracies was Alexander Ross's English rendering of the 1647 French translation published by André du Ryer. Ross offered no claim to scholarly impartiality, urging in his preface that the Qur'an was a repository of 'follies' which would confirm the 'health' of Christianity. In 1649 the Arabic text of the Qur'an was published in Hamburg; availing himself of this as well as a new Latin version (1698) by Ludovico Maracci, George Sale produced a more accurate English version in 1734. Again, Sale's endeavours were polemical regarding both Islam and Catholicism: he viewed the exposure of the 'imposture' of Islam and its overthrow as a 'glory' reserved for Protestants. This version stood behind Edward Gibbon's ambivalent assessment of Muhammad. This reading of Sale and Western translators has been challenged by Ziad Elmarsafy.

The methods of the Higher Criticism, applied to the Christian Gospels in the 19th c., eventually made their impact on Qur'anic translation and exegesis: J. M. Rodwell's translation changed the order of the *suras* or Qur'anic chapters and his assessment of Muhammad as inspired by a sincere monotheism was certainly more impartial and 'scientific' than that of his predecessors. Other notable translations have included those by Henry Edward Palmer (1880) and Marmaduke Pickthall (1930), an English convert to Islam. A. J. Arberry's version (1955) attempts to recapture the rhetorical and rhythmical patterns which lie behind the splendour of the original. Since then, numerous other renderings have appeared, notably by M. A. S. Abdel Haleem (2004) and by scholars such as Tarif Khalidi (2008): these have attempted to grapple with the problems enumerated above in the light of increasingly sophisticated historical and philological research, as well as of the need to translate the spirit of the Qur'an into idioms of relevance to the 20th and 21st c.. *See also* ALLEGORY; SACRED BOOKS.

R

Rabelaisian From the name of François Rabelais (c. 1490–1553). The term usually denotes ribald humour, but can also cover fantastical and exuberant writing.

rabinal achí A form of ballet-drama found among the Quiché Indians of Guatemala. Its theme is the heroic exploits and legend of the princes of Rabinal. It is performed at traditional festivals.

Rahmenerzählung (G 'frame story') Some of the better known are Ovid's *Metamorphoses*, *The Arabian Nights*, Boccaccio's *Decameron* and Chaucer's *Canterbury Tales*. Goethe, Hoffmann and Tieck all used the frame story, or stories within a story. The Swiss writers C. F. Meyer and Gottfried Keller are regarded as the most accomplished users of the frame story in recent times. Among their main works are: Meyer's *Der Heilige* (1880) and *Die Hochzeit des Mönchs* (1884); Keller's *Züricher Novellen* (1876) and *Das Sinngedicht* (1881). *See also* NOVELLA; STORY WITHIN A STORY.

raisonneur (F 'reasoner') An equivalent of confidant (*q.v.*).

Rāmāyana ('Story of Rama') The later of the two major Sankrit epic poems, the earlier and much larger one being the *Mahābhārata* (*q.v.*). It is traditionally classified as belonging to the genre of *kāvya* (*q.v.*) and *itihāsa* or traditional historical epic. Its composition (during the period 500–100 BC) is attributed to the sage Vālmīki. The *Rāmāyana* recounts the story of Prince Rama, who embodies the ideal of conduct and heroic courage, and his bride Sita. The epic also narrates the history of Rama's dynasty, beginning with his father King Dasaratha and his three queens. In the first book, Rama alone lifts a giant bow and wins the hand of Sita, the daughter of King Janaka. But as a result of a plot against him, Rama is sent into exile, living as a hermit in the forest, while his half-brother Bharata is urged onto the throne. Sita is kidnapped by the demon Ravana, and Rama undertakes a heroic quest to rescue her. Eventually, Rama defeats the demon and his army and, after Sita's purity is proved, they return from exile and Rama ascends the throne. In recounting Rama's story, the epic also expresses, often allegorically, the fundamental wisdom of the Hindu sages and philosophers in the realms of ethics, the ideals of government and ideal family roles, hence its great religious significance. *See also* MAHĀBHĀRATA.

rannaigheacht An Irish syllabic verse form. The *rannaigheacht ghairid* is a quatrain (*q.v.*) stanza in which the first line has three syllables and the rest seven. It rhymes aaba, and the third line cross-rhymes with the fourth. There are variations. For example, if lines end in disyllables instead of monosyllables, the form is called *rannaigheacht chetharchubaid garit recomarcach. Rannaigheacht mhor* is a quatrain stanza of heptasyllable lines which consonate abab. In this form there are at least two cross-rhymes in each couplet and the final word of the third line rhymes with a word in the middle of the fourth. In the second couplet rhymes must be exact. In each line two words alliterate.

RAPP An acronym for Russian Association of Proletarian Writers. This organization was created in 1929 and was an off-shoot of the *proletarskaya kul'tura* (*q.v.*) movement during the first Five-Year Plan. It was violently anti-bourgeois and strongly in favour of proletarian culture and literature. Its militant chairman was Leopold Averbakh (1903–38). RAPP was disbanded in 1932 and merged with the Union of Soviet Writers (*q.v.*).

rasa A Sanskrit term for one of the nine so-called flavours of a work of art. The desirable nine are: the erotic, heroic, furious, piteous, comic, fearful, repulsive, marvellous and peaceful.

rationalism At least three basic meanings may be distinguished: (a) the theory or doctrine that human reason can provide *a priori* knowledge without intermediary sense data; (b) the theory or doctrine that reason can pursue and attain truth for its own sake; (c) the idea or conviction that a rational order can be found in reality; and, alternatively, that reason can impose an order on reality.

Rationalism, rationalist and rational are often used fairly loosely. For example, the 18th c. is referred to as a period of rationalism; a rationalist may be a person who depends on reason rather than feeling and intuitive perception; being rational may mean using the brain and ratiocinative processes rather than any others. All three terms are occasionally used pejoratively.

Raumbühne The German term for theatre-in-the-round (*q.v.*).

readerly/writerly Terms devised by Roland Barthes (1915–80), the French critic, to make a distinction between two basic kinds of text: the *lisible* ('readerly') and the *scriptible* ('writerly'). He expounds on this in his book *S/Z* (1970). By a 'readerly' text he means a book (a novel, say) to which a reader's response is more or less passive. For example, a 'realistic' novel (or any 'classic text' as Barthes terms them), presents to us a recognizable world with easily recognizable characters and events. The reader accepts the meaning without needing to make much effort. A 'writerly' text, however, makes demands on the reader; he or she has to work things out, look for and provide meaning. Obvious examples of writerly texts are Joyce's *Ulysses* and *Finnegans Wake*. A writerly text tends to focus attention on how it is written, on the mechanics of it, the particular use of language. A writerly text tends to be self-conscious; it calls attention to itself as a work of art. It also makes the reader into a producer. Barthes makes the point that the writerly text is of value because the goal of literary work (of literature as work) is to make the reader no longer a consumer, but a producer of the text. However, as Barthes demonstrates in his analysis of Balzac's short story *Sarrasine* (which is basically a readerly story but which Barthes discusses as a writerly one), a critic may, if he or she wishes, read any story as either writerly or readerly. A readerly or writerly reading is not inherent in the text but may be a part of the reading. *See also* AUTHOR, DEATH OF; CODE; LISIBLE; POSTSTRUCTURALISM; STRUCTURALISM.

reader-oriented theory *See* READER-RESPONSE THEORY; RECEPTION THEORY.

reader-response theory Theory concerned with the relationship between text and reader and reader and text, with the emphasis on the different ways in which a reader participates in the course of reading a text and the different perspectives which arise in the relationship Thus, reader-response theory is concerned with the reader's contribution to a text, and it challenges, with varying degrees of plausibility and conviction, the text-oriented theories of Formalism and the New Criticism (*qq.v.*), which have tended to ignore or underestimate the reader's role.

Fundamentally, a text, whatever it be (poem, short story, essay, scientific exposition), has no real existence until it is read. Its meaning is *in potentia*, so to speak. A reader completes its meaning by reading it. The reading is complementary; it *actualizes potential meaning*. Thus, the reader does not have a passive role, as has been traditionally thought; on the contrary, she is an active agent in the creation of meaning. By applying codes and strategies the reader decodes the text.

Various theories about this 'collaboration' have been advanced since the mid- to late 1970s. For example, in his book *The Act of Reading: A Theory of Aesthetic Response* (1976, trans. 1978) Wolfgang Iser puts the proposition that all literary texts have *Leerstellen* ('blanks', 'gaps' or 'lacunae'). These blanks have to be filled in or 'concretized' by the reader in order to interpret the text. But this proposition poses a basic question: is the text itself the cause of the reader's interpretation, or does the reader impose, as it were, an interpretation on the text? A possible answer to this is that the reader supplies a set of social, historical and cultural norms but the text calls them forth and in a sense contains them.

In 1979 Umberto Eco, the Italian semiotician and novelist, published *The Role of the Reader*. In this he proposes a distinction between what he calls 'open' and 'closed' texts. An 'open' text (e.g. *Finnegans Wake*, Eliot's *The Waste Land* or Jacques Lacan's theories of the unconscious) requires the reader's close and active collaboration in the creation of meaning; whereas a 'closed' text (e.g. a whodunnit by Agatha Christie, a thriller by Frederick Forsyth or a scientific treatise on lice) more or less determines or predetermines a reader's response; though, of course, in a detective story the interpretation of clues would be an important part of a reader's response.

Yet another reader-response theory is that advanced by the Americans Norman Holland and David Bleich. In their view reading is a form of covert wish-fulfilment, so the reader engages with a text as with any other form of desire. In their books – *Five Readers Reading* (1975) by Holland and *Subjective Criticism* (1978) by Bleich – they analyse in depth the reading habits and responses of individual readers.

In *Semiotics of Poetry* (1978) Michael Riffaterre postulates what he describes as the 'Superreader', who analyses a text in a search for meanings beyond and below surface meanings. The 'Superreader' represents the sum of reactions to the language of a text manifested in the published work of its interpreters, translators and so on. Riffaterre believes that the stylistic function of a text can be analysed objectively, that style has a constant trans-subjective tone. He suggests that the task of the stylistician is to reveal what is ungrammatical or in any other way unconventional or 'abnormal' in the way a text (e.g. a poem) is composed.

In examination of the conventions of reading, Jonathan Culler (in *The Pursuit of Signs: Semiotics, Literature, Deconstruction*, 1981) attempts a structuralist theory of interpretation in the analysis of readers' strategies, with an emphasis on the operation of interpretive moves rather than the content of the moves.

Another theory about the reader and reader responses has been proposed by Gerald Prince, who coins the term 'narratee' (*q.v.*). The 'narratee' is not the reader but the kind of person who is addressed by the narrator.

The American critic Stanley Fish evolved a reader-oriented theory which he calls 'affective stylistics'. He is concerned with the ways a reader's responses develop and change in relation to the words or sentences *as they succeed each other in time*.

Yet another aspect of reader-response theory is contained in what is known as 'reception theory' (*q.v.*), discussed by Hans Robert Jauss in connection with what he calls the 'horizon of expectations' (*q.v.*).

Reader-oriented theory is fundamental to phenomenology (*q.v.*) and phenomenological criticism and also to theories of hermeneutics (*q.v.*). *See also* IMPLIED READER/ACTUAL READER; READERLY/WRITERLY.

realism Fundamentally, in literature, realism is the portrayal of life with fidelity. It is thus not concerned with idealization, with rendering things as beautiful when they are not, or in any way presenting them in any guise as they are not; nor, as a rule, is realism concerned with presenting the supranormal or transcendental.

The use of the terms real and realistic clearly implies their antitheses, like unreal, unrealistic, fantastic, improbable, fanciful, of the dream world. The imaginative flights of bizarre invention that we find in some of Lucian's works, in Rabelais, in Voltaire's *Candide*, in H. G. Wells's *The War of the Worlds*, in Ray Bradbury's science fiction (*q.v.*) stories, are not realistic, though they are excellent fantasy based on reality. Occasionally a writer (e.g. Roald Dahl) manages to keep a beautiful and breathtaking balance on that high wire that joins both worlds.

In the end realism, as a literary term, is about as clear and bendable a term as, say, romanticism (*q.v.*) and, as it happens, they are the -isms of two very different camps – if not campuses. In the last hundred years or so there have developed a large number of theories about realism, and about what is to be regarded as realistic or not. We can hardly avoid using the term on occasions, particularly when we mean to state or suggest that a work of literature has verisimilitude (*q.v.*) or in some way possesses that kind of authenticity which is generally believed to be an essential quality in a work of literature, however fantastic or improbable (in some cases) it might be – or *seems* to be.

The issue has been much confused by the fact that in the 19th c. – a period almost too fertile in antinomies, schools, movements and, to use the current jargon, 'cultural fissiparation' – there was a recognizable and conscious movement in literature which was subsequently tagged 'realism'. The French were responsible for this movement. It began sometime in the 1830s and had gathered momentum by the 1850s. During the latter part of the century realism was a definite trend in European literature.

One of the earlier instances of the use of the term *le réalisme* is to be found in the *Mercure français du XIXe siècle* (1826). Here it refers to a point of view or doctrine which states that realism is a copy of nature and reveals to us the literature of truth. Realism rejects classicism (*q.v.*), romanticism and the doctrine of art for art's sake (*q.v.*).

It is clear that, according to the realist, an artist should concern herself with the here and now, with everyday events, with her own environment and with the movements (political, social, etc.) of her time. The anti-Romantic movements in Germany also concentrated attention on the lot of the common person and on the need to present life with all its warts. In general we can see clearly enough in the works of Immermann, Balzac and Dickens, for instance, what forms the realist attitude was likely to take.

Theory combined with practice in the 19th c. to produce a large body of literature which presented an altogether different view of the so-called *condition humaine*. The practice was almost certainly influenced by philosophical thought, and most notably by Comte's *Cours de philosophie positive* (1830). Comte's positivism made sociology a prime science. Later, the inquiries of Feuerbach and Darwin induced many people to reappraise assumptions about their origin and to take a very different view of the environment. Later, also, Comte's theories were applied by Taine to the sphere of literature, especially in *Histoire de la littérature anglaise* (1863–4) and in *Nouveaux essais de critique et d'histoire* (1865). One may also suppose that the invention of photography in 1839 had an immense effect on the way people looked at the world and existence in general. Here was precision; the scene, the fact, the episode were faithfully recorded. The paintings of Courbet, too, had an incalculable influence. Courbet was strongly opposed to any kind of idealization in art. He rejected both Classical and Romantic precepts and tastes, and maintained that only realism was democratic. For him the peasant and the worker were the fittest and most estimable subjects for a painter. Champfleury, in *Le Réalisme* (1857), applied Courbet's point of view to literature and suggested that the hero in the novel should be an ordinary man. Here, no doubt, we have the egg of the so-called anti-hero (*q.v.*) whose genesis *appears* to have been of a later date.

It is a noteworthy curiosity of this realistic movement that in the first place realism was either defined negatively or rejected as undesirable. Courbet himself did not like it as a label though he used it himself. Champfleury expressed disapproval of it in his essays *Le Réalisme*. Baudelaire described it as an 'injure dégoutante' and as a 'mot vague et élastique'. Edmond de Goncourt also expressed dislike of it in his preface to *Les Frères Zemganno* (1879). Distaste for the term seems to have arisen from a fear that realism would be regarded as a school or movement, which is how we are inclined to think of it now. As it happened, Champfleury was the prime mover behind a trend already very apparent in the novels of Balzac and Stendhal. *Le Réalisme* was virtually a manifesto of a new doctrine.

In the same year in which Champfleury published this, Flaubert produced *Madame Bovary*, which was greeted as a great work of realism (later it was greeted as a great work of naturalism, *q.v.*). Flaubert, too, disliked the label. Other so-called realistic novels to appear at this period were *Germinie Lacerteux* (1865) by Edmond and Jules de Goncourt, and minor works by Ernest Feydeau, who wrote *Fanny* (1858), and Duranty, who wrote *Le Malheur d'Henriette Gérard* (1860).

The realist novelists paid particular attention to exact documentation, to getting the facts right, and in many ways were continuing in a more intensive and conscientious fashion what Balzac had been doing years before in *La Comédie humaine*. Balzac regarded human beings (and analysed character) as a zoologist might and he expressed the intention of following Buffon's work on zoology in order to write a natural history of man. This was a scientific approach which, at times, came near to the method of the field guide quoted above.

Zola and Maupassant have also been taken as exponents of realism but it is perhaps more correct to regard them as the supreme analysts of the school of naturalism. Zola's essays in *Le Roman expérimental* (1880) are one of the main statements about naturalism.

Outside France the effects of realism are to be seen in the works of Tolstoy, Gogol and Gorky, and, to a lesser extent, in Turgenev. Also in the work of Gissing and the American novelist William Dean Howells.

As far as drama is concerned, realism in the 19th c. was a less extreme form of naturalism. Playwrights who favoured realism – Ibsen is a key figure – rejected the concept of the well-made play (*q.v.*) with its mechanical artifices and its altogether too slick plotting, and rejected also exaggerated theatricalism. Ibsen's influence was very great, especially on Shaw and Strindberg, and subsequently on a whole generation of prominent 20th c. dramatists; not to mention Stanislavsky and the various adaptations of his teachings in method acting.

What is known as socialist realism (*q.v.*) in the theatre is largely a Russian phenomenon. Anatoli Lunacharsky (1875–1933) invented the theory of it. This involved the development of specifically Soviet theatre. Classics were to be interpreted in contemporary terms so that they became more relevant to the people. New plays should be about life lived by ordinary people. The effects of his teachings in Communist countries have been considerable, even where the Kremlin faith has been thrown over with consequent excommunication – as in Albania. Now, socialist realism suggests the committed propaganda (*q.v.*) of writers submissive to a particular political regime.

Realism occurs in another important context, namely psychological realism. This denotes fidelity to the truth in depicting the inner workings of the mind, the analysis of thought and feeling, the presentation of the nature of personality and character. Such realism also requires a fictional character to behave *in* character. The ultimate in psychological realism is the use of the stream of consciousness (*q.v.*) method. This kind of realism, too, has often resulted in a kind of decadence (*q.v.*) as authors dig deeper and further and with greater relish into the scatological and orectic chaos of the conscious and subconscious territories.

In the light of the broad historical background outlined above, it is clear that realism has comprised not just a literary technique but a vast historical phenomenon with economic, ideological, philosophic and religious ramifications. This is neatly indicated in Fredric Jameson's statement that 'the realistic mode . . . is one of the most complex and vital realizations of Western culture, to which it is . . . well-nigh unique'. *See also* ROMAN DOCUMENTAIRE; SLICE OF LIFE; VERISM.

reality effect A term used by Roland Barthes to describe the strategy of some forms of literary realism which attempt to present an interpretation of reality as reality itself, effectively suppressing one part of the overall sign (the signified) and purporting to offer a direct relationship between the signifier and the object (or reality) itself.

recension A critical revision of a literary work.

reception theory A school of literary theory which is associated particularly with the University of Konstanz and the journal *Poetik und Hermeneutik* (published from 1964). One theorist, namely Hans Robert Jauss, is especially associated with the theory. He is concerned with the general response to literature in terms of reception-aesthetics rather than the individual's response, and he suggests that literary work should be studied in terms of the impression or impact it makes on its contemporary audience, and that literary value is judged according to how much the view of a text alters over time. 'Aesthetic distance' (*q.v.*) is the term used by Jauss to denote the difference between the contemporary view of a work of art (at the time of its first publication) and the present-day view. But still the idea holds that the reader has a contribution to make in the process. So there is a kind of balance and cooperation between text and what it provides and what the reader contributes. However, all readers are different and therefore may be supposed to bring a different response to any text.

More recently a number of American critics (e.g. Edward Said, Jonathan Culler and Stanley Fish) have become interested in 'reading communities' and institutions as determining forces in the reading of texts. Fish, for instance, holds that it is only within a given community or institution that the facts of literary study (i.e. genres, periods, authors, texts) are available, and that these 'facts' are as much a product of the community as they are of the interpreters. Fish contends that all interpreters are extensions of communities. His collection of essays *Is There a Text in This Class?* (1980) is relevant. *See* FORMALISM, RUSSIAN; HORIZON OF EXPECTATIONS; PHENOMENOLOGY; READER-RESPONSE THEORY.

receptor A jargon term for the person (or group of persons) experiencing a work of art.

recessive accent This occurs when a word usually accented on its final syllable is followed by another heavily accented word. For the sake of meter and rhythm the accent is shifted to the beginning of the preceding word. A common practice in writing blank verse.

récit (F 'narration, narrative, accounts of events, recital') A form of fictional narrative which is related to the *novella*, the *Novelle*, the *roman* and the *nouvelle* (*qq.v.*). André Gide, one of its most notable practitioners, made a clear distinction between his *romans* and his *récits*. *Les Faux-monnayeurs* (1926), for instance, is a *roman*; *L'Immoraliste* (1902) and *La Porte étroite* (1909) are outstanding examples of the *récit*. Gide theorized about both forms, and debate as to precisely what a *récit* is and is not continues. Typically, a *récit* has a high degree of compression and concentration and the narrative is related from one point of view (two in *La Porte étroite*). It has a single theme and very few characters, apart from the central character on whom attention is focused almost exclusively. Events and actions should speak for themselves and the reader is left to draw his or her own conclusions. Thus, there is no intervention on the part of the author to explain motives, pass judgements or draw conclusions. Gide's *récits* combine intimate personal experience with a technique which is aimed to exclude the presence of the author. His elimination of the author in some ways prefigures Roland Barthes's celebrated exposition *The Death of the Author* (*see* AUTHOR, DEATH OF). In order to achieve the required effacement he uses the first-person narrator device, but the first person is 'borrowed'. The author effaces himself behind his narrator (who is also his hero/heroine or one of the main characters). Whereas in a novel events tend to unfold in a chronological sequence and are described as they occur, the events in a *récit* are depicted by an oblique, reflective and associative method. *Récits* may be as long as novels and a plot may extend over a longer period of time than does the single and significant episode of the *nouvelle*. The *récit* seems to have a kind of intermediary position between novel and *nouvelle*. Apart from those cited, examples which might fall into the *récit* category are Samuel Beckett's *Malone Dies* (1951) and Albert Camus's *La Chute* (1956). *See also* NARRATOLOGY.

recognition *See* ANAGNORISIS.

recoil A term used when speaking of tragedy (*q.v.*) to indicate that the protagonist has brought about his own doom.

recto and verso The *recto* is the right-hand page in a book; the *verso* the left-hand page.

redaction The editing or revising of a work for publication.

redondilla (Sp 'little round', diminutive of *redondo*, 'round, clear, straightforward'; or 'a round, ring, circle') An eight-syllable quatrain (*q.v.*) rhyming either abba or abab, but in the latter rhyme scheme it is usually called *serventesio*. Sometimes *redondilla* is referred to as *redondilla mayor*, *cuarteta* and *cuartilla*. Formerly the term included the *quintilla* (*q.v.*) and was also applied to any eight-syllable strophe in which all the verses rhymed in consonance. This is an important form because it was adapted by one poet after another until Lope de Vega and Calderón used it very widely and often for specific purposes (for example, to create mood) in drama. In the verses of King Alfonso the Wise *redondillas* of *pie cruzado* are also to be found.

redundant verse *See* ACATALECTIC.

reduplicatio *See* ANADIPLOSIS.

reference, point of An idea developed by Coventry Patmore (*Principle in Art*, 1889) and first applied to painting. It was gradually adopted as a literary term, partly owing to Quiller-Couch, and as such now denotes a figure, a character, who may be regarded as 'normal' or balanced in the sense that he keeps a sense of proportion amidst excesses. A sound example is the sane, good and pragmatic Kent in *King Lear*. *See also* IDEAL SPECTATOR.

referent *See* SIGNIFIER/SIGNIFIED.

referential language *See* EMOTIVE LANGUAGE.

reflexive novel A novel in which the author calls the reader's attention to the fact that he or she is writing (or has written) a novel. Thus, what Roland Barthes would call a 'writerly' novel. A classic and early example of such a work is Laurence Sterne's *Tristram Shandy* (1760–7), an attempt at autobiography in which virtually no progress is made. Sterne uses many devices to show that there is a discrepancy between reality/life and art, and that it is not possible to provide a coherent and rational picture of anything so complex as life and reality. Other reflexive novels of that period are Fielding's *Joseph Andrews* (1742) and his *Tom Jones* (1749).

In the 19th c. most novelists tried to give form, shape and rationality to their versions of reality, though this often tended to falsify reality in the cause of artistic and aesthetic coherence. Periodically, one can see that novelists were well aware of the inherent shortcomings of the endeavour to impose form on the disorderly or chaotic.

In the 20th c. numerous novelists developed various forms of reflexive novel. James Joyce (with *Ulysses*, 1922) is an outstanding example. So is Gide's *Les Faux-monnayeurs* (1926). Since the 1950s we should also mention the work of Vladimir Nabokov, Flann O'Brien, William Burroughs, Christine Brooke-Rose, Samuel Beckett, Alain Robbe-Grillet, Thomas Pynchon, John Fowles and Salman Rushdie. This kind of fiction is also sometimes called 'self-conscious' or 'self-referential'. *See also* ANTI-NOVEL; METAFICTION; NOUVEAU ROMAN; READERLY/WRITERLY; STREAM OF CONSCIOUSNESS.

reflexivity (L *reflectere*, 'to bend back') Writing which is reflexive (or self-referential) draws attention to its own textuality, that is, its own origins, history, and literary and rhetorical techniques and processes of construction. The concept has its root in the linguistic notion of language which refers to itself. *See also* METAFICTION; REFLEXIVE NOVEL.

refrain A phrase, line or lines repeated at intervals during a poem and especially at the end of a stanza. A device of great antiquity, it is found in the Egyptian Book of the Dead, the Bible, Greek and Latin verse, in Provençal and Renaissance verse and in many ballads (*q.v.*). Very often it is an exact repetition. Sometimes it serves to work out an 'argument' (*q.v.*) in a poem, in which case it will undergo a slight modification, as in this fine lyric by Sir Thomas Wyatt:

> Disdain me not without desert,
>   Nor leave me not so suddenly;
> Since well ye wot that in my heart
>   I mean ye not but honestly.
>   Disdain me not.
>
> Refuse me not without cause why,
>   Nor think me not to be unjust;
> Since that by lot of fantasy
>   This careful knot needs knit I must.
>   Refuse me not.

See REPETEND; REPETITION.

regional novel A regional writer is one who concentrates much attention on a particular area and uses it and the people who inhabit it as the basis for his or her stories. Such a locale is likely to be rural and/or provincial. Among the earliest of regional novelists was Maria Edgeworth (1767–1849), an Anglo-Irish woman who was one of the first to perceive the possibilities of relating characters to a particular environment. Her most notable novels were *Castle Rackrent* (1800), *Belinda* (1801) and *The Absentee* (1812).

Castle Rackrent is generally believed to have been the first of its kind. It was followed quite soon by novels by the Irish writer Lady Morgan (1776–1859). The Scottish novels of John Galt (1779–1839) and Sir Walter Scott (1771–1832) were also closely dependent on regional study and atmosphere. Once established, the regional novel began to interest a number of writers, and soon the regions described became smaller and more specifically defined. For example, the novels of Mrs Gaskell (1810–65) and George Eliot (1819–80) centred on the Midlands, and those of the Brontë sisters were set in Yorkshire. Other novelists to concentrate on particular areas were Charles Kingsley (1819–75) and R. D. Blackmore (1825–1900), who set their scenes in Devon, Richard Jefferies (1848–87), who concentrated on his native Hampshire (and Wiltshire), Robert Louis Stevenson (1850–94), who wrote about the Highlands and Lowlands, and J. M. Barrie (1860–1937), who was devoted to Angus.

The four outstanding regional novelists were: Thomas Hardy (1840–1928), who re-created the West Country (especially Dorset) in many of his novels and short stories and revived the name Wessex; Arnold Bennett (1867–1931), who centred many of his stories on the Potteries – 'the five towns'; D. H. Lawrence (1885–1930), who evoked his native Nottinghamshire; and William Faulkner (1897–1962), whose main focus was the Deep South in the USA.

There were also 'urban' or 'industrial' novels, set in a particular town or city, some of which had considerable fame in the 19th c. and some of which remain major novels. Notable instances are Mrs Gaskell's *Mary Barton* (1848) and her *North and South* (1854–5), Charles Dickens's *Hard Times* (1854) and George Eliot's *Middlemarch* (1871–2).

The tradition of the regional novel in Britain is by no means defunct. Latterly, Stanley Middleton and Stanley Barstow have both written a number of such novels; the former about his native Nottinghamshire and the latter about his native Yorkshire. Alan Sillitoe has also contributed to this form of fiction.

Other distinguished writers of this kind were the Spanish Countess Emilia Pardo Bazán, who wrote about Galician life in the 19th c.; Grazia Deledda (1871–1936), who wrote mostly about Sardinia and its people; Ivan Cankar (1876–1918), the Slovene dramatist and writer of short stories whose native Slovenia was the scene of much of his work; Ivo Andrić (1892–1975), a number of whose novels and short stories are about his native Bosnia, and in particular the small townships of Travnik and Višegrad; and Jean Giono (1895–1970), who re-created the region of Provence in several of his books. *See* CONDITION OF ENGLAND NOVEL; LOCAL COLOUR; NOVEL; REALISM.

register A list of facts or names. A precise record. A volume into which information is entered systematically. Early examples of registers were the *Doomsday Book* and a bead-roll. *See* ROLL.

regressio *See* EPANADOS.

reification (L *res* + *facere*, 'to make a thing' of) Refers in general to the treating of an idea or concept as a thing or object possessing fixity. Marx used the term to denote the viewing of human products and social relations as fixed objective or natural entities. Money or gold, for example, can embody the reification of human labour, as can the products of that labour. Likewise, in capitalist society, human subjectivity can be reified, treated as a fixed and identified with its productive value or relations. As such, reification is an instance of alienation (*q.v.*) and is related to commodity fetishism.

Reification has been an important concept in the work of Lukács, the Frankfurt School (*q.v.*), and modern theorists such as Roland Barthes, Jacques Derrida and the Frankfurt philosopher Axel Honneth, who has recently attempted to rethink the concept in terms of intersubjective struggles for recognition. *See also* ALIENATION; FETISHISM; MARXIST CRITICISM.

rejet A term in French prosody which denotes that the sense in one line of verse is completed in the next; that part 'run over' is the *rejet*. *See also* ENJAMBEMENT; RUN-ON LINE.

relativism In aesthetics the term refers to a situation in which it is logically possible for two contradictory 'value judgements' to be true and known to be true. For instance: (a) this is a good novel; (b) this novel is bad. Apart from the subjective nature of the critic's opinion and tastes it must be remembered that sensibility changes from age to age, and what was regarded as a good novel in 1900 may be thought much otherwise fifty years later. *See* ABSOLUTISM.

remate (Sp 'end, finish, finishing touch', from the verb *rematar*, 'to end, to stop, to finish off') The last and shortest stanza of a *canción* or song. It goes under other names: *commiato, despido, envio, contera, ripressa. See also* ENVOI.

Renaissance (F 'rebirth', from Italian *rinascenza, rinascimento*) The original meaning of the Italian *rinascimento* for those who actually took part in it was the 'rebirth' of Classical Greek and Latin literature. The term is commonly applied to the historical period which follows the Middle Ages, but when the Middle Ages ended and when the Renaissance began has been a source of much debate. A long-accepted view was that the Renaissance began in the latter half of the 14th c. and that it continued throughout the 15th and 16th c. and perhaps even later. In order to make the issues more manageable historians have identified periods within the period; hence, early, middle, high and late Renaissance.

In the course of time a variety of misconceptions about the Middle Ages (as opposed to the Renaissance) developed. These became particularly apparent in the 19th c. when, among some, there evolved an image of the Middle Ages as being ignorant, narrow, priest-ridden, backward, superstitious, uncultured and inhibitied by dogmatic theology. By contrast, the Renaissance was extolled as learned, civilized, broadminded, progressive, enlightened and free-thinking. The derogatory view of the Middle Ages was encouraged by such writers as Jules Michelet (1798–1874), J. A. Symonds (1840–93) and G. G. Coulton (1858–1947). J. A. Symonds was even capable of saying that: 'The arts and the inventions, the knowledge and the books which suddenly became vital at the Renaissance, had long been neglected on the shores of the Dead Sea which we call the Middle Ages.' Moreover, misconceptions about the Renaissance (and, *ipso facto*, the Middle Ages) were presented by Jacob Burckhardt (1818–97) and Walter Pater (1839–94).

Nor have the terms 'medieval' and 'Middle Ages' by any means lost their pejorative connotations. People still use them to suggest the backward and the primitive. The late Sir Julian Huxley was capable of doing so. Such implied attitudes overlook the facts that the period 1100–1400 produced such men as (and this is a random selection): Abelard, Hartmann von der Aue, Walther von der Vogelweide, Wolfram von Eschenbach, Albert the Great, St Bernard, Thomas Aquinas, Peter Lombard, Roger Bacon, Guinicelli, Ramon Llull, Giovanni Pisano, Vincent of Beauvais, Meister Eckhart, William Langland and Chaucer . . . And such cathedrals as those of Piacenza, Rochester, Chartres, Mainz, Lisbon, Modena, Verona, Siena, Notre Dame de Paris, Rheims, Amiens, Salisbury, Burgos, Toledo and Cologne . . .

Opinions like those of J. A. Symonds have been totally discredited during the 20th c., and in recent years historians' views about the Renaissance have been considerably modified. Moreover, there has been a tendency to think in terms of several renaissances, each succeeding the other and each gathering a kind of momentum from its predecessor(s). Such a view has, for instance, been put persuasively by Irwin Panofsky in *Meaning in the Visual Arts* (1955). The beginnings of the Renaissance have been pushed further and further back, even as far as the 12th c. – and not without justice. At that time Romanesque architecture was at a high point of development and Gothic architecture was beginning. Vernacular literatures were developing. There was a revival of the Latin classics, Latin poetry and Roman law. Greek philosophy and Greek and Arab scientific discoveries were becoming known. The first European universities were being founded. In short, intellectual and creative activity abounded.

Italy is customarily taken as the starting place of the Renaissance but authorities differ as to when. As far as literature is concerned, some settle for the 14th c. (even though this omits a considerable part of Dante's life, 1265–1321). Others prefer the 13th c. and cite the Sicilian School (*q.v.*), that group of talented poets who flourished at the Palermo court of the Hohenstaufen monarchs from *c.* 1200. We should also note that there was a modest literary renaissance in Bohemia (and other parts of what is now Slovakia and the Czech Republic) during the 14th c.

It may be that attempts to identify a beginning to the Renaissance are not particularly helpful or fruitful. We might cite the problems inherent in tracing the development of painting from *c.* 1150. For instance, Cimabue (*c.* 1240–*c.* 1302), Duccio (*c.* 1255/60–*c.* 1318/19) and Giotto (*c.* 1266/7–1337) are often taken to be important pioneers of the Renaissance in Italy (and so they were), but what they attempted and achieved in their work had *already* been anticipated by court painters (e.g. Dimitrije, Djordje and Teodor) in the churches built under the Nemanjić dynasty in the Balkans (usually referred to as the 'Raška School') late in the 12th c. and early in the 13th c., and was later often excelled by the successors (e.g. Astrapas, Mihajlo and Eutihije) of those painters in the late 13th c. and early 14th c.

Broadly speaking it may be said that between *c.* 1200 and *c.* 1600 man's opinions about the nature and structure of the universe (and the role of man in it) brought about profound and far-reaching changes. But the gradualness of these changes must be emphasized. Many attitudes, beliefs and convictions which were commonplace in, say, the 15th c. were still widespread in the 17th. Whether these changes were for good or evil can be argued endlessly.

The gradualness may perhaps be underlined by referring to two outstanding personalities: Ramon Llull and Sir Thomas More. Llull was a Catalan; a gifted poet, a scholar, philosopher, linguist, theologian and encyclopaedist, a prolific author in many fields (his extant works number 243). He spent between 30 and 40 years of his, for those days, exceptionally long life, in travelling over Europe and North Africa in the promotion of the cause of Catholicism. Sir Thomas More's achievements are too well known to need reiteration. Ramon Llull was born in 1235 and died *c.* 1315. More was born in 1478 and executed in 1535. Llull was beatified by the Church and More was canonized. One cannot help feeling that, had they been contemporaries, they would have found much in common. They were both 'Renaissance men'.

Again, broadly speaking, it may be suggested that a survey of the achievements of painters, writers, sculptors and architects (not to mention scientists, philosophers and astronomers) between say, 1200 and 1600, reveals almost continuous creative and intellectual activity of an excellence which may never be equalled. To catalogue the names is to intone a litany of geniuses.

Among writers those invariably mentioned are: Dante, Petrarch, Boccaccio, Machiavelli and Sanazzaro in Italy; Erasmus in the Netherlands; Montaigne, Rabelais and the poets of the Pléiade (*q.v.*) in France; Lope de Vega and Cervantes in Spain; Sir Thomas More, Sir Thomas Wyatt, Edmund Spenser, Sir Philip Sidney, Shakespeare and Sir Francis Bacon in England. *See* HUMANISM; SCHOLASTICISM.

Renaissance humanism   In the first place, the humanists of the Renaissance period were students of *literae humaniores* (*q.v.*); the literature of the Greek and Latin poets, dramatists, philosophers, historians and rhetoricians. At the

Renaissance (*q.v.*) there was a great revival of interest in Classical literature and thought and this revival was, to some extent, at the expense of medieval scholasticism (*q.v.*). The long-term influences of this revival were immense and incalculable, and they led to an excessive devotion to Classical ideals and rules in the late 17th c. and 18th c.

Humanism (*q.v.*), a European phenomenon, was a more worldly and thus more secular philosophy; and it was anthropocentric. It sought to dignify and ennoble man.

In their more extreme forms humanistic attitudes regarded man as the crown of creation; a point of view marvellously expressed in *Hamlet*, by Hamlet:

> ... What a piece of work is a man. How noble in reason, how infinite in faculty. In form and moving how express and admirable in action, how like an angel in apprehension, how like a god. The beauty of the world. The paragon of animals.

It would have been inconceivable that anyone in the 14th c. should have expressed such a view. Then Hamlet adds: 'And yet, to me what is this quintessence of dust?' And in that one line he summarizes another attitude or feeling, which a man in the 14th c. would have responded to instantly.

At its best, humanism helped to civilize man, to make him realize his potential powers and gifts, and to reduce the discrepancy between potentiality and attainment. It was a movement that was at once a product of and a counteraction to a certain prevalent scepticism; a way of dealing with the disequilibrium created by the conflict between belief and doubt. Humanism turned out to be a form of philosophy which concentrated on the perfection of a worldly life, rather than on the preparation for an eternal and spiritual life.

The popularity of the courtesy book (*q.v.*) in the 16th and 17th c., for instance, suggests what a radical change there had been in man's view of himself. He was increasingly regarded as a creature perfectible on earth. Hence the secular emphasis in courtesy books.

Humanistic ideas and beliefs pervade much other literature of the Renaissance period. Ficino (1433–99); Pico della Mirandola (1463–94); Erasmus (1466–1536); Guillaume Budé (1468–1540); Sir Thomas More (1478–1535); Juan Luis Vives (1492–1540); and Montaigne (1533–92) were outstanding humanists.

renga A Japanese verse form; a kind of linked verse in which successive half *tanka* (*q.v.*) are composed by different poets.

repartee A witty or clever rejoinder, as in the story of Bernard Shaw meeting a very fat man on a narrow staircase. Shaw shoved his way past him. 'Pig!' said the fat man angrily. Shaw raised his hat and replied: 'Shaw. Good afternoon.'

repetend A repeated element in a poem; a word, a phrase or a line. The term can be used as a synonym for a refrain (*q.v.*), but a repetend is usually more varied than a refrain and occurs at different and unexpected points in a poem. It is a kind of echo and a common device. A number of excellent examples are to be found in T. S. Eliot's *The Love Song of J. Alfred Prufrock*. See INCREMENTAL REPETITION; REPETITION.

repetitio *See* ANAPHORA.

repetition An essential unifying element in nearly all poetry and much prose. It may consist of sounds, particular syllables and words, phrases, stanzas, metrical patterns, ideas, allusions and shapes. Thus refrain, assonance, rhyme, internal rhyme, alliteration and onomatopoeia (*qq.v.*) are frequent in repetition. *Hoarding* by Roger McGough contains some ordinary repetitive elements:

> all too busy boarding
> thirty year old numbskull
> with a change of dirty coats
> every single day gets porridge
> but never gets his oats
>
> all too busy boarding
> the xmas merry-go-round

replevin (OF *replevir*, from *plevir*, 'to pledge') Of legal origin, it denotes an inquiry intended to restore to the owner goods which have been in some way wrongfully distrained. As a literary term it denotes an inquiry intended to secure for a writer recognition which has been denied.

resolution Those events which form the outcome of the climax of a play or story. The equivalent of falling action (*q.v.*).

rest A metrical term adopted from music. It indicates where a pause seems to compensate for the absence of an unstressed syllable (or syllables) in a foot.

Restoration comedy That kind of drama which prevailed between the restoration of the English monarchy in 1660 and the advent of sentimental comedy (*q.v.*) early in the 18th c. It is also referred to as artificial comedy or comedy of manners (*q.v.*) and was chiefly concerned with presenting a society of elegance and stylishness. Its characters were gallants, ladies and gentlemen of fashion and rank, fops, rakes, social climbers and country bumpkins. Witty, urbane and sometimes licentious, it dealt with the intricacies of sexual and marital intrigue and therefore also with adultery and cuckoldry. A five-star constellation of gifted playwrights were largely responsible for this resurgence of theatrical life after the Puritan period. They were Wycherley, Etheredge, Congreve, Vanbrugh and Farquhar. The main plays were: Wycherley's *The Country Wife* (1672 or 1673) and *The Plain Dealer* (1674); Etheredge's *The Man of Mode* (1676); Congreve's *The Double Dealer* (1694), *Love for Love* (1895) and *The Way of the World* (1700); Vanbrugh's *The*

Relapse (1697) and *The Provoked Wife* (1697); Farquhar's *The Recruiting Officer* (1706) and *The Beaux' Stratagem* (1707). These last two were somewhat less mannered and artificial than their predecessors. *See* COMEDY; RESTORATION PERIOD.

Restoration period   It is usually taken to apply to the period from 1660 (the year Charles II was re-established as monarch) to the end of the century. The outstanding writers in this age were John Aubrey, Dryden, Congreve, Sir John Vanbrugh, Farquhar, Etheredge, Wycherley, Pepys, George Savile Marquess of Halifax, Otway, Samuel Butler, the Earl of Rochester, and Sir William Temple. Dryden was the major writer of the period in both verse and prose. *See also* RESTORATION COMEDY.

resumptio   *See* EPANALEPSIS.

revenge tragedy   A form of tragic drama in which someone (usually a hero or a villain) rights a wrong. Perhaps the earliest instance of a kind of revenge tragedy is the *Oresteia* of Aeschylus. During the Renaissance period two main 'revenge' traditions are discernible: first, the French–Spanish tradition, best exemplified in the work of Lope de Vega (1562–1635), Calderón (1600–81) and Corneille (1606–84). In their treatment of revenge themes the emphasis is on the point of honour (*see* CALDERONIAN HONOUR) and the conflict between love and duty. English revenge tragedy owed much to Senecan tragedy (*q.v.*). The Elizabethan dramatists took Seneca as a model and the Roman stoic's influence can be seen in a considerable body of drama between *c.* 1580 and *c.* 1630. His plays were sensational, melodramatic and savage, and emphasized bloodshed and vengeance. One of the earliest English Senecan-type tragedies was *Gorboduc* (1561), in which there is a revenge element: Porrex, one of the sons of King Gorboduc and Queen Videna, kills his brother Ferrex. The mother avenges the murder by killing Porrex. However, it was Thomas Kyd who established the genre of revenge tragedy in England with *The Spanish Tragedy* (*c.* 1586). This play contains many of the basic features of the genre. It begins with the introduction of a ghost and with the character of Revenge. In the course of the play they function as Chorus (*q.v.*) to an elaborate intrigue in which Hieronomo seeks revenge for his murdered son. Hieronomo pretends to be mad and presents a play in dumb show (*q.v.*) at court. *The Spanish Tragedy* was a sensational play which pleased the Elizabethan taste for blood, melodrama and rhetoric. It was popular (though ridiculed by writers of the period) and had a wide influence.

Shakespeare's first attempt at the genre was *Titus Andronicus* (1594). This is similar in construction to *The Spanish Tragedy* and deeply under its influence. It is one of the bloodiest and most horrific of all plays. Later, Shakespeare was to raise the genre to its highest level with *Hamlet* (1603–4). He may have been influenced by what is known as the *Ur-Hamlet*, a play not extant.

A different kind of revenge tragedy was Marlowe's *The Jew of Malta* (*c.* 1592), a kind of chronicle history concerned with the siege of Malta in which the central character is Barabas, a revengeful Jew, and a Machiavel (*q.v.*) type. John Marston's *Antonio's Revenge* (1600) carried on the Kyd tradition and was unmarked by Marlowe's influence; but Marston's play *The Malcontent* (1604) – a rare example of comedy involving revenge in the tragic tradition – has a plurality of revenging characters and also a revenger in disguise. In *Hoffman* (1602), Henry Chettle had already achieved a further development by making his hero revenger a villain (*q.v.*) who has no good cause, who is morally corrupt and exults in his villainous deeds rather as Iago does in *Othello* (1604). *Othello* is not a revenge tragedy but Iago is the supreme villain of the period and much of the play is concerned with the way in which he takes his revenge on the Moor. Cyril Tourneur's *The Revenger's Tragedy* (1607) is the last of the major tragedies in the tradition of Kyd but the villain revenger is a different kind of person from any of the villains hitherto. From about this time the villain became more and more prominent. In many plays the protagonist was a villain and the themes of revenge and motives of revenge became more and more complex.

In its decadence revenge tragedy became increasingly sensational and macabre. Ghosts, apparitions, graveyards, charnel houses, incest, insanity, adultery, rape, murder, infanticide, suicide, arson, poisoning and treachery were commonplace elements. Moral and political corruption were displayed in lurid detail. The characters inhabited microcosms of hell in which the plotting villains went about their work with sardonic relish, devising ever more bizarre methods of destroying people. Death was the main subject on their syllabus and murder their recreation.

Among other major works which have revenge themes mention should be made of: George Chapman's *The Revenge of Bussy D'Ambois* (1607); Tourneur's *The Atheist's Tragedy* (1611); Webster's *The White Devil* (1612) and *The Duchess of Malfi* (*c.* 1613–14); and Middleton and Rowley's *The Changeling* (1622).

Of the many minor works in this tradition, some of the more outstanding are: John Fletcher's *The Bloody Brother* (*c.* 1616); Thomas Drue's *The Bloody Banquet* (1620); Massinger's *The Duke of Milan* (1620); James Shirley's *The Maid's Revenge* (1626); and Henry Glapthorne's *Revenge for Honour* (1640).

This kind of drama did not become wholly extinct. Shelley's closet drama (*q.v.*) *The Cenci* (1819) is in the revenge tradition. So are Victor Hugo's *Hernani* (1830) and his *Ruy Blas* (1838). In more recent times Lorca's *Blood Wedding* (1933) continued the form. Arthur Miller's *A View from the Bridge* (1955) treated of the Sicilian point-of-honour revenge in a modern setting. David Rudkin's *Afore Night Come* (1962) also contained revenge elements. *See* TRAGEDY.

reverdie An OF dance form which celebrated the advent of spring. In structure it is similar to the *chanson* (*q.v.*) and has five or six stanzas without a refrain (*q.v.*).

reversal *See* PERIPETEIA.

reversio *See* ANASTROPHE.

Revesby play A remarkable example of English folk drama which comes from Revesby, Lincolnshire. It is akin to the Mumming Play and the Plough Monday play (*qq.v.*). The characters are the Fool and his sons (Pickle Herring, Blue Breeches, Pepper Breeches and Ginger Breeches) and Mr Allspice and Cicely. The Fool has a battle with a hobby-horse and a dragon. The sons perform a ritual killing of the Fool. But the Fool is revived and there follows a sword dance (*q.v.*) and the wooing of Cicely by the Fool and his sons. In all probability this is a dramatic survival of a fertility rite which symbolizes the death of the old year and the resurrection in the spring. *See also* PACE-EGGING PLAY.

review (a) A short notice or discussion or critical article in a paper, journal or periodical; (b) A journal or periodical containing articles on literature, art and philosophy. The *Edinburgh Review* is a famous example: so is the *Quarterly Review*. Publications like *Horizon, Scrutiny,* the *London Magazine, Essays in Criticism* and *Encounter* might well be placed in this category. *See also* PERIODICAL.

revolving stage Often called merely a 'revolve', it is a turntable stage which dates from Roman theatres in the 1st c. BC. In modern times it was first used *c.* 1760 in the Japanese *kabuki* (*q.v.*) theatre. In Europe, the first dates from 1896 in Munich. Such a stage is now a standard piece of equipment in most large theatres and is a great help in bringing about rapid scene changes.

revue A theatrical entertainment comprising dance, song, sketches, mime (*q.v.*) and improvisation. It is usually satirical and topical. Reference to the form is first found in Planché's *Recollections* (1872) when he claims to have been responsible for the first revue on the English stage: a work called *Success: or, a Hit if You Like It* (1825). But this was no more than a review (*q.v.*) of productions in the previous season. The first revue in the modern sense of the term was *Under the Clock* (1893), by Seymour Hicks and Charles Brookfield. In the early 20th c. this kind of entertainment became very popular, and so it continued to be during the First World War. In America revue started up with the *Ziegfeld Follies* in 1907. Since then the vogue for revue has waned little. Famous names associated with it have been C. B. Cochran, Noël Coward and Herbert Farjeon. Notable successes have been *Apple Sauce* (1940); *New Faces* (1940); *Rise Above It* (1941); *Sweet and Low* (1943); *Oranges and Lemons* (1949); *Airs on a Shoestring* (1953).

In 1961 was produced *Beyond the Fringe*, a highly successful attempt at satirical revue which had considerable influence; especially, for instance, on *The Royal Commission Revue* (1964).

Other well-known instances have been *At the Drop of a Hat* (1956) and *At the Drop of Another Hat* (1962), both devised and performed by Michael Flanders and Donald Swann. *See also* EXTRAVAGANZA.

rhapsody (Gk 'stitch song') In ancient Greece a rhapsodist was an itinerant minstrel who recited epic poetry. Part came from memory: part was improvised. A rhapsodist was thus a poet who 'stitched' together various elements.

In a more general sense a rhapsody may be an effusive and emotional (perhaps even ecstatic) utterance in verse or, occasionally, in prose. *See also* GUSLAR; SCOP; SKALD; TROUBADOUR; TROUVÈRE.

rhetoric (Gk *rhētōr*, 'speaker in the assembly') Rhetoric is the art of using language for persuasion, in speaking or writing; especially in oratory. The Classical theoreticians codified rhetoric very thoroughly. A knowledge and command of it was regarded as essential. The major textbooks included Aristotle's *Rhetoric*; Quintilian's *Institutio Oratoria*; Cicero's *De Invertione*, *De Optimo Genere Oratorum* and *De Oratore*. Cicero himself was an accomplished rhetorician. So great was the influence of these men (and, later, of Longinus in the work ascribed to him, *On the Sublime*) that in the Middle Ages rhetoric became part of the *trivium*, together with logic and grammar.

The rules for oral and written composition (these rules altered little from Cicero's day until well on in the 19th c.) were divided into five processes in a logical order: invention, arrangement (or disposition), style, memory and delivery (each had a large number of subdivisions). 'Invention' (*q.v.*) was the discovery of the relevant material; 'arrangement' was the organization of the material into sound structural form; under 'style' (*q.v.*) came the consideration of the appropriate manner for the matter and the occasion (e.g. the grand style, the middle and the low or plain); under 'memory' came guidance on how to memorize speeches; the section devoted to 'delivery' elaborated the technique for actually making a speech.

rhetorical figure An artful arrangement of words to achieve a particular emphasis and effect, as in apostrophe, chiasmus and zeugma (*qq.v.*). A rhetorical figure does not alter the meanings of the words, as a metaphor (*q.v.*) may do. *See* RHETORIC.

rhetorical irony A form of irony (*q.v.*) in which the attitude and tone of the speaker or writer is the exact opposite of what is expressed. Such irony is common in the work of Swift, Voltaire, Samuel (*Erehwon*) Butler and Anatole France.

rhetorical question Basically a question not expecting an answer, or one to which the answer is more or less self-evident. It is used primarily for stylistic effect, and is a very common device in public speaking – especially when the speaker is trying to work up the emotional temperature.

Writers might also use rhetorical questions when arguing with themselves, as in the 47th sonnet of Sir Philip Sidney's *Astrophil and Stella* ('What, have I thus betrayed my libertie?'); or when they intend to supply immediate answers to the questions posed, as in Falstaff's disquisition on 'honour' in *King Henry IV*, Pt I (V, i, 131).

Two other kinds of rhetorical question (both have something in common with the above) are (a) a series of questions in quick succession for emphasis (e.g. 'Can we make it? If so, will it work? Where can we market it? Where can we market it cheaply?' and so on); (b) a question put to another person or oneself which expresses surprise, astonishment or anger and which is not easily answered. A good example is Bolingbroke's outburst in *Richard II* (I, iii, 294) after he has been banished, beginning with the lines:

> O, who can hold a fire in his hand
> By thinking on the frosty Caucasus?

See also RHETORIC; RHETORICAL FIGURE; RHETORICAL IRONY.

rhétoriqueurs A group of French poets who flourished late in the 15th and early in the 16th c. at the court of Burgundy and in Paris. They were obscure, difficult poets who went in for complex allegory, intricate rhyme and meter, involved rhetoric and a high degree of formalism. Among the better known are Alain Chartier, Jean Lemaire de Belges, Molinet, Crétin and Jean Marot. They have no counterparts in England or elsewhere.

rhizome Derived from botany, the term 'rhizome' refers to kinds of plants whose roots grow horizontally and may spread across the ground to develop new plants from several points rather than from a single root. The term was adopted by Gilles Deleuze (1925–95) and Félix Guattari (1930–92) in their book *A Thousand Plateaus: Capitalism and Schizophrenia* (1980) as a model for non-hierarchical, relational and decentred structures. Deleuze and Guattari seek to reconceptualize the whole notion of the intellectual discipline and established Western forms of knowledge, in particular their basis in binary, chronological, genealogical and hierarchical thought. They call such forms of knowledge 'arborescent'– solid, tree-like systems and ideas that spring from a single base/root and branch into concepts, categories and subcategories acknowledging a common origin. Rhizomatic thought, on the other hand, is opposed to hierarchical, systematic and disciplinary forms of knowledge. It is open, anarchic and in a manner of becoming rather than being rooted in a single point. That is, the rhizome produces anti-disciplinary forms of knowledge; it is against categories and classifications, and links and networks can be forged with disparate elements in the system with no specific origin through diverse affective encounters at any given point.

Deleuze and Guattari thus develop a number of related concepts that favour instability and multiplicity, such as 'deterritorialization', 'nomadism', 'schizoanalysis' and 'assemblage'. These 'assemblages' are always already contingent and temporary. The rhizome *par excellence* today would be the internet, or the hypertext (*qq.v.*). Deleuze and Guattari's concept of minor literature not as literature that comes from a minor language, but as 'that which a minority constructs within a major language', and hence introduces ruptures and heterogeneity into the system, parallels the characteristics of the rhizome. While some have been sceptical as to whether a system can be changed through unpredictable assaults and ruptures, and have questioned whether the rhizome offers effective strategies for resistance, Deleuze and Guattari's ideas have profoundly shaped media studies and critical theory (*qq.v.*).

The term has also been used in postcolonial theory (*q.v.*) to discuss the ways in which imperial power is dispersed not only through colonial institutions with violence, but also 'rhizomatically' through other less visible forms such as psychological domination. *See also* DISSEMINATION; POSTSTRUCTURALISM.

rhozzum A word of obscure origin which denotes a short humorous tale (*q.v.*), often about a local character. They tend to belong (or to *have* belonged) to oral tradition (*q.v.*). Students of folklore, historians of folk literature, and anthropologists (among others) have recorded many of them. They tend also to belong to rural communities and some are very old indeed. Like many other kinds of folk tale they have been classified into types and enjoy a degree of universality. A well-known example is 'The Irishman's Hat' (also called 'The Hat that Paid' and 'The Hat that Pays for Everything'). The theme is guile and gullibility. In various forms it is known all over Europe, Asia and the New World. Other instances fairly widespread in Britain are: 'The Farmer and the "Parson"'; 'The Three Foreigners' (also widely known in Europe, India and the New World); 'The Deaf Man and the Pig Trough' (also known in India and North America); 'The Borrowdale Cuckoo' (a very funny story which has variants in different parts of Britain and varies in length considerably); and 'Growing the Church', known in Somerset, Herefordshire, Oxfordshire and Suffolk as well as in New York. The rhozzum is a relative of, among other things, the tall story, the shaggy dog story, fable, *fabliau*, *Märchen* and *fatrasie* (*qq.v.*).

rhyme The formalized consonance of syllables, rhyme probably originated in prehistoric ritual, but only in the last millennium has it come to dominate verse architecture. Most classical verse is blank (unrhymed), and Old English verse uses assonance and alliteration; but the Humanist dissemination of Italian stanza-forms prescribing rhyme established rhyme as, for many people, a defining feature of both verse and poetry. In the 20th c. prescribed rhyme-schemes (*q.v.*) were often disavowed, but rhyme has remained a feature of much elite poetry, and continues to dominate popular verse.

A general caution must be taken with regard to regional and national accents: rhyme in the mouth and ear is not always as it may seem on the page, but (with that allowance) may be analysed by degree, type and position. **Full** (or *perfect*) rhyme is the identity of the last stressed vowel and all following sounds of two or more words or phrases (fish/dish, smiling/filing). If one or more of the sounds preceding the last stressed vowel are also identical, it is **rime riche** (or *identical* rhyme) (catfish/cat-dish, designing/resigning), as are homophones (there/their) and homographs (well [of water]/well [not ill]) (*qq.v.*). Conversely, if the sounds following the last stressed vowel are not identical it is **vowel** rhyme (fish/finger, smiling/smiting); and if the last stressed vowels differ, but the following sounds are identical, **pararhyme** (fish/dash, smiling/falling): both are **half-rhyme** (or *near* or *slant* rhyme). Weakened further, rhyme frays into the repetition of the same vowel(s), in **assonance,** or consonant(s), in **alliteration**.

Eight major types of rhyme are distinguished. If the last stressed vowel is in the last syllable, the rhyme is **stressed** (or *masculine*) (smile/file, design/resign); whereas if there are unstressed following sounds the rhyme is **unstressed** (or *feminine*) (smiling/filing, designing/resigning). Rhyme on a wrenched accent (me/surgery [surgeree], dam/wománi) is also **wrenched**. Non-rhyming homographic endings create **eye-rhyme** (or *printer's* rhyme) (cough/dough), and rhymed phrases **mosaic** rhyme (lot o' news/hypotenuse, Light Brigade/sight they made). Notably silly (often unstressed or wrenched mosaic) rhymes (philosopher/gloss over, opposite/God for spite) are **hudibrastic**. The perfect (non-)rhyme of a word with itself creates **autorhyme** (or *null* rhyme), and the rhyming of words with related meanings **semantic** rhyme.

Positionally, there are **internal** rhyme, within a line (or other unit), and **external** rhyme, between successive lines/units; though **anaphoric** rhyme, the web of autorhymes created by continued repetition of a word or phrase (verbal formulae in psalms, for example) is liable to blur the distinction. The only internal rhyme now usually distinguished is **leonine** rhyme, between the word preceding the caesura (*q.v.*) and the end-word ('I met a man with a skin of tan', 'His only cloak it was the smoke'), but external rhyme is extensively classified. It is usually **terminal,** on the last words of lines, but may also be **initial** or **medial**. Successive terminal rhymes create first **couplets** (cat/sat), then **triplets** (cat/sat/bat); longer sequences form **monorhyme**. The principal patterns created by separating rhyming lines with non- or otherrhyming lines are **single-rhyme** (cat/dog/ bat/sheep), **cross-rhyme** (cat/dog/bat/frog), and **arch-rhyme** (or *chiasmic* rhyme) (cat/dog/frog/bat). Rhymes separated by more than three places are **delayed,** and both delayed and **accelerated** rhyme may be created by varying an established pattern. **Irregular** rhyme weakens into **dispersed** and finally **scattered** (or *occasional*) rhyme.

Particular degrees, types or positions of rhyme have reasonably particular consequences (though poets are of course always at liberty to try to work against the grain). Full rhyme will tend to harmonize with or confirm the sense, while half-rhyme will tend to dissonance and interrogation of the sense. Stressed (especially monosyllabic) rhyme will tend to be assertive, martial, or grave, while unstressed rhyme (especially when extended) tends to levity. The other types all draw attention to themselves: wrenched rhyme is commonest in forms for oral performance, while eye-rhyme is restricted to print; mosaic and hudibrastic rhyme are largely tools of mock-epic, satire, or broad comedy; autorhyme (of which Shakespeare and Eliot were particular masters, and which is prescribed by refrains) is among the most powerful and delicate controls on tone; and semantic rhyme is a principal skill of poetry. The greater the proximity of rhymes the greater the acceleration they induce (consider leonine rhyme or the dimetric couplet in limericks); and even in couplets the thump of certainty is a constant danger, while extended monorhyme rapidly becomes comic or grotesque. Conversely, cross-rhyme sets a steady pace, arch-rhyme creates a sequence of tightly closed units, and more delayed rhymes a drag which usually slows the pace. Even scattered rhymes will echo and bind for the attentive reader.

Any of these effects may (at least in theory) be combined, but the terminology may equally be combined in pursuit. The long-standing rhyme of 'love' with 'move' or 'prove', for example, perhaps full rhymes in the early seventeenth century, are now eye-pararhymes; the ten lines of Shakespeare's sonnet 87 which end in '-ing' form wrenched monorhyme (as well as the prescribed cross-rhyme); and a sequence such as fell/Cerberus/barbarous/Hell is a stressed arch-rhyme enclosing an unstressed pararhyme, the whole semantic. *See also* RHYME SCHEME; RIME.

rhyme counterpoint   A poetic device in which line length is opposed to rhyme scheme. The rhymed lines are of unequal length; the unrhymed of equal length.

rhyme royal   A stanza form of seven decasyllabic lines rhyming ababbcc and so called, in all probability, from its use by James I of Scotland in *Kingis Quair* (1423). Because Chaucer was the first to use it in *Complaint unto Pity* it is also known as the Chaucerian stanza. Chaucer employed it in *Troilus and Criseyde*, *The Parlement of Foules* and several of *The Canterbury Tales*. Other poets who have experimented with it include Sir Thomas Wyatt, Edmund Spenser, Shakespeare, Michael Drayton, William Morris and John Masefield. *See* HEPTASTICH; RHYME; SCOTTISH CHAUCERIANS; SEPTET.

rhyme scheme   The abstract pattern of end-rhymes in a stanza, usually notated with lower-case letters: the first line and all subsequent lines that rhyme with it are 'a', the first line not to rhyme with 'a' (and all subsequent lines that rhyme with *it*) are 'b', and so on. Thus heroic couplets (*q.v.*) are 'aabbcc' and so on, a limerick (*q.v.*) is 'aabba', and rhyme royal (*q.v.*) is 'ababbcc'.

Prescribed line lengths may also be annotated, by writing the number of beats after the rhyme-letter: thus a limerick might also be notated as 'a9a9b6b6a9', and the hymnal stanza (*q.v.*) as 'a8b6a8b6'. If stressed and unstressed rhymes are prescribed, they may also be annotated, by using the sequence of consonants (bcdfghj . . .) for the stressed rhymes, and of vowels (aeiou) for the unstressed.

rhyming slang   A form of cryptic speech devised and used by cockney people. It is based on a trick rhyme, in which a phrase is substituted for the word; as in 'apples and pears' for 'stairs'. Occasionally the word is twice removed from its name in rhyming slang, as in 'use your loaf' from 'use your head' which rhymes with 'bread'. Other well-known examples are: trouble and strife/wife; plates of meat/feet; Hampstead Heath/teeth; titfor (titfortat)/hat; tea-leaf/thief; north and south/mouth. There are hundreds of such phrases, many of which have been gathered in Julian Franklyn's *A Dictionary of Rhyming Slang* (1960). *See also* CANT; COCKNEY RHYMES; SLANG.

rhythm (Gk 'flowing') In verse or prose, the movement or sense of movement communicated by the arrangement of stressed and unstressed syllables and by the duration (q.v.) of the syllables. In verse the rhythm depends on the metrical pattern. In verse the rhythm is regular: in prose it may or may not be regular. See CADENCE; FALLING RHYTHM; METER; RISING RHYTHM; ROCKING RHYTHM; SPRUNG RHYTHM.

rhythmical pause By some used as the equivalent of a caesura (q.v.), and thus it occurs during a line of verse rather than at the end of it.

riddle (OE 'opinion, advice') An ancient and universal form of literature, in its commonest form it consists of a puzzle question: the equivalent of a conundrum or an enigma. For example:

> Brothers and sisters have I none.
> This man's father is my father's son.
> Who am I?

The earliest known English riddles are recorded in the *Exeter Book* (8th c.). Some are brief, while others run to many lines of verse.

There are collections of riddles also in Sanskrit, Hebrew, Arabic and Persian literature, not to mention Greek riddles in the *Greek Anthology* and the Latin riddles of Symphosius. Other authors of Anglo-Latin riddles were Aldhelm of Sherborne, Tatwine, Archbishop of Canterbury, and Eusebius, Abbot of Wearmouth. One of the largest collections is Nicolas Reusner's *Aenigmatographia* (1602).

riding rhyme A term for the heroic couplet (q.v.) and its meter. So named in all probability because Chaucer used it for *The Canterbury Tales*, related by the pilgrims while riding to the shrine at Canterbury.

rime The word derives from the Greek *rhythmos*. In Late Latin the word *rithmi* was used of accented verse and *metra* of quantitative verse. The word *rithmus* (conceivably influenced by the OHG word *rim*, 'number') became *rime*. By the 17th c. there was a clear distinction between rhyme and rhythm. But the term *rime* is by no means defunct. See RHYME.

rime couée See TAIL-RHYME STANZA.

rimes croisées In French prosody, the alternation of masculine and feminine rhymes (qq.v.) for an abab rhyme scheme. See also ALTERNANCE DES RIMES.

rimes embrassées In French prosody, the alternation of masculine and feminine rhymes (qq.v.) for an abba rhyme scheme. See also ALTERNANCE DES RIMES.

rimes équivoquées In French prosody, a scheme in which the rhyming syllables are identical in spelling and sound but the words they make up in various combinations are puns. *Les rhétoriqueurs* (q.v.) were fond of this kind of wordplay.

rimes mêlées In French prosody this denotes a random rhyming scheme. Even so, the rule pertaining to the alternation of masculine and feminine rhymes (*qq.v.*) is still observed. It is common in light verse, madrigal, fable and *chanson* (*qq.v.*) in the 17th c.

rimes plates *See* ALTERNANCE DES RIMES.

rimes riches In French (and later English) prosody rhyming syllables in which accented vowels and the consonants before and after them sound identical. When spelt the same they are homographs (e.g. well/well); when spelt differently they are homophones (e.g. stare/stair). Also known as identical rhyme. *See* PERFECT RHYME; RHYME.

rimes suffisantes In French prosody, rhyming syllables in which the accented vowel and one identical consonant sound. *See* RIMES RICHES.

rimes suivies *See* ALTERNANCE DES RIMES.

rímur A form of Icelandic metrical romance (*q.v.*) which originated in the 14th c. They were narrative poems based on heroic tales and composed, for the most part, in alliterative four-line stanzas. They were complex in meter and the kenning (*q.v.*) occurs frequently.

rising action That part of a play which precedes the climax (*q.v.*). *See* FALLING ACTION; FREYTAG'S PYRAMID.

rising rhythm This occurs when the stress pattern is thrown *forward* in a line of verse, so that it falls on the last syllable of the feet. Iambic and anapaestic feet are basic to rising rhythm. Most English verse is composed in it. The following example comes from the Prologue to Vernon Watkins's *The Ballad of the Mari Lwyd*. 'Midnight' is trochaic, then he moves into a mixture of iambics and anapaests:

> Mídnĭght. | Mídnĭght. | Mídnĭght. | Mídnĭght.
> Hárk | ăt thĕ hánds | ŏf thĕ clóck:
> Nŏw déad | mĕn ríse | ĭn thĕ fróst | ŏf thĕ stárs
> Ănd físts | ŏn thĕ cóf|fĭns knóck.
> Thĕy drópped | ĭn theĭr gráves | wĭthóut | óne sóund:
> Thén thĕy wĕre | stéadў | ănd stíff.
> Bŭt nów | thĕy téar | thrŏugh thĕ fróst | ŏf thĕ gróund
> Ăs hérĕtĭc, drún|kărd ănd thíef.

See ANAPAEST; FALLING RHYTHM; IAMB; TROCHEE.

rispetto (It 'respect') An eight-line stanza, usually rhyming abababcc. Probably of Tuscan origin, it is now general in Italy. Well-known Italian poets who have used this form (the themes are often related to love, honour and respect) are Lorenzo de Medici, Carducci and Pascoli. *See* SICILIAN OCTAVE.

Ritter- und Räuberroman (G 'knight and robber novel') As the term suggests, such novels were tales of adventure and derring-do; basically historical novels, which were elaborately contrived, melodramatic and sensational. Some of them were extremely successful. The *Sturm und Drang* (*q.v.*) movement had some influence on their development. Their closest counterpart in Britain was the Gothic novel (*q.v.*). Some of the main authors were Benedikte Naubert (1756–1819), one of the few female novelists of the period, Friedrich Schlenkert (1757–1826), who wrote *Das Petermannchen* (1791–2), Karl Cramer (1758–1817), author of *Hasper a Spada* (1792–3), and Christian Vulpius (1762–1827), who wrote the very popular *Rinaldo Rinaldini, der Räuberhauptmann* (1798). *See* PICARESQUE NOVEL.

Robinsonade The German term for stories which derived from Defoe's ever popular *The Life and Strange and Surprising Adventures of Robinson Crusoe* (1719). The first German translation appeared the following year and there were numerous imitations. Among the more notable examples were Johann Schnabel's *Die Insel Felsenburg* (1751–43), Johann Campe's *Robinson der Jüngere* (1779–80) and Johann Wyss's *Der schweizerische Robinson* (1812–27), which, as *The Swiss Family Robinson*, became a much loved classic in Britain. *See* DESERT ISLAND FICTION.

rocking lineation *See* CAESURA.

rocking rhythm A term used by Gerard Manley Hopkins in his *Preface* to *Poems* (1918). A metrical device which occurs when a stressed syllable comes between two unstressed syllables, as in the first of these two lines from the poet's *The Wreck of the Deutschland*:

> Bŭt hĕ scóres ĭt ĭn scárlĕt hĭmsélf ŏn hĭs ówn bĕspókĕn,
> Bĕfóre-tíme-tákĕn, déarĕst prízĕd ănd prícĕd –

See RUNNING RHYTHM; SPRUNG RHYTHM.

rococo (F *rocaille*, 'rock work') An architectural term used to describe decorative scrollwork. As a literary term it may be used judiciously to describe something which is light, gay and graceful, and perhaps embellished by elegant twirls and flourishes of wit, image or verbal dexterity. The rococo period belongs to the 18th c. Pope's *The Rape of the Lock* might qualify as a specimen.

rogue literature A genre concerned with the underworld and thus with criminal and quasi-criminal life and activities. It was particularly popular in the 16th and 17th c. and at its best gives a vivid and memorable impression of the seamier side of existence among vagrants, vagabonds, beggars, cutpurses, conmen *et al.* – the Autolycuses of this world. Some fairly renowned examples are *Hye Way to the Spytell House* (16th c.) by Robert Copland, *Caveat for Common Cursetors* (1567) by Thomas Harman, *A Notable Discovery of Coosnage* (1592) by Robert Greene, and *Lanthorne and Candle-light* (1608) by Thomas Dekker. In the field of modern criminology there is a plentiful literature in the 'rogue' tradition. Jean Genet's *Journal du voleur* (1949) is a well-known instance.

roll A piece of parchment made into a cylindrical form which usually bears official records. Thus, a kind of register (*q.v.*). Rolls are to be found in any public-record office. Famous examples are *The Ragman Roll*, the *Pipe Rolls*, and the *Rolls Series* (or *Chronicles and Memorials of Great Britain and Ireland from the Invasion of the Romans to the Reign of Henry VIII*).

roman A word used in most European languages (including the Slav languages) to denote a novel. French in origin, it first denoted a common language, as opposed to Latin. There is a reference in 1813 to *roman* meaning the vernacular tongue, while Latin was the learned language. In literary history, one of the earliest dates it appears is 1140 when *roman* denoted a story in verse adapted from Latin legends. Originally, *roman* referred to imaginative works in the vernacular, mainly the medieval French verse epics. By the 16th c. it was applied to works in prose.

In French there are various categories of *roman*: *roman-fleuve*, *roman à tiroirs*, *roman noir*, *roman-feuilleton*, *roman policier*, *roman documentaire*, *nouveau roman* (*qq.v.*), *roman à clef* (*see* LIVRE À CLEF) and *roman d'aventure*. The French also use the terms *récit* and *nouvelle* (*qq.v.*) to denote particular kinds of novel. Various other classifications came into use in the 20th c.: (a) *roman réaliste* – which covers *romans sur la guerre*, *romans réalistes à thèse révolutionnaire*, *romans documentaires*, *romans populistes et prolétariens*, *romans régionalistes* and *romans documentaires sur le pays de l'Union Française et sur les pays étrangers*; (b) *roman psychologique* – which covers *psychologues catholiques*, *psychologues humanistes* and *psychologues de la passion et de la volonté*; (c) *roman d'imagination* – which covers *roman merveilleux*, *roman d'aventure*, *roman historique* and *roman policier*. There is also the *roman existentialiste* which was influenced by the French existentialist philosophers such as Jean-Paul Sartre and Simone de Beauvoir. *L'Étranger* (1942) by Albert Camus is a notable example.

roman à clef *See* LIVRE À CLEF.

roman à deux sous French equivalent of a penny dreadful (*q.v.*).

roman à tiroirs (F 'novel with drawers') A novel (*q.v.*) which consists of a series of episodes which have no very obvious connecting link or theme. A noteworthy instance is Lesage's *Gil Blas de Santillane*, a picaresque (*q.v.*) romance which came out in four volumes between 1715 and 1735.

romance (i) (MedL *romanice*, 'in the Romantic tongue') In OF *romaunt* and *roman* meant, approximately, 'courtly romance in verse' or a 'popular book'. Thus romances in verse (and to start with most of them were in verse) were works of fiction, or non-historical. In the 13th c. a romance was almost any sort of adventure story, be it of chivalry or of love. Gradually more and more romances were written in prose.

Whatever else a romance may be (or have been) it is principally a form of entertainment. It may also be didactic but this is usually incidental. It is a European form which has been influenced by such collections as *The Arabian Nights*. It is usually concerned with characters (and thus with events) who live in a courtly world somewhat remote from the everyday. This suggests elements of fantasy, improbability, extravagance and naivety. It also suggests elements of love, adventure, the marvellous and the 'mythic'. For the most part the term is used rather loosely to describe a narrative of heroic or spectacular achievements, of chivalry, of gallant love, of deeds of derring-do.

The medieval metrical romances were akin to the *chansons de gestes* and to epic (*qq.v.*). There were a very large number of them, as we might expect in a form of popular literature. Chrétien de Troyes, who flourished in the latter half of the 12th c., was one of their most distinguished composers. His works were widely translated and imitated and he showed remarkable skill in combining the love story with the adventure story. Popular medieval romances in England were *Lay of Havelok the Dane* and *Sir Gawain and the Green Knight* in the 14th c. and Sir Thomas Malory's prose work *Le Morte d'Arthur* in the latter half of the 15th c. The traditions and codes of romance remained evident during the Renaissance period, in the poems of Ariosto and Tasso, in Spenser's *Faerie Queene*, in Sidney's *Arcadia* and in numerous other works.

Near the end of the 14th c. Chaucer satirized romance by means of burlesque (*q.v.*) in his *Tale of Sir Thopas*. Occasionally, after Chaucer, we find examples of satire on the conventions and sensibilities of the romance, but not until Cervantes's *Don Quixote* was the whole idea and tradition 'sent up'. The book displays the incongruities of romance by making fun of the conventions of chivalry and contrasting them with the realities of ordinary life.

Cervantes's masterpiece had considerable influence on the later romances as well as on the picaresque (*q.v.*) narrative of adventure and on the novel in general during the 19th c. In the 17th c. Samuel Butler modelled his splendid mock-heroic (*q.v.*) poem *Hudibras* (1663, 1664, 1678) on *Don Quixote*. And in the following century Fielding described his novel *Joseph Andrews* (1742) as an imitation of *Don Quixote*.

In the 18th c. romance elements are still evident, but the novel is already tending to concentrate on the everyday, the social and domestic – except when picaresque. With the advent of the Gothic novel (*q.v.*) a new kind of romance appears, one which makes use of the more bizarre and extravagant characteristics of the medieval romance.

During the Romantic period the concept of the romance (and what is romantic) underwent a further modification. In the 18th c. the term 'romantic' meant something that could happen in a romance, but towards the end of the 18th c. and at the beginning of the 19th it becomes clear that romance connotes those flights of fancy and imagination (*q.v.*) which had been regarded with suspicion in the Augustan age (*q.v.*). Hence the renewed interest in ballads, folk tales and fairy tales and in *The Arabian Nights*. At this time a number of major works illustrate a new conception of the romance as a revitalizing force. The poets re-create a remote past, an 'old world' of romance which reveals a potent nostalgia.

In the 19th c. influences of the medieval romance are evident in Tennyson's poem *The Idylls of the King* and in William Morris's *The Earthly Paradise*. The novels by Sir Walter Scott, Nathaniel Hawthorne and George Meredith can also be variously classified as kinds of romance. By this time realism, to be followed by naturalism (*qq.v.*), was the main trend in fiction, and romance was scarcely compatible with it. The more popular kinds of 'romance', an entertainment and form of escapist literature, remained in demand, but more serious novelists, like H. G. Wells, for example, attempted a reconciliation between romance and realism. A score of other writers in the 20th c. might be cited as using the conventions of romance. There are also contemporary romance novels (also known as Mills & Boon/Harlequin romances); however, these popular love stories are less connected to the romance tradition. *See also* CHANTE FABLE; GESTA; LAI.

romance (ii) This Spanish term should not be confused with the English and French words similarly spelled (though the same derivation is common to all three). In Spanish it is pronounced approximately *ro – mahn – thay*, with the middle syllable stressed and the last very short.

In Spanish the original use of the word was for the language, as in the English 'Romance languages'. When literary poetic forms of Provençal or French or other Latin-language origin arrived in Spain they were referred to as *romance* for that reason. The term can also refer to the type of meter used in the medieval poems.

The background to the *romance* is essentially popular, being generally connected with oral tradition (*q.v.*), and there is some similarity with the English ballad and the French *ballade* (*qq.v.*). As to the origin of the first romances, there are two main schools of thought. Both Menéndez y Pelayo and Menéndez Pidal support the suggestion put forward in 1874 by Milá y Fontanals that they are surviving fragments of medieval epic songs. This fits in with the lack of division into strophes, as well as with the type of assonance. Before 1874 it was thought that the romances had been the precursors of the *cantares de gesta* – the counterpart of the French *chansons de gestes* (*qq.v.*). It seems probable that the form developed concurrently with the Spanish language itself, yet the first mention of the term appears to be *c.* 1445–8 when the Marqués de Santillana referred to 'those songs and romances the lower classes so much enjoy'. It may well be that the romances developed along with the growth of Spanish national feeling. From the second half of the 16th c. onwards a number of poets have composed romances. They can be broadly classified as follows: *romance viejo* (the popular type); *romance artístico* (those composed by cultured poets); *romance histórico* (on various historical periods, in cycles); *romance fronterijo* (concerned with the 'frontier wars' in which the Arabs were beaten back from Granada); *romance morisco* (similar to the preceding); and *romance juglaresco* (on subjects about which the *juglares* sang). Some of the better-known writers have been Castillejo,

Montemayor, Silvestre and Espinel. Lope de Vega, Cervantes, Quevedo and, later, the Duque de Rivas and Zorrilla, also composed romances.

Romance languages A collective term for the group of languages descended from Latin. The main ones are: French, Italian, Spanish, Portuguese, Provençal, Romanian and Romansch.

romancero (Sp 'collection of romances') A collection of ballads which had previously been gathered on loose sheets known as *pliegos sueltos* (*q.v.*). The first of these was Sepúlveda's in 1551. There were many different types of collection from the highly specialized (e.g. *Poema de mío Cid*) to *romanceros generales* (1600 onwards).

roman cycle A series of interconnected novels (but each novel is independent and self-contained) with a central hero, heroine or family. It is kin to the *roman-fleuve* and the saga novel (*qq.v.*). Well-known examples are Georges Duhamel's five Salavin novels, *Vie et Aventures de Salavin* (1920–32), and his *Chronique des Pasquier* (1933–45).

roman documentaire This form of fiction was invented by the Goncourt brothers, Edmond (1822–96) and Jules (1830–70), in the 1860s. The brothers, in collaboration, set out to write history 'which might have happened'. It was a form of realism and naturalism (*qq.v.*), and the Goncourts are often cited in connection with those two -isms. Using the research methods of the historian and also of the anthropologist working in the field, they aimed for the highest possible degree of fidelity to life, to fact. They describe their approach in their famous *Journal*, which was begun in 1851 and continued by Edmond after Jules died. An entry for 24 Oct. 1864 reads: 'Le roman actuel se fait avec des *documents* racontés, ou relevés d'après nature, comme l'histoire se fait avec des documents écrits.' For the most part the novels were not well received, but they are important in the development of fictional techniques. The brothers developed a particular style which they called *écriture artiste* (*q.v.*). The main novels are *Les Hommes de lettres* (1860), *Sœur Philomène* (1861), *Renée Mauperin* (1864), *Germinie Lacerteux* (1864), *Manette Salomon* (1867) and *Madame Gervaisais* (1869). In 1879 Edmond published *Les Frères Zemganno*, a study of circus life. *Germinie Lacerteux* remains one of the best known; it is a detailed history of their faithful servant who led a double life: off duty she devoted her time to debauchery and corruption. *Sœur Philomène* is a remarkable account of hospital life. Later, Émile Zola was to apply comparable methods of documentary 'fieldwork' to achieve maximum realism and accuracy.

roman-feuilleton A novel published in instalments in a daily paper. The fashion began *c.* 1830. In 1836 a translation of the Spanish picaresque novel *Lazarillo de Tormes* first appeared in the newspaper *Le Siècle*. In the late 19th c. many authors took advantage of such serialization. It is still done occasionally when a newspaper is absolutely sure that an author's book is going to sell well.

roman-fleuve A term used in modern fiction for a series of novels, each of which exists as a separate novel in its own right but all of which are inter-related because the characters (some or all) reappear in each succeeding work. The vogue for this kind of encyclopaedic and epic chronicle was established in the 19th c. Balzac planned and in part executed his vast scheme of *La Comédie humaine*; Zola wrote his twenty-volume series *Les Rougon-Macquart* (1871–93) and the Spaniard Perez Galdos produced his monumental *Episodios nacionales* (1873–1912), a cycle of historical novels covering the history of Spain from Trafalgar (1805) to the Restoration (1875). In the 20th c. four Frenchmen undertook works on a similar scale. Romain Rolland wrote *Jean-Christophe* (1906–12) in ten volumes. Later he returned to the *roman-fleuve* scheme with *L'Ame enchantée* (1922–33) in seven volumes. Proust's monumental *A la recherche du temps perdu* (1913–27) consists of seven interrelated sections and occupied him for at least twelve years. Georges Duhamel began with the *Vie et aventures de Salavin* (1920–32) in five novels, and followed this with *Chronique des Pasquier* (1933–45) in ten volumes. Jules Romains was even more ambitious with his *Les Hommes de bonne volonté* (1932–47), the generic title of a series of twenty-seven novels covering a wide range of French life from 1908 to 1933. Galsworthy attempted the same sort of thing with *The Forsyte Saga* (1922). The 20th c. also saw C. P. Snow's *Strangers and Brothers* sequence (1940–70), which gives a documentary chronicle of English social history from 1925; Henry Williamson's *A Chronicle of Ancient Sunlight* (1951–69) in fifteen volumes; and Anthony Powell's *A Dance to the Music of Time* (1951–76) in twelve volumes. A number of other novelists have used the trilogy and the tetralogy (*qq.v.*) to achieve a comparable continuity. *See* BILDUNGSROMAN; NOVEL; SAGA NOVEL

roman héroïque A form of fiction especially popular in France in the seventeenth century. The novels (often in several volumes) were of love and adventure. Marin Le Roy de Gomberville (1600–74), Gaulthier de Coste la Calprenède (1610–63), and Madeleine de Scudéry (1608–1701) were the most eminent practitioners in the genre. Madeleine de Scudéry's *Artamène, ou le Grand Cyrus* (1649–53) is particularly well known. *See* NOVEL.

roman noir This term was originally used in France as an equivalent of the Gothic novel (*q.v.*) but now tends to denote some form of thriller (*q.v.*). They are often fairly sensational and violent and are concerned with criminals and criminal organizations which the 'heroes' of the story hunt down and destroy. See ROMAN POLICIER.

roman policier The French equivalent of the detective story and novel about crime. It is generally agreed that the first practitioner was Émile Gaboriau (1832–73). Gaboriau was ahead of his time, for he created a policeman as his detective, namely Lecoq. He also had an amateur sleuth in the shape of an old pawnbroker, Père Tabaret, called 'Tir-au-clair'. Gaboriau's long-term influence on British and American writers of detective fiction was considerable, and in some ways he was the first to see the possibilities of the police procedural (*q.v.*), which was not to be fully developed until the 1950s. His *Le Crime d'Orcival* (1867) was the first full-length detective novel. In the 20th c. there was Sébastien Japrisot (1931–2003), a prolific writer of ingenious crime novels, many of which have been filmed. Jacquemard-Sénécal is the pseudonym of Yves Jacquemard (1943–80) and Jean-Michel Sénécal (1943–), who collaborated on crime novels. Easily the most famous writer of the *policier* is Georges Simenon (1903–90), whose detective inspector Jules Maigret has become universally famous, almost as famous as Sherlock Holmes himself. The Maigret novels were written between 1931 and 1973. Maigret finally 'retired' from fiction on 7 February 1973, after he had become Commissaire at the Quay des Orfèvres, the headquarters of the Paris police. Simenon also wrote a large number of crime novels in which there is no particular hero. His total output was huge. *See* CRIME FICTION.

romans bretons   Romances (usually in octosyllabic couplets) composed in the period *c.* 1150–1250. Their subjects for the most part are 'the matter' of Brittany. Two of the most famous authors were Marie de France and Chrétien de Troyes. *See also* METRICAL ROMANCE; ROMANCE; ROMANS COURTOIS; ROMANS D'ANTIQUITÉ; ROMANS D'AVENTURE.

romans courtois   A general term which denotes medieval romances, *romans bretons*, *romans d'aventure* (*qq.v.*). Such works were nearly always in verse and composed in octosyllabic couplets. They were usually intended to be read aloud. *See also* METRICAL ROMANCE; ROMANS D'ANTIQUITÉ.

romans d'antiquité   Medieval metrical romances (*q.v.*) whose themes and subjects were mostly taken from the works of Roman authors. Notable examples from the 12th c. are *Roman de Troie*, *Roman de Thèbes* and *Enéas*. *See also* ROMANS BRETONS; ROMANS COURTOIS; ROMANS D'AVENTURE.

romans d'adventure   Fictional narratives of the 12th and 13th c. They were usually in verse (commonly octosyllabic couplets), but were sometimes composed in prose, or in a mixture of prose and verse. The principal themes were love and chivalry and, like most romances (*q.v.*), they were intended solely as entertainment (largely for women). In this period some of the more distinguished works were: *Ipomedon*; *Partenopeu*; *Guillaume de Dole*; *Aucassin et Nicolette*; *Le Châtelain de Coucy*; *Guillaume de Palerme*; *Floire et Blanche-flor*; *Robert le Diable*. *Aucassin et Nicolette* is an outstanding instance of the mixture of prose and verse. Two well-known prose romances were *Conte du roi Constant l'empereur* and *Le Roi Flore et la belle Jeanne*. *See also* METRICAL ROMANCE; ROMANS BRETONS; ROMANS COURTOIS; ROMANS D'ANTIQUITÉ.

romantic comedy   A somewhat vague term which denotes a form of drama (it may, occasionally, be applied to a novel) in which love is the main theme – and love which leads to a happy ending, as in Shakespeare's *A Midsummer Night's Dream*, *As You Like It* and *Twelfth Night*. *See* COMEDY.

romantic irony   Novalis (alias Friedrich von Hardenberg, 1772–1801) described irony as 'genuine consciousness, true presence of mind'. The writer who employs what is called romantic irony (a concept for which Schlegel was largely responsible) exhibits true presence of mind by showing an awareness, a sensibility, that he does not expect his work to be taken wholly seriously – and does not wish it to be. He conveys this tone and attitude (thus inviting a complementary tone and attitude in his reader) by being at once critically aware of what he is doing and why he is doing it, even while he may be impelled by a strong dynamic creative purpose. Thus he is fully conscious of the comic implication of his own seriousness.

This form of irony is often at its best when the author is *showing* us what he is doing while he is doing it, so to speak. It may occur, for instance, when he comments on literary composition and perhaps also on the composition in hand. The novel is the main vehicle of romantic irony, but dramatists and poets have also used it. Notable examples are: (a) Fielding's interruptions and comments as author in *Tom Jones* and *Joseph Andrews*; (b) Pirandello's awareness of the ambivalent nature of drama in *Six Characters in Search of an Author*; and (c) Byron's continual breaking of the serious tone in *Don Juan*.

Among other outstanding exponents of this kind of irony are Aristophanes, Chaucer, Cervantes, Marivaux, Sterne, Diderot, Goethe, Hoffmann, Heine, Henry James, Gide and Nabokov. Perhaps the most accomplished of all is Thomas Mann, especially in *Joseph und seine Brüder* and *Der Zauberberg* where the ironic tone produces a gradual and cumulative joke, a growing sense of comic innuendo. It is mirth brought about by subtle and elaborate teasing. *See* COMEDY; DRAMATIC IRONY; IRONY; SATIRE.

romanticism The American scholar A. O. Lovejoy once observed that the word 'romantic' has come to mean so many things that, by itself, it means nothing at all. The variety of its actual and possible meanings and connotations reflects the complexity and multiplicity of European romanticism.

The word *romantic(ism)* has a complex and interesting history. In the Middle Ages 'romance' denoted the new vernacular languages derived from Latin – in contradistinction to Latin itself, which was the language of learning. *Enromancier*, *romancar*, *romanz* meant to compose or translate books in the vernacular. The work produced was then called *romanz*, *roman*, *romanzo* and *romance* (*q.v.*). A *roman* or *romant* came to be known as an imaginative work and a 'courtly romance'. The terms also signified a 'popular book'. There are early suggestions that it was something new, different, divergent. By the 17th c. in Britain and France, 'romance' had acquired the derogatory connotations of fanciful, bizarre, exaggerated, chimerical. In France a distinction was made between *romanesque* (also derogatory) and *romantique* (which meant 'tender', 'gentle', 'sentimental' and 'sad'). It was used in the English form in these latter senses in the 18th c. In Germany the word *romantisch* was used in the 17th c. in the French sense of *romanesque*, and then, increasingly from the middle of the 18th c., in the English sense of 'gentle', 'melancholy'.

Friedrich Schlegel is generally held to have been the person who first established the term *romantisch* in literary contexts. However, he was not very clear as to what he meant by it. That which is romantic depicts emotional matter in an imaginative form, he said. It would not be easy to be much vaguer than that. At the same time, in fairness, it should be said that the baffling and, very often, irritating part about anything to do with the romantic and romanticism is that it *is* vague and formless. Schlegel also equated 'romantic' with 'Christian'. His brother August implied that romantic literature is in contrast to that of classicism, thus producing the famous antinomy (*see* CLASSICISM/ROMANTICISM).

Madame de Staël knew the Schlegels and she appears to have been responsible for popularizing the term *romantique* in literary contexts in France. She made a distinction between the literature of the north and of the south. The northern was medieval, Christian and romantic; the southern, Classical and pagan.

Many hold to the theory that it was in Britain that the Romantic movement really started. At any rate, quite early in the 18th c. one can discern a definite shift in sensibility and feeling, particularly in relation to the natural order and Nature. This, of course, is hindsight. When we read Keats, Coleridge and Wordsworth, for instance, we gradually become aware that many of their sentiments and responses are foreshadowed by what has been described as a 'pre-Romantic sensibility'.

The British influence travelled to the continent via Thomson's *Seasons* (1726–30), Young's *Night Thoughts* (1742–5), Blair's *The Grave* (1743), Hervey's *Meditations among the Tombs* (1748), Gray's *Elegy* (1750), Macpherson's Ossianic poetry, much of which was published in the 1760s, and Percy's *Reliques* (1765). Most of these works (and especially Young's *Night Thoughts*) show a preoccupation with death and decay, with ruins and graveyards; they display a grieving melancholy, a mournful reflectiveness and a quantity of self-indulgent sentimentality. Hence the title 'Graveyard school of poetry' (*q.v.*).

New modes of feeling are also evident in sentimental comedy, *comédie larmoyante* and the sentimental novel (*qq.v.*). The novel is particularly important in tracing the history of romanticism. Especially the following works: Richardson's *Pamela* (1740), *Clarissa Harlowe* (1747) and *Sir Charles Grandison* (1754); Goldsmith's *The Vicar of Wakefield* (1766); Sterne's *Sentimental Journey* (1768); Henry Mackenzie's *The Man of Feeling* (1771); and Henry Brooke's *Juliet Grenville; or the History of the Human Heart* (1774). On the continent three major works of fiction are a counterpart – namely, Prévost's *Manon Lescaut* (1735), Rousseau's *La Nouvelle Héloïse* (1761) and Goethe's *Die Leiden des jungen Werthers* (1774). One should add that the Gothic novel (*q.v.*) and a considerable revival of Shakespeare's plays round about the middle of the 18th c. also contributed to the movement subsequently known as 'Romantic'.

Other aspects of romanticism in the 18th c. are (a) an increasing interest in Nature, and in the natural, primitive and uncivilized way of life; (b) a growing interest in scenery, especially its more untamed and disorderly manifestations; (c) an association of human moods with the 'moods' of

Nature – and thus a subjective feeling for it and interpretation of it; (d) a considerable emphasis on natural religion; (e) emphasis on the need for spontaneity in thought and action and in the expression of thought; (f) increasing importance attached to natural genius and the power of the imagination; (g) a tendency to exalt the individual and his needs and emphasis on the need for a freer and more personal expression; (h) the cult of the Noble Savage (q.v.).

In all these connections Rousseau is the major figure in the 18th c. and his influence in the pre-Romantic period was immense; especially through the following works: *Discours sur l'origine de l'inégalité parmi les hommes* (1755); *Du contrat social* (1762); *Rêveries du promeneur solitaire* (1778); and *Les Confessions* (published after his death, in 1781 and 1788). *La Nouvelle Héloïse* has been mentioned above.

Notable works by other authors which expressed a new vision of man and his role in the world are Goethe's *Götz von Berlichingen* (1773); Herder's *Stimmen der Völker* (1778); Schiller's *Die Räuber* (1781); Bernardin de Saint-Pierre's *La Chaumière indienne* (1790) and *Paul et Virginie* (1788); Chateaubriand's *Atala* (1801) and his *René* (1805).

To these should be added the extremely influential *Conjectures on Original Composition* by Young, which was published in 1759 and published in a German translation the following year. Young's aesthetic theories considerably affected the so-called *Sturm und Drang* (q.v.) movement.

The German Romantics belong to roughly two generations known as the *Frühromantik* ('Early Romantics') and the *Hochromantik* ('High Romantics'). The *Frühromantik* formed a group from the late 1790s until early in the 19th c. which was based first on Berlin and then on Jena. The two central figures of the group were the brothers Schlegel: Friedrich (1759–1805) and August Wilhelm (1767–1845). The other main personalities in the group were Wackenroder (1773–98), Tieck (1773–1853) and Novalis (1772–1801). These were all poets. There were also the philosophers Schelling and Baader, the theologian Schleiermacher and the physicist Ritter.

The *Hochromantik* group comprised principally Arnim (1781–1831), Brentano (1778–1842), Chamisso (1781–1838), Eichendorff (1788–1857), Fouqué (1777–1843), Heine (1797–1856), Hoffmann (1776–1822) and Mörike (1804–75).

Grossly to simplify the matter one can say that the earlier group were the philosophers and aestheticians of the new movement and revolution; while their followers practised as poets and writers of stories more than they preached. Both were movements of intense activity and national importance.

In Britain romanticism was much more diffused and never really associated with a movement, but then literary movements have been rare in Britain. There was no British Romantic campaign and the literary and cultural revolution was a much more gradual and informal affair than on the continent. The main figures associated with it are Coleridge, Wordsworth, Keats, Shelley, Byron and Sir Walter Scott. The political and social beliefs of Wordsworth, Coleridge and Shelley were quite often expressed in their poems as well as their prose works.

Partly because of the Revolution and partly because of the French devotion to classicism and neoclassicism, the Romantic movement came considerably later to France. There the works of Lamartine, Victor Hugo and de Vigny were the main influence to start with; later came de Musset and Dumas *père*.

In general, then, the ideals of romanticism included an intense focus on human subjectivity, an exaltation of Nature which was seen as a vast repository of symbols, of childhood and spontaneity, of primitive forms of society, of human passion and emotion, of the poet, of the sublime, and of imagination as a more comprehensive and inclusive faculty than reason. The most fundamental literary and philosophical disposition of romanticism was irony, an ability to accommodate conflicting perspectives of the world. Developing certain insights of Kant, the Romantics often insisted on artistic autonomy and attempted to free art from moralistic and utilitarian constraints. *See* PARNASSIANS; PRE-RAPHAELITES; REALISM.

Romantic period *See* ROMANTIC REVIVAL.

Romantic revival A term loosely applied to a movement in European literature (and other arts) during the last quarter of the 18th c. and the first twenty or thirty years of the 19th c. It was marked by a rejection of the ideals and rules of classicism and neoclassicism (*qq.v.*) and by an affirmation of the need for a freer, more subjective expression of passion, pathos and personal feelings. As its narrowest, the Romantic period in Britain is usually taken to run between 1798, the year in which Coleridge and Wordsworth published the first edition of *Lyrical Ballads*, and 1832, when Sir Walter Scott and Goethe died and the Reform Bill was passed. The major British writers in this period, apart from Coleridge, Wordsworth and Scott, were Byron, Shelley, Keats, Jane Austen, Hazlitt and de Quincey. Abroad, the movement was widely embracing: Goethe, Schlegel, Wackenroder, Tieck, Schelling, Novalis and Hölderlin in Germany; Chateaubriand and Madame de Staël in France; Leopardi, Manzoni and Foscolo in Italy; Espronceda in Spain; Slowacki in Poland; Pushkin and Lermontov in Russia; Petöfi in Hungary; and Oehlenschläger in Denmark. *See* ROMANCE; ROMANTICISM.

romería Of 12th c. Galician origin, a kind of festival at a local shrine. The *cantiga de romería* is a type of *cossante* composed by local minstrels in honour of their shrine.

rondeau (OF *rond*, 'round') An OF form, consisting of a thirteen- or fifteen-line poem, usually octosyllabic, in three stanzas. The opening words became the refrain (*q.v.*). Usually there were only two rhymes. It was popular in 16th c. France. Among distinguished French poets who have since used it one may mention Clément Marot, Alfred de Musset and Théodore de Banville. The form did not catch on in England until late in the 19th c. when Dobson and

Swinburne, among others, experimented extensively with it. The following example, *In Rotten Row*, by W. E. Henley, illustrates the basic principles:

> In Rotten Row a cigarette
> I sat and smoked, with no regret
>   For all the tumult that had been.
>   The distances were still and green,
>
> And streaked with shadows cool and wet.
> Two sweethearts on a bench were set,
> Two birds among the bows were met;
> So love and song were heard and seen
>   In Rotten Row.
>
> A horse or two there was to fret
> The soundless sand; but work and debt,
>   Fair flowers and falling leaves between,
>   While clocks are chiming clear and keen,
> A man may very well forget
>   In Rotten Row.

See also RONDEAU REDOUBLÉ; RONDEL.

rondeau redoublé A rare poetic form akin to OF forms but little used, apparently, before the 16th c. It consists of six quatrains and only two rhymes are worked, as in the *rondeau* (*q.v.*). Marot, La Fontaine and Théodore de Banville are among the few poets known to have experimented with it. A good, witty modern example is Wendy Cope's *Rondeau Redoublé* (in the collection *Making Cocoa for Kingsley Amis*, 1986).

rondel A French fixed form of considerable antiquity and known from the 13th c. In its earliest form it appears to have been an eight-line poem rhyming AB aA ab AB (A and B represent repeated lines). A variation was the *rondel doublé* rhyming ABBA abBA abba ABBA. The most usual *rondel* form consisted of three stanzas working on two rhymes, thus: ABba abAB abba (B); a thirteen-line poem in which the refrain came twice in the first eight lines and the opening line was repeated as the last line. If it was of fourteen lines, the refrain was repeated three times. Among British poets who attempted the form were W. E. Henley, Edmund Gosse, Austin Dobson and R. L. Stevenson. *See also* RONDEAU; ROUNDEL.

rondelet A short fixed form, usually consisting of one stanza of five or seven lines, on two rhymes. If of seven lines, the first part of the opening line is used as a refrain (*q.v.*) thus: abRabbR (R is the refrain).

round character *See* FLAT AND ROUND CHARACTERS.

roundel As developed by Swinburne and published in his *A Century of Roundels* (1883), this form was an eleven-line poem in three stanzas, the twice repeated refrain consisting of the opening lines of the poem, and rhyming thus: abaR, bab, abaR (R is the refrain). Swinburne at once described and illustrated the form in *The Roundel*:

> A Roundel is wrought as a ring or a starbright sphere,
> With craft of delight and with cunning of sound unsought,
> That the heart of the hearer may smile it to pleasure his ear
> A roundel is wrought

See also RONDEAU; RONDEL.

roundelay A short simple song with a refrain. A kind of ditty (*q.v.*) popular in medieval times, to which people danced. The term also covers, variously, fixed forms like *rondeau*, *rondel* and *villanelle* (*qq.v.*) where refrain and repetition are used extensively.

roundlet A short form of roundel (*q.v.*).

Royal Literary Fund A benevolent society founded in 1790 to help authors and their dependants. It began as the Literary Fund Society and in 1818 was granted a royal charter. It added 'Royal' to its title in 1845. The fund has always depended on donations of one kind and another. Well-known beneficiaries have been Coleridge, Thomas Love Peacock, James Hogg, John Clare, James Joyce, D. H. Lawrence and Dylan Thomas. In 1999 the society launched the Royal Literary Fund's Fellowship scheme for writers in partnership with UK universities and higher education colleges.

Royal Shakespeare Company Thanks to the initiative and financial backing of a brewing family, the Flowers, the first Shakespeare Memorial Theatre in Stratford-upon-Avon, Warwickshire, was opened in 1879, and F. R. Benson (1858–1939) was appointed as director of an annual Shakespeare festival there. He remained associated with the theatre until 1919. The original theatre was destroyed by fire in 1926 and a second one was opened on the same site in 1932. After the Second World War the theatre prospered under three distinguished directors: Barry Jackson, Anthony Quayle and Glen Byam Shaw. In 1960 the Royal Shakespeare Company was formed and Peter Hall was made director. The RSC then took on the Aldwych Theatre in London. In 1970 Trevor Nunn replaced Peter Hall, who, in 1973, became artistic director of the National Theatre (*q.v.*). In the 1990s, the Company underwent financial difficulties, but Michael Boyd, who became artistic director in 2003, was able to rebuild the Company's reputation and success in the 21st c. The RSC also has the Swan Theatre, and a smaller theatre – the Other Place (reopened as the Courtyard Theatre in 2006) – at Stratford, plus the theatres in the Barbican Centre, London (opened in 1982). For the most part the company has concentrated on presentations of Shakespeare, often with great success (e.g. *The Wars of the Roses* cycle in 1963, devised by Peter Hall and John Barton); but at the Other Place and at the Barbican a wide range of work by other playwrights, ancient and modern, has been produced.

Royal Society of Literature   Founded in 1823 under the patronage of George IV. It awarded pensions to 'Associates' who were elected by the Society's council. It had regular meetings at which papers were read to members and thereafter published as *Transactions*. The Society has Members and Fellows, and also Companions (dating from 1961).

rubai   (A pl. *rubáiyát*) A 'quatrain', written usually in the rhyme scheme aaba. Notable authors of *rubáiyát* include the Persian poets Rumi (1207–73) and Hossein Ghods-Nakhaï (1911–77). Readers of English are most familiar with the *rubáiyát* or quatrains of the Persian poet Omar Khayyam (1048–1131; better known in Iran as an astronomer and algebraist) through Edward Fitzgerald's translation (1859). Here are three samples of Fitzgerald's rather liberal but distinctive rendering:

> Come, fill the Cup, and in the Fire of Spring
> The Winter Garment of Repentance fling:
>   The Bird of Time has but a little way
> To fly – and Lo! the Bird is on the Wing.

> Here with a Loaf of Bread beneath the Bough,
> A Flask of Wine, a Book of Verse – and Thou
>   Beside me singing in the Wilderness –
> And Wilderness is Paradise enow.

> The Worldly Hope men set their Hearts upon
> Turns Ashes – or it prospers; and anon,
>   Like Snow upon the Desert's dusty Face
> Lighting a little Hour or two – is gone.

See also OMAR KHAYYAM QUATRAIN.

rubá'iyat   *See* RUBAI.

rules   In literary theory and history, those precepts and conventions which by custom and usage have come to be regarded and accepted as norms, if not actually ordained and thus taken as a body of dogma. For instance, those concerned with the dramatic unities (*q.v.*), with the composition of epic and tragedy, eclogue and sonnet (*qq.v.*), with the kind of subject matter suitable for, say, comedy, with the appropriateness of style to subject matter (e.g. the grand and fully canonical manner for epic; a much 'lower' style for farcical comedy).

  Many of the rules originated in Classical theory: for instance, Aristotle's *Poetics*, Horace's *Ars Poetica*; and, later, in that work ascribed to Longinus called *On the Sublime*. The 'rules' of many forms and genres were established during the Middle Ages and in the 16th c., but it was during the 17th c. especially and in the first half of the 18th that writers paid particular attention to the 'rules'. Witness Racine's devotion to the conventions governing the Classical form of tragedy, or Pope's exacting and professional regard for decorum (*q.v.*) in language and genre (*q.v.*).

Since the end of the 18th c. fidelity to the rules has been taken to be of less and less importance. However, the best writers still tend to be those who have learnt the rules so thoroughly (this is particularly true of poets) that they are then in a position to modify them (and break them) and make rules of their own.

rune (ON and OE *run*, 'whisper, mystery') A character of the earliest Germanic alphabet, *run* denoted a cryptic sign signifying something secret, mysterious or pertaining to hidden lore. It thus had associations with magic. The runic alphabet, consisting of twenty-four letters, was adapted from Greek and Latin and devised by the Scandinavians and Anglo-Saxons for carving on slabs of beechwood. The 9th c. poet Cynewulf 'signed' his name by means of runes in four of his poems. The rune names were: *cen*, 'torch', *yr*, 'bow', *ned*, 'need', *eoh*, 'horse', *wyn*, 'joy', *ur*, 'bison', *lagu*, 'sea', *feoh*, 'wealth'.

running rhythm A term used by Gerard Manley Hopkins in his *Preface* to *Poems* (1918). It denotes a rhythm measured by feet of two or three syllables (excluding imperfect feet at the beginning and end of lines, and feet which seem to be paired together and double or composite feet which seem to arise). Each foot has one main stress or accent. The remaining one or two unaccented syllables are known as 'the slack'. The term is synonymous with common English rhythm. Hopkins distinguishes this from sprung rhythm (*q.v.*). *See* FALLING RHYTHM; RISING RHYTHM; ROCKING RHYTHM.

run-on line A line of verse which runs into the next line without any grammatical break. Also known as *enjambement* (*q.v.*), it is common in English poetry. This example is from Auden's *Letter to Lord Byron*:

> It is a commonplace that's hardly worth
> A poet's while to make profound or terse,
> That now the sun does not go round the earth,
> That man's no centre of the universe.

See also REJET.

Russian Formalism Along with movements in futurism and symbolism, the Russian Formalists were a group of writers who flourished during the period of the Russian Revolution of 1917. These two groups were active in the fierce debates of this era concerning art and its connections with ideology. The Formalists and Futurists found a common platform in the journal LEF (Left Front of Art). The Formalists, focusing on artistic forms and techniques on the basis of linguistic studies, had arisen in pre-revolutionary Russia but now saw their opposition to traditional art as a political gesture, allying them somewhat with the revolution. However, all of these groups were attacked by the most prominent Soviet theoreticians, such as Trotsky, Nikolai Bukharin (1888–1937), Anatoly Lunacharsky (1875–1933) and Aleksandr Voronsky (1884–1937), who decried the attempt to break completely with the past and what they saw as a reductive denial of the social and cognitive aspects of art. V. N. Volosinov (1895–1936) and Mikhail Bakhtin (1895–1975) later attempted to harmonize the two sides of the debate, namely formal linguistic analysis and sociological emphasis, by treating language itself as the supreme ideological phenomenon, as the very site of ideological struggle. Other groups, called 'Bakhtin Circles', formed around this enterprise.

There were two schools of Russian Formalism. The Moscow Linguistic Circle, led by Roman Jakobson, was formed in 1915; this group also included Osip Brik and Boris Tomashevsky. The second group, the Society for the Study of Poetic Language (*Opoyaz*), was founded in 1916, and its leading figures included Viktor Shklovsky, Boris Eichenbaum and Yuri Tynyanov. Other important critics associated with these movements included Leo Jakubinsky and the folklorist Vladimir Propp.

It should be said that the Russian Formalists' emphasis on form and technique was different in nature from that of the later New Critics. The Formalists' analyses were far more theoretical, seeking to understand the general nature of literature and literary devices, as well as the historical evolution of literary techniques; the New Critics were more concerned with the practice (rather than the theory) of close reading of individual texts. Though Russian Formalism as a school was eclipsed with the rise of Stalin and the official Soviet aesthetic of socialist realism (*q.v.*), its influence was transmitted through figures such as Jakobson and Tzvetan Todorov to their own structuralist analyses and those of writers such as Roland Barthes and Gérard Genette. Even reception theorists such as Hans Robert Jauss have drawn upon Shklovsky's central notion of defamiliarization, which holds that art has the power to override our habitual perceptions and to give represented objects and ideas a renewed unfamiliarity.

S

saber   A Provençal term which, in origin, probably meant 'wisdom' and then came to mean 'poetic skill'. It refers to the art of the troubadour (*q.v.*), which was codified in the Toulouse treatise *Leys d'amours* of the 14th c. *See* TROUVÈRE.

sacra rappresentazione   (It 'sacred representation') A dramatic form originating in medieval Italy, and akin to the Mystery Plays (*q.v.*) in England and elsewhere. Its usual subjects were the passion of Christ. It was a devotional entertainment or diversion which was presented after Mass and might be accompanied by sermons.

sacred books   Literature connected with any specific religion; works of spiritual guidance, rules, hymn books, liturgies, any kind of record made of the utterances of holy men, prophets or sages. Obvious and well-known examples are: the Old and New Testaments; *Vedas, Brahmanas* and *Upaniṣads*; the *Kijoki* and *Nihongi*; the *Talmud*; the Qur'an (or Koran); the *Analects* of Confucius; *The Rule of St Benedict*; Walter Hilton's *The Scale of Perfection*; Thomas à Kempis's *Imitation of Christ*. To which might be added *The Confessions* of St Augustine, *The Cloud of Unknowing, The Steps of Humility* by St Bernard of Clairvaux, the works of Meister Eckhart and Jakob Boehme, Nicolas of Cusa's *Vision of God*, the Tibetan *Book of the Dead*, Thomas Traherne's *Centuries of Meditation*, and the works of St François de Sales and William Law. *See also* HAGIOGRAPHY; BIBLE; QUR'AN; VEDAS.

saga   (ON 'saw, saying') The sagas were medieval Icelandic and Scandinavian prose narratives usually about a famous hero or family or the exploits of heroic kings and warriors. Until the 12th c. most of them belonged to the oral tradition (*q.v.*) and thereafter scribes wrote them down. They can be divided into approximately five groups: (a) Sagas of the Kings, mainly about the early Norwegian kings; for instance, *Heimskringla* and *Sverris saga*. But

A Dictionary of Literary Terms and Literary Theory, Fifth Edition. J. A. Cuddon.
© 2013 The Estate of J. A. Cuddon. Published 2013 by Blackwell Publishing Ltd.

there are some about the earls of Orkney known as the *Orkneyinga saga*. Others are about the Danish kings, like *Skjöldunga saga* and *Knýtlinga saga*. One, the *Jómsvíkinga saga*, treats of both Danish and Norwegian kings. (b) The Icelandic sagas, concerned with the period when Iceland was first settled; that is *c*. 930–*c*. 1030. Some of the more famous Icelandic sagas are: *Gísla saga Súrssonar*; *Víga-Glúms saga*; *Grettis saga*; *Hallfreðar saga*; *Egils saga*; *Laxdœla saga*; *Vatnsdœla saga*; *Njáls saga*; *Eyrbyggja saga*; *Hrafnkels saga*; and *Bandamanna saga*. These are anonymous works and are believed to have been first written down in the first half of the 12th c. (c) Contemporary sagas, about Icelandic chieftains and bishops. They date from the end of the 12th c. and later, and in some cases the authors are known. Moreover the authors were contemporaries of the people they wrote about. The main works are: the *Sturlunga saga*, the *Islendinga saga* and the *Hungrvaka*. There are also separate sagas devoted to several bishops whose episcopal reigns covered the period *c*. 1178 to *c*. 1330. (d) What are known as the For-naldarsögur, about legendary times, with little historical basis. The best known is the *Völsunga saga*. (e) During the 12th and 13th c. a number of romances were translated into Norse. The main works are: *Alexander's saga* (a version of a Latin poem on Alexander the Great; the *Þiðriks saga* (from a German original); and *Karlamagnús saga* (which stems mostly from stories in French about Charlemagne). There have been many versions of these sagas in English literature, especially by William Morris. Longfellow, too, used the *Heimskringla saga* as a basis for his *Saga of King Olaf*. *See also* SCOP; SKALD.

saga novel So called from the Icelandic sagas (*q.v.*) because it is a narrative about the life of a large family. The most notable example in English literature is Galsworthy's *Forsyte Saga*, a series of novels – written over a long period – which are all linked together by the Forsyte family. The main ones are: *The Man of Property* (1906), *In Chancery* (1920), *To Let* (1921) and *A Modern Comedy* (1929). One of the most remarkable saga novels of European literature is Thomas Mann's tetralogy (*q.v.*) *Joseph und seine Brüder* (1933, 1934, 1936, 1942). *See also* BILDUNGSROMAN; ROMAN CYCLE; ROMAN-FLEUVE.

sainete (Sp diminutive of *saín*, 'piquant sauce') A term used to describe one-act sketches which were developed to form the main kind of *género chico* (*q.v.*). They remain popular in Spain.

salon (F 'reception room') A social gathering *and* the place where it occurs. An informal meeting of writers, artists, scientists *et al.* at a private house. The *salon* was particularly popular in France in the 17th and 18th c. The prototype was very probably the Hôtel de Rambouillet (that is, town house) where, between 1610 and 1650, literary men and aristocrats were wont to assemble in the 'Blue Room' of the Marquise de Rambouillet. Other famous *salons* were run by Mesdames de Scudéry, Scarron, de Tencin and Récamier. After the French Revolution the influence and importance of the *salon* declined. In England it was never a popular institution, though Mrs Vesey and Mrs Elizabeth Montagu tried to establish it. In England the pub, the club and the coffee house were preferred.

samizdat   (R *sam*, 'self' + *izdatelstvo*, 'publishing') The term now denotes a form of underground writing ('self-publication') and has been in general use since *c.* 1966 to denote articles and books which are circulated in typescript (or are run off on duplicating machines and then circulated) without the knowledge of the authorities and certainly without their approval. *Samizdat* is literature which expresses views contrary to those of the state. In 1966 the trial of Andrei Sinyavsky revealed the existence of a large body of underground literature (*q.v.*) in the Soviet Union. In that year Sinyavsky and another writer, Yuri Daniel, were sent to prison for publishing works abroad under pseudonyms. More famous writers than these have incurred the disapproval of the state by making use of *samizdat*. They included Solzhenitsyn and Andrei Sakharov. Solzhenitsyn's *The First Circle*, published in English in 1968, started life as underground literature. Sakharov published his political treatise *Progress, Coexistence and Intellectual Freedom* in the same way.

A reverse process named *tamizdat* (R *tam*, 'there' + *izdatelstvo*, 'publishing') is the publication of work in Russian in the West. This is then taken into the Soviet Union secretly. Pasternak's *Dr Zhivago* was banned in the Soviet Union, then published in Russian in Milan in 1957. Later, copies found their way back into the USSR.

Magnitizdat denotes material recorded on tapes which are then circulated illegally.

Sapphic ode   Named after the poetess Sappho (7th c. BC). An ode (*q.v.*) written in regular stanza form. Sapphics, as they are called, are written in quatrain (*q.v.*) stanza with a particular metrical scheme thus:

$$/ \cup | / \bar{\ } | / \cup \cup | / \cup | / \bar{\ } |$$

repeated thrice, and a fourth line:

$$/ \cup \cup | / \bar{\ } |$$

In the fourth and eleventh syllables of the first three lines the foot may be trochaic or spondaic; and on the last syllable of the fourth line the same applies.

Despite (or, perhaps, because of) the difficulties of this form a large number of European poets have used it. Among Englishmen the best known are Sir Philip Sidney, Cowper, Watts, Southey, Tennyson, Swinburne and Ezra Pound. This example is Pound's *Apparuit*, and it shows the strain of using dactyls and trochees as the basic feet in English verse:

> Gólděn | róse thě | hóuse, ǐn thě | pórtǎl Í sǎw |
> thée, ǎ | márvěl, | cárvěn ǐn | súbtlě | stúff, ǎ |
> pórtěnt. | Lífe diéd | dówn ǐn thě | lámp ǎnd | flíckěred, |
> cáught ǎt thě | wónděr. |

Crimson, frosty with dew, the roses bend where
thou afar, moving in the glamorous sun,
drinkst in life of earth, of the air, the tissue
    golden about thee.

Green the ways, the breath of the fields is thine there,
open lies the land, yet the steely going
darkly hast thou dared and the dreaded æther
    parted before thee.

Swift at courage thou in the shell of gold, casting
a-loose the cloak of the body, camest
straight, then shone thine oriel and the stunned light
    faded about thee.

Half the graven shoulder, the throat aflash with
strands of light inwoven about it, loveliest of all things, frail alabaster, ah me!
    swift in departing.

Clothed in goldish weft, delicately perfect,
gone as wind! The cloth of the magical hands!
Thou a slight thing, thou in access of cunning
    dar'dst to assume this?

See also ALCAICS; ODE.

satanic school The term was originated by Southey in his preface to *A Vision of Judgment* (1821), a poem which made a fairly violent attack on Shelley and Keats and, especially, on Byron. In the preface Southey refers to Byron's works as 'monstrous combinations of horrors and mockery, lewdness and impiety'. Southey attacked these poets because he thought them immoral (in their lives as well as in their work), because they rejected orthodox Christianity and because he strongly disapproved of their interest in the exotic and passionate. Byron got his own back with a splendid satirical parody (*q.v.*) called *The Vision of Judgment* (1822). However, Southey was poet laureate (*q.v.*) and the law was on his side. Byron's publisher was fined.

satire (L *satira*, later form of *satura*, 'medley') It may be a cooking term in origin or, as Juvenal called it, *ollapodrida*, 'mish-mash', 'farrago'.

According to Johnson, Swift and Pope, the satirist is a kind of self-appointed guardian of standards, and ideals; of moral as well as aesthetic values. He is a man (women satirists have been *very* rare) who takes it upon himself to correct and ridicule the follies and vices of society and thus to bring contempt and derision upon aberrations from a desirable and civilized norm.

The history of satire begins with the early Greek and Roman literature. The great satirist of Greece was Aristophanes (*c.* 448–*c.* 380 BC), who used ridicule and abuse to great effect in several plays. In Rome, Horace wrote tolerant, urbane and amused satire of the human scene, while Juvenal's satires were bitter and misanthropic.

Notable instances of satire in medieval literature are Chaucer's *Canterbury Tales* and Langland's *Piers Plowman* (late 14th c.). From late in the 16th c. and early in the 17th we find an increasing propensity towards satirical modes and means, rather than the *occasional* satire of Dante or Cervantes. Examples in English literature are Thomas Lodge's *A Fig for Momus* (1595), the satires of Donne, Marston and Hall in Juvenal's manner, and the satirical comedy (*q.v.*) of Ben Jonson.

The major English satirist of the second half of the 17th c. was Dryden, with his poetic satires *Absalom and Achitophel* (1681), *The Medal* (1682) and *Mac Flecknoe* (1682). Samuel Butler's mock-heroic poem *Hudibras* (1663, 1664, 1687) is another notable example. In France Molière produced a succession of satirical comedies which have become classics.

In European literature, the 17th c. and the 18th c. is regarded as the golden age of satire. Various reasons are adduced for this. Those commonly put forward are that it was a period of fairly highly developed civilization and culture (at any rate, for a minority) which bred the satirists whose need and purpose was to protect this culture from abuse, aberration and corruption. Thus we find Pope satirizing materialism, excess and bad writing; Swift ferociously attacking hypocrisy, pride, cruelty and political expedience; Voltaire ridiculing credulity, religious humbug and naive optimism. With their moral weight and unblinking scrutiny of the truth, such men sought to be the cleansers and guardians of civilization – such as it was; for there can be no doubt that the 18th c. was, for the majority, from China to Peru, an era of poverty, misery and pain.

In the first half of the 18th c. there flourished the two greatest satirists in the history of literature, namely, Swift and Pope. Swift excelled in prose, Pope in verse. The Dean's principal works were *A Tale of a Tub* (1704), *The Battle of the Books* (1704), *Gulliver's Travels* (1726) and *A Modest Proposal* (1729). Pope's main works were *The Rape of the Lock* (1714) and *The Dunciad* (1728, 1729, 1742 and 1743). In France the greatest prose satirist of the period was unquestionably Voltaire.

For the most part, during the 19th c. (and thereafter), prose was the chosen medium for satire. The principal writers were Thackeray, Flaubert, Anatole France and Samuel Butler.

During the 20th c. satire was rare. Two of the main reasons for this lack were that it was a period of much instability and violent change, and the humour industry grew to such an extent that the satirist could hardly make himself felt except in the caricature and the cartoon. The only poet to attempt satire on a considerable scale was Roy Campbell in *The Georgiad* and *The Wayzgoose*.

To these instances we should add some of Aldous Huxley's early novels (e.g. *Antic Hay*), several novels by Evelyn Waugh (e.g. *Vile Bodies*, *Black Mischief*, *A Handful of Dust*) and George Orwell's *Animal Farm* – a political satire in the beast-fable tradition. Anti-utopianism or dystopianism also produced a kind of satire: the creation of a futuristic society whose shortcomings and evils are then exposed. The most famous examples of these in English literature are Huxley's *Brave New World* and Orwell's *Nineteen Eighty-Four*. John Betjeman also wrote several satirical poems.

Late 20th c. and contemporary writers have used satire for a wide range of purposes. Martin Amis's *Money* (1984), Iain Sinclair's *Landor's Tower* (2001) and Will Self's satirical novels are notable examples in contemporary British fiction. Satire has also played a prominent role in postcolonial literature (*q.v.*), for instance in V. S. Naipaul's travel book (*q.v.*) *The Middle Passage* (1962), and in the novels of Achebe and Rushdie. There is a great deal of satire in modern journalism, for instance London's *Private Eye*, and in TV programmes such as *Have I Got News for You*. See also CARICATURE; HORATIAN SATIRE; INVECTIVE; JUVENALIAN SATIRE; LAMPOON; LUCILIAN SATIRE; MENIPPEAN SATIRE; PARODY; UTOPIA.

satirical comedy A form of comedy (*q.v.*), usually dramatic, whose purpose is to expose, censure and ridicule the follies, vices and shortcomings of society, and of individuals who represent that society. It is often closely akin to burlesque, farce and comedy of manners (*qq.v.*). Some of the best and earliest examples of satirical comedy are to be found in the plays of Aristophanes, especially his *Acharnians*, *Knights*, *Clouds*, *Wasps*, *Birds*, *Frogs* and *Lysistrata*. In English literature classic examples of the genre are Ben Jonson's *Volpone* (1606) and *The Alchemist* (1610); Sheridan's *The School for Scandal* (1777); Shaw's *The Doctor's Dilemma* (1906). Apart from Aristophanes and Jonson, the supreme exponent of satirical comedy in the theatre is Molière, as in *Les Précieuses ridicules* (1659); *Le Misanthrope* (1666); *Le Médecin malgré lui* (1666); *Tartuffe* (1669); *L'Avare* (1669); *Le Bourgeois Gentilhomme* (1670); *Le Malade imaginaire* (1673). Other such works include Machiavelli's *Mandragola* (c. 1520); Gogol's *The Government Inspector* (1836); Benavente's *Gente conocida* (1896), *La noche del sábado* (1903), *Los intereses creados* (1907); Kanin's *Born Yesterday* (1946); and Sartre's *Nekrassov* (1955). Since the Second World War there have been Nigel Dennis's *Cards of Identity* (1956), *The Making of Moo* (1957) and *August for the People* (1961); Alan Bennett's *Forty Years On* (1968); Tom Stoppard's *Jumpers* (1972) and *Dirty Linen* (1976); David Hare's *Teeth 'n' Smiles* (1975); David Mamet's *American Buffalo* (1975) and *Glengarry Glen Ross* (1983); Michael Frayn's *Liberty Hall* (1979); David Hare and Howard Brenton's *Pravda* (1985); and Caryl Churchill's *Serious Money* (1987).

satura *See* SATIRE.

Saturnian meter An early Latin meter chiefly used by Livius Andronicus and Naevius, and so called because Roman writers related it to the age of Saturn. There are about 160 examples of it. Whether it was scanned accentually or by quantity is not certain.

satyr play The Greek tragic poet was expected to present four plays at once: three tragedies (whether a trilogy or not) and a satyr play, which came as a kind of after-piece (*q.v.*). It was a form of burlesque (*q.v.*) in which a mythical hero (perhaps the hero of the foregoing tragedies) was presented as a ridiculous personage with a chorus of satyrs, perhaps led by Silenus. The satyrs were creatures that were half man and half goat, or half man and half horse, and bore prominent, erect phalluses. In Greek art and pottery, satyrs were often depicted thus; and the goat has for centuries been regarded as a symbol of lust. The satyr plays were ribald in speech and action as well as in costume, and their dramatic function was clearly a form of comic relief (*q.v.*) after matters of high seriousness. Such a play had the effect of 'earthing' an audience, so to speak, after it had had the exalting spiritual experience of tragedy. It was a reaffirmation of the senses and of the sensual pleasures of life. Their origin is obscure, though Aristotle contends that tragedy developed out of the satyric. It is possible that the satyr play first formed part of the tragic contest instituted by Pisistratus at the festival of Dionysus.

There were a great many satyr plays. Aeschylus is believed to have written ninety plays altogether, including about twenty satyr plays. Sophocles's output is believed to have been 123 plays all told, including perhaps thirty satyr plays. And Euripides probably wrote eighty plays, fifteen of which were satyr plays. Only one play survives complete, namely the *Cyclops* of Euripides. Fragments of Sophocles's satyr play the *Ichneutai* were discovered in 1907 by the Oxford Classical scholars Grenfell and Hunt.

In 1987 Tony Harrison's play *The Trackers of Oxyrhynchus* was presented at Delphi. This free adaptation of Sophocles's *Ichneutai* was also performed in 1990 at the National Theatre, London.

There is no connection of any kind between satyric drama and satire (*q.v.*); or, apparently, between it and Greek comedy. *See* TETRALOGY.

saudosismo A Portuguese term for a blend of pantheism and the cult of the Portuguese sentiment *saudade* or 'yearning'. The movement, such as it was, to which the term refers was initiated shortly before the First World War by Teixeira de Pascoais (1878–1952). It was inspired by a kind of mystical nationalism and was retrogressive in that it harked back to folklore, fantasy and national myth. Neither realistic nor rational, it promoted the bizarre idea that a 'new world' would emerge under the leadership of Portugal, and was so far out of touch with reality that its more eccentric advocates actually thought that King Sebastian (killed in Morocco in 1578) was destined to return and lead Portugal to greatness in the putative new era. The poet Fernando Pessoa (1885–1935) was closely associated with it and his collection of poems *Mensagem* (1934) expressed some of the cult's fundamental yearnings.

savoyard In the 18th c. natives of Savoy (near Lake Geneva) were well known as itinerant musicians with hurdy-gurdy and monkey. Today the term is more likely to denote a devotee of Gilbert and Sullivan operas, for which, in 1881, D'Oyly Carte built the Savoy Theatre in London. He opened it with a production of *Patience*.

scansion (L *scandere*, 'to climb') The analysis of the metrical patterns of verse. It includes the arrangement of accented and unaccented syllables into metrical feet and the grouping of lines according to the number of feet. Also, the classification of stanza according to rhyme scheme and the number of lines per stanza.

There are three basic methods of scanning English verse: graphic, musical and acoustic. The graphic is the most commonly used. The conventional symbols are: × or ∪ to denote a syllable which is unstressed (or short); / or – to denote a stressed (or long) syllable; | to indicate a foot division; || to indicate a caesura (*q.v.*).

When scanning, the normal practice is to mark in the stressed and unstressed syllables according to the natural emphasis in the words. Thus, this first stanza from Kingsley Amis's *Beowulf* reads:

> Só, || bóred wĭth drágŏns, || hĕ láy dówn tŏ sléep,
> Lóckĭng fŏr góod || hĭs mássĭve hóard ŏf wórds
> (Dĭscúss ănd íllŭstrăte), || fŏrgéttĭng nów
> Thĕ hópe ŏf héathĕns, || múddlĕd thóughts ŏn fáte.

Scansion helps to reveal rhythm and gives the reader a representation of the 'tune' underlying and supporting the words.

Stanzaic structure may be analysed by indicating the rhyme scheme in letters and the number of feet per line in the numbers. For example, the following stanza from Thomas Hood's *A Reflection*:

> When Eve upon the first of Men
>   The apple press'd with specious cant,
> Oh, what a thousand pities then
>   That Adam was not Adamant.

may be notated thus: abab – $a^4b^4a^4b^4$.

Some prosodists prefer musical symbols, using eighth for unstressed syllables and quarter or half notes for stressed syllables. Caesuras may be indicated by musical rests of varying lengths. The acoustic method has been developed by linguists using the kymograph and the oscillograph. A small minority prefer to indicate rhythmical movements and sound units by wavy lines and brackets. *See* FOOT; METER; SPRUNG RHYTHM.

scatology (Gk 'dung knowledge') In pathology, diagnosis by a study of the faeces. As a literary term, used occasionally for obscene or bawdy literature. *See* LOW COMEDY; PORNOGRAPHY.

scattered rhyme *See* RHYME.

scenario An outline of a theatrical or cinematic work, giving the sequence of scenes, the characters involved and so forth.

scene A subdivision of an act (*q.v.*) in a play or an opera or other theatrical entertainment.

scène à faire French for 'obligatory scene' (*q.v.*).

Schauspiel (G 'spectacle, sight') A term for any public performance or visual entertainment. More specifically it denotes a play which is neither comedy nor tragedy (*qq.v.*) but which is a serious play whose resolution is positive and hopeful or optimistic. It does not end with the death of the hero or heroine. The term was first used for the performance of a stage play by Niklaus Manuel (1484–1530). During the 18th c. it acquired its modern sense. Examples of a *Schauspiel* are Goethe's *Iphigenie auf Tauris* (1779), Schiller's *Die Räuber* (1782) and Brecht's *Leben des Galilei* (1943). *See also* DRAME; TRAGICOMEDY.

Schicksalstragödie (G 'fate/destiny tragedy') A form of tragedy (*q.v.*) which had some vogue in Germany early in the 19th c. In such a play the hero or heroine (in some instances a complete family) was driven towards crime or destruction by a kind of fate or nemesis from which there was no escape. The sequence of tragic events might be the result of some crime. The victims might be destroyed on a particular fated day or through a fated/fatal weapon (or both). The sombre and doom-laden quality of these plays owes something to Greek tragedy, the Gothic novel (*q.v.*) and to the more bizarre extravagances of Gothic-type romances. Crime and its disastrous consequences were themes that were to become of increasing interest to writers during the 19th c., as may be seen in a variety of fiction (e.g. Newgate fiction and the detective story, *qq.v.*). The first example of *Schicksalstragödie* is generally believed to be Moritz's *Blunt, oder der Gast* (1781). Later came Zacharias Werner's *Der vierundzwanzigste Februar* (1806). Others are *Der neunundzwanzigste Februar* (1815) by Adolf Müllner and his *Die Schuld* (1816). Baron von Houwald wrote *Das Bild* (1821), *Die Heimkehr* (1821) and *Der Leuchtturm* (1821). Grillparzer's *Die Ahnfrau* (1816) has also been regarded as a fate tragedy. After the 1820s this form of drama fell into desuetude.

scholasticism The teachers of the liberal arts in the medieval schools were known as *doctores scholastici*; theologians and philosophers were also so called. Scholasticism now refers, loosely, to the methods and matter of theological and philosophical thought in the Middle Ages. St Thomas Aquinas, Duns Scotus, Peter Lombard and Albertus Magnus were all scholastics – the principal luminaries in an exceptional constellation of metaphysicians. They drew on Boethius's logic to attempt a rational and coherent interpretation of Christian doctrine as derived from Scripture, the Church Fathers and the decrees of the Church. They were typically concerned with proving the existence of God, the connection between faith and reason, the relation of will and intellect, and the problem of universals (whether universals actually existed or were merely names for classes of objects). The scholastics attempted to establish a systematic and hierarchical synthesis of the various branches of learning, at the apex of which stood theology. Though the influence of scholasticism after the Middle Ages was eclipsed by the empirical impetus of modern philosophy and science, its spirit has been kept alive in more recent times by T. E. Hulme, Jacques Maritain, Étienne Gilson and Gabriel Marcel. *See also* HUMANISM; RENAISSANCE.

school The term may be applied to a group of writers who combine as an influential unit and who are broadly agreed on the principles upon which their work should be based. Sometimes the principles are published as a manifesto (*q.v.*). A school may produce a movement whose influence spreads to several countries. Schools are usually short-lived but their fertilizing impact may last many years, especially when the principles which guided them have been of a revolutionary nature. Well-known examples of literary schools are: the Pléiade, the Göttinger Dichterbund, the Pre-Raphaelite Brotherhood, the Parnassians, the school of Spenser and the Bloomsbury Group (*qq.v.*).

school drama A term applied to an academic and educational genre of plays which were written by scholars and performed by schoolboys. Early in the 16th c. there was a great deal of dramatic activity in schools and colleges in England. In *c.* 1553 *Ralph Roister Doister* was written by Nicholas Udall or Uvedale, headmaster of Westminster, and performed by the boys of the school. In 1566 *Gammer Gurton's Needle*, of uncertain authorship, was acted at Christ's College, Cambridge. The tradition of the annual school play very probably derives from school drama. One of the best-known examples is the annual Greek play at Bradfield. Originally the plays were in Latin; then the vernacular was used more and more. The Jesuits, above all, were responsible for the popularization of this form in Europe and were the major influence in the 17th c.; Jesuit drama (*q.v.*) is a genre of its own. *See* ACADEMIC DRAMA; JESUIT DRAMA.

school of Spenser A group of English poets who, in the earlier part of the 17th c., were considerably under the influence of Edmund Spenser. The main poets were: Browne, Wither, Giles and Phineas Fletcher, and the Scots Drummond of Hawthornden and Sir William Alexander. In imagery, meter and diction, as well as in theme and subject matter, they were imitators of Spenser.

science fiction A science fiction (SF) story is a narrative set in an alternative or altered reality. Many SF stories describe experiences beyond the confines of normal human experience, such as space exploration or time travel; others imagine the familiar human world transformed by new technology, ecological change or alien visitation. Some SF stories are concerned with utopia (*q.v.*) and utopian visions, while others are dystopian or apocalyptic. Science fiction often provides straightforward escapism, but equally imagines scenarios which provoke serious questions about what it is to be human, the nature of reality, perception and power. Concepts such as atomic energy, cyberspace and robotics were all first conceived in science fiction stories.

The term 'science fiction' was first used, it seems, in 1851, the year of the Great Exhibition, in William Wilson's *A Little Earnest Book upon a Great Old Subject*. Having cited Thomas Campbell's remark that 'Fiction in Poetry is not the reverse of truth, but her soft and enchanting resemblance', Wilson goes on to say: 'Now this applies especially to Science-Fiction, in which the revealed truths of Science may be given, interwoven with a pleasant story which itself may be poetical and true . . .' The term was eventually put into circulation by Hugo Gernsback (1894–1967), who had originally coined the word 'scientifiction'. 'Science fiction' gradually replaced the term 'scientific romance'.

Notable predecessors of modern SF are too numerous to list in full. An early example is the *Vera Historia* or 'True History' (*c.* AD 150) of Lucian of Samosata, a parody (*q.v.*) of the tall stories of adventure presented as truth by former historians. The hero of this work visits the moon and the sun and is involved in interplanetary warfare. The 'vision literature' of the Middle Ages was popular and widespread in Europe. It is about the exploration of metaphysical worlds: heaven, purgatory, and especially hell. Gradually, the attraction of such escapist tales palled, to be replaced by utopianism. Thomas More's *Utopia*, published in 1516, was to be a kind of prototype for all sorts of utopian schemes and adventure quests, including expeditions into space. A particular curiosity is the publication in 1661 by Margaret Cavendish, Duchess of Newcastle, of *The Description of a New World, called the Blazing World* – an extraordinary Wellsian fantasy in the course of which the Duchess advanced the then improbable idea that mankind might be ruled by a non-human, animal 'intelligence'. The 18th c. was no less fecund in the creation of other worlds and fictional voyages of discovery. Two key works were Defoe's *Robinson Crusoe* (1719) and Swift's *Gulliver's Travels* (1726).

A major text in the evolution of science fiction was Mary Shelley's *Frankenstein* (1818). The anonymous creature that is constructed from bits of corpses by Dr Frankenstein, who then rejects his creation, prompting its vengeful and murderous rampage, is the classic cautionary tale of the scientist whose ambition overreaches his humanity. Another influential figure (who like Shelley's *Frankenstein* is closely associated with the Gothic) is Poe (1809–49), who published a number of stories, such as *The Conversation of Eiros and Charmion* and *The Unparalleled Adventures of One Hans Pfaall*, in which one can see him feeling his way towards science fiction. The ever popular Jules Verne (1828–1905), who was considerably influenced by Poe, made a major contribution to a new kind of fiction which combined adventure and exploration and the popularization of science. Immensely prolific, he is now best remembered for *Voyage au centre de la terre* (1864) and *Vingt mille lieues sous les mers* (1869). A major part of Verne's success was his ability to make scientific expertise plausible. In the 1890s H. G. Wells, one of the great originators of science fiction ideas, made an impact with such stories as *The Time Machine* (1895), *The Island of Dr Moreau* (1896), *The War of the Worlds* (1898) and the *First Men in the Moon* (1901). Wells was prophetic, showing the way to many possibilities in SF. He had the advantage of being a trained scientist with a profound understanding of scientific matters (he prophesied the atom bomb and lived to see it a reality).

Much SF written in the early to mid 20th c. took a more pessimistic direction in response to the multiple threats of world war, totalitarianism, the atom bomb and mass consumerism. Dystopian visions abounded, for example Zamyatin's *We* (1920–1), Aldous Huxley's *Brave New World* (1932), Orwell's *Nineteen Eighty-Four* (1949) and Anthony Burgess's *A Clockwork Orange* (1962). At the same time, the numbers of SF publications and readers soared, first as a result of pulp magazines (*see* PULP LITERATURE) and then, in the postwar period, the paperback. These formats provided a platform for some of the most celebrated SF writers, including Isaac Asimov, Arthur C. Clarke and Philip K. Dick. In the late 20th c. many female and gay writers, for example Ursula Le Guin, Doris Lessing and Samuel R. Delaney, produced important works of science fiction. The end of the 20th c. saw the rise of the cyberpunk (*q.v.*) subgenre, which is particularly focused on the possibilities of information technology.

scolion A type of Greek lyric poetry. Its etymology and origin are uncertain, but it seems to have been a kind of drinking song, sung by choruses and accompanied by a lyre. Tradition ascribes the invention of the *scolion* to a famous musician called Terpander, a native of Lesbos, who lived in the first half of the 7th c. BC.

scop (OE 'jester, one who scoffs') An Anglo-Saxon minstrel; also known as a gleeman. A professional entertainer (poet and singer) of an ancient and honoured calling. The *scopas* were the conservers of the OE oral tradition (*q.v.*) and they were makers of poetry as well as reciters. A number of them were members of royal households, like the *skalds* (*q.v.*). Few are known by name, but in the OE poem *Widsith* 'far traveller' we see the *scop* travelling from court to court and reciting his lays. The poem *Deor* 'animal brave' also affords us glimpses of the *scop's* life. The art of the *scop* is still perpetuated by ballad-makers in many parts of the world, and especially by the *guslar* (*q.v.*) in the South Slav lands. *See also* EPIC; SAGA; TROUBADOUR; TROUVÈRE.

Scottish Chaucerians The traditional title of a group of Scottish poets whose work apparently shows the influence of Chaucer. In fact, the influence was slight, though it is true that in his poem *The Kingis Quair* King James I (1394–1437) did use the rhyme royal (*q.v.*) scheme that Chaucer had used in *Troilus and Criseyde* and elsewhere, and Robert Henryson (1424?–1506?) wrote a fine sequel to Chaucer's poem in the shape of *The Testament of Cresseid*. Henryson and the King were two of the main Scottish Chaucerians. The others were William Dunbar (1456?–1513?) and Gawin Douglas (1475–1522). *See also* SCOTTISH RENAISSANCE.

Scottish Enlightenment The term denotes an intellectual movement which originated in Glasgow early in the 18th c. and was thereafter at its most active in Edinburgh from *c.* 1750 to 1800. It is mostly associated with philosophers and scientists, and the leading lights in the movement had considerable influence in Britain, France and America. Some of them were: Francis Hutcheson (1694–1746); Thomas Reid (1710–96); David Hume (1711–76); Adam Smith (1723–90); Adam Ferguson (1723–1816); and Dugald Stewart (1753–1828). *See* ENLIGHTENMENT.

Scottish renaissance A movement in Scottish literature which was at its most active between the two world wars. Those who belonged to it wished to revive Scots (or Lallans as it is now called) as a literary language. They aimed to achieve the revival through the use of regional dialects and also by harking back to the styles and traditions of the Scottish poets of the 15th and 16th c. The principal moving spirit of the movement was Hugh MacDiarmid (1892–1978) – his actual name was C. M. Grieve – who was politically committed (he was a Communist) and wanted to re-create Scots as a national language. He also wanted to reanimate Scottish political and social institutions. By these means he aimed to counter what he described as the 'English ascendancy'. Other prominent members of the movement were William Soutar (1898–1943), Lewis Grassic Gibbon (1901–35) and Sorley Maclean (1911–96). *See also* SCOTTISH CHAUCERIANS.

scribe (L *scriba*, 'clerk') A copyist, especially one who copied manuscript before the invention of printing. In England the term was used in the 18th c. to denote a secretary or taker of notes. The term also denotes a public writer, not uncommon in modern society where there is a high incidence of illiteracy. They may ply for custom on the pavement or in a booth for example. In 1947 in England the editor acted as a public scribe to illiterate fellow recruits in the army who wanted to write home. Sometimes journalists describe themselves jokingly as scribes. *See* HACK; SCRIBBLER.

Scriblerus Club A club founded *c.* 1713 whose principal members were Pope, Swift, Gay, Congreve, Arbuthnot, Parnell and Lord Oxford. It was so called after an imaginary antiquarian Martinus Scriblerus, a German of Münster, who had the reputation of being a man who had read almost everything but who had no judgement at all. He became the subject of 'memoirs', mostly written by Dr John Arbuthnot, and published in 1741. The 'memoirs' were a kind of satire (*q.v.*) against pretentious learning and false tastes.

script (L *scriptum*, 'written') There are five main meanings: (a) the characters used in a writing system (e.g. cuneiform script); (b) handwriting; (c) the text of a manuscript; (d) the text of a play or film or television or radio broadcast; (e) to write a script for a play or film. *See* MANUSCRIPT.

scriptible *See* LISIBLE; READERLY/WRITERLY.

scriptio continua (L 'continuous script') Writing without word-separation or marks of punctuation, astringoflettersrepresentingastringofsounds. All Western writing before the late 7th c. was in *scriptio continua*; word-separation was then introduced in Ireland, and over the next century or so spread into the Germanic and Romance vernaculars, and into Latin. *See* PUNCTUATION.

scriptorium (L 'writing room') A room in a monastery or abbey which is devoted to the writing and copying of books.

scripture (L *scriptura*, 'writing') A sacred text such as the Old Testament, the New Testament, the Qur'an and the Hindu *Vedas*.

Scythians A group of Russian writers and intellectuals led by the socialist revolutionary Ivanov-Ruzumnik (pseudonym of R. V. Ivanov, 1878–1945) who, with various followers, supported the Bolsheviks in the 1917 October Revolution. They stressed the fundamental differences between Russia and the West and maintained that the Russians were not Europeans but Scythians: that is, half Asiatic and half European. They sought to do away with European influence and purge Russia of it. They had mystical beliefs in the nature and future of Russia and the Russians, and they greatly admired the poetry of Yesenin (1895–1925) and Klyuyev (1885–1937), which presented a kind of mystical acceptance of the Russian Revolution as the ultimate destiny of the Russian people. A number of notable writers were influenced by the Scythians' point of view, including Alexander Blok (1880–1921) and Andrei Bely (1880–1934). *See also* SLAVOPHILES; WESTERNERS.

sea shanty (F *chantez* (imperative) 'sing!') Sea shanties were the working songs of sailors aboard the old square-rigged sailing vessels. Their origins are not known, but it would not be too fanciful to suppose that sailors have chanted songs to ease their labour since early times. One can easily imagine the Vikings doing so. The shanty *Haul on the Bowline* dates from Tudor times. Most of the best shanties were recorded in the 19th c., the age of the clippers. Their function was to co-ordinate group activity and to maintain morale. Their rhythms and words are therefore dictated by the kind of work being done. Negroes and Irishmen were particularly good at devising them. Some famous examples are *Hanging Johnny, Blow the Man Down, Boney, Haul Away* and *The Fair Maid of Amsterdam*. *See also* ORAL TRADITION.

secentismo (An Italianism from *seicento*, 'six hundred' = 17th c.) Connoting a reaction against classicism and a taste for the elaborate conceit (*q.v.*). It was the counterpart of baroque (*q.v.*) and its literary relations are Gongorism, *préciosité* and euphuism (*qq.v.*). In Italian *secentismo* is more or less synonymous with Marinism – from Marino (1569–1625), who wrote *L'Adone*, a long poem full of flamboyance and stylistic conceits; a bizarre work in every respect. Marinism is evident in the work of English writers like Richard Crashaw and Sir Thomas Browne.

seci A Turkish term for a feature of prose style in which the last words of a clause or sentence rhyme. The Qur'an contains a number of examples of it.

sedoka A Japanese verse form comprising two *katautas* (*q.v.*) with a syllable count of five, seven, seven, five, seven, seven.

seer One who sees visions of divine things; and, in a broader sense, a person endowed with precognitive and prophetic powers. Virgil was credited with the vatic gift because he would seem to have foretold the birth of Christ in his *Fourth Eclogue*:

> Cumaei venit iam carminis aetas;
> Magnus ab integro saeclorum nascitur ordo.
> Iam redit et virgo . . . (ll. 4–6)

('The last age, heralded in Cumean song, is come, and the great march of the centuries begins anew. Now the Virgin returns . . .')

William Blake was often vouchsafed a visionary gleam of the supranormal and the divine. H. G. Wells was a prophet in his writings in a more literal sense. One of the most remarkable of all prophetic writers (at any rate outside the Old Testament) was Nostradamus (1503–66), the Provençal astrologer. His work in verse named *Centuries* achieved considerable popularity in his time, and because of the fulfilment of some of his forecasts of major events in the 20th c. (e.g. the rise of Hitler, the assassination of the Kennedys, the flight of yellow men over London and the death of two Popes in quick succession) his predictions are again under scrutiny.

seguidilla (Sp 'little series', diminutive of *seguida*, 'series') A Spanish poetic form of popular origin which may have begun life as a dance song. To start with, it probably consisted of a four-line strophe with alternating long and short lines (seven or eight syllables in the long lines; five or six in the short). Later, very probably during the 17th c., three lines were added and it became established as a seven-line form, alternating seven and five syllables in the first part, and five, seven, five in the second. It is regarded as the most elegant of the popular Spanish metrical forms and is the only generalized form of the seven-line verse. *See* FOLÍA.

self-referential A statement or text which is self-referential (or reflexive) refers to itself, drawing attention to its own techniques and artifice. *See also* METAFICTION; REFLEXIVE NOVEL.

semantics A branch of linguistics (*q.v.*) which deals with the meanings of words, and particularly with changes in the meanings. It involves, moreover, the study of the relationship between words and things; and between language, thought and behaviour. That is, how behaviour is influenced by words uttered by others or to oneself.

semantic rhyme *See* RHYME.

semic code *See* CODE.

semiotics/semiology The terms have a common Greek root: *semeion*, 'sign'. Hence, the science of signs. The basic founders of modern semiotics and semiology were the philosopher C. S. Peirce (1839–1914) and the linguistician Ferdinand de Saussure (1857–1913). Strictly speaking, semiology is the science of signs (and signals) in general; semiotics refers to the theory of sign systems in language. For all practical purposes they are both concerned with the means of communication as conventions, with particular emphasis on language. But, *not just language*. The study of animal behaviour is known as *zoosemiotics*. Human bodily communication (*kinesics* and *proxemics*) and

643

communication by olfactory signs (i.e. the codes of scent) are branches of semiotics.

The term 'semiology' was taken over and used by Saussure in a manuscript dated 1894. He defines semiology as 'a science that studies the life of signs within a society'. Semiotics is the older of the two terms and its use is traceable to the ancient Greeks. Broadly speaking, semiotics is associated with the North American tradition of sign study, whereas semiology is associated with the European tradition. In literary criticism semiotics is concerned with the complete signifying system of a text and the codes and conventions we need to understand in order to be able to read it.

Peirce made two main contributions to the science: (a) he demonstrated that a sign can never possess or arrive at a definite meaning; definition has always to be qualified; (b) he distinguished between various types of sign; for example, as summarized by Raman Selden in *A Reader's Guide to Contemporary Literary Theory* (1985): (i) the 'iconic' – a sign which resembles its referent (*see* SIGNIFIER/SIGNIFIED), as in a road sign for a double bend; (ii) the 'indexical' – when the sign is associated with its referent: for instance, smoke = fire; (iii) the 'symbolic' – when sign and referent have an arbitrary relationship. Language signs are arbitrary, except in ideographic/ideogrammatic signs (e.g. those used in Chinese) or in onomatopoeic signs. The above examples of Peirce's system (which come under his heading of 'triadic relations of performance') are only three of his nine types of sign, all of which are susceptible to various possible combinations which would produce, all told, ten classes of sign. Ogden, I. A. Richards, Wimsatt and the behaviourist and semiotician Charles Morris have all discussed semiotic schemes related to Peirce's theories.

Saussure's classic work is *Cours de linguistique générale* (1915) – a text constructed from students' notes. It was his belief that beyond language there lies a range of sign systems. He made the primary distinctions of: (a) *langue* and *parole* (*q.v.*); (b) signifier and signified (*q.v.*). His theories have been fundamental to all developments in structuralism and poststructuralism (*qq.v.*) and have also influenced psychoanalytic criticism as developed by, for instance, the French philosopher Jacques Lacan (1901–81). Julia Kristeva, in *The System and the Speaking Subject*, tries to describe a semiotics which goes beyond Saussure, Peirce and structuralism towards a displacement of the subject – *à la* Freud. 'Semanalysis', as Kristeva calls it, conceives of meaning not as a sign system but as a signifying process. Jonathan Culler argues that a semiotics of literature should be concerned with signifying practices and interpretative conventions which make it possible for literary texts to communicate with readers. *See* NARRATOLOGY.

senarius   A metrical line which has six feet or six stresses. The Roman equivalent of the Greek iambic trimeter (*q.v.*) and the meter commonly used for dramatic dialogue. The alexandrine (*q.v.*) is its 'descendant'. *See also* HEXAMETER.

Senecan tragedy The closet dramas (*q.v.*) of the Roman Seneca (4 BC–AD 65) had a considerable influence on the Elizabethan tragedians, who accepted them as stage plays.

The themes of Seneca's plays *Hercules Furens, Medea, Troades, Phaedra, Agamemnon, Oedipus, Hercules Oetaeus, Phoenissae* and *Thyestes* were taken from the whole field of Greek drama and contained little or no action in the true sense of the word. The characters rarely voiced feelings similar to those experienced by most human beings, and Seneca was better fitted to express ideas than put life into his characters. The illusion of action was evoked by words, and the whole burden was thrown onto the language. Rhetorical devices were plentiful: stichomythia (*q.v.*) was a favourite device.

The plays had a five-act structure with a Chorus (*q.v.*) marking the end of each act. The subject matter of these choric speeches, often little more than mythological catalogues, was often remote from the action of the play.

Other and important features were: the theme of revenge, usually introduced by the ghost of a wronged person (obvious Shakespearean parallels are Hamlet's father and Banquo's ghost in *Macbeth*); the messenger figure, whose speeches usually report the culminating activity or disaster and fall into a stereotyped pattern, e.g. the bleeding captain in *Macbeth*; and a striving to extract the utmost effect from the spoken word.

One of the earliest Senecan tragedies was *Gorboduc* (1561) by Thomas Norton and Thomas Sackville. With its bloody plot, long, static and declamatory speeches, sensational events and high emotions, its debt to Seneca was obvious; and nowhere more so than in the purely mechanical juxtaposition of speeches and the constant striving for balance and counterbalance in language. Thomas Kyd's *The Spanish Tragedy* (*c.* 1586) also owed much to Seneca. But Kyd did not allow Seneca's influence to overcome his own sense of theatrical technique. The Senecan elements were all present: the revenge theme was supplied by the death of Horatio, though other characters also called for revenge; the characters were disproportionate and the emotions were taken too far (Hieronomo kills innocent people as well as those deserving death); the language was heavily rhetorical. Unlike Seneca, Kyd presented his atrocities on stage, and he had a good instinct for ironic juxtapositions. Shakespeare's *Titus Andronicus* (1594) was considerably influenced by Kyd's play and has a full complement of blood-curdling deeds.

Tudor and Jacobean dramatists owed many other debts to Seneca, whose influence extended through Marlowe and Shakespeare to Webster, who, like him, was fascinated by states of extreme suffering and by stoic virtues. For example, in *The Duchess of Malfi* (*c.* 1613–14) Webster followed Seneca in investigating the role of madness in society; as did Middleton and Rowley in *The Changeling* (1622). *See* REVENGE TRAGEDY; TRAGEDY; VILLAIN.

sensation novel *See* NOVEL OF SENSATION.

sense In the first place it concerns what is said and the meaning of what is said (e.g. 'What is the sense?'; 'Does it make sense?'). In critical terminology 'sense' has acquired some more flexible connotations. When we speak of a 'man of good sense' we imply someone whose judgement is sound, a man who has some capacity for appreciation. Good sense equals more or less the French *bon sens*. Jane Austen contrasted sense with sensibility (*q.v.*), in *Sense and Sensibility*.

The 18th c. has been described as 'the age of good sense' – for its balance, its feeling for proportion, its regard for the superiority of reason, its good taste and awareness of decorum (*q.v.*). *See also* NEOCLASSICISM; PROPRIETY.

sensibility The term became popular in the 18th c., when it acquired the meaning of 'susceptibility to tender feelings'; thus, a capacity not for feeling sorry for oneself so much as being able to identify with and respond to the sorrows of others – and to respond to the beautiful. This quality of empathy was probably a reaction against 17th c. stoicism and Hobbes's theory that man is innately selfish and motivated by self-interest and the power drive. In sermon, essay (*qq.v.*), fiction and philosophical writing (in the early 18th c.) it was averred, on the contrary, that man was innately benevolent and thus wished others well. The Earl of Shaftesbury's *Characteristicks* (1711) proclaimed this view. In the periodical *The Prompter* (1735) a writer defended the human attitude that is not content merely with good-natured actions 'but feels the misery of others with inward pain'. This was deservedly termed 'sensibility'. By mid-century such feelings were an accepted part of social ethics and public morality. It was a sign of good breeding and good manners to shed a sympathetic tear, as indeed in Gray's *Elegy* (1750), Goldsmith's *The Deserted Village* (1770) and Cowper's *The Task* (1785), not to mention the various odes to sensibility from the 1760s onwards. Two other relevant works in the history of this attitude were Sterne's *A Sentimental Journey* (1768) and Mackenzie's *The Man of Feeling* (1771). 'Dear sensibility!', writes Sterne (in an almost ode-like tone), 'source inexhausted of all that's precious in our joys, or costly in our sorrows!' In *The Man of Feeling* sensibility became self-indulgent. It declined into sentimentalism, and showed a propensity for 'the luxury of grief'. Jane Austen and Dr Johnson both criticized it; particularly Austen in *Sense and Sensibility* (1811).

In the 19th c. the term was more or less replaced by 'sensitivity', but the latter never established itself as a literary term. In fact, sensibility received a renewed and vigorous life in the critical essays of T. S. Eliot, for whom it represented the creative faculty and the quality of temperament in a poet. *See also* SENTIMENTAL COMEDY; SENTIMENTALITY; SENTIMENTAL NOVEL.

sentence *See* PERIOD (3).

sententia (L 'feeling, opinion, judgement') Closely related to, if not actually synonymous with, the apophthegm, maxim and aphorism (*qq.v.*), a *sententia* is customarily a short, pithy statement which expresses an opinion; hence the term 'sententious', now as a rule used pejoratively. One of the most famous collections of *sententiae* is that by Peter Lombard, who was known as *Mag-*

ister sententiarum. His *Sententiae* (12th c.) was an important theological textbook in the later Middle Ages. *See also* PENSÉE.

sentimental comedy   Also known as the drama of sensibility, it followed on from Restoration comedy (*q.v.*) and was a kind of reaction against what was regarded as immorality and licence in the latter. Jeremy Collier (1650–1726) severely criticized Restoration comedy in *A Short View of the Immorality and Profaneness of the English Stage* (1698). Sentimental comedy was rather anaemic by comparison and is seldom produced now. It arose because a rising middle class enjoyed this kind of drama, in which, as Goldsmith put it, 'the virtues of private life are exhibited, rather than the vices exposed, and the distresses rather than the frailty of mankind . . .'. The characters, both good and bad, were luminously simple; the hero was ever magnanimous and honourable and hypersensitive to the sensibilities of other people – rather like the hero in Hampton's *The Philanthropist* (1971). Good representative examples from the period are Richard Steele's *The Conscious Lovers* (1722), Hugh Kelly's *False Delicacy* (1768), Goldsmith's *The Good-Natured Man* (1768) and several works by Richard Cumberland – notably *The Brothers* (1769) and *The West Indian* (1771). In the same period Sheridan was attempting to revive comedy of manners (*q.v.*). *See also* COMÉDIE LARMOYANTE; SENSIBILITY; SENTIMENTAL NOVEL.

sentimentality   For the most part a pejorative term to describe false or superficial emotion, assumed feeling, self-regarding postures of grief and pain. In literature it denotes overmuch use of pathetic effects and attempts to arouse feeling by 'pathetic' indulgence. It was not often found earlier than the 18th c., though Crashaw might fairly be described as sentimental at times. It showed itself in Cowper and Gray and, later, in Shelley. It was also evident in sentimental comedy (*q.v.*) and in *comédie larmoyante* (*q.v.*) and in the sentimental novel (*q.v.*). It was particularly apparent in the thinking and attitudes of Rousseau and Shaftesbury. Cowper's poem *To Mary* illustrates some of its more obvious characteristics:

> The twentieth year is well-nigh past,
> Since our first sky was overcast;
> Ah would that this might be the last!
> My Mary!

> Thy needles, once a shining store,
> For my sake restless heretofore,
> Now rust disus'd, and shine no more,
> My Mary!

> Partakers of thy sad decline,
> Thy hands their little force resign;
> Yet, gently press'd, press gently mine,
> My Mary!

sentimental novel A form of fiction popular in 18th c. England. It concentrated on the distresses of the virtuous and attempted to show that a sense of honour and moral behaviour were justly rewarded. It also attempted to show that effusive emotion was evidence of kindness and goodness. The classic example was Richardson's *Pamela, or Virtue Rewarded* (1740), the story of a servant girl who withstood every attack on her honour. Comparable but more readable novels in this category were Goldsmith's *The Vicar of Wakefield* (1766), Henry Brooke's *The Fool of Quality* (1765–70), Mackenzie's *The Man of Feeling* (1771) and Maria Edgeworth's *Castle Rackrent* (1800). Sentimentality (*q.v.*) was very apparent in Sterne. In this period scores of sentimental novels were published and read avidly. *See also* BATHOS; COMÉDIE LARMOYANTE; PATHOS; SENSIBILITY; SENTIMENTAL COMEDY.

septenarius (L 'of seven each') A metrical line consisting of seven feet or seven stresses. More commonly known as the septenary, which is the same as the heptameter and fourteener (*qq.v.*). The term is now usually restricted to MedL verse and to ME poems like *Orm*, *Poema Morale* and Robert of Gloucester's *Chronicle*.

septet A seven-line stanza (Italian *septette* and French *septain*) of varying meter and rhyme. A large number of English poets have used it, including Chaucer, Lydgate, Hoccleve, Skelton, Sir Thomas Wyatt and William Morris – plus the Scot, Dunbar. *See* RHYME ROYAL.

sequence A composition sung after the Epistle at Mass. Sequences were incorporated into the Liturgy at an early stage and certainly by the end of the 19th c. Many sequences were of impressive beauty.

Serapionovy bratya (R 'Serapion brothers') A group of young Soviet writers formed in 1921. They were followers of Zamyatin (author of *We*) and took their name from E. T. A. Hoffmann's story *The Serapion Brothers*, about an individualist who dedicates himself to non-conformist art. The Serapion fraternity claimed a right to create literature independent of political ideology. Their articles of faith were drawn up by Lev Lunts in 1922. Other members of the group were Zoshchenko, Tikhonov, Fedin, Vsevolod Ivanov, Nikolay Nikitin and Slonimiski.

serenade (It *serenata*, 'made serene, purified', associated with *sera*, 'evening') Traditionally a song sung at night beneath a lady's window; or an imitation of such a song, like Shelley's *Indian Serenade*. Its meaning has now become vague, but it is a musical rather than a literary term. One should mention Mozart's *Serenata notturna*, Vaughan Williams's *Serenade to Music*, and Benjamin Britten's *Serenade*.

serial (L *series*, 'row, chain, succession') The term serial derived from Neo-Latin *serialis* in the 1830s. There are three basic usages: (a) a story occurring in sections in a magazine; (b) a work published or broadcast on television or radio in parts; (c) a periodical like a scientific journal which has numerous parts and is catalogued. In the 19th c. and the earlier part of the 20th c. many novels were serialized in magazines. Dickens and Hardy, for instance, made regular use of serialization.

sermon (L *sermo*, 'talk, discourse') As a form of literature the sermon dates from the sub-Apostolic age. One of the earliest examples is the so-called *Second Epistle* of Clement (*c.* 100–200). Throughout the Middle Ages many of the Fathers (Origen, Basil, Gregory of Nazianzus, John Chrysostom, Ambrose, Augustine *et al.*) helped to develop the sermon into something like a work of art, with definite rules of composition. By the late Middle Ages the *ars predicandi* was something which had to be learnt and worked at (as Chaucer's Pardoner implied). Hence, in part, the growth of the preaching orders, like the Dominicans and Franciscans; and also the number of manuals for preachers. John Bromyard's *Summa Praedicantium* (printed in 1485), for instance, was an encyclopaedic reference work for the preacher.

The sermon became one of the principal sources of instruction and 'entertainment' in a period when the Church had much control over the diversions available to the public. The great age of sermon literature runs from the 13th to the 17th c., and throughout Europe the 'literature of the pulpit' had considerable influence on the establishment of ethnic languages and the development of allegory, *exemplum*, fable, dialogue (*qq.v.*), verse and drama. Religious reformers like Wycliffe and Luther used the sermon to publicize their beliefs. The invention of printing allowed countless volumes of sermons to be published, though there are vast collections of manuscript sermons still lying unread in the cathedral libraries of Europe.

Between 1550 and 1700 the sermon attained its apogee in England and France. Notable preachers of the period were Latimer, Lancelot Andrewes, Joseph Hall, John Donne and Jeremy Taylor in England; Bossuet, Bourdaloue and Massillon in France. John Donne, as Dean of St Paul's Cathedral in London, could command an audience of perhaps 10,000 at St Paul's Cross, in the open air, with an extremely learned and closely argued sermon lasting two hours or more.

Since those times sermons have been published in large quantities and have been much read. Among many famous preachers one should mention John Wesley (reputed to have preached over 40,000 sermons), Frederick Robertson, Cardinal Newman and Cardinal Manning. As a literary form the sermon is almost defunct today, and the extent to which the art of preaching has deteriorated is shown by the fact that the average contemporary preacher has difficulty in keeping the interest of a few hundred people for ten minutes in a church equipped with a public-address system. *See* HOMILY.

sermon joyeux A kind of mock sermon which was popular in medieval times, especially in France. It was delivered in churches during the period associated with the traditional Feast of Fools (i.e. between Christmas and the Octave of the Epiphany – Jan. 13th). In this period revels, sometimes of a semi-dramatic nature, were permitted in church. A *sermon joyeux* played a part in these and was often a satirical and/or ribald diversion. Later (by the 15th c.) these profane interpolations in the Mass and the Liturgy were abolished and were eventually succeeded in the developing drama by farces, Morality Plays and *soties* (*qq.v.*). *See also* CARNIVALIZATION/CARNIVALESQUE.

serpentine verse A line or a stanza of poetry which begins and ends with the same word.

sestet The subdivision or last six lines of the Italian sonnet (*q.v.*) following the octet or octave (*q.v.*). Sometimes the sestet resolves the proposition made in the octave, just as the final couplet in the Shakespearean sonnet (*q.v.*) rounds off the propositions in the three preceding quatrains (*q.v.*). *See* HEXASTICH; SESTINA; SEXAIN.

sestina A complex verse form first worked out by the troubadours (*q.v.*), it consists of six stanzas of six lines apiece with an *envoi* (*q.v.*) of three lines. The rhyming scheme requires that the same six end words occur in each stanza but in a different order according to a fixed pattern. The invention of the form is attributed to Arnaut Daniel (*c.* 1200). It was practised by many Provençal poets and also by Dante and Petrarch. Examples are to be found in Sir Philip Sidney's *Arcadia* (1590). From time to time since then various European and English poets have used it. One of the best-known examples in English verse is Swinburne's *Complaint of Lisa*. Kipling, Pound, Eliot and Auden have also cultivated it. *See* HEXASTICH; SESTET; SEXAIN.

setting The where and when of a story or play; the locale. In drama the term may refer to the scenery or props.

sevdalinke Bosnian love-songs. The word is Serbian, based on the Turkish *sevda*, 'love'. *Sev* is love as a verb, *sevdali* means 'one who is in love'; so, *sevda, sevdali*. There are at least two other words for each meaning. Reminiscent of the Moorish love-songs, *sevdalinke* are fatalistic in mood and tone, and sometimes bitter. They often express a helpless or hopeless yearning and lament the pangs of unrequited or disprized love. Their influence on music and song in the Balkans has been considerable, as any traveller there can verify. In Bosnia itself, in such towns as Foča and Sarajevo, one may easily hear modern *sevdalinke*. Similarly in Serbia and across Bulgaria and in other parts where the Ottoman Empire prevailed.

seven arts, the *See* QUADRIVIUM.

7:84 Theatre Company Founded in 1971 by John McGrath (1935–2002) and so called on the basis of a then current statistic that 7 per cent of the British population owned 84 per cent of the wealth. The first production was McGrath's *Trees in the Wind* at the 1971 Edinburgh Festival. He followed that up with several other plays in the 1970s. Other notable dramatists to have work performed by the company were John Arden (1930–2012) and David Edgar (1948–). In 1973 the company was divided into two groups: 7:84 England and 7:84 Scotland. Avowedly political and left-wing, the company sought to bring drama to working-class audiences. *See also* AGIT-PROP DRAMA; THEATRE WORKSHOP; UNITY THEATRE.

sexain A six-line stanza, also known variously as a sixain, sextain, sextet, sestet (*q.v.*) and hexastich.

sextilla A Spanish verse form of six octosyllabic or shorter lines with a varying rhyme scheme.

shadow show A puppet show in a shadow theatre. The puppets are manipulated between a strong light and a translucent screen. *See also* KARAGÖZ.

shaggy dog story An improbable kind of yarn, often long and spun out, which, as a rule, does *not* have a witty or surprise ending; but comes, rather, to a deflating and quasi-humorous conclusion. Colloquially, 'a groaner'. A tolerably well-known example concerns the Australian bee which had a consuming ambition to become a ballet dancer. It presented itself to the authorities in Sydney and was advised to go to Covent Garden, London. But how was it to get there? Eventually it persuaded a racing pigeon bound for London to transport it. After many hazards (all detailed in the story) they arrived and the bee made a 'bee-line' for the Covent Garden Opera House. It explained its ambition and the powers that be were so impressed that they decided that a 'pigeon-towed' bee would be a unique addition to the corps. In fiction, Joseph Heller's digressive and crazily funny novel *Catch-22* (1961) might be taken as an example. *See also* TALL STORY.

Shakespearean sonnet A fourteen-line poem in iambic pentameters (with subtle variations on the iambic pattern) consisting of three quatrains (*q.v.*) and a concluding couplet. It is so named because Shakespeare was its greatest practitioner. Also known as the English sonnet, it is a variant of the Petrarchan sonnet (*q.v.*). It was developed, particularly, by Sir Thomas Wyatt and the Earl of Surrey during the Tudor period. The rhyme scheme is normally (a) abab, cdcd, efef, gg; or (b) abba, cddc, effe, gg. The following example is Shakespeare's 46th Sonnet:

> Mine eye and heart are at a mortal war,
> How to divide the conquest of thy sight;
> Mine eye my heart thy picture's sight would bar,
> My heart mine eye the freedom of that right.
> My heart doth plead that thou in him dost lie
> A closet never pierc'd with crystal eyes;
> But the defendant doth that plea deny,
> And says in him thy fair appearance lies.
> To 'cide this title is impanelled
> A quest of thoughts, all tenants to the heart;
> And by their verdict is determined
> The clear eye's moiety and the dear heart's part –
>> As thus: mine eye's due is thine outward part,
>> And my heart's right thine inward love of heart.

It will be seen from this that each quatrain deals with a separate aspect of the theme introduced in the first line, and that the 'argument' (*q.v.*) is resolved in the final couplet. *See* SONNET.

sharacans (Ar 'rows of gems') Armenian verse forms which consist of chants and hymns. Composed either in free verse (*q.v.*) or according to metrical schemes, they constitute the main part of Armenian church music. Most of them were composed between the 5th and the 7th c. but occasional additions were made up until *c.* 1500. Some of the poets are known by name.

Shavian Characteristic of the style, tone and attitudes of George Bernard Shaw (1856–1950). Thus, witty, irreverent, paradoxical, eloquent, stimulating and socialist. However, Shaw could also be verbose.

shih (Ch 'songs') In Chinese there is no word for poetry, but there are words for different kinds of poetry. *Shih* is the basic Chinese verse, and the term was first used to designate folksongs, hymns and libretti. The earliest examples of *shih* in regular five-word lines date from *c.* 1st c. BC.

shimpa A form of Japanese dance drama which developed late in the 19th c. and derives in some respects from *kabuki* (*q.v.*).

short couplet A tetrameter (*q.v.*) couplet, usually either iambic or trochaic, like the following from Belloc's *Henry King*:

> The Chief Defect of Henry King
> Was chewing little bits of String.
> At last he swallowed some which tied
> Itself in ugly Knots inside.

short measure Often abbreviated to SM, in Anglican hymn books, it consists of a quatrain (*q.v.*) rhyming abab or abxb. The first, second and fourth lines are iambic trimeters (*q.v.*), the third an iambic tetrameter (*q.v.*), as in the opening stanza of this hymn by Edwin Hatch (1835–89):

> Breathe on me, Breath of God,
> Fill me with life anew,
> That I may love what thou dost love,
> And do what thou wouldst do.

See also HYMNAL STANZA; POULTER'S MEASURE.

short meter *See* SHORT MEASURE.

short novel A work of fiction which is longer than a short story (*q.v.*) and shorter than a novel (*q.v.*). We tend to use the Italian word *novella* (*q.v.*) for this 'middle-distance' type of book. Novelette is another term sometimes used. Examples are: Conrad's *Heart of Darkness* and Aldous Huxley's *Two or Three Graces*. However, many people would classify these as merely long short stories.

short story A prose narrative of indeterminate length, but too short to be published separately as novels or novellas (*qq.v.*) usually are. According to Edgar Allan Poe, it is a story that concentrates on a unique or single effect and one in which the totality of effect is the objective. A short story may be concerned with a scene, an episode, an experience, an action, the exhibition of a character or characters, the day's events, a meeting, a conversation, or a fantasy. In the preface to his *Complete Short Stories* Somerset Maugham remarks that the shortest item runs to about 1,600 words (although there have been shorter ones) and the longest to about 20,000 words. The vast majority of short stories would fall somewhere between the two.

It may be argued that the forefathers of the short story are myth, legend, parable, fairy tale, fable, anecdote, *exemplum*, essay, character study and *Märchen*; plus the *lai*, the *fabliau* and even the ballad (*qq.v.*). The term 'short story' has relatives in the shape of the French *conte* and *nouvelle*, the Spanish *novela*, the Italian *novella*, the German *Novelle* and *Kurzgeschichte* (a word used to translate the English 'short story'), the yarn, the sketch, the tale and the Russian *skaz* (*qq.v.*).

Historically, we find many inset stories or digressions in Classical literature which amount to short stories, for instance in biblical stories, the Norse sagas and in many other tales. In the second half of the 18th c. the short story was being developed and established in Britain, partly as a result of the popularity of the oriental tale (*q.v.*) but more so as a result of the popularity of the Gothic novel (*q.v.*). In the opening years of the 19th c. the short story as a form was highly evolved, especially in the shape of the ghost story (*q.v.*) and the horror story, and stories which had to do with the supernatural.

Edgar Allan Poe (1809–49) was long regarded (inaccurately) as the originator of the modern short story. He was affected by the German Romantics and their Gothic stories, and particularly by E. T. A. Hoffmann. Poe excelled in the detective story and a kind of Gothic spine-chiller. In the mid 19th c. he was a major influence. Among his most famous works are *The Fall of the House of Usher* (1839) and *The Black Cat* (1843).

Later, more realistic stories were written and they became highly developed in Russia. Pushkin, Gogol, Turgenev and Chekhov are regarded as the greatest practitioners of this form of short story. In France the short story was established in 1829–31 with the publication of a dozen *contes* by Balzac, Gautier and Guy de Maupassant. In America, during the second half of the 19th c., numerous writers made a considerable name for themselves in the short story form, including Herman Melville, Mark Twain, Stephen Crane and Jack London. Meanwhile, another American, Henry James, made a lasting contribution to the genre with his short story *The Turn of the Screw* (1898) and his numerous collections. In Britain, during the 1890s and across the turn of the century, many writers were active practitioners of the form. Arthur Conan Doyle established the detective story with *The Adventures of Sherlock Holmes* (1892) and Katherine Mansfield was another important figure in the evolution of the genre.

Scores of other writers were equally industrious at the turn of the 20th c. exploiting the possibilities of the form and often producing original work. In 1914 Joyce published *Dubliners*, something of a landmark. Two notable European short story writers in the early part of the 20th c. were the Slovene Ivan Cankar and the Czech Franz Kafka. Kafka's weird and enigmatic vision makes his stories unlike anything else in the genre. He remains especially famous for *Metamorphosis* (1915) and *In the Penal Colony* (1919). The ghost and the horror story continued to be very popular at this time; however, for the most part, short story writers have settled for realistic and naturalistic conventions. Since *c.* 1920 numerous British, Irish, American, German and other authors have made memorable contributions. Two Spanish-American authors who attained international renown in the second half of the 20th c. are Luis Borges and Gabriel García Márquez.

In the mid-1990s there were well over a hundred general anthologies of short stories available in English alone (including a fair number of translations into English). Well-established stories, or classics of the genre, are regularly recycled in new anthologies.

Short-Title Catalogue Published by the Bibliographical Society in 1926; an indispensable guide and reference work to English books published between 1475 and 1640.

sic (L 'so') Put in brackets after a word or expression or even perhaps a sentence from a quoted passage to indicate that it is quoted accurately even though it may be incorrect, absurd or grotesque.

Sicilian octave An eight-line Italian stanza (rhyming abababab) of hendecasyllabic (*q.v.*) verses. Also called *strambotto popolare*, it is believed to have been used in Southern Italy and Sicily in the 13th c., and also in Tuscany. It is related to the medieval French *estrabot* and to *ottava rima* (*q.v.*), which may have developed from it. It was in fairly general use in the 15th c. *See also* RISPETTO; SONNET.

Sicilian School A term applied to a group of poets associated with the court of Emperor Frederick II (1220–50) in Palermo. The poets used the vernacular and were very probably the first to establish Italian as a literary language. The school flourished for about fifty years.

sick verse Sick verse (the term is a modern neologism) is kin to black comedy (*q.v.*); it is queasily, uneasily funny, mordant, sardonic and occasionally macabre. Its themes are misfortune, death, disease, cruelty, love-sickness and morbid preoccupations related to mental illness (sometimes masochistic and sadistic). It is the product of melancholy, ennui, despair and nausea of the world. At its strongest it displays horror and necrophiliac urges. It ranges from the apocalyptically sombre vision of James Thomson's *City of Dreadful Night* to the comparatively light-hearted jingle of W. S. Gilbert's *Nightmare*.

A very large number of poets have written verse which qualifies as sick. Some would find parts of Juvenal's more misanthropic satires fairly sick, but there is little of note until the 15th c. when the disastrous wars and plagues which devastated Europe inspired poets to express disgust and regret. Some notable examples from this period of what we might now describe as sick verse are: Villon's *Regrets de la belle heaulmière*, *Ballade des dames du temps jadis*, and *Ballade des pendus*; Chastellain's *Le Pas de la Mort*; and Olivier de la Marche's *Parement et Triumphe des Dames*. A preoccupation with death, decay and disease sometimes inspired Elizabethan and Jacobean dramatists (especially Webster and Tourneur) to write appropriately sick verse for some scenes. A macabre and 'sick' element is particularly noticeable in revenge tragedy (*q.v.*).

Sick verse becomes rare after the middle of the 17th c., but a certain blackness of spirit and a dwelling upon the gloomy and horrific reappears towards the middle of the 18th c. in the Graveyard School of Poetry (*q.v.*), and during the 19th c. sick verse of one kind and another is common. Out of the many examples available one should mention George Crabbe's *Peter Grimes* and *Sir Eustace Grey*; many works by Thomas Lovell Beddoes (especially his play *Death's Jest-Book*); *The City of Dreadful Night* by James Thomson, already referred to, and the same author's *Insomnia*; Edgar Allan Poe's poems *The Raven*, *The Bells*, *The Conqueror Worm*, *The Sleeper*; Robert Browning's poems *Madhouse Cells*, *Soliloquy of the Spanish Cloister*, *The Laboratory*, *Sibrandus Schafnaburgensis* and *Childe Roland to the Dark Tower Came*; Swinburne's *Faustine* and *After Death*. The works of some 19th c. French poets also qualify as sick. For instance, Baudelaire's *Les Fleurs du mal* and *Spleen*; Rimbaud's *Le Bateau ivre* and *Une saison en enfer*. In more recent years some of the more notable contributions have been made by Robert Graves (*The Halls of Bedlam*, *The Castle*, *The Suicide in the Copse*); Robert Service (*The Cremation of Sam McGee*); W. H. Auden (*Miss Gee*); John Betjeman (*Death in Leamington*; *Late-Flowering Lust*); Sylvia Plath (*Surgeon at 2 a.m.*, *In Plaster*). One should also mention Tom Lehrer's witty 'sick' lyrics. *The Penguin Book of Sick Verse* (1963), edited by George MacBeth, is a sufficiently emetic collection. *See also* NONSENSE.

sigmatism A term deriving from the Greek letter *sigma*, 's'. It denotes the marked use (or repetition) of the letter 's'. In English it is a very common letter and the use of sibilance, especially in verse, in order to achieve certain effects is also very common. From among many well-known instances one may cite Wordsworth's celebrated description of skating in *The Prelude*:

> All shod with steel,
> We hissed along the polished ice in games
> Confederate, imitative of the chase
> And woodland pleasures – the resounding horn,
> The pack loud chiming, and the hunted hare.
> So through the darkness and the cold we flew,
> And not a voice was idle; with the din

Smitten, the precipices rang aloud;
The leafless trees and every icy crag
Tinkled like iron; while far distant hills
Into the tumult sent an alien sound
Of melancholy not unnoticed, while the stars
Eastward were sparkling clear, and in the west
The orange sky of evening died away.

See ONOMATOPOEIA.

signature The printer's original sheet with four or more pages printed on it. Folded and bound, this forms a section. *See* GATHERING.

signifiant *See* SIGNIFIER/SIGNIFIED.

signifié *See* SIGNIFIER/SIGNIFIED.

signifier/signified In his classic work *Cours de linguistique générale* (1915) Ferdinand de Saussure describes a language system as 'a series of differences of sound combined with a series of differences of ideas'. In elaboration, he makes the famous distinction between *signifiant* ('signifier') and *signifié* ('signified'). Each sign in language is a union of *signifier* (i.e. a sound image or its graphic equivalent) and a *signified* (i.e. the referent; the concept referred to). The letters or marks *h-o-u-s-e* form a signifier which evoke the signified 'house'. There is no inherent reason why the letters or marks should mean 'house'. The association of signifier and signified is the product of linguistic convention and not of any natural link. The relation between the whole sign and what it refers to (i.e. the referent, or actual house with walls, roof, doors, windows, etc.) is arbitrary in that there is no natural link between the sign and the actuality to which it refers. Each sign in a linguistic system possesses 'meaning' by virtue of the fact that it is different from any other sign rather than because of any linguistic reason why this should be so. House is different from 'louse' and 'mouse'. Thus a word can be identified because of how it is related to, and differentiated from, other words in the linguistic system. As Saussure puts it: 'in language there are only differences without positive terms'. *See* DECONSTRUCTION; LANGUE AND PAROLE; POSTSTRUCTUR-ALISM; STRUCTURALISM.

sijo (K 'melody of the times') A Korean verse form, originally sung or chanted to the accompaniment of music. A complex form, the conventional *sijo* comprised three lines, each being composed of four groups of syllables. The first two lines had either fourteen or fifteen syllables, the third fifteen. There were slight variations, but a *sijo* was usually of forty-three, forty-four or forty-five syllables. Head rhyme (*q.v.*) is common. The *sijo* is of great antiquity and dates back at least to the 14th c. It is still used by Korean poets.

sillographer A writer of *silloi* (Gk 'squint-eyed') pieces: poems which satirize particular schools of thought or an individual's doctrines. A famous sillographer of antiquity was Xenophanes of Colophon who satirized the mythology of Homer and Hesiod. Samuel Butler's *Hudibras* (1663–78) might be described as a sillographic work. So might Pope's *Dunciad* (1728–43). Belloc and Chesterton were other writers who excelled at trenchant debunking of this kind. *See also* SATIRE.

silva A Spanish poetic form, apparently first developed in the 16th c. and related to the *canción* (*q.v.*). It consisted of hendecasyllabic or heptasyllabic lines arranged in strophic form and with a variable rhyme scheme. Lope de Vega wrote a number of them.

silver fork school *See* FASHIONABLE NOVEL.

simile (L neuter of *similis*, 'like') A figure of speech in which one thing is likened to another, in such a way as to clarify and enhance an image. It is an explicit comparison (as opposed to the metaphor, *q.v.*, where the comparison is implicit) recognizable by the use of the words 'like' or 'as'. It is equally common in prose and verse and is a figurative device of great antiquity. The following example in prose comes from Graham Greene's *Stamboul Train*:

> The great blast furnaces of Liège rose along the line like ancient castles burning in a border raid.

And this instance in verse from Ted Hughes's poem *February*:

> The wolf with its belly stitched full of big pebbles;
> Nibelung wolves barbed like black pine forest
> Against a red sky, over blue snow . . .

See also EPIC SIMILE.

similiter desinens *See* HOMEOTELEUTON.

similitude (from L 'likeness') For all practical purposes a synonym for parable and allegory (*qq.v.*); and thus in the sense 'in the guise of'. As the prophet Hosea put it (12: 10): 'I have multiplied visions, and used similitudes'. Occasionally it is used to mean a simile (*q.v.*), as Macaulay intended in his attack on Robert Montgomery's poems (1830); he derides the poet for a comparison: 'We take this to be, on the whole, the worst similitude in the world.'

simulacra The terms 'simulacra' and its singular form 'simulacrum' were coined by the French poststructuralist theorist Jean Baudrillard (1929–2007) in his discussion of the changing relationship between the real and the original in postmodern culture. Baudrillard distinguishes three orders of simulacra throughout history: counterfeit, production and simulation. In the first order, associated with the Renaissance period, the image is recognized as an imitation of the real; however, in the second order, associated with the industrial revolution, this distinction begins to get blurred because of the mass production of copies. Finally, in the third order, associated with the late 20th c., we are confronted with what Baudrillard terms 'a precession of simulacra'. In the postmodern age, there is a complete breakdown between representation and reality and we are left with signs and symbols that come to precede and substitute for the real. In other words, there are no originals, only copies without referents or origin. *See also* HYPERREAL.

simultanéisme A short-lived movement in French poetry early in the 20th c. The writers aimed at a kind of 'simultaneousness' of image and sound to represent or reproduce human sounds mingled with other sounds (e.g. those made by animals, birds), and also the sounds of cities (e.g. traffic). It was an attempt at a complex form of onomatopoeia (*q.v.*) and also at a form of synaesthesia and the kinaesthetic image (*qq.v.*). Representative examples are to be found in *La Trilogie des forces* (1908–14) by H.-M. Barzun, the leader of the movement, and *Naissance du poème* (1918) by Fernand Divoire. *See also* KINETIC POEM; PHANOPOEIA; UNANIMISME.

sincerity A term commonly used in the 19th c. to denote a criterion of aesthetic excellence and truthfulness, even of moral integrity. Matthew Arnold, for example, held that the test of greatness in poetry was whether or not it possessed the 'high seriousness which comes from absolute sincerity'. Later critical thinking dispensed with the term as being too vague, and because it implied or presupposed a knowledge of the author's intentions and feelings which no one but the author himself could be fully aware of. *See* PERSONAL HERESY; SPONTANEITY.

single-moulded line An end-stopped line, fairly frequent in early blank verse (*q.v.*). Three of the following lines from Marlowe's *Jew of Malta*, III, iv (*c.* 1592) are end-stopped:

> Barabas: O trusty Ithamore; no servant, but my friend!*
> I here adopt thee for mine only heir,
> All that I have is thine when I am dead,
> And, whilst I live, use half; spend as myself;
> Here take my keys, I'll give 'em thee anon.*
> Go buy thee garments; but thou shalt not want.*
> Only know this, that thus thou art to do:
> But first go fetch me in the pot of rice
> That for our supper stands upon the fire.

single rhyme A one-syllable or masculine rhyme (*q.v.*). For instance: stuff/muff. *See* RHYME.

Singspiel A German term for a simple form of opera in which strophic songs are linked by spoken dialogue. In Germany it dates from the 18th c. with imitations of John Gay's *The Beggar's Opera* (1728). The term also denotes musical comedy. Bertolt Brecht experimented with *Singspiel*; for instance, *Mahagonny* (1927), described as a *Songspiel*. *See* BALLAD OPERA.

skald An ON word of unknown origin. A Scandinavian bard or court singer. Many of them were Icelanders who settled in Norway. Skaldic poetry differs from the Elder Edda lays because most of the authors are known by name.

Much of the poetry deals with the deeds of contemporary chieftains and kings. The verse forms are complicated; mostly the *dróttkvætt* (*q.v.*). The kenning (*q.v.*) was used liberally. Among the better-known *skalds* are: Bragi Boddason (*c.* 800–50); Þjóðólfr ór Hvini (9th c.); Þorbjörn Hornklofi (*c.* 900); Eyvindr Finnson (10th c.); Egill Skallagrímsson (9th c.); Kormákr Ögmundarson (10th c.); Gunnlaugr Ormstunga Illugason (10th–11th c.); Hallfreðr Ottarsson Vandrae Askald (10th–11th c.); Þórmóðr Kolbrúnarskáld (11th c.); Sigvatr Þórðarson (*c.* 995–1045); Arnórr Þórðarson Jarlaskáld (11th c.). From late in the 11th c. the *skald* became less and less important. The oral tradition (*q.v.*) declined and poetry came to be written down more and more. *See also* GUSLAR; SAGA; SCOP; TROUBADOUR; TROUVÈRE.

skaz A Russian term (from *skazat*, 'to tell') applied to a genre of folk literature. It usually consists of an eyewitness account of an episode in peasant or provincial life. More specifically it is a narrative related by a fictitious narrator rather than by the author directly. Such a device allows the author considerable scope in the use of speech forms such as dialect, slang, neologism (*qq.v.*), mispronunciation and so forth, which give a naturalistic vigour and colourfulness which might not be attainable in a more conventional narrative told solely from the author's viewpoint (*q.v.*). The possibilities of this technique were exploited very successfully by Nikolai Leskov (1831–95), many of whose tales are told in *skaz*. Early in the 20th c. the *skaz* style was often used as a form of ornamentalism (*q.v.*) and Leskov's influence is apparent in the work of such authors as Remizov, Babel and Zoshchenko. *See also* TALL STORY.

skazka Russian folk tales. *See* SKAZ.

sketch Two basic categories of sketch may be distinguished: (a) a short piece of prose (often of perhaps a thousand to two thousand words) and usually of a descriptive kind. Commonly found in newspapers and magazines. In some cases it becomes very nearly a short story (*q.v.*). A well-known example is Dickens's *Sketches by Boz* (1839), a series of sketches of life and manners; (b) a brief dramatic piece of the kind one might find in a revue (*q.v.*) or as a curtain raiser (*q.v.*) or as part of some other kind of theatrical entertainment. A good example is Harold Pinter's *Last Bus*.

The sketch has also been developed into a particular dramatic form, as a kind of monodrama (*q.v.*) by monologists like Hetty Hunt, Ruth Draper and Joyce Grenfell. The solo mime Marcel Marceau worked out his own form of dramatic sketch. *See also* CHARACTER.

skit (ON 'shooting') A skit aims to 'shoot' or caricature a person or a style of writing or a mode of performance and interpretation. It is thus very closely related to, if not actually synonymous with, parody and burlesque (*qq.v.*). It is common in musical revue (*q.v.*) and comparable entertainments where famous people are 'taken off' by humorous impersonation, or where the style of a composer or author is 'guyed'.

slack The unaccented syllable(s) in a metrical foot. In a dactyl (*q.v.*) like *métrĭcăl*, the slack consists of the second and third syllables.

slang (ON *slyngva*, 'to sling') The present meaning comes close to Norwegian dialect *sleigeord*, 'offensive language'. *Slengjenamn* means 'nickname', and the phrase *slengje kjoeften* means 'to sling the jaw' or utter offensive language – which smacks of slang.

Common to many languages, it is the lingo of the gutter, the street, the market-place, the saloon, the stable, the workshop, the theatre, the fo'c'sle, the barrack room and the ranch – indeed almost anywhere where men work or play. It is the poetry of the common man, the tuppence-coloured of every-day life, and is indispensable to the well-being of a language. A thriving and developing language has plentiful slang. Slang provides its calories, its energy and its vigour.

One can readily distinguish between slang, formal language and colloquial (*q.v.*) language: 'He dresses in a contemporary fashion' is formal; 'He's always got the latest clothes' is colloquial; 'He's a snappy dresser' is slangy.

Again: 'We have had a week of many misfortunes'; 'It's been a bad week'; 'It's been a dark seven'. In the growth of language the movement is thus: – colloquialism > standard speech > idiom > cliché > archaism (*qq.v.*). Take the phrase 'our withers are unwrung' which Shakespeare uses in *Hamlet* (III, ii, 255). Shakespeare may have heard this, or invented it himself. It could have been a slang phrase. At any rate, as a result of his usage it became colloquial and passed into standard speech. Persistent usage gave it the rank of idiom; overusage has put it in the cliché class; and it may soon become a dead metaphor (*q.v.*) or an archaism (*q.v.*).

So slang is the language of intimacy, of everyday conversation, and much of it is ephemeral. However, if it passes the hard tests of vitality and original-ity it may survive for centuries. It *can* date very rapidly, like fashions in clothes, and the writer, therefore, is obliged to be judicious in using current slang in order to remain natural and unaffected. Examples of long-established slang phrases are: smudge = plumber's black; chancellor's egg = a day-old barrister; bear = broker who works to lower the price of stock; butter boys = fledgling cabbies; yell play = a bad play which relies on jokes to keep it going; a man with muscles on his eyebrows = a strong man.

Sex, money, food and drink are responsible for a large proportion of slang terms. Those relating to sex are so plentiful and many of them so commonly used that most people may be expected to know them. Money may be referred to as cash, dough, rhino, folding, green, cabbage, ready, bread, off, splosh, chink, dibs, plunks, bucks, bones, siller, dust, tin, the necessary, the needful. And food as nosh, grub, scoff, chop, prog, chow, chuck, toke. A man may be intoxicated or drunk, or he may be canned, smashed, stoned, pissed, plastered, sloshed, sozzled, under the table, drunk as a piper, drunk as a fiddler's bitch, or drunk as a lord.

Much slang from trades and professions 'graduates' from being private and esoteric to becoming public and open. However, school slang has a habit of remaining private. English public schools are well known for their domestic or parochial slang. Slang was studied in some detail in the 20th c. and the most celebrated expert on the subject was Eric Partridge, one of whose main works is *A Dictionary of Slang and Unconventional English* (1937, 1961). *See also* ARGOT; CANT; EUPHEMISM; JARGON; KING'S ENGLISH; PATOIS; RHYMING SLANG; STANDARD ENGLISH.

slant rhyme A rhyme that is not true. It may be deliberate or the result of incompetence. In this stanza from Peter Redgrove's *The Archaeologist* the second and third line contain a form of slant rhyme, and the first and fourth have pure rhymes:

> So I take one of those thin plates
> And fit it to a knuckled other,
> Carefully, for it trembles on the edge of powder,
> Restore the jaw and find the fangs their mates.

See RHYME.

slapstick Low, knockabout comedy, involving a good deal of physical action and farcical buffoonery like the throwing of custard pies. A slapstick consisted of two pieces of wood which, when applied, for instance, to somebody's buttocks, produced a cracking or slapping sound. It was used by the Harlequin in *commedia dell'arte* (*q.v.*). There *may* be some connection between this and the tradition of the Vice (*q.v.*) cudgelling the devil; and, further back, the demons of the medieval Mystery Plays (*q.v.*) coming on with firecrackers exploding from their tails. *See also* FARCE; LOW COMEDY.

slave narrative The autobiographical narrative of a (former) slave, usually based on his or her experience of chattel slavery in the New World. One of the earliest was Olaudah Equiano's *The Interesting Narrative of the Life of Olaudah Equiano, or Gustavus Vassa, the African* (1789). It recounts Equiano's memories of African society, his enslavement and harrowing passage across the Atlantic in a slave ship and subsequently his life in bondage; it also describes the terrible treatment and suffering of countless black slaves that he witnessed first-hand. Importantly, the narrative also depicts his emancipation and his personal and social development as a free individual. *The Interesting Narrative* went through eight editions in five years in England and was translated into many European languages; it had a profound effect on the anti-slavery debate in Great Britain. It also markedly influenced the shape of writings of American fugitives during the antebellum era, including Frederick Douglass, William Wells Brown and Harriet A. Jacobs. These narratives were similarly geared towards the abolitionist cause and made their case by emphasizing both the inhumanity of slavery and the humanity of black slaves.

A great number of slave narratives were written after the Civil War, though many did not find commercial publishers. Some of these emphasized how surviving slavery prepared the author well for the rigours of living a free life in a racist nation; others, like Booker T. Washington's *Up from Slavery* (1901), recount individual success stories and stress interracial cooperation. In the 1930s Federal Writers' Project workers interviewed over two thousand surviving ex-slaves to produce the remarkable body of testimony that is the Slave Narrative Collection.

In recent years many writers have produced fictional slave narratives. Sometimes called 'neo-slave narratives', these stories typically seek to depict the consciousness and culture of chattel slaves in ways the earlier narratives did not or could not, or instead examine the lasting psychological and social effects of slavery. Toni Morrison's *Beloved* (1987) is one of the most widely read and highly regarded of these. *See also* ABOLITIONIST LITERATURE; AFRICAN-AMERICAN STUDIES; AUTOBIOGRAPHY; BILDUNGSROMAN.

slavophiles Members of a Russian intellectual movement active from *c.* 1840 to the 1860s. They were in favour of preserving and nurturing Russian cultural roots and of maintaining tradition. They were opposed to many of the influences of Western Europe (its culture, rationalism, materialism and democratic systems) and were thus opposed to the contrary movement of the 'Westerners' (*q.v.*) in Russia. *See* SCYTHIANS.

slice of life A direct translation of the French phrase *tranche de vie* (attributed to the French playwright Jean Jullien, 1854–1919), and applied to the works of Zola and other 'realistic' writers. It suggests that a work presents life 'in the raw', factual, visceral and unadulterated by art. It is not a particularly helpful or clear term since it might be variously applied to Chaucer's *Miller's Tale*, Defoe's *Journal of the Plague Year* (1722), George Gissing's *New Grub Street* (1891), Walter Greenwood's *Love on the Dole* (1933) and John Braine's *Room at the Top* (1957), without telling us very much about any of them. *See* NATURALISM; REALISM.

Slipslop After Mrs Slipslop, a character in Fielding's *Joseph Andrews* (1742). She had a habit of misusing words in a ridiculous way: 'delemy' for dilemma; 'confidous' for confident; 'indicted to wenching' for addicted to wenching; and 'ragmaticallest mophrodites' – which is anyone's guess. This is better known as a Malapropism (*q.v.*).

slogan The term derives from the Gaelic compound *sluagh-ghairm*; *sluagh*, 'host' or 'army', *ghairm*, 'cry' or 'shout'. Thus, a war-cry; the cry of a political party. It is related to watchword and motto.

šloka A Sanskrit verse form consisting of two hemistichs (*q.v.*), each of sixteen syllables organized in four units of four syllables each. It was used in many epic Sanskrit works.

smithy poets A pejorative term applied to a group of Soviet poets (formed about 1920) who wrote crude verse as a sort of jingoistic propaganda (*q.v.*) on behalf of the proletariat. The *kuznitsa*, 'the smithy', was a branch of the *proletarskaya kul'tura* (*q.v.*). There were also 'Cosmists' who believed in universal power for the 'proles'. The Smithies could be better described as 'hammer and tongs' poets.

soap opera A television or radio drama serial with an open-ended structure which typically focuses on family life and personal relationships. The term 'soap opera' derives from the 1930s when many American radio serials were sponsored by soap manufacturers. Soap operas were originally broadcast in the daytime and targeted female audiences. As many more women entered the workforce towards the end of the 20th c., most soaps came to be broadcast in 'prime time', i.e. in evening slots which attracted the largest audiences. Many American TV soaps, such as *Dallas* (1978–91) and *Dynasty* (1981–9), abandoned modest budgets and a focus on the home life of ordinary people for glamorous depictions of the tribulations of the very wealthy.

Another key change in American TV soaps was the move by the 1970s to recording shows on tape. Previously, shows had often been broadcast live, and since most cast members were professional theatre actors, many soaps had the feel of stage plays. Despite their predominantly naturalistic settings, the plotting of soaps sometimes strains at plausibility. Their emotional intensity, which makes them compelling viewing for some, but off-putting for others, is inherited from the tradition of melodrama (*q.v.*). The intersecting story arcs and dependence on ensemble casts which are characteristics of the soap opera have given shape to many critically acclaimed TV shows, including the police dramas *Hill Street Blues* (1981–7) and *The Wire* (2002–8).

The longest-running soaps in the world on both radio and television are British – *The Archers* (1951–) and *Coronation Street* (1960–) (The American soap *Guiding Light*, which started out as a radio serial in 1937 before transferring to screen in 1952, ended in 2009.) In contrast to their American counterparts, British soaps tend to be set in working-class communities. Soaps are produced and watched around the world, notably in Australia, India and parts of Europe. In the Spanish- and Portuguese-speaking world, however, the *telenovela* ('TV novel') is predominant. In terms of setting and themes the *telenovela* is similar to the soap opera (in America it is called 'Spanish soap opera'), but it lacks the open-ended structure and typically concludes after about a hundred episodes broadcast over a single year.

social formation This term is used by most theorists (including Marx and Engels) to designate a given type of society such as feudal or bourgeois. It is given a more specific import in the tradition of structuralist Marxist theorists which includes Maurice Godelier, Louis Althusser, Barry Hindess and Paul Hirst: as opposed to the humanist readings of Marx offered by Lukács, Gramsci and others which stress the role of human agency and history in social development, the structuralist Marxists have contended that what Marx primarily points the way to is a 'scientific' structural analysis of social formations. These are not centred on human agencies but comprise a structure of hierarchies relatively autonomous but determined in the last instance by the economic infrastructure. Some of these theorists have attempted to distinguish between the usage of 'social formation' and 'society'; but Althusser's understanding of 'social formation' as the total complex of superstructure and economic infrastructure contains perhaps the most practical potential for the application of this term.

socialist realism   This aesthetic achieved predominance in Russia from around 1930 to 1956. Both prior to and beyond the Bolshevik revolution of 1917, Russia witnessed a series of heated debates, involving Lenin, Trotsky, Formalists, Futurists and constructivists, over the connection between art and political commitment: this subsumed such questions as Party control of the arts, the need to create a proletarian culture, the relations between socialism and its bourgeois cultural inheritance, and the formulation of an appropriate socialist aesthetic. A Communist Party resolution of 1925 refused to stand behind any one literary faction. But by the time of the first Soviet Writers' Congress of 1934, socialist realism emerged, in an atmosphere of Stalinist repression of all other factions, as the victorious official Party aesthetic, sanctioned by Maxim Gorky, N. Bukharin and A. A. Zhdanov, Secretary of the Central Committee for 'ideology'.

Zhdanov defined socialist realism as the portrayal of 'reality in its revolutionary development'. Such art, he argued, must contribute to the project of ideological transformation and education of the working class. Other features of socialist realism, as designated by its various proponents, were an emphasis on factuality, the integration of scientific and technical detail, the application of later 19th c. realist techniques to Soviet heroes, and the literary projection of a socialist future.

Socialist realism traced its authority back through Lenin's notions of *partinost* (partisanship) and literature as *reflection* of reality to the statements of Marx and Engels themselves, especially Engels's comments on the importance of expressing 'typical' individuals and forces. But this alleged lineage is somewhat misleading. While Marx and Engels certainly saw literature as performing an ideological function, they stressed its highly mediated connection with economic formations, and Engels spoke of its 'relative autonomy'. It is true that they both praised realism but they did not centralize it in any coherent interventionist formulation. In fact, the first generation of Marxist theorists such as Antonio Labriola (1843–1904) and Georgi Plekhanov (1856–1918) articulated essentially contemplative accounts of the connection between art and social reality. It was only with Lenin and Trotsky that literature was ascribed an interventionist and partisan function in a broader revolutionary approach. But the interventionism championed by both men was highly complex and flexible, qualified by its reference to particular historical circumstances. The more immediate impulses behind socialist realism included *Proletkult*, a left-wing group of writers led by A. A. Bogdanov (1873–1928) who, dedicated to creating a proletarian culture which would displace bourgeois art, viewed art as an instrument of class struggle. The Association of Proletarian Writers (VAPP; later RAPP) also insisted on achieving Communist cultural hegemony. But these movements were merely prefatory to the official triumph of socialist realism. This was essentially a result of the adoption under Stalinism, during the periods of the first and second Five-Year

Plans (1928–36), of a more politically committed artistic attitude, embodied in the Writers' Union, whose first congress in 1934 officially adopted socialist realism.

For all its crudities, socialist realism found a powerful advocate in Georg Lukács (1885–1971), whose version of realism elaborated on Engels's notion of typicality. While Lukács opposed the alleged modernism and experimentalism of Bertolt Brecht (1898–1956), Brecht too claimed to be a socialist-realist, also equating realism with the expression of what is typical in human relationships. In the 1930s Brecht's work evoked considerable hostility among the Marxist faithful, though he has subsequently been accepted. *See also* MARXIST CRITICISM.

Society of Authors It was founded in 1884 by Sir Walter Besant (1836–1901) to help authors stand up for their rights, especially in matters of copyright (*q.v.*). Within thirty years the society had achieved a good deal in the protection of authors, more particularly in dealing with publishers' contracts. George Bernard Shaw became a militant supporter, especially over the rights of dramatists. In 1931 the League of Dramatists was created as an autonomous section of the society. Other sections were formed in due course. Membership of the society enables an author to receive help in such matters as taxation, contracts, libel and social security. The society made an outstanding contribution in the campaign (which lasted for twenty-eight years) to establish the Public Lending Right (*q.v.*).

society verse *See* VERS DE SOCIÉTÉ.

sociological novel *See* THESIS NOVEL.

sociometry The study and measurement of attitudes in various groups. As far as literature is concerned, study of what sort of readers buy particular books and why.

Socratic irony So called after Socrates whose favourite device was to simulate ignorance in discussion, especially by asking a series of apparently innocuous questions in order to trap his interlocutor into error. *See* IRONY.

solecism (Gk *soloikismos*, from *soloikos*, 'barbarous') A deviation from conventional usage in grammar, syntax or pronunciation. For example: 'I ain't done nothing'; 'I never ought to have come'; 'You didn't ought to do it'.

soliloquy It is possible that St Augustine of Hippo coined this compound in Latin: *soliloquium*, from *solus*, 'alone' and *loqui*, 'to speak'.

A soliloquy is a speech, often of some length, in which a character, alone on the stage, expresses his thoughts and feelings. The soliloquy is an accepted dramatic convention (*q.v.*) of great importance and the various uses it has been put to show the strengths and advantages of such a convention. Its advantages are inestimable because it enables a dramatist to convey direct to an audience important information about a particular character: his state of mind and heart, his most intimate thoughts and feelings, his motives and intentions.

In Classical drama the soliloquy is rare, but the playwrights of the Elizabethan and Jacobean periods used it extensively and with great skill. They achieved an excellence in the use of this convention which has not been equalled. *Hamlet, Macbeth* and *Othello* all have major soliloquies (those in *King Lear* are somewhat less important), and so does Marlowe's *Dr Faustus*.

A particular use of the convention is to be found in the development of the villain (*q.v.*) at this time. The soliloquies given to the villains are more like prolonged asides and often take the form of a direct address to the audience. The villains are manipulators of the plot and commentators on the action. Often they deliver these self-revelatory statements of invention rather in the manner of the devils in the Morality Plays (*q.v.*). Examples are to be found in *Othello* (from Iago), *The Jew of Malta* (from Barabas), in *Titus Andronicus* (from Aaron), *Richard III* (from Gloucester), *The Duchess of Malfi* (from Bosola), *The White Devil* (from Flamineo), *The Revenger's Tragedy* (from Vendice), *Antonio's Revenge* (from Piero) and *Lust's Dominion* (from Eleazar).

In a modified form dramatists continued to use the soliloquy during the Restoration period and during the 18th and 19th c. With the advent of a more naturalistic drama towards the end of the 19th c. it was no longer feasible, though dramatists who persisted in writing verse plays still exploited its possibilities. In the last eighty-odd years it has been very rare. However, fairly recent exceptions may be found in Auden's *The Ascent of F6*, Eliot's *Murder in the Cathedral* and Robert Bolt's *A Man for All Seasons. See* MONOLOGUE.

somonka A Japanese syllabic verse form. It comprises two *tankas* (*q.v.*) with a syllable count of five, seven, five, seven, seven. It is a kind of epistolary love poem, usually composed by two authors. The first part is a declaration or statement of love, the second part is a reply.

son et lumière French in origin. A form of theatrical, mixed-media entertainment, usually out of doors, in which spectacular lighting and sound effects are combined with music, narration and dramatic presentation, sometimes with an element of pageant (*q.v.*). Not infrequently used to present major historical events (e.g. the French Revolution). A famous building, such as Windsor Castle or the Tower of London, which has a long and colourful history, lends itself particularly well to *son et lumière*.

song Many poems, even if not set to music, may be called songs (e.g. Smart's *A Song to David*; Blake's *Songs of Innocence*; Robert Service's *Songs of a Sourdough*), but the term, in its literary sense, usually denotes a poem and its musical setting; a poem for singing or chanting, with or without musical accompaniment. Music and words may be composed together; or the music may be 'fitted' to the words and vice versa.

It seems that in the earlier stages of civilization (in many parts of the world) much of the poetry created was designed to be sung or chanted (much of it still is) and the oral tradition (*q.v.*) sustained the union of music and poetry. In fact, up until the 16th c. in Europe, poet and composer/musician were often one and the same. The epic (*q.v.*), the war-song, the ballad (*q.v.*), the madrigal (*q.v.*) and the lyric (*q.v.*) were in many cases the works of professional musician/poets who were also composers (for example, the *skalds*, *scops*, troubadours, *trouvères* and Minnesingers, *qq.v.*). During the 16th c. (or perhaps a little earlier) a kind of fissiparation took place. The poet and composer/musician began to part company, and the classifying of literary forms or genres put the song in an individual category. Lyrics were written in the expectation of their being set to music and composers made extensive use of the great variety of poetry available.

Paradoxically, though the poet and composer/musician were parting company (and the term 'song' increasingly meant a literary composition in verse form rather than words for music) the 16th and 17th c. in England produced a great many good songs for music. Sir Thomas Wyatt, for example, an important innovator in the Tudor period, wrote some beautiful songs, one of them including the following stanza:

> My lute awake! perform the last
> Labour that thou and I shall waste,
> The end that I have now begun;
> For when this song is sung and past,
> My lute be still, for I have done.

Many of the poets of the Elizabethan and Jacobean periods wrote fine songs as well as poems that might be set to music. The two most famous composer/poets of the period were Thomas Campion (1559?–1619) and John Dowland (1563?–1626?).

In the 17th c. many poets composed songs. Suckling, Herrick, Lovelace, Jonson, Milton and Dryden created some of the best known of all. These lines come from Milton's masque (*q.v.*) of *Comus* (1634) – the song to Echo:

> Sweet Echo, sweetest nymph that liv'st unseen,
> > Within thy airy shell
> By slow Meander's margent green,
> And in the violet-embroidered vale
> > Where the love-lorn nightingale
> Nightly to thee her sad song mourneth well.

The dramatists of the period 1580–1640 often used songs in their plays to sustain or create a particular mood. In many cases the song was an integral – one might say an essential – part of the dramatic structure (e.g. Desdemona's 'Willow' song in *Othello;* Ophelia's songs in *Hamlet;* Iago's drinking song in *Othello*). A large number of the best and most famous Elizabethan and Jacobean songs are to be found in Shakespeare's drama.

The influence of the masque on song-writing in the 1620s and 1630s was considerable. Many masques contained good songs (or lyrics) and the authors were fortunate in having two English composers who well understood the techniques of allying music and words. They were Henry Lawes (1596–1662) and his brother William (1602–45). Later Purcell was to make an even greater contribution in setting words to music.

When the theatres reopened after the Puritan ban, Dryden sustained the tradition of the Elizabethans and Jacobeans in song-writing. However, by the end of the 17th c. the poet no longer used the theatre. Dramatic prose was the desired medium for comedy of manners (*q.v.*) and the art of song-writing very nearly died in the 18th c., except, of course, in opera and ballad opera (*qq.v.*). This is not to say that the song in general was defunct, but if we compare the 18th with the 17th c. the former has little to show for its efforts – except two major collections of earlier songs: namely, Thomas D'Urfey's *Pills to Purge Melancholy* (1719), which contained over a thousand songs, and Bishop Percy's *Reliques of Ancient English Poetry* (1765).

A handful of poets, only, kept the tradition of song-writing alive. Notable examples are Thomas Moore, Robert Burns, William Blake, Thomas Haynes Bayly, plus the anonymous makers of ballad and folksong (*qq.v.*). Thomas Moore (1779–1852) was a musician as well as poet, and became the national lyrist of Ireland through the publication of his *Irish Melodies* (1807–35). Burns (1759–96) did for Scotland what Moore did for Ireland, and wrote some of the finest songs ever created. Many of them were published in James Thomson's *Scots Musical Museum* (1787–1803) and George Thomson's *Select Collection of Scottish Airs* (1793–1805).

In the 19th c. there was no revival of song-writing in England, though Thomas Lovell Beddoes and Thomas Hardy both showed a considerable gift for the song lyric. In the 20th c. dramatists again became aware of the importance of songs in plays. The work of W. B. Yeats, Sean O'Casey, T. S. Eliot, W. H. Auden, Brendan Behan and John Arden – among a number of others – illustrates the point. *See* DITTY; LYRIC.

songbook As a rule a collection of verses set to music. A famous instance is the *Carmina Burana*. Scores of manuscript collections survive in Europe and many have been printed. *See* AIR; CAROL; DITTY; LAUDA; MADRIGAL; MINNESINGER; SONG; TROUBADOUR.

sonnet The term derives from the Italian *sonetto*, a 'little sound' or 'song'. It was Petrarch, more than anyone, who established the sonnet as one of the major poetic forms. Except for the curtal sonnet (*q.v.*) the ordinary sonnet consists of fourteen lines, usually in iambic pentameters (*q.v.*) with considerable variations in rhyme scheme. The three basic sonnet forms are (a) the Petrarchan (*q.v.*), which comprises an octave (*q.v.*) rhyming abbaabba and a sestet (*q.v.*), rhyming cdecde or cdccdc, or in any combination except a rhyming couplet (*q.v.*); (b) the Spenserian (*q.v.*) of three quatrains and a couplet, rhyming abab, bcbc, cdcd, ee; (c) the Shakespearean, again with three quatrains and a couplet, rhyming abab, cdcd, efef, gg.

The Italian form is the commonest. The octave develops one thought; there is then a 'turn' or *volta*, and the sestet grows out of the octave, varies it and completes it.

In the other two forms a different idea is expressed in each quatrain; each grows out of the one preceding it; and the argument, theme and dialect (*qq.v.*) are concluded, 'tied up' in the binding end-couplet.

The sonnet came into the English language via Sir Thomas Wyatt and the Earl of Surrey early in the 16th c. and it was the Petrarchan form which they imported. However, it was not until the last decade of the 16th c. that the sonnet was finally established in England.

The first major sonnet cycle was *Astrophil and Stella*, written by Sir Philip Sidney (*c.* 1580–3) and printed in 1591. The greatest sequence of all was Shakespeare's sonnets, not printed until 1609, but some had circulated in manuscript for at least eleven years before. He wrote 154 sonnets, from which No. 94 is given below to illustrate the form:

> They that have power to hurt, and will do none,
> That do not do the thing they most do show,
> Who, moving others, are themselves as stone,
> Unmovèd, cold, and to temptation slow;
> They rightly do inherit heaven's graces,
> And husband nature's riches from expense;
> They are the lords and owners of their faces,
> Others, but stewards of their excellence.
> The summer's flower is to the summer sweet,
> Though to itself, it only live and die,
> But if that flower with base infection meet,
> The basest weed outbraves his dignity:
> >   For sweetest things turn sourest by their deeds;
> >   Lilies that fester, smell far worse than weeds.

By early in the 17th c. the vogue for love sonnets was already over. Ben Jonson was not interested in the form, and hardly any lyric poet in the Jacobean and Caroline periods (*qq.v.*) wrote a sonnet of note. However, Donne did write nineteen very fine sonnets on religious themes, grouped together under the title of *Holy Sonnets*.

Thereafter it was not until Milton that the sonnet received much attention. Milton did not write a sequence and he did not write about love. His sonnets belong to the genre of occasional verse (*q.v.*), and thus are about a particular event, person or occasion, like *To the Lord General Cromwell* and *On the Late Massacre in Piedmont*. After Milton the sonnet was virtually extinct for well over a hundred years.

There was a very considerable revival of interest during the Romantic period. Wordsworth, Keats, Shelley and Baudelaire all wrote splendid sonnets. Wordsworth's are generally thought to be the best, especially his *Composed upon Westminster Bridge, September 3, 1802, To Toussaint L'Ouverture* and

On the Extinction of the Venetian Republic. Shelley also wrote two splendid sonnets: *Ozymandias* and *England in 1819.*

During the Victorian period (*q.v.*) a large number of poets re-established the sonnet form, and in particular the sonnet sequence about love. The major works are Elizabeth Barrett Browning's *Sonnets from the Portuguese* (1847–50), Christina Rossetti's *Monna Innominata* (1881) and her brother Dante Gabriel Rossetti's *The House of Life* (1881). Christina Rossetti's and Elizabeth Barrett Browning's sonnets have significantly modified sonnet convention by introducing female desire into a form traditionally written from a male point of view.

In the 20th c. a number of poets writing in English composed a variety of sonnets on many different themes. Robert Frost, John Crowe Ransom and W. H. Auden all composed memorable sonnets. Dylan Thomas and George Barker also wrote notable sonnets, as did Robert Lowell (e.g. his sequence *The Dolphin*). Two other distinguished modern poets who have composed sequences are Geoffrey Hill and Seamus Heaney. In the late 1970s Tony Harrison emerged as an outstandingly talented sonneteer.

During over seven hundred years the 'narrow room of the sonnet' has been adapted to a remarkable variety of experiment and development and an astonishing range of feeling and themes. One of the most remarkable of all modern experiments in sonnet form is Vikram Seth's *The Golden Gate* (1986). The recent anthology *The Penguin Book of the Sonnet: 500 Years of a Classic Tradition in English* (2001), edited by Phillis Levin, collects over six hundred sonnets from Wyatt to 20th c. poets. *See also* CROWN OF SONNETS; QUATOR-ZAIN; SONNET CYCLE.

sonnet cycle A series of sonnets on a particular theme to a particular individual. Love is the commonest theme and the advantages of the cycle are that it enables the poet to explore many different aspects and moods of the experience, to analyse his feelings in detail and to record the vicissitudes of the affair. At the same time each individual sonnet lives as an independent poem. Of the many cycles the following are the most famous: Dante's *Vita Nuova* (1292–4), in which there are extensive prose links; Petrarch's *Canzoniere* (c. 1328–74); du Bellay's *L'Olive* (1549); Ronsard's *Amours* (1552); Sidney's *Astrophil and Stella* (1591); Spenser's *Amoretti* (1595); Shakespeare's *Sonnets* (1609); Donne's *Holy Sonnets* (1635–9); Wordsworth's *Ecclesiastical Sonnets* (1822); Dante Gabriel Rossetti's *The House of Life* (1881); Elizabeth Barrett Browning's *Sonnets from the Portuguese* (1850); Rilke's *Sonette an Orpheus* (1923). *See also* CROWN OF SONNETS; CURTAL SONNET; SONNET.

sophism/sophistic A philosophical tendency which arose in 5th c. BC Athens, whose major exponents were Protagoras, Gorgias (c. 485–380 BC), Antiphon (c. 480–411 BC), Lysias (c. 458–380 BC) and Isocrates (436–338 BC). It was closely related to rhetoric, the art of public speaking. Both the Sophists and the rhetoricians offered training in public debate and speaking, often for very high fees; their curriculum aimed to prepare young men of the nobility for political life. While the Sophists were the first teachers of rhetoric, there was a distinction between the two disciplines: rhetoric was, strictly speaking, restricted to the techniques of argument and persuasion; the more ambitious Sophists promised a more general education extending over the various branches of philosophy: morality, politics, as well as the nature of reality and truth.

Sophistic accounts of the world were essentially secular, humanistic and relativistic. These accounts rejected the authority of religion and viewed truth as a human and pragmatic construct. In other words, there was no truth which ultimately stood above or beyond human perception. Rhetoric also was concerned not with truth but merely with persuasion, often preying on the ignorance of an audience and merely pandering to its prejudices rather than seeking a moral and objective foundation. Protagoras argued that 'man is the measure of all things', an essentially a secular humanistic and individualistic idea that each person constructs his own view of reality on the basis of sensations individually received. He also taught the very influential notion that every argument or position had two sides, which could be equally rational. The other Sophists held similarly humanistic and relativistic views. Clearly, the attitudes of sophistic and rhetoric arise in a democratic environment: just as in our modern-day democracies, the concept of truth as some kind of transcendent datum is extinguished; in our law courts, we can argue only that one version of events is more probable, more supported by evidence and more internally coherent than another. We do not claim that this superior version somehow expresses an infallible truth.

Plato's philosophy was generated in part by his stern opposition to both sophistic and rhetoric, which he saw as expressing a vision of the world that had long been advanced by the much older art of poetry. It is not only his dialectical method but the content of his philosophy that arises in the sharpest opposition to that vision. This was a vision of the world as ruled by chance, a world subject to the whims and caprice of the gods. It could be argued that Greek philosophy began as a challenge to the monopoly of poetry and the extension of its vision in more recent trends such as sophistic and rhetoric.

soraismus (Gk 'mingle-mangle') A mixture of terms from various tongues, usually used for comic effect. A particularly good example is Skelton's *Speak, Parrot* (1521), from which this example comes:

> *Moderata juvant*, but *toto* doth exceed:
> Discretion is mother of noble virtues all.
> *Myden agan* in Greeke tongue we read.
> But reason and wit wanteth their provincial
> When wilfulness is vicar general.
> *Haec res acu tangitur*, Parrot, *par ma foy*:
> *Taisez-vous*, Parrot, *tenez-vous coy!*

See FATRASIE; MACARONIC.

sotie (or sottie) The term derives from the French *sot, sotte*, 'fool', and applies to a kind of dramatic entertainment which was popular in France in the late

Middle Ages. Not genuine farce (*q.v.*) but a knockabout satirical jollification which sometimes served as a curtain raiser (*q.v.*) to Mystery and Morality Plays (*qq.v.*). The actors wore fool's costume and derided society, manners and political events. Two well-known *soties* were: *Le Jeu du Prince de Sots et Mère Sotte* (1512) and *Les Trois Pèlerins* (*c.* 1521). At the end of the 19th c. André Gide brought his individual genius to the creation of a new kind of *sotie*; a type of *récit* (*q.v.*) 'arbitraire et volontiers bouffon'. Examples are *Paludes* (1896), *Le Prométhée mal enchaîné* (1899) and *Les Caves du Vatican* (1914).

source-book Any work from which an author has 'lifted' or borrowed an idea, plot or story. Holinshed's *Chronicles* (1577) was a much used source-book for Elizabethan dramatists. *See also* PLAGIARISM.

southern Gothic *See* GROTESQUE.

spasmodic school A group of minor 19th c. poets who achieved considerable popularity in England and America in the 1840s and 1850s. The three main ones were P. J. Bailey, Sydney Dobell and Alexander Smith. Among their better-known works are Bailey's epic drama *Festus* (1839), Dobell's *The Roman* (1850) and Alexander Smith's *A Life Drama* (1853). These turgid verse plays of inordinate length were written in an extravagant, bombastic 'neo-romantic' verse and they had little formal discipline or structure. In 1853 Charles Kingsley described their work as 'spasmodic'. Later William Aytoun parodied and derided them successfully in *Firmilian, or, The Student of Badajoz: A Spasmodic Tragedy* (1854). He also attacked them in *Blackwood's Magazine*.

speech acts *See* PERFORMATIVE UTTERANCE.

speech, divisions of These divisions were first laid down by the Classical rhetoricians. They did not all agree, but the basic parts are: (a) introduction (proem or exordium); (b) statement of the case; (c) argument (or agon); (d) conclusion (epilogue or peroration). Some subdivided 'statement' into: (i) agreed points; (ii) points in controversy; (iii) points the speaker intends to establish. 'Argument' is sometimes subdivided into: (i) proof; (ii) refutation. These divisions are still taught today. *See* ARGUMENT; RHETORIC.

Spenserian sonnet Developed by and named after Edmund Spenser, it has a rhyme scheme abab, bcbc, cdcd, ee. It is also known as the link sonnet – because of the rhyme scheme. It has the binding couplet of the Shakespearean sonnet (*q.v.*) at the end. This example is No. LXX from Spenser's sonnet cycle *Amoretti* (1595):

> Fresh spring, the herald of love's mighty king,
> In whose coat-armour richly are displayed
> All sorts of flowers, the which on earth do spring,
> In goodly colours gloriously arrayed;
> Go to my love, where she is careless laid,

> Yet in her winter's bower not well awake;
> Tell her the joyous time will not be stayed,
> Unless she do him by the forelock take;
> Bid her therefore herself soon ready make,
> To wait on Love amongst his lovely crew;
> Where every one, that misseth then her make,
> Shall be by him amerced with penance due.
>> Make haste, therefore, sweet love, whilst it is prime;
>> For none can call again the passèd time.

See PETRARCHAN SONNET; SONNET; SONNET CYCLE.

Spenserian stanza A form invented by Edmund Spenser and an important innovation in the history of English poetry. It consists of nine iambic lines, the first eight being pentameters and the last a hexameter or alexandrine (*qq.v.*), with a rhyme scheme ababbcbcc. Spenser invented it for his long allegorical poem *The Faerie Queene* (1589, 1596). This is the last stanza from Canto III in Book I:

> Nought is there under heaven's wide hollowness,
> That moves more dear compassion of mind,
> Than beauty brought to unworthy wretchedness
> Through envy's snares, or fortune's freaks unkind.
> I, whether lately through her brightness blind,
> Or through allegiance, and fast fealty,
> Which I do owe unto all womankind,
> Feel my heart pierced with so great agony,
> When such I see, that all for pity I could die.

Oddly enough, this stanza form, which is related to *ottava rima* (*q.v.*), and the octave used by Chaucer in *The Monk's Tale*, was little used in the 17th c., though the Fletcher brothers, Giles and Phineas, attempted it; and it was not until the 18th c. that its possibilities in narrative were fully appreciated. Three works from that period display notable use of it: namely, Shenstone's *The Schoolmistress* (1742), James Thomson's *Castle of Indolence* (1748) and James Beattie's *The Minstrel* (Book I, 1771; Book II, 1774). The Romantic poets proved its most successful exponents, their major works being Byron's *Childe Harold's Pilgrimage* (1812, 1816, 1818); Keats's *Eve of St Agnes* (1820); Shelley's *Revolt of Islam* (1818) and *Adonais* (1821). See also MONK'S TALE STANZA.

Spielmannsdichtung (G 'minstrel poetry') A general term for medieval German epics of the more popular kind which, it was formerly believed, were composed and written down by itinerant and professional poet minstrels. Well-known examples are *Herzog Ernst*, *König Rother*, *Orendel*, *Ortnit* and *Salman und Morolf* (12th and 13th c.).

spondee (Gk 'libation') A metrical foot of two stressed or long syllables, so named because it was used in Greek melodies accompanying libations. Not particularly common in accentual verse (poems written wholly or mostly in spondaics are very rare), but often used sparingly to slow the rhythm of a line, thus making it 'heavier' for a particular effect. There is skilful use of spondees to suggest dead weight in this extract from Ted Hughes's *View of a Pig*:

> Thĕ píg | láy ŏn ă | bárrŏw déad.
> Ĭt wéighed, | thĕy sáid, | ăs múch | ăs thrée mén.
> Ĭts éyes | clósed, pínk | whíte éye|láshĕs.
> Ĭts trót|tĕrs stúck | stráight óut.
>
> Sŭch wéight | ănd thíck | pínk búlk
> Sét ĭn déath | séemed nót | jŭst déad.
> Ĭt wăs léss | thăn lífelĕss, | fúrthĕr óff.
> Ĭt wăs líke | ă sáck | ŏf whéat.

See also DISPONDEE; FOOT; SCANSION.

spontaneity   As a critical term, linked with the idea that the creative act is (or should be) unpremeditated, a sudden precipitation of verse or prose. Perhaps what Shelley had in mind when he described the skylark pouring forth its full heart in 'profuse strains of unpremeditated art'. In fact, poets of the Romantic period (*q.v.*) regarded spontaneity as one of the more reliable marks of the true poet. The most celebrated remark on the matter was Wordsworth's, that 'Poetry is the spontaneous overflow of powerful feelings'. Coleridge, rather more cautiously, distinguished between poets who write from inspiration and those who do it by an act of will.

This attitude has long been unfashionable and has been replaced by the view that the poet is much more like a patient and painstaking artificer or craftsman; that the poem is shaped, worked at, revised over and over again until it is well wrought. Auden averred you may have a few lines 'given' to you, but the rest is just 'plugging away': a point of view that Shelley would have deplored. It was error, Shelley claimed, to assert that 'the finest passages of poetry are produced by labour and study'.

The term may still be used judiciously, perhaps to describe what *appears* to be unpremeditated. *See* DONNÉE; INSPIRATION; LIGNE DONNÉE; SINCERITY.

spoof   A neologism (*q.v.*) invented by the comedian Arthur Roberts (1852–1933). Originally it described any sort of hoaxing game, or jape. Also applied to a round game of cards in which certain cards when occurring together are called 'spoof'. As a literary term it may be used of the sort of hoax that pokes fun by use of parody, satire and burlesque (*qq.v.*). Well-known examples are: *1066 and All That* (1931) by W. C. Sellar and R. J. Yeatman; Richard Armour's *It All Started with Columbus* (1953), and several other 'it all started' books by that author; R. M. Myer's *From Beowulf to Virginia Woolf* (1952); Robert Nathan's *The Weans* (1960); and Nabokov's novel *Pale Fire* (1962).

Spoonerism So called after the Rev. W. A. Spooner (1844–1930), dean and warden of New College, Oxford. It consists of a transposition between the consonant sounds (especially the initial sounds) of two words; a practice to which Spooner was addicted. 'The queer old dean', for 'the dear old queen' is a famous example attributed to him. So are these valedictory words he is alleged to have addressed to an undergraduate pupil: 'You have tasted your worm, hissed my mystery lectures, and you must catch the first town drain.'

sporting verse/fiction There is a modest corpus of such verse in British and American literature. In view of the fact that the British have been responsible for the invention and development of a high proportion of the world's games and sports, the surprising thing is that there is not more of it; and also that it is not of better quality.

If we except the splendid description of the hunt in *Sir Gawain and the Green Knight* (14th c.), there is not much of note until the 18th c., from which period date a few anonymous poems on curling, boxing and bowls. The only memorable poem of the period about a game is *Cricket* by James Love (1722–74). It celebrates Kent's victory over All-England at the Artillery in June 1744. The poem comprises three short books each prefaced by an argument (*q.v.*). Love adopts an epic 'stance' and, naturally, writes in the standard heroic couplets (*q.v.*) of the period in which the influence of Pope's *Rape of the Lock* (1714) is easily discernible.

Most sporting verse is about cricket, hunting, curling, swimming, running, football and boxing. From the 19th c. date a number of broadside (*q.v.*) poems about pugilism and notable prize-fights of the era, and such legendary pugilists as Tom Cribb, Dick Curtis, Mendoza, John Randall, James Burke, 'Bendigo' Thomson, William Perry 'the Tipton Slasher', Charles Freeman, Brassey, Caunt, Tom Sayers and John Heenan.

The most prolific sporting poet of the 19th c. was George Whyte-Melville (1821–78), who was an authority on field sports and wrote copiously about them, especially fox-hunting. He was a facile versifier capable of the occasional memorable descriptive piece.

Many distinguished poets have sometimes composed on a sporting theme, or a theme very closely related to a sport or game. A roll-call of names is impressive: Wordsworth (on skating), Coleridge (climbing), Byron (swimming), Swinburne (swimming), Andrew Lang (cricket), Francis Thompson (cricket), W. B. Yeats (horse-racing), John Masefield (fox-hunting), Alfred Noyes (swimming), J. C. Squire (rugby union), Ezra Pound (fencing), Hart Crane (swimming), John Betjeman (golf), Louis MacNeice (cycling), John Arlott (cricket), Norman Nicholson (cricket), Gavin Ewart (cricket), Vernon Scannell (boxing), Alan Ross (cricket), Dannie Abse (football), James Kirkup (rugby league), Ted Hughes (football), Douglas Dunn (running) and Roger McGough (tennis).

There are some quite ingenious examples of concrete poetry (*q.v.*) on sports and games. For example, Roger McGough's *40-Love*, Maxine Kumin's

400-Meter Freestyle, Stephen Morris's *High Jump Poem* and *Long Jump Poem* and Michael Horowitz's *The Game*.

Only two sportsmen of national or international fame have displayed any facility whatever as poets. They are John Snow, the Sussex and England fast bowler, and Muhammad Ali, whose jingles are no more than self-advertisements for 'the Greatest'.

A handful of writers have written sporting novels. There have been few of distinction. However, R. S. Surtees made the world of fox-hunting his own and produced a number of fine comic novels (which at their best rival those of Dickens), including *Handley Cross* (1843), *Mr Sponge's Sporting Tour* (1853) and *Mr Facey Romford's Hounds* (1865). Of his many comic characters three are outstanding: Jorrocks, the sporting cockney grocer, James Pigg, his dour and morose huntsman, and Mr Soapy Sponge. George Whyte-Melville also wrote a number of sporting novels of merit, especially *Market Harborough* (1861); like Surtees he was especially interested in and knowledgeable about the hunting scene.

In the 20th c. there was little of note in fiction (apart from a few good short stories such as Edmund Blunden's *The Flower Show Match*), but David Storey's *This Sporting Life* (1960) was a novel of considerable distinction. He also wrote *The Changing Room* (1972), a play which, like *This Sporting Life*, is set in the world of rugby league football.

Sprachgesellschaften German literary societies founded in the 17th c. Their aim was to 'purify' the German language and encourage its use in poetry. The main ones were: the Fruchtbringende Gesellschaft (founded 1617); the Tannengesellschaft (1643); the Teutschgesinnte Genossenschaft (1643); the Hirten- und Blumenorden an der Pegnitz (1644) and the Elbschwanenorden (1660). It should be noted that Latin and French prevailed in Germany early in the 17th c.

Sprechspruch *See* SPRUCH.

Spruch (G 'saying, epigram') A short lyrical poem set to music. Walther von der Vogelweide (c. 1170–1230), generally regarded as the best of the Minnesingers (*q.v.*), wrote a number of them.

The *Spruch* has to be distinguished from the *Sprechspruch*, a form for gnomic verse (*q.v.*) designed to be spoken and read. The *Sprüche* first appear in the 12th c., and there was a 13th c. collection called *Bescheidenheit*, 'modesty', which remained popular until the 16th c. Other poets who composed *Sprüche* were Goethe and Stefan George.

sprung rhythm The thing is old but the term is comparatively new. The term was invented by Gerard Manley Hopkins to describe his own metrical system, and his rediscovery of the techniques involved in sprung rhythm have had a wide influence on the development of English poetry. Hopkins's own words on the subject (in *Preface* to *Poems*, 1918) can hardly be improved upon:

[It] is measured by feet of from one to four syllables, regularly, and for particular effects any number of weak or slack syllables may be used. It has one stress, which falls on the only syllable, if there is only one, or, if there are more, then scanning as above, on the first, and so gives rise to four sorts of feet, a monosyllable and the so-called accentual Trochee, Dactyl, and the First Paeon [*qq.v.*]. And there will be four corresponding natural rhythms; but nominally the feet are mixed and any one may follow any other. And hence Sprung Rhythm differs from Running Rhythm [*q.v.*] in having or being only one nominal rhythm, a mixed or 'logaoedic' one, instead of three, but on the other hand in having twice the flexibility of foot, so that any two stresses may either follow one another running or be divided by one, two, or three slack syllables ... It is natural in Sprung Rhythm for the lines to be *rove over*, that is for the scanning of each line immediately to take up that of the one before, so that if the first has one or more syllables at its end the other must have so many the less at its beginning ... Two licences are natural to Sprung Rhythm. The one is rests, as in music ... The other is *hangers* or *outrides*, that is one, two, or three slack syllables added to a foot and not counted in the nominal scanning. They are so called because they seem to hang below the line or ride forward or backward from it in another dimension than the line itself ...

Some analysis of his poem *Harry Ploughman* may help to clarify the main points:

Hárd as hurdle árms, with a bróth of góldish flúe
Breáthed round: the ráck of ríbs; the scoóped flank; lank
Rópe-over thígh; knée-nave; and bárrelled shánk –
       Héad and fóot, shoúldér and shánk –
By a gréy eye's heed steéred wéll, one créw, fall to;
Stand at stréss. Each límb's bárrowy bráwn, his théw
That onewhere cúrded, onewhere súcked or sánk
         Soared ór sánk –,
Though as a beéchbóle firm, finds his, as at a róll cáll, rank
And feátures, ín flesh, whát deéd he each must dó –
       His sínew-sérvice where do.

He leans to it, Harry bends, look. Back, elbow, and liquid waîst
In him, all quaíl to the wallowing o' the plough: 'S cheék
  crímsons; cúrls
Wág or cróssbrídle, in a wind lífted, wíndláced –
       Seé his wind-lilylocks-láced;
Chúrlsgrace, too, child of Amansstrength, how it hangs or húrls
Them – broad ín bluff híde his frówning feét láshed! raced
With, along them, crágiron under and cóld fúrls –
        With-a-fountain's shíning-shót
         furls.

The symbols used by Hopkins indicate the following:

(a) ´ = metrical stress.
(b) ∧ = strong stress.
(c) ⌢ = a pause or dwelling on a syllable.
(d) ~ = a quiver or circumflexion; a drawing out of one syllable to make it almost two.
(e) ⌣ = slur; a tying or binding together of syllables into the time of one.
(f) ⌣ = hanger or outride.
(g) ⌐ over adjacent words indicates that, though one word has the metrical stress and the other has not, in recitation they are to be taken as more or less equal.

This rediscovery of Hopkins (sprung rhythm was not unknown in OE and ME alliterative verse) had a considerable influence on the work of, among others, T. S. Eliot, Dylan Thomas and Ted Hughes. *See also* FOOT; ICTUS; INSCAPE AND INSTRESS; SCANSION.

spy story A form of fiction devoted to various kinds of espionage. Since late in the 19th c., and increasingly since the 1920s, it has been kin to novels of adventure (e.g. Anthony Hope's *The Prisoner of Zenda*, 1894), the thriller (e.g. the stories of Edgar Wallace), and the politico-military thriller (e.g. some works by Eric Ambler, some of Graham Greene's 'entertainments', *q.v.*, and novels by Lionel Davidson, Frederick Forsyth and Francis Clifford). In fact, the spy story has subsumed many of the best elements of such tales, and has evolved into a specialized and sophisticated form of fiction which, at its best, is skilfully plotted and contains well-drawn characters, exciting action and a high degree of suspense and tension.

The use of spies is an ancient practice. There is evidence of it in the Bible, in Classical and Byzantine history; and it becomes more evident in the history of the late Middle Ages and the Renaissance period. From that time onwards espionage of all kinds has proliferated in most countries, until, in the 21st c., we find huge secret service agencies and secret police organizations operating all over the world.

The First World War produced a number of spy stories of nationalistic and right-wing tone in Britain, in which, inevitably, the Germans were the 'baddies'. Best-known spy stories of this period are John Buchan's *The Thirty-Nine Steps* (1915) and Sapper's – pseudonym of Herman Cyril McNeile (1888–1937) – *Bulldog Drummond* (1916). In 1928 Somerset Maugham (1874–1965) published his *Ashenden* stories, a landmark in the genre. They were based on the author's experiences as an intelligence officer. Maugham presented spies who were very ordinary and quite amiable people doing a job. There is a complete absence of anything sensational.

Between the wars some of the very best spy stories were those by Eric Ambler (1909–98) – especially *The Dark Frontier* (1936) and *Epitaph for a Spy* (1938). Ambler's books remain compulsively readable. He was original because of his detachment and his exceptional gift for creating and sustaining tension without being melodramatic. As good, but different in his approach, was Graham Greene (1904–91), who classified his spy stories as 'entertainments'. *Ministry of Fear* (1943) showed Greene as a supremely capable contriver of a wholly realistic spy story. Together, Maugham, Ambler and Greene deglamorized the spy and the whole business of espionage, but, even so, the realism begun by Maugham was somewhat reversed during the Second World War, which produced much third-rate 'nationalistic' spy fiction.

From the 1950s the spy story burgeoned, and it continue to thrive for the next thirty or so years. Dozens of writers (most of them British) applied themselves to tales of espionage. Many produced good or excellent novels, but there were quantities of run-of-the-mill derivative stuff in which there was far too much gratuitous violence and brutality – plus gratuitous sex. There were lurid stories of defection, treachery and exposure. Numerous books about the CIA, MI5, MI6 and secret service activities in general were published.

In the 1950s there began the James Bond era of spy fiction written by Ian Fleming (1908–64). The Bond stories achieved enormous success, first as books, then as films. Some of Fleming's books were *Casino Royale* (1953), *Diamonds are Forever* (1956) and *From Russia with Love* (1957). By 1960, if not earlier, many people had had more than enough of James Bond. During the 1960s an anti-Bond image developed; in fact a kind of anti-hero (*q.v.*) agent/spy/operator evolved. This was noticeable in the fiction of Len Deighton (1929–) and John le Carré (David Cornwell) (1931–). Both excellent writers, they established between them an even more realistic form of spy story than that conceived by Maugham, Ambler and Greene. They revealed the squalor, cynicism, treachery, expediency and corruption of the world of espionage and in their novels confirmed the actualities of that world in real life. Other notable writers who turned their hand to this genre included Peter Cheyney (1876–1951), Dennis Wheatley (1897–1977) and Leslie Charteris (1907–93).

Very surprisingly, the spy story has not flourished in other languages and literatures. In fact, the British (and, to a lesser extent, the Americans) have been and are overwhelmingly the main practitioners. One Communist-bloc author has made some name in this genre. Around 1960 Andrei Gulyashki, a Bulgarian novelist, was 'invited' by the KGB to refurbish the image of Soviet espionage which had been tarnished by the successes of James Bond (a figure who, incredible though it may seem, was actually taken seriously by some members of the KGB). Gulyashki created a proletarian Bond in the shape of a spy Avakum Zakhov whose main mission was to liquidate 007. Gulyashki's most successful novel was *Avakum Zakhov versus 07* (*sic*), published in 1966.

Since the late 1950s numerous other writers have produced notable spy fiction, detective stories, thrillers and miscellaneous tales of mystery and suspense. *See* CRIME FICTION; THRILLER.

stage directions Notes incorporated in or added to the script of a play to indicate the moment of a character's appearance, character and manner; the style of delivery; the actor's movements; details of location, scenery and effects. Printed texts of Elizabethan and Jacobean dramatists keep them to an absolute minimum (e.g. Enter two servants; Music; Dies; *Exit*; Sings; *Manet*; *Exeunt omnes*; Stabs him). Over the years they became more detailed and complex and by the end of the 19th c. dramatists were providing elaborate directions and instructions. Shaw, perhaps more than anyone, exploited their possibilities very skilfully and usually at considerable length, often indicating *exactly* how he wanted anything to be said or done. In recent years there has been a reaction against this kind of elaboration. Some dramatists have gone to the other extreme and pared direction to an austere simplicity. A notable exponent of such frugal practice was Harold Pinter.

standard English That English, spoken or written, which is regarded as generally accepted and correct in grammar, syntax and spelling, and which is a fit model for imitation. *See* COLLOQUIALISM; KING'S ENGLISH; SLANG.

stanza (It 'standing, stopping place') A group of lines of verse. It may be of any number but more than twelve is uncommon; four is the commonest. A stanza pattern is determined by the number of lines, the number of feet in each line and the metrical and rhyming schemes. The stanza is the unit of structure in a poem and most poets do not vary the unit within a poem. Exceptions can be found in Spenser's *Epithalamion* and Coleridge's *Rime of the Ancient Mariner*. Earlier English terms are batch, fit and stave (*qq.v.*). *See also* CANTO; OTTAVA RIMA; PUNCTUATION; QUATRAIN; RHYME ROYAL; SPENSER-IAN STANZA; TERZA RIMA; VERSE PARAGRAPH.

stasimon (Gk 'stationary song') An ode (*q.v.*) sung by the Chorus (*q.v.*) in a Greek play after it has taken its position in the orchestra. The *stasima* alternated with dialogue delivered by other actors.

statement A division of a speech (*q.v.*). Also used by I. A. Richards in a special sense to refer to a scientifically verifiable discourse. *See* PSEUDO-STATEMENT.

Stationendrama (G 'station drama') The walls of Roman Catholic churches are usually adorned by pictures or carvings (customarily fourteen in number) which represent the stages of Christ's journey to Calvary, the 'Stations of the Cross'. Thus, they are a series of tableaux; separate but interrelated episodes. This form of representation is analogous to the *Stationendrama*, which was basically expressionist. Among the better-known exponents were Georg Kaiser (1878–1945), Reinhard Sorge (1892–1916) and Ernst Toller (1893–1939).

Stationers' Company The London craft guild of printers, incorporated by Mary in 1557. The Stationers had exclusive right to print anything that was intended for sale in the realm. Members were required by the Company to record prospectively in the Stationers' Register any publications they proposed to print; not everything so recorded was published. The Register is an important source of information about literary activity from its inception through the 17th c. The original purpose of the incorporation of the Stationers and the keeping of their Register had been to prevent the spread of seditious publications, but during Elizabeth's reign Register entries became (not very effective) attempts to secure copyright; in 1709 the descendant of the Register, in the form of the first English Copyright Act, started to establish more formally the rights of writers and publishers.

stave A back formation from *staves*, plural of *staff*. A synonym for stanza (*q.v.*). *See* BATCH; CANTO; FIT; VERSE PARAGRAPH.

stemma (Gk 'garland') The term has come to denote the recorded genealogy of a family; hence, family tree. By transference, it also denotes the tree of descent or lineage of a text (*q.v.*). A manuscript (*q.v.*) may exist in several versions. There are 'good' texts and 'bad' (or 'corrupt') texts. A scholarly edition of a text will take into account all the available data, readings, versions and emendations. A published text may in turn be subject to re-editing, hence recession and redaction (*qq.v.*). *See also* FOLIO; TEXTUAL CRITICISM.

stichomythia (Gk 'line talk') Dialogue of alternate single lines, especially in drama. Usually a kind of verbal parrying accompanied by antithesis (*q.v.*) and repetitive patterns. It is highly effective in the creation of tension and conflict. It is frequent in Classical drama, not so common since. Well-known examples occur in *Hamlet* (III, iv) and *Richard III* (IV, iv) and in many scenes in *Love's Labour's Lost*. Molière used it several times in *Les Femmes savantes* (III, v) and he sometimes used double lines. The following example comes from Milton's *Comus* (1634):

> COMUS: What chance good lady hath bereft you thus?
> LADY: Dim darkness, and this leavy labyrinth.
> COMUS: Could that divide you from near-ushering guides?
> LADY: They left me weary on a grassy turf.
> COMUS: By falsehood, or discourtesy, or why?
> LADY: To seek i' the valley some cool friendly spring.
> COMUS: And left your fair side all unguarded lady?
> LADY: They were but twain, and purposed quick return.
> COMUS: Perhaps forestalling night prevented them.

See ALTERCATIO; AMOEBEAN; HEMISTICH; SENECAN TRAGEDY.

stichos (Gk 'line, row') A line of Greek or Latin verse. A single line or a poem of one line. Verse is stichic when composed in homogeneous lines (e.g. iambic pentameters) in which case it is not stanzaic. *See* STANZA.

stock The identical line which ends each stanza of the *refrein* in the poetry of the *rederijkers*. It contains the main theme of the poem.

stock character A recurrent type, like the *miles gloriosus* in Roman drama, the *Bomolochos*, or buffoon, in Greek Old Comedy (*q.v.*), the characters in *commedia dell'arte* (*q.v.*) and the villain and heroine in melodrama (*q.v.*). Other examples are the golden-hearted whore, Colonel Blimp, the oaf, the clown, the coward, the hypochondriac, the procrastinator, the nagging wife, the absent-minded professor and the man whose life is always beset with misfortune. A writer of creative originality can take such stock figures and transform them into individuals. Falstaff was the outstanding example of the braggart soldier; the braggadocio (*q.v.*). Jonson's Volpone was the supreme instance of the miser. *See also* ARCHETYPE; FABULA; FLAT AND ROUND CHARACTERS.

stock response A reaction on the part of a reader or spectator according to a standard pattern of behaviour. No critical judgement is involved. Obvious examples are cheering the hero and booing the villain.

stock situation A well-tried, recurrent pattern in fiction or drama. For example: mistaken identity; the eternal triangle; dramatic irony (*q.v.*); deception based on disguise; imposture. *See also* ARCHETYPE.

storm and stress *See* STURM UND DRANG.

storm of association A phrase used by Wordsworth in connection with the power of inspiration (*q.v.*). He suggests that a kind of external force impels or compels the poet to write. In this respect he believes in the traditional idea of the Muse (*q.v.*).

story within a story An enclosed narrative; a story which occurs as part of, or as a digression in, a longer story. Of many examples one may mention *The Arabian Nights*, Voltaire's *Zadig* and Dickens's *Nicholas Nickleby*. *See* FRAME STORY; RAHMENERZÄHLUNG.

stracittà (It 'over or across city') A form of literary movement in Italy which developed after the First World War. The leader of the movement was Massimo Bontempelli (1878–1960), who elaborated a literary creed known as *novecentismo*. He advocated a break with traditional 19th c. forms and attitudes and sought for what he called 'magic realism'. Yet another attempt to elucidate the essence of reality. *See also* STRAPAESE.

strapaese (It 'across, over country') An Italian literary movement which attained some prominence in the 1920s. Its origins appear to have been related to the Nationalist Party manifesto of 1904 by Giovanni Papini. Its principal periodical was *Il Selvaggio*, and one of its leading lights was the Roman novelist Curzio Malaparte (1878–1957). *See also* STRACITTÀ.

strategy A jargon (*q.v.*) term which appears to have come into literary criticism some time in the 1930s. It can mean either (a) an author's attitude towards his theme and subject; or (b) his method or technique of dealing with it. *See* SYMBOLIC ACTION.

stream of consciousness A term coined by William James in *Principles of Psychology* (1890) to denote the flow of inner experiences. Now an almost indispensable term in literary criticism, it refers to that technique which seeks to depict the multitudinous thoughts and feelings which pass through the mind. Another phrase for it is 'interior monologue' (q.v.). Something resembling it is discernible in Sterne's *Tristram Shandy* (1760–7), and long self-communing passages to be found in some 19th c. novels (e.g., those of Dostoevsky) are also kin to interior monologue (q.v.). In 1901 the German playwright and novelist Arthur Schnitzler published a *Novelle* called *Leutnant Gustl*, a satire on the official code of military honour. In this the interior monologue technique is highly developed. However, it seems that it was a minor French novelist, Edouard Dujardin, who first used the technique (in a way which was to prove immensely influential) in *Les Lauriers sont coupés* (1888). James Joyce, who is believed to have known this work, exploited the possibilities and took the technique almost to a point *ne plus ultra* in *Ulysses* (1922), which purports to be an account of the experiences (the actions, thoughts, feelings) of two men, Leopold Bloom and Stephen Daedalus, during the twenty-four hours of 16 June 1904, in Dublin. The following lines give some idea of the method:

> Yes. Thought so. Sloping into the Empire. Gone. Plain soda would do him good. Where Pat Kinsella had his Harp theatre before Whitbread ran the Queen's. Broth of a boy. Dion Boucicault business with his harvest-moon face in a poky bonnet. Three Purty Maids from School. How time flies eh? Showing long red pantaloons under his skirts. Drinkers, drinking, laughed spluttering, their drink against their breath. More power, Pat. Coarse red: fun for drunkards: guffaw and smoke. Take off that white hat. His parboiled eyes. Where is he now? Beggar somewhere. The harp that once did starve us all.

The climax to this extraordinary work is the forty-odd page interior monologue of Molly Bloom, a passage which has only one punctuation mark.

The beginning of Joyce's *A Portrait of the Artist as a Young Man* (1916) is an early indication of his interest in this technique.

Meantime, Dorothy Richardson had begun to compile her twelve-volume *Pilgrimage* (1915–67) and Marcel Proust was at work on the equally ambitious *A la recherche du temps perdu* (1913–27). Henry James and Dostoevsky had already indicated, through long passages of introspective writing, that they were aware of something like the stream of consciousness technique. So it seems that several original minds had been working, independently, towards a new method of writing fiction.

Since the 1920s many writers have learned from Joyce and emulated him. Virginia Woolf (*Mrs Dalloway*, 1925; *To the Lighthouse*, 1927) and William Faulkner (*The Sound and the Fury*, 1931) are two of the most distinguished developers of the stream of consciousness method. There have been hundreds of others and it has long been a commonplace literary technique. *See also* ANTI-NOVEL; DRAMATIC MONOLOGUE; FREE ASSOCIATION; IMPRESSIONISM; NOUVELLE VAGUE; VIEWPOINT.

street songs Most of these are anonymous and some are very old, though not many are extant from earlier than the 17th c. Unhappily, they are also dying out though traditional ones may still be heard very occasionally in markets or in the old-fashioned pub where locals gather for a sing-song. Cockneys tend to know them more than most people. At their best they are racy, witty and slangy, as this first stanza from *A Leary Mot* suggests:

Rum old Mog was a leary flash mot, and she was round and fat,
With twangs in her shoes, a wheelbarrow too, and an oilskin round her
   hat;
A blue bird's-eye o'er dairies fine – as she mizzled through Temple Bar,
Of vich side of the way, I cannot say, but she boned it from a Tar – Singing
   tol-lol-lol-lido.

Other fairly well-known ones are *The Ploughman's Wooing, Unfortunate Miss Bailey, The Ratcatcher's Daughter, She was poor but she was honest, Under the Drooping Willow Tree, Bung Your Eye, Polly Perkins, Darky Sunday School, The Man on the Flying Trapeze* and *Wot Cher! or, Knocked 'em in the Old Kent Road.* The last two were certainly music-hall songs. *See* BALLAD; FOLKSONG; JINGLE; NONSENSE; PATTER.

stress As a metrical term, stress is interchangeable with accent (*q.v.*). A metrical foot usually comprises one stressed syllable and one or more unstressed syllables; for example, the dactyl (*q.v.*) $-\cup\cup$. *See* BEAT; FOOT; ICTUS; PRIMARY AND SECONDARY ACCENT; QUANTITY; SCANSION.

stressed rhyme *See* RHYME.

strict meter poetry A 14th c. Welshman, Einion the Priest, is regarded as the first person to have analysed the meter of Welsh peotry. He defined twenty-four different meters and classified them under three categories: *awdl, cywydd, englyn.* These are known as strict meter poetry. *See* FREE METER.

strophe (Gk 'turning') Originally the first part of a choral ode (*q.v.*) in Greek drama which the Chorus chanted while moving from one side of the stage to the other. It was followed by the antistrophe (*q.v.*), a reverse movement, and then by the epode (*q.v.*), of a different metrical structure, which was chanted by the Chorus when standing still. The term came to be used as a synonym for stanza (*q.v.*), especially in the ode (*q.v.*). More recently it has been applied to a unit or verse paragraph (*q.v.*) in free verse (*q.v.*).

structural metaphor *See* ORGANIC METAPHOR.

structuralism A movement of thought in the human sciences, widespread in Europe, which has affected a number of fields of knowledge and inquiry – especially philosophy, anthropology, history, sociology and literary criticism. It has led to a fundamental reconsideration of mankind's and womankind's position, behaviour, function and attitude historically – and now.

   Broadly speaking it is concerned with 'language' in a most general sense: not just the language of utterance in speech and writing. It is concerned with signs and thus with signification. Structuralist theory considers all conventions and codes of communication; for example, all forms of signal (smoke, fire, traffic lights, Morse, flags, gesture), body language, clothes, artefacts, status symbols and so on. In theory, at any rate, it is to do with any or all of the means by which human beings convey information to each other: from a railway timetable to a thumbs-up sign; from a PR brochure to a siren.

The biologist's and zoologist's study of animal, insect, fish and bird behaviour, for instance, is equally concerned with 'language' signs and signification (zoosemiotics (*q.v.*)). In the non-human order communication is astonishingly refined and complex, not least through scent. For example, the female silk moth (*Bombyx mori*) secretes a chemical substance (a pheromone) into the air whose scent is so alluring that it can attract a male moth over a distance of half a mile; and the secretion weighs but the thousandth part of a gram. Indeed, even the *antennae of a disembodied male*, monitored by electrodes, will respond to a mere molecule of *Bombykol*.

Everything, then, in the theory of structuralism, is the product of a system of signification or code (*q.v.*). The relationships between the elements of the code give it signification. Codes are arbitrary (all signs are arbitrary) and without them we cannot apprehend reality.

As far as literature and literary criticism are concerned, structuralism challenges the long-standing belief that a work of literature (or any kind of literary text) reflects a given reality; a literary text is, rather, constituted of other conventions and texts.

Structuralism began in the science of linguistics and, more particularly, in the work of Ferdinand de Saussure (1857–1913), whose most influential text is *Cours de linguistique générale* (1915), a treatise which formed the basis of 20th c. linguistics and which has ultimately influenced much literary criticism.

Saussure made a number of important original contributions: (a) the concept of language as a sign system or structure whose individual components can be understood only in relation to each other and to the system as a whole rather than to an external 'reality'; (b) a distinction between *langue* and *parole* (*q.v.*), *langue* representing a language as a whole (e.g. French, English, German), and *parole* representing utterance, a particular use of individual units of *langue*; (c) a distinction between diachronic and synchronic (*q.v.*), diachronic denoting the historical study of the growth and development of a language (namely through philology), and synchronic denoting the study of a language as a system at any given moment of its life (Saussure put most emphasis on synchronic study); (d) a distinction between the signifier and signified (*q.v.*).

The concept of language as a sign system was developed in the science of semiotics (*q.v.*), and especially by the American founder of semiotics, C. S. Peirce (1839–1914). Saussure's ideas were further developed by Charles Bally (1865–1947), by the Geneva School (*q.v.*) of phenomenology (*q.v.*) and by the Prague Linguistic Circle (*q.v.*). The theories of Russian Formalism (*q.v.*) are also associated with structuralist theory.

Claude Lévi-Strauss (1908–2009) developed a structural theory in a consideration of myth, ritual and kinship, especially in his classic work *Anthropologie structurale* (1958), and in his earlier *Elementary Structures of Kinship* (1949). He sees social structure as a kind of model and is at pains to show that the behaviour patterns of kinship and the existence of institutions depend on methods of communication that are all characteristic of how the human mind works. Thus, he analyses modes of thought as well as modes of action, looking for the system of differences which underlie practice, rather than their origins and causes. His theories about myths had considerable influence in the development of the theory of narratology (*q.v.*), a further aspect of structuralism.

The structuralist theories of Roland Barthes (1915–80), expressed in, for example, *Mythologies* (1957) and *Système de la mode* (1967), reveal a very general interpretation of the term 'language' as social practice. Early Barthes is Marxist and he had a rather different view of myth and kinship – perhaps more as bourgeois ideology. He is also concerned with, for instance, *haute cuisine* and clothes. His quest is for a kind of 'grammar' and 'syntax' of such modes of communication. He interprets social practices involving food and clothes as sign systems which function on the same model as language. Thus, he elaborates the idea that there is a 'garment system' which works like a language. Garments in general are the system (what Saussure would call *langue* and Chomsky would call 'competence'); a particular set of garments is the equivalent of a 'sentence' (what Saussure denotes as *parole* and Chomsky as 'performance'). The same distinction applies to food. Foodstuffs in general constitute the system; a particular menu and meal constitute the 'sentence'. It should be added that after 1968 and his celebrated discourses *S/Z* (1970) and *The Death of the Author* (1968), Barthes was associated with poststructuralism.

Noam Chomsky (1928–) made another contribution to structuralist theory which is of importance in linguistics and should be mentioned here. He made a distinction between 'surface structures' and 'deep structures'. A surface structure consists of the collection of words and sounds that we articulate and hear in a sentence; a deep structure is the abstract and underlying structure in language. A single sentence may have many different surface forms and features and yet have the same meaning. The underlying or deep structure regulates the meaning. These are central theoretical distinctions in generative grammar (*q.v.*). The main current theory, as summarized by David Crystal, is that 'a grammar operates by generating a set of abstract deep structures in its phrase-structure rules, subsequently converting these underlying representations into surface structures by applying a set of transformational rules'. Crystal points out that this two-level conception of grammatical structure has been questioned.

A theory of structuralist poetics has been developed by Jonathan Culler in his book *Structuralist Poetics: Structuralism, Linguistics and the Study of Literature* (1975). He advances the idea that the real object of poetics 'is not the work itself but its intelligibility. One must attempt to explain how it is that works can be understood; the implicit knowledge, the conventions that enable readers to make sense of them, must be formulated . . .' Culler focuses on the reader rather than the text, suggesting that whereas it is possible to determine the rules which govern the interpretation of texts, it is not possible to determine the rules which govern the composition of texts. Thus, the structure resides in the system that underlies the reader's interpretation or 'literary competence' rather than in the text. The idea of 'literary competence' is questionable, but Culler does not seek to identify a set of predictable rules of reading through it; as an articulation of a theory of codes and conventions it is internalized.

The work of Roman Jakobson (1896–1982), especially his two essays *Linguistics and Poetics* (1960) and *Two Aspects of Language* (1956), provides other forms of structuralist theory. He developed a theory based on the concept of binary opposition (*q.v.*) in the structure of language. He was particularly concerned with the metaphor/metonymy (*q.v.*) opposition and its implication in the analysis of realism and symbolism. In *The Modes of Modern Writing* (1977) Professor David Lodge applies the theory to modern literature, and in his fine comic novel *Nice Work* (1988) he makes some drolly witty 'play' with the concept. *See also* DECONSTRUCTION; POSTSTRUCTURALISM.

structuralist poetics *See* STRUCTURALISM.

structure The sum of the relationships of the parts to each other; thus, the whole. Even as Germans speak of *Gestalt* (*q.v.*), we can speak of the structure of a word, a sentence, a paragraph, a chapter, a book, and so forth. The formal structure of a play consists of its acts and scenes and their interdependent balance. The non-formal structure comprises the events and actions which take place. John Crowe Ransom makes a distinctive use of the term when he holds that the structure of a poem is its central statement or argument (its logical structure) while everything else (the words, their sounds, the images, the connotations suggested by the 'inload' of the words, etc.) is texture (*q.v.*) or 'local texture'. *See* FORM; STYLE.

structures of feeling A term used by Raymond Williams in several works including *A Preface to Film* (with Michael Orrom, 1954), *The Long Revolution* (1961) and *Marxism and Literature* (1977) to characterize the lived experiences of people in a given epoch, denoting the common values and attitudes of that epoch, as expressed especially in literary and artistic forms and conventions. Williams distinguished 'structures of feeling' from what he considered to be more formally 'fixed' categories such as 'ideology' or 'world view'. Typically, he observes, we reduce social formations and elements of culture (*q.v.*) and society to fixed forms; we convert lived experience into finished products and speak of them in the past tense. But practical social consciousness is 'lived, actively, in real relationships'; it exists in the *present*.

It is this articulation of *presence* that most distinguishes the term 'structures of feeling' from formally held or systematic beliefs. Although the term refers to structure in as much as this entails a 'specific set of internal relations', it denotes 'a social experience which is still in process' and usually in its 'emergent' phase. Such structures concern 'meanings and values as they are actively lived and felt'. Art or literature also characteristically articulates presence – as experience that is not yet fully categorized or finished – and hence is an especially germane repository and index of structures of feeling. It should be noted that many of these insights had already been articulated by the neo-Hegelian philosophers at the turn of the century. *See also* DOMINANT/ EMERGENT/RESIDUAL; SOCIAL FORMATION.

Stuart period   1603–1714, during which time the Stuart family ruled England (except for the Cromwellian period). *See* CAROLINE; CAVALIER; JACOBEAN; RESTORATION (PERIODS).

Sturm und Drang   (G 'storm and stress') The phrase first occurred in the title of the play *Der Wirrwarr, oder Sturm und Drang* (1776) by Friedrich Maximilian von Klinger (1752–1831). It gave its name to the revolutionary literary movement which was stirring in Germany at that time. Adherents of anti-Enlightenment and anti-Classicism, its supporters preferred inspiration to reason. They were also unduly nationalistic. A number of famous German authors were influenced by the movement, including Goethe, Schiller, Herder and Lenz. *See* CLASSICISM/ROMANTICISM; ENLIGHTENMENT; GÖTTINGER DICHTERBUND; ROMANTICISM.

style   The characteristic manner of expression in prose or verse; how a particular writer says things. The analysis and assessment of style involves examination of a writer's choice of words, his figures of speech, the devices (rhetorical and otherwise), the shape of his sentences (whether they be loose or periodic), the shape of his paragraphs – indeed, of every conceivable aspect of his language and the way in which he uses it. Style defies complete analysis or definition (Remy de Gourmont put the matter tersely when he said that defining style was like trying to put a sack of flour in a thimble) because it is the tone and 'voice' of the writer himself; as peculiar to him as his laugh, his walk, his handwriting and the expressions on his face. The style, as Buffon put it, *is* the man.

However, styles have been roughly classified and these crude categories are sometimes helpful: (a) according to period: Metaphysical, Augustan, Georgian, etc.; (b) according to individual authors: Chaucerian, Miltonic, Gibbonian, Jamesian, etc.; (c) according to level: grand, middle, low and plain; and (d) according to language: scientific, expository, poetic, emotive, referential, journalistic, etc. *See also* DECORUM; PROPRIETY.

stylistics   Akin to linguistics and semantics (*qq.v.*), it is an analytical science which covers all the expressive aspects of language: phonology, prosody, morphology, syntax and lexicology.

subaltern   The word 'subaltern' denotes a person holding a subordinate or inferior position. Italian Marxist thinker Antonio Gramsci (1891–1937) used the term in his discussion of the hegemony (*q.v.*) of the ruling classes over the subordinate classes, such as the workers and the peasants, in the late 19th c. and early 20th c. The term has since been used in postcolonial studies, most notably by the Subaltern Studies Collective, a group of South Asian historians formed by Ranajit Guha in the 1980s, and the postcolonial critic Gayatri C. Spivak (1942–).

The Subaltern Studies scholars initially adopted Gramsci's term to examine the history of peasant insurgency in colonial India and its representation in colonialist texts, which, they argued, was as important as those of the dominant classes, thus shifting the focus from the colonial and postcolonial elites to the peasantry and rural gentry. Ranajit Guha has also broadened the term to refer to 'the general attribute of subordination in South Asian society whether this is expressed in terms of class, caste, age, gender and office or in any other way'.

The term has since been misappropriated to refer to any marginalized group, a usage which Spivak has criticized. In her well-known (and often misinterpreted) essay *Can the Subaltern Speak? Speculations on Widow Sacrifice* (1985), Spivak develops a gendered analysis of the subaltern by looking at the situation of Indian women and their representation in Western discourses, particularly in the context of 'sati' or widow sacrifice. Spivak argues that 'subaltern as female is even more deeply in shadow', concluding famously that 'the subaltern cannot speak'. What Spivak is suggesting is not that the subaltern does not have a voice; rather, her critical project is to question the whole representational system which attempts to retrieve the voice of the subaltern. In other words, even when intellectuals are trying to give voice to the oppressed, this act remains implicated in Western discourse – it produces subalternity and the subaltern as a passive object who is spoken for. By examining these uneven transactions between speaker and listener, Spivak wants to challenge the very production of the condition of subalternity. *See also* POSTCOLONIALISM.

subculture   A community united by a specific identity or particular set of cultural practices and values not shared by the dominant culture. The term is particularly associated with youth subcultures such as hippies, mods and punks. During the late 1970s much work within cultural studies (*q.v.*) focused on the forms of symbolic resistance enacted by youth subcultures to real or imagined authority.

Literary subcultures abounded in the 20th c. Many are associated with countercultural currents, the most famous and influential being the Beat generation (*q.v.*). Feminist critics such as Elaine Showalter have argued that many women authors operate within a female subculture, and that the history of women's writing is characterized by attempts to negotiate dominant patriarchal values and structures. The cultural materialist critic Alan Sinfield understands gay and lesbian subculture to be constituted by cultural interventions which examine the conflicts and tensions faced by gay and lesbian people. In this context subculture is a forum and an essential resource for the expression of a minority's concerns.

Some literary genres and subgenres have developed into fully fledged subcultures, sometimes with their own argot (*q.v.*) and sartorial codes – steampunk (*see* CYBERPUNK/STEAMPUNK) is one such example. The rise of the internet has helped subcultures to proliferate, but has also caused them to become more fluid and amorphous. *See also* ALTERNATIVE LITERATURE; CULTURE; FEMINIST CRITICISM; GAY AND LESBIAN CRITICISM.

subdued metaphor *See* TELESCOPED METAPHOR.

subintellectio *See* SYNECDOCHE.

subjectivity and objectivity The terms subjective and objective were imported into England from the post-Kantian German critics of the late 18th c. and are, in many ways, as Ruskin put it, 'two of the most objectionable words . . . ever coined by the troublesomeness of metaphysicians'. Subjectivity, when applied to writing, suggests that the writer is primarily concerned with conveying personal experience and feeling – as in autobiography (*q.v.*) or in fiction which is thinly concealed autobiography (e.g. Joyce's *A Portrait of the Artist as a Young Man*, Samuel Butler's *The Way of All Flesh* and Thomas Wolfe's *Look Homeward, Angel*). Objectivity suggests that the writer is 'outside' of and detached from what he is writing about, has expelled himself from it, is writing about other people rather than about himself, and by so doing is exercising what Keats called 'negative capability' (*q.v.*), and preserving what is described as 'aesthetic distance' (*q.v.*). The novels of Henry James and, to a certain extent, the poems of Philip Larkin show marked objectivity.

In fact, any writer of any merit is simultaneously subjective and objective. He is subjectively engrossed in his work and the quality and intensity of his personal vision will be dictated in a subjective way. At the same time he must be removed from and in control of his material. Thus he is involved in a paradoxical activity: an intellectually creative balancing act in which invention (*q.v.*) and judgement coalesce or co-ordinate to achieve and preserve equilibrium. *See also* PERSONAL HERESY; VIEWPOINT.

subject of enunciation/subject of enunciating Terms used in linguistic theory to denote two concepts of the pronoun 'I'. For instance, in the sentence 'I am writing this sentence' there are two 'I's: (a) in one sense 'I' is a point of reference, a self-designation by the use of the pronoun ('I' here is the 'subject of enunciation'); (b) in another sense the 'I' stands for what might be called the *aggregate of the self*, the sum total of the entire being – of all that 'I' am (this is the 'subject of enunciating'). This second 'I' is self-evidently permanently elusive by virtue of the fact that it is 'plurisignificative' (i.e. it bears meanings which are multiple).

The French linguist Emile Benveniste discusses the matter at length in *Problems in General Linguistics* (1966). He distinguishes between the 'personal' and 'apersonal' aspects of language. In one sense 'I' is personal; in another, apersonal. When apersonal, '*I*' is nothing other than 'the person who utters the present instance of discourse containing the linguistic instance "*I*"'.

Roland Barthes elaborates on Benveniste in his discourse *The Death of the Author*, pointing out that linguistically the author is never more than 'the instance writing, just as *I* is nothing other than the instance saying *I*: language knows a "subject", not a "person", and this subject, empty outside of the very enunciation which defines it, suffices to make language "hold together", suffices, that is to say, to exhaust it'.

It is perhaps worth noting that this is a matter of narrative theory, and also of psychoanalytic/ideological criticism. The 'theory of the subject' in literary theory is anti-Cartesian. The 'I' is an ideological construct associated with the individualist ethos of capitalistic and bourgeois society; so, the redefinition of the 'I' is part of a critique of a realist aesthetic. *See also* NARRATOLOGY.

subjunctio *See* EPIZEUXIS.

sublime (L 'elevated, lofty') As a critical and aesthetic term it owes its existence to a treatise, *On the Sublime*, originally entitled in Greek *Peri Hypsous* (*hypsos*, 'height', 'elevation'), ascribed to Longinus.

The idea of sublimity stems from the rhetoricians' distinctions of various styles of speech: namely, high, middle and low. From the 17th c. onwards it held a particular fascination for people. As an intellectual concept and as an attainable quality in art and literature it was especially attractive to writers during the 18th c. and during the Romantic period (*q.v.*). Sublimity came to connote a surpassing excellence, an Everest of achievement, where great thoughts, noble feeling, lofty figures (i.e. figurative language), diction and arrangement (the five sources of sublimity established by Longinus) all coincided. Edmund Burke's *A Philosophical Inquiry into the Origin of our Ideas of the Sublime and the Beautiful* (1757) was an important contribution to thinking on the subject and the ideas were of great interest to literary critics and those concerned with aesthetics. Burke distinguished between the sublime and the beautiful. The former is associated with the infinite, solitude, emptiness, darkness and terror; the latter with brightness, smoothness and smallness.

The sublime also came to be associated with powerful emotions, with spiritual and religious awe, with vastness and immensity, with the natural order in its grander manifestations and with the concept of genius (*q.v.*).

What Burke had to say about terror and the inspiration of terror and the terrible in his *Inquiry* excited people's imaginations and this was to have some influence on the Gothic novel (*q.v.*), which became extremely popular in the last forty-odd years of the 18th c. During that time there was a kind of cult of the sublime, considerably stimulated by Macpherson's Ossianic poems. James Macpherson (1736–96) created a sensation with these fake poems in Gaelic and, in company with Homer and Milton, he was regarded as one of the great poets of the sublime. His works were widely read, not least in Germany, where Goethe, Schiller and Klopstock, among others, praised them loudly. Artists, too, were inspired by the sublime (e.g. Fuseli, Barry, Mortimer, Salvator Rosa and the mad John Martin). The Grand Tour (*q.v.*)

introduced people to sublime scenery: the Alps, abysses, forests, mountain ravines and torrents. Travellers waxed lyrical on the grandeurs of Nature: the more awe-inspiring it was the better.

Many writers were affected by the cult, which was to have a far-reaching influence during the Romantic revival (*q.v.*). In 1781 Kant developed Burke's ideas in his *Critique of Pure Reason* and equated beauty with the finite and the sublime with the infinite. As Byron was to put it later in *Childe Harold*:

> Dark-heaving – boundless, endless, and sublime,
> The image of eternity.

Shelley and Wordsworth were particularly susceptible to intimations of the sublime and were profoundly stirred by the mysteries and dynamic forces of Nature.

submutatio *See* HYPALLAGE.

subplot A subsidiary action in a play or story which coincides with the main action. Very common in Tudor and Jacobean drama, it is usually a variation of or counterpoint to the main plot. For example, the comic subplot involving Stefano and Trinculo in *The Tempest*; and the serious one involving Gloucester, Edmund and Edgar in *King Lear*. The subplot became increasingly rare after the 17th c. *See* PLOT.

subscription publishing A method or system by which authors get together a list of buyers who are prepared to pay for their books in advance. In other words, before publication and, conceivably, before they even embark on writing. William Caxton (*c.* 1422–91), the English printer, is known to have got advances, or at any rate promises, of money for some of his major works. Early in the 17th c. John Minsheu achieved the same for his lexicographical *Guide into Tongues* (1617). The system became popular in the 18th c. and worked tolerably well, partly through the influence of patronage (*q.v.*). In this period writers issued what were called 'Proposals' for books and touted for subscribers. Pope and Johnson both did this; so did many others. Subscription publishing has worked sporadically since then with varying success and is still used by authors who produce specialist books on, perhaps, arcane subjects which would have a very limited readership.

substitution In verse, the replacement of one kind of metrical foot (*q.v.*) by another. Usually done as a deliberate variation in order to produce a particular counterpoint (*q.v.*) effect of sound and sense. A common form of substitution in English verse is putting a trochee (*q.v.*) for an iamb (*q.v.*) at the beginning of a line. In this first stanza of Geoffrey Hill's *God's Little Mountain* the basic foot is an iamb (though there are one or two variations), but the first word of the third line is a trochee carefully placed for emphasis:

> Bĕlów, | thĕ rí|vĕr scrám|blĕd líke | ă goát
> Dĭslód|gĭng stónes. | Thĕ móun|taĭn stámped| ĭts fóot,

Shákĭng, | ăs fróm | ă tránce. | Ănd Í | wăs shút
Wĭth wáds | ŏf sóund | ĭntŏ ă súd|dĕn quíĕt.

See also DEMOTION.

subtext The 'under' or 'below' text; what is not said or done. The term has a
wide application to literature in general; particularly, perhaps, to the novel
and short story, and other fictional genres, and to poetry. A reader tends to
construct a subtext for herself or himself, imagining or interpreting what is
not said or *not* done (and *how* it is not said or done), what may be implied,
suggested or hinted, what is ambiguous, marginal, ambivalent, evasive,
emphasized or not emphasized – and so on. In doing all this the reader exercises insight into the 'unconscious' elements in the work itself and thus elicits
additional meanings. Psychoanalytical criticism involves a quest for such
concealed or partially concealed meanings.

The term is often associated with drama to denote the unspoken in a play;
what is implied by pause and by silence. And perhaps also what Harold
Pinter means by 'the pressure behind the words'. The term may also apply
to the shape of the plot and the patterns of imagery.

Another and perhaps somewhat arcane concept of the subtext is to be
found in the work of two prominent Marxist critics: Pierre Macherey and
Fredric Jameson. Macherey is concerned with the 'silences' or 'gaps' in a text
which both conceal and expose ideological contradictions, and he believes
that the critic's task is to reveal the text's unconscious content. Jameson is
concerned with the 'political unconscious' of a text: that subtext which, historically and ideologically, constitutes the 'unspoken', the concealed and
repressed. *See* HERMENEUTIC OF SUSPICION; INDETERMINACY; MARXIST CRITI-
CISM; RECEPTION THEORY; THEATRE OF SILENCE.

succès (F 'success') A *succès d'estime* means that the critics have given their
blessing; *succès fou* is a popular hit; *succès de scandale*, a popular hit because
of some notoriety or scandalous element. A *roman à clef* or *livre à clef* (*q.v.*)
might produce a *succès de scandale*.

suggestion The term covers those ideas, feelings and impulses that a word or
an arrangement of words may evoke over and above their actual sense and
sound. Suggestion may be achieved by literary association (and, perhaps,
allusion) as well as through subjective links in the receptor (*q.v.*) – to use a
jargon (*q.v.*) term. Much writing is 'suggestive' in various ways for different
people, especially in the use of allegory (*q.v.*), symbol (*q.v.*), and particular
images. Both the poet and the writer of prose may 'suggest'. It is largely a
matter of subjectivity (*q.v.*). These lines from John Berryman's *The Dispossessed* might trigger all sorts of associations through suggestion for various
readers:

> 'and something that . . . that is their – no longer ours'
> stammered to me the Italian page. A wood
> seeded & towered suddenly. I understood. –

The Leading Man's especially, and the Juvenile Lead's,
and the Leading Lady's thigh that switches & warms,
and their grimaces, and their flying arms:

our arms, our story. Every seat was sold.
A crone met in a clearing sprouts a beard
and has a tirade. Not a word we heard.

Movement of stone within a woman's heart,
abrupt & dominant. They gesture how
fings really are. Rarely a child sings now.

My harpsichord weird as a koto drums
adagio for twilight, for the storm-worn dove
no more de-iced, and the spidery business of love.

The Juvenile Lead's the Leader's arms, one arm
running the whole bole, branches, roots, (O watch)
and the faceless fellow waving from her crotch,

Stalin-unanimous! who procured a vote
and care not use it, who have kept an eye
and care not use it, percussive vote, clear eye.

See also CONNOTATION.

summary A précis (*q.v.*) or résumé of the main points of a book or part of it. Also known as a synopsis. To be found in abridged works and also by way of introduction. It used to be a common practice but is now fairly rare. *See* ARGUMENT.

superfluous man (R *lishni chelovek*) The name given to an important and recurrent character type in 19th c. Russian literature. It denotes an idealistic but inactive hero who is aware of and sensitive to moral and social problems but who does not take action; in part because of personal weakness and lassitude, in part because of social and political restraints on freedom of action. Pushkin was the first to use the word *lishni* in this sense, in so describing the character Onegin in *Eugene Onegin* (1823–31). Eugene is regarded as the prototype, closely followed by Griboyedov's Chatski in *Woe from Wit* (1825). Pushkin's Onegin influenced Lermontov in his creation of Pechorin in *A Hero of Our Times* (1840). A development of the type was achieved by Turgenev in Rudin (*Rudin*, 1856). Turgenev's short story *The Diary of a Superfluous Man* (1850) popularized the term. His character Rakitin in his play *A Month in the Country* is a comparable type, as is the character in *The Hamlet of the Shchigrovsky District* in *Sketches from a Hunter's Album*. Turgenev tried to document and justify the existence of this type in Russian society, seeing him as a kind of tragi-comic figure, a compound of Hamlet and Don Quixote, unable to reconcile the impulses of heart and head, given to overmuch introspectiveness, intellectualizing and indecision. Perhaps the most famous of all superfluous men is the endearing and totally ineffectual

Oblomov in Goncharov's *Oblomov* (1859). Descendants of Onegin *et al.* are to be found in Tolstoy (e.g. Count Vronski in *Anna Karenina*, 1875–6) and in Chekhov's plays and stories, where they abound. By contrast, the heroines involved with superfluous men were strong, determined and decisive (e.g. Tatyana in *Eugene Onegin* and Natalya in *Rudin*). A contrast was aesthetically desirable and necessary anyway; hence the energetic and ebullient figure, Stolz, in *Oblomov. See also* CHARACTER; FABULA; STOCK CHARACTER.

supernatural story A very comprehensive term which may be applied to any sort of story which in some way makes use of ghosts, ghouls, spectres, apparitions, poltergeists, good and evil spirits and things that go bump in the night; not to mention magic, witchcraft, marvels, talismans, the eerie atmosphere and the presence of the uncanny; anything supranormal and beyond sensory perception; what makes the flesh creep and the hair stand on end; the 'spooky', the numinous; that which conveys the sense of the preternatural (to use Coleridge's word) powers.

In verse, of the thousands of examples available, one may mention the supernatural and supranormal elements in *Beowulf, Sir Gawain and the Green Knight, Sir Orfeo,* Spenser's *Faerie Queene,* Milton's *Paradise Lost* and *Comus,* Coleridge's *Rime of the Ancient Mariner* and *Christabel,* Keats's *La Belle Dame Sans Merci,* E. A. Poe's *The Raven,* Browning's *Childe Roland to the Dark Tower Came,* Walter de la Mare's *The Listeners,* W. W. Gibson's *Flannan Isle,* Alfred Noyes's *Sherwood,* Vernon Watkins's *The Ballad of the Mari Lwyd,* as well as a large number of ballads (e.g. *The Wee Wee Man, The Wife of Usher's Well, The Daemon Lover*).

Two classic collections of supernatural stories are *The Arabian Nights* and the brothers Grimm *Fairy Tales.* Mention should also be made of Perrault's collection of fairy stories which includes *Sleeping Beauty, Cinderella* and *Red Riding Hood;* Defoe's *True Relation of the Apparition of one Mrs Veal;* Horace Walpole's *Castle of Otranto;* Ann Radcliffe's *Mysteries of Udolpho;* M. G. ('Monk') Lewis's *The Monk* and *The Castle Spectre;* C. R. Maturin's *Melmoth the Wanderer;* Mary Shelley's *Frankenstein;* Hoffmann's *Tales;* Poe's *Tales of Mystery and Imagination;* Hawthorne's *The Scarlet Letter;* James Hogg's *Confessions of a Justified Sinner;* Dostoevsky's *The Possessed;* Dickens's *A Christmas Carol;* Stevenson's *Dr Jekyll and Mr Hyde* and *The Bottle Imp;* Oscar Wilde's *The Picture of Dorian Gray;* Ambrose Bierce's *An Occurrence at Owl Creek Bridge;* W. W. Jacobs's *The Monkey's Paw;* Sheridan Le Fanu's *In a Glass Darkly* (a collection which contains the famous *Green Tea*); Henry James's *The Turn of the Screw;* Conan Doyle's *The Hound of the Baskervilles;* H. G. Wells's *The Invisible Man.* Plus a large number of stories by French and Russian 19th c. writers – principally Gautier, Mérimée, Villiers de l'Isle-Adam, Huysmans, Balzac, Gogol, Pushkin and Turgenev.

More recent writers of note who have made memorable use of supernatural elements are: G. K. Chesterton, Walter de la Mare, Algernon Blackwood, H. P. Lovecraft, W. F. Harvey, A. M. Burrage, A. N. L. Munby, Georges Bernanos, L. P. Hartley, M. R. James (his *Ghost Stories of an Antiquary* is a classic),

Dennis Wheatley, Ray Bradbury and Roald Dahl. *See also* GHOST STORY; GOTHIC NOVEL/FICTION; HORROR STORY.

superreader *See* READER-RESPONSE THEORY.

superstructuralism A term coined by Richard Harland in *Superstructuralism: The Philosophy of Structuralism and Post-Structuralism* (1987). He uses it to cover the whole field of structuralism, poststructuralism, semiotics (*qq.v.*), Althusserian Marxists, Foucauldians, etc. He suggests that in relation to structuralism, 'superstructuralism' appears as '*super*-Structuralism' – a larger intellectual phenomenon over and above structuralism (taking 'super' in its strict Latin sense). He also suggests that the term can be read in another and more important sense, as '*superstructure*-alism', and elaborates the idea that 'superstructuralists' invert our ordinary 'base-and-superstructure models until what we used to think of as superstructural takes precedence over what we used to think of as basic'.

supplément The French word *suppléer* means 'to take the place of, to substitute' as well as 'to supplement'. The noun *supplément* can mean 'substitute' as well as 'addition'. The term *supplément* is used by the French philosopher Jacques Derrida to denote, for example, the unstable equilibrium and thus a constantly shifting relationship which exists between speech and writing. Each term both replaces and supplements the other. But not only this relationship or opposition. The idea of '*supplément*' is part of a Derridean critique of the simple structuralist binary opposition (*q.v.*) in which a term is defined by its opposite. Derrida uses the idea of the supplement to emphasize that there is no priority in any of these oppositions but only *différance* (*q.v.*). Speech, nature, truth, for instance, are themselves supplements, substitutions and deferrals of traces; they are not stable or logocentric in the way that structuralists use them. In *Of Grammatology* (1967, trans. 1976) Derrida writes: 'It is the strange essence of the supplement not to have essentiality: it may always not have taken place. Moreover, literally, it has never taken place: it is never present, here and now. If it were, it would not be what it is, a supplement, taking and keeping the place of the other.' In the same book his reading of Rousseau depends on the ambiguity of the word *supplément*, in relation to the nature/culture opposition which Rousseau discusses. In *Deconstructive Criticism: An Advanced Introduction*, Vincent B. Leitch clarifies: 'Derrida notes the emergence of an undecidable concept (the supplement), tracing its pervasive operations throughout the text of Rousseau. The effect is to deconstruct nature and culture, showing that culture does not supplement nature but that nature [*sic*] is always already a supplemented entity.' The point is that since the term 'nature' needs its opposite 'culture' in order to exist, the supplement is always already there. It is not simply that the supplement *comes after* but that the supposed priority of the term nature is itself supplementary (i.e. the process of the supplement is an aspect of *différance*, difference and deferral). *See* DECONSTRUCTION; LOGOCENTRISM.

sura A chapter in the Qur'an, which is composed of 114 *suras*. *See also* QUR'AN.

surface structure *See* DEEP STRUCTURE; LINGUISTICS.

surfiction A term coined in 1973 by Raymond Federman. His original statements titled 'Surfiction – A Position' were reprinted in a collection of essays called *Surfiction: Fiction Now . . . and Tomorrow* (1975). Broadly speaking, the term denotes fiction which makes little or no attempt to be realistic or naturalistic, and it emphasizes its fictional status. It may not be intended to 'mean' anything.

surprise ending The twist in the tail of a story; a sudden and unexpected turn of fortune or action. Some writers of the short story (*q.v.*) have proved expert at this device; notably, O. Henry and Maupassant.

surrealism This movement originated in France in the 1920s and was a development of Dadaism (*q.v.*). The surrealists attempted to express in art and literature the workings of the unconscious mind and to synthesize these workings with the conscious mind. The surrealist allows his work to develop non-logically (rather than illogically) so that the results represent the operations of the unconscious.

The term 'super-realism' was coined by Guillaume Apollinaire (1880–1918), but it was not until 1924 that the poet André Breton issued the first manifesto (there were three altogether) of surrealism, which recommended that the mind should be liberated from logic and reason. Breton had been influenced by Freudian analysis and had experimented with automatic writing under hypnosis. The surrealists were particularly interested in the study and effects of dreams and hallucinations and also in the interpenetration of the sleeping and waking conditions on the threshold of the conscious mind, that kind of limbo where strange shapes materialize in the gulfs of the mind. In his second manifesto (1929) Breton explained how the surrealist idea was to revitalize the psychic forces by a 'vertiginous descent' into the self in quest of that secret and hidden territory where all that is apparently contradictory in our everyday lives and consciousness will be made plain. There was a 'point' in the mind, he thought, where, beyond realism, one attained a new knowledge.

Distinguished writers who experimented with surrealistic methods were mostly Frenchmen: principally (apart from Breton) Louis Aragon, Paul Eluard, Benjamin Péret and Philippe Soupault. The main surrealistic painters have become much more famous: chiefly, Chirico, Max Ernst, Picasso and Salvador Dali.

The long-term influence of surrealism all over the world has been enormous. Apart from poetry, it has affected the novel, the cinema, the theatre, painting and sculpture. A great many writers have continued to explore the territories of the conscious and semi-conscious mind; delving into and exposing the private chaos, the individual hell. In doing so they have often experimented with stream of consciousness (*q.v.*) techniques. Surrealistic poetry is now rare, but plays and novels often show the influence of surrealism. From the scores of examples available, one may mention the work of Antonin Artaud, Eugène Ionesco, Jean Genet, Samuel Beckett, William Burroughs, Julien Gracq, Alain Robbe-Grillet, Nathalie Sarraute, Alan Burns and B. S. Johnson. *See also* EXPRESSIONISM; NONSENSE; PATAPHYSICS; REALISM; THEATRE OF THE ABSURD; VORTICISM.

suspended rhyme When the final consonants of two words are the same but their vowel sounds differ, e.g. 'rude' and 'broad'.

suspense A state of uncertainty, anticipation and curiosity as to the outcome of a story or play, or any kind of narrative in verse or prose. The suspense in *Hamlet*, for instance, is sustained throughout by the question of whether or not the Prince will achieve what he has been instructed to do and what he intends to do. *See* PLOT.

sutra A Sanskrit term for (a) a mnemonic rule; (b) a poetic treatise in verse.

sweetness and light A phrase probably used for the first time by Swift in his preface to *The Battle of the Books* (1697): 'Instead of dirt and poison we have rather chosen to fill our hives with honey and wax; thus furnishing mankind with the two noblest of things, which are sweetness and light.' Matthew Arnold, in *Culture and Anarchy* (1869), regarded these as the basic contributions of the artist: '. . . He who works for sweetness and light united, works to make reason and the will of God prevail.'

sword dance A dramatic ritual of ancient origin; in the first place probably a fertility rite symbolizing the death and resurrection of the year. It is widespread in central Europe. In England also, especially in Yorkshire, Durham and Northumberland. Often enough the practice of the dance survives in mining areas. There are many variations. An element common to a large number of them is the symbolic death of one of the characters and his revival. There are some stock characters (*q.v.*): notably a Fool and a man dressed in woman's clothes. The sword dance is one of the origins of the Mumming Play (*q.v.*). A famous European example is the *Moreška*, a traditional dramatic spectacle at least a thousand years old, performed on the Adriatic island of Korčula (it also used to be done at Split, Zadar, Dubrovnik, Vis and Budva). It is performed by the young men of the island (boat-builders, farmers, masons *et al.*) and is basically an amalgam of masque, melodrama (*qq.v.*) and dance. One form of it symbolizes the war between the Christians and Arabs, to which there is a more or less peaceful ending; the other a struggle between Moorish forces (hence the name *Moreška*) and the Turks, at the end of which the Moorish leader is conquered. The latter version is the one staged on Korčula. *See* FOLK DRAMA; PLOUGH MONDAY PLAY; REVESBY PLAY.

syllaba anceps (L 'twofold, fluctuating syllable') A syllable that may be read as either long or short according to the requirements of the meter. This especially refers to a syllable at the end of a line of verse.

syllabic verse Verse measured not by stress (*q.v.*) or quantity (*q.v.*) but by the number of syllables in each line. The more conservative English poets, like Dryden, Pope and Johnson, were fairly strict about the number of syllables they would allow in the pentameter (*q.v.*) line. The term is also applied to a type of verse which became fairly common in the late 1950s and 1960s which was based merely on a syllable count, regardless of duration (*q.v.*). Among well-known poets who experimented were W. H. Auden, Thom Gunn and George MacBeth. Roy Fuller's *Owls and Artificers* (1971) is a discussion of syllabics. *See also* FOOT; SCANSION.

syllepsis (Gk 'a taking together, comprehension') A figure of speech in which a verb or an adjective is applied to two nouns, though appropriate only to one of them. A well-known example occurs in *Henry V* when Fluellen says, 'Kill the poys and the luggage'. The verb 'kill' cannot apply to luggage. *See* ZEUGMA.

syllogism (Gk 'reckoning together') Deduction, from two propositions containing three terms of which one appears in both, of a conclusion that is true *if* they are true. A stock example is: All men are mortal; Greeks are men; so all Greeks are mortal. 'Men' is the middle term. 'Mortal', the second term in the conclusion, is the major term and the premise in which it occurs is the major premise. 'Greeks' is the minor term and its premise the minor premise.

symbol and symbolism The word symbol derives from the Greek verb *symballein*, 'to throw together', and its noun *symbolon*, 'mark', 'emblem', 'token' or 'sign'. It is an object, animate or inanimate, which represents or 'stands for' something else. As Coleridge put it, a symbol 'is characterized by a translucence of the special [i.e. the species] in the individual'. A symbol differs from an allegorical (*see* ALLEGORY) sign in that it has a *real* existence, whereas an allegorical sign is arbitrary.

Scales, for example, symbolize justice; the orb and sceptre, monarchy and rule; a dove, peace; a goat, lust; the lion, strength and courage; the bulldog, tenacity; the rose, beauty; the lily, purity; the Stars and Stripes, America and its States; the Cross, Christianity; the swastika (or crooked Cross) Nazi Germany and Fascism; the gold, red and black hat of the Montenegrin symbolizes glory, blood and mourning. The scales of justice may also be allegorical; as might, for instance, a dove, a goat or a lion.

Actions and gestures are also symbolic. The clenched fist symbolizes aggression. Beating of the breast signifies remorse. Arms raised denote surrender. Hands clasped and raised suggest suppliance. A slow upward movement of the head accompanied by a closing of the eyes means, in Turkish, 'no'. Moreover, most religious and fertility rites are rich with symbolic movements and gestures, especially the Roman Mass.

A literary symbol combines an image with a concept (words themselves are a kind of symbol). It may be public or private, universal or local. They *exist*, so to speak. As Baudelaire expressed it in his sonnet *Correspondances*:

La Nature est un temple où de vivants piliers
Laissent parfois sortir de confuses paroles;
L'homme y passe à travers des forêts de symboles . . .

In literature an example of a public or universal symbol is a journey into the underworld (as in the work of Virgil, Dante and James Joyce) and a return from it. Such a journey may be an interpretation of a spiritual experience, a dark night of the soul and a kind of redemptive odyssey. Examples of private symbols are those that recur in the works of W. B. Yeats: the sun and moon, a tower, a mask, a tree, a winding stair and a hawk.

Dante's *Divina Commedia* is structurally symbolic. In *Macbeth* there is a recurrence of the blood image symbolizing guilt and violence. In *Hamlet* weeds and disease symbolize corruption and decay. In *King Lear* clothes symbolize appearances and authority; and the storm scene in this play may be taken as symbolic of cosmic and domestic chaos to which 'unaccommodated man' is exposed. The poetry of Blake and Shelley is heavily marked with symbols. The shooting of the albatross in Coleridge's *Rime of the Ancient Mariner* is symbolic of all sin and stands for a lack of respect for life and for a proper humility towards the natural order. In his *Four Quartets* T. S. Eliot makes frequent use of the symbols of Fire and the Rose. To a lesser extent symbolism is an essential part of Eliot's *Ash Wednesday* (especially Pt III) and *The Waste Land*.

In prose works the great white whale of Melville's *Moby-Dick* (the 'grand god') is a kind of symbolic creature – a carcass which symbol-hunters have been dissecting for years. Much of the fiction of William Golding (especially *Lord of the Flies*, *Pincher Martin* and *The Spire*) depends upon powerful symbolism capable of more interpretations than one. To these examples should be added the novels and short stories of Kafka, and the plays of Maeterlinck, Andreyev, Hugo von Hofmannsthal, Synge and O'Neill.

In all these works we find instances of the use of a concrete image to express an emotion or an abstract idea; or, as Eliot put it when explaining his term 'objective correlative' (*q.v.*), finding 'a set of objects, a situation, a chain of events, which shall be the formula of that particular emotion'.

There is plentiful symbolism in much 19th c. French poetry. In *Oeuvres complètes* (1891) Mallarmé explained symbolism as the art of evoking an object 'little by little so as to reveal a mood' or, conversely, 'the art of choosing an object and extracting from it an *état d'âme*'. This 'mood', he contended, was to be extracted by 'a series of decipherings'.

Mallarmé's follower Henri de Régnier made the additional point that a symbol is a kind of comparison between the abstract and the concrete in which one of the terms of the comparison is only suggested. Thus it is implicit, oblique; *not* spelt out.

As far as particular objects are concerned, this kind of symbolism is often private and personal. Another kind of symbolism is known as the 'transcendental'. In this kind, concrete images are used as symbols to represent a general or universal ideal world of which the real world is a shadow. Sir

Thomas Browne, long before theories of symbolism were abundant, suggested the nature of this in his magnificent neo-Platonic phrase: 'The sun itself is the dark simulacrum, and light is the shadow of God.'

The 'transcendental' concept is Platonic in origin, was elaborated by the neo-Platonists in the 3rd c. and was given considerable vogue in the 18th c. by Swedenborg. In the 19th c. there developed the idea that this 'other world' was attainable, not through religious faith or mysticism, but, as Baudelaire expressed it in *Notes nouvelles sur Edgar Poe*, 'à travers la poésie'. Through poetry the soul perceives 'les splendeurs situées derrière le tombeau'.

Baudelaire and his followers created the image of the poet as a kind of seer (*q.v.*) or *voyant*, who could see through and beyond the real world to the world of ideal forms and essences. Thus the task of the poet was to create this 'other world' by suggestion and symbolism; by transforming reality into a greater and more permanent reality.

The attainment, in transcendental symbolism, of the vision of the essential Idea was to be achieved by a kind of deliberate obfuscation or blurring of reality so that the ideal becomes clearer. This, according to symbolist theory, could be best conveyed by the fusion of images and by the musical quality of the verse; by, in short, a form of so-called pure poetry (*q.v.*). The music of the words provided the requisite element of suggestiveness. Verlaine, in his poem *Art poétique* (1874), for instance, says that verse must possess this musical quality 'avant toute chose'. Such a point of view was also expressed, in other words, by Mallarmé, Valéry and Rimbaud.

Theory and practice led the French symbolist poets to believe that the evocativeness and suggestiveness could best be obtained by verse forms that were not too rigid. Hence *vers libérés* and *vers libre* (*qq.v.*). Rimbaud and Mallarmé were the main experimenters in these forms; Rimbaud the chief practitioner of the 'prose poem' (*q.v.*). Such verse enabled the poet to achieve what Valéry described as 'cette hésitation prolongée entre le son et le sens'.

The definitive manifesto of symbolism was published in September 1886 in an article in *Le Figaro* by Jean Moréas, contending that romanticism, naturalism and the movement of *les Parnassiens* were over and that henceforth symbolic poetry 'cherche à vêtir l'idée d'une forme sensible'. Moréas founded the Symbolist School whose progenitors were Baudelaire, Mallarmé, Verlaine and Rimbaud; and whose disciples were, among others, René Ghil, Stuart Merrill, Francis Viélé-Griffin and Gustave Khan.

Some of the major symbolist poems by Baudelaire are *Correspondances*, *Harmonie du soir*, *Spleen*, *La Chevelure*, *L'Invitation au voyage*, *Bénédiction*, *Au lecteur*, *Moesta et Errabunda*, *Elévation*, *Les Sept Vieillards*, *Le Voyage*, *Le Cygne*. His main work is the collection known as *Les Fleurs du mal* (1857).

From Verlaine's work one should mention *Poèmes saturniens* (1866), *Fêtes galantes* (1869), *La Bonne Chanson* (1872), *Romances sans paroles* (1874) and *Sagesse* (1881). From Rimbaud *Le Bateau ivre* (1871), *Une saison en enfer* (1873) and *Les Illuminations* (1886). From Mallarmé, these poems particularly: *Apparition*, *Les Fenêtres*, *Sonnet allégorique de lui-même*, *Ses purs ongles*, *Un coup de dés*, *Grand oeuvre*. His main collection is *Poésies* (1887).

These poets were later to influence the work of Valéry very considerably, as can be seen from a study of *Le Cimetière marin*, *L'Abeille*, *Le Rameur*, *Palme*, *Les Grenades*, *La Jeune Parque* and in various poems in the collection *Charmes* (1922).

Other influences of symbolist theory and practice are discernible in Lautréamont's prose poem *Chants de Maldoror* (1868, 1869), in several works by Laforgue, in a number of plays by Villiers de l'Isle Adam, Maurice Maeterlinck and Claudel, in J.-K. Huysmans's novel *A rebours* (1884), and, most of all, in Proust's *A la recherche du temps perdu* (1913–27).

The main 'heirs' of the symbolist movement outside France are W. B. Yeats, the Imagist group of English and American poets (especially T. E. Hulme and Ezra Pound), and T. S. Eliot; and, in Germany, Rainer Maria Rilke and Stefan George. The ideas of the French symbolists were also adopted by Russian writers in the 1870s and the early years of the 20th c.; notably by Bryusov, Volynsky and Bely. *See also* ALLEGORY; CORRESPONDENCE OF THE ARTS; IMAGERY; IMAGISTS; IMPRESSIONISM; METONYMY; PARNASSIANS; PRIMITIVISM; SUGGESTION; SYMBOLIC ACTION; SYNECDOCHE; TROPE.

symbolic action This jargon term denotes the conscious or unconscious 'ritual' which the writer experiences while creating a work. The work is a 'strategy' (*q.v.*) for controlling his own problems. The writer disguises his identity and, by so doing, performs a symbolic action. For example, a writer may 'write out of himself' aggressive impulses, guilt complexes, sex complexes, through the symbolic action. These theories were introduced and elaborated by Kenneth Burke in *Attitudes towards History* (1937) and *The Philosophy of Literary Form: Studies in Symbolic Action* (1941).

symbolic code *See* CODE.

symbolistes, les *See* SYMBOL AND SYMBOLISM.

sympathy *See* EMPATHY.

symposium (Gk 'drinking together') The term derives from the most famous of Plato's Dialogues, *The Symposium*, and, by transference, it now applies to a collection of essays or articles by various scholars on some special topic. Sometimes such a collection of monographs is presented to a person as a homage volume. *See also* FESTSCHRIFT.

synaeresis (Gk 'seizing together') It occurs when two normally separate vowels are combined into one syllable. For example: 'see-est' becomes 'seest'. *See* CONTRACTION; ELISION.

synaesthesia (Gk 'perceiving together') The mixing of sensations; the concurrent appeal to more than one sense; the response through several senses to the stimulation of one. For instance: 'hearing' a 'colour', or 'seeing' a 'smell'.

Dr Johnson once remarked on the discovery of a blind man that scarlet represented 'the clangour of a trumpet'.

It is probable that the word was first used by Jules Millet in 1892 in a thesis on *Audition colorée*. Before that, Huysmans's character Des Esseintes and Rimbaud had consciously attempted synaesthetic effects. Earlier, Baudelaire had deliberately attempted the same sort of impression in many of his poems. As he put it in his sonnet *Correspondances*:

> Les parfums, les couleurs et les sons se répondent.
> Il est des parfums frais comme des chairs d'enfants,
> Doux comme les hautbois, verts comme les prairies

Synaesthetic effects are frequent in Baudelaire's *Les Fleurs du mal*, especially in those poems addressed to Jeanne Duval. But there was nothing new about synaesthesia, except that it had not been theorized over so intensely before or so consciously used. Homer, Aeschylus, Horace, Donne, Crashaw, Shelley and dozens of other poets had used synaesthetic effects. We use them in everyday speech when we talk of 'a cold eye', 'a soft wind', 'a heavy silence', 'a hard voice', 'a black look', and so forth. *See also* CORRESPONDENCE OF THE ARTS; LOGOPOEIA; ONOMATOPOEIA; TONE COLOUR.

synaloepha (Gk 'coalescence') In Classical prosody the contraction of a long vowel or diphthong at the end of one word with a vowel or diphthong at the beginning of the next. Thus, the making of one long syllable. In effect, elision (*q.v.*). In Spanish verse *sinalefa* is more complex and has been known to combine six vowels. Spanish has rather more words *beginning* with vowels and ending with them than other languages.

synathroesmus (Gk 'collection, union') An accumulation of words of different meaning in a sentence or a sequence of clauses, as in these lines from *Macbeth* (II, iii):

> Who can be wise, amaz'd, temp'rate and furious,
> Loyal and neutral, in a moment?

synaxarion In the Eastern Church, a brief account of a saint or feast appointed to be read at the early morning service of *Orthros*. It also denotes the book which contains such passages, arranged according to the Calendar (the Greater Synaxarion). Synaxaries therefore belong to hagiography (*q.v.*). *See also* CALENDAR.

synchronic *See* DIACHRONIC/SYNCHRONIC.

syncopation (MedL 'striking together') In verse and in music it occurs when the metrical pattern goes contrary to the natural stress of normal speech. Common in ballad meter, as in these two opening stanzas from *Sir Patrick Spens*:

> The King sits in Dumfermline toune,
> Drinking the blude-red wine:

> 'O whar will I get a skeely skipper
> To sail this ship o' mine?'
> Up and spak an eldern knicht,
> Sat at the king's richt kne:
> 'Sir Patrick Spens is the best sailor
> That sails upon the se.'

'Sailor' in line 7 is a trochaic word, but the meter clearly requires the stress to fall upon the second syllable, making it iambic. *See* FOOT; RHYTHM; SCANSION; WRENCHED ACCENT.

syncope (Gk 'cutting') The cutting short of a word by omitting a letter or syllable, as in 'e'er' for 'ever', 'e'en' for 'even'. *See* CONTRACTION; ELISION.

synecdoche (Gk 'taking up together') A figure of speech in which the part stands for the whole, and thus something else is understood within the thing mentioned. For example: in 'Give us this day our daily bread', 'bread' stands for the meals taken each day. In these lines from Thomas Campbell's *Ye Mariners of England*, 'oak' represents the warships as well as the material from which they are made:

> With thunders from her native oak,
> She quells the flood below.

Synecdoche is common in everyday speech. In 'Chelsea won the match', Chelsea stands for the Chelsea Football Team. *See also* ANTONOMASIA; METALEPSIS; METONYMY.

syneciosis (Gk 'lining of opposites') An antithetical device quite frequent in satire (*q.v.*) which was often used by practitioners of the heroic couplet (*q.v.*). This example comes from part of Dryden's description of Shimei in *Absalom and Achitophel*:

> His Cooks, with long disuse, their Trade forgot;
> Cool was his Kitchen, tho' his Brains were not.

See ANTITHESIS; OXYMORON; ZEUGMA.

synizesis *See* SYNALOEPHA.

synonym (Gk 'together name') A word similar in meaning to another. It is rare to find an exact synonymous meaning. It is usually a matter of 'shades' of meaning, as in: insane, mad, demented, daft, loopy, psychotic, barpoo, crazy, nutty, maghnoon, off one's coconut, etc. *See* ANTONYM.

synonymous parallelism Jargon for a couplet in which each line expresses the same idea in different terms.

synopsis *See* SUMMARY.

syntagmatic/paradigmatic The structuralist Ferdinand de Saussure (1857–1913) described language as 'a system of interdependent terms in which the value of each term results solely from the simultaneous presence of the others'. From this principle or premise he elaborates the idea that there are two dimensions in the relationships of words: (a) the syntagmatic or 'horizontal' relations; (b) the associative or 'vertical' relations, more usually described as paradigmatic. By this distinction he means that each word has a linear relationship with the words that may go before it and come after it. It is axiomatic that in any linguistic communication terms are arranged in sequences. For example, in the sentence 'The batsman hit the ball to the boundary' there is a perceptible relationship between each word. The paradigmatic relationship entails a consideration of the fact that each word in, say, a sentence (like the one above) has a relationship with other words that are *not* used but are *capable of being used* – and by being capable are thus associated. Obvious associative words in this instance would be pads, gloves, bat, bowler – or even the whole concept of cricket.

In *A Survey of Structural Linguistics* (1972) G. C. Lepschy analyses the distinction very concisely:

> A sign is in contrast with other signs which come before and after it in a sentence. It has with the preceding and following signs a syntagmatic relationship. This is a relationship *in praesentia*, i.e. between elements (the sign in question, and the preceding and following ones) which are all present in the message. But a sign is also opposed to other signs not because they are in the message but because they belong to the language; it is associated (through similarity or difference) with these other signs, it has with them an associative relationship. This is a relationship *in absentia*, i.e. between the element in question which is there, and other elements, which are not there in that particular message.

Thus, the syntagmatic is concerned with combination; the paradigmatic with substitution.

The concept of the 'language of presence' and the 'language of absence' creates a kind of fundamental opposition or antinomy (*q.v.*), which Jacques Derrida has been at pains to question; he sees no resolution, only an instability. *See* DIACHRONIC/SYNCHRONIC; DIFFÉRANCE; GRAMMATOLOGY; METAPHOR/METONYMY; SIGNIFIER/SIGNIFIED.

syntax   (Gk 'together arrangement') Sentence construction.

synthesis   *See* ANALYSIS.

synthetic rhyme   This occurs when words are distorted in any way in order to give an approximate phonetic identity. It is common in humorous verse. For example, Odgen Nash's *Requiem*:

> There was a young belle of old Natchez
> Whose garments were always in patchez.
>   When comment arose
>   On the state of her clothes,
> She drawled, 'When Ah itchez Ah scratchez'.

And:

> For the over-fifties
> And the not-so-nifties
> A discotheque
> Is a risk to tek. (J. A. Cuddon)

synthetic rhythm The repetition of a word or phrase to fill up a line. It is common in folksong, nonsense verse and ballad (*qq.v.*). The second and third stanzas from *The Wife of Usher's Well* illustrate the effect:

> They hadna been a week from her,
>   A week but barely ane,
> When word came to the carline wife
>   That her three sons were gane.
> They hadna been a week from her,
>   A week but barely three,
> When word came to the carline wife
>   That her sons she'd never see.

See also INCREMENTAL REPETITION; REFRAIN.

system In Greek prosody, a sequence of *cola* (*q.v.*) in the same meter (*q.v.*).

systems theory An interdisciplinary theory of self-regulating systems (including, for example, the physiological systems of the body, ecosystems) that seeks to conceptualize and understand the principles that govern their operation. Emerging in the mid 20th c. – with Karl Ludwig von Bertalanffy's 'An Outline of General System Theory' (1950) published in the *British Journal for the Philosophy of Science* – the discourse has expanded its application to various fields including software and computing, biology, and sociology. Among the major exponents of systems theory was the German sociologist Niklas Luhmann (1927–98), a student of Talcott Parsons, who engaged in salient debates with figures such as Jürgen Habermas and whose work exerted a worldwide influence.

systrophe A rhetorical device which contains an accumulation of definitions, or repetition by definition. A classic example is Macbeth's apostrophe (*q.v.*) to Sleep (*Macbeth*, II, ii.).

syzygy (Gk 'yoke') A term in Classical prosody to describe the combination of two feet into a single metrical unit. Phonetic *syzygy* describes consonant sound patterns and repetitions not covered by alliteration (*q.v.*). *See also* CONSONANCE; IAMBIC TRIMETER.

T

tableau (F 'little table, picture') Primarily a theatrical term, though deriving from graphic art. Current from the 19th c. and frequently used in stage directions in 19th c. plays. To create a tableau actors took up positions and held them until the curtain came down or applause finished. Sometimes, when the curtain went up again, the actors would be regrouped into another tableau. Sometimes an actual picture was copied and there would be a copy of the picture on stage for rehearsal to guide the performers. The musical *My Fair Lady* (adapted from Shaw's *Pygmalion*) has a fine tableau for the Ascot scene, which is not in the original play. *See also* DUMB SHOW.

tableaux vivants A development of the tableau (*q.v.*) in the theatre in the 19th c. and also frequent as a form of elegant private entertainment (in a drawing room, for instance). A mythical topic, a notable work of art or a famous historical event was 'dramatized' in a series of fixed tableaux. The whole thing was highly 'theatrical'. Attitudes and groupings were exaggerated and authentic costume was an important part of the presentation. A kind of static choreography was needed. Vivid animation was essential. Nelson's mistress, Lady Hamilton, was a well-known presenter of *tableaux vivants* and as a form of private entertainment they became popular. Frances Trollope (mother of the novelist Anthony) in *The Mother's Manual* (1842) actually recommends the *tableau vivant* as an acceptable way of luring suitors to marriageable daughters. In the theatre James Robinson Planché (1796–1880), who designed extravaganzas (*q.v.*) for Madame Vestris (1797–1856), and Gilbert and Sullivan made use of them. In the 1820s Andrew Ducrow presented 'living statues' at Astley's Amphitheatre. During the 1830s *tableaux vivants* were a feature of music-hall entertainments, where they were called *poses plastiques*. In the long run their influence is easily discernible in 20th c. musicals, in chorus-line routines and in the kind of film musicals that Busby Berkeley excelled at creating.

A Dictionary of Literary Terms and Literary Theory, Fifth Edition. J. A. Cuddon.
© 2013 The Estate of J. A. Cuddon. Published 2013 by Blackwell Publishing Ltd.

table-talk A form of literary biography (*q.v.*) which consists of a person's sayings, opinions, *obiter dicta* (*q.v.*), *aperçus*, etc. These are recorded by the person to whom they are addressed. Table-talk may constitute extremely valuable material for biographers.

This type of literature (often known as '-ana', *q.v.*, as in *Walpoliana*) is of great antiquity. A notable paradigm in Greek literature is *Deipnosophistai* ('Sophists at Dinner' or 'Connoisseurs in Dining'), by Athenaeus (*c.* AD 200), a work of fifteen books in which twenty-three learned men meet at dinner in Rome on various occasions and discuss food and other subjects. In Latin literature the *Noctes Atticae* of Aulus Gellius (*c.* 200) is a collection of writings in 'essay' (*q.v.*) form based on quotations, conversations, discourses.

By far the most important of the early records of table-talk in modern European literature, brutally frank and intimate, were Martin Luther's *Tischreden* or *Colloquia Mensalia* (1566).

In 1618 Ben Jonson visited (on foot) William Drummond of Hawthornden in Scotland. The laird recorded many of his observations and left them in manuscript. Though not published in full until 1833, they comprise one of the earliest and most valuable instances of table-talk in English literature.

A vogue for recording table-talk established itself during the 17th c. Clearly, by now, table-talk and '-ana' were 'in'. It is also worth noting that during the 17th c. the practice of keeping diaries, journals and notebooks became widespread. To this time belong the famous diaries of Pepys and John Evelyn, also various collections of apophthegms, *pensées* and aphorisms (*qq.v.*). Even John Aubrey's *Brief Lives* are almost a form of table-talk because Aubrey, as a biographer, depended so much on his ears and therefore on what people said, rather than on books and what people wrote. The greatest table-talker of the 17th c. was John Selden (1584–1654), a friend of Jonson's.

In 1763 Boswell began laying down the vintage Johnsoniana and, not to be outdone, also bottled his own *Boswelliana* – as well as the abrasive remarks of his caustic wife which he titled *Uxoriana*. At Strawberry Hill Horace Walpole had his Boswell in the shape of J. Pinkerton, who published *Walpoliana* in 1799. Two other famous 18th c. English writers went into the books of the 'Ana-ists'. Samuel Foote was recorded by William Cooke, who published *Memoirs of the Life of Samuel Foote* (1778) and *Memoirs of Samuel Foote Esq.* (1805). The dramatist Sheridan was reported by Kelly, who published *Sheridaniana; Or, Anecdotes of the Life of Richard Brinsley Sheridan; his Table-Talk, and Bon Mots* in 1826.

Sydney Smith, one of the wittiest of all English talkers, had much reported by his daughter Lady Holland in *A Memoir of the Reverend Sydney Smith* (1855), and by Thomas Moore, whose *Memoirs, Journal, and Correspondence* was published in 1856. At about the time that Smith was most famous, Eckermann arrived in Weimar (*c.* 1823), when Goethe was already an old man. However, Eckermann was able to jot down many of the sage's most interesting observations before the poet died in 1832. The first two volumes of the *Conversations* were published in 1836, the third in 1848. Again at about the same period H. N. Coleridge was recording the table-talk of

S. T. Coleridge. Specimens of this came out in 1835. Apart from Selden, Johnson and Goethe, Coleridge was about the best table-talker of all time.

Three other notable collections of table-talk dating from the first half of the 19th c. are Hazlitt's conversations with the painter James Northcote (which Hazlitt had published in 1830 under the title *Conversations of James Northcote, Esq., RA*), Thomas Medwin's record of things said by Byron when the poet was at Pisa in 1821–2 (which was published in 1824) and Leigh Hunt's *Table-Talk* (1851). *See also* ANECDOTE.

tabloid (a conflation of *tabl/et* and *-oid*) A newspaper whose pages are half the size of a broadsheet. The term derives from the pharmaceutical industry where it is used to describe a form of pill. Lord Northcliffe introduced the term to describe the *Daily Mirror* when it was relaunched in 1904 in half size. Originally the term implied that the contents of a tabloid newspaper were a concentrate of good things (like a tabloid pill), and the term 'tabloid journalism' (which actually pre-dates the *Daily Mirror*'s relaunch by a few years) was complimentary. Gradually, and especially since the 1960s, it has become a pejorative term for sensationalism, scandal-mongering and celebrity gossip. In the UK, many broadsheets switched to tabloid format in the 2000s (sometimes the term 'compact' is used to distinguish them from traditional tabloids, though the term broadsheet is still used). The tabloid has been a feature of the American newspaper scene since the 1920s, though it is less common elsewhere. In Europe most newspapers use the 'Berliner' format, a size halfway between the tabloid and the broadsheet – though the German tabloid *Bild* (1952–) is a notable exception.

tag Something added to a piece of writing by way of ornament; commonly a quotation. It may also apply to a saying, proverb or adage. The addition of a quotation is quite a common device among modern poets. T. S. Eliot made good use of it. Ezra Pound was addicted to the practice, as can be seen in his *Cantos*.

tail-rhyme A tailed caudate rhyme is our term for F *rime couée* (L *rhythmus caudatus*). It denotes a unit of verse in which a short line, followed by a group of longer lines, e.g. couplet, triolet or stanza (*qq.v.*), rhymes with a preceding short line. The tail-rhyme stanza has a number of variants. Well-known instances can be found in Chaucer's *Sir Thopas*, Drayton's *Ballad of Agincourt* and Shelley's *To Night*, from which the following example is taken:

> Swiftly walk o'er the western wave,
>   Spirit of Night!
> Out of the misty eastern cave,
> Where, all the long and lone daylight,
> Thou wovest dreams of joy and fear,
> Which make thee terrible and dear, –
>   Swift be thy flight!

See CAUDA; CAUDATE SONNET.

tale A narrative, written (in prose or verse) or spoken. When in prose, barely distinguishable from a short story (*q.v.*). If there *is* a difference, then a tale perhaps suggests something written in the tone of voice of someone speaking. Usually the theme of a tale is fairly simple but the method of relating it may be complex and skilled. Much depends on the writer's viewpoint (*q.v.*). One might perhaps say that the kind of narratives which R. L. Stevenson, Rudyard Kipling, W. W. Jacobs, Joseph Conrad, Somerset Maugham and William Faulkner liked to write and excelled at are tales, whereas the kind preferred by Henry James, E. M. Forster, Aldous Huxley, Katherine Mansfield and Elizabeth Bowen are short stories. However, any such classifications may be wholly misleading, and such a division would not be serviceable in classifying the shorter works of Poe, Saki, Chekhov, Maupassant and D. H. Lawrence or a dozen other writers.

The tale in verse has a long and venerable history in English literature (the term includes ballad, epic and lay, *qq.v.*) from Chaucer's *Canterbury Tales* to C. Day Lewis's *The Nabara*. Among shorter tales the following are notable: Thomas Parnell's *The Hermit*, William Cowper's *John Gilpin*, George Crabbe's *Peter Grimes*, Robert Burns's *Tam o'Shanter*, Wordsworth's *Michael*, Coleridge's *Ancient Mariner*, Byron's *Prisoner of Chillon*, Keats's *Eve of St Agnes*, Macaulay's *The Keeping of the Bridge*, Tennyson's *Maud* and *Morte d'Arthur*, Browning's *Childe Roland to the Dark Tower Came*, Matthew Arnold's *Sohrab and Rustum*, Dante Gabriel Rossetti's *The White Ship*, Swinburne's *St Dorothy*, Dobson's *The Ballad of 'Beau Brocade'*, Hardy's *The Sacrilege*, R. L. Stevenson's *Ticonderoga*, Kipling's *Tomlinson*, Robert Service's *The Shooting of Dan Macgrew*, Laurence Binyon's *The Battle of Stamford Bridge*, Masefield's *The Rider at the Gate* and *Reynard*, Alfred Noyes's *The Highwayman* (not to mention many by Sir Walter Scott and William Morris) – plus: Edmund Blunden's *Incident in Hyde Park*, 1803, W. S. Graham's *The Nightfishing*, Patrick Kavanagh's *The Great Hunger*, Anthony Cronin's *RMS Titanic*, Vernon Watkins's *The Ballad of the Mari Lwyd*, and a considerable number of poems by Robert Frost. *See also* CONTE; FAIRY TALE; FOLK TALE; NARRATIVE VERSE; SHORT STORY; TALL STORY; YARN.

tall story A story which is extravagant, outlandish or highly improbable. Usually regarded as false, however good it may be. It is of the same family as fantasy and fairy tale (*q.v.*). The epic (*q.v.*) tradition, and especially the primary epic, contains a good many episodes which are classifiable as tall stories: e.g. the deeds of Odysseus, Beowulf's swimming match with Breca, the feats of Marko Kraljević in the South Slav *narodne pesme* (*q.v.*) and the exploits of Skanderbeg in the Albanian epic cycles. They abound in legend and hagiography (*qq.v.*). Often enough the 'traveller's tale' is virtually the same as a tall story. Early and very entertaining examples of these are to be found in Pliny the Elder's *Natural History* (1st c. AD), and in Lucian's *Dialogues* (2nd c. AD), particularly Icaromenippus. Medieval 'Vision' literature is full of splendid tall stories (e.g. the 12th c. *Vision of Tundale*), and medieval collections of *exempla*, like the *Gesta Romanorum*, also contain many. Some of the early authors (especially Pliny) believed them. Sir John Mandeville's *Book of Travels* (14th c.) is a classic of its kind. Chaucer's *Miller's Tale* is as good an example as one can hope to meet. In Rabelais's *Gargantua* and *Pantagruel* (1534, 1532) we find some of the more prodigious instances of the tall story. Utopian literature also provides memorable instances, for example Gabriel de Foigny's *La Terre Australe connue* (1676). But for sustained invention, wit and panache it is difficult to find anything to equal Voltaire's *Zadig* (1747) and, even better, *Candide* (1759). That age which, for all its devotion to reason, took much delight in fantasia also produced Raspe's *Baron Munchausen: Narrative of his Marvellous Travels* (1785). There have been few taller stories than Munchausen's tale of the horse that was cut in two, drank from a fountain, and was sewn up again.

More recent examples are: T. B. Thorpe's *The Big Bear of Arkansas*; Sheridan Le Fanu's *The Ghost and the Bone-Setter*; Francis Bret Harte's *Plain Language from Truthful James*; Mark Twain's *The Celebrated Jumping Frog of Calaveras County*; Jack London's *One Thousand Dozen* (i.e. eggs); John Russell's *The Price of the Head*; T. F. Powys's *Lie Thee Down, Oddity*; William Faulkner's *A Rose for Emily*; Stephen Vincent Benét's *The Devil and Daniel Webster*; Marcel Aymé's *The Ubiquitous Wife*; James Thurber's *The Catbird Seat*; and J. G. Ballard's *The Lost Leonardo* – a brilliant tour de force (q.v.) of the genre.

Ambrose Bierce wrote twenty-three 'tall tales' which he called 'negligible' stories. They are satirical, blackly comic and inclined to the grotesque and in some cases are extremely funny. Other notable contributors to the genre are O. Henry, J. C. Powys and William Saroyan.

The tall story has also flourished in the environments and atmospheres of frontier life, 'bad lands', pioneering endeavours (e.g. the Gold Rush in the Yukon and Australia), among sporting fraternities, among fishermen and sailors, and often in rural areas (hence, for instance, the rhozzum, *q.v.*, which is kin to the tall tale).

The ghost story (*fact* rather than fiction), the Russian *skaz* and the Chinese *p'ing hua* (*qq.v.*) are also sources of tall tales. See *also* FOLK LITERATURE; SHAGGY DOG STORY; WESTERN; YARN.

tamizdat *See* SAMIZDAT.

tanka A Japanese lyric form of thirty-one syllables, in lines of five/seven/five/seven/seven syllables. Also known as a *Waka* or an *uta*, it originated in the 7th c. and is regarded as the classic Japanese poetic form. It has not had so much influence on Western poetry as the *haiku* (*q.v.*). A few poets (e.g. Amy Lowell and Adelaide Crapsey) have imitated it.

tantra (Skt 'thread, fundamental doctrine') Any of a number of Hindu and Buddhist writings of a religious didactic nature. They give ritual instructions, including the use of incantations and diagrams. Many *tantras* are ascribed to Buddha and thousands have been composed since *c.* 500 AD. The Tibetan

Book of the Dead (8th c.) – a spiritual guide for the dying – contains numerous *tantras*.

tapinosis (Gk 'lowering') A figurative device, expression or epithet which belittles by exaggeration; for instance, Pope's lines about Timon's villa in *Moral Essays, Epistle IV*:

> Greatness, with Timon, dwells in such a draught
> As brings all Brobdingnag before your thought.
> To compass this, his building is a Town,
> His pond an Ocean, his parterre a Down:
> Who but must laugh, the Master when he sees,
> A puny insect, shiv'ring at a breeze!
> Lo, what huge heaps of littleness around!

See HYPERBOLE.

taste We first find the word used as a critical term towards the end of the 17th c. La Bruyère, for example, in *Les Caractères* (1688) argued that in artistic matters 'il y a donc un bon et un mauvais goût'. Joseph Addison, in his *Spectator* papers on taste (1712), defined it as 'that faculty of the soul which discerns the beauties of an author with pleasure, and the imperfections with dislike'. The term became well established in the 18th c. and, in criticism, was thereafter used in a bewildering variety of senses especially in the philosophy and science of aesthetics. How bewildering may be gauged from Coleridge's definition of it as 'the intermediate faculty which connects the active with the passive powers of our nature, the intellect with the senses; and its appointed function is to elevate the *images* of the latter, while it realizes the *ideas* of the former'. In fact, the history of the word exemplifies the truism: *quot homines, tot sententiae*.

Every man may be expected to possess at any rate an inchoate idea of taste, about which, in all probability, there can be no dispute – or a great deal. To establish a polarity: some hold that matters of taste are subjective; others that they are objective. In either case the judgements may be universally valid, but it is more than likely that, owing to what Dr Johnson referred to as 'the wild vicissitudes of taste', few works survive to pass a hypothetical absolute test of excellence or inferiority; that is, the test of universality (*q.v.*). Even Shakespeare's works have been regarded as lacking in taste, and have suffered a period of being 'out of fashion'. The issue is further complicated by the fact that any arbiter is immediately vulnerable when he arrogates to himself the power of discriminating between what is in good or bad taste. *See* VULGARITY.

tautology (Gk 'the same saying') A sentence (composed of subject and predicate) in which the predicate merely repeats the content of the subject, as in: 'This man is a man' or 'The child is young'. The concept of 'child' already implies that he or she is young, and so the predication of youth to the child is superfluous. *See also* PERIPHRASIS.

telescoped metaphor Also known as a complex metaphor. In such a figure of speech the vehicle of one metaphor becomes the tenor of another (*see* TENOR AND VEHICLE). Consider the following lines from *King Lear* (IV, vi, 141–8):

> And the creature run from the cur? There thou mightst behold
> The great image of authority: a dog's obeyed in office . . .
> . . . The usurer hangs the cozener.
> Through tatter'd clothes small vices do appear;
> Robes and furr'd gowns hide all. Plate sin with gold,
> And the strong lance of justice hurtless breaks;
> Arm it in rags, a pigmy's straw does pierce it.

The vehicle here may be taken as the image or concept of authority whose shortcomings can be concealed by rich apparel (a thematic image in *King Lear* and an idea central to the tragedy; thus it is doubly an organic metaphor, *q.v.*). This vehicle becomes the personification of sin armoured in gold like a knight at tourney; or, again, like a beggar. Thus we have one vehicle elaborated in three tenors.

The passage also contains what are sometimes called 'subdued metaphors'; in this case they are implied images of justice in a court of law, and the conflict in a jousting tournament. The interlocking images support each other; the 'sword' of justice becomes a lance and then a straw. *See* IMAGERY; METAPHOR.

telescope word *See* PORTMANTEAU WORD.

telestich *See* ACROSTIC.

Tel Quel school In 1960 the French novelist and critic Philippe Sollers (1936–67) founded the literary periodical *Tel Quel*, and later he outlined its objectives in his discourse *Logiques* (1968). The aims are basically ideological and activist, as well as aesthetic. One of its aims is to restore to language its original revolutionary power; and it advances the principle that 'literature is language made with language'. The school, which has been influenced by, among others, Roland Barthes, and also by theories of semiotics and semiology (*q.v.*), has been particularly concerned to promote interest in and more understanding of such French writers as the Marquis de Sade (1740–1814), Stéphane Mallarmé (1842–98), Lautréamont (1846–70) and Antonin Artaud (1896–1948), who had a considerable influence on theatre and drama in the 20th c. *See also* POÈTE MAUDIT; THEATRE OF CRUELTY.

tenor and vehicle Terms coined by I. A. Richards. By 'tenor' he meant the purport or general drift of thought regarding the subject of a metaphor; by 'vehicle', the image which embodies the tenor. In these lines from R. S. Thomas's *A Blackbird Singing* the tenor is the bird's song, its tune; the vehicle is the fine smelting image in the fifth and sixth lines:

> It seems wrong that out of this bird,
> Black, bold, a suggestion of dark

Places about it, there yet should come
Such rich music, as though the notes'
Ore were changed to a rare metal
At one touch of that bright bill.

tension A term used in a particular sense by Allen Tate to designate the totality of meaning in a poem. He derives it from the logical terms 'extension' and 'intension' by removing the prefixes. Extension = literal meaning; intension = metaphorical meaning. The simultaneous coexistence of these sets of meaning constitutes tension. It may also refer to 'conflict structures'. For example, the counterpoint (q.v.) between the rhythm and meter of a poem and speech rhythms; or between the concrete and the abstract. Some critics, following the theories of Anaximander and Heraclitus, take it to mean the balance of mental and emotional tensions which help to give shape and unity to a work.

tenson A type of poetic composition (also known as *tenzone* and *tencon*) which originated in Provence in the 12th c. It usually consisted of a debate between two poets, or with a poet versus an imaginary opponent. The subjects were various: love, politics, literary criticism. It developed into the *partimen* (q.v.) and the *jeu parti* (q.v.) and as a poetic device spread to Italy and Sicily. See DÉBAT.

ten-year test A term devised by Cyril Connolly to denote a book (usually a novel) which, ten years after its first publication, is still regarded as being of unusual literary merit, is still being widely read, and is still well thought of in literary and critical circles. Instances in English have been William Golding's *Lord of the Flies* (1954), Kingsley Amis's *Lucky Jim* (1954), V. S. Naipaul's *A House for Mr Biswas* (1961), J. G. Farrell's *The Siege of Krishnapur* (1973), Malcolm Bradbury's *The History Man* (1975) and Iris Murdoch's *The Sea, the Sea* (1978). See also BEST-SELLER.

tercerilla In Spanish prosody a three-line stanza of *arte menor* (q.v.): two to eight syllables of one or more rhythmic stresses.

tercet (F 'triplet') A stanza of three lines linked by rhyme, as in *terza rima* (q.v.). Also as one of a pair of triplets which makes up the sestet (q.v.) of a sonnet (q.v.) or as three consecutive rhyming lines (known as a triplet in a poem which is largely written in couplets). These tercets are from Tennyson's *Two Voices*:

A still small voice spake unto me:
'Thou art so full of misery,
Were it not better not to be?'

Then to the still small voice I said:
'Let me not cast in endless shade
What is so wonderfully made.'

terminal rhyme See RHYME.

tern A group of three stanzas, especially in a *ballade* (*q.v.*) consisting of a tern and an *envoi* (*q.v.*). See TERCET.

ternaire (F 'three at one time') A three-line stanza on one rhyme. The French poet Auguste Brizeux (1803–55) claimed to be the first to use it.

terror/horror A distinction made by one of the most successful authors of Gothic fiction, Ann Radcliffe, in her essay *On the Supernatural in Poetry* in 1826. 'Terror' and 'horror' correspond to two different kinds of Gothic writing, the first commendable (such as her own novels), the second danger- ous (such as Matthew Lewis's salacious novel *The Monk* (1796), which parodies Radcliffe). Terror is produced by suggestion, implication and uncer- tainty; horror is felt when one suffers full exposure to something awful, for instance, a howling ghost or a bloody corpse. For Radcliffe, the difference has moral implications. She writes: 'Terror and horror are so far opposite that the first expands the soul, and awakens the faculties to a high degree of life; the other contracts, freezes, and nearly annihilates them.' Thus terror inspires: it makes us better people by encouraging us to realize that fear is just in our minds and can be overcome. By contrast, horror paralyses: it leaves us power- less and confused, at the mercy of forces we can't fully comprehend. In short, horror makes us frightened of life. *See also* GOTHIC NOVEL/FICTION; HORROR STORY.

tertulia A type of Spanish literary salon (*q.v.*) which gradually replaced the formal literary academy of the 18th c. The term is believed to derive from the word *tertuliantes* – the educated classes and clergy among theatre-goers. They were so called because they frequently quoted Tertullian, and the *ter- tulia* in a theatre was an upper circle or gallery. Tertullian (born *c.* 150) was one of the most famous early Christian writers in Latin. He wrote *Apologet- icus* (197) and a number of treatises on the Christian life.

terza rima (It 'third rhyme') The measure adopted by Dante for his *Divina Commedia*, consisting of a series of interlocking tercets (*q.v.*) in which the second line of each one rhymes with the first and third lines of the one suc- ceeding, thus: aba, bcb, cdc. At the end of the canto (*q.v.*) a single line rhymes with the second from last: wxyx, as in the conclusion of the first canto of the *Inferno*:

> Ed io a lui: Poeta, io ti richieggio
>   per quello Dio che tu non conoscesti,
>   acciocch'io fugga questo male e peggio
> Che tu mi meni là dov' or dicesti,
>   sì ch'io vegga la porta di san Pietro,
>   e color cui tu fai cotanto mesti.
> Allor si mosse, ed io li tenni retro.

Terza rima was also used by Petrarch and Boccaccio. Chaucer used it for part of *A Complaint to his Lady*, but it was Sir Thomas Wyatt who pioneered its use in England. This example comes from the beginning of his *Second Satire*:

My mother's maids, when they did sew and spin,
They sang sometimes a song of the field mouse,
That for because her livelihood was but thin

Would needs go seek her townish sister's house.
She thought herself endured to much pain:
The stormy blasts her cave so sore did souse . . .

Because it is a difficult form to manage (few Italian poets have used it successfully) it has never been very adaptable or popular outside Italy. A few 19th and 20th c. Dutch and German poets employed it; some French (notably Gautier); and some English – principally Byron in *The Prophecy of Dante*, Shelley in *Prince Athanese*, *The Triumph of Life* and *Ode to the West Wind*, Browning in *The Statue* and *The Bust*. More recently, Auden attempted it (with variations) in *The Sea and the Mirror*. See also TERZA RIMA SONNET.

terza rima sonnet A term occasionally used to describe a quatorzain (*q.v.*) whose rhyme uses the interlocking method of *terza rima* (*q.v.*). The rhyme pattern of aba, bcb, cdc, ded, ee (the same form as the sections in Shelley's *Ode to the West Wind*) is similar to the Spenserian sonnet (*q.v.*).

terzina An Italian term for a stanza of three lines, especially in *terza rima* (*q.v.*). Also applied to a continuous (non-stanzaic) poem rhymed aba, bcb, cdc, and so on. Fairly common in early Romance languages (*q.v.*), but rare in English.

testament (L 'witnessing') A document which bears witness; an affirmation. For instance, the Old and New Testaments. A number of well-known secular works come into the category. Among the better known are: Thomas Usk's allegorical prose work *The Testament of Love* (1387); Henryson's beautiful *Testament of Cresseid* (15th c. but printed in 1593); Villon's highly personal *Petit Testament* (1456) and *Grand Testament* (c. 1461), both of which (and especially the first) contain a strong element of mockery; Bridges's philosophical poem *The Testament of Beauty* (1929). In view of the general meaning of the term, numerous other writings might be put into this genre. For example, St Augustine's *Confessions*, or Newman's *Apologia pro Vita Sua*, or Camus's remarkable *Lettres à un ami allemand*. See also CONFESSIONAL LITERATURE.

tetralogy (Gk 'set of four') Four plays (three tragedies and a satyr play) were submitted for the prize in tragedy (*q.v.*) at the drama competitions in Athens in the 5th c. The term may now be applied to any four connected works. Eight of Shakespeare's ten History Plays are sometimes divided into two tetralogies: (a) *Henry VI* (Pts I, II and III) and *Richard III*; (b) *Richard II*, *Henry IV* (Pts I and II) and *Henry V*. See also SATYR PLAY; TRILOGY.

tetrameter (Gk 'of four measures') A line of four metrical feet. In English verse usually iambic or trochaic. Used extensively by many English poets, including Milton, Scott and Byron. These lines are from Milton's *L'Allegro*:

> Haste thee nymph, and bring with thee
> Jest and youthful Jollity,
> Quips and Cranks, and wanton wiles,
> Nods, and becks, and wreathed smiles

tétramètre The twelve-syllable French Classical alexandrine (*q.v.*). It was already in use in the 12th c. and is seen at its best in the tragedies of Corneille and Racine. *See also* TRIMÈTRE.

tetrapody (Gk 'four feet') A group or line of four feet.

tetrastich (Gk 'four lines') A group, stanza or poem of four lines. A synonym for quatrain (*q.v.*).

text (L *texere*, *textum*, 'to weave') A number of meanings may be distinguished: (a) the actual words of a book in their original form or any form they have been transmitted in or transmuted to; (b) a book of such words; (c) the main body of matter in a book – apart from notes, commentary, glosses, index, appendices, etc.; (d) a short passage taken from the Bible as the theme or subject or a sermon. *See* MANUSCRIPT; TEXTUAL CRITICISM.

textual criticism A branch of scholarship which is devoted to the study and analysis of extant texts in order to determine authorship and authenticity and, where there is a multiplicity of texts of one work, to determine which one is the 'best' or the 'original'.

texture A jargon term derived from the plastic arts which denotes the surface qualities of a work, as opposed to its shape and structure. In modern literary criticism it tends to designate the concrete qualities of a poem as opposed to its ideas; thus, the verbal surface of a work, its sensuous qualities, the density of its imagery. In these lines from John Crowe Ransom's *Dog* (Ransom, incidentally, uses 'texture' to refer also to the variations on the basic metrical pattern or structure) the texture varies a good deal:

> Cock-a-doodle-doo the brass-lined rooster says,
> Brekekekex intones the fat Greek frog –
> These fantasies do not terrify me as
> The bow-wow-wow of dog.
>
> I had a little doggie who used to sit and beg,
> A pretty little creature with tears in his eyes
> And anomalous hand extended on his leg;
> Housebroken was my Huendchen, and so wise.

Tentative analysis suggests that the general springiness and resilience of the rhythms is varied by a certain abrasiveness in 'brekekekex', a plumpness in 'fat Greek frog', and a pronounced brittleness in 'a pretty little creature'. The alliteration in the fourth line of the second stanza helps to knot the line together; while the nap on the mellifluous third line of that stanza is relieved by slight asperity of 'intertexture' in the word 'extended'.

Théâtre de Complicité   A London-based theatrical company founded in 1983 by Annabel Arden, Simon McBurney and Marcello Magni. The company has developed a highly experimental form of total theatre (*q.v.*) which makes extensive use of mime, clown techniques, improvisation, the techniques of *commedia dell'arte* (*q.v.*), acrobatics and most traditional theatrical styles and modes, including *Nō* (*q.v.*). Movement is taken to be as important as the text, and performance makes much use of the absurd. Tragedy (*q.v.*) is regarded as basic material – for that is where the comedy lies. In 1988 a notable version of Dürrenmatt's *The Visit* (1956) was presented. *See also* THEATRE OF THE ABSURD.

theatre-in-the-round   A form of theatrical presentation in which the acting area is surrounded by the audience. It is far from being a new idea, though it has had some vogue since the 1930s. It seems very probable that some of the Cornish Mystery Plays were performed in the open air with an audience ranged round the actors on banks. One may suppose, too, that Mumming Plays (*q.v.*) and related dramatic entertainments were thus presented. In modern times theatre-in-the-round achieved prominence in Russia in the 1930s where Okhlopov, using his realistic theatre, even involved the audience in the drama. At that time, too, Robert Atkins was producing Shakespeare in The Ring at Blackfriars. In America it has been a particularly popular form of presentation, especially in the universities. Margo Jones was the main American exponent. In France, also, it has had some success, particularly in the hands of André Villiers who, in 1954, founded the Théâtre en Rond in Paris. In England the leading light and dedicated crusader was Stephen Joseph, who established something of a tradition for theatre-in-the-round at Stoke-on-Trent. Joseph also worked on it in London, Southampton and Scarborough.

Theatre Laboratory   A Polish theatre company founded in 1959 under the directorship of Jerzy Grotowski (1933–99). It was highly experimental and many of the productions were adaptations of classic Polish works little known outside Poland. Grotowski created a troupe with avant-garde (*q.v.*) attitudes and his techniques had considerable influence on the Living Theater and the Third Theatre (*qq.v.*), and on such directors as Peter Brook. The company became defunct in 1984. *See also* TOTAL THEATRE.

Théâtre Libre   A theatre company created by André-Léonard Antoine (1858–1943) in Paris in 1887. It lasted for ten years and was to have an immeasurable influence on playwrights, directors and actors for a very long time; it was thus an important landmark in the evolution of the modern theatre. It was highly naturalistic in presentation and performance and concentrated on 'slice-of-life' (*q.v.*) plays known as *comédies rosses* ('cynical comedies'). Eugène Brieux (1858–1932) wrote a number of these. Antoine also presented work by Ibsen, Strindberg, Verga and Hauptmann, and his achievement helped to bring about the formation of similar theatres – such as Otto Brahm's Freie Bühne (*q.v.*) in Berlin.

Théâtre National Populaire   The theatre was founded in 1920, when Firmin Gémier (1865–1933) chose it as the name of his touring company. In 1937 it was established at the Palais de Chaillot. Jean Vilar (1912–71) became director in 1951. As a state-subsidized theatre it was and is expected to provide a wide variety of 'popular' theatre in many parts of France. Georges Wilson was director from 1963 to 1971, and in 1972 Roger Planchon (1931–2009) took the post. In 1986, Georges Lavaudant replaced Patrice Chéreau and shared the leadership with Roger Planchon until 1996. Then in 2002, the current director, Christian Schiaretti left the Comedy of Reims to lead the TNP.

theatre of cruelty   This derives from the theories of the French dramatist Antonin Artaud (1896–1948), who, in 1938, published *Le Théâtre et son double*, in which he formulated his principles. In his view the theatre must disturb the spectator profoundly, pierce him heart and soul in such a way as to free unconscious repressions and oblige men to view themselves as they really are. In it mime (*q.v.*), gesture and scenery are more important than words, and the director is a kind of maker of magic, 'a master of sacred ceremonies'. Much depends on spectacle, lighting effects and the exploitation of the full range of the 'theatrical'. Prior to 1938 Artaud had published two manifestos (in 1923 and 1933) and also had produced *Les Cenci* (1935), based on versions by Shelley and Stendhal, which was an attempt to put his theories into practice. Artaud's influence has been very considerable, especially on the work of Adamov, Genet, Camus and Audiberti. English dramatists have not been affected anything like as much. A recent and well-known example of *Théâtre de la cruauté* is Weiss's drama *The Persecution and Assassination of Marat as Performed by the Inmates of the Asylum of Charenton under the Direction of the Marquis de Sade* (1964). *See also* GRAND GUIGNOL; MELODRAMA.

theatre of panic   The term *théâtre panique* was invented in 1962 by the Spanish-born dramatist Fernando Arrabal (1932–), a playwright of the theatre of the absurd (*q.v.*) who writes in French. Arrabal, who was much influenced by Samuel Beckett and Antonin Artaud, sought to create a kind of ritualistic drama which combines elements of tragedy and buffoonery with religious (or quasi-religious) ceremonial. It is intended to surprise and frighten as well as to arouse laughter. Two notable examples of such drama have been *The Architect and the Emperor of Assyria* (1967) and *And They Handcuffed the Flowers* (1969). *See also* GRAND GUIGNOL; THEATRE OF CRUELTY.

theatre of silence   A theory of drama, more accurately called the theatre of the unspoken (*Théâtre de l'inexprimé*), devised by Jean-Jacques Bernard (1888–1972) in the 1920s. In his view dialogue was not sufficient; equally important was what characters *could* not and *did* not say. Though this may always have been obvious, and certainly has been since Bernard's experiments, very few dramatists had deliberately exploited the possibilities of silence before. Chekhov is a clear exception. Bernard's influence has been considerable.

Some of his main works are: *Le Feu qui reprend mal* (1921), *Martine* (1922), *Le Printemps des autres* (1924), *L'Ame en peine* (1926). Among recent English dramatists the master of the prolonged pause (*q.v.*) and sustained silence is unquestionably Harold Pinter (especially in *Landscape* and *Silence*, 1970). *See* SUBTEXT.

theatre of the absurd A term applied to many of the works of a group of dramatists who were active in the 1950s: Adamov, Beckett, Genet, Ionesco and Pinter. Among the less known were Albee, Arrabal, Günter Grass, Pinget and N. F. Simpson. The phrase 'theatre of the absurd' was probably coined by Martin Esslin, who wrote *The Theatre of the Absurd* (1961).

The origins of this form of drama are obscure, but it would be reasonable to suppose that its lineage is traceable from Roman mime plays, through to aspects of comic business and technique in medieval mid-Renaissance drama and *commedia dell'arte* (*q.v.*), and thence to the dramatic works of Jarry, Strindberg and Brecht. The work of Jarry is vital and the possibilities of a theatre of the absurd are already apparent in *Ubu Roi* (1896), *Ubu Cocu* (1897–8) and *Ubu enchainé* (c. 1898); as they are also in Apollinaire's *Les Mamelles de Tirésias* (completed in 1917). Moreover, it is conceivable that the increasing popularity of nonsense verse (*q.v.*) from about the mid 19th c. onwards is connected with this concept of the absurd. Almost certainly Dadaism and surrealism (*qq.v.*) influenced the development of the theatre of the absurd, and so have Artaud's theories on the theatre of cruelty (*q.v.*).

In the evolution of a new vision of mankind in relation to his environment and the universe one may expect to see a large number of cross-fertilizing influences. Clearly, the idea that man is absurd is by no means new. An awareness of the essential absurdity of much human behaviour has been inherent in the work of many writers. Aristophanes, Chaucer, Erasmus, Cervantes, Molière, Swift, Pope, Balzac, Dickens, Goncharov – to cite only a handful – have all shown an acute feeling for man's comicality.

However, the concept of *homo absurdus* has acquired a rather more specific meaning in the last hundred years or so. This is partly, no doubt, owing to the need to provide an explanation of man's apparently purposeless role and position in a universe which is popularly imagined to have no discernible reason for existence. Mathematically, a surd is that which cannot be expressed in finite terms of ordinary numbers or quantities; hence it embodies what is irrational rather than ridiculous.

In his *La Tentation de l'occident* (1926) André Malraux, who expatiated at length about 'the human condition', remarked that 'at the centre of European man, dominating the great moments of his life, there lies an essential absurdity'. The theme recurs in a number of works by Malraux, and is apparent, particularly, in the works of Sartre and Camus. The latter's collection of essays *The Myth of Sisyphus* (1942) contains some of the most interesting statements on the theme. Camus expounded in some detail a vision of life which was essentially absurd, without apparent purpose, out of harmony with its surroundings, sad to the point of anguish, and at the same time, in a laconic fashion, funny. He stresses the destructive nature of time, the feeling of solitude in a hostile world, the sense of isolation from other human beings. The dominant symbolism of the title is perfectly appropriate.

In the early 1950s many diffused conceptions of the absurd began to be resolved and articulated in a series of remarkable plays which dramatized the kind of vision which Camus had projected – fundamentally, human beings struggling with the irrationality of experience, in a state of what has been described as 'metaphysical anguish'. The plays themselves lack a formal logic and conventional structure, so that both form and content support (while emphasizing the difficulty of communicating) the representation of what may be called the absurd predicament. Some of the major works are (the dramatists in alphabetical order): *La Parodie* and *L'Invasion* (1950) by Adamov; *Waiting for Godot* (1953) and *Endgame* (1957), by Beckett; *Le Balcon* (1957) and *Les Nègres* (1959) by Genet; *La Cantatrice chauve* (1950) and *Le Roi se meurt* (1961) by Ionesco; *Lettre morte* (1960), *La Manivelle* (1960) by Pinget; *The Birthday Party* (1958) and *The Dumb Waiter* (1960) by Pinter. *See also* FARCE; HAPPENING; PATAPHYSICS.

Theatre Workshop A theatrical company founded in 1945 by Joan Littlewood (1914–2002) and Ewan MacColl (1915–89). From 1953 its headquarters were at the Theatre Royal, Stratford East, London. It was a notable success and proved a life-giving force in the theatre for over twenty years. The policy was that left-wing writers and writers with working-class backgrounds were given special encouragement. One of its most famous and memorable productions was *Oh! What a Lovely War* (1963).

theatricalism A concept and theory of dramatic presentation which developed in Russia and Germany in the early years of the 20th c. It was strongly opposed to naturalism (*q.v.*) and was in favour of the principle that theatre *is* theatre and is a representation of life – and is *not* life itself. Nevertheless, naturalistic drama (*q.v.*), like the well-made play (*q.v.*), has continued to be popular.

theme Properly speaking, the theme of a work is not its subject but rather its central idea, which may be stated directly or indirectly. For example, the theme of *Othello* is jealousy. *See* LEITMOTIF; MOTIF.

theogony A Greek term for an account of the origin and genealogy of the gods. Probably the most famous is the *Theogonia*, a poem in hexameters attributed to Hesiod (8th c. BC). In it he recounts the genealogy and mythological history of the gods.

theory *See* CRITICISM AND THEORY.

thesaurus (Gk 'treasure') A repository of information, like a dictionary or encyclopaedia (*qq.v.*). Well-known examples are: the *Thesaurus Linguae Latinae*, the German dictionary of the Latin language begun in 1900. Roget's *Thesaurus of English Words and Phrases*, first published in 1852, has been revised and enlarged many times since.

thesis   Three meanings may be distinguished: (a) a long essay (*q.v.*) or treatise (*q.v.*) presented for a degree; (b) a proposition to be proved; (c) the unstressed syllable of a metrical foot (e.g. *thesis* itself is a trochaic word on which the second syllable is unstressed). *See* ARSIS.

thesis novel   One which treats of a social, political or religious problem with a didactic and, perhaps, radical purpose. It certainly sets out to call people's attention to the shortcomings of a society. Some outstanding examples of the genre are: Charles Kingsley's *Alton Locke* (1850); Harriet Beecher Stowe's *Uncle Tom's Cabin* (1852); Dickens's *Hard Times* (1854); Charles Reade's *Hard Cash* (1863); Samuel Butler's *The Way of All Flesh* (1903); Upton Sinclair's *The Jungle* (1906); Robert Tressell's *The Ragged Trousered Philanthropists* (1914, abbreviated text; full text, 1955); Walter Greenwood's *Love on the Dole* (1933); Winifred Holtby's *South Riding* (1936); John Steinbeck's *The Grapes of Wrath* (1939); and Alan Paton's *Cry, the Beloved Country* (1948). Some would include William Golding's *Lord of the Flies* (1954) in this category. Utopian and dystopian visions in fictional form might also be included. *See also* PROLETARIAN NOVEL; THESIS PLAY; UTOPIA.

thesis play   A drama which deals with a specific problem and, very probably, offers a solution. This form appears to have originated in France in the 19th c. Both Dumas *fils* and Brieux wrote a considerable number between 1860 and 1900. Elsewhere Ibsen was a major influence on the genre, for example *A Doll's House* (1879). In England Shaw (*Widowers' Houses*, 1892, *Mrs Warren's Profession*, 1902, *Major Barbara*, 1905) and Galsworthy (*The Silver Box*, 1907, *Strife*, 1909, *Justice*, 1910) made notable contributions. This type of drama is also known as a problem or propaganda play. Arnold Wesker has also written something approximating to thesis plays (e.g. *Chicken Soup with Barley*, 1958, *Roots*, 1959, and *I'm Talking about Jerusalem*, 1960). A subspecies of the problem play is what has been called the 'discussion play'. This is more like a debate in which characters put forward different points of view. Shaw employed this method of dramatizing issues in *Getting Married*, *The Apple Cart* and in Act III of *Man and Superman* – perhaps the best-known example.

During the 1960s and from then onwards, some playwrights developed a rather different approach to the problem play about a social issue, very different from the intense but narrow focus achieved by, for instance, Ibsen in *An Enemy of the People* (1882). They have been concerned with broad political and social issues and have been influenced by the example of agitprop drama, the Living Theater, documentary theatre and the Living Newspaper (*qq.v.*) and by such dramatists as Brecht and Ewan MacColl. The dramatists have addressed themselves (often in a spirit of protest and reform) to such matters as the class system in Britain, racism, sexism, chauvinism, Thatcherism, crime, violence, moral values, poverty and the condition of the deprived, the press, and political corruption and hypocrisy. Many of the plays have thus been about 'the state of Britain'. Outstanding among these playwrights are John McGrath, David Edgar, Howard Brenton, David Hare, Edward Bond, Howard Barker and Caryl Churchill.

third space A theoretical term coined by the postcolonial critic Homi Bhabha (1949–) to describe a space in which we can overcome the problematic claims to cultural purity and homogeneity, and embrace the hybridized nature of cultures. According to Bhabha, this is a potentially productive space which may 'open up the way to conceptualizing an *inter*national culture, based not on the exoticism of multiculturalism or the *diversity* of cultures, but on the inscription and articulation of culture's *hybridity*'. *See also* HYBRIDITY; POSTCOLONIALISM.

third theatre A term coined in 1976 by Eugenio Barba (1936–) to describe his own theatrical group, the Odin Teatret founded in 1964 in Oslo. So called by analogy with the term 'Third World' – deprived, neglected and short of money and resources. It is a kind of fringe (*q.v.*) theatre company and has a good deal in common with Theatre Laboratory and Total Theatre (*qq.v.*).

threnody (Gk 'wailing song') Originally a choral ode (*q.v.*), it changed to a monody (*q.v.*) which was strophic in form. It can now be applied to any lamentation; for instance, Tennyson's *In Memoriam* (1850) has been described as 'the great threnody of our language'. *See* COMPLAINT; DIRGE; ELEGY; EPICEDIUM; LAMENT; UBI SUNT.

thriller A broad term, perhaps no longer particularly useful for purposes of categorization, yet frequently used for a wide variety of fiction, and also for plays and films. In fiction it is a tense, exciting, tautly plotted and sometimes sensational type of novel (occasionally a short story) in which action is swift and suspense continual. Sex and violence may often play a considerable part in such a narrative, and they have tended to do so since the 1960s. *Very* broadly speaking, such fiction might include the crime novel, the police procedural, the *roman policier*, the cloak-and-dagger story, some ghost and horror stories, a multitude of novels of adventure (*qq.v.*) and, of course, what is known as the politico-military (thriller). Most of the best spy stories (*q.v.*) are *ipso facto* thrillers. Some detective stories, or forms of detective story, might also be described as thrillers.

In the broad sense the thriller is one of the most remarkable literary phenomena of the 20th c. Since the turn of the 19th c. more than six hundred writers (the vast majority of them British and American) have written thrillers of one kind and another. Some of them have been immensely prolific, publishing a hundred or more titles in their professional careers. Not a few have used several pseudonyms. Some thriller writers who were famous in the first half of the 20th c. have been out of print for many years.

The origins of the thriller go back to the Gothic novel (*q.v.*) and the 'literature of terror' which was so popular during the latter part of the 18th c. and at the beginning of the 19th c. From that period its evolution can be plotted via the development of the crime story, the ghost, horror and detective story, the so-called novel of sensation (*q.v.*) and what came to be known as Newgate fiction (*q.v.*). It was particularly developed by Edgar Allan Poe in his short stories and by Wilkie Collins in such novels as *The Woman in White* (1860) and *The Moonstone* (1868).

Near the turn of the century the modern thriller was coming of age, so to speak. Richard Haggard, A. E. W. Mason, and E. W. Hornung were prolific writers in the genre. During the early part of the 20th c. the supreme exponent of the 'pure' thriller was Edgar Wallace, who made his name with *The Four Just Men* (1906) and followed this up with a succession of gripping stories. In his era the novel of espionage and the detective story were fully established and the pulp (*q.v.*) magazines featured miscellaneous kinds of thriller.

An outstanding talent that came to the fore in the 1930s and 1940s was Eric Ambler. Regarded by many as master of the genre, he produced, over a period of fifty years, a succession of finely written and well-constructed thrillers. He remains particularly famous for *The Mask of Dimitrios* (1939). In America, in the 1920s, Dashiell Hammett established the private-eye type of crime thriller. His novel *The Maltese Falcon* (1930) has gradually established itself as a classic of its kind. His most distinguished 'successor' in the private-eye thriller form was Raymond Chandler with his seven novels, notably *The Big Sleep* (1939) and *The Long Good-Bye* (1953).

The 1950s was the era of Ian Fleming's James Bond stories, a species of cloak-and-dagger and espionage. Their enormous success was compounded by the universally popular Bond films. Many of the best thrillers from the 1950s onwards have been concerned with espionage. Pre-eminent in this field are Len Deighton and John Le Carré. During the 1960s Lionel Davidson made a big impact with several well-written and witty thrillers, such as *The Night of Wenceslas* (1960) and *Making Good Again* (1968). In the 1970s Frederick Forsyth achieved enormous success with several brilliantly constructed, well-researched and complex thrillers, notably *The Day of the Jackal* (1971) and *The Dogs of War* (1974). A consistently high standard was set by Patricia Highsmith in her suspense thrillers: stories which feature the anti-hero (*q.v.*) Tom Ripley. Scores of other writers active, with varying degrees of success, since the 1950s might be cited. More recent notable works include *The Silence of the Lambs* by Thomas Harris (1988), *The Blue Nowhere* by Jeffery Deaver (2001), *The Avenger* by Frederick Forsyth (2003), *Whiteout* by Ken Follett (2004), and Lee Child's *One Shot* (2005). The public demand for such fiction appears unabated.

In the theatre the thriller derived from the 19th c. tradition of melodrama (*q.v.*). There were a large number of successful plays of the thriller kind in the 20th c. Here again Edgar Wallace excelled with *The Ringer* (1926) and *The Case of the Frightened Lady* (1931). Other notable instances were John Willard's *The Cat and the Canary* (1922) and Agatha Christie's *Ten Little Niggers* (1943) and *The Mousetrap* (1952) – a play still running fifty-nine years later. Since the 1950s good stage thrillers have been rare, but Simon Gray's comedy thriller *Stage Struck* (1979) was a success. *See* CRIME FICTION.

time novels A term used occasionally to denote those novels which employ the stream of consciousness (*q.v.*) technique and in which the use of time, and time as a theme, is of pre-eminent importance. Famous instances are: Proust's *A la recherche du temps perdu* (1913–27), Dorothy Richardson's *Pilgrimage* (1915–67), Joyce's *Ulysses* (1922) and Thomas Mann's *Der Zauberberg* (1924). More recently there has been Anthony Powell's twelve-volume series *A Dance to the Music of Time* (named after Poussin's painting), which began with *A Question of Upbringing* (1951) and concluded with *Hearing Secret Harmonies* (1975). Time is thematically central to the sequence. Nicholas Jenkins, the narrator, observes that all human beings are driven 'at different speeds by the same Furies'. *See also* BILDUNGSROMAN; KÜNSTLER-ROMAN; ROMAN CYCLE; ROMAN-FLEUVE; SAGA NOVEL; TIME PLAY.

time play A loose category for a form of drama which in some way exploits chronological sequence by various means: the flashback, and what might be called the 'flash-forward'. It entails the exploitation of dramatic convention (*q.v.*). Numerous playwrights have used various devices. For instance, in *The Winter's Tale* the Chorus asks us to accept the fact that sixteen years have elapsed since Perdita was 'lost'. J. B. Priestley (1894–1984) is the most notable example of a dramatist who experimented with the space/time continuum. In this he was influenced by J. W. Dunne's theories expounded in *An Experiment with Time* (1927) and *The Serial Universe* (1934). Priestley wrote four plays in which he experimented with space/time: *I Have Been Here Before* (1937), *Time and the Conways* (1937), *Johnson over Jordan* (1939) and *An Inspector Calls* (1946). In *Time and the Conways*, for instance, he ingeniously allows eighteen years to elapse between Acts I and II, and in the third act reverts to 1919. Many writers have been deeply interested in the nature of time. H. G. Wells is an obvious example. Another is Graham Greene, who, in his autobiographical *Ways of Escape*, wonders whether or not it is possible to take symbols from the future as well as from the past. Writers of science fiction (*q.v.*) are particularly preoccupied with the question of time.

tirade (F 'volley of words') A long speech, usually vehement, and perhaps abusive and censorious. Timon delivers several remarkable tirades in Act IV of Shakespeare's *Timon of Athens* (*c.* 1607).

tmesis (Gk 'a cutting') The separation of the parts of a word by the insertion of another word or words. Not unusual in abusive speech. For example: 'Neverthebloodyless, I won't accept that.'

tonada *See* TONADILLA.

tonadilla *Tonada* is a Spanish term for a type of ballad poem performed in the intervals between acts of *autos sacramentales* (*q.v.*). They were often bawdy or obscene. The diminutive *tonadilla* came to denote an operetta with two to four characters and lasting about fifteen minutes. They were presented between the acts of serious plays in the 18th c. *See also* ENTREMÉS.

tone The reflection of a writer's attitude (especially towards his readers), manner, mood and moral outlook in his work; even, perhaps, the way his personality pervades the work. The counterpart of tone of voice in speech, which may be friendly, detached, pompous, officious, intimate, bantering and so forth. For example, in the following poem by David Holbrook *Living? Our Supervisors Will Do That For Us!* the skilfully contrived rhythm almost slouches and preserves the tune of slightly jerky, elliptical speech. The shrugging, 'throw-away' language, very colloquial, suggests laconic detachment. As a sketch of two contrasting characters it is most adroit in its economy and largely sympathetic to both:

> Dankwerts, scholarship boy from the slums,
> One of many, studied three years for the Tripos,
> Honours, English; grew a beard, imitated the gesture
> And the insistent deliberate (but not dogmatic)
> 'There!' of his supervisor. For a time
> The mimesis was startling. Dankwerts knew
> Uncannily what was good, what bad.
> Life and earning a living, extra muros, for a time afterwards,
> Left him hard up: people in their ambiguity
> Nuisances. A bracing need for self-justification
> (And spot cash) drove some of the nonsense out of him:
> He found a foothold in films, the evening papers,
> With his photograph, up to the ears in steaks, or ivy,
> In 'art' magazines. Passing over the metropolis
> He ejaculates like a satellite, evaporates, and falls,
> Albeit on to a fat bank balance of amoral earnings.
>
> Whereas his supervisor can be seen any Friday
> Walking up Trumpington Street with an odd movement of the feet,
> Still looking like an old corm, lissom, and knowing
> Uncannily what's good, what's bad,
> And probably rather hard up out of the bargain.

tone colour Jargon for the auditory quality of speech sounds, what Ezra Pound meant by melopoeia (*q.v.*). It covers kinaesthetic and synaesthetic experience. For instance, despair may be a 'black' word; hope, a 'white'. We speak of a 'hard' tone and a 'soft' tone. Words may seem 'smooth' or 'rough'. *Mellifluous* is 'soft' and euphonious, whereas *crag* is 'hard' and harsh. *See* EUPHONY; LOGOPOEIA; ONOMATOPOEIA; SYNAESTHESIA.

tongue-twister Associated with nonsense verse, nursery rhyme and patter songs (*qq.v.*) the tongue-twister is an alliterative jingle (*q.v.*) of some antiquity. Also known as a tongue-tripper. The following is a fairly well-known example:

> Theophilus Thistledown, the successful thistle sifter,
> In sifting a sieve of unsifted thistles,

Thrust three thousand thistles
Through the thick of his thumb.
If, then, Theophilus Thistledown, the successful thistle sifter,
In sifting a sieve full of unsifted thistles,
Thrust three thousand thistles
Through the thick of his thumb,
See that thou, in sifting a sieve of unsifted thistles,
Do not get the unsifted thistles stuck in thy tongue.

topographical poetry   Writing of Denham in *Lives of the Poets* (1779–81) Johnson aptly described this genre as 'local poetry, of which the fundamental subject is some particular landscape, to be poetically described, with the addition of such embellishments as may be supplied by historical retrospection, or incidental meditation'. One of the earliest examples was, in fact, Sir John Denham's *Cooper's Hill* (1642). In the next 150 years the genre flourished in England (it seems to be a very English phenomenon) like a counterpart to landscape painting. Not a few of them are what are known as 'prospect poems': the poet views a broad scene from a high vantage point and describes, for instance, a park or estate (perhaps in the hope of gaining patronage from a rich and powerful owner who was very likely to belong to the peerage). Apart from one or two slight pieces by Lady Winchilsea (e.g. *Fanscomb Barn* (1713)), some of the principal works were: Pope's *Windsor Forest* (1713); Samuel Garth's *Claremont* (1715); Dyer's *Grongar Hill* (1726), one of the most agreeable poems of the kind; James Thomson's delightful poem *The Seasons* (1726–30), which Wordsworth later remarked offered new images of 'external nature'; Gray's *Ode on a Distant Prospect of Eton College* (1742); Collins's *Ode on the Popular Superstitions of the Highlands of Scotland* (written in 1749, but not published until 1788); Richard Jago's *Edge-hill* (1767); Goldsmith's *The Deserted Village* (1770); plus several works by George Crabbe, who might be described as a regional poet of East Suffolk: most notably, *The Village* (1783), *The Parish Register* (1807), *The Borough* (1810), *Tales* (1812) and *Tales of the Hall* (1819). Wordsworth also wrote topographical poetry; an obvious example is *Tintern Abbey* (1798). After Wordsworth and Crabbe few seriously attempted the form on any scale. However, one encounters the occasional poem which is in the general tradition, not infrequently displaying nostalgia and elegiac regret for a vanishing rural scene, and in the 20th c. Sir John Betjeman (who remarked on his 'topographical predilection') achieved something of a revival of such poetry with many evocative descriptions (tinged with melancholy) of rural, urban, suburban and provincial scenes. Ted Hughes also wrote two memorable poems of the topographical type in the shape of *Remains of Elmet* (1979) and *River* (1983). *See also* PASTORAL; CHOROGRAPHY; TOPOTHESIA.

topothesia   (Gk 'description of a place') The description of an imaginary place. *See* CHOROGRAPHY.

tornada A short concluding stanza, similar to the *envoi* (*q.v.*), added to Old Provençal poems by way of complimentary dedication to a patron or friend. *See also* CHANSON.

total theatre The German term *Totaltheater* was first used in the mid-1920s for a form of theatrical presentation planned by Walter Gropius for the director Erwin Piscator (1893–1966). Piscator's approach was highly individual. He altered texts to suit his own ends and was the first to introduce film and animated cartoons on stage to speed up the action. He was in favour of spectacle to get his messages (often propagandist) across. The text was subordinated to effects which could be achieved by arresting lighting, music, dance, acrobatics, startling sets and costumes. All the mechanical resources of the theatre were put to use. Total theatre developed into epic theatre (*q.v.*). In France the concept of total theatre was put into practice by Jean-Louis Barrault in the 1950s. One of his notable productions was Claudel's *Christophe Colombe* (1953). More recently the Italian director Luca Ronconi has enlarged the possibilities of total theatre by involving spectators and audience in the action. For example, his travelling version of Ariosto's *Orlando Furioso* (1970). In England the leading exponent was Joan Littlewood at the Theatre Workshop. One of her most successful productions was *Oh! What a Lovely War* (1963). There have been many others in the total theatre style. One of the most brilliant and spectacular was Bill Bryden's version of the *Wakefield Mystery Plays* in the promenade productions at the National Theatre and the Lyceum in 1985–6.

touchstone A touchstone is a dark flinty schist, jasper or basanite, and so called because gold is tried by it. Matthew Arnold used the word in his essay *The Study of Poetry* (1880) in connection with literary criteria and standards:

> Indeed there can be no more useful help for discovering what poetry belongs to the class of the truly excellent, and can therefore do us most good, than to have always in one's mind lines and expressions of the great masters, and to apply them as a touchstone to other poetry. Of course we are not to require this other poetry to resemble them; it may be very dissimilar. But if we have any tact we shall find them, when we have lodged them well in our minds, an infallible touchstone for detecting the presence or absence of high poetic quality, and also the degree of this quality, in all other poetry which we may place beside them.

Arnold goes on to quote lines from Homer, Dante, Shakespeare and Milton to demonstrate his point. He suggests that his touchstone method should be the basis of a 'real' rather than a 'historic' or 'personal' estimate of poetry. He also contends that a passage has 'high poetic quality' if it has high seriousness and the grand style. Such a view is now regarded as somewhat limiting and exclusive.

Arnold was by no means the first critic to have suggested such criteria. John Dennis (1657–1734) had presented a comparable point of view in *The*

Advancement and Reformation of Modern Poetry (1701) and *The Grounds of Criticism in Poetry* (1704).

tour de force (F 'turn of force') As a literary term it may be applied to a work which provides an outstanding illustration of a writer's skill and mastery; a sort of 'one-off' brilliant display. Among modern examples one might suggest: Hemingway's short story *The Short and Happy Life of Francis Macomber* (1938); Arthur Koestler's novel *Darkness at Noon* (1940); Orwell's fable *Animal Farm* (1945); Anthony Burgess's novel *A Clockwork Orange* (1962); Daniel Keyes's short story *Flowers for Algernon* (1965); and Vikram Seth's extraordinary 'novel' *The Golden Gate* (1986) – a narrative which consists of 590 sonnets in rhyming tetrameters.

trace A term used in a particular sense by the French philosopher Jacques Derrida (1930–2004) to signify his view that there is no simple sense in which linguistic signs are either present or absent. According to Derrida, every sign (e.g. a word such as 'dwelling') contains a 'trace' of other signs which differ from itself. But, paradoxically, the 'trace' is *not* there; it is *potentially inherent*, or *present by virtue of its absence*, just as absence denotes the possibility of presence. No sign is complete in itself. One sign leads to another via the 'trace' – indefinitely. The word/sign 'dwelling' carries with it scores of traces (i.e. connotations) and other signs associated with dwelling. The 'trace' is one aspect of Derrida's theory of *différance* (*q.v.*). In the series of interviews published as *Positions* (1972, trans. 1981) he elaborates:

> The play of differences involves syntheses and referrals [*renvois*] which prevent there from being at any moment or in any way a simple element which is *present* in and of itself and refers only to itself. Whether in written or spoken discourse, no element can function as a sign without relating to another element which itself is not simply present. This linkage means that each element – phoneme or grapheme – is constituted with reference to the trace in it of the other elements of the sequence or system . . . Nothing, in either the elements or the system, is anywhere ever simply present or absent.

See CONNOTATION; DECONSTRUCTION; DENOTATION; DISSEMINATION; POSTSTRUCTURALISM; SIGNIFIER/SIGNIFIED; STRUCTURALISM; SYNTAGMATIC/PARADIGMATIC.

tract Usually a short pamphlet (*q.v.*) on a religious or political subject. Two famous examples are the *Marprelate Tracts* issued in 1588–9, which were an attack on the bishops and a defence of Presbyterian discipline, and *Tracts for the Times* (1833–41), a series on religious subjects written by, among others, Cardinal Newman, Keble, R. H. Froude and Pusey. Their object was to revive certain doctrines of the Church. *See* OXFORD MOVEMENT.

tractarian movement *See* OXFORD MOVEMENT.

tradition This denotes the inherited past which is available for the writer to study and learn from. Thus, the writer's native language, literary forms, codes, devices, conventions (*q.v.*) and various cultures from the past. We may, for example, refer to the neoclassical tradition or the French Classical tradition or to the tradition of the English essay, or the Irish tradition of dramatic comedy, or the Scottish ballad tradition, or the Welsh tradition of religious lyric poetry and many others, and in each case mean something fairly specific in spirit, matter and style. Anything traditional is established, has often been tried and is constantly returned to.

And all writers begin with some sort of tradition behind them (even if only that provided by their own language) and every writer in some way modifies or influences that tradition, even when being imitative. Though some poems by Keats might have been written by Milton, and some by Dylan Thomas are almost indistinguishable from work by Gerard Manley Hopkins, there are differences.

Arbitrary classification of writers according to differing traditions is obviously a more perilous undertaking, but, bearing in mind the primary meaning of tradition (that which is passed down from generation to generation through custom and practice), we may distinguish certain traditions in English poetry (or poetry written by English-speaking peoples). Basically, there are (a) the native tradition, as exemplified in the work of Chaucer and the Scottish Chaucerians, Wyatt, Shakespeare (and the majority of his contemporary poets and dramatists), Donne and most of the 17th c. lyric poets, and, thereafter, Burns, Blake, Clare, Barnes, Browning, Hopkins, Yeats, Pound, Eliot, W. H. Auden, Dylan Thomas and Ted Hughes – to mention only some of the major writers, and; (b) the Italianate tradition of Surrey, Sidney, Spenser, Milton, Keats, Shelley, Tennyson, Matthew Arnold and Francis Thompson. Linking these two, and owing a good deal to both, is the neoclassical tradition from the Renaissance through to the 18th c., whose finest representatives are Dryden, Pope, Johnson and Crabbe, though all four are peculiarly *English* poets. Pope, for example, is much nearer in spirit and style to Donne than to Tennyson. As always there are poets who appear not to belong to (or who are not easily identified with) any specific tradition. Wordsworth, Coleridge and Byron are obvious examples.

Among prose writers definite traditions are much less distinguishable. For example, in the novel the main tradition seems to lie through the work of Jane Austen, George Eliot, Charles Dickens, Thomas Hardy, Henry James, Conrad, Arnold Bennett and D. H. Lawrence, but clearly this is not a tradition in which one could include major writers like James Joyce, Dorothy Richardson, Virginia Woolf, William Faulkner and Samuel Beckett, and dozens of others who have flourished recently.

traductio *See* PARONOMASIA; PUN.

tragedy (Gk 'goat song') In the first place it almost certainly denoted a form of ritual sacrifice accompanied by a choral song in honour of Dionysus, the god of the fields and the vineyards. Out of this ritual developed Greek dramatic tragedy. The Greeks were the first of the tragedians and it was upon their work only that Aristotle formed his conclusions.

In his *Poetics*, Aristotle defined tragedy as:

The imitation of an action that is serious and also, as having magnitude, complete in itself; in language with pleasurable accessories . . . ; in a dramatic, not in a narrative form; with incidents arousing pity and fear, wherewith to accomplish its catharsis of such emotions.

Aristotle saw plot as the most crucial element of tragedy, more important than character. He spoke of the tragic hero as:

a man not pre-eminently virtuous and just, whose misfortune, however, is brought upon him not by vice and depravity but by some error of judgement, of the number of those in the enjoyment of great reputation and prosperity; e.g. Oedipus, Thyestes, and the men of note of similar families.

(Bywater's translation)

Since then, Classical Greek and Renaissance tragedy has tended to be a form of drama concerned with the fortunes and misfortunes, and, ultimately, the disasters, that befall human beings of title, power and position. For example, Oedipus, Antigone, Hamlet, Romeo and Juliet. By participating vicariously in the grief, pain and fear of the tragic hero or heroine, the spectator, in Aristotle's words, experiences pity and fear and is purged.

The principal writers of Greek tragedy were Aeschylus, Sophocles and Euripides. Aeschylus wrote about ninety plays, of which only a few are extant, namely *Persians*, *Prometheus Bound*, and the Oresteian trilogy which comprises *Agamemnon*, *Choephori* and *Eumenides*. Sophocles was even more prolific. He is credited with 120 plays; however, only seven of his works are extant, namely *Antigone*, *Oedipus Rex*, *Electra*, *Ajax*, *Trachiniae*, *Philoctetes* and *Oedipus at Colonus*. The output of Euripides was almost as great. Eighty or ninety plays are ascribed to him, and eighteen of these survive.

By 400 BC Greek tragedy seems to have run itself out. There is relatively little of note in Roman tragedy except for the work of Seneca, which, fifteen hundred years after his death, was to have a very considerable influence on Elizabethan tragedy.

During the latter part of the 16th c. and until approximately 1640, dramatists paid less attention to the Classical rules and conventions and worked out what was suitable for their individual needs. In rough chronological order some of the more famous and notable works are Marlowe's *Dr Faustus* (c. 1588); several major works by Shakespeare, namely, *Romeo and Juliet* (c. 1595), *Othello* (1604), *King Lear* (1606), *Macbeth* (c. 1606) and *Antony and Cleopatra* (c. 1606–7); Ben Jonson's *Sejanus* (1603) and his *Catiline* (1611); Webster's *The Duchess of Malfi* (c. 1613–14); Beaumont and Fletcher's *The Maid's Tragedy* (c. 1610); John Ford's *'Tis Pity She's a Whore* (1633).

During approximately the same period tragedy burgeoned in Spain, where the main writers were Lope de Vega (1562–1635), Molina (1571–1648) and

Calderón (1600–81), and in France, where the two finest exponents were Corneille and Racine.

From c. 1700 onwards relatively little tragedy of note was written. Nevertheless, during the 18th and 19th c. a large number of European playwrights did experiment with tragic formulae. Among the more notable achievements, one should mention Addison's *Cato* (1713); Johnson's *Irene* (1749); Schiller's *Don Carlos* (1787); Shelley's *Cenci* (written in 1818, but first performed in 1886); Victor Hugo's *Hernani* (1830); Büchner's incomplete *Woyzeck* (1836–7).

Near the end of the 19th c. two Scandinavian dramatists brought about a wholly unexpected revolution of tragic form and subject. Their tragedies were unlike anything written hitherto, and, like many that followed, far removed from Classical and Aristotelian concepts. Their tragic vision revealed a society that was spiritually and morally corrupt and decadent. Some of their major works in the tragic mode were: Strindberg's *The Father* (1887) and *Miss Julie* (1889); Ibsen's *A Doll's House* (1879) and *Hedda Gabler* (1891).

Since then a large number of dramatists have attempted different kinds of tragedy; or serious plays which are tragic in tone, import and intention. Two powerful influences in the 20th c. theatre were the theatre of the absurd and the theatre of silence (*qq.v.*). Other notable instances are: Synge's *Riders to the Sea* (1904); Eugene O'Neill's *Emperor Jones* (1920); Lorca's *Blood Wedding* (1933); T. S. Eliot's *Murder in the Cathedral* (1935); Anouilh's *Antigone* (1944); Tennessee Williams's *A Streetcar Named Desire* (1947); Arthur Miller's *Death of a Salesman* (1948); and John McGrath's *Events while Guarding the Bofors Gun* (1966).

The concept of tragedy has changed greatly since the 16th c. We now have the grief, the misery, the disaster, of the ordinary person. Not a king or a queen or a prince, but an everyday mother, tramp, peasant or salesman. Nowadays the potentially tragic dramatist is more likely to express the sadness and wretchedness of man's position by understatement; even to the point of saying nothing. For further reading, see Clifford Leech, *Tragedy* (2002). *See* ANAGNORISIS; DRAME; HAMARTIA; HUBRIS; METATHEATRE; PERIPETEIA; TRAGIC FLAW.

tragedy of blood *See* REVENGE TRAGEDY.

tragic flaw Traditionally that defect in a tragic hero or heroine which leads to their downfall. To all intents and purposes a synonym for the Greek *hamartia* (*q.v.*). The *locus classicus* is *Hamlet*, I, iv, 23–36. *See also* HUBRIS; TRAGEDY.

tragic irony *See* IRONY.

tragicomedy The term derives from a reference by Plautus (254–184 BC) to the unconventional mixture of kings, gods and servants in his own play *Amphitruo* as *tragico-comoedia*. However, the idea of tragicomedy was not new even then since Euripides's *Alcestis* and *Iphigenia* (both tragedies) had happy endings; and Aristotle had made it clear in *Poetics* that audiences preferred the kind of endings where poetic justice (*q.v.*) was seen to be done.

From the late Middle Ages (or early Renaissance) there are two roughly identifiable genres of tragicomedy in drama: the neoclassical and the popular. Some Italian playwrights, of whom the best known is Giraldi Cinthio, wrote several tragedies with happy endings, which he called *tragedie miste* ('mixed tragedies'). By the end of the 16th c. these two kinds had drawn together and were more or less indistinguishable. By this time, anyway, we find an increasing mingling of tragic and comic elements, the use of comic relief (*q.v.*) in tragedy, and what might be called tragic aggravation or heightening in comedy.

A different kind of tragicomedy was that devised by the Italian Guarini (1537–1612), author of the pastoral drama *Il pastor fido* (*c.* 1585). Guarini drew on the pastoral (*q.v.*) tradition. Like Cinthio he had characters of rank and nobility and also tragic elements; but he also presented comic episodes and characters and used appropriate comic diction. *Il pastor fido* had a considerable vogue in England in the 17th c. It was often translated and also acted in a Latin version at Cambridge. The dramatist most influenced by Guarini in England was John Fletcher, whose version of Guarini was *The Faithful Shepherdess* (*c.* 1608). Beaumont and Fletcher between them created several tragicomedies for courtly audiences in private theatres.

Shakespeare also wrote tragicomedies. All are different from each other and from anything that preceded them: namely, *Troilus and Cressida* (1602), *All's Well that Ends Well, Measure for Measure* (1604), *The Winter's Tale* (1609–10), *Cymbeline* (*c.* 1610) and *The Tempest* (*c.* 1611). Other works of note were Beaumont and Fletcher's *Philaster or Love Lies Bleeding* (*c.* 1610) and Chapman's *The Widow's Tears* (1612). John Marston, Thomas Heywood, Massinger, Shirley, Dryden and Davenant also wrote tragicomedies.

It is noticeable that by the turn of the 16th c. something like a theory of tragicomedy is evolving. We find John Florio referring to 'tragi comedia' and Sir Philip Sidney, in his *Apologie for Poetrie* (1595) speaking of 'mungrell Tragi-comedie'. And William Drummond of Hawthornden refers to 'this tragi-comedy, called life'.

The pioneer of tragicomedy in France was Robert Gamier (1544–90), who wrote *Bradamante* (1582). Something like two hundred tragicomedies were produced in France in the period *c.* 1620–70. Outstanding examples were Rotrou's *Don Bernard de Cabrère* (1647), Corneille's *Don Sanche d'Aragon* (1649) and Molière's *Le Misanthrope* (1666).

With the demise of verse drama, dramatic tragicomedy virtually disappeared, but occasionally a playwright has combined tragic and comic elements in such a way as to warrant his work being called tragicomedy. Notable examples are Rostand's *Cyrano de Bergerac* (1897); Chekhov's *Uncle Vanya* (1900) and *The Cherry Orchard* (1904); J. M. Synge's *The Shadow of the Glen* (1903); and Samuel Beckett's *Waiting for Godot* (1955), which the author described as a tragicomedy. More recently, David Hare's *Secret Rapture* (1989) might also come into the category.

But distinctions between tragicomedy, black comedy (*q.v.*) and what Jean Anouilh calls *pièces noires* and *pièces grinçantes* are difficult to make. From the 18th c. onwards the French have tended to use the term *drame* (*q.v.*) to denote a serious play which contains some comedy; and there are literally hundreds of plays extant from, say, 1800 which are now loosely called 'dramas' because they do not fit into any easily identifiable category.

One may conclude that the Elizabethan and Jacobean conception of life as a tragicomedy was an attempt to balance and reconcile a conflict of vision. This would help to explain the mordant wit and the more macabre elements; also the sudden and sombre events which unexpectedly overshadow the radiance of plays like *Much Ado about Nothing*. It is a commonplace that surprisingly little tragedy of note has been produced since the 17th c. whereas there have been many excellent plays with tragic qualities and tragic potentialities.

It should also be noted that since early in the 20th c. the theatre of the absurd (*q.v.*) has been a major influence in drama; perhaps partly as a result of this, the 'darker' comedies of the Elizabethan and Jacobean playwrights have become particularly popular.

transatlantic   Recently the term has been used in relation to modernism (*q.v.*) as offering a more expansive framework across national boundaries than an isolated study of British or American modernism. It thus emphasizes transnational networks, circulation and exchange of ideas on both sides of the ocean in modernist cultural production. The term 'transatlantic' also refers to the transatlantic slave trade in which both Britain and America were heavily involved from the 16th c. to the abolition in the 19th c. The term also invites consideration of other transatlantic routes, such as the Caribbean, Africa and Latin America, which point beyond canonical works of modernism, thus providing a more complex picture of the intersection and literary exchange of ideas during the period. For example, the work of some black intellectuals may be read comparatively in relation to Irish literary nationalism. In his book *The Black Atlantic: Modernity and Double Consciousness* (1993), Paul Gilroy has examined African-American travels to Europe. His notion of 'the black Atlantic' – a diasporic space of historical and cultural ruptures, and subsequent cultural and artistic links created between the people of African descent dispersed by the slave trade – has been highly influential. Finally, when the term 'transatlantic' is coupled with modernism, it may also enable a critical examination of the ways in which the so-called 'primitive' cultures and artefacts of Africa or Native Americans played a central role in the development of European and American modernist aesthetics. *See also* ABOLITIONIST LITERATURE; MODERNISM; WORLD LITERATURE.

transcendentalism   A New England movement which flourished from *c.* 1835 to 1860. It had its roots in romanticism (*q.v.*) and in the post-Kantian idealism by which Coleridge was influenced. It had a considerable influence on American art and literature. Basically religious, it emphasized the role and importance of the individual conscience, and the value of intuition in matters of moral guidance and inspiration. The actual term was coined by opponents of the movement, but accepted by its members (e.g. Ralph Waldo

Emerson, 1803–82, one of the leaders, published *The Transcendentalist* in 1841). The group were also social reformers. Some of the members, besides Emerson, were famous and included Bronson Alcott, Henry David Thoreau and Nathaniel Hawthorne.

transferred epithet   *See* HYPALLAGE.

transgender studies   Meaning 'across gender', the term 'transgender' has since the early 1990s been used to denote a broad range of non-normative gendered identities and behaviours, including transsexuals, butch lesbians, transvestites, drag queens/kings and intersexed people. Previously the term, which first began to be used in the early 1980s, denoted a more narrowly based identity category, being the preferred term of males who chose to live full-time in female roles without seeking gender-reassignment surgery. Since the 1990s, transgender studies has flourished, particularly in the US. In a similar fashion to gay and lesbian criticism (*q.v.*), the discipline takes transgender identities and experience to be its primary object of inquiry, and conceives of itself as being at the service of transgender communities.

One of the key motivations of transgender studies has been to challenge the dominance of the medical establishment, which has tended to view transsexuality as a condition needing correction. Transgender theorists have drawn readily from queer theory (*q.v.*), and particularly the concept of performativity (*q.v.*), for this line of thinking has helped to challenge received notions about the stability and coherence of normative gender categories. However, theorists such as Jay Prosser have argued that queer theory's usefulness is limited, for it is too little concerned with the materiality of the body, something which transgender subjects all too often experience in traumatic ways. Prosser argues that the distinctiveness of transgender studies has to do with the special attention it pays to how gender is *experienced* (*see* AFFECT). Some theorists, such as Leslie Feinburg, have sought to challenge the presumption in the West of the naturalness of gender dimorphism by exploring the roles of alternatively gendered figures in other societies and historical periods, such as the *hijras* of India and Native American *berdaches*.

Examples of influential cultural material by transgender artists are the writings and performance art (*q.v.*) of activist Kate Bornstein, Del LaGrace Volcano's photography depicting female masculinity, and Feinburg's semi-autobiographical *Stone Butch Blues* (1992), which combines a lesbian coming-out story (*q.v.*), an account of transsexual 'passing', and a transgender identity narrative. Many works of fiction depicting transgender characters and themes have been written by non-transgender authors. Two recent examples are Jeffrey Eugenides's *Middlesex* (2002) and Jackie Kay's *Trumpet* (2004). Some earlier novels, including Radclyffe Hall's *The Well of Loneliness* (1928), which is usually seen as a landmark lesbian novel, have been reappraised as articulating transgender experience. *See also* GAY AND LESBIAN CRITICISM; QUEER THEORY.

transgressio   *See* HYPERBATON.

transhumanism *See* POSTHUMANISM.

translatio *See* METAPHOR.

translation Despite the truth of the Italian aphorism 'traduttore traditore', there have been many praiseworthy and successful (and, in some cases, super-lative) translations across a large number of languages – not least from foreign tongues into English. Three basic kinds of translation may be distinguished: (a) a more or less literally exact rendering of the original meaning at the expense of the syntax, grammar, colloquialism and idiom of the language into which it is put (e.g. Lang, Leaf and Myers's famous translation of the *Iliad*, 1883); (b) an attempt to convey the spirit, sense and style of the original by finding equivalents in syntax, grammar and idiom (e.g. Dryden's *Virgil*, 1697); (c) a fairly free adaptation which retains the original spirit but may consider-ably alter style, structure, grammar and idiom (e.g. Edward FitzGerald's free versions of six of Calderón's plays, 1853; the same author's version of *Omar Khayyám*, 1859).

Notable landmarks in the history of translation are: King Alfred's transla-tion of Boethius's *De Consolatione* and of Bede's *Ecclesiastical History* (9th c.); Luther's version of the Bible (1522–34); William Adlington's translation of *The Golden Ass* by Apuleius (1566); North's version of *Plutarch's Lives* (1579); Marlowe's of Ovid's *Elegies* (1590); George Chapman's of the *Iliad* (1598–1611); Florio's of Montaigne's *Essays* (1603); The English Authorized Version of the Bible (1611); Dryden's *Virgil* (1687); Pope's *Iliad* (1715–20); Schlegel's *Shakespeare* (1797–1810); Jowett's version of Plato (1871); Seamus Heaney's *Beowulf* (1999). Other outstanding translators are: C. M. R. Leconte de Lisle, Ezra Pound, Arthur Waley, Scott Moncrieff, E. V. Rieu and Robert Graves.

transmutatio *See* METONYMY.

trauma theory An interdisciplinary theoretical body that draws from psychoanalytic, feminist, and poststructuralist discourses and focuses on the study of both personal trauma (e.g. abuse, mental illness) and collective experiences of trauma (e.g. the Holocaust, slavery, genocide). The theory offers a framework for understanding experiences that – by definition – over-whelm the coping mechanisms of individuals, and involves enquiry into the relationship between memory and truth and the ways that testimony can aid the recovery process. Key theorists in the field include Cathy Caruth, Shoshana Felman, Dori Laub and Dominick LaCapra. *See also* FEMINIST CRITICISM; POSTSTRUCTURALISM; PSYCHOANALYTIC CRITICISM.

travel book A neglected and much varied genre of great antiquity to which many famous, more or less professional or 'full-time' writers have contrib-uted, but which has also been enriched by a number of occasional writers. For the most part these have been diplomats, scholars, missionaries, soldiers of fortune, doctors, explorers and sailors. The genre subsumes works of exploration and adventure as well as guides and accounts of sojourns in foreign lands.

Some of the earliest records of travels come from Egypt; for instance, an anonymous 14th c. BC record known as *The Journeying of the Master of the Captains of Egypt*. From China we have early accounts of travels in India by Fa-Hian (*c.* AD 399–414), and by Shaman Hwui-Li (*c.* AD 630) of journeys in the Far East. A notable Arabian traveller was Ibn Battutah (1304–78), who for twenty-eight years travelled round the Far East, India, Africa, South Russia, Egypt, Spain and elsewhere and who in 1354 compiled a copious description of his journeyings.

These are only a handful of the many who, in Classical times, in the Middle Ages and during the Renaissance period, explored the then known world and opened up the unknown.

From the 16th c. onwards the Near East, the Middle East and the Far East, Asia and parts of Africa were increasingly explored and colonized by the Europeans, and the world of the Americas was gradually charted. As the world became more navigable, so travel books of every kind proliferated.

In the last half of the 16th c. a number of accounts of exploratory journeys began to appear. A notable example is Hakluyt's *Principall Navigations, Voiages, and Discoveries of the English Nation* (1598). In the 18th c. travel became easier (hence the popularity of the Grand Tour, *q.v.*) and thus there is a steadily increasing number of works. The following are a few of the more notable instances: Montesquieu's *Lettres Persanes* (1721); Defoe's *A Tour through the Whole Island of Great Britain* (1724–6); Lady Mary Wortley Montagu's *Letters . . . During Travels in Europe, Asia and Africa* (1763–7); Smollett's *Travels in France and Italy* (1766); Sterne's *Sentimental Journey through France and Italy*; plus many other works by European writers.

Early in the 19th c. Alexander von Humboldt, the great German explorer, geographer, botanist and mineralogist, began to publish the voluminous accounts of his global travels. All told they amount to the biggest body of travel literature in existence composed by a single person. Between 1808 and 1827 he published thirty-five volumes, finally gathered together under the title *Voyage aux régions équinoxiales du Nouveau Continent*.

In the 19th and 20th c. there was a positive flood of one sort and another which shows no signs of abating. Since the Second World War, 'armchair' travelling has become an occupation for many people; and, as travelling has become easier and easier, so people read more books about the places they have heard of, have been to or are going to.

Here follow just a few of some of the outstanding works of the last 200-odd years: Nikolai Karamzin's *Letters of a Russian Traveller* (1801), translated into English in 1957; Lamartine's *Souvenirs, impressions, pensées et paysages pendant un voyage en Orient* (1835); Charles Darwin's *Voyage of the Beagle* (1839); Sir Henry Stanley's *How I Found Livingstone* (1872) and *Through the Dark Continent* (1878); Mary Kingsley's *Travels in West Africa* (1897); Edith Durham's *High Albania* (1909); Rebecca West's *Black Lamb and Grey Falcon* (1942); Eric Newby's *A Short Walk in the Hindu Kush* (1958), which he followed with *Slowly Down the Ganges* (1966) and *The Big Red Train Ride* (1978); V. S. Naipaul's *An Area of Darkness* (1964), which he followed with *A Turn in the South* (1989); Bruce Chatwin's *In Patagonia* (1978) and *The Songlines* (1987); Pico Iyer's *Video Night in Kathmandu: And Other Reports from the Not-so-Far East* (1988); Bill Bryson's *Neither Here nor There: Travels in Europe* (1991); Cees Nooteboom's *Berlijn 1989/2009* (2009); and their numerous other travel books. This selection suggests the remarkable richness and variety of travel literature.

In 1997, Tim Youngs launched a journal *Studies in Travel Writing*, and has played an important role in the development of travel writing studies as a discipline. Scholarly research on travel texts has blossomed over the last couple of decades. Of particular note has been the research concerned with women's travel writing and the relationship between travel books and European colonial expansion. Mary Louise Pratt's *Imperial Eyes: Travel Writing and Transculturation* (1992) and Sara Mills's *Discourses of Difference: Analysis of Women's Travel Writing and Colonialism* (1991) are notable examples. *See also* CONTACT ZONE; GUIDEBOOK.

travesty *See* BURLESQUE.

treatise A formal work containing a systematic examination of a subject and its principles. The commonest subjects are philosophical, religious, literary, political, scientific and mathematical. Notable examples of the genre are: Aristotle's *Poetics* and *Metaphysics* (4th c. BC); Quintilian's *Institutio* (1st c. AD); Peter Lombard's *Sententiae* (*Liber Sententiarum*) (1145–50); Calvin's *Institution de la religion chrétienne* (1535); Sir Philip Sidney's *Apologie for Poetrie* (1595); Francis Bacon's *Novum Organum* (1620); William Harvey's *Exercitatio Anatomica de Motu Cordis et Sanguinis in Animalibus* (1628); Isaac Newton's *Principia Mathematica* (1687); Locke's *Essay concerning Human Understanding* (1690); Bossuet's *Traité de la connaissance de Dieu et de soimême* (1722); David Hume's *Treatise of Human Nature* (1739–40); Montesquieu's *Esprit des lois*; Rousseau's *Du contrat social* (1762); Bentham's *Introduction to Principles of Morals and Legislation* (1789); Malthus's *An Essay on the Principle of Population* (1798); J. S. Mill's *System of Logic* (1843) and his *Principles of Political Economy* (1848); Darwin's *Origin of Species* (1859); A. N. Whitehead's *A Treatise of Universal Algebra* (1898) and his *The Concept of Nature* (1920); Louis Aragon's *Traité du Style* (1928). *See also* TRACT; PAMPHLET.

tremendismo A characteristic of some Spanish fiction since the late 1940s. Authors using *tremendista* techniques stress violence and terror, the violent tendencies of modern society and the damaging influences of social and religious upbringing on behaviour. Early notable examples of novels of this kind are Camilo José Cela's *La familia de Pascual Duarte* (1942) and Carmen Laforet's *Nada* (1944).

triad (Gk 'three') In Classical Greek poetry a group of three lyric stanzas: strophe, antistrophe and epode (*qq.v.*). This arrangement was probably introduced by Stesichorus (*c.* 650–*c.* 555 BC) and was followed by Simonides and Pindar. *See* ODE.

tribe of Ben Or the sons of Ben. A title adopted by a group of English poets early in the 17th c. who were considerably influenced by Ben Jonson – and thus by Classicism (*q.v.*). Their lyrics were often epigrammatical, witty and satirical and were modelled on the lyrics of *The Greek Anthology*. The main members of the 'tribe' were Herrick, Carew, Sir John Suckling, Lovelace, Randolph and Godolphin. *See also* METAPHYSICAL; SCHOOL OF SPENSER.

tribrach (Gk 'three short') A metrical foot containing three unstressed syllables: ◡ ◡ ◡. Usually a resolved iamb or trochee (*qq.v.*) and seldom found as an independent foot.

trilogy (Gk 'set of three') A group of three tragedies presented by individual authors at the drama festivals in Athens in the 5th c. BC. The practice was introduced by Aeschylus, whose *Oresteia* is the only complete trilogy extant from that time. More recent examples are Shakespeare's *Henry VI* (*c.* 1592); Schiller's *Wallenstein* (1799); Eugene O'Neill's *Mourning Becomes Electra* (1931), which was a reworking of the Oresteian theme; and Arnold Wesker's *Chicken Soup with Barley, Roots* and *I'm Talking about Jerusalem* (1960). The term may also be applied to a group of three novels linked by a common theme and characters. Good 20th c. examples are Joyce Cary's *Herself Surprised, To be a Pilgrim* and *The Horse's Mouth* (1941–4) and Philip Pullman's award-winning trilogy of fantasy novels *His Dark Materials* (1995–2000; published as *The Golden Compass* in America). See TETRALOGY.

trimeter (Gk 'three measure') A line of verse containing three metrical feet, as in the second and fourth lines of these verses from W. S. Gilbert's *The Yarn of the 'Nancy Bell'*:

> 'Twas on the shores that round our coast
> Frŏm Déal | tŏ Ráms|găte spán,
> That I found alone on a piece of stone
> ăn él|dĕrlў návăl mán.
>
> His hair was weedy, his beard was long,
> ănd wée|dў ănd lóng | wăs hé,
> And I heard this wight on the shore recite,
> Ĭn ă sín|gŭlăr mí|nŏr kéy:

Line 2 contains three iambs; line 4 an iamb, an anapaest and an iamb; line 6 is the same as line 4; line 8 is anapaest, anapaest, iamb. *See* ANAPAEST; IAMB.

trimètre A French metrical term for the twelve-syllable alexandrine (*q.v.*) which has *three* divisions to the line. Common in the 16th c., it was later used by Molière and La Fontaine, and extensively revived by the 19th c. romantic poets.

triolet (F 'little three') A French fixed form, it has eight lines and two rhymes. The first line is repeated as the fourth, and the second and eighth are alike. The first and fourth lines are repeated in the seventh. It has been used occasionally by various poets, mostly French: Deschamps and Froissart in the late Middle Ages, La Fontaine in the 17th c., Daudet and Théodore de Banville in the 19th c. Few English poets have attempted it, but Austin Dobson, W. E. Henley and Robert Bridges all experimented quite successfully. The following piece is by Bridges:

> When first we met, we did not guess
>   That Love would prove so hard a master;
> Of more than common friendliness
> When first we met we did not guess
> Who could foretell the sore distress,
>   The inevitable disaster,
> When first we met? We did not guess
>   That Love would prove so hard a master.

An agreeable recent example is Wendy Cope's *Triolet* (in *Making Cocoa for Kingsley Amis*, 1986).

triple meter This occurs when a metrical scheme requires a three-syllable foot. It is common in anapaestic meter, and also with dactyls; though dactylic metrical schemes are fairly rare. *See* ANAPAEST; DACTYL; DUPLE RHYTHM.

triple rhyme Multiple or polysyllabic rhyme. A three-syllable rhyme, like prettily/wittily, rosily/cosily. Rare except in comic and bawdy verse. Four-syllable rhymes, like risibility/visibility, are rarer still but can be found or invented.

triple rhythm A synonym for triple meter (*q.v.*).

triplet A run of three lines in the same pattern, as a stanza, an individual poem, or, in particular, in a poem whose basic scheme is different: especially three successive rhyming lines in a poem of rhyming couplets. Dryden was fond of the occasional triplet, as in *Absalom and Achitophel*, Pt I, 150:

> Of these the false Achitophel was first,
> A name to all succeeding ages curst:
> For close designs and crooked counsels fit,
> Sagacious, bold, and turbulent of wit,
> Restless, unfixed in principles and place,
> In power unpleas'd, impatient of disgrace;
> A fiery soul, which working out its way, ⎫
> Fretted the pigmy body to decay   ⎬
> And o'er-informed the tenement of clay. ⎭

The interlinking *sestine* of Dante's *Divina Commedia* is the major example of triplet composition. Other notable users of it are Donne, in his verse epistles; Shelley, in *Ode to the West Wind* and *The Triumph of Life*; and William Carlos Williams in *The Desert Music*. *See* RHYME; TERCET; TERZA RIMA; TERZINA.

tripody   A line of three feet or three feet treated as one unit. *See* TRIMETER.

trisemic   (Gk 'of three time units') The term denotes the principle whereby three syllables are equivalent to three morae. *See* MORA.

tristich   (Gk 'three rows') A group of three lines of verse or a stanza of three lines, as in a triplet (*q.v.*).

tritagonist   (Gk 'third contestant') The third actor in Greek tragedy, probably introduced by Sophocles. *See* ANTAGONIST; PROTAGONIST; TRAGEDY.

triversen stanza   A stanza with three lines which comprise a complete sentence. The sentence is broken into three parts, each part being one line. This form was developed by William Carlos Williams (1883–1963).

trivium   *See* QUADRIVIUM.

trobar   (Pr) The profession, act or art of composing poetry. The word appears to derive from the Latin *tropare*, 'to make tropes'. *See* TROPE.

trochee   (Gk 'running') A metrical foot containing a stressed, followed by an unstressed, syllable: / ⌣. The reverse of an iamb (*q.v.*) and thus producing a falling rhythm (*q.v.*) as opposed to a rising rhythm (*q.v.*). In Classical verse trochaics were used from the time of Archilochus onwards, especially in lyric and drama. The commonest form was the trochaic tetrameter (*q.v.*) catalectic – known as the *septenarius* by the Romans. Not much used in English verse before the 16th c., the trochee (also known sometimes as a *choree*) was used increasingly thereafter in blank verse to provide variations in the iambic line. Many subtle examples of this substitution (*q.v.*) can be found, for instance, in Milton's *L'Allegro* and *Il Penseroso*. It is rare to find English verse composed exclusively of trochaics. When employed as the basic foot, as in Longfellow's *Hiawatha*, the effect can become monotonous. In these two lines from Robert Lowell's *The Holy Innocents* the first words are trochaic:

> Lístĕn, | thĕ háy-bélls | tínklĕ | ăs thĕ cárt
> Wávĕrs | ŏn rúb|bĕr týres | ălóng | thĕ tár

Troilus stanza   *See* RHYME ROYAL.

trope   (Gk 'turn') In general it still denotes any rhetorical or figurative device, but a special development in its use occurred during the Middle Ages when it came to be applied to a verbal amplification of the liturgical text. An early example was the elaboration of the *Kyrie eleison*:

> Kyrie,
> magnae Deus potentiae,
> liberator hominis,
> transgressoris mandati,
> eleison.

However, the most famous instance of such an interpolation was the *quem quaeritis* trope (*q.v.*) preceding the *Introit* on Easter Sunday. This developed into a dramatized form and became detached from the sacred Liturgy. *See* LITURGICAL DRAMA; MYSTERY PLAY.

tropism A term popularized by the French novelist Nathalie Sarraute (1902–99) which refers to mental and imaginative life as perceived by her. Thus perceived, it comprises millions of tiny little responses to innumerable stimuli. In her experimental fictional narratives, such as *Tropismes* (1939) – regarded as one of the prototypes of the *nouveau roman* (*q.v.*) – she attempts to translate her vision of reality with a highly unconventional use of language to give the impression of a different kind of reality. *See also* STREAM OF CONSCIOUSNESS.

troubadour (Pr 'finder, inventor') The troubadours were poets who flourished in the South of France between *c.* 1100 and 1350. They were attached to various courts and were responsible for the phenomenon known as courtly love (*q.v.*). Most of their lyrics were amorous; some satirical and political. They cultivated five main genres: the *canso d'amor* (*see* CHANSON); the *pastorela* (*see* PASTOURELLE); the *alba* (*see* AUBADE); the *tenso*, *partimen* or *jeu parti* (*q.v.*); and the *sirventes*. Some troubadours were known by name: Guillaume d'Aquitaine, Arnaut Daniel and Bertrand de Born. The troubadours (who composed in *langue d'oc*) had a very considerable influence on Dante and Petrarch, and indeed on the whole development of the lyric (*q.v.*), especially the love lyric, in Europe. *See* MINNESINGER; PAYADA; TROUVÈRE.

trouvère (OF 'finder, inventor') A medieval poet of northern France, especially Picardy. The *trouvères*, who were contemporary with the southern troubadour poets, wrote lyrics on similar topics in *langue d'oïl*. They also composed *chansons de gestes* (*q.v.*) and *romans bretons* (*q.v.*). As with the troubadours, some were known by name: for instance, Jean Bodel, Blondel de Nesle, Conon de Béthune. *See* MINNESINGER; PAYADA; TROUBADOUR.

truncation *See* CATALEXIS.

Tudor period The period of 1485–1603 during which the Tudor family ruled England. Among the hundreds of writers who flourished during this time of almost unparalleled creative activity in literature, the following are some of the most famous: John Lydgate, William Caxton, John Skelton, William Dunbar, Alexander Barclay, William Tyndale, Sir Thomas More, Sir David Lindsay, John Bale, John Heywood, Sir Thomas Elyot, Sir Thomas Wyatt, Nicholas Udall, Roger Ascham, the Earl of Surrey, George Puttenham, Thomas Sackville, George Gascoigne, Thomas Deloney, Sir Philip Sidney, Richard Hakluyt, Edmund Spenser, Sir Walter Ralegh, John Florio, John Lyly, Richard Hooker, Robert Greene, Thomas Kyd, George Peele, Thomas Lodge, George Chapman, Sir Francis Bacon, Robert Southwell, Samuel Daniel, Michael Drayton, Christopher Marlowe, William Shakespeare, Thomas Campion, Thomas Nashe, Henry Chettle, Barnabe Barnes, Thomas Dekker, Thomas Middleton, Ben Jonson, John Donne, Thomas Heywood, John Marston, Robert Burton, Cyril Tourneur, John Fletcher, John Webster.

tumbling verse A term apparently first used by James VI of Scotland in *Reulis and Cautelis* (1585) to describe a four-foot line of trisyllabic feet (dactyls and anapaests); a line form which developed from the alliterative verse (*q.v.*) of the Middle Ages. Skelton, among others, experimented with this. The following stanza comes from *Speak, Parrot* (1521):

> My name is Parrot, a bird of Paradise,
> By nature deviséd of a wonderous kind,
> Daintily dieted with divers delicate spice
> Till Euphrates, that flood, driveth me into Ind;
> Where men of that countrý by fortune me find
> And send me to greatë ladyés estate:
> Then Parrot must have an almond or a date.

Most of the feet are dactylic or anapaestic.

However, the term is also applied to another kind of verse at which Skelton again was particularly adept. It consists of short lines of two or three stresses which move at a brisk, almost helter-skelter (one might say helter-Skelton) pace, as in his *Colin Clout* (1519–20). *See* DOGGEREL.

turning point The observable moment when, in a story or a play (and indeed in many kinds of narrative), there is a definite change in direction and one becomes aware that it is now about to move towards its end. This is a change of fortune; what Aristotle described as *peripeteia* (*q.v.*), or reversal. It is the equivalent of reaching a peak and beginning the descent beyond. In tragedy (*q.v.*), especially, one is conscious of this crucial or fulcral point. Thomas Hardy, for example, underlines the moment in *The Mayor of Casterbridge*:

> Small as the police-court incident had been in itself, it formed the edge or turn in the incline of Henchard's fortunes. On that day – almost at that minute – he passed the ridge of prosperity and honour, and began to descend rapidly on the other side.

In the same way, Chaucer, when he begins Book IV of *Troilus and Criseyde*, makes it clear that the wheel of fortune is about to turn:

> From Troilus she [Fortune] gan hire brighte face
> Awey to writhe, and tok of hym non heede,
> But caste hym clene out of his lady grace,
> And on hire whiel she sette up Diomede;
> For which right now myn herte gynneth blede,

> And now my penne, allas! with which I write,
> Quaketh for drede of that I moste endite.

See CLIMAX; FREYTAG'S PYRAMID.

typological *See* ALLEGORY; CONCEIT.

tz'u A Chinese poetic form created during the T'ang period. It was a kind of song libretto with a tonal pattern similar to that found in the *lü-shih* (*q.v.*), and its meters were irregular.

U

ubi sunt   (L 'where are they?') The opening words of a number of MedL
poems, they are now used to classify a particular kind of poem that dwells
on and laments the transitory nature of life and beauty. Sometimes the words
open a poem, or begin each stanza, or serve as a refrain (*q.v.*). The elegiac
mood to which they are a keynote is present in some early OE poems like
The Seafarer and *The Wanderer*, and in ME lyrics like the 13th c. *Ubi Sount
Qui Ante Nos Fuerount*, which begins:

> Uuere be þey beforen us weren,
> Houndes ladden and hauekes beren
> And hadden feld and wode?
> þe riche leuedies in hoere bour,
> þat wereden gold in hoere tressour
> Wiþ hoere briȝtte rode . . .

A number of French poets made considerable use of the motif. In the 14th
c. Deschamps composed several *ballades* on the theme. In the 15th c. Chastellain used it in a long poem called *Le Pas de la Mort*, and in the same period
Olivier de la Marche worked it through the allegorical *Parement et triumphes
des dames*. Probably the best known of all is Villon's *Ballade des dames du
temps jadis* (also of the 15th c.) with its famous refrain 'Mais où sont les neiges
d'antan?' The motif recurs regularly in Tudor and Elizabethan lyric poetry,
and nowhere more eloquently than in Thomas Nashe's magnificent *In Time
of Pestilence* whose third stanza runs:

> Beauty is but a flower
> Which wrinkles will devour:
> Brightness falls from the air,
> Queens have died young and fair,
> Dust hath closed Helen's eye.

A Dictionary of Literary Terms and Literary Theory, Fifth Edition. J. A. Cuddon.
© 2013 The Estate of J. A. Cuddon. Published 2013 by Blackwell Publishing Ltd.

Followed by the knell-like refrain:

> I am sick, I must die.
> Lord have mercy on us!

The motif is present in many elegies, but today one is unlikely to find it except in a fixed form; as in, for example, Edmund Gosse's *Ballade of Dead Cities*. *See also* CARPE DIEM; CORONACH; DANSE MACABRE; DIRGE; ELEGY; EPICEDIUM; LAMENT; THRENODY.

Ultra Grupo A group of seven Spanish poets who began the *ultraísmo* movement in 1919 and published a manifesto the following year. The name was invented by Guillermo de Torre, one of the poets. The others were Xavier Bóveda, César A. Comet, Pedro Garfias, Fernando Iglesias Caballero, J. Rivas Panedas and J. de Aroca. Like many such movements of that period it aimed at a complete break with the past and traditionalism, and advocated the creation of the 'pure' poem without formal or narrative structure and without any eroticism.

ultraism A radical attitude whose quest and objective in literature (and art) is for a kind of *reductio ad absurdum*, or for an expression of experience which seeks to go beyond the limitations of the medium. Hence phenomena like 'happenings', the use of different-coloured pages in a novel to suggest tone and mood, gimmick books in which the pages can be rearranged as the reader wishes. In the 20th c. there were many experiments in ultraistic modes. If we accept that language is 'public' but that 'private' languages are also possible, then Joyce, in *Finnegans Wake*, was pushing language near the limits of comprehensibility in the 'public' sense. Orwell was clearly experimenting 'ultraistically' in *Nineteen Eighty-Four*. Likewise Anthony Burgess with *nadsat* in *A Clockwork Orange*; and B. S. Johnson in several of his novels. Ultraism is particularly noticeable in the Theatre of the Absurd (*q.v.*). *See also* DADAISM; EXPRESSIONISM; SURREALISM.

Ultraismo A literary movement originating in Spain at the end of the First World War. Proclaimed by the critic Rafael Cansinos Assens and articulated in the manifesto and journal writings of Guillermo de Torre, adherents of Ultraismo rejected the tenets of traditional literary and poetic practice such as rhyme, regular meter and conventional typography on the page. In its quest for unadorned simplicity and succinctness, the movement advocated the synthesis of multiple images resulting in associative rather than objective or easily identifiable connections. Having encountered the Ultraists in Spain, Jorge Luis Borges returned to his native Argentina and became an important exponent of their ideas in Buenos Aires in the early 1920s. *See* MODERNISM.

unanimisme A French poetic movement developed *c*. 1908–11 by Jules Romains. It was probably inspired by Whitman's concepts of universal brotherhood and had a kind of didactic and reforming purpose and spirit: to reveal the soul of the group and the collective society. Hence the idea of unanimity. There were several poets involved, principally Georges Duhamel

(1884–1966), Luc Durtain, Charles Vildrac, René Arcos and Georges Chennevière. They favoured what was called 'poésie immédiate', a poetry shorn of anything symbolic or allegorical, without assonance (*q.v.*) or end-rhyme (*q.v.*) and possessing distinctive accentual rhythms. The main statements of intention and practice were *Notes sur la technique poétique* (1910) and *Petit traité de versification* (1923). Jules Romains explained his ideas in *Les Hommes de bonne volonté* (1932–47).

uncanny *See* PSYCHOANALYTIC CRITICISM

unconscious, the A region or state of mind assumed to exist without any evidence other than that adduced by conscious action. Alternatively, by assumption, the sum of the dynamic elements which constitute a personality (the individual may be aware of some of these and unaware of others). Or, again by assumption, a mental process wholly different from a conscious process but at the same time one which influences and modifies the conscious processes; also known as endopsychic processes.

The term 'unconscious', like subconscious and, to a much lesser extent, pre-conscious, co-conscious and extra-conscious, has become a part of literary critical jargon; for example, in the phrase 'creative unconscious', which Koestler says works by a 'bisociation of matrices'.

underground literature/poetry The adjective 'underground' suggests something illegal, subversive and clandestine. This is all true of *samizdat* (*q.v.*) literature but does not accurately describe the work of a number of British writers active from the late 1950s to the 1970s to which the term 'underground' has been applied. Some of the writers so classified are Alexander Trocchi (1925–84), Adrian Mitchell (1932–2008), Jeff Nuttall (1933–2004), Heathcote Williams (1941–) and Tom Pickard (1946–). Plus the Liverpool Poets (*q.v.*), whose works have for many years been esteemed in the most conservative classrooms. There was a time when the writings of the Beat generation (*q.v.*) might easily have been described as 'underground'. They have long since been 'mainstream'.

The so-called underground poets were predominantly anti-war, anti-establishment, non-traditional and experimental, and quite often wrote a kind of poetry of protest which was clearly influenced by traditional folksong. The poets tended to reach their audiences through public readings and they published their work in little magazines (*q.v.*). This was deliberate policy; they declined to go through the standard publishing channels. A notable one was *New Departures*, founded in 1959 and edited by Michael Horowitz. He also published an anthology of their work titled *Children of Albion: Poetry of the 'Underground' in Britain* (1969). *See also* JAZZ POETRY; SUBCULTURE.

understatement *See* LITOTES.

Union of Soviet Writers Formed in April 1932 by order of the Central Committee of the Communist Party. By decree all existing literary organizations were abolished, and a new, uniform, literary policy was established. Socialist realism (*q.v.*) was to be the dogma. Those who did not conform were to be expelled from the union. If you were expelled you could not function as a writer. If you toed the Party line then you could expect good working conditions, a high salary, rewards and respect. *See also* IDEYNOST; NARODNOST; PARTYNOST.

unities Aristotle was the first to consider the problem of the dramatic unities of action, time and space, but he did not invent them. In *Poetics* (writing of action) he says: 'The fable should be the imitation of one action, since it is the imitation of action, and of the whole of this, and that the parts of the transactions should be so arranged, that any one of them being transposed, or taken away, the whole would become different and changed.' Of time he writes: 'Tragedy endeavours... to confine itself to one revolution of the sun, or but slightly to exceed this limit.' On space he is less explicit, merely saying (when contrasting epic and tragedy, *qq.v.*) that tragedy should be confined to a narrow compass.

In the 16th and 17th c. neoclassical critics of the drama in Italy and France required adherence to the unities. In all probability it was Jean Mairet (1604–86) who established the doctrine of unities (though Ronsard and Jean de la Taille had made earlier statements) which French dramatists were to follow (almost unquestioningly) for two hundred years. Mairet's play *Sophonisbe* (1634) was the first French play to conform strictly to the unity rules.

The supporters of the Classical precepts required that a play should be a unified whole, that the time of action should be limited to twenty-four hours (though some allowed thirty-six) and that the scene should be unchanged (or at any rate confined to one town or city).

These rules were largely ignorerd by English and Spanish dramatists – probably to the lasting gain of drama – though, oddly, the French called them *les unités scaligériennes* after Julius Caesar Scaliger, the eminent classical scholar, who had referred to them in *Poetices Libri Septem* (1561) when speaking of verisimilitude (*q.v.*). *See* CONVENTION; UNITY.

unity The concept of artistic unity was first worked out by Plato in *Phaedrus*. A work which possesses the quality of unity has an internal logic of structure wherein each part is interdependent. The work coheres, is self-contained and is free of any element (digression, ornament or episode) which might distract attention from its main purpose. The concept of perfect unity presupposes a work from which nothing can be taken away without marring it, and to which nothing can be added without introducing a blemish. *See also* PLATONISM; UNITIES.

Unity Theatre An amateur membership theatre group of great enterprise founded in 1935–6 as a result of a merger of Red Radio and the Rebel Players. It was a left-wing company, part of the Labour movement, and based in London. The policy was to present socialist and Communist plays and the group pioneered the Living Newspaper (*q.v.*) in England. Its first production was a version of Clifford Odets's *Waiting for Lefty* (1935). In 1937 the group took over and converted a missionary hall at St Pancras, London, where, in

1938, they presented Brecht's *Señora Carrar's Rifles* – the first Brecht play to be produced in Britain. In the war members of Unity gave entertainments to people sheltering from the blitz in London tube stations. During and after the war numerous regional branches were established. Notable productions were: *Black Magic* (1947), *Matchgirls* (1947), *Cyanamide* (1957), British premières of plays by Brecht and Sartre, and Adamov's *Spring '71*. In 1975 Unity became defunct when its theatre was burnt down. *See* AGITPROP DRAMA; COMMITMENT; PROPAGANDA.

universality That quality in a work of art which enables it to transcend the limits of the particular situation, place, time, person and incident in such a way that it may be of interest, pleasure and profit (in the non-commercial sense) to all people at any time in any place. As it was expressed in the treatise *On the Sublime* – 'lofty and true greatness in art pleases all men in all ages'. The writer who aspires to universality therefore concerns himself with, primarily, aspects of human nature and behaviour which seldom or never change. Thus the good satirist concentrates on the major diseases of the mind and spirit – like pride and avarice, envy, hypocrisy and lust for power. This explains why the satires of Aristophanes, Juvenal, Erasmus, Ben Jonson, Molière, Dryden, Swift, Voltaire, Pope and Samuel (*Erewhon*) Butler are so successful. *See also* QUOD SEMPER QUOD UBIQUE; TASTE.

university wits A name given to a group of writers who flourished in London in the last twenty years or so of the 16th c. The most notable members (all Oxford or Cambridge men) were: Marlowe, Nashe, Greene, Lyly, Lodge and Peele. They are reputed to have used the Mermaid Tavern in Bread Street off Cheapside. Shakespeare was not a university man and in his romantic comedy *Love's Labour's Lost* (c. 1595) there is a certain amount of mirth and wit at the expense of the university wits.

unstressed rhyme *See* RHYME.

untranslatableness A word used by Coleridge in a fairly famous passage in *Biographia Literaria* (Chap. XXII): 'In poetry, in which every line, every phrase, may pass the ordeal of deliberation and deliberate choice, it is possible, and barely possible, to attain that *ultimatum* which I have ventured to propose as the infallible test of a blameless style; namely; its *untranslatableness* in words of the same language without injury to the meaning.'

Upaniṣads *See* VEDAS.

urbinatas *See* ASTEISMUS.

Ur-text The German term for an original version of a text. The prefix 'Ur' denotes 'first', 'original' and carries with it the idea of earlier/primitive. It is likely to denote a version of a text that is lost but which may be reconstructed by textual criticism. For example, Shakespeare's *Hamlet* may have been based on an earlier text not extant; this is called the 'Ur-*Hamlet*'.

usage The generally accepted mode of expression in words, as established by custom, tradition and practice. Words, idioms, colloquialisms, syntax, grammar in common everyday use. Two classic works on the subject are H. W. and F. G. Fowler's *The King's English* (1906) and H. W. Fowler's *A Dictionary of Modern English Usage* (1926). *See* KING'S ENGLISH.

utopia Sir Thomas More was the first to apply this word (from Gk *ou*, 'not' + *topos*, 'place') to a literary genre when he named his imaginary republic *Utopia* (1516), a pun on *eutopia*, 'place (where all is) well'.

The idea of a place where all is well is of great antiquity. We find descriptions of earthly paradise in the Sumerian epic of *Gilgamesh* (2nd c. BC) as well as in the *Odyssey*. Christianity reinforced the notion of an attainable paradise which, in St Augustine's terms, was the heavenly city (as opposed to the earthly city), and for the next thousand years at least, in both 'official' and popular literature, the kingdom of heaven was a more than possible objective. The Church exhorted the faithful to lead holy lives in order to go there. Many of the paradises are reminiscent of garden cities and the descriptions are materialistic in tone.

It is probably no coincidence that as traditional religious beliefs were modified, so the number of earthly utopian schemes proliferated. Since More's *Utopia*, which can probably be taken as the first of modern times, there have been at least a hundred similar ideas. Some are mere pipe-dreams; others are carefully thought-out working models.

Long before More, however, the very first ideal commonwealth was devised by Plato. In his *Republic* (4th c. BC), Plato depicted a state in which the rulers are philosophers, goods and women are communally owned, slavery is taken for granted, and the breeding of children is controlled on eugenic lines. There was to be no art or drama and almost no poetry. It was a Spartan utopia.

More's welfare state was also communistic. No private property, free universal education, six hours' manual work a day, utility clothes, free medical treatment, meals in civic restaurants (meals accompanied by reading or music). All religions were to be tolerated, but the penal code, especially in sexual matters, was harsh; adultery led to slavery; repeated offences to death.

The next utopian plan of note was the *Christianopolis* (1619) of Andreae and this was not dissimilar to More's conception. In 1626 Francis Bacon published his *New Atlantis*, which is particularly noteworthy because it contains the 'blueprint' for the Royal Society and mentions inventions which suggest the future development of aeroplanes, submarines and telephones. From this period also date Hobbes's *Leviathan* (1651) and Harrington's *Oceana* (1656). Hobbes's work is a treatise on political philosophy; *Oceana* a counter and a contrast to it, a kind of political romance (*q.v.*).

From this time on, many contributions to utopian literature were made but there is nothing of great importance or merit until the 19th c. when there was not only a spate of literary utopias, but an increasing number of experiments in putting utopian schemes into actual practice.

The influence of the French and industrial revolutions suggested again that some form of earthly paradise was attainable. For example, Southey and Coleridge were stimulated by the concept of Pantisocracy (a utopia in which all rule and all are equal).

The most original utopias were created towards the end of the century: Bulwer Lytton's *The Coming Race* (1817); Edward Bellamy's *Looking Backward* (1888); William Morris's *A Dream of John Bull* (1888). But the major contribution was H. G. Wells's *A Modern Utopia* (1905). Wells was the first to conceive utopia as a world state: international government; central bureaucracy; state-controlled land, capital and industry; and population control. This global utopia was ruled by a voluntary 'nobility' called Samurai – the equivalent of Plato's guardian philosophers.

The seeming impossibility of utopia (and the many failures to create it) has produced its converse: dystopia or anti-utopia; in some cases almost chiliastic forecasts of the doom awaiting humankind. They range from the whimsical fantasy of Joseph Hall's *Mundus Alter et Idem* (1600), very probably the first of its kind, to the unrelievedly depressing vision of Orwell's *Nineteen Eighty-Four* (1949), and to Aldous Huxley's *Brave New World* (1932), the wittiest and most urbane of all anti-utopian worlds.

In some instances utopian worlds are almost indistinguishable from those in SF, desert island fiction and travellers' tall tales (*qq.v.*). Some works which owe a good deal to the classic examples of utopia are Samuel Butler's *Erewhon* (1872), Evelyn Waugh's *Love among the Ruins* (1953), William Golding's *Lord of the Flies* (1954) and John Wyndham's *From Pillar to Post* (1956).

Since the 1950s new visions of dystopia have flourished in the cinema and in somewhat apocalyptic fiction, often of considerable and disturbing power. Examples in fiction are Kurt Vonnegut's *Player Piano* (1952), Anthony Burgess's *A Clockwork Orange* (1962), William Burroughs's *Nova Express* (1964) and J. G. Ballard's *The Terminal Beach* (1964). More recent utopian or dystopian fiction has included *Always Coming Home* (1985) by Ursula K. Le Guin, Margaret Atwood's *Oryx and Crak* (2003) and Kazuo Ishiguro's *Never Let Me Go* (2005). *See also* APOCALYPTIC LITERATURE.

ut pictura poesis (L 'as is painting so is poetry') A phrase invented by Horace (*Ars Poetica* 361), though the idea was not new, suggesting that painting and poetry are comparable or similar arts. The idea provoked some discussion during the 16th, 17th and 18th c. Shaftesbury may well have been right when, in *Plastics* (1712), he remarked that comparisons 'between painting and poetry are almost ever absurd and at best constrained, lame and defective'. As an aesthetic theory (it was probably little more than a casually tentative *obiter dictum* by Horace – like Aristotle's remarks on the dramatic unities, *q.v.*) it is not often held now. *See* CORRESPONDENCE OF THE ARTS; EKPHRASIS.

V

vade mecum (L 'go with me') A manual (*q.v.*) or handbook carried for frequent and regular reference. For example, *The Fisherman's Vade Mecum* (1942) by G. W. Maunsell. Field guides for birds, trees, mammals, insects, etc. are also *vade mecums*. *See also* GUIDEBOOK.

variable syllable One which may be stressed or unstressed according to the needs of the metrical pattern. Also known as 'distributed stress' and 'hovering accent'. Take these lines from the beginning of Pope's *Second Epistle: Of the Characters of Women*:

> Nothing so true as what you once let fall,
> Most Women have no Characters at all.
> Matter too soft a lasting mark to bear,
> And best distinguish'd by black, brown or fair.

The first line is regularly iambic, except for the substituted trochaic foot at the beginning ('nothing' is trochaic) and scans thus:

> Nóthĭng | sŏ trué | ăs whát | yŏu ónce | lĕt fáll,

The second line, however, might be scanned in three different ways, according to where the emphases are placed, in order to get a particular sense:

> Móst Wó|mĕn hăve nŏ | Chárăctĕrs | ăt áll.

That is: spondee/tribrach (which is rare)/dactyl/iamb. Or:

> Mŏst Wó|mĕn hăve nó | Chárăctĕrs | ăt áll.

That is: iamb/anapaest/dactyl/iamb. Or:

> Móst Wó|mĕn háve nó | Chárăctĕrs | ăt áll.

That is: spondee/bacchius (which is rare)/dactyl/iamb.

A Dictionary of Literary Terms and Literary Theory, Fifth Edition. J. A. Cuddon.
© 2013 The Estate of J. A. Cuddon. Published 2013 by Blackwell Publishing Ltd.

The third line is exactly the same as the first, with a substituted trochaic 'matter'. The fourth has a variable syllable in 'distinguish'd'. The line may be scanned either:

ănd bést | dĭstíngúish'd | bў́ bláck, | brówn ŏr fáir.

That is: iamb/bacchius/iamb/cretic (or amphimacer). Or:

ănd bést | dĭstíngŭish'd | bў́ bláck, | brówn ŏr fáir.

In this version 'distinguish'd is an amphibrach.

It should be noted that each of the above lines has ten syllables and that in each the basic stress pattern tends to comprise five stresses per line – as one would expect in iambic pentameters. But Pope had such a sensitive ear for the delicate nuances of words that he often eludes scansion, and technical exegesis of the kind displayed here verges on impertinence. *See* DURATION; FOOT; HOVERING STRESS; SUBSTITUTION.

variorum (Short for, 'an edition with the notes of various persons' from L *editio cum notis variorum*) A *variorum* contains the complete works of an author accompanied by the notes of previous commentators and editors; and, in all probability, indications of the textual changes made during successive printings. An outstanding recent example is the *Twickenham Edition* of Pope's works.

Varronian satire *See* MENIPPEAN SATIRE.

vates (L 'poet, bard') Especially one of the theopneustic or prophetic kind. Hence *vatic* means characteristic of a prophet or seer. A class of Gaulish druids were known as *vates*. Perhaps the most famous of Classical times was the Sibyl. Virgil has been credited with vatic powers because, in the *Fourth Eclogue*, he prophesied the birth of a boy under whose rule the world would be peaceful. This was later interpreted as a prophecy of the birth of Christ.

vaudeville (Shortened alteration of OF *chanson du vau de Vire*, 'song of the vale of Vire') In all probability the term derives from the fact that, in the 15th c., Olivier Basselin, who lived in the valley of the river Vire in Calvados, Normandy, wrote satirical songs. Such songs were later incorporated in comedies; thus, comedy with vaudevilles. Later, it was adopted in America to describe comic, musical and acrobatic turns in the theatre; the equivalent of the British music hall. The period of its greatest popularity coincided with that of the music hall (*c.* 1890–1930). Thereafter vaudeville could not compete with the cinema. The term is still used in France and England to describe light, theatrical entertainment of a knockabout kind, with musical interludes. *See also* ZARZUELA.

Vedas (Skt *véda*, 'knowledge, wisdom') The most fundamental scriptures of Hinduism, regarded as revealed texts. Composed between 1500 and 1000 BC and redacted around 1000 BC, they are the oldest form of Sanskrit literature. There are four canonical Vedas or vedic collections (known as *samhitās*):

Rigveda, Yajurveda, Samaveda and *Atharvaveda*. They are composed in meter and an individual verse is called a *mantra*. The *Rigveda* is the oldest of these scriptures and comprises 1,028 hymns, addressed to various gods, including Indra, Varuna and Agni; it deals with the basic themes of creation, birth and death. Here are some lines from the hymn to Ratri, goddess of the Night:

> When night comes on, the goddess shines
> In many places with her eyes:
> All glorious she has decked herself.
>
> Immortal goddess far and wide,
> She fills the valleys and the heights:
> Darkness she drives away with light.
>
> The goddess now, as she comes on,
> Is turning out her sister, Dawn:
> Far off the darkness hastes away.

> (Translated by A. A. Macdonell)

The other Vedas, each of which has two major recensions, serve a more liturgical purpose. The *Yajurveda* or Veda of the Formulae is composed of mantras and ritual incantations used by priests at sacrifices. The *Samaveda* or Veda of the Chants consists of numerous verses taken from the *Rigveda* and rearranged for song. The *Atharvaveda* or Veda of the Priest is a book of hymns and also magical spells for protection against disease, misfortune and death.

The Vedas are complemented by three main forms of later canonical texts: the *Brahmanas* which explain the correct performance and meaning of rituals described in the four Vedas; the *Aranyakas* (Books of the Forest), composed by sages who meditated in the wilderness, detailing esoteric rituals that needed to be practised in the wild; and the *Upaniṣads* (produced from the 9th c. BC until the modern era), which are collections of philosophical texts and didactic poetry, centring on the concepts of *Brahman* (the Absolute, or universal spirit) and *Atman* (individual self), concepts which are ultimately identified.

The Vedas and the thirteen principal *Upaniṣads* have exerted a widespread influence on Indian thought, culture and literature. The philosophical traditions of *Vedanta* had their roots in the *Upaniṣads*. The word *Vedanta* ('appendix' or 'end' of Vedas) initially referred to the *Upaniṣads* which offered an exegesis of the earlier scriptures. *Vedanta* – through its numerous inflections over various periods – was essentially a philosophy of realization of one's true self through renunciation of the phenomenal world as illusory, and identification with *Brahman*, the ultimate reality. *See also* BHAGAVAD GITA.

vehicle *See* TENOR AND VEHICLE.

venedotian code An extremely complex code dating from the 15th c. which lays down the rules of Welsh versification and classifies twenty-four different measures.

Venus and Adonis stanza So named because Shakespeare used it for *Venus and Adonis* (1593). A six-lined stanza rhyming ababcc. But a number of poets had used it earlier, e.g. Sidney in *Arcadia* (1590). However, it has a 'curiosity' interest because Shakespeare used it in *Love's Labour's Lost* (c. 1595) and *Romeo and Juliet* (c. 1595) where its effect is to produce dramatic stylization of an almost operatic kind.

verbocrap A type of jargon (*q.v.*) language commonly used by verbocrats, and thus dear to bureaucrats and semi-literate officials of all kinds. It is marked by polysyllabic circumlocutions, crude syntax, faulty grammar and a self-important, orotund tone; what A. P. Herbert called 'Jungle English' or 'Dolichologia'. An example (from an ILEA educational publication) is:

> Due to increased verbalization the educationist desires to earnestly see school populations achieve cognitive clarity, auracy, literacy and numeracy both within and without the learning situation. However, the classroom situation (and the locus of evaluation *is* the classroom) is fraught with so many innovative concepts (e.g. the problem of locked confrontation between pupil and teacher) that the teaching situation is, in the main, inhibitive to any meaningful articulacy. It must now be fully realized that the secondary educational scene has embraced the concept that literacy has to be imparted and acquired via humanoid-to-humanoid dialogue. This is a break-through.

One may well ask – from what and to what. *See also* OFFICIALESE; PERIPHRASIS.

Verfremdung *See* ALIENATION EFFECT.

verisimilitude Likeness to the truth, and therefore the appearance of being true or real even when fantastic. But then fantasy is, or should be, rooted in reality. What might be called the inherent authenticity of a work (as well as its intrinsic probability), having made allowances for premises, conventions and codes, will be the criterion by which its 'truth' can be assessed. If the writer has done his work well, then the reader will find the result an acceptable presentation of reality. Thus, works which may strain ordinary credulity (e.g. Rabelais's *Gargantua* and *Pantagruel*, Swift's *Gulliver's Travels*, Voltaire's *Candide*, Wells's *The First Men in the Moon*) will be as credible as those which purport to be mundanely realistic (e.g. most of the novels of writers like Jane Austen, Zola, Thomas Hardy, Henry James and Arnold Bennett). In the end, verisimilitude will depend as much on the reader's knowledge, intelligence and experience (and his capacity for make-believe) as upon the writer's use of those same resources. *See* BIENSÉANCES; MIMESIS; VRAISEMBLANCE.

verism The doctrine that literature or art should represent the truth (reality), however disagreeable that truth might be. A verist believes this. *See* REALISM; VERISMO.

verismo A literary movement in Italy which occurred late in the 19th c. and early in the 20th c. In part it derived from the movement of naturalism (*q.v.*) in France. Theories of naturalism had been discussed by Francesco De Sanctis (1817–83) in his two works *La scienza e la vita* (1872) and *Studio sopra Emilio Zola* (1878), but the chief theorist in the *verismo* movement was Luigi Capuana (1839–1915). The main emphasis was on 'truthfulness', truth at any price, so to speak. This in effect meant a great deal of stress on the more squalid aspects of life: poverty, despair and violence, among other things. The main novelists involved were Giovanni Verga (1840–1922), De Roberto (1866–1927) and Capuana himself. The term *verismo* was also applied to the rather violent and melodramatic operas composed by Puccini and Mascagni c. 1900.

vernacular (L *vernaculus*, 'domestic, native, indigenous') Domestic or native language. Now applied to the language used in one's native country. It may also be used to distinguish between a 'literary' language and a dialect; for instance, William Barnes's 'vernacular poems', an outstanding example of dialect (*q.v.*) poetry.

vers A kind of song in Old Provençal. Almost indistinguishable from the *chanson* (*q.v.*), but *vers* is the older term.

vers de société Literally 'society verse', a subspecies of light verse (*q.v.*). It is usually epigrammatic or lyrical verse dealing with the superficial problems and events of a sophisticated and polite society. It is often satirical and characterized by technical virtuosity, wit, elegance and a conversational tone. Often intricate forms like *triolet*, *villanelle* and *rondeau* (*qq.v.*) are used. The ballads, the limerick and the clerihew (*qq.v.*) are also favourite forms. A great many English poets have produced such verse; outstanding among them are Alexander Pope, Matthew Prior, Winthrop Mackworth Praed, Theodore Hook, C. S. Calverley, W. E. Henley, Andrew Lang, Austin Dobson, W. S. Gilbert, Hilaire Belloc, G. K. Chesterton, A. P. Herbert, John Betjeman and W. H. Auden. Less notable contributions have been made by George Wither, the Cavalier Poets (*q.v.*), John Wilmot Earl of Rochester, and Thomas Gray. Among Americans the better known are Ogden Nash, Morris Bishop, Phyllis McGinley and Richard Armour. Many French poets have essayed *vers de société*, including Léon-Paul Fargue, Jules Laforgue, Tristan Corbière and Théophile Gautier.

Betjeman's *In Westminster Abbey* is a good modern example of the genre. The first verses run:

> Let me take this other glove off
> As the *vox humana* swells
> And the beauteous fields of Eden

Bask beneath the Abbey bells.
Here, where England's statesmen lie,
Listen to a lady's cry.

Gracious Lord, oh bomb the Germans.
    Spare their women for Thy Sake,
And if that is not too easy
    We will pardon Thy Mistake.
But gracious Lord, whate'er shall be,
Don't let anyone bomb me.

Keep our Empire undismembered
    Guide our Forces by Thy Hand,
Gallant blacks from far Jamaica,
    Honduras and Togoland;
Protect them Lord in all their fights,
And, even more, protect the whites.

Think of what our Nation stands for,
    Books from Boots, and country lanes,
Free speech, free passes, class distinction,
    Democracy and proper drains.
Lord, put beneath Thy special care
One-eighty-nine Cadogan Square.

A more recent witty example is Philip Larkin's *Vers de Société* (in *High Windows*, 1974).

verse Three main meanings may be distinguished: (a) a line of metrical writing; (b) a stanza (*q.v.*); (c) poetry in general.

verse-novel A narrative poem, often in several books (*q.v.*), chapters or cantos (*q.v.*), which deals with the substance of everyday modern life in much the same way as a work of prose fiction (*q.v.*). Most verse-novels are set in a contemporary world with characters who are naturalistic rather than mythical or heroic; there is usually a good deal of quotidian detail, some attempt at credible dialogue and interest in the issues of the day; the conventions of the prose novel are often to be felt in the plot construction.

The genre probably owes a debt to those poets of the ancient world who chose to stress the domestic at the expense of the heroic. (One thinks of the *epyllia*, *q.v.*, of Theocritus and Ovid.) But the genre seems to have arisen during the Romantic period in response to the new success of the prose novel. In some examples of the genre there is evident anxiety to compete with the novelist and envy of the larger canvas available to him or her. At the same time, most verse-novelists recognize the necessity of retaining the emotional power of poetry through music, imagery and concentration if the work in question is to remain a poem. It must be said that few verse-novels wholly avoid diffuseness, dilution and a tendency to fall between two stools.

The earliest example of the genre is probably Goethe's bourgeois idyll (*q.v.*) *Hermann und Dorothea* (1797). Though not consistently novelistic, Byron's *Don Juan* (1824) possesses many of the key characteristics and undoubtedly influenced many of the major practitioners, notably Pushkin in his *Eugene Onegin* (1831) and the Polish master Adam Mickiewicz in his *Pan Tadeusz* (1834). The most fully developed English example is Elizabeth Barrett Browning's *Aurora Leigh* (1857), which is written in 11,000 lines of blank verse (*q.v.*) divided into nine books. It purports to be the autobiography of a woman poet, struggling to establish herself as an independent writer in the largely hostile circumstances of a man's world. There is also a subplot (*q.v.*) which deals with the class conflicts of mid 19th c. England. Both Wordsworth's autobiographical poem *The Prelude* (1850) and Charlotte Brontë's prose novel *Jane Eyre* (1847) are intermittently evident as sources.

Barrett Browning has two main rivals among her contemporaries. Her husband Robert Browning's *The Ring and the Book* (1868–9), a book-length murder mystery in verse, is novelistic in scope, though not in method. It is in fact a series of dramatic monologues (*q.v.*), each dealing with the same narrative material from a different point of view. As such, it was an important influence on prose fiction (*q.v.*) through the novels and tales of Henry James, an avowed admirer. It also slightly anticipates the stream of consciousness (*q.v.*) method, as employed in (for instance) William Faulkner's *As I Lay Dying* (1930). Barrett Browning's other rival, Arthur Hugh Clough, wrote two verse-novels in an imitation of the Latin hexameter (*q.v.*): *The Bothie of Tober-na-Vuolich* (1848) and *Amours de Voyage* (1858). These achieve greater concision, and therefore more poetic consistency, by appropriating the method of the epistolary novel (*q.v.*), a method which, like Robert Browning's, provides opportunities for playing with point of view. This is especially true of *Amours de Voyage*, an ironic tale of English tourists in Rome, which uncannily anticipates both the international novels of Henry James and the ineffectual *personae* (*q.v.*) who speak the poems of Jules Laforgue and the young T. S. Eliot.

Despised by the Modernists for its supposed prolixity, the genre went into eclipse in the early 20th c. but has been successfully revived in recent years. Notable examples of this late flowering are Les Murray's *The Boys Who Stole the Funeral* (1980), Vikram Seth's *The Golden Gate* (1986), Derek Walcott's *Omeros* (1990) and Bernardine Evaristo's *Lara* (1997, 2009). *See* AUTOBIOGRAPHY; EPIC; NARRATIVE VERSE; NOVEL; ONEGIN STANZA; SONNET CYCLE.

verse paragraph A group of lines (often in blank verse) which forms a unit. Common in long narrative poems, like Milton's *Paradise Lost* and Wordsworth's *Prelude*. In fact, Milton developed the verse paragraph so skilfully that it is unlikely that anyone will ever surpass him. *See* LAISSE; VERSET.

verset A form derived from the kind of verse formations to be found in the Old Testament (e.g. *The Song of Songs*). Usually several long lines forming a group or 'paragraph', the whole characterized by a strong rhythm and many figurative and rhetorical devices. A number of European poets have explored the possibilities of this flexible form. Notable instances are Hölderlin, Péguy, Rimbaud and Claudel. Among poets writing in English: Walt Whitman, T. S. Eliot and D. H. Lawrence. These lines from Lawrence's *Kangaroo* give some idea of the verset:

> Still she watches with eternal, cocked wistfulness!
> How full her eyes are, like the full, fathomless, shining eyes of an Australian black-boy
> Who has been lost so many centuries on the margins of existence!
>
> She watches with insatiable wistfulness.
> Untold centuries of watching for something to come,
> For a new signal from life, in that silent lost land of the South.
>
> Where nothing bites but insects and snakes and the sun, small life.
> Where no bull roared, no cow ever lowed, no stag cried, no leopard screeched, no lion coughed, no dog barked,
> But all was silent save for parrots occasionally, in the haunted blue bush.
>
> Wistfully watching, with wonderful liquid eyes.
> And all her weight, all her blood, dripping sack-wise down towards the earth's centre,
> And the live little-one taking in its paw at the door of her belly.
>
> Leap then, and come down on the line that draws to the earth's deep, heavy centre.

See VERSE PARAGRAPH.

versicle Usually a liturgical term. Four meanings can be distinguished: (a) a short sentence said or sung antiphonally; (b) a little verse; (c) a verse of the Psalms or Bible; (d) a short or single metrical line.

versification Three meanings may be distinguished: (a) the action of composing a verse (*q.v.*) or the art or practice of versifying; (b) the form of a poetical composition – its structure and meter; (c) a metrical version of some prose work.

vers libéré (F 'freed verse') The French *symbolistes*, most notably Verlaine, ᵉ 1880, introduced new metrical forms and modifications of traditional one The intention was to free French versification from Classical conventio But this 'liberated' verse was still syllabic and still rhymed. *See also* ᵉ VERSE; VERS LIBRE; SYMBOL AND SYMBOLISM.

vers libre (F 'free verse') (1) A term used to denote verse forms com employed in the 17th c. in which there were subtle variations of li stanza length and alternations of masculine and feminine rhymes in achieve special effects. La Fontaine's *Fables* (1668–94) contain mai ples. *See also* FREE VERSE; VERS LIBÉRÉS.

(2) An important innovation in French prosody dating, like (*q.v.*), from *c.* 1880. It abandoned certain traditional principles; e

rules which prescribed recurrent metrical patterns and a certain number of syllables per line. Rhythm, together with the division of verse into rhythmical units, was held to be the essential foundation of poetic form. This rhythm was to be personal, the particular expression of the individual poet. Thus, his own voice or tune. The rhythm had also to be appropriate to the subject. Any poet worthy of the name had always been keenly aware of the nature and importance of rhythm, and any poet anyway has his own voice and tune. The theories of the French poets and prosodists helped to enforce a heightened awareness of the essential; and the innovations were, in many cases, beneficial.

Among the earliest poems to be written in *vers libre* were two by Rimbaud: namely, *Marine* and *Mouvement* (c. 1872–3). Other important *vers-libristes* were Paul Verlaine, Jules Laforgue, Edouard Dujardin, Francis Jammes, Henri de Régnier and Emile Verhaeren. The innovations had considerable influence upon American and English poets. How much is a matter of dispute; but it is a fact that Walt Whitman, Ezra Pound, T. S. Eliot and D. H. Lawrence (among many others) were all, at some stage or another, affected by them. Poets continue to experiment with *vers libre*. For example: Gregory Corso, Lawrence Ferlinghetti, Allen Ginsberg, Roger McGough, John Berryman, Ted Hughes, Michael Hamburger, Peter Redgrove, Thom Gunn, Sylvia Plath and Anne Sexton – to name a handful of American and English poets. Their counterparts on the European continent are as numerous.

verso piano (It 'plain verse') In Italian prosody, any line that has a feminine ending (q.v.) with the stress on the penultimate syllable. *Verso piano* is the basic narrative line in Italian verse, corresponding to our iambic pentameter. *See* IAMB; PENTAMETER; VERSO SCIOLTO; VERSO TRONCO.

verso sciolto (It 'free, easy, loose verse') An unrhymed hendecasyllabic line with the main accent on the tenth syllable. Italian poets were using it in the 13th c. and by the Renaissance period it was established as the equivalent of the Classical hexameter (q.v.) used for epic poetry. It served as the basis for ...k verse (q.v.) in English poetry. *See also* VERSO PIANO; VERSO TRONCO.

...nco (It 'truncated verse') In Italian prosody, any line ending with an ... syllable, especially one with the principal accent on the tenth syl... masculine ending. *See also* VERSO PIANO; VERSO SCIOLTO.

...erman term used from late in the 19th c. to denote under-... d from within by means of empathy (q.v.). It is commonly ...rmeneutics (q.v.).

...l or buffoon who appeared as a character in the Inter-... ...vs (qq.v.) in the 16th c. The Vice was often borne ... he carried a dagger of lath or a stick. *See also*

...een Victoria's reign (1837–1901). The period ...(the passage of the first Reform Bill). A period of intense and prolific activity in literature, especially by novelists and poets, philosophers and essayists. Dramatists of any note are few. Much of the writing was concerned with contemporary social problems; for instance, the effects of the industrial revolution, the influence of the theory of evolution, movements of political and social reform. The following are among the most notable British writers of the period: Thomas Love Peacock, Keble, Carlyle, William Barnes, Cardinal Newman, Disraeli, R. S. Surtees, Bulwer Lytton, J. S. Mill, Elizabeth Barrett Browning, Kinglake, Tennyson, Charles Darwin, Thackeray, Robert Browning, Edward Lear, Dickens, Aytoun, Charles Reade, Trollope, Charlotte Brontë, Emily Brontë, Anne Brontë, Charles Kingsley, George Eliot, Ruskin, Matthew Arnold, Wilkie Collins, T. H. Huxley, George Meredith, Dante Gabriel Rossetti, Christina Rossetti, Lewis Carroll, William Morris, Lord Acton, Samuel Butler, Swinburne, Pater, Dobson, Thomas Hardy, Gerard Manley Hopkins, Andrew Lang, Alice Meynell, W. E. Henley, Robert Louis Stevenson, Henry Arthur Jones, Oscar Wilde, Pinero, Francis Thompson, Rudyard Kipling, Synge.

Famous American writers of the period were Emerson, Hawthorne, Longfellow, Melville, Mark Twain and Henry James.

vidalita A Spanish verse form common in gaucho literature (q.v.). It consists of four- or six-line stanzas of four, six or eight syllables each. The rhymes are customarily on the second and fourth lines, or the third and sixth.

viewpoint The position of the narrator in relation to his story; thus the outlook from which the events are related. There are many variations and combinations but three basic ones may be distinguished. Firstly, the omniscient – the author moves from character to character, place to place, and episode to episode with complete freedom, giving himself access to his characters' thoughts and feelings whenever he chooses and providing information whenever he wishes. This is probably the commonest point of view and one which has been established for a very long time. Chaucer used the method very successfully in *Troilus and Criseyde* (c. 1385); Fielding employed it in *Tom Jones* (1749); Huxley in *Brave New World* (1932); Gabriel Fielding in *The Birthday King* (1962). Such a point of view does not require the author to stay outside his narrative. He may interpolate his own commentaries. Secondly, the third person – the author chooses a character and the story is related in terms of that character in such a way that the field of vision is confined to him or her alone. A good example of this is Strether in Henry James's *The Ambassadors* (1903). Thirdly, first person narrative – here the story is told in the first person by one of the characters. Well-known examples are Defoe's *Moll Flanders*, Melville's *Moby-Dick*, Dickens's *Great Expectations*, Mark Twain's *The Adventures of Huckleberry Finn*, Conrad's *Heart of Darkness* and Scott Fitzgerald's *The Great Gatsby*. This method has become increasingly popular and was used by many authors during the 20th c. A recent instance is Graham Greene's *Travels with My Aunt* (1969). Various combinations of these methods have been attempted by many authors; in some cases deliberately; in some, apparently, haphazardly. For example: Dickens shifts his viewpoint continually in *Bleak House* (1852–3). So does Tolstoy in *War and Peace* (1865–72). In many cases the viewpoint is restricted to a minor character within the story. Examples of this method are to be found in Emily Brontë's *Wuthering Heights* (1847), Conrad's *Victory* (1915) and Somerset Maugham's *The Razor's Edge* (1944).

Percy Lubbock's *The Craft of Fiction* (1926), E. M. Forster's *Aspects of the Novel* (1927) and Henry James's prefaces to his novels (eventually collected and published as *The Art of the Novel*, 1934) are important discourses on the matter of point of view. Since those days theory on this aspect of the novelist's art, and, indeed, of the story-teller's art in general, has proliferated. *See also* AESTHETIC DISTANCE; CONFESSIONAL NOVEL; EPISTOLARY NOVEL; NARRATOLOGY; NARRATOR; NOVEL; PERSONA; RÉCIT; STREAM OF CONSCIOUSNESS; SUBJECTIVITY AND OBJECTIVITY.

vignette (F 'little vine') A small ornamental design on a blank page in a book, especially at the beginning or end of a chapter. Today it may also be applied to a sketch or short composition which shows considerable skill (e.g. Virginia Woolf's short story *Kew Gardens*). Moreover, it may describe part of a longer work (e.g. Faulkner's extraordinary description of the wild spotted horses in *The Hamlet*). A further example is Turgenev's *Sketches of a Sportsman* (1847–51), vignettes of country life in Russia.

villain The wicked character in a story, and, in an important and special sense, the evil machinator or plotter in a play. Not to be found in Classical literature, the villain, as a particular character type, was developed in the 16th c. in drama. During this period the devils who played a prominent part in the medieval Mystery Plays (*q.v.*) and the Tudor Moralities (*q.v.*) suffered a kind of metamorphosis into the full-scale villains of Elizabethan and Jacobean tragedy (the majority of the villains are to be found in revenge tragedy, *q.v.*). In effect the devils were humanized and the villains diabolized. This process of evolution, in which two of the major formative influences were the concept of 'Senecal man' and the philosophy of expediency culled from Machiavelli (hence Machiavel, *q.v.*, Machiavellian), can be seen in the *Digby Plays* (*c.* 1512), *The Castell of Perseverance* (1425), *Mind, Will and Understanding* (1460), in Bale's *The Temptation of Our Lord* (1547), in Wever's *Lusty Juventus* (*c.* 1559), in *The Conflict of Conscience* (1563), in Fulwell's *Like Will to Like* (1568), in Lupton's *All For Money* (1578) and in Marlowe's *Dr Faustus* (*c.* 1588) – plus a number of other works. In most of these (and in similar plays) the devils are comic or semi-comic figures – devils continued to appear as devils in comedy until late in the 16th c. and early in the 17th c., e.g. Greene's *Friar Bacon and Friar Bungay* (1594), Haughton's *Grim the Collier of Croydon* (1600), the anonymous *The Merry Devil of Edmonton* (1608), Dekker's *If This be not good the Devil is in it* (1610), Ben Jonson's *The Devil is an Ass* (1616) and the anonymous *The Witch of Edmonton* (1623); but *Dr Faustus* is one of the few tragedies of the period in which the Devil appears *as* a devil. Other examples are Barnabe Barnes's *Devil's Charter* (1607) and Chapman's *Bussy D'Ambois* (1607).

The villains (and some of the villainous characters) of Elizabethan and Jacobean tragedy (*q.v.*) exhibit the characteristics of devils incarnate. Of the many instances that might be cited the following are among the most notable: Barabas in Marlowe's *The Jew of Malta* (*c.* 1592), Aaron in Shakespeare's *Titus Andronicus* (1594), and Gloucester in his *Richard III* (*c.* 1594), Piero in John Marston's *Antonio's Revenge* (1599), Hoffman in Chettle's *Tragedy of Hoffman* (*c.* 1600), Eleazar in *Lust's Dominion* (1600), Iago in Shakespeare's *Othello* (1604), Vendici in Tourneur's *The Revenger's Tragedy* (1607), Flamineo in Webster's *The White Devil* (*c.* 1608), the husband in the anonymous *Yorkshire Tragedy* (1608), D'Amville in Tourneur's *The Atheist's Tragedy* (1607–11), Bosola in Webster's *The Duchess of Malfi* (*c.* 1613–14), De Flores in Middleton and Rowley's *The Changeling* (1622) and Eleazar in William Heminge's *The Jewe's Tragedy* (*c.* 1637).

In these plays, and in many others of the period, the dramatists explored and exploited the possibilities of the evil antagonist as something like an incarnate devil, thus achieving an increased realism.

The summit and apotheosis, so to speak, of the villain in literature (and a devilish villain at that) is attained in Milton's portrayal of Satan in *Paradise Lost* (1667). Satan, as a figure and character, combines many of the characteristics of the devils and villains of the preceding three hundred years.

Thereafter, the villain as a character is not prominent until 19th c. melodrama when, for the most part, he has deteriorated into a grotesque if not buffoonish 'baddy' to be hissed and booed. The outstanding exception to this generalization is the Mephistopheles of Goethe's *Faust* (Pt I: 1808; Pt II: 1832), but this character does not really belong to the same tradition of the Elizabethan and Jacobean villain. *See* SENECAN TRAGEDY; SOLILOQUY.

villancico A Spanish song and verse form believed to derive from the Arabic *zéjel* (*q.v.*) and often used by Spanish court poets in the early Renaissance period. The term derives from *villano*, 'villein, peasant' and so we may suppose that it has a rustic origin. It is a popular poetic form often with a religious content which is sung in churches at Christmas and on other feast days. In some cases it can be taken as a kind of carol, though, properly, a Christmas carol is *verso de Nochebuena* or *verso de Navidad*.

villanelle (It 'rural, rustic' from *villano*, 'peasant') Originally used for pastoral (*q.v.*) poetry in various forms. Jean Passerat (1534–1602) very probably fixed the standard form: five three-lined stanzas or tercets (*q.v.*) and a final quatrain (*q.v.*). The first and third lines of the first tercet recur alternately in the following stanzas as a refrain (*q.v.*) and form a final couplet. A number of English poets have experimented with it, notably Oscar Wilde, W. E. Henley and W. H. Auden. Auden's *If I Could tell You* is a good example:

> Time will say nothing but I told you so,
> Time only knows the price we have to pay;
> If I could tell you I would let you know.

If we should weep when clowns put on their show,
If we should stumble when musicians play,
Time will say nothing but I told you so.

There are no fortunes to be told, although,
Because I love you more than I can say,
If I could tell you I would let you know.

The winds must come from somewhere when they blow,
There must be reasons why the leaves decay;
Time will say nothing but I told you so.

Perhaps the roses really want to grow,
The vision seriously intends to stay;
If I could tell you I would let you know.

Suppose the lions all get up and go,
And all the brooks and soldiers run away;
Will Time say nothing but I told you so?
If I could tell you I would let you know.

See CHAIN VERSE.

virgule, virgula A slanting stroke / often used to mark foot divisions in a line of verse. *See* PUNCTUATION; SCANSION.

vísa Half-line unit in ON poetry.

vocalic assonance *See* VOWEL RHYME.

voice *See* NARRATOR; PERSONA; VIEWPOINT.

Volapük An artificial international language invented by J. M. Schleyer in 1879. It was superseded by Esperanto (*q.v.*). *See also* BASIC ENGLISH; IDO.

Volksbuch A German term for 'popular' literature of the prose narrative type. The term was coined by Johann Görres, who in 1807 published *Die teutschen Volksbücher. Volksbücher* were very popular during the 16th c. and remained so until well on in the 18th c. Many derived from French and German verse romances of the Middle Ages. During the Romantic revival (*q.v.*) there was renewed interest in them.

Volksbühne (G 'people's stage') A German theatre association founded in 1890 by Bruno Wille which was of considerable importance in the 'people's theatre' movement of the period. It opened a theatre in 1914 in Berlin, where Erwin Piscator (1893–1966), the pioneer of epic and documentary theatre (*qq.v.*), became director in 1924. The Nazis suppressed the theatre but it reopened after the war. Until October 1990 there was one *Volksbühne* in West Berlin and one in East Berlin.

Volkslied (G 'folk poem/song') A poem of unknown origin belonging to oral tradition (*q.v.*). Usually in a simple stanza (*q.v.*) form rhyming abab, abcb.

The term was invented by the great German scholar Johann Herder and first used in his essay *Auszug aus einem Briefwechsel über Ossian und die Lieder alter Völker* (1773). Interest in this kind of poetry became widespread in the late 18th c. (it was an aspect of nationalism) and was to continue in the 19th c. Percy's *Reliques of Ancient English Poetry* (1765) had a considerable influence in Germany and elsewhere. Herder published a collection of folksongs in 1778–9 and many were to follow through the work of others.

Volksmärchen (G 'folk tale') A tale which belongs to the oral tradition (*q.v.*), and thus differs from the *Kunstmärchen*, which is written down.

Volksstück (G 'folk play') A play in local dialect for 'popular' audiences. *Volksstücke* originated in Vienna early in the 18th c. There were two main forms: the 'magic play' or *Zauberstück*; and the *Lokalstück*. The former presented a somewhat extravagant and fairy-like world in which the central character was the 'common man'; perhaps an ordinary Viennese tradesman, somewhat dim-witted or something of a comic, who would experience various adventures. The latter tended to be broad or knockabout comedy, with plentiful jokes at the expense of local society, characters, celebrities, fashions, customs, language and so forth. A development of the genre was the *Besserungsstück* (*q.v.*)

Such plays (which were often presented with elaborate stage machinery and scenic splendour and often included music and song) remained popular until the turn of the 19th c., and were always particularly associated with Vienna and its environs. Karlweis (1850–1901), a Viennese railway inspector, was one of the last dramatists to write them successfully.

volta (It 'turn') The change in thought or feeling which separates the octave (*q.v.*) from the sestet (*q.v.*) in a sonnet (*q.v.*). *See also* MILTONIC SONNET.

Vorticism A movement in art and literature begun *c.* 1912 by the painter and writer Wyndham Lewis. It produced a magazine, *Blast: The Review of the Great English Vortex*, which came out twice, in 1914 and 1915. These publications carried the manifestoes of Wyndham Lewis, the poet Ezra Pound and the sculptor Henri Gaudier-Brzeska. Some of the early poems of Pound and T. S. Eliot were also published in *Blast* and Pound used it to elaborate his theory of the image. The movement lost momentum after 1920. *See also* IMAGISTS; SURREALISM.

vowel rhyme When two words rhyme because their vowel or vowels are the same. For instance: boot/roof; ease/peace. Some accept it as a form of rhyme in which any vowel sound is allowed to agree with any other. Emily Dickinson used it quite often, as in these two stanzas from *A bird came down the walk*:

> . . . Cautious,
> I offered him a Crumb,
> And he unrolled his feathers
> And rowed him softer home –

> Than Oars divide the Ocean,
> Too silver for a seam –
> Or Butterflies, off Banks of Noon,
> Leap, plashless, as they swim.

See also ASSONANCE; RHYME.

vraisemblance The French equivalent of verisimilitude (*q.v.*). 17th c. French criticism distinguished between *vraisemblance ordinaire* and *extraordinaire*. The former covered appropriateness of behaviour and motive; the latter, supernatural or extraneous action – the element of surprise in plot or word. *See* BIENSÉANCES.

vulgarity Of the large number of synonyms available in English for vulgar, 'loud' is one of the most suitable, partly because of its sartorial associations. Vulgarity in literature usually occurs when a writer strains himself and protests too much. He then becomes boorish, ill-bred, bullying, crude, conceivably tawdry, or just plain silly or absurd. Thus vulgarity occurs where there is a serious discrepancy between tone, matter and form; where there is incongruity; where the feelings are contrived or forced; where the language is not apt for the emotional content; where there is pretension or self-indulgence in the shape of meretricious ornament, effect for the sake of effect, and 'display' of emotions which are not really felt.

A good deal of dramatic verse written during the Elizabethan and Jacobean periods is in poor taste because it is bombast (*q.v.*). This kind of vulgarity was skilfully parodied by Shakespeare on a number of occasions (especially, for example, in the Players' speeches in *Hamlet*, and in Pistol's rant in *Henry IV* and *Henry V*). Crashaw is also guilty of vulgarity. For example, these lines from *The Weeper*:

> Upwards thou dost weep,
> Heav'n's bosom drinks the gentle stream,
> Where the milky rivers creep
> Thine floats above, and is the cream.

Crashaw was a poet susceptible to the more bathetic forms of vulgarity, and so were a number of poets and novelists during the 18th c., a period when writers were particularly sensitive to what was fitting, and to aberrations from decorum (*q.v.*). The attitude and sensibility (*q.v.*) were conveyed in Lord Chesterfield's remark that audible laughter was illiberal and ill-bred, and in Johnson's *obiter dictum* that cow-keeper and hog-herd were not to be used in our language (though, he added, there were no finer words in the Greek language). Thomas Parnell, a minor 18th c. poet, conveys the then prevailing view tersely at the beginning of his *Essay on the Different Styles of Poetry* (1713):

> I hate the vulgar with untuneful mind;
> Hearts uninspir'd, and senses unrefin'd.

Some lines at the beginning of the second book are a good example of a discrepancy between style, tone and matter:

> Through all the brute creation, none, as sheep,
> To lordly man such ample tribute pay.
> For him their udders yield nectareous streams;
> For him the downy vestures they resign;
> For him they spread the feast; ah! ne'er may he
> Glory in wants which doom to pain and death
> His blameless fellow creatures.

The vulgarity of overmuch sentimentality is a notable feature of some 18th c. novels, especially Richardson's *Pamela* (1740) and Mackenzie's *The Man of Feeling* (1771).

Many other examples can be found. Swinburne often tries strenuously to be 'poetical'. Balzac, frequently a bad writer, is quite often guilty of vulgarity (for example, in *Séraphita*, 1834–5). So is Dickens, especially in the death scene of Little Nell in *The Old Curiosity Shop* (1841). Hardy comes perilously near to 'overdoing it' in the horrors of *Jude the Obscure* (1895). Among more recent writers examples can be found in the work of Henry Miller, Lawrence Durrell, William Burroughs and Ian Fleming; not to mention many instances in the purveyors of cheap, popular 'pulp' (*q.v.*) literature: the third-rate erotica and the fourth-rate thrillers. *See* TASTE.

W

waka A Japanese verse form related to the *tanka* (*q.v.*) consisting of alternate five- and seven-syllable lines. The *waka* form was standard for hundreds of years and survives.

Waldeinsamkeit (G 'forest loneliness') A 'mode' word (apparently coined by Tieck) during the German Romantic period, which was frequently used. It implies a turning away from reality into a dream world, a yearning for distant countries (of the mind as well as of actuality), a yearning for remoteness of time and place. The concept of the forest is important because forests are remote, wild, dark, lonely places where the spirit may commune with Nature. A good deal of poetry and fiction of the period dwells on this quasi-mystical longing. It is apparent in the work of, among others, Novalis (1772–1801), Ludwig Tieck (1773–1853) and Clemens Brentano (1778–1842). Goethe's poem *Wanderers Nachtlied* is a well-known example of the expression of the feelings involved. *See also* ROMANTICISM; ROMANTIC REVIVAL.

Wappendichtung (Also *Heroldsdichtung*) A form of Heraldic poetry dating from the 13th c.

war literature *See* WAR POETS.

war poets, the A title ultimately bestowed on, primarily, a number of writers who 'soldiered' in various capacities during the First World War and who recorded very memorably their feelings about their experience. Some seventy British poets wrote about that war and more than fifty of them were actively engaged in it. Not a few of them were killed. A handful (e.g. Rupert Brooke and Julian Grenfell) expressed patriotic and quasi-romantic views. The majority expressed varying degrees of disgust, disenchantment, cynicism, revulsion, anger and horror. It was often poetry of protest and it deglamorized war for ever. The strongest feelings were often leavened by a grim and

---

A Dictionary of Literary Terms and Literary Theory, Fifth Edition. J. A. Cuddon.
© 2013 The Estate of J. A. Cuddon. Published 2013 by Blackwell Publishing Ltd.

laconic humour. Pre-eminent among the poets were (and are) Wilfred Owen, Siegfried Sassoon, Edmund Blunden, Charles Sorley, Isaac Rosenberg, W. N. Hodgson, Edward Shanks, Edward Thomas, Robert Nichols, Wilfred Gibson, Alan Seeger, Herbert Asquith and David Jones. One of the major poems is *In Parenthesis* (1937) by David Jones. It is on an epic scale and was begun by him in 1927. Passages of prose are combined with the verse.

The Second World War, and its aftermath, were recorded (somewhat less memorably) by another generation of writers: notably, Sidney Keyes, Keith Douglas, Alun Lewis, Roy Fuller, Roy Campbell, Charles Causley and Alan Ross.

Most of the poets of both world wars have been well represented in a number of fine anthologies. Two of the best concerned with the First World War are *Up the Line to Death* (1964), edited by R. B. Gardner, and *Men Who March Away* (1965), edited by I. M. Parsons. The Second World War yielded *The Poetry of War: 1939–1945* (1965), edited by I. Hamilton, *The Components of the Scene* (1966), edited by R. Blythe, and *The Terrible Rain* (1966), edited by R. B. Gardner. It is noticeable that all five anthologies appeared within two years of each other in the 1960s, nearly fifty years after the First World War ended and twenty years after the end of the Second World War. This is some indication of the length of the shadow that both cataclysms cast across the world. In 1988, the seventieth anniversary of the original armistice year, half a dozen volumes of verse and prose about the 1914–18 war were published.

Not a few of those classed as war poets also contributed to a copious quantity of literature (novels, short stories, autobiography, biography, diaries, journals, *qq.v.*, memoirs, and stories of escape from prisoner-of-war camps) which appeared steadily in the interwar period and continued unabated from the late 1940s onwards. Three writers in particular published memoirs of the First World War which, over the years, have become more or less established as classics of their kind: namely, *Undertones of War* (1928) by Edmund Blunden, *Goodbye to All That* (1929) by Robert Graves and *Memoirs of a Fox-Hunting Man* (1928) by Siegfried Sassoon. Two lesser-known works of considerable merit are Frank Richards's *Old Soldiers Never Die* (1933) and *With a Machine Gun to Cambrai* (1969) by George Coppard (a brother of A. E. Coppard). *See also* LITERATURE OF ESCAPE; LOST GENERATION.

weak-ending One that is unaccented. *See* FEMININE ENDING.

well-made play Eugène Scribe (1791–1861), the French dramatist, is usually credited with the concept of the well-made play. The term is now normally pejorative and refers to a neatly and economically constructed play which works with mechanical efficiency. Scribe was a very successful dramatist and exerted considerable influence in the theatre for many years. Well-made plays were still common in the 1930s and not infrequent until the late fifties. There may always be a commercial market for them. Witness the phenomenal run of Agatha Christie's *The Mousetrap* (1952).

Weltanschauung (G 'world outlook') As a literary term it may be used judiciously in reference to a particular author's attitude to the world, or to the
prevailing spirit and vision of a period. For instance, Thomas Hardy's view
of the human being as the victim of fate, destiny, impersonal forces and circumstances; or the disillusioned and laconic cynicism so often expressed by
poets in the 1930s. W. H. Auden, Louis MacNeice, Stephen Spender, Cecil
Day Lewis, William Empson, Francis Scarfe, Michael Roberts, Bernard
Spencer, Norman Cameron, David Gascoyne and others.

Weltliteratur A term coined by Goethe which means, approximately (Goethe
did not define it), that literature which is of all nations and peoples, and
which, by a reciprocal exchange of ideas, mediates between nations and helps
to enrich the spirit of man. Carlyle spoke of 'World literature'. This notion
has been theorized in several recent works, including Edward Said's *The
World, the Text, and the Critic* (1983), David Damrosch's *What is World
Literature?* (2003) and Pascale Casanova's *The World Republic of Letters*
(2004). *See also* COMPARATIVE LITERATURE; WORLD LITERATURE.

Weltschmerz (G 'world pain') Vague yearning and discontent, a weariness of
life, and a melancholy pessimism. Many of the poems of Giacomo Leopardi
(1798–1837) suggest such a feeling of unease and despair. The term may also
apply to the spirit of a period like the 15th c. when there was widespread
despondency and pessimism throughout Europe: feelings frequently manifest
in the literature and art of that time. *See also* WELTANSCHAUUNG; ZEITGEIST.

wên and wu The two main classes of traditional Chinese drama. *Wên* denotes
civil and *wu* military drama. The 'book' for these plays is more like a roughly
outlined scenario than a dramatic text as we understand it in the West. In
China the actors fill out the scenario framework as required, and this gives
flexibility. The plays are a mixture of dialogue in prose and verse, acrobatics,
dancing, mime and operatic singing. They are divided into many different
scenes of variable length and are usually performed on a square stage. The
dramatic conventions are prescribed and elaborate. Stage props are simple
and symbolic: a table, for instance, may represent variously an altar, a wall,
a bridge, a hill or a judge's bench; four black flags waved vigorously represent a strong wind; a hat done up in red cloth signifies a decapitated head; a
cube wrapped in yellow silk is an official seal – and so on.

There are four main types of character: *shêng* – males in general; *tan* –
females in general; *ching* or *hua-lien* – strong, vigorous men whose faces are
painted like masks; *ch'ou* – comedians. Within these categories there are a
number of subdivisions.

Both speech and song are delivered in a high-pitched voice, though the
comedians render a kind of bass. The noises are reinforced by not dissimilar
musical accompaniment from a fiddle; but the Chinese orchestra (which is
on stage) also has brass and percussion instruments.

Costume and make-up are of the greatest importance. Costumes tend to
be lavish and are adapted from the styles of the T'ang, Sung, Yüan and Ming

dynastic periods. Convention prescribes the significance of particular colours (emperors wear red, important officials yellow, and so forth) and also prescribes particular uses of the clothes (for example, a sleeve held up to the eyes denotes weeping). Comparable rules apply in the use of complicated make-up. Character and temperament are expressed by lines on the face and varied combinations of colour. For instance, white denotes a treacherous disposition; red, loyalty and courage; black, candour and integrity; yellow, guile; green for demons, brigands and outlaws . . . and so on. The beard, an important prestige and status symbol in ancient China, is also an integral part of make-up. A very long beard signifies heroism and wealth; a blue or red beard signifies a supernatural being.

The movements of the actors are according to convention and their tempo is set by the orchestra.

Most of the *wên* and *wu* plays are based on traditional material like legends and historical events. They tend to point a moral, or give that impression. They possess a timeless quality in that they depict Chinese life over many centuries, and they are as stylized as *Nō* (*q.v.*) and puppet-theatre like *karagöz* (*q.v.*).

Wendepunkt (G 'turning point') An important element in the theory and practice of the *Novelle*. See NOVELLA.

Wertherism An *-ism* deriving from the title of Goethe's *Die Leiden des jungen Werthers* (1774), an autobiographical and epistolary novel and also a kind of *Künstlerroman* (*qq.v.*). The hero, Werther, is a hypersensitive, highly strung and melancholy young man who is a social misfit and is engaged in a hopeless love affair; the prototype of the pale, love-lorn, romantic, 'interesting' youth. The novel was an enormous success in Europe and created a cult which influenced male fashion (a blue coat and yellow breeches were *de rigueur* among young men who were well-off) and such artefacts as China tea-sets, which were decorated with scenes and motifs from the story. 'Wertherism' became a popular term in English. A young man suffering from 'Wertherism' was subject to fits of melancholia, and what Goethe described (in the novel) as *Weltschmerz* ('a feeling of being ill-at-ease with the world') and *Ichschmerz* ('a feeling of self-dissatisfaction').

Western A genre of fiction – usually in short story or novel (*qq.v.*) form – associated with the western states of the USA (sometimes called the 'Wild West'), and more particularly the South-west (i.e. the region encompassing the border states of Arizona, New Mexico and Western Texas) and what was known as the 'Old South-west', which included the area between the Savannah River and the Mississippi which formed the south-western frontier from colonial times to the 19th c. It is also associated with the great plains and prairies of Nebraska, Kansas, Oklahoma and Texas, plus parts of Montana, Wyoming, Colorado, the western parts of North and South Dakota, and New Mexico. These territories were inhabited by famous tribes of American Indians. White pioneer settlers (some of whom were called 'crackers' because their chief diet was cracked corn) created a folklore of the regions. This in turn produced frontier stories and sketches about hunting, trapping, ranching, cowboys, conflicts with Indians, cattle-rustling, sheriffs, gun-law, prospecting, brigandage and so forth. There were also ballads and other verse which were part of local gaucho literature (q.v.), and many a tall story (q.v.) or tall tale.

James Fenimore Cooper (1789–1851) was one of the first to write of such ways of life memorably – especially in his *Leatherstocking Tales* (q.v.) – between 1823 and 1841. A number of other lesser-known writers contributed numerous stories, sketches and yarns which were forerunners of the traditional and timeless Western that proved such a boon to the cinema industry. Some of these writers were cowboys. Among the better known were Davy Crockett (1786–1836), A. B. Longstreet (1790–1870), Sol Smith (1801–69), J. M. Field (1810–56), G. W. Harris (1814–69), author of the *Sut Lovingwood Yarns* (1867), Joseph Baldwin (1815–64), J. J. Hooper (1815–62) and T. B. Thorpe (1815–78), author of the famous tall story *The Big Bear of Arkansas*.

Francis Bret Harte (1836–1902) made a considerable contribution to the genre. In 1868 he helped to establish *Overland Monthly* as an outlet for Western writers and he printed a number of his own stories in it. In 1870 he published *The Luck of Roaring Camp and Other Sketches* – a collection of Western stories about frontier life and the fortunes and misfortunes of the individual in frontier society. Harte (and the other writers mentioned above) were eventually to have some influence on Mark Twain and, much later, William Faulkner.

One of the best-known writers of a traditional type of Western was Andy Adams (1859–1935), author of *The Log of a Cowboy* (1903), *The Outlet* (1905) and *Cattle Brands* (1906). Eugene Manlove Rhodes (1869–1934) wrote ten or more novels on comparable themes. Another who became popular was Harold Bell Wright (1872–1944), author of *The Shepherd of the Hills* (1907), *The Calling of Dan Matthews* (1909) and *When a Man's a Man* (1916). The most famous in the 20th c. was Zane Grey (1872–1939), who wrote over sixty novels and is particularly remembered for *Riders of the Purple Sage* (1912), *To the Last Man* (1922), *Nevada* (1928), *Wild Horse Mesa* (1928) and *Code of the West* (1934). He presents the West as a kind of moral landscape in which and against which characters fight and struggle. Their destruction or salvation/redemption depends on how they cope with and respond to the codes of violence which prevail. Over a hundred Western films were based on Grey's stories, and during the 1920s and 1930s he was the most popular author in America. Latterly Jack Schaefer has written books in the same tradition; for instance, *The Big Range* (1953). Other recent writers who have contributed are: Winfred Blevins, Bill Gulick, Donald Hamilton, Dorothy M. Johnson, Louis L'Amour and Peggy S. Curry.

Westerners   Russian intellectuals who created a movement *c.* 1840. They were opposed to the ideology of the Czar and to the Russian Slavophiles (q.v.).

These two groups were in contention over the matter of Russia's relationship with the West. The Westerners maintained that it was essential to belong to European civilization, to be a part of its culture and to use its progressive forms of government and technological progress. Turgenev's novel *Smoke* (1867) depicts the controversy from the point of view of the Westerners. Other 'Westernist' writers were Nikolai Ogaryov (1813–77), Yakov Polonski (1891–98) and Alexander Druzhinin (1824–64).

wheel *See* BOB AND WHEEL.

whodunnit An illiterate form of 'who did it?' (i.e. the crime). A crime story closely akin to the thriller, the detective story and the *roman policier* (*qq.v.*), and often synonymous with these terms. *See* CRIME FICTION.

willing suspension of disbelief One of the most famous phrases ever coined. Like 'negative capability' and 'dissociation of sensibility' (*qq.v.*) it has almost the utility of an indispensable talisman. Coleridge invented it and used it in Chapter XIV of *Biographia Literaria* to describe that state of receptivity and credulity desirable in a reader or member of an audience (in current jargon, 'the receptor'). The reader must 'grant' that he or she is about to read a story; a person in the audience is 'asked' to accept the dramatic conventions of the theatre and stage. In explaining one of the more remarkable *aperçus* in literary criticism Coleridge writes:

> In this idea [he has been speaking of two possible subjects for poetry] originated the plan of the LYRICAL BALLADS; in which it was agreed, that my endeavours should be directed to persons and characters supernatural, or at least romantic; yet so as to transfer from our inward nature a human interest and a semblance of truth sufficient to procure for these shadows of imagination that willing suspension of disbelief for the moment, which constitutes poetic faith.

It is possible that Coleridge got the original idea from the French sceptic François de La Mothe le Vayer (1588–1672), who composd a number of dialogues and discourses (e.g. *Les Problèmes sceptiques*, 1666, *Les Solitudes sceptiques*, 1670) and referred to the wisdom of the sceptic in his phrase 'cette belle suspension d'esprit de la sceptique'. *See also* ALS OB.

wit (OE *witan*, 'to know') The word has acquired a number of accretions in meaning since the Middle Ages, and in critical and general use has changed a good deal. Wit formerly meant 'sense' or 'the five senses'; thus common sense. (Cf. the phrase 'out of one's wits'.) During the Renaissance period it meant 'intelligence' or 'wisdom'; thus intellectual capacity; even, perhaps, 'genius' (*q.v.*). Roger Ascham and Lyly, for example, associated quick wit with intellectual liveliness. To Sir Philip Sidney it suggested an aptitude for writing poetry. Later, during the 17th c., the word came to mean 'fancy', dexterity of thought and imagination. Boyle and Locke understood it in those terms. Hobbes, however, in *Leviathan* (1651) thought that judgement rather than fancy was the main element. 'Judgement without fancy is wit, but fancy without judgement not.' Dryden, Cowley and Pope (among others) held that wit was primarily a matter of propriety. As Pope put it in his *Essay on Criticism* (he uses the term forty-six times in at least five different senses):

> True wit is Nature to advantage dressed,
> What oft was thought, but ne'er so well expressed.

Johnson, however, growled disapprovingly at Cowley's conception and referred to his 'heterogeneous ideas ... yoked by violence together ...' Hazlitt distinguished between wit, which is artificial, and imagination, which is valid. During the 19th c., imagination was the term generally used to designate the ability to invent and find resemblances. Wit was associated with levity. Matthew Arnold would not allow Chaucer or Pope on his list of the greatest poets because of their wittiness, and lack of 'high seriousness'. T. S. Eliot adjusted the balance by preferring witty poets like Donne and Marvell because they were able to combine wit with seriousness. The majority of modern critics agree with Eliot. For the most part wit now suggests intellectual brilliance and ingenuity; verbal deftness, as in the epigram (*q.v.*). Wit is commonly verbal, while humour need not be. *See* FANCY AND IMAGINATION; JEU D'ESPRIT.

women's studies A term that has often been used coterminously with feminist studies and has in some institutions recently been renamed 'gender studies'. Having originated in the 1970s, largely through the impetus of the second-wave feminism spurred by Betty Friedan and the National Organization of Women founded in 1966, women's studies comprises a wide range of programmes and courses, which are taught at university and college level, as well as through professional organizations and centres of research. Women's studies has been promoted by a number of devoted presses.

The first women's studies programmes were established in the 1960s, not in universities but in independent schools such as the New Orleans Free School and the Susan Koppelman's School for Women. The Boston Women's Health Collective produced a widely influential book *Our Bodies, Ourselves* (1971; first published as *Women and their Bodies* in 1970). Since then, such programmes have proliferated enormously in universities, complemented by pedagogical resources such as the series of Female Studies sponsored by the Modern Language Association (MLA) in the 1970s, and the growth of research centres such as the National Women's Studies Association (founded in 1977) and the Center for Women's Policy Studies in Washington, DC.

The goals of women's studies, as defined by Catherine Stimpson, Sandra M. Gilbert, Susan Gubar and others, include the detailed study of women on many levels, biological, psychological, historical and literary; an attempt to contribute to the attainment of gender equality in education, as well as in domestic, social and political life; a critique and reconceptualizing of university curricula and of male epistemic paradigms in general; the reinterpretation of women's roles in history and culture; and a large-scale reassessment not only of gender relations but also of the very notion of gender as a social construction in its intersections with race and class. In the later 20th c., influenced by postmodernism and poststructuralism, women's studies increasingly examined the ideological and psychological formation of subjectivity as well as the operations of language and power. Since the 1980s and 1990s women's studies has come to embrace gender studies and queer theory, and has striven for greater ethnic and global inclusiveness, with black, Chicana, Asian-American, Native American and Islamic feminists articulating their own feminist visions, as integrally shaped by race, class, region and religion.

In pedagogical terms, women's studies has fostered a collaborative and consensual, rather than authoritative, approach to learning; it has resisted the binarism of Aristotelian logic and the coercive implications of substance or essence (οὐσία) as descended from Aristotle all the way down the male philosophical tradition through Locke and Hume to modern positivism; like much philosophy in the heterological tradition (running from Schopenhauer through Nietzsche and Bergson to poststructuralism), it has challenged the binary oppositions of body and soul, intellect and sensation, extending this challenge to the fundamental opposition of masculine and feminine; finally, it has encouraged outreach into community programmes and social activism.

Women's studies has been promoted by a number of presses, including the Feminist Press, Virago, Kitchen Table, Women's Press, Persephone Books and Pergamon; major journals include *Signs*, *Women's Studies*, *Feminist Studies*, and the more recently established *Journal of Feminist Scholarship*. Mainstream university presses almost all have a section devoted to women's studies.

Some of the important publications in this field are: Paul Lauter, *Reconstructing American Literature* (1983); Susan Koppelman, *Images of Women in Literature* (1972); Gerda Lerner, *Black Women in White America* (1972); Gloria Hull, Patricia Bell Scott and Barbara Smith, *All the Women Are White, All the Blacks Are Men But Some of Us Are Brave: Black Women's Studies* (1982); Gayle Linch, Eleanor Holmes Norton, Maxine Williams, Frances M. Beale and Linda La Rue, *Black Women's Manifesto* (1970); Gloria Anzaldúa and Cherrie Moraga (eds), *This Bridge Called My Back: Writings by Radical Women of Color* (1981); AnaLouise Keating and Gloria Anzaldúa (eds), *This bridge we call home: radical visions for transformation* (2002); Roberta Rosenberg (ed.), *Women's Studies: An Interdisciplinary Anthology* (2001); Elizabeth Lapovsky Kennedy and Agatha Beins, *Women's Studies for the Future: Foundations, Interrogations, Politics* (2005). *See also* FEMINIST CRITICISM; POSTSTRUCTURALISM.

working-class novel Occasionally referred to as the 'proletarian novel' (*q.v.*), the working-class novel may be defined as a novel that is written by a working-class author and which focuses on the experiences of working people. Some would argue that the term is an oxymoron (*q.v.*), since the novel (*q.v.*) is a bourgeois form which privileges individual over collective experience. Moreover, the act of writing a novel inevitably distances an author from the community he or she presumes to represent. However, this is to ignore the variety of formal innovations working-class authors have developed to engage with working-class life, and also distinct working-class traditions of novel reading.

While the poor and dispossessed featured regularly in 19th c. realist novels written by middle-class authors, working-class people were usually only permitted a narrow range of experiences; and political activity, if represented at all, was shown to be deeply suspect. However, some Chartist fiction of the mid 19th c., such as Ernest Jones's *De Brassier: A Democratic Romance* (1850–1) and Martin Wheeler's *Sunshine and Shadow* (1849–50), attempted to combine realistic depictions of working lives with insurrectionary messages. The rise of the labour movement in the late 19th c. saw the publication of a few socialist novels in Britain, notably those of Margaret Harkness (who used the pen-name John Law).

The most influential and celebrated working-class novels in English were all published in the early to mid 20th c. The most salient examples are Robert Tressell's anti-capitalist *The Ragged Trousered Philanthropists* (1914); Walter Greenwood's *Love on the Dole* (1933), about working-class poverty in northern England during the Depression; John Dos Passos's trilogy *U.S.A.* (1930–6), which employs a variety of experimental narrative techniques; Pietro di Donato's modernist *Christ in Concrete* (1939), about Italian immigrant bricklayers in New York City; John Steinbeck's migrant novel *The Grapes of Wrath* (1939); and the so-called 'angry young man' (*q.v.*) novels, for example, Alan Sillitoe's *Saturday Night and Sunday Morning* (1958), about the travails of a disaffected lathe operator, and John Braine's *Room at the Top*, published the same year. Braine's novel is rather a narrative about social mobility: its protagonist abandons his working-class roots for a life of wealth and privilege. From the 1960s onwards, far fewer recognizably working-class novels were published in the English-speaking West, mainly due to sociological and political change (the decline of industries which sustained the working classes; the rise of neoliberalism). However, many writers, such as Irvine Welsh and Niall Griffiths, have continued to write about the disenfranchised communities from which they hail. *See also* SOCIALIST REALISM.

world literature   A concept originally formulated by Goethe, who asserted:

> poetry is the universal possession of mankind, revealing itself everywhere and at all times in hundreds and hundreds of men. . . . National literature is now a rather unmeaning term; the epoch of world literature is at hand, and everyone must strive to hasten its approach.
>
> (Eckermann, *Conversations with Goethe*, 1835)

It is obvious that for a considerable time the efforts of the best writers and authors of aesthetic worth in all nations have been directed to what is common to all mankind. In every field, whether the historical, the mythological, the fabulous, or the consciously imagined, one can see, behind what is national and personal, this universal quality becoming more and more apparent ... and although it can hardly be hoped that universal peace will be achieved by this means we may trust that conflict will decrease, war become less cruel and victory less arrogant ... One must learn to note the special characteristics of every nation and take them for granted, in order to meet each nation on its own ground.

(Quoted in Fritz Strich, *Goethe and World Literature*, 1949)

Noticeably, Goethe does not desire the special characteristics of each nation's writing to be effaced but merely to be situated within a larger scheme where its connections with other literatures can be explored, to their common benefit.

The 19th c. Danish writer Georg Brandes authored a renowned essay on world literature (1899). He argued that many scientific works, such as those by Pasteur, Darwin, Bunsen and Helmholtz, unconditionally belong to world literature since they have enriched all humanity. He is more sceptical about the contributions of historians who are necessarily bound in various ways by their personal and national contexts. He sees only a few literary figures – such as Dante, Cervantes and Shakespeare – who transcend their own settings to rise to the status of world literature. And he is scathing about translations, which he calls a 'pitiful expedient'. He also doubts that world renown is necessarily a sign of genuine artistic or intellectual worth, given the perennial popularity of mediocre writers. Finally, he sees Goethe's vision of world literature as undermined by the advance of 'bellicose nationalism'. He ends his essay with this statement:

The world literature of the future will become all the more interesting the more the mark of the national appears in it and the more heterogeneous it becomes, as long as it retains a universally human aspect as art and science. That which is written directly for the world will hardly do as a work of art.

Other 19th c. writers who propounded the idea of a culturally comprehensive approach to literature include Matthew Arnold who, while he did not speak of world literature as such, pointed out the insularity of English letters and advocated recourse to a broader, European tradition.

In the late 19th and early 20th c. literary nationalism (largely in relation to both imperial and domestic ideological agendas) was still strong, in Europe and Ireland, and in some cases, such as America, was still being forged. In the 20th c. modernists such as Eliot and Pound – notwithstanding their parochialism in other respects – had recourse to a more global literary context which included works in Sanskrit and Chinese. But nationalistic literary paradigms have endured intact in terms of both pedagogy and scholarship, with notable exceptions such as Erich Auerbach's culturally and historically wide-ranging study *Mimesis* (1946). 'World literature', as reflected in generations of anthologies used in teaching, has denoted largely the European tradition. Sometimes literary comparatists such as Albert

Guérard expressed the hope that comparative literature would eventually abrogate literary nationalism.

In the 1980s Edward Said argued that literary texts suffered from what he called 'filiation' (given ties of family, home, class and country); he advocated a 'secular criticism' that would focus on a text's 'worldliness' in as much as it had implications in real social and political conditions. For Said, the European canon represented 'only a fraction of the real human relationships and interactions now taking place in the world. . . . New cultures, new societies, and emerging visions of social, political and aesthetic order now lay claim to the humanist's attention'.

But it was not until the heated debates concerning multiculturalism in the 1990s that literary canons were (sometimes) opened up to include minority and foreign literatures. The literary anthologies produced thereafter were more comprehensive in their international cultural and ethnic range but often lacked any foundation of coherence and were indeed tainted by a perhaps unavoidable amateurism, as for example in the use of inaccurate and uncontextualized translations or of unrepresentative figures (the work of Rushdie, for example, is sometimes used to 'represent' the literature of India while the major writers who are truly experts in the languages and literatures of the Indian subcontinent, such as Premchand and N. M. Rashed, remain largely unheard of).

More recently, the concept of 'world literature' has been examined in depth by theorists such as David Damrosch, Pascale Casanova and Graham Huggan. Damrosh argues that 'world literature' is an 'elliptical refraction' of national literatures, which, as they circulate among other cultures, retain only some marks of their national origin and gain other qualities in the receiving cultures. The dilemma of needing to know about two or more cultures can be addressed by collaboration, even among graduate students. In this way, certain translated works can actually gain in translation. Arguing against, or rather contextualizing, Robert Frost's comment that poetry is 'what gets lost in translation', Damrosch points out that certain works such as *The Epic of Gilgamesh* or Joyce's *Dubliners* achieve an increased depth as their range of world circulation is extended; not only can certain stylistic features – such as epic qualities or attributes of realism – continue to be examined but the texts can be situated in a far richer context, among other texts sharing such qualities, thereby actually heightening the creative and interpretative element in reading. Translation has an important and mediating role in world literature. Finally, for Damrosch, 'world literature' is not a canon of texts but a mode of reading, in a detached manner, engaging with a world beyond our own. We encounter the work not in its home culture but in a different field of force, one generated by diversity of culture and era.

Pascale Casanova and Graham Huggan talk in their own ways about how world literature is not some kind of equalizing melting pot but a series of hierarchical regimes where certain cultures and ideologies are privileged and others are marginalized and reduced to forms of exoticism.

The imperative to look seriously at literature in a world context has been fuelled partly by studies in the operations of globalization. For example, the philosophers Michael Hardt and Antonio Negri argue that in the postmodern world sovereignty is beginning to take a new form, composed 'of a series of national and supranational organisms united under a single logic of rule'. The name for this new global form of sovereignty is 'Empire'. *See also* COSMO-POLITAN LITERATURE; POSTCOLONIALISM; TRANSATLANTIC; WELTLITERATUR.

wrenched accent This occurs in verse when the requirements of metrical stress prevail over the natural stress of a word or words. Common in ballads, as in this verse from the 18th c. Scots ballad *Mary Hamilton*:

> He's courted her in the kitchen,
> He's courted her in the ha',
> He's courted her in the laigh cellar,
> And that was warst of a'.

Cellar is a trochaic word, but for the sake of the stress pattern is here made iambic – thus *cellár*. A rhyme dependent on a wrenched accent is known as a wrenched rhyme. *See* RHYME.

writerly *See* READERLY/WRITERLY.

Writers' Guild of Great Britain Founded in 1959 as the Screenwriters' Guild. It is the writer's trade union, affiliated to the TUC, and represents writers' interests in film, radio, theatre, publishing and television. It is by constitution non-political, has no involvement with any political party and does not pay a political levy. There is an executive council of twenty-nine members, and regional committees represent Scotland and Wales and the North and West of England.

X

Xanaduism   A form of academic research which entails the quest for sources behind works of imagination. John Livingston Lowes set a fashion for it in 1927 with the publication of *The Road to Xanadu*, which was inspired by Coleridge's 'visionary' poem about Xanadu.

Xenophanic   Xenophanes (6th c. BC) was a native of Ionia and an itinerant poet who visited many parts of the Greek world. He was also a sillographer (*q.v.*). Thus 'Xenophanic' may be used to describe a wandering poet with a witty and satirical talent. The Goliards were Xenophanic. *See also* GOLIARDIC VERSE.

Y

Yale School A group of literary critics associated with deconstruction (*q.v.*) in America, centred on Yale University, Connecticut, and also, more recently, at Irvine, California (Irvine is a branch of the University of California). The Yale School flourished particularly during the 1970s. The chief luminaries were Harold Bloom, Paul de Man, Geoffrey Hartman, J. Hillis Miller and the French philosopher Jacques Derrida. The so-called Yale Manifesto, to which all five contributed essays, was published in 1979 under the title *Deconstruction and Criticism*. The essays were all initially responses to Shelley's poem *The Triumph of Life*. They were much influenced by Freud and by the deconstruction theories of Derrida.

yarn A story or tale (*q.v.*). The term derives from the nautical slang phrase 'to spin a yarn'. It often has the connotation of a tallish or slightly improbable story. One who 'yarns' is inclined to be a romancer, with the attitude of 'believe it if you will'. Among the many distinguished yarners in English and American literature one should mention R. L. Stevenson, Rudyard Kipling, W. W. Jacobs, Joseph Conrad, Somerset Maugham, A. E. Coppard, John Masefield, T. F. Powys, Mark Twain and William Faulkner. Some poets, too, have been fine yarners. For example: John Masefield, Robert Frost, Robert Service; plus the Australian poets Charles Harpur, Adam Lindsay Gordon, A. B. 'Banjo' Paterson, Henry Lawson and Christopher Brennan. *See* SHORT STORY; TALL STORY.

year book In particular the reports of English Common Law cases for the period 1292–1534. These were succeeded by the Law Reports. In general a year book is an annual publication; usually a reference work – like *The Writers' and Artists' Year Book*.

yellow-backs Cheap editions of novels bound in yellow boards, including the 'railway novels' of the latter years of the 19th c.

A Dictionary of Literary Terms and Literary Theory, Fifth Edition. J. A. Cuddon.
© 2013 The Estate of J. A. Cuddon. Published 2013 by Blackwell Publishing Ltd.

Yellow Book, The An illustrated quarterly which appeared in 1894–7. Many distinguished writers and artists contributed. Among the better known were Aubrey Beardsley, Max Beerbohm, Henry James and Walter Sickert.

yellow journalism A name given to a particularly sensational kind of journalism which flourished in America in the 1880s. The term derives from an 1895 number of the *New York World* in which a child in a yellow dress ('The Yellow Kid') was the central figure of a cartoon. This was an experiment in colour printing. In England the term 'yellow press' is applied to sensational periodicals.

yüeh-fu (Ch 'music bureau') A form of Chinese poetry so named because the music bureau collected popular songs and ballad-type lyrics. The *yüeh-fu* poems were in mixed meters and short lines (a five-word line was common), and the number of stanzas was variable. The poem usually consisted of monologue or dialogue which presented, in dramatic form, some misfortune.

Z

zany (It *zani*, *zanni*; a Venetian form of Gianni or Giovanni) A servant-clown in *commedia dell'arte* (*q.v.*). More generally, any kind of jester or clown; also a comedian's stooge. Currently used on occasions to describe an idea (or person) which is off-beat, odd, crazily funny.

zapadnichestvo *See* WESTERNERS.

zarzuela (Sp, after la Zarzuela, a hunting lodge near the Pardo Palace near Madrid) A form of 17th c. Spanish drama first composed by Calderón de la Barca with the help of composers such as Juan Risco. *Zarzuelas* were a form of musical comedy (*q.v.*) in one to three acts. Thus a sort of hybrid of drama and opera. Music became an increasingly important element in which recitative alternated with song. The themes were usually mythological and the plays were stylized in structure and language. Early examples (both by Calderón) were *El mayor encanto amor* (1635) and *El jardín de Falerina*. In the 1650s the plays were performed at the hunting lodge. *Zarzuelas* became particularly popular in the 17th c. After a period of desuetude in the 18th c. they were revived in the 19th and continue to be popular to this day.

zaum A Russian term for 'trans-sense' language (*zaumny yazyk*), a language which would be 'beyond sense'. For example, neologisms (*q.v.*), onomatopoeic effects, arbitrary combinations of sounds, and play with the morphological components of ordinary words. It was a notable feature of work produced by Russian Futurist poets, especially Khlebnikov and Kruchenykh. *See* FUTURISM; NONSENSE.

Zeitgeist (G 'spirit of the time') The trend, fashion or taste of a particular period. For instance, a preoccupation with the more morbid aspects of dying and death was characteristic of some English literature in the Jacobean period (*q.v.*), especially in the works of dramatists like Webster and Tourneur. *See also* DECADENCE; WELTANSCHAUUNG.

A Dictionary of Literary Terms and Literary Theory, Fifth Edition. J. A. Cuddon.
© 2013 The Estate of J. A. Cuddon. Published 2013 by Blackwell Publishing Ltd.

Zeitroman (G 'era, period, times, novel') In German the term denotes a novel which is mainly concerned with an author's critical analysis of the age in which he or she lives. There are many such novels. Notable examples in German literature are Gutzkow's *Die Ritter vom Geiste* (1850-1), Freytag's *Soll und Haben* (1855), Thomas Mann's *Der Zauberberg* (1924), and Günter Grass's *Die Blechtrommel* (1959) and his *Aus dem Tagebuch einer Schnecke* (1972). *See also* BILDUNGSROMAN.

zéjel A Spanish poetic form (believed to be of Arabic origin) which was popular in Spain in the late Middle Ages. It consists of an introductory strophe (*q.v.*) followed by a series of strophes. At its simplest the strophic form is four verses rhyming aaab, cccb. The b rhyme runs throughout. *See also* ESTRIBILLO; MUDANZA.

ženske pesme (S 'women's songs') Songs or poems of oral tradition and of the ballad (*qq.v.*) type frequently sung and chanted by South Slav women, especially peasant women. Their themes are often love, death, marriage, home life and romance. *See* NARODNE PESME.

zeugma (Gk 'yoking, bonding') A figure of speech in which the same word (verb or preposition) is applied to two others in different senses. For example: 'she looked at the object with suspicion and a magnifying glass'; or 'Miss Bolo went home in a flood of tears and a sedan chair' (Charles Dickens); or Evelyn's description of Charles I as 'Circled with his royal diadem and the affections of his people'. *See also* SYLLEPSIS.

Zhdanovshchina (R 'the Zhdanov time') The period of 1946-8, during which Andrei Zhdanov, secretary of the Central Committee in control of ideology, brought heavy pressure to bear on prominent Soviet writers who were deemed not to be following Party doctrine. Among the most prominent were Anna Akhmatova, Mikhail Zoshchenko and Boris Pasternak. Later, comparable pressures were put on Alexander Solzhenitsyn, who in 1969 was expelled from the Union of Soviet Writers (*q.v.*) and in 1974 was deported to West Germany. *See also* DISSIDENT WRITERS.

Penguin Language

SHAKESPEARE'S WORDS
DAVID CRYSTAL AND BEN CRYSTAL

A vital resource for scholars, students and actors, this book contains glosses and quotes for over 14,000 words that could be misunderstood by or are unknown to a modern audience. Displayed panels look at such areas of Shakespeare's language as greetings, swear-words and terms of address. Plot summaries are included for all Shakespeare's plays and on the facing page is a unique diagrammatic representation of the relationships within each play.

'This is a fascinating guide to Shakespeare's language, a more or less indispensable treasure-chest for anyone who loves watching or reading the plays and is curious about the meaning, use and derivation of the language' Sir Richard Eyre

'Detailed, comprehensive – fascinating' Kenneth Branagh

'*Shakespeare's Words* is one of the very few works of reference that deserves a place on the shelves of all Shakespeare lovers and for that matter all lovers of the English language' Professor Jonathan Bate, author of *The Genius of Shakespeare*

PENGUIN REFERENCE LIBRARY

THE PENGUIN DICTIONARY OF ART AND ARTISTS

EDITED BY PETER AND LINDA MURRAY

'A vast amount of information intelligently presented, carefully detailed, abreast of current thought and scholarship and easy to read'
The Times Literary Supplement

Why exactly did Van Gogh cut off his ear? Was Warhol an original, or was he just a copyist? The answers to all this and more are found in *The Penguin Dictionary of Art and Artists*, the essential guide to over 700 years of creative endeavour. A brilliant, updated seventh edition of an essential reference work, it charts the lives of over 1200 painters, as well as a wide range of periods, ideas, processes and movements. Any artist or student of the arts will not be able to survive without one. Each entry features extensive cross-referencing and listings of galleries where the artist's work can be seen.

- Short, incisive biographies on every notable (and not so notable) artist of the past seven centuries, from *Caravaggio* to *Picasso* to *Zoffany*, citing their location in the world's museums

- Descriptions of artistic techniques (*collage*), styles (*nocturne*) and materials (*stump*)

- Definitions of artistic movements, from *Cubism* to *Impressionism* to *Dada*

ONLY PENGUIN GIVES YOU MORE

PENGUIN REFERENCE LIBRARY

THE PENGUIN DICTIONARY OF BUILDING

EDITED BY JAMES H. MACLEAN & JOHN S. SCOTT

'Should be recommended reading to anyone interested in building'
Technical Education

Do you need to know your *lime putty* from your *lime plaster*? Want to improve your *flatness tolerance*? Stuck with an incomprehensible DIY manual? *The Penguin Dictionary of Building* is your answer. Ably steering you through the confusing maze of jargon and technical terms, this ever-popular text has sold over 150,000 copies and is invaluable for anyone interested in construction: students, professional architects, bricklayers, carpenters, glaziers, plasterers, plumbers or DIY enthusiasts. From *abrasives* to *Z-purlin* via the *murder clause*, this clear and comprehensive dictionary provides succinct and accurate explanations of the techniques, equipment and issues of the building world.

- Explains all aspects of construction from *foundations* to *roof tiles*, including international variants for a truly universal text

- Provides detailed coverage of methods (*construction joint*), materials (*acrylic paints*, *spatterdash*) and tools (*bench grinder*, *water gauge*)

- Clarifies fire, health & safety, insulation and noise regulations

- Is a splendid cross-referenced companion to *The Penguin Dictionary of Civil Engineering*

ONLY PENGUIN GIVES YOU MORE

PENGUIN REFERENCE LIBRARY

THE PENGUIN DICTIONARY OF CLASSICAL MYTHOLOGY

EDITED BY PIERRE GRIMAL

'An essential source' *Library Journal*

Who bore children by a bear and was transformed into a bird as punishment?
Why exactly did Zeus turn his lover into a cow? Classical myth is a vibrant and
entertaining world, and Pierre Grimal's seminal text *The Penguin Dictionary of
Classical Mythology* is indisputably the finest guide available. Meticulously
researched and thoroughly cross-referenced, the text is accessible and informative,
sweeping in its breadth and comprehensive in its detail. You will find the no less
than *four* versions of the beautiful *Helen*'s birth, as well as lengthy explanations
of all the major figures and events – from *Odysseus* to *Heracles* to *Troy* to the
Jason and the *Argonauts*.

- Discusses all the heroes and heroines of Homer, Sophocles, Aeschylus and
  Euripides (amongst many others), from *Venus* to *Pandora* via *Apollo* and
  Aphrodite

- Demonstrates how and where classical mythology has resurfaced and
  influenced the works of later painters and writers, from Freud to James Joyce

- Includes comprehensive cross-referencing and genealogical tables to show the
  complex links between different characters and myths

ONLY PENGUIN GIVES YOU MORE

PENGUIN REFERENCE LIBRARY

THE PENGUIN DICTIONARY OF ECONOMICS

EDITED BY GRAHAM BANNOCK, R. E. BAXTER & EVAN DAVIS

'Another winner from the Penguin Reference shelf' John David Charles Hilton

An undoubted classic, *The Penguin Dictionary of Economics* has enlightened over half a million economics students over the last thirty years. From *Hotelling's Law* to *hyperinflation*, this now fully updated dictionary explains a host of economic terms in accessible yet detailed entries for both local and international markets. Wide-ranging and illuminating, this comprehensive practical guide is an absolute must for students of economics and professionals (in business, finance or the public sector), and for anyone wishing to follow economic discussions in the media today.

- Has sold more than 600,000 copies worldwide

- Provides entries on major individual economists, from *Joseph Stiglitz* to *John Maynard Keynes* to *Adam Smith*

- Discusses economic theory, including development economics, industrial organisation, finance and game theory, as well as international monetary and welfare economics

- Surveys applied economics, major financial institutions and the history of economics

ONLY PENGUIN GIVES YOU MORE

PENGUIN REFERENCE LIBRARY

THE PENGUIN DICTIONARY OF INTERNATIONAL RELATIONS

EDITED BY GRAHAM EVANS & JEFFREY NEWNHAM

'Cogently argued and lucidly expressed. The scholarship is impeccable'
Professor J. E. Spence

It's the twenty-first century, and the political landscape has never been so explosive. Will history repeat itself, or are we entering a new phase of governmental relations? No one can say for sure, but *The Penguin Dictionary of International Relations* provides the clues. A must for any student or teacher of politics, this exceptional text is the only guide on the market to this complex and constantly shifting subject. The entries are lucid, wide-ranging and lengthy, offering detailed explanation of the *Arab–Israeli conflict*, *weapons of mass destruction* and much more.

- Covers major events, from the *Cold War* to *Hiroshima*

- Includes substantial articles on fundamental political and philosophical concepts, such as *intervention*, *nationalism* and *just war*

- Describes key organizations in detail, from the *ANC* to *UNO*

- Explains specialist terms, from *agent-structure* to *zero-sum*

ONLY PENGUIN GIVES YOU MORE

PENGUIN REFERENCE

THE PENGUIN DICTIONARY OF ISLAM
AZIM NANJI

Islam today is a truly global faith, yet it remains an enigma to many of us. Each and every day our newspapers are saturated with references to Islam: Quran, Taliban, Hijab, Fatwa, Allah, Sunni, Jihad, Shia, the list goes on. But how much do we really understand? Are we, in fact, *mis*understanding?

The Penguin Dictionary of Islam provides complete, impartial answers. It includes extensive coverage of the historical formations of the worldwide Muslim community and highlights key modern Muslim figures and events. Understanding Islam is vital to understanding our world and this dictionary is the definitive authority, designed for both general and academic readers.

An informative and invaluable book that provides clear and definitive explanations of key terms relating to Islam, it is essential for truly understanding the world in which we live.